1001 TV SERIES
YOU MUST WATCH BEFORE YOU DIE

1001 TV SERIES
YOU MUST WATCH BEFORE YOU DIE

GENERAL EDITOR
PAUL CONDON

FOREWORD BY
STEVEN MOFFAT

CASSELL
ILLUSTRATED

A Quintessence Book

First published in Great Britain in 2015 by Cassell Illustrated
A division of Octopus Publishing Group Limited
Carmelite House
50 Victoria Embankment
London EC4Y 0DZ
www.octopusbooks.co.uk

An Hachette UK Company
www.hachette.co.uk

ISBN: 978-1-84403-833-6
QSS.TVS

A CIP catalogue record for this book is available from the British Library.

This book was designed and produced by
Quintessence Editions Ltd.
The Old Brewery
6 Blundell Street
London N7 9BH

Project Editor	Sophie Blackman
Editors	Rebecca Gee, Bruno MacDonald, Fiona Plowman, Frank Ritter, Henry Russell, Dorothy Stannard
Proofreader	Liz Jones
Designers	Damian Jaques, Josse Pickard
Picture Researchers	Hannah Phillips, Kate Symondson
Production Manager	Anna Pauletti
Editorial Directors	Jane Laing, Ruth Patrick
Publisher	Philip Cooper

Colour reproduction by Portland Media Print Services Ltd.
Printed in China by Printplus Ltd.

Contents

Foreword
By Steven Moffat

Back in the smoky brown world of the distant past, when instead of the Internet we had to go on a bus ride to a library, and a three-bar electric fire wasn't just a super-modern way to heat your room but counted as a decent evening's viewing, television programs just vanished. It's true—you can check. If you happened to miss a particular show, it just disappeared from the screen like smoke from a chimney, never to be seen again.

In those early days we didn't have DVDs, or downloads, or Netflix. We didn't even have a video recorder. Programs came and went, and if you missed one because your train was delayed, or your mum and dad wouldn't stop talking to the man in the shop, or you were at someone else's house and your friend's parents changed the channel (the horror of that happening!), that was that. The movie you had planned to see, or, worse, the last episode of the series you had been watching, was gone forever, like a missed sunset, or a kiss that you never knew was yours for the taking.

It was these circumstances that spawned books of the sort you are reading now. In a way, they also explain why they have never gone away. Because, back in the mists of time, what television viewers had instead of the means to record everything were opinions. Yes, opinions! I sometimes think that forming an opinion about what is playing out there in front of you is the best bit of all.

As a little boy, I would be watching *Doctor Who*, which launched in 1963, with my dad. And he would nod along, and smile, and point out mistakes in the physics—hopefully those are eliminated now—and when it was over we would agree that it was a great show.

"But of course," my dad would say, as he always did, "it's not as good as *Quatermass*." Now, the *Quatermass* shows had been made and broadcast before I was even born. Which meant, back in those days, there was no chance I would ever see them. Those old serials were as lost as ships at the bottom of sea, and every bit as thrilling. I was haunted by them. My dad told me the best one was *Quatermass and the Pit* (1958), and that everybody stayed home to watch it. Over and over again, he told me every beat of the plot, but only because I made him do it. In the course of these re-tellings, my dad, of course, elaborated, misremembered, and allowed himself any flight of fancy that he thought would entertain me. (Inevitably, when I finally saw the real thing many years later, I was disappointed that they had gotten so much of my dad's account of it wrong.)

But, while I was still a child, a magical thing happened. In a bookshop, flicking through some old tome about science-fiction movies, I stumbled across a photograph from *Quatermass and the Pit*. I stared at it, as though it was a forbidden wonder. An entirely gray man with a moustache (clearly identifiable as *Quatermass*, just by the sheer wisdom of his hat) stood in confrontation with an angry colonel, who was obviously wrong about everything he was saying. Next to the pair was a spaceship that had been buried in the ground. And there, in clear print, was a brief account of the show; it corroborated my father's story, albeit with a few disappointing errors.

And so began my fascination with books like this one. I knew that the actual TV show was out of my grasp forever, but that didn't stop me forming opinions about it; indeed, it made it easier. I read book after book, usually unpurchased, still in the bookshop—which I hope is not what you are doing now. I discovered that three different men played Quatermass, a different actor for each serial. I was terribly upset by that, so I decided to appoint one—he would be the only one who counted. After reading and absorbing as many opinions as I could, I decided it had to be André Morell.

I clung fiercely to this opinion and regularly argued about it with other kids who, of course, hadn't seen the show either, and only knew about it from me. And then, when the movie version came on the television (oh, the confusion that caused me!), I concluded that Andrew Keir as Quatermass wasn't quite as good as André Morell—whom I'd never seen. And as far as I knew, I never would see him. But, thanks to all those books and forbidden pictures, I already knew what I thought, and that was good enough for me.

It wasn't just *Quatermass* that had my attention. I was off and reading all those books, and oh, I enjoyed a lot of shows I never saw. I became a particular fan of Basil Rathbone's Sherlock Holmes years before I saw him in action. I was enraged by the decision, in the third movie, to update him. Update Sherlock Holmes: what kind of lunacy was that? I was also a particular devotee of *The Prisoner* (1967), which I read about endlessly. I was especially thrilled that it was a direct sequel to another show, called *Danger Man* (1960), featuring the same character (John Drake), but I did feel very let down by the confusing and chaotic last episode. None of this turned out to be true, when I saw the actual show a few years later—but, to be honest, the version of *The Prisoner* I invented for myself still feels more real than the actual production. Similarly, *Quatermass and the Pit* itself will never be as good as the original version—the one my father told me about after every single episode of *Doctor Who*.

All madness, of course. But it is a wonderful madness, and that is why books like this matter. In the end, all TV shows are just noise and colour; it is what goes on in your brain afterward that matters. The theories you concoct, the sequels you imagine, the glorious opinions you develop for the exact purpose of slightly annoying your friends. The conversations the next day that go on for longer than the show. In fact, the only place a TV show really comes alive is in the minds and hearts of the audience, as expressed in their watercooler chats, in their shared joy or outrage, their scorn, and their excitement. Oh, and in their disagreements, above all.

Scanning the list of writers in this book is a pleasant shock to me because I know so many of them, but that isn't because there is a secret cabal where all media matters are decided. There is certainly no such thing, so please don't mention it again. No, if you'll forgive me bringing up the subject one more time, it's sort of because of *Doctor Who*. That show was once lost at the bottom of the sea, no more than the punchline to a joke or a *Trivial Pursuit* question. On the first Thursday of every month, a number of us old fans showed up at the same pub to talk and laugh about that daft old TV program—and, in time, every other TV program, too. And because the word spread, as the word always does, people started showing up who had never even heard of the TARDIS. And for many, many years, on every first Thursday, in that one little pub, there were more opinions expressed about TV shows than you would ever have thought possible.

Eventually I got too busy, and I don't go there any more. I was writing episodes of *Doctor Who*, then *Sherlock Holmes*, and suddenly there was never any time. I don't even know if it still happens—I hope it does. But if it doesn't, well, there's always the book you're holding right now to give you a flavour of our discussions.

This book is full of opinions; it is seething with them. And it's time you got in there and disagreed. Pick a show you hate and read the entry; you will be pacing up and down arguing with it. If you want to get really cross (and who doesn't?), pick a show you love and read someone praising it for all the wrong reasons. Because that is what television is for. Not the shows themselves, but all the mad, passionate, bonkers conversation afterward. The real show is what you think it is, not just what you have seen on the screen.

A little while ago, I was cornered at a party by someone who wanted to scold me for everything I had ever written. This happens now and then, and usually ends with my critic asking for a selfie. But this particular guy said to me: "Your shows—the fridge logic is terrible." This was a new concept to me. "Um. I'm not sure there's all that many fridges in them," I replied, privately reflecting that he'd have been better off choosing his *Sherlock* tee shirt in a larger size.

"No, no, no. Fridge logic."

"Do fridges have that now?"

"You've never heard of fridge logic?" He laughed at me, and the image of Benedict Cumberbatch wobbled in sympathy.

"No. But I do own a fridge, if that helps. It's green."

He decided to enlighten me. "It's when you get to the fridge after watching a show, and realise that the show doesn't make any sense. I can't enjoy your shows because of their lack of fridge logic. For me, that damages the entertainment."

I thought for a bit. "Okay," I said, brightly, "But on the plus side, it improves your trip to the fridge!"

S. M.

Introduction
By Paul Condon

Hello, and thanks for wanting to discover more about the wonderful world of TV. Now, before you rush off to your DVD collection, streaming service, or PVR, I should issue a brief word of warning. Watching every single episode of each of the 1001 TV shows included in this book is quite a tall order. For example, watching the first 8,630 episodes of *Coronation Street* would take up the best part of thirty days. Next month, you could start on 1980s American medical drama *St Elsewhere* and all of its spin-offs. But more on this in a moment . . .

I should mention something from the off—this book is not a tick-list. For every great TV event mentioned here, there are hundreds more you could jump onto and never run out of things to enjoy. This is more of a tourist information guide. You see, if you did start with *St Elsewhere*, you might slowly discover that some of the regular characters from *St Elsewhere* made guest appearances on other shows—such as on *Homicide: Life on the Streets*. Now, *Homicide* featured the detective character John Munch, who also appeared in *The X Files*. In fact, Munch also appeared in *Law and Order*, *The Wire*, *Unbreakable Kimmy Schmidt*, and five other major shows. Thanks to him, almost ninety percent of US TV output from the 1990s and beyond can be considered the fantastical imaginings of a visiting patient who appeared in the final episode of *St Elsewhere*. In other words, you're about to embark on a long journey. A very long journey.

The countries with the most successful TV export businesses are of course the United States and the UK—and that's why the vast majority of entries here are from those countries. We've selected a good cross-section of US and UK programs from across the decades. Some are universally acknowledged as important works (*Fawlty Towers*, *The Sopranos*, *Upstairs Downstairs*, *I Love Lucy*)—but tucked away among the big hitters are a handful of obscure cult titles that may be new to you. However, you'll also find unforgettable classics from Scandinavia, France, Germany, Brazil, and even South Korea—programs that will command your attention, even if you're only used to watching shows in the English language.

Any list like this is of course going to be fairly subjective—rest assured that this isn't just a list of one person's favourites. We took on board suggestions from people on both sides of the Atlantic and right around the world. Still, I'm sorry if your most heartfelt favorite show isn't here. It's gone but not forgotten.

Our main focus here is TV shows that can be binge-watched, from short series through to programs lasting many seasons. As most significant US TV shows consist of long-running successful series, we've focused on those. In the UK and in many other countries, there's a long tradition of much shorter programs, and even one-off plays from renowned directors and playwrights, so we've chosen a representative cross-section of those. Sadly, we had to make the choice not to include children's programs. Though many cross the generations, they don't often travel beyond the borders of their own countries. We've retained one or two programs that have a significance outside of their original target audience. See if you can spot why.

The idea of doing a "1001" book about TV has been circulating for nearly a decade, but it's only now, when streaming technology has caught up, that the time is right. Unlike with feature films, which enjoy global strategic releases, until recently it would have been difficult for readers in other countries to gain access to the very best and latest programs from around the world. Thankfully, with the rise of streaming sites like Netflix, Amazon Prime, YouTube, and BBC Store (and they're just the legitimate sources), programs that seemed out of reach forever are now available instantaneously to viewers anywhere on the planet. As a fan of TV in all its forms, it's increasingly pleasing to see a lot of older, archive material being made available. It means classic television can be classed as "new" to modern viewers who were unlucky enough to be born a little late. Now, *I Love Lucy* or *I, Claudius* can stand alongside *30 Rock* or *Game of Thrones* and still surprise us.

Since we drew a line under the list of 1001 shows for this edition, I've already seen some amazing new series that would definitely warrant an entry in this book: *Grace & Frankie*, *Daredevil*, *Black Sails*, *Jonathan Strange & Mister Norrell*, *Wayward Pines*, *1864*, *The Casual Vacancy*, and the revival of *Poldark*, to name but a few. And with more exciting new programs already announced for the future, one thing is certain: we're never likely to run out of great things to watch!

Index by Title

Television had existed for more than a decade but in the 1950s it became universal. The launch of satellites made our planet a smaller place: millions tuned in to see Brazil win the 1958 soccer World Cup; the European Broadcasting Union created a song contest that continues to baffle outsiders to this day; and viewers in the United States began to suspect that something odd was going on with their quiz shows. Television became a genre in its own right, not just cinema on a small scale or radio with pictures, as Lucille Ball, Rudolph Cartier, and many others invented a new art form that was purely televisual.

Pre 1960s

Sergeant Ernie Bilko (on table), played by US comedian Phil Silvers, in the popular sitcom *The Phil Silvers Show* (1957).

The Ed Sullivan Show

Variety | USA | 1948–71

*Ladies and gentlemen, enjoy
"a really big shew"*

Cast | Ed Sullivan
Original broadcaster | CBS
Awards | 1 Emmy, 1 Golden Globe
For fans of . . . | *The Tonight Show* (1954), *Late Show
with David Letterman* (1993)

With stilted delivery, idiosyncratic pronunciation, and
an appearance that won him the nickname "The Great
Stone Face," writer-turned-broadcaster Ed Sullivan
wasn't an obvious TV host. However, his Sunday variety
show—titled *Toast of the Town* until 1955—introduced
a galaxy of stars, from Broadway to Hollywood and
from circus tents to opera halls, to a riveted audience.

Iconic appearances by Elvis Presley in 1956 and 1957
and The Beatles and The Supremes in 1964 were the
biggest in the show's history. However, Edsullivan.com
notes, "The Stones were banned (temporarily, it turned
out) after their rowdy first appearance, and the show's
director asked The Doors to leave out the line "Girl we
couldn't get much higher" from "Light My Fire" (they
agreed, sang it anyway, and likewise got banned)."

Viewers also enjoyed mouse puppet Topo Gigio,
Ethel Merman, the Muppets, Richard Pryor, and many
more. An *Ed Sullivan* slot was often a shortcut to fame,
with the kingmaker—hailed as "a brilliant tracker and
arranger of talent"—holding court on-screen and off.
A true variety show, it mixed the mundane with the
bizarre, the comic with the dramatic.

The show's New York venue—once Hammerstein's
Theatre, then CBS-TV Studio 50, and, from 1967, The Ed
Sullivan Theater—is now a registered historic location.
The sitcom *Kate & Allie* was shot there from 1984 to 1989,
as was David Letterman's *Late Show* from 1993. **ATB**

❯ (L–R) Sullivan with The Beatles' John Lennon, Ringo Starr, and
Paul McCartney, during rehearsals for the show.

Hopalong Cassidy

Western | USA | 1949–54

A true Western pioneer

Cast | William Boyd, James Ellison, Russell Hayden, George Reeves, Rand Brooks, George Hayes, Britt Wood, Andy Clyde, Edgar Buchanan **Original broadcaster** | NBC **For fans of . . .** | *The Lone Ranger* (1949)

Created by writer Clarence E. Mulford in 1904, Hopalong Cassidy was a gritty sort, unsuited to children's stories. By the 1930s, however, he had grown more personable, especially once he was embodied by William Boyd in sixty-six movies through the 1930s and '40s; he even drank sarsaparilla instead of anything alcoholic. Cliché dictated that good guys wore white, but "Hoppy" dressed in black, setting him apart from his fellow cowboy heroes. His horse, Topper, however, was white.

Savvy businessman Boyd acquired the rights to his movies. With judicious editing, he and NBC created a series to fill half-hour and hour-long slots. Its popularity eventually prompted the production of fifty-two new episodes, featuring sidekick Red Connors (Edgar

Buchanan). (Cassidy's exploits also ran in a radio show on two successive networks from 1950 to 1952.)

A legend in his own time, Boyd made the covers of *Time* and *Life*. Long after his death in 1972, his character's legacy was honored by museum exhibits and a 2009 U.S. Postal Service stamp commemorating Cassidy's contribution to the early history of TV. **ATB**

Classic episode

Black Waters | *Season 1, episode 21*. Hoppy is asked to persuade an Indian chief to give up his land's oil. Character actor Rick Vallin guests, as he also did on other Westerns such as *The Gene Autry Show, Cowboy G-Men,* and *The Lone Ranger.*

🌀 William Boyd with Topper, after whose death the actor said he would never ride another horse.

The Lone Ranger
Western | USA | 1949–57

Who was that masked man?

Cast | Clayton Moore, Jay Silverheels, John Hart, Chuck Courtney, Marshall Bradford
Original broadcaster | ABC **For fans of . . .** | *Hopalong Cassidy* (1949)

Created for radio in 1933, the Lone Ranger came to TV in the form of Clayton Moore. He played a Texas Ranger who, having surviving an ambush, donned a mask to serve as an unknown agent of justice with the help of Tonto (Jay Silverheels), an American Indian who had helped him cheat death. The Lone Ranger shot silver bullets only to wound, and—on horses Silver and Scout—the duo patrolled the West with an eye out for danger. Their exploits, guided by a strict code, were heralded by Rossini's *William Tell Overture*, and The Lone Ranger rode into adventure with the cry, "Hi-Yo, Silver! Away!"

Moore's distinctive, smoky voice led some viewers to wonder how anyone couldn't identify the man behind the mask, to say nothing of seeing through the disguises he used to baffle the bad guys. But the enduring friendship of the two leads gave the show an irresistible emotional core. (John Hart took over the lead role in the 1950s, but was poorly received and duly replaced by his predecessor.) Moore and Silverheels graced two movies, *The Lone Ranger* (1956) and *The Lone Ranger and the Lost City of Gold* (1958). **ATB**

Classic episode
The Angel and the Outlaw | *Season 5, episode 37*.
With the show still going strong at the end of its life, this 1957 tale was directed by Oscar Rudolph, who also helmed *The Donna Reed Show, My Favorite Martian, Batman,* and *The Brady Bunch.*

Jay Silverheels (Tonto) and Clayton Moore (The Lone Ranger) pose with the latter's trusty steed, Silver.

The George Burns and Gracie Allen Show

Comedy | USA | 1950–58

Celebrated gag show that was one of the first on television to break the "fourth wall"

Cast | George Burns, Gracie Allen, Bea Benaderet, Harry von Zell, Larry Keating, Ronnie Burns
Original broadcaster | CBS
For fans of . . . | *The Jack Benny Program* (1950), *I Love Lucy* (1951), *Hazel* (1961), *Roseanne* (1988)

Husband-and-wife team George Burns and Gracie Allen won success on the vaudeville stage, graduated to a self-titled radio program, then transferred their signature take on married life to TV. Hitting airwaves a full year before Lucille Ball's flighty redhead, Allen's ditzy character paved the way for all screwball wives to come. Costarring Bea Benaderet as Blanche and Harry von Zell as an announcer, the show broke the fourth wall when George would look into the camera to address the TV audience directly, commenting on the action or silently begging for salvation or sympathy.

Filmed on a set that resembled the Burns' own home, and populated with characters either named after or based on their own friends and family (including their children, Ronnie and Sandra), the show took reality to zany peaks as viewers watched the Hollywood couple's daily lives play out both on TV and the stage on the TV show. Both relied heavily on Allen's impeccable timing and deadpan delivery of her often rambling, but always hilarious, stories about her family. One of the most popular gags involved a closet filled with the hats of guests who, because of confusion or fear, left the home too quickly to collect them. The show often ended with the leads trading banter on the proscenium of the stage for the "show" that had just been staged. Allen died in 1964, but Burns performed on stage , on TV, and in films, until his death at age one hundred. He attributed his success to his late wife and partner—who had been the brains of the operation all along. **RP**

Classic episode
The Girl Behind the Perfume Counter | *Season 7, episode 14*. In a case of mistaken identity, Gracie believes Ronnie is dating a much older woman. Eleanor Audley—later better known as Mother Eunice Douglas in *Green Acres* (1965)—guests.

⬥ A Hitchcockian shot with George Burns and Gracie Allen.

The Jack Benny Program

Comedy | USA | 1950–65

Well . . . Immensely popular sitcom starring one of the comedy greats

Cast | Jack Benny, Eddie "Rochester" Anderson, Don Wilson, Dennis Day, Mary Livingstone, Mel Blanc
Original broadcaster | CBS
Awards | 6 Emmys, 1 Golden Globe
For fans of . . . | *Hancock's Half Hour* (1956)

Jack Benny became a star in the 1930s and '40s thanks to a clever radio series set "behind the scenes" of his "real" life. His dry wit, slow-burn delivery, and painful violin playing became trademarks, but it was his depiction of a miser that really captured listeners' imaginations. In the 1950s he developed a TV version of the show and found a formula that proved equally successful. Recurring characters from the radio show— his valet Rochester (Eddie Anderson) and announcer Don Wilson—also made the transition to TV.

It was a sitcom norm at the time for the biggest stars to play heightened variations of their real selves and to retain their real names (*The George Burns and Gracie Allen Show*, *The Abbott and Costello Show*) and the public would often confuse the on-screen persona with the real-life characters. Benny personified this more than anyone else and rarely lapsed out of character when offscreen. A master of timing, his confidence and fearlessness meant he was willing to hold a pause longer than others would dare—often resulting in audience hysteria.

Eddie Anderson also became a star because of the show and was one of the first African-Americans to have a regular, major part on radio and television. His role as a servant was stereotypical and earlier (radio) episodes included dubious references to his color and creed, but, later, Benny helped ensure the character was treated with more dignity and that any racial references would only ever come from Rochester himself. **DF**

Classic episode
The Murder of Clayton Worthington | *Season 13, episode 18*. Fellow comedian Dick Van Dyke— then starring in his own CBS show—guests in multiple roles, offering a rare opportunity to see the old master with a brilliant emerging talent.

◉ The perpetually thirty-nine-year-old Jack Benny on set in 1951.

What's My Line?

Game show | USA | 1950–67

The longest-running prime-time game show in US network history

Cast | John Daly, Johnny Olson, Hal Simms, Lee Vines, Arlene Francis, Bennett Cerf, Dorothy Kilgallen
Original broadcaster | CBS
Awards | 3 Emmys, 1 Golden Globe
For fans of . . . | *I've Got a Secret* (1952)

Spawning adaptations around the world, the stylish and formal *What's My Line?* featured four celebrities attempting to determine a mystery guest's occupation via a series of yes or no questions. Audiences became accustomed to one of the show's most oft-posed inquiries: "Is it bigger than a breadbox?" Produced by powerhouse duo Mark Goodson and Bill Todman (also responsible for, among many others, *The Price Is Right*) and provisionally titled *Occupation Unknown*, the show offered a maximum $50 prize for anyone who confounded the panel (they did, however, receive a $500 appearance fee regardless of the outcome).

While contestants came from all walks of life, the final round involved a celebrity whom the now blindfolded panel would have to identify. Many of these mystery guests, notably Lucille Ball, returned over the years.

The show's network run ended in 1967 with a celebratory set of clips, returning contestants, and a final mystery guest: John Daly himself. It was resurrected in syndication—and color—from 1968 to 1975. (Many of the black-and-white episodes were lost—some victims of editing mistakes made during preparations for a twenty-fifth anniversary special in 1975.)

The most controversial panelist, journalist Dorothy Kilgallen, appeared on a live *What's My Line?* broadcast just hours before she was found dead under mysterious circumstances in 1965. Her death has often been linked to conspiracy theories concerning her investigation of President Kennedy's assassination. **ATB**

Your Show of Shows

Variety | USA | 1950–54

Training ground for some of the greatest comedy writers of the 1960s

Cast | Sid Caesar, Imogene Coca, Howard Morris, Carl Reiner, James Starbuck, Tom Avera
Original broadcaster | NBC
Awards | 2 Emmys
For fans of . . . | *Saturday Night Live* (1975)

This ninety-minute live broadcast broke new ground by adding recurring comedy scenes and characters to the variety show format (much as *Saturday Night Live* does today). It was tightly written by some of the greatest comics in TV history, including future movie director Mel Brooks, playwright-to-be Neil Simon (who celebrated *Your Show of Shows* in 1993's *Laughter on the 23rd Floor*), Mel Tolkin (later story editor on *All In the Family*) and his writing partner Lucille Kallen, and future *Dick Van Dyke Show* creator Carl Reiner. The latter was also a member of the hilarious cast, headed by Sid Caesar, Imogene Coca, and Howard Morris.

The show was originally part of the two-hour *Saturday Night Review*, before the first thirty minutes—filmed in Chicago—were dropped in 1951. The resultant New York–based creation drew comedy from the foibles of human nature and served laugh-out-loud satire of current events and parodies of American culture. Caesar's multiple roles relied on his quick verbal chops, versatile facial expressions and body language, and considerable charm. He shared a spectacular chemistry with Coca, who could play subtle, sweet, absurd, sometimes vaudevillian. Together they expanded and redefined the variety show format, while adding recurring characters that the audiences grew to love.

Your Show of Shows built a foundation for American TV comedy, but it's tricky to find full episodes as they originally aired. However, clips collected by museums, on DVD, and online are more than worth the effort. **RP**

Dragnet

Crime/Mystery | USA | 1951–59; 1967–70; 1989–91; 2003–04

A realistic midcentury police procedural drama that led to a new style of TV cop show

Cast | Jack Webb, Ben Alexander, Harry Morgan
Original broadcaster | NBC
Awards | 5 Emmys
For fans of . . . | *Law and Order* (1990), *Homicide: Life on the Street* (1993), *CSI* (2000)

The progenitor of the modern police procedural drama, *Dragnet* captured not just the excitement and adventure of catching criminals, but also the gritty reality of police work for the first time. The series was the brainchild of Jack Webb, a radio voice actor who became interested in producing such a show after performing a small role in the 1948 movie *He Walked by Night*. Webb, who played *Dragnet*'s central character, Sergeant Joe Friday, for decades, believed the show should portray police work as accurately as possible, and sent scripts to the Los Angeles Police Department for endorsement. Scripts were written in the understated, clipped fashion of hard-boiled detective fiction, and the show made every effort to avoid melodrama.

Dragnet began life as a radio drama before moving into television in the 1950s, where it was an immediate success. In its heyday, only *I Love Lucy* could compete with *Dragnet*'s ratings. The show influenced generations of police procedurals to come, including shows such as *The French Connection* and *Homicide: Life on the Streets*. It is famously associated with the phrase "Just the facts, ma'am," even though this was never actually said on the show (the closest version was "all we want are the facts, ma'am"). The catchphrase is still in use decades after it was first included in a *Dragnet* parody called *St. George and the Dragnet*, a 45 rpm single released by Stan Freberg for Capitol Records in 1953. **AP**

Classic episode
The Big Cast | Season 1, episode 5. Lee Marvin gave such a powerful performance as a serial killer in this early episode that he landed a starring role in his own copycat police procedural, *M Squad*.

⊘ Jack Webb as Sergeant Joe Friday in *Dragnet*.

I Love Lucy

Comedy | USA | 1951–57

The sitcom that helped define the future of TV. Waaaaah!

Cast | Lucille Ball, Desi Arnaz, William Frawley, Vivian Vance, Joseph A. Mayer, Michael Mayer
Original broadcaster | CBS
Awards | 4 Emmys
For fans of . . . | *The Carol Burnett Show* (1967)

The premise was simple: the misadventures of homemaker Lucy Ricardo, played by film star Lucille Ball, married to Cuban bandleader Ricky, portrayed by Ball's husband, Desi Arnaz, based on her radio comedy *My Favorite Husband* (1953). ("We decided," she said, "that instead of divorce lawyers profiting from our mistakes, *we'd* profit from them.") But it didn't simply fill a half hour on the fledgling CBS network: magic was born.

It is impossible to ponder the history of TV without focusing on *I Love Lucy*. The production was flawless, the laughs boundless, the core cast—completed by William Frawley and Vivian Vance as cantankerous neighbors Fred and Ethel Mertz—one of TV's finest quartets. At its heart was a pioneer who would become the queen of American TV; the quintessential clown.

Instead of being broadcast live from New York, it was filmed on three cameras in Hollywood, preserving it for posterity and essentially inventing the TV rerun. Shot with a studio audience, its laugh track was live and reactive, and is still sampled today. Skyrocketing ratings provided Ball and Arnaz with clout, raising the profile of their company, Desilu Productions. Later acquired by Paramount, Desilu—with Ball firmly at the helm—shepherded TV icons, including *Star Trek* (1966) and *Mission: Impossible* (1966), into the spotlight.

I Love Lucy only ran six seasons as a weekly sitcom, followed by three years of sporadic one-hour specials. But it has run in syndication for over sixty years, creating one of TV's most celebrated legacies. **SL**

Sue Vida Me Pertence

Soap opera | Brazil | 1951–52

This slightly racy serial pioneered a new TV genre that was exported all over the world

Cast | Vida Alves, Walter Forster, Lia de Aguiar, José Parisi, Lima Duarte, Dionisio de Azevedo, Néa Simões, João Monteiro, Astrogildo Filho
Original broadcaster | TV Tupi
For fans of . . . | *The Girl Watchers* (1969)

The Portuguese-language *Sua Vida Me Pertence* (*Your Life Belongs to Me*) was the first telenovela, a genre that took off in Latin America and then spread to other parts of the globe. Though often described as Spanish soap opera, the telenovela differs from the usual soap format in that it focuses on one main story and reaches a conclusion after a set number of episodes. Like American TV soap, which had its origins on the radio, the telenovela was a natural evolution of the radionovela.

Sua Vida Me Pertence was broadcast in black and white just over a year after the launch of TV Tupi, Brazil's first TV station, in São Paulo. The series debuted in December 1951 and lasted for just fifteen episodes, shown twice a week and performed live. The story centered on an attractive young girl, played by Vida Alves, and her "will they, won't they" romance with a respectable and enamored young man, played by Walter Forster. Controversially, the couple showed the first mouth-to-mouth kiss on Brazilian television. As well as spawning many more telenovelas, a genre that has now grown into a huge industry, with its modern successors running for eight months to a year, *Sua Vida Me Pertence* proved a launching pad for the career of Forster. He went on to star in many TV series and movies, including *Amor Estranho Amor* (1982), *The Girl Watchers* (1969), and *Aventuras com Tio Maneço* (1971) for which he was best known. Forster worked right up until his death in 1996, aged seventy nine. **JA**

◉ Lucille Ball on the cutting edge in the 1953 episode, "Lucy Tells the Truth."

American Bandstand

Variety | USA | 1952–89

"It's got a good beat and you can dance to it"

Cast | Bob Horn, Dick Clark, Charlie O'Donnell
Original broadcasters | WFIL-TV, ABC, syndication, USA Network
Awards | 2 Emmys
For fans of . . . | *Top of the Pops* (1964)

"American Bandstand," marveled John Oates of Hall & Oates, "spread the gospel of American pop music and teenage style that transcended the regional boundaries of our country and united a youth culture that eventually spread its message throughout the entire world." Originating in Philadelphia and expanding nationally by 1957, the show (originally just *Bandstand*) featured live, usually lip-synched, performances from both popular and up-and-coming singers and bands, with teens grooving to the latest tunes. (The dancers won fans of their own—and, in 1979, invented The Village People's "Y.M.C.A." hand movements.) When disc jockey Dick Clark took over from the first host Bob Horn in 1956, he transformed America's relationship with Top 40 pop music with weekday episodes that ran for ninety minutes (although some network affiliates cut episodes to an hour or even thirty minutes, and the main show eventually moved to Saturdays only).

Memorable moments included a 1970 appearance by The Jackson Five, Prince's national TV debut in 1980, and, in 1985, rising star Madonna's answer to Clark's question about her future plans: "To rule the world."

The advent of MTV signaled the end of *Bandstand*'s reign. Clark left in 1987, and the show's final incarnation—hosted by David Hirsch—lasted only six months. However, a fiftieth anniversary celebration in 2002 starred Michael Jackson, and Clark's death in 2012 occasioned tributes from luminaries such as Motown founder Berry Gordy and President Obama. **ATB**

This is Your Life

Reality | USA | 1952–61

Shining a spotlight on stars and ordinary Joes

Cast | Ralph Edwards
Original broadcaster | NBC
Awards | 2 Emmys, 1 Golden Globe
For fans of . . . | *Person to Person* (1953), *This is Your Life* (UK, 1955)

It could have been you. Every time producer and host Ralph Edwards appeared at the beginning of an episode of *This is Your Life* (which originally ran on the radio from 1948 to 1952), the book of someone's life in hand, no one knew whom he might select as the subject of that day's story. From big-name actors to people from all walks of life, including survivors of the Holocaust and the Hiroshima bombing, anyone might become the star of his or her own biographical drama. Over the course of an hour, relatives, friends, and associates might join the subjects on stage as Edwards narrated their life and times.

Most people were surprised at becoming the focus of an episode, but not all enjoyed or even tolerated the attention. Some were angered, including Lowell Thomas and Stan Laurel, but most enjoyed their time in the spotlight. The one person who would never become the subject of the show—under the threat of mass crew firings—was Edwards himself. The show did suffer from criticism of its limited research that often failed to reveal the full details of a subject's life, as well as its reliance on tearful histrionics. Edwards produced short-lived follow-up series in the 1970s and '80s. Two attempts to revive the show in the 2000s didn't go into production. In the UK, Irish presenter Eamonn Andrews hosted a British version of the show from 1955 to 1964 and again from 1969 to 1987. The series continued with new host Michael Aspel until 2003, and it was briefly revived in 2007 by Trevor McDonald. **ATB**

Adventures of Superman

Action/Adventure | USA | 1952–58

High-flying superhero series that brought an American icon to TV for the first time

Cast | George Reeves, Phyllis Coates, Noel Neill, Jack Larson, John Hamilton, Robert Shayne
Original broadcaster | Syndication
For fans of . . . | *Batman* (1966)

It's hard to think about this series without allowing the mysterious details of star George Reeves' final days to color one's perception. Although tragedy may have befallen the man who wore the cape, the character he embodied through six seasons became a hero for a generation and continues to inspire new fans today.

The show was developed by Whitney Ellsworth and Robert J. Maxwell from the *Superman* comics published by DC Comics since 1938, and was preceded by an hour-long feature film—*Superman and the Mole Men* (1951)—later adapted into a two-part episode. The series built up several clichés, such as the fact that one pair of glasses was sufficient to convince everyone that Clark Kent and Superman were two different people. While there were mad scientists and other fantasy threats, budgetary limitations usually meant that the show was most often a police procedural with tights.

The show went through several changes, from a Lois Lane swap (Noel Neill for Phyllis Coates) to the then-spectacular shift from black-and-white to full color. That also meant trading in Reeves' original suit—in brown and gray—for one in the red, blue, and yellow of the comic book Superman. Even without the trademark "S" spit curl that usually accompanied other versions of the character, Reeves was a natural with his square-jawed determination and winning smile. And for the children who watched him battle for truth, justice, and the American way, as well as countless fans for decades after that, Reeves was Superman . . . and always will be. **ATB**

Classic episode
Superman's Wife | *Season 6, episode 9*. In the series' 100th episode, Lois is heartbroken when Superman decides to marry Sergeant Helen J. O'Hara, but the wedding is a sham designed to force the hand of a foe known as Mr. X.

◮ Don't mess with the Man of Steel (George Reeves).

Academy Awards

Awards show | USA | 1953–present

A promotional vehicle for the latest movies gives Hollywood stars the chance to dress up and make embarrassing acceptance speeches

Classic episode
77th Academy Awards, 2005. Chris Rock hosted. George Clooney won Best Supporting Actor for *Syriana* and made a speech about Hattie McDaniel that was memorable but, not universally well received.

◑ The twenty-fifth-anniversary event was the first to be televised, in 1953.

Hosts | Bob Hope, Jerry Lewis, Jack Lemmon, Frank Sinatra, Johnny Carson, Walter Matthau, Billy Crystal, Whoopi Goldberg, Ellen DeGeneres
Original broadcaster | NBC
For fans of . . . | *Golden Globe Awards* (1958)

The first Academy Awards ceremony was held in May 1929 at the Hollywood Roosevelt Hotel. Thirteen Oscars were handed out, including one for Best Title Writing (that is, subtitles)—a category that did not reappear, thanks to the success of *The Jazz Singer* (1927) and the rapid decline of the silent pictures. Since 1940, when the *LA Times* leaked the identities of the winners ahead of the ceremony, Price Waterhouse has been "the guardian of secrets," ensuring that the names inside those "winner" envelopes remain secret until they're announced live on-screen. That was the year in which Hattie McDaniel became the first African American to win an Oscar (as Best Supporting Actress for *Gone with the Wind*); Sidney Poitier was the second, in 1964, for *Lilies of the Field*, by which time the ceremony was being shown on television.

The twenty-fifth ceremony in 1953 was the first to be televised. The live show was soon attracting forty million viewers in the United States and an estimated one billion viewers for the highlights shown later worldwide, and thus became established as the single biggest advertisement a film could have.

Television has even influenced when the awards actually happen; having traditionally been held on Monday nights, the ceremony shifted back a day in 1999 to take advantage of the potentially larger Sunday night audience. It also takes up a big chunk of the schedule—over three hours of it (the event in 2000 even passed the four-hour mark). **JS**

The Quatermass Experiment

Fantasy/Horror/Sci-Fi | UK | 1953

British TV's first sci-fi hero tackles aliens—live!

Cast | Reginald Tate, Isabel Dean, Hugh Kelly, Paul Whitsun-Jones, Duncan Lamont, John Glen, Ian Colin
Original broadcaster | BBC
For fans of . . . | *The Twilight Zone* (1959), *The Outer Limits* (1963), *Doctor Who* (1963)

Playing on the fears and paranoias of postwar Britain, writer Nigel Kneale's Quatermass series terrified the nation and inspired British sci-fi dramas for years to come. In *The Quatermass Experiment*, scientist Bernard Quatermass takes responsibility when his experimental rocket launch results in the disappearance of two of its three-man crew and the survivor begins a murderous transformation into something horrifically alien. A sequel, 1955's *Quatermass II*, targeted the phenomenon of new towns and shady government complexes that appeared overnight, and was preceded by a warning for "viewers of a nervous disposition." A third case, 1958's *Quatermass and the Pit*, postulated that an alien craft uncovered beneath London could be the last remnant of an invasion that took place millions of years before.

The Quatermass Experiment was a result of the rise in TV ownership after the coronation of Queen Elizabeth II (most early TV output had been merely radio programs with pictures). With little to keep this nascent audience entertained, executives decided to create a new, visual form of drama and called upon writer Kneale and director Rudolph Cartier. Broadcast live from tiny studios in West London, the performances can seem a little stagy to modern eyes, yet the ambition of the production cannot be faulted.

All three *Quatermass* serials were adapted for the big screen by Hammer Studios, while the first was also remade as a live TV event in 2005. A fourth *Quatermass* series, starring John Mills, aired on ITV in 1979. **JS**

The Good Old Days

Variety | UK | 1953–83

Reviving the raucous glamour of the music hall

Cast | Leonard Sachs, Don Gemmell
Original broadcaster | BBC
For fans of . . . | *Come Dancing* (1949), *Top Hat Rendezvous* (1951), *The Music Box* (1957), *The Black and White Minstrel Show* (1958)

As the band played "Down at the Old Bull and Bush", the audience, dressed in period costume, jostled for position in the packed City Varieties Music Hall in Leeds, England. The master of ceremonies, in his place in a pulpit to the side of the stage, began a soliloquy of melodious magnificence, then made way for an hour of variety acts.

Eternally nostalgic, *The Good Old Days* took viewers back a century to the time when popular entertainment was a communal affair in a theater. Novelty acts like magicians and acrobats would share the stage with the top comedians and light entertainers of the time to delight and enthrall—all in the spirit of the age they attempted to re-create. Don Gemmell was the first master of ceremonies, but it was in Leonard Sachs (also an actor, with turns in *Doctor Who* (1963) among his credits) that the series found its true frontman. Oozing charm, he constructed gushing, alliterative introductions to each act, prompting the audience to whoop and cheer at each contrived link.

Popular comedians Les Dawson and Larry Grayson could almost have stepped out of time, such was the ease with which they transformed their own act into something more imperial. Occasionally guests would surprise as they abandoned their popular image—Edward Woodward, familiar as the hardboiled hero of *Callan* (1967), proved to be a singer with an engaging baritone voice. By keeping the format the same, but the guests up to date, the series survived for thirty years. **JS**

Make Room for Daddy

Comedy | USA | 1953–65

How a man balanced his family life with his nightclub career

Cast | Danny Thomas, Jean Hagen, Angela Cartwright, Marjorie Lord, Louise Beavers, Amanda Randolph
Original broadcasters | ABC, CBS
Awards | 5 Emmys
For fans of . . . | *The Brady Bunch* (1969)

Modeled on the life of entertainer Danny Thomas, *Make Room for Daddy* documented the struggles of Danny Williams, whose successful nightclub career made him miss out on the daily lives of his wife and children. Fun-loving Danny ceded most of the parenting of his children, Terry and Rusty (Sherry Jackson and Rusty Hamer), to his more serious wife, Margaret (Jean Hagen), and their housekeeper, Louise (Louise Beavers).

The series took a sharp turn in its fourth season when Hagen left the show. Rather than replace her with a new actress, the character was killed off and the series focused on Danny's new status as a single and dating widower. Daddy, and the family, eventually made room for a new wife, Kathy (Marjorie Lord), and her adorable daughter, Linda (Angela Cartwright). In due course, Kathy adopted Terry and Rusty, Danny adopted Linda, Amanda Rudolph replaced Louise Beavers, and they all moved into a new apartment. This new and higher-rated family unit would be so solidified in viewers' minds that most forgot about the first three seasons—a testament to the on-air chemistry of the cast.

The show remains a prime example of how characters—and actors—can evolve over the course of a series. (A sequel, *Make Room for Granddaddy*, lasted one season in 1970–71.) Danny Thomas' personal legacy, fueled as much by his own talents as by the popularity of *Make Room For Daddy*, was sealed by his founding of St. Jude Children's Research Hospital, now a leader in the treatment of children's cancers. **RP**

Fabian of the Yard

Crime/Mystery | UK | 1954–56

A glossy police drama based on real-life British crime cases

Cast | Bruce Seton, Robert Raglan, Philip Dale, Jack Melford, John Boxer
Original broadcaster | BBC
For fans of . . . | *Dixon of Dock Green* (1955), *Z Cars* (1962), *The Bill* (1984)

The casebooks of the man who was—in the words of the show's regular introduction—"hailed by the press as one of England's greatest detectives" formed the basis of the BBC's first ongoing police serial. Robert Fabian (Bruce Seton) presented each case and then explained precisely how he cracked it, using "routine, detailed, science, and tenacity"—the best weapons available at the "brain of Great Britain's manhunting machine," the Metropolitan Police Service's headquarters, Scotland Yard.

At the end of each episode, the fictional Fabian was replaced by the real thing (a retired detective superintendent who, when he visited the United States, was irritated to find that people expected him to look and act like Sherlock Holmes). This quirk reinforced the factual accuracy of the production, even if Fabian himself was more than a little wooden in his delivery.

Fabian of the Yard stands out in part because it was shot on film, allowing for fast editing and location shoots that were particularly handy for showing off the detective's beautiful black Humber Hawk squad car. It also enabled the BBC to re-air the series, while a few episodes were edited together to make feature-length productions released in movie theaters: *Fabian of the Yard* (1954) and *Handcuffs, London* (1955).

The series was titled *Fabian of Scotland Yard* in the United States and *Patrol Car* in Australia. Sadly, fewer than a third of the thirty-six episodes produced between 1954 and 1956 survive in the archives. **JS**

◀ Father and son bonding with Danny Thomas and Rusty Hamer.

Father Knows Best

Comedy | USA | 1954–60

Featuring an all-American family from the Midwest, this was the first family sitcom

Cast | Robert Young, Jane Wyatt, Elinor Donahue, Billy Gray, Lauren Chapin
Original broadcaster | CBS **Awards** | 6 Emmys
For fans of . . . | *Make Room for Daddy* (1953), *The Donna Reed Show* (1958)

Never controversial or edgy, *Father Knows Best* knew what it did best—showing an almost-perfect vision of what an American family should—or could—be. One of several popular 1950s television shows that started out on radio, the pilot of *Father Knows Best* was called *Keep It in the Family* and produced for The Ford Television Theatre slot in 1954. Robert Young, who played the father Jim Anderson, was the only actor in the pilot to also appear in the series, which was picked up by CBS later the same year. During the course of the long-running series Young won two Emmy awards.

In the show, Jim spent his days as an insurance agent, but his evenings were spent in the company of his loving wife, Margaret, played by Jane Wyatt (who also won Emmys), daughters Betty and Kathy (Elinor Donahue and Lauren Chapin), and son Bud (Billy Gray). Whether suffering from sporting disappointments or dating heartbreak, the Anderson children were comforted by the fact that their parents, especially their father, could be counted on for sound advice.

In 1977, the show spawned two made-for-television reunion movies, *Father Knows Best Reunion* and *Father Knows Best: Home For Christmas*, becoming one of the first TV shows to make the transition to the big screen. The movies, in which the Anderson children had offspring of their own, didn't break new ground, but they provided the public with what they were looking for—an escape to a time when all the world's problems could be solved in less than thirty minutes. **RP**

The Tonight Show

Talk show | USA | 1954–present

The legendary king at the heart of late-night talk TV

Cast | Steve Allen, Jack Paar, Johnny Carson, Jay Leno, Conan O'Brien, Jimmy Fallon (current)
Original broadcaster | NBC
For fans of . . . | *Parkinson* (1971), *Late Show with David Letterman* (1993)

Late-night TV in the United States has been a cavalcade of talk shows, variety hours, news features, and game shows for decades, but at its heart is *The Tonight Show*. Conceived as a vehicle for light entertainment and chat, along with comedy sketches and musical numbers, the program debuted in 1954 with host Steve Allen. Little did he know a TV legacy had been born.

The Tonight Show emerged as the place Americans wrapped up their day; everybody who was somebody would venture on to the show, from the latest starlet to the biggest stars Hollywood had to offer. Alternatively broadcast from New York, then Los Angeles and now back in the Big Apple, it was a reflection of its times, but never more so than with Johnny Carson as its popular host. It was also not without its controversies, such as longtime guest host Joan Rivers going up against Carson on the fledgling Fox network, Jay Leno's appointment as host in 1992 (eschewing Carson's preferred successor David Letterman, who went on to score big competing against *The Tonight Show* with his own late-night talk show on rival CBS), or the departure of Conan O'Brien after six months to be replaced by his predecessor, Jay Leno.

From classic characters such as Carnac the Magnificent to bizarre moments such as the wedding of Tiny Tim and Miss Vicki, *The Tonight Show* has remained a vital part of American entertainment and a mainstay of late-night fun for more than sixty years. There is no end in sight, nor should there be. **SL**

Alfred Hitchcock Presents

Drama | USA | 1955–65

The master of suspense himself lent his name and image to this iconic anthology series of spine-chilling mystery stories

Cast | Alfred Hitchcock
Original broadcaster | CBS
Awards | 3 Emmys, 1 Golden Globe
For fans of . . . | *The Twilight Zone* (1959), *The X-Files* (1993), *American Horror Story* (2011)

When it comes to anthology series, none is more memorable than *Alfred Hitchcock Presents*, a weekly dose of suspense drama to which Alfred Hitchcock famously lent his name. From the menacing opening to the twist endings and concluding remarks by Hitchcock himself, the half-hour slot mesmerized audiences. The stories ranged from psychological horror to traditional thrillers and midcentury noir mysteries.

A success from the start, *Alfred Hitchcock Presents* attracted top creative talents, including director Robert Altman, writer Roald Dahl, and actors Steve McQueen and Walter Matthau. The show also generated spin-off books, including mystery anthologies written in the style of the TV series and stories based on scripts that had failed to get past the censors and so had not made it onto the screen. The series continued for seven years, then turned into *Alfred Hitchcock Hour* in 1962. When the show went off the air in 1965, it remained a ratings success in syndication, and an updated version of the series was shown by NBC in 1985.

Perhaps the most enduring memory of the program was its opening sequence, when Hitchcock would walk on-screen and eclipse his own rotund caricature to the unforgettable strains of Charles Gounoud's "Funeral March of a Marionette." After this, Hitchcock would wish the viewers good evening and introduce that week's story. More than half a century later, the combination of image and sound signifies one thing: Alfred Hitchcock. **AP**

Classic episode
Lamb to the Slaughter | *Season 3, episode 28.*
Written by Roald Dahl and directed by Hitchcock himself, this episode features a meek housewife ridding herself of a philandering husband and ensuring the murder weapon will never be found.

⊙ Hitchcock in a promotional portrait for *Alfred Hitchcock Presents*.

Dixon of Dock Green

Crime/Mystery | UK | 1955–76

"Evenin', all." Parochial charm and mild peril in "stories of a London policeman"

Classic episode
The Roaring Boy | *Season 2, episode 11.* In this 1956 helping, a soldier (Kenneth Cope) on the run winds up with a hostage, a gun, and Dixon in his sights. Cope later found fame in *Coronation Street* and *Randall and Hopkirk (Deceased)*.

◎ Jack Warner in the role for which he is best remembered. He played George Dixon for more than twenty years.

Cast | Jack Warner, Peter Byrne, Geoffrey Adams, Arthur Rigby, Jeanette Hutchinson, Nicholas Donnelly
Original broadcaster | BBC
For fans of . . . | *Fabian of the Yard* (1954), *Z Cars* (1962), *The Bill* (1984), *Law & Order: UK* (2009)

George Dixon first featured in the Ealing Studios movie *The Blue Lamp* (1950), in which he was shot dead by Dirk Bogarde's trigger-happy villain. Resurrected by his creator, Ted Willis, for this BBC series, Dixon was again played by former music-hall star Jack Warner.

Dixon reassured the viewers that they could sleep safe in their beds, regardless of activities planned by London's criminals. Solid, dependable, and paternal toward the younger officers, Dixon was a family man with principles and a good, old-fashioned attitude. He spoke to viewers—literally, as each episode began with a little introduction from him, delivered straight to the camera, and ended with a similar homily. Such was the close relationship between Dixon and his fans—among whom were many police officers—that he even closed one season by warning them he wouldn't be around for a while as he was going on holiday.

Early episodes were broadcast live, which is why so few of them survive in the archives. Later seasons faced stiff competition from the harder-hitting *Z-Cars* (1962) and ITV's glossy *Special Branch* (1969), but the show lasted until 1976, clocking up 430 episodes.

Aged fifty-nine when the series began, Warner was eighty when the show finished. At a royal award ceremony in 1965, he recalled in his autobiography, he had been hailed as a part of the fabric of Britain. But this coziness looked out of touch in a world where the police were more likely to face terrorists and gangsters than petty thieves and wayward teens. **JS**

Gunsmoke

Western | USA | 1955–75

Longest-running prime-time, scripted, live-action drama in the twentieth century

Cast | James Arness, Milburn Stone, Amanda Blake, Dennis Weaver, Ken Curtis, Glenn Strange, Buck Taylor
Original broadcaster | CBS
Awards | 5 Emmys
For fans of . . . | *Bonanza* (1959)

For many, *Gunsmoke* remains *the* Western series, if only by virtue of its longevity. No other prime-time, scripted, live-action drama ran for longer, and—alongside *The Life and Legend of Wyatt Earp* (1955)—it ushered in a veritable gold rush of TV Westerns for adult viewers. Central to its success was James Arness' earnest performance as craggy-faced Marshal Dillon of Dodge City, Kansas—a hero and paternal figure whose relationship with saloon owner Miss Kitty (Amanda Blake) was implicit but chaste. John Wayne — who, legend has it, was considered for the role—recommended his good friend Arness for the job, and subsequently introduced the pilot episode.

Created by John Meston and Norman Macdonnell, *Gunsmoke* began on radio in 1952, with William Conrad as Dillon, then made the transition to TV. The series began with thirty-minute, black-and-white episodes in its first six seasons (1955–61, later rerun as *Marshal Dillon*), expanded to an hour for five seasons (1961–66), and evolved into color for the final nine years.

When ratings dropped in the late 1960s, a move from Saturday to Monday sent the show surging back into the top ten. When it was finally canceled, the cast had no warning and learned their fate from press reports. Nonetheless, *Gunsmoke* helped establish a standard for adult Western storytelling that has rarely been matched on the small or big screen. A little-known comedy spin-off, *Dirty Sally*, aired in 1974, and Arness returned for five TV-movie sequels that aired from 1987 to 1994. **ATB**

Classic episode
The Jailer | *Season 12, episode 3.* Hollywood legend Bette Davis appears as a deranged matriarch seeking revenge for her husband's hanging. This 1966 episode also stars Bruce Dern, Tom Skerritt, and future director Zalman King.

◉ (Clockwise, from top left) Glenn Strange, Ken Curtis, Roger Ewing, Milburn Stone, Amanda Blake, and James Arness.

The Adventures of Robin Hood

Historical drama | UK | 1955–59

Robbing from the rich, giving to the poor, the Merry Men reinvent an enduring English legend

Cast | Richard Greene, Bernadette O'Farrell, Patricia Driscoll, Alan Wheatley, Alexander Gauge, Archie Duncan, Rufus Cruikshank, Paul Eddington **Original broadcaster** | ITV **For fans of . . .** | *Robin of Sherwood* (1984)

Taking its cue (and title) from a 1938 film starring Errol Flynn, this lavish series ran for four years and, for some, became the definitive version of the Robin Hood legend. Its closing theme song, a jolly folk song, has passed into popular culture to the point that many wouldn't recognize its origins from a TV show: "Robin Hood, Robin Hood, riding through the glen. . . ."

The BBC had televised the tale in 1953 with Patrick Troughton in the lead, but it was Richard Greene's jovial hero who really left his mark. Amid the familiar band of outlaws, including Friar Tuck, Little John, and Will Scarlet, a significant divergence from the legend was Maid Marian—less a damsel in distress, more an action heroine, and Robin's best female friend.

However, Alan Wheatley as the Sheriff of Nottingham stole every episode. Keeping to the right side of camp, Wheatley's wicked sheriff was a joy to behold as he suffered repeated defeats, but survived to scheme another day. The series paved the way for serials such as *Ivanhoe* and *The Adventures of William Tell* (both 1958), though none made quite as big an impact. **JS**

Classic episode

The Trap | *Season 2, episode 14*. Exasperated by the resilience of the Merry Men, the Sheriff of Nottingham dispatches a spy (Alfred Burke, best known for 1965's *Public Eye*) to infiltrate the gang and undermine Robin's authority from within.

◈ Richard Greene's Robin Hood—the Katniss Everdeen of his day—with his reliable band of merry men.

The Benny Hill Show

Comedy | UK | 1955–89

Slapstick, mime, and sauciness are the trademark ingredients of this massive global hit

Cast | Benny Hill **Original broadcaster** | BBC **Awards** | 2 BAFTAs
For fans of . . . | *The Two Ronnies* (1971)

Although many series carried this title over the years, the two must-see periods are the black-and-white BBC shows from 1955 to 1968, which made the young Benny Hill a smash hit in the United Kingdom, and the widely exported ITV color shows from 1969 to 1989, which made him a global star. The BBC series often included spoofs of other TV shows. Using clever camerawork and split-screen techniques to play all the parts himself, Hill would lampoon game shows such as *What's My Line?* (1950) and the BBC pop show *Juke Box Jury* (1959). Another hallmark was his comic deconstruction of the making of film and television, with sketches about faulty microphones, actors performing to the wrong camera, and singers miming to records that get stuck.

Hill's twenty-year run of commercial television shows developed his love of musical comedy, mime, and slapstick, often with an underlying sauciness. Although elements of this comedy were later regarded as sexist and outdated, at the time the shows were phenomenally popular and made Hill the most successful global comedian since Charlie Chaplin. **DF**

Classic episode
Season 19, episode 3, 1 May, 1989. What turned out to be Hill's final TV show featured ingenious takeoffs of the title sequences of various popular programs, including *The Bill* and *Tales of the Unexpected.*

⬙ A young Benny Hill poses with the medium that was to make his name, in his London apartment, in 1955.

The Honeymooners

Comedy | USA | 1955–56

Working-class comedy that established a long-lasting sitcom template

Cast | Jackie Gleason, Art Carney, Audrey Meadows, Joyce Randolph   **Original broadcaster** | CBS
Award | 1 Emmy   **For fans of . . .** | *I Love Lucy* (1951)

The 1950s sitcom *The Honeymooners* only aired for thirty-nine episodes, but made a lasting impact on pop culture. The show captured a postwar image of working-class people striving to achieve the American dream while clinging to love, friendship, and everyday triumphs over adversity. Brooklyn bus driver blowhard Ralph Kramden (Jackie Gleason) and his best friend, sewer worker Ed Norton (Art Carney), contended with their assertive wives, Alice (Audrey Meadows) and Trixie (Joyce Randolph), while chasing get-rich-quick schemes and tripping over their own ambitions.

Although episodes were filmed, they were performed as if live with minimal rehearsal; to cover lapses in scripted action, Gleason would touch his stomach to signal he had forgotten a line, and Meadows would eye the refrigerator if someone was meant to use it. The claustrophobic single-room apartment set reinforced the show's focus on character, with the Kramden bedroom never glimpsed. Animated fireworks and a theme song composed by Gleason, "You're My Greatest Love," heralded the start of every episode. **ATB**

Classic episode

The $99,000 Answer | *Season 1, episode 18*. Ralph is going on a game show where he will have to answer questions about popular songs. He eventually faces the $99,000 question about a song he knows very well . . . but cannot name.

⊘ Gleason, Carney, Meadows, and Randolph in the sparsely furnished apartment where most of the action took place.

Was bin ich?

Game show | Germany | 1955–58;1961–89

Germany embraced this long-running panel quiz show based on What's My Line?

Cast | Robert Lembke, Björn Hergen
Original broadcaster | ARD **For fans of . . .** | *To Tell the Truth* (1956), *Would I lie to You?* (2007)

Such was the success of *What's My Line?*, on CBS network, that the format for the celebrity panel game was sold to TV broadcasters in twelve other countries, including Germany. Each TV channel produced its own version of the show.

Bavarian Robert Lembke, head of the news division of Bayerischer Rundfunk, sought the rights to the show after seeing the British version during a visit to the BBC in 1954. *Was Bin Ich?* (*What Am I?*) launched on Germany's ARD TV channel the following year, with Lembke as the host. In it, a panel of four celebrities were tasked with deducing the occupation of a guest by asking questions to which the guest could answer only yes or no. For the "celebrity guest of honor" round,

the panelists had to identify a well-known guest by name while blindfolded. After every "no," Lembke would deposit five Deutsche Marks, in one of several colored piggy banks, and questioning passed to the next panelist. This gave rise to Lembke's catchphrase, "Which piggy would you like to have?" The sound of the coin dropping into the pig was a ritual of the show.

The lineup occasionally changed, but the best-known panelists were district attorney Hans Sachs, actress Marianne Koch, TV announcers Annette von Aretin and Anneliese Fleyenschmidt, and Guido Baumann, head of the Swiss TV station DRS. The show was canceled in 1958, but returned in 1961, still hosted by Lembke, and lasted until his death in 1989. **JA**

◉ Quizmaster Robert Lembke and his mascot, Jacky, who guarded the all-important piggy banks in *Was bin ich?*

The Phil Silvers Show
Comedy | USA | 1955–59

Sergeant Bilko schemes to get rich quick—
"Look alive!"

Cast | Phil Silvers, Harvey Lembeck, Allan Melvin, Paul Ford
Original broadcaster | CBS
Awards | 8 Emmys
For fans of . . . | *Blackadder* (1983)

Comic actor Phil Silvers made a name for himself when he won a Tony award for Broadway's *Top Banana* (1951), but he is best known as Master Sergeant Ernest G. Bilko in the self-titled *The Phil Silvers Show*. It was a vehicle for Silvers' ability to imbue his rakish character with enough heart for the audience to want him to get away with his various shenanigans. By setting the series on an army base in Kansas, rather than in an active military zone, the program was able to parlay post-Korean War patriotism without having to worry about actual warfare.

Winning three consecutive Emmys for comedy, *The Phil Silvers Show* centered around Bilko taking advantage of his soldiers, but it was his superior, Colonel Hall (Paul Ford), who was most often the target of his machinations. Silvers became so associated with his performance as the lovable rogue that its sweet-yet-salty veneer followed him to other roles, most notably as a cunning producer on *Gilligan's Island* (1964), a greedy racer in the all-star comic romp *It's a Mad, Mad, Mad, Mad, World* (1963), and on Broadway in 1972 as the Machiavellian slave, Pseudolus, in Stephen Sondheim's *A Funny Thing Happened on the Way to the Forum*.

After the show relocated to California, the base was frequented by characters played by the most popular stars of the day, but none could hold a candle to Bilko—without him trying to sell them matches. **RP**

❯ Phil Silvers (seated center) and his right-hand men.

Eurovision Song Contest

Music/Musical | Various | 1956–present

International competition known for outlandish performances and controversial voting

Cast | Performers included: ABBA, Bucks Fizz, Celine Dion, Dana, Johnny Logan, Julio Iglesias, Katrina and the Waves
Original broadcaster | Various
For fans of . . . | *Jeux Sans Frontières* (1965)

The Eurovision Song Contest is an annual music competition seen by nearly two hundred million people, making it one of the most watched TV shows in the world. Over five decades, fifty-one countries have competed for the prize: a trophy and the chance to host the following year's contest.

Just seven nations took part in the first show, hosted in and won by Switzerland in 1956. Before satellite technology, and in a Europe still recovering from the Second World War, a live entertainment show broadcast across multiple countries was groundbreaking.

The voting is controversial. Each country gives points to ten songs, with twelve points going to its favorite. Countries aren't allowed to vote for their own song, but many vote for one another every year, perhaps through shared politics and history or similar musical tastes and cultures. Nevertheless, winning the contest requires support from across the continent.

The show reaches well beyond the borders of Europe—Israel and Azerbaijan have both been victorious. With so many countries involved, the contest exhibits a range of languages and musical styles, although power ballads are particularly well represented. Winners have ranged from Celine Dion and ABBA, who reached worldwide stardom after their victories, to Lordi, a Finnish hardrock band who wear monster masks while performing. But it's the eclectic range of songs and kitsch performances that make *The Eurovision Song Contest* event television. **WH**

The Nat King Cole Show

Variety | USA | 1956–57

The first TV variety show hosted by an African American

Cast | Nat King Cole with Nelson Riddle and the Randy Van Horne Singers
Original broadcaster | NBC
For fans of . . . | *The Judy Garland Show* (1963), *Saturday Night Live* (1975)

As the reigning monarch of jazz piano, Nat King Cole commanded stages of all sizes across the globe. The next logical kingdom for him to conquer lay on the TV landscape. Cole's blend of personality and musicality was perfect for the intimate experience of TV viewing. With a smooth, easygoing style and hits such as "Nature Boy" and "Straighten Up and Fly Right," King's vocal styling and guests, including such heavyweights as Peggy Lee, Harry Belafonte, and Ella Fitzgerald, was a surefire recipe for success.

Although *The Nat King Cole Show* started with a modest fifteen-minute running time, it soon expanded to thirty minutes, thanks to King's unique talents. Unfortunately, despite the positive audience response, national sponsors feared that 1956 was not the ideal time for an African American to be beamed into US living rooms and refused to put their money toward keeping the show on the air. Local sponsors were slightly more generous (and forward-thinking), but the production was never able to overcome the financial barriers, and the show ended a little more than a year after it first hit the small screen.

Cole was able to recover from the failure of the show, and went on to perform on other people's TV shows, as well as in films and on stages around the world for years to come. His legacy as a brilliant and charismatic musician—kept alive in part by his daughter, entertainer Natalie Cole—is further brightened by his historic mark on the TV landscape. **RP**

Hancock's Half Hour

Comedy | UK | 1956–61

The morose musings of a much-challenged pessimist—
"Stone me, what a life!"

Cast | Tony Hancock, Sid James, Bill Kerr,
Andrée Melly, Kenneth Williams, Hattie
Jacques, Patricia Hayes
Original broadcaster | BBC
For fans of . . . | *The Jack Benny Program* (1950)

Transferring from a popular BBC radio series, *Hancock's Half Hour* was the product of a golden collaboration between actor Tony Hancock and writers Ray Galton and Alan Simpson. In Galton and Simpson's hands, Hancock played an exaggerated form of himself; he was pompous, paranoid, and seemingly bewildered and exasperated by every aspect of modern life. For much of the series, Hancock played off Sid James, who played his best friend and confidante. James could be guaranteed to prick his pomposity and bring him down to earth.

At a time when variety was still in fashion, *Hancock's Half Hour* was truly groundbreaking in its approach to the serious business of comedy. Galton and Simpson's scripts didn't merely consist of line after line of brilliant dialogue, but they also appreciated the importance of the gaps; the sighs and pauses might remind the viewers of the works of contemporary playwrights such as John Osborne or Harold Pinter. The final, seventh season (titled simply *Hancock*) consisted of six episodes that all stand out as classics, and was broadcast between May 26, 1961, and June 30, 1961. The most memorable of these is "The Blood Donor," in which Tony decides to do his civic duty at a local hospital, only to discover that the doctor wants more than just a pinprick of blood: "A pint? That's very nearly an armful!" He later telephones the hospital to attempt to find out the recipient of his blood and in a comedic twist he cuts himself with a bread-knife, resulting in a transfusion of his own blood. **JS**

Classic episode
Twelve Angry Men | *Season 5, episode 4.* In a parody of the 1957 film, Hancock is the foreman of a jury who persuades his fellow jurors to find the defendant not guilty, only to change his mind and work equally hard for a guilty verdict.

◭ A gloomy Tony Hancock enjoys a cup of tea, March 18, 1960.

The Price Is Right

Game show | USA | 1956–65; 1972 –present

A crowd-pleaser of a game show packed with bidding, buying, and bargaining—
"Come on down" for fun and prizes!

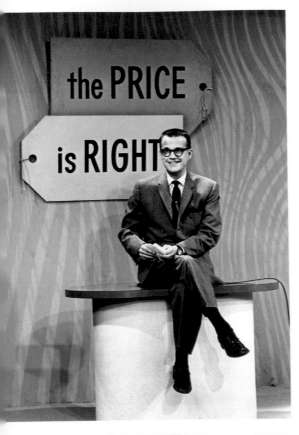

Classic episode
Season 1, episode 1. The first episode to be hosted by Bob Barker in 1972 was originally called *The New Price is Right*. Prizes included a fur coat, a self-cleaning oven, a Mazda sedan, a sewing machine, and a dishwasher.

◉ The original host Bill Cullen introduces the show in 1962.

Cast | Bill Cullen, Bob Barker, Drew Carey
Original broadcaster | CBS (current iteration)
Awards | 37 Emmys
For fans of . . . | *Let's Make a Deal* (1963), *Deal or No Deal* (2005)

"Come on down," cries the announcer, "you're the next contestant on *The Price Is Right*!" One of TV's most enduring and beloved game shows is a revival of an earlier attempt (featuring host Bill Cullen) that aired alternately on NBC and ABC in the late 1950s and early 1960s and was summarily canceled thereafter.

It returned in 1972 with the man who would become forever tied to its legacy: Bob Barker. *The Price Is Right* (originally touted as *"New,"* but later shortened to the current title) has changed little over its long history: a series of contestants, constantly rotating but never more than four at a time, compete by naming the approximate price of a prize package, with the winner then going on to play one of a series of pricing games. Universally tied to product placement, both major (the new model of a car, no matter the brand, is always a crowd-pleaser) and minor (each food or medical or cleaning product is identified and advertised), *The Price Is Right* remains, perhaps, the most adored long-running advertising franchise on TV.

Comedian Drew Carey replaced the retiring Barker in 2007 and remains its host, guiding wildly excited contestants through games such as Safe Crackers and Plinko, as well as the equally nerve-wracking Showcase Showdown final contest, with tens of thousands of dollars in products at stake. The popular format has been duplicated in more than forty countries, and in its hour-long format, it remains a popular staple on US morning TV to this day. **SL**

Emergency Ward 10
Soap opera | UK | 1957–67

British commercial TV's first successful soap opera

Cast | Jill Browne, Charles Tingwell, Glyn Owen, Joan Hooley, John White, John Alderton
Original broadcaster | ITV
For fans of . . . | *Casualty* (1986), *ER* (1994), *Grey's Anatomy* (2005)

Originally entitled *Calling Nurse Roberts* and only scheduled for a limited run, *Emergency Ward 10* (created by Tessa Diamond) went on to become a ratings phenomenon and the first successful UK super-soap. Although the soap-opera genre was developed in the United States, the notion of successful evening soaps in prime time was realized in the United Kingdom (beginning in 1954 with the BBC's *The Grove Family*) and reached true fruition with ITV's *Emergency Ward 10* and its crowd-pleasing mix of drama and romance set against the plot-heavy landscape of a busy hospital, Oxbridge General.

The series concentrated on the staff rather than the patients, although individual cases could provide plot strands and introduce a life-and-death factor into the narrative. Viewers, though, were hooked on the characters and their interactions and romantic entanglements. The very nature of the setting meant that the program reflected the real-life diversity of the National Health Service with an ethnic mix that was unusual elsewhere on UK TV. The program courted controversy in 1964 with an interracial romance between Dr. Louise Mahler (Joan Hooley) and Dr. Giles Farmer (John White) that featured the couple kissing (causing ripples in the newspapers at the time). The series pioneered the idea of two half-hour episodes per week, which proved to be a highly successful audience ploy and led to the show attracting 24 million viewers at its peak. **DF**

Il Musichiere
Game show | Italy | 1957–60

Name that Tune struck gold in Italy with its winning combination of quiz and song

Cast | Mario Riva, Gorni Kramer, Johnny Dorelli, Nuccia Bongiovanni, Paolo Bacilieri
Original broadcaster | RAI
For fans of . . . | *Name That Tune* (1953), *Lascia* (1955), *Face the Music* (1980)

Every week for three years, Italians sat down to play, laugh, and sing with *Il Musichiere*, the Italian version of NBC's *Name that Tune* (1953). The show came to an abrupt end when a fatal accident killed host and actor Mario Riva.

The rules were the same as those for the US version: Players had to guess the names of various tunes in order to accumulate money, and in the last test, one contestant had the chance to win the total prize money. The viewers' favorite part of the show was when the VIP guest—there was one per episode—was made to sing. Guests included Italian celebrities such as Totò, Marcello Mastroianni, Mina, Fausto Coppi, and Gino Bartali, and also international stars such as Gary Cooper, Jayne Mansfield, Perry Como, and Louis Armstrong.

The theme song, "Domenica è sempre domenica" ("Sunday is always Sunday"), became popular, and the show was so successful that *Il Musichiere* weekly magazine followed, which gave readers a free flexi disk (thin vinyl record). This was also the first Italian periodical to publish the music charts and to produce, in 1959 and 1960, *Il Festival del Musichiere*, a live show that gave aspiring writers the chance to have their poetry sung by professionals. The beautiful Verona Arena was the location of the festival, and it was there that, during the last rehearsal of the second festival, Mario Riva fell into a hole in the stage and died a few days later. A similar TV show, *Sarabanda*, aired from 1997 to 2004 on Italia 1, and then again in 2009 on Canale 5. **SDG**

Leave It to Beaver

Comedy | USA | 1957–63

Stereotypical ideal of 1950s American suburban life preserved as TV amber

Classic episode
The Last Day of School | *Season 3, episode 38.*
The Beaver asks June to pick out a gift for him to give to his teacher Miss Landers. A store mix-up leaves him with an uncomfortable decision to make.

◉ Tony Dow (above) and Jerry Mathers (below), c. 1957.

Cast | Jerry Mathers, Tony Dow, Hugh Beaumont, Barbara Billingsley, Ken Osmond, Robert Stevens, Stanley Fafara, Stephen Talbot, Frank Bank
Original broadcasters | CBS, ABC
For fans of . . . | *The Adventures of Ozzie and Harriet* (1952)

Living out their lives in a creepily pristine neighborhood, the fictional Mayfield, the Cleavers embodied the essence of postwar American conformity with their endless cycle of daily meals, firmly embedded middle-class values, crises managed within a half-hour, and a list of lessons intoned by the parents, Ward and June (Hugh Beaumont and Barbara Billingsley) and accepted with a nod and "gee whiz" by the boys, Theodore "Beaver" (Jerry Mathers) and older brother Wally (Tony Dow).

Created by Joe Connelly and Bob Mosher, who drew on their own children for inspiration and authentic slang, the show recast the father and Beaver roles between the pilot and first episode. The series moved to multiple time slots and ran on two networks, then ended when Mathers left acting for high school. A final retrospective episode designed to bid farewell to the Cleavers—a rarity for sitcoms at the time—aired on June 20, 1963, but the show's true popularity began in countless reruns over the next two decades.

Reality finally crashed completely into the Cleavers' world when Beaver came home after separating from his wife in the 1983 TV movie *Still the Beaver*. That reunion did well enough to launch a 1984–89 revival, *The New Leave it to Beaver*, although a divorced Beaver raising two sons in his parents' home with widowed grandma June's help didn't click with viewers in quite the same way as the cult classic original. A 1997 feature film adaptation similarly failed to capture the audience's attention—gee whiz. **ATB**

Maverick

Western | USA | 1957–62

Subversive, satirical Western that turned the genre cliché on its head

Cast | James Garner, Jack Kelly, Roger Moore, Robert Colbert, Efrem Zimbalist Jr., Diane Brewster
Original broadcaster | ABC
Award | 1 Emmy
For fans of . . . | *The Rockford Files* (1974)

As opposed to most other Western heroes of the era, Bret Maverick (James Garner) was a charming rogue who preferred playing cards and tricking his way out of danger rather than engaging in gun play—not that he couldn't handle himself when the occasion called for it.

Created by Roy Huggins, *Maverick* was a lighthearted antidote to the grittier world of other TV Westerns. A grueling production schedule, however, meant that Garner couldn't carry the show himself, so the Maverick family grew to include his brother Bart (Jack Kelly). Different crews shot the Garner and Kelly episodes, with occasional crossovers uniting the brothers. As Kelly's Bart handled more standard action adventure, Garner's Bret was more of a lovable con artist with an eye on the door.

The show relied on source material from the likes of Robert Louis Stevenson and Louis L'Amour, as well as presenting parodies poking fun at the competition. Recurring guest star Ben Gage played variations of *Gunsmoke*'s Marshal Matt Dillon, most memorably in an episode spoofing that show and *Have Gun—Will Travel*, titled "Gun-Shy." Huggins left the series after the second season. After the third year, Garner too was gone, and third brother Brent (Robert Colbert) and cousin Beau (Roger Moore) turned up to assist Bart. A 1978 TV movie, *The New Maverick*, and revival of Garner's Maverick in 1981 to 1982 kept the character alive, while a 1994 big screen adaptation featured Mel Gibson as Maverick, with Garner appearing in a supporting role. **ATB**

Classic episode
Shady Deal at Sunny Acres | *Season 2, episode 10*. This episode by series creator Roy Huggins (which he believed inspired the first half of *The Sting*) unites all of the recurring characters in a complex con against an unscrupulous banker.

⊙ James Garner and Jack Kelly in character as Bret and Bart Maverick.

Perry Mason

Drama | USA | 1957–66

The long-running courtroom drama that defined its genre—
it's all about the confession

Classic episode
*The Case of the Perjured Parrot | Season 2,
episode 11.* This was the first TV show to use an
outline on the ground to show where a body had
been found. Mel Blanc (the voice of Bugs Bunny),
voiced the parrot; the only witness to a murder.

⊚ Raymond Burr as Perry Mason, the crime-solving attorney who
always knew how to tease out a confession.

Cast | Raymond Burr, Barbara Hale, William Hopper,
William Talman, Ray Collins, Wesley Lau
Original broadcaster | CBS
Awards | 3 Emmys
For fans of . . . | *Dragnet* (1951), *Law and Order* (1953)

Each episode of *Perry Mason* unfolded with precision.
From the unmistakable first bars of "Park Avenue
Beat," the swinging theme song, until the point where
the guilty party broke down in confession, the main
pleasure of *Perry Mason* did not lie in who did it, or how
it was done, but in how Mason (Raymond Burr), defense
attorney extraordinaire, would get the villain to confess.

Following a murder—or a suggestion that someone
might commit one—the wrong man was arrested.
Mason then investigated the crime himself, assisted by
his secretary, Della Street (Barbara Hale), and his private
investigator, Paul Drake (William Hopper). Occasionally
they would even find a body, before spending the
second half of the episode in court, attempting to prove
to a judge that there was not enough evidence for a
trial. Usually, Mason demonstrated that someone other
than his client had committed the crime, a revelation
that often resulted in the guilty party breaking down
on the witness stand, or making a break for freedom,
only to get caught by the bailiff.

Perry Mason was the creation of Earl Stanley Gardner,
a lawyer who wrote in his spare time. Gardner invented
the crusading defense attorney—and the legal
procedural—on TV as we now know it. With his hulking
physique and craggy goodlooks, Burr was not CBS's first
choice to play Mason. But Gardner insisted, so Burr was
cast in a role that he would play for 271 episodes and
25 TV movies. *Perry Mason* defined the way that the US
justice system is portrayed on TV today. **AP**

The Army Game
Comedy | UK | 1957–61

Mining the ready-made sitcom of National Service, The Army Game *struck a chord among postwar Brits*

Cast | William Hartnell, Bernard Bresslaw, Michael Medwin, Alfie Bass, Bill Fraser
Original broadcaster | ITV
For fans of . . . | *Dad's Army* (1968), *It Ain't Half Hot Mum* (1974)

First broadcast in 1957 when the Second World War was still a recent memory, *The Army Game* revolved around a gang of British soldiers undergoing National Service. Its popularity over the course of five seasons spilled into other media and made stars of many of its cast.

If *The Army Game* lacked a certain sophistication, its audience didn't seem to mind. They warmed to the work-shy antics of the soldiers billeted in Hut 29 of a Surplus Ordnance Depot in the county of Warwickshire. These conscripts included Private Montague "Excused Boots" Bisley (Alfie Bass), Private "Popeye" Popplewell (Bernard Bresslaw), and Corporal Springer (Michael Medwin). The gang's increasingly inventive methods of making light of their conscription were kept in check by a pre–*Doctor Who* William Hartnell as Sergeant Major Bullimore, and later Bill Fraser as Sergeant. Major Snudge. Viewers loved it—many had family members who were away on National Service, which was still in place in Britain until 1960—and 154 episodes were produced in just four years.

The *Army Game* was an early success of the still-young television medium. A film version, *Only Arsked!*, was released in 1958, and its theme song (sung by the cast) reached number five in the British charts. Meanwhile, Bass and Fraser took their characters to civvy street for the spin-off series, *Bootsie and Snudge* (1960). Only fifty of the 154 episodes of *The Army Game* survive to this day, which may be why it is not as well regarded as it deserves. **MW**

Classic episode
Emergency Hut 29 | Season 4, episode 38. Fears of "Banana Flu" spread through the camp and the men queue up to be inoculated. But Snudge and Bootsie claim there is nothing to fear—until they end up in the sick bay.

⊙ The cast: top, Ted Lune; below him (L–R) Mario Fabrizi, Dick Emery. Harry Fowler; bottom (L–R) William Hartnell, Geoffrey Summer.

Zorro

Western | USA | 1957–59

Spirited and lavish adaptation of the swashbuckling hero—"Out of the night/When the full moon is bright/Comes the horseman known as Zorro!"

Cast | Guy Williams, Gene Sheldon, Henry Calvin, Don Diamond, George J. Lewis, Nestor Paiva
Original broadcaster | ABC
For fans of . . . | *The Swamp Fox* (1955)

A pulp hero who first appeared in 1919 with stories by Johnston McCulley, Zorro (Spanish for "fox") was the wealthy Don Diego de la Vega, who donned mask and cape to become the daring swordsman defending the rights of those struggling under tyrannical Spanish rule in early 1800s Los Angeles. Zorro inspired film adaptations starring silver-screen legends Douglas Fairbanks and Tyrone Power before Walt Disney turned his attention to acquiring the rights to the man in black.

Guy Williams was already well versed in fencing when he took on the lead role, although he would endure an extensive training regimen to turn him into a capable adventurer worthy of riding his horse, Tornado, into battle. He also learned how to play the guitar. Disney spent a great deal of money on the production, making it the most expensive Western TV show at the time, and teased its premiere during the *Disneyland* TV series. The first year presented serialized, multipart stories, while the second loosened up on that format; both seasons featured half-hour episodes.

A legal wrangle between Disney and ABC over the series rights brought a premature end to this Zorro's exploits, although Disney honorably kept Williams on the payroll the entire time and also produced four hour-long specials. Two feature film compilations of Williams' Zorro episodes were released, and although Williams considered wearing the mask again in a 1982 revival, *Zorro and Son*, he declined to participate when he discovered that it was a sitcom. **ATB**

Classic episode

El Bandido | *Season 3, episode 1*. Mexican bandits led by skilled swordsman El Culchillo (The Knife) ride into Los Angeles, intending to steal a shipment of silver. Zorro intercepts the plan and a sword fight ensues between the pair.

◍ Guy Williams, as Zorro, showcasing his swordsmanship.

Wagon Train

Western | USA | 1957–65

A hybrid of anthology and ongoing series that helped define the Western genre

Cast | Ward Bond, John McIntire, Robert Horton, Frank McGrath, Terry Wilson, Denny Miller, Michael Burns
Original broadcasters | NBC
For fans of . . . | *Rawhide* (1959), *Laramie* (1959), *The Virginian* (1962)

Based on the 1950 film *Wagon Master* that also featured Ward Bond, *Wagon Train* built upon a simple but solid basis for a Western series. Although the trek across the United States undertaken by settlers in the post-Civil War era proved a perfect premise for an ongoing TV show, it wouldn't be the journey itself or those taking it that would drive the plot. Guest stars were the focal point of every episode, and *Wagon Train* boasted a wide array of present and future stars, including Ronald Reagan, Ernest Borgnine, Lee Marvin, Bette Davis, Lon Chaney Jr., Barbara Stanwyck, Charles Laughton, Leonard Nimoy, Dennis Hopper, and Angie Dickinson. Bond, a seasoned veteran of the genre, was often at odds with younger star Horton. When Bond died in 1960, John McIntire stepped in as the new wagon master and rode it out until the series ended.

Wagon Train rose from number two to number one in the ratings by 1961, but two changes weakened its position: an ill-fated shift from black-and-white one-hour installments to color hour-and-a-half episodes, and a move from NBC to ABC. Even then the journey went on for another three seasons, although a return to black and white devastated the series' ratings. ABC ran earlier Bond episodes in the daytime under the title *Trailmaster* in order to differentiate them from the current run.

With its edgier exploration of geography and human nature that led Gene Roddenberry to invoke its name when pitching *Star Trek* to NBC, *Wagon Train* and its cavalcade of stars continues its journey in repeats. **ATB**

The Sky at Night

Documentary | UK | 1957–present

This late-night show about astronomy had everyone gazing at the stars

Cast | Patrick Moore, Lucie Green, Chris Lintott, Maggie Aderin-Pocock
Original broadcaster | BBC
For fans of . . . | *Cosmos* (1974), *Hyperspace* (2001), *Through the Wormhole* (2010)

When Sir Patrick Moore died in December 2012, *The Sky at Night* was, at more than fifty-five years, the longest-running series with the same host in global television history. It could have ended there, but affection for the show was such that it continued with new hosts—Lucie Green, Chris Lintott, and Maggie Aderin-Pocock. Not bad for a monthly factual program that is solely about astronomy.

It's easy to forget that when the series started, there was no space race, and no expectation that a man might one day stand upon the surface of the Moon. Since then, every discovery and scientific development in the universe has been charted by the program, from the launch of Sputnik to the first Moon landing. It was Moore who first told British viewers with absolute certainty that life on the Moon was a fantasy (even into the early 1960s, this was a matter of debate).

The program is open-minded enough to allow for speculation, which appeals to viewers' imagination. But it is the engaging and involving presentation of simple facts that have held the show's core audience for so long. Many keen amateurs learned how to read the night sky through Moore's discussions, while news of phenomena such as forthcoming meteor showers or a solar eclipse lend the show topical appeal too.

The Sky at Night continues to be a regular fixture on the BBC, and it still opens with the same stirring theme music—"At the Castle Gate," a segment from the opera *Pelléas et Mélisande* by Jean Sibelius. **JS**

Zum Blauen Bock

Music/Musical | Germany | 1957–87

How a weekly dose of folk music, chat, and nostalgia entranced the German nation

Cast | Otto Höpfner, Heinz Schenk, Lia Wöhr
Original broadcaster | Hessische Rundfunk
For fans of . . . | *The Ed Sullivan Show* (1948), *Musikantenstadl* (1981)

The Saturday evening talk show *Zum Blauen Bock* (*To the Blue Ram*) brought a traditional Hessian beer garden, complete with *Äppelwoi* (apple wine) and music, into German living rooms. It was a simple but successful concept that persuaded a substantial section of the German public to sit in front of their televisions every Saturday evening for thirty years. After Heinz Schenk took over from Otto Höpfner as host in 1966, the show regularly attracted up to twenty million viewers, and almost all the great representatives of German folk music were guests on the show.

Unusually, the show was a traveling production that moved from one small town in Hesse to another, causing a sensation wherever it erected its half-timbered set. The show's charm lay partly in this regional dimension, but also in its folksy *Gemütlichkeit*—coziness. The mayor and personalities of each town were interviewed as guests, and in a short establishing shot at the start of each show the host appeared dressed as a well-known folk figure.

Music (mainly folk and pop but also opera and operetta) punctuated the interviews and sketches. Guests were served apple wine from the celebrated "Bembel," a little jug that guests could take home as a souvenir. Although *Blaue Bock* is now mainly appreciated in an ironic way, its place in the history of German TV is undisputed. Its successor, *Musikantenstadl*, in which music and chat are presented in a mocked-up ski lodge, is still going strong today. **NK**

Canzonissima

Music/Musical | Italy | 1958–74

Singing competition that propelled some of its contestants to stardom

Cast | Corrado, Nino Manfredi, Delia Scala, Pippo Baudo, Raffaella Carrà, Mina, Walter Chiari, Dario Fo, Franca Rame
Original broadcaster | RAI
For fans of . . . | *The Voice* (2011)

Canzonissima was a singing competition produced in association with the New Year's Lottery. It was a spin-off from *Le Canzoni della fortuna* (*Songs of Fortune*), a radio music competition first broadcast in 1956. A constant feature of the show was that the public took part in voting for the best song, sending in their votes on cards supplied with tickets for the lottery. None of the shows had fewer than twenty million viewers.

The contests between singers (such as the historic ones between Claudio Villa and Gianni Morandi, and between Iva Zanicchi and Ornella Vanoni) influenced record sales. The two best known and most popular seasons of *Canzonissima* were those of 1959 and 1968. In 1959 the hosts were Delia Scala, Paolo Panelli, and Nino Manfredi. Manfredi invented the character Bastiano, the man from Ciociaria, who, referring to the lottery, declaimed the words "*Fusse che fusse la volta bona*" ("Let's hope we'll get it right this time"). This catchphrase entered the Italian language.

In 1968 the program was presented by Mina, Walter Chiari, and Paolo Panelli and, thanks to the unforgettable singing performance of the candidate, together with the sketches involving the three hosts, it achieved record viewing figures. As well as making many singers famous, *Canzonissima* turned many of its hosts into stars, such as Raffaella Carrà, who through the songs "*Ma che musica maestro*" and "*Tuca Tuca*," in which she sings and dances, became a legend of international television. **SM**

77 Sunset Strip

Crime/Mystery | USA | 1958–64

Quintessential prototype for the glamorous private-eye series—but the parking lot attendant stole the show

Cast | Efrem Zimbalist Jr., Roger Smith, Edd Byrnes, Richard Long, Louis Quinn, Robert Logan
Original broadcaster | ABC
For fans of . . . | *The Rockford Files* (1974), *Moonlighting* (1985)

Emerging at the end of the 1950s when the Western was still the dominant genre on US TV, *77 Sunset Strip* brought a welcome splash of modern-day glitz to the schedules and established a blueprint of sorts for many similar shows that would follow.

The series featured the adventures of two handsome private eyes, Stu Bailey (Efrem Zimbalist Jr.) and Jeff Spencer (Roger Smith), both former government agents now plying their investigative skills out of a glamorous Sunset Strip office. Their clientele, often moneyed and with prestigious positions, embroiled them in cases involving attractive people and exotic locations. In spite of the charismatic leads, it was actually one of the support characters who caught the public imagination and propelled the series to the heights of the ratings. Gerald Lloyd "Kookie" Kookson III (Edd Byrnes) was a wannabe private eye, working as a parking-lot attendant in the restaurant next door to the detective agency. Kookie was a good-looking, jive-talking youth who instantly clicked with the younger members of the audience, turning Byrnes into a teenage heartthrob of Elvis Presley proportions. He even released a hit novelty record ("Kookie, Kookie, Lend Me Your Comb"), which referenced the character's habit of constantly combing his hair.

By 1963 the glitz of the series had started to fade and—despite a radical change of format and location with Zimbalist as the only survivor from the earlier days—the show bowed out in 1964. **DF**

Classic episode
The Rice Estate | *Season 3, episode 16.*
Stu is assigned to protect a recluse, but ends up falling for her. The private-eye series meets the haunted-house genre in an episode of thrills, chills, and clever comedy.

◬ "Violence for Your Furs" aired on March 30, 1962, and guest starred Phil Carey and Mala Powers.

The Donna Reed Show

Comedy | USA | 1958–66

America's sweetheart Donna Reed is an every-mom steering her husband and children through the trials and tribulations of middle-class life

Classic episode
How the Other Side Lives | *Season 3, episode 5.*
Having stayed with a friend, Mary returns home full of praise and admiration for her friend's amazing house. Donna begins to feel that her own home is inadequate.

◉ Head of the household Donna Reed shows on-screen husband Carl Betz how it's done.

Cast | Donna Reed, Carl Betz, Shelley Fabares, Paul Peterson, Patty Peterson
Original broadcaster | ABC
Award | 1 Golden Globe
For fans of . . . | *The Lucy Show* (1962)

Premiering two years before the squeaky-clean 1950s morphed into the counterculture of the 1960s, *The Donna Reed Show* was one of the first US sitcoms to be anchored by a strong-minded woman. Numerous previous TV shows such as *Make Room for Daddy* (1953) and *Father Knows Best* (1954) had been built around male authority figures, but here, it was Academy Award winning Donna Reed who took center stage as the unflappable and impeccably dressed Donna Stone.

Her husband Alex (Carl Betz), a respected town pediatrician, filled his traditional role as man of the house, but it was Donna who, with good humor and quiet resolve, was the driving force of the family. The show's focus on a strong, capable woman allowed it to tackle topical, and at the time controversial, issues such as women's rights, adoption, and, in its last season, drugs. As the children, Mary (Shelley Fabares) and Jeff (Paul Peterson), grew up, their misadventures matured along with them. They displayed their musical talents on the show, which led to actual chart-topping hits and may have paved the way for the other kid singing groups that showcased on subsequent shows including *The Brady Bunch* (1969) and *The Partridge Family* (1970).

A delightful look at the traditional and expanding role of wife and mother as seen through the rosy lens of 1950s optimism, *The Donna Reed Show* is a prime example of how TV shows are shaped by, and shape, public opinion. **RP**

Golden Globe Awards

Awards show | USA | 1958–present

The great and the good of the big and small screens gather for this prequel to the Oscars

Cast | Tina Fey, Amy Poehler
Original broadcaster | NBC
For fans of . . . | *The Academy Awards* (1953), *The British Academy Film Awards* (1967), *The Hollywood Film Awards* (2014)

The Golden Globes is the cheeky little sister to the Oscars. Inaugurated by the Hollywood Foreign Press Association in 1944, in a ceremony televised since 1958, the awards celebrate film and television alike. In the case of the former, they are considered to be a strong indication of success at the Oscars six weeks later.

Due to their range, the categories are slightly arbitrary, with musical and comedy judged separately from drama when it comes to best actor and best film, but not for best supporting roles, resulting in tongue-twisting titles such as Best Supporting Actress in a Series, Limited Series or Motion Picture made for Television. This can also lead to multiple wins, as it has for Kate Winslet, Sigourney Weaver, Joan Plowright, and Helen Mirren. Over the years, Barbra Streisand has won the most awards, with ten over six categories, while Meryl Streep has had the most nominations (twenty-nine).

The ceremony is sometimes controversial, with the producers of the Algerian political thriller *Z* refusing to accept their award for Best Foreign Language Film in 1970, on the grounds that it should not have been considered separately from the Best Motion Picture. In 1973, Marlon Brando refused his award for Best Actor, in a stance against American "imperialism and racism."

Watched in 167 countries, the ceremony had no host (except for the fifty-first awards in 1994) until the sixty-seventh awards in 2010, when Ricky Gervais stepped into the role, repeating it for two years before being replaced by Tina Fey and Amy Poehler in 2012. **EB**

Sea Hunt

Action/Adventure | USA | 1958–61

Educational and ecologically minded marine adventure

Cast | Lloyd Bridges, Ken Drake, Courtney Brown, Jan Harrison, William Boyett, Richard Probert
Original broadcaster | Syndication
For fans of . . . | *Sky King* (1951), *Dragnet* (1951), *Voyage to the Bottom of the Sea* (1964)

One of the most extensively syndicated series in the United States, *Sea Hunt* drew about forty million people every week to watch Mike Nelson (Lloyd Bridges), an expert diver formerly with the U.S. Navy. Unable to sell the concept to any major network, creator Ivan Tors took the show to the choppy waters of first-run syndication and found himself with a near-instant hit.

For four seasons, Nelson—in his boat *The Argonaut*—was regularly recruited for all manner of missions from rescues to salvage operations. Bridges' matter-of-fact voice-overs during the diving scenes became a trademark of the series and ripe for parody, once by Bridges himself in the film *Hot Shots! Part Deux* (1993). Although Bridges was trained in diving for the role, accomplished divers handled much of the stunt work until, by the show's end, Bridges himself was tackling nearly all of his character's underwater action. Much of the diving footage was shot at Marineland of the Pacific, California, as well as locations on both coasts.

Guest stars included future famous faces of film and TV, including Larry Hagman (*Dallas*' J. R.) and Leonard Nimoy (*Star Trek*'s Spock). Jack Nicholson had one of his earliest roles in *Sea Hunt*'s final episode. While the show often focused on educational and environmental topics concerning diving and the sea, Bridges decided to depart when the production changed course toward more predictable procedural stories. A brief 1987 remake starred former TV Tarzan Ron Ely as Nelson, but the new *Sea Hunt* sank out of sight quickly. **ATB**

Naked City
Drama | USA | 1958–63

Filmic crime drama with a gritty take on police procedurals

Cast | James Franciscus, John McIntire, Horace McMahon, Paul Burke, Harry Bellaver, Nancy Malone,
Original broadcaster | ABC
Awards | 3 Emmys
For fans of . . . | *Peter Gunn* (1958)

It might not seem likely for a landmark show to derive from a volume of photographs, but it was Arthur H. "Weegee" Fellig's 1945 book that inspired the 1948 film *Naked City*, which in turn led to the creation of this series. Although the stories were based around the activities of the NYPD's 65th Precinct, it was the opposite side of the equation—the underworld figures that the police pursued and the people upon whom they preyed—that served as the show's primary focus.

Part of *Naked City*'s charm was its use of verisimilitude. The series was shot entirely on the streets of New York, and the documentary-like approach to storytelling gave the series a grittier mood. The high caliber of writing, insisted upon by creator and lead writer Stirling Silliphant, also attracted top talents from the world of TV and film. The series did have its share of creative pitfalls, losing one of its original stars, John McIntire, when he decided to move back to Montana midway through production of the first season. Canceled after that first year, the show was revived thanks to support from sponsor Brown & Williamson, and expanded to twice its run time with an almost entirely new cast.

In 1959, the episode "Four Sweet Corners" led to the creation of the series *Route 66*, which ran one year longer than its parent show. *Naked City* featured thirty-minute episodes in its first season, but shifted to a full hour for the remainder of its run. There were ultimately 138 episodes in the *Naked City*, leaving many of the show's "eight million stories" left to tell. **ATB**

Peter Gunn
Drama | USA | 1958–61

Musically experimental detective series with a sophisticated twist

Cast | Craig Stevens, Lola Albright, Herschel Bernardi, Hope Emerson, Minerva Urecal
Original broadcasters | NBC
Award | 1 Emmy
For fans of . . . | *The Rockford Files* (1974)

It was the propulsive opening theme by composer Henry Mancini that drew viewers into the smoky world of suave Peter Gunn, private eye, and the musical aspect of the show didn't end there. Created by Blake Edwards (later known for the *Pink Panther* films), this moody detective series is perhaps more memorable for its innovative use of modern jazz to underscore Gunn's sophisticated exploits than for the atmospheric stories it told.

Based on *Richard Diamond, Private Detective* (1957)—also created by Edwards for a radio series starring Dick Powell and a TV adaptation featuring *The Fugitive*'s David Janssen—Peter Gunn (Craig Stevens) operated out of a club called Mother's and charged $1,000 a case. Although the city on the river that he called home was never mentioned by name, Gunn spent most of his time working cases there, with occasional adventures that took him to other parts of the United States or even abroad. Friend and police Lieutenant Jacoby (Herschel Bernardi) would sometimes recommend Gunn for a case, while information often came via Mother herself (Hope Emerson and later Minerva Urecal) or other sources like pool-playing Babby (Billy Barty).

Episodes were directed by some of the best in the business, including Boris Sagal and Robert Altman. Two *Peter Gunn* soundtrack albums were released by RCA Victor, featuring music by Mancini with piano performances by future legend of film composition John Williams. The first of those albums made it to No. 1 on the *Billboard* pop chart. **ATB**

Craig Stevens as the sophisticated private detective Peter Gunn. ❯

The Rifleman

Western | USA | 1958–63

Nontraditional family Western with a strong moral streak

Cast | Chuck Connors, Johnny Crawford, Paul Fix, Joe Benson, Bill Quinn, Hope Summers, Joan Taylor, Patricia Blair
Original broadcaster | ABC
For fans of . . . | *Bonanza* (1959)

Widower and Civil War veteran Lucas McCain (Chuck Connors) was a man of morals, a dedicated crusader for justice, and an ambidextrous straight shooter with his Winchester rifle, but all he wanted was a quiet life on his North Fork, New Mexico ranch with son Mark (Johnny Crawford). Whenever someone needed help or a crime was committed, however, Marshal Micah Torrance (Paul Fix) and the townsfolk inevitably turned to Lucas to save the day. Through every adventure, Lucas was guided by his strong sense of ethics, cool approach to danger, and his desire to set a worthy example for his son through simple life lessons.

Created by Arnold Laven, who championed the core father-son relationship and Lucas' use of the modified rifle, the show was further shaped by writer and director Sam Peckinpah, whose attention to realistic storytelling and nuanced characterization helped define the tone of the series and presaged Peckinpah's work in Western feature films. A more cinematic approach in the show's visual style, especially with atmospheric lighting provided by prolific series director Joseph H. Lewis, set *The Rifleman* apart from its competitors.

Although it did not have the longevity of other Western series, *The Rifleman* pioneered a nontraditional look at the struggles of a widowed parent within the framework of the familiar Western action-adventure format. Lucas also refreshingly favored finding nonviolent solutions and allowing second chances for reformed gunfighters and lawbreakers. **ATB**

Bonanza

Western | USA | 1959–73

First color Western TV series—"We chased lady luck, 'til we finally struck Bonanza"

Cast | Lorne Greene, Pernell Roberts, Dan Blocker, Michael Landon, Victor Sen Yung, Ray Teal
Original broadcaster | NBC
Awards | 3 Emmys
For fans of . . . | *The Big Valley* (1965)

Bonanza stood out almost instantly among its many Western competitors, debuting in color with flames engulfing a map of the show's setting: Virginia City, Nevada. With a memorable opening theme, the show centered on Ponderosa ranch owner Ben Cartwright (Lorne Green), who lived with his three sons: educated Adam (Pernell Roberts), warmhearted Eric or "Hoss" (Dan Blocker), and impetuous Little Joe (Michael Landon). Together with cook Hop Sing (Victor Sen Yung), the Cartwrights were constantly embroiled in other people's lives, upholding strong standards of morality and ethics as well as racial equality; Ben, in particular, always saw the best in everyone and strived to make sure justice was upheld.

Created by David Dortort, the show cemented its success as a character-driven Western after it moved from Saturday to Sunday; there it became number one in the ratings for three years in a row. Viewers noted that none of the sons ever kept a girlfriend and none of the leads changed clothes (allowing for frequent shuffling of stock footage from previous episodes). The show often employed a somewhat innovative nonlinear storytelling style, devoting episodes to flashbacks that filled in the story of Ben's three wives, each a mother to one of his sons. Roberts left in the sixth season after growing tired of the production grind and what he saw as limiting artistic opportunities. The show suffered a double blow in 1972: Blocker's sudden death and a move to Tuesdays, leading to its cancellation. **ATB**

(L–R) Dan Blocker, Michael Landon, and Lorne Greene as the Cartwrights of *Bonanza*. ❯

The Untouchables

Drama | USA | 1959–63

Controversial, high-rating gangster series set in the 1930s

Cast | Robert Stack, Jerry Paris, Abel Fernandez, Nicholas Georgiade, Bruce Gordon
Original broadcaster | ABC   **Awards** | 2 Emmys   **For fans of . . .** | *Peaky Blinders* (2013)

The Untouchables, a fast-paced, bullet-laden, all-action, period-piece crime drama, caused waves because of its intense violence, but scored heavily with viewers, and was the number eight TV show of the 1960–61 season.

Set in the early 1930s, the series told the story of organized crime fighter Eliot Ness, who worked for the Bureau of Prohibition and led a team of incorruptible, unbribable agents known as the Untouchables.

Following the huge success of a one-off Desilu Playhouse special depicting Ness' real-life pursuit of Al Capone, the series continued the story of the team's attempts to bring down various crime lords. Robert Stack portrayed Ness as a humorless and virtuous type, introverted and composed, in direct contrast to many

of the colorful, flamboyant, and noisy villains he faced. To counteract the comic-book violence of the piece, the show featured an atmospheric voice-over narration from famed radio broadcaster Walter Winchell.

The series burned brightly, but ended after four seasons. Ness' book, *The Untouchables*, also inspired the 1987 Brian De Palma film of the same name. **DF**

Classic episode

The Rusty Heller Story | *Season 2, episode 1*.
Elizabeth Montgomery guest stars as the nightclub jazz singer named in the episode title, playing a dangerous game with members of the mob. A cracking opener to season 2.

⊘ (L–R) Agents Youngfellow (Abel Fernandez), Hobson (Paul Picerni), Ness (Robert Stack), and Rossi (Nicholas Georgiade) in 1961.

The Twilight Zone

Fantasy/Horror/Sci-Fi | USA | 1959–64

The most popular and influential sci-fi anthology series in TV history

Cast | Rod Serling, Robert McCord   **Original broadcaster** | CBS
Awards | 3 Emmys, 1 Golden Globe   **For fans of . . .** | *Alfred Hitchcock Presents* (1955)

Among the sitcoms and news reports and adaptations of stage and audio plays of 1950s TV, one show took viewers on a journey to another dimension. There, reality warped to the needs of the storyteller from week to week, presenting unsettling morality tales and disturbing diatribes on cogent social issues, from a region known only as the Twilight Zone.

Creator Rod Serling cagily claimed he wasn't making meaningful TV, but he knew that through allegory he could explore deeper issues that would slip past censors and pundits alike. The five-season series ran the gamut from psychological thriller to far-flung fantasy, almost always with a twist ending, and featured memorable opening credits iconography and creepy musical themes composed by Bernard Herrmann and Marius Constant.

Through sharp storytelling, incisive psychological exploration of character, and countless stars anchoring even the most fanciful of plots, *The Twilight Zone* became a time capsule of transformative television that continues to enlighten and entertain. **ATB**

Classic episode
To Serve Man | Season 3, Episode 24. A benevolent alien race, the Kanamits, lands on Earth. Initial suspicion of them is revealed to be unjustified after the title of a book in their language is translated as "To Serve Man."

◬ Plane passenger William Shatner comes face-to-face with a "Nightmare at 20,000 Feet" in this well-loved episode.

Rawhide

Western | USA | 1959–65

A star-studded Western adventure that's always "Rollin', rollin', rollin'!"

Cast | Eric Fleming, Clint Eastwood, James Murdock, Paul Brinegar, Steve Raines, Rocky Shahan, Sheb Wooley, Robert Cabal, Raymond St. Jacques
Original broadcaster | CBS
For fans of . . . | *Gunsmoke* (1955)

Like one of its contemporaries in the Western genre, *Wagon Train* (1957), *Rawhide* put its stories in motion by following a Texas-to-Kansas cattle drive. The series was based on several sources, including the Borden Chase novel *Red River: Blazing Guns on the Chisholm Trail* (1948), the movie *Cattle Empire* (1958), and the diaries of George C. Duffield, whose experiences grounded the show and influenced Eric Fleming's opening narration for every episode.

Long before he was riding stoically through Sergio Leone films or asking dirtbags to make his day, Clint Eastwood costarred on *Rawhide* as Rowdy Yates, a ramrod who took the mantle of trail boss when Fleming departed in the show's final year. However, Eastwood was not alone in solving the problems that the drive encountered, as a never-ending parade of notable guest stars turned up, including Barbara Eden, DeForest Kelley, Charles Bronson, Dean Martin, Peter Lorre, Debra Paget, Harry Dean Stanton, and Eastwood's future *The Good, The Bad and the Ugly* costar Lee Van Cleef.

Making its mark by featuring the first black regular in a Western (Raymond St. Jacques), *Rawhide* was one of the longest-running shows in the genre, spanning eight seasons. In 1964, the future creators of *Mission: Impossible* took the reins temporarily. Bernard Kowalski and Bruce Geller reinvented the show as a progressive commentary on modern issues, enraging CBS president William S. Paley. After firing the team, Paley instructed their successors to "put the cows back in." **ATB**

Laramie

Western | USA | 1959–64

Lauded Western series from the golden age of television

Cast | John Smith, Robert Fuller, Spring Byington, Dennis Holmes, Robert Crawford Jr., Stuart Randall, Hoagy Carmichael
Original broadcaster | NBC
For fans of . . . | *Wagon Train* (1957)

In nineteenth-century Wyoming, Slim Sherman and his teenage brother Andy joined together to run the family ranch, assisted by their father's old friend Jonesy, after their father was shot and killed by a land grabber. After initial tensions with Slim, drifter Jess Harper reluctantly joined the group to help in running the ranch as a stagecoach station for Great Central Overland Mail, just outside the eponymous town of Laramie.

Despite the primal animosity between the two men, the developing friendship of Slim and Jess became a driving point of the show. Now considered a classic Western that stands up in its own right against some of the flashier, big-budget movies of the time, *Laramie* had an arsenal of skilled directors, including Joseph Kane and Lesley Selander.

Andy and Jonesy were written out in the second season; Andy was sent to boarding school in Missouri, with Jonesy accompanying him. To restore the show for its third season, new characters were introduced: Daisy Cooper, a potential love interest, and Mike Williams, a young orphan. This, alongside the move into color in 1961, helped to reinvigorate the show. NBC's new "living color" logo, premiered in 1962, quickly became known as "the Laramie peacock," and remained long after the show's run had ended.

The show attracted a range of guest stars—some established, such as Charles Bronson, Ernest Borgnine, and Brett King; others up-and-coming, including Leonard Nimoy and Adam West. **EB**

◆ (L–R) Raymond St. Jaques, Eric Fleming, Clint Eastwood, Paul Brinegar, and Sheb Wooley in *Rawhide*.

It was time for TV to stop being safe. It took its first timid steps to challenge the traditional values of previous generations, and viewers became aware of civil rights movements, counter-cultures, and the power of pop, rock, and soul. Thanks to TV, the viewers grew more critical of the establishment; the age of deference was over, as television brought our political leaders into sharp focus and comedians made them flinch before our eyes. By the end of the decade, color broadcasts and new high-definition systems were commonplace. More than 700 million people watched the moon landings, a feat so baffling that some still refuse to accept the evidence.

1960s

◄ Leonard Nimoy (Mr. Spock), Nichelle Nichols (Uhura), and William Shatner as Captain James T. Kirk in *Star Trek* (1966).

The Andy Griffith Show

Comedy | USA | 1960–68

Not a typical cop show: a down-home sheriff and virtually no crime

Cast | Andy Griffith, Don Knotts, Ron Howard, Frances Bavier, Jim Nabors, George Lindsey, Aneta Corsaut
Original broadcaster | CBS **Awards** | 6 Emmys **For fans of . . .** | *The Dick Van Dyke Show* (1961)

The Andy Griffith Show was created by Sheldon Leonard and Arthur Strander, and built around Andy Griffith, the comedic actor who made a splash in the 1955 teleplay *No Time for Sergeants* (1955) and its 1958 movie adaptation. In his own series, as Sheriff Andy Taylor, Griffith was a contemplative and capable straight man, with the wilder comedy handled by his inept sidekick and cousin, Deputy Barney Fife (Don Knotts), who was only trusted to keep one bullet in his shirt pocket.

A warm relationship between Taylor and his son, Opie (Ron Howard), the domestic ministrations of Aunt Bee (Frances Bavier), and an array of authentic townsfolk living a languid, nostalgic lifestyle made the series a welcome respite from viewers' own fast-paced modern lives. When five-time Emmy Award winning Knotts left in 1965, the show was never the same again. Griffith also decided to depart in 1968. In what may be one of the most successful reunion TV movies ever made, most of the cast returned for a heartwarming *Return to Mayberry* in 1986, which perfectly recaptured the series' blend of bucolic comedy and character. **ATB**

Classic episode

Opie the Birdman | *Season 4, episode 1*. Opie accidentally kills a mother bird and decides to raise her three babies until they're ready to fly the nest. The message is simple but powerful, summed up by a father's love for his son.

◉ Andy Griffith and Ron Howard have a father-and-son heart-to-heart in the episode titled "Opie's Girlfriend."

The Flintstones

Animation | USA | 1960–66

The adventures of a suburban couple and their neighbors in the prehistoric town of Bedrock

Cast | Alan Reed, Mel Blanc, Daws Butler, Jean Vander Pyl, Bea Benaderet, John Stephenson, Harvey Korman
Original broadcaster | ABC **For fans of . . .** | *The Honeymooners* (1955), *Bewitched* (1964), *The Simpsons* (1989)

The first animated series to be broadcast at prime time on US TV, *The Flintstones* was a weekly half–hour comedy in which the eponymous married couple, Fred and Wilma, and their neighbors Barney and Betty Rubble lived in a cozy modern suburbia millions of years ago when dinosaurs roamed the Earth.

Devised by William Hanna and Joseph Barbera, the series spent some time in the planning stages as the producers considered the possibilities offered by hillbilly, Roman, and pilgrim families as the basis for their sitcom before realizing that prehistory offered the greatest number of sight gags and comically anachronistic takes on contemporary US life. Although it was not initially easy to sell the idea to broadcasters,

the series' success was responsible for the subsequent plethora of themed sitcoms, from *The Beverly Hillbillies* in 1962 to *I Dream of Jeannie* in 1965.

Fred Flintstone, the loud, somewhat boorish but essentially well-meaning patriarch with his life-affirming catchphrase "Yabba-dabba-do!", became an iconic character throughout the Western world. With the series' growing popularity, Hollywood stars such as Tony Curtis and Ann-Margret lent their vocal talents to play prehistoric versions of themselves (Stoney Curtis and Ann Margrock, respectively). Anachronistic technology, such as the gramophone, was provided by dinosaurs, while stone automobiles were powered solely by the feet of the drivers and passengers. **JJJ**

⌂ Fred, Barney, Wilma, and Betty with their kids Pebbles and Bamm-Bamm and Dino the dinosaur.

Coronation Street

Soap opera | UK | 1960–present

One small street. One big drama

Cast | William Roache, Eileen Derbyshire, Barbara Knox, Helen Worth, Violet Carson, Jean Alexander, Pat Phoenix
Original broadcaster | ITV **Awards** | 8 BAFTAs **For fans of . . .** | *Emmerdale* (1972), *Talking Heads* (1987)

"Corrie" is almost a genre in itself, turning the spotlight on working-class folk in Industrial north-west England. It was created by actor-turned-writer Tony Warren, raised on a similar street in Salford (fictionalized as Weatherfield). From the beginning, it was a story of women fighting poverty, jealousy, snobbery, and men—all lazy, deceitful, or too clever for their own good.

In the early years, Pat Phoenix played Elsie Tanner, a tough divorcée whose nemesis was Violet Carson's Ena Sharples, a widow with one hand on a Bible and the other on a glass of beer. University graduate Ken Barlow aspired to change the world, yet was still on the same street fifty years later, making William Roache the longest-serving actor in a continuous role in TV history.

Coronation Street regularly introduces fresh stars and often triumphs over its rivals by making the youngsters behave like world-weary retirees while the older characters act like randy teens. Such is its ongoing popularity that if the *Street*'s residents have affairs, it becomes front-page news and, when they die, the gates to the studios are often lined with flowers. **JS**

Classic episode
Episode 1 | December 9, 1960. As Ena Sharples, Violet Carson paints years of backstory in just a few lines. "I was a pianist, a singer, and an actress," the star rued in 1980. "I even played Shakespeare. Now I have become Ena Sharples forever."

⊘ Violet Carson as Ena Sharples (seated, center), in 1968.

Danger Man

Action/Adventure | UK | 1960–61; 1964–67

I spy . . . a British icon in the making

Cast | Patrick McGoohan, Richard Wattis, Lionel Murton, Warren Mitchell, Peter Madden, Earl Cameron
Original broadcaster | ITV **For fans of . . .** | *The Avengers* (1961), *I, Spy* (1965), *The Prisoner* (1967)

Danger Man followed the adventures of John Drake, a quick-thinking NATO operative as adept with his fists as with the ingenious paraphernalia with which he was issued. At the vanguard of the spy genre booming on both sides of the Atlantic, the show propelled Patrick McGoohan from respected character actor to leading man (and the highest-paid actor on British television).

A half-hour in its original 1960–61 run (an hour on its 1964–67 return), the series—created by Ralph Smart—placed Drake in often exotic and always hazardous environments. McGoohan played him with a grim determination, terse delivery, and bone-dry humor. He encountered many glamorous ladies, but McGoohan insisted on eschewing Bond-style sexual shenanigans.

Later aired in the United States as *Secret Agent*, the series enjoyed consistently good writing. But the main factor in its success was McGoohan, who turned in a considered, charismatic performance as one of 1960s TV's most memorable lone wolves. One episode—"Colony Three", from 1964—is cited as an inspiration for his next TV project, the cult classic *The Prisoner*. **DF**

Classic episode
Don't Nail Him Yet | *Season 2, episode 2*. Drake comes up with an unusual strategy to trap a suspected spy. The cast included Jacqueline Pearce (later Servalan in *Blake's 7*) and Wendy Richard (later Pauline Fowler in *EastEnders*).

⊘ Patrick McGoohan, who played two TV icons in the 1960s.

Car 54, Where Are You?

Comedy | USA | 1961–63

Ooh, ooh! A fast-paced, genuinely funny cop comedy

Cast | Joe E. Ross, Fred Gwynne, Bea Pons, Paul Reed, Al Lewis, Hank Garrett, Jack Healy, Charlotte Rae
Original broadcaster | NBC
Award | 1 Emmy
For fans of . . . | *The Phil Silvers Show* (1955)

New York patrol officers Gunther Toody (Joe E. Ross) and Francis Muldoon (Fred Gwynne) were the *Dumb and Dumber* of the early 1960s. Toody was short, noisy, enthusiastic, and gullible, while Muldoon was tall, quiet, and suspicious but, in the end, equally gullible. Their assignments (escorting a visiting dignitary, going undercover as a bank robber) invariably ended in chaos and confusion—an assortment of misunderstandings and misdirection adding to the woes of their already frazzled boss, Captain Block (Paul Reed).

The series was the brainchild of Nat Hiken, the man behind *The Phil Silvers Show* (a.k.a. *Bilko*). Alumni of that show turned up on both sides of the *Car 54* camera, including leads Ross (whose character was very similar to his *Bilko* role of Rupert Ritzik) and Gwynne, who had scored a memorable role in *Bilko* as a recruit with a huge appetite, nicknamed The Stomach. Now Gwynne proved he could carry a starring role, making full use of his long face and downbeat attitude to squeeze every comical moment from his partnership with the mercurial Ross. Also good value was Al Lewis as the sarcastic Officer Schnauser (he and Gwynne would go on to costar in 1964's *The Munsters*).

With its catchy theme ("There's a holdup in the Bronx, Brooklyn's broken out in fights / There's a traffic jam in Harlem, that's backed up to Jackson Heights") and location filming in New York City, *Car 54* was a viewer favorite that featured well-delivered slapstick comedy and warm, likable characters. **DF**

Classic episode
Get Well, Officer Schnauser | *Season 1, Episode 14.*
The usual misunderstandings result in Toody accidentally robbing a bank. This was the first of eleven episodes to feature Charlotte Rae, who later found fame in *Diff'rent Strokes* and *The Facts of Life*.

◉ New York's finest funny men, Joe E. Ross and Fred Gwynne.

Dr. Kildare

Drama | USA | 1961–66

Medical drama, anchored by the dynamic between a young intern and his mentor

Cast | Richard Chamberlain, Raymond Massey
Original broadcaster | NBC
Award | 1 Golden Globe
For fans of . . . | *Ben Casey* (1961), *Casualty* (1986),
ER (1994)

Based on the characters from a successful series of movies that starred Lionel Barrymore from 1937 to 1947, and a radio program in the 1950s, the television version of *Dr. Kildare* followed a medical intern, Dr. James Kildare (Richard Chamberlain) as he handled the problems of his patients and staff at Blair General hospital, while trying to gain the respect of Dr. Leonard Gillespie (Raymond Massey).

Featuring a cast anchored by Chamberlain and Massey, the show featured a roster of recurring characters played by stars such as Leslie Nielsen, Fred Astaire, James Earl Jones, Martin Balsam, William Shatner, Robert Reed, and Jack Nicholson. Kildare's easy bedside manner and the show's soapy story lines were enough to endear the show to the viewing public, as was the veritable "who's who" of guest stars, including Robert Redford, Lauren Bacall, Douglas Fairbanks Jr., Leonard Nimoy, John Cassavetes, Olympia Dukakis, and James Caan, all of whom had their medical issues solved in a tidy thirty to sixty minutes.

NBC's *Dr. Kildare* premiered at the same time as ABC's *Ben Casey* (1961), which starred Vince Edwards. Perhaps this double dose of dreamy doctors inspired other medical dramas in which doctors, nurses, and administrators get too close to their patients such as *General Hospital* (1963), *St. Elsewhere* (1982), and *Grey's Anatomy* (2005). In 1972, *Young Dr. Kildare*, starring Mark Jenkins as Kildare, premiered, but failed to garner the interest of viewers and lasted only one season. **RP**

Classic episode
One Clear, Bright Thursday Morning | *Season 3, episode 7*. Kildare discovers that the pregnant wife of a Japanese American had been contaminated by radiation in the US nuclear attack on Nagasaki.

◉ Richard Chamberlain as the conscientious Dr. Kildare.

Mr. Ed

Comedy | USA | 1961–66

You never heard of a talking horse? Well, listen to this . . .

Cast | Alan Young, Connie Hines, Allan Lane (voice)
Original broadcasters | Syndication, CBS
Award | 1 Golden Globe
For fans of . . . | *Lassie* (1954), *The Beverly Hillbillies* (1962), *The Addams Family* (1964)

Mr. Ed was created by Arthur Lubin (based on a character invented by writer Walter R. Brooks), who directed early Abbott & Costello films and the Francis the Talking Mule movies, the latter of which had a very similar premise. Produced by George Burns and Gracie Allen's McCadden Corporation, it began as a syndicated series in January 1961 before, unusually, being picked up as a prime-time series by CBS in October 1961.

Mr. Ed was a horse who would speak only to his owner, Wilbur Post (Alan Young), for whom he would initiate wacky misadventures by talking on the phone or leaving the barn. Famous guest stars included Mae West, Zsa Zsa Gabor, George Burns, and Clint Eastwood.

The horse, Bamboo Harvester, was trained by Les Hilton, who had apprenticed under Roy Rogers and worked on the Francis the Talking Mule films. (It has been suggested that a zebra was used in some scenes as a stunt animal.) Multiple explanations have been provided for how the horse's mouth was made to move so it looked as if he were talking, from nylon threads to peanut butter. But, as Young explained in his autobiography, "By our second season, Ed was so adept at his lip movements that as soon as he heard me stop talking, he would start jawing."

Allan "Rocky" Lane, who provided Mr. Ed's speaking voice, received no on-screen credit, despite requesting it as the show's popularity grew. The producers, reportedly, did not want to disillusion children who believed the horse was really talking. **KB**

Classic episode
Clint Eastwood Meets Mister Ed | *Season 2, episode 25.* Long before Clyde the orangutan, Eastwood met the talking horse. Coincidentally, his first credited big-screen role had been in the Talking Mule movie *Francis in the Navy* (1955).

⊘ The long-suffering Alan Young (Wilbur Post) and his mischievous costar.

Hazel

Comedy | USA | 1961–66

Magic but no sorcery

Cast | Shirley Booth, Don DeFore, Whitney Blake, Ray Fulmer, Bobby Buntrock, Lynn Borden, Julia Benjamin
Original broadcaster | NBC
Awards | 2 Emmys
For fans of . . . | *The Jetsons* (1962), *Bewitched* (1964)

Hazel was as much a fantasy as its contemporary sitcom *Bewitched*, though its heroine was not a witch, but a lovable live-in maid played by Oscar-winner Shirley Booth. Hazel was loud, nosy, and cheeky, but so wise and thoughtful that she might as well have been a fairy godmother. (The two shows were filmed at the same studios, and the house next to that of Hazel's family was Darrin and Samantha's in *Bewitched*.) Booth won two Emmys for her performance, which in its first year became the fourth highest rated in the United States.

Brought to TV by producer James Fonda (no relation to the acting dynasty), *Hazel* was based on a *Saturday Evening Post* comic strip by Ted Key. It featured the title character trying to ensure all ran smoothly in the home of the Baxter family: lawyer George (Don DeFore), wife Dorothy (Whitney Blake), and young son Harold (Bobby Buntrock). Episodes revolved around conflict between Hazel and "Mr. B," whose attempts to assert his authority ended with Hazel proving who was boss.

After four seasons the show was dropped by NBC, but CBS took it on. To snare younger viewers, middle-aged George and Dorothy were shunted off to the Middle East and Hazel moved in with George's younger, hipper brother Steve (Ray Fulmer) and his family, taking little Harold with her. This incarnation lasted just a year.

But Booth's warmth keeps Hazel fondly remembered, and the show continues to be rerun in the United States. Her legacy also includes inspiring Rosie, the robot maid in *The Jetsons*, which premiered a year later. **IK**

The Rudi Carrell Show

Music/Musical | Germany | 1961–73

Musical numbers and slapstick comedy

Cast | Rudi Carrell, Petula Clark, Heidi Kabel, Heinz Erhardt
Original broadcaster | ARD
For fans of . . . | *Zum Blauen Bock* (1957), *Am laufenden Band* (1974), *Verstehen Sie Spass?* (1980)

Those who claim that "German sense of humor" is an oxymoron may point to the closing moments of any episode of *The Rudi Carrell Show* and rest their case. Named after its host, a Dutch entertainer who had presented a similar program in the Netherlands, the show consisted of musical performances and sketches, and always ended with Carrell being drenched in water.

In a country that appreciated slapstick, this never failed to amuse, and the enjoyment was heightened by the fact that the direction of the assault varied each time. It was a comedy of its time, during a period when the relationship between Germany and the Netherlands was uneasy. Carrell, who attracted millions of viewers on both sides of the border, arguably reconciled the two countries more than any other individual. Despite his deliberate Dutch accent, he was considered an honorary German, and when he received a lifetime achievement award in 2001, he told his adopted nation, "I owe this wonderful country my life."

The Rudi Carrell Show was his first foray on TV after a disastrous result in the *Eurovision Song Contest* in 1960 that, nevertheless, didn't hamper his success as a singer in Germany and the Netherlands. Each of the twenty-seven episodes broadcast in Germany had a different setting, such as a department store, station, or market. As well as inviting established musicians, Carrell regularly showcased new talent and swore by the maxim that several short sketches were better than a single long one. **DH**

The Avengers
Action/Adventure | UK | 1961–69

Eccentric, sexy, and extraordinarily British spy drama

Cast | Patrick Macnee, Diana Rigg, Honor Blackman, Linda Thorson, Ian Hendry
Original broadcaster | ITV **Award** | 1 BAFTA **For fans of . . .** | *The Man from U.N.C.L.E.* (1964), *The Prisoner* (1967)

In the early 1960s the United Kingdom and the United States went spy crazy. James Bond came to movie screens and TV audiences had shows such as *The Man from U.N.C.L.E.* and *The Avengers*. The latter was wonderfully British, capturing perfectly the stereotypical British gentleman in John Steed (Patrick Macnee), the independent (and ahead of their time) female characters, and the eccentric story lines and villains. It remains one of only a handful of British TV shows to have properly conquered the United States. Its success was partly due to its evolution, starting life as a vehicle for actor Ian Hendry as Dr. Keel, who along with John Steed tried to avenge the murder of his wife. After Dr. Keel left, Steed became the focal point and he

was joined by a succession of mold-breaking female sidekicks. These women were not only eye candy; they were Steed's equals, often doing more of the fighting than Steed himself. When Diana Rigg replaced Honor Blackman, the show went stratospheric; the will they/won't they flirtatious chemistry between Steed and Emma Peel is electric. **LH**

Classic episode
The Town of No Return | Season 4, episode 1.
Classic Avengers territory: a mysterious seaside town with eccentric locals, people disappearing and ending up dead, and a dollop of megalomania. Notable as Diana Rigg's debut as Emma Peel.

⊕ Honor Blackman and Patrick Macnee in a promotional shot for *The Avengers*.

The Dick Van Dyke Show
Comedy | USA | 1961–66

Classic, showbiz-based comedy

Cast | Dick Van Dyke, Mary Tyler Moore, Morey Amsterdam, Rose Marie, Carl Reiner **Original broadcaster** | CBS
Awards | 15 Emmys, 2 Golden Globes **For fans of . . .** | *30 Rock* (2006)

Brilliant young comedian Dick Van Dyke found this TV series a perfect vehicle for his many comedic talents (verbal, facial, physical). His casting as Rob Petrie, head writer for *The Alan Brady Show*, was a major factor in the show's success, but he was very strongly supported by an equally well-cast troop, especially Mary Tyler Moore as his beautiful wife, Laura. Tyler Moore proved that she could hold her own in the comedy stakes against Van Dyke's prodigious talents, and later she would graduate to her own groundbreaking series, *The Mary Tyler Moore Show* (1970). Rob's cowriters (and coconspirators) were wisecracking couple Sally (Rose Marie) and Buddy (Morey Amsterdam)—quick-thinking, fast-talking veterans who were more cynical than the sometimes naive Rob. Story lines revolved around Rob's professional and home lives and how each would impact on the other. Smarter than most contemporary shows, it exuded a classy, sophisticated air and, after bedding in for a season or two, became massively popular with the public and a frequent winner of a variety of awards. **DF**

Classic episode
My Husband Is Not a Drunk | *Season 2, episode 6*. Brilliantly sustained half-hour of classy comedy as Rob is compelled (by a posthypnotic suggestion) to act drunk every time he hears the sound of a bell.

Mary Tyler Moore and Dick Van Dyke in the episode titled "It May Look Like a Walnut," February 1963.

Dr. Finlay's Casebook

Soap opera | UK | 1962–71

The adventures of a country doctor in a simpler time

Cast | Bill Simpson, Andrew Cruickshank, Barbara Mullen, Eric Woodburn, Effie Morrison, Neil Wilson
Original broadcaster | BBC **For fans of . . .** | *All Creatures Great and Small* (1978), *Doctors* (2000)

For a decade, *Dr. Finlay's Casebook* defined the medical genre for British viewers. A highly popular drama of its day, its generation-gap tales of young Dr. Alan Finlay (Bill Simpson) clashing with elder mentor Dr. Cameron (Andrew Cruickshank) were taken to the nation's hearts.

Based on stories by A.J. Cronin, the show was a throwback to simpler times in rural Scotland. It made stars of Simpson, Cruickshank, and Barbara Mullen, who played no-nonsense receptionist Janet MacPherson. It was deft casting; the difference in age and outlook between Finlay and Cameron created tension at the heart of relationships that were ultimately affectionate. And in their interactions with patients, there were lessons to be learned, with Janet as the voice of reason.

In 1970, as the show neared its end, the trio moved to radio, and many TV scripts were adapted. ITV revived *Doctor Finlay* with David Rintoul in 1993 and, in 2001, John Gordon Sinclair took on the title role in new adaptations of Cronin's stories for BBC Radio 4. However, these later incarnations could never hope to eclipse the popularity of the fondly remembered original. **MW**

Classic episode
The Greatest of These Is Charity | *Season 7, episode 5*. Required to give an impassioned sermon from a pulpit, Cruickshank was dismayed to find that his character's views ran contrary to his own, and fought to change them.

◉ (L–R) Dr. Cameron (Andrew Cruickshank), Dr. Finlay (Bill Simpson), and Janet MacPherson (Barbara Mullen) at work.

Steptoe and Son

Comedy | UK | 1962–74

A father and son in a failing junk yard

Cast | Harry H. Corbett, Wilfrid Brambell   **Original broadcaster** | BBC
For fans of . . . | *Sanford and Son* (1972), *Porridge* (1974), *Arrested Development* (2003)

When their partnership with comedian Tony Hancock ended, writers Ray Galton and Alan Simpson turned to a series of one-off plays under the banner of *Comedy Playhouse*. For "The Offer," about junk men, they altered the series' approach of casting comedians, preferring stage actors Wilfred Brambell and Harry H. Corbett, who they felt would add reality to the situations.

The scripts and stars brought Pinteresque despair and claustrophobia to up to 28 million viewers a week. Albert Steptoe became one of TV's great grotesques—a skinny old man in a tin bath eating pickled onions from a jar, or cutting pastry with his dentures. Yet the skillful Brambell evoked sympathy for a lonely man terrified of being abandoned. Meanwhile, Corbett's Steptoe Jr.,

forever dreaming of a better life denied him by an emotionally manipulative parent, actually needed his father just as much as the "dirty old man" needed him.

The show spawned two movies and was successfully exported to the Netherlands as *Stiefbeen en zoon* (1963), to the United States as *Sanford and Son* (1972), and to Sweden as *Albert och Herbert* (1974). **JS**

Classic episode
The Desperate Hours | *Season 7, episode 7*.
Criminals Leonard Rossiter (*Rising Damp*) and J.G. Devlin (formerly shortlisted to play Albert Steptoe) break into the junk yard, only to learn that the owners are worse off than they are.

◉ Harry H. Corbett and Wilfred Brambell loathed each other but created TV gold.

Intervilles

Game show | France | 1962–present

Towns play silly games against each other in a bid for national supremacy

Cast | Guy Lux, Léon Zitrone, Jean-Pierre Foucault, Cécile de Ménibus
Original broadcaster | RTF
For fans of . . . | *It's a Knockout* (1966), *Treasure Hunt* (1982), *Fort Boyard* (1990)

In 1962, a contractual dispute between the organizers of the Tour de France and the television companies meant that that year's cycle race would not be broadcast live in its home country. That left a vast, gaping hole in the summer schedule. Producers Guy Lux and Pierre Brive stepped into the breach with a knockout tournament in which the people of various French towns played specially devised games against each other. The idea was based on a format previously used by the Italian station RAI on *Campanile sera* (1959).

Apart from a tug-of-war, most of the events were developed specially for visual appeal—instead of conventional, established sports like tennis or boules, competitors faced challenges with varying degrees of wackiness. In one event, they had to race each other along conveyor belts that were moving in the opposite direction to their own. In another, competitors stood on narrow pedestals while dodging a rubber demolition ball that revolved faster and faster in circles; their objective was to be the last one standing.

The Tour de France returned to French screens the following year, but demand for *Intervilles* was so great that it came back every year thereafter, apart from a three-season hiatus between 2010 and 2012. The show is currently broadcast by the Gulli network.

Having seen that the original Italian format worked just as well in France, other countries then followed suit. This gave rise to the *Jeux sans frontières* franchise, whose British iteration was entitled *It's a Knockout* (1966). **GL**

Sábado Gigante

Variety | Chile/USA | 1962–present

The world's longest-running variety show

Cast | Veronica Milagros, Mario Kreutzberger, Pedro de Pool, Javier Romero, Gloria Benavides
Original broadcasters | Canal 13, Univision
Award | 1 Emmy
For fans of . . . | *The Gong Show* (1976)

In 2006, Guinness World Records declared that *Sábado Gigante* was the world's longest-running variety show. It has been entertaining Spanish-speaking audiences for three hours every Saturday since August 8, 1962. Host and creator Don Francisco (Mario Kreutzberger) presents a frenetic mix of on-screen competitions, recurring comedy skits, guest acts, beauty contests, and human interest stories.

The show launched in Chile and gained a loyal following in Latin America before being acquired by Univisión, the American Spanish-language network, in 1986. The show has now reached one hundred million viewers in forty-two countries.

The show is popular for its on stage competitions, where contestants win prizes ranging from a six-pack of Coca-Cola to a brand-new car. Games include "El Chacal de la Trompeta," where the hooded character of El Chacal eliminates singers by blowing a trumpet in their face; "Póngale Ritmo," a freestyle dance competition; and the "Miss Colita" beauty pageant. The show has an unabashed approach to product placement, with Don Francisco inviting audiences to sing the jingles for various brands. Regular characters, such as La Cuatro (Gloria Benavides), appear in comedy skits set in hospitals, space stations, hotels, and a TV office.

The show is also an influential platform for reaching Latino audiences. Both Enrique Iglesias and Shakira performed here early in their careers—and even Barack Obama has made an appearance. **WML**

The Andy Williams Show

Variety | USA | 1962–71

Cozy musical variety show punctuated with zany comedy—
something for everyone

Cast | Andy Williams
Original broadcaster | NBC
Awards | 3 Emmys
For fans of ... | *The Judy Garland Show* (1963),
Des O'Connor Tonight (1977)

Showcasing Andy Williams' easy charm and warm voice interspersed with comedic interludes, *The Andy Williams Show* bridged the generation gap between those who enjoyed traditional easy-listening American pop music, and fans of the rock and psychedelic era.

The long-running variety show existed in two discrete incarnations. The first version, which aired after a series of popular specials, ran regularly from 1962 to 1967, and featured a wholesome US songbook vibe accompanied by novelty acts and comedy sketches. In 1967, Williams switched to occasional specials, including his very popular Christmas shows. Regular episodes of the series returned to the airwaves in 1969 and included rock music and flower-power psychedelia, featuring artists such as Elton John, The Rascals, Davy Jones, Ray Stevens, Creedence Clearwater Revival, and Blood, Sweat & Tears. One of the cultural touchstones created during this later era was a recurring sketch involving Williams and the Cookie Bear, played by stunt actor Janos Prohaska. The Cookie Bear would aggravate Williams, begging for a cookie, until Williams lost his usual composed demeanor and shouted the catchphrase, "Not now ... not ever ... never!"

After *The Andy Williams Show* was canceled in 1971, Williams returned with three specials a year, including at Christmas. Audiences welcomed him back into their living rooms to hear "It's the Most Wonderful Time of the Year," to admire his Christmas sweaters, and to visit with his family and famous friends. **RP**

Classic episode
Episode 17 | December 20, 1962. This introduced the viewers to The Osmonds. Andy Williams discovered Alan, Jay, Merrill, and Wayne Osmond on stage at Disneyland, and invited them to perform on his show.

◉ Jonathan Winters (left) acts up with host Andy Williams.

The Beverly Hillbillies

Comedy | USA | 1962–71

Fabulous fish-out-of-water fun with the mountain dwellers turned millionaires

Cast | Buddy Ebsen, Irene Ryan, Donna Douglas, Max Baer Jr., Raymond Bailey, Nancy Kulp
Original broadcaster | CBS
For fans of . . . | *The Real McCoys* (1957), *Petticoat Junction* (1963), *Green Acres* (1965)

The Beverly Hillbillies' premise—reiterated each week via its memorable theme song—was that a poor mountain man struck oil and, newly rich, transplanted his family from the backwoods of the Ozark Mountains to the millionaires' playground of Beverly Hills. Despite their fabulous wealth, the Clampett clan—father Jed, "Granny" Daisy, beautiful tomboy Elly May, and hulking dimwit Jethro—maintained their mountain ways, clashing comically with their new surroundings. They caused constant headaches for banker Mr. Drysdale, who tolerated the chaos to keep hold of Jed's fortune, while his secretary—game spinster Miss Hathaway—was often forces to deal with the Clampetts and the problems arising from their naive grasp of "city ways."

Created by Paul Henning, writer of many episodes of *The Bob Cummings Show* (1955), *The Beverly Hillbillies* was panned by critics, but proved a hit with audiences. (Henning considered siting the show in New York, but realized the cost of on-location shooting would be prohibitive.) It topped US ratings in its first season, and took up residence in annual top tallies for the rest of the 1960s. Henning's brand of cheerfully simplistic, culture-clash comedy continued with the hits *Petticoat Junction* (1963) and *Green Acres* (1965), while like-minded shows such as *Gomer Pyle: USMC* (1964) bolstered this vibrant subgenre—of which the Clampetts were the kings.

A big-screen version appeared in 1993, featuring an all-new cast and with Buddy Ebsen guesting as another of his TV alter egos, Detective Barnaby Jones. **DF**

Classic episode
Another Neighbor | Season 2, episode 26.
A countess (Jean Willes) moves in next door and falls for mountain-man Jed's charms. Ultimately, however, she marries her chauffeur (Burt Mustin, later seen in *Petticoat Junction*).

◭ The Hillbillies' 1921 Oldsmobile was modified by George Barris, the man behind the similarly iconic Batmobile and Munster Koach.

The Saint

Drama | UK | 1962–69

Man of mystery—less shaken not stirred, more suave and sophisticated

Cast | Roger Moore, Ivor Dean, Arnold Diamond
Original broadcaster | ITV
For fans of . . . | *Danger Man* (1960), *The Avengers* (1961), *The Persuaders!* (1971), *Return of the Saint* (1978), *The Saint in Manhattan* (1987)

Had he not gone on to play James Bond, Roger Moore would still have earned an immortal place in pop culture. Having made a name for himself in *Maverick* (1957) and *Ivanhoe* (1958), he inhabited the role of Simon Templar—aka the Saint—as if it were made for him. His suave performance as the enigmatic antihero embodied the essential cool of 1960s Britishness and proved popular on both sides of the Atlantic.

Based on books by Leslie Charteris, *The Saint* evolved from black-and-white to color midway through a seven-year, 118-episode run. The adventures of the modern-day Robin Hood proved a perfect mix of glamour and action as he took on underworld heavies to protect the vulnerable. For a supposed man of mystery, the character was oddly well-known. Most episodes began with a character identifying the "infamous" Simon Templar—the cue for an animated halo to appear above Moore's head and the catchy theme to kick in. Many episodes were adapted from Charteris' novels, but later the series moved into original territory.

Moore eventually became a producer of the show, and directed several episodes. Whether he would have been offered the role of Bond without it is debatable, but *The Saint* made him recognizable worldwide.

Attempts to revive the character largely fell flat, with the Ian Ogilvy starring *Return of the Saint* (1978) lasting just one season. Moore himself produced a pilot for a 2013 reboot starring Adam Rayner and Eliza Dushku, but this too failed to take flight. **MW**

Classic episode
Vendetta for the Saint | *Season 6, episodes 15 and 16.* A two-parter that received a theatrical release in Europe. Simon Templar becomes involved with the Sicilian Mafia when he investigates a murder. Former *Avengers* star Ian Hendry guests.

⏺ Roger Moore proved an exemplary Templar years before he became known for playing the role of James Bond.

The Virginian

Drama | USA | 1962–71

An everyday story of 1890s ranching folk in the Wild West of Wyoming

Cast | James Drury, Doug McClure, Lee J. Cobb, Roberta Shore, Clu Gulager, Sara Lane, Randy Boone
Original broadcaster | NBC **For fans of . . .** | *Gunsmoke* (1955), *Bonanza* (1959), *The High Chaparral* (1967)

It's no mean feat to secure a nine-season hit centered on an anonymous cowboy. But just as in Owen Wister's 1902 novel, which gave its title and broad outline to this colorful saga, nobody ever named the ranch foreman called "The Virginian." Far from harming the show, this enigmatic aura and the strength of the lead characters drove it into the top three longest-running TV Westerns, behind only *Gunsmoke* and *Bonanza*.

The ranch in question, Shiloh, was amid Wyoming's sparsely populated plains. In this isolated turn-of-the-century setting, great friendships and rivalries were forged around how men deal with women, horses, and cattle (perhaps not in that order). James Drury first played the tough but principled title character—often

referred to as "Ramrod"—in a one-off pilot in 1958. When NBC's *Wagon Train* relocated to ABC, a season of *The Virginian* was commissioned. Unusually, its episodes ran to ninety minutes of airtime including commercials.

The only major character to endure throughout was amiable ranch hand Trampas (Doug McClure), a lighter foil to the sober-minded, upstanding Virginian. **MWy**

Classic episode

The Horse Fighter | *Season 4, episode 13*. The Virginian hires Willock, a much-admired veteran horse tamer, but comes to regret his decision when when he realizes that his new employee is in cahoots with a gang of robbers.

⊘ (L–R) James Drury as The Virginian, Doug McClure as Trampas, and Gary Clarke as Steve Hill.

Z Cars

Crime/Mystery | UK | 1962–78

Heroes and villains on the streets of northern England

Cast | Stratford Johns, Frank Windsor, Joseph Brady, James Ellis, Brian Blessed, Jeremy Kemp, Colin Welland
Original broadcaster | BBC **For fans of . . .** | *Softly Softly* (1966), *Second Verdict* (1976), *The Bill* (1984)

Z Cars became the benchmark against which British cop shows were measured. Like *Dixon of Dock Green* (1955), its first few years were broadcast live. Unlike *Dixon*, these cops were flawed, and not all were heroes.

The "Z" referred to the call signs of patrol cars in the fictional Newtown. In the first episode, as a result of the death of an officer, new mobile patrols are set up, and Inspector Barlow (Stratford Johns) and Detective Sergeant Watt (Frank Windsor) seek suitable recruits. The series introduced future stars, such as Brian Blessed of *Flash Gordon* fame and Colin Welland, who later won a screenwriting Oscar for *Chariots of Fire*. It also attracted writers who became notable in British TV, including James Mitchell (*Callan*) and Alan Plater (*A Very British*

Coup). In the first few years alone, plots touched on arson, domestic abuse, blackmail, and homosexuality.

Z Cars' popularity led to a spin-off, 1966's *Softly Softly* (later *Softly Softly: Taskforce*), while Johns and Windsor reprised their roles for two curious series in which Barlow and Watt investigated notorious old cases: *Jack the Ripper* (1973) and *Second Verdict* (1976). **JS**

Classic episode
Loyalties | *Season 7, episodes 68 and 69*.
Sergeants Stone (*Passport to Pimlico* star John Slater) and Lynch (James Ellis, who had played a policeman in a *Morecambe & Wise Show* sketch) have a falling out in this two-parter.

⌖ (L–R) Frank Windsor, James Ellis, Stratford Johns, Joseph Brady, Colin Welland, Robert Keegan, and Donald Gee in 1965.

Wild Kingdom
Documentary | USA | 1963–present

I'll wait here while you look at these dangerous animals . . .

Cast | Marlin Perkins, Jim Fowler, Peter Eros, Tom Allen, Stan Brock, Stephanie Arne
Original broadcasters | NBC, syndication, Animal Planet
Awards | 4 Emmys
For fans of . . . | *Life on Earth* (1979), *Nature* (1982)

Viewers of *Wild Kingdom* in its heyday remember insurance company Mutual of Omaha's sponsorship and its American Indian head logo, the grandfatherly tones of narrator and host Marlin Perkins (who often resembled a gray Walt Disney), and the occasionally death-defying exploits of man in the field Jim Fowler. The show pioneered a hybrid approach; over the years cohosts, including Tom Allen, Stan Brock, and Peter Eros, taught viewers about an array of animals, filmed at zoos and in the wild. Other naturalists sometimes joined the *Wild Kingdom* team, including primatologist Dian Fossey. A 1984 episode, "Reunion with the Gorillas," followed Fossey back to Rwanda, where she had encountered the great apes. (The episode aired a year before her murder.)

Marlin Perkins had hosted a show called *Zoo Parade* (1950) and, with its producer Don Meier, devised this follow-up, never realizing the impact it would have on pop culture. A long-standing joke, pioneered by *The Tonight Show*'s Johnny Carson, involved Perkins remaining at a safe distance while Fowler tackled a predator for the camera. However, an encounter with an anaconda proved the host could hold his own.

Perkins fronted the show until 1985, when Fowler took over and remained through the end of the original series in 1988. (It was revived on Animal Planet in 2002.) *Wild Kingdom*'s impact on awareness of ecology and programming on networks like the Discovery Channel cannot be overestimated. **ATB**

Dinner for One
Comedy | West Germany | 1963

The black-and-white sketch that became an annual institution

Cast | Freddie Frinton, May Warden
Original broadcaster | NDR
For fans of . . . | *Meet the Wife* (1963), *Billy Liar* (1973), *ChuckleVision* (1987), *The Fast Show* (1994), *The League of Gentlemen* (1999), *Little Britain* (2003)

If the New Year's Eve practice of watching a ball drop is baffling to anyone outside of North America, there's a European staple that's even odder: *Der 90. Geburtstag* (*The Ninetieth Birthday*), aka *Dinner for One*.

Performed in English, the short sketch is set on the birthday of the aristocratic Miss Sophie (May Warden). Her butler, James, serves her dinner. As all her friends are dead, he pretends to be them. He serves the soup, the fish, the chicken, then the dessert—each course accompanied by a different wine. As the meal wears on, James becomes more and more drunk. At its close, Miss Sophie announces that she would like to retire to bed. Then comes the punchline. And that's it.

Initially a staple of British theaters, *Dinner for One* was recorded by a German TV producer. Audiences took to the piece, and it became a New Year's Eve fixture in West Germany. Then East Germany. Then Finland, Norway, the Faroe Islands, and South Africa. It is now a tradition worldwide (albeit virtually unknown in the United States, Canada, and Britain), and earned a *Guinness Book of Records* listing as the world's most repeated program. (Warden and Frinton received several thousand Deutsche Marks for their performance but the latter had cannily bought the rights to the sketch itself several years earlier, thus ensuring repeat fees.)

Over the years people have objected to its depiction of heavy drinking, its whiff of nonagenarian sex, and even the tiger-skin rug on the floor. But there is no stopping *Der 90. Geburtstag*. **JG**

Ready, Steady, Go!

Music/Musical | UK | 1963–66

"The weekend starts here"—seminal 1960s pop series that inspired the BBC to fight back with its own version

Cast | Keith Fordyce, Cathy McGowan
Original broadcaster | ITV
For fans of . . . | *American Bandstand* (1952),
Juke Box Jury (1959), *Top of the Pops* (1964),
Beat-Club (1965)

In the early 1960s, as pop music became the vanguard of a newly developing and revolutionary artistic and cultural movement, TV producers struggled to tackle the task of inventing a format to cover the emerging scene in a "hip" and "happening" way. *Ready, Steady, Go!* cracked the problem with an intoxicating blend of performances (lip-synched and live), celebrity interviews, competitions, and dance demonstrations, which cashed in on the growing popularity of pop music from artists on both sides of the Atlantic.

The show's main host was the avuncular Keith Fordyce (who had the air of a trendy uncle), but it was with the arrival of cohost Cathy McGowan—a pretty, miniskirted ingenue, who had answered an ad to become a teenage adviser on the show—that the series really took off. In its prime, the Friday night show lived up to its catchphrase—"the weekend starts here"—presenting the hottest acts and the most up-to-the-minute chart hits. The ramshackle nature of the production—with cameras in shot, dancers gathered close to the acts, and performances and interviews taking place in different areas of the studio—gave it a chaotic but appealing style. Featuring homegrown talents (The Beatles, The Rolling Stones, Dusty Springfield) alongside American superstars, the series coincided with, and exploited, the tremendous explosion of pop talent that was taking the world by storm. It covered the waterfront musically and offered a constantly innovative take on the music scene. **DF**

Classic episode
Motown Special | April 28, 1965. Dusty Springfield produced and hosted this special, introducing soul music to the wider British public. The Temptations, The Supremes, and Stevie Wonder were among the guests.

◉ The Rolling Stones appear on *Ready, Steady, Go!* in 1964.

Doctor Who
Fantasy/Horror/Sci-Fi | UK | 1963–present

Legendary show that has stood the test of time (and space)

Cast | William Hartnell, Patrick Troughton, Jon Pertwee, Tom Baker, Peter Davison, Colin Baker, Sylvester McCoy, Paul McGann
Original broadcaster | BBC
For fans of . . . | *Star Trek* (1966), *Farscape* (1999)

From humble beginnings (half-hour, semi educational adventures on a minuscule budget, shot originally in black-and-white in a tiny studio), *Doctor Who* captured the hearts of generations of British viewers and became the longest-running sci-fi TV show in history. The Doctor is a human-looking benevolent alien, who traveled through time and space (more often than not late twentieth-century Britain, for budgetary reasons), accompanied by a succession of companions (usually attractive young women), fighting scary villains and monstrous life forms. His conveyance, the TARDIS (Time and Relative Dimension in Space) should camouflage itself whenever it lands on a new planet, but it was stuck in the form of a 1950s London police box.

The reason for the program's longevity is a very clever trick, one that came about through necessity. In 1966, when William Hartnell was too ill to continue, the producers decided simply to morph Hartnell into his replacement, Patrick Troughton. Over time, viewers discovered that the Doctor was a 750-year-old Time Lord from the planet Gallifrey, able to regenerate his form when his body grew old or he was seriously injured.

After twenty-six seasons during which the Doctor fought such enemies as the Master, the Cybermen, and most famously the Daleks, ratings slumped and the series was dropped in 1989. However, the demand was such that it returned with a bang in 2005. **PC**

◁ William Hartnell as the Doctor meets his archenemies, the Daleks, for the first time, in this rehearsal photograph.

Let's Make a Deal

Game show | USA | 1963–76

Dream prizes and unwanted gifts

Host | Monty Hall
Original broadcaster | NBC
For fans of . . . | *Queen for a Day* (1956),
The Price Is Right (1956), *Sale of the Century* (1969),
Deal or No Deal (2005)

Like many popular game shows, *Let's Make a Deal*, created by Stefan Hatos and host Monty Hall, has lived many lives beyond its first incarnation—prime-time revivals, retitlings, relaunchings, new hosts, and revised formats—but the original version with Hall was what made it great. The host selected a person (or sometimes more than one) from the audience and made them an offer, typically presenting them with a choice between a cash prize or a prize that was hidden behind a curtain or door, or under a large prop box. Often the deal-making went from one contestant to another with Hall giving the prize not chosen from the first deal to another person, and giving them a chance to trade it for yet another unknown prize.

One key idea that made *Let's Make a Deal* exciting was the anticipation of a contestant trading something valuable for something useless. These booby prizes, which came to be called "zonks," were not always worthless, but they were usually impractical or undesirable, examples including a live camel or an oxcart. Winners of zonks could accept a cash amount in lieu of the unwanted prize. The other fascinating thing about *Let's Make a Deal* was the costumes that were worn by audience members to catch the host's eye. The costumes were not part of the original show until viewers began to notice what attracted Hall's attention. The outrageous accoutrements and costumes rapidly became one of the program's most well-known identifiers. **SWH**

The Judy Garland Show

Variety | USA | 1963–64

A showcase for a national treasure

Host | Judy Garland, Jerry Van Dyke,
Mel Tormé
Original broadcaster | CBS
For fans of . . . | *The Andy Williams Show* (1962),
The Mary Tyler Moore Show (1970)

After a series of successful specials, CBS offered mega star Judy Garland, who was struggling to keep her career alive, the chance to lead a weekly series.

Produced by George Schlatter (*Laugh-In*, 1967), Norman Jewison (*Fiddler on the Roof*, 1971), and Bill Colleran (*The Bing Crosby Show*, 1959), the series was to feature musical performances, comedy sketches, and recurring segments in which Garland addressed the audience and interviewed guests. The first guest was her old friend and co-star, Mickey Rooney. Garland was respected by her peers in the entertainment community, so was able to approach people such as Ethel Merman, Steve Allen, Count Basie, Tony Bennett, Barbra Streisand, Peggy Lee, and Lena Horne, as well as Ray Bolger, her old *Wizard of Oz* (1939) co-star, and Liza Minnelli, and Lorna and Joe Luft. The program showcased their talents, while putting her own sense of musicality, comedy, and pathos into the spotlight.

Garland would close each episode by singing the song "Maybe I'll Come Back," but after the show's original producers left, the program evolved into more of a Judy-in-concert show and it didn't come back for a second season. This could have been due to one or more of several factors: perhaps it was because the show was broadcast at the same time as the popular Western *Bonanza* (1959) on rival station NBC; maybe Garland had been away from the spotlight for too long. For whatever reason, *The Judy Garland Show* marks the beginning of the end of variety shows of its type. **RP**

The Fugitive

Action/Adventure | USA | 1963–67

A murdered wife. A one-armed man. An obsessed detective. A thriller that captivated viewers

Cast | David Janssen, Barry Morse, Paul Birch, Bill Raisch, William Conrad
Original broadcaster | ABC
Awards | 1 Emmy, 1 Golden Globe
For fans of . . . | *The Incredible Hulk* (1978)

Inspired by Victor Hugo's *Les Misérables*, *The Fugitive* popularized what became a TV thriller trope: a man falsely accused of a crime escapes police custody and sets out to prove his innocence. Created by Roy Huggins—also responsible for the hits *Maverick* (1957), *77 Sunset Strip* (1958), and *The Rockford Files* (1974)— *The Fugitive* was the perfect continuing drama. In the show, Richard Kimble—wonderfully played by *Richard Diamond, Private Detective* (1957) star David Janssen— was falsely convicted of his wife's murder, but escaped when the train carrying him to prison crashed. Kimble went on the run to hunt the one-armed man (Bill Raisch) he thought was the real murderer and was in turn pursued by Lieutenant Gerard (Barry Morse), who was fixated to the point of obsession on capturing his prey. Within this arc, individual episodes offered stand-alone stories featuring guests, including Robert Duvall, Telly Savalas, Dabney Coleman, and Ed Asner.

Key to the show's success was Kimble, a caring and brilliant doctor, feeling compelled to help those he encountered despite the risks to himself. Allied to the pursuit arc, each situation contributed to a powder-keg atmosphere. The story-resolving finale was watched by the United States' highest audience until the 1980 episode of *Dallas* that revealed who shot J.R.

The series inspired a successful movie in 1993 (with Harrison Ford as Kimble and Tommy Lee Jones as a less maniacal Gerard) and, in 2000, a CBS remake with Tim Daly and Mykelti Williamson. **DF**

Classic episode
Fear in a Desert City | *Season 1, episode 1*. In this opener, Kimble—who has been on the run for six months—jeopardizes his freedom to help an abused woman (Vera Miles, who later appears in another Huggins show, 1965's *Run for Your Life*).

◭ Janssen captured on film, if not in the story, during season one.

Thierry La Fronde
Action/Adventure | France | 1963–66

A dashing French version of the Robin Hood legend

Cast | Jean-Claude Drouot, Robert Bazil, Fernand Bellan, Jean Gras, Robert Rollis, Jean-Claude Deret
Original broadcaster | ORTF
For fans of . . . | *William Tell* (1958), *Robin Hood* (1984)

France has always hated any invasion by the English. In the 1960s the French were appalled to find their schoolchildren excitedly pretending to be Robin Hood, the English outlaw who struggled so valiantly against oppression. If they weren't pretending to be Robin Hood, they were playing at William Tell, another brave outlaw who was notionally Swiss (yet curiously, thoroughly British). The French answer was to invent their own hero, and in 1963 *Thierry La Fronde* debuted.

Oddly enough, the show was about how completely beastly *les Anglais* were. It was set during the Hundred Years' War (1337–1453) when France was occupied by the English and ruled by the cruel Black Prince. In Sologne, in the heart of France, lived Thierry of Janville (Jean-Claude Drouot), the noblest of young noblemen. He fought galliantly against the English occupation, but was betrayed by his steward, Florent (Jean-Claude Deret), and lost both his titles and his lands. Living in the woods, he took the name "Thierry La Fronde" and, with the help of his ragtag band of faithful companions, he continued his fight undercover. And so, the Alliance Française was formed.

Thierry La Fronde was an enormous success. It made the most of limited outdoor filming (a couple of streets were made to look like an entire town and a field doubled as a forest). Good deeds were done, nothing too gruesome happened, and the English were beaten every week. Fast-paced and with a stirring theme, the series was followed in 1965 by *Robinson Crusoe*. **JG**

The Outer Limits
Fantasy/Horror/Sci-Fi | USA | 1963–2002

Classic sci-fi series with tales of horror and wonder

Cast | Vic Perrin, Bob Johnson, Ben Wright, Alex Diakun, Eric Schneider
Original broadcaster | ABC
For fans of . . . | *Alfred Hitchcock Presents* (1955), *The Twilight Zone* (1959)

"There is nothing wrong with your television set. Do not attempt to adjust the picture." So went the opening narration for *The Outer Limits,* which, like its earlier CBS counterpart *The Twilight Zone*, would bring dramatic stories of science fiction and horror into American homes on a weekly basis.

Creator Leslie Stevens devised the anthology series to remain untied to any specific actor (unlike Rod Serling's appearances in *The Twilight Zone*), and the only common ground between each episode was Vic Perrin's haunting narration. However, it was very much grounded in the speculative fiction genre, written by top names in the field, and it was really quite serious and dramatic. Bug-eyed monsters, savage creatures, and terror from the dark were commonplace; there was little room for whimsy and lightness, or obvious morals to the story. Contemporaneous dramas were no match for the raw horror and hard science-fiction *The Outer Limits* provided; it was only the unstoppable curse of low ratings that halted the series in its tracks.

Considered a major influence on science fiction TV and film that followed—especially on TV shows such as *Star Trek* (1966) and films including *Close Encounters of the Third Kind* (1977)—it was no surprise that the format was brought back by the Showtime network and Canadian partnership in 1995. This revived series also presented tales by well-known science fiction and horror writers, and enjoyed a seven-year run (its final two on the Sci Fi Channel). **SL**

Jill Haworth and David McCallum star in the episode "The Sixth Finger," of *The Outer Limits*, broadcast in 1963. ❷

Bewitched

Comedy | USA | 1964–72

Suburban life was turned upside down by glamorous witch Samantha, her meddling mother Endora, and her baby daughter Tabitha

Classic episode
Man's Best Friend | *Season 2, episode 34.* A warlock, played by Richard Dreyfuss, turns himself into a dog so that he can be adopted by Samantha, whom he loves, and be taken into her home and break up her marriage.

◉ The female characters work their magic in *Bewitched.*

Cast | Elizabeth Montgomery, Dick York, Dick Sargent, Agnes Moorehead, Larry Tate
Original broadcaster | ABC
Awards | 3 Emmys   **For fans of . . .** | *The Addams Family* (1964), *I Dream of Jeannie* (1965)

In 1964, the supernatural sitcom captured the public's imagination. *The Munsters* and *The Addams Family* crept onto US screens, but neither was as successful as the story of a witch called Samantha, who tried to put aside her powers to become a housewife, but usually failed. She cast spells by twitching her nose.

Bewitched followed a familiar format, generating comedy from misunderstandings with friends, nosy neighbors, and the classic sitcom boss. The plot was driven by the need to keep Samantha's powers a secret. Not helping the situation was Endora, the mother-in-law from hell, who disapproved of Samantha's mortal husband, Darrin.

Bewitched peaked at second place in the Nielsen ratings during its first year. Perhaps part of its success was the subversive situation. Though a stay-at-home mother, Samantha was much more powerful than her husband. In creating the role, Elizabeth Montgomery brought lightness and charm.

The show had its problems. Regular actors Marion Lorne and Alice Pearce died, while Dick York (Darrin) collapsed on set during the fifth season and was replaced by Dick Sargent. Montgomery's marriage to producer William Asher had broken down by 1972, hastening the end. That came after 254 episodes, and the series has been repeated and syndicated ever since. In 2005, Nora Ephron directed a mediocre postmodern movie inspired by and called *Bewitched*, starring Nicole Kidman, Will Ferrell, and Shirley MacLaine. **WH**

Crossroads

Soap opera | UK | 1964–88; 2001–03

Much-mocked yet much-loved motel antics—drama was never far away from the ringing of the reception bell

Cast | Noele Gordon, Tony Adams, Ronald Allen, Susan Hanson, Paul Henry, Sue Lloyd, Jane Rossington
Original broadcaster | ITV
For fans of . . . | *Howards' Way* (1985), *Victoria Wood: As Seen on TV* (1985)

With unsteady sets and disaster-prone dialogue, the *Crossroads* motel had barely opened before the critical kickings began. Its daily format took an inevitable toll on production values, yet the show proved the British public's enduring fondness for the underdog, at its peak earning ratings that threatened the supremacy of the nation's soap heavyweight *Coronation Street* (1960).

Shepherded to screens by producer Reg Watson—who later gifted the world *Prisoner* (1979)—the show initially centered on the contrasting lives of motel owner Meg Richardson (Noele Gordon) and her down-at-the-heels sister Kitty Jarvis (Beryl Johnstone). However, viewers made it clear whom they preferred: such was Gordon's soaring popularity that there were headlines and protests when, exhausted by the filming schedule, she attempted to resign in 1968. Johnstone's death in 1969 put an end to the original concept, and other popular characters emerged—most memorably simpleminded handyman Benny Hawkins (Paul Henry).

Gordon was fired in 1981, a move variously attributed to a desire to steer the show in a grittier direction, to kill it off entirely, or to punish the actress for her on-set demands. With her character's demise, *Crossroads'* fate was sealed, and it was axed in 1988—living on in spirit in comedian Victoria Wood's "Acorn Antiques" sketches.

The show was revived in 2001, but initial curiosity failed to translate into enduring ratings. Scheduled against another Reg Watson production, *Neighbours*, it flagged further and was canceled in 2003. **DJ**

Classic episode
Episode 4,928 | May 30, 2003. In the final episode, new motel owner Jane Asher is revealed to be a checkout girl who has dreamed the entire series. The show "didn't take me into the realm of high art," the actress admitted, "but I had a lot of fun."

⬣ Noele Gordon with *Crossroads'* cocreator and writer Peter Ling.

Gilligan's Island

Comedy | USA | 1964–67

"Sit right back and you'll hear a tale . . . a tale of a fateful trip"

Cast | Bob Denver, Alan Hale Jr., Jim Backus, Natalie Schafer, Tina Louise, Russell Johnson, Dawn Wells
Original broadcaster | CBS   **For fans of . . .** | *The Beverly Hillbillies* (1962), *Survivor* (2000)

It was supposed to be a three-hour tour, but for the crew and passengers of the S.S. *Minnow*, a leisurely trip at sea turned into three seasons (one black-and-white) of high jinks. A storm swept them to an unknown island, three TV movie reunions, and a pop culture legacy that continues to entertain generations.

Created by Sherwood Schwartz, who later gave us *The Brady Bunch* (1969), the series was ideal for a long afterlife in syndication. From week to week, little progressed in the lives of the castaways (although the TV movies did see them rescued, only to return to the island to open a resort). For three years they faced threats like headhunters and extreme weather, and welcomed countless visitors to the impossible-to-find island—only to foul up their chances for rescue every time, usually thanks to the bumbling Gilligan (Bob Denver). The castaways entertained themselves with homespun pop music and waited for the Professor (Russell Johnson) to concoct a coconut-based invention to solve whatever problem they faced.

The slapstick routines of Gilligan and The Skipper (Alan Hale Jr.) were lifted from the likes of Laurel and Hardy, while there were jokes aplenty at the expense of upper-crust couple Thurston Howell III and his wife, Lovey (Jim Backus and Natalie Schafer).

The characters and most of the original cast returned in two cartoon follow-ups, *The New Adventures of Gilligan* (1974) and *Gilligan's Planet* (1982). **ATB**

⦿ Bob Denver as the much-loved Gilligan, a role he reprised on *Baywatch* in 1992.

Peyton Place

Drama | USA | 1964–69

Interconnected lives and loves in a New England idyll with a clapboard church and picket fences

Cast | Dorothy Malone, Ryan O'Neal, Mia Farrow, Barbara Parkins, Ed Nelson, Christopher Connelly, Lee Grant
Original broadcaster | ABC **Award** | 1 Emmy **For fans of . . .** | *All My Children* (1970)

Although continuing dramas had been a staple of American daytime schedules for some years, *Peyton Place* was the first such drama intended for a prime-time evening slot. Based upon the best-selling 1956 novel of the same name by Grace Metalious and the subsequent 1957 film adaptation, starring Lana Turner, the series of twice-weekly, half-hour episodes was intended to emulate the success of the British series *Coronation Street*, which had then been running for three years with considerable success.

Viewers were introduced to *Peyton Place* and its characters by the incoming Dr. Michael Rossi (Ed Nelson), who had moved his practice there from New York. It quickly became apparent, however, that small-town life wasn't necessarily simple. When love blossomed between Allison McKenzie (Mia Farrow) and Rodney Harrington (Ryan O'Neal), other intrigues and infidelities soon unfolded.

The producer and writer Paul Monash eschewed much of what he considered the tawdry sensationalism in Metalious' novel and sought, instead, to craft what he described as a "novel for television" about "people evolving toward the light." In an article for *New York Times Magazine* in 1965, he said, "Though an episode ends in a cliff-hanger, you can await the sequel without anxiety. For unlike the world we live in, villains will always be punished, justice will always be done, character will be improved by adversity. You are among friends." JJJ

◓ The cast of *Peyton Place* in 1966, when the townsfolk were preoccupied with secrets, scandals, and a murder trial.

Le inchieste del commissario Maigret

Drama | Italy | 1964–72

*TV adaptations of George Simenon's stories about Inspector Maigret—
the author's favorite renderings of his books*

Cast | Gino Cervi, Andreina Pagnani, Mario
Maranzana, Franco Volpi, Oreste Lionello,
Original broadcaster | RAI
For fans of . . . | *Sherlock Holmes* (1968), *I racconti
di padre Brown* (1970)

Wrapped in a winter coat with a velvet collar, trademark
pipe in his mouth, Gino Cervi in Italian TV's *Le inchieste
del commissario Maigret* (*The Inquiries of Inspector
Maigret*) was the essence of the fictional detective.
While Cervi nailed the enigmatic central character,
Maigret, the moody ambience of the Parisian *quartiers*
where he unraveled the crimes was captured by the
series' black-and-white photography—most of which
was filmed in the studio due to budget constraints.

Maigret was the creation of Belgian crime writer
Georges Simenon, and was probably inspired by the
real-life Chief Inspector Marcel Guillume, considered to
be the best French detective of his time and a friend
of Simenon. The author wrote seventy-five novels and
twenty-eight stories about Maigret between 1931 and
1972. The books were adapted for TV, film, and radio in
many countries, and were even released in comic form
in Japan as manga *Juzo Megure*.

The Italian series comprised of four seasons with
sixteen episodes, and the last episode, in 1972, peaked
with 18.5 million viewers. An earlier British version
produced in 1960 starred Rupert Davies, and another
British production, starring Michael Gambon, was
released in 1992. Meanwhile, German, Dutch, Japanese,
and Russian adaptations appeared, as well as a French-
Swiss-Belgian coproduction. Many excellent actors
have interpreted Maigret worldwide, but Simenon
himself always seemed to prefer Cervi, whom he called
"his" Maigret. **AC**

Classic episode
*L'innamorato della signora Maigret (Madame
Maigret's Lover)* | *Season 2, episode 4.* Mrs.
Maigret has a faithful suitor who sits every day in
the gardens in front of Maigret's house. One day
he is found dead with a shotgun wound.

◉ Gino Cervi as Inspector Maigret in 1959.

The Likely Lads

Comedy | UK | 1964–66

*Northern lads put the world to rights . . .
in the pub*

Cast | James Bolam, Rodney Bewes, Bartlett Mullins,
Don McKillop, Sheila Fearn, Olive Milbourn
Original broadcaster | BBC
For fans of . . . | *Steptoe and Son* (1962), *Whatever
Happened to the Likely Lads?* (1973)

Writers Dick Clement and Ian La Frenais created *The
Likely Lads* in the wake of British theater's wave of "angry
young men": young, working-class, and disillusioned.
In Terry Collier (James Bolam) and Bob Ferris (Rodney
Bewes), the viewers saw the trials of modern young
men played out in double dates, work at the local
factory, and pseudophilosophy in the pub. While Bob
was a cautious dreamer, Terry's wilder side often got
them into trouble. *The Likely Lads* ran for just twenty
episodes over three seasons, ending with Bob in love
and Terry accidentally signed up to join the army.

  Seven years later, the duo returned in *Whatever
Happened to the Likely Lads?* (1973), which began with
Terry returning from his tour of duty to find Bob on the
verge of marriage. The latter's fiancée quickly identified
Terry as a bad influence, while he realized he'd never
quite rescue his old friend from her domineering grasp.

  With most of the 1960s series being wiped from
the BBC archives and the remaining episodes being
black-and-white, *The Likely Lads* has been somewhat
eclipsed by its sequel. (The latter's melancholy yet
memorable theme song, "Whatever Happened to
You," was written by La Frenais and Manfred Mann's
Mike Hugg.) However, the BBC made radio adaptations
of both series, and a movie version appeared in 1976.

  The legacy of *The Likely Lads* is evident in later
comedies, such as *Men Behaving Badly* (1992) and *Red
Dwarf* (1988), in which the answers to life's mysteries
could be solved by a discussion over a drink. **JS**

Seven Up!

Documentary | UK | 1964–present

*"A glimpse of England in the year 2000" . . .
from 1964*

Cast | Bruce Balden, Jackie Bassett, Symon Basterfield,
Andrew Brackfield, John Brisby, Peter Davies
Original broadcaster | ITV
Awards | 3 BAFTAs
For fans of . . . | *Age 7 in America* (1991)

"Give me a child until he is seven and I will give
you the man." This Jesuit belief inspired a series of
interviews that, to date, has spanned half a century.
Beginning in 1964, fourteen children from different
backgrounds across Britain were asked about life and
their understanding of the world around them. In 1970,
the researchers returned to see how the children had
progressed, and continued to do so every seven years.

  Researcher-turned-director Michael Apted (whose
résumé ranges from James Bond to C.S. Lewis) has
followed his subjects through adulthood. Not all of
the original fourteen continued to participate (Charles
Furneaux, producer of the TV show *Panorama* and
documentary movie *Touching the Void*, declined), but
most stayed with the project through *56 Up* in 2012.

  Consequently, viewers have seen early hopes
dashed, families raised, and life-threatening illnesses
faced. Perhaps most dramatically, Neil Hughes' arc has
stretched from high-flying student to homelessness,
then standing for election as a Member of Parliament.

  The experiment has been tried across the globe
with versions launched in the Soviet Union in 1990,
the United States in 1991, and South Africa in 1992. A
second generation of seven-year-olds were recruited
for a new British cycle that began with *Entourage*
director Julian Farino's *7Up 2000* (2000) and *14Up 2000*
(2007). Selected from across the United Kingdom,
they represented a much more diverse sample than
the originals, yet faced an equally uncertain future. **JS**

The Addams Family

Comedy | USA | 1964–66

"They're creepy and they're kooky, mysterious and spooky . . . They're altogether ooky . . .
We're gonna pay a call on the Addams family"

Classic episode
Christmas with the Addams Family | Season 2,
episode 15. When a mean neighbor tells Pugsley
and Wednesday that there's no Santa Claus, the
family rally around to prove that there is. The
episode aired on Christmas Eve in 1965.

◈ Gomez (John Astin), Fester (Jackie Coogan), and Itt (Felix Silla).
◉ Morticia (Carolyn Jones, center) proves weird is relative.

Cast | Carolyn Jones, John Astin, Jackie Coogan, Lisa
Loring, Ken Weatherwax, Ted Cassidy, Blossom Rock
Original broadcaster | ABC
For fans of . . . | *The Munsters* (1964), *Scooby-Doo,*
Where Are You! (1969), *The League of Gentlemen* (1999)

Adapted from Charles Addams' series of single-panel
cartoons in *The New Yorker*, this sitcom combined the
homespun family values of *The Dick Van Dyke Show*
(1961) with the macabre charms of *The Twilight Zone*
(1959). Amid sadomasochistic innuendos and morbid
humor, it offered an inspirational vision of family unity
and a marriage in which passion flourished despite the
presence of two school-age children and often irksome
relatives. But what made *The Addams Family* the cooler
cousin of *The Munsters* (also 1964) was the opportunity
it offered to revel in the ghoulish, the sinister, and—
in the case of matriarch Morticia—the downright
seductive, without worrying about the consequences.
(Carolyn Jones had starred in the horror movies *House
of Wax* (1953) and *Invasion of the Body Snatchers* (1956).)

The central relationship between the upbeat Gomez
and his paramour Morticia was enchanting, although
their offspring, Wednesday and Pugsley, were more
unsettling, playing on a fear of children akin to *The
Bad Seed* (1956) or *Children of the Damned* (1964). Butler
Lurch ("You rang?") and disembodied hand Thing
provided domestic support, while the extended family
included the hirsute Cousin Itt, the electrocution-prone
Uncle Fester, and the wackily witchy Grandmama.

Less popular than *The Munsters* at the time, *The
Addams Family* has arguably proved more influential
and enduring, thanks to animated, live-action,
cinematic, and theatrical adaptations that have kept
the inventively disturbing clan close to our hearts. **JS**

Jeopardy!

Game show | USA | 1964–present

The answer is . . . a game show where the answer is a question

Cast | Art Fleming, Alex Trebek, Don Pardo, John Harlan, Johnny Gilbert **Original broadcasters** | NBC, syndication
Awards | 17 Emmys **For fans of . . .** | *Rock & Roll Jeopardy!* (1998), *Who Wants to be a Millionaire?* (2002)

Alongside *Wheel of Fortune* (1975) and *The Price Is Right* (1956), *Jeopardy!* is one of the holy trinity of game shows. Conceived by singer-turned-TV star Merv Griffin, it tests three contestants' knowledge of trivia, the twist being that their answers must be in the form of a question. (This format has been traced, by tvtropes. org among others, to 1941's *CBS Television Quiz*.)

In its original NBC and syndicated incarnations, the show was hosted by Art Fleming—a role he reprised in the 1982 movie *Airplane II: The Sequel*. After a five-year break from 1979, it was revived in 1984 and Canadian game show veteran Alex Trebek took the reins. Known for his soft-spoken, witty banter with contestants, Trebek is still at the helm over three decades later.

Contestants tackle topics ranging from geography and politics to art and literature. Two games are played with variable amounts of money at stake, followed by a final question involving as much risk as the player wishes. (The show's theme song, played over the deciding moments of the final round, is called "Think!"—composed by Merv Griffin as a lullaby for his son.) The format made stars of champions Ken Jennings and Brad Rutter, who both faced IBM's computer Watson.

Syndicated in prime time across America, *Jeopardy!* has spawned international variants, catchphrases ("Daily Doubles," "I'll take . . ."), and parodies—notably *Saturday Night Live*'s "Celebrity Jeopardy," with appearances aplenty by Darrell Hammond as Sean Connery. **SL**

◬ Alex Trebek with Julia Collins, the record-breaking contestant who became the biggest female money-winner in show history.

Top of the Pops

Music/Musical | UK | 1964–2006

Charting the risers, fallers, and nonmovers of the hit parade for more than four decades

Cast | Every successful pop act of the last half-century
Original broadcaster | BBC **For fans of . . .** | *Ready, Steady, Go!* (1963), *Later With Jools Holland* (1992)

It took executives at BBC Radio a while to catch on to the passion for pop music among British teens, but their colleagues in TV were quicker off the mark. Every week from 1964 until 2006, a changing roster of DJs would introduce *Top of the Pops*, featuring acts rising up the pop singles charts. Some acts performed live, but most lip-synched, while a studio audience danced.

It was by no means the first pop music show—*Six-Five Special* (1957) and *Ready, Steady, Go!* (1963) had focused on chart acts—but its countdown structure, building to the unveiling of that week's number one, added drama. This formula served every music trend, from Merseybeat and glam rock, to punk and New Wave, through to a new century. However, in 2006,

BBC managers decided that the program's time had passed. A *Top of the Pops* special, featuring the year's biggest releases, still forms part of the BBC schedule on Christmas Day, but its main function is now as a heritage brand, with compilation programs broadcast under the "TOTP2" banner. Repeats of the show are shown on BBC Four, though those featuring Jimmy Savile, the program's most enduring host, were banned after a long history of sexual abuse perpetrated by Savile came to light after his death in 2011.

International versions appeared in Germany, France, the Netherlands, and New Zealand. Attempts to create a version in the United States failed against stiff competition from the *American Top 40* radio show. **JS**

⏴ The Beatles' only live *Top of the Pops* appearance. They performed their new single, "Paperback Writer," on June 16, 1966.

The Man from U.N.C.L.E.

Action/Adventure | USA | 1964–68

1960s espionage antics that went from the sublime to the ridiculous

Cast | Robert Vaughan, David McCallum, Leo G. Carroll
Original broadcaster | NBC
Award | 1 Golden Globe
For fans of . . . | *The Avengers* (1961), *Mission: Impossible (1966)*

In the early 1960s, movies led and TV followed. With the success of the first James Bond movie, *Dr. No*, in 1962, it wasn't long before TV produced its own spy franchise in *The Man From U.N.C.L.E.*, a slick, often irreverent drama, in which Bond writer Ian Fleming had a hand.

Fleming worked with television producer and *U.N.C.L.E.*'s cocreator Norman Felton on fleshing out secret agent Napoleon Solo. Legal wranglings with Bond's movie producers ended Fleming's association, but the similarities with Bond remained. Solo (Robert Vaughn) was a member of the U.N.C.L.E. organization (United Network Command for Law and Enforcement), working alongside Russian agent Ilya Kuryakin (David McCallum). Assigned missions by Alexander Waverley (Leo G. Carroll) from U.N.C.L.E.'S secret headquarters in New York (famously accessed through Del Floria's Tailor Shop), the agents thwarted the sinister T.H.R.U.S.H. with an array of gadgets, guns, and guile.

The Man from U.N.C.L.E. was popular during its first, monochrome season. By the third season, though, ratings had slipped, as camp slapstick took hold (though a spin-off, *The Girl from U.N.C.L.E.*, starring Stephanie Powers, ran in 1966 and was canceled in 1968). But rumors of a new mission for the men from U.N.C.L.E. are never far away. Although *The Return of the Man from U.N.C.L.E.*, featuring Vaughn and McCallum, failed to catch on in 1983, a movie headlined by Henry Cavill and Armie Hammer as Solo and Kuryakin was released in 2015. **MW**

Classic episode
The Mad, Mad Tea Party Affair | *Season 1, episode 18*. On the eve of an important conference, Solo and Kuryakin must stop attacks on the base's security systems and prevent a T.H.R.U.S.H. infiltrator from assassinating world leaders.

◬ David McCallum (Kuryakin) and Robert Vaughn (Solo) in 1964.

The Munsters

Comedy | USA | 1964–66

The infamous inhabitants of 1313 Mockingbird Lane

Cast | Fred Gwynne, Yvonne De Carlo, Al Lewis,
Butch Patrick, Beverley Owen, Pat Priest
Original broadcaster | CBS
For fans of . . . | *The Addams Family* (1964), *The
Munsters Today* (1988), *Mockingbird Lane* (2012)

It's hard to believe that the arrival on screens of two horror-themed sitcoms could have been coincidence, yet the idea for *The Munsters* had long been in development. In any event, *The Addams Family* beat it to air by less than a week, but *The Munsters* offered broader laughs, and duly beat its rival in the ratings.

The Munsters benefited from access to Universal Studios' horror back catalog. Head of the household Herman (*Car 54, Where Are You?*'s Fred Gwynne) caricatured Frankenstein's monster, as played by Boris Karloff and Lon Chaney Jr., in a costume so heavy that the actor began to lose weight and dehydrate. His wife, Lily (Yvonne De Carlo, told to play the role like Donna Reed), and father-in-law, Sam "Grandpa" Dracula (Al Lewis, another *Car 54* veteran), were vampires, while young Eddie (Butch Patrick, who had graced the pilot of *General Hospital*) had the look of a young werewolf. Lily's niece Marilyn (Beverley Owen for the pilot and first thirteen episodes, then Pat Priest) was conventionally beautiful in the style of a 1950s scream queen—yet the family pitied what they saw as her plain appearance.

The family were resurrected in 1988 for *The Munsters Today*. Now in color, with an all-new cast, it racked up more episodes than the original, but ultimately won less exposure and never threatened the definitive status of the original. Another reboot, *Mockingbird Lane*, failed to get past the pilot stage despite the directorial talents of Bryan Singer and the presence of stars such as Portia de Rossi and Eddie Izzard. **JS**

Classic episode
Munster Masquerade | *Season 1, episode 1.*
Marilyn wants to introduce her boyfriend to the family, so he suggests inviting Herman and Lily to his parents' fancy dress party. Unfortunately, Grandpa wants to come, too.

⊘ (L–R) Beverley Owen, Al Lewis, Fred Gwynne, and Yvonne De Carlo.

Voyage to the Bottom of the Sea

Fantasy/Horror/Sci-Fi | USA | 1964–68

Aquatic adventures and monsters of the week

Cast | Richard Basehart, David Hedison, Bob Dowdell, Henry Kulky, Terry Becker, Del Monroe, Paul Trinka
Original broadcaster | ABC   **Awards** | 4 Emmys   **For fans of . . .** | *Lost in Space* (1965), *SeaQuest DSV* (1993)

Piloting the *Seaview* wasn't plain sailing for Admiral Harriman Nelson (Richard Basehart) and Captain Lee Crane (David Hedison); the research-oriented submarine encountered a ceaseless parade of aliens, mad scientists, and creatures of all shapes and sizes.

Created by producer Irwin Allen (*Lost in Space, The Time Tunnel, Land of the Giants*), *Voyage to the Bottom of the Sea* was based on his 1961 movie of the same name. To save money, the show recycled footage, costumes, and props from its big-screen antecedent.

Set in the 1970s and '80s, the series began with more plausible stories of Cold War-inspired international espionage and environmental threats. Increasingly, however, werewolves and lobster men took the place of foreign agents. This monster-of-the-week format became a hallmark, as did the *Flying Sub* introduced in the second season and the way the crew lurched to simulate battle, dubbed the "Seaview Rock and Roll."

The *Seaview* docked for the last time at the end of its fourth year, by which time *Star Trek* had taken over both its *Wagon Train*-esque remit and its lurching. **ATB**

Classic episode

The Sky's on Fire | *Season 2, episode 18*. Using material shot for, and the plot of, the movie that preceded the series, the crew of the *Seaview* fight the clock and sabotage from within to save the world from an explosive atmosphere.

⊘ Richard Basehart (Nelson) and David Hedison (Crane) prepare themselves for the creatures of the deep.

The Big Valley
Western | USA | 1965–69

The lives and loves of a wealthy Wild West family

Cast | Barbara Stanwyck, Lee Majors, Richard Long, Linda Evans, Peter Breck, Napoleon Whiting
Original broadcaster | ABC **Award** | 1 Emmy **For fans of . . .** | *Gunsmoke* (1955), *Dallas* (1978)

One of the most reliable actresses of any generation, Barbara Stanwyck proved her mettle as Victoria, the matriarch of California's Barkley family, overcoming obstacles and adversaries with every bit as much muscle and ingenuity as the cowboy heroes of the time, in this Western from the producers of *The Rifleman*.

Victoria's adult children were lawyer Jarrod (Richard Long, formerly of *77 Sunset Strip*), ranch manager Nick (Peter Breck, another *77 Sunset Strip* bit player), and Audra (Linda Evans, later Krystle in *Dynasty*), who followed her mother's tough yet tender lead. Brawling his way into the family in the first episode was Heath (future *Six Million Dollar Man* Lee Majors), the eventually accepted bastard son of Victoria's late husband.

The most exciting aspect of *The Big Valley* was watching Stanwyck hold her own against an array of threats. She clearly relished the opportunity to—as she once said in an interview—"go where the boys go" and in the course of four seasons was the only Barkley not to be shot at least once, despite regularly putting herself in harm's way to protect her family. **SWH**

Classic episode
The Profit and the Lost | *Season 4, episode 9.*
Robert Loggia stars as Vern Hickson, a killer sent to dispatch Heath Barkley. When Heath saves Hickson's life, the story gives way to an exploration of conflicting interests and loyalties.

Outlaw Sam Beldon (Harold J. Stone) kidnaps Victoria (Stanwyck) so that she can teach him to read, in "Teacher of Outlaws," 1966.

I Dream of Jeannie

Comedy | USA | 1965–70

Well-executed fantasy comedy with just the right amount of mischief

Cast | Barbara Eden, Larry Hagman, Bill Daily, Hayden Rorke, Barton MacLane, Emmaline Henry, Vinton Hayworth
Original broadcaster | NBC
For fans of . . . | *Bewitched* (1964)

When astronaut Tony Nelson (Larry Hagman) was stranded on a Pacific island and discovered a bottle that conjured an alluring two-thousand-year-old genie (Barbara Eden), he did what any man would do—he resisted her advances and tried to prevent her from using her magic for his benefit. He also attempted to obscure her existence and abilities with varying success. Created by Sidney Sheldon to combat ABC's *Bewitched* (1964) and partly inspired by the film *The Brass Bottle* (1964), which also featured Eden, *I Dream of Jeannie* was supposed to star a brunette in order to differentiate Jeannie from *Bewitched*'s blonde star Elizabeth Montgomery. Eden's audition changed this.

The first season was in black and white and the rest followed in color. National contests determined the outcome of multipart stories. When Tony and Jeannie married in the final season, this change contributed to a drop in viewers and ultimate cancellation. But Jeannie had not disappeared for good: in two TV movies—*I Dream of Jeannie . . . Fifteen Years Later* (1985) and *I Still Dream of Jeannie* (1991)—Eden reprised the role, but without Hagman on both occasions.

The show made a lasting impact on pop culture, confirmed by the inclusion of Jeannie's harem outfit and iconic genie bottle in the Smithsonian Institution in Washington, D.C. In fact, Eden donned a version of her costume at the age of seventy-eight for the 21st Life Ball charity event, proving that she still had what it took to be Jeannie. **ATB**

Classic episode
Happy Anniversary | *Season 2, episode 1*. Tony finds himself stranded on the same island exactly one year after he found Jeannie on the beach. There he finds another genie who enslaved Jeannie two thousand years ago.

◍ Barbara Eden as the mischievous genie, Jeannie.

Green Acres

Comedy | USA | 1965–71

The pig-friendly place to be

Cast | Eddie Albert, Eva Gabor, Pat Buttram, Tom Lester, Frank Cady, Alvy Moore, Hank Patterson, Barbara Pepper, Sid Melton, Mary Grace Canfield
Original broadcaster | CBS
For fans of . . . | *Petticoat Junction* (1963)

When Oliver Douglas (Eddie Albert) tired of life as a New York lawyer, he and his hotcake-baking, Hungarian wife, Lisa (Eva Gabor, sister of Zsa Zsa), quit the city for the country . . . only to find loony sight gags, defiantly dopey down-home wisdom, and a school-going, piano-playing, newspaper-delivering pig named Arnold (name-dropped in the 1994 movie *Pulp Fiction*).

Drawn from creator Jay Sommers' *Granby's Green Acres* radio comedy, the series shared a rural subgenre with *The Andy Griffith Show* (1960), *Petticoat Junction* (1963, on which Sommers served as producer and writer), and *The Beverly Hillbillies* (1962,for which he wrote two episodes). It even shared *Petticoat Junction's* location, Hooterville, and, occasionally, its characters.

When CBS ill-advisedly purged its schedules of shows that appealed principally to older viewers, the series was brought to an end in 1971. Many of its stars reunited for the 1990 TV movie *Return to Green Acres*, which followed a somewhat predictable pattern by threatening the residents of Hooterville with a real-estate swindle. But all was right by the movie's end . . . and, yes, Arnold was there, too.

Using in-jokes (the title sequence parodied Grant Wood's iconic painting *American Gothic*, 1930), avant-garde editing (the characters noticed the on-screen credits), and surreal twists to finesse even the silliest jokes into a whirlwind of whimsy, *Green Acres* was later embraced as a show well ahead of its time. Maybe that pig knew something all along. **ATB**

Jeux Sans Frontières

Game show | Various countries | 1965–99

Crazily contrived physical game show

Cast | Guido Pancaldi, Gennaro Olivieri, Eládio Clímaco, Simone Garnier, Stuart Hall, Claude Savarit
Original broadcasters | Various
For fans of . . . | *Eurovision Song Contest* (1956), *Takeshi's Castle* (1986), *Total Wipeout* (2009)

Thanks to *Takeshi's Castle*, *Total Wipeout*, and their international variants, obstacle-based game shows are now so common that no one blinks on seeing padding-clad contestants toppling into water. In the 1960s and 1970s, however, such sights were a novelty. Sadly, history does not record whether that's quite what French President Charles De Gaulle had in mind when he mooted an Olympics-style tournament that would unite the youth of France and Germany.

Its antecedents were Britain's *Top Town* and Italy's *Campanile sera*, which pitted those nations' towns against each other in sports-style events. The latter evolved into France's *Intervilles* (1962), one of the most enduring nonsport game events. The international version, *Jeux Sans Frontières* (*Games Without Frontiers*), began courtesy of the European Broadcasting Union.

Britain weighed in with *It's a Knockout* (1966), whose winners represented the country in *Jeux Sans Frontières*, competing against contestants from similar shows in countries including Germany, Spain, Belgium, and Portugal. (A 1987 British edition, *The Grand Knockout Tournament*, featured members of the country's royal family. Despite raising over £1 million for charity, it was so poorly received that neither the show nor the royals were ever again regarded with the same affection.)

At its peak, with oversized inflatable characters and ever-more-ludicrous obstacles, *Jeux Sans Frontières* drew a reported one hundred million viewers. But ultimately, it fell victim to prohibitive production costs. **JS**

Hogan's Heroes

Comedy | USA | 1965–71

A group of POWs attempt to bring down the Axis powers from the inside

Cast | Bob Crane, Werner Klemperer, John Banner, Robert Clary, Richard Dawson, Larry Hovis, Cynthia Lynn, Sigrid Valdis   **Original broadcaster** | CBS   **Awards** | 2 Emmys   **For fans of . . .** | *M*A*S*H* (1972), *'Allo 'Allo* (1982)

Hogan's Heroes followed a group of prisoners of war inside fictional Stalag 13. Using the camp as a base to coordinate resistance groups, Colonel Robert Hogan (Crane) and his group of American, British, and French soldiers were unintentionally assisted by incompetent camp leaders Colonel Klink (Klemperer) and Sergeant Schultz (Banner), who regularly said, "I see nothing," to avoid trouble. The duo's ineptitude often caused Hogan to defend their roles, lest skilled soldiers replaced them.

Two decades after the Second World War, the show ushered in a new way of thinking about the conflict and the absurd comic situations that could arise. It was criticized for its farcical interpretation of significant events, but the actors playing the German soldiers were all Jewish, and had fled Germany during the rise of Hitler; Clary had spent three years in a concentration camp. It eventually aired in Germany in the 1990s, with the characters exaggerated to caricatures. The show's impact on modern culture was confirmed when Klink appeared as Homer's conscience in *The Simpsons*. In 2013, a movie adaptation was announced. **EB**

Classic episode
War Takes a Holiday | *Season 3, episode 21*. In order to free a group of prisoners from the Gestapo, Hogan tricks the prison guards into believing that armistice has been declared and that the Second World War is finally over.

⊕ (L–R) John Banner (Schultz), Bob Crane (Hogan), and Werner Klemperer (Klink) in "The Great Impersonation" in 1965.

Lost in Space

Fantasy/Horror/Sci-Fi | USA | 1965–68

One small step for solemnity, one giant leap for silliness

Cast | Guy Williams, June Lockhart, Mark Goddard, Marta Kristen, Angela Cartwright, Billy Mumy, Jonathan Harris, Dick Tufeld, Bob May **Original broadcaster** | CBS **For fans of . . .** | *Voyage to the Bottom of the Sea* (1964)

Created by Irwin Allen, *Lost in Space* followed the Space Family Robinson as they set off from Earth in 1997 to colonize a distant planet. Sabotaged by stowaway Dr. Zachary Smith (Jonathan Harris), the Robinsons found themselves roaming the stars in the saucer-shaped ship *Jupiter 2*, occasionally taking refuge on alien planets and encountering bizarre creatures and technology.

Initially, Smith was a genuine threat and the focus was firmly on Robinson patriarch John (Guy Williams) as he led his family through the perils of space survival. But noting how much viewers enjoyed the comedic combination of Smith, his foil the Robot (Dick Tufeld and Bob May), and the brilliant young Will (Billy Mumy), producers began to marginalize the rest of the cast.

Smith became a bumbling troublemaker with a penchant for alliteratively berating the Robot and manipulating Will into schemes to obtain money or a way home, even if it meant risking everyone's lives.

Late attempts to restore the balance did not assuage Williams' dismay and few in the cast were disheartened when the show was axed. Oh, the pain, the pain! **ATB**

Classic episode
Visit to a Hostile Planet | *Season 3, episode 2*. The *Jupiter 2* returns to Earth . . . in 1947. As the family wrestles with staying in an unfamiliar time or heading back into space, Smith plots to destroy the ship and keep everyone home.

⊘ (Clockwise from left) Angela Cartwright, Billy Mumy, Marta Kristen, Jonathan Harris, Guy Williams, and June Lockhart.

Not Only . . . But Also . . .
Comedy | UK | 1965–70

The genius of Peter Cook and Dudley Moore

Cast | Peter Cook, Dudley Moore
Original broadcaster | BBC
Awards | 2 BAFTAs
For fans of . . . | *Rowan & Martin's Laugh-In* (1968),
Monty Python's Flying Circus (1969)

Conceived as a vehicle for mischievously humorous everyman Dudley Moore—whose talent for comedy was matched by his mastery of jazz piano—this sketch show was intended to have been billed as *Not Only (Dudley Moore) But Also [that week's guests]*.

However, among contributors to the 1964 pilot (alongside John Lennon and Diahann Carroll) was mercurial improviser Peter Cook, Moore's partner in the stage revue *Beyond the Fringe*. The chemistry between the two was irresistible and the series became a home for their double act. They created a host of characters—notably pontificating idiots Pete and Dud, whose "Film Stars" sketch set a benchmark for their future collaborations. Combining sophisticated satire with sexual innuendo and absurd premises, the pair conjured a free-flowing, surreal mélange in which they could often be seen stifling their own laughter.

In-studio and filmed sketches were complemented by musical guests ranging from Dionne Warwick to Mel Tormé, and interludes featuring Moore and his band. Producers/writers Joe McGrath (who won a BAFTA for his work on the show, and went on to direct 1967's *Casino Royale*), and Dick Clement and Jimmy Gilbert (both of whom went on to *Whatever Happened to the Likely Lads?*, 1973) created a space for Cook and Moore to explore the more lunatic side of their shared sense of humor. Sadly, much of the series fell victim to the BBC's wiping of its tape archives, although a classic episode with Peter Sellers resurfaced in 2004. **DF**

The White Horses
Action/Adventure | Yugoslavia | 1965

Popular equestrian-themed children's drama

Cast | Helga Anders, Helmuth Schneider,
Franz Muxeneder
Original broadcasters | RTV (Yugoslavia),
Südwestfunk (Germany)
For fans of . . . | *Belle, Sebastian and the Horses* (1968)

A German–Yugoslav coproduction, this series was originally filmed with German dialogue and Serbo-Croat subtitles. It comprised only thirteen twenty-five-minute episodes, but it has lived on in the collective memory of children of the 1960s, particularly in Britain, because of its haunting theme song. "White Horses," written by Michael Carr and Ben Nisbet, was originally used and intended only for the dubbed, English-language version of the show, but such was its appeal that it was later adopted in all markets. Released as a single in 1968, it became a UK Top Ten hit for singer Jacky (Irish vocalist Jackie Lee).

The main story line concerned the adventures of Julia (Helga Anders), a teenager from Belgrade, Yugoslavia (modern Serbia), who spent a summer holiday with her uncle, Dmitri (Helmuth Schneider), who was raising white thoroughbred Lipizzaner horses on a stud farm in Lipica, the town in modern Slovenia for which these animals are named.

Shortly after her arrival, a stallion named Boris was stolen, and Julia set off with the head groom, Hugo (Franz Muxeneder), to find him.

The thieves dyed the horse's coat brown to conceal his true identity, but that didn't fool the intrepid pair, who recognized him immediately and returned him to his rightful owner. Julia and Boris subsequently formed a strong affinity, and horse and rider had several other outings together before the end of what turned out to be the only season. **GL**

I Spy
Action/Adventure | USA | 1965–68

Espionage with attitude—and the first black lead in an American drama

Cast | Bill Cosby, Robert Culp
Original broadcaster | NBC
Awards | 4 Emmys, 1 Golden Globe
For fans of . . . | *The Man from U.N.C.L.E.* (1964),
The Greatest American Hero (1981)

Best known as a stand-up comedian, Bill Cosby was cast in a surprisingly serious role as Alexander Scott, a secret agent for the Pentagon masquerading as a tennis pro's trainer. Posing as tennis player Kelly Robinson was Robert Culp, whose résumé included *The Man from U.N.C.L.E.* and *The Outer Limits*. With exotic international locations serving as the backdrop for gritty adventures leavened by lively and humorous byplay between the two leads, *I Spy* staked out a unique spot in the booming world of TV secret agents.

Created by Sheldon Leonard (executive producer of *The Andy Griffith Show* and *The Dick Van Dyke Show*), the groundbreaking show never made Cosby's race a factor in the show itself, which depicted the two agents as equals, with mutual respect and a lighthearted but dedicated attitude to their careers. The rapport between Cosby and Culp—which was mirrored in their personal lives and led to ad-libbing on the set—made the show magnetic, and a precursor to later buddy cop movies (including Cosby and Culp's *Hickey & Boggs* in 1972).

I Spy went to great lengths to capture the global scope of James Bond's escapades by filming on location in countries such as Japan, Greece, Italy, and Spain. It spawned tie-in books, comics, soundtrack albums featuring the music of series composer Earle Hagen, and a 2002 movie starring Eddie Murphy and Owen Wilson. Cosby and Culp reprised their roles in the 1994 TV movie *I Spy Returns* and again in "My Spy", an episode of Cosby's self-titled 1999 series. **ATB**

Classic episode
The Tiger | *Season 1, episode 15*. Scripted by star Robert Culp and loosely based on the show's pilot, this 1966 episode dared to take the viewers to the controversial setting of Vietnam. Guest star France Nuyen married Culp a year later.

◉ Robert Culp and Bill Cosby had a novel approach to disputing line calls.

Days of Our Lives
Soap opera | USA | 1965–present

This long-running daytime serial revolves around lives and loves in the small town of Salem

Cast | Deirdre Hall, John Aniston, Lauren Koslow, Bryan Dattilo, Josh Taylor, Alison Sweeney
Original broadcaster | NBC **Awards** | 39 Emmys **For fans of . . .** | *General Hospital* (1963)

From its modest beginnings as a peek into the lives of several families in the community of Salem (never quite precisely identified in a particular state, but with all the trappings of a New England hamlet), *DOOL*, as *Days of our Lives* is dubbed, became one of the longest-running shows on US TV. It has followed multiple formats over the decades and aired as both half-hour and hour-long episodes.

The show was the birthplace of the modern soap "supercouple," in which much of the action focuses on the romantic tangles of a particular couple, in this case Dr. Marlena Evans (Deirdre Hall) and John Black (Drake Hogestyn), which are then extensively hyped in the media. In the 1990s, the show boosted viewing figures by embracing the supernatural, with Marlena Evans floating above her bed when she became possessed, and the character Jack Deveraux (Matthew Ashford) returning from the dead three times. Story lines can be convoluted with outlandish developments to overcome the problem of actors leaving and returning to the show.

The show has long united the generations by bringing back beloved characters from different periods in its history, and many of its current cast have been with the program since the 1970s and 1980s.

Days of Our Lives is aired in many countries throughout the world, on various networks. It is currently NBC's only daytime drama series. **SL**

⬥ Lauren Koslow (Kate Roberts) and John Aniston (Victor Kiriakis) formed a treacherous partnership in the 1990s.

The Dating Game

Game show | USA | 1965–80

The contestant asks the questions; the prize is a date

Cast | Jim Lange
Original broadcaster | ABC   **For fans of . . .** | *Singled Out* (1995), *Take Me Out* (2010)

Created by Chuck Barris and hosted by Jim Lange, *The Dating Game* reflected the state of American relationships through the sexual revolution of the 1960s and early 1970s. The show was first shown in black-and-white, but in 1966, a color version ran in prime time. The daytime edition updated to color concurrently, becoming the first regular ABC daytime show broadcast in color.

In most episodes, the audience was introduced to three bachelors and a bachelorette, who were seated on opposite sides of a panel; therefore they could not see one another. The bachelorette lobbed softball and mildly risqué questions at the bachelors, who attempted to impress her with funny, clever, and romantic answers. Based on their responses and voices, the bachelorette chose a winner, and the show paid for the pair to go on a sponsored date. Occasionally, the sexes were switched and a bachelor questioned three bachelorettes. A surprising number of celebrities appeared as contestants early in their careers, including Burt Reynolds, Farrah Fawcett, Michael Jackson, Tom Selleck, Lindsay Wagner, Steve Martin, and Arnold Schwarzenegger. Each episode signed off with Lange and the contestants blowing the audience a kiss.

In the United Kingdom, *The Dating Game* was reworked slightly to become *Blind Date*. It enjoyed a hugely successful eighteen-year run from 1985, hosted by former pop star Cilla Black. **RP**

⊙ The best bit of *The Dating Game* was the fact that the contestants could not see one another—and the audience could see them all.

Thunderbirds

Action/Adventure | UK | 1965–66

Thunderbirds are go! . . . F.A.B.

Cast | Peter Dyneley, Sylvia Anderson, David Graham, Shane Rimmer, Jeremy Wilkin, David Holliday, Ray Barrett, Matt Zimmerman, Christine Finn **Original broadcaster** | ITV **For fans of . . .** | *Stingray* (1964), *Joe 90* (1968)

Millionaire and former astronaut Jeff Tracy shared a tropical island home with his sons Scott, John, Virgil, Gordon, and Alan, father–daughter domestic staff Kyrano and Tin-Tin, and a scientist, Brains. Beneath the island was an impressive array of vehicles that could carry the boys across land, sea, or air, and even into space—for Tracy was the head of a secret outfit called International Rescue, who intervened in dangerous situations to avert crisis. They were helped by their London agent Lady Penelope and her chauffeur, Parker.

Creators Gerry and Sylvia Anderson had captured imaginations with "supermarionation" thrillers *Supercar* (1961), *Fireball XL5* (1962), and *Stingray* (1964). With *Thunderbirds*, they reached an iconic pinnacle: thirty-two ambitious, fifty-minute disaster movies involving film-standard scale-model work. The Andersons' trademark hardware here yielded an aircraft, a submarine, and a space station, in addition to the Tracy Island complex. Coupled with catchphrases "*Thunderbirds* are go!" and "F.A.B.," these—and the impeccable puppetry—made the show iconic. **JS**

Classic episode

Trapped in the Sky | *Season 1, episode 1.* Terrorists have planted a bomb on a new aircraft—aboard which is Tin-Tin, the daughter of Jeff Tracy's manservant Kyrano. Looks like the perfect situation for International Rescue's first mission.

◆ The pilot of *Thunderbird 2*, Virgil Tracy.

Till Death Us Do Part

Comedy | UK | 1966–75

Backfiring satire with iconic antihero Alf Garnett

Cast | Warren Mitchell, Dandy NIchols, Una Stubbs, Anthony Booth, Patricia Hayes, Bill Maynard, Alfie Bass
Original broadcaster | BBC **Award** | 1 BAFTA **For fans of . . .** | *All in the Family* (1971)

From Al Bundy to Barney Stinson, TV is full of characters whose reprehensible behavior and views have made them favorites. Blazing this trail was a working-class bigot from London's East End, brought to life by writer Johnny Speight. "I did not create Alf Garnett," Speight said. "Society created him. I just reported him."

Garnett's worldview, formed by Speight keeping his ears open while "standing around in pubs," was harsh on immigrants and women; his description of wife Else (Dandy Nichols) as a "silly moo" has entered the British lexicon. Jewish actor Warren Mitchell delivered lines about Hitler ("Granted, he had his faults"), "the Jews," and other targets with such conviction and charisma that Garnett became an icon. (Guests in the series

included comedian Spike Milligan and soccer legend Bobby Moore, while Garnett's son-in-law was played by Tony Blair's father-in-law, Anthony Booth.)

Garnett returned in 1981's short-lived *Till Death . . .*, the better-received *In Sickness and In Health* (1985), and a handful of TV specials, and is best known internationally for inspiring *All in the Family's* Archie Bunker. **BM**

Classic episode

Three Day Week | *Season 5, episode 5*. Alf's wife, Else, decides to follow the reduced working week imposed by Britain's government In early 1974. Dandy NIchols' finest hour, this was repeated in tribute when she passed away in 1986.

⊘ Else (Nichols) and her bigoted husband Alf (Mitchell) in 1967.

Batman

Action/Adventure | USA | 1966–68

Tongue-in-cheek capers with the Caped Crusader

Classic episode
The Thirteenth Hat/Batman Stands Pat | Season 1, episodes 13 and 14. Using a hypnotic ray, the Mad Hatter (Jervis Tetch) kidnaps the jurors who convicted him. His final target is Batman, whom he traps inside a plaster statue.

🅐 Adam West (Batman) leaps into history.

Cast | Adam West, Burt Ward, Alan Napier, Neil Hamilton, Madge Blake, Stafford Repp, Frank Gorshin, Cesar Romero, Julie Newmar, Eartha Kitt
Original broadcaster | ABC
For fans of . . . | *Wonder Woman* (1975)

Batman was the first TV adaptation of Detective Comics' "Dark Knight." Light, colorful, and funny, it was this show that Tim Burton and Christopher Nolan kicked against with their respective movie franchises. But for many who grew up watching Adam West and Burt Ward "THWACK!" and "POW!" their way through a litany of criminals, they were the definitive Dynamo Duo.

Lifting the Caped Crusader from the page, creator William Dozier (also the series' emphatic narrator) chose a comedic approach. The show's design was bright and cartoonish, and guest actors—many of them Hollywood stars—enjoyed camping it up as the "Special Guest Villain." But despite the anarchy around them and their absurd superhero costumes, West and Ward played their roles with complete commitment.

To begin with, each two-part story followed a rigid formula, with some scenes almost identical from week to week. A crime would be committed; Commissioner Gordon would recognize the calling card of a malevolent mastermind and summon Batman; millionaire Bruce Wayne and his ward Dick Grayson would head to the Bat Poles to adopt their alter egos; and at the end of part one, one or both of our heroes would be in deadly peril.

The format was changed in the third season with longer, self-contained episodes and the introduction of Batgirl. A fourth season was mooted after the series was canceled, but by then the Batcave set had been dismantled and it was too late. **WH**

Raumpatrouille Orion

Fantasy/Horror/Sci-Fi | Germany | 1966

An international spaceship patrols the universe

Cast | Dietmar Schönherr, Eva Pflug, Claus Holm, Wolfgang Völz, Ursula Lillig, Frederich George Beckhaus
Original broadcaster | ARD
For fans of . . . | *Star Trek* (1966), *UFO* (1969)

Broadcast over four months in 1966, the seven black-and-white episodes of *Raumpatrouille Orion* (*Spaceship Orion*) was West German television's first foray into science fiction. Beginning with a groovy mid-60s theme song by Peter Thomas, the series represented optimism and internationalism, with nations reaching jointly into space. However, nothing was straightforward for Major Cliff McLane and his crew. They contended with intergalactic disasters and the warlike "Frogs"—dimly seen, shimmering humanoids whose malevolence was never in doubt.

The show is often described as a European riposte to *Star Trek*, and there are similarities. However, the West German series had been in the pipeline for some time when *Star Trek* first aired in the United States—a mere nine days before the first broadcast of *Raumpatrouille Orion* in West Germany. It is likely that both series were simply inspired by the zeitgeist of the period.

From time to time, Orion's crew returned to the spacecraft's base, on the seabed of planet Earth, where they relaxed in the imaginatively realized officers' mess, the "Star-light Lounge," with its outsized marine life swimming overhead. Although the series' design and effects appear, to modern eyes, somewhat less than special, the work of Götz Weidner and Rolf Zehetbauer represented the height of West German filmmaking at the time, and the series' budget—a substantial DM 3.4 million—required a collaboration with French public television station ORTF. **JJJ**

Softly Softly

Crime/Mystery | UK | 1966–76

Crime-busting duo who wouldn't go quietly

Cast | Stratford Johns, Frank Windsor, Norman Bowler, John Barron, David Lloyd Meredith, Terence Rigby
Original broadcaster | BBC
For fans of . . . | *Z Cars* (1962), *Second Verdict* (1976), *The Bill* (1984), *Inspector Morse* (1987)

The BBC's *Z Cars* (1962) took a two-year break in 1965, but there was life for the detectives in spin-offs that endured into the next decade. In *Softly Softly* (from the proverb, "Softly, softly, catchee monkey"), Inspectors Charles Barlow (Stratford Johns) and John Watt (Frank Windsor) were assigned to head a new plainclothes division tackling crime on the streets of Great Britain.

For five seasons from 1966, many of its episodes were broadcast live, as *Z Cars* had been. *Softly* was one of the final BBC dramas to use this outmoded practice and, consequently, few episodes are held in the archives.

Johns' and Windsor's contrasting performances as the domineering Barlow and soft-spoken Watt were at its heart, but an ensemble joined them, including Norman Bowler as the popular Sergeant Harry Hawkins. With the BBC's move to color broadcasting, the show was retooled in 1969: Barlow, Watt, and Hawkins were promoted to a new unit and, one week after *Softly Softly* ended, *Softly Softly: Taskforce* was on the beat.

After four seasons, Johns departed for *Barlow at Large* (1971), though he was reunited with Windsor in *Second Verdict* (1976), in which Watt and Barlow investigated historical cases. Both iterations of *Softly* were hits, but, in 1975, a harder-edged police drama arose: *The Sweeney* and, the following year, *Taskforce* ended. However, Windsor had a final opportunity to revive his character in the last *Z Cars* in 1978. He had played Watt in over three hundred episodes of five different shows. **SL**

Dark Shadows

Soap opera | USA | 1966–71

The daytime soap opera with the heartthrob vampire

Cast | Jonathan Frid, Kathryn Leigh Scott, Nancy Barrett, Grayson Hall, Lara Parker, David Selby, Joan Bennett, Roger Davis, Alexandra Moltke, Jerry Lacy **Original broadcaster** | ABC **For fans of . . .** | *Sunset Beach* (1997)

Early episodes of *Dark Shadows* mined works of popular nineteenth-century fiction, such as *Jane Eyre*. By the end of its run, five years and 1,225 episodes later, the show had become the strangest soap opera on television.

The Collins family lived in a mansion overlooking the town of Collinsport. Matriarch Elizabeth was a recluse who lived with her daughter Carolyn, her alcoholic brother Roger, and his wayward son David.

There was spookiness from the start, but the show followed standard soap opera tropes—acrimonious rivalries and long-lost relatives. Ratings were poor until the writers introduced Barnabas Collins (Jonathan Frid). Audiences loved him and the actor received the adulation normally reserved for rock stars.

Innovations continued. Characters moved through time and into a parallel universe. Other supernatural creatures joined, including the witch Angelique and heartthrob werewolf Quentin Collins.

With daily episodes recorded as live shortly before broadcast, *Dark Shadows* remains an impressive imaginative and organizational achievement. **WH**

Classic episode

Season 1, episode 212. Elizabeth meets visitor Barnabas Collins, who introduces himself as a cousin from England. He claims descent from the Barnabas Collins whose portrait hangs in her hall, but he doesn't just look like him. . . .

⊘ Jonathan Frid as the 175-year-old vampire Barnabas Collins.

Mission: Impossible

Action/Adventure | USA | 1966–73

Your mission, should you choose to accept it . . .

Cast | Steven Hill, Peter Graves, Martin Landau, Barbara Bain, Greg Morris, Peter Lupus, Leonard Nimoy
Original broadcaster | CBS **Awards** | 10 Emmys, 3 Golden Globes **For fans of . . .** | *The Avengers* (1961)

Shadowy agents using elaborate techniques to pull off "impossible" missions on foreign soil, the Impossible Missions Force knew that, if they were captured, the government would "disavow all knowledge of them."

Their leader—Dan Briggs (Steven Hill) in the first season, then Jim Phelps (Peter Graves)—received assignments via tapes that promptly self-destructed. Then femme fatale Cinnamon Carter (Barbara Bain), master of disguise Rollin Hand (Martin Landau), technical wizard Barney Collier (Greg Morris), and "muscle" Willy Armitage (Peter Lupus) carried out fabulously complicated plots to topple dictators, initiate coups, or free dissidents. (Leonard Nimoy came on board in 1969, as another disguise expert.)

Opening with a burning fuse allied to Lalo Schifrin's Grammy-winning theme, the show was a hit, thanks to its stylized set pieces (the playing of the tape, the choosing of the team, the carrying out of the caper). It returned to TV (on ABC) in 1988, with Graves leading a new cast, and inspired a blockbuster movie franchise that began in 1996, starring Tom Cruise. **DF**

Classic episode
The Mind of Stefan Miklos | *Season 3, episode 13*.
On a rare US-based mission, the team's attempts to foil an enemy agent contain all the usual shenanigans, but with everything notched up a level. Ed Asner is among the guest stars.

⊘ (L–R) *Mission*-aries Peter Graves, Martin Landau, and Greg Morris.

Star Trek

Fantasy/Horror/Sci-Fi | USA | 1966–69

To boldly go into a new era of science fiction—warp speed ahead

Cast | William Shatner, Leonard Nimoy, DeForest Kelley, Nichelle Nichols, James Doohan, George Takei
Original broadcaster | NBC
For fans of . . . | *Lost in Space* (1965), *Battlestar Galactica* (2004)

Captain Kirk. Mr. Spock. Dr. McCoy. The USS *Enterprise*. It's hard to imagine a time in which these icons, these symbols of pop culture, were not present in our psyche. But, in 1966, *Star Trek* was anything but universal.

Created by TV writer (*Have Gun—Will Travel*, *The Lieutenant*) Gene Roddenberry, *Star Trek* was envisioned as a "Wagon Train to the Stars." It met resistance from networks, financial and technical obstacles, and even refusal by NBC to broadcast its first pilot (starring Jeffrey Hunter). Granted a rare second shot with a new pilot starring William Shatner, *Star Trek* headed into history, but only after a fight. The blend of philosophy, humor, and heroics earned it a loyal audience, but not a vast one. It faced cancellation threats at the end of each of its three seasons, the third proving fatal. The adventures of the *Enterprise* seemed to be at an end.

But then the legacy began. Syndication propelled it into more homes than ever. An animated series launched in 1973, and a mooted live-action revival in the 1970s—*Star Trek: Phase II*—instead led to twelve blockbuster movies, and spin-offs *The Next Generation* (1987), *Deep Space Nine* (1993), and *Voyager* (1995).

Today, the world remains captivated by the show's mission, "To boldly go where no man has gone before." As star Leonard Nimoy remarked, "I thought it could have a long future. It is set in the future, so it wouldn't outdate itself very quickly." **SL**

> The *Enterprise*, after which the first space shuttle was named.

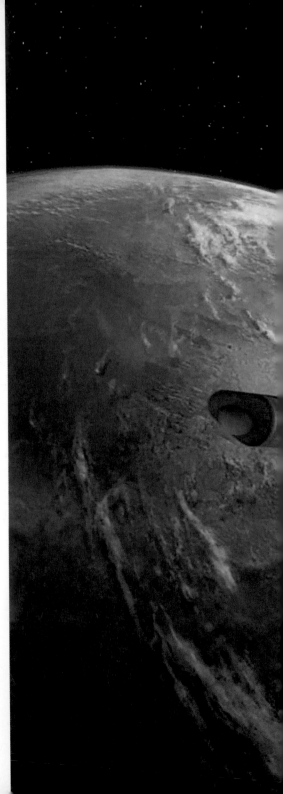

The Monkees
Music/Musical | USA | 1966–68

The crazy antics of a manufactured band who were just monkeying around

Cast | Davy Jones, Micky Dolenz, Michael Nesmith, Peter Tork   **Original broadcaster** | NBC
Awards | 2 Emmys   **For fans of . . .** | *Monty Python's Flying Circus* (1969), *The Goodies* (1970)

Bob Rafelson and Bert Schneider created The Monkees as both a band and a TV show, each promoting the other. Heavily inspired by The Beatles—specifically the loose, partly improvised style of their movies *A Hard Day's Night* (1964) and *Help!* (1965)—the show followed the adventures of a folk-rock band forever on the verge of stardom. They lived together in a crazy apartment and were frequently drawn into the lives of California's many eccentrics. These adventures were interrupted by songs (courtesy of some of the best writers around), which meant that fans were familiar with the band's catalog when a new album came out.

The Monkees ran for fifty-eight episodes across two seasons, living on in syndication. The band also starred in a movie, *Head* (1968), a nonlinear celebration of the counterculture that alienated many of their fans.

The quartet imploded in 1971, but later reunited in various combinations, even after Davy Jones' death in 2012. What began as a constructed act for TV left a pop legacy that allowed The Monkees to be discussed in the same breath as The Beatles they emulated. **JS**

Classic episode
Monkees Get Out More Dirt | *Season 1, episode 19.* Julie Newmar—better known as Catwoman in *Batman* (1966)—plays a beautiful woman for whom all four boys fall at a laundromat. Wally Cox, the voice of Underdog, also guests.

◉ Here they come . . . Davy Jones, Micky Dolenz, Peter Tork, and Mike Nesmith.

The Time Tunnel

Fantasy/Horror/Sci-Fi | USA | 1966–67

Irwin Allen casts his heroes into the time vortex with fairly typical results

Cast | James Darren, Robert Colbert, Lee Meriwether, Whit Bissell, John Zaremba
Original broadcaster | ABC **For fans of . . .** | *Quantum Leap* (1989), *Sliders* (1995)

With *The Time Tunnel*, visionary producer Irwin Allen focused on scientists Doug Phillips (Robert Colbert) and Tony Newman (James Darren) who were lost in time as a result of a covert US governmental experiment. Supported by colleagues who were able to communicate with them, Tony and Doug tried to find their way back to their own time—but were unable to control where, or when, they would end up next.

The focus was on Tony and Doug traveling to past events, such as the sinking of the *Titanic*, the eruption of Krakatoa, and the attack on Pearl Harbor. There was a practical reason behind this decision—Allen used stock footage from Fox—which meant that the show didn't fully exploit its time travel concept. There were

excursions to the future, and the occasional appearance of aliens livened up episodes. The show benefited from the stylized art direction that was Allen's trademark, and from a memorable theme by John Williams.

Despite being well received, ABC dropped the series after thirty episodes. There were several attempts to revive the program, but none came to fruition. **SO**

Classic episode

The Day The Sky Fell In | *Episode 4*. Tony and Doug arrive in Pearl Harbor the day before the 1941 Japanese attack, in which Tony's father died. Tony has the opportunity to prevent the impending attack and learn what happened to his father.

◉ Time travelers James Darren (Dr. Newman) and Robert Colbert (Dr. Phillips).

The Baron

Action/Adventure | UK | 1966–67

One of Britain's first full-color dramas was snapped up on both sides of the Atlantic

Cast | Steve Forrest, Sue Lloyd, Colin Gordon, Paul Ferris
Original broadcaster | ITV
For fans of . . . | *Danger Man* (1960), *The Avengers* (1961), *The Saint* (1962)

By the mid-1960s, monochrome was slowly giving way to color, with American networks leading the way. In Britain, *The Baron*, from the ITC production stable, was one of the first dramas to be produced entirely in color. It made the undercover investigations of British-based Texan antiques dealer John Mannering (Steve Forrest) even more exciting.

The series was based on the spy novels of John Creasey (under the pseudonym Anthony Morton). In developing the series, some strategic liberties were taken with the source. By establishing Mannering as a Texan and casting American actor Forrest, ITC presold the series to ABC.

Frequently coopted by British Intelligence, Mannering was initially partnered with David Marlowe (Paul Ferris). But after a handful of episodes had been made, ABC expressed doubts about the character and requested the reintroduction of a female character from the first episode. Cordelia, played by Sue Lloyd, brought glamour to the series and her partnership with Forrest completed a very appealing package. Ferris departed the series after appearing in just eight episodes.

The Baron was an engaging drama, produced at a time when ITC was honing its particular brand of jet-setting, action adventure that would serve the production company well into the next decade. Its thirty episodes were slick and watchable, even if they are not as well remembered as the series' stablemate, *The Saint*, starring Roger Moore. **MW**

Ultraman

Fantasy/Horror/Sci-Fi | Japan | 1966–67

State-of-the-art special effects made this superhero fantasy a hit

Cast | Susumu Kurobe, Akiji Kobayashi, Bin "Satoshi" Furuya, Hiroko Sakurai, Sandayū Dokumamushi, Masanari Nihei, Corinne Orr
Original broadcaster | TBS
For fans of . . . | *Mighty Morphin Power Rangers* (1993)

The red and silver alien superhero known internationally as Ultraman has become one of the most recognizable figures in Japanese pop culture. And the series that made his name, created by Eiji Tsuburaya (with Ultraman himself designed by Toru Narita), is the foremost TV example of the *tokusatsu* (special effects) genre that also includes the Godzilla movies.

Indeed, anyone familiar with Godzilla will recognize *Ultraman*'s premise of scientists trying to halt the rampages of gigantic, bizarre *kaiju* (monsters). These eggheads were the orange-clad Science Special Search Party, one of whom—Shin Hayata (Susumu Kurobe)—was secretly able to transform into Ultraman. He matched the monsters in size and powers, but had to defeat them quickly, owing to a "color timer" on his chest that turned from blue to red as his stores of solar energy depleted (and which kept his screen time, and hence the show's production costs, down). If the light went out, Ultraman would be destroyed forever.

His outlandish adversaries included Dada, a sort of op-art Tiki god; the rocklike Jamila; and Pestar, an inspired cross between a bat and a starfish. They were usually played by Haruo Nakajima, who had been the first Godzilla and donned that creature's costume again (with a neck frill added) to create *Ultraman* foe Jirass.

The show spawned ever more elaborate sequels, spin-offs, and rip-offs that introduced a whole family of Ultra beings. Internationally, its most familiar legacy is the deathless *Power Rangers* franchise. **IK**

Callan

Drama | UK | 1967–72

An assassin with a conscience was at the heart of this action-packed and brutal Cold War spy thriller

Cast | Edward Woodward, Russell Hunter, Anthony Valentine, Lisa Langdon
Original broadcaster | ITV
Award | 1 BAFTA
For fans of . . . | *The Equalizer* (1985), *Spooks* (2002)

First seen in James Mitchell's TV play *A Magnum for Schneider* (1967), government assassin David Callan survived four seasons, a feature film (1974), and a one-off reunion (1981's *Wet Job*). Played with steely ruthlessness by Edward Woodward, Callan was a convict turned killer, hired by a shadowy wing of the security service to perform acts of extortion, blackmail, and even murder on behalf of the state. The best in his field, Callan was, nonetheless, cursed with a conscience—he had to know that his targets deserved their fate and was always disappointed to discover just why they did.

Woodward's skill was in making such a blunt tool so compelling. Through voice-over, we discovered his inner turmoil as he wrestled with each case, handed to him by a succession of superiors, all called Hunter. Every hero needs a sidekick, and Callan's was Lonely (Russell Hunter), a master housebreaker afflicted with body odor and a cowardly streak. The opening titles were particularly memorable, accompanied by haunting theme song "Girl in the Dark" (credited to Jack Trombey), a swinging bulb was shattered by a gunshot.

Another victim of the poor archiving policies of many broadcasters at the time, not all of *Callan's* first two seasons survived. Still, the extant episodes possessed a brutality and willingness to sacrifice major characters not seen on British TV again until *Spooks*. Woodward would later star in the US action series *The Equalizer*, in which he also played a hit man for hire with a troubled conscience. **JS**

Classic episode
Let's Kill Everybody | *Season 2, episode 5*. In this 1969 installment, Callan learns that an assassin has been dispatched to execute his entire department. Hilary Dwyer, later a film and TV producer, stars as his doomed girlfriend.

⊘ Have gun—will travel: Edward Woodward stars as David Callan.

The Phil Donahue Show

Talk show | USA | 1967–96

Pioneering talk show tackling issues of the day

Classic episode
Four episodes in 1994 | Phil Donahue interviews Holocaust revisionists Bradley Smith and David Cole, maker of the documentary *One Third of the Holocaust*, who were questioning whether gas chambers were ever used to kill Jews and others.

⊘ Talk show ringmaster Phil Donahue holds court, discussing controversial issues with sensitivity, as here in 1985.

Cast | Phil Donahue
Original broadcasters | WLWD, syndication
Awards | 20 Emmys
For fans of . . . | *ABC's Nightlife* (1964), *The Oprah Winfrey Show* (1986)

Blazing a TV trail, *The Phil Donahue Show* actively involved a studio audience in the exploration of its topics. Unlike late-night talk shows full of celebrities making promotional appearances or Sunday morning political discussions, *Donahue* secured a niche on the daytime schedule, amid soaps and game shows.

Former TV news anchor and radio talk show host, Donahue—in his early thirties when the show began—was a remarkably astute interviewer. He unflinchingly tackled such subjects as abortion, religion, incest, and homosexuality without resorting to sensationalism. And when Donahue did get "name" guests, they were people like Ayn Rand, Nelson Mandela, Jesse Jackson, Ralph Nader, Muhammad Ali, Noam Chomsky, and Gloria Steinem. (In 1985, he teamed up with Russian journalist Vladimir Pozner to host *Space Bridge*, telecast discussions between Americans and Soviets credited with contributing to the new era of openness between the two superpowers. As Donahue put it in an interview, "We reached out instead of lashed out.")

Oprah Winfrey said, "Phil opened the door for all of us," but his show's success was key to its downfall; it paved the way for more brazen daytime shows, such as *Geraldo* (1987) and *The Jerry Springer Show* (1991), which promptly ran away with the ratings. Undeterred, Donahue continues to write and produce media on topical issues in his own style: intimate, careful, and aggressively questioning but never sacrificing taste or tact. **SWH**

Ironside

Crime/Mystery | USA | 1967–75

Ensemble cop show with the chief confined to a wheelchair—a brave move for 1967

Cast | Raymond Burr, Don Galloway, Don Mitchell, Elizabeth Baur, Barbara Anderson
Original broadcaster | NBC
Awards | 2 Emmys
For fans of . . . | *Cannon* (1971), *Kojak* (1973)

Many cop shows had gimmicks. Kojak had his lollipops, cowpoke McCloud had a horse in Manhattan, and Cannon offered proof that obesity was no hindrance to catching bad guys. However, the forerunner to these was Robert T. Ironside (Raymond Burr), San Francisco's chief of detectives, gunned down and confined to a wheelchair. Aided by detectives Ed Brown (Don Galloway), Fran Belding (Elizabeth Baur), Eve Whitfield (Barbara Anderson), and con-turned-bodyguard Mark Sanger (Don Mitchell), Ironside was almost an American equivalent of Sherlock Holmes, as he masterfully pieced together mysteries by looking beyond the obvious.

For Burr, this was a natural follow-up to his acclaimed run as Perry Mason (which ran for nine years before he started his eight-year run as Ironside). Charming, loyal and witty, Ironside could be equally grumpy, sardonic, and downright rude when dealing with criminals or the perceived ineptitude of those around him in the police department. His supporting characters also offered the actors substantial roles: Ed, Fran, Eve, and especially Mark, had their own moments, real progression, individual lives, and story lines. Despite Burr playing the titular character, he and his writers allowed the program to become more of an ensemble show as the eight seasons rolled on. Equally surprising was the fact that the quality rarely dropped. Fashions, hairstyles, and cars aside, there is little to differentiate between the first and eighth seasons in terms of good solid storytelling, mystery, and excitement. **GR**

Classic episode
The Gambling Game | *Season 5, episode 4*. Fran Belding's introduction as a policewoman determined to prove that Ironside is corrupt makes this a standout episode, because you start to wonder if she could be right.

◭ Raymond Burr impressed viewers with his dramatic and comedic range as wheelchair-bound Robert T. Ironside.

The High Chaparral

Western | USA | 1967–71

Family feuds and territorial conflicts on the wild American Frontier

Classic episode
Too Many Chiefs | *Season 3, episode 23*. Chaos ensues when Buck, Mantolito, and Buck's son Blue are left in charge of the ranch after an exhausted Big John takes a break by going on a belated honeymoon with Victoria.

◉ Three Cannons firing: (L–R) Mark Slade (Billy Blue), Leif Erickson (Big John), and Cameron Mitchell (Buck).

Cast | Leif Erickson, Cameron Mitchell, Henry Darrow, Linda Cristal, Mark Slade, Frank Silvera
Original broadcaster | NBC
For fans of . . . | *Gunsmoke* (1955), *Bonanza* (1959), *The Wild Wild West* (1965)

The love of the Western still held firm on prime-time TV in the 1960s, with powerhouses *Gunsmoke* (1955) and *Bonanza* (1959) captivating audiences. The introduction of *The High Chaparral* in 1967 proved that the love of this genre showed no signs of waning.

The show took its name from the Arizona cattle ranch run by the Cannon family, who managed relations with Apache Indians and rival ranchers in order to save their business. "Big" John Cannon (Leif Erickson) was the head of the family, who entered into an uneasy alliance with rival rancher Montoya (Henry Darrow)—by marrying Montoya's daughter, Victoria (Linda Cristal). Much of the action was driven by Cannon's brother, Buck (Cameron Mitchell), and Victoria's brother, Manolito (Henry Darrow). Their maverick behavior quickly made them the most popular characters with audiences. Creator David Dortort had a powerful track record in TV Westerns, having created *Bonanza*. *The High Chaparral* trod a similar path, but differed in its attempt to explore interracial tensions between white Americans, American Indians, and Mexicans. As the series progressed, spanning ninety-eight episodes across its four-year run, it placed more emphasis on the high-spirited antics of Buck and Manolito, but the tension remained a constant backdrop.

It is sometimes lost among the many Western shows produced by US TV, but *The High Chaparral* was a solid and entertaining drama that took an authentic look at a pivotal period in US history. **SO**

The Invaders

Fantasy/Horror/Sci-Fi | USA | 1967–68

Architect David Vincent attempts to alert the world to an alien invasion, but no one is listening

Cast | Roy Thinnes, Kent Smith
Original broadcaster | ABC
For fans of . . . | *The Twilight Zone* (1959), *The Fugitive*
(1963), *The Outer Limits* (1963), *Mission: Impossible*
(1966), *Dark Skies* (1996)

David Vincent (Roy Thinnes) stops for a rest one night on a long drive home. He's woken by a spacecraft and there begins a solo mission to raise the alarm about an alien invasion.

The Invaders was a replacement for *The Fugitive*, which it resembles inasmuch as both series were stories of one man against the world. Vincent's friends didn't believe him when he told them Earth was in danger. So he travels the country alone, tracking the aliens, upsetting their plans, and attempting to convince authority figures of the threat to humanity.

The invaders were mysterious and nameless. When they burned away, a pile of ash was the only evidence they existed. They assumed human form and inveigled themselves into positions of power. Only a lack of circulation (no pulse and no bleeding) and a malformed little finger gave them away. It was easy to draw parallels between this creepy, invisible foe and the "reds under the bed" McCarthyism of the 1950s.

As the series progressed, Vincent gradually recruited supporters. The show ended after just two seasons, and although the invaders weren't defeated outright, the last episode suggested that the government would start to take the threat seriously.

Despite its relatively short run, *The Invaders* was fondly remembered by its many fans. A 1995 follow-up miniseries starring Scott Bakula saw the return of David Vincent to pass the baton to a new generation of the resistance movement. **WH**

Classic episode
Labyrinth | *Season 2, episode 12.* A doctor examines a captured alien and gives David his first incontrovertible evidence that Earth really has been invaded. But then the radiographer claims the X-rays she took are fakes.

◉ Roy Thinnes as David Vincent, self-appointed defender of the planet.

Super Bowl

Sports | USA | 1967–present

The spectacular halftime show famously eclipses the game itself

Cast | Ray Scott, Jack Whitaker, Curt Gowdy, Jack Buck, Pat Summerall, Dick Enberg, Frank Gifford
Original broadcasters | CBS, NBC, ABC, Fox
Award | 1 Emmy
For fans of . . . | *Monday Night Football* (1970)

At the first Super Bowl, on January 15, 1967, the Green Bay Packers triumphed over the Kansas City Chiefs, and the halftime entertainment was simple fare, featuring trumpeter Al Hirt and marching bands. Sadly, both CBS and NBC later wiped their tapes of this first game.

The season-ending football game is now an international event, and often tops year-end lists of the most watched shows of American origin (at home, it regularly breaks its own record for the most watched program of all time). Advertisers compete to secure costly slots and produce themed commercials for the occasion, making them events in themselves. Unusually, just as the game is hosted by a different city each year, networks rotate the broadcast rights.

Since Michael Jackson's ratings-boosting performance in 1993, the halftime entertainment has become a huge draw. The Rolling Stones, Bruce Springsteen, and Madonna have performed, while the lighting design for Beyoncé in 2013 secured the show's only Emmy. A new phrase was born when Justin Timberlake explained his exposing of Janet Jackson's nipple in 2004 as a "wardrobe malfunction." Football fans and nonsports viewers get caught up in the spectacle and excitement of the Super Bowl, as the game is only part of the greater whole ("Americana at its most kitsch and fun," suggested Sting). It doesn't matter if you don't understand the rules—this is event TV in its purest sense. **AS**

⦉ Christina Aguilera sings at the Super Bowl in 2011.

Les Enquêtes du commissaire Maigret

Drama | France | 1967–90

Impeccable realization of the Maigret stories

Cast | Jean Richard, François Cadet, Christian Rémy, Jean-François Devaux, Jean-Pierre Maurin, André Penvern, Maurice Coussonneau, Jean Lanier
Original broadcaster | ORTF
For fans of . . . | *Maigret* (1960)

One of the most common traps into which dramatic adaptations of period pieces fall is anachronism: audiences have sharp eyes and ears for anything that did not exist or which could not possibly have been said at the time the events depicted are supposed to have taken place, and as soon as they notice the flaws, the magic starts to wear off.

The beauty of *Les Enquêtes du commissaire Maigret* (*The Investigations of Inspector Maigret*) was that it avoided all such pitfalls by updating the original novels by Georges Simenon—which were set in the period between the First and Second World Wars—to the time of filming. This was the idea of the creators, Claude Barma and Jacques Rémy.

The basic stories required little emendation— they are timeless—so worked just as well in postwar settings as they would have done in their original context. The show was further strengthened by strong performances in the leading roles, notably by Jean Richard in the title role, and François Cadet as Inspector Lucas. Also notable was Richard's real-life wife Annick Tanguy, who took over as Madame Maigret after the death in 1968 of the original actress, Micheline Francey.

The show ran periodically for almost a quarter of a century: eighty-eight ninety-minute episodes were made in total. In spite of all the subsequent iterations of *Maigret*, this series is still frequently revived on French cable channels today because it is widely regarded as the definitive version. **GL**

The Mothers-in-Law

Comedy | USA | 1967–69

Squabbling in-laws—what a treat!

Cast | Eve Arden, Kaye Ballard, Herbert Rudley, Jerry Fogel, Deborah Walley
Original broadcaster | NBC
For fans of . . . | *The Brady Bunch* (1969), *The Golden Girls* (1985)

Created by Bob Carroll Jr. and Madelyn Davis, *The Mothers-in-Law* starred Academy Award-nominated Eve Arden as the mother of a straight-laced family, and TV and stage personality Kaye Ballard as the mother of a fun-loving family. They lived next door to each other and became in-laws when their children eloped.

Eve and Herb Hubbard and Kaye and Roger Buell were neighbors and friends. Roger was a TV writer and Herb was a lawyer. While in college, the Hubbards' daughter, Suzie, ran off and married the Buells' son, Jerry, and they returned to live in the Hubbards' garage, which had been converted into a small apartment. The parents, especially the mothers, squabbled and meddled in their children's lives, approaching the youngsters' marriage from different points of view. When Suzie and Jerry had twins—a boy (Joey) and a girl (Hildy)—the mothers-in-law had more reasons to bicker.

Although it aired in a prime slot between *Walt Disney's Wonderful World of Color* (1954) and *Bonanza* (1959), the show did not perform to expectations. The network considered canceling the show after the first season, and when ratings continued to slump, it was canceled at the end of its second season. Although its run was brief, the show, and especially the performances of stars Arden and Ballard—considered to have been over the hill at the time—are often regarded as prime examples of mature talent, and perhaps inspired other female-led sitcoms such as *Maude* (1972) and *The Golden Girls* (1985). **RP**

The Prisoner

Drama | UK | 1967–68

One man's endurance is tested to the limit in a series of psychological experiments designed to break him

Cast | Patrick McGoohan, Angelo Muscat, Leo McKern, Peter Swanwick
Original broadcaster | ITV
For fans of . . . | *Danger Man* (1960), *The Avengers* (1961)

Having played secret agent John Drake in ITV's *Danger Man* (1960), Patrick McGoohan hoped to escape typecasting when he took on the central role in *The Prisoner*. In fact, he failed. Thanks to *The Prisoner*'s bold visuals, and a determination to be as perplexing as possible, McGoohan was forever associated with a nameless man trapped in a sinister village.

Superficially, *The Prisoner* was a simple concept. After resigning from his job as a secret agent, McGoohan's character was kidnapped and taken to a strange village whose inhabitants had numbers instead of names. He was dubbed "Number Six," a title he emphatically rejected: "I am not a number, I am a free man!" In each episode he challenged the establishment, which was represented by changing characters called "the new Number Two." Few of the stories made complete sense—but that wasn't their goal. Their psychological concepts challenged the idea of individuality. A rare thing in television drama, *The Prisoner* commanded viewers to think.

It was the look of the program people remember most. Villagers wore black jackets with white piping on the lapels and badges showing penny farthings and their number. The village itself (an Italianate folly in Portmeirion, North Wales) was policed by a gigantic weather balloon called "Rover," which prevented dissenting inhabitants from escaping. A 2009 remake starred Jim Caviezel and Ian McKellen; it played with the paranoia of the original, but lacked its style and wit. **JS**

Classic episode
Free For All | *Episode 3*. Number Six is invited to stand for election as the next Number Two. He uses his campaign to challenge his mysterious jailers, posing such questions as "Where are we?" and "Who is in charge?"

◈ Patrick McGoohan, as Number Six, is held prisoner—but why? And by whom?

The Carol Burnett Show

Variety | USA | 1967–78; 1991

Classic comedy from a champion of variety and queen of the comic sketch

Cast | Carol Burnett, Harvey Korman, Vicki Lawrence, Lyle Waggoner, Tim Conway **Original broadcaster** | CBS
Awards | 25 Emmys, 8 Golden Globes **For fans of . . .** | *The Morecambe & Wise Show* (1968)

A staple of US TV schedules in the 1950s and 1960s, variety shows were waning in popularity by the 1970s. However, *The Carol Burnett Show* was a family-friendly variety series that bucked this trend. It was nominated for a variety of Emmy awards every year and won twenty-five in all, making it one of the most honored shows in TV history.

The format of the show remained much the same over the years and included Burnett interacting with the studio audience, interviews with the week's guest star, wacky and elaborate comedy sketches, and guest performances. It always ended with Burnett tugging her ear, a nod to her beloved grandmother who had raised her. The show succeeded because it was funny. Very funny. The chemistry of the cast was visible on-screen, led by the vibrant energy of Burnett. A long list of high-caliber guest stars appeared on the show. The sketches led to some memorable and often-recurring characters, and even a spin-off show, *Mama's Family*, in 1983. The show was briefly brought back in 1991, but was short-lived. **KB**

Classic episode
Went With the Wind | *Season 10, episode 8.*
A memorable parody of *Gone With the Wind* provides plenty of humor, with Bob Mackie's green curtain "dress"—complete with pole across the shoulders—a highlight.

◍ Carol Burnett in a nudist camp sketch shown in 1967.

The Forsyte Saga
Historical drama | UK | 1967

Intergenerational struggles among a privileged and expansive English family

Cast | Kenneth More, Eric Porter, Nyree Dawn Porter, Margaret Tyzack, Terence Alexander, Susan Hampshire
Original broadcaster | BBC   **Awards** | 2 BAFTAs, 1 Emmy   **For fans of . . .** | *Upstairs Downstairs* (1971)

The Forsytes were an influential upper-middle-class family all too aware of their position in society. "Young Jolyon" Forsyte was a painter and portrait artist who felt disconnected from his relatives and his wife. His ruthless and ambitious cousin, Soames, was a man of property whose cold neglect of his wife, Irene, sent her into Jolyon's arm. The two branches of the family became further intertwined in the next generation when Soames' daughter fell for Jolyon's son.

This twenty-six-part adaptation of John Galsworthy's novels was a lavish period piece of a type for which the BBC is renowned, and up to that point was the corporation's costliest serial. Its soaplike cliff-hangers and tangled relationships had viewers gripped: after moderate success on the nascent BBC Two channel, it was repeated on BBC One in 1968 and peaked at over eighteen million viewers for the finale. A similar hit in the United States, it sparked a passion for literary adaptations that paved the way for *Masterpiece Theatre*.

In 2002, the UK's ITV network rebooted the saga, with *Homeland*'s Damian Lewis as Soames. **JS**

Classic episode
Decisions | *Episode 6*. Soames has learned of the relationship between his wife (Nyree Dawn Porter) and a young architect. Frustrated and enraged by her infidelity and the growing distance between them, he rapes her.

⏷ Terence Alexander and Margaret Tyzack suffer period pains.

The Morecambe & Wise Show

Comedy | UK | 1967–83

"What do you think of it so far?" "Rubbish!"

Cast | Eric Morecambe, Ernie Wise **Original broadcaster** | BBC **Awards** | 6 BAFTAs
For fans of . . . | *The George Burns and Gracie Allen Show* (1950), *The Two Ronnies* (1971)

Eric Morecambe and Ernie Wise first teamed up in 1941 and made their name as a duo in the music halls of Britain. Their first attempt to transfer to television was a flop, but they learned from the experience and when they returned with this show they quickly became the most popular comedians in the UK.

The format was a series of comedy sketches in which Eric played the lazy and unsophisticated one and Ernie played the pompous and ambitious one—but both were idiots. They were often joined by guests who became more famous as the series set more and more viewing records. Among the stars who submitted willingly to their ridicule were the actresses Vanessa Redgrave and Glenda Jackson and singer Tom Jones.

Eric and Ernie were the last hurrah for old-fashioned vaudeville, but their perfectly balanced relationship was popular with all generations. A move in 1978 to the BBC's rival, ITV, did little to dull their popularity, but Morecambe's ill-health slowed their work rate: a raucous 1983 Christmas special was aired just five months before he died of a heart attack. **JS**

Classic episode

1971 Christmas Show | Season 6, episode 7.
Conductor André Previn, exasperated by Eric's piano skills, accuses him of playing "all the wrong notes." "I'm playing all the right notes," Eric retorts, "but not necessarily in the right order."

Irrepressible comic duo Ernie Wise and Eric Morecambe—the kings of British TV in the 1970s.

Dad's Army

Comedy | UK | 1968–77

Don't panic! It's only the Home Guard . . .

Cast | Arthur Lowe, Clive Dunn, John Le Mesurier, John Laurie, Arnold Ridley, Ian Lavender, James Beck
Original broadcaster | BBC **Award** | 1 BAFTA **For fans of . . .** | *Blackadder Goes Forth* (1989)

The idea of a Second World War platoon consisting of retirees and other men unfit for regular service came from cocreator Jimmy Perry's memories of being a teenage volunteer in the Home Guard. In 1940 it was oversubscribed, but in the ensuing decades the efforts of these brave men had been all but forgotten.

As leader Captain Mainwaring, Arthur Lowe was patriotic but pompous. Second-in-command Sergeant Wilson (John Le Mesurier) routinely undermined him with a weary, "Do you think that's wise, sir?" But what Wilson lacked in enthusiasm was more than made up for by Lance-Corporal Jones (Clive Dunn, aged forty-eight, playing eighty), keen to show he was still capable of action even if his body suggested otherwise. Jones'

catchphrases have lived on—"They don't like it up 'em," "Permission to speak, sir!" and "Don't panic!"—as has Mainwaring's withering "Stupid boy!"

Perry and cocreator David Croft opted not to end the war in the last episode, but to have the platoon raise a toast to the Home Guard—a scene that effortlessly brings a tear to the eye. **JS**

Classic episode
The Deadly Attachment | *Season 6, episode 1*. The platoon guards a prisoner—an arrogant U-boat captain who, when mocked by a young private, demands to know his name. "Don't tell him, Pike!" blurts Captain Mainwaring.

⚓ (Clockwise from top) Ian Lavender, James Beck, Arnold Ridley, Arthur Lowe, John Laurie, John Le Mesurier, and Clive Dunn.

Hawaii Five-0

Action/Adventure | USA | 1968–80

Tight writing, compelling acting, and a gorgeous setting made this long-running police procedural a beacon of popular culture

Classic episode
Hookman | *Season 3, episode 15*. A man with a grudge against the police attacks several officers, including McGarrett's father. The villain is played by Peter Weller, who later became one of the stars of *24*.

⊘ "Book 'em, Danno!" Jack Lord as Steve McGarrett in this long-standing police drama.

Cast | Jack Lord, James MacArthur, Kam Fong Chun
Original broadcaster | CBS
Award | 1 Emmy
For fans of . . . | *Cannon* (1971), *Magnum, P.I.* (1980), *Miami Vice* (1984)

Hawaii Five-O ran for a record-breaking twelve seasons, taking police procedural into an exotic new locale in Hawaii. Created by Leonard Freeman, who had moved to Hawaii to recuperate after an illness, it was named in honor of Hawaii's status as America's fiftieth state.

The series centered on a fictional police force led by Steve McGarrett (Jack Lord), who answered directly to the state governor. The attractive landscape gave Freeman's series a different vibe from the majority of US crime dramas of the day. Combined with Lord's powerful central performance, it made the show a top-thirty hit for much of its run. Morton Stevens' theme song and McGarrett's "Book 'em, Danno," catchphrase (James McArthur played McGarrett's number two, Danny "Danno" Williams) soon entered the pop culture lexicon around the world.

After Leonard Freeman died from complications following heart surgery in 1974, Lord took a controlling interest in *Hawaii Five-O*, becoming executive producer until the series finished due to waning popularity in 1980. Its final episode saw McGarrett finally bring recurring nemesis Wo Fat (Harry Endo) to justice.

A revival pilot featuring Gary Busey, with James McArthur as Hawaii's governor, failed to go to series in 1996, but a more successful reboot, with Alex O'Loughlin as McGarrett, premiered on CBS in 2010. As of the 2014–15 television season, this new version has clocked up five seasons and, like the original, often appears in the ratings top thirty. **MW**

Julia

Comedy | USA | 1968–71

The first sitcom to star an African American woman. Diahann Carroll played a widowed mother working as a nurse

Cast | Diahann Carroll, Lloyd Nolan, Marc Copage, Michael Link
Original broadcaster | NBC
Award | 1 Golden Globe
For fans of . . . | *Diff'rent Strokes* (1978)

Julia was a gentle workplace and family comedy that nevertheless courted controversy because it addressed the then-dangerous subject of race.

Diahann Carroll, who had first emerged in the movie *Carmen Jones* (1954), starred as Julia Baker, a nurse raising her son, Corey (Marc Copage), on her own after her husband was killed in the Vietnam War. Her boss, Dr. Morton Chegley (Lloyd Nolan), ran his practice in a relatively suburban area, while Julia and Corey lived together in an urban apartment building, where Corey's best friend, Earl J. Waggedorn (Michael Link) was also a resident.

Although the show and its star attracted much adverse criticism for not tackling racial politics strongly enough, many also felt that the show made great strides in the movement toward equality by simply allowing black viewers, for the first time, the opportunity to see people who looked like them on television. That these men and women were portrayed as smart, responsible, accomplished professionals may have given audiences a jolt, but also led to the widening of who could be featured—and enjoyed by everyone—in popular entertainment.

Carroll went on to further success in movies, theater, concerts, and on television, where she became one of the first African-American female leads on the top-rated glitz-a-thon *Dynasty* (1981), where she showed that anyone, regardless of color, can be as rich, manipulative, and devious as anyone else. **RP**

Classic episode
Unloneliest Night of the Week | *Season 1, episode 5*. Julia finds herself inundated with visitors when the Waggedorn children and an army friend of her late husband all arrive at the same time.

⬙ Golden Globe–winning Diahann Carroll with Fred Williamson as Steve Bruce in the episode "Magna Cum Lover," in 1970.

Land of the Giants

Fantasy/Horror/Sci-Fi | USA | 1968–70

Humans crash-land on a giant Earth-like planet

Cast | Gary Conway, Don Marshall, Don Matheson, Stefen Arngrim
Original broadcaster | ABC
For fans of . . . | *Voyage to the Bottom of the Sea* (1964), *The Time Tunnel* (1966), *The Invaders* (1967)

For his final genre hit of the 1960s, producer Irwin Allen combined aliens and space travel with miniature humans to create the memorable *Land of the Giants*.

Set in the then-future year of 1983, where orbital travel was a reality, *Land of the Giants* focused on the crew and passengers of the *Spindrift* spaceship as it hit a spacewarp and crash-landed on a world similar to Earth—except that everything was twelve times bigger. The now-miniature humans, led by Captain Steve Burton (Gary Conway), had to fight to survive in this frightening world, while they tried to repair their stricken ship in order to escape. A concept such as this hangs together on its realization, and the show delivered on this front. Bolstered by a large budget, the sets and props were lavishly mounted, and still pack a punch for a show of its vintage. More serious than Allen's previous shows, the lack of explanation of the alien world was disconcerting, and made the audience fear for the protagonists. Furthermore, Captain Burton was prepared to sacrifice the group's chances of escape to prevent the Giants from making their way to Earth, which added to the pervading sense of hopelessness.

The plot relied on kidnaps, rescues, and the introduction of other outlandish elements, such as robots, time travelers, and doppelgängers. But *Land of the Giants* also successfully tapped into the themes of paranoia and persecution found in several other contemporaneous shows, such as *The Invaders*. Overall, it was a big, unsettling, yet interesting show. **SO**

Rowan & Martin's Laugh-In

Variety | USA | 1968–73

A comic take on 1960s hippie culture

Cast | Dan Rowan, Dick Martin, Henry Gibson, Lily Tomlin, Goldie Hawn, Judy Carne
Original broadcaster | NBC
Awards | 8 Emmys, 2 Golden Globes
For fans of . . . | *Saturday Night Live* (1975)

The comedy team of Dan Rowan and Dick Martin, in their nightclub-perfected personae as, respectively, exasperated straight man and loquacious "dumb" guy, were the hosts, ringleaders, and cat herders on their self-titled show. *Laugh-In* based its format on the now-defunct vaudeville and burlesque model of populist satirical entertainment, and packed each episode with a string of rapid-fire sketches, quick gags, non sequiturs, and enough sexual innuendo and political jabs to keep censors, politicians, and the public talking for years to come.

Originally aired as a one-off special on September 9, 1967, the show was such a success that it was brought back as a series in January the following year. Each episode began with Rowan and Martin chatting about current events (or whatever they wished), until Rowan ended Martin's often rambling intro with "C'mon Dick, let's go to the party." The stage would then transform into a mod dance hall, with the music periodically interrupted by snappy jokes delivered by guests and cast members, including a ditzy, bikini-clad blonde (Goldie Hawn).

Other regulars played in running sketches and one-off topical scenes. At the end of each episode the entire cast would wind up at the Joke Wall, where they would open the windows in a psychedelic backdrop to spout topical or surreal words of wisdom. Many enduring catchphrases started life here, including "Sock it to me," "Very interesting," and "Here come de judge." **RP**

Sammy Davis Jr. with Dan Rowan and Dick Martin. ❯

Súper Sábado Sensacional

Variety | Venezuela | 1968–present

Musical acts for Latin American audiences

Cast | Amador Bendayan, Gilberto Correa, Daniel Sarcos, Leonardo Villalobos
Original broadcaster | Radio Caracas Television
For fans of . . . | *The Ed Sullivan Show* (1948), *Sábado Gigante* (1962)

The highest-rated variety show in Venezuela, *Súper Sábado Sensacional* has been a fixture in Latin American households on Saturday nights for almost half a century. A weekly five-hour broadcast in its native country and two hours abroad, the glossy Spanish-language show features regional and international musical acts and competitions and game-show segments involving members of the public and a range of stars that have included Michael Jackson, John Travolta, and Shakira.

Created by Amador Bendayán, its host for the first two decades, the show is currently presented by Leonardo Villalobos, who links interviews, comedy skits, music and dance performances, and numerous competitions before a panel of judges. Some of these events have self-explanatory titles: "Dancing with the Stars," and "Yes I Can Sing"; in "Mini-Stars," children imitate musical celebrities.

Some segments became spin-off shows, such as *Mega Match Sensacional* (high school teams compete in physical and verbal challenges) and *La Guerra de Los Sexos* (*The War of the Sexes*), which pits three male celebrities against three female celebrities. In 1982, the show's producers launched the Festival Internacional de la Orquídea, an annual live international musical competition in Maracaibo that is broadcast as part of the series.

The show ceased transmission in the United States in 2009, but still plays an important role in Venezuelan— and Pan-Latin American—popular culture. **WML**

Whistle and I'll Come to You

Fantasy/Horror/Sci-Fi | UK | 1968

A chilling telling of M.R. James' ghostly tale

Cast | Michael Hordern
Original broadcaster | BBC
For fans of . . . | *The Stalls of Barchester* (1971), *A Warning to the Curious* (1972), *The Signalman* (1976), *The Tractate Middoth* (2013)

First broadcast as part of the BBC's arts strand, *Omnibus,* this show replaced the usual mix of interviews and cultural events with one of TV's most haunting hours.

Published in 1904, M.R. James' *Oh Whistle and I'll Come to You, My Lad* tells the story of a professor's holiday on a windswept British coast. Finding a medieval whistle engraved with a warning, he blows it and summons something that confronts the formerly skeptical academic with absolute proof of the supernatural.

Director and producer Jonathan Miller's adaptation distilled the story to its bare bones, dispensing with its wry humor and focusing on an atmosphere of sustained terror. Stark, static, black-and-white shots allowed the viewers to absorb the period details. The soundtrack consisted of whistling wind and the haunted professor's mumbling, making the sudden, indistinct appearance of the ghost—accompanied by a weird, electronic screaming—horrifyingly powerful.

Michael Hordern's performance as Professor Parkins was inspired. Apparently improvising his limited dialogue, Hordern made him repressed, unable to relate to staff or guests at his hotel, and happiest in his own company. But he was helpless in the face of forces he could not understand, and his disintegration was more disturbing than the ghost itself.

Paving the way for *A Ghost Story for Christmas,* an annual series of James adaptations, and remade with John Hurt as Parkins in 2010, *Whistle and I'll Come to You* remains a high-water mark in TV terror. **MM**

The Champions

Fantasy/Horror/Sci-Fi | UK | 1968–69

Three superhuman espionage agents combat neo-Nazis, South American dictators, and other despicable villains

Cast | Stuart Damon, Alexandra Bastedo, William Gaunt, Anthony Nicholls
Original broadcaster | ITV
For fans of . . . | *Randall and Hopkirk (Deceased)* (1969), *Sapphire and Steel* (1979)

Three agents of the international espionage agency Nemesis crash-land in the Himalayas, where they are brought back to health and endowed with superhuman abilities by mysterious rescuers. With enhanced strength, extraordinary cognitive abilities, and shared telepathy, they strike out to save the world from a long string of villains.

The Champions broke the action-adventure mold of the 1960s, embracing science fiction and ushering in a period of fantastical concepts. Its creator, Dennis Spooner, had form in fantasy drama, having supplied scripts for *Doctor Who* and *Thunderbirds* before coming to *The Champions* via the espionage drama *The Baron*.

Plots often featured neo-Nazis or South American dictators, though the exotic locations were achieved on a British backlot, employing production company ITC's usual budget-friendly, smoke-and-mirrors approach. Unusually, the female character of the three protagonists, Sharron Macready (Alexandra Bastedo), was on equal footing with the two men—Richard Barrett (William Gaunt), and Craig Stirling (Stuart Damon).

The influence of *The Champions* can be seen in a variety of sci-fi fantasies, from the children's series *The Tomorrow People* (1973) to *Sapphire and Steel* (1979). In 2007, the Mexican movie director Guillermo del Toro was reportedly attached to a big-screen update of the series, but this has failed to materialize, leaving Sterling, Macready, and Barrett in superpowered limbo for now. **MW**

Classic episode
The Interrogation | *Season 1, episode 18*.
A budget-saving flashback episode, incorporating frames from past shows, sees Stirling subjected to investigation from an unnamed interrogator, played by Colin Blakely.

⊙ William Gaunt and Stuart Damon as two of the Champions of the espionage agency Nemesis.

The Dick Cavett Show

Talk show | USA | 1969–75

The thinking person's talk show

Cast | Dick Cavett
Original broadcaster | ABC
Awards | 3 Emmys
For fans of . . . | *Parkinson* (1971),
Late Show with David Letterman (1993)

When American viewers light up nostalgically at the mention of Dick Cavett's name, they're usually thinking of his best-remembered program, this late-night ABC series that aired from 1969 until 1975, going head-to-head with *Johnny Carson's Tonight Show*.

Hailed as an intelligent alternative to fluffier interview shows, *The Dick Cavett Show* gave air time to a wide range of guests—novelists, critics, politicians—in addition to the usual movie, music, and TV stars. Guests included Marlon Brando, Norman Mailer, Gore Vidal, Muhammad Ali, Groucho Marx, Fred Astaire, Bette Davis, and Orson Welles. Cavett helped discover Woody Allen after he came across him doing stand-up comedy and invited him on to the show.

Unusually for the time, the show frequently booked rock acts, which *Tonight* tended to ignore. Jimi Hendrix, Janis Joplin, Jefferson Airplane, and Paul Simon were just some of them. John Lennon and Yoko Ono gave Cavett their first interview after the break-up of The Beatles, and when a "wired" David Bowie sat down with an unflappable Cavett, it led to some of the most surreal repartee in television history.

Despite critical acclaim, Cavett ran behind Johnny Carson and Merv Griffin in ratings. After his contract with ABC ended in 1975, he briefly had a summer show on CBS. Next came a half-hour PBS interview program running from 1977 until 1982. He returned to ABC in 1986. His longest-running gig was on CNBC, from 1989 to 1996. **JGT**

Civilisation

Documentary | UK | 1969

Pioneering cultural documentary—in color

Cast | Kenneth Clark (narrator)
Original broadcaster | BBC
Awards | 2 BAFTAs
For fans of . . . | *The Ascent of Man* (1973), *Life on Earth* (1979), *Human Universe* (2014)

When the BBC set up its second TV channel (BBC Two), it was used as a test bed for technical innovation. The first to raise its resolution and the first to broadcast in color, it also had a remit to cater to an inquisitive audience. When David Attenborough became BBC Two's controller, he commissioned programs that would appeal to an intelligent audience, but also showcase the new color and "high-definition" technology.

One such commission was *Civilisation*, which took three years to make and, afforded the luxury of 35mm film stock, was "future-proofed." The only shame was that, when it reached screens, few among the available audience in Britain even owned a color TV set.

From the outset, art historian Kenneth Clark conceded that the program's aim was limited by time and resources. He began his thirteen-part epic with the Viking influence on northern Europe, but referenced classical cultures only in regards to their rediscovery in the fourteenth century. He explained the cultural and religious context of artists like Michelangelo and Rembrandt, and the musical achievements of Mozart and Handel. In the final episode, he went to New York to illustrate the legacy of industrialists such as Brunel.

The series led to an equally successful book, at a time when such a tie-in wasn't a foregone conclusion. Its influence can be seen in the lavish, personality-led documentaries that followed, from Jacob Bronowski's *The Ascent of Man* and Attenborough's own *Life on Earth* to Brian Cox's *Human Universe*. **JS**

Department S
Action/Adventure | UK | 1969–70

Oddball crime caper that introduced a TV icon

Cast | Peter Wyngarde, Joel Fabiani, Rosemary Nicols, Dennis Alaba Peters, Basil Dignam
Original broadcaster | ITV
For fans of . . . | *Danger Man* (1960), *The Avengers* (1961), *The Saint* (1962), *Jason King* (1971)

From Dennis Spooner and Monty Berman, the creative minds behind *The Champions* (1968) and *Randall and Hopkirk (Deceased)* (1969), *Department S* was a similarly fantastical take on the 1960s international crime genre.

The department's responsibility was to investigate crimes that had baffled the authorities. Cases included an astronaut found dying in the middle of London, a plane landing at Heathrow without its passengers and crew, and a murder in a country house—built inside a factory. Having hooked the viewers with these wacky premises, the writers conjured solutions that were rational but ingenious. Even more stylish than other ITC Entertainment shows (including *The Saint* and *Danger Man*), many of its episodes were directed by Hammer Films, alumni including Cyril Frankel and John Gilling.

The team's chief (Joel Fabiani) was a conventional leading man, but his colleagues were diverse: a computer expert and mistress of disguise (Rosemary Nicols); a mysterious diplomat (Dennis Alaba Peters); and a louche playboy (Peter Wyngarde), replete with flamboyant ruffled shirts—many the actor's own—and an impeccably unflappable manner.

Always ready with a droll aside or inspired deduction, and providing both most of the show's comic relief and glamor, Wyngarde was an instant hit, even being voted best-dressed man in Europe. The producers opted to bring *Department S* to a close after just one season and promote Wyngarde's character of Jason King to his own, self-titled show. **MM**

Classic episode
The Pied Piper of Hambledown | *Episode 4*.
A woman wakes to discover that everybody in a sleepy English village has been abducted during the night: a characteristically bizarre premise for one of the show's most stylish installments.

⬤ Jason King (Peter Wyngarde) belonged to an era when a camp manner was considered indispensable in a playboy.

Monty Python's Flying Circus

Comedy | UK | 1969–74

And now for something completely different

Classic episode
Full Frontal Nudity | *Season 1, episode 8.* Written by John Cleese and Graham Chapman, and performed by Cleese and Michael Palin, this episode's "Dead Parrot" sketch (originally about a faulty toaster) became Python's greatest hit.

◉ Cleese in season 2's "The Ministry of Silly Walks" sketch.
❷ (Clockwise from top) Cleese, Palin, Jones, Idle, and Chapman.

Cast | Graham Chapman, John Cleese, Terry Gilliam, Terry Jones, Eric Idle, Michael Palin, Carol Cleveland
Original broadcaster | BBC
Awards | 2 BAFTAs
For fans of ... | *The Goodies* (1970), *The Fast Show* (1994)

Much like William Shakespeare, Winston Churchill, and Groucho Marx, the Monty Python team have left an indelible mark on our use of language. Phrases such as "No one expects the Spanish Inquisition," "Nudge nudge, wink wink, say no more," and "It is an ex-parrot" have become so commonplace that it's possible to use them without being aware of their origins.

This sketch show, comprising forty-five half-hour episodes over four seasons, veered wildly from erudite philosophical discussions to men in drag wrestling in mud. The characters vented frustrations with authority, pomposity, and conformity. Sketches were interrupted if they had run their course (often by an army colonel complaining they were "silly"), while animated sequences by Terry Gilliam expanded on the show's surrealism. (Seen on-screen less often than his colleagues, Gilliam—the team's sole American—nonetheless played a central role as Cardinal Fang in the oft-quoted "Spanish Inquisition" sketch.)

The writer-performers, now known as the Pythons, became a global phenomenon with stage shows, albums, and hit movies, such as *Monty Python and the Holy Grail* (1975) and *Life of Brian* (1979). Individually, they've enriched our culture with children's books, riotous comedies, travel documentaries, and cinematic fantasies. But it was as a collective that they etched themselves into legend. "You can start any Monty Python routine and people finish it for you," observed Robin Williams. "Everyone knows it like shorthand." **JS**

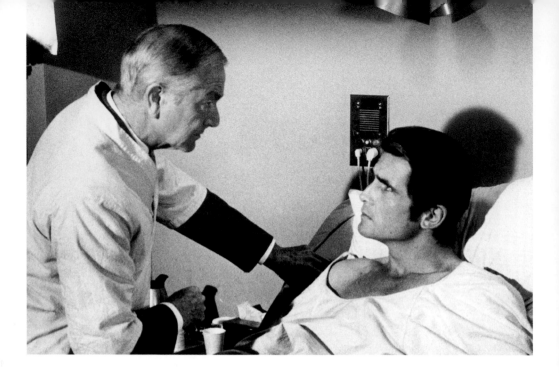

Marcus Welby, M.D.

Drama | USA | 1969–76

A much-loved medical drama that pitted orthodox medical training against good old intuition

Cast | Robert Young, James Brolin, Elena Verdugo
Original broadcaster | ABC **Awards** | 4 Emmys, 4 Golden Globes **For fans of . . .** | *Dr. Kildare* (1961)

Starring Robert Young, of *Father Knows Best* (1954) as Dr. Welby, and young heartthrob James Brolin as Dr. Kiley, *Marcus Welby, M.D.* was about two general practitioners with conflicting attitudes toward their patients. The generation gap between the pair was underlined at the start of each episode, when Dr. Kiley rode up on a motorcycle while Dr. Welby arrived in his sedan.

Welby and Kiley had several love interests during the series, including their nurse Consuelo Lopez (Elena Verdugo), Dr. Welby's sometime girlfriend, Myra Sherwood (Anne Baxter), and Dr. Kiley's girlfriend and later wife, PR director Janet Blake (Pamela Hensley). Other characters included office secretary Kathleen Faverty, played by Sharon Gless years before her success on *Cagney & Lacey*. Story lines focused on a myriad of medical issues, which were checked for accuracy by the American Academy of Family Physicians.

In 1975, previous episodes went into syndication under the title *Robert Young, Family Doctor*. Soon after, the popularity of medical dramas waned and *Marcus Welby, M.D.* flatlined after 169 episodes. **RP**

Classic episode

Designs | Season 5, episode 25. Robert Young is here reunited with Jane Wyatt, his wife from *Father Knows Best*, who guest stars as a fashion designer suffering from nervous fatigue and secretly married to a paraplegic.

◉ Robert Young (Dr. Welby) helps his younger colleague James Brolin (Dr. Kiley) when he becomes the patient.

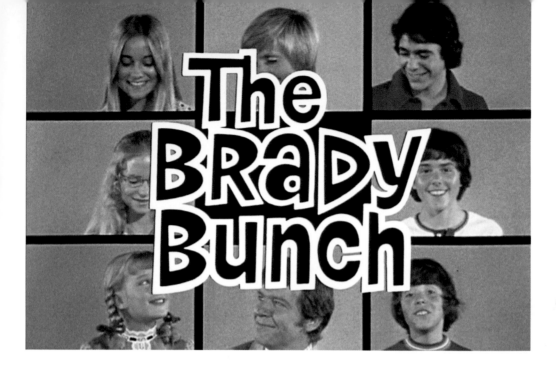

The Brady Bunch

Comedy | USA | 1969–74

This cheerful suburban sitcom enraptured successive generations of American kids

Cast | Robert Reed, Florence Henderson, Ann B. Davis, Barry Williams, Maureen McCormick, Christopher Knight, Eve Plumb, Mike Lookinland, Susan Olsen   **Original broadcaster** | ABC   **For fans of . . .** | *Modern Family* (2009)

It's a well-known story: A man named Brady, father to three sons, marries a lovely lady with three daughters, blending into a single family unit (with the help of cheerfully irascible maid Alice, of course). The show received a solid reception during its initial airing, but developed into a bona fide classic when, after going into syndication, it became essential after-school viewing for two generations of kids.

Two decades after it first aired, a seemingly forgettable sitcom transformed into a cultural juggernaut. The show's dated aesthetic, cheerful attitude, and insistence on positive lessons lent it an old-fashioned, hokey appeal. (In a late-period episode of *The X-Files*, "Sunshine Days," a reclusive young man

takes refuge from his lonely life by re-creating *The Brady Bunch* with his telekinetic powers.)

When, in 1995, *The Brady Bunch* migrated to the big screen in a gentle satire of modern life, it seemed the show had come full-circle. The film was a hit, and yet another generation found itself using *The Brady Bunch* to access a seemingly more innocent time. **AP**

Classic episode

Her Sister's Shadow | *Season 3, episode 10*.
This is the origin of the famous "Marcia, Marcia, Marcia!" line, when Jan complains to her parents about always being second-best to her older sister Marcia.

⌂ This image of the Brady family was used in the opening sequence of the show to introduce the characters.

Wünsch dir was

Game show | Austria/Germany/Switzerland | 1969–72

I'm family, get me out of here! European forerunner of a familiar modern game show

Cast | Vivi Bach, Dietmar Schönherr
Original broadcaster | ZDF
For fans of . . . | *Ich wünsch mir was* (1968), *Family Fortunes* (1980), *I'm a Celebrity, Get Me Out Of Here!* (2002)

Teenage nudity, political partisanship, and near-drowning are just three reasons *Wünsch dir was* (*Make a Wish*) lingered in the memory of viewers. In a game show format that rings bells today, competing families from three countries had to demonstrate both harmony and bravery by completing outlandish tasks, such as handling huge snakes and crossing thin ice. The winners were decided by the audience, who expressed their preferences by pressing toilet flushes or light switches.

The game show was an Austrian-German-Swiss co-production, conceived by Austrian writer Peter Hajek, subsequently the creator of German-Austrian police procedural drama *Kommissar Rex* (1994), and Swiss journalist Guido Baumann, a veteran of *Was bin ich?* (*What Am I?*, 1955). It was hosted by Danish actress Vivi Bach and her Austrian husband Dietmar Schönherr. Aired on Saturday evenings, it attracted up to thirty million viewers, and even spawned a soundtrack album in 1970.

In one episode, Schönherr wore a red carnation, which the Austrian regulators interpreted as a gesture of support for a socialist political candidate. In another, teenager Leonie Stöhr wore a transparent blouse that left little to the imagination, scandalizing some German viewers. In March 1971, contestants were lowered into a pool of water—in a car. The escape of the admirably unshaken family had to be assisted by a swiftly deployed team of frogmen. **BM**

Classic episode
Series 3, episode 8. A painter shows his skills on the outside window of a house but omits to ask the owner's permission. The ensuing disputes were grist to the producers' mill: the greater the controversy, the higher the viewing figures.

⊛ Dual hosts Vivi Bach and her husband Dietmar Schönherr in 1972.

Riten

Drama | Sweden | 1969

Art and obscenity on a small-screen stage

Cast | Gunnar Björnstrand, Anders Ek, Ingrid Thulin, Erik Hell, Ingmar Bergman
Original broadcaster | SVT
For fans of . . . | *Aus dem Leben der Marionetten* (1980), *Efter repetitionen* (1984), *Riget* (1994)

Riten (*The Rite*) was Ingmar Bergman's first project made especially for TV. It is also dark, twisted, and more explicit than his previous work—perhaps because this tale of actors brought before a judge on charges of staging an obscene play was made during his tenure as head of the Swedish Royal Dramatic Theatre. According to Bergman (who has a cameo as a priest), it was a way for him to channel his fury with this role and his wider issues with Swedish theater and cinema at the time.

Many consider this his most innovative period and here he proves it with a cast of just four. "There's always such a lot of pretentiousness surrounding films," he noted. "Such a lot of apparatus. Shooting takes forty-five days, fifty days, sixty-five days . . . There's a hell of a hullabaloo and [it] costs God knows how much. So I thought, 'Hell, I'll gather four of my close friends and we'll rehearse for four weeks and then we'll shoot it.'"

Filmed to look like a play on a stage, the drama unfolded relentlessly as the judge interrogated the actors and, in doing so, uncovered dark secrets and twisted relationships. But the actors convinced him to let them perform the play, which upset the balance of power. This battle of wills could easily be interpreted as the struggle between the creative arts and censorship.

With strong performances, explicit dialogue, and nudity, *Riten* was an uncomfortable yet alluring viewing. It may not be among Bergman's more accessible work, but leaves a lasting impression—and proves just how lenient Swedish TV censors were in the late 1960s. **JH**

Randall & Hopkirk (Deceased)

Fantasy/Horror/Sci-Fi | UK | 1969–70

One of them is dead. The other's lucky to be alive

Cast | Mike Pratt, Kenneth Cope, Annette Andre
Original broadcaster | ITV
For fans of . . . | *Danger Man* (1960), *The Avengers* (1961), *The Saint* (1962), *Department S* (1969), *Jason King* (1971), *Due South* (1994)

Murdered by the subject of one of his investigations, detective Marty Hopkirk (Kenneth Cope) returned as a ghost visible only to his partner, Jeff Randall (Mike Pratt). The pair tracked down the killer, but Marty was doomed to walk the Earth for one hundred years. As he came to terms with this state of existence, he used his new powers to aid Jeff, with variable results.

The 1960s were a high point for stylish and quirky detective shows, but this made *Randall and Hopkirk (Deceased)* a tongue-in-cheek blend of *The Avengers* (1961), and *Blithe Spirit* (1945). (Stateside, it was known as *My Partner The Ghost*.) "The techniques we used were primitive," Cope confessed to retrosellers.com. "I would stand in front of a black piece of velvet and my mirror image would be reflected to obtain the ghost illusion. We had to innovate and make lots of things up."

Many episodes played on trends of the time: Marty wore a mod-style suit, his grieving widow, Jeannie (Annette Andre) was every inch the trendy It Girl, and the bad guys included hippies and psychics alongside more conventional gangsters and thugs.

A revival in 2000 featured comedians Vic Reeves and Bob Mortimer in the title roles, with Emilia Fox as Jeannie and *Doctor Who* star Tom Baker as Marty's spiritual guide. They tried hard to balance the comedy and drama of the original, but suggested the show's writers would rather have been remaking *The Avengers*. The original installments, however, were—Cope recalled —"very pleasant and . . . a joy to work on." **JS**

The rise of the blockbuster in cinemas was matched by TV's thirst for spectacle. British TV host David Frost persuaded former US president Richard Nixon to apologize to more than 45 million viewers, while *Roots* became the highest-rated miniseries of the decade. *Monty Python's Flying Circus* went from being a niche comedy on the verge of cancellation to a worldwide smash, while a four-piece band from Sweden won the 1974 Eurovision Song Contest and became one of the biggest music acts in history. Meanwhile, moderately successful shows from the 1960s, such as *The Addams Family* and *Star Trek*, were syndicated and became huge cult hits.

1970s

◀ Mike Farrell (Captain B.J. Hunnicutt), Loretta Swit ("Hot Lips" Houlihan), and Alan Alda ("Hawkeye" Pierce) in *M*A*S*H* (1972).

All My Children
Soap opera | USA | 1970–2013

A strong commitment to social issues and a humorous script: what's not to like?

Cast | Susan Lucci, Julia Barr, David Canary, Michael E. Knight, Jill Larson, Debbi Morgan, Darnell Williams
Original broadcasters | ABC, TOLN **Awards** | 92 Emmys **For fans of . . .** | *One Life to Live* (1968)

Prolific soap writer Agnes Nixon's greatest creation, *All My Children* was the definitive daytime soap for several generations. In its pre-lunchtime slot, it was unusually popular across a wide demographic as audiences found it easy to relate to self-made woman Erica Kane (played by Susan Lucci for forty-one years) as she underwent every conceivable challenge in life, always emerging on top. Nixon envisioned the soap as a vehicle to explore social issues. In fact, the show racked up a number of firsts: Erica had an abortion in 1973, only weeks after the US Supreme Court's decision to legalize abortion. It was also the first soap to tackle homosexuality, with the character Devon McFadden, in 1983. The decision to deal openly with a character with

AIDS in 1988 also proved controversial, as did Bianca's (Erica's daughter) wedding to her civil partner in 2009. Balancing heavy story lines with more lighthearted fare, not to mention an outstanding team of scriptwriters, led to soaring ratings and numerous awards. However, as with most US daytime soaps, ratings declined in the 2010s, and *All My Children*'s last episode aired in 2013. **LN**

Classic episode
Episode 9,781 | January 7, 2008. High drama as Ryan is rushed to hospital after being shot by Hannah. She confesses that she has been working as a double agent and reveals that she plans to kill both Zach and Josh.

⊘ Erica's rival Brooke English (Julia Barr) has an affair with Mark Dalton (Mark La Mura), Erica's half-brother.

UFO

Fantasy/Horror/Sci-Fi | UK | 1970–71

Look out, the aliens are coming—from all directions

Cast | Ed Bishop, Michael Billington, George Sewell, Gabrielle Drake, Wanda Ventham, Dolores Mantez
Original broadcaster | ITV   **For fans of . . .** | *The Invaders* (1967), *Space:1999* (1975)

In the futuristic setting of 1980, Earth's defenses were alerted to a series of incursions by alien spacecraft. The aliens were harvesting human organs in an attempt to prolong their own crippled race. A secret organization, led by Commander Straker (Ed Bishop), protected the Earth with armed vehicles on land, sea, and air, and it also had a base on the Moon that gave early attack warnings.

Having dipped his toe into working with real actors in his feature film *Journey to the Far Side of the Sun* (1969), Gerry Anderson stepped away from the puppet stars of *Stingray* (1964) and *Thunderbirds* (1965) with his first live-action TV drama for adults. Although the lead characters were humans, the special effects were still impressive. Past masters at making futuristic

vehicles look full-scale, the team created land-based tanks, submarines, and UFO-blasting spacecraft. A few episodes proved too extreme for the ITV network and were banned after original transmission; drug use and sexual references were used to mix post-euphoria with paranoia and the kind of psychedelia that, at the time, would have been called "trippy." **JS**

Classic episode
A Question of Priorities | *Episode 8.* With his son fighting for his life, Straker uses a transporter to obtain life-saving medicine. But the same transporter is needed to investigate a potential alien defector, and Straker's loyalties are tested.

⏏ Commander Straker (Ed Bishop) and Colonel Paul Foster (Michael Billington) repel another alien attack.

The Odd Couple

Comedy | USA | 1970–75

Oil-and-water friendships are the best

Cast | Jack Klugman, Tony Randall, Al Molinaro, Penny Marshall, Elinor Donahue
Original broadcaster | ABC   **Awards** | 3 Emmys, 1 Golden Globe   **For fans of . . .** | *Laverne & Shirley* (1976)

Can lightning strike twice? When the Neil Simon-scripted film *The Odd Couple* (1968, based on his own play) introduced audiences to sloppy sports writer Oscar Madison and fastidious news writer Felix Ungar—mismatched friends thrown together in an apartment when Felix's wife kicks him out—there was no question that Walter Matthau and Jack Lemmon embodied their characters with comedic perfection. Surely no one else would ever be able to duplicate that combination? When the time came to adapt the film into a TV series, the impossible happened and viewers met Oscar and Felix (now a photographer) again, this time in the form of Jack Klugman and Tony Randall. The series began with the same apartment set seen in the film, but

the layout was altered drastically and redecorated in the second season. A number of continuity problems arose during the course of the show's run, including the circumstances of Oscar and Felix's first meeting. The opening narration clarified the premise of the show because the network feared viewers might believe that the friends were actually a gay couple. **ATB**

Classic episode
Password | *Season 3, episode 11.* When Oscar appears on *Password*, Felix begs to play too, but their fundamental differences in knowledge and temperament lead to tragic and hilarious results. Guest stars game show host Allen Ludden.

◉ In the episode "Gloria Moves In," Oscar (Jack Klugman) helps Felix (Tony Randall) attempt to get his ex-wife, Gloria, back.

The Partridge Family

Comedy | USA | 1970–74

Let's sing our way across the country on a musical adventure, man!

Cast | Shirley Jones, David Cassidy, Susan Dey, Danny Bonaduce, Jeremy Gelbwaks, Brian Forster
Original broadcaster | ABC **For fans of . . .** | *The Monkees* (1966), *The Brady Bunch* (1969)

How many American families thought that life would be better if they formed a traveling band? Following the template of *The Monkees*, which created a fictional group that quickly became a real one, *The Partridge Family* followed the exploits of a family band led by a widowed mother (Shirley Jones). Based loosely on the group The Cowsills, and moving in and out of the family members' lives as they traveled and performed, the Partridges faced many of the trials and tribulations of their personal and professional lives from the vantage point of their repainted psychedelic school bus.

Jones and teen heartthrob David Cassidy sang on the Partridge Family records, which were released in conjunction with the show, but the other cast members were replaced in the recordings, and session musicians provided the music itself. Their eight albums sold millions of copies. The TV theme song, "Come On, Get Happy", was well known, but the group's biggest success was the No.1 Billboard hit "I Think I Love You." In the show's final season, a move to Saturday from its original Friday time slot led to a ratings decline. **AB**

Classic episode
Soul Club | Season 1, episode 18. The Partridge Family arrive at a Detroit nightclub to substitute for The Temptations in a tone-deaf but well-meaning episode that tries to address racial issues through music.

⊕ "Come on, get happy, a whole lotta lovin' is what we'll be bringin'," sang the Partridge family.

McCloud

Drama | USA | 1970–77

Sparks flew when a cowboy cop brought his homespun brand of law and order to the NYPD

Cast | Dennis Weaver, J.D. Cannon, Terry Carter, Ken Lynch, Diana Muldaur
Original broadcaster | NBC
For fans of . . . | *Cannon* (1971), *Kojak* (1973), *NYPD Blue* (1993)

In the 1970s, New York was a city in decline. Crime was on the rise, and the police were under investigation for corruption on a large scale. The city, and its protectors, needed a new start. What it got, in the TV version of events at least, was Sam McCloud, a cowboy from Taos, New Mexico, played by Dennis Weaver.

Inspired by Don Siegel's 1968 movie *Coogan's Bluff*, NBC commissioned *McCloud* in 1970. It was the story of a deputy sheriff—complete with Stetson, sheepskin coat, and occasional horse—assigned to the 21st Precinct of the New York Police Department. The show became a ratings hit with movie-length episodes ranging from sixty minutes to two hours. McCloud's unflappable attitude, southern charm, and determination to do things his own way contrasted brilliantly with the cynicism of the NYPD at the time. His spiky relationship with Chief of Detectives, Peter B. Clifford (J.D. Cannon), highlighted the different policing styles, but at the end of each episode McCloud's ability to solve crimes earned him the grudging respect of his hard-boiled colleagues. Weaver was nominated for two Primetime Emmys for the role.

McCloud was a cop show in the best traditions of its genre, mixing bold action with high comedy and conflict. Its central character was everything the viewer hoped the NYPD, and the city itself, would be. The writing was vibrant, the shows exciting, and the timing perfectly judged. In cowboys, viewers decided, we trust. **PPW**

Rischiatutto

Game show | Italy | 1970–74

Attracting audiences of thirty to forty million, this Italian quiz show was a runaway success

Cast | Mike Bongiorno
Original broadcaster | Secondo Canale RAI/ Programma Nazionale
For fans of . . . | *The $64,000 Question* (1955), *Jeopardy!* (1984)

Presented by the well-known Italian TV host Mike Bongiorno, known in Italy as *Il Re del Quiz* (*Quiz King*), *Rischiatutto* was based on the format of the quiz show *Jeopardy!* Each episode had three rounds—a warm-up individual challenge when each of the three contestants answered questions from their chosen category in order to win an initial prize and a more exciting second round in which contestants challenged each other in front of an electronic board, selecting one of six categories, each with a monetary value that reflected the difficulty of the question. (A correct answer earned the stated sum, but if a contestant gave an incorrect response, or failed to answer in time, the amount was deducted from their accrued total.) In the final round, each contestant had to answer multiple questions in less than one minute. At the end of the show, the contestant with the biggest earnings was pronounced champion and had the right to return the following week to claim the title again.

The show was closely linked with Bongiorno, who was a character and an innovator. Born in New York, he moved back and forth between the United States and Italy during his early years before settling permanently in Italy in 1953. Under his influence, *Rischiatutto* became the first quiz program to show videos and pictures as clues on an electronic board. A new edition of the show, which was to be called *RISKYtutto*, was scheduled to air on SKY Uno in 2009, but it was canceled after the host's death that year at the age of eighty-five. **SDG**

The Goodies

Comedy | UK | 1970–82

Anarchic and wonderfully silly, The Goodies *was a madcap British comedy that viewers either loved or loathed*

Cast | Graeme Garden, Tim Brooke-Taylor, Bill Oddie
Original broadcaster | BBC One
For fans of . . . | *Monty Python's Flying Circus* (1969), *Fawlty Towers* (1975), *The Young Ones* (1982), *Bottom* (1991)

Hilarious cruelty and extreme silliness are two strains that have run throughout the history of British television humor and they've never been mixed quite so brilliantly as in *The Goodies*, an anarchic comedy show that was the brainchild of stars and former Cambridge University pals Graeme Garden, Tim Brooke-Taylor, and Bill Oddie. The trio were contemporaries of the Monty Python crew, and it's easy to see the similarities in the two groups' surreal humor. But where the Pythons often had bite to their satire, the Goodies were always most interested in having fun—and their audience had an enormous amount of fun with them.

Graeme, Tim, and Bill play housemates who ran a somewhat vaguely defined agency that would do anything the absurd story of the week required—the more absurd the better. Their madcap adventures ranged from holding a séance that resulted in Graeme becoming a witch who brazenly advertised for sacrificial virgins, to selling their "trandem" (a bicycle made for three) in exchange for a magical beanstalk that led them to a surprisingly small giant.

The series was hugely popular, its songs hummed in playgrounds (and offices) throughout Great Britain, with "The Funky Gibbon" actually reaching number four in the UK single charts. To this day *The Goodies* remains perhaps the craziest thing ever to have been broadcast on British television. It shouldn't work—it should be too self-indulgent, just too daft—but it does, and it's glorious. **RL**

Classic episode
The Music Lovers | *Season 2, episode 5*. After the Goodies witness a string quartet being dragged offstage midconcert, they set out to foil an evil plot to replace all live performances with recorded music.

◎ Riding their trandem (front to back): Tim Brooke-Taylor, Graeme Garden, and Bill Oddie.

Tatort

Crime/Mystery | Germany/Austria/Switzerland | 1970–present

These weekly murder investigations have become essential viewing for three generations

Cast | Götz George, Manfred Krug, Ulrike Folkerts, Jan Josef Liefers, Martin Wuttke
Original broadcaster | ARD
For fans of . . . | *Der Bulle von Tölz* (1996), *Criminal Minds* (2005)

This crime drama has become an iconic part of Germany's TV landscape, remaining popular with those who have watched it since the start more than forty years ago, while also gaining cult status among their children and grandchildren.

Each episode is produced independently by one of the nine regional TV channels that make up the state broadcaster ARD. This means that *Tatort* (*Crime Scene*) is an umbrella term for several almost identical TV series, as it follows a recurring cast of fictional police inspectors in different parts of the country who have never met. These detectives investigate murder cases that frequently reference recent news stories. This current affairs angle occasionally puts *Tatort* at odds with organizations that have a particular agenda, but it has also proved so popular in German-speaking countries that Austria's and Switzerland's public-service broadcasters produce their own episodes, too.

Although *Tatort*—unlike virtually any other TV series—doesn't have any omnipresent cast members, many of them have become household names in Germany. However, one actor has appeared in each of the nearly 1,000 episodes, but isn't well known at all: Horst Lettenmayer, whose eyes and legs appear in the opening sequence, which has remained virtually unchanged since 1970. This has helped *Tatort* to forge a distinct identity, and it also epitomizes the drama's enduring success in finding the right balance between innovation and tradition. **DH**

Classic episode
Strahlende Zukunft (Bright Future) | *Episode 671*.
This episode about a distraught, gun-wielding woman who blames her daughter's leukemia on a cell phone mast antagonized network operators when it aired in 2007.

◬ The late Ivan Desny appeared in early *Tatort*, before being taken up by movie directors David Lean and Rainer Werner Fassbinder.

The Mary Tyler Moore Show

Comedy | USA | 1970–77

The gold standard of US sitcoms, the Mary Tyler Moore Show *broke new ground by showing a feisty and funny female with no man or kids in tow*

Cast | Mary Tyler Moore, Edward Asner, Valerie Harper, Gavin MacLeod, Ted Knight, Cloris Leachman
Original broadcaster | CBS
Awards | 29 Emmys, 3 Golden Globes
For fans of . . . | *Lou Grant* (1977), *The Golden Girls* (1985)

Mary Richards (Mary Tyler Moore) was a single, career-focused woman. Her determination impressed the local TV news editor, Lou Grant (Edward Asner), and he offered her a job on his team, which included head writer Murray (Gavin MacLeod) and anchorman Ted (Ted Knight). Mary lived in an apartment block, where her neighbors included wisecracking Rhoda (Valerie Harper) and the domineering Phyllis (Cloris Leachman).

Costar of the hugely successful *The Dick Van Dyke Show* (1961), Tyler Moore, along with lead writers James L. Brooks and Allan Burns, took a big risk with her first star vehicle, despite a lack of confidence from the network. Belief in her vision resulted in one of the most influential sitcoms ever to have aired: Mary was an independent career woman, and the character was never defined by a husband, significant boyfriend, or children—something even Lucille Ball never achieved (*I Love Lucy*, 1951). More than this, the comedy was driven by the characters: if the drama dictated that a scene end without a laugh, so be it. Suddenly, the sitcom became real.

Politics provided a subtle undercurrent to the series, from the handling of topics such as divorce, equal pay, and homosexuality to the kind of issues that Lou and the news team would class as a "good story." Lou's suggestion that they should investigate how easy it is to buy a gun in Milwaukee clearly showed which side of the gun debate the team fell; Murray saw it as a good chance to put Ted in front of a loaded gun. **JS**

Classic episode
Chuckles Bites the Dust | *Season 6, episode 7*. The bizarre circumstances of the death of Chuckles the Clown provide the opportunity for a raft of workplace jokes in the newsroom. Mary finally sees the funny side at the funeral.

◉ Mary Tyler Moore wonders which time zone she should use to set her watch.

Flip

Variety | USA | 1970–74

The first successful network variety series starring an African-American comedian

Cast | Flip Wilson
Original broadcaster | NBC
Award | 1 Golden Globe
For fans of . . . | *Saturday Night Live* (1975), *The Richard Pryor Show* (1977)

In a radical departure from the norm, *Flip*, starring stand-up comedian Flip Wilson, one of the most popular African-American performers of the time, presented comedy monologues, skits, and musical performances in a theater-in-the-round. His character, Geraldine Jones, may have gotten her start on *Rowan & Martin's Laugh-In*, but her popularity soared thanks to *Flip*. Sassy, modern, and unapologetic, the DNA of Wilson's drag performance can be clearly seen in contemporary characters such as Tyler Perry's Madea and Martin Lawrence's Big Momma. Though she may have been his most talked-about creation, Flip also created Reverend Leroy, the minister of the Church of What's Happening Now. Wilson's catchphrases, such as "What you see is what you get," and "The devil made me do it!" became part of the American vernacular.

Wilson's popularity, and eye for spotting talent in others, brought the show such on-camera guest stars and backstage writers as Richard Pryor, Joan Rivers, Lily Tomlin, and George Carlin. The show was also a desired platform for musical acts of the day, ranging from Ella Fitzgerald to Roberta Flack, James Brown, Stevie Wonder, and The Jackson 5. Singers often took part in sketches with Wilson. In late 1971, gospel legend Mahalia Jackson made one of her final public performances on *Flip*

After the show's end, Wilson went on to continued success on stage, and guest-starring on other television shows, often in character as Geraldine Jones. **RP**

Hey Hey It's Saturday

Variety | Australia | 1971–99

Anything can happen on live TV . . . and that was this show's charm

Cast | Daryl Somers, Ernie Carroll, Jacki MacDonald, Livinia Nixon, Ian "Molly" Meldrum, Russell Gilbert, Wilbur Wilde, Andrew Fyfe, John Blackman
Original broadcaster | Nine Network
For fans of . . . | *The Tonight Show* (1954)

For nearly thirty years Australian audiences sat down every Saturday to relax, laugh, and be entertained by a variety of comedy and performance acts over a period of three hours. The acts ranged from the strictly amateur to the professional. The show also boasted a regular stable of performers, including saxophonist Wilbur Wilde and instant cartoonist Andrew Fyfe. A hallmark was John Blackman's double entendre laden voice-overs. Blackman also voiced characters Dickie Knee (a soccer ball on a stick with a wig and school cap) and Mrs. McGillicuddy (a stock photograph of an old woman). "Red Faces," "Plucka Duck," "Chook Lotto," "Celebrity Head," and "Molly's Melodrama" were all popular segments of the show.

The show originally ran on Saturday mornings, when Daryl Somers and Ernie Carroll would introduce cartoon programs. Although *Hey Hey It's Saturday* stayed in the morning time slot until 1984, the program evolved quickly from its humble beginnings into a full show created and performed by Somers, Carroll, Jacki MacDonald, and John Blackman, as well as the production crew. Its mocking, tongue-in-cheek humor laced with naughty references and knowing winks to the audience established it as a must-watch program for a wide family audience.

When it moved to Saturday nights, it brought in numerous guests and some of the regulars changed, but it retained its edgy sense of humor and witty take on popular culture. **SJG**

Dalli Dalli

Game show | Germany | 1971–86

For many families in 1970s Germany, Saturday evening viewing kicked off with this celebrity game show loved for its carnival atmosphere and fun

Cast | Hans Rosenthal
Original broadcaster | ZDF
For fans of . . . | *Jeopardy!* (1964), *Am laufenden Band* (1974), *Auf los geht's los, Wetten, dass . . . ?* (1986), *Wheel of Fortune* (1988)

"Sie der Meinung das was . . . Spitze!" ("You believe that was . . . great!") There is no one who grew up in Germany in the 1970s who does not associate this catchphrase with cozy Saturday evenings around the television watching *Dalli Dalli*. The phrase was used by Hans Rosenthal, the charming host of the game show, in which pairs of celebrities were pitted against one another in a mix of word games and activities. A typical word game might ask, "What sort of things do you keep on your bedside table?" while activities might be as trivial as hanging out laundry or as absurd as stuffing bratwurst into sausage casing. The deciding factor was usually speed (players had one minute to perform each task). At the end of the show, there was a short sketch of a famous play in which the competitors had to spot deliberate mistakes, and from mid-1975 a cult game called Dalli-Klick, in which players had to identify a picture as quickly as possible, as different parts of the whole were revealed. The show contained lots of running gags and visual devices that were repeated each week. Each time the audience shouted "Spitze!" in response to *"Sie der Meinung das was . . .,"* for example, Rosenthal jumped into the air.

Rosenthal's game show is one of the classics of German television. As well as being parodied many times over the years, it has been remade twice. But the remakes have never achieved the popularity and appeal of the original show. Only Hans Rosenthal was *Spitze!* **NK**

Classic episode
September 5, 1985 | The well-known actor Helmut Berger participated in this episode, but failed to acquit himself to his own satisfaction, a fact attributed to his runaway alcohol and substance abuse at the time.

◉ Every time the audience shouted *"Spitze!"* ("Great!"), Hans Rosenthal, the popular host of *Dalli Dalli*, jumped into the air.

Upstairs, Downstairs

Historical drama | UK | 1971–75

The original Downton Abbey—*with laughs*

Cast | Gordon Jackson, David Langton, Jean Marsh, Angela Baddeley, Simon Williams
Original broadcaster | ITV **Awards** | 2 BAFTAs, 6 Emmys, 1 Golden Globe **For fans of . . .** | *Downton Abbey* (2010)

The lives of the Bellamy family and staff at London's 165 Eaton Place made for compelling appointment TV that has rarely been matched. The show was conceived by actresses Jean Marsh and Eileen Atkins as a comedy that followed the exploits of two housemaids. At Sagitta Productions, John Hawkesworth and John Whitney saw drama potential and handed the concept to writer Alfred Shaughnessy, who developed it into *Upstairs, Downstairs*. The program immediately took off and was a popular mainstay in the schedules. Of the five seasons, the second and fourth stand among the finest drama ever produced in the world. *Upstairs, Downstairs* spanned 1903 to 1930, documenting the sweeping social, political, and economic changes that transformed Great Britain. Drama and history—the death of Edward VII, the sinking of the *Titanic*, and the outbreak of the First World War—meshed together with direst consequences for much-loved characters. In the final episode, 165 Eaton Place is sold, and the last moments feature housekeeper Rose (Jean Marsh) alone, hearing voices from the past. **MW**

Classic episode

I Dies from Love | *Season 1, episode 8*. Thought-provoking and shocking, "I Dies from Love" takes the infatuation of kitchen maid Emily (Evin Crowley) with another household's footman and turns it into abject tragedy with her suicide.

◉ The Bellamys' butler, Hudson (Gordon Jackson), is intrigued by the contents of a small envelope.

The Two Ronnies

Comedy | UK | 1971–87

Comic timing and comic expression at its best—sheer genius

Cast | Ronnie Barker, Ronnie Corbett   **Original broadcaster** | BBC One
Awards | 4 BAFTAs   **For fans of . . .** | *The Carol Burnett Show* (1967)

First coming to prominence (as a pair) in the weekly lightly satirical show *The Frost Report* (1966), Ronnies Corbett and Barker scored a massive hit when they fronted their own sketch and variety show, in which their marked physical differences (Barker was tall and somewhat portly; Corbett was very short) added a visual comedic content to the high-quality material.

Barker and Corbett excelled at inventing characters, and it was their versatility and acting skills that made their sketches so memorable. The format of the show changed rarely over the years; it opened with the pair sitting behind a desk delivering one-liners disguised as spurious news items before unleashing a slew of extravagant sketches, many based on complicated verbal routines, sprinkled with innuendo and double entendre. A filmed serial sketch often played over a number of weeks, but the highlight of each episode was the lavish, grand production, comedy music-and-dance number that closed the show. Both stars also appeared in various solo projects, thereby further establishing themselves as comedy royalty. **DF**

Classic episode
Season 5, episode 3 | September 18, 1976. This typically strong entry features the well-known "Four Candles" sketch, in which the brilliant use of wordplay in a simple shopping list results in one of the funniest UK sketches of all time.

Ronnies Corbett and Barker chew the fat in their local pub; the setting for some of their best wordplay-based sketches.

Jason King

Action/Adventure | UK | 1971–72

Suave action-adventure from a hero who defined a decade

Cast | Peter Wyngarde, Anne Sharp   **Original broadcaster** | ITV
For fans of . . . | *The Avengers* (1961), *Department S* (1969), *The Protectors* (1972)

Few TV characters epitomize an era more than Jason King. The playboy novelist and adventurer possessed a sartorial elegance that captured the essence of the dandified energy crackling through popular culture as the 1960s grooved into the 1970s.

Jason King first appeared in the ITC thriller series *Department S* (1969), but the character outgrew the format and launched in his own series. In *Department S*, King had a sideline writing novels featuring adventurer Marc Caine, the plots based on cases the department investigated. In *Jason King*, the novelist credentials were front and center; the debonair dilettante was firmly part of the literary set. King's research often took him to international locations, which brought a distraction of exotic beauties and a mystery to be solved. Despite the character's phenomenal popularity, Peter Wyngarde worked infrequently on-screen in the years following his rise to celebrity status. However, the legacy of the character is seen today in everything from the *Austin Powers* movies (1997–2002) to the *X-Men* comics (1963–present): a tag for an era in which elegance ruled. **MW**

Classic episode

As Easy as A.B.C. | *Episode 6.* King comes to the attention of the police when two criminals commit copycat robberies. Things go wrong, putting King and his girlfriend of the week, Arlene (Yutte Stensgaard), in danger.

⊘ Jason King (Peter Wyngarde) was an international man of mystery long before Austin Powers unleashed his mojo.

McMillan & Wife

Drama | USA | 1971–77

A high-society cocktail of crime and comedy

Cast | Rock Hudson, Susan Saint James, John Schuck, Nancy Walker, Martha Raye, Richard Gilliland
Original broadcasters | NBC, CBS   **For fans of . . .** | *Hart to Hart* (1979), *Castle* (2009)

Built on the tradition of mystery-solving couples, such as Nick and Nora Charles of *The Thin Man* series (1957), *McMillan & Wife* paved the way for future crime, and, comedy combinations. The series also brought movie star Rock Hudson to the small screen as Police Commissioner Stewart McMillan, a dedicated investigator with a long-standing reputation as a ladies' man. Susan Saint James played his wife, Sally, the daughter of a celebrated criminologist. Together the couple hit the streets and ferreted out crime while also living the high life. Although the mysteries were often offbeat, if not completely ridiculous and lacking in accuracy with regard to law enforcement procedures, the comedic chemistry between the leads electrified every episode. In the final season, drastic changes took place when Saint James fell out with the production company; Sally was written out via a plane crash and the series was reinvented with a now-widowed lead. Retitled *McMillan*, the show followed the investigator as he found a new place to live, a new housekeeper, and a new girlfriend in every one of the final six episodes. **AB**

Classic episode

Till Death Us Do Part | *Season 1, episode 6*. A crazed killer spikes the drinks of Mac and Sally and orders a pest control company to pump poisonous gas into their family home. Mac must outwit the killer before the pair suffocate.

◉ Rock Hudson and Susan Saint James brought a quirky charm and sophistication to 1970s sleuthing.

All in the Family

Comedy | USA | 1971–79

Frank and progressive portrait of clashing generations and changing ideologies—
"Those were the days!"

Cast | Carroll O'Connor, Jean Stapleton, Rob Reiner, Sally Struthers, Danielle Brisebois
Original broadcaster | CBS
Awards | 22 Emmys, 8 Golden Globes
For fans of . . . | *The Jeffersons* (1975)

Loosely based on UK sitcom *Till Death Us Do Part* (1965), *All in the Family* was a razor-sharp cut across the complacency of American home life. Created by Norman Lear and Alan "Bud" Yorkin, the series tackled controversial topics without shying away from uncomfortable language, sharp but troubling humor, deft shifts into drama, and aggravatingly ambiguous resolutions. *All in the Family* also pioneered taping episodes in front of a live studio audience.

Iconic bigot Archie Bunker (Carroll O'Connor) was the arch conservative pontificating with malapropism-laden monologues from his easy-chair throne, facing the audience and challenging them to love as much as hate him as he railed against the changes in his country and his own house. Long-suffering, good-hearted Edith Bunker (Jean Stapleton) held her own against Archie's onslaught, while daughter Gloria (Sally Struthers) and her politically liberal activist boyfriend/husband Mike Stivic (Rob Reiner) kept the Bunker home loud and controversial.

The series was so successful—it remained number one in the ratings for five consecutive years—that it spawned its own mini TV universe, generating a record number of spin-offs including *Maude* (1972), *The Jeffersons* (1975), and *Gloria* (1982). Furthermore, Archie and Edith's original chairs joined the Smithsonian National Museum of American History collection in 1978. The show's impact on pop culture is immeasurable . . . "ya meathead!" **ATB**

Classic episode
Gloria Discovers Women's Lib | *Season 1, episode 11.* Gloria decries Archie's treatment of Edith, demanding equality in her own relationship. Mike defends antiquated gender roles, endangering his marriage as Gloria leaves home.

⬤ Golden Globe winner Carroll O'Connor stars as Archie Bunker.

Budgie

Drama | UK | 1971–72

A down-on-his-luck jailbird tries to do the right thing, kind of . . .

Cast | Adam Faith, Iain Cuthbertson, Lynn Dalby
Original broadcaster | ITV
For fans of . . . | *Callan* (1967), *Shoestring* (1979), *Bergerac* (1981)

Ronald "Budgie" Bird (Adam Faith) just could not get a break. Recently released from prison, he tried to get by, but was frequently involved in shady crime capers that invariably went wrong and put the young man in deeper trouble. In each self-contained episode, Budgie was out of his depth and often in thrall to gangster Charlie Endell (Iain Cuthbertson), and it was only a matter of time before Budgie ended up back behind bars.

Adam Faith was one of the United Kingdom's most successful solo music artists of the 1960s. Throughout the decade, he made occasional sidesteps into acting, and, in 1971, was chosen to headline his own series: *Budgie*. The program was created by writers Keith Waterhouse and Willis Hall. Parallels could be seen between Budgie and the character of Billy Liar, which they had previously adapted for the big screen, in 1963, from Waterhouse's original novel. *Budgie* was a light-hearted drama, albeit with an air of melancholy running through it. Faith gave the character a winning charm, which was enhanced by the pairing with Cuthbertson's suavely spoken but dangerous Glaswegian gangster.

Overseen by acclaimed TV producer Verity Lambert, *Budgie*'s first season was popular, with its final episode ending with Budgie back in prison. In season two, the jailbird was back on the streets and involved with Endell once more, while dealing with pregnant girlfriends, estranged wives, and the usual battle to keep going. A potential third season was never realized after Faith was seriously injured in a car crash. **MW**

Cannon

Drama | USA | 1971–76

Gravel-voiced authority and sardonic humor make this detective one to watch—in bulk

Cast | William Conrad
Original broadcaster | CBS
For fans of . . . | *Ironside* (1967), *The Streets of San Francisco* (1972), *Barnaby Jones* (1973), *Jake and the Fatman* (1987)

In the field of 1970s TV crime fighters, Frank Cannon (William Conrad) looms large—literally. The actor's formidable bulk became the character's trademark, and when not bringing to justice the crooks of Southern California, Cannon could usually be found enjoying his own gourmet cooking. Conrad, previously best known as Matt Dillon in the radio version of *Gunsmoke* (1952; his physical appearance was considered unsuitable for the Wild West hero's TV incarnation), was working mainly as a director when he took on the role that made his physique as familiar as his voice. The unlikelihood of a man as unfit as Cannon chasing after criminals became a favorite joke of comedians, but while the show got humor out of his appearance, it still gave Conrad plenty of rough stuff to do, occasionally even using his impressively huge stomach as a weapon.

The series was another hit from Quinn Martin Productions, which had given the world *The Fugitive* (1963; narrated by Conrad), *The Invaders* (1967), and *The Streets of San Francisco* (1972). It commenced with the widowed LA cop going solo as a private eye, and the opener of the show's final season offered a rare insight into Cannon's private life, as the detective finds the man responsible for killing his wife and son years before. *Cannon* also regularly offered a contrast between the shabby detective and his glamorous guest star clients: Joan Fontaine, Vera Miles, Anne Baxter, and Leslie Nielsen are some of those who turned up on the show. **IK**

Bless This House

Comedy | UK | 1971–76

Mega-popular generation-gap comedy with some cracking one-liners

Cast | Sid James, Diana Coupland, Sally Geeson, Robin Stewart
Original broadcaster | ITV **For fans of . . .** | *Wait Till Your Father Gets Home* (1972)

In the United Kingdom, the BBC has always produced the most critically acclaimed and universally admired sitcoms, but for a while in the 1970s, the commercial channel ITV enjoyed unprecedented success with a series of sitcoms that struck a chord with the public and attracted some of the biggest ratings of all time. The family comedy *Bless This House* was one of the best.

Comedy actor Sid James, well-known star of the *Carry On . . .* film series, played Sid Abbott, a forty-something traveling salesman married to a ditzy but unflappable housewife, Jean. They had two teenaged children: Sally, a flirtatious type who Sid worried might be promiscuous; and Mike, his flamboyantly dressed, rather effete son who Sid worried might be

gay. Although faithful to wife, Sid was an old-school type who struggled against the temptations of a permissive society, while, at the same time, deploring the fact that his children were growing up as a part of it. The ever-widening gap between the generations and Sid's penchant for jumping to the wrong conclusions provided the basis for most of the plots. **DF**

Classic episode

The Generation Gap | *Season 1, episode 1.* The opening episode of the first season neatly encapsulates all the themes that would drive the show for its six-season run. Sid does not seem to understand any of them.

◉ Sid Abbott (Sid James) turns his back on Jean (Diana Coupland)—a familiar sight.

Parkinson

Talk show | UK | 1971–2007

The undisputed British champion of chat

Cast | Michael Parkinson **Original broadcaster** | BBC One
Award | 1 BAFTA **For fans of . . .** | *The Jonathan Ross Show* (2011)

Michael Parkinson began his career as a journalist, and broke into television as a reporter for local news before joining ITV's flagship current-affairs program *World in Action*. His self-titled talk show arrived in 1971 and within only a few years, he proved himself the king of talk, attracting huge stars and introducing new faces.

Parkinson's skill was to be complimentary enough to warm up his guest, to interrupt only if it helped to provide context to the anecdote, and to know when to sit back and let his guests ramble. Self-deprecating, he was often at his most charming when he knew he was being outclassed. His interviews with Muhammad Ali are infamous; he brought the boxing legend into British homes and provided him with a space to show off.

Hollywood stars were known to flirt with the gruff Yorkshireman, as he became visibly shy at the slightest flutter of an eyelid. Although Parkinson might cite Shirley MacLaine as his most flirtatious guest, few would deny the sexual energy oozing from the Muppet diva Miss Piggy. Another puppet, Emu, provided the interview for which he is best remembered. **JS**

Classic episode
Muhammad Ali | *Season 1, episode 13*. On their first meeting, Parky introduces "the most beautiful and complete athlete I've ever seen," and then spends an hour basking in his magnificence. One of the greatest sports interviews ever.

⊘ Actress Raquel Welch took a quick break from filming *The Last Sheila in Nice* to join Michael Parkinson for a chat in November 1972.

Rio das Mortes

Comedy/Drama | Germany | 1971

This made-for-TV farce was the work of mighty German movie director Rainer Werner Fassbinder

Cast | Hanna Schygulla, Michael König, Günther Kaufmann, Katrin Schaake, Harry Baer
Original broadcaster | ARD **For fans of . . .** | *Liebe ist kälter als der Tod* (1969), *Detectorists* (2014)

When the German writer and movie director Rainer Werner Fassbinder began shooting *Rio das Mortes* (*River of the Dead*) in 1970 he was just twenty-four years old, yet he already had seven films to his name. Themes of bleakness, repression, and homoeroticism informed much of his life's work—he died in 1982 at the age of thirty-seven—yet were largely absent from this droll farce, making it a fascinating footnote to Fassbender's filmography.

Actors Günther Kaufmann (who featured in Fassbinder's final film, *Querelle*) and Michael König played friends trapped in the mundane reality of existence. Günther (Kaufmann) has recently left the army, while Michel (König) tiled floors. However, a map

of South America's Rio das Mortes galvanized them into action, and they became fixated with seeking treasure in Peru—in vain, given that the region is in Brazil (apparently an oversight by Fassbinder rather than a comedic flourish). This plan was resisted by Michel's girlfriend Hanna—played by Hanna Schygulla, whose long association with Fassbinder placed her in the vanguard of the New German Cinema of the late 1960s and 1970s. Hanna is key to the best remembered sequences in the movie: a dance with the director himself to Elvis Presley's "Jailhouse Rock" that prefigured John Travolta and Uma Thurman's routine in *Pulp Fiction* (1994), and a climactic scene in which she took drastic action against her errant lover. **BM**

⚋ Hanna Schygulla (Hanna) takes aim in *Rio das Mortes*.

Soul Train

Music/Musical | USA | 1971–2006

All aboard the hippest trip in America

Cast | Don Cornelius (1971–93), Mystro Clark (1997–99), Shemar Moore (1999–2003), Dorian Gregory (2003–06)
Original broadcaster | WCIU-TV **Award** | 1 Emmy **For fans of . . .** | *American Bandstand* (1951)

For over forty years *Soul Train* brought urban music and dance into America's living rooms, from joyous pop to gritty funk, slick disco, and edgy hip-hop. The show was synonymous with the best in black entertainment.

Soul Train began as a series of concerts held at high schools around Chicago, emceed by local news reporter and DJ Don Cornelius. In 1970, with Sears, Roebuck & Co. as a sponsor, Cornelius began hosting *Soul Train* on the Chicago station WCIU-TV.

Within a year, the show moved into national syndication, airing on a weekly basis, and production moved to Los Angeles. Smooth and dapper, Cornelius introduced the hottest soul acts. The first episode shown nationally featured Gladys Knight & the Pips,

Eddie Kendricks, Honey Cone, and Bobby Hutton, and the *Soul Train* dancers getting down to prerecorded cuts by artists such as James Brown and Wilson Pickett. The famous "Soul Train Line," formed from two lines of dancers, down which a couple would perform inventive moves, came later.

Production was halted at the end of the 2005–6 season. The show staggered on for two more years showing repackaged episodes under the title *The Best of Soul Train*, but syndication distribution ended in 2008. A good train can't be stopped, however, and the *Soul Train Music Awards* broadcast, honoring the very best in black music and entertainment, continues to be aired annually on the BET network. **RBA**

🎵 Godfather of soul James Brown performing live in 1971.

Columbo

Drama | USA | 1971–2003

Slow but masterful, frustrating but suspenseful: the detective series that turns the traditional whodunit on its head

Classic episode
Troubled Waters | *Season 4, episode 4.* Columbo is on a cruise with his wife (unseen, of course) when a singer is murdered. The killer (Robert Vaughn) fakes a heart attack to create an alibi and tries to frame the victim's band mate (Dean Stockwell).

◐ Singer Johnny Cash (Tommy Brown) in "Swan Song" (season 3).
◑ Peter Falk (Columbo) weaves a verbal web to outsmart his prey.

Cast | Peter Falk, with guest stars Billy Connolly, Faye Dunaway, Janet Leigh, Leonard Nimoy, William Shatner
Original broadcasters | NBC, ABC
Awards | 13 Emmys, 2 Golden Globes
For fans of . . . | *Murder, She Wrote* (1984)

Columbo broke the mold of the whodunit by revealing the killer up front. It usually was not until the second act that we would meet Columbo (Peter Falk): a detective who lulled his suspects into a false sense of security with his crumpled trench coat, childlike curiosity, and anecdotes about his never-seen wife, before trailing after his suspect and uttering the fateful words "Just one more thing . . ."

The show was an immediate success when it first aired as part of NBC's Mystery Movie series. The character of Columbo—he gives his first name only as "Lieutenant"—had first been played by Bert Freed in an episode of *The Chevy Mystery Show* in 1960. Richard Levinson and William Link then reworked their script into a stage play, *Prescription: Murder*, which eventually returned to TV as a pilot starring Peter Falk, the actor now synonymous with the role. The appeal was not the mystery itself, but watching Columbo circle and then catch his prey. These were high-society types: politicians, military commanders, and well-known authors. A gentle class war ran throughout the series as the working-class cop sparred with suspects who looked down on him. Columbo would cling to his targets like a limpet, upping the pressure until their lies and evasions unravelled before him.

The show attracted numerous celebrity guest stars. Honor Blackman, Johnny Cash, Donald Pleasance, and Roddy McDowall all took their turns. Patrick McGoohan wrote, directed, produced . . . and murdered! **WH**

The Onedin Line

Historical drama | UK | 1971–80

This period piece captained by Peter Gilmore was appointment viewing for Britain in the 1970s

Cast | Peter Gilmore, Anne Stallybrass, Michael Billington, Jill Gascoigne
Original broadcaster | BBC One   **For fans of . . .** | *Poldark* (1975)

Chronicling the trials of James Onedin (Peter Gilmore) as he set up his own shipping company in Liverpool in the late nineteenth century, *The Onedin Line* was a staple of the BBC's Sunday evening schedules for close on a decade. It was a classy affair that made a star of Gilmore.

The series opened with James acquiring a derelict schooner through his marriage to Anne Webster (Anne Stallybrass), the owner's daughter. Though it was a marriage of convenience, true love blossomed when the Onedin Line took sail and Anne showed herself to be a shrewd businesswoman.

Liverpool-born Cyril Abraham, who created the series, had intimate knowledge of ships from his days in the Merchant Navy. He blended a family saga with period detail and attractive locations. Anne was killed off in season two, her place eventually taken by Jill Gascoigne as James' second wife Letty (off–screen, Gilmore and Stallybrass married in 1977). Gilmore feared typecasting but was persuaded to return after a two-year gap in 1976. *The Onedin Line* sailed on for another five seasons before dropping anchor for good.   MW

Classic episode
Pound and Pint | *Season 2, episode 2*. James' underhand response to a sailors' strike causes conflict with Anne, who is shocked by his callousness and leaves him. Passions run high between the series' lead characters.

⬥ Peter Gilmore as James Onedin set sail in a series of epic tales of seafaring and trading on the high seas.

The Persuaders!

Action/Adventure | UK | 1971–72

Two of Hollywood's biggest names starred in this fun and frothy adventure romp

Cast | Roger Moore, Tony Curtis, Laurence Naismith
Original broadcaster | ITV   **For fans of . . .** | *Danger Man* (1960), *The Saint* (1962)

Of all the action series from Lew Grade's ITC production company, *The Persuaders!* ranks as the most audacious. Grade took two giant stars, Roger Moore and Tony Curtis, and added a heady cocktail of action and adventure. The concept of a Brit and an American in an adventure romp was inspired by an episode of *The Saint*, in which Simon Templar (Roger Moore) was partnered with a Texan oilman in Monte Carlo.

The story that Grade and producer Robert S. Baker came up with revolved around wayward and wealthy playboys Lord Brett Sinclair (Moore) and Danny Wilde (Curtis), who were blackmailed by Judge Fulton (Laurence Naismith) into working as investigators in order to avoid a jail sentence. With a budget of £100,000 per episode, partly spent on foreign locations, it was the most expensive TV show in Britain at the time. Though successful in Britain and Europe, the show received a lukewarm reception in North America. A mooted second season was derailed by Moore being cast as James Bond in 1972, a role for which Lord Brett Sinclair was the perfect warm-up. **MW**

Classic episode

Greensleeves | *Season 1, episode 4.* Brett Sinclair discovers that a mysterious group is using his mothballed family estate for nefarious purposes. With Danny's help, he impersonates the actor hired to portray him and infiltrates the group.

⬆ Tony Curtis and Roger Moore created a strong and watchable dynamic in *The Persuaders!*

La Maison des bois

Drama | France | 1971

A poetic yet authentic depiction of life in the French countryside during the First World War

Cast | Pierre Doris, Albert Martinez, Michel Terrazon, Jacqueline Dufranne, Agathe Natanson, Henri Puff, Hervé Lévy, Fernand Gravey, Maurice Pialat **Original broadcaster** | ORTF **For fans of . . .** | *Clochemerle* (1972)

Commissioned by the Office de Radiodiffusion Télévision Française (ORTF), *La Maison des bois (The House in the Woods)* is French film director Maurice Pialat's one and only contribution to television. It came on the back of his first full-length feature, *L'Enfance nue (Naked Childhood)*, which, despite a good public reception and critical acclaim, had left him penniless. This miniseries turned out to be a key moment in the director's career, and is regarded as one of his most important achievements.

The seven episodes are each fifty-two minutes long and tell the story of the day-to-day life of three Parisian children who were forced to relocate to the countryside during the First World War. Hervé (Hervé Lévy), Bébert

(Albert Martinez), and Michel (Michel Terrazon) all have to find refuge with Papa Albert (Pierre Doris), a gamekeeper, and his wife, Maman Jeanne (Jacqueline Dufranne), whose house in the woods is far from the turbulence of the frontline. Hervé was placed there by his own mother; she then left without a trace. He quickly became Maman Jeanne's favorite.

The show was slow-paced and had no particular narrative thrust; it focused merely on mundane village life. It has been praised for its humanism and its excellent depictions of the characters' lives. Pialat worked with the themes he was drawn to and to which he would return in his subsequent films—childhood and the abandonment of children. **MS**

◬ (L–R) Michel Tarrazon, Albert Martinez, Hervé Lévy, and Agathe Natanson in the character-driven *La Maison des Bois*.

The Waltons

Drama | USA | 1971–81

Homespun saga of the perfect all-American family

Cast | Ralph Waite, Michael Learned, Richard Thomas, Jon Walmsley, Mary Beth McDonough, Eric Scott, Judy Norton
Original broadcaster | CBS **Awards** | 13 Emmys, 3 Golden Globes **For fans of . . .** | *Little House on the Prairie* (1974)

In January 1992, incumbent President George Bush delivered a speech on family values in which he expressed a desire to "make American families a lot more like the Waltons and a lot less like the Simpsons." The Virginian Walton family stood for good, old-fashioned values—unsurprisingly, as the story began in the Depression and continued to the Second World War. Creator Earl Hamner Jr. took inspiration from his semiautobiographical novel. He also narrated the series, playing eldest son John-Boy as an adult. Head of the family was John (Ralph White), whose household contained his elderly parents, wife Olivia (Michael Learned), and seven children. The youngsters provided tales of growing pains and sibling rivalry in

an overcrowded home. *The Waltons* rarely settled for a saccharine solution; episodes were heartwarming and reassuring, not melodramatic—even when young Elizabeth experienced the effects of a poltergeist. Whatever they faced, each night the family would discuss the day's events, and installments ended with a shot of the house at night, as viewers eavesdropped on their good-night blessings.

The Waltons was canceled in 1981, but the viewers revisited Walton's Mountain for six TV movies between 1982 and 1997. By the final film, the story had moved to 1969, marking John and Olivia's fortieth wedding anniversary surrounded by their children and awaiting the birth of John-Boy's first child with wife Janet. **JS**

⚠ We're not listing all of the Walton family members—we'd be here all night.

Emmerdale

Soap opera | UK | 1972–present

Character-driven plots with a labyrinth of story lines and occasional high-octane drama

Cast | Sheila Mercier, Andrew Burt, Frazer Hines, Patrick Mower, Shirley Stelfox, Richard Thorp, Chris Chittell
Original broadcaster | ITV **Award** | 1 BAFTA **For fans of . . .** | *McLeod's Daughters* (2001)

Emmerdale is an institution of British television and the nation's second longest-running soap opera. It developed from modest beginnings as a rural-set drama titled *Emmerdale Farm*, but has grown over four decades into a rich, detailed soap that embraces the best traits of the genre. Originally the show focused on three generations of the Sugden family, who ran a Yorkshire Dales farm. Unusually for a soap of the period, many of the farm sequences were shot on location, Yorkshire Television having consulted with the producers of the groundbreaking Irish-set soap *The Riordans* (1965) on how this could be achieved.

Year-round production of *Emmerdale Farm* was instigated in 1988, and the series became *Emmerdale* the following year, thereby reflecting the gradual widening of focus away from the Sugdens toward the daily life of the local village and its inhabitants. Today the show is barely recognizable from the series created by Kevin Laffan in 1972. Although there are still Sugdens farming the land, it is the lives and loves of the villagers of Emmerdale that now entertain millions. **MW**

Classic episode
The Plane Crash | *Episode 1,829.* This story line featured some of the most dramatic scenes ever seen in a British soap opera. An airliner explodes in the sky over the village and fuel and fire rain down. Not every villager makes it through the night.

◬ Frazer Hines as Joe Sugden and Andrew Burt as Jack Sugden on location in rural Yorkshire.

Kung Fu

Action/Adventure | USA | 1972–75

A Shaolin monk takes on gun-toting America with his bare hands

Cast | David Carradine, Keye Luke, Radames Pera, Philip Ahn, James Hong, Tad Horino
Original broadcaster | ABC **Awards** | 3 Emmys **For fans of . . .** | *The Water Margin* (1973, Japan; 1976, UK)

ABC's *Kung Fu* was born out of a growing enthusiasm for martial arts, popularized during the period by Bruce Lee in films such as *Enter the Dragon* (1973). It followed the exploits of a Shaolin monk, Kwai Chang Caine (David Carradine), who left his monastery after the murder of his teacher, Master Po (Keye Luke). He traveled to the United States, where he battled evildoers and tried to keep to the path of his Shaolin teachings. During its run, *Kung Fu* became one of the most popular shows on TV, making a star out of Carradine. The show's trademarks—fighting in slow motion, Carradine fighting barefoot, and Master Po having white, eggshell-like eyes—have all become tropes of the genre. There is some controversy over who created the series, as actor Bruce Lee (who was actually considered for the role of Caine) has claimed that it was his idea. However, it seems that writer Ed Spielman can take the credit because in the 1960s he developed the ideas and format that underpinned the show. The show eventually stopped, allegedly because Carradine had sustained too many injuries during filming. **DJH**

Classic episode
The Ancient Warrior | *Season 1, episode 15*. Caine supports an elderly American Indian in his quest for burial rights on his ancestral land, now occupied by an unruly "white man" civilization. A touching episode—superb storytelling.

◬ Watched by a serene Master Po (Keye Luke), Caine (David Carradine) learns the arts of the Shaolin monk.

Love Thy Neighbour
Comedy | UK | 1972–76

This suburban culture clash rang true in postwar Britain, but appears controversial to modern eyes

Classic episode
The Housewarming Party | Season 2, episode 1.
Bill and his wife Barbie (Nina Baden-Semper) are throwing a housewarming party but Eddie, fearing that any West Indian celebration is likely to turn into a riot, calls the police before it does.

⬥ Rudolph Walker (Bill) and Jack Smethurst (Eddie) living up to one another's expectations.

Cast | Jack Smethurst, Rudolph Walker, Nina Baden-Semper, Kate Williams
Original broadcaster | ITV
For fans of . . . | *George and Mildred* (1976), *Mind Your Language* (1977)

Love Thy Neighbour was a popular element of 1970s British TV, but as social outlooks changed, it became taboo, so has rarely been repeated. A white husband and wife are aghast when a West Indian couple move in next door. This premise seems hackneyed when viewed from a modern perspective, but for 1970s Britain adapting to the upheaval of mass postwar immigration, it, no doubt, felt like deft social commentary in a comic setting, and it must have struck a chord.

Eddie Booth (Jack Smethurst) was a dyed-in-the-wool socialist, his bigotry exploding with the arrival of neighbor Bill Reynolds (Rudolph Walker), a Conservative West Indian. The comedy stemmed from the polar opposites of their racial and social outlooks, but episodes frequently descended into name-calling, both characters hurling racial slurs at the other with abandon. Writers Vince Powell and Harry Driver claimed that balance was inherent within the format, but Eddie frequently came out on top. *Love Thy Neighbour* could be considered progressive in its depiction of the feuding mens' wives, Joan (Kate Williams) and Barbara (Nina Baden-Semper). They were strong, intelligent, capable women who knew they were married to idiots.

After eight seasons, *Love Thy Neighbour* was dropped by Thames Television, but it made a transfer to cinemas in 1974. Smethurst starred in a short-lived Australian version in 1979, but *Love Thy Neighbour* is remembered for the many things it did poorly, rather than the few things it did well. **MW**

Colditz

Historical drama | UK | 1972–74

Tense, steely Second World War drama set in the "escape-proof" Colditz castle

Cast | Jack Hedley, David McCallum, Bernard Hepton, Robert Wagner, Anthony Valentine, Edward Hardwicke
Original broadcaster | BBC One
For fans of . . . | *Secret Army* (1977), *Band of Brothers* (2001)

During the Second World War, it was the duty of every captured officer to make an escape attempt or die trying. For the repeat escapee, the Germans maintained a castle near Leipzig: Colditz. Imprisoned there, the British and Allied officers spent their time concocting and testing various escape plans. While some of them successfully found their way out (few managed to make it all the way home in one piece), for others it was the strategic planning for future escapes that gave them the hope they needed to carry on.

Brian Degas and producer Gerald Glaister based this drama on true accounts from officers who survived the real Colditz Castle (including Major Pat Reid, whose story had also inspired a feature film). Nearly thirty years after the end of the war, some revisionist theories were becoming popular—detached from the propaganda and the need to demonize the enemy—and Glaister and his team took the brave decision to allow for a broadly sympathetic portrayal of the German officers, in particular the Kommandant (Bernard Hepton), who faced not only resistance from his prisoners but also interference from the SS, represented in the second season by the over-efficient, opportunistic Major Mohn (Anthony Valentine).

International stars Robert Wagner and David McCallum stood alongside British character actors Jack Hedley and Edward Hardwicke to create a real ensemble in which anyone could disappear suddenly and nobody was bigger than the drama itself. **JS**

The Stone Tape

Fantasy/Horror/Sci-Fi | UK | 1972

Unsettling ghost story—will anyone survive with their lives or their sanity intact?

Cast | Michael Bryant, Iain Cuthbertson, Michael Bates, Jane Asher
Original broadcaster | BBC Two
For fans of . . . | *The Quatermass Experiment* (1953), *Dead of Night* (1972)

A ghost story for Christmas was something of a tradition on the BBC in the 1970s, with the works of M.R. James often adapted for the small screen. *The Stone Tape* was something different, based on an original script from Nigel Kneale, the creator of *The Quatermass Experiment*, science fiction serials that had captivated and terrorized TV audiences in the 1950s.

Jill Greeley (Jane Asher) arrives to join her scientist colleagues, who have just moved into a new facility in a renovated country house. She is freaked out immediately by a series of sounds and apparitions, and soon her skeptical colleagues discover that their equipment is registering something strange. Is Jill really seeing and sensing the ghost of a girl who plunged to her death, or could something be hidden in the stonework? The team moves in to conduct experiments on this "stone tape," but only succeed in "wiping it." However, Jill is drawn to the room once more and discovers a much older malevolent presence.

The Stone Tape was successful because it combined the horrific with the everyday. Sensibly avoiding pyrotechnics and special effects, the thrills and scares came from the sound effects and the fact that the cast played it absolutely straight. Music from the BBC's avant-garde Radiophonic Workshop, masters at making the everyday unworldly, greatly added to the spooky atmosphere. The drama popularized T.C. Lethbridge's stone tape theory: ghosts are merely recordings of the past left in the fabric of buildings. **DJ**

M*A*S*H

Comedy/Drama | USA | 1972–83

Groundbreaking comedy that lasted three times longer than the war in which it was set

Cast | Alan Alda, Loretta Swit, Harry Morgan, David Ogden Stiers, Mike Farrell, Jamie Farr
Original broadcaster | CBS
Awards | 14 Emmys
For fans of . . . | *Scrubs* (2001), *House* (2004)

On February 28, 1983, 106 million Americans watched the final episode of *M*A*S*H* (twice as many as tuned in for the *Friends* finale). Rather than the usual half-hour, it ran for two and a half hours—the New York Sanitation Department reported a leap in water usage as millions rushed to the bathroom after the show ended.

The ridiculous and comic were always peripheral to a series that won awards as a comedy, but was propelled by the underlying grim reality of war. The first episode was broadcast in 1972, when the Vietnam conflict was uppermost in the minds of the US public, and easy answers were hard to come by. The tales of committed army doctors in the Korean War were simply frames upon which larger issues were laid. The conceit worked brilliantly, and brought enduring success. In the final five of its remarkable eleven seasons, the writing grew ever more serious. Alan Alda—who played star of the show Hawkeye—was largely responsible for this, and the shows he produced are notable for an often somber undertone.

Nonetheless, *M*A*S*H*—an acronym for Mobile Army Surgical Hospital—had memorably comic moments. Corporal Maxwell Q. Klinger (Jamie Farr) organizing the wounded wearing a chiffon dress is an enduring image, as are Hawkeye's ongoing attempts to get the girl. However, the image that most viewers recall is the final shot of the final episode: the melancholy view as a helicopter pulls away and the audience sees "GOODBYE" spelled out on the ground. **PH**

Classic episode
Goodbye, Farewell, and Amen | *Season 11, episode 16.* Directed and cowritten by star Alan Alda, this became the single most watched TV episode in US history, overtaking the *Dallas* episode in which "who shot J.R.?" is revealed.

⬆ Alan Alda (seated) with his longest-standing costars.
➡ Gary Burghoff as Radar and Harry Morgan as Sherman T. Potter.

Are You Being Served?

Comedy | UK | 1972–85

Hilarious farce set in a British department store—"Ground floor: perfumery, stationery, and leather goods, wigs and haberdashery, kitchenware and food—going up!"

Cast | Mollie Sugden, Frank Thornton, John Inman, Wendy Richard, Nicholas Smith, Trevor Bannister
Original broadcaster | BBC One
For fans of . . . | *Hi-De-Hi!* (1980), *Mrs. Brown's Boys* (2011)

Many of British TV's great ensemble sitcoms carry the name of writer/creator David Croft, either with Jimmy Perry (on *Dad's Army*, 1968, and *It Ain't Half Hot, Mum*, 1974) or, as here, with former actor Jeremy Lloyd. Although the series was criticized for its gender stereotyping, and some of the double entendres made your toes curl, its parody of the British class system was second to none.

Are You Being Served? was set in Grace Brothers, an old-fashioned department store owned by two rarely seen decrepit siblings. On the shop floor was Captain Peacock (Frank Thornton), a proud ex-officer with a stern attitude and little patience for nonsense. Senior staffer on the women's garments counter was Mrs. Slocombe (Mollie Sugden), whose improbably colored hair changed from episode to episode and whose never-seen pet cat provided some of the crudest innuendo in 1970s comedy: "My central heating broke down. I had to light the oven and hold my pussy in front of it." Miss Brahms (Wendy Richard) was her young assistant, forever the focus of attention from the randy young gent in menswear, Mr. Lucas (Trevor Bannister). However, the star of the show was undoubtedly John Inman as Mr. Humphries, an effeminate man who lived with his mother and whose campiness (particularly the way he would call "I'm free!" across the shop floor) caused concern for upper management at the BBC until David Croft explained that the character was a "mummy's boy" and not, in fact, homosexual. **JS**

Classic episode

Dear Sexy Knickers . . . | *Season 1, episode 1.*
Riotous episode in which the ever flirtatious Mr. Lucas tries to woo the buxom Miss Brahms. His love note falls into the wrong hands, and Captain Peacock receives a very unexpected phone call.

⊙ Haughty Captain Peacock (Frank Thornton) checks the order book before inevitably calling out, "Are you free?"

Crown Court

Drama | UK | 1972–84

Fictional court cases in which the verdict was decided by real members of the public

Cast | Peter Wheeler, William Mervyn, Bernard Gallagher, John Barron, Richard Wilson, Charles Keating, Edward Jewesbury, Richard Warner
Original broadcaster | ITV
For fans of . . . | *Rumpole of the Bailey* (1978)

Crown Court was an anthology with a difference. Screened on weekday afternoons (usually Wednesdays, Thursdays, and Fridays), the series brought viewers into the fictional Fulchester Crown Court to witness a dramatized trial. Each week the three episodes saw the prosecution set out their case against the accused, the defense counteract, and the delivery of the verdict. It was most often played straight, only occasionally veering into lighthearted territory and rarely featuring humor. A successful format, *Crown Court* ran for 879 episodes over twelve years.

Although most of the participants were actors, the jury consisted of members of the public who were eligible for jury service. Each episode began with the court reporter (Peter Wheeler) explaining the details of the offense, or summarizing the events so far, accompanied by photographs of the key individuals concerned. The jury would then be presented with all of the evidence as if for a real trial, and their unscripted verdict decided how each story would conclude (alternative endings were written to cover either outcome).

As in a real court, the judge and the lawyers were not the same every week, although some characters recurred over the years, such as Jonathan Fry QC (Bernard Gallagher) and The Hon. Mr. Justice Campbell (William Mervyn). A number of the defendants and witnesses were played by actors who later achieved great fame, including Colin Firth, Ben Kingsley, Peter Capaldi, and Bob Hoskins. **JS**

Maude

Comedy | USA | 1972–78

Maude presented the liberal political flipside of its parent show, All in the Family

Cast | Bea Arthur, Bill Macy, Conrad Bain, Rue McClanahan, Adrienne Barbeau, Esther Rolle
Original broadcaster | CBS
Awards | 1 Emmy, 1 Golden Globe
For fans of . . . | *The Golden Girls* (1985)

Maude centered around Maude Findlay, a liberal, independent, middle-aged woman who lived in the suburbs of Tuckahoe, NY, with her fourth husband, Walter Findlay. Maude was played by the perennial star of stage and screen, Bea Arthur. She strongly supported women's liberation, civil rights, and other equality causes, which sometimes got her into hot water. The program was a spin-off of *All in the Family* (1971), in which Maude first appeared as Edith Bunker's cousin.

Maude's catchphrase, "God'll getcha for that, Walter," stemmed from her many arguments with her husband. Another catchphrase arose as she answered the phone, declaring, "No, this is not Mr. Findlay, this is Mrs. Findlay. Mr. Findlay has a much higher voice." Maude had a divorced daughter from her first marriage, Carol Traynor, played by 1970s It girl Adrienne Barbeau. Carol was a liberal feminist, like her mother, but, although they had the same core values, they often bickered. Radically, several episodes featured only Maude and Walter in dialogue. Taking this minimalism a step further in season four, the groundbreaking episode "The Analyst" featured Maude alone for the entire episode speaking to a silent psychiatrist.

In 1978, CBS revamped the final season. The governor of New York appointed Maude as a Democratic congresswoman, after the previous congresswoman died unexpectedly in Maude's house. Maude and Walter relocated to Washington, D.C., taking their liberal views with them. **RP**

The Protectors

Drama | UK | 1972–74

Fast-paced espionage thriller with a hit theme song: "Every city's got 'em, Can we ever stop 'em, Some of us are gonna try"

Cast | Robert Vaughn, Nyree Dawn Porter, Tony Anholt
Original broadcaster | ITV
For fans of . . . | *Mission: Impossible* (1966), *Spooks* (2002)

Harry Rule, Contessa Caroline di Contini, and Paul Buchet were wealthy and talented, and they operated a private organization to troubleshoot and help wherever they were needed. They traveled the world, cutting through red tape and international frontiers to tackle murder, extortion, kidnap, and blackmail with unconventional methods. They were the Protectors.

The Protectors had a troubled genesis. Lew Grade, head of the ITC production stable, reportedly gave producer Gerry Anderson a vague outline for a new show; it amounted to little more than a line about a brotherhood of detectives acting outside the law. Anderson, best known for puppet-based series such as *Thunderbirds* (1965), developed the idea as his first live-action show, featuring two male leads. He was, therefore, dismayed when Grade signed former *The Man from U.N.C.L.E.* star Robert Vaughn to headline the series, along with Nyree Dawn Porter, thereby forcing the format to be tweaked for three leads. Joining Vaughn as group leader Harry Rule and Porter as Contessa Caroline di Contini was Tony Anholt as gadget man Paul Buchet. A larger-than-average budget, thanks to financial assistance from fragrance company Fabergé, afforded *The Protectors* the luxury of overseas filming, with Malta doubling as various Mediterranean locations. A twenty-five-minute episode format allowed for fast-paced scripts, and the first season of *The Protectors* proved so popular on broadcast that the second was commissioned with ease. **MW**

Classic episode
With a Little Help from My Friends | *Season 1, episode 21.* When the president's son is kidnapped, Harry is blackmailed into assassinating the leader, forcing the Protectors into an elaborate charade in which Harry appears to be killed by Caroline.

⦿ Robert Vaughn picks his moment as detective Harry Rule.

A Warning to the Curious

Drama | UK | 1972

Ghost story and moral tale in a single package

Cast | Peter Vaughan, Clive Swift, Julian Herrington, John Kearney, David Cargill, George Benson, Roger Benson, Gilly Fraser, David Pugh, Cyril Appleton
Original broadcaster | BBC One
For fans of . . . | *The Ghost & Mrs. Muir* (1968)

This spine-chilling tale was written and directed by Lawrence Gordon Clark, whose subsequent credits included the movie *Romance on the Orient Express* (1985). *A Warning to the Curious* was based on a ghost story of the same name by the English author M.R. James, originally published in 1925, about a young man who, on a visit to East Anglia, stumbled across some hidden treasure including an Anglo-Saxon crown that, according to ancient legend, would protect Britain from invasion. After he had dug up his find, he felt that he was being followed by an invisible and possibly malign presence. The following day, after he failed to attend a rendezvous with two friends, they went looking for him on the nearby beach. A mist descended on them, and they found him lying on the shore; it was clear from the state of his corpse that he had met a violent end. The men put the treasure back where it had been found, and vowed never to speak a word of what had happened to anyone. The murder remained unsolved.

Clark's adaptation updated the tale to the 1930s, and dwelt on the privations of the Great Depression. It also turned the protagonist from the original ingénue into an older, ambivalent, and altogether more intimidating figure (Peter Vaughan). It also brought in a character from another James story, "The Stalls of Barchester," the scholar Dr. Black (Clive Swift).

A Warning to the Curious has since been reshown on Channel 4; it has lost none of its eerie power. **GL**

Semnadtsat mgnoveniy vesny

Drama | Russia | 1973

Russia's best-loved spy series

Cast | Vyacheslav Tikhonov, Leonid Bronevoy, Ekaterina Gradova, Rostislav Plyatt, Oleg Tabakov, Nikolai Prokopovich, Yuriy Vizbor, Wilhelm Burmeier
Original broadcaster | Programme One
For fans of . . . | *Tinker Tailor Soldier Spy* (1979)

Repeated every year since its debut, the TV miniseries *Semnadtsat mgnoveniy vesny* (*Seventeen Moments of Spring*) features Stierlitz (aka Maxim Isaev), the Russian equivalent of James Bond. Actor Vyacheslav Tikhonov, who played Stierlitz/Isaev, was even awarded a medal in honor of the character's achievements. On the death of the series' director, Tatyana Lioznova, in 2011, President Vladimir Putin declared Russia had lost a "brilliant and extraordinary woman."

The series was set at the end of the Second World War, and told how Isaev, posing as SS Standartenführer Stierlitz, had worked his way up the Nazi ranks. He wants to undermine a potential alliance between Germany and the United States, but had to first overcome the suspicions of Hitler's officers.

The story was based on a novel by Yulian Semyonov, who was encouraged to create work that reflected positively on the KGB. Lioznova added female roles and cinematic flair; she accurately predicted that it would bring Tikhonov stardom overnight.

Aired over consecutive nights in August 1973, the fourteen-hour series was, in the words of historian Stephen Lovell, "a massive success, with each episode gathering between fifty and eighty million Russian viewers and emptying city streets." Remarkably, it appealed to Soviet officials, who admired Stierlitz's sacrifice and patriotism, while also being seen, as Lovell noted, as "a progressive statement against bureaucratic oppression." **BM**

Kojak

Crime/Mystery | USA | 1973–78

Police thriller centered on street-smart but straight Detective Lieutenant Theo Kojak, investigating crime in the NYPD's Eleventh Precinct

Cast | Telly Savalas, Dan Frazer, Kevin Dobson, George Savalas, Mark Russell, Vince Conti
Original broadcaster | CBS
Awards | 2 Emmys, 3 Golden Globes
For fans of . . . | *NYPD Blue* (1993), *NCIS* (2003)

This series of largely stand-alone episodes followed the work and, occasionally, the personal lives of Kojak and his colleagues as they investigated homicides, robberies, and drug crime in the grim world of Lower Manhattan from their dilapidated headquarters.

Although ostensibly a police procedural, the series concentrated on the interplay of Kojak (Telly Savalas) with his superior, Captain Frank McNeill (Dan Frazer), his younger subordinates Crocker (Kevin Dobson) and Saperstein (Mark Russell), and their primarily office-bound sergeant, Stavros, played by Savalas' younger brother, George. In this male-dominated world, glamour and occasional romantic possibilities were provided by the weekly guest stars.

The series followed on from a pilot TV movie, *The Marcus-Nelson Murders*, developed by Academy Award–winning producer Abby Mann, which was loosely based on a notorious 1963 murder case. The plots were largely the stuff of standard crime drama, but *Kojak* elevated them through the strength of its gritty NYC locations, frequently shot after dark or covered by a thick blanket of snow, and the easy charm of its star, who became a worldwide phenomenon. Savalas, well known for his frequently unsympathetic or villainous performances in films such as *The Dirty Dozen* (1967) and *On Her Majesty's Secret Service* (1969), became a cultural icon through his portrayal of the slick, bald, fedora-wearing cop with a penchant for Tootsie Roll lollipops and his catchphrase, "Who loves ya, baby?" **JJJ**

Classic episode
No Immunity for Murder | *Season 3, episode 10.*
A bookkeeper is murdered by a prostitute and her pimp. It looks like a lowlife crime, but Kojak's investigation is obstructed by powerful individuals and the FBI.

◉ Kojak chewed Tootsie Pops as he tried to quit smoking.

An American Family

Documentary | USA | 1973

Before the Kardashians . . .

Cast | Bill Loud, Pat Loud, Lance Loud, Kevin Loud, Grant Loud, Delilah Loud, Michelle Loud
Original broadcaster | PBS
For fans of . . . | *Seven Up!* (1964), *The Real World* (1992)

Today, reality TV offers viewers the chance to be a fly on the wall, vicariously experiencing the supposedly unscripted lives of everyone from real housewives to has-been celebrities. However, back in the 1970s, the members of the Loud family of Santa Barbara, California, were unique TV stars. Filmed for seven months in 1971 by producer Craig Gilbert and his two-member crew and airing on PBS in 1973, *An American Family* was intended to be a portrait of a typical family, but the results were far from typical.

Bill Loud was the president of American Western Foundries, seemingly happily married and raising five children. The producers could not have expected to capture such dramatic moments as the breakup of his marriage and the revelation that his son, Lance, was homosexual. Lance Loud was the first gay person on TV to publicly declare his orientation, and he subsequently wrote for *The Advocate* magazine. The oddest thing may have been that the Loud family could not have had a more ironic name, since ultimately the show captured the lack of meaningful communication in the American home endemic to families in any era.

The series ran for only twelve episodes, but forever altered the TV landscape. In the years that followed, the family commented on what they felt was an unfair portrayal, produced by creative editing of the three hundred hours of footage shot for the series. The Louds endured further ups and downs, some of which were chronicled in a tenth-anniversary special. **ATB**

Some Mothers Do 'Ave 'Em

Comedy | UK | 1973–78

Meet a well-intentioned, walking disaster

Cast | Michael Crawford, Michele Dotrice, Jessica Forte, Jane Hylton, Glynn Edwards, Hazel Bainbridge
Original broadcaster | BBC One
For fans of . . . | *Fawlty Towers* (1975), *One Foot in the Grave* (1990)

Frank Spencer (Michael Crawford) was a well-meaning idealist with the enthusiasm and outlook of a child and the ability to cause chaos and destruction in any situation. His home was full of half-finished DIY projects, the result of him crashing through ceilings or knocking out supporting walls, while his natural good manners ensured he was always shocked at just how rude other people could be to his face. His attempts to better himself with a varied vocabulary often left him prone to malapropisms like "ejaculated" instead of "ejected."

Before the days of risk assessment or health-and-safety reports, Crawford had audiences on the edges of their seats as each elaborate stunt offered the very real possibility of severe maiming or death, whether that was being hoisted up by a rope during an amateur production of the Nativity, or hanging from his car while teetering on the edge of a clifftop.

What potentially could have been a hugely irritating character was saved by Crawford's ability to play up Frank's childlike charm and innocence, an element only strengthened by the arrival of baby Jessica in the second season. Thanks to Frank's distinctive voice, every impressionist of the time merely had to tilt their head, straighten their arms, and say "Ooh, Betty, the cat's done a whoopsie on the carpet!"

Crawford completely inhabited the role of Frank Spencer, even performing most of his own stunts. Later he became a megastar in the United States in Andrew Lloyd Webber's *Phantom of the Opera* (1986). **JS**

The Tomorrow People

Fantasy/Horror/Sci-Fi | UK | 1973–95

Nosy kids with superpowers on supernatural adventures in space

Cast | Nicholas Young, Philip Gilbert, Elizabeth Adare, Peter Vaughan-Clarke, Michael Holoway, Stephen Salmon, Misako Koba, Sammie Winmill
Original broadcaster | ITV
For fans of . . . | *Doctor Who* (1963)

For a generation of Brits in the 1970s, this show brought teatime adventures in outer space. The Tomorrow People were young people in their teens and early twenties who "broke out" and began to display supernatural powers, such as telepathy, telekinesis, or teleportation—a skill they called "jaunting." Led by John (Nicholas Young), the gang lived in a secret lab in the care of an alien computer called TIM. Each story was told across multiple episodes. The more impressive ones involved alien incursions on modern-day Earth: "The Blue and the Green" was a gang-culture satire, only a few years after the infamous mods-versus-rockers riots, whereas "The Living Skins" looked at mindless obsessions with fashion.

The Tomorrow People was problematic, though: its ambition far outstretched its budget, and some of the adventures—particularly those set in space—were decidedly cheesy. There was also an unsettling number of episodes that required teenage boys to appear in underwear or loincloths, which made uncomfortable viewing. However, at heart it was a deeply moral production. The ideal of nonviolent coexistence with humanity was a sound metaphor for the young audience to grasp, especially when presented by a multiracial, working-class cast who reflected the audience better than the BBC's middle-class children's dramas. The series was revived in 1992, and a 2013 US remake fused characters from the original with a conspiracy plot, but it ran for only one season. **JS**

The World at War

Documentary | UK | 1973–74

Definitive documentary about the Second World War

Cast | Laurence Olivier
Original broadcaster | ITV
Award | 1 BAFTA
For fans of . . . | *All Our Yesterdays* (1960), *Secret History* (1991), *The Untold History of the United States* (2012)

In 1973, the events of the Second World War were still a living memory for many, but a generation was coming to adulthood for whom the conflict was only a narrative told to them by their parents and grandparents. If a definitive television account of the conflict was ever to be made, the time was now, while there were still enough surviving veterans to provide a rounded picture.

Producer Jeremy Isaacs was determined to move beyond the simple descriptions of single campaigns attempted by most previous documentaries on the subject. With twenty-six episodes to fill, his ambition was to tell a truly world history of the global conflict. The director of the Imperial War Museum was asked to name the fifteen key military campaigns, and an episode was devoted to each. But the program had broader ambitions than to be a purely military history, and the remaining episodes were devoted to the civilian side of the conflict, from the impact of occupation on Continental Europe to a harrowing study of the Nazis' Final Solution. Extensive interviews gave both sides of every story; there is even a revealing discussion with Hitler's architect, Albert Speer. Extensive research uncovered raw film footage that had never before been broadcast and which was more revealing than any edited contemporary newsreel.

The World at War couldn't be made now; too many eyewitnesses are dead. We are lucky to have it, and everyone should see at least part of it. **JL**

Ein Herz und eine Seele
Comedy | Germany | 1973–76

Meet the German cousin of Alf Garnett and Archie Bunker in this popular satire derived from the British comedy Till Death Us Do Part

Cast | Heinz Schubert, Hildegard Krekel, Elisabeth Wiedemann, Diether Krebs
Original broadcaster | ARD
For fans of . . . | *Till Death Us Do Part* (1965), *All in the Family* (1971), *Familie Heinz Becker* (1992)

Proving that xenophobia and bigotry have no geographical boundaries, Johnny Speight's popular satirical comedy *Till Death Us Do Part* for the BBC was replicated from Britain to Brazil. In the United States, the antihero Alf Garnett became the equally popular Archie Bunker in *All in the Family* (1971), while in Germany he was reborn as Alfred Tetzlaff, in *Ein Herz und eine Seele* (*One Heart and One Soul*). Heinz Schubert, who played Tetzlaff, never escaped the shadow of the iconic reactionary, despite an award-winning role in the 1993 miniseries *Der große Bellheim*. Fiercely conservative, racist, and never short of a conspiracy theory, Tetzlaff was a caricature who provided catharsis for millions of viewers.

Ein Herz und eine Seele retained the names of Speight's core characters—long-suffering wife Else, daughter Rita, and son-in-law Michael—but added uniquely German twists, such as Tetzlaff's suspicion of anyone from what was then East Germany. Playing Else, Elisabeth Wiedemann, acclaimed for her part in the 1966 TV movie *Spätere Heirat erwünscht oder Pallü ist ein Spiel*, proved as popular as her British counterpart Dandy Nichols. Writer Wolfgang Menge regarded Wiedemann as the key to the show's success, and viewers agreed: When she and Diether Krebs (Michael) left, ratings waned and the show was canceled after two seasons. A revival in 1976 lasted just four episodes, but the show remains among the most enduringly popular in Germany, with one 2004 poll even judging it the best German comedy show of all time. **BM**

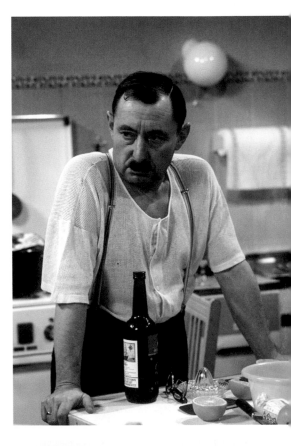

Classic episode
Sylvesterpunsch | *Season 2, episode 1.* Originally broadcast on New Year's Eve, 1973, this is one of two episodes—alongside the winter carnival-themed *Rosenmontagszug*—to become seasonal staples of German TV.

ⓐ Heinz Schubert as Alfred Tetzlaff, whose Hitleresque mustache was just the tip of the show's vicious satire.

The Water Margin

Drama | Japan | 1973–74 (Japan); 1976–78 (UK)

One of the great novels of Chinese literature is adapted for Japanese TV

Cast | Atsuo Nakamura, Sanae Tsuchida, Kei Satô, Isamu Nagato   **Original broadcaster** | China Central Television, Nippon Television Company   **For fans of . . .** | *Kung Fu* (1972), *Monkey* (1978)

Chinese culture was very popular in the 1970s, epitomized in part by the increase in TV shows featuring kung fu and other Asian stylings. *The Water Margin* played to this trend, presenting the story of one man's struggle against a corrupt Chinese government during the Song dynasty.

The original Japanese series was made in 1973, but it was the David Weir BBC version in 1976 that brought the show to a Western audience. Weir took the basic plot of each episode and then wrote English dialogue to fit the mouth movements of the cast, rather than translating the Japanese script word for word. This led to the show having near-perfect lip synchronization, which made it more accessible to the UK audience.

The UK voice artists involved were many, but the prime actors were Burt Kwouk (narration), with Michael McClain (Lin Chung), Miriam Margolyes (Hu San-Niang) Peter Marinker, Sean Lynch, David Collings, and Simon Lack. The series followed Lin Chung (Atsuo Nakamura) in his struggles against a corrupt government official Kao Chiu (Kei Satô). As the series progressed, more people fell foul of Kao Chiu and joined Lin Chung to fight against the government. The series featured numerous fights and battles, humans with apparent superpowers—expert fighters, unbelievable strength, and so on—and captured the hearts and minds of a generation. More serious in tone than the whimsical *Monkey*, *The Water Margin* is a classic of its time. **DJH**

❷ "These men riding are outlaws . . . each fights tyranny with a price on his head, in a world very different from our own."

Welt am Draht

Fantasy/Horror/Sci-Fi | Germany | 1973

Stylish dystopia from German cinema's wunderkind

Cast | Klaus Löwitsch, Barbara Valentin, Mascha Rabben, Karl-Heinz Vosgerau, Wolfgang Schenck, Günter Lamprecht, Ulli Lommel   **Original broadcaster** | WDR   **For fans of . . .** | *Edge of Darkness* (1985)

Director Rainer Werner Fassbinder died aged thirty-seven, but packed an extraordinary number of film, TV, stage, and radio projects into his fifteen-year career. The two-part miniseries *Welt am Draht* (*World on a Wire*), his only venture into the sci-fi genre, prompted its audience to question the very nature of reality.

Simulacron is a whole world inside a computer, populated by thousands of "identity units" who believe they are human beings living in the real world. When Simulacron's creator mysteriously dies after making a shocking discovery about the project, Fred Stiller (Klaus Löwitsch) takes over as director. His investigation leads him to discover that, just as people can plug themselves into Simulacron, its identity units can enter our world,

too. And that is only the beginning of the revelations. *Welt am Draht* had its share of action, but it was mostly a philosophical thriller, with a sleek aesthetic inspired by Jean-Luc Godard's *Alphaville* (1965) and the melodramas of Fassbinder's hero Douglas Sirk.

Welt am Draht was an early screen depiction of simulated reality, a concept that would become familiar to audiences in films such as *Tron* (1982) and *The Matrix* (1999). However, its direct influence was limited; unavailable for many years, it became one of the most obscure Fassbinder works. In 2010 a restored version was shown at the Berlin Film Festival, which led to it being reclaimed as a major work both of one of Europe's most distinctive directors and of sci-fi TV. **IK**

⬥ Plugged in: *Welt am Draht* explored the idea of virtual realities decades before the sci-fi classic *The Matrix*.

Je später der Abend

Talk show | Germany | 1973–78

This early incarnation of the late-night talk show in Germany soon woke up the nation

Cast | Dietmar Schönherr, Hansjürgen Rosenbauer, Reinhard Münchenhagen   **Original broadcaster** | WDR
For fans of . . . | *The Tonight Show* (1962), *The Dick Cavett Show* (1968)

With a title coined from the German aphorism *"Je später der Abend, desto schöner die Gäste"* ("The later the evening, the more beautiful the guests"), this pioneering talk show was created by Dietmar Schönherr and Peter Hajek. Having collaborated on *Wünsch dir was* (1969), they were keen to bring American-style talk shows to German screens.

The first episode opened with Schönherr introducing the talk show concept to German audiences. "What that is, you do not know, and," he admitted, "we do not know exactly." Despite the intention to, as one of the editors declared, "unravel guests to the limits," the show made only a minor impact initially, and some commentators were hostile to it. Thanks to Schönherr,

carped a critic, viewers could "safely dispense with the sleeping pill."

In 1974, however, the show provoked the first of several stirs when beloved German actress Inge Meysel casually described losing her virginity at the age of twenty-one—"I was a real late bloomer." That set the stage for the show dubbed "Beauty and the Driest," when Romy Schneider, star of the 1955 Austrian movie *Sissi* told fellow guest, bank-robber-turned-author Burkhard Driest, "I like you a lot," in a way that suggested more than a passing acquaintance. Actor Klaus Kinski and punk poetess Nina Hagen also raised eyebrows before the show lost out to talk shows that sacrificed serious discussion for trivia. **BM**

⊕ (L–R) Actress Uschi Glas, writer Gregor von Rezzori, and feminist Alice Schwarzer debate on *Je später der Abend* in 1975.

Scenes from a Marriage

Drama | Sweden | 1973

A master class in uncomfortable but compulsive viewing

Cast | Liv Ullman, Erland Josephson, Gunnel Lindblom, Bibi Andersson **Original broadcaster** | SVT
Award | 1 Golden Globe **For fans of . . .** | *Pennies from Heaven* (1978), *Berlin Alexanderplatz* (1980)

Marriage might seem like a cakewalk at first in Ingmar Bergman's *Scener ur ett äktenskap* (*Scenes from a Marriage*) when viewers meet happily married couple Marianne (Liv Ullman) and Johan (Erland Josephson). They have been together for ten years, but how happy are they? Their relationship cracks when Johan admits to having an affair and over the next ten years they continuously drift apart, flow back together, and drift apart again. Does Johan's affair make him a happier person than when he was with Marianne? Marianne finds new freedom, but does that make her a happier person than when she was with Johan? *Scener ur ett äktenskap* asked the questions but didn't give the answers. That was for the viewer to decide.

The result was an uncompromising examination of a marriage in meltdown and made for some of the strongest TV viewing in history. The drama was vivid and delivered through very powerful performances. Long monologues and intense dialogue, in which Johan and Marianne verbally tore each other to shreds, each blaming the other for the failure of their marriage, was utterly merciless and the audience found themselves squirming in their seats yet unable to look away. Many therefore consider this show as the standard against which all other dramas should be measured, and it is often cited by directors and writers, such as Woody Allen, as a source of their inspiration. Even today, the show feels contemporary and has a lot to teach us. **JH**

Johan (Erland Josephson) and Marianne (Liv Ullman): friends, lovers, or neither?

Barnaby Jones

Crime/Mystery | USA | 1973–80

Silver-haired private eye always gets the bad guy—slowly but surely

Cast | Buddy Ebsen, Lee Meriweather, Mark Shera, John Carter
Original broadcaster | CBS
For fans of . . . | *Cannon* (1971), *Matlock* (1986)

Barnaby and Betty Jones (Buddy Ebsen and Lee Meriwether) had an unusual relationship for a private-eye duo: they were father- and daughter-in-law. Their partnership began when veteran investigator Barnaby came out of retirement to investigate the murder of his son Hal, with the widowed Betty's assistance. After the killer was brought to justice, Barnaby realized how much he had missed detective work, and the pair decided to carry on working together.

Barnaby Jones shared the same Los Angeles setting as its fellow Quinn Martin production *Cannon*, with which it twice crossed over. Originally, the characters of Barnaby and Betty were to be tried out in an episode of *Cannon*, but in the end, their own show was commissioned by CBS to fill a scheduling gap. The intended *Cannon* script served as *Barnaby Jones'* first episode, with William Conrad's portly detective Frank Cannon coaxing the title character back to work. Like Cannon, the character of Barnaby was a conscious attempt to create something different from the stereotypical tough-guy image of the private detective: Cannon's quirk was his size; Barnaby's was his age. Moreover, the latter's seemingly naive, folksy manner (he eschewed alcoholic drinks in favor of milk) led criminals to underestimate his abilities. In fact, he was an extremely shrewd forensics expert with his own office lab. The combination of Ebsen's homely charm and Meriwether's sophisticated glamour proved popular enough to keep *Barnaby Jones* running for eight seasons. **IK**

Classic episode

Sing a Song of Murder | *Season 1, episode 8.* When a rock star is found murdered in a pool of blood, his managers decide to conceal the truth and invent a kidnapping scenario. Unfortunately there is a witness to the real crime. . . .

◉ Buddy Ebsen as forensics expert Barnaby Jones, in 1973.

Last of the Summer Wine

Comedy | UK | 1973–2010

Witty scripts and masterful physical comedy

Cast | Peter Sallis, Bill Owen, Brian Wilde, Michael Aldridge, Frank Thornton, Kathy Staff, Michael Bates
Original broadcaster | BBC One
For fans of . . . | *Keeping Up Appearances* (1990), *Dinnerladies* (1998)

The influence of *Last of the Summer Wine* should not be underestimated. Following the misadventures of a trio of friends in their twilight years, contemplating their place in the world while living in the countryside of West Yorkshire, it had a good heart. Over thirty-seven years it mined a rich seam of visual comedy and was praised for its positive depiction of senior citizens.

Last of the Summer Wine debuted as an episode of the BBC's Comedy Playhouse, titled *Of Funerals and Fish*, and brought together old friends Norman Clegg (Peter Sallis), Compo (Bill Owen), and Blamire (Michael Bates) on the anniversary of Clegg's wife's death. As they wandered around town, the world was put to rights. This set the template for the entire series; the trio may have changed over the decades, and an ensemble grown around it, but the show's durability was testament to the wit of writer Roy Clarke's scripts. A positive response to the debut led to a series commission.

Following the departure of Bates due to ill health, Brian Wilde completed the trio as Foggy Dewhurst. The series continued in the same enjoyable manner, the friends interacting with a growing list of supporting characters, chiefly Nora Batty (Kathy Staff), the subject of Compo's unrequited affections. Exterior sequences were filmed in the West Yorkshire town of Holmfirth, which became a popular tourist destination as the popularity of the series grew. Although the show was canceled in 2010, considered by some to be past its prime, it remains a true classic of TV comedy. **MW**

The Magician

Drama | USA | 1973–74

A magician solves crimes with sleight of hand

Cast | Bill Bixby, Julian Christopher, Keene Curtis
Original broadcaster | NBC
For fans of . . . | *Jason King* (1971), *Hart to Hart* (1979), *Jonathan Creek* (1997)

By the early 1970s, series such as *The Persuaders!* (1971) and *The Saint* (1962) had established a successful template for glamorous jet-setters who dabbled in crime. US network television looked to these shows as it moved on from the solid professionalism of series such as *Mission: Impossible* (1966). Heroes didn't have to be dull; they could have a great job and fight crime.

Cue *The Magician*. Tony Blake (Bill Bixby) was a wildly successful magician who lived on a private jet. Hanging around the built-in bar sipping cocktails were his live-in pilot, his wheelchair-bound buddy, and his gossip columnist friend. At any moment crime would come calling, usually in a rather contrived manner that would allow Tony to get involved, thwarting plots and showing off his magic skills. Bixby, a keen amateur magician, insisted on doing his own magic stunts rather than relying on trick photography. While a laudable sentiment, in practice this meant that the magic was mostly limited to sleight of hand and card tricks. Also, while Tony's life was full of Vegas dazzle, the criminals he became involved with were a disappointingly pedestrian mix of smugglers, blackmailers, and thieves.

A victim of the writer's strike in 1973, *The Magician* never had a chance to find its feet, but the notion of a glamorous amateur sleuth continued to churn away over the next decade, with shows such as *Hart to Hart* (1979) and *Remington Steele* (1982). Producer Bruce Lansbury went on to create the genre's supreme example: *Murder, She Wrote* (1984), starring his sister Angela. **JG**

Am laufenden Band

Game show | Germany | 1974–79

A critical success for a charismatic host

Cast | Rudi Carrell
Original broadcaster | Deutsche Fernsehen
For fans of . . . | *Jeopardy!* (1964), *The Generation Game* (1971), *The Price is Right* (1972), *Wheel of Fortune* (1988)

The entertainer Rudi Carrell, already popular from the German talent show *The Rudi Carrell Show* (1961), was casting around for a new game show concept when he came across *Eén van de acht* (1969, *One of the Eight*) in his Dutch homeland. The key ingredient of the show was that it was intergenerational, with four pairs of family members from different generations, or sometimes identical twins, competing in memory games or psychological challenges—for instance, contestants might have to predict the behavior of their family member in a certain situation. The show included prominent guests from the world of German television and pop music. At the end of each show various prizes were paraded on the *Laufenden Band*, a conveyor belt, in front of one member of the winning couple. The more objects that the contestant could remember afterward, the more of them they won. Initially, the studio set was simple, but after twenty-five episodes it became a feature of the show that the setting changed to reflect that week's theme.

Carrell's talents as an entertainer and host made *Am laufenden Band* (*On the Conveyor Belt*) one of the few programs that won over television critics as well as mainstream audiences. It was the first of Carrell's shows to be sold abroad: In Britain, the program became a massive hit for Bruce Forsyth, who hosted it as *The Generation Game* from 1971 to 1982. In Germany, a board game based on the program was even produced. **NK**

Kolchak: The Night Stalker

Fantasy/Horror/Sci-Fi | USA | 1974–75

An atmospheric chiller with flashes of humor

Cast | Darren McGavin, Simon Oakland, Jack Grinnage, Ruth McDevitt
Original broadcaster | ABC
For fans of . . . | *The X-Files* (1993), *Fringe* (2008), *Being Human* (2008)

Later acknowledged by the writer and director Chris Carter as a major inspiration for his creation *The X-Files* (1993), *Kolchak: The Night Stalker* brought a welcome dose of horror fantasy to an American TV schedule that was full of sitcoms and quiz shows in the mid-1970s. The show centered on the exploits of crusading reporter Carl Kolchak (Darren McGavin), a noir-style gumshoe whose investigations inexplicably brought him into deadly contact with all manner of supernatural beings: vampires, zombies, mummies, and so on.

The Kolchak character had appeared previously in the ABC TV movie *The Night Stalker* (1972), which had been a smash hit. Its success spurred a sequel, *The Night Strangler* (1973), and a projected third entry in the franchise morphed into this twenty-part, one-season TV series. McGavin co-produced the show, liking the sardonically humorous edge to the Kolchak character that had developed in the second movie. Simon Oakland, who played Kolchak's boss, Tony Vincenzo, also made the transition from the movies to the TV show.

Despite McGavin's reluctance to describe it as such, the series was a monster-of-the-week show, in which a new set of supernatural villains was vanquished each time. It was rescued from cliché by the masterful acting, especially from the two leads, and the clever story lines that mixed aspects of crime noir with traditional horror. Disappointing ratings and litigation from the original creator ensured it ran for only one season, but it is remembered fondly by cult TV fans. **DF**

Planet of the Apes

Fantasy/Horror/Sci-Fi | USA | 1974

Much more than an ape-versus-human adventure series: these apes have feelings!

Cast | Roddy McDowall, Ron Harper, James Naughton, Mark Lenard
Original broadcaster | CBS
For fans of . . . | *The Fugitive* (1963), *Star Trek* (1966), *The Incredible Hulk* (1977)

Pierre Boulle's science-fiction novel has had an impressive life span on-screen. The first *Planet of the Apes* film arrived in 1968, starring Charlton Heston as an astronaut trapped on Earth—in the distant future—where apes are the dominant species. Four sequels followed before the concept came to TV.

Here, three more astronauts leave Earth in 1980 and arrive on the ape-run planet. One dies, but the two survivors, Alan Virdon (Ron Harper) and Pete Burke (James Naughton), befriend an inquisitive chimp called Galen (Roddy McDowall, once again playing simian as he had in four of the five films). Galen's interest in human history causes him to be denounced as a heretic. He and the two humans go on the run, pursued by General Urko (Mark Lenard), a sadistic, military gorilla intent on seeing them dead. The episodes followed a familiar formula: like *The Fugitive* (1963), or *The Incredible Hulk* (1977), the heroes found the time each week to help other citizens, while evading capture themselves.

Surprisingly, *Planet of the Apes* was canceled after only fourteen episodes due to poor ratings. It was not the end, though. *Return to the Planet of the Apes* (1975) was a short-lived animated series, much closer in vision to Pierre Boulle's source novel, in which the apes lived in a more technologically advanced age than our own. In the twenty-first century, the franchise was resurrected on the big screen with a new run of prequels, beginning with *Rise of the Planet of the Apes* (2011) and *Dawn of the Planet of the Apes* (2014). **JS**

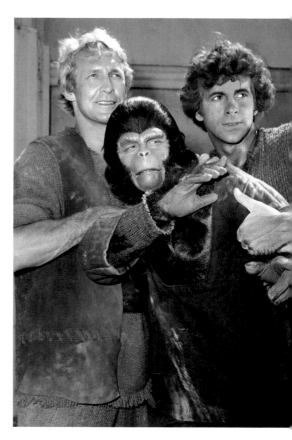

Classic episode
The Deception | *Season 1, episode 8.* Burke unintentionally inspires a crush from a blind female chimpanzee, Fauna, whose father has been killed by a violent group of apes. Fauna does not know that Burke is human.

◬ The two astronauts and Galen (Roddy McDowall) unite against the enemy.

Happy Days

Comedy | USA | 1974–84

"Goodbye gray sky, hello blue"—an upbeat slice of Americana, sitcom-style

Classic episode

Dance Contest | *Season 3, episode 15.*
Unbeknown to Howard, Marion and Fonzie are meeting in secret to practice for a dance contest. Howard gets suspicious, Arnold makes it worse, and no one keeps their cool.

◭ Suzi Quatro joins Ron Howard and Anson Williams in the band.
❯ Henry Winkler as " Fonzie"—"Correctamundo."

Cast | Ron Howard, Henry Winkler, Tom Bosley, Marion Ross, Anson Williams, Don Most, Scott Baio
Original broadcaster | ABC
Awards | 1 Emmy, 3 Golden Globes
For fans of . . . | *Modern Family* (2009)

In the 1970s, the longing for simpler times in the United States manifested itself in nostalgia, and *Happy Days* was, by far, one of the most prominent and long-lasting examples on TV. A sitcom set in Milwaukee in the 1950s, it began life as a one-episode drama in the anthology series *Love, American Style*, and introduced audiences to the Cunningham family: a middle-class, suburban clan headed by hardware store owner Howard; his wife, Marion; their awkward young daughter, Joanie; and the teenage son, Richie (Ron Howard), who longs to find his place in life.

At first a cautious tale of Richie trying to blend in with his new high-school buddies, *Happy Days* needed a bit of color to make the series truly gel—and that came in the form of Arthur "Fonzie" Fonzarelli, a white knight with a motorcycle, played to perfection by Henry Winkler, who rapidly became one of TV's true icons. In the beginning, Fonzie was a tangential character, then he moved into the apartment over the Cunningham's garage. Before long, his friendship with Richie and his dedication to the Cunningham family—not to mention, his deeply moral foundation—became key components of the series' success. Eventually, *Happy Days* became Fonzie's show when Ron Howard departed (later he became an award-winning filmmaker), and the revolving cast circled around his legacy. *Happy Days* remained a staple of ABC's TV success well into the 1980s and spawned a legacy of spin-offs, including *Laverne & Shirley* (1976) and *Mork & Mindy* (1978). **SL**

Good Times

Comedy | USA | 1974–79

First spin-off from a spin-off, focusing on a working-class black family

Cast | Esther Rolle, John Amos, Jimmie Walker, BernNadette Stanis, Ralph Carter, Ja'net Dubois, Johnny Brown, Moses Gunn, Janet Jackson, Ben Powers   **Original broadcaster** | CBS   **For fans of . . .** | *All in the Family* (1971)

Part of the extensive *All in the Family* universe of television shows and created by Eric Monte and Mike Evans, *Good Times* followed the Evans family in the Chicago inner-city projects. Originally intended to focus on the parents, James and Florida Evans (John Amos and Esther Rolle), and their struggle to eke out a living despite low income and frequent unemployment, the series shifted to showcase the breakout performance of Jimmie Walker as their son J.J., much to Amos and Rolle's chagrin. Rolle in particular felt that J.J.'s comical exploits made him a poor role model for young black viewers.

After ongoing disputes and before the start of the fourth season, James was killed off in an off-camera car crash and Florida was now a widow. Rolle herself left

the show one year later, with the show now focused entirely on the children as they fended for themselves with support from neighbor Willona (Ja'net Dubois).

Rolle returned for the sixth year to boost the now-failing series; she, in turn, demanded that they improve J.J.'s character. Sadly the show's ratings had already declined enough that it was canceled that season. **ATB**

Classic episode
The Gang (Parts 1 & 2) | *Season 2, episode 9/10.* J.J. joins the Satan's Knights, a gang in a turf war with the Warlords. When J.J.'s reluctance to participate threatens the safety of the Evans family, James makes a dangerous decision.

🔺 (L–R) J.J. (Jimmie Walker), James Evans (John Amos), Michael Evans (Ralph Carter), and Thelma Evans (BernNadette Stanis).

Derrick

Crime/Mystery | Germany | 1974–98

Stories of Munich's top detective and his faithful sidekick Klein ran and ran

Cast | Horst Tappert, Fritz Wepper **Original broadcaster** | ZDF
For fans of . . . | *Columbo* (1971), *Inspector Morse* (1975), *Midsomer Murders* (1997)

A phenomenally long-lasting and successful procedural crime drama, *Derrick* revolved around the casebook of Detective Chief Inspector Stephan Derrick and his more junior colleague, Inspector Harry Klein, of the Munich police force. Nearly three hundred episodes were made, all written by Herbert Reinecker, a prolific author of tough crime dramas.

Early episodes of *Derrick* perfectly captured the flavor of the mid-1970s. There was a synthesizer theme tune, blondes were murdered stylishly, and Derrick and Klein were rough, tough detectives forever on the case. *Derrick* was still on the air in 1998, by which time its star, Horst Tappert, was sixty-five years old and now liked to solve murders by sitting down for a chat rather than

chasing suspects through the streets of Munich. By the time *Derrick* went off the air in 1998, it had evolved from a German *Sweeney* to a *Columbo*, with Derrick gently wearing down his suspect until he was so revolted by the sins of his past that he would break down and confess. Inspector Derrick fought for his country's soul.

One of the reasons the program is no longer shown in Germany is on account of revelations about Tappert's own dark past. He had long claimed to have spent the Second World War as a medic, but in 2013 it was revealed that he had been a commander in the Waffen-SS. Reinecker, too, had worked in the Propaganda Unit of the SS, and edited the Hitler Youth training manual, but at least that he had been honest about it. **JG**

◬ (L–R) Derrick (Horst Tapper) and his assistant Klein (Fritz Wepper) prepare to bust the bad guys in *Derrick*.

The Six Million Dollar Man
Action/Adventure | USA | 1974–78

Superhuman Steve Austin fought crime and the paranormal in this cult drama of the 1970s

Cast | Lee Majors, Richard Anderson, Martin E. Brooks   **Original broadcaster** | ABC
For fans of . . . | *Charlie's Angels* (1976), *The Bionic Woman* (1976), *Knight Rider* (1982)

Based on *Cyborg* (1972), a novel by Martin Caidin, *The Six Million Dollar Man* presented the adventures of Steve Austin, a former astronaut rebuilt with bionic implants (costing six million dollars), who worked for a fictional government office called the O.S.I. (Office of Scientific Intelligence). The show starred Lee Majors, husband of *Charlie's Angels* star Farrah Fawcett. Its opening voice over ("We can rebuild him... we have the technology"), the slow-motion action sequences, and the electronic sound effects became cultural touchstones.

Austin used his enhanced strength, speed, and vision to battle spies, criminals, and paranormal threats. The slow-motion action sequences, a hallmark of the show, indicated to viewers that Austin was running or using his bionic arm. When Austin used his bionic eye, the camera switched to his perspective, including a visible crosshair and a beeping sound effect.

A spin-off series, *The Bionic Woman*, ran from 1976 to 1978, and was remade in 2007. Several television movies featuring both bionic characters were produced between 1987 and 1994. **RP**

Classic episode
The Secret of Bigfoot (Part 1) | *Season 3, episode 16.* Steve Austin confronts a monster while setting up a warning system for earthquakes . . . and then meets its masters. Stefanie Powers guest stars as ill-fated love interest Shalon.

⊗ "We can rebuild him! We have the technology." Lee Majors as bionic miracle Steve Austin.

Rhoda

Comedy | USA | 1974–78

Sassy New York girl finds love and a new career

Cast | Valerie Harper, Julie Kavner, Nancy Walker, David Groh, Ron Silver, Lorenzo Music
Original broadcaster | CBS **Awards** | 2 Emmys, 2 Golden Globes **For fans of . . .** | *Sex and the City* (1998)

Rhoda Morgenstern (Valerie Harper) pops back to New York to visit her sister for a couple of weeks and meets Joe, a divorced father of two. The pair quickly fall in love and marry. Moving back to New York is not easy, though, especially when Rhoda's mother takes every opportunity to point out her many mistakes.

A spin-off of *The Mary Tyler Moore Show* (1970), *Rhoda* had a similarly strong supporting cast, each member elbowing his or her way forward to steal the scene. Nancy Walker, as Rhoda's mother, tended to get the best lines but Julie Kavner really shone as Rhoda's sister, Brenda, while everything that Lorenzo Music's never-seen doorman Carlton said was priceless. Kavner later became a regular performer for Woody Allen and

also voiced TV's most enduring sitcom mom, Marge Simpson. Music voiced Carlton once more for an animated special in 1980, before becoming the voice of cartoon cat Garfield. Harper reunited with Mary Tyler Moore in 2000 in a TV movie, *Mary and Rhoda*, in which the characters catch up and share stories of their children and ex-husbands. **JS**

Classic episode

Kiss your Epaulets Goodbye | *Season 2, episode 1.*
Carlton lets burglars into the building and Rhoda's apartment is robbed; she reports him and gets him fired. Carlton's mother comes to plead his case—and steals some more of Rhoda's things.

⬥ Emmy-winning actresses Julie Kavner (left) and Valerie Harper star as the Morgenstern sisters.

Little House on the Prairie

Drama | USA | 1974–83

Charming chronicle of family life in the Wild West—as cozy as a cup of cocoa and a pair of slippers

Cast | Melissa Sue Anderson, Melissa Gilbert, Karen Grassle, Michael Landon
Original broadcaster | NBC **Awards** | 4 Emmys **For fans of . . .** | *The Waltons* (1971)

This TV series was based on the semi-autobiographical novels of Laura Ingalls Wilder. After his success in *Bonanza* (1959), Michael Landon was asked to direct the pilot episode and star as family man Charles, who moved with his wife and children to the quaint town of Walnut Grove, Minnesota. Cue lots of adventures about poverty, religion, bullying, racism, and alcoholism: moral tales told in an entertaining way, with sugar on top and order inevitably restored at the end of each episode. Melissa Gilbert, who played Laura Ingalls, was arguably the show's star. Cute in a gap-toothed kind of way, she was often at the center of the story. Humor was supplied by the Oleson family: the local storekeeper Nels; his harridan of a wife, Harriet; and

their spoiled brats, Nellie and Willie, who more often than not clashed with the Ingalls children. Mary Ingalls evoked pathos as she coped with her developing blindness. When Landon left at the end of season eight, the focus shifted to a grown-up Laura and her husband, Almanzo. With the introduction of new characters, audience figures dwindled and the ax fell. **DJ**

Classic episode

I'll Be Waving as You Drive Away | *Season 4, episode 21.* Struggling to cope with life away from Walnut Grove at the school for the blind, Mary finds companionship and hope in her new teacher, Adam. Get the tissues!

◑ Pa, Ma, Mary, Half-pint, and Carrie may have lived a simple life, but their tight family bond touched the hearts of many.

Porridge

Comedy | UK | 1974–77

Inmates in a British prison serve time while running rings around the wardens

Cast | Ronnie Barker, Richard Beckinsale, Fulton Mackay, Brian Wilde, Sam Kelly, Tony Osoba
Original broadcaster | BBC One   **Awards** | 3 BAFTAs   **For fans of . . .** | *Auf Wiedersehen, Pet* (1983), *Red Dwarf* (1988)

Prison is an unlikely setting for a sitcom, but Dick Clement and Ian La Frenais crafted *Porridge* into a critically acclaimed British TV comedy. The pilot, "Prisoner and Escort," was one of six half-hour plays commissioned as potential starring vehicles for Ronnie Barker. He played Norman Stanley Fletcher, a convicted career criminal being accompanied on a train to Slade Prison by two wardens, the humorless Scot Mr. Mackay and the kind but woolly Mr. Barraclough. Both characters were retained for the series as Fletcher's main foils.

In the first episode proper, Fletch shared a cell with a first-timer called Lenny Godber (Richard Beckinsale), and took him under his wing. Fletch was a father figure for several inmates, including illiterate Bunny

Warren, camp chef Lukewarm, and uneducated Cyril. Occasional menace came from privileged prisoner and big-time gangster Harry Grout. After three well-received seasons and a short spin-off, *Going Straight* (1978), came the inevitable feature film. Unlike most TV-to-movie comedies, it successfully matched the brilliant wit of the series. **JS**

Classic episode

Men Without Women | Season 1, episode 6. Fletch discovers that his wife has been "unfaithful" and is granted a weekend of compassionate leave—or rather a weekend of watching sports and enjoying home comforts with his very loving wife.

⚓ Fulton Mackay (center) lays down the rules for Fletcher (Ronnie Barker, R) and Godber (Richard Beckinsale, L). Completely pointless!

Land of the Lost

Fantasy/Horror/Sci-Fi | USA | 1974–76

A family goes over a waterfall and into the land time forgot . . .

Cast | Spencer Milligan, Wesley Eure, Kathy Coleman, Ron Harper
Original broadcaster | NBC
For fans of . . . | *Gilligan's Island* (1964), *Shazam!* (1974)

NBC's Saturday morning lineup for children in 1974 included the adventures of the Marshall family—father Rick and his two teenaged children, Will and Holly—in a spirited, and sometimes surprisingly adult-themed, voyage. Produced by well-known TV pioneers Sid and Marty Krofft, and developed for television by acclaimed science fiction writer David Gerrold, *Land of the Lost* became a popular fixture on Saturday mornings as the Marshall family endeavored to survive in an "other" world and find a way home.

Although the series lasted only three seasons, the series was repeated endlessly in syndication packages; children and their families tuned in for the latest chapter of the adventures of the time-lost family and their battles against the elements, the savage dinosaurs whose land they had breached, and the Sleestaks: bulb-eyed lizard men with a sophisticated backstory and abandoned technology. Week after week, the Marshalls attempted to piece together clues about the mysterious pylons and their crystal technology, meeting allies (such as the Neanderthal-like Pakuni) and enemies in their quest to escape from the Land of the Lost.

Lead actor Spencer Milligan was written out for the third season due to a dispute over merchandising rights, and Ron Harper replaced him as the children's Uncle Jack, who had been searching for them. The series was later revived briefly in 1991 (a loose adaptation that lasted two seasons) and for a comedy film, in 2009, starring Will Ferrell. **SL**

Police Woman

Drama | USA | 1974–78

Groundbreaking cop drama that brought a female lead to prime-time US TV

Cast | Angie Dickinson, Earl Holliman, Charles Dierkop
Original broadcaster | NBC
Award | 1 Golden Globe
For fans of . . . | *Charlie's Angels* (1976), *Cagney & Lacey* (1982)

Until the 1970s, crime dramas were male-dominated affairs, with female characters playing second fiddle to the heroic male leads. Then, along came *Police Woman,* and it all changed. A spin-off from NBC's *Police Story* (1973), *Police Woman* focused on undercover cop Sergeant "Pepper" Anderson (Angie Dickinson) as she and her colleagues placed themselves in dangerous situations to bring criminals to justice. These assignments saw Pepper adopt a range of covers, including a showgirl, a prison inmate, and a casino hostess. The story was told in a similar vein to other detective shows, but the female detective protagonist was refreshing.

Launching a prime-time series with a female lead was a brave step at the time, but it was still the 1970s, and there was too much reliance on Dickinson's sex appeal. Dickinson has commented on the amount of shower scenes she had to film, saying that she felt exploited. However, her gutsy performance proved she was more than just a pretty face, and was able to make Pepper the equal of her male colleagues. Holliman—Sergeant Bill Crowley—proved a good counterpoint for Dickinson, and the wisecracking between the two was a highlight.

Running for four seasons, *Police Woman*'s success must be attributed to Dickinson; the impact she and Pepper had on the audience—and TV—cannot be underestimated. She proved that viewers better responded to the equal representation of women's importance in society, and paved the way for the many successful female-led dramas that followed. **SO**

Rising Damp
Comedy | UK | 1974–78

A fondly remembered sitcom made great by the comic genius of its star—
"Myyyyyyy God!"

Cast | Leonard Rossiter, Frances de la Tour,
Don Warrington, Richard Beckinsale
Original broadcaster | ITV
Award | 1 BAFTA
For fans of . . . | *Man About the House* (1973)

There is a thread of grimy bleakness that runs through British comedy. The BBC series *Hancock's Half Hour* (1956) and *Steptoe and Son* (1962) showed a postwar Britain living in squalor and aspiring to something better. Yet ITV's *Rising Damp* made its debut more than a decade later, and showed that for many, poor-quality housing was still an unavoidable fact of life, especially in overcrowded inner-city dwellings such as the apartment block run by Rigsby (Leonard Rossiter). The series was developed for TV by Eric Chappell from his own stage play, *The Banana Box* (1971).

Rossiter somehow made Rigsby a rather likable character. He was mean, refusing to pay for minor apartment repairs and trying to blame them on his tenants. He was predatory, forever looking for an opportunity to pounce on the oblivious spinster Miss Jones (Frances de la Tour). He was a snob, resentful of the money being spent on the education of long-haired layabouts such as Alan (Richard Beckinsale), and he was also deeply suspicious of the motives of the handsome, suave Philip (Don Warrington), who, upon his arrival, pretended to be African royalty and continued to make Rigsby aware of his own superior education. Despite this, viewers loved Rigsby's persistence with Miss Jones and wanted him to woo her. They hoped he would not fall into whatever situational traps Philip had set, and they also prayed that one day he would have a more successful love life than his snowy white cat, Vienna. **JS**

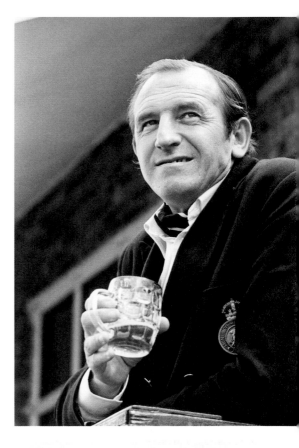

Classic episode
The Prowler | *Season 1, episode 6.* When Miss Jones reports seeing a strange man through her window, Rigsby's prejudices come to the fore as all of his male residents become suspects. His suspicions are way off the mark.

◉ Leonard Rossiter as Rigsby on the set of the spin-off feature film that was released in 1979.

The Rockford Files

Crime/Mystery | USA | 1974–80

Easygoing, amiable ex-con turned private investigator solves crime and dodges punches on the West Coast

Cast | James Garner, Noah Beery Jr., Joe Santos, Gretchen Corbett
Original broadcaster | NBC
Awards | 5 Emmys
For fans of . . . | *Magnum P.I.* (1980)

Jim Rockford, played by James (Maverick) Garner, was a dry, cynical private investigator who lived and worked from his beat-up trailer home by a beach in Malibu, near Los Angeles. An ex-con who had been imprisoned for a crime that he did not commit, Jim drove a gold Pontiac Firebird Esprit, got his work through a small ad that he ran in the local paper, and had an answering machine that played the message: "This is Jim Rockford. At the tone leave your name and message and I'll get back to you." The messages were almost always from people who owed Rockford money, or who were owed money by Rockford, or from women who were owed an explanation.

Each episode followed the same formula: Jim would encounter a client who retained his services and then get drawn into a dangerous situation he knew nothing about, usually involving the Southern California underworld. There was usually at least one car chase or fist fight, which Rockford was as likely to lose as win. Over the course of the show, Rockford would crack the case, and it would end with a joyful freeze-frame and a reprise of Mike Post's memorable theme song.

The *Rockford Files* aired on the NBC television network from 1974 through 1980, starting with a TV movie. The series run included a number of two-part episodes, as well as feature-length episodes that were split into two parts for syndication. In the 1990s, *Rockford* returned to the air in a series of eight TV movies on CBS. **JG**

Classic episode
The Oracle Wore a Cashmere Suit | *Season 3, episode 2*. Written by David Chase, the creator of *The Sopranos*, this was a tightly plotted murder mystery in which Garner himself is accused of the crime by a psychic.

⚫ James Garner as Jim Rockford, a TV icon of the 1970s on both sides of the pond.

Within These Walls

Drama | UK | 1974–78

The lives and loves of female prisoners and the staff tasked with looking after them

Cast | Googie Withers, Mona Bruce, Katharine Blake, Jerome Willis, Sarah Lawson
Original broadcaster | LWT
For fans of . . . | *Prisoner* (1979), *Bad Girls* (1999), *Tenko* (1981), *Wentworth* (2013)

The concept of a program in which 95 percent of the characters are strong, powerful women was pretty much unheard of before the prison drama *Within These Walls*. Whether creator David Butler intended to break down such barriers or whether he simply thought a woman's prison was a great place for drama is anyone's guess—but both proved to be the case. Coming out of Britain's ITV network, in which most drama was genteel or period during the 1970s, *Within These Walls* took the viewers by the collar and shook them up. Drugs, sex, lesbianism, riots, and violence perpetrated by women were controversial subjects for Saturday night television.

In the first few seasons, Googie Withers, as Faye Webber, governor of H.M.P. Stone Park, developed the kind of matriarchal character that would be commonplace five years later, but was groundbreaking at the time. She showed a cynical male-dominated TV industry that female-led shows could not only hold their heads up against the more typical series, but could outclass them. When Withers departed at the end of the third season, Katharine Blake stepped forward to fill the hole, as Governor Forrester.

By the fifth season, the glory days of the show were over, as was Blake. For the fifth and final run, Sarah Lawson played Governor Marshall, but by then the show had lost its focus and become more like a soap with convoluted story lines. No one was surprised when ITV pulled the plug in 1978. **GR**

Zatôichi monogatari

Historical drama | Japan | 1974–79

Blind swordsman walks the land, righting wrongs and seeking redemption

Cast | Shintaro Katsu, Shintaro Akatsuki, Renji Ishibashi
Original broadcaster | Fuji TV
For fans of . . . | *Kung Fu* (1972), *The Incredible Hulk* (1978), *Daredevil* (2015)

An archetype of the lonely, wandering hero who simply wants to be left alone, but cannot help but get involved in local troubles, the character of Zatôichi was first introduced in a novel by Kan Shimozawa. Played by Shintaro Katsu, the character soon moved to the big screen in one of film's longest-running franchises, with twenty-six films from 1962 to 1989. During that period Katsu also played the character in one hundred TV episodes of *Zatôichi monogatari* (*The Tale of Zatôichi*).

After losing his sight at the age of two, Zatôichi zealously studied the sword arts of Japan, using other heightened senses to compensate for his loss of sight. He became a yakuza for three years, but realized the folly of his ways and attempted to atone for his brief period as a criminal. As a blind man, Zatôichi's social status in Japan could not have been lower, but his low caste and blindness ensured that his enemies underestimated him, at their peril. As he wandered through Japan during the late Edo period (1830s and 1840s), Zatôichi earned a living both as a humble masseuse and as a gambler. His blindness could serve him well when he became involved in fights, during which he would extinguish the candles in a room and intone his catchphrase, "Darkness is my advantage."

Zatôichi monogatari appealed because it combined admiration of samurai skills with the pleasure of seeing an apparent underdog triumph. It effectively combined martial arts action with travelogue settings, and as such became a hit not just in Japan but globally. **RBA**

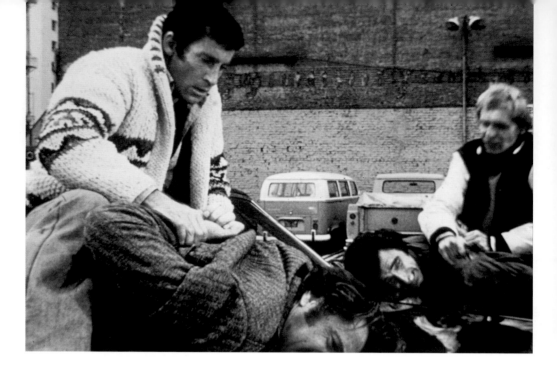

Starsky & Hutch

Drama | USA | 1975–79

By far the coolest cop show of the 1970s

Cast | Paul Michael Glaser, David Soul, Antonio Fargas, Bernie Hamilton
Original broadcaster | ABC **For fans of . . .** | *The Sweeney* (1975), *Miami Vice* (1984)

David Starsky (Paul Michael Glaser) and Kenneth "Hutch" Hutchinson (David Soul) brought a fresh blast of 1970s cool to the US cop show format. As undercover detectives—with leather jackets, belt-tie cardigans, and flares—they stormed their way into the viewers' homes, bringing crime-solving action from the fictional town of Bay City, California. Alongside the two stars were Bernie Hamilton as their put-upon boss, Captain Dobey, and the unforgettable Antonio Fargas as their informant Huggy Bear, the streetwise bar owner with a style all his own. The fact that neither of these characters was white may not seem special now, but at the time it was the mark of a show that reflected the times. The other star of the show was the car: Starsky's

Ford Gran Torino. Bright red with its signature white stripe running down the side, it was the car that kids of all ages desired.

The series paved the way for grittier dramas, such as *Hill Street Blues* (1981). Michael Mann, who scripted several episodes went on to write and produce the big buddy cop show of the 1980s, *Miami Vice*. **DJO**

Classic episode

The Fix | *Season 1, episode 6*. Hutch dates a girl who is on the run from her mobster boyfriend. When Hutch is abducted and refuses to give up her whereabouts, he is forcibly given heroin and turned into an addict. Starsky to the rescue.

⊙ Paul Michael Glaser as Starsky and David Soul as Hutch make a typical arrest.

Barney Miller

Comedy | USA | 1975–82

Character-driven ensemble comedy show with an undeniable charm—addictive

Cast | Hal Linden, Ron Glass, Steve Landesberg, Abe Vigoda, Max Gail   **Original broadcaster** | ABC
Awards | 3 Emmys, 2 Golden Globes   **For fans of . . .** | *Reno 911!* (2003), *Brooklyn Nine-Nine* (2013)

Barney Miller eschewed guns, gangsters, and high-octane crime scenes, instead opting for a considered exploration of the relationships of a group of city cops trying to do a workman-like job despite the flaws in the system and the pressures of the urban environment.

Central to the series was the character of Miller (Hal Linden) himself, an unexceptional Jewish guy who, nonetheless, commanded respect because of his fairness, impartiality, and determination to do a good job. His men (it was a very male show) were a typical New York ethnic mix, but it was Detective Sergeant Phil Fish (Abe Vigoda), a decrepit and ancient figure, frail and seemingly always on the verge of retirement (or death), who was the unlikely hit of the series.

Barney Miller was a slow-burn success that spent years in development and defied simple analysis. It was well written, featured complex relationships, and was often leisurely paced. It was never afraid of portraying its characters as less than perfect, with their own sets of prejudices, and it never shied away from tackling thorny, sometimes controversial, issues. **DF**

Classic episode
Quarantine | *Season 3, episodes 2 and 3.* A memorable two-parter in which all the regulars are confined to the precinct house with a handful of miscreants after a perpetrator they have bought in collapses with a mystery illness.

⬥ Guest star William Windom (left) threatens to blow up Miller (Hal Linden) and his team unless he can speak to President Nixon.

The Naked Civil Servant

Drama | UK | 1975

A poignant journey from self-discovery to cult camp icon

Cast | John Hurt, Liz Gebhardt, Patricia Hodge, Stanley Lebor, Katharine Schofield
Original broadcaster | ITV
Award | 1 BAFTA
For fans of . . . | *Oranges Are Not the Only Fruit* (1989)

Based on Quentin Crisp's autobiography, *The Naked Civil Servant* arrived only a few years after homosexuality was partially decriminalized in England (and some time before the rest of the United Kingdom caught up). The TV play looked back on Crisp's turbulent life, his unhappy relationships, and his uncanny knack for irritating authority wherever he went. Crisp's decision to be as flamboyant as possible—flame-red hair, almost blind with mascara, lips covered with lipstick—was as foolhardy as it was brave, especially during the very conservative 1930s and 1940s. His bare insolence in refusing to conform resulted in frequent beatings and abuse in the streets, yet he also found support from surprising quarters.

John Hurt impressed viewers (and Crisp) in the way he inhabited the role of an effeminate man with a singsong drawl, whose mere presence in public inspired primal hatred and disgust. Little did they know that punk was only around the corner, or that Crisp would later be lauded as a great British character. As Crisp himself put it, "You cannot touch me now; I am one of the 'stately homos' of England."

Hurt returned to Quentin Crisp in 2009 for a follow-up drama, *An Englishman in New York*. It focused on Crisp's later years in the United States, where he fell out of fashion because of his insensitive and poorly received comments about AIDS, before being rediscovered and ultimately recognized as a tenacious pioneer of gay rights. **JS**

The Sweeney

Crime/Mystery | UK | 1975–78

The blunt weapons of London's police have their own methods of catching thieves

---

Cast | John Thaw, Dennis Waterman, Garfield Morgan, John Alkin
Original broadcaster | ITV
For fans of . . . | *Starsky & Hutch* (1975), *Widows* (1983), *Miami Vice* (1984)

In Cockney rhyming slang, "Sweeney Todd" is the "flying squad": quick-dispatch police detectives in fast cars chasing down villains and responding to major crimes. *The Sweeney* was as much a reaction against the BBC's cozy *Z Cars* (1962) as that series had been to *Dixon of Dock Green* (1955). Shot on film in London, *The Sweeney* was aggressive and unglamorous, with guaranteed car chases and fight scenes in every episode. Jack Regan (the exceptional John Thaw) was a hard-drinking old-school cop, more likely to swing a punch than read a suspect his rights. His methods might have been old-fashioned and boorish, but he often got results and his superiors considered him a necessary risk. Aided by the naive but loyal George Carter (Dennis Waterman), Regan did not always get his man; *The Sweeney* was not afraid to allow some criminals to escape. Viewers loved the irreverence of the scripts, too—when Regan's squad pulls a suspect from his bed, the latter is told, "Get your trousers on—you're nicked!"

Hugely popular, *The Sweeney* became the kind of show that actors wanted to be a part of, and the guest cast is made up of the era's best-known names and faces. Even Eric Morecambe and Ernie Wise played themselves in one episode. *The Sweeney* also threw a spotlight on many of the problems that dogged the police force. Although Regan was a hero to some, he was also a relic of the type of arrogant, thuggish policing that the London Metropolitan Police has spent the subsequent forty years trying to wipe out. **JS**

Space: 1999

Fantasy/Horror/Sci-Fi | UK | 1975–77

An adventure as big as the universe—the inhabitants of a base on the Moon come to terms with a future in outer space

Cast | Martin Landau, Barbara Bain, Barry Morse, Catherine Schell, Tony Anholt, Nick Tate
Original broadcaster | ITV
For fans of . . . | *Star Trek* (1966), *Buck Rogers in the 25th Century* (1979)

A series of nuclear explosions on the dark side of the Moon sends it careering out of Earth's orbit and into deep space, along with several hundred inhabitants of Moonbase Alpha, a lunar research station. With little chance of being able to pilot the Moon back home, the station personnel must work together for survival and protect one another from dangerous space phenomena and alien encounters.

The two seasons of *Space: 1999* could be described as two separate series with some of the same cast. The first was a serious attempt at doing *Star Trek* (1966) on a British budget; the second was closer to *Lost in Space* (1965), with a contrived, shape-shifting alien among the crew and an increase in outlandish plots. Following on from Gerry Anderson's *UFO* (1969), *Space: 1999* was a remarkable, big-budget, sci-fi epic for the small screen. Its regular cast was headed up by *Mission: Impossible* husband-and-wife team Martin Landau and Barbara Bain, and its guest cast was a who's who of British character actors, including Peter Cushing, Peter Bowles, and Brian Blessed, among many others.

The visual effects were inspired by *2001: A Space Odyssey* (1968), and the model work was as impressive as would be expected from a Gerry and Sylvia Anderson production. The spaceships—known as "Eagles"—were popular toys while the show was on the air, and although *Space: 1999* ran for only two seasons, it was the most expensive British series produced up to that time. **JS**

Classic episode
The Metamorph | *Season 2, episode 1*. The Moonbase Alpha team encounters a father and daughter with the power of transforming into animals. After her father's death, Maya elects to join the Alphans on their journey through space.

◬ Catherine Schell and Martin Landau assess an oncoming threat.

The Good Life

Comedy | UK | 1975–78

A couple turn their suburban garden into a small farm much to the dismay of their neighbors—"Jerry, do something!"

Classic episode
Pig's Lib | Season 1, episode 4. Margo is horrified when the Goods install pigs in their garden and enlists the help of a local politician to get the animals removed. But then she learns that the only way out for them is to the abattoir.

◉ Richard Briers and Felicity Kendal as Tom and Barbara Good.

Cast | Richard Briers, Felicity Kendal, Paul Eddington, Penelope Keith
Original broadcaster | BBC One
Award | 1 BAFTA
For fans of . . . | *Butterflies* (1978)

The 1970s in the United Kingdom saw a series of strikes and frequent power outages, which reinforced how reliant the public was on basic services such as transportation and electricity. Advocating the advantages of self-sufficiency, John Esmonde and Bob Larbey's *The Good Life* introduced Tom Good (Richard Briers), a bored forty-year-old who persuaded his wife, Barbara (Felicity Kendal), that they should give up the trappings of modern consumerism, and live only from things they grew or made themselves. Their neighbors, ambitious Jerry (Paul Eddington) and his snobbish wife Margo (Penelope Keith), were appalled—at the notion of self-sufficiency itself, at the state of the Goods' suburban garden, and at the noise from their animals.

For many, the Goods were British TV's perfect married couple. Tom was fun but practical, Barbara was plucky and determined, and they got through their hardships thanks to their shared sense of humor. In contrast, a sense of humor was something that Margo sadly lacked, which often made her the butt of their affectionate jokes. Yet it was Margo's snootiness and impracticality that were the highlight of most episodes—particularly on the rare occasions when she attempted to muck in with some manual labor.

The Good Life (shown in the United States as *Good Neighbors*) ran for four glorious seasons. Its final episode became a royal event when it was recorded in the company of Queen Elizabeth II and Prince Philip, Duke of Edinburgh. **JS**

Wonder Woman

Action/Adventure | USA | 1975–79

Comic strip brought to life—"Woman of the hour, with your superpowers, we're so glad you're on our side! You're a wonder! Wonder Woman!"

Cast | Lynda Carter, Lyle Waggoner, Tom Kratochvil, Beatrice Colen
Original broadcasters | ABC, CBS
For fans of . . . | *I Dream of Jeannie* (1965), *Batman* (1966), *Charlie's Angels* (1976)

After a very lame *Wonder Woman* pilot in 1974, starring Cathy Lee Crosby in a star-spangled jumpsuit, ABC tried again a year later with another pilot episode—*The New Original Wonder Woman*, a more faithful take on the comic-strip superhero—casting Lynda Carter in a lead role that she would make her own.

The first ABC season had a naive charm. The episodes opened with a glorious animated title sequence where the comic-strip representations of the characters transformed into their actor counterparts; literally, the comic strip came to life. Wonder Woman's alter ego, Diana Prince, was a yeoman in the War Office, under Major Steve Trevor (Lyle Waggoner). Stories, therefore, generally pitted her against various Nazi villains, but there was also room for mad encounters with cattle rustlers, an alien sent in judgment on the human race, and Gargantua, a giant gorilla.

With a change of network to CBS, the show was updated in 1977 as *The New Adventures of Wonder Woman*, and it became a more generic, light-hearted adventure. In the two CBS seasons, Wonder Woman took on mad scientists creating volcanoes, a crazy toy maker, a hired assassin in drag, and a modern-day Nazi cell trying to resurrect Hitler. The wartime ABC episodes have perhaps aged better, but the whole series was an entertaining romp, and Lynda Carter's performance was judged perfectly. There was also the joy of waiting for those explosive spinning transformations as Diana Prince became our heroine. **PV**

Classic episode
The New Original Wonder Woman | *Season 1, episode 1.* The pilot is terrific fun and sets up the show perfectly. It is worth catching for the camp performances of Kenneth Mars as the Nazi bad guy and Cloris Leachman as Queen of the Amazons.

⬥ Lynda Carter in superheroine garb.

Saturday Night Live

Variety | USA | 1975–present

Late-night comedy sketch show—"Live from New York, it's Saturday Night!"

Cast | Various
Original broadcaster | NBC
Awards | 45 Emmys
For fans of . . . | *The Tonight Show* (1954),
30 Rock (2006)

If there is something that can truly be called an American institution on TV, it is *Saturday Night Live*. A staple of late-night weekend TV since 1975, filmed in front of a live studio audience in New York, *Saturday Night Live* has launched the careers of dozens of actors, brought countless bands and musicians their day in the sun, made headlines for its controversial items, and held up a mirror to each moment in time.

Created by Lorne Michaels, *Saturday Night Live* has been on air for forty years, hosted by a major celebrity and supported by the comedy stylings of a rotating cast of regulars, many of whom have launched careers in the process: it has brought viewers the likes of John Belushi, Dan Aykroyd, Will Ferrell, Chevy Chase, Bill Murray, Julia Louis-Dreyfus, Eddie Murphy, Phil Hartman, Kristen Wiig, and Amy Poehler; the list goes on. The sketches are usually timely and topical, blending satire with biting social commentary, whereas the long-running "Weekend Update" segment presents a look at the latest news topics in a wry and sometimes quite stunning fashion. World news events can often become fixed in our minds, and so too can *Saturday Night Live*. For example, viewers can remember not only where they were in September 2001, but also how *Saturday Night Live* dealt with the aftermath. Whether it is Sinead O'Connor tearing up a photograph of the Pope, or Tina Fey impersonating candidate Sarah Palin and changing the course of a presidential election, *Saturday Night Live* remains a true TV monument. **SL**

Classic episode
Betty White with Jay-Z | Season 35, episode 21.
Octogenarian Betty White lives up to the hype (and the Facebook campaign) and hosts a cracking episode, with a stellar supporting cast.

◔ Fred Armisen and Kristen Wiig in season 39 as their characters from *The Lawrence Welk Show*.
◑ All smiles: Tina Fey (left) as Sarah Palin and Amy Poehler as Hillary Clinton.

Fawlty Towers

Comedy | UK | 1975–79

Mishap after mishap in a seaside hotel—"A satisfied customer. We should have him stuffed"

Cast | John Cleese, Prunella Scales, Andrew Sachs, Connie Booth
Original broadcaster | BBC Two
Awards | 3 BAFTAs
For fans of . . . | *The Office* (2001)

Bored with *Monty Python's Flying Circus* (1969) and inspired by an unpleasant stay at a hotel, John Cleese left his castmates to work on what is now perceived as the most perfectly structured British sitcom of all time. Each episode was crafted by Cleese and his then-wife Connie Booth like a Harold Pinter play squeezed into half an hour. Whether or not you find it funny depends on your threshold for embarrassment, because the hotel antics are often toe-curling in the extreme.

In truth, Basil Fawlty (Cleese) was not the right man to run a hotel. He might have enjoyed it if it were not for the residents, who had the audacity to expect so much of him: good service, politeness, and privacy. He might also have once loved his wife, Sybil (Prunella Scales), although they had both long since reduced their relationship to barbed comments and low expectations (Fawlty suggested his wife could be a contestant on *Mastermind*, specialist subject "the bleeding obvious"). The resourceful maid Polly (Connie Booth) was Basil's confidante, especially when he needed help removing himself from a potentially catastrophic situation. Sadly, the waiter Manuel (Andrew Sachs) was less useful. Somehow acquired from Barcelona, Manuel was a gullible buffoon with barely enough knowledge of English to be a credible asset to anyone.

Although *Fawlty Towers* is now cited as the inspiration for almost every British sitcom that followed, on its first broadcast it was not a success, perhaps as a backlash against Cleese leaving the Pythons. **JS**

Poldark

Historical drama | UK | 1975–77

Landmark TV that set the benchmark for historical drama

Cast | Robin Ellis, Angharad Rees, Ralph Bates, Mary Wimbush
Original broadcaster | BBC One
For fans of . . . | *The Onedin Line* (1971), *North and South* (1985)

The *Poldark* novels by Winston Graham provided material for one of the BBC's most popular historical dramas. The romantic backdrop of eighteenth-century Cornwall provided fertile ground for the romance between Captain Ross Poldark (Robin Ellis) and servant Demelza (Angharad Rees). Potent plotlines of family rivalry, underhand business, smuggling, and a turbulent romance made *Poldark* unmissable viewing.

Struggling to make his Cornish tin mine a success, Ross Poldark lost fiancée Elizabeth to his cousin, but romance blossomed between brooding Poldark and tempestuous Demelza. Between 1945 and 2002, Graham wrote twelve Poldark novels, and the first seven provided material for two seasons of the TV show. Ratings grew throughout early episodes, and the historical detail, high drama, and strong characters lured audiences worldwide. The relationship between Ross and Demelza struck the major chord, making stars of Ellis and Rees and creating a fervent fan base.

When Graham's eighth novel, *The Stranger from the Sea,* was adapted in 1996 with John Bowe and Mel Martin as Ross and Demelza, a furious contingent of loyal fans marched to the ITV headquarters protesting against this slight to the original stars. The original show was broadcast in the United States as part of PBS's Masterpiece Theatre. With *Poldark's* lasting popularity, it was only a matter of time before a revival. In 2014, the BBC began production on a new *Poldark*, starring Aidan Turner as Ross and Eleanor Tomlinson as Demelza. **MW**

◀ Fawlty (Cleese) appears to give his guests a warm welcome.

Wheel of Fortune

Game show | USA | 1975–present

Contestants solve word puzzles to win cash and prizes in this stalwart of the game show

Cast | Chuck Woolery, Susan Stafford, Pat Sajak, Vanna White
Original broadcaster | NBC **Awards** | 5 Emmys **For fans of . . .** | *The Price Is Right* (1972)

Wheel of Fortune was created by Merv Griffin and premiered as a daytime series. Its popularity led to a syndicated version being developed for the evening, which premiered in 1983 and continues to air today.

The format derives from the old pen-and-paper guessing game called hangman. Contestants work out hidden phrases (the general theme is hinted at) by suggesting letters, one at a time. For each correct consonant, the contestants win money or prizes, as determined by a spin of a giant carnival wheel. They have to "buy" vowels, however. The contestant who collects the most winnings moves onto a bonus round, in which he or she can win larger cash sums and more expensive prizes, including cars and vacations.

The network version was originally hosted by Chuck Woolery and Susan Stafford, with Charlie O'Donnell as its announcer. O'Donnell left in 1980, Woolery in 1981, and Stafford in 1982; they were replaced by Jack Clark, Pat Sajak, and Vanna White, who are still in place.

Wheel is the longest-running syndicated US game show and has been sold to sixty countries. **RP**

Classic episode
Season 32, episode 74. Contestant Matt DeSanto started off by guessing "The Lone Ranger" when only a single "E" was visible and rode his luck to walk away with nearly $92,000, the biggest win in the show's history.

⊗ Contestants try to make it from the spinning wheel to the steering wheel of one of the show's top prizes.

The Jeffersons

Comedy | USA | 1975–85

An All in the Family *spin-off that followed the Bunkers' neighbors to Manhattan*

Cast | Isabel Sanford, Sherman Hemsley, Marla Gibbs, Roxie Roker, Franklin Cover, Paul Benedict
Original broadcaster | CBS **Awards** | 2 Emmys **For fans of . . .** | *All in the Family* (1971), *The Cosby Show* (1984)

One of the longest-running sitcoms on American television, *The Jeffersons* was about an affluent African-American family living in New York City. There was George (Sherman Hemsley), who would affectionately call his wife "Wheezie," but would bristle anytime anyone else used the pet name; said wife Louise (Isabel Sanford), who often clashed with George's know-it-all mother, Mother Jefferson (Zara Cully); son Lionel (Damon Evans); and housekeeper Florence (Marla Gibbs).

George's fortune was based on his chain of dry cleaners. In their upscale apartment building, his stubbornness often bordered on arrogance, while Louise, who liked to consider herself an "ordinary person," made friends with neighbors Tom and Helen Willis (Franklin Cover and Roxie Roker), an interracial couple with two adult children. The Jeffersons' lives were further enriched, and complicated, by their British neighbor, Mr. Bently, and doorman Ralph.

The sitcom was less political than other shows created by Norman Lear, especially *All in the Family*, from which it was spun. It had one short-lived spin-off, *Checking In*, which centered on the Jeffersons' housekeeper, Florence. To the annoyance of audiences, *The Jeffersons* was canceled after four seasons without having had a proper ending. But the 1996 finale of the sitcom *The Fresh Prince of Bel-Air* rectified that by having George and Louise make guest appearances to buy the house from the Banks family. **RP**

◬ Sherman Hemsley (George Jefferson) and Isabel Sanford (Louise Jefferson) in an episode from 1975.

Baretta

Crime/Mystery | USA | 1975–78

Leading light of the unconventional cop canon

Cast | Robert Blake, Michael D. Roberts
Original broadcaster | ABC
Awards | 2 Emmys, 1 Golden Globe
For fans of . . . | *Ironside* (1967), *Columbo* (1971), *Kojak* (1973)

American TV cops of the 1970s were distinguished by unconventional policing styles and idiosyncratic quirks. Columbo had his shabby raincoat and beaten-up car; Kojak was bald and sucked lollipops; Ironside was grumpy; and Tony Baretta was no exception, with his street-style fashion sense and his pet cockatoo, Fred.

Essentially, this was a reboot of the earlier less successful show *Toma* (1973), which itself owed a debt to the film *Serpico* (1973). *Baretta* starred Robert Blake as an undercover cop, who used his skill at disguise and method acting ability to immerse himself into a different character to infiltrate dangerous underworlds and bring about justice. Baretta was a maverick and a loner, eschewing the idea of a partner to pursue cases alone and off the grid. Although he did touch base occasionally with his masters (initially Inspector Schiller, later Lieutenant Brubaker), his only other consistent acquaintance—and his closest thing to a friend—was his stylish informant Rooster (Michael D. Roberts). The series was enlivened by humorous moments in between the tense drama and by Blake's brilliant Emmy Award–winning performance as the driven cop.

The series originated during a particularly healthy period for US crime shows, and *Baretta* could hold its own against the best of them. However, memories of the show have often been overshadowed by Blake's arrest for the murder of his second wife, which understandably caused a media sensation at the time, although he was subsequently acquitted. **DF**

Survivors

Fantasy/Horror/Sci-Fi | UK | 1975–77

Post-apocalyptic drama that tells it how it is

Cast | Carolyn Seymour, Ian McCulloch, Lucy Fleming, Denis Lill
Original broadcaster | BBC One
For fans of . . . | *The Day of the Triffids* (1981), *The Walking Dead* (2010)

Terry Nation may be remembered as the creator of *Doctor Who*'s iconic Daleks, but his skill as a dramatist was never bleaker than in *Survivors*: the former comedy writer's vision of humanity brought to the brink by a devastating virus. There were no laughs here as the survivors came to terms with the end of civilization.

Through an economical—and terrifying—title sequence, the downfall of the world was conveyed in stark imagery: a vial falling, shattering in slow motion; a scientist collapsing in an airport lounge; a montage of passport stamps. The opening episode ratcheted the bleakness, providing an apocalyptic fifty minutes of TV. The familiar and domestic became deadly: hospitals overrun, death toll rising. There were survivors, namely Abby Grant (Carolyn Seymour), who provided the narrative thrust of the first season in her search for her son, Peter. With a road-movie aesthetic, Abby teamed with architect Greg Preston (Ian McCulloch) and young woman Jenny (Lucy Fleming), eventually forming the beginnings of a small community in a stately home.

Nation departed after one season (as did Seymour), citing creative differences with producer Terence Dudley. Later episodes showed a world rebuilding, centered on the day-to-day life of the Whitecross community, led by Charles Vaughan (Denis Lill). Under Dudley, *Survivors* eschewed Nation's bleak outlook for a more homespun feel, although the bleakness returned in the final season as Jenny and Charles embarked on a journey to find the missing Greg. **MW**

I, Claudius

Historical drama | UK | 1976

Dynastic epic covering five emperors of the Roman Empire

Cast | Derek Jacobi, John Hurt, Siân Phillips, Brian Blessed, George Baker, Margaret Tyzack, Patrick Stewart
Original broadcaster | BBC Two
Awards | 3 BAFTAs, 1 Emmy
For fans of . . . | *Rome* (2005), *House of Cards* (2013)

Inflicted with a pronounced stammer, a limp, and an incurable belief in a future republic, Tiberius Claudius Caesar Augustus Germanicus was perceived by many to be an idiot. An embarrassment to his family, he was kept out of public sight, leaving him free to indulge his passion for history. For Claudius was not the fool his murderous relatives believed him to be; fate would see him outlive them all.

Presented through the eyes of an elderly Claudius, this show was the bloody history of the Roman emperors Augustus, Tiberius, Caligula, Claudius himself, and his successor, Nero. Nephew to Augustus and grandson of Augustus' wife, the arch manipulator Livia, Claudius was witness to the political machinations, the treachery, and sadistic madness that ran through his family and threatened to bring Rome to its knees.

A lavish BBC production for the time, *I, Claudius* was an acting master class. Brian Blessed, now famous for his bombastic, shouty performances, delivered an Augustus comfortable in his role as emperor. For Derek Jacobi as Claudius, it was a career-defining role that took him from youth to old age. Despite the unpleasantness, the violence, and the degrading sexual exploits of the Roman royals, *I, Claudius* was also surprisingly funny, albeit rather blackly. Hurt appears to be pulling all the stops out to make his performance as over the top as possible, not least in the scene where Caligula declared himself a god, which was by turns cringeworthy, gloriously camp, and chillingly terrifying. **JS**

Classic episode
Waiting in the Wings | *Episode 3*. While Tiberius serves out his exile, Emperor Augustus discovers his daughter has enjoyed a string of lovers, forcing him to cry: "Is there nobody in Rome who hasn't slept with my daughter?!"

◭ Derek Jacobi's Claudius—a "fool" destined for greatness.

Laverne & Shirley

Comedy | USA | 1976–83

The fabulous 1950s and 1960s from a female perspective

Cast | Penny Marshall, Cindy Williams, Michael McKean, David L. Lander
Original broadcaster | ABC **For fans of . . .** | *Happy Days* (1974)

A truly successful spin-off of the ABC powerhouse sitcom *Happy Days*, *Laverne & Shirley* focused on two guest characters who had appeared on the former show as double dates for Fonzie and Richie Cunningham: the earthy Laverne DeFazio (Penny Marshall) and her fastidious best friend Shirley Feeney (Cindy Williams), both bottlecappers at the Shotz Brewery in Milwaukee. Following their antics and those of their neighbors, the rather crazy and slightly creepy greasers Lenny Kosnowski (Michael McKean) and Squiggy Squigman (David L. Lander), *Laverne & Shirley* helped ABC create a one-two punch on its Tuesday night lineup.

At its core, *Laverne & Shirley* focused on the funniest trials and tribulations of the two young women, who balanced their dull jobs with their daydreams. Their evenings were spent fending off Lenny and Squiggy, or hanging out at the local pizzeria (run by Laverne's father). Many crossover episodes with the show's progenitor filled the first several seasons.

However, the series was not without its controversies, most notably a midseries shift in tone and setting from Milwaukee to Southern California; later shifts by ABC in the show's broadcast schedule; and a final-season departure of Cindy Williams, ostensibly removing half of the title characters from the narrative. While the show quietly petered out during its eighth season, it, nevertheless, remained popular in reruns for many years thereafter. **SL**

◉ Cindy Williams (left) and Penny Marshall in the episode "Excuse Me, May I Cut In," broadcast in 1976.

Charlie's Angels

Action/Adventure | USA | 1976–81

They're beautiful, they're brilliant, and they work for Charlie

Cast | David Doyle, Farrah Fawcett, John Forsythe, Kate Jackson, Chery Ladd, Jaclyn Smith
Original broadcaster | ABC **For fans of . . .** | *The A-Team* (1983)

"Once upon a time there were three little girls . . ." went John Forsythe's introduction to every episode, thus launching the audience into memorable split-screen titles, accompanied by a catchy theme, and a series featuring three beautiful women and plenty of action.

Plucked from dull jobs after graduation from the L.A. Police Academy by mystery millionaire Charlie (Forsythe), Sabrina Duncan (Kate Jackson), Jill Munroe (Farrah Fawcett), and Kelly Garrett (Jaclyn Smith) were recruited as private detectives. Add to the mix screwball comedy and outrageous undercover identities, accents, and outfits and producer Aaron Spelling had a hit on his hands. Yes, there were accusations of sexism, but the Angels were always firmly in control and provided

the series with "something for the dads," but also acted as role models for young girls. The fact that Forsythe never appeared on-screen—only at the end of the telephone in Bosley's office—added a sense of mystery.

When Fawcett left after only one season, a lawsuit followed, and she was replaced by Chery Ladd as Jill's sister, Kris. Shelly Hack and Tanya Roberts were later Angels, but by then the show's popularity had begun to wane and it was canceled. Two films were made in the 2000s. Despite playing it for laughs, they didn't stray too far from the show's formula and were made with love, with Forsythe voicing Charlie and Jaclyn Smith making a brief return as Kelly in the sequel. A remake in 2011 aired for just four episodes following harsh criticism. **DJ**

⬥ (L–R) Kate Jackson, Farrah Fawcett, and Jaclyn Smith on the set of *Charlie's Angels* in 1977.

Loriot

Comedy | Germany | 1976–78

Skits and sketches satirizing society

Cast | Loriot, Evelyn Hamann, Heinz Meier, Bruno Pannek
Original broadcaster | ARD
For fans of . . . | *Rudi Carrell Show* (1961), *Ein Herz und eine Seele* (1973)

Vicco von Bülow, aka Loriot, was voted Germany's greatest comedian a few years before his death in 2011, but this accolade barely did him justice. During the height of his popularity, from the 1970s to the early 1990s, his sharp wit and dry sense of humor set him apart from his peers, and many of the phrases he coined entered common parlance. "I am interested most in people who lack communication skills," he said, and *Loriot*, his first foray into TV, proved that he wasn't just perceptive, but was also skilled at satirizing society.

Born in 1923 to an aristocratic family, von Bülow served in the Second World War before studying graphic design and becoming a cartoonist. He adopted "Loriot" as his pen (and later stage) name, the French word for "oriole," the bird on his family's coat of arms. Another influence from his privileged upbringing could be seen in his humorous portrayals of Germany's postwar middle class, which included conversations based on the formal interactions and repressed behavior he witnessed in upper-class families growing up.

Loriot, a six-episode show, consisted of skits and cartoons based on everyday situations presented by Loriot and, in the last two episodes, Evelyn Hamann. Almost twenty years younger than von Bülow, the grumpy-looking German actor became a fixture as the wife, employee, or a relative of Loriot. They both appeared in other TV shows and two hugely successful movies (*Ödipussi*, 1988, and *Pappa ante Portas*, 1991) over the fifteen years that followed. **DH**

Mary Hartman, Mary Hartman

Comedy | USA | 1976–77

Postmodern comedy and social commentary

Cast | Louise Lasser, Greg Mullavey, Dody Goodman, Mary Kay Place, Graham Jarvis, Debralee Scott
Original broadcaster | Syndication
Awards | 2 Emmys
For fans of . . . | *Soap* (1977)

Creator Norman Lear parodied the TV soap opera genre with this series; its very title poked fun at the tendency of soaps to repeat dialogue. Despite its satirical side and relatively short life—it ran for two seasons, but produced more than three hundred episodes due to its daily weekday schedule—*Mary Hartman, Mary Hartman* was a complex show about a beleaguered housewife (Louise Lasser) that featured powerful dramatic moments and sharp commentary on sexual and cultural issues. This surreal blend earned it a lasting cult status and established a fictional universe that continued into several other TV series.

One of the show's greatest strengths was its female creative staff, including writers Gail Parent and Ann Marcus, and director Joan Darling. When all three networks turned down the pilot, Lear took the show to syndication. Lasser's performance in particular made the series a fast-growing favorite. Its habit of piling on tragedy after tragedy, including deaths by mass murder, and its barbed attacks on the very medium on which it aired soon drew critical praise that has lasted decades after the end of its run.

The Mary Hartman universe rippled into the music world when cast member Mary Kay Place received a Grammy nomination for an album she recorded as her character, country singer Loretta Haggers. Local Los Angeles station KTTV also joined in the fun by running a parody of its own Metronews under the title "Metronews, Metronews." **ATB**

Domenica In

Talk show | Italy | 1976–present

Conceived by the Italian government to keep people at home during a period of austerity

---

Cast | Corrado, Raffaella Carrà, Pippo Baudo,
Lorella Cuccarini, Mara Venier
Original broadcaster | RAI 1
For fans of . . . | *Festival di San Remo* (1951),
Buona Domenica (1985)

Domenica In was the first all-day program broadcast on
Italian TV. It was transmitted for the first time on October
3, 1976, and was hosted by Corrado. He gave the
program its name, a play on words—"In" meaning both
"fashionable" and "at home." The show was intended to
encourage Italians to stay home on Sunday afternoons
instead of taking the car for a drive in the country. At the
time, gas companies had increased the price of fuel, so
the Italian government imposed a period of austerity.
The show soon became a great success.

    Domenica In lasted for six hours—a revolution in
Italian TV, as programs had never been more than
one hour long. It featured films made for TV, musical
performances, the Italian lottery, and a sports slot
for the soccer championship matches that took
place on Italian fields. In 1979, Corrado retired due to
disagreements with Paolo Grassi, the chairman of the
Italian network RAI. He was replaced by the talented
and versatile Pippo Baudo, who hosted the show until
1985. Baudo introduced several changes to the original
format and made *Domenica In* the most successful
program on Italian TV. Many hosts have succeeded
her with varying degrees of success. From 1985 the
rival program *Buona Domenica* (which has since been
known by various names) was broadcast by Canale 5,
and introduced new and different editorial strategies.
The competition between the two channels prevailed
over the rich offering of entertainment that *Domenica
In* began in the mid-1970s. **SM**

Classic episode
Annual Special. From 1995 onward, on the Sunday
following the Festival of San Remo, the show was
broadcast from the Ariston Theatre, San Remo, and
was devoted to the singing contest that had just
taken place there.

⌾ Celine Dion was one of Pippo Baudo's guests in 1997.

The Bionic Woman

Action/Adventure | USA | 1976–78

*Female-led action adventure that helped build a bionic dynasty—
better, stronger, faster*

Classic episode
The Vega Influence | *Season 2, episode 9.* In a dark
and unsettling episode, Jaime is pushed to her
limits when she and a deaf girl are the only people
left unaffected after everyone at a remote island
base is zombified by an alien meteorite.

⊘ Jaime (Lindsay Wagner) is unable to convince anyone of her true
identity in the episode "Deadly Ringers."

Cast | Lindsay Wagner, Richard Anderson, Martin
E. Brooks, Sam Chew Jr., Ford Rainey, Martha Scott
Original broadcasters | ABC, NBC
Award | 1 Emmy
For fans of . . . | *The Six Million Dollar Man* (1974)

Being the girlfriend of a hero can be dangerous, but
for tennis pro Jaime Sommers (Lindsay Wagner), it was
also her salvation. A former love of Six Million Dollar
Man Steve Austin (Lee Majors), Jaime first appeared
in a two-parter on that show, but died after rejecting
the bionic limbs that she received after a parachuting
accident. Viewer reaction to her death was so negative
that the character was resurrected and given a spin-off
show of her own.

Like Austin, Sommers had bionic legs and a bionic
right arm; unlike Austin, she had a bionic right ear
instead of a bionic eye. Working as a teacher on an Air
Force base, Jaime was assigned top-secret missions by
the head of the Office of Scientific Intelligence, Oscar
Goldman (Richard Anderson), which took her all over
the world in a variety of cover identities. Wagner's
earnest, naturalistic portrayal contrasted with many
of her costars and lent her character an honesty that
balanced the fantastic elements of her adventures. She
joined other 1970s female TV leads, such as *Wonder
Woman*'s Lynda Carter, in a welcome wave of more
empowered women on the small screen. Not every
young girl at home could leap tall buildings or bend
steel, but she might realize that the future could be
bright thanks to the Bionic Woman.

Wagner reprised her role in three reunion TV movies.
In the last of these, *Bionic Ever After?* (1994), Jaime and
Steve were married, presumably to run in slow motion
together for as long as they both shall live. **ATB**

Ripping Yarns

Comedy | UK | 1976–79

Celebrated send-up of prewar English adventure stories

Cast | Michael Palin, Ian Ogilvy, Roy Kinnear, John Le Mesurier, Jan Francis, Denholm Elliott, Joan Sanderson, David Griffin
Original broadcaster | BBC One
For fans of . . . | *Fawlty Towers* (1975)

When *Monty Python's Flying Circus* (1969) ended in 1974, the six members went off and started other projects. *Ripping Yarns* was the first outing of two of them, Michael Palin and Terry Jones. While the Pythons were widely reputed to have dealt a knockout blow to traditional British comedy, this new show targeted traditional English-language modes of literary and screen fiction in nine self-contained stories. The opening episode took a swipe at private schools, which it depicted not as establishments in which callow youths were turned into men, but as havens for sociopaths of all kinds, particularly bullies. The second tale, about an old bore who got caught up in a bank raid and joined the robbers, satirized Ealing film comedies such as *Kind Hearts and Coronets* (1949). The third, a parody of prisoner-of-war fiction, involved a captured British officer who built a network of escape tunnels so complex that after the war it became the Munich subway. The fourth took the already far-fetched concept of the locked-room mystery so strongly associated with the novels of Agatha Christie and raised it to a farcical level. The series' other targets were explorers, ghost stories, colonialists, spies, and tales of achievement on the sports field. Palin appeared in every episode, Jones in only one.

Ripping Yarns was not satire: it had no savage indignation, and did not disapprove of its source material. It was affectionate and nostalgic, but it had the effect of banishing the old genres into history. **GL**

Open All Hours

Comedy | UK | 1976–85

Golden comedy about a miserly shopkeeper and his put-upon nephew

Cast | Ronnie Barker, David Jason, Lynda Barron, Stephanie Cole, Barbara Flynn
Original broadcaster | BBC Two
For fans of . . . | *Steptoe and Son* (1962), *Last of the Summer Wine* (1973), *Porridge* (1974)

It wasn't edgy or groundbreaking, yet *Open All Hours*, about a man and his nephew who run a corner store, was voted the eighth-best comedy of all time in 2004's Britain's Best Sitcom poll. Much of that was due to the performances of its two leads—Ronnie Barker and David Jason, two giants of British comedy.

The show was created by Roy Clarke. It was Ronnie Barker's own idea to play shopkeeper Arkwright with a stutter, which he used for maximum comic effect. Many of the funniest moments involved Arkwright's attempts at delivering a speech, or his nephew, Granville (David Jason), mimicking him. Supporting characters included Nurse Gladys Emmanuel (Lynda Baron), Arkwright's one interest beyond the walls of his shop (he is often found up a ladder outside her window, trying to woo her), Delphine Featherstone (Stephanie Cole), aka Black Widow, and Milk Woman (Barbara Flyn), with whom Granville has a fling.

The store where the action was set was of a kind that belonged to another era, so nostalgia was another factor in the show's success. Arkwright's adherence to postwar austerity values gave rise to humor, as did his violent cash register, unique salesmanship, and the savings tin that he kept under an old sink.

In 2013, the BBC revived the show as *Still Open All Hours*, with Granville now running the shop in a manner similar to that of his late uncle, and ordering his own son Leroy around. A high-rating Christmas show in 2014 kicked off a full series at the beginning of 2015. **LH**

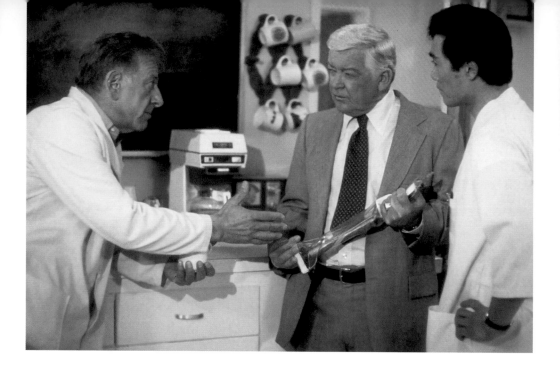

Quincy, M.E.

Crime/Mystery | USA | 1976–83

The cases of a crime-solving coroner bringing justice to the people of Los Angeles

Cast | Jack Klugman, Robert Ito, John S. Ragin, Garry Walberg, Val Bisoglio, Lynette Mettey, Anita Gillette
Original broadcaster | NBC **For fans of . . .** | *Silent Witness* (1996), *CSI: Crime Scene Investigation* (2000)

Nominated for numerous Emmy Awards, *Quincy, M.E.* remains one of the best-loved crime and medical dramas of the 1970s and 1980s. Created by Glenn A. Larson, it was one of the first medical-examiner-plays-sleuth TV series, and launched as part of the NBC Mystery Movie series, which also created *Columbo* (1971). Like the character of Columbo, Dr. Quincy investigated mysterious deaths in and around Los Angeles. Not all of Quincy's cases were the result of murder; the series covered numerous health and social issues, including drug abuse, diseases, hazardous waste, and anorexia. Quincy cared about the victims and was passionate about bringing justice and exposing injustice. In fact, Quincy gave up a lucrative private medical practice

to work in the public service. He lived on a boat in a dry dock, which he was forever working on, and drove around in the coroner's vehicle. Although he frequented Danny's, the bar on the harbor, he was more often either in his medical lab or out and about pursuing leads.

Golden Globe- and Emmy-winning actor Jack Klugman played the irascible title role, whose full name was never given. Dr. Quincy often changed his mind during the course of the investigation and expressed impatience as others were slow to catch up, but Klugman's comic genius and lovable nature shone through. He appeared in all but one of the one hundred and forty-eight episodes, missing only from "Has Anybody Here Seen Quincy?" in season two. **SJG**

⬛ (L–R) Jack Klugman (Quincy), Garry Walberg (LAPD Lieutenant Frank Monahan), and Robert Ito (lab assistant Sam Fujiyama).

The Krofft Supershow

Variety | USA | 1976–78

Action-packed anthology aimed at a teen audience

Cast | Michael Lembeck, Jay Robinson, Billy Barty, Ted Eccles, Deirdre Hall, Judy Strangis, Norman Alden, Frank Welker, Lennie Weinrib   **Original broadcaster** | ABC   **For fans of . . .** | *Shazam!* (1974)

Saturday mornings were a magical time for any kid watching US network affiliates in the 1970s, as the lineups were packed with cartoons and entertainment aimed directly at them. Sid and Marty Krofft, designers on *The Banana Splits* (1968) and producers of beloved children's TV classics such as *H.R. Pufnstuf* (1969) and *Land of the Lost* (1974), provided a great deal of the programming, with many of their most memorable characters and shows airing on the anthological series *The Krofft Supershow*.

Hosted by the fictional glam band Kaptain Kool and the Kongs (with many of their songs provided by the Osmonds), the show ran a number of ongoing serials in fifteen-minute segments in its first season,

including "Dr. Shrinker," "Electra Woman and Dyna Girl," and "Wonderbug." Segments of "The Lost Saucer" ran early in the first year when the series debuted at ninety minutes, but that story line was dropped when the show moved to a one-hour format.

Perhaps the best-remembered segment of *The Krofft Supershow* remains "Electra Woman and Dyna Girl," a female counterpart to the *Batman* (1966) TV series; Judy Strangis, who played Dyna Girl, was *Batman* production manager and director Sam Strangis' sister. The sixteen segments of the superhero series were later syndicated as eight full episodes and featured notable guest villains such as Malachi Throne (who also played a *Batman* foe) and horror-film icon Sid Haig. **ATB**

⬥ Kaptain Kool and the Kongs in their glam rags, broadcast on September 11, 1976.

The Muppet Show

Comedy | USA/UK | 1976–81

*The Muppets take over a dilapidated theater
and face a critical mauling every night*

Cast | Jim Henson, Frank Oz, Dave Goelz, Jerry Nelson,
Richard Hunt, Louise Gold
Original broadcasters | Syndication (USA), ITV (UK)
Awards | 3 BAFTAs, 4 Emmys
For fans of . . . | *Jim Henson's The Storyteller* (1987)

Surprisingly perhaps, *The Muppet Show* was a British
production, funded by Lew Grade of ATV. Having failed
to trade on the success of *Sesame Street* (1969) in the
United States, Jim Henson brought his idea of an old-
fashioned vaudeville pastiche to Elstree Studios, near
London. Kermit the Frog, Henson's most enduring
character, was given the job of host and frantic producer
of an inventive and unhinged array of cabaret acts,
including the divalike Miss Piggy (who was an amalgam
of certain Hollywood stars of the time), the pedestrian
stand-up comic Fozzie Bear, the Great Gonzo (whose
escapology acts always ended in disaster), plus funky
house band Dr. Teeth and The Electric Mayhem.

Regular sketches included ballroom dancing, in
which the competitors would deliver cheesy one-liners;
a cooking slot starring the Swedish Chef (speaking a
made-up language that was not remotely Swedish);
the medical soap "Veterinarian's Hospital"; and pun-
laden sci-fi epic "Pigs in Space." From the royal box
of the theater, critics Statler and Waldorf heckled and
provided a running commentary on just how lame the
productions were. Self-deprecation has always been a
huge part of the muppet charm. Special guests, such
as Diana Ross, Elton John, and John Cleese, also battled
the furry characters for screen time. Being mistreated
by the muppets became the most wanted guest spot
for Hollywood stars. **JS**

◗ Miss Piggy, Fozzie Bear, Kermit the Frog, and Gonzo were the
stars of the show; here with guest Liza Minnelli.

The Gong Show

Game show | USA | 1976–80

Bizarre amateur hour that featured some of the weirdest acts in TV history

Cast | Chuck Barris, Gary Owens, Trixie Dejonge
Original broadcaster | NBC, syndication
For fans of . . . | *Treasure Hunt* (1982), *Britain's Got Talent* (2007)

Chuck Barris, producer of game shows such as *The Dating Game* (1965) and *The Newlywed Game* (1966), stepped in front of the camera to host an insane cavalcade of amateur acts (and some professional performances) that ran the gamut from mildly strange to truly surreal. Despite his embarrassment at appearing as emcee, he was endearing in the extreme. If an act impressed the panel of three celebrity judges—over the years, the show featured the likes of Jaye P. Morgan, Arte Johnson, Jamie Farr, and Rip Taylor—contestants could win $516.32 on the daytime incarnation of the show and $712.05 on the syndicated episodes. If they did not win over the panel, they were "gonged" via a large gong and mallet wielded by one of the judges. The audience would often start screaming and chanting for a judge to gong the act long before they finally did, giving everyone from recurring performer Gene Gene the Dancing Machine to future Broadway Annie Andrea McArdle their time in the TV spotlight. The paper bag-headed Unknown Comic (Murray Langston) frequently taunted "Chuckie" during his many appearances, and when Christmas rolled around, acts were allowed to perform with no threat of a gong at all.

Despite its popularity, the show was canceled due to what some believed was mounting concern about the bawdy nature of certain acts, including an infamous appearance by the "Popsicle Twins." Various revivals were attempted over the years, but none lasted very long before the gong rang out once again. **ATB**

Classic episode
Episode 501 | *July 21, 1978.* In the final episode on NBC, after the show had been axed, Chuck Barris appeared as a contestant and sang "Take This Job and Shove It." He was gonged by Jamie Farr, and the network censored his response.

◉ Chuck Barris hosts *The Gong Show*, in his own special way.

The Fall and Rise of Reginald Perrin

Comedy | UK | 1976–79

A suburban midlife crisis takes a surreal turn

Cast | Leonard Rossiter, Pauline Yates, John Barron, Sue Nicholls
Original broadcaster | BBC One
For fans of . . . | *The Good Life* (1975), *A Very Peculiar Practice* (1986)

The repetition of Reginald Iolanthe Perrin's daily life drove him mad. Every morning, he walked to the station, caught the same train alongside the same suits, arrived at his job late, by the same number of minutes, and went through the same routine of meetings and reports. Eventually, he ended it all by leaving his clothes on a beach and faking his own death.

Adapted by David Nobbs from his own novels, and starring Leonard Rossiter, who beautifully captured the comic desperation of the character, the show was the story of a man obsessed with the idea of escaping the machine in which he is just a cog. In the second season, Reggie returned from his fake death and opened a shop called Grot, which he stocked with useless items in the hope that it would fail. This backfired when customers snapped up the novelty items. The third and final season saw Reggie and his friends start a commune. It also failed, and Reggie was back to square one.

In 1996, twelve years after Rossiter's death, a less successful follow-up series was made: *The Legacy of Reginald Perrin*. Again written by Nobbs, and also adapted from a novel, the seven episodes reunited many of the characters from the original series, brought together after Reggie is killed by a falling billboard advertising accident insurance.

Satirical and surreal, *The Fall and Rise of Reginald Perrin* was an ingenious study of middle-class, middle-aged frustration. **WH**

The Duchess of Duke Street

Historical drama | UK | 1976–77

Period drama with an ambitious lead

Cast | Gemma Jones, Christopher Cazenove, June Brown, Richard Vernon, Victoria Plunkett
Original broadcaster | BBC One
For fans of . . . | *Upstairs, Downstairs* (1971), *Downton Abbey* (2010)

The award-winning team that created *Upstairs, Downstairs* (1971) served up another period piece focusing on the rags-to-riches journey of a feisty Cockney cook. Like *Upstairs, Downstairs*, the writers continued the successful formula of life above and below stairs, this time following the day-to-day dramas of the hotel staff and the rather colorful guests. Using the real-life exploits of hotel-owner and society hostess Rosa Lewis (allegedly, the mistress of the Prince of Wales) as the basis of the series added fascinating insight into the comings and goings of the fictional Bentinck Hotel on Duke Street, London.

Gemma Jones (later known for TV series *Spooks* (2002), the *Harry Potter* films (2001–11), and as Bridget Jones' mom) gave great depth to cook Louisa Trotter, whose tough, no-nonsense ambitious exterior only masked her vulnerability. With the on–off relationship blossoming between commoner (Louisa) and aristocracy (Lord Charlie Haslemere, played beautifully by Christopher Cazenove)—despite doomed marriages to other people, an ill-timed pregnancy, and other scandals that threatened their union—there was enough meat to this delicious concoction to keep viewers transfixed until the series came to a natural end after two seasons, having taken viewers through Victorian London right up to postwar England in the 1920s. For British viewers watching the show today, the surprise turn is the regular appearances by June Brown (*EastEnders*' Dot Cotton) as Louisa's mother. **JV**

The Sullivans

Soap opera | Australia | 1976–83

Soap opera set during the Second World War and told in close to real time

Classic episode
The Court Martial | *1977*. Sub-Lieutenant Ray Henderson (Mel Gibson) visits the Sullivan home to inform them that Kitty's boyfriend is to be court-martialed on Kitty's birthday. Geoff Sullivan starts at the boys' school and is bullied.

⬥ Lorraine Bayly as Grace, the Sullivan matriarch.

Cast | Paul Cronin, Lorraine Bayly, Andrew McFarlane, Vivean Gray, Susan Hannaford
Original broadcaster | Nine Network
For fans of . . . | *Sons and Daughters* (1982), *Neighbours* (1985), *The Pacific* (2010)

The Sullivans was unique for being both a soap opera and a war drama. It followed the events and effects of the Second World War through the eyes of a middle-class Melbourne family and their friends. Set amid a backdrop of often-genuine 1930s and 1940s furniture and props, the highs and lows of domestic drama were broadcast four nights a week in half-hour episodes for most of its seven-year run in Australia. It became incredibly popular in Gibraltar in the 1980s, where it was shown in a prime-time slot, and the phrase "doing a Sullivan" was synonymous with having a tough life.

Much of the program's initial audience had survived the Second World War or were the next generation who wanted to understand it. Because the story was told in as close to real time as possible, the audience had to wait for news to travel, and finding out what was happening to sons Tom, John, and Terry became nail-biting stuff. The home front was just as fraught. Episodes dealt with racism, politics, spousal abuse, pacifism, and bittersweet memories of the First World War. The last few years of the series examined the effects of war on its survivors.

The blend of kitchen sink drama and real-time war action in *The Sullivans* made it special. The attention to detail and the newsreels shown about real battles and events were more thorough than many serious dramas. These elements alone made *The Sullivans* worth watching. However, it also showcased performers such as Mel Gibson, Sam Neill, and Kylie Minogue, who would later become international stars. **SJG**

The Signalman

Fantasy/Horror/Sci-Fi | UK | 1976

Eerie adaptation of a short story by Dickens

Cast | Denholm Elliott, Bernard Lloyd
Original broadcaster | BBC One
For fans of . . . | *Whistle and I'll Come to You* (1968),
The Stalls of Barchester (1971), *A Warning to the
Curious* (1972)

An annual Christmas treat in the UK in the 1970s,
A Ghost Story for Christmas put fear into the festive
season. In 1976, the sixth in the series was a spooky
drama called *The Signalman,* based on a short story
by Charles Dickens. Creepy and disturbing it was the
perfect antidote to sleigh bells and mince pies.

Made by Lawrence Gordon Clark, *The Signalman*
starred Denholm Elliott and was adapted by British
screenwriter Andrew Davies, whose later successes
included scripts for *A Very Peculiar Practice* (1986), *House
of Cards* (1990), *Pride and Prejudice* (1995), and *Bridget
Jones's Diary* (2001). The story had been produced on
radio several times previously and dramatized with
Boris Karloff as part of the US TV series *Suspense* (1949).

The tale featured a lonely, middle-aged signalman
(Elliott) and an ominous traveler (Bernard Lloyd) who
is invited into the signal box. There, the signalman tells
the traveler about an apparition he sometimes sees
at the entrance to the railway tunnel, after which an
awful tragedy always ensues—first a crash in the tunnel
(Dickens was likely inspired by the 1861 Clayton Tunnel
rail crash) and then a bride who fell from a train. The
final victim turned out to be the signalman himself.

Clark was a master of quiet, atmospheric dramas
with a twist in the tail. Elliott captured the protagonist's
increasing desperation, while the tone of the piece
was supported by the atmospheric Victorian setting.
Even when you knew what was coming, the end was
a shock. **WH**

Children of the Stones

Drama | UK | 1977

Haunting drama set inside a stone circle

Cast | Gareth Thomas, Iain Cuthbertson, Freddie
Jones, Veronica Strong, Ruth Dunning
Original broadcaster | ITV
For fans of . . . | *Ace of Wands* (1970), *Catweazel* (1970),
The Ghosts of Motley Hall (1976)

The creators of *Children of the Stones* were not afraid of
being frightening, and the result was one of the most
haunting kids' shows ever broadcast. The story began
with astrophysicist Adam Brake (Gareth Thomas, later to
become famous as the titular character of *Blake's 7*) and
his son, Matthew (Peter Demim), arriving at their new
home in Milbury, a picturesque British village located
inside a megalithic stone circle. The show was actually
filmed in the English village of Avebury, in Wiltshire,
which sits inside just such a circle. The realism of the
setting enhanced the scary vibe—much assisted by
the deeply creepy soundtrack.

Needless to say, all was not as it seemed. The locals
were hiding an ancient secret and the local lord of the
manor, Hendrick (a sinister Iain Cuthbertson), went to
almost any lengths to keep it.

The story that unraveled over seven episodes was
remarkably complex for a show aimed at children, with
a time loop that stretched back millennia. It verged on
impenetrability at times, but gave its young viewers
just enough understanding to leave them intrigued
rather than frustrated. Oblique and intellectual rather
than in-your-face and gory, its chills haven't dated in
the years since it first broadcast. It's a show for children
that might send even adults scurrying behind the sofa.

A belated sequel, *Return to the Stones*, by original
writers Jeremy Burnham and Trevor Ray, was released
in 2012, revealing what happened when a now grown-
up Matthew returned to Milbury. **RL**

Roots

Drama | USA | 1977

Highly rated adaptation of Alex Haley's blockbuster slavery saga

Cast | Olivia Cole, Ben Vereen, LeVar Burton, John Amos, Leslie Uggams, Carolyn Jones, Louis Gossett Jr.
Original broadcaster | ABC **Awards** | 9 Emmys, 1 Golden Globe **For fans of . . .** | *Queen* (1993)

Alex Haley's *Roots: The Saga of an American Family* was first published in 1976, and although based on what Haley believed to be a real sequence of events, the details and conversations were fictionalized.

The TV adaptation of the book in the following year probably did more to open the world's eyes to the history and injustices of slavery than any TV program or movie before or since. The story began in 1767 with the kidnap of the son of an African chief by slave traders and his transport to America. Beaten and sold at auction, Kunta Kinte (LeVar Burton) was forced to accept the slave name Toby Reynolds. His foot was cut off after he attempted to escape. In time, Toby had a daughter named Kizzy (Leslie Uggams), who was sold to a

neighboring slave owner who raped and impregnated her. Kizzy's son, George (Ben Vereen), grew up to be a trainer of fighting birds, earning him privileges and the nickname "Chicken George" until he is sold to a visiting Englishman. The Civil War brought freedom for the slaves, but George's sons soon discovered how empty this freedom could be. **JS**

Classic episode
Episode 2 | January 24, 1977. Kunta Kinte endures the violent and torturous journey to the New World on the slave ship. He is then bought at auction by Fiddler, with whom he strikes up a tense friendship.

⚉ Sam Bennett (Richard Roundtree) tries to introduce some cheer into the troubled life of Kizzy Reynolds (Leslie Uggams).

Lou Grant

Drama | USA | 1977–82

Fast-paced drama set in a Los Angeles newspaper office

Cast | Edward Asner, Robert Walden, Nancy Marchand, Linda Kelsey, Mason Adams, Daryl Anderson
Original broadcaster | CBS **Awards** | 13 Emmys, 3 Golden Globes **For fans of . . .** | *Cagney & Lacey* (1981)

While popular characters may find themselves spun off into their own series, it is usually within the same genre. It is rare for a sitcom to produce a sequel that is a drama. Lou Grant (Edward Asner) had been the head of a TV newsroom in *The Mary Tyler Moore Show* (1970), and in his own show he was the city editor for a newspaper. He inherited a team of old hands and ambitious newcomers, who learned to rely on his no-nonsense demeanor and avuncular compassion. Presiding over all was the owner of the paper, wealthy widow Mrs. Pynchon (Nancy Marchand), whose uncompromising attitudes were often at odds with Lou's values. Just as *The Mary Tyler Moore Show* had never been afraid to allow room for the drama to breathe, *Lou Grant* could be very funny, with characters making wisecracks and ironic observations at the pace of a sassy sitcom—without the laugh track. The social commentary was surprisingly left-leaning with a strong liberal conscience, often played out in debates between Lou and Mrs. Pynchon. Although the thread of the series was a battle around the ethics of good journalism, it never became preachy. **JS**

Classic episode

Hostages | Season 1, episode 2. Rossi is praised for his coverage of an attempted robbery in which the shop owner shot the young thief dead. His celebrations are curtailed when the brother of the dead boy holds the news team at gunpoint.

⊕ Golden Globe winner Edward Asner in the title role of Lou Grant.

Citizen Smith

Comedy | UK | 1977–80

Debut comedy from John Sullivan that brought the world Robert Lindsay

Cast | Robert Lindsay, Mike Grady, Cheryl Hall, Peter Vaughan, Hilda Braid
Original broadcaster | BBC One
For fans of . . . | *Whatever Happened to the Likely Lads?* (1973), *Just Good Friends* (1983)

John Sullivan was one of the most successful comedy writers in the United Kingdom and wrote some of the most popular sitcoms in TV history, but in 1977 he was unknown. *Citizen Smith*, his first show, has all the qualities for which he would become renowned: wordplay, realistic dialogue, and sympathetic, but not necessarily likable, characters. It is not as polished as his later work, but is immensely enjoyable and funny.

Citizen Smith was about "Wolfie" Smith (Robert Lindsay)—a Che Guevara-esque revolutionary wannabe who ran the Tooting Popular Front—all six members of it. As Shirley (Cheryl Hall), his long-suffering girlfriend, pointed out, it wasn't very popular. Wolfie was really an unemployed petty criminal. He accidentally got engaged to Shirley and had to contend with her disapproving parents—her Dad called him the "flaming Yeti." Most of the episodes revolved around plans for revolution going disastrously wrong, as well as encounters with the local gangster.

Citizen Smith had a memorable title sequence as Wolfie emerged from Tooting Broadway tube station shouting "Power to the people!" The moment was ruined every time, for example, as he woke up a baby and was hit by the mother. *Citizen Smith* was Lindsay's big break and he has since starred in multiple films, dramas, plays, and sitcoms. He exuded charm, charisma, and vulnerability as Wolfie, a man who thinks he is cleverer than he is. Watching *Citizen Smith* is the perfect way to see how Sullivan and Lindsay made it big. **LH**

Abigail's Party

Comedy | UK | 1977

A cringeworthy comedy of social etiquette— "We've got whiskey gin, vodka whatever you like"

Cast | Alison Steadman, Tim Stern, Janine Duvitski, John Salthouse, Harriet Reynolds
Original broadcaster | BBC One
For fans of . . . | *The Good Life* (1971), *Absolutely Fabulous* (1992), *Gavin & Stacey* (2007)

When mild-mannered middle-aged mom Susan (Harriet Reynolds) allows her fifteen-year-old daughter Abigail to throw her first party, Susan's neighbors—Beverly (Alison Steadman) and Laurence (Tim Stern)—invite her to join them for drinks with their new neighbors, the timid Angela (Janine Duvitski) and her sullen ex-soccer player husband, Tony (John Salthouse). Although Beverly believes herself to be the height of sophistication, her overt bullying of Laurence—"You're a boring little bugger, Laurence"—and a lack of tact or self-awareness doom the gathering from the start.

Mike Leigh's use of improvisation is legendary; he presents a situation to each of his actors and allows his stories to develop organically based on how the cast react in character during long rehearsal periods. This particular production had been a stage play performed at the Hampstead Theatre before being adapted for the BBC's "Play for Today" strand. It subsequently became a favorite among drama students thanks to the hugely quotable dialogue, which references Greek singer Demis Roussos—"We don't want to listen to that fat Greek caterwauling all night"—and the virtues of olives.

Tucked away on the BBC's second TV channel (at the time watched predominantly by educated middle-class viewers), *Abigail's Party* gained some critical acclaim. When a repeat was broadcast two years later, while the BBC's sole rival ITV was off the air due to job action, sixteen million viewers tuned in, making Mike Leigh and Alison Steadman household names. **JS**

Auf los geht's los

Game show | Germany | 1977–86

This Saturday evening game show took the German version of the genre up a notch or two by attracting international guest stars and introducing significant prizes

Cast | Joachim Fuchsberger
Original broadcaster | Südwestfunk/ARD
For fans of . . . | *Wetten, dass . . . ?* (1981), *The Price Is Right* (1972), *The Tonight Show with Jay Leno* (1992), *Ant & Dec's Saturday Night Takeaway* (2002)

Joachim Fuchsberger was one of the first television hosts in Germany to present world-famous stars effectively. Catherine Deneuve, Barbra Streisand, Christopher Lee, Robert de Niro—the list of guest stars on *Auf los geht's los* (*On Your Marks, Get Set, Go*) was impressive. As a result, the format took off, and was the prototype for *Wetten, dass . . .?*, with which it later competed.

In the show, ordinary people competed in word games, interspersed with chat between Fuchsberger and the celebrity guests and interaction with the audience. There was always a musical guest, who would play requests from the studio audience. A central strand was the "A–Z" game, when contestants had to guess the letters of a particular word, as in the popular word game Hangman. At the end of this, the winner's points were multiplied by 100 and converted to Deutschmarks. Long-distance travel tickets could also be won, and the journey offered was always extensively described before and after the trip, reflecting the boom in foreign travel at this time.

For Joachim Fuchsberger, the game show was all about the people and his conversations with interesting personalities. Technical gimmicks, such as those later introduced in *Wetten, dass . . .?* (1981), were limited to a dot matrix scoring machine placed behind the contestants: He believed in creating a potpourri of entertainment, which he smoothly adapted to the public's changing taste, a recipe for success that remained popular for almost ten years. **NK**

Classic episode
1984. Fuchsberger hosts Tami Stronach, Barret Oliver, Wolfgang Petersen, and Bernd Eichinger as stars of *The Neverending Story* (1984). Fellow star Noah Hathaway was not invited because he had demanded an increase in his movie fee.

◐ Joachim Fuchsberger, who died in 2014, stamped his own personality on *Auf los geht's los*.

The Richard Pryor Show

Variety | USA | 1977

Cutting-edge, controversial, and clever comedy that lasted only four episodes

Cast | Richard Pryor, Robin Williams, Edie McClurg, Jimmy Martinez
Original broadcaster | NBC
Award | 1 Emmy
For fans of . . . | *Saturday Night Live* (1975)

Radical and brilliantly hilarious comedian Richard Pryor was hired to star in his own variety show after a special he hosted was a hit. Broadcast in a prime-time slot on Tuesdays against ABC's popular TV shows *Laverne & Shirley* (1976) and *Happy Days* (1974), the show consisted of Pryor performing a range of characters, including a money-seeking priest, a wino, and a racist rock star. The rest of the cast comprised the most cutting-edge comedians of the day, some of whom went on to have impressive careers in Hollywood, particularly Robin Williams, Paul Mooney, Tim Reid, Sandra Bernhard, Edie McClurg, and Marsha Warfield.

Pryor filmed only four episodes of the show and there were controversies and fights with the network concerning nearly every scene. A skit in which Pryor appeared as a machine-gun-toting rocker who kills all of his white fans caused quite a stir. The second episode also featured a controversial sketch that showed a woman in a park describing what her first lesbian experience was like. Probably one of the most shocking and revealing skits of the series came during the last episode, which featured a roast of Pryor, who sat with his head down and laughed mildly while the regular comedians on the show either overpraised him or tore him apart with insults.

The decision to air the edgy *The Richard Pryor Show* during weekday prime time may have doomed it from the start, although Pryor was probably too honest and too wild for TV viewers at any hour. **RP**

Classic episode
Pilot episode | *September 13, 1977*. The original opening had Pryor explaining that he'd given up nothing to have a network TV show, while the camera pulled back to reveal that he was naked and had no genitals. That opening never aired.

Ⓐ Straight-talking Richard Pryor came to prominence in the 1970s with a pertinacious brand of comedy.

Secret Army

Historical drama | UK/Belgium | 1977–79

Nerve-shreddingly tense story of the Belgian "evasion lines" during the Second World War

Cast | Bernard Hepton, Angela Richards, Juliet Hammond-Hill, Clifford Rose, Michael Culver
Original broadcasters | BBC One (UK), BRT (Belgium)
Award | 1 BAFTA
For fans of . . . | *Colditz* (1972), *Tenko* (1981)

Secret Army was the story of Brussels café owner Albert Foiret (Bernard Hepton) and his friends as they dealt with life under German occupation. However, under the noses of Nazi customers, Albert ran "Lifeline"—a network throughout Belgium and France created to hide crashed British airmen and smuggle them home to Britain. Anyone caught helping the evaders faced being handed to the sadistic Gestapo officer, Sturmbannführer Kessler (Clifford Rose).

Secret Army was a cat-and-mouse thriller. Would the airmen get home? (Not always.) Would the heroes survive? (Definitely not always.) Supporting characters were killed regularly, so the viewers constantly feared for the safety of the heroes. As the characters and plot were based on real people and events, *Secret Army* emphasized just how traumatic living under occupation was, and the viewers questioned what they would have done in similar circumstances.

The three seasons of *Secret Army* were among the best British TV drama ever made. Boosted by location filming in Belgium and by a flawless cast at the top of their game, the show was gripping (even though the pace was more leisurely than modern shows). At its best, it was unbeatable, and its portrayal of characters was groundbreaking—in particular showing Germans and Gestapo officers with personal lives and consciences. Unfortunately, due to the 1980s parody *'Allo 'Allo* that used an almost identical setup, *Secret Army* isn't always remembered as it deserves to be. **PC**

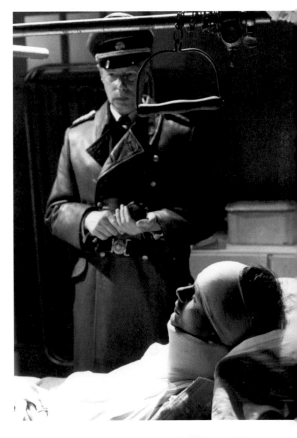

Classic episode
Collaborator | *Season 3, episode 10.* The Nazis retreat, but the secret army are in peril: from Belgians suspecting collaboration, Communists out for revenge, and Luftwaffe Major Reinhardt who realizes that Albert was in charge of Lifeline.

⬥ Clifford Rose (Major Kessler) interrogates Martin Burrows as a captured airman.

Three's Company

Comedy | USA | 1977–84

King of the jiggle shows

Cast | John Ritter, Suzanne Somers, Joyce DeWitt, Priscilla Barnes, Don Knotts, Norman Fell, Audra Lindley
Original broadcaster | ABC   **Awards** | 1 Emmy, 2 Golden Globes   **For fans of . . .** | *Charlie's Angels* (1976)

Eligible bachelor lands a swanky apartment deal with two beautiful roommates: for many a terrific dream, but it's actually the premise of this sitcom. Based on the British series *Man About the House* (1973), *Three's Company* was both a staple of Tuesday evening TV viewing in the United States and a vehicle for comedian John Ritter. As aspiring chef Jack Tripper, a pratfall-laden charlatan, he pretended to be gay in order to live with his two lovely roommates. *Three's Company* was also known for contributing to (in fact being the centerpiece of) the success of the "jiggle" shows: late 1970s TV series that featured buxom women in order to attract male viewers in large numbers. The series was supposed to last only six episodes, but a midseason debut achieved

such strong ratings (one of the highest midseason debuts of all time) that the show was brought back in the fall. During its run several cast changes occurred: Suzanne Somers and Joyce DeWitt had a well-publicized falling-out when Somers left in 1980; after taping their scenes separately, the two actresses did not speak to each other for more than thirty years. **SL**

Classic episode

Lee Ain't Heavy, He's My Brother | *Season 4, episode 21*. Jack is on edge when his brother Lee comes to visit and starts impressing the girls. Things are complicated further when Lee and Chrissy (Suzanne Somers) decide to date.

⊘ (L–R) Joyce DeWitt, John Ritter, and Suzanne Somers in the episode "Lee Ain't Heavy, He's My Brother" in 1980.

CHiPs

Drama | USA | 1977–83

A cheesy buddy cop show—heavy on the stunts

Cast | Erik Estrada, Larry Wilcox, Robert Pine, Bruce Jenner, Tom Reilly **Original broadcaster** | NBC
For fans of . . . | *Starsky & Hutch* (1975), *T.J. Hooker* (1982), *The A-Team* (1983)

Created by Rick Rosner, *CHiPs* was an action drama that included a surprising amount of comedy. Although the show was well known for its over-the-top freeway pileups, there was no real violence. *CHiPs* starred Larry Wilcox as Officer Jon Baker, trying to steer his macho partner Frank "Ponch" Poncherello (Erik Estrada) out of trouble as they patrolled the California highways. Occasionally the team was reprimanded by the stern but supportive Sergeant Joseph Getraer (Robert Pine).

Typically, an episode began with Ponch and Jon on routine patrol or being given a specific assignment, in which they would discover suspects racing away, thus leading them into a high-speed chase. Sometimes a few moments of darker emotion would interrupt the fun. Despite their chemistry on the show, Wilcox and Estrada reportedly clashed behind the scenes, and Wilcox lost patience with his costar's greater popularity. In season five, Estrada was replaced by Bruce Jenner as Officer Steve McLeish, and Wilcox refused to return for the final season and was replaced by Tom Reilly as Officer Bobby Nelson. **RP**

Classic episode
Supercycle | *Season 2, episode 11*. A daredevil rider continues to outsmart and outride the CHiPs team. Whiz-kid mechanic Harlan develops a "supercycle" so that Ponch can try and catch him. Loads of stunts.

⊘ Larry Wilcox as Officer Jon Baker and Erik Estrada as Officer Francis Llewellyn 'Ponch' Poncherello.

The Love Boat

Comedy | USA | 1977–87

Sailing the oceans blue in search of romance and adventure

Cast | Gavin MacLeod, Lauren Tewes, Bernie Kopell, Ted Lange, Fred Grandy, Jill Whelan
Original broadcaster | ABC   **For fans of . . .** | *Fantasy Island* (1977)

"Attention! Captain Merrill Stubing and the crew of the *Pacific Princess* would like to welcome you aboard, as we set a course for adventure . . . "

For ten years, *The Love Boat* was not only the centerpiece of ABC's Saturday night entertainment block, but also a showcase for Hollywood's company of TV stars and acclaimed screen giants of yesteryear. Under the direction of well-known executive producer Aaron Spelling, *The Love Boat* combined a regular cast — including the ship's captain, memorably portrayed in his trademark white Bermuda shorts by Gavin MacLeod, and the senior members of his crew—with a rotating sample of guest stars each week, each of whom would board the *Pacific Princess* in search of fun and romance.

Multiple story lines were the hallmark of nearly every episode: tales that would begin with the weekly arrival of passengers and end with disembarkation. Only occasionally did the stories overlap, and usually this was only when dealing with the show's lead characters.

The Love Boat was often a ratings champion for its time slot, but the passing of time and multiple cast changes—not to mention a gradual shift in audience tastes—eventually led to a permanent berth. The kitsch element of the series, however—not to mention, its catchy theme song sung by Jack Jones—would continue to keep it remembered fondly by its viewers. A brief UPN revival in 1998 was not quite enough to rekindle old flames. **SL**

⚓ (L–R) Gavin MacLeod, Patricia Klous, Bernie Kopell, and Jill Whelan in "The Crew's Cruise Director/What a Drag/Doc's Slump" in 1984.

The Life and Times of Grizzly Adams
Drama | USA | 1977–78

"Maybe, there's a time we'll call our own / Livin' free in harmony and majesty"

Cast | Dan Haggerty, Denver Pyle, Don Shanks **Original broadcaster** | NBC
For fans of . . . | *The Fugitive* (1963), *Gentle Ben* (1967), *Little House on the Prairie* (1974)

A real-life mountain man was turned into a modern-day legend more than a hundred years after his death with *The Life and Times of Grizzly Adams*. John "Grizzly" Adams lived from 1812 to 1860. In his early twenties, he became a zoological collector, learning to hunt, capture, and then release wild animals in several New England states. He joined the California gold rush in 1849 and traveled west, becoming a miner and trader. In 1852, he lost his ranch to creditors and opted to become a mountain man in the Sierra Nevada range, where he began capturing and training grizzly bears.

In 1974, a highly successful independent film, *The Life and Times of Grizzly Adams*, was made. In order to heighten the drama, it posited that Grizzly Adams fled for the mountains because he was unjustly accused of murder. A few years later, after a showing of the film on US network television led to high ratings, NBC opted to create a TV show. Viewers were thrilled to see Grizzly Adams (Dan Haggerty), his ever-present companion bear Ben, fellow mountain-man Mad Jack (Denver Pyle), and American Indian Nakoma (Don Shanks), as they helped travelers lost in the mountains and protected the local wildlife. Although *The Life and Times of Grizzly Adams* lasted only two seasons as an episodic TV show, the character of Grizzly remained popular, and two further TV movies were made: *Once Upon a Starry Night* (1978) and *The Capture of Grizzly Adams* (1982), in which Grizzly finally proved his innocence. **RBA**

◐ Bozo the Bear as Ben and Dan Haggerty as James "Grizzly" Adams on location.

Soap

Comedy | USA | 1977–81

The first comedy to burst the bubble of the soap opera

Cast | Billy Crystal, Katherine Helmond, Robert Guillaume
Original broadcaster | ABC
Awards | 4 Emmys, 1 Golden Globe
For fans of . . . | *The Carol Burnett Show* (1967)

These days, *Soap*'s satirical take on the soap opera genre may seem tame. The shows it lampooned have become their own self-parodies, and cable drama has pushed absurdity even farther. But the style of comedy that *Soap* pioneered has yet to be bettered.

The comedy centered on two families at the opposite ends of the class spectrum—the Campbells and the Tates—and the rival sisters who headed them. Secret affairs and crimes were standard, but alien abduction, amnesia, mob hits, and South American guerrillas also featured. Decades ahead of its time, the show had an out gay lead character, an African American butler smarter than anyone around him (Robert Guillaume), and a sly knowingness about the conventions of TV genres that blazed a trail for later comedies. (The Catholic Church and Southern California's Board of Rabbis protested before it even aired.)

Soap succeeded by telling its insane stories using characters so well drawn that viewers couldn't help but care about them. Guillaume's sarcastic butler, Benson, was so popular that he was given his own spin-off, while Billy Crystal had his first taste of screen fame playing gay character Jodie. But the best comic creation wasn't even human. Unassuming ventriloquist Chuck expressed his anger through his dummy, Bob, and over time the other characters—and the audience—came to see Bob as the real person and Chuck as his sidekick. **JL**

❯ Caroline McWilliams (Sally) gets very close to Richard Mulligan (Burt) in season 2, 1978.

Jesus of Nazareth

Historical drama | UK/Italy | 1977

*This no-expense-spared miniseries about the life of Christ was filmed
by Franco Zeffirelli and featured a cast of major international stars*

Cast | Robert Powell, Anne Bancroft, James Farentino,
James Mason, Ian McShane, Laurence Olivier, Donald
Pleasence, Christopher Plummer, Anthony Quinn
Original broadcaster | ITV, RAI
For fans of . . . | *I, Claudius* (1976)

Filmed in Morocco and Tunisia over three years,
with a budget of some £18 million, Sir Lew Grade's
dramatization of the life of Christ was one of the
first television productions to blur the lines between
cinema and television. It offered a cinematic grandeur,
but at a more sedate and considered pace.

Following the success of Grade's 1974 miniseries
Moses, The Lawgiver, the television impresario was
invited to meet Pope Paul VI, who encouraged him
to commission a television drama on a similar scale
about the life of Christ. Entering into a partnership
with Radiotelevisione Italiana (RAI), Grade appointed
Franco Zeffirelli to direct the project. He gathered a
cast of internationally renowned movie stars to portray
the New Testament characters, in a script by Anthony
Burgess, writer of *A Clockwork Orange*.

While the majestic sweep of the production was
lent additional weight by Academy Award-winner
Maurice Jarre's epic score, Zeffirelli and Burgess were
keen to present Christ as "an ordinary man—gentle,
fragile, simple," to make the character more easily
accessible to those of all beliefs. Although a regular
face on British television, Robert Powell, who starred
as Christ, was largely unknown outside the UK, which
removed the preconceptions involved in casting a
major international star in the role. In addition to an
endorsement by the Pope during his public address
on Palm Sunday in 1977, the serial was well received
by critics and viewers alike. **JJJ**

Classic episode
Episode 4. Jesus enters Jerusalem. After
celebrating the Last Supper with his disciples, he
is betrayed by Judas and taken before Pontius
Pilate. Unlike in the Gospels, Judas's motives are
presented as political.

⬥ Robert Powell's piercing blue eyes gave Christ an intensity that
contrasts with the ordinariness that the series also stressed.

Fantasy Island

Drama | USA | 1977–84

Set on a remote island resort where fantasies may or may not come true:
"Smiles everyone, smiles!"

Cast | Ricardo Montalban, Hervé Villechaize,
Wendy Schaal, Christopher Hewett
Original broadcaster | ABC
For fans of . . . | *Charlie's Angels* (1976), *The Love Boat*
(1977), *The Fall Guy* (1981)

Beginning with two TV movies and derived from a network pitch by producers Aaron Spelling and Leonard Goldberg that was meant to be a joke, *Fantasy Island* took viewers to a beautiful Pacific island resort where customers could experience whatever fantasy they wished, although the results were often not as they intended. Presided over by the mysterious Mr. Roarke (Ricardo Montalban) and his assistant, Tattoo (Hervé Villechaize), events on Fantasy Island appeared to take their own path, but Roarke often influenced the results to teach his guests valuable lessons in life and morality by the end of their sometimes harrowing stay. He could not actually stop a fantasy once things were set in motion, but he often intervened to prevent fatal consequences.

The show utilized an approach to anthological storytelling that was common at the time, focusing on celebrity guest stars in multiple stories per episode, with elements of romance, comedy, and drama. There were even darker aspects to some fantasies. Roarke's true origins and the extent of his powers were never revealed, but he had some intriguing acquaintances, including a mermaid and the Devil (Roddy McDowall); there were even indications that he might be immortal or somehow connected directly to God. A revival of *Fantasy Island* in 1998 cast Malcolm McDowell as a far more sinister Mr. Roarke, with the implication that the island activities might be taking place in a form of purgatory. **ATB**

Classic episode
The Wedding | Season 3, episode 7. In this format-breaking installment that featured a single moving tale, Helena Marsh (Samantha Eggar) comes to the Island to live out her fantasy of marrying her longtime love Mr. Roarke.

◉ Ricardo Montalban (left) and Hervé Villechaize (right) star in the episode "Return to Fantasy Island," broadcast on January 20, 1978.

The Professionals

Action/Adventure | UK | 1977–83

Explosive drama that defined 1970s action aesthetics

Cast | Gordon Jackson, Martin Shaw, Lewis Collins
Original broadcaster | ITV **For fans of . . .** | *The Sweeney* (1975), *Minder* (1979)

The spiky, on-the-nose action of *The Professionals* responded to a hard edge that seeped into British TV in the late 1970s. The investigations of the Intelligence unit CI5 were embodied in operatives Bodie (Lewis Collins) and Doyle (Martin Shaw) and the abrasive relationship they had with commanding officer George Cowley (Gordon Jackson). It was a ratings winner, and its success hinged on the interactions of Bodie and Doyle, influenced by the ambivalence of the actors toward each other.

The Professionals marked a contrast to the whimsy of *The Avengers* (1961), for which creator Brian Clemens was known. The show was charged with guns, fast cars, leather jackets, and overt violence. British TV was moving beyond studio-bound drama to glossy shows

shot on film. Among the directors was future James Bond helmer Martin Campbell.

A revival in 1998, *CI5: The New Professionals*, failed to find an audience, but a new movie is often rumored. Often parodied as shorthand for the testosterone-fueled aesthetics of 1970s crime drama, *The Professionals* is remembered as a document of TV past. **MW**

Classic episode
Foxhole on the Roof | *Season 5, episode 1*. An ex-convict holds a hospital ward to ransom from a machine gun on a roof. The tense siege narrative and perilous climax provides a challenge for CI5, showcasing the three leads at their best.

◉ The famous three in action (L–R): Martin Shaw (Doyle), Gordon Jackson (Cowley), and Lewis Collins (Bodie).

Diff'rent Strokes

Comedy | USA | 1978–85

Humor ensues when a wealthy but kindly old gent adopts two young kids from Harlem

Cast | Conrad Bain, Gary Coleman, Dana Plato, Todd Bridges
Original broadcaster | NBC **For fans of . . .** | *The Facts of Life* (1979)

A sitcom staple of the 1980s, *Diff'rent Strokes* revolved around a controversial topic: the adoption of two African-American boys by a wealthy white man. Conrad Bain's Philip Drummond might have had money, but he was portrayed as a loving, caring father taking in young Arnold Jackson (the breakout role for actor Gary Coleman, who would become one of the 1980s' most prominent child stars) and his older brother Willis, whose mother, Drummond's former housekeeper, had died unexpectedly.

Comedy came from Drummond's inexperience of New York street life as well as Arnold and Willis' response to their new environment. Among the many recurring players in the series was future international recording star Janet Jackson, in the role of Charlene, Willis' girlfriend for much of the first four seasons.

Diff'rent Strokes was a popular part of NBC's family lineup, and included special episodes that educated its audience in particular topics. In 1983, for example, First Lady Nancy Reagan appeared on the show to promote the "Just Say No" anti-drug crusade. **SL**

Classic episode
Arnold's Tangled Web | *Season 8, episode 15*.
After gaining an F in geometry, Arnold takes home a fake report card. Impressed by his excellent grades, Philip decides to enrol him on an honors program.

◉ Gary Coleman as Arnold Jackson receives a word of fatherly advice from Conrad Bain as Philip Drummond in 1987.

Saiyûki

Action/Adventure | Japan | 1978–80

"Born from an egg on a mountain top . . . the punkiest monkey that ever popped"

Cast | Masaaki Sakai, Masako Natsume, Shirô Kishibe, Toshiyuki Nishida, Tonpei Hidari, Shunji Fujimura
Original broadcaster | NTV
For fans of . . . | *Saiyuki* (1960), *The Water Margin* (1973), *Saiyuki* (2006)

As *Saiyûki*—a live-action version of a 1960 animation—this cult favorite was broadcast in Japan from 1978, a two-season telling of Wu Cheng'en's sixteenth-century Chinese novel *Journey to the West*. In 1979 it was sold overseas, and selected episodes were dubbed into English with dialogue. As *Monkey*, it won an audience of British children who were attracted to the larger-than-life characters, slapstick action, and broad comedy.

Born from an egg on a mountaintop, as the theme song related, Monkey (Masaaki Sakai)—arrogant king of a simian tribe—fell foul of Buddha and was imprisoned for five hundred years. He was freed by a monk (Masako Natsume) to join a pilgrimage to retrieve holy scriptures. The party was completed by water monster Sandy (Shiro Kishibe) and lustful pig creature Pigsy (Toshiyuki Nishida/Tonpei Hidari). Along the way, they encountered power-mad emperors, crazed demons, and supernatural threats, but learned valuable lessons.

Monkey's vocal tics as he was subjected to Tripitaka's pain headband, his blowing air through fingers to summon a cloud, and the knockabout fight sequences were all easily copied by a school-yard audience.

Thirty-nine of the fifty-two episodes were dubbed into English; the voices including noted British actress Miriam Margolyes. The remaining thirteen episodes were completed after high VHS and DVD sales of the original run. The series introduced oriental fantasy action to Western audiences who have since revealed an insatiable appetite for the genre. **MW**

Classic episode
Monkey Goes Wild About Heaven | *Season 1, episode 1*. With a title that may ring bells for fans of alt-rock legend the Pixies, this perfect introduction to the madcap series fills in the backstory of the quartet of pilgrims.

◉ Monkey magic: Masaaki Sakai and Masako Natsume.

Grange Hill

Drama | UK | 1978–2008

Sex, drugs, bullying, and racism—it's just a normal day at school

Cast | Todd Carty, Michelle Herbert, Michael Percival, Michael Cronin, Gwyneth Powell, Susan Tully, Mark Savage, Lee Macdonald, Erkan Mustafa
Original broadcaster | BBC One
For fans of . . . | *Waterloo Road* (2006)

Writer Phil Redmond created children's drama *Grange Hill*, set in a British state school, as a reaction to the old-fashioned, privately educated posh kids that populated children's literature. Stories were told from the children's point of view, with the cameras set at their eye level. The teachers were a mix of personalities, from the cheery Mr. Hargreaves and long-serving headmistress Mrs. McCluskey to disciplinarians, such as "Bullet" Baxter, and the humorless, wig-wearing Mr. Bronson, who became something of a cult hero.

Grange Hill tackled difficult subjects and refused to patronize its viewers. In age-appropriate ways, it took on AIDS, teen pregnancy, date rape, homosexuality, and bullying. Children died as a consequence of dangerous dares, while the popular character Zammo was selected by the writers to become a drug addict who descended into lies, deception, and violence before counseling and recovery. Outside the show, the cast worked on a campaign to warn children about the dangers of drugs and were even invited to Washington, D.C. to meet First Lady Nancy Reagan, who was spearheading an anti-drugs campaign.

For its final years, *Grange Hill* went back to basics with stories aimed at younger children, but it still managed to keep in mind the importance of being a bridge between children's drama and adult series, such as *EastEnders* and *Neighbours*. When it came to an end in 2008, *Grange Hill* had been a major player on British television for thirty years. **JS**

Blake's 7

Fantasy/Horror/Sci-Fi | UK | 1978–81

Low-budget black holes and apocalyptic revelations—"The place is full of criminals"

Cast | Gareth Thomas, Paul Darrow, Michael Keating, Jan Chappell, Sally Knyvette, Jacqueline Pearce, Peter Tuddenham, Josette Simon, Steven Pacey
Original broadcaster | BBC One
For fans of . . . | *Doctor Who* (1963), *Firefly* (2002)

On a future Earth, rebel leader Roj Blake (Gareth Thomas) was found guilty of fabricated charges and sentenced to serve the rest of his life on a prison planet. En route, he met other criminals—among them the smuggler Jenna (Sally Knyvette), computer fraudster Avon (Paul Darrow), and gentle giant Gan (David Jackson). They escaped their captors and took command of an advanced alien ship, which they named *Liberator*. They were later joined by Cally (Jan Chappell), a telepath from the planet Auron, and together they battled the oppressive forces of the Federation and its tyrannical leader, Servalan (Jacqueline Pearce).

The writer, Terry Nation, introduced the Daleks to *Doctor Who* (1963), and in this show he reworked *The Magnificent Seven* (1960) and set it in space. He scripted the first two seasons, which focused on the *Liberator* crew's various quests either to obtain useful technology—such as the sentient supercomputer Orac—or to sabotage the Federation's infrastructure.

In contrast to the idealized vision of the future seen in *Star Trek* (1966), *Blake's 7* offered a bleaker view. Guest characters often died, and the crew of the *Liberator* were not immune from this, either. Fans found their allegiances torn between earnest Blake and cynical, self-serving Avon, who remained a fascinating character thanks to a charismatic performance from Darrow. The final season saw Avon and Vila without the *Liberator*, instead taking command of another craft, *Scorpio*. **JS**

All Creatures Great and Small

Drama | UK | 1978–90

The heartwarming story of a Yorkshire vet

Cast | Christopher Timothy, Robert Hardy, Peter Davison, Carol Drinkwater, Lynda Bellingham
Original broadcaster | BBC One
For fans of . . . | *Heartbeat* (1992), *Peak Practice* (1993), *Doc Martin* (2004)

There was a charm to *All Creatures Great and Small* that was hard to resist. Adapted from the novels of James Herriot (the pseudonym of veterinary surgeon turned novelist Alf Wight), the stories were based on Wight's experiences as a vet in the Yorkshire Dales at the tail end of the 1930s.

The heart-warming drama was a perennial in the BBC's weekend schedules for over a decade. The first three seasons followed the young vet as he found his feet in the practice of Siegfried Farnon, married, and became a partner in the practice, before leaving the village in 1939, at the outbreak of the Second World War. The series made household names of Christopher Timothy as Herriot and Peter Davison as Siegfried's wayward brother Tristan, with the more experienced actor Robert Hardy completing the trio as Siegfried himself. Shrewd casting, humor, beautiful countryside, and animals proved a winning formula. Following two seasonal specials between 1983 and 1985, the show returned in 1988 with original writing, the stories in the books having been exhausted by then.

The series came to a close in 1990 after ninety episodes. A reunion episode, based on an unproduced script, was proposed in 2007, but didn't come to fruition, and the BBC showed *Young James Herriot*, a three-part prequel, in 2011. *All Creatures Great and Small* set the template for a particular brand of gentle Sunday evening drama that remains idiosyncratic to British television schedules to this day. **MW**

The Kenny Everett Video Show

Comedy | UK | 1978–87

"It's all done in the best POSSIBLE taste!"

Cast | Kenny Everett, Cleo Rocos, Hot Gossip, Billy Connolly, Lionel Blair, Sheila Steafel, Terry Wogan
Original broadcaster | ITV **Awards** | 2 BAFTAs
For fans of . . . | *The Kids in the Hall* (1988), *Little Britain* (2003), *The Catherine Tate Show* (2004)

As a radio DJ in the 1960s and 1970s, Kenny Everett broke taboos and created an aural soundscape unlike anything heard before. When he finally got his own TV show in 1978, he blended musical guests and saucy routines from dance troupe Hot Gossip with the kind of off-the-wall characters that had made his name on the radio. Aided by top writers, such as Barry Cryer, and utilizing the latest in TV technology, Kenny preempted the look of MTV with rapid edits, video captions, and televisual effects. But it was Kenny's huge roster of recurring characters that stuck in the mind: 1950s rocker Sid Snot, French champagne-swilling Marcel Wave, silent comic Maurice Mimer, animated space hero Captain Kremmen (a cartoon adaptation of Kenny's radio serial), dim-witted punk Gizzard Puke, US preacher with giant hands Brother Lee Love, half-transvestite businessman Angry of Mayfair—the list is endless.

After four years and a BAFTA, a dispute with ITV bosses saw Cuddly Ken move his show to the BBC, where musical acts were cut to one per episode, but the sketches became more spectacular. Kenny's creations for the BBC included pneumatic Hollywood starlet, Cupid Stunt; the host of religious show "Up Your Way," Verity Treacle; and bumbling TV handyman, Reg Prescott, who was more likely to sever his own fingers in a spray of comedy blood than correctly build a shelf.

Kenny returned to radio before his early death in 1995, which robbed the world of an innovative, driven, and irreplaceable comedy talent. **PC**

Dallas

Drama | USA | 1978–91; 2012–14

You can't strike oil without getting your hands dirty

Cast | Larry Hagman, Patrick Duffy, Linda Gray, Ken Kercheval, Barbara Bel Geddes, Victoria Principal
Original broadcasters | CBS, TNT
Awards | 4 Emmys, 1 Golden Globe
For fans of . . . | *The Big Valley* (1965), *Revenge* (2011)

Sometimes our greatest enemies aren't those we face on the battlefield. Sometimes they're rivals in big business, and occasionally they're members of our family. And few TV shows have proved this like *Dallas*.

Conceived as a CBS miniseries, *Dallas* instead ran for fourteen years in its original run, spearheaded by one of the most popular characters of a generation: the villainous J.R. Ewing, played with grandeur by *I Dream of Jeannie*'s Larry Hagman. At the center of the Ewing oil dynasty, J.R. battled his brother Bobby (Patrick Duffy) and brother-in-law Cliff Barnes (Ken Kercheval), while wooing his long-suffering wife-cum-nemesis Sue Ellen (Linda Gray). (Brother Gary—Ted Shackelford—left for his own long-running spin-off, *Knots Landing*, 1979.)

Dallas elevated the soap archetype to new heights. Plot lines ranged from dark and sullen to outright fantastic (one entire season was all a dream), and a cliff-hanger at the end of the third season—"Who shot J.R.?"—kept millions on tenterhooks for eight months until the fourth episode of the following season.

Though ratings flagged as the series ran its course, *Dallas* refused to go quietly. After three TV movies, it returned in full force on TNT, in 2012, to showcase a new generation of Ewings alongside the returning Hagman, Duffy, and Gray. Hagman's passing during the production of the second season was handled with dignity and grace as part of the narrative, proving once more that the heart of *Dallas* was the timeless legacy of J.R. Ewing—oil baron, patriarch, and legend. **SL**

Classic episode
Blast From the Past | *Season 9, episode 31*. In what might be TV's most notorious twist, Pam Ewing (Victoria Principal) wakes to find her dead husband Bobby greeting her from the shower. Life, it turns out, really can be a dream.

◉ The initial cast's only Texas native, Larry Hagman played J.R.

Mork & Mindy

Comedy | USA | 1978–82

Nanu-nanu!

Cast | Robin Williams, Pam Dawber, Elizabeth Kerr, Conrad Janis, Ralph James, Robert Donner, Jonathan Winters
Original broadcaster | ABC **Award** | 1 Golden Globe **For fans of . . .** | *Happy Days* (1974)

In the wake of *Star Wars* (1977), sci-fi became big business. A 1978 episode of *Happy Days* introduced a visiting alien called Mork, played by stand-up comedian Robin Williams. The character proved a hit who was ripe for a spin-off, although a syndicated press preview grumbled about a "tired idea" with a "goofy premise," and sniped, "Not another *My Favorite Martian*, we hope."

Mork—sent to Earth to help his leader Orson (a nod to Orson Welles) understand human behavior—befriended Mindy (Pam Dawber), who tutored him about life. A relationship akin to curious child and patient parent eventually blossomed into love.

Accommodating Williams' breathless, often drug-fueled mix of cultural references, impressions, and improvisation, the show made him a star. "He used to call me Sister Mary St. Patience," Dawber recalled. "Because it was *crazy*." Williams' catchphrases—"Nanu-nanu," "Shazbot," "Mork calling Orson"—became ubiquitous. "It's weird," he reflected later. "A week after I won the Academy Award (for 1997's *Good Will Hunting*), there were still people going, 'Mork!'"

In their final year, Mork and Mindy married and found themselves with child—who, owing to Orkan biology, was a middle-aged man (comedian Jonathan Winters) with the mind of a child. After this protracted shark-jumping, there was a more dignified conclusion three decades later, when Dawber guested in an episode of Williams' final TV show, *The Crazy Ones* (2013). **JS**

◉ Robin Williams and Pam Dawber in the first season's "Mork Goes Public."

Taxi

Comedy | USA | 1978–83

Driving into the dawn of a new golden age of US sitcom

Cast | Judd Hirsch, Danny DeVito, Marilu Henner, Tony Danza, Andy Kaufman, Jeff Conaway **Original broadcasters** | ABC, NBC **Awards** | 18 Emmys, 4 Golden Globes **For fans of . . .** | *The Mary Tyler Moore Show* (1970)

The Mary Tyler Moore Show introduced a new kind of ensemble comedy, with top-quality writing ensuring that the humor grew from character rather than from situation. When its writers/producers James L. Brooks, Stan Daniels, David Davis, and Ed Weinberger quit, they created *Taxi,* which was even more successful.

Taxi charted the lives of the rich mix of personalities working for (or hanging around) a New York taxi depot. All but one of them believed that driving a cab was no more than a fill-in until they went on to a better life someplace else. The sole exception was Alex (future *Numb3rs* star Judd Hirsch), who knew he was a lifer and became the Everyman at the center of the action. The other two main characters were Alex's confidante,

Elaine (Marilu Henner), and his mean and moody boss Louie (Danny DeVito).

In any other series Louie would have been the best-remembered character, but here he had strong competition from the Reverend Jim (Christopher Lloyd)—a spaced-out casualty of the 1960s—and Eastern European immigrant Latka (off-the-wall stand-up comedian Andy Kaufman).

The multi-award-winning *Taxi* ran for five seasons and 114 episodes. It was a hard act to follow, but the writers and producers who took over the final episodes—the brothers Glen and Les Charles and James Burrows—went on to fashion an even bigger hit, the phenomenal *Cheers* (1982). **DF**

◬ (L–R) Randall Carver, Jeff Conaway, Judd Hirsch, Tony Danza, and Marilu Henner; (front, left) Danny DeVito; (kneeling) Andy Kaufman.

Holocaust

Historical drama | USA | 1978

The story of man's inhumanity to man in the Second World War

Cast | Fritz Weaver, Tovah Feldshuh, Rosemary Harris, Meryl Streep, Michael Moriarty, Ian Holm
Original broadcaster | NBC
Awards | 8 Emmys,, 2 Golden Globes
For fans of . . . | *The Winds of War* (1983)

A number of programs and movies had tried to capture just a fraction of the horror that was the Holocaust: 1961 alone saw the *Twilight Zone* episode "Deaths-Head Revisited" and the Oscar-winning film *Judgment at Nuremberg*. But when NBC presented the four-part *Holocaust* miniseries under its umbrella title *The Big Event*, nothing like it had ever been seen on TV before.

Gerald Green wrote the controversial story, focusing on a family's fight to evade the growing threat of the Nazis, but, one by one, being lost to Hitler's forces. The show also examined the effect on Germans in the form of young lawyer Erik Dorf (based on SS officer Rudolf Hermann Brandt and played by Michael Moriarty), who sank into corruption and villainy after joining the party.

Harrowing material set in the concentration camps riveted US viewers, but some of the series' most profound effects were felt in Germany. "Holocaust" was named "Word of the Year" in 1979 by the Society for German Language, and, more significantly, many viewers called in to a postshow panel of historical experts, objecting that they had never heard of their country's involvement in the events depicted. In contrast, others reportedly confessed to participating in *Kristallnacht* in November 1938, when Jewish businesses and synagogues were vandalized. Though condemned by some for its perceived blend of shocking fact and soap-opera drama, there couldn't be a more profound proof of the power of TV than a program that moved people to bare their very souls. **ATB**

Matador

Drama | Denmark | 1978–82

A local business whose success is inversely proportional to its popularity

Cast | Jørgen Buckhøj, Ghita Nørby, Holger Juul Hansen, Malene Schwartz, Helle Virkner, Buster Larsen, Ove Sprogøe, Karin Nellemose, Kirsten Olesen
Original broadcaster | DR
For fans of . . . | *Dallas* (1978), *Dynasty* (1981)

The classic board game Monopoly is called "Matador" in Danish. It's also a term used to describe a successful businessman. This made *Matador* a perfect title for a show about a salesman who arrived in the small fictitious small town of Korsbæk in 1929, opened a clothing store, and upset the town's delicate power balance as his shop evolved into a business empire.

The show was laced with all the power struggles, intrigue, and romance that you would expect—yet no one could be singled out as a bad guy because the characters were different shades of gray: some painted in lighter shades, but none dark and twisted. Over the course of the series, the show cleverly toyed with the viewers' perceptions of them, and loyalties shifted as characters revealed new sides to themselves.

Matador remains one of the Danes' most beloved TV shows. Much of its success and longevity is attributed to creator Lise Nørgaard's ability to create unique characters that viewers could relate to and who remained endearing even if their actions were sometimes questionable.

It is also a show of significant cultural importance, with the town of Korsbæk often seen as a microcosm of Danish society at the time. For better or worse, a lot of the values and issues raised in the show still ring true for Danes today. Perhaps that is why *Matador* remains such a success, rerun six times since its original broadcast in 1978, and why it continues to draw in new viewers across generational and cultural gaps. **JH**

◀ Meryl Streep in the role for which she earned her first Emmy.

1970s 271

The Sandbaggers

Drama | UK | 1978–80

A British spy who's the cerebral antithesis of all-action James Bond

Cast | Roy Marsden, Richard Vernon, Ray Lonnen, Alan MacNaughton, Elizabeth Bennett, Jerome Willis, Diane Keen
Original broadcaster | ITV
For fans of . . . | *Callan* (1967)

There was a vogue for hard-nosed, violent action drama in British television in the late 1970s, but *The Sandbaggers* was different. A cerebral depiction of the British intelligence services, it owed more to the works of thriller writer John le Carré. Taut and tense, it showed that sometimes the most dangerous place for a spy was behind a government desk.

Created by former Royal Navy officer Ian Mackintosh, *The Sandbaggers* had an authentic feel, with tight scripts and a complex performance by Roy Marsden as Neil Burnside, Director of Special Operations. Burnside assigned elite spies—sandbaggers—to operations across the world, often behind the Iron Curtain.

The meat of *The Sandbaggers* came from office-based dialogue. There were deals with CIA ally Jeff Ross (Bob Sherman), confrontations with direct superior Peele (Jerome Willis), and personal attachments to sandbagger Laura Dickens—a liaison destined for a brutal end. Burnside's only real friend was Willie Caine (Ray Lonnen), his longest-serving operative.

The end of *The Sandbaggers* was shrouded in mystery. During production of season three in 1979, the small plane in which Mackintosh was flying went missing over the Pacific Ocean, leading to speculation that the writer may have had firsthand experience of espionage. With the remaining scripts having to be handled by other writers, and arguably of a lower quality, the series was curtailed. The final episode ended with Caine shot on assignment in Malta, his fate unknown. **MW**

Rumpole of the Bailey

Drama | UK | 1978–92

The law according to Rumpole—an irascible but lovable lawyer

Cast | Leo McKern, Peggy Thorpe-Bates, Marion Mathie, Peter Bowles, Patricia Hodge, Julian Curry
Original broadcaster | BBC One
For fans of . . . | *Perry Mason* (1957), *Crown Court* (1972), *This Life* (1996)

Featuring a bravura performance from Leo McKern in the title role, *Rumpole of the Bailey* mined the rich seam of comedy to be found in the English criminal justice system. Through a mire of legal pomposity and low life tottered the dogged, cigar-smoking figure of Rumpole, who was irascible and cynical but, nonetheless committed to his clients and the concept of justice. He was also devoted to his formidable wife, Hilda—"She Who Must Be Obeyed."

Audiences were first introduced to Horace Rumpole in a one-off play for the BBC's prestigious *Play for Today* slot broadcast in 1975. Critical praise for the play was such that producer Irene Shubik hoped the BBC would want a series, but she ended up taking the property, its writer, and star to Thames Television. Mortimer penned six more hour-long episodes, which would expand to fill the next thirteen years.

The series became something of a national institution, as beloved by lawyers as the rest of the British public. It featured a plethora of sparkling British acting talent, and McKern, a regular face on British stage and television for some decades, became an icon of lovable English irritability. But it was the quality of John Mortimer's scripts that was the series' chief strength. As a Queen's Counsel, Mortimer had considerable experience in the legal world and it seems likely that a great deal of Mortimer himself existed in Rumpole, especially in his predilection for championing the underdog. **JJJ**

Pennies from Heaven

Music/Musical | UK | 1978

"Into each life some rain must fall"—if you want the things you love, you must take the showers with the sunshine . . .

Cast | Bob Hoskins, Cheryl Campbell, Gemma Craven, Kenneth Colley, Dave King
Original broadcaster | BBC One
Award | 1 BAFTA
For fans of . . . | *The Singing Detective* (1986)

The first of Dennis Potter's musical fantasies—followed by *The Singing Detective* and *Lipstick on Your Collar* (1993)—*Pennies from Heaven* merged the tragic escapades of a Great Depression–era sheet-music salesman with nods to classic Hollywood film romances. Characters stepped out of the story to address the camera, and lip-synched and danced to 1930s songs that darkly illustrated their own innermost thoughts and predicaments.

Bob Hoskins plays Arthur Parker, trapped in a loveless marriage to the repressed Joan (Gemma Craven). On the road, he meets a disturbed, accordion-playing vagrant (Kenneth Colley), whom he ditches, and naive schoolmistress Eileen (Cheryl Campbell) with whom he becomes obsessed. His search for her draws the attention of police investigating a rape and murder, while the real culprit, the accordion man, escapes. When Arthur and Eileen run away together, an overzealous inspector convinces Joan that her husband is a dangerous sex maniac. Fleeing to the countryside, Arthur is damned by another fateful coincidence.

Each of the six seventy-five-minute episodes was structured like a musical, with a sinister undercurrent. Potter and director Piers Haggard maintained an unreal quality that prevented the tragedy from becoming too oppressive—and even managed to go out on a song.

Three years later, Hollywood remade *Pennies* as a movie, with Steve Martin and Bernadette Peters. Sadly, it wasn't a patch on the original miniseries. **JS**

Classic episode
Easy Come, Easy Go | Episode 3. Arthur happens upon a blind girl in a field. He has lustful thoughts about her, but goes on his way. Shortly afterward, she is raped and murdered and he is the obvious number one suspect.

◉ Bob Hoskins and Cheryl Campbell dance away their troubles.

WKRP in Cincinnati

Comedy | USA | 1978–82

Living (and laughing) on the air in Cincinnati . . .

Cast | Gary Sandy, Gordon Jump, Howard Hesseman, Loni Anderson, Richard Sanders, Frank Bonner, Tim Reid, Jan Smithers **Original broadcaster** | CBS **Award** | 1 Emmy **For fans of . . .** | *Taxi* (1978)

Based at a struggling radio station in the Midwest, this quirky sitcom focused on a lovably dysfunctional work family. Andy Travis (Gary Sandy), young and ambitious, was brought in by owner Mr. Carlson (Gordon Jump) to update WKRP's unprofitable format. This was complicated by Carlson's tough-as-nails mother (Sylvia Sidney in the pilot, then Carol Bruce) and oddball employees. These included slimy salesman Herb Tarlek (Frank Bonner), forever attempting to woo curvaceous secretary Jennifer Marlowe (Loni Anderson); newsman Les Nessman (Richard Sanders); stoner DJ Dr. Johnny Fever (Howard Hesseman in a career-making role); shy but savvy reporter Bailey Quarters (Jan Smithers); and smooth-tongued DJ Venus Flytrap (Tim Reid).

Produced by MTM (*The Mary Tyler Moore Show*), *WKRP* was created by Hugh Wilson, whose experiences at an Atlanta station inspired many of the characters and stories. Creating endless subsequent clearance headaches, the show incorporated genuine songs; one of which—Blondie's "Heart of Glass"—topped the real-life chart a month after it aired on *WKRP*. **KB**

Classic episode
Turkeys Away | *Season 1, episode 7.* "As God is my witness, I thought turkeys could fly." Based on a real event, this spun its horrifying inspiration into a classic half-hour that regularly shows up on lists of the best episodes in TV comedy.

🅐 (L–R) Tim Reid, Jan Smithers, Richard Sanders, Gary Sandy, Frank Bonner, Loni Anderson; (seated) Howard Hesseman.

The Incredible Hulk

Drama | USA | 1977–82

A man with anger management issues puts his rampaging id to good use

Cast | Bill Bixby, Lou Ferrigno, Jack Colvin
Original broadcaster | CBS   **Award** | 1 Emmy   **For fans of . . .** | *The Fugitive* (1963)

An innocent man on the run was the staple plot device for Alfred Hitchcock and had kept *The Fugitive* as a top-rated show in the mid-1960s. Here, the hero was Dr. David Banner, whose experiments with gamma rays had left him with a terrifying curse—at times of stress or anger, he would transform into the Hulk, a raging muscle-bound giant with green skin and glaring white eyes. David was pursued by McGee, a dogged tabloid reporter convinced that the doctor was somehow connected to the Hulk, who he believed was responsible for the deaths of two people. David moved from town to town, making friends and doing his best to help people out when he could, all the while hoping for a cure for his affliction.

In casting Bill Bixby as Banner, producer Kenneth Johnson managed to find an actor who brought gravitas to the role, making it a serious adult drama that coincidentally appealed to children, who loved those moments when David's eyes would change to white and former bodybuilder Lou Ferrigno would take his place to trash the set. **WH**

Classic episode

Married | *Season 2, episode 5.* While working as a groundskeeper at an elementary school, David sides with a little boy against a gang of bullies, who have no idea how bad things can get if he loses his temper.

Ⓐ Lou Ferrigno as The Hulk saves a blind woman from drowning in an episode entitled "Prometheus."

Butterflies

Comedy | UK | 1978–83

Daring, downbeat comedy about the dullness of family life

Cast | Wendy Craig, Geoffrey Palmer, Bruce Montague, Andrew Hall, Nicholas Lyndhurst
Original broadcaster | BBC Two
For fans of . . . | *Solo* (1981), *Ever Decreasing Circles* (1984), *One Foot in the Grave* (1990)

Actress Wendy Craig had cornered a market as a likable, scatterbrained mom in *Not in Front of the Children* (1967) and *And Mother Makes Three* (1971). But writer Carla Lane, keen to evolve from the broad strokes of *The Liver Birds* (1969) and *Bless This House* (1971), created a more mature role that reflected where she—then approaching age forty—was at that stage of her life.

Ria Parkinson (Craig) was in a loving but staid marriage, with teenage sons (Andrew Hall and future *Only Fools and Horses* star Nicholas Lyndhurst) going nowhere. Husband Ben (Geoffrey Palmer) was in a dull job and collected butterflies, a solitary hobby. When Ria met separated businessman Leonard (Bruce Montague), he offered an escape from the drudgery.

Over four seasons (the show seemed to end in its third, with Leonard moving to America, but came back three years later), the viewers followed Ria's temptations, as fate seemed determined to push her into Leonard's eager arms. The redemptive climax, however, offered a different take on domestic bliss.

For Lane, seemingly already at the top of her game, *Butterflies* proved a watershed. The show shot her into the stratosphere and, after two further midlife crisis–style series—*Solo* (1981) and *The Mistress* (1985)—she returned to her working-class roots with her most successful comedy-drama of all, *Bread* (1986).

The series ended in 1983, but a sweet reunion mini episode, as part of 2000's Comic Relief, provided an opportunity to catch up with all the characters. **GR**

Salem's Lot

Fantasy/Horror/Sci-Fi | USA | 1979

Stephen King adapatation that brings big evil to a small town

Cast | David Soul, James Mason, Lance Kerwin, Bonnie Bedelia, Lew Ayres, Ed Flanders, Geoffrey Lewis, Fred Willard, Bonnie Bartlett, Reggie Nalder
Original broadcaster | CBS
For fans of . . . | *True Blood* (2008)

Novelist Ben Mears (*Starsky & Hutch*'s David Soul) grew up in the New England town of Jerusalem's Lot—or, as locals call it, Salem's Lot. He returned home seeking inspiration for his next work and discovered that an old house that has stood empty for decades has been purchased by an antiques dealer called Barlow. None of the townsfolk had seen Barlow, but met his charming representative, Straker. But then people started dying—including a young boy—and Ben learned that the dead didn't stay dead for long in Salem's Lot.

Stephen King's 1975 novel became the stuff of nightmares for a generation who caught this two-part miniseries, directed by Tobe *The Texas Chainsaw Massacre* Hooper. Two sequences in particular were especially chilling: a teenage horror movie fan awakes as if from a dream to find a recently deceased friend floating outside his window, scratching the glass with sharp fingernails, begging to be let in; and Barlow's true self is revealed to be a bald, steel-blue-skinned, Nosferatu-esque vampire. Also of note was James Mason's portrayal of Straker, turning a rather one-note character into something more chillingly urbane.

The miniseries was also released theatrically in a cut-down form, losing much of the atmospheric buildup in the process. A 2004 remake for TNT starred Rob Lowe as Ben, Donald Sutherland as Straker, and Rutger Hauer as Barlow. The latter was much closer to the character as drawn in the novel, but much less scary than Reggie Nalder's hissing beast. **JS**

(L–R) Lance Kerwin, Reggie Nalder, and James Mason scare it up.

The Dukes of Hazzard

Action/Adventure | USA | 1979–85

*Southern-fried action adventure
with modern Robin Hoods*

Classic episode
The Ghost of General Lee | **Season 2, episode 6.**
Rosco thinks the Dukes have met their maker
when he witnesses the General Lee driving into
a lake—giving the duo a chance to use the car's
"ghost" to shame Boss Hogg into a confession.

⚠ John Schneider, Catherine Bach, and Tom Wopat duke it out.

Cast | Tom Wopat, John Schneider, Catherine Bach,
Denver Pyle, Sonny Shroyer, Ben Jones, James Best,
Sorrell Booke, Rick Hurst, Waylon Jennings
Original broadcaster | CBS
For fans of . . . | *Starsky & Hutch* (1975), *Enos* (1980)

You weren't a child of the 1980s if you didn't think
about firing a flaming arrow from a crossbow while
leaning out the window of an orange Dodge Charger.
The Dukes of Hazzard followed former Georgia
moonshiners Luke (Tom Wopat) and Bo Duke (John
Schneider), and their cousin Daisy (Catherine Bach)
and Uncle Jesse (Denver Pyle), as they challenged the
authority of corrupt Hazzard County commissioner
Boss Hogg (Sorrell Booke) and inept sheriff Rosco
P. Coltrane (James Best). The Dukes were invariably
framed for crimes they didn't commit, but all was well
by the end of every episode.

Created by Gy Waldron and former moonshiner
Jerry Rushing (who later sued owing to extensive use
of details from his own life), the series was inspired by
the former's 1975 movie *Moonrunners*. Its biggest star,
and the subject of the most fan mail, was the General
Lee, the Duke boys' 1969 Dodge Charger with its
Confederate flag motif and "Dixie"-blaring horn.

When contract disputes led to Schneider and
Wopat's departure prior to the fifth season, they were
replaced by poorly received Duke-alikes Coy (Byron
Cherry) and Vance (Christopher Mayer). The originals
returned before the season was over, but the damage
was done; the increasingly formulaic show was axed
after two more years. Short-lived spin-off *Enos* ran from
1980 to 1981, and the animated *The Dukes* aired in 1983.
TV movie reunions aired in 1997 and 2000, and a movie
reboot in 2005 led to a TV movie sequel in 2007. **ATB**

Life on Earth

Documentary | UK | 1979

*Natural history classic that set
the template for the entire genre*

Cast | David Attenborough
Original broadcaster | BBC
For fans of . . . | *The Living Planet* (1984), *The
Blue Planet* (2001), *Planet Earth* (2006),
Frozen Planet (2011)

Nowadays, natural history programs are synonymous with David Attenborough, and this is the one that started it all. *Life on Earth* remains an outstanding accomplishment, with stunning filming and sharp writing. It is the yardstick against which all other shows of its type are still measured. Decades later, when the theory of evolution remains contentious, this show presents a coherent and compelling argument for how all life on Earth came to be.

When *Life on Earth* first aired in 1979, the UK's increasingly urban population was disconnected from the natural world. City-dwellers might never have seen a living example of the animals they consumed. Watched by an estimated half-a-billion people worldwide, it introduced a generation to the marvel of the natural world, and kickstarted an environmental consciousness that continues to impact government policy today. Its thirteen-episode-long guided tour of the development of life on this planet, from bizarre yet beautiful single-celled organisms to humanity itself, presented the argument for the value of all natural things, and for our place within the natural order as simply another product of evolution.

Attenborough has since been knighted, embraced by the British public as a national treasure, and has made a slew of natural history programs covering the entirety of life on this planet. *Life on Earth* is the foundation on which that work rests, and is an enduring masterpiece of natural history TV. **RL**

Shoestring

Crime/Mystery | UK | 1979–80

Mystery solving by request

Cast | Trevor Eve, Michael Medwin, Doran Godwin,
Liz Crowther, Colin Maitland
Original broadcaster | BBC
For fans of . . . | *Columbo* (1971), *Bergerac* (1981),
Luther (2010)

There was something of the noir about Eddie Shoestring, despite his private investigations taking place in the unlikely British city of Bristol. Writer/producer Robert Banks Stewart gave his creation all the traits for a compelling character study: he was shambolic but brilliant, vulnerable yet possessed of inner strength, and, like all good detectives, haunted by inner demons. Trevor Eve's performance as this down-at-the-heels detective was nothing short of remarkable, so it's frustrating that only two seasons of *Shoestring* were made when there were many stories left to tell.

A former computer programmer, Shoestring was in recovery after a breakdown when he turned his hand to detective work. His first client was an entertainer for a local radio station, which gave the series its twist: following a successful case, he became the station's "private ear," and listeners called in with cases for him to solve. These ranged from missing persons and robberies to miscarriages of justice and blackmail, and Shoestring reported back to listeners on his progress. Though there were dashes of humor, the results were bleak, their noirish tone helped by being shot on film.

Shoestring made Eve an overnight star and unlikely sex symbol. A second season was commissioned after stellar ratings for the first, and a long, high-rating run seemed on the cards. However, fearing typecasting, Eve opted not to return for a third season. Banks Stewart and many of the production team duly developed a new BBC detective drama: the mighty *Bergerac*. **MW**

Prisoner

Drama | Australia | 1979–86

Power struggles on Cell Block H

Cast | Elspeth Ballantyne, Betty Bobbitt, Sheila Florance, Val Lehman, Maggie Kirkpatrick, Patsy King
Original broadcaster | Network Ten **For fans of . . .** | *Bad Girls* (1999), *Orange Is the New Black* (2013)

Wentworth Detention Centre had a poor record. Escapes were common, as were the varied deaths suffered by prisoners and wardens. Riots resulted in fires, drugs and alcohol were rife, and armed gangsters once broke *in* to aid an escape. The result? A massacre.

Inspired by British drama *Within These Walls* (1974), *Prisoner* began as an uncompromising examination of life in a women's prison. It tackled serious issues and addressed the difficulties faced by women who spent their formative years in institutions. These lofty aims soon gave way to constant battles between whoever was the leader of the women—their "top dog"—and the staff. Among the latter, none was more corrupt than Joan "The Freak" Ferguson (Maggie Kirkpatrick),

while the long-standing top dog was Bea Smith (Val Lehman). The years in which these two were locked in a war of attrition marked the golden age of *Prisoner*.

Prisoner became an international cult hit, particularly in Britain. In 2013, *Wentworth Prison*—a gritty reimagining of the series—gave several popular characters from the original a modern reworking. **JS**

Classic episode

Episode 326 | November 9, 1982. In a fight, Joan savagely beats Bea, but a fire in the prison triggers security gates that trap her in a corridor filling with smoke—while, on the other side, Bea falls into unconsciousness, holding Joan's keys.

⬤ Bea (Val Lehman, left) and Chrissie (Amanda Muggleton, right) beat a confession out of Margo (Jane Clifton).

Not the Nine O'Clock News

Comedy | UK | 1979–82

Satirical alternative to the actual nine o'clock news

Cast | Rowan Atkinson, Pamela Stephenson, Mel Smith, Griff Rhys Jones, Chris Langham
Original broadcaster | BBC Two **Awards** | 2 BAFTAs **For fans of . . .** | *Alas Smith & Jones* (1984)

Making a virtue of its scheduling on the BBC's second channel—against the actual *Nine O'Clock News* on BBC One—this series laced its satire with real footage. News clips mocked politicians and royals, sports reports acquired new commentaries (show jumping became upper-class idiots being thrown from horses), and advertising was parodied (sexual favors were offered to credit card users). "I wanted to see a show which was twenty years 'younger' than *The Two Ronnies*," creator John Lloyd told *Mustard* magazine, "and had a sense of going to your favorite rock concert, with girls and music and a terrific sense of excitement and joy."

The cast settled in the second season, when Griff Rhys Jones replaced Chris Langham alongside Mel Smith,

Pamela Stephenson, and future *Mr. Bean* star Rowan Atkinson. Episodes concluded with musical numbers, such as the gleeful "Trucking Song" ("I like trucking and I like to truck") and the pop-skewering "Nice Video, Shame About the Song," while the show's roll call of writers included future stars Richard Curtis, Douglas Adams, Clive Anderson, Nigel Planer, and Ruby Wax. **JS**

Classic episode

Season 2, episode 5 | April 28, 1980. A professor takes a gorilla on TV to discuss communication between animals and humans. "When I caught Gerald in '68," he explains, "he was wild." "Wild?" exclaims the gorilla. "I was absolutely livid!"

⬖ (L–R) Rowan Atkinson, Pamela Stephenson, Mel Smith, and Griff Rhys Jones in the final season's "Nice Video, Shame About the Song."

The Facts of Life

Comedy | USA | 1979–88

You take the good, you take the bad . . .

Cast | Charlotte Rae, Lisa Whelchel, Nancy McKeon, Kim Fields, Mindy Cohn, Mackenzie Astin, Cloris Leachman
Original broadcaster | NBC **For fans of . . .** | *Diff'rent Strokes* (1978), *The Wonder Years* (1988)

A spin-off of *Diff'rent Strokes*, *The Facts of Life* relocated that show's beloved housekeeper Edna Garrett (Charlotte Rae) to a posh prep school for girls in New York. After a lackluster debut season—whose large cast included a young Molly Ringwald before her "Brat Pack" movie days—the show was retooled. The cast was trimmed as Mrs. Garrett became a dietician and supervisor of four girls who needed her special touch: vainglorious Blair Warner (Lisa Whelchel), tomboy Jo Polniaczek (Nancy McKeon), bubbly Tootie Ramsey (Kim Fields), and spirited Natalie Green (Mindy Cohn).

Together, the five tackled teenage pregnancy, abortion, drug use, and crushes. Supporting cast members included Cloris Leachman (Rae's replacement when she departed after six seasons), comic Geri Jewell (whose battle with cerebral palsy became a key and groundbreaking story line), and a young George Clooney as a capable handyman.

Never among TV's top ten shows, *The Facts of Life* was nonetheless key to NBC's family programming and remains a beloved artifact of 1980s Americana. **SL**

Classic episode
The First Time | Season 9, episode 16. One of the girls finally loses her virginity (to *Fast Times at Ridgemont High*'s Robert Romanus), but, owing to Lisa Whelchel's religious convictions, it's not the character the writer intended.

⬥ (L–R) Nancy McKeon as Jo, Cloris Leachman as Beverly Ann, Kim Fields as Tootie, Lisa Whelchel as Blair, Mindy Cohn as Natalie.

Minder

Drama | UK | 1979–94

A sharp-edged drama with a soft center, Minder *created one of television's greatest characters*

Cast | George Cole, Dennis Waterman, Patrick Malahide, Glynn Edwards, Gary Webster, Michael Povey
Original broadcaster | ITV **For fans of . . .** | *The Sweeney* (1975)

Debuting in 1979, just after Margaret Thatcher came to power, *Minder* blew in on the wind of political change in the United Kingdom. Thatcher sought to empower entrepreneurs, and car salesman Arthur Daley (George Cole), looked after by his "minder" Terry McCann (Dennis Waterman), symbolized opportunity (and opportunism). *Minder* was floated by Euston Films as a vehicle for Waterman, following his success in the police drama *The Sweeney* (1975). Creator Leon Griffiths' inspiration came from stories heard in the pubs of north London.

George Cole, a British movie star of the 1950s, was cast as Daley, which was originally envisioned as a supporting role. However, Cole's deft comedy and on-screen chemistry with Waterman led to equal spread for the two characters, with most plots revolving around Arthur's latest scheme. Glynn Edwards played Dave, owner of the Winchester Club, a drinking haunt, and there were various police antagonists, notably DS "Cheerful Charlie" Chisholm (Patrick Malahide).

Minder ran for seven seasons and two specials. Waterman's decision not to return after season seven in 1989 could have brought it to a close were it not for the viewers' love of Arthur. Gary Webster was subsequently cast as nephew Ray Daley, leading to three more seasons. In the last episode, the police catch up with Arthur. A revival, without Cole, starring Shane Richie as another Daley nephew, failed to win over the public in 2009, confirming their lasting love for the original. **MW**

⚓ The world was their lobster: (L–R) George Cole as Arthur, Glynn Edwards as Dave, and Dennis Waterman as Terry.

Tinker Tailor Soldier Spy

Historical drama | UK | 1979

The evil empire strikes back in show that builds at a leisurely pace through psychological insight into stomach-tightening suspense

Classic episode
Smiley Tracks the Mole | **Season 1, episode 3.**
As Smiley's old friend Connie Sachs ("Queen of the filing cabinets," sniped TV critic Clive James), Beryl Reid delivers a powerhouse performance for which she earned a BAFTA nomination.

⊙ Obi who? Alec Guinness as George Smiley, a role for which he earned both a BAFTA and a Broadcasting Press Guild award in 1980.

Cast | Alec Guinness, Beryl Reid, Bernard Hepton, Michael Jayston, Ian Richardson, Hywel Bennett
Original broadcaster | BBC Two
Awards | 2 BAFTAs
For fans of . . . | *Smiley's People* (1982), *Spooks* (2002)

As a spy-thriller hero, *Tinker Tailor Soldier Spy*'s George Smiley could not be more different from the action-packing James Bond. As played by movie star Alec Guinness, he barely spoke in many scenes, letting the dialogue flow around him or allowing blustering characters to exhaust themselves.

Control, head of the secret intelligence service MI6, suspects there is a mole in the top ranks of his organization. Among the suspects is Smiley, Control's deputy. But after a botched attempt in Czechoslovakia to unmask the traitor, Smiley is called in by the government to find out what went wrong with that operation and who is handing secrets to the Soviets.

The screenplay, by Arthur Hopcraft, was adapted from John le Carré's novel of the same name, his fifth to feature Smiley. The story was based on le Carré's own time in the intelligence service and on the unmasking of British spies "The Cambridge Five" as KGB agents.

More than five hours long (re-edited for the US market), *Tinker Tailor Soldier Spy* was gloriously slow, ensuring that the viewers got to know the suspects and their idiosyncrasies. The series was full of British character actors, with Ian Richardson, Bernard Hepton, Terence Rigby, and Michael Aldridge as Control's suspects and memorable cameos by Beryl Reid and Patrick Stewart. The gradual unraveling was immensely satisfying and Guinness exuded experience, patience, and intelligence. The book was also turned into a successful movie in 2011, starring Gary Oldman as Smiley. **WH**

Sapphire and Steel

Fantasy/Horror/Sci-Fi | UK | 1979–82

Popular show that demonstrated that not all mysteries need neat solutions

Cast | David McCallum, Joanna Lumley, David Collings
Original broadcaster | ITV
For fans of . . . | *Doctor Who* (1963), *A Ghost Story for Christmas* (1971), *The Invisible Man* (1975), *The Omega Factor* (1979)

Sapphire and Steel were beings with superpowers who took human form to investigate and, when possible, fix cracks in time. David McCallum played Steel with the cold absence of emotion that his name suggested. He was the rationalist while Joanna Lumley's Sapphire was sensitive and able to detect irregularities in time. Often, the conundrums facing the pair were moral ones: First World War soldiers killed after the 1918 cease-fire wanting a second chance, or animals slaughtered for human consumption terrorizing time travelers from the future. (In the final episode, they were confronted with a problem so convoluted that it seemed they might be trapped forever.)

Creator P.J. Hammond—who had honed his TV storytelling on the likes of *Z Cars* (1962)—combined the creepiest elements of science fiction and ghost fantasy to create something genuinely unsettling, preying on our collective fears of sinister forces lurking just out of sight. Each story played out across multiple half-hour episodes, with the causes of the time disturbances often veiled for weeks. The menace could be hidden in a meme—such as the recitation of a nursery rhyme— or in photographs. Indeed, with such an abstract menace as the ever-menacing time, and few easy explanations, *Sapphire and Steel* was a strong contender for the strangest British prime-time drama since *The Prisoner* (1967). "People liked it because it scared them a little bit, and confused them a little bit," McCallum observed. "It was a good show." **JS**

To the Manor Born

Comedy | UK | 1979–81; 2007

Riches to rags comedy that drew laughter from the British class structure

Cast | Penelope Keith, Peter Bowles, Angela Thorne, Daphne Heard, John Rudling, Michael Bilton
Original broadcaster | BBC One
For fans of . . . | *The Good Life* (1975), *A Fine Romance* (1981), *Jeeves and Wooster* (1990)

It's easy to dismiss *To the Manor Born* as middle-of-the-road. However, that does a disservice to the quietly subversive writing of Peter Spence and the playfulness of stars Penelope Keith and Peter Bowles. There was a sparkle to the tale of widowed Audrey fforbes-Hamilton (Keith) falling from lofty heights when forced to sell Grantleigh Manor to pay off her late husband's debts and move into the estate lodge. The buyer was debonair, foreign-born businessman Richard DeVere (Bowles)—and, inevitably, romantic frissons ensued (although, amid the comedy, there were messages about class divide and erosion of country values.)

The show's origins can be traced to the early 1970s, when Spence married into a family that owned a sprawling country estate. Meanwhile, Keith enjoyed success as suburban snob Margo Leadbetter in *The Good Life*, and Spence's newly hatched concept was considered a good fit for the actress. A radio pilot, recorded in 1976 by Keith and Canadian actor Bernard Braden, went unbroadcast when the BBC realized the tale had TV potential. However, by the time Keith was available (after the end of *The Good Life* in 1978), Braden wasn't and Bowles was drafted in. *To the Manor Born* was a hit; the first season finale earned British comedy's highest audience figures of the 1970s.

The story returned to its roots in 1997 for a ten-part series on BBC Radio 2. And in 2007, the cast reunited for a one-off Christmas special, whose ratings confirmed the show's place among Britain's best-loved sitcoms. **MW**

Buck Rogers in the 25th Century

Fantasy/Horror/Sci-Fi | USA | 1979–81

Pulp (science) fiction

Cast | Gil Gerard, Erin Gray, Tim O'Connor, Felix Silla, Mel Blanc, Eric Server, Pamela Hensley
Original broadcaster | NBC
Award | 1 Emmy
For fans of . . . | *Battlestar Galactica* (1978)

Star Wars created a thirst for fast-paced, effects-heavy sci-fi. TV was quick to catch on, especially producer Glen A. Larson, who had made his name with *The Six Million Dollar Man* (1974). In quick succession, he launched *Battlestar Galactica* (1978) and *Buck Rogers in the 25th Century* into orbit, even reusing props from the former in the latter—a spacey smorgasbord of cute robots, tight jumpsuits, and exotic princesses.

The source for *Buck Rogers* was a character who had debuted in pulp adventure stories in 1928 and adapted for comic strips, radio, and a serial starring *Flash Gordon*'s Buster Crabbe. Originally intended as a series of TV movies, Larson's *Buck Rogers* first took flight on the big screen as a film that earned $21 million at the box office. NBC duly green-lit the TV series.

The first season featured threat-of-the-week stories in which Buck fought both the mighty Draconians and the amorous attentions of Princess Ardala (Pamela Hensley). In the second and final season, the focus switched to the adventures of Buck, his colleague Colonel Wilma Deering (Erin Gray), and robot sidekick Twiki (voiced by Mel Blanc, who also voiced Daffy Duck's alter-ego Duck Dodgers), and the core crew of the starship *Searcher*.

Buck Rogers in the 25th Century bridged the gap between big- and small-screen sci-fi, and its space battle sequences still hold up today. It was canceled after two seasons, but is fondly remembered for colorful stories, a strong female role model in Wilma Deering, and, in the form of Twiki, TV's cutest space robot. **MW**

Hart to Hart

Drama | USA | 1979–84

When they met, it was murder

Cast | Robert Wagner, Stefanie Powers, Lionel Stander
Original broadcaster | ABC
Award | 1 Golden Globe
For fans of . . . | *Murder, She Wrote* (1984), *Dempsey and Makepeace* (1985), *Diagnosis Murder* (1993)

Created by bestselling writer Sidney Sheldon and produced by Aaron Spelling and Leonard Goldberg, *Hart to Hart* featured movie star Robert Wagner as Jonathan Hart and Stefanie Powers as Jennifer Hart, a rich Californian couple who often found themselves in close proximity to crime.

Shows such as *The Brady Bunch* (1969) and *The Addams Family* (1964) explained the premise of the show in their theme song, but *Hart to Hart* opened each episode with the now-classic introduction by Max (Lionel Stander), the Harts' deep-voiced, faithful butler, chauffeur, and cook: "This is my boss: Jonathan Hart, a self-made millionaire. He's quite a guy. This is Mrs. H. She's gorgeous. What a terrific lady. By the way, my name is Max. I take care of them, which ain't easy, 'cause when they met, it was murder." The show's iconic opening, complete with Max's monologue, was replicated in one of the *The Greatest Event in Television History* (2012) specials.

The glamorous Harts, aided by Max and their dog, Freeway, stumbled into episodes of theft, smuggling, and espionage, and, more often than not realized they were the ones with more resources and wit than the local authorities, therefore able to solve the crime. The easy banter and tactile relationship of the fun-loving Harts kept audiences rooting for them throughout.

In 1993, Jonathan, Jennifer, and Max returned for the first of eight two-hour *Hart to Hart* movies. Wagner and Powers then portrayed the couple three more times. **RP**

☉ Gil Gerard—"A beefy sort," said *TV Guide*, "squarish of jaw, stuffed into a tight white suit and looking rather like a Polish sausage."

The wedding of a British prince to a shy young girl captured hearts around the world. British pop acts starred in innovative videos that were created solely to promote them on MTV in the United States, while a news report from famine-struck Ethiopia inspired pop's defining moment as an estimated 1.9 billion people worldwide tuned in for *Live Aid*. We said goodbye to *M*A*S*H*, which broke records for a TV finale with more than 105 million viewers, while a new British soap opera, *EastEnders*, began a tradition of grim Christmas specials that has brilliantly blighted the season ever since.

1980s

◄ Homer and his family are alarmed to meet apparitions of their former selves in an episode of *The Simpsons* (1989).

Berlin Alexanderplatz

Drama | Germany | 1980

A harrowing account of life in Germany between the two World Wars

Cast | Günter Lamprecht, Hanna Schygulla, Barbara Sukowa, Elisabeth Trissenaar, Gottfried John, Brigitte Mira
Original broadcaster | TeleCulture **For fans of . . .** | *Acht Stunden sind kein Tag* (*Eight Hours Are Not a Day*, 1972)

Based on the celebrated 1929 novel by Alfred Döblin, this fifteen-hour film, directed by Rainer Werner Fassbinder, was divided for television into fourteen demanding episodes.

The protagonist, Franz Biberkopf (Günter Lamprecht), was a petty criminal who had just completed a jail sentence for murdering his girlfriend, a prostitute. On reentering normal life, he found that Berlin had been transformed since he last saw it from an austere imperial capital into an anarchic jungle in which Nazis and communists vied for power in a rapidly failing state.

With poor employment prospects, Franz drifted from job to job and from personal disaster to catastrophe. He lost an arm after having been thrown out of a getaway car by a fellow robber, then discovered that his one true love had been murdered.

The plot is minimal, but the atmosphere is all-consuming. *Berlin Alexanderplatz* demonstrates how people with no interest in politics can be swept away by the tide of global events. It's a masterpiece of cinema reedited for the small screen. **GL**

> **Classic episode**
> *How is One to Live if One Doesn't Want to Die?* |
> *Episode 2.* With few decent jobs available to him, Franz agrees to sell a Nazi newspaper. He meets an old Jewish friend, and reassures him that he is not an anti-Semite.

◬ A strained encounter between Frau Bast (Brigitte Mira) and former jailbird Franz Biberkopf (Günter Lamprecht).

Yes, Minister / Yes, Prime Minister

Comedy | UK | 1980–87

Political sitcom satirizing the complexity of British government

Cast | Paul Eddington, Nigel Hawthorne, Derek Fowlds **Original broadcaster** | BBC Two **Awards** | 3 BAFTAs
For fans of . . . | *Fawlty Towers* (1975), *The Thick of It* (2005)

The problem with political satire is that it often dates incredibly quickly. One of the strengths of *Yes, Minister* was that it didn't satirize political times, events, or people so much as the machines, processes, and practices of government. It followed Jim Hacker MP (Paul Eddington), who was appointed to the (fictional) Department of Administrative Affairs, and two civil servants: his permanent secretary, Sir Humphrey Appleby (Nigel Hawthorne) and his principal private secretary, Bernard Woolley (Derek Fowlds). Most of the humor revolved around Hacker trying to make a change for the good, Sir Humphrey thwarting him because he believed the real power lay with the civil service, and Bernard getting caught somewhere in the middle.

Throughout the entire run Antony Jay and Jonathan Lynn's writing remained as sharp as on first broadcast. The linguistic dexterity on display was unparalleled. One of Sir Humphrey's speeches, as he tried to win Hacker around while obfuscating his real point and motives, combined with the wonderfully supercilious performance of Hawthorne; it was a joy to watch. **LH**

Classic episode
Party Games | *Season 3, episode 8*. The prime minister has resigned, the home secretary has quit after being arrested as part of his own anti-drink-driving initiative, and Sir Humphrey is promoted. Who will be the next prime minister?

⬀ Nigel Hawthorne (Sir Humphrey), Derek Fowlds (Bernard Woolley), and Paul Eddington (Jim Hacker) spin the daily news.

Juliet Bravo

Crime/Mystery | UK | 1980–85

*A woman in charge of a police station?
Whatever next?*

Cast | Stephanie Turner, Anna Carteret, David Ellison,
Noel Collins
Original broadcaster | BBC One
For fans of . . . | *The Gentle Touch* (1980),
Cagney & Lacey (1981)

Change was in the air on British TV in the early 1980s as the small screen finally—albeit slowly—embraced changes in gender politics. *Juliet Bravo* was the BBC's contribution to this sweeping social change: a police procedural featuring a strong female protagonist who must overcome the prejudices of her predominantly male colleagues.

Stephanie Turner brought an honest, good-humored charm to the role of Inspector Jean Darblay, arriving in the fictional northern town of Hartley to take up position as senior officer in the all-male-staffed police station. In the series creator Ian Kennedy Martin's opening episode, "Shot Gun," Darblay dealt with an estranged father who abducted his daughter at gunpoint, while overcoming the sexist ambivalence of her subordinates. There was a starkness to *Juliet Bravo*, epitomized in the domestic nature of many of the crimes and the depiction of Darblay's home life. The series had pedigree, too: Kennedy Martin had created *The Sweeney* (1975), while Turner played the first regular speaking female police officer in *Z Cars* (1962), a drama with which *Juliet Bravo* clearly shared DNA.

After three seasons, Turner departed, fearing typecasting. Her replacement was Anna Carteret as Inspector Kate Longton, who provided a tough contrast to Darblay's softer approach. The show continued for another three seasons before coming to an end in 1985 as the last of a breed of BBC police dramas that had begun with *Dixon of Dock Green* (1955). **MW**

Hi-de-Hi!

Comedy | UK | 1980–88

*"Good morning, campers!"
Join the holiday rock 1950s style*

Cast | Ruth Madoc, Paul Shane, Su Pollard, Jeffrey
Holland, Diane Holland, Felix Bowness, Simon Cadell
Original broadcaster | BBC One
Award | 1 BAFTA
For fans of . . . | *Are You Being Served?* (1972)

Following their success with *Dad's Army* (1968) and *Some Mothers Do 'Ave 'Em* (1973), writers David Croft and Jimmy Perry launched another sitcom with an ensemble cast, this time taking viewers back to the 1950s. Perry drew on his postwar experience working at a Butlins holiday camp for inspiration for the tales of the staff and entertainers of the fictional Maplins.

Memorable characters and broad comedy combined with genuinely touching moments as those on the bottom of the entertainment ladder interacted with old stalwarts past their prime. Central to the action was the camp announcer and sports manager, Gladys Pugh (Ruth Madoc), who was forever pursuing the posh, and out-of-his-depth, new entertainment manager Jeffrey Fairbrother (Simon Cadell), who provided much of the earlier series' drama. Camp comic Ted Bovis (Paul Shane) was always on the make, and together with his sidekick, would-be stand-up Spike (Jeffrey Holland), and chalet maid Peggy (Su Pollard), he provided not only the belly laughs, but also some lump-in-the-throat moments. In the final episode, the staff heard the sad news that the camp was closing down, just after Peggy had been awarded her much sought-after yellow coat. Returning to her day job to help with a final clean, she waved off a bus full of campers. "Hi-de-Hi!" she muttered in possibly the finest example of tragic comedy. The nation wept. A stage show spin-off, featuring some of the cast, later took the campsite comedy, appropriately enough, to Blackpool. **DJ**

Shogun

Historical drama | USA | 1980

A miniseries that kept Americans glued to their armchairs—and also got them interested in all things Japanese

Cast | Richard Chamberlain, Toshiro Mifune, Yoko Shimada, Furanki Sakai
Original broadcaster | NBC
Awards | 3 Emmys, 3 Golden Globes
For fans of . . . | *The Thorn Birds* (1983)

Based on the best-selling novel by James Clavell and the adventures of English navigator William Adams, who journeyed to feudal Japan in 1600 and rose to a high rank in the service of the shogun, this miniseries followed Englishman John Blackthorne's experiences and intrigues in Japan in the early seventeenth century. After his Dutch trading ship ran aground in a violent storm on the east coast of Japan, Blackthorne (Richard Chamberlain), the ship's navigator, was taken prisoner by samurai warriors. When he was released, he had to adapt to the alien Japanese culture in order to survive. A Protestant, Blackthorne forged an alliance with Lord Toranaga (Toshiro Mifune), who mistrusted the Catholics gaining a foothold in Japan. In order to help Blackthorne assimilate into Japanese culture, Toranaga assigned him a teacher and interpreter: the beautiful Lady Mariko (Yoko Shimada). Blackthorne became infatuated with her, but Mariko was already married, and their budding romance was doomed.

NBC had the highest weekly Nielsen ratings in its history with *Shogun*. Its 26.3 average rating was the second highest in TV history after ABC's with *Roots* (1977). In fact, so many viewers stayed home to watch the miniseries that restaurants and movie theaters reported an enormous decrease in business. An average of 32.9 percent of all TV households watched at least part of the series, and its success caused the mass-market paperback edition of Clavell's novel to become the best-selling paperback in the United States. **RP**

Classic episode
Season 1, episode 1 Shipwrecked Blackthorne finds himself in the middle of a conflict between the two most powerful men in Japan as they struggle to be Shogun, the supreme military leader of the nation.

⬥ Richard Chamberlain in a publicity shot for *Shogun*.

Magnum P.I.

Drama | USA | 1980–88

Tom Selleck played the seductive lead in this Hawaii-based detective show about a Ferrari-driving private eye who solves the islands' crimes

Cast | Tom Selleck, John Hillerman, Roger E. Mosley, Larry Manetti
Original broadcaster | CBS   **Awards** | 2 Golden Globes
For fans of . . . | *Hawaii Five-0* (1968), *Moonlighting* (1985), *Midnight Caller* (1988)

Magnum P.I.'s biggest draw was its lead actor. Cast to play the eponymous private eye, six-foot-four Tom Selleck brought charm, comic timing, and sex appeal in spades. Signing up to the show cost him the chance to play Indiana Jones in *Raiders of the Lost Ark* (1987), as production schedules clashed. Steven Spielberg's loss was television's gain. From 1980 until 1988, *Magnum P.I.* was an enormous hit.

The show was the brainchild of American producer Donald P. Bellisario, known for *Quantum Leap* (1989) and *NCIS* (2003). His central character was a Vietnam veteran Thomas Magnum, who lived in Oahu, Hawaii, on a 200-acre estate owned by novelist Robin Masters, who was never seen, but voiced by Orson Welles. The estate manager was Higgins, an uptight Englishman who was antagonistic toward Magnum until a mutual respect developed. Magnum had two sidekicks: T.C., a helicopter pilot, and Rick, the suave manager of a members-only club. The stories were a mix of the silly and the serious, but all were set in the sunny world of Hawaii. Magnum zipped around in a Ferrari 308 GTS, wore colorful shirts, and had a new woman on his arm every week.

Using a classic detective story device, the show featured dry voice-overs from Selleck, such as "I know what you're thinking, and you're right. . ." There were parodies of genre conventions, even spoofing *Raiders of the Lost Ark* (1981) at one point, ghosts from time to time, and even a crossover episode with *Murder, She Wrote* (1984). It was escapist fun of the highest order. **IF**

Classic episode
Flashback | Season 3, episode 7. Magnum dreams that he has been teleported back to the 1930s—versions of his friends are there, as are the clues he needs to solve his latest case—the framing of a union leader for murder.

◎ Tom Selleck's contract as Magnum meant he had to turn down the role of Indiana Jones.

Verstehen Sie Spass?

Variety | Germany | 1980–present

The spectacular success of this long-running German prank show had as much to do with its likable hosts as its well-worn format

Cast | Paola and Kurt Felix, Harald Schmidt, Frank Elstner
Original broadcaster | ARD
For fans of . . . | *Candid Camera* (1960), *Wetten dass …?* (1981), *Surprise Surprise* (1984)

During the 1980s heyday of Saturday night variety shows, *Verstehen Sie Spass?* (*Can You Take a Joke?*), a potent mix of slapstick and schadenfreude, was one of Germany's must-see TV programs. Hosted by its likable Swiss creator, Kurt Felix, and his wife, Paola, it featured prerecorded clips of unsuspecting celebrities and ordinary people being provoked into losing their temper in front of hidden cameras. Once this had been achieved, the presenters would appear out of nowhere and ask the title question: "Can you take a joke?"

At its peak, the program attracted around thirty million viewers across all German-speaking countries, and in 1988 its hosts were voted Germany's favorite TV presenters. However, the couple quit the show (and presenting) in 1990. After a two-year gap, the up-and-coming comedian Harald Schmidt took up the reins. His quick wit and irreverent humor attracted younger viewers, but many older people felt alienated by Schmidt's ego and audience figures declined. Schmidt left and subsequently established himself as Germany's answer to David Letterman.

Since then, many well-known presenters (including Frank Elstner, the creator of another popular German variety show, *Wetten, dass . . .?*, 1981) have hosted the program. However, none has had the same success as Paola and her late husband Kurt, who died in 2012. A full sixteen years after retiring from television, the pair were voted "Germany's perfect couple" by viewers of the state-run channel ARD. **DH**

Classic episode
1987: TV host Rudi Carrell claimed he would never fall for the hidden-camera routine. But when his marital bed is awarded to the winners of his own game show, he is perplexed as to how the show could have got hold of it.

⊙ Kurt Felix, the Swiss creator and cohost of the big German hit *Verstehen Sie Spass?*

Cosmos

Documentary | USA | 1980

Landmark science documentary with mass-market appeal

Cast | Carl Sagan **Original broadcaster** | PBS **Awards** | 3 Emmys
For fans of . . . | *Through the Wormhole* (2010)

Created by cosmologist Carl Sagan, astrophysicist Steven Soter, and producer Ann Druyan, *Cosmos* was a landmark documentary that covered the origins of life, the principles of physics, and the biographies of scientists who contributed to our understanding of the universe. It even speculated about what we might discover in the future. Although much of the series utilized extensive special effects—the most for a documentary at that time—the production also traveled the globe to film Sagan as he journeyed through time and space in his "Ship of the Imagination." The musical accompaniment to Sagan's endeavor was itself mesmerizing, blending work by Greek composer Vangelis with classical pieces.

There were some members of the scientific community who would always say that Sagan sold out, preferring popularity and stardom to the "serious" pursuit of science, but to many viewers he offered one of the most compelling and entertaining introductions to the world of scientific inquiry ever made. By bringing science to TV in an easily understandable way, while never talking down to his audience, Sagan opened minds and inspired many to pursue their dreams in scientific fields and contemplate their existence not just as human beings, but as "star stuff." A truncated special edition of the series released in 1986 updated the special effects, and it was accompanied by a specially written soundtrack, again by Vangelis. **ATB**

◔ Carl Sagan attempted to explain theories of the universe without losing his television audience.

A Town Like Alice

Drama | Australia | 1981

She survived the Japanese death marches in Malaya, but can she survive love in the Aussie outback?

Cast | Helen Morse, Bryan Brown, Gordon Jackson, Yuki Shimoda   **Original broadcaster** | Seven Network
Award | 1 Emmy   **For fans of . . .** | *Tenko* (1981), *The Flying Doctors* (1986)

In the early 1980s, *A Town Like Alice* was the most ambitious and successful TV miniseries produced in Australia. In three two-hour parts, it traveled from wartorn Malaya to dreary postwar London and the harsh Australian outback. Novelist Nevil Shute's epic love story was told boldly and beautifully.

Englishwoman Jean Paget (Helen Morse) was caught in Malaya in 1941 by the invading Japanese army. She and other English women and children were forced to march from one side of the country to the other for six grueling months. The trek took a heavy toll and by the time they met Aussie prisoner of war Joe Harman (Bryan Brown), only half their number survived. Joe helped them, but was caught and brutally punished. The remaining women survived the war because of Jean's resilience. In 1948 Jean met solicitor Noel Strachan (Gordon Jackson) to discuss a healthy inheritance. While Noel fell in love with her, she was determined to repay villagers who helped her, so traveled back to Malaya. She learned that Joe survived and headed to Alice Springs to find him. Life in the outback Queensland town where Joe worked was far from the idyllic scene that he had described. Jean was treated poorly by the people there until she earned their respect by virtue of her conduct during a life-threatening flood. This version of *A Town Like Alice* was credited with revitalizing the Australian love of the miniseries format, and was easily one of the best of the genre. **SJG**

◉ Bryan Brown and Helen Morse as the lovers Jean Paget and Joe Harman.

Dynasty

Drama | USA | 1981–89

Glitz and glamor, sex, and superbitches

Cast | John Forsythe, Linda Evans, John James, Joan Collins   **Original broadcaster** | ABC   **Award** | 1 Emmy,
5 Golden Globes   **For fans of . . .** | *Knots Landing* (1979), *Falcon Crest* (1981), *The Colbys* (1985)

In 1978, CBS launched *Dallas*, an expensive glossy saga about a huge family and their oil empire, and it created a whole new subgenre: the prime-time soap. In 1981, ABC launched a rival, *Dynasty*, following the story of the Carrington family, their oil empire, and the marriage of magnate Blake Carrington (John Forsythe) to his secretary, Krystle Jennings (Linda Evans). Standard story-of-the-week fare included betrayal, homosexuality (groundbreaking for US prime-time TV in 1981), snobbery, fast cars, and fast girls. And then the producers trumped all that at the end of season one by introducing a new character, Alexis (Joan Collins).

Alexis changed *Dynasty* forever. Each season got progressively more outlandish, yet *Dynasty* was more than just Alexis proving that women on TV could be strong, sexy, and fun: it ran the gamut of every soap staple. The Carringtons and Colbys married time and time again, swapping wives and husbands like coat-check tickets. Murders, affairs, long-lost unheard-of-relatives, and a two-season spin-off (*The Colbys*, 1985) were just part of what kept the audience coming back. **GR**

Classic episode

The Vendetta | *Season 6, episode 30*. Blake has lost everything; Alexis has Denver-Carrington, she has the mansion, and she has money—"Take this junk, and your blonde tramp, and get out of my home!"—so Blake throttles her.

Linda Evans, John Forsythe, Michael Nader, and Joan Collins in the episode "The Proposal," broadcast in 1988.

Bergerac

Crime/Mystery | UK | 1981–91

A recovering alcoholic cleans up crime, and his own life, on the wealthy island of Jersey

Cast | John Nettles, Terence Alexander, Louise Jameson, Sean Arnold, Annette Badland
Original broadcaster | BBC One   **Award** | 1 BAFTA   **For fans of . . .** | *Shoestring* (1979), *Midsomer Murders* (1997)

The cop who doesn't do things by the book is a classic crime drama trope, and in Jim Bergerac, writer Robert Banks Stewart and actor John Nettles created the perfect specimen. In fact, Bergerac came into being by default. Banks Stewart already had a success with the series *Shoestring* (1979), so when its star, Trevor Eve, quit, Stewart used his leftover ideas to develop *Bergerac*, set on the picturesque Channel Island of Jersey.

A recovering alcoholic, Bergerac drove a classic car (a 1947 Triumph Roadster), had an ex-wife called Deborah and a daughter, Kim. He also had a string of girlfriends, in particular estate agent Susan Young (Louise Jameson), who died at the start of season eight. Many of the crimes Bergerac investigated involved Jersey's wealthy residents. His way into this stratum of society was often through his father-in-law, the cigar-chomping Charlie Hungerford, endearingly portrayed by Terence Alexander.

As well as drawing in big audiences, *Bergerac* turned Jersey into a tourist hot spot, and tours of key locations continue to this day. **WH**

> **Classic episode**
> *Ice Maiden* | *Season 3, episode 4*. Jewel thief, and recurring love-interest/villainess Philippa Vale (Liza Goddard) raises Bergerac's suspicions when she visits the island just before a major diamond auction is to be held.

◉ Sean Arnold as Crozier and John Nettles as Jim Bergerac fight crime on the streets of a small island.

Brideshead Revisited

Historical drama | UK | 1981

A throwback to a lost age of TV drama with big ideas and big budgets

Cast | Jeremy Irons, Anthony Andrews, Diana Quick, John Gielgud, Laurence Olivier
Original broadcaster | ITV
Awards | 7 BAFTAs, 1 Emmy, 2 Golden Globes
For fans of . . . | *The Jewel in the Crown* (1984)

Jeremy Irons was the perfect Charles Ryder, his extensive and consistently weary narration running throughout ITV's big-budget adaptation of Evelyn Waugh's best-known literary work, *Brideshead Revisited*. Ryder's tale of his two-decade connection to Brideshead Castle and the attendant members of the Marchmain family was brought to life on-screen in rich fashion. Adding veteran gravitas to the large and superlative cast were John Gielgud and Laurence Olivier, with Castle Howard in Yorkshire serving as Brideshead itself.

However, *Brideshead Revisited* had an uncertain gestation, with strike action halting production after the completion of location shoots abroad, and Irons' subsequent commitment to *The French Lieutenant's Woman* (1981) causing further delay. During these pauses, the serial expanded by degrees from an original six-hour running time. Where many literary adaptations are, by their nature, cut to the quick to accommodate swift running times, *Brideshead Revisited* was afforded a rare opportunity to linger on every syllable of Waugh's novel at eleven hours. Much of the narration was lifted verbatim from the book, while the homosexual undertones present in the text were emphasized here: an atypical choice for a prime-time British drama in 1981.

Decades after its transmission, *Brideshead Revisited* is still lauded among the finest small-screen dramas ever made. Whether TV drama will ever again be this sumptuous, rich, and detailed remains to be seen. **MW**

The Borgias

Historical drama | UK | 1981

Political and religious intrigue centered around one of the most notorious Italian families

Cast | Oliver Cotton, Anne-Louise Lambert, Adolfo Celi, Louis Selwyn
Original broadcaster | BBC Two
For fans of . . . | *I, Claudius* (1976), *The Cleopatras* (1983), *The Borgias* (2011)

BBC Two built its reputation partly on the quality of its historical dramas, and it is highly likely that producer Mark Shivas, when coming up with the idea behind *The Borgias*, was thinking of enhancing that reputation by emulating past TV dynastical glories such as Philip Mackie's *The Caesars* (Granada, 1968) and Jack Pulman's flawless *I, Claudius* (BBC Two, 1976). Although the subject didn't offer the generational scope of those previous two watershed moments of British TV, it was thought that most people would be intrigued by the evil reputation of the family, particularly Lucretia and Rodrigo Borgia, and would want to know more about them. The suits at BBC Two were persuaded; this production would be expensive and beautifully shot, with amazing sets and a beautiful cast.

In the event, much of this came to be, but the critics were unsatisfied. One issue was Adolfo Celi's key performance as Rodrigo, with the audience struggling to understand what he was saying through his thick Sicilian accent. BBC One's production of *Jamaica Inn* (2014) caused a minor storm for the same reason, and the virtues of both shows were overlooked as a consequence. The audience certainly did get to know more about the Borgias, too, but no amount of sex and violence compensated for a script, produced by the usually amazing Ken Taylor and historian John Prebble, that was long on history but short on action. The lesson carried away from *The Borgias* was that good storytelling is now more important than ever. **SO**

◀ (L–R) Jeremy Irons as Charles Ryder and Anthony Andrews as Sebastian Flyte: icons of 1980s British drama.

Hill Street Blues

Drama | USA | 1981–87

Complex cop drama that redefined the genre—
"Let's be careful out there"

Cast | Daniel J. Travanti, Veronica Hamel, Michael Conrad
Original broadcaster | NBC
Awards | 26 Emmys, 3 Golden Globes
For fans of . . . | *L.A. Law* (1986)

No one who has seen the first episode of *Hill Street Blues* can forget it, and TV itself never forgot the lessons the show taught about the exciting possibilities inherent within a genre that had long languished in what had seemed like its formulaic senescence. Previously, cop dramas had been about the crime. *Hill Street Blues* showed the world that they could also be about the cops who fought it, their personal lives, their professional struggles, and the grim, compromised moral world in which they were forced to function.

The show's city setting was left deliberately vague: it could be South Central Los Angeles, or the Bronx, or the rough district of Pittsburgh, where show creator Steven Bochco once studied. Its dramas were both specific and universal, and its portrayal of gang culture was unprecedented, as was its depiction of the fraught race relations in the urban jungle. Yet what *Hill Street Blues* said about men and women and their intersecting desires rang true all around the world. Although the show struggled to find its audience, it was critically acclaimed almost from the start, and it launched the career of Bochco, one of the most influential producers in US TV history. It is hard to overstate the influence of *Hill Street Blues* on the subsequent TV landscape. Episodes-long story arcs, human drama mixed with procedural stories, a revolving cast of actors chosen for their authenticity—all these and more are the legacy of a show whose artistic decisions seem even more correct in retrospect. **RL**

Classic episode
Hill Street Station | *Season 1, episode 1*. The show hit the ground running, introducing the precinct and its officers as they respond to a hostage crisis, try to calm an aggressive SWAT team, and find a compromise with troubled gang members.

◉ Betty Thomas as Sgt. Bates and Ed Marinaro as Officer Coffey.
◉ Bruce Weitz (right) as undercover cop Sgt. Belker.

Only Fools and Horses

Comedy | UK | 1981–2003

Lovable rogues on the make; scriptwriting on the money—"Viva la France as they say in Rome"

Cast | David Jason, Nicholas Lyndhurst, Lennard Pearce, Buster Merryfield, Roger Lloyd Pack
Original broadcaster | BBC One   **Awards** | 5 BAFTAs   **For fans of . . .** | *Steptoe and Son* (1962)

More than thirty years after it was first broadcast, *Only Fools and Horses* remains one of Britain's most popular sitcoms. The reason for its success? John Sullivan's comedy writing was unparalleled in the 1980s, and the casting was spot-on. Sullivan captured situations, people, and relationships perfectly in his portrayal of brothers Derek "Del Boy" and Rodney Trotter and their long-suffering Grandad (and in later seasons, Uncle Albert). As market traders, Del Boy (David Jason) and Rodney (Nicholas Lyndhurst) were constantly trying to find the deal that would take them away from the streets of Peckham. "This time next year, we'll be millionaires!" Del promised his world-weary brother. Sullivan explored the use of pathos better in his

comedies than many dramatists: try keeping a dry eye as Del is left standing alone on the dance floor as Rodney gets married. But even in its saddest moments *Only Fools and Horses* made the viewers laugh, and it was this ability of Sullivan that made *Only Fools and Horses* stand above its peers. Who didn't cheer when Del and Rodney finally became "millyonaires"? **LH**

> **Classic episode**
> *The Longest Night* | *Season 5, episode 3.* Del, Rodney, and Uncle Albert are mistakenly held as shoplifters at a supermarket at the same time as a robbery takes place and they all end up having to spend the night in the shop.

⊘ Nicholas Lyndhurst, David Jason, and Lennard Pearce, wheeling and dealing, ducking and diving, and so on.

Das Traumschiff

Drama | Germany | 1981–present

Still cresting the waves after more than thirty years

Cast | Heide Keller, Sascha Hehn, Nick Wilder, Harald Schmidt, Heinz Hoenig, Gaby Dohm, Evelyn Hamann
Original broadcaster | ZDF   **For fans of . . .** | *The Love Boat* (1977), *Hotel* (1983), *Die Schwarzwaldklinik* (1985)

Inspired by the American series *The Love Boat* (1977), set on a cruise ship, *Das Traumschiff* (*The Dream Ship*) didn't fall far from the tree. Action revolves around the love affairs and problems of the ship's passengers and crew, who seek guidance from the ship's triumvirate—the captain, doctor, and chief stewardess. The latter, a mother figure called Beatrice, played by Heide Keller since day one of the show, dispenses advice on everything from finding a life partner to terminal illness.

Visits to far-flung places, such as Thailand, Kenya, and Tahiti, make up almost half of each episode. The combination of exotic landscapes, light drama, happy endings, and familiar actors (it attracts guest performances from some of Germany's biggest stars)

has proved enduringly popular, with ten million viewers tuning in to episodes lasting up to two hours.

Given that *Das Traumschiff*'s core audience is of a certain vintage, it seems unlikely that the series will be able to match other long-established German dramas such as *Tatort* (1970), a police procedural that proved enduringly popular with all ages. **DH**

Classic episode
Season 1, episode 23. Against the backdrop of the Chinese New Year festivities in Hong Kong, steward Klaus has a disastrous altercation with a passenger whose heroin-addict daughter he helped several years ago.

⬣ Siegfried Rauch (Captain Paulsen), Heide Keller (Chief Stewardess Beatrice), and Nick Wilder (Dr. Wolf Sander).

The Fall Guy

Action/Adventure | USA | 1981–86

Good ol' boy action with a truck-driving stuntman turned bounty hunter

Cast | Lee Majors, Douglas Barr, Heather Thomas, Jo Ann Pflug, Markie Post, Nedra Volz
Original broadcaster | ABC **For fans of . . .** | *The Six Million Dollar Man* (1974)

After the success of stunt movie *Hooper* (1978), starring Burt Reynolds, prolific TV producer Glen A. Larson developed *The Fall Guy* centered on Colt Seavers (Lee Majors), a stuntman who made extra money working as a bounty hunter. Joined by stuntwoman Jody Banks (Heather Thomas) and fledgling stunt performer Howie "Kid" Munson (Douglas Barr), Colt juggled toiling on movie sets with tracking down criminals trying to jump bail, all the while pulling off spectacular stunts in both jobs. Thanks to the huge volume of stunts involving Colt's pickup truck, many of which caused lasting damage, the show ran through numerous vehicles.

Celebrity cameos were common in *The Fall Guy*—Richard Burton, Buzz Aldrin, La Toya Jackson—as were nods to Major's previous bionic exploits on *The Six Million Dollar Man* (1974). Although much of the show was formulaic, run-of-the-mill 1980s action adventure with the requisite car and physical stunts, the series is also remembered for featuring Majors as the lead vocalist for the somewhat incongruously heartfelt theme song "The Unknown Stuntman." **ATB**

> **Classic episode**
> *Reluctant Traveling Companion* | *Season 2, Episode 6*. Colt must accompany a difficult woman to the East Coast. On the train they find themselves next to Richard Burton. There is also a killer who wants Colt's disruptive charge dead.

⌾ Guest star Judith Chapman joins Lee Majors as stuntman Colt Seavers in the episode "Goin' For It," broadcast in 1982.

Wetten, dass. . . ?

Game show | Germany | 1981–2014

Talent, celebrities, and danger proved a winning formula for this long-running game show

Cast | Frank Elstner, Thomas Gottschalk, Wolfgang Lippert, Markus Lanz
Original broadcaster | ZDF **For fans of . . .** | *Deal Or No Deal* (2005), *America's Got Talent* (2006)

One of the most successful game shows of all time, *Wetten, dass . . . ? (Wanna Bet?)* was a cornerstone of German television for over thirty years. Broadcast live from a glamorous location that changed weekly, it drew A-list guests (Tom Cruise, Bill Gates, and Angelina Jolie) and top singers (Madonna, Lady Gaga, One Direction, Luciano Pavarotti). But the meat of the show was a string of audacious stunts performed by the public.

The role of the celebrities was to bet on whether the feats could be pulled off. Did Megan Fox believe that Marion and Michael could recognize their dog's teeth marks on a frisbee? Did Jennifer Lawrence and Liam Hemsworth think Alexander's friends could build a tower of beer crates under him while he flipped somersaults?

Tragedy triggered the show's decline. In 2010, a contestant was paralyzed live on air while jumping over moving cars. The broadcast ended abruptly and host Thomas Gottschalk resigned. A softer format and a new host, Markus Lanz, proved unpopular and the show ended in 2014. But is this the end for the format? Markus's last words were: "Life goes on. Wanna bet?" **JG**

Classic episode

October 7, 1995. A typically bizarre and compelling edition of the show in which thirteen swimmers took on the challenge of hauling a boat weighing 312 tons over a distance of 80 feet (25 m).

◉ The stunts on *Wetten, dass...?* were often spectacular, sometimes crazy, and frequently just weird.

The Chinese Detective

Crime/Mystery | UK | 1981–82

A British-born Asian cop with complex motives solves cases on the streets of London

Cast | David Yip, Derek Martin, Robert Lee, Arthur Kelly
Original broadcaster | BBC One
For fans of . . . | *Shoestring* (1979), *Juliet Bravo* (1980), *Bergerac* (1981)

Devised and created by writer Ian Kennedy Martin, whose distinguished track record included ITV's popular police drama *The Sweeney* (1975), *The Chinese Detective* marked the first and only time a Chinese actor had played the lead role in a British television series.

David Yip played John Andrew Ho, a Detective Sergeant in the Limehouse district of London. A second-generation immigrant born and brought up in the Chinese community of London's East End, Ho had joined the police in an effort to find an identity outside this strict community. When asked where he is from, Ho replied simply, "I'm Cockney." However, Ho had another reason for joining the police force—he was determined to nail the ex-cop who had framed his father, and this dark backstory ran like a thread through the first season.

Although the identity of this ex-cop was eventually revealed, fresh cases took precedence each week in classic police procedural style. Ho often solved these through his connections in the Asian community in Limehouse, which was evocatively portrayed. Ho's cheerfully racist superior, Detective Inspector Berwick (Derek Martin) couldn't stand his detective sergeant, but had a grudging respect for the fact that Ho got results. However, *The Chinese Detective* never shied away from representing racism and other pressures faced by ethnic minority officers, from both fellow policemen and the public. The program is well-remembered by older viewers to this day. **JGT**

The Day of the Triffids

Fantasy/Horror/Sci-fi | UK | 1981

John Wyndham's sci-fi classic brought to life for the small screen

Cast | John Duttine, Emma Relph, Maurice Colbourne, Jenny Lipman, Desmond Adams
Original broadcaster | BBC One
For fans of . . . | *Doctor Who* (1963), *Survivors* (1975), *The Walking Dead* (2010)

A brilliant meteor shower blinded the majority of the United Kingdom, perhaps even the world. Bill Masen (John Duttine) was one of the lucky ones, having spent the night of the shower in the hospital with his eyes bandaged after suffering a minor sting from a triffid. Grown for their oil, triffids were walking, thinking plants. They also had projectile stings that, at full strength, could be lethal. With most of humanity unable to see, everyone was vulnerable both to the growing triffid menace and to one another.

Playing on the same kind of apocalyptic "what if" that later powered *The Walking Dead* (2010), *The Day of the Triffids* made for chilling viewing. Viewers saw and heard people panicking, stumbling through the streets as they ran out of basic necessities such as food, fuel, and hope. Each episode revealed a different attempt at rebuilding society: academics elected themselves to the top of an elitist hierarchy, but soon succumbed to a plague; chain gangs of blind people led by a sighted guide quickly proved impractical; even when Bill and his girlfriend Jo (Emma Relph) set up home in a remote cottage protected by an electric fence, they found that they were still not safe from those who wanted security for themselves. What made this miniseries linger in the mind was the lack of resolution, with Bill and his friends determined to carry on while the triffids massed around them, in scenes reminiscent of Alfred Hitchcock's *The Birds* (1963). For fans of the original novel, this was a faithful attempt to bring it to screen. **JS**

Tenko

Historical drama | UK | 1981–85

A harrowing and uplifting dramatization of a real-life story about European women held in Japanese prison camps during the Second World War

Cast | Ann Bell, Stephanie Cole, Stephanie Beacham, Louise Jameson, Burt Kwouk, Claire Oberman, Veronica Roberts, Elizabeth Chambers
Original broadcaster | BBC One **For fans of . . .** |
Secret Army (1977), *Orange Is the New Black* (2013)

Tenko (Japanese for "roll-call") was rooted in a true story—how Western women living in Singapore during the outbreak of the Second World War were captured by the Japanese forces and thrown into prisoner-of-war camps for almost four years. A powerful and mesmerizing TV drama, it burned long in the minds of everyone who saw it.

The series initially followed the story of Marion Jefferson (Ann Bell), a colonel's wife who reluctantly became leader of the British prisoners and had to deal directly with stern-yet-fair Camp Commandant Major Yamauchi (Burt Kwouk). Along with fellow internees Sister Ulrica, formidable Dr. Beatrice Mason, good-time girl Blanche, spoiled snob Rose, the feisty Aussie nurse Kate, and elderly troublemaker Joss, Marion tried to hold herself and her friends together in the hope that they would survive long enough to be rescued.

Some of the characters the audience came to love died of malaria, malnutrition, or the punishments meted out by the guards, and viewers were rocked to their core. No character was safe. If anything, however, the producers toned down some story lines, afraid that viewers wouldn't be able to handle the brutality of the historical facts.

Only small parts of each series were filmed in Singapore; the realistic prison camp set was built in a quarry in Dorset, England. The uniformly magnificent, mainly female, cast forged a strong bond during filming and hold regular reunions to this day. **PC**

Classic episode
Season 2, episode 10. The women have been held for nearly two years and conditions are getting worse. The revelation that Red Cross parcels have been hoarded by the duplicitous Verna Johnson leads to a near riot.

⬥ Rose (Stephanie Beacham) discovers what is in store for the European women and children arriving at the prisoner-of-war camp.

The Hitchhiker's Guide to the Galaxy

Fantasy/Horror/Sci-Fi/Comedy | UK | 1981

The story of the worst Thursday ever

Cast | Peter Jones, Simon Jones, David Dixon, Mark Wing-Davey, Sandra Dickinson, Stephen Moore
Original broadcaster | BBC Two
Awards | 3 BAFTAs
For fans of . . . | *Monty Python's Flying Circus* (1969)

The impact of writer Douglas Adams on popular culture, beginning with his landmark radio drama *The Hitchhiker's Guide to the Galaxy* and including occasional writing credits on *Doctor Who* (1963) and *Not the Nine O'Clock News* (1979), cannot be understated. Adapted into an internationally best-selling series of novels, a computer game, and eventually a feature film, the unique story he crafted was one of the first truly British sci-fi tales to make mainstream impact in the United States and beyond.

The TV version of *The Hitchhiker's Guide to the Galaxy* covered roughly the same material as the first radio series—hapless Englishman Arthur Dent (Simon Jones) is rescued from Earth's destruction at the hands of the sinister Vogons, and is subsequently dragged across the universe by his alien friend, Ford Prefect (David Dixon). It was filmed on a limited budget as a six-episode miniseries, and it united members of the radio cast with several new performers, including Sandra Dickinson as Trillian. Groundbreaking visual effects were combined with animatronics and outlandish costumes, as well as occasionally dodgy special-effects sequences, serving perhaps as a reminder to the audience of the often hilarious farce playing out on their TV screens. Although Adams, who made several cameo appearances in the series (including stark naked from behind in episode two), has since passed, *The Hitchhiker's Guide to the Galaxy* retains its cult classic status. **SL**

Attenti a noi due

Variety | Italy | 1982–83

A variety and comedy extravaganza

Cast | Sandra Mondaini, Raimondo Vianello
Original broadcasters | Channel 5, TVS
For fans of . . . | *The Colgate Comedy Hour* (1950), *The Generation Game* (1971), *Saturday Night Live* (1975), *Noel's House Party* (1991)

If you can get your head around an Italian version of Britain's *The Morecambe & Wise Show* (1968) presented by Johnny Carson and Lady Gaga, then you'll be right at home with *Attenti a noi due* (*Beware of Us*). Husband-and-wife team Raimondo Vianello and Sandra Mondaini presented a mix of music, dance, sketches, and taffeta.

An enthusiastic studio audience applauded every twitch of a spangly curtain. Typically, elaborate dance numbers alternated with sketches, with Sandra frequently striding off for a costume change, pausing for applause on her return. The curtain might pull back for a disco version of a routine from *West Side Story* (1961) or there might be a surreal but genial game show round with a concert pianist and a gunk tank. Guests ranged from Sheena Easton to Sacha Distel. It was variety without mercy.

Sandra and Raimondo were the king and queen of Italian television for more than fifty years. Raimondo was a prolific actor, comedian, host, sports commentator, and movie star, while Sandra had a separate thriving career as a stage and screen comic actor (she voiced Winona Ryder's part as Lisa's rival in the Italian dub of *The Simpsons*; 1989). As a screen duo, however, they were unstoppable, beginning with *Un Juke Box per Dracula* (*Dracula's Jukebox*, 1958) through to the last episode of the sitcom *Casa Vianello* (1988), in which the couple essentially played themselves, in 2008. Sandra died in 2010, five months after Raimondo. **JG**

Cagney & Lacey

Drama | USA | 1982–88

Witty female-led cop show with heart—and a "black belt in mouth karate"

Cast | Sharon Gless, Tyne Daly, John Karlen, Dick O'Neill, Al Waxman, Carl Lumbly, Martin Kove
Original broadcaster | CBS
Awards | 11 Emmys, 1 Golden Globe
For fans of . . . | *Charlie's Angels* (1976)

Devised as a reaction against the male-dominated detective shows of the 1970s and early 1980s, *Cagney & Lacey* had a difficult birth. It was commissioned originally as a TV movie starring Loretta Swit (from *M*A*S*H*, 1972) as Christine Cagney and Tyne Daly as Mary Beth Lacey, two very different New York City police detectives. A series was then optioned, with Meg Foster replacing Swit. After six episodes the series was canceled, and it was only the efforts of producer Barney Rosenzweig and the promise of a recast Cagney, in the form of Sharon Gless, that saved it.

In Gless and Daly, the show had two accomplished star performers, capable of running the gamut from drama to comedy. Uniquely, though, never before had a detective series "gone home" with its lead characters and shown their personal lives and families. Alongside the obligatory police story lines, the show tackled domestic abuse, rape, child pornography, alcoholism (Cagney), and breast cancer (Lacey), while at the same time drawing on the two leads' strengths in comedy. The contrasting characters of Cagney—with her relentless dedication to her job and troubled relationships—and Lacey—with her strong morals, husband, and family—together with a talented and diverse supporting cast provided a rich seam of material that kept the show fresh. Surviving a second cancelation after its second season, *Cagney & Lacey* went from strength to strength, garnering Emmys for either Gless or Daly every year of its life. **PV**

Classic episode
Matinee | *Season 3, episode 1.* A perfect mix of an interesting, dramatic case and a lot of character humor, the show properly hit its stride with this episode involving the murder of a wealthy housewife, and a very funny scene in a strip club.

◉ (L–R) Emmy-winning actress Tyne Daly as Mary Beth Lacey and Golden Globe winner Sharon Gless as Christine Cagney.

Remington Steele

Comedy/Drama | USA | 1982–87

*Charming detective drama with a
"will they, won't they" romantic twist*

Cast | Stephanie Zimbalist, Pierce Brosnan,
Doris Roberts
Original broadcaster | NBC
For fans of . . . | *Hart to Hart* (1979),
Moonlighting (1985)

Remington Steele has sometimes been seen as merely
a precursor to the better remembered *Moonlighting*
(1985), but it had unique charms of its own and a wit
and inventiveness that had aged exceptionally well.
The show attempted something bold and new—a
detective drama that doubled as a romantic comedy—
and its success hinged on the chemistry of its leads.
Fortunately, Stephanie Zimbalist sparkled opposite
Pierce Brosnan, in the role that would first put him in
the frame to play James Bond.

The premise was quite brilliant: Laura Holt (Zimbalist)
was a private detective whom no one would employ
because she was a woman. However, when she devised
a fictional male boss, Remington Steele, and posed as
his assistant, the work came flooding in. Her troubles
began when a man walked through her office door
pretending to be the boss she had invented, and she
was in no position to expose him as an imposter. The
show had fun with its central mystery—just who was
the man claiming to be Remington Steele, and could
he really be trusted?—and teased out the solution over
the course of its five seasons. Also extended, but never
over-extended, was the question of whether Steele and
Laura would find the love they so clearly craved with
each other. It would be easy to undervalue *Remington
Steele*'s innovative blend of playful romance and serious
crime, because it made it seem so effortless, but with
dialogue as sharp as its mysteries, the show is as fresh
today as the day it was first broadcast. **RL**

'Allo, 'Allo!

Comedy | UK | 1982–92

*The ultimate catchphrase-heavy sitcom: "Good
moaning!" "Oooh René!" "You stupid woman!"*

Cast | Gorden Kaye, Carmen Silvera, Vicki Michelle,
Richard Marner, Sam Kelly, Kim Hartman, Guy Siner,
Richard Gibson, Arthur Bostrom, Kirsten Cooke
Original broadcaster | BBC One
For fans of . . . | *Dad's Army* (1968)

René Artois's war was not going well. Despite the Nazi
occupation of France, all he wanted was to be left alone
to run his café and have affairs with his waitresses. But
there were several impediments—the crashed British
airmen hiding in his café, the local Resistance leader
who was determined to turn him into a patriotic
French hero, the bumbling German officers who
used the café to hide priceless stolen artwork, and
the undercover British policeman who spoke French
with a ridiculous English accent. Not to mention the
resistance, the Gestapo, and the Fallen Madonna With
The Big Boobies.

At first sight, *'Allo 'Allo* seemed like a low-rent
sitcom. Old men lusted after beautiful French maids,
shameless double entendres littered the script,
and blatant stereotyping of European nationalities
pandered to the worst Little Englander mentality.
But the show was much more subtle than that. All
nationalities were painted as idiots or scoundrels,
especially the British, and the concept of war as a
heroic act was gently mocked through liberal doses
of smut, giant knockwurst sausages, and comedy
Gestapo officers.

Essentially *'Allo 'Allo* was a brutally accurate parody
of the BBC One drama series *Secret Army* (1977), right
down to the balding café owner with a mustache, the
beret-wearing French Resistance workers, and even the
plotlines. Ridiculously successful, the show lasted nearly
twice as long as the Second World War itself. **PC**

Police Squad!

Comedy | USA | 1982

A tour de force of ridiculous humor that is ridiculously clever—from the makers of Airplane!

Cast | Leslie Nielsen, Alan North, Rex Hamilton, Peter Lupus, Tessa Richarde
Original broadcaster | ABC
For fans of . . . | *Sledge Hammer!* (1986), *Duckman* (1994), *Due South* (1994)

There had never been another TV comedy like it, but the swiftly and unjustly canceled *Police Squad!* went on to spawn the hugely successful *Naked Gun* (1988) movie franchise from creators David Zucker, Jim Abrahams, and Jerry Zucker, who had already showcased their uniquely silly humor with the film *Airplane!* (1980). They originated a comedy style that has been imitated, but never bettered: a frequency and diversity of jokes that guaranteed laughs for every minute of the show.

A pastiche of cop dramas such as *Felony Squad* (1966), *Police Squad!* relied not on recognition for its laughs, but on absurdist humor and razor-sharp verbal and visual gags. It followed the exploits of the squad cops as they bumbled their way through every noir detective drama cliché in the book, hindering far more often than helping, and solving crimes more by luck than judgment. Every line was meticulously crafted to wring out each possible laugh. There were recurring jokes, such as the cast's inept attempts to freeze in place at the end of each episode, and some very low humor, but the genius of the show lay most of all in its central character, Detective Frank Drebin (Leslie Nielsen). "We're sorry to bother you at a time like this," he told a recently widowed woman in one episode. "We would have come earlier, but your husband wasn't dead then." Drebin was so inept that he barely functioned as a human being, let alone a police officer, and his straight-faced careening from disaster to disaster was never less than hilarious. **RL**

Classic episode
Rendezvous at Big Gulch (Terror in the Neighborhood) | *Season 1, episode 5.* Not a second goes by without humor of all types, from blink-and-you'll-miss it sight gags to wonderfully absurd wordplay.

⊘ Tongue-in-cheek detectives: (L–R) Leslie Nielsen (Drebin) and Alan North (Ed Hocken) on the case with Tessa Richarde (Mary).

Knight Rider

Action/Adventure | USA | 1982–86

Knight fights crime with the help of his talking car, KITT

Classic episode
KITT vs KARR | *Season 3, Episode 6.* Mechanic John Stanton finds prototype car KARR buried in sand and is persuaded to reboot and revamp it. KARR embarks on revenge against Michael and KITT.

⊙ David Hasselhoff gets tough as Michael Knight.

Cast | David Hasselhoff, William Daniels, Edward Mulhare, Patricia McPherson
Original broadcaster | NBC
For fans of . . . | *Magnum P.I.* (1980), *The A-Team* (1983), *Airwolf* (1984)

Created by TV producer Glen A. Larson—*Battlestar Galactica* (1978), *The Fall Guy* (1981), *Magnum P.I.* (1980)—*Knight Rider* was pure 1980s-style action and adventure. Fast cars, exciting stunts, nail-biting crime stories, and a charismatic lead character meant that audiences were gripped. In the first episode, billionaire Wilton Knight was looking for a head agent for his crime-fighting organization, the Foundation for Law and Government. So he co-opted policeman Michael Long (David Hasselhoff), who had just survived a near-fatal shooting. With a new appearance thanks to plastic surgery, the renamed Michael Knight led a team that included chief technician Dr. Bonnie Barstow (Patricia McPherson), with whom he developed a flirtatious relationship, and Devon Miles (Edward Mulhare), who ran the missions. The star of the show, however, was Michael's car. KITT (Knight Industries Two Thousand) was a sleek, black Pontiac Firebird Trans Am that had been heavily modified. It included many special features, such as turbos, armor, tracking devices, and most famously an artificial intelligence. Urbanely voiced by William Daniels, KITT became the star of *Knight Rider* as it calmly advised Michael—often during chaotic action scenes.

The show was the start of a franchise that ran for many years. After a pair of TV movies in the early 1990s, there were two attempts at revival series. Neither *Team Knight Rider* (1997) nor *Knight Rider* (2008) lasted very long, but Hasselhoff appeared in the latter to hand over the baton to Michael's son. **IF**

The Comic Strip Presents . . .

Comedy | UK | 1982–2012

Launchpad for a new generation of comics

Cast | Adrian Edmondson, Dawn French, Rik Mayall, Nigel Planer, Peter Richardson, Jennifer Saunders, Alexei Sayle
Original broadcaster | Channel 4
For fans of . . . | *Saturday Live* (1985)

This show pooled the talents of a group of young comedians who had been making names for themselves in the comedy clubs of Central London. Their first episode, "Five Go Mad in Dorset," a parody of the Famous Five novels of Enid Blyton, polarized the viewers: most found it hilarious, but a vocal few thought it disrespectful to the children's classics. However, the objections were good for publicity, making viewers curious to see what all the fuss was about.

The Comic Strip Presents . . . never pulled its punches or shied away from addressing sensitive and sometimes even taboo topics. In the course of its long but sporadic run, it tackled international problems, such as apartheid, and domestic matters, such as the closure of the British coal mines, together with a range of thorny social issues, such as sexism and racism.

In 1990, the show transferred to BBC Two, whose bigger budgets permitted more expansive productions. One of the most ambitious of these was a celebrated episode about the Greater London Council (the British capital's local government assembly), in which the comedians played Hollywood stars playing the roles of English politicians: , for example, Jennifer Saunders played Brigitte Nielsen playing Margaret Thatcher.

The comedians all went on to even greater success in their own right, but for many years they would always happily regroup for further episodes of the show that had propelled them from London's Soho to stardom. **GL**

The Maurizio Costanzo Show

Talk show | Italy | 1982–2009

Italy's longest-running talk show

Cast | Maurizio Costanzo
Original broadcasters | Rete 4, Canale 5, Canale 5 Plus
For fans of . . . | *Face to Face* (1959), *Parkinson* (1971), *Late Night with David Letterman* (1982), *Wogan* (1982), *So Graham Norton* (1998)

Maurizio Costanzo began his career as a journalist, and in 1982 created *The Maurizio Costanzo Show*, the most important and longest-running talk show in Italy. In each episode, a group of illustrious guests discussed a topic that was introduced and moderated by Costanzo. Celebrities, politicians, Nobel Prize laureates, artists, comedians, writers, and the general public all participated. The show soon grew in popularity and became a must-see for millions of Italians. It also enhanced celebrity careers and launched new names. The topics varied from health, politics, gossip, current affairs, money, and crime to culture, art, and literature, and discussions were interspersed with light comedy sketches. Among the topics that had a wider appeal were the role and importance of aid worldwide and the fight against the Mafia.

Costanzo campaigned aggressively against the Mafia and, on May 14, 1993, he and his partner, Maria De Filippi, were victims of an assassination attempt: a car bomb exploded. They escaped unharmed because Costanzo's usual driver was ill, so they were in a different car. Costanzo interrupted his show in 2004, but it came back in 2005. It finally ended in 2009 after twenty-seven successful years. In 2014, Mediaset Extra aired *Maurizio Costanzo Show—The History*, rerunning selected episodes introduced by Costanzo.

The secret of the show's success was its mixture of serious and light moments, so even niche topics could reach a mainstream audience. **SDG**

Cheers

Comedy | USA | 1982–93

The bar "where everybody knows your name"

Classic episode

Thanksgiving Orphans | Season 5, episode 9.
A true ensemble showcase that allows every
character to shine, it mixes sentiment with
cynicism and classic screwball comedy. Naturally,
it culminates in a food fight.

ⓐ The stars of the show won a raft of awards between them.
ⓑ Exterior shots were filmed at the Bull & Finch Pub in Boston.

Cast | Ted Danson, Shelley Long, Rhea Perlman, Kirstie
Alley, George Wendt, John Ratzenberger
Original broadcaster | NBC
Awards | 28 Emmys, 6 Golden Globes
For fans of . . . | *Taxi* (1978), *Frasier* (1993)

Sweet and sour, cutting yet poignant, *Cheers* was
a life-affirming sitcom about the small tragedies of
half-lived lives and the friendships that make them
bearable. It was as near to perfect as any show could
be: hilarious and moving and as emotionally engaging
as any earnest drama. *Cheers* was a show that helped to
redefine its genre, and retains a timeless quality even
thirty years on.

Set in the titular bar where a ragtag band of misfits
regularly gathered, the show found its strength
in its characters: womanizing bartender Sam (Ted
Danson); Diane (Shelley Long), the aspiring poet and
appalling intellectual snob; bitter Carla (Rhea Perlman);
slobbish, work-shy Norm (George Wendt); and Cliff
(John Ratzenberger), a bore who was never boring to
watch. For five seasons, the "will they, won't they" or
even "should they" romance between Sam and Diane
drew in viewers. But the departure of Long, and her
replacement with another love interest for Sam (Kirstie
Alley as Rebecca) did not lessen the show's popularity.
And when Nicholas Colasanto, who played lovable
moron Coach, died, he was ably succeeded by Woody
Harrelson as a younger but no-less-lovable fool.

The setting, the writing, the wit, and the warmth
were the show's true stars and they saw it through
eleven superb seasons. After a slow start in its first
season, the comedy began an inexorable ratings
climb and received an unprecedented 117 Emmy
nominations. **RL**

Sons and Daughters

Soap opera | Australia | 1982–87

Family soap chronicling the lives, loves, and warfare between the Palmers and the Hamiltons

Cast | Leila Hayes, Peter Phelps, Ian Rawlings, Tom Richards, Rowena Wallace   **Original broadcaster** | Seven Network   **For fans of . . .** | *Dynasty* (1981), *Neighbours* (1985), *Home and Away* (1988)

This series started off as a riff on *Romeo and Juliet*, with the rich, Sydney-based Hamiltons disapproving of their daughter Angela dating the decidedly working-class John Palmer from Melbourne. This being a soap, the two were revealed to be twins, separated at birth!

But soon it was another staple of drama, the relationship triangle, that kept us watching. Sexy, working-class David cheats on frumpy, dependable earth mother Beryl with the delightfully acidic Patricia, whom he had dated twenty years previously.

Patricia captured the imagination of viewers, who nicknamed her Pat the Rat. Her scheming was moved to center stage, and became the staple ingredient of every end-of-season cliff-hanger.

In spite of some ridiculously far-fetched story lines, the show was for a time Australia's highest-rated soap in the 1980s. It even spawned a cast album, or at least half of one, with actors from *A Country Practice* (1981) warbling on the B-side. Germany, Sweden, Greece, Italy, Bulgaria and Croatia have all remade the drama in their own languages. **DJ**

> **Classic episode**
> *Episode 545 | 1985.* Pat lies in hospital. "Believe me, Mrs. Stone," says the doctor, "by the time you leave the clinic, you'll look exactly as you always did." "But doctor," calls Pat, "I don't want to look like I did before. I want a whole new face."

⬥ Belinda Giblin and Ian Rawlings play the arch-schemers Alison Carr and Wayne Hamilton in a dramatic showdown.

The Young Ones

Comedy | UK | 1982–84

Anarchic student comedy with a lot of shouting—"heavy"

Cast | Rik Mayall, Adrian Edmondson, Nigel Planer, Christopher Ryan, Alexei Sayle
Original broadcaster | BBC Two   **Award** | 1 BAFTA   **For fans of . . .** | *Blackadder* (1983), *Bottom* (1991)

For a certain generation in the United Kingdom, *The Young Ones* might be the most memorable comedy ever. Taking the fragmented oddness of *Monty Python* (1969) and the antiauthority attitude of punk, it marked the point where alternative comedy finally pushed its way into the mainstream. Avoiding the traditional route of working men's clubs, *The Young Ones'* cast had honed their skills in the trendy comedy clubs of London during university. For them, the orchestrated stupidity was a definite choice. The exaggerated violence was straight out of *Tom and Jerry* (1940), while the sexual content was filtered through the minds of grubby schoolboys, all theoretical and a little embarrassing. This was a comedy of snot, spit, swearing, and shouting.

Most episodes featured a musical guest star—Madness, Dexy's Midnight Runners, Motörhead, for example—while interludes were provided by puppet rats and other animals. One episode even experimented with flash frames of random images, designed to confuse the viewer. In two seasons, the sitcom rule-book was ripped apart. **JS**

Classic episode
Interesting | Season 1, episode 5. The housemates throw a house party. Their record player is smashed by overzealous police officers, gatecrashers trash the house, and pop act Rip Rig + Panic perform in the front room.

⊛ Rik Mayall, Adrian Edmondson, Nigel Planer, and Christopher Ryan in a perfect parody of student life.

Brookside

Drama | UK | 1982–2003

British soap opera that tackled taboos and kept it real

Cast | Ricky Tomlinson, Sue Johnston, Dean Sullivan, John McArdle, Gabrielle Glaister, Sue Jenkins, Claire Sweeney, Alexandra Fletcher, Anna Friel
Original broadcaster | Channel 4
For fans of . . . | *EastEnders* (1985), *Revenge* (2011)

Created by Phil Redmond, *Brookside* was designed to reflect the politics of the time in the form of a drama set on a new housing development on the outskirts of Liverpool. By the early 1980s, The Beatles were a distant memory in their hometown. Long-term unemployment was a reality for many, especially the city's youth, and this was reflected in the daily struggles of the drama's characters, young and old. Realism was key: rather than spending money on production facilities, Redmond bought a real housing estate and converted it into everything he needed to make a twice-weekly soap.

The realism informed the stories. It was said that only in *Brookside* would two characters put a kettle on and the scene would allow it time to boil. But soon realism gave way to sensationalism: the first same-sex kiss in a soap generated tabloid headlines; the first soap incest story only revulsion. A sensational domestic abuse plot resulted in the now infamous "body under the patio" case. When the soap began to lose its way, *Brookside* was shifted to a late-night slot and cancellation beckoned. Its last great shout involved the community coming together to execute a drug dealer who was terrorizing them all. That done, and with the fictional Brookside Close earmarked for redevelopment, the characters left, one by one, until only Jimmy Corkhill and a young friend were left to discuss the politics of the land and the worrying state of British TV. It might have been too late to save the show, but it was great to see *Brookside* finish as it had begun. **JS**

Classic episode
Episode 1,521 | *January 30, 1995*. Mandy Jordache and her daughters escape to Ireland after Mandy kills her abusive husband. Back home, excavation work leads to the discovery of a body under Mandy's patio.

⚲ Anna Friel as Beth Jordache and Sandra Maitland as Mandy Jordache give evidence in 1995.

Fame

Music/Musical | USA | 1982–87

"Fame costs and right here's where you start paying . . . in sweat"

Cast | Debbie Allen, Lee Curreri, Erica Gimpel, Valerie Landsburg, Gene Anthony Ray, Lori Singer
Original broadcaster | NBC
Awards | 9 Emmys, 2 Golden Globes
For fans of . . . | *Glee* (2009)

Long before *Glee* (2009), there was another TV show that centered on the lives and struggles of a group of talented teenagers, and it took the world by storm. After the huge success of Alan Parker's hit film in 1980, it was a no-brainer for Warner Brothers to launch a TV version of *Fame*, also set in the New York City High School for the Performing Arts. But it wasn't all legwarmers and tantrums; this show had soul, wit, and charm. It also had a likable ensemble cast—with most viewers able to identify with at least one of the students—and a chart-busting soundtrack, which included "Fame," "Starmaker," "Hi-Fidelity," and "Life is a Celebration."

Not only did *Fame* win two consecutive Golden Globes for Best TV Series (Comedy/Musical), but it was also a huge hit around the world. In fact, its popularity abroad ensured its survival, when broadcasters, including the BBC, invested in a syndicated run following its cancellation after two seasons.

As a testament to *Fame*'s enduring appeal, there have been attempts to revive it, and a loose remake of the original film was released in 2009. A UK special, *Bring Back Fame* (2008), also attempted to reunite the students and teachers. Of the cast, Debbie Allen has had the most success, mainly as a choreographer (including ten consecutive Academy Awards ceremonies). She was also the only original cast member to appear in all three versions. Lori Singer (Julie) went on to star in *Footloose* (1984), and Valerie Landsburg (Doris) carried on making her own music. **DJ**

Classic episode
A Special Place | *Season 1, episode 16*. Budget cuts lead to the dismissal of Mr. Crandal, the drama teacher. The students decide to put on a show to try to reverse the decision, but the decision stands. A tearful ending.

◉ Cast of *Fame* in season one. Long-serving choreographer and cast member Debbie Allen is in the second row down, at right.

St. Elsewhere

Drama | USA | 1982–88

Eccentric medical drama set in a run-down teaching hospital in Boston

Cast | Ed Flanders, Christina Pickles, Denzel Washington, Ed Begley Jr., Bonnie Bartlett
Original broadcaster | NBC
Awards | 13 Emmys
For fans of . . . | *Grey's Anatomy* (2005)

St. Elsewhere was one of a handful of US TV series that redefined TV drama during the 1980s, especially medical drama. Its stablemate, *Hill Street Blues* (1981), did likewise for police drama. *St. Elsewhere* centered around St. Elegius in Boston, a run-down hospital known colloquially and derisively as St. Elsewhere. The stories revolved around the doctors, nurses, medical students, and orderlies, as well as their families—played by an ensemble cast that included many actors who went on to successful careers. It was one of the first TV series to feature HIV and AIDS, and the first to have a main character contract the virus. It dealt with domestic violence, organ donation, rape, drug use, and mental health issues. A running story line involved Dr. Westphal (Ed Flanders) and his autistic son, Tommy, exploring the difficulties of a single father, two-children family.

In-jokes and dark humor abounded. For example, a recurring character, amnesiac John Doe, believed he was Mary Richards from *The Mary Tyler Moore Show* (1970) and interacted with a character played by an actor from that show. And a Dr. Gwyneth Paltrow was paged in several episodes; in reference to the actress who was the daughter of the executive producer of the series, Bruce Paltrow. Finally, came the controversial, divisive end. In keeping with the eccentric, pushing-the-boundaries style of *St. Elsewhere*, the final scenes suggested that the hospital, its staff, and patients were all in the imagination of Tommy Westphal playing with a snow globe. **SJG**

Classic episode
Time Heals | Season 4, episodes 17 and 18. The hospital celebrates its anniversary and key moments. A thread is the tricky diagnosis of a long-term patient. *Star Trek* fans should look out for Kate Mulgrew and a very young William Russ.

⬥ Cast members in season four.

Boys from the Blackstuff

Drama | UK | 1982

Desperate and depressed—"Gizza job!"

Cast | Michael Angelis, Bernard Hill, Alan Igbon, Peter Kerrigan, Tom Georgeson, Gary Bleasdale
Original broadcaster | BBC Two
Awards | 3 BAFTAs
For fans of . . . | *Auf Wiedersehen, Pet* (1983)

The Black Stuff was an installment of Play for Today, by Liverpool writer Alan Bleasdale, broadcast in 1980. The plot told of a gang of workmen who left their homes in Liverpool and crossed the north of England for the promise of work laying tarmac (the "black stuff") for a contractor. The gang comprised animal-loving Chrissie, elderly socialist George, hot-tempered Yosser, selfish Loggo, and gang leader Dixie and his teenage son Kev. Largely through their own stupidity, the men lost their jobs and had to return home empty-handed.

This mix of characters was extremely strong, and Bleasdale concocted a six-part series around them. For political reasons, an episode about the contractor was dropped from the series and reworked as a separate Play for Today installment, but the five-part serial began with the men working together again on a construction site. Due to their financial situations, they were also claiming benefits illegally and, therefore, constantly dodging the menace of the authorities.

Two stars emerged from this series. Bernard Hill was one; although born in Manchester, his perfect Scouse accent and his tragically comical portrayal of the increasingly unhinged Yosser—"Gizza job. I can do that . . . "—made the people of Liverpool claim him as one of their own. The second star was the city of Liverpool itself. Many viewers saw the series as a biting criticism of the Conservative government at the time, but Bleasdale revealed that most of the episodes were plotted before they came to power in 1979. **JS**

Bauer sucht Frau (Bäuerin)

Reality | Germany/Austria | 1983

A niche dating show that was a surprise hit

Cast | Inka Bause, Arabella Kiesbauer
Original broadcasters | RTL, ATV
For fans of . . . | *The Dating Game* (1965), *Blind Date* (1985), *The Bachelor* (2002), *Bachelor Pad* (2010)

Bauer sucht Frau (*Farmer Wants a Wife*) is a reality dating show with a difference. Based on an original concept first shown on Swiss television as *Bauer sucht Bäuerin* in 1983, it helps farmers find a life partner, the premise being that they are too busy or shy to do so themselves. The twist is that a lot of the potential candidates, who dream of escaping city life, are not cut out for the role, as they quickly discover when they start mucking out the stables and milking the cows on an exploratory visit to the farm. The German version has been hosted by Inka Bause since it started in 2005; the Austrian show is hosted by veteran presenter Arabella Kiesbauer, who had her own talk show, *Arabella*, on German TV from 1994 to 2004.

There are as many as twenty international versions, including *Farmer Wants a Wife* (2001) in the UK and in the USA, *Granjero busca esposa* in Spain, and shows in the Netherlands, Belgium, Denmark, France, Greece, Croatia, and Hungary. The concept varies slightly from country to country and has evolved to include female farmers looking for a partner. In the American version, ten women compete for the attention of just one farmer, and fictionalized elements are incorporated. The show features interviews and hidden camera sequences, and regularly revisits couples who have married. A special ten-year-anniversary show with highlights from past episodes summarized the show's success stories. It featured twenty-nine couples, thirteen marriages, and nine babies. **KH**

The A-Team

Action/Adventure | USA | 1983–87

Fugitives turned heroes for hire

Cast | George Peppard, Dirk Benedict, Dwight Schultz, Mr. T
Original broadcaster | NBC   **For fans of . . .** | *Mission: Impossible* (1966), *MacGyver* (1985)

Writer/producer Stephen J. Cannell—*Columbo* (1968), *The Rockford Files* (1974), *21 Jump Street* (2012)—loved it when things fell into place. After losing his job at ABC, he switched to a rival network and helped develop *The A-Team*. Over five seasons, the show gave viewers a weekly dose of action-driven crime stories and pulled in huge viewing figures for NBC. It was so successful, in fact, that any discussion of 1980s popular culture is incomplete without its mention.

The backstory was summed up at the start of each episode. During the Vietnam War, four US commandos were accused of a crime they didn't commit. So they fled to LA and offered their vigilante services to people with nowhere else to turn. Action and comedy went hand in hand. There was plenty of violence—car chases, explosions, gun fights—but the producers always kept it on the cartoonish side, with no one being seriously hurt. Meanwhile, a roster of running jokes—centered on B.A. ("Bad Attitude") Baracus, played by Mr. T—and the team's ability to build weaponry from discarded scrap kept things lighthearted. **IF**

Classic episode
The Bend in the River | *Season 2, episodes 2 and 3*.
In this two-part story from 1984, the team travel to the Peruvian jungle to go up against river pirate El Cajon, who has captured a female member of an archaeology expedition.

◉ (L–R) Dirk Benedict, Mr. T, Dwight Schultz, and George Peppard in the season five opening episode "Dishpan Man."

Auf Wiedersehen, Pet

Comedy/Drama | UK | 1983–84; 2002–04

"Working on the site, from morning till night, that's livin' alright"

Cast | Timothy Spall, Jimmy Nail, Tim Healy, Kevin Whately, Christopher Fairbank, Pat Roach, Gary Holton
Original broadcasters | ITV (1983–84), BBC One (2002–04) **For fans of . . .** | *Boys from the Blackstuff* (1982)

Seven manual laborers found themselves billeted together in Düsseldorf, Germany, for a big construction job. Three of the gang hailed from the northeast of England: recently married Neville (Kevin Whately) pined for his bride, levelheaded Dennis (Tim Healy) faced a divorce, and boorish loudmouth Oz (Jimmy Nail) didn't even bother to tell his wife he was leaving the country. The rest of the gang comprised Moxey, from Liverpool; Wayne, a lothario from London; Bomber, a former wrestler and gentle giant from the West Country; and Barry, from Birmingham, who considered himself well-read, but was really just a sponge for useless trivia.

Although *Auf Wiedersehen, Pet* tackled the issues of unemployment, it also focused on the daily interactions between the men and the sacrifices they were making just to keep their families fed. Mostly written by the successful pairing of Dick Clement and Ian La Frenais (*The Likely Lads*, 1964, *Porridge*, 1974)—the show was a surprise hit for ITV, and the broadcaster even reedited some episodes to remove the more adult elements to make it suitable for a prime-time repeat. **JS**

Classic episode
The Fugitive | *Season 1, episode 8*. On a fishing trip, the men pick up a young hitchhiker from London (Ray Winstone), who claims to be a student, but later confesses to being a soldier, absent without leave.

◉ Timothy Spall, Tim Healy, Christopher Fairbank (partly hidden), Pat Roach, Gary Holton, and Kevin Whately in season one.

Just Good Friends

Comedy | UK | 1983–86

A witty and warm "will they, won't they" story

Cast | Jan Francis, Paul Nicholas, Sylvia Kay, John Ringham, Ann Lynn, Shaun Curry
Original broadcaster | BBC One
Award | 1 BAFTA
For fans of . . . | *Dear John* (1986), *Gavin & Stacey* (2007)

Where would UK TV comedy be without John Sullivan? Although better known for his work on *Only Fools and Horses* (1981), for many *Just Good Friends* is his best work. He was inspired to write it for two reasons: firstly he was hurt by criticism that he gave his best comedy roles to men, and secondly he had read a newspaper letter from a woman jilted at the altar. And so Jan Francis was cast as Penny, and her frosty, yet vulnerable performance established great chemistry in tandem with Paul Nicholas' working-class charmer, Vince.

It was a strength of Sullivan's writing that he made viewers care so deeply about the characters he created, and this was especially true in *Just Good Friends*. From the moment we met Penny and Vince, as they bumped into each other for the first time in five years, the spark between them was electric and viewers knew they wanted them to get back together. That dynamic was the crux of the series: each week the pair went on dates and Vince messed things up unintentionally.

Just Good Friends was also one of Sullivan's funniest comedies; the wordplay was stunningly good: "Of course he knows what a vegan is, don't you, Vince?" "Absolutely, I never missed an episode of *Star Trek*." Equally admirable was the small supporting cast of regulars; the shame Penny's posh parents felt at the re-emergence of Vince was beautifully played comedy about extreme snobbery. Vince's working-class, but in the money, family worked well in contrast and provided a great insight into Vince's own behavior. **LH**

Return to Eden

Soap opera | Australia | 1983–86

Prime-time soap opera—with added bite

Cast | Daniel Abineri, Rebecca Gilling, Wendy Hughes, James Smilie, Peta Toppano, Daniel Abinieri
Original broadcaster | Network Ten
For fans of . . . | *Dallas* (1978), *Dynasty* (1981), *The Thorn Birds* (1983)

Playing out like a soapier, antipodean cousin of *The Life and Loves of a She-Devil* (1986), *Return to Eden* told the everyday story of wealthy heiress Stephanie Harper (Rebecca Gilling), who survived the honeymoon from hell when her new husband threw her—quite literally—to the crocodiles. Stephanie's luck changed when she was rescued from the crocodiles by a miner who gave her some precious gems. Using the gems to fund plastic surgery, she then set out to rebuild her face and get her home (the "Eden" of the title) back. Along the way, she fell in love with her plastic surgeon, whose talents enabled Stephanie to embark on a career as a supermodel.

With its bonkers plot and high production values, the success of the initial miniseries in 1983 led to a full series in 1986. The accent was firmly on glamour and high drama, in an attempt to capture the audiences of American super-soaps *Dallas* (1978) and *Dynasty* (1981).

Despite being successfully transmitted in many countries, ratings dwindled in Australia, so *Return to Eden* was axed after one season. It ended on a double cliff-hanger: Dennis was knocked unconscious by an unknown figure, and Jake was shot, while wrestling a gun from Jilly, who was trying to kill Stephanie. Stephanie then picked up the gun, with blood truly on her hands. Some showings of the season featured an alternate ending. Fondly remembered, a remake was announced in 2012 by the Nine Network, although at the time of writing, this was yet to enter production. **DJ**

Taggart

Crime/Mystery | UK | 1983–2010

Long-running Scottish crime drama with a bleak outlook—"There's been a murder"

Cast | Mark McManus, James MacPherson, Alex Norton, Blythe Duff, Colin McCredie, Alistair Duncan
Original broadcaster | ITV
Award | 1 BAFTA
For fans of . . . | *Midsomer Murders* (1997), *Luther* (2010)

It may have provided the world at large with an unfair view of Glasgow as a lawless city, with detectives as tough as the villains they investigated, but *Taggart* was part of the TV landscape for more than twenty-five years. Audiences in the region of eighteen million regularly tuned in, despite some haphazard scheduling. First produced as *Killer* in 1983, it was written by Glenn Chandler and introduced the craggy visage of DCI Jim Taggart, played by former boxer Mark McManus. It was a compelling performance and utterly believable, and the character's experience was leavened in the pairing with Sgt Peter Livingstone (Alistair Duncan), a university graduate. *Killer* struck a chord, and in 1985 the series returned, named after its beguiling protagonist. Chandler wrote many episodes over the next decade, injecting scripts with a gallows humor to complement the often-brutal murder investigations. Severed body parts were not unusual, and *Taggart* had a noirish tint long before anybody had heard of *The Killing* (2007).

Duncan departed in 1987, and was replaced by James MacPherson as DCI Mike Jardine. McManus died suddenly in 1994, partway through production of new episodes. It is a testament to the mark he made in the role that the series continued as *Taggart* for a further fifteen years, his presence never far away. The show may have endured an ignoble cancellation in 2010, in the wake of financial disputes between STV and ITV, but its reputation as the best Scottish crime drama ever produced is not in doubt. **MW**

Classic episode
Funeral Rites | *Season 3, episode 2.* A typically grisly discovery of a charred corpse in a railway tunnel leads Taggart, Livingstone and Jardine into a multilayered investigation, involving black magic and a series of murder attempts.

⊘ Mark McManus as the eponymous hero.

Blackadder

Comedy | UK | 1983–89

Historical sitcom with many a "cunning plan"

Cast | Rowan Atkinson, Tony Robinson, Tim McInnerny, Hugh Laurie, Miranda Richardson, Stephen Fry
Original broadcaster | BBC One
Awards | 3 BAFTAs
For fans of . . . | *Fawlty Towers* (1975)

Historical records purged by Tudor propaganda revealed the hitherto unknown son of York, King Richard IV, and his son Edmund, known as the "Black Adder." In fact, "Edmund Blackadder" was a name that cropped up throughout history: in the court of Queen Elizabeth I; in the household of George IV, the Prince Regent; and on the French battlefields during the Great War. This family line was intertwined with the Baldricks—a dynasty of lowly serfs—and the Percys, who at some point in their family tree became the Darlings.

In a similar vein to spoof history *1066 and All That* (1938) by R.J. Yeatman and W.C. Sellar, the many incarnations of Blackadder played very loosely with historical detail. Rowan Atkinson's first interpretation—the bastard son of a forgotten king—was a cowardly idiot. By the Elizabethan *Blackadder II* (1986), Atkinson had settled on a less manic, more sarcastic portrayal that he kept for subsequent installments. Each season witnessed Blackadder scheme and manipulate anew, often aided by a deeply flawed cunning plan from Baldrick (Tony Robinson). The last scene of each season showed Baldrick and his associates brutally murdered, yet somehow the Blackadder line continued.

Written by Atkinson, Richard Curtis, and Ben Elton, the show was a riot of very clever wordplay, unfettered sarcasm, and absurdist humor. The scripts were matched by the brilliance of the characterizations: Tim McInnerny twitching as Captain Darling and Hugh Laurie simpering as Prince Regent were priceless. **JS**

V

Fantasy/Horror/Sci-fi | USA | 1983–85

"V" is for "Visitors"—the alien kind

Cast | Jane Badler, Marc Singer, Faye Grant, Michael Durrell, Michael Ironside, Blair Tefkin, Michael Wright, Jennifer Cooke
Original broadcaster | NBC
For fans of . . . | *The Twilight Zone* (1959)

Kenneth Johnson's attempts to adapt a novel about a fascist takeover of America had proven a difficult sell for TV executives until he switched the threat to invading aliens. Johnson wrote, directed, and produced the two-part miniseries, *V*, about a fleet of huge alien flying saucers that appeared over some of the Earth's key cities. The inhabitants, a seemingly human and benign race soon dubbed the "Visitors," claimed to be in desperate need of water. In return, they offered technology and cures for common illnesses. They became celebrities, dominating the media and charming their way to the very top of the social hierarchy.

Then the "scientists" began to disappear. The Visitors began to recruit Earth's youth into their own militia, and soon families turned against families in fear that they might be next. When a war correspondent managed to explore the aliens' ship, he uncovered their true nature: a race of lizards, in masks, intent on harvesting humans for food. The "V" of the title carried a second meaning; adopted as shorthand for the Visitors, it also became a symbol of the resistance—for "victory."

Johnson produced a second miniseries, *The Final Battle* (1984), in which humanity developed a red dust that was deadly to the aliens. When NBC pushed for a longer ongoing serial, Johnson left the production. Sadly, with squeezed budgets and a more formulaic approach, the series was not as impressive as its creator's initial vision, and *V* rapidly degenerated into a hybrid of a Western and *Dynasty* (1981) in space. **JS**

◔ Miranda Richardson as the demented "Queenie," Elizabeth I, alongside Rowan Atkinson's Edmund Blackadder.

Brass

Comedy | UK | 1983–84, 1990

Satire of the haves and have-nots in a "grim-up-north" British mining community

Cast | Timothy West, Caroline Blakiston, James Saxon, Gail Harrison, Emily Morgan, Barbara Ewing, Shaun Scott, Gary Cady, David Ashton, Robert Reynolds
Original broadcaster | ITV
For fans of . . . | *To the Manor Born* (1979)

While US TV depicted the power struggles of the boardroom in glossy soaps like *Dallas* and *Dynasty*, the British took the comedic approach in this production from Granada, ITV's northern franchise holder. *Brass* was a beautifully observed mockery of literary adaptations and the grand traditions of theatrical farce. Up in the manor house were the Hardacres, led by domineering self-made businessman Bradley Hardacre (Timothy West), who married Lady Patience as a means to lift his social standing. His children were the cocky heir Austin, rampant, sex-mad Isobel, idealistic feminist Charlotte, and effete Morris, who clutched his teddy bear in a nod to Sebastian from *Brideshead Revisited* (a critically acclaimed hit for Granada just two years before).

Down in the slums lived the Fairchilds. Agnes was a political animal who espoused socialism, yet whose secret affair with Bradley cast doubt on the true lineage of her younger son, the delicate poet Matthew. Meanwhile, her elder son, earnest miner Jack, despaired of his father's subservient gratitude to the bullying Bradley Hardacre, whom he plotted to undermine while also conducting a love affair with Isobel.

Creators Julian Roach and John Stevenson had been writers on *Coronation Street* (1960) and the pair had a real talent for the particulars of the British class system, making much fun of the persistent patronizing clichés that pollute depictions of the North of England. *Brass* came to an end after just two series, but was revived for one final run in 1990, this time airing on Channel 4. **JS**

Widows

Drama | UK | 1983–95

The female of the species is even more criminal than the male

Cast | Ann Mitchell, Maureen O'Farrell, Fiona Hedley, Eva Mottley, Kate Williams, Dudley Sutton, Debby Bishop, Stephen Yardley
Original broadcaster | ITV
For fans of . . . | *Prime Suspect* (1991)

Writer Lynda La Plante first made her mark on British television with this acclaimed series about three women whose husbands were killed while committing a robbery. The death of Harry Rawlins, leader of the gang, left rivals and the police vying to get their hands on his ledgers, which contained plans for future jobs and the names of all his contacts.

The widows then did Harry's next intended job themselves. They stashed most of the money in lockers at a local convent, and flew off to Rio de Janeiro. And there Harry's widow Dolly revealed to the gang that her husband was still alive and now wanted "his" money.

Due to public demand and critical success, a sequel followed in 1985 with the widows forced to return to England. Harry's determination to regain his position in the criminal underworld led to tragedy for the women and a tense confrontation with his wife.

Once again, fan pressure inspired La Plante to write another follow-up, *She's Out* (1995), in which Dolly's plans to open a children's home were disrupted when she was forced to undertake another job. Throughout all three series was Ann Mitchell, who made Dolly Rawlins one of the most memorable characters in television history. She brought a chilling edge to a woman who refused to be a victim, a strong character who inspired others, albeit toward a life of crime.

A 2002 US remake starring Mercedes Ruehl and Brooke Shields changed the basic premise and failed to achieve the success of the original. **JV**

The Thorn Birds

Drama | USA | 1983

Multigenerational epic tale of forbidden love—desire, passion, and scandal

Cast | Richard Chamberlain, Rachel Ward, Barbara Stanwyck, Christopher Plummer, Jean Simmons
Original broadcaster | ABC
Awards | 6 Emmys, 4 Golden Globes
For fans of . . . | *Shogun* (1980)

The 1980s was the decade of the lush TV miniseries, and the genre reached its zenith in *The Thorn Birds*: an adaptation of the 1977 best-selling novel by Colleen McCullough. A generation had fallen in love with the tale of a tortured Catholic priest and the girl he helplessly adores, and they fell in love all over again with Richard Chamberlain as Father Ralph de Bricassart and Rachel Ward in her defining screen role as Meggie Cleary, the young woman who captivated him.

The narrative was richly layered, as viewers watched the friendship between a young priest and a neglected girl transform into something more perilous when she grew up to be a beautiful woman wed to another. The story stretched across decades, and the look of the show matched its grand ambitions, with the United States ably doubling for the Australian outback in cinematography worthy of a Hollywood blockbuster. The film was desaturated during early scenes, lending the past the washed-out, not-quite-real atmosphere of hazy memories, while shots of later times were filled with sharp, vibrant color. The story was undoubtedly a melodramatic one, but the seriousness of its treatment and the commitment of its cast kept it from descending into kitsch. Chamberlain has never been better as troubled Father Ralph, and the love story was played just right, with consummation of Ralph and Meggie's desire held off for eight hours while they pined for each other and the audience became increasingly desperate for them to surrender to their passions. **RL**

Classic episode
Episode 4 | March 30, 1983. Meggie is distraught that her son, Dane, has decided to enter the priesthood. History seems to be repeating itself as he chooses the church over her. A tragedy forces her to realize what is truly important.

⬙ (L–R, seated) Jean Simmons, Rachel Ward, and Barbara Stanwyck pose with Richard Chamberlain.

Spitting Image

Comedy | UK | 1984–96

No public figure was safe from the long arm of this satirical puppet show

Cast | Chris Barrie, Harry Enfield, Louise Gold, Steve Coogan, Peter Serafinowicz
Original broadcaster | ITV
Award | 1 BAFTA
For fans of . . . | *Headcases* (2008)

If respect for one's betters had ever been a British value, it was in steep decline by the dawn of the 1980s, and *Spitting Image* delivered the *coup de grâce*. Perhaps for this reason, the show was hugely popular, even with those it lampooned. Some of its targets claimed to be pleased with the grotesque puppets that depicted them, but this wasn't a show whose mockery came from affection.

The concept of a sketch show based on Peter Fluck and Roger Law's puppet caricatures provoked skepticism in some quarters when it was mooted—weren't puppets for kids?—but the first show in 1984 dispelled doubts. The show's ire wasn't reserved for politicians—big-name celebrities and the Royal Family were also targets—but it was at its sharpest when aimed at the governing elite. Its depiction of Margaret Thatcher as a steely shrew ruling her Cabinet ("the vegetables") with a rod of iron did much to cement her image in the public's mind. The show had chart success, too, with "The Chicken Song"— a parody of dreadful novelty records that reached number one in Britain in 1986.

Spitting Image got pretty much everything right. The puppets were marvelous creations, grotesquely exaggerated yet instantly recognizable. But that would have been nothing if the writing and voice acting hadn't been so sharp, and many stalwarts of British comedy, from Harry Enfield to Peter Serafinowicz, were given a leg up by the show. Its references may now be dated but its laughs are as plentiful as ever. **RL**

The Bill

Drama | UK | 1984–2010

Police drama knee-deep in villains of every persuasion

Cast | Graham Cole, Trudie Goodwin, Jeff Stewart, Simon Rouse, Mark Wingett, Eric Richard
Original broadcaster | ITV
Awards | 2 BAFTAs
For fans of . . . | *Hill Street Blues* (1981)

The world's longest-running police procedural TV drama, *The Bill* was created by Geoff McQueen from his one-off drama *Woodentop* (1983). The original show was broadcast as hour-long episodes in twelve-part seasons, but this format gave way to twice-weekly half-hour episodes running all year around. Generally, each episode was self-contained, and the story lines were divided between uniformed officers on the beat and plainclothes detectives.

Despite a sizable regular cast, befitting an inner-city police station, early episodes had the feeling of an anthology, with guest characters introducing their own plots when they came into contact with the investigating officers. Some of the writers took the show in interesting directions, notably *Sapphire and Steel* (1979) creator P.J. Hammond, whose episodes led to some particularly chilling early evening viewing.

However, in a bid to battle falling ratings, the format was adjusted over time, predominantly to follow the private lives of the officers, and it became more like a soap opera. When that failed, producers tried to ape the success of US police dramas such as *NYPD Blue* (1993) and *CSI: Crime Scene Investigation* (2000) by introducing faster pacing and a completely different, more superficial tone. Despite this, the doors of Sun Hill police station closed for the final time in 2010, after the series had racked up 2,400 episodes and spawned two short-lived spin-off series, *Burnside* (2000) and *M.I.T.: Murder Investigation Team* (2003). **JS**

❹ *Spitting Image* targets Colonel Gaddafi and Ronald Reagan, 1986.

1980s 333

The Adventures of Sherlock Holmes

Crime/Mystery | UK | 1984–94

"What one man can invent another can discover"

Cast | Jeremy Brett, David Burke, Edward Hardwicke, Charles Gray, Colin Jeavons, Rosalie Williams
Original broadcaster | ITV
For fans of . . . | *Sherlock* (2010), *Elementary* (2012)

Like Tarzan and Robin Hood, the character of Sherlock Holmes is a perennial literary classic. Every generation has one. There had been other attempts at a TV Holmes — Douglas Wilmer and Peter Cushing played him for the BBC in the 1960s—but Jeremy Brett, a fan of Arthur Conan Doyle's original stories, took the role to another level. Blessed with a decent budget and made on film, Granada's impressive production seduced even the most ardent Holmes enthusiasts, despite certain dramatic liberties taken with the text.

Brett's personal issues, including a battle with bipolar disorder, informed his portrayal; his Holmes was aloof and vague one minute, razor-sharp and manic the next. His passionate belief in the character compelled him to continue despite health issues, but it also led him to make some interesting choices, such as a scene in the episode "The Devil's Foot" in which Holmes was seen on a beach, burying the equipment he'd used to inject cocaine. His associate, Dr. Watson, had often been portrayed as a buffoon, but in this series he was shown to be a man of intelligence. David Burke (and later Edward Hardwicke) ensured that the viewer was never left in any doubt of Watson's contributions.

Two-thirds of the original canon made it to the screen, plus feature-length adaptations of five stories, including *The Sign of Four* (1890) and *The Hound of the Basker-villes* (1902). More would have followed had it not been for Brett's death. For anyone interested in the original Holmes, this series is essential viewing. **JS**

MTV Video Music Awards

Awards show | USA | 1984–present

The "Super Bowl for youth"

Cast | Various
Original broadcaster | MTV
For fans of . . . | *Primetime Emmy Awards* (1949), *The Academy Awards* (1953), *The BAFTA Awards* (1955), *The Brit Awards* (1977)

It is the show that brought twerking into the public consciousness, showed Madonna and Britney Spears kiss in front of an audience of millions, and played host to Lady Gaga wearing a meat dress. Yes, the *MTV Video Music Awards*—a big-budget by-product from the pioneering music-video channel—has become more notorious over the decades for its controversial moments than for its actual prizes, which honor the best of the year's music videos. And this is why it has become a global viewing phenomenon; while viewers may have a passing interest in knowing who won what, chances are they will be watching the show to see how it can outdo itself from one year to the next.

The awards show was conceived in 1984 as a younger, hipper alternative to the Grammy Awards (at a time when music videos were still a relatively new invention), with recipients awarded a spaceman-themed statue in deference to the channel's early logo. The first ceremony, at New York's Radio City Music Hall, set the tone for what was to come as Madonna took to the stage in a saucy bridal costume and proceeded to give an eye-opening performance of "Like A Virgin." It was the first of many memorable performances, but the show reached new levels of notoriety in 2013 when Miley Cyrus shed her cutesy Hannah Montana image, donned a nude latex bikini, and twerked with Robin Thicke. It was the kind of once-seen-never-forgotten performance that assured the show's place in the annals of TV history. **CW**

Miss Marple

Crime/Mystery | UK | 1984–92

These novels have had several adaptations, but the firm favorite is the TV series in which the little-old-lady detective is played by the marvelous Joan Hickson

Cast | Joan Hickson, David Horovitch, Ian Brimble
Original broadcaster | BBC One
For fans of . . . | *The Adventures of Sherlock Holmes* (1984), *Murder, She Wrote* (1984), *Agatha Christie's Poirot* (1989), *Foyle's War* (2002)

Despite dedicating her novel *The Mirror Crack'd from Side to Side* (1962) to Margaret Rutherford, Agatha Christie professed discontent with the 1960s Rutherford-led adaptations of her famous Miss Marple novels. Christie was not alone in finding Rutherford's bluff and hearty portrayal a far cry from the sharp-eyed octogenarian detective she had created.

Had she still been alive, Christie surely would have approved of Joan Hickson's deliberate, faithful portrayal of the character in the BBC adaptations of the Miss Marple novels in the 1980s. Indeed, following Hickson's appearance in a stage adaptation of *Appointment with Death* (1938) in 1946, Christie sent Hickson a note: "I hope one day you will play my dear Miss Marple." When Hickson did so, at age 78, she was the oldest actress ever to take the lead in a major television series.

Miss Jane Marple is an eagle-eyed, quick-witted spinster who wishes only to live a quiet life in the small town of St. Mary Mead. But trouble seems to follow her wherever she goes and she finds herself tested by baffling murders. Although secondary characters tend to underestimate or ignore the amateur sleuth, they do so at their peril; her beady eyes and insight into human nature inevitably provide the key to the mystery at hand.

Lovingly filmed against a backdrop of quiet English villages, and country house interiors, this series of Miss Marple adaptations brought all twelve Marple novels to the screen. **AP**

Classic episode
The Mirror Crack'd from Side to Side | *Episode 15*.
An innocent woman dies after drinking poison intended for a fading Hollywood star. Miss Marple is called in to solve the mystery and nail the perpetrator.

◬ Joan Hickson captured the essence of Christie's Miss Marple.

Murder, She Wrote

Crime/Mystery | USA | 1984–96

A mix of folksy charm and high-quality murder mysteries

Classic episode

Capitol Offense | *Season 1, episode 12*. When Jessica's US congressman dies, she is appointed as his temporary replacement. Caught up in the machinations of Washington, D.C., she needs to find out what happened to her predecessor.

⬥ Golden Globe winner Angela Lansbury as Jessica Fletcher.

Cast | Angela Lansbury, Tom Bosley, Ron Masak, William Windom
Original broadcaster | CBS
Awards | 2 Emmys, 6 Golden Globes
For fans of . . . | *Midsomer Murders* (1997)

Amateur detective and mystery writer Jessica Fletcher (Angela Lansbury) was the perfect auntie. She was warm, creative, and shrewd, and had a talent for discovering and solving murders. She could not resist investigating these crimes—"I know it's none of my business, but . . . I believe I know what happened"—and was often chastized by the police for being meddlesome.

Murder, She Wrote was created by Richard Levinson, William Link, and Peter S. Fischer, who had previously worked together on *Columbo* (1971). It originated from *Ellery Queen* (1975), another series about a mystery writer who solved murders. When that show ended after a year, the writers switched the lead from a young man to a middle-aged woman and started again. The title comes from the Miss Marple film *Murder, She Said* (1961), and the show's catchy theme song was composed by Emmy Award winner John Addison.

Starring as Jessica Fletcher was film and Broadway legend Lansbury, whose credits included *The Manchurian Candidate* (1962) and *Bedknobs and Broomsticks* (1971). Her charismatic central performance made even weaker episodes of the show very watchable. She also occasionally played Jessica's identical English cousin. Recurring guest actors included Tom Bosley and Ron Masak as successive town sheriffs and William Windom as Jessica's friend Dr. Seth Hazlitt. Jerry Orbach, later of *Law & Order*, appeared as a private eye in several episodes and even earned a short-lived spin-off, *The Law & Harry McGraw* (1987). **WH**

Mickey Spillane's Mike Hammer

Drama | USA | 1984–85

Crime series with film noir undercurrents

Cast | Stacy Keach, Don Stroud, Donna Denton, Kent Williams
Original broadcaster | CBS
For fans of . . . | *The Rockford Files* (1974), *Veronica Mars* (2004)

American TV had seen a previous version of crime writer Mickey Spillane's hard-boiled private detective Mike Hammer in the late 1950s, but what made Stacy Keach's version so interesting was that while the series was set in the 1980s, Hammer's appearance and attitude were firmly rooted in the film noir genre of the 1940s, a reference underlined by the melancholy strains of the saxophone from the start of the show. Keach made for a magnetic leading man, owning the screen in his fedora and trench coat, constantly throwing punches at villains, and with a string of glamorous women at his beck and call.

The clever juxtaposition of eras was further underlined by Keach's dry narration, and the knowing use of humor to show the gap between Hammer and the modern world he finds himself in. Hammer's various cases see him face up to corrupt organizations, Chinese Triads, and gangsters. The series was masterminded by executive producer Jay Bernstein, who was friends with Spillane and purchased the TV rights to Hammer for one dollar.

Preceded by two TV movies, the series initially ran for 24 episodes although production was halted when Keach was imprisoned in the UK for carrying drugs. He returned to the role for another TV movie in 1986, and a new series, entitled *The New Mike Hammer*, followed the same year, but only ran for one season. A further revival—also starring Keach—hit the screens in 1997, but again lasted for just one season. **SOB**

La Piovra

Crime/Mystery | Italy | 1984–2001

Where fact and fiction coincide

Cast | Michele Placido, Patricia Millardet, Remo Girone, Raoul Bova, Vittorio Mezzogiorno
Original broadcaster | RAI Cinema
For fans of . . . | *Paolo Borsellino* (2004), *Il capo dei capi* (2007), *L'ultimo padrino* (2008), *Gomorra, la serie* (2014)

Lasting over ten seasons, each with forty-eight episodes, *La Piovra* (*The Octopus*) was a big beast. It told the complex and intertwining stories of warring mafia families, as they eluded the law in the form of Commissioner Cattani (Michele Placido). A determined opponent, whose own family is murdered by the mafia, Cattani seeks to destroy La Piovra. Its links with organized crime, freemasonry, politics, and business unfold, as does the organization's relentless brutality. The last three series were actually prequels to the first seven, fleshing out the background of the main characters during the 1960s and 1970s.

During the seventeen years in which the series aired, accounts of real-life mafia activities were unfolding in Italy's courts and media. Because of this, the series came under strong political pressure to end. The second and third series aired in 1986 and 1987, while the Maxi Trial against Cosa Nostra was taking place in Palermo, Sicily (lasting 22 months and leading to life sentences for nineteen mafia bosses and 342 convictions). Later, the killing of Cattani in the program's fourth series anticipated the real-life murders of the anti-mafia judges Giovanni Falcone and Paolo Borsellino in 1992. During this time viewing figures for *La Piovra* in Italy peaked at 17 million.

La Piovra was successfully exported to 80 countries, and was particularly popular in Russia, Bulgaria, and Albania. In the UK, the first three series were broadcast by Channel 4. **AC**

Night Court

Comedy | USA | 1984–92

*Raunchy comedy set in a late-night New Y
ork courtroom*

Cast | Harry Anderson, Karen Austin, John Larroquette,
Paula Kelly, Richard Moll, Selma Diamond, Ellen Foley
Original broadcaster | NBC
Awards | 7 Emmys
For fans of . . . | *Barney Miller* (1974)

Creator Reinhold Weege did not plan to build his
courtroom-based sitcom around fast-talking magician
and comedian Harry Anderson, whose appearances on
Saturday Night Live (1975) and *Cheers* (1982) had already
made him familiar with TV audiences. However, once
Night Court began, it was impossible to believe that
anyone else could have embodied the disarmingly
madcap but very capable Judge Harold T. Stone.

With wild and off-color humor, balanced by infrequent
but seriously dramatic moments, *Night Court* became
a solid performer in NBC's long-standing, unbeatable
Thursday night lineup. Initially based in reality, like
Weege's previous series *Barney Miller* (1974), the show
evolved into what could be called a live-action cartoon,
with a bawdy approach to comedy. In particular, John
Larroquette's iconic turn as unrepentant bad boy
prosecutor Dan Fielding earned him an astonishing run
of four Emmys for Best Supporting Actor in a Comedy
Series; Larroquette actually requested that he no longer
be nominated to allow others a chance at the award.

The show weathered several cast changes over
the years, some as a result of untimely deaths (Selma
Diamond, Florence Halop). There were also a number of
memorable recurring and guest characters, including
Harry's father Buddy, played by John Astin; future
Star Trek: The Next Generation (1987) star Brent Spiner
as perpetually unlucky Yugoslav hick Bob Wheeler;
and singer Mel Tormé, who was Harry's idol in character
and in real life. **ATB**

Ever Decreasing Circles

Comedy | UK | 1984

*Sharp writing and acting added bite
to familiar sitcom territory*

Cast | Richard Briers, Penelope Wilton, Peter Egan,
Stanley Lebor, Geraldine Newman
Original broadcaster | BBC One
For fans of . . . | *The Good Life* (1975), *Butterflies* (1978),
One Foot in the Grave (1990)

This show reunited actor Richard Briers with writers
John Esmonde and Bob Larbey, who together had
turned *The Good Life* (1975) into one of Britain's best-
loved all-time comedies. *Ever Decreasing Circles* had the
same suburban setting as that series but the jolly and
optimistic Tom Good character Briers had played there
was replaced by Martin Bryce—controlling, obsessive,
even unpleasant. The tension between Martin and his
new neighbor Paul, and the response of Martin's wife
Ann, created four seasons of painfully funny comedy.

Martin had good intentions, but always felt
compelled to take charge and force everyone to obey
him. Paul, charmingly played by Peter Egan, was the
opposite: laid-back, charming, and ready to challenge
Martin. Penelope Wilton brought Ann's contradictions
to life: she loved Martin but was attracted to Paul.

Completing the cast were Howard and Hilda (Stanley
Lebor and Geraldine Newman), a married couple in
matching outfits who represented the community at
large. They could have been a two-dimensional pair,
but their inner steel flashed whenever one felt the
other had been slighted.

The series was hugely popular in the UK and has
withstood the test of time. Esmonde and Larbey's
sparkling scripts haven't lost their bite. By bringing
Martin Bryce to life, Richard Briers demonstrated his
skill and versatility. His understanding of character, and
comedy, was such that he could get a laugh simply by
rearranging a telephone receiver. **WH**

Heimat

Drama | Germany | 1984–2004

This epic drama follows one family through twentieth-century German history, from the dark days of Nazism to the fall of the Berlin Wall

Cast | Marita Breuer, Noemi Steur, Salome Krammer, Henry Arnold, Frank Roth, Jan Dieter Schneider, Lena Lessing
Original broadcaster | ARD
For fans of . . . | *The Mill* (2013), *The Village* (2013)

Heimat (*Homeland*) was one of the most ambitious shows ever made: a sequence of thirty-two films across three series, following one German family from the end of the First World War to the turn of the millennium. Its claim to greatness lay not just in its scope and technical artistry but in its sympathetic depiction of ordinary lives being played out against a backdrop of major social and political change.

Set in the town of Schabbach in West Germany's Hunsrück area, the first series followed the life of Maria Simon from adolescence, through marriage and motherhood, to her death as an old woman. The rise and fall of Nazism and the changing face of Germany were seen through this prism. By focusing on the small-scale and the everyday, *Heimat* showed a much bigger picture. The series was also notable for being shot in both black and white and color, with the gentler, more lyrical black-and-white sequences abruptly giving way to bolder color scenes as life in Schabbach was disrupted by the forces shaping the wider world.

The second series was the story of Maria's youngest son, Hermann, as he moved to Munich and became a composer in the 1960s. The third series saw Hermann return to Schabbach after the fall of the Berlin Wall.

The films that made up the three series were originally released in theaters, but their episodic structure made them perfect for the small screen. *Heimat* reliably features in polls of the best television ever made. **HE**

Classic episode
Heimatfront (Home Front) | *Episode 6*. Anton Simon, fighting on the Eastern Front in the Soviet Union, marries Martha Hanke by telephone. Back in Schabbach, the people learn about the evils of Nazism.

◭ Jan Dieter Schneider as Jakob Simon and Marita Breuer as Maria Simon.

Robin of Sherwood

Action/Adventure | UK | 1984–86

The finest screen depiction of the Robin Hood legend—"Nothing is ever forgotten"

Cast | Michael Praed, Jason Connery, Judi Trott, Ray Winstone, Nickolas Grace, John Abineri, Mark Ryan
Original broadcaster | ITV **Awards** | 2 BAFTAs **For fans of . . .** | *Game of Thrones* (2011)

Of the many screen variants of this centuries-old legend, *Robin of Sherwood* could lay arguable claim to being the finest iteration of the outlaw's adventures. A deft blending of swords, adventure, and romance with fantasy and magic, punctuated by an award-winning soundtrack from Clannad, made memorable TV.

Creator Richard Carpenter had a good track record in children's fantasy-adventure series, having developed *Catweazle* (1970), *The Ghosts of Motley Hall* (1976), and *Dick Turpin* (1979). The last's high-quality adventure credentials set much of the template for *Sherwood*, in which the core elements of the Robin Hood legend were very much on display: Robin of Loxley (Michael Praed) took to Sherwood Forest with a band of outlaws

to fight the oppression of King John, represented by the ruthless Sheriff of Nottingham (Nickolas Grace). Carpenter embellished the myth with fantastical elements, as Robin became the instrument of the pagan god figure, Herne the Hunter (John Abineri).

Robin of Sherwood ended prematurely when financial backer Goldcrest Films pulled out of the production. The influence of the series could be seen in other screen outings of the legend, most notably in *Robin Hood: Prince of Thieves* (1991). There were parallels between that film's Moorish character Azeem and Sherwood's sword-wielding Saracen Nasir (Mark Ryan), while Alan Rickman's overstated performance as the Sheriff of Nottingham evoked that set down by Grace. **MW**

◉ (L–R) Ray Winstone (Will Scarlet), Oliver Cotton (Lord Owen of Clun), and Jason Connery (Robert of Huntingdon).

The Jewel in the Crown

Historical drama | UK | 1984

The last days of the British Empire in India

Cast | Tim Pigott-Smith, Art Malik, Susan Wooldridge, Geraldine James, Wendy Morgan, Peggy Ashcroft
Original broadcaster | ITV **Awards** | 5 BAFTAs, 2 Emmys, 1 Golden Globe **For fans of . . .** | *Brideshead Revisited* (1981)

When a young British lady, Daphne Manners (Susan Wooldridge), moves to India to live with her aunt, she attracts the attention of two suitors: a coldhearted British army officer Ronald Merrick (Tim Pigott-Smith) and an attractive Indian Hari Kumar (Art Malik). Hari had been educated at one of the best schools in England, but returned to India after his father's suicide. Neither able to speak Urdu nor welcome among the British, Hari found himself caught between two cultures, so was grateful for the friendship Daphne offered. When he and Daphne were attacked one night, the sadistic Merrick arrested Hari and brutally tortured him, in spite of Daphne's insistence that he was innocent of her rape.

The repercussions of that night, and of Merrick's actions, cast long shadows across the rest of this fourteen-part epic. Even though Hari was barely seen after the first few episodes, his role remained significant in the way that others treated Merrick. The injustice had tainted Merrick's reputation, and he spent the rest of his life trying to rebuild it. When an act of bravery left him horrifically disfigured, he visibly became the monster he always knew himself to be.

With scripts co-written by Paul Scott, author of the original novel, stunning location filming in India, and outstanding performances by established and emerging stars, *The Jewel in the Crown* still features in polls of the best TV series ever made. **JS**

⊘ Ronald Merrick (Tim Pigott-Smith) looks down on Daphne Manners (Susan Wooldridge) and her suitor Hari Kumar (Art Malik).

The Cosby Show

Comedy | USA | 1984–92

A show that helped define the 1980s and reinvigorated the family sitcom

Cast | Bill Cosby, Phylicia Rashad, Sabrina Le Beauf, Malcolm-Jamal Warner, Lisa Bonet, Tempestt Bledsoe, Keshia Knight Pulliam **Original broadcaster** | NBC **Awards** | 6 Emmys, 3 Golden Globes **For fans of . . .** | *Family Ties* (1982)

Incorporating comedian Bill Cosby's stand-up material about his own family, *The Cosby Show* followed the triumphs and travails of the Brooklyn-based Huxtable family—Dr. Heathcliff "Cliff" Huxtable (Cosby), his lawyer wife Clair (Phylicia Rashad), and their five children.

Created by Ed Weinberger and Michael Leeson together with Cosby, the show was a comedic take on family life in the 1980s, but also dealt with serious issues such as teen pregnancy and dyslexia. The series was so successful—the highest ratings for five consecutive years from 1985–89—that it almost single-handedly revived the all-but-dead family sitcom format.

Over the years the show progressed conversation on racial matters with its depiction of black culture blended with color-blind characterization that appealed to viewers across the board, although it drew criticism for avoiding the more troubling aspects of race in America. Decades later, sordid accusations against Cosby affected the show's syndication, and diminished Cosby's personal reputation. Nonetheless, *The Cosby Show* itself remained a landmark achievement in television. **ATB**

Classic episode

Happy Anniversary | *Season 2, episode 3*. Cliff's parents mark 49 years of marriage with a cruise and then a dinner at the Huxtable home. The evening ends in a memorable musical number as the children perform an array of classic songs.

⚘ Phylicia Rashad as Clair Huxtable with Bill Cosby, the show's creator and her on-screen husband, Cliff, in June 1990.

Threads

Drama | UK | 1984

What would happen if a nuclear bomb hit the United Kingdom?

Cast | Karen Meagher, Reece Dinsdale, David Brierly, Rita May, Jane Hazlegrove, Nicholas Lane, Henry Moxon
Original broadcaster | BBC Two **Awards** | 4 BAFTAs **For fans of . . .** | *The Walking Dead* (2010)

A crisis in the Middle East was just background noise on the radio and TV. Most people remained oblivious to the international situation until late on, when the government broadcast information films about what to do in the event of an attack. One Thursday, Britain was hit by 200 megatons of nuclear explosives. Nothing could have prepared the survivors for what came next.

Presented as a dramatized documentary, *Threads* was broadcast as part of a series about a potential nuclear war. The drama was interspersed with footage from news reports and the actual public information films that had been prepared in the event of an attack. The cast worked alongside more than 1,000 volunteers locally recruited, playing panicked shoppers on the streets of Sheffield prior to the attack and desperate survivors in the weeks, months, and years after, as they tried to cope with radiation sickness, hypothermia, hunger, and fatigue. The attack itself remains one of the most harrowing dramatic sequences ever made for TV.

Writer Barry Hines used the latest information from the World Health Organization, which had estimated that half the world's population would be immediate casualties in the event of nuclear war and that essential infrastructures would collapse in weeks. He and director Mick Jackson spent a week at the Home Office training center for official survivors, which inspired the character of Clive Sutton, the peacetime chief executive who coordinates supplies weeks ahead of the attack. **JS**

⌼ Rita May and David Brierly as Mr. and Mrs. Kemp in the aftermath of a nuclear attack.

Miami Vice

Crime/Mystery | USA | 1984–90

A hyperstylized cop show for the MTV generation

Cast | Don Johnson, Philip Michael Thomas, Edward James Olmos, Saundra Santiago, Olivia Brown
Original broadcaster | NBC
Awards | 4 Emmys, 2 Golden Globes
For fans of . . . | *Hill Street Blues* (1981)

Miami Vice made it acceptable for men to wear pastel T-shirts beneath expensive white suit jackets. It also proved that style and substance could go hand in hand. It centered on undercover cops Sonny Crockett (Don Johnson) and Ricardo Tubbs (Philip Michael Thomas), who battled evil drug lords, partied at expensive nightclubs, and raced powerboats while eyeing up scantily clad bikini babes.

The show was conceived by NBC executive Brandon Tartikoff, who wanted a cop show for younger viewers. He turned to *Hill Street Blues* writer Anthony Yerkovich, who took the idea of "MTV cops" and ran with it.

Miami Vice's unique aesthetic enticed viewers with its pioneering use of fast cuts and stylish cinematography. Equally praiseworthy was its soundtrack, which featured works by such artists as Glenn Frey (the once and future guitarist of the Eagles), Phil Collins (solo star and lead singer of Genesis), and Kate Bush, and original music by Jan Hammer, the former keyboardist for the Mahavishnu Orchestra. Frey and Collins made cameo appearances in some episodes of the series.

Miami Vice also influenced the video game *Grand Theft Auto: Vice City* (2002), which was basically a homage to the show, and Thomas voiced one of the characters. The show is remembered almost exclusively for its style, which sadly makes it easy to forget that it was a solid crime drama, with gritty story lines and noticeable guest appearances by the likes of Bruce Willis, Helena Bonham Carter, and Liam Neeson. JH

Classic episode
Calderone's Return Part I | *Season 1, episode 4.*
Drug lord Calderone returns with a vengeance. It ends in tragedy for Crockett and Tubbs, but paves the way for one of the show's iconic characters: no-nonsense lieutenant Martin Castillo.

◉ Don Johnson (Sonny Crockett) stays cool under pressure.

Anzacs

Historical drama | Australia | 1985

Underrated wartime drama from Australia—
"Our heritage, our story, our legend"

Cast | Paul Hogan, Bill Kerr, Andrew Clarke, Jon Blake, Megan Williams
Original broadcaster | Nine Network
For fans of . . . | *Band of Brothers* (2001), *The Pacific* (2010)

Anzacs remains one of the most popular and fondly remembered miniseries ever broadcast in Australia. It showcased the volunteers enlisting in the Eighth Battalion of the First Australian Imperial Force and their role on the Western Front during the First World War. The story followed young soldiers from the outbreak of war, through training, the Gallipoli Campaign in 1915, the Battle of the Somme in 1916, and a reunion of the survivors back home in 1919.

At close to nine hours, it was a lengthy buddy movie told across five episodes with a large ensemble cast, among them a pre-*Crocodile Dundee* (1986) Paul Hogan, displaying credible dramatic acting skills, away from the comedy he was well known for in Australia. Between the battle sequences, there was an emphasis on the interpersonal relationships of the men making up the battalion, with themes of kinship and larrikinism—from an Australian term for a young hoodlum or hooligan—pushed to the fore.

The historical accuracy and period detail were to be lauded, and the hefty budget spent by Nine Network was very much in evidence on-screen. Punctuating the character drama, there was a momentum and energy to the battle sequences that could be held up against the best Hollywood had to offer. Thirty years after the transmission of *Anzacs*, these sequences hold their own in the face of modern-day examples of the genre, including the budget-heavy *Band of Brothers* (2001) as the series' most obvious offspring. **MW**

Die Schwarzwaldklinik

Drama | Germany | 1985–89, 2004–05

A popular German medical drama that
could cause drowsiness in large doses

Cast | Klausjürgen Wussow, Gaby Dohm, Sascha Hehn, Barbara Wussow, Evelyn Hamann
Original broadcaster | ZDF
For fans of . . . | *General Hospital* (1963), *Casualty* (1986)

"Thousands of people wanted me to operate on them," said Klausjürgen Wussow, *Die Schwarzwaldklinik*'s lead actor, in 2004, summing up the impact that one of Germany's most popular medical dramas had on him.

Die Schwarzwaldklinik (*The Black Forest Hospital*) reached peak audiences of 28 million. Almost half the German nation lapped up its mix of medical and relationship issues. Although inspired by the US *General Hospital* (1963) and the Czech TV series *Hospital at the End of the City* (1977), the series was also a throwback to the West German *Heimatfilme* (homeland movie) genre of the 1950s, in which characters led carefree lives in the mountains. As such, *Die Schwarzwaldklinik* reflected the prosperity of Germany in the 1980s, and its title became a byword for the days before the reunification of East and West tightened the purse strings.

The story begins with Wussow's Professor Klaus Brinkmann returning to his hometown to become senior consultant at its hillside hospital. His son Udo, a headstrong philanderer, already works there, so they share the farmhouse where Brinkmann was born. They also have the same taste in women and both fall for Nurse Christa, who eventually marries the older man, while Udo marries a young nurse played by Wussow's real-life daughter Barbara.

Die Schwarzwaldklinik's seventy episodes were shown in almost forty countries. They sparked many more German medical dramas and established the show's actors as household names. **DH**

Das Boot

Historical drama | Germany | 1985

Gut-wrenchingly tense drama set on board a German U-boat during the Second World War

Cast | Jürgen Prochnow, Herbert Gronemeyer, Klaus Weinnemann, Hubertus Bengsch, Martin Semmelrogge
Original broadcaster | Cinema release **For fans of . . .** | *Colditz* (1972), *Secret Army* (1977), *Tenko* (1981)

Set in 1941, *Das Boot* (*The Boat*) was a dramatized account of life on board a German submarine during the Second World War. When a war correspondent joined the beleaguered crew he discovered not only the claustrophobia, brutality, and sheer terror of life under the sea, but also the moral complexities involved. As the drama unfolded, it became clear that the captain (Jürgen Prochnow) and some of his more experienced crew had become jaded and embittered toward the war. Tension built as the conflict between morality and duty was played out.

Most of the drama took place on board the German U-boat. Conditions were shown in a stark and terrifyingly real manner. The crew often engaged in gallows humor and were as quick to mock Hitler as they were to deprecate Churchill.

Originally given a cinematic release (which garnered six Academy Award nominations), an extended version in three parts was broadcast on the BBC in 1984 and later all over Europe. Critically acclaimed, it was accepted into modern culture as a stunning war epic. Its significance seeped into the popular cultural psyche and was often used as a metaphor for claustrophobia and terror. It was even parodied by the British comedian and actor Eddie Izzard, who used *Das Boot* as metaphor for pips trapped in an orange. There have been few better dramatizations of tension, fear, tragedy, and humanity than this justly praised war epic. **CR**

◉ Jürgen Prochnow (left) as the German U-boat captain facing the risks and moral dilemmas of war in a submarine.

Edge of Darkness

Crime/Mystery | UK | 1985

The murder of a policeman's daughter leads to the exposure of an industrial eco-crime

Cast | Bob Peck, Joe Don Baker, Charles Kay, Ian McNeice, Joanne Whalley, Hugh Fraser
Original broadcaster | BBC Two **Awards** | 6 BAFTAs **For fans of . . .** | *State of Play* (2003)

Police detective Ronald Craven (Bob Peck) had been involved in many investigations in his time, including corruption and informers in Northern Ireland, so when his daughter Emma (Joanne Whalley) was shot dead in front of him, his first assumption was that he had been the intended target. When he later discovered Emma's links with a group of environmental activists, he grew suspicious and decided to investigate the murder.

Troy Kennedy Martin was the creator of *Z Cars* (1962) and had also written for *The Sweeney* (1975), a show created by his brother, Ian. Frustrated by a perceived lack of enthusiasm for political drama among TV executives, Kennedy Martin crafted a subtle thriller that merged ecological concerns with fantasy.

By public demand, *Edge of Darkness* was repeated from the beginning almost immediately after the final episode had first been broadcast. Things might have been different if Kennedy Martin had had his way—in his original ending, Craven had been petrified by radiation as he slowly turned into a tree. But Peck objected, and the ending was rewritten. **JS**

Classic episode
Into the Shadows | *Season 1, episode 2*. Craven continues to track down those responsible for his daughter's murder, and his investigations lead him to Emma's boyfriend. But was she an innocent victim?

◉ Bob Peck as Ronald Craven and Joanne Whalley as Emma Craven in the cult eco-thriller.

Moonlighting
Drama | USA | 1985–89

Romantic capers and fourth-wall fun in this detective drama

Cast | Bruce Willis, Cybill Shepherd, Allyce Beasley, Curtis Armstrong   **Original broadcaster** | ABC
Awards | 6 Emmys, 3 Golden Globes   **For fans of . . .** | *Remington Steele* (1982)

With one established star (Cybill Shepherd as Maddie Hayes) and one new discovery (Bruce Willis as David Addison), *Moonlighting* played on one of the oldest procedural tropes in the book: an unlikely pair working together at a detective agency. Although the agency belonged to Hayes, a retired model, Addison was the experienced detective—or was he just an opportunist, able to talk his way out of anything? She was uptight; he was laid back. She was hard-working; he was hard-shirking. She didn't trust herself enough, and he thought way too much of himself. The chemistry and style were reminiscent of 1930s screwball comedies— *Bringing up Baby* (1938), with Willis as Katharine Hepburn and Shepherd as Cary Grant, for example.

Although Hayes and Addison flirted their way through the series, the show's appeal extended beyond the extreme watchability of its cast. Never afraid to play with the audience, it often broke the fourth wall, with characters commenting on the action, the believability of the plot, the responses of the audience, and the show's relationship with the network. **RL**

Classic episode
Atomic Shakespeare | *Season 3, episode 7*. A kid who is daydreaming about the show *Moonlighting* when he's supposed to be doing his homework imagines David and Maddie as the lead characters in Shakespeare's *Taming of the Shrew*.

◉ David (Bruce Willis) and Maddie (Cybill Shepherd) are all tied up on their latest case.

Lindenstrasse

Soap opera | Germany | 1985–present

Classic soap opera with enduring appeal

Cast | Marie-Luise Marjan, Ludwig Haas, Andrea Spatzek, Sybille Waury, Philipp Neubauer   **Original broadcaster** | Das Erste   **For fans of . . .** | *Coronation Street* (1960), *EastEnders* (1985), *Neighbours* (1985)

Inspired by the UK's *Coronation Street* (1960), *Lindenstrasse* numbers more than 1,500 episodes to date. Broadcast every Thursday, with a short but memorable theme tune and cliff-hanger endings, the show chronicles the lives of a number of interconnected families and individuals in a fictional quarter of Munich. Chief among them is the indomitable matriarch Helga Beimer (Marie-Luise Marjan), initially a happily married housewife who over the years has had to deal with divorce, the endless personal dilemmas of her children and grandchildren, unexpected romance, and a late career as a travel agent while her ex-husband, Hans, started a second family.

Lindenstrasse strives for a realistic portrayal of everyday problems as well as wider issues; over the years it has covered immigration, homosexuality, environmental debates, euthanasia, unemployment, and depression. It is also known for incorporating current affairs such as elections into story lines as much as possible, with some scenes being reshot shortly before broadcast or alternative versions being prepared to chime with unfolding events. **KH**

Classic episode

Räumaktionen (Removals) | *Episode 225*. Helga has to decide whether to attempt to win back her ex-husband in this 1990 broadcast that featured the first gay kiss to be shown on prime-time German TV.

Helga (Marie-Luise Marjan) looks on as a story line related to disability in a younger demographic begins to unfold.

Neighbours

Soap opera | Australia | 1985–present

"Neighbours, should be there for one another. That's when good neighbours become good friends"

Cast | Alan Dale, Anne Haddy, Stefan Dennis, Jackie Woodbourne, Alan Fletcher
Original broadcasters | Seven Network, Network Ten   **For fans of . . .** | *Home and Away* (1988), *Hollyoaks* (1995)

After years of fairly engaging if unadventurous soaps— *The Sullivans* (1976), *A Country Practice* (1981), *Sons and Daughters* (1982)—Australia tried to modernize its TV output with *Neighbours*. Full of color, charm, and simple but emotional plots, it served almost as a tourist guide to the country. However, the show nearly fell at the first hurdle when Seven Network ditched it. Fortunately Network Ten saw the potential to sell the show abroad and took it over. With revamped story lines and several recast characters, the network had its biggest stroke of luck by casting unknowns Kylie Minogue and Jason Donovan, who swiftly appealed to the masses.

Set in the fictional district of Erinsborough, *Neighbours* is idyllic, aspirational, and fun. When it started the sets wobbled, the cameras shook, and not all the cast were at the top of their game. But these days it's slick and professional, and creates an engaging balance of everyday family stories and occasional big events (tornadoes, bushfires, arson, armed sieges). It has also produced young stars with lasting potential, such as Guy Pearce and Radha Mitchell. **GR**

Classic episode
April 6, 2001. Deaths in *Neighbours* provide the most emotionally gut-wrenching moments. But none can match the sheer sadness of matriarch Madge Bishop succumbing to cancer in her bed, with Harold by her side.

◉ Jason Donovan as Scott Robinson and Russell Crowe as Kenny Larkin in 1987.

EastEnders

Soap opera | UK | 1985–present

Prime-time soap set in London's gritty East End

Cast | Lesley Grantham, Anita Dobson, Adam Woodyatt, Wendy Richard, June Brown, Steve McFadden
Original broadcaster | BBC1 **Awards** | 8 BAFTAs **For fans of . . .** | *Coronation Street* (1960), *Emmerdale* (1972)

EastEnders first hit screens in February 1985, devised by Julia Smith and Tony Holland to be the BBC's answer to ITV's long-running and successful soaps *Coronation Street* (1960) and *Emmerdale* (1972). Smith and Holland agreed that they wanted to make a much grittier drama, a world away from the glamour of US soaps and the cozy charm of ITV's offerings. It was to feature true-to-life characters going through hard-hitting, life-changing events. The early years were hugely successful; the daily lives of the Beale, Fowler, and Watts families regularly pulled in twenty million viewers.

Some of *EastEnders'* best story lines have influenced how British society views a certain topic: for example, Stacey and Jean Slater's battles with bipolar disorder brought the effects of that illness to the viewers at home. Today, *EastEnders* is still one of British TV's most watched programs. Mick and Linda Carter (Danny Dyer and Kellie Bright) are worthy successors to Den and Angie as owners of the Queen Victoria pub, while old hands, such as Ian (Adam Woodyatt), Dot (June Brown), and Phil (Steve McFadden), continue to entertain. **LH**

> **Classic episode**
> *Christmas Day 1986*. More than thirty million viewers tuned in to watch Arthur Fowler's nervous breakdown and Den Watts giving Angie divorce papers after discovering she'd lied about having terminal cancer. "'Appy Christmas, Ange."

◉ Sibling rivalry: Jessie Wallace as Kat Slater, Elaine Lordan as her sister Lynne.

Victoria Wood: As Seen on TV

Comedy | UK | 1985–87

Sketch show by the queen of British comedy

Cast | Victoria Wood, Julie Walters, Celia Imrie, Duncan Preston, Susie Blake, Kenny Ireland
Original broadcaster | BBC Two
Awards | 4 BAFTAs
For fans of . . . | *Dinnerladies* (1998)

"Acorn Antiques," Victoria Wood's soap parody, has eclipsed almost everything she has done since. A deliberately ropy production with wobbly sets, melodramatic plots, and knowingly shoddy acting, it eventually transferred to the stage as a successful musical, but it began as just another recurring sketch among many in this surprisingly short-lived comedy.

Victoria Wood first paired up with Julie Walters for an ITV comedy, *Wood and Walters* (1981), before they jumped to the BBC for *As Seen on TV*. Although Wood wrote the sketches and hosted the show, she created a brilliant ensemble around her. Many of the best sketches gave Walters the chance to create stunningly realized and hilarious comic grotesques, from Mrs. Overall in "Acorn Antiques" to a variety of shopgirls and an elderly waitress struggling to carry "two soups." Susie Blake played an in-vision continuity announcer with little patience for the audience—"We'd like to apologize to viewers in the north, it must be awful for them"—while Patricia Routledge guest starred as Kitty in a series of monologues that showcased Wood's ear for trivial gossip and also provided the inspiration for Routledge's role as Hyacinth Bucket in *Keeping Up Appearances* (1990). Episodes also featured fly-on-the-wall-style documentaries about rather sad individuals, such as a teenage girl who went off unprepared to swim the English Channel and never returned, or an elderly couple who won a million pounds in a magazine competition. **JS**

The Secret Diary of Adrian Mole, Aged 13¾

Comedy | UK | 1985–87

A teenage boy examines his intimate thoughts

Cast | Gian Sammarco, Stephen Moore, Bill Fraser, Lindsey Stagg, Steven Mackintosh, Julie Walters, Lulu, Beryl Reid, Chris Gascoyne, Louise Jameson
Original broadcaster | ITV
For fans of . . . | *The Inbetweeners* (2008)

Adrian Mole (Gian Sammarco) was a humorless, pompous thirteen-year-old, who was convinced that he was a misunderstood intellectual, as proven by his mounting collection of rejection letters from the BBC for his poems. He was oblivious to the marital problems of his parents, until his mother left the family for a neighbor. Instead, Adrian was more concerned with the outbreaks of acne that plagued his chin and his obsession with the politically minded Pandora (Lindsey Stagg), whose parents were free-spirited communists.

Sue Townsend's fictional diaries were essential reading in the 1980s. Although not commanding the style or importance of Samuel Pepys, Adrian, nevertheless documented the world around him, including the Royal Wedding of 1981 and Germaine Greer's feminist tract *The Female Eunuch* (1970). He also wrote about the usual adolescent changes that boys experience (some of which he kept track of with a ruler and a wall chart).

In these faithful adaptations of Townsend's first two novels for the screen, Sammarco was cast as Adrian, a perfect embodiment of the character that saw him typecast in similar geeky roles for the rest of his short TV career. The diarist returned for another series in 2001—*Adrian Mole: The Cappuccino Years*—in which Adrian has reached adulthood. Stephen Mangan and Helen Baxendale starred as Adrian and Pandora, involved with the rise of New Labour and their victory at the General Election in 1997. **JS**

Dempsey and Makepeace

Action/Adventure | UK | 1985–86

New York Cop and British detective tackle violent crime on the streets of London

Cast | Michael Brandon, Glynis Barber, Ray Smith, Tony Osoba
Original broadcaster | ITV
For fans of . . . | *Department S* (1969), *The Persuaders!* (1971), *The Professionals* (1977), *Bones* (2005)

Dempsey and Makepeace was created by Ranald Graham, who had previously written scripts for *The Sweeney* (1975) and *The Professionals* (1977). His new series was overshadowed to some extent by these slicker action predecessors, but it still pulled in enough viewers in its time to have lasted for three seasons. Its success was founded mainly on the appeal of the two leading actors, American Michael Brandon and South African Glynis Barber, whose on-screen chemistry blossomed into a true-life romance that was extensively covered in the popular news media.

Elite Scotland Yard crime unit SI 10 receives a new recruit in the form of Lieutenant James Dempsey, a New York cop forced to flee to London after his partner is murdered. His unorthodox working methods—and his ostentatious firearm—are deplored by his tough commanding officer Gordon Spikings (Ray Smith), who pairs him with icy English aristocrat Harriet Makepeace to keep him in check.

The mismatched partner set-up is a familiar television trope, but Brandon and Barber here refreshed it with a playful spikiness and a constant will-they-won't-they tension. The action was slick and the plots were well constructed, so there was much to like about this series. There was also a high quota (for its time) of often brutal violence, which attracted criticism from some quarters but only increased the series' popularity with younger viewers, who became its core audience. Two years after the show ended, Brandon and Barber married. **MW**

Classic episode
Makepeace, Not War | *Season 1, Episode 7*.
Dempsey impersonates a hit man to infiltrate a drug-smuggling ring, placing him in the position of eliminating Makepeace when she finds evidence of the gang's activities.

Michael Brandon and Glynis Barber: a love match in art and life.

The Golden Girls

Comedy | USA | 1985–92

Groundbreaking US comedy series focusing on four older women

Cast | Bea Arthur, Betty White, Rue McClanahan, Estelle Getty   **Original broadcaster** | NBC
Awards | 11 Emmys, 4 Golden Globes   **For fans of . . .** | *Waiting For God* (1990), *Modern Family* (2009)

Picture Miami, 1985. Four older women live together and share their stories (bawdy, memorable, or merely fantastic), more often than not over cheesecake. How such a pitch would be received at the networks today is debatable, but in the mid-1980s, *The Golden Girls* was truly golden in every sense.

Immediately after its pilot episode, the show was a staple of NBC's Saturday night lineup for seven seasons. The key to its success was its cast. Bea Arthur and Betty White had both become sitcom legends during the 1970s: Arthur as the titular character of *Maude* (1972); White as the wily vixen Sue Ann Nivens in *The Mary Tyler Moore Show* (1970). They were joined by long-time character actress Rue McClanahan and Estelle Getty,

a stage veteran who achieved fame on Broadway. Although lighthearted in tone, *The Golden Girls* dealt with issues both public and personal: menopause, elder care, homosexuality, AIDS, and the ever-present shadow of loved ones dearly departed. Together, the foursome achieved magic on the small screen that still persists in daily reruns. **SL**

> **Classic episode**
> *Henny Penny, Straight No Chaser* | *Season 6, episode 26*. Dorothy enlists Rose and Blanche to join her students' play; nothing is more priceless than the ladies in their stage costumes, and they milk every moment for laughs.

⊘ (L–R) Rue McClanahan, Estelle Getty, and Bea Arthur all won Emmys for their roles in *The Golden Girls*, along with Betty White.

Larry King Live

Talk show | USA | 1985–2010

How one man and his nightly talk show became an American institution

Cast | Larry King **Original broadcaster** | CNN
For fans of . . . | *Parkinson* (1971), *The Oprah Winfrey Show* (1986), *Piers Morgan Live* (2011)

For fifteen years, *Larry King Live* was CNN's most-watched program, regularly reaching over one million viewers nightly, and making King one of the most recognizable celebrities in the United States. Dressed in signature suspenders, and facing a non-functional vintage RCA microphone as a prop, King would engage his guests in casual conversation. Politicians, royalty, movie stars, or former prisoners, they all received courtesy and respect, though his centrist approach meant that the far left and the far right regularly accused him of favoritism.

King was often criticized for only asking softball questions. He expressed bewilderment at this, saying that the best way to get a guest to open up was to allow them to speak about themselves. He was also criticized for not preparing properly for interviews; he admitted that he never read the books of guest authors.

The last episode of *Larry King Live* aired on December 16, 2010, but 19 months later King began hosting *Larry King Now* four nights a week on streaming service Hulu and the cable and satellite channel RT America. **RBA**

Classic episode
July 11, 1995. Special guest Hugh Grant plugs his latest movie, *Nine Months*, but—more interestingly—does much to regain public sympathy after his arraignment in Los Angeles for lewd conduct.

◉ King interviews actor Hugh Grant, after Grant's arrest for soliciting a prostitute in a public place in 1995.

North and South

Historical drama | USA | 1985–94

Set before, during, and immediately after the American Civil War, this emotionally charged trio of miniseries was studded with high-voltage stars

Cast | Patrick Swayze, James Read, Lesley-Anne Down, Wendy Kilbourne, Kirstie Alley, David Carradine, Genie Francis, Morgan Fairchild, Forest Whitaker
Original broadcaster | ABC **Award** | 1 Emmy
For fans of . . . | *Roots* (1977), *The Winds of War* (1983)

This Civil War saga of the lasting friendship between Orry Main of South Carolina (Patrick Swayze) and George Hazard of Pennsylvania (James Read) gripped the American nation in the mid-1980s. Adapted from a trilogy by John Jakes, it spread over three miniseries, aired in 1985, 1986, and 1994, the first of which was the seventh-highest rated miniseries in TV history.

After meeting at military academy, the young protagonists fight together in the Mexican War, where George saves Orry's life. Their friendship spreads to their families—the Hazards who have made their fortune in a northern steel town, and the Mains, who are southern plantation owners with slaves—and love blossoms. Then the two men find themselves fighting on opposite sides of the Civil War.

The epic story tracks the families' vacillating fortunes at home and the men's experiences on the battlefields. When the South surrenders the families are reunited in friendship.

North and South was particularly popular for its heartbreaking romantic scenes and impressive cinematography, as well as its sweeping battles, which paid close attention to Civil War verisimilitude. It attracted a roster of guest stars, such as Olivia de Havilland, Johnny Cash, and Elizabeth Taylor. It even led to several marriages between members of the cast and crew, including James Read and Wendy Kilbourne; Jonathan Frakes and Genie Francis; and Lesley-Anne Down and cameraman Don E. FauntLeRoy. **RP**

Classic episode

Season 1, episode 6. After the election of Abraham Lincoln as US President, secessionist feelings reach fever pitch. The Hazards and their rivals patch up their differences and prepare for war against the Union.

◉ David Carradine (Justin LaMotte) and Lesley-Anne Down (Madeline Fabray) in *North and South*.

Mapp & Lucia

Comedy | UK | 1985–86

Acidic comedy of manners set against a picturesque 1930s backdrop

Cast | Geraldine McEwan, Prunella Scales, Denis Lill, Nigel Hawthorne
Original broadcaster | Channel 4
For fans of . . . | *Jeeves and Wooster* (1990), *Agatha Christie's Marple* (2004)

Beneath a mannered exterior, there is a deceptively dark heart to the novels of E.F. Benson. This was successfully adapted to the screen in the series *Mapp & Lucia*, concerning the social rivalries of Emmeline Lucas (Geraldine McEwan) and Miss Mapp (Prunella Scales).

In the United Kingdom, Channel 4 was barely three years into its life when it broadcast *Mapp & Lucia*, and the comedic drama was a welcome addition to its schedules. The series occupied similar territory to the works of P.G. Wodehouse, set in the picturesque coastal town of Tilling in the 1930s, where the recently widowed Lucia rented a house from Miss Mapp. So began a sharply observed comedy of social manners as Mapp and Lucia enter into a contest of one-upmanship. Lucia was vain, selfish, and possessed of an appreciation of her place in society bordering on arrogance. Spinster Mapp hid her desire for social mastery behind a frumpy exterior, but those who crossed her should beware. McEwan and Scales were perfect embodiments of their fictional counterparts; plots might have revolved around the removal of a piano from a sitting room or who had claim to the vegetables in Mapp's garden, but they were played as matters of life and (social) death. The fey Georgie Pillson (Nigel Hawthorne) and golf-obsessed Major Benjy (Denis Lill) were frequent collateral in this war of social graces. The episodes were given extra dimension with location filming in Rye, where Benson lived for many years. A new version of the stories was produced by BBC One in 2014. **MW**

Quelli della notte

Variety | Italy | 1985

In this Italian parody of the talk show, comic characters played the part of guests

Cast | Renzo Arbore, Nino Frassica, Riccardo Pazzaglia, Maurizio Ferrini, Andy Luotto
Original broadcaster | RAI 2
For fans of . . . | *Knowing Me, Knowing You with Alan Partridge* (1994), *The Daily Show* (1996)

Quelli della notte (*Those of the Night*) was a satirical variety show hosted by Renzo Arbore, a multitalented musician, actor, and showman who delighted in sending up popular culture and trash TV. In a parody of the talk show, Arbore invited his "guests," comic characters, many of whom made regular appearances, to sit on a couch in a mocked-up living room. Their surreal chat was interspersed with comedy sketches and songs played by the New Pathetic Elastic Orchestra.

Arbore was an excellent scout as well as a great host: He wanted spontaneous and unique personalities, able to improvise on the screen. Among the comedians who regularly appeared were Nino Frassica (who went on to star alongside Arbore in the 1987 show *Indietro Tutta!/ Full Astern!*), who played the role of Father Antonino di Scasazza, a friar who couldn't help twisting words ("It was a glacial hot night"), and Riccardo Pazzaglia, who played an intellectual who kept trying, unsuccessfully, to knock sense into all others. Other names that became popular thanks to the show were Maurizio Ferrini, Andy Luotto, and Marisa Laurito.

Arbore once revealed that the idea for the show came to him during a meeting with residents of his apartment building, who inspired him with their colorful chat and discussions. The show only lasted two months, but it quickly reached a fifty-one percent audience share, while its theme tune, *"Ma la notte no,"* became a hit. Arbore's show changed the history of Italian television. **SDG**

The Flying Doctors

Drama | Australia | 1985–93

The outback comes to our screens

Cast | Andrew McFarlane, Liz Burch, Robert Grubb, Lenore Smith
Original broadcaster | Nine Network
For fans of . . . | *All Creatures Great And Small* (1978), *Neighbours* (1985)

In the mid-1980s, worldwide popular culture suddenly became infatuated with all things Australian, from *Crocodile Dundee* (1986) and Yahoo Serious through, eventually, to *Home and Away* (1988) and *Neighbours*. (1985). *The Flying Doctors* is an early relic of that era.

It began as a miniseries that focused on the work of the Flying Doctor Service of Australia and was successful enough to be spun off into a whole series. Its subsequent format generally featured standalone stories each week (as the medics flew to the rescue of unfortunates all over the Australian outback), although various ongoing plot lines, such as the romance between Dr. Geoff Standish (Robert Grubb) and nurse Kate Wellings (Lenore Smith), punctuated the action throughout the whole run.

There was always something a bit rough-and-ready about *The Flying Doctors*, with its occasionally far-fetched story lines and its view of the outback which, to outsiders, fit all the stereotypes they might ever have imagined: it was an Australia for people who have never been there. Yet it was a hugely successful show and remains eminently watchable (not to mention oddly escapist), possibly because it was the antithesis of *Dynasty* (1981) and other glamorous, shoulder-padded American soaps of the same period. If you want a reminder of just how entertaining 1980s TV could be, while at the same time tapping in to the pop culture of the day, then you may find that *The Flying Doctors* sums it all up perfectly. **CW**

Bread

Comedy | UK | 1986–91

"We'll make it and we'll take it home—bread!"

Cast | Jean Boht, Peter Howitt, Nick Conway, Victor McGuire, Jonathon Morris, Gilly Coman, Kenneth Waller, Ronald Forfar, Bryan Murray, Graham Bickley
Original broadcaster | BBC One
For fans of . . . | *The Liver Birds* (1969), *Shameless* (2004)

In the 1960s, Liverpool was perceived internationally as a glamorous place thanks to its music scene and its football. Two decades later, it experienced mass unemployment as industry moved away. Tabloid newspapers depicted the city as a den for scroungers and thieves, a view that was compounded when writer Carla Lane, a Liverpudlian by birth, characterized the reputation in the form of the Boswells, a large Catholic family living on the outskirts of the city center. Each of the Boswell clan had unrealistic ambitions and an unorthodox method of achieving them.

Bread acts as a counterpoint to the harder-hitting drama of the early 1980s, such as *Boys from the Blackstuff* (1982) and the ongoing saga *Brookside* (1982). A rather traditional ensemble sitcom, it charmed its way into the hearts of the British public, most of whom appreciated the core values of family and of working together against adversity. Or perhaps they just tuned in to see how Joey Boswell would once again make the life of social security officer Pamela a living hell by putting in another outlandish claim for welfare benefits. Viewers adored her exasperated sigh before she pointed out just how many times he'd tried a similar tactic. It should be noted though that while the people of Liverpool rolled their eyes in exasperation at the stereotypes, exactly the same basic premise powered *Only Fools and Horses* (1981), in which London trader Del Boy performed similarly shifty deals to support his family. **JS**

ALF

Comedy | USA | 1986–90

An average suburban family adopt a wise-cracking extraterrestrial being—"Haaa! I kill me"

Cast | Paul Fusco, Max Wright, Anne Schedeen,
Andrea Elson, Benji Gregory
Original broadcaster | NBC
For fans of . . . | *The Muppet Show* (1976),
Mork & Mindy (1978)

The Tanners are a pretty ordinary Californian family until the day ALF comes to stay. Ham radio enthusiast Willie Tanner (Max Wright) unwittingly attracts the attention of the sole survivor of the destroyed planet Melmac, an alien who then crashes his ship into their garage. The alien in question is a furry, aardvark-like biped with a long segmented snout. Named Gordon Shumway, he has a gift for dry one-liners and his favorite food is cat. The Tanners take to their new visitor and decide that he can stay (on the condition he doesn't eat the family cat). The Tanners dub him ALF—"alien life form"—and Gordon's new name sticks.

Comedian Paul Fusco was the voice behind ALF, and during its four-year run the show became a major hit. The core concept of ALF—an alien stuck among human beings—had worked before in the 1970s (as *Mork & Mindy*, 1978) and would work again in the 1990s (as *3rd Rock From the Sun*, 1996), but in both of those shows the aliens could pass as human. There was no chance of that with ALF. The puppet made the series unique, and cemented the character as a firm favorite with children and adults alike.

Perpetually bemused by humans, ALF struggled to get to grips with the complexities of social mores and manners. But he was always warm and funny, and not without his sardonic, worldly side—a pleasant contrast to the other big "stranded alien" story, *E.T.* (1982). The character was a big hit with merchandisers, and the series spun off into a Saturday morning cartoon. **WM**

Classic episode
Consider Me Gone | *Season 4, episode 24*. ALF makes contact with other Melmacians and decides to leave for good. After a tearful farewell, the US government turns up, and ALF is surrounded by agents as the Tanners look on, helpless.

⌂ Paul Fusco voiced the alien life form ALF, seen here in Season 3.

The Life and Loves of a She-Devil

Drama | UK | 1986

A feminist classic, this adaptation of a best-selling novel about sex and revenge reveled in its gripping plot, terrific central character, and wicked sense of humor

Cast | Julie T. Wallace, Dennis Waterman, Patricia Hodge
Original broadcaster | BBC Two
Award | 1 BAFTA
For fans of . . . | *Revenge* (2011)

Some themes never get stale: the deceptions of love, the destructions of love, and the burning need for revenge—the subjects of Fay Weldon's 1983 novel and this brilliant 1986 TV adaptation, which preceded the movie starring Roseanne Barr by three years.

Ruth (Julie T. Wallace) was the plain but loyal wife of Bobbo (Dennis Waterman), a financial advisor. When Bobbo had an affair with a client, the romantic novelist Mary Fisher (Patricia Hodge), Ruth realized she no longer loved her husband, who had only ever treated her like a despised servant, and set out to take revenge. Instead of a "good wife," she became a she-devil.

Ruth's machinations in pursuit of that revenge were worthy of *The Count of Monte Cristo* (1844). She saddled Mary and Bobbo with unwanted relatives, drained Bobbo's bank accounts, framed him for embezzlement, and finally revealed him for exactly what he was. "I let in reality," she said, "and love cannot survive reality."

Wallace, by turns sexy and dowdy, competent and submissive, brazen and demure, as her various "lives" demanded, delivered a tour de force. Waterman, often cast as a sex symbol, gamely sported a seedy moustache as philanderer Bobbo. Refusing to walk his wife home late at night, he uttered the line, "I don't think Ruth is a natural rape victim," with repellent conviction.

Utterly damning of how women are sold a vision of impossible romantic love instead of the myriad other ways to find fulfillment, the series was a brilliant jewel of 1980s feminism. **RL**

Classic episode

Episode 4. Ruth's revenge reaches its climax as heartbroken novelist Mary turns to her local priest for emotional comfort. But Ruth has seduced the priest, and there is no love left for Mary, the woman who destroyed Ruth's life.

◉ Julie T. Wallace as Ruth, faithful wife turned she-devil.

La Dama de Rosa

Drama | Venezuela | 1986–87

Melodrama led to more melodrama in this quintessential telenovela of the 1980s

Cast | Jeannette Rodríguez, Carlos Mata, Miguel Alcantara, Jaime Araque, Amalia Pérez Díaz, Gigi Zanchetta
Original broadcaster | Radio Caracas Television
For fans of . . . | *Revenge* (2011), *La Patrona* (2013)

For five nights a week in the mid-1980s, *La Dama de Rosa* (*The Lady in Pink*) gripped audiences in Venezuela and abroad, with its classic story of a poor girl seeking revenge on the wealthy womanizer who wronged her. Now a distinct relic of its era, it may display less than polished production values and clichéd characters, but it remains a quintessential Latin American telenovela.

The series was created by prominent Venezuelan writer José Ignacio Cabrujas, a master of telenovelas. It began with Gabriela Suárez (Jeannette Rodríguez), a spirited young cheerleader and theater student, starting a job at a car wash to help her poor family, after the death of her father. Tito Clemente (Carlos Mata), the handsome businessman who owned the car wash, wooed Gabriela, but abandoned her when she was falsely accused of drug trafficking. Pregnant with Tito's child, she served seven years in prison before escaping, driven by vengeance against Tito. She changed her appearance, renamed herself, and reintroduced herself to Tito, with the sole aim of making him fall in love with her so she can engineer his downfall.

The show succeeded because, like many telenovelas, it addressed key issues in Latin American society: the importance of family, the perils of the drug industry, the gulf between wealth and poverty. Audiences rooted for the female protagonist from a humble background, who must rely on her own wits, while exciting plot elements like the prison break and Gabriela's secret identity added tension and bite. **WML**

A Very Peculiar Practice

Comedy/Drama | UK | 1986–88

Dark comedy and surreal academic drama

Cast | Peter Davison, Graham Crowden, Barbara Flynn, David Troughton, Amanda Hillwood, Joanna Kanska, John Bird, Lindy Whiteford, Michael Shannon
Original broadcaster | BBC One   **Award** | 1 BAFTA
For fans of . . . | *One Foot in the Grave* (1990)

Scriptwriter Andrew Davies is best known for his literary adaptations for TV, such as *Pride and Prejudice* (1995), but he also created this original drama as a satire of the British university system. It starred former Doctor Who Peter Davison as another doctor, this time working at a medical practice in a highly dysfunctional university, where the lecturers appeared to be mad and those in charge just wanted to find ways to make a fast buck.

When Dr. Stephen Daker arrived at Lowlands University he found chaos. The layout of the university campus seemed designed to perplex the unwary traveler; his new boss, Jock McCannon (Graham Crowden) was an alcoholic conspiracy theorist; and his colleagues, the manipulative Rose Marie (Barbara Flynn) and the highly stressed and ruthless Bob Buzzard (David Troughton), were locked in an eternal power game. Eventually, when Jock was considered unfit for work, Stephen was appointed as his replacement, which further antagonized Rose Marie and Bob. The only sane voice among the babble was Lyn, a postgraduate student who helped Stephen overcome his recent divorce but refused to commit to a relationship. In the second series, he met visiting Polish academic Grete Grotowska (Joanna Kanska). Grete was fiery and initially her relationship with Stephen was rocky, but somehow, they fell in love. A one-off feature-length episode in 1992 showed Stephen trying to adapt to life with Grete in her native Poland. There, he discovered a health service no less chaotic than the one he had left behind. **JS**

The Monocled Mutineer

Historical drama | UK | 1986

A charismatic chancer finds himself leading a rebellion in the trenches

Cast | Paul McGann, Bill Fellows, Matthew Marsh, Anthony Calf, Jane Wood, Ron Donachie, Timothy West, Dave Hill, Penelope Wilton, Jerome Flynn
Original broadcaster | BBC One **Award** | 1 BAFTA
For fans of . . . | *The Crimson Field* (2014)

Whether the actual events of this drama took place, or the historical truth was enhanced for dramatic effect, it did not reduce the impact of *The Monocled Mutineer*. Paul McGann starred as the charming Percy Toplis, who escaped the mines of Nottingham for the trenches of France. After witnessing an officer being executed for cowardice, Percy stole the dead man's uniform and absconded, taking over his identity and using it for personal gain. Eventually, he was arrested and sent for retraining to Etaples, where he and his fellow soldiers were treated so cruelly that they began to riot. In an attempt to bring order, Percy was pushed into representing the men in negotiations with the officers. Although the men won their dispute, Percy knew the officers would use him as a scapegoat, so he absconded again and saw out the rest of the war in England. Not one for a quiet life, he re-enlisted in the army under a fake name and was drawn into gang-related rackets that resulted in him being accused of murder.

The source book *The Monocled Mutineer* was written by William Allison and John Fairley and published in 1978. When approached to adapt it, Alan Bleasdale (*Boys from the Blackstuff*, 1980) was reluctant, preferring to develop original ideas. He eventually gave in after finding an emotional connection to the story. The series, however, attracted criticism from the press, which accused the BBC of left-wing bias and Bleasdale of perpetuating a lie. The BBC stood by the production, stating that it represented "a wider truth." **JS**

The Oprah Winfrey Show

Talk show | USA | 1986–2011

The most influential talk show in history, with a media star at the helm

Cast | Oprah Winfrey
Original broadcaster | Syndication
Awards | 47 Emmys
For fans of . . . | *Donahue* (1967), *Parkinson* (1971), *So Graham Norton* (1998)

There are few people in the world with the reach and power of Oprah Winfrey, and even fewer shows as successful as hers. Quickly outgrowing its origins as a simple Chicago talk program, *The Oprah Winfrey Show* became the highest-rated television talk show in the United States. It redefined the talk show genre, and Winfrey's engaging and honest style propelled her to international fame. By the time her final episode aired in 2011, she had become the confidante of 145 nations.

Winfrey's ability to connect with people meant the show could be all things to all people. It didn't matter if they were black or white, gay or straight, ordinary or famous, Oprah talked to them all. She attracted huge audiences—90 million people watched Michael Jackson's first interview in fourteen years—yet she made her couch feel like the safest place on Earth. Her best shows were often those in which ordinary people shared their extraordinary stories. Her sensitivity made discussions about race and sexuality commonplace on television and thus easier for families to have at home.

Throughout the show's 4,500 episodes, Winfrey also shared her own life—the books she loved, the joy of charity, and the experiences that had shaped her life. Her intimate connection with her audience was extraordinary. She opened her nineteenth season by handing out little boxes to all 276 members of her studio audience. One, she implied, would contain the keys to a brand-new car. They all did. "You get a car! You get a car! You get a car! Everybody gets a car!" she said. **PPW**

Liebling Kreuzberg

Comedy/Drama | Germany | 1986–98

The casebook of a brilliantly lazy German lawyer who cannot be bothered to work

Cast | Manfred Krug, Anja Franke, Corinna Genest, Roswitha Schreiner
Original broadcasters | SFB, NDR, WDR
For fans of . . . | *Boston Legal* (2004), *The Beiderbecke Affair* (1985)

People have an idea of the Germans as ruthlessly efficient, hard-working, and, above all, serious. And yet, there is lawyer Robert Liebling. He is a lazy slob and also one of the great heroes of German TV. Liebling's work ethic would bring Angela Merkel out in hives. As played by Manfred Krug, he is a perpetually feckless genius. Don't bother looking for him in his office; he's more likely to be feeding the ducks from the comfort of a deckchair. With his shabby clothes and a generally rumpled air, Liebling is no catch but he is never without a girlfriend (or several). The only things he is devoted to are his vast range of hobbies: yoga, model-making, and long baths with a nice cigar. However, if you can succeed in piquing his interest, Liebling will devote his brilliant legal mind to your problem, schlepping to your rescue on his motorbike or in his vintage Mercedes-Benz. Set in the district of Kreuzberg, Liebling's world straddles immigrant slums and shabby chic. The pace is gentle, the resolutions convivial, and the incidental music is jazz.

Created by Jurek Becker (whose novel *Jakob the Liar*, 1969, became an Oscar-nominated film), the show ran for five seasons, which appeared over thirteen years, as and when they felt like it. Utterly charming, *Liebling Kreuzberg* finally petered out in 1998, following Becker's death. However, it remains a warm-hearted and genuinely charming show, and also depicts a district of Berlin that has changed almost beyond recognition. Kreuzberg is now infamously hipsterish. **JG**

Classic episode

Ein Dringender Fall (An Urgent Case) | *Season 1, episode 2.* Robert is planning a day in bed with his girlfriend, but a young man called Bodo has other plans. Can Liebling defuse a hostage crisis at a supermarket in his pants? Of course he can.

⊛ Manfred Krug as the work-shy lawyer Robert Liebling with Natascha Bonnermann in the role of Tanja.

It's Garry Shandling's Show

Comedy | USA | 1986–90

Laid-back comedy that delighted in breaking the "fourth wall"

Cast | Garry Shandling, Barbara Cason, Molly Cheek   **Original broadcaster** | Showtime
For fans of . . . | *The Larry Sanders Show* (1992)

In the United States in the 1980s cable channels were beginning to make an impact on the TV landscape, and they fared especially well with comedic talents that were considered too "difficult" for network TV. Garry Shandling was one of these talents.

After making an impression with two one-off comedy specials for the Showtime channel, the comedian graduated to his own cable sitcom, which was a marked departure from the offerings elsewhere in the schedules. In *It's Garry Shandling's Show* (co-created by Shandling and Alan Zweibel), Shandling played himself as a nerdy, nervy, but amiable type encountering difficulties with dealing with the modern world. He would regularly break off mid plot to talk directly to the camera, and his awkward, hesitant, shambling delivery and presentation proved exceptionally endearing. Critics and young audiences, hungry for something different, soon latched on. After the show ended its run, Shandling went on to greater success with another series that toyed with the notions of reality and fiction, *The Larry Sanders Show* (1992). **DF**

Classic episode
No Baby, No Show | *Season 2, episode 2*. Garry's plan for hosting a live birth on the show does not run smoothly, but events are enlivened by a guest appearance from nearby neighbor Tom Petty.

⊘ Garry Shandling won an American Comedy Award in 1988 for funniest male performer in a TV series.

Casualty

Drama | UK | 1986–present

Accidents will happen . . .

Cast | Derek Thompson, Patrick Robinson, Suzanne Packer, Amanda Mealing **Original broadcaster** | BBC One
For fans of . . . | *Cardiac Arrest* (1994), *ER* (1994), *Holby City* (1999), *Grey's Anatomy* (2005)

Casualty, currently the world's longest-running medical drama series, tells the story of the staff of the accident and emergency ward of the fictional Holby City Hospital. It started out as a gritty show that addressed important political issues, such as the funding of the British National Health Service (NHS). Over the years, however, it has softened considerably. The soap opera elements have increased, and the cast and the sets are better looking and more realistic because more money has been spent on their construction.

What hasn't changed is that *Casualty* still brings important issues into the nation's homes. The audience might be watching to see what happens to the man stuck up a ladder, or to find out which nurse a doctor will choose from his current love triangle, but they're also seeing racial and gender issues, HIV, the consequences of smoking and drinking, teenage pregnancy, and much more.

Such was the success of *Casualty* and the demand for more in a similar vein that BBC One came up with the no-less-successful spin-off, *Holby City* (1999). JL

Classic episode
Boiling Point | *Season 7, Episode 24*. An old man is beaten up in a rough part of town and a vigilante group seeks revenge. Characters from both sides of the ensuing fight end up in the hospital. And then someone starts a fire.

◬ A child in a hospital bed? Concerned medical technician?
Your remote has almost certainly found an episode of *Casualty*.

La Corrida

Variety | Italy | 1986–2011

An ironic take on a popular talent show that proved tremendously popular

Cast | Corrado Mantoni, Gerry Scotti, Flavio Insinna, Antonella Elia
Original broadcaster | Canale 5
For fans of . . . | *Ant and Dec's Saturday Night Takeaway* (2002), *The X-Factor* (2004)

"If you can't dance, sing, or act, you should be on the show." That was the tagline for *La Corrida*, which was created in 1968 as a radio program and moved to TV in 1986, where it was presented by much-loved veteran Corrado Mantoni for Silvio Berlusconi's Canale 5. In each episode, contestants performed an act, a song, or a dance, and were either applauded or ridiculed by the studio audience. Unlike in shows such as *The X-Factor* (2004) or the *Got Talent* franchise (2006), contestants did not audition—they simply sent in a postcard saying they would like to take part.

Corrado's initial fear that contestants would feel embarrassed on camera and lose their spontaneity proved unfounded. Most of the "performers" simply wanted to meet celebrities and greet their families from TV. The audience, not judges, had the power to make or break the contestants. If the audience liked the performance, they applauded; if not, they hissed or slammed pots and other objects.

A traffic light signaled to the audience when they should vote, and the show introduced phone lines in 1992, so that people at home could call in to guess, for example, the name of a song mimed by a person chosen by Corrado from the audience.

Corrado was loved by Italians for his simplicity, humility, and self-irony, and his death in 1999 was mourned by Italian TV. He was then replaced by Gerry Scotti and Flavio Insinna, who kept the show going for another twelve years. **SDG**

L.A. Law

Drama | USA | 1986–94

Groundbreaking drama both legal and personal

Cast | Harry Hamlin, Corbin Bernsen, Susan Dey, Jill Eikenberry, Michael Tucker
Original broadcaster | NBC
Awards | 15 Emmys, 5 Golden Globes
For fans of . . . | *Moonlighting* (1985)

Just as *Hill Street Blues* (1981) revolutionized the cop drama, *L.A. Law* rewrote the rules of the legal show. This was not surprising because both were brain children of executive producer Steven Bochco. Unlike its gritty predecessor, *L.A. Law* had a sense of the absurd, its humor wound into its DNA. It told serious stories and silly stories, and sold them all to its audience with the same verve. Today, its blend of soap opera theatrics and procedural drama is commonplace, but in the 1980s it was pioneering.

Los Angeles law firm McKenzie, Brackman, Chaney, and Kuzak took on a range of cases every week, but the real drama came from its lawyers. Harry Hamlin as Michael Kuzak and Susan Dey as Grace Van Owen provided the sexual tension in the form of their on-off romance; Arnold Becker (Corbin Bernsen) was a "pickup artist" before the term was fashionable. In addition, *L.A. Law* was never afraid to tackle serious issues. Jill Eikenberry and Michael Tucker—married in real life—played married lawyers Ann Kelsey and Stuart Markowitz, dealing with the anti-Semitism of Kelsey's mother and both families' hostility to their mixed marriage. The show also featured an openly bisexual lawyer, C.J. Lamb (Amanda Donohoe), and Jimmy Smits as the fiercely principled Victor Sifuentes, a rare positive portrayal of a Hispanic character on TV at the time. The ground *L.A. Law* broke is now well trodden, but the progenitor of the modern workplace drama is certainly worth revisiting. **RL**

Matlock

Crime/Mystery | USA | 1986–95

Well-crafted courtroom drama with a cantankerous lead—"I'd sooner eat a live chicken than be your lawyer!"

Cast | Andy Griffith, Linda Purl, Kene Holliday, Nancy Stafford, Julie Sommars, Kari Lizer, Clarence Gilyard, Jr.
Original broadcasters | NBC (1986–92), ABC (1992–95)   **Award** | 1 Emmy
For fans of . . . | *Perry Mason* (1957), *Columbo* (1971)

It is rare for a TV star to strike lightning twice as the lead in two different series, but Andy Griffith's popularity with the US public gave him two well-earned shots, with his role as Sheriff Andy Taylor in *The Andy Griffith Show* (1960), generally considered one of the greatest shows in US TV history, and with his performance as folksy but high-priced attorney Ben Matlock in *Matlock*.

Thrifty to a fault, known for preferring cheap gray suits and hot dogs, Matlock charged his clients $100,000 in advance of working their cases, only occasionally making exceptions for poor clients. Although he had private investigators at his beck and call to discover facts and clues, he wasn't above visiting crime scenes himself and proved to have keen insights regarding evidence overlooked by the police. His primary penchant for unmasking a murderer was by questioning them on the stand, in the courtroom. Despite his great skill, he tended to lose one or two cases a week, a deliberate choice by the production team so that Matlock wasn't seen as infallible. A revolving cast of characters aided the lawyer both in the office and in the courtroom, but Andy Griffith was the only actor to star in all 195 episodes. His many years on TV made him part of the United States' extended family, especially among senior citizens. This deep fondness for the character has been parodied for years on *The Simpsons* (1989), where Grandpa Simpson and other elderly Springfield residents watch *Matlock* with near-religious fervor and believe Ben Matlock to be a real person. **RBA**

Classic episode
The Sisters | *Season 1, episode 8*. Two sisters concoct a callous plot to frame their uncle, Harold Scully, for the murder of their wealthy aunt. Matlock must defend Scully and break down the seemingly solid alibis of the sisters.

⌾ Andy Griffith stars in the episode "The Witness Killings."

The Singing Detective

Music/Musical | UK | 1986

A dark journey through a labyrinth of fiction, memories, and paranoia

Cast | Michael Gambon, Patrick Malahide, Janet Suzman, Jim Carter, Alison Steadman, Joanne Whalley
Original broadcaster | BBC One
Awards | 3 BAFTAs
For fans of . . . | *Pennies from Heaven* (1978)

In Dennis Potter's most lauded work, Michael Gambon starred as Philip Marlow, a noir fiction writer, trapped in hospital with an attack of psoriatic arthritis. Trying to work through writer's block and a medication-induced delirium, Marlow tried to adapt one of his novels, *The Singing Detective*, as a screenplay. Barely able to move and reliant on help from a nurse (Joanne Whalley), he tried to construct the script within the confines of his mind, but found himself plagued with memories of childhood—notably his mother's adultery and suicide, and his own betrayal of a classmate. Soon he came to suspect his ex-wife of conspiring to steal his script.

Potter took viewers through his metatextual tale, mixing literary allusion and clashing genres. The sexual content shocked the audience and drew complaints, but this was nothing new for Potter. In among the fantasy, though, Marlow was shown in extreme distress with a condition similar to Potter's own. As he slipped between medicated and lucid states, Marlow saw himself as his fictional hero on a trail of espionage and murder that remained largely unresolved. Potter's script was wilfully confusing as it flitted from fantasy to a perceived reality. At one point characters discuss Marlow's script, only for them to start also reading out the punctuation marks in their dialog; we realize that the scene is probably imagined by Marlow in his bed.

In 2003, an unsuccessful movie adaptation of Potter's story, starring Robert Downey Jr., Robin Wright Penn, and Mel Gibson, tanked at the Box Office. **JS**

Classic episode
Heat | *Episode 2.* After several weeks in hospital, Marlow has not improved and his doctor thinks that his condition is psychological. The patient must recall distrubing events from his childhood in order to be rid of his demons.

◉ Michael Gambon as the singing detective . . . but is he real, or a figment of his own imagination?

Hot Metal

Comedy | UK | 1986–88

Satirical comedy about the tabloid press

Cast | Geoffrey Palmer, Richard Wilson, Robert Hardy, Richard Kane
Original broadcaster | ITV
For fans of . . . | *Whoops Apocalypse* (1982), *One Foot in the Grave* (1990)

Hot Metal is probably the funniest sitcom that nobody remembers. It is a wickedly cutting, humorous look at the tabloid press in the United Kingdom, and despite being nearly thirty years old, it holds up remarkably well. It is extraordinarily prescient about the state of the British tabloids and the tactics they use to get their story. Indeed, the journalists at *The Daily Crucible* sink to new levels: hiding in the wardrobe of members of the royal family and stealing medical records to print.

The show's main strength is its gag rate, both verbal and visual. You'd have to have a heart of stone not to laugh as they print a Braille version of naked ladies or a three-dimensional version of the same page. There is also a retired army sergeant allegedly channeling the words of God: silly stuff, but rip-roaringly funny. Unlike most sitcoms, both series of *Hot Metal* have an ongoing plot, and both story lines involve a deep conspiracy that could rock the establishment. In true *Hot Metal* style these conspiracies nod toward reality and truth while remaining deeply ridiculous and hilarious.

The cast is excellent: in series one Geoffrey Palmer is wonderful as a man pushed to the brink by stress; in series two Richard Wilson takes over as editor and test-drives a prototype of the character that would prove so popular not long after in *One Foot in the Grave*. However, the standout is Robert Hardy as both Twiggy Rathbone and Russell Spam. Viewers are sure the fact that one actor is playing two characters is going to be a joke and it is all the funnier for usurping those expectations. **LH**

Dear John

Comedy | UK | 1986–87

Finds the humor in being single

Cast | Ralph Bates, Belinda Lang, Peter Blake, Peter Denyer, Rachel Bell, Lucinda Curtis, Jean Challis, Kevin Lloyd
Original broadcaster | BBC
For fans of . . . | *Only Fools and Horses* (1981)

Recently separated, middle-aged schoolteacher John Lacey (Ralph Bates) attends a weekly encounter group —the 1-2-1 Club—for divorcees and singletons. It is organized by the prying Louise (Rachel Bell), a handsome woman who can be relied upon to ask each new attendee if there were "any sexual problems" that led to their breakup. The other regulars include Ralph (Peter Denyer), a spectacularly boring and gullible man, the spiky, three-times-divorced Kate (Belinda Lang), and boorish fantasist Kirk (Peter Blake), who claims to be a spy (prompting Kate to suggest his life story could be called "Tinker, Tailor, Soldier, Dickhead").

Dear John is often overshadowed by writer John Sullivan's bigger hits, *Just Good Friends* (1983) and *Only Fools and Horses*, yet it is packed with engaging characters, hilarious dialogue, and a few ingenious twists. The group members are broadly drawn without ever slipping into the grotesque, and even the obnoxious Kirk elicits viewers' sympathies when John discovers that he is a nobody—real name Eric—who still lives with his sadistic bully of a mother. Ralph Bates, as the frustrated optimist John, is at his best when confronted both by the harsh realities of other people's selfishness and by his own inability to grasp victory from the jaws of defeat.

This masterful sitcom ran for only fourteen episodes across two series. A US remake for the NBC network, starring Judd Hirsch, racked up ninety episodes from 1988 to 1992. **JS**

Married . . . with Children

Comedy | USA | 1987–97

"Domestic bliss was never like this!"

Cast | Ed O'Neill, Katey Sagal, Christina Applegate, David Faustino, Amanda Bearse, David Garrison, Ted McGinley
Original broadcaster | Fox   **For fans of . . .** | *The Simpsons* (1989), *Family Guy* (1999), *American Dad!* (2005)

The Bundys were not your average sitcom fodder, with zany misadventures and social commentary on family life. They were drawn instead from the realm of outrageous, familial stereotypes run completely amok: Al, the weary, unappreciated father with a keen eye for the ladies; Peggy, the lazy, unemployed housewife dreaming of a rich man to take her away; Kelly, the air-headed blond bombshell teenage daughter without supervision; and Bud, the slightly sinister post-pubescent son.

Today such political incorrectness might make a TV executive blush, but in the late 1980s it was comedy gold. On paper *Married . . . with Children* should never have achieved the success it did, but it had the right

credentials at the right time. Its cast was flawless, including brilliant character actor Ed O'Neill as Al; up and coming actress Katey Sagal as Peggy (later of *Sons of Anarchy* (2008) fame); and as Kelly, Christina Applegate, who went on to become a breakout comedic actress in her own right. The show was placed within the fledgling Fox network's Sunday night lineup, where the attraction of the slightly less racy *The Simpsons* helped provide new viewership. Two years into its run, it became the target of a boycott over inappropriate subject matter, but fans remained loyal and Fox renewed the show for eleven seasons. *Married . . . with Children* remains the network's longest-running live-action series—not bad for a sitcom. **SL**

🔺 Ed O'Neill as Al Bundy and Katey Sagal as his long-suffering wife, Peggy.

Talking Heads

Drama | UK | 1987–98

A series of monologues by one of the UK's leading playwrights

Cast | Thora Hird, Julie Walters, Patricia Routledge
Original broadcaster | BBC One   **Awards** | 2 BAFTAs   **For fans of . . .** | *Monologues* (1993)

Alan Bennett was already one of the UK's most celebrated playwrights when the BBC produced *Talking Heads*, a series of monologues set in his native Leeds. His characters were mostly female and middle-aged or elderly, although Bennett himself played a closeted gay man caring for his elderly mother in "A Chip in the Sugar," and David Haig starred in the most controversial play, "Playing Sandwiches," as a pedophile trying—and ultimately failing—to reform himself.

At their core, the plays were about loneliness: These people talked to themselves because they had no one else to talk to. Bennett's eye was at once unsparing and compassionate, simultaneously exposing his characters' delusions and their vulnerability. Their lives were mostly

lived in the margins, colored by disappointment and even shame: A vicar's wife found solace in drink and an affair with a young grocer; a widow had to come to terms with her unexpected impoverishment and the discovery that her husband abused their daughter; a woman who spied on her neighbors and wrote letters of complaint landed on the wrong side of the law.

The second season, made ten years later, skewered Bennett's undeserved reputation for coziness. Much darker, these plays covered domestic abuse, murder, and pedophilia, while remaining rooted in Bennett's familiar world. The monologue may be a dramatic form rarely seen on television, but in *Talking Heads* Bennett and an impeccable cast delivered the peak of the art. **HE**

◈ Thora Hird as Doris in the once-seen, never-forgotten episode "A Cream Cracker Under the Settee."

French and Saunders

Comedy | UK | 1987–2004

Idiosyncratic sketch show from Britain's premier female double act

Cast | Dawn French, Jennifer Saunders   **Original broadcaster** | BBC Two
Award | 1 BAFTA   **For fans of ...** | *The Comic Strip* (1987), *Absolutely Fabulous* (1992)

Having risen to fame through live performances and appearances on the Channel Four series *The Comic Strip*, Dawn French and Jennifer Saunders were offered their own starring series by the BBC in 1987 and delivered a winning hybrid of traditional slapstick and off-kilter comedy. Considered part of the "alternative comedy" new wave, the double act pioneered a style that avoided the "isms" that featured in the material of many earlier practitioners—sexism, racism—instead utilizing observational comedy of a more contemporary bent. They wrote the sketches themselves, which resulted in a quirky combination of satire, slapstick, and sparky impressionism from a female perspective. Superbly executed musical pastiche played a big part in the show, and another hallmark was the appearance of guest stars often playing against type or acting as exaggerated clichéd versions of themselves. Arguably the most memorable skits were the spot-on film and TV spoofs, beautifully realized satirical takes on well-known titles such as *Baywatch* (1991), *Batman* (1966), and *Whatever Happened to Baby Jane?* (1962). **DF**

Classic episode
The Silence of the Lambs | *Season 4, episode 2.*
Among the usual mix of clever sketches is a wonderful film spoof, lampooning (with affection) *The Silence of the Lambs*. With guest appearances from veteran comedy stars.

⬥ (L–R) Dawn French and Jennifer Saunders in an early 1990s' episode of the long-running show.

Tutti Frutti

Comedy/Drama | UK | 1987

Wop bop a loo bop a lop bam boom!

Cast | Robbie Coltrane, Emma Thompson, Richard Wilson   **Original broadcaster** | BBC Scotland
Awards | 6 BAFTAs   **For fans of . . .** | *Thompson* (1988), *Your Cheatin' Heart* (1990), *One Foot in the Grave* (1990)

Tutti Frutti is the funny but bitter-sweet tale of The Majestics, a washed-up rock 'n' roll band trying in vain to recapture their fleeting moment of success. Director Tony Smith likened it to a Greek tragedy because, as scriptwriter John Byrne explained, "all the violence happens offscreen."

The six-part story is strong, the settings are powerfully unglamorous, and the acting is outstanding. Robbie Coltrane and Emma Thompson had come to prominence in, respectively, the 1986 movie *Mona Lisa* and the 1987 TV series *Fortunes of War*, but it was in *Tutti Frutti* that they became stars. Richard Wilson's performance as the band's untrustworthy manager Eddie Clockerty led him on to his career-defining role as Victor Meldrew in the long-running comedy series *One Foot in the Grave*.

Byrne went on to write *Your Cheatin' Heart*, but after its failure he was never again asked to work for TV. Meanwhile, *Tutti Frutti*'s release on video/DVD was delayed for twenty years by contractual squabbles. But, as Byrne noted, "Success isn't everything." **BM**

Classic episode
Love Hurts | *Episode 5*. Danny McGlone (Coltrane) exacts revenge on the abusive ex-husband of his paramour Suzi Kettles, a dentist played by David Dixon (Ford Prefect in *The Hitchhiker's Guide to the Galaxy*).

🔊 Robbie Coltrane as Big Jazza (flanked by Stuart McGugan as Bomba and Jake D'Arcy as Fud) in the Majestics' heyday.

The New Statesman

Comedy | UK | 1987–92

Rude, crude, and utterly scathing

Cast | Rik Mayall, Michael Troughton, Marsha Fitzalan
Original broadcaster | ITV
Award | 1 BAFTA
For fans of . . . | *Yes Minister* (1980), *The Young Ones* (1982), *Birds of a Feather* (1989)

Rik Mayall was never afraid to take his comedy to the darkest, most grotesque places, and in the comic creation of Alan B'Stard—a posh, right-wing MP during Margaret Thatcher's ascendancy—he found the ideal character to invest with loathsomeness. Writers Laurence Marks and Maurice Gran were known for a slew of rather cozy award-winning sitcoms. But there was nothing cozy about the media's relationship with the Conservative "nasty party" under Thatcher, and *The New Statesman* had a vicious edge of class- and wealth-based humor.

Alan B'Stard is greedy, selfish, promiscuous, sadistic, cruel, and megalomaniacal. His wife, Sarah (Marsha Fitzalan, a genuine aristocrat) is constantly cheating on him with an army of lovers, and he on her. He treats his hapless sidekick Piers Fletcher-Dervish (Michael Troughton) with utter contempt: a relationship that owes more than a little to the pioneering work of *Blackadder* (1983) in the genre of sitcoms with charmingly awful leads. B'Stard thinks he can write his way out of any problem by signing a few cheques, and often he can. While the show loved to back him into corners, it also loved to see him fight his way out, and it was this ambiguity that was its triumph. Through its satirical gaze, *The New Statesman* examined the British class system and exactly how one can love to hate the ruling elite. By channeling a great deal of public anger about the Conservative government, the show prefigured modern attitudes toward politicians of all stripes, and the move from reflexive respect to outright mockery. **RL**

Indietro Tutta!

Variety | Italy | 1987–88

Satire mocking Italy's penchant for trash TV

Cast | Renzo Arbore, Nino Frassica, Alfredo Cerruti, Arnaldo Santoro
Original broadcaster | RAI 2
For fans of . . . | *The Daily Show* (1996), *InfoMania* (2007)

On the face of it, *Indietro Tutta!* (*Full Astern!*) was a game show like many others. In reality, it was one of the first variety shows to criticize and parody Italian television itself, whose output of very commercial, culturally poor shows soared during the 1980s. Hosts Renzo Arbore and Nino Frassica brought spontaneity and unpredictability to the show. In a subtle and intelligent way, with songs, gags, fake games, and fake sponsors, they made fun of the trash TV that was invading people's lives, and, some said, changing Italian society itself. The scantily dressed showgirls who populated commercial television at the time were replaced by Ragazze Coccodè, a comic character who wore a variety of chicken costumes.

The show was free from advertising breaks or promotions, though there was an imaginary sponsor in the form of Cacao Meravigliao, a cocoa powder available in three flavors, Delicassao (delicate), Spregiudicao (impudent), and Depressao (depressed). The Cacao Meravigliao jingle became so popular that Italians went looking for the product in supermarkets and corner shops all over Italy, for a long time. It confirmed how powerful television was—and still is—if even a fake product could be perceived as real and create demand.

Indietro Tutta! is still considered to have been a groundbreaking show. Its success was mostly thanks to Arbore, a smart, multitalented figure (director, singer, actor, host), whose name was long synonymous with quality TV. **SDG**

Porterhouse Blue

Comedy/Drama | UK | 1987

Dark comedy based on Tom Sharpe's novel about the self-preservation of ancient institutions

Cast | David Jason, Ian Richardson, Barbara Jefford, John Sessions, Charles Gray
Original broadcaster | Channel 4
Awards | 2 BAFTAs
For fans of . . . | *House of Cards* (1990)

One of the striking things about *Porterhouse Blue* is that at times it could be mistaken for a period drama: from the clothes that David Jason wears as Skullion to the opulence and centuries-old traditions that the academic staff at Porterhouse College, Cambridge, are desperate to preserve. Ian Richardson—showing hints of what would make him so intimidating as Francis Urquhart in *House of Cards*—plays Sir Godber Evans, the new master of the college. He wants to make radical reforms, but is fought every step of the way. This is the source of much of the humor and drama.

Porterhouse Blue very much plays with the fight between modernity and tradition, and this comedy of juxtaposition offers some of the funniest moments. For example, the scene in which Skullion is desperately trying to pop inflated condoms that are flying around the quad at night demonstrates fabulously the dark edge that permeates *Porterhouse Blue*. The condoms cause an explosion that kills two college residents, but Skullion won't let the emergency services through before the condoms are burst for fear of tarnishing the college's reputation. A thoroughly devious, and at times, despicable character, Skullion stands for everything that many people in modern Britain despise. However, Jason brings warmth, vulnerability, and passion to him in, arguably, a career best performance. *Porterhouse Blue* is a faithful adaptation of Tom Sharpe's novel—there are no winners here except tradition, as the superbly macabre ending testifies. **LH**

Classic episode
Episode 4 | June 24, 1987. Skullion humiliates everyone in a TV interview. Sir Godber tries to limit the damage but, as everything hurtles toward the shocking and downbeat denouement, everyone falls into place.

⊙ David Jason is mesmerizing as Skullion.

thirtysomething

Comedy/Drama | USA | 1987–91

Chatty and snappy, but heart-wrenching at times

Cast | Ken Olin, Mel Harris, Melanie Mayron, Timothy Busfield, Patricia Wettig, Peter Horton, Polly Draper
Original broadcaster | ABC
Awards | 1 Emmy, 2 Golden Globes
For fans of . . . | *Cold Feet* (1997)

Created by Edward Zwick and Marshall Herskovitz, and influenced by the films *Return of the Secaucus Seven* (1979) and *The Big Chill* (1983), *thirtysomething* follows a group of baby boomers in their thirties as they go about their daily lives. At the center of the circle are Hope and Michael Steadman and their young children, close relatives, and friends.

Although the show focused on Hope and Michael, *thirtysomething* was an ensemble drama, and the stories followed the lives of Michael's cousin, photographer Melissa Steadman; his business partner Elliot Weston, who has a troubled marriage with Nancy; Michael's best friend, English professor Gary Shepherd; and Hope's best friend Ellyn Warren. They are bonded by their youthful association with the counterculture of the 1960s, a past that contrasts with their adult suburban lives. The show was one of the first to unexpectedly kill off a main character, to deal realistically with the painful process of battling cancer, to acknowledge homosexuality by showing two men in bed (they were only talking), and to address the concerns felt by yuppies in the United States during the 1980s. Such story lines, unfurled via chatty, literate, intricately constructed scripts, attracted a cult audience of loyal viewers. Furthermore, the *Oxford English Dictionary* added "thirtysomething" as a word in 1993, defining the term as an undetermined age between thirty and forty, specifically applied to members of the "baby boom" generation entering their thirties in the mid 1980s. **RP**

Classic episode
Fighting the Cold | Season 4, episode 15.
The sudden, surprising death of a main character in this episode traumatized viewers and shocked them into facing their own mortality. Get the tissues ready.

◑ The opening episode introduces the seven friends in their Philadelphia setting.

Ramayan

Historical drama | India | 1987–88

Blockbuster adaptation of a mythological epic

Cast | Arun Govil, Deepika Chikhalia, Sunil Lahri, Sanjay Jog, Arvind Trivedi, Dara Singh, Vijay Arora, Sameer Rajda, Mulraj Rajda, Lalita Pawar
Original broadcaster | Doordarshan
For fans of . . . | *Mahabharat* (1988)

Created by acclaimed film director, producer, and writer Ramanand Sagar, *Ramayan* brought to life the story of Shri Rama, the seventh incarnation of Lord Vishnu, based largely on the Hindu literary classics *Ramayana* by Valmiki and *Ramcharitmanas* by Tulsidas. Rama's complete life story was dramatized as authentically as possible over seventy-eight episodes, which reconciled many different versions of the story to avoid offending any part of the audience. A combination of good casting, makeup, and costume ensured that the look of the many legendary characters from Hindu mythology lived up to the popular perception of how they should appear.

An undisputed landmark of Indian TV, *Ramayan* was an instant hit and became appointment viewing for the whole of India, with viewing figures reaching 40 million on its first national screening. For many, watching the series became a religious experience in itself, bathing early before the Sunday morning broadcast of each episode, and burning incense while it was on. The newspaper *India Today* proclaimed that the nation had been gripped by "*Raymayan* fever," and stories abounded of weddings delayed, funerals postponed, and religious services re-scheduled, all to ensure that nobody missed a single episode. Made on video and with many of its locations and visual effects realized by the most basic video trickery, the majority of *Ramayan*'s loyal viewers were oblivious to its technical shortcomings and allowed themselves to become immersed in the emotional drama. **JA**

Full House

Comedy | USA | 1987–95

There's a lotta love in that house

Cast | Bob Saget, John Stamos, Dave Coulier, Candace Cameron, Jodie Sweetin, Mary-Kate Olsen, Ashley Olsen, Lori Loughlin, Andrea Barber, Scott Weinger
Original broadcaster | ABC
For fans of . . . | *The Brady Bunch* (1969)

There's always room on TV for a completely inoffensive family sitcom. Shows such as *The Brady Bunch* and *Growing Pains* (1985) were safety zones for parents, whereas edgier family sitcoms such as *Family Ties* (1982) and the dysfunctional *Roseanne* (1988) tackled harder topical issues. *Full House* remained popular by remaining squarely in the safety zone, becoming the poster child for wholesome family entertainment into the 1990s.

At the start of the series new widower and TV reporter Danny Tanner (Bob Saget) needs help raising his three daughters. His solution is to have his best friends—wannabe rocker Jesse Katsopolis (John Stamos) and comedian Joey Gladstone (Dave Coulier)—move into his cramped, narrow two-story Victorian house in the Lower Pacific Heights neighborhood of San Francisco. The three men attempt to follow their chosen media-related careers and at the same time provide rock-solid examples for Danny's daughters: D.J., Stephanie, and Michelle. The show featured the usual family sitcom tropes of misunderstandings, sibling rivalry, and innocent lies that grow out of proportion, but by the end of every episode, almost every problem had been solved by the power of love and understanding.

In 1995 the decision was made to stop production on the series due to high production costs, largely because of the higher salaries for cast members. However, in 2014, Warner Bros. Television was considering a series reboot, and the majority of the original cast members had announced their interest in returning. . . . **RBA**

Star Trek: The Next Generation

Fantasy/Horror/Sci-fi | USA | 1987–94

Boldly going with a new generation of the sci-fi great

Cast | Patrick Stewart, Jonathan Frakes, LeVar Burton, Denise Crosby, Michael Dorn, Gates McFadden, Marina Sirtis
Original broadcaster | Syndication **Awards** | 18 Emmys **For fans of . . .** | *Star Trek* (1966)

There was much pressure placed on *Star Trek: The Next Generation*. How could an update of sci-fi royalty hope to succeed? Not only did the show succeed, it did so in style, and while it may not have eclipsed the original voyages of the *Enterprise*, it came to be equally loved.

Paramount had wanted to bring *Star Trek* back to TV for some years, but this desire had evolved into a successful movie franchise with the original cast. By 1986, moves to create a new TV incarnation were in motion, and original creator Gene Roddenberry was lured aboard. The new concept was set 100 years after the original, featuring a redesigned USS *Enterprise* and a different crew, whose interpersonal relationships were founded on cooperation rather than conflict.

One of the masterstrokes was casting Patrick Stewart as Captain Jean-Luc Picard, a more considered and cerebral commanding officer, and a necessary contrast to William Shatner's headstrong James T. Kirk. This set the tone, while other popular casting included LeVar Burton as the blind Geordi La Forge and Brent Spiner as the android Data—an early hit with viewers. **MW**

Classic episode
The High Ground | *Season 3, episode 12*. A perfect example of an issue-led episode that manages to be an exciting adventure thriller. It's a tour de force for Gates McFadden and provides Patrick Stewart with his finest moment as Picard.

◬ Patrick Stewart in "The Next Phase," a season five episode.

Max Headroom

Fantasy/Horror/Sci-fi | USA | 1987–88

A computerized talking head with a slick presenting style

Cast | Matt Frewer, Amanda Pays, Jeffrey Tambor, Chris Young   **Original broadcaster** | ABC
Awards | 3 Emmys   **For fans of . . .** | *Beavis and Butt-Head* (1993), *Utopia* (2013)

Occasionally, TV characters epitomize a vital quality of their era, and one of the most successful examples of this is Max Headroom in the 1980s. With his neatly sculpted hair, sharp suits, and shades, he was the perfect star for a generation part-raised by TV: a virtual host who had no existence outside of the TV set. His rapid-fire presenting style was complete with a trademark computer glitch stutter and the over-friendly manner of a million real-live chat show hosts. However, his TV genesis is rather complex. He made his debut in 1985 on Channel 4 in the United Kingdom in the TV movie *Max Headroom: 20 Minutes into the Future*. In this feature, the fearless reporter Edison Carter (Matt Frewer) is investigating a TV network that has devised a fiendish new form of

subliminal advertising. He is almost killed in a motorcycle crash, but his personality is re-created inside a virtual reality environment—pretty forward-thinking stuff for 1985. Ironically, Max wasn't computer generated at all: Frewer was fitted with cumbersome latex prosthetics, and his image and the ever-changing patterns behind him were manipulated electronically.   **MW**

Classic episode

The Blanks | *Season 1, episode 6*. This fast-paced cyberpunk adventure sees Edison caught up in an investigation into a terrorist plot to hack the city's central computer systems. An anarchic gang—the Blanks—is to blame.

◭ Matt Frewer as Max Headroom—icon of the 1980s.

Inspector Morse

Drama | UK | 1987–2000

Cerebral detective who loves vintage cars, real ale, and a spot of culture—"When I'm thinking, I get thirsty"

Classic episode

Last Bus to Woodstock | Season 2, episode 4. When Morse and Lewis investigate the death of a young woman, whose body is found in a parking lot, they uncover a complex set of relationships. Includes one of Colin Dexter's cameos.

◉ (L–R) John Thaw as Morse and Kevin Whately as Lewis: an unsurpassed detective pairing.

Cast | John Thaw, Kevin Whately, James Grout, Clare Holman
Original broadcaster | ITV
Awards | 6 BAFTAs
For fans of . . . | *Lewis* (2006), *Endeavour* (2013)

Based on the novels of Colin Dexter, each self-contained episode of *Inspector Morse* occupied a two-hour time slot, eschewing the standard sixty-minute format that was the norm in the United Kingdom. It gifted a languorous pace that allowed plots and character to breathe and for the camera to linger on the backdrop of the university town of Oxford. For John Thaw, it demonstrated his astonishing range as an actor.

Each week a single murder investigation is carried out by Chief Inspector Morse (John Thaw) and Sergeant Lewis (Kevin Whately). Their work often takes them into the privileged environment of Oxford's universities. This sits in contrast to Thaw's other best-known role—as Jack Regan in *The Sweeney* (1975). Morse is a weary, cynical, and flawed human being; his idiosyncratic love of opera, ale, and his vintage Jaguar the signs of a complex character. Whately brings a sensible demeanour to Lewis, and together they create one of the great screen detective pairings.

The craftsmanship oozes from every episode of *Inspector Morse*. The pace, trappings, and performances offered an atypical viewing experience for the period, leading to a slew of feature-length crime dramas in its wake. Morse was killed off in 2000—dying alone of a heart attack—but the show was so loved that it was never going to be the end. Whately accepted promotion to inspector for the popular spin-off *Lewis*, while the early investigations of young Morse continue to pull in big ratings in *Endeavour*. **MW**

Home and Away

Drama | Australia | 1988–present

Family-friendly sun, surf, and sex

Cast | Ray Meagher, Emily Symons, Lynne McGranger, Ada Nicodemou
Original broadcaster | Seven Network
For fans of . . . | *Neighbours* (1985), *Paradise Beach* (1994), *Hollyoaks* (1995), *H₂O: Just Add Water* (2006)

In the late 1980s, Britain's children were gripped by Australian soap opera *Neighbours* (1985). Broadcast on BBC One it gave a generation the opportunity to watch young sexy Australian teens having exciting lives in a suburbia where people had swimming pools. Nothing could beat that, surely? And then ITV bought and broadcast a rival Australian soap, *Home and Away*.

Neighbours was about nice families in suburbia. The main family in *Home and Away* were, originally, Pippa, Tom, and their foster children. Basically, the bad boys and girls who occasionally featured as antagonists in *Neighbours* were the main protagonists in *Home and Away*—a setup that has continued throughout the show's history. Whereas *Neighbours* is set in a lovely Melbourne suburb, *Home and Away* is set in the surfing community of Summer Bay. This means that the characters get to wear very little for most of the time (recent characters the Braxton brothers have literally never worn anything more substantial than tank tops and shorts). And that's the thing about *Home and Away*. It's sexy, not in a boy-next-door way but in a bad-boy way. And it isn't just the characters. In *Neighbours* there's the occasional car accident. *Home and Away* has earthquakes and floods and Summer Bay stalkers and ghosts coming out of fridges.

It's also spawned the careers of numerous international stars—Heath Ledger, Chris Hemsworth, Ryan Kwanten, Melissa George, and Julian McMahon, among many others. **JL**

Mystery Science Theater 3000

Comedy | USA | 1988–99

Good-natured rapid-fire riffing on bad movies

Cast | Joel Hodgson, Trace Beaulieu, J. Elvis Weinstein, Jim Mallon, Kevin Murphy, Frank Conniff, Michael J. Nelson, Mary Jo Pehl, Bill Corbett, Patrick Brantseg
Original broadcaster | KTMA
For fans of . . . | *Futurama* (1999)

Created by Joel Hodgson, *Mystery Science Theater 3000* repurposed Z-grade movies with a framing sequence inspired by the sci-fi film *Silent Running* (1972) and the cartoon *Beany and Cecil* (1962). Joel Robinson (Hodgson) has been shot into space and is stranded on the Satellite of Love. There he builds robot friends Crow T. Robot (Trace Beaulieu, then Bill Corbett), Tom Servo (J. Elvis Weinstein, then Kevin Murphy), and Gypsy (Weinstein, Jim Mallon, then Patrick Brantseg) and is forced to endure movie "experiments" sent to him by evil Dr. Clayton Forrester (Beaulieu again) and Dr. Laurence Erhardt (Weinstein again).

The movies are interspersed with wisecracking host segments and skits, and there are silhouettes of Joel and the robots sitting in front of the movie they are riffing. One of the first TV shows to benefit from Internet fan support and the open, encouraged trading of videotaped episodes, the series became a cult phenomenon. Mike Nelson replaced Hodgson in the fifth year, with other cast changes occurring throughout the show's run. The series leapt to the big screen in 1996 with *Mystery Science Theater 3000: The Movie*, riffing sci-fi classic *This Island Earth* (1955).

Many cast members later pursued similar projects such as *Total Riff Off* (2014) and *Cinematic Titanic* (2007). In 2013, the series' annual tradition of a Thanksgiving marathon was revived online as a live streaming event, with Hodgson back to provide new linking segments. "We've got movie sign!" **ATB**

Mahabharat

Historical drama | India | 1988–90

An epic saga of feuding Indian princes based on the world's longest poem

Cast | Rishabh Shukla, Kiron Juneja, Mukesh Khanna, Gajendra Chouhan, Arjun, Praveen Kumar, Roopa Ganguly, Nitish Bhardwaj, Puneet Issar **Original broadcaster** | Doordarshan **For fans of . . .** | *Ramayan* (1987)

After the phenomenal success of *Ramayan* (1987), Hindu mythology became a rich vein for Indian TV drama. With the *Ramayana* being one of India's two great Sanskrit epics, it was obvious choice to adapt the other, the *Mahabharata* which, at more than 200,000 lines, is believed to be the world's longest poem. Even at ninety-four episodes, the epic story was still considerably condensed for its TV audience. Like *Ramayan*, *Mahabharat* was screened on Sunday mornings for a family audience. The story was a timeless one of good versus evil and concerned the family conflict between royal cousins, the Pandavas and the Kauravas, whose rivalry ultimately results in the devastating Kurukshetra War.

The series was produced by award-winning Bollywood mogul Baldev Raj Chopra and directed by his son Ravi. Each episode opened with a song, sung by Mahendra Kapoor, that included two verses from the Bhagavad Gita (part of the *Mahabharata*). This was followed by narration that revealed the spiritual significance of the story to follow. **JA**

Classic episode
Shakuni Provokes Ashwathama Against Arjun | *Episode 47*. Having lost a gamble, the Pandavas are to be humiliated when their wife is brought to court to be publicly disrobed. Desperate to preserve her dignity, she prays to Lord Krishna.

⊙ Painstaking historical research did not necessarily inform the extraordinary beards and costumes of *Mahabharat*.

Roseanne

Comedy | USA | 1988–97

A blue-collar woman's novel approach to parenting and relationships

Cast | Roseanne Barr, John Goodman, Laurie Metcalf, Sara Gilbert, Alicia Goranson   **Original broadcaster** | ABC
Awards | 4 Emmys, 3 Golden Globes   **For fans of . . .** | *Everybody Loves Raymond* (1996)

This show was a phenomenon; it ranked in the top five in the Nielsen ratings for each of its first six seasons, and every season but its last was in the top twenty. Its creator and star, Roseanne Barr, turned herself from a stand-up comedian into one of the most powerful women in television.

Roseanne revolved around the title character, a blue-collar worker with a smart mouth and a demanding family. At the start of the series she and her husband Dan (John Goodman) had three children: teen daughters, girly Becky (Alicia Goranson) and tomboy Darlene (Sara Gilbert), whose relationship mirrored that of Roseanne and her own sister, and young son D.J. (Michael Fishman). Their fourth child, Jerry, came along

later. The parents rejoice in tormenting their children and outwitting any attempt they make to trick them.

Having two overweight, poorly dressed leading actors was groundbreaking, and the jokes always felt natural, as part of normal conversations. And as Barr's influence grew, she forced ABC to incorporate a degree of social realism by including some gay characters. **JS**

Classic episode
Scenes from a Barbecue | *Season 3, episode 24.*
Family and friends descend on the Connor household for a Mother's Day party, and Roseanne's free-spirited Nana Mary (Shelley Winters) pays a visit.

⊙ John Goodman (behind the couch) with Rosanne Barr (on its arm next to him), surrounded by their on-screen family.

Murphy Brown

Comedy | USA | 1988–98

Situation comedy known for its potent political satire and willingness to tackle current events

Cast | Candice Bergen, Pat Corley, Faith Ford, Robert Pastorelli, Joe Regalbuto, Grant Shaud, Lily Tomlin
Original broadcaster | CBS
Awards | 18 Emmys, 5 Golden Globes
For fans of . . . | *The Newsroom* (2012)

Created by Diane English, *Murphy Brown* starred Candice Bergen as a famous investigative journalist and news anchor for *FYI*, a fictional television news magazine show in Washington, D.C. Murphy was ambitious, sarcastic, stubborn, and hot-tempered, but she was also dedicated, clever, and ethical.

An unabashed liberal critic of the then Republican US administration, Murphy was unafraid to ask tough questions. At the start of the series, she was a recovering alcoholic returning from the Betty Ford Clinic, free of booze and cigarettes, and cranky. She had to deal with a new producer, Miles, a brilliant neurotic half her age; Corky, a naive but well-meaning Miss America hired to replace her; Jim, an aging and staid anchorman; and her best friend Frank, a danger-loving investigative reporter. Her coworkers tried to keep her balanced, but Murphy was a whirlwind of fascinating trouble, and she clashed with them often, although they eventually settled into mutual respect.

Over forty years old and single, Murphy had a private life that contained nothing more than a laid-back, philosophical house painter named Eldin, who was endlessly repainting the interior of her townhouse, until she had a baby and raised her child as a single mother.

With its sophisticated, smart scripts and tight ensemble, *Murphy Brown* established itself as one of television's strongest sitcoms. For all its effective comedy, the show tackled serious topics, including aging, feminist choices, and breast cancer. **RP**

Classic episode
You Say Potatoe, I Say Potato | *Season 5, episode 1.*
Murphy Brown hits back at Dan Quayle, the real-life vice president of the United States, who had denounced her decision to become a single parent.

⊘ Murphy (Candice Bergen) always gets to the point.

The Wonder Years

Comedy/Drama | USA | 1988–93

Innovative drama in which the protagonist moves from childhood to maturity

Cast | Fred Savage, Dan Lauria, Alley Mills, Olivia D'Abo, Jason Hervey, Danica McKellar, Daniel Stern
Original broadcaster | ABC
Awards | 4 Emmys, 1 Golden Globe
For fans of . . . | *Freaks and Geeks* (1999)

In *The Wonder Years*, the viewers watched Kevin Arnold (Fred Savage) go through the joy and heartbreak of growing up while the country around him was growing up, too. The show followed Kevin through the tumultuous years of adolescence during the 1960s and early 1970s, with Vietnam, the racial divide, and a clash of generations complicating his childhood.

Creators Neil Marlens and Carol Black conceived this journey back to a transformative time as an ode to the baby boomers, but it was as universal as it was nostalgic in depicting family issues that remain the same in any era. There were Kevin's parents, his bullying brother, his flowerchild sister, his dorky best friend, and Winnie, the girl of his dreams. Together they made their way through a changing cultural landscape in suburban Anytown USA, guided by the raspy strains of Joe Cocker's cover of The Beatles' "With a Little Help From My Friends," which opened every episode, and a lilting guitar score provided by W. G. Snuffy Walden. The show's preview debut right after the 1988 Super Bowl didn't hurt its chances, but it didn't need the help.

A gently bittersweet tone, enhanced by narration from an adult Kevin (Daniel Stern), made *The Wonder Years* a heartwarming blend of rose-colored memories and deeper revelations about the truths that define us all. While some criticized the final episode with its unexpected twists and the shocking fate of one of the main characters, it rang truer than a happier ending might have done. **ATB**

Classic episode
My Father's Office | *Season 1, episode 3*. Kevin visits his father's workplace and makes a troubling discovery about his dad's aspirations in life. A talk over coffee and an evening of stargazing enable them to bond in a new way.

◉ Kevin (Savage) with his on-screen best friend Paul (Saviano).

Red Dwarf

Comedy | UK | 1988–99, 2009, 2012–present

A sci-fi parody that was even a hit with those uninterested in the form it satirized

Cast | Craig Charles, Chris Barrie, Danny John-Jules, Robert Llewellyn, Norman Lovett, Chloë Annett, Hattie Hayridge
Original broadcaster | BBC Two
For fans of . . . | *Doctor Who* (1963), *Being Human* (2008)

Dave Lister is a slacker, a slob, and a lowly maintenance operative aboard the Jupiter Mining Corporation's *Red Dwarf* spaceship. Convicted of smuggling a pregnant cat, he was placed in suspended animation. Due to a radiation leak contaminating the ship and wiping out its entire crew, the ship's computer, Holly, elected to leave Dave in stasis for three million years. When he emerged he discovered that he is the last surviving human in the universe and that his only companions are a pedantic hologram, a humanoid cat, a neurotic android, a corrupted onboard computer, and a dimension-hopping ex-girlfriend.

Writers Rob Grant and Doug Naylor created something that was part *The Odd Couple* (1970) and part *Lost in Space* (1965), playing loosely with science fiction clichés and bending the rules for comic effect. Their scripts were rich in cultural references and sci-fi in-jokes, such as a *Star Wars*–style intro of scrolling text that could be read only on freeze-frame. From the third season, Kryten, the mechanical butler from season two, was promoted to lead cast status and was given many of the best lines. Chloë Annett joined in season seven as Lister's ex-girlfriend from a parallel universe.

Regular production ended in 1999, but in 2009, the series was revived for an anniversary miniseries by the digital comedy channel Dave. In 2013, *Red Dwarf* returned to Dave for its first full season in a decade. **JS**

❷ Robert Llewellyn as robot servant Kryten and Danny John-Jules as The Cat.

The Kids in the Hall

Comedy | Canada | 1988–95

Sketch comedy that picked up where Monty Python *left off and took its format deeper into the world of the grotesque*

Classic episode
Season 1, episode 1. The Headcrusher agonizes about his calling. A ballet school principal humiliates a hopeless pupil. Dave Foley forces Bruce McCulloch to apologize to the audience for causing cancer.

◉ The kids in … the street.

Cast | Dave Foley, Bruce McCulloch, Kevin McDonald, Mark McKinney, Scott Thompson
Original broadcaster | CBC Television
For fans of . . . | *Monty Python's Flying Circus* (1969), *Saturday Night Live* (1975), *The Fast Show* (1994)

The Kids in the Hall (*KITH*) had much in common with *Monty Python's Flying Circus*. Both featured a group of male writers/performers teaming up to do sketch comedy in which they take most of the female roles and play with the format, commenting on the show's own sketches and processes (and both were accused of blasphemy, with *KITH* attracting criticism for its "Dr. Seuss Bible" sketch). However, *KITH* was no rip-off; it had its own identity and went far deeper into the grotesque than Python—witness Bruce McCulloch's cigarsmoker Cabbage Head, ever on the lookout for sympathy sex due to having a cabbage for a head, and Mark McKinney's Chicken Lady, who offered her date an omelette, "straight out of my body and on to your plate".

The original *KITH* went through several incarnations as a live troupe, but it was the lineup of McCulloch, McKinney, Dave Foley, Kevin McDonald, and Scott Thompson that was spotted by *Saturday Night Live* creator Lorne Michaels, who masterminded its transfer to TV. The resulting show was broadcast initially in Canada and then in the United States, with a brief appearance on Britain's Channel 4 in the early 1990s.

KITH ended after five seasons, but was followed by a film, *Brain Candy* (1996), and a miniseries, *Death Comes to Town* (2010), as well as several live tours. Thompson's gay monologuist Buddy Cole has continued to have a life outside of *KITH*. With most of its comedy being absurdist rather than topical, the show itself remains as funny today as when it was first broadcast. **JR**

Les guignols de l'info

Comedy | France | 1988–present

Satire in which puppets are ruder than real people would dare to be

Cast | Yves Lecoq, Daniel Herzog, Jean-Eric Bielle, Nicolas Canteloup, Sandrine Alexi, Bruno Gaccio
Original broadcaster | Canal+
For fans of . . . | *Le Bébête Show* (1982), *Spitting Image* (1984)

Les guignols de l'info (*News Puppets*) is a satirical show in which latex puppets depict the rich and famous. It was originally entitled *Les Arènes de l'info* (*News Arena*), but changed to its current name in 1990.

Its main targets are French politicians: former presidents Jacques Chirac, Valéry Giscard d'Estaing, and Nicolas Sarkozy are depicted as, respectively, an inveterate beer-swilling swindler who can turn himself into a superhero when he needs to tell a particularly big lie; a transcendentally conceited pseudointellectual who is too stubborn to admit that he is dead; and a man with a complex about his short stature who keeps trying to distract the public from his violent temper by drawing attention to his beautiful wife, Italian singer Carla Bruni. Right-wing political leader Jean-Marie Le Pen is a pitbull terrier and remained a prominent character in the show even after he handed over leadership of the Front National to his daughter, Marine.

Foreign politicians are also pilloried, none more so than US presidents George H. W. Bush and George W. Bush, who sit around at home playing war games against terrorists at whom they lob beer cans that they imagine to be hand grenades. They have no real control over foreign policy, which is run by faceless agents in the Pentagon. US commerce is represented by a caricature of Sylvester Stallone in the *Rambo* movies.

The show has been criticized for left-wing bias, but despite—or perhaps because of—that, it has been essential viewing for almost thirty years. **GL**

Bangkok Hilton

Drama | Australia | 1989

Australian drug-smuggling drama set in a dynastic framework

Cast | Nicole Kidman, Denholm Elliott, Hugo Weaving, Joy Smithers, Norman Kaye, Jerome Ehlers, Noah Taylor, Gerda Nicholson, Pauline Chan, Lewis Fiander
Original broadcaster | Network Ten
For fans of . . . | *Tenko* (1981)

Bangkok Hilton was bold and original. It painted a picture of a man running from his past, of people separated by the actions of others, and of both the misfortune and the fortune that trusting a stranger can bring.

Among the stars of the series was Nicole Kidman, who was then somewhere between appearing in the low-budget film *BMX Bandits* (1983) and making her name in the blockbuster *Days of Thunder* (1990). She was joined here by Hollywood-bound Hugo Weaving. Top billing, however, went to British actor Denholm Elliott. The plot focused on his character and how, as a British soldier, he was discharged in disgrace. He moved to Australia and fell in love with a woman, but her parents broke up the relationship and he left her pregnant. Years later the product of their union (Nicole Kidman) tried to find her father. She became involved with a photographer, who duped her into carrying drug-filled luggage into Bangkok. She was caught and imprisoned, enduring the harrowing reality of a Thai prison. Then she finally discovered her lost parent.

The show's dynastic backstory was completely in keeping with US TV dramas; what distinguishes this series was the juxtaposition of exotic locations and the brutal realism of life behind bars in Bangkok. The viewers were not spared its grim harshness. Kidman's character befriended a female prisoner and her mentally disabled brother. They were both executed in a scene that is bleak and dark, showing the sheer cruelty of the Thai justice system. **RJH**

Alien Nation

Fantasy/Horror/Sci-Fi | USA | 1989–90

Mismatched cop show with an original twist

Cast | Gary Graham, Eric Pierpoint, Michele Scarabelli, Terri Treas
Original broadcaster | Fox **For fans of ...** | *Starsky & Hutch* (1975), *Miami Vice* (1984)

In the 1980s, there were many shows about unlikely law-enforcement partnerships, but none was as imaginative or as touching as *Alien Nation*.

The viewers learned in the first episode that Newcomers' spaceship crash-landed in the desert near Los Angeles and disgorged a group of aliens, who were the hapless slaves of another unknown extraterrestrial race. In an effort to integrate these Tenctonese into American society, they were invited to join the police force, and as the show began, xenophobic human Detective Matthew Sikes (Gary Graham) was assigned a Newcomer partner known as George Francisco (Eric Pierpoint). Their initially prickly relationship mellowed as they investigated cases ranging from a Newcomer

prostitution ring to the abuse of a performance-enhancing alien hormone.

Alien Nation was one of the first TV shows to use a season-long story arc, and thus prefigured a form that became the norm in cable drama. However, it failed to find an audience and its first season was its last, although it was later resurrected in five TV movies. **RL**

Classic episode
Three to Tango | *Episode 9.* Newcomer procreation requires three distinct genders, and someone is murdering the third. Francisco and Sikes hunt the perpetrators in order to prevent an attempted genocide of the Tenctonese race.

◐ (L–R): James Caan (Det. Sgt. Matthew Sykes) shakes with Mandy Patinkin (alien Detective Samuel "George" Francisco).

Agatha Christie's Poirot

Drama | UK | 1989–2013

A great literary detective brought to vivid life on-screen

Cast | David Suchet, Hugh Fraser, Philip Jackson, Pauline Moran   **Original broadcaster** | ITV
Awards | 3 BAFTAs   **For fans of . . .** | *The Adventures of Sherlock Holmes* (1984)

Of all the television adaptations of classic works of detective fiction, none is a match for ITV's *Agatha Christie's Poirot*, which featured every major story about the eccentric Belgian detective and brought from David Suchet one of the finest performances of all time.

Although the original stories on which this series was based were written and set over almost half of the twentieth century, producer Brian Eastman and screenwriter Brian Exton both agreed that they would set all of the episodes in the 1930s so that they could make use of the art deco style of that decade.

Suchet's casting had the blessing of the Christie estate following his performance as Blott in *Blott on the Landscape* (1985), an adaptation of Tom Sharpe's

novel, and he was joined by Hugh Fraser as Poirot's confidante Hastings, Philip Jackson as Inspector Japp, and Pauline Moran as Miss Lemon, Poirot's secretary. The early seasons took the short stories as their basis, embellishing the narrative to fill a 50-minute running time. Later episodes were often feature-length to accommodate full-length novel adaptations. The series came to an end in 2013 with four TV movies. The whole series is the most complete adaptation of a fictional canon in TV history.

The distinctive title sequence, the memorable theme music, the period detail, and the finely honed performances all helped the show to become one of the most popular on British TV. **MW**

◉ David Suchet gets to exercise more than his "little gray cells"
as Agatha Christie's meticulous detective Hercule Poirot.

Mother Love

Drama | UK | 1989

Sinister psychological thriller about the mother-in-law from hell

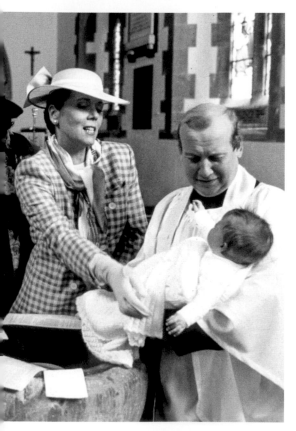

Classic episode
Episode 3. Helena's psychosis, until now seen only in flashes and flashbacks, comes to the fore as she plots to murder her ex-husband's new wife. From here on, the series accelerates toward its frightful denouement.

⊘ Diana Rigg as Helena moves to take possession of her grandchild.

Cast | Diana Rigg, David McCallum, James Wilby, Isla Blair
Original broadcaster | BBC One
Award | 1 BAFTA
For fans of . . . | *House of Cards* (1990)

A four-part adaptation by Andrew Davies from a novel of the same title by Roger Longrigg, *Mother Love* detailed the extreme lengths to which a mother will go to protect what she believes—in this case deludedly—is exclusively hers.

Divorced from her husband, concert musician Alex (David McCallum), Helena Vesey (Diana Rigg) has invested all her love and attention in their only son, Kit (James Wilby). But she wanted Kit to reciproacate this exclusivity. She forbade him to see his father and interfered in his life long after he became a man. Matters reached a head when Kit proposed to his girlfriend, and threatened his mother's hold over him.

Intensely jealous, Helena obsessed over petty and largely imagined slights, which she perceived as evidence of betrayal. Her relationship with Alex's new wife was also fraught with tension because, although she did not want him back, she did not want anyone else to have him either. When she learned that Kit was not quite so easy to control as he once was, mounting paranoia led Helena to plot her revenge against those who she thought had scorned her. Through stylish black-and-white flashbacks, we learned that Helena was dangerously unstable as a child—her anger had little to do with her current situation; it was a lifelong characteristic.

Culminating in a race against time to prevent history from repeating itself, *Mother Love* was a modern take on the classical Greek story of Medea. **MM**

Around the World in 80 Days

Documentary | UK | 1989

A Python in pursuit of a French classic

Cast | Michael Palin
Original broadcaster | BBC One
Award | 1 BAFTA
For fans of . . . | *Full Circle with Michael Palin* (1997),
The Amazing Race (2001)

A veteran of *Monty Python's Flying Circus* (1969) Michael Palin might have seemed an unlikely choice to front a travel documentary series, but his genial-yet-knowledgeable charm made this show work supremely well. *Around the World in 80 Days* set the actor/writer on a new career that continued with more seasons of assorted travelogue documentaries over the next twenty years.

The concept was simple—follow in the footsteps of Phileas Fogg, the protagonist of Jules Verne's *Around the World in 80 Days* (1873), and circumnavigate the globe in the same time or less. The only restriction was that none of the travel could be by aircraft, because that mode of transport was not available to Fogg in the novel. Palin and a five-person crew (known collectively as Passepartout, after Fogg's manservant) embarked on their quest on September 25, 1988, traveling through countries on foot and by balloon, ship, train, and other methods, keeping to Fogg's itinerary whenever possible. En route, Palin met a wide range of people and provided commentary on local culture. He displayed an apparently effortless mastery of the genre.

Palin and his crew arrived back in London on December 12, 79 days and 7 hours after leaving.

Around the World in 80 Days was such a critical and ratings success that it was followed by *Pole to Pole* (1992), *Full Circle* (1997), *Michael Palin's Hemingway Adventure* (1999), *Sahara* (2002), *Himalaya* (2002), *Michael Palin's New Europe* (2007), and *Brazil* (2012). **MW**

Dekalog

Drama | Poland | 1989–90

Ten philosophical tales with biblical origins

Cast | Henryk Baranowski, Aleksander Bardini, Daniel Olbrychski, Adrianna Biedrzyńska, Mirosław Baka, Grażyna Szapołowska, Anna Polony
Original broadcaster | TVP
For fans of . . . | *Talking Heads* (1988)

Long before Krzysztof Kieślowski won international awards for *La double vie de Véronique* (*The Double Life of Véronique*, 1991) and the *Trois couleurs (Three Colors)* trilogy (1993), he earned acclaim in his native Poland for TV movies, documentaries, and films. The director secured his reputation with *Dekalog*, coauthored by lawyer-cum-writer Krzysztof Piesiewicz, with whom he had worked on 1984's fiercely political *Bez końca* (*No End*) about state repression.

The miniseries was loosely based on the Ten Commandments—aka The Decalogue—and jettisoned the political material with which he had become associated. "We knew it was important, but could do nothing about it," he noted, "so we decided it wasn't important at all." In its place was muted philosophy concerning issues faced by his countrymen—"People who," he suggested, "didn't know why they were living." (The exception was a blackly comic closing installment, in which Jerzy Stuhr and Zbigniew Zamachowski played brothers who inherit a valuable art collection.)

Of the ten tales, some related more obliquely to their biblical origins than others, but all were suffused with magnetic melancholia and impeccable performances. Providing tenuous continuity was an angel figure played by Artur Barciś; all the films were made as one production. The director told documentary makers Eileen Anipare and Jason Wood, "Sometimes we were shooting three different films in one day." **BM**

The Simpsons

Animation | USA | 1989–present

The world's most enduring sitcom has maintained high standards throughout its run

Cast | Dan Castellaneta, Julie Kavner, Nancy Cartwright, Yeardley Smith
Original broadcaster | Fox
Awards | 31 Emmys
For fans of . . . | *Family Guy* (1999)

There had been animated sitcoms before, such as *The Flintstones* (1960) and *Wait Till Your Father Gets Home* (1972), but there had never been anything like *The Simpsons*. The growing cable channels were bringing a new type of darker, more risqué comedy to TV, shows like *Hard Knocks* (1979), but the most significant of them all was this brilliant, subversive family sitcom that seemed to get away with so much more because it was animation.

Beginning life as short segments on *The Tracey Ullman Show* (1987), this groundbreaking series centers on the adventures of the Simpson family: food-and-beer obsessed simpleton Homer; his practical wife, Marge; their delinquent son, Bart; their precocious, child-prodigy daughter, Lisa; and the newborn comforter-addicted, Maggie. They are surrounded by a colorful array of other characters in their hometown of Springfield, but it is Homer's crass ways that fuel most of the plots.

The series was the brainchild of cartoonist Matt Groening, whose comically twisted worldview had first come to light in his "Life is Hell" cartoon strip series. *The Simpsons* soon became established in the American consciousness, but never lost its capacity to court controversy. A full-length feature film released in 2007 had much to commend it, but it never quite rose to the heights of the glorious original. **DF**

❯ The Simpson family are shocked to discover that a channel exists that isn't screening early episodes of their show in reruns.

Navarro

Drama | France/Switzerland | 1989–2006

A police commissioner who must balance his caseload against the demands of fatherhood

---

Cast | Roger Hanin, Maurice Vaudaux, Emmanuelle Boidron
Original broadcaster | TF1
For fans of . . . | *Maigret* (1960), *Kojak* (1973), *Derrick* (1974)

Navarro was one of France's longest-running drama series, spanning seventeen years and eighteen seasons. Set in Paris, the show centered on the life of police commissioner Antoine Navarro (Roger Hanin), a single parent who balanced his criminal investigations with the upbringing of his daughter, Yolande (Emmanuelle Boidron). Navarro was strong and incorruptible, a role model in the police force; his authority was manifest. Yet the depiction of his private life revealed his softer side: he was also a loving father and a faithful friend.

The show never found much favor with critics, who regarded it as slow, poorly scripted, and unoriginal in plotting. But if it had any such faults, it always seemed that viewers were blind to them. The audience regularly exceeded ten million, and no detective series achieved anything like this level of popularity in France until the influx of US imports began in the late 1970s.

Still today there is great enthusiasm for the show and enduring affection for its leading man Hanin, who died in 2015. The series largely contributed to his fame, and he was acclaimed by the public for his accessible and human portrayal of the struggles of a lone father, as well as for the credibility of his depiction of a cop. As a result of this faithful following, a spin-off, *Brigade Navarro*, was made after the original series ended in 2006. This sequel retained the totemic central character, but broadened its canvas and concentrated increasingly on the exploits of Navarro's fellow officers. **MS**

The Arsenio Hall Show

Talk show | USA | 1989–94; 2013–14

Breathing new life into an old format, this talk show was so good, they made it twice

---

Cast | Arsenio Hall
Original broadcaster | Syndication
For fans of . . . | *The Chris Rock Show* (1997), *The Graham Norton Show* (2007), *Late Night with Jimmy Fallon* (2009), *Lopez Tonight* (2009)

The late-night talk show is a staple of American television, and each of the four biggest network channels has its own well-funded, celebrity-packed version. Launching a competing show in syndication is therefore an ambitious venture, but that didn't stop comedian Arsenio Hall from reviving a show in 2013 that had been successful in 1989. His goal was to "have fun, make people laugh, and send viewers to bed with a smile on their face."

The original *Arsenio Hall Show* was much lauded for bringing an urban sensibility to an old format. Hall's vibrant personality and light touch appealed to viewers who wanted something different from the approach of talk show giants David Letterman and Johnny Carson. Hall's show had a house band, an opening monologue of topical jokes, and lots of audience participation—a section of the audience known as the Dog Pound, located near the band, would interact with Hall throughout the show, and frequently shout, "Woof! Woof!" Guests ranged from Eddie Murphy and Paula Abdul to wrestler Hulk Hogan, with space on the sofa often given to talented individuals ignored by the networks. As such, it attracted a younger—and crucially, more diverse—audience.

Unfortunately, Hall's 2013 off-network revival, while sharing many of the ingredients of the original show, and attracting guests such as Chris Tucker, Lisa Kudrow, and Magic Johnson, didn't maintain its initial high ratings. Despite being commissioned for a second season, the show was pulled. **SO**

Baywatch

Action/Adventure | USA | 1989–2001

A byword for beautiful bodies, surf, and sunshine, Baywatch *was one of the most popular shows in the world in the 1990s*

Cast | David Hasselhoff, Pamela Anderson, Billy Warlock, Erika Eleniak, Monte Markham, Yasmine Bleeth, Nicole Eggert, Jeremy Jackson
Original broadcaster | NBC
For fans of . . . | *Pacific Blue* (1996)

Baywatch taught the world two important things—firstly, that running in slow motion can solve almost any crisis; secondly, this is especially true if the aforementioned running is done by attractive, buxom women in inappropriate workwear. As referenced by Chandler in that other powerhouse of 1990s television, *Friends*, "This is the brilliance of the show. I say, always keep them running."

When it first aired in 1989, *Baywatch* was canceled after just one season, but one of its stars, David Hasselhoff, led a push to revive the show, believing it still had potential. The program centered on a team of stunningly beautiful Californian lifeguards, who not only saved lives, but also defused nuclear bombs, birthed babies, and fought sharks. The notable exception within the blonde and bronzed cast, epitomized by C.J. Parker, played by Pamela Anderson, was Michael Newman, a real lifeguard who was also the technical advisor on the show. In the late 1990s, *Baywatch* moved to Hawaii for its last two seasons.

At its peak, *Baywatch* was declared the most watched show in the world, with a global audience of over one billion across 140 countries. Its popularity led to spin-offs, most notably *Baywatch Nights*. Running from 1995 to 1997, it followed a local police officer who quit the force to form his own detective agency—assisted by Mitch, David Hasselhoff's lifeguard character. The show even aped *The X-Files* (1993), featuring vampires and mummies. **EB**

Classic episode
Shark Derby | *Season 1, episode 18.* When a number of sharks are spotted in the bay, Mitch becomes concerned by their prevalence, particularly when a local restaurant owner offers $25,000 to whoever kills the biggest one.

◙ Pamela Anderson as C.J. Parker and Yasmine Bleeth as Caroline Holden, lifeguards extraordinaire.

Quantum Leap

Fantasy/Horror/Sci-Fi | USA | 1989–93

An American scientist bounces back and forth across time, taking control of people's lives to avert crisis after crisis

Classic episode
The Color of Truth | *Season 1, episode 7.* Sam Beckett leaps into the body of a black chauffeur in the Deep South in the late 1950s. He battles against institutionalized racial prejudice in his efforts to save a woman's life.

⊘ (L–R) Dean Stockwell as Admiral Al Calavicci and Sam Bakula as his scientific colleague Sam Beckett.

Cast | Scott Bakula, Dean Stockwell
Original broadcaster | NBC
Awards | 6 Emmys, 2 Golden Globes
For fans of . . . | *The Twilight Zone* (1959), *Doctor Who* (1963), *The X-Files* (1993)

Dr. Sam Beckett (Scott Bakula) worked on a secret government project to explore the possibilities of time travel. He'd theorized that it might be possible to travel within his own lifetime, no farther forward than the present day and only as far back as his own birth. With the funding for his project about to be pulled, he tested the machine before it was finished and disappeared into the past. He found himself inhabiting the body of a test pilot in the late 1950s who had no knowledge of how to fly a plane. Fortunately, his colleague Al (Dean Stockwell) managed to send a hologram of himself to Sam's location. Using information collated by their computer, Ziggy, Al predicted that Sam needed to fix a problem—to save the pilot's life by getting right what he'd gotten wrong. Only then could Sam return home.

Except that it wasn't that simple. Sam leaped into another body—and then another. Each time, with Al's help, he had to work out what had happened in the life of whoever's body he was inhabiting and put it right. As soon as that life was back on course, he'd move on to his next time and place.

Writer Donald P. Bellisario concocted *Quantum Leap* as a means of getting an anthology series onto the network by having a small regular cast who linked each story. The episodes gave him an opportunity to tackle social issues—racism, sexism, homosexuality—within the context of a time-travel fantasy, although the science fiction was less of a focus than the social commentary on three decades of American history. **JS**

Press Gang

Drama | UK | 1989–93

A newspaper is staffed by teens whose personal problems are bigger than any of their stories

Cast | Julia Sawalha, Dexter Fletcher, Paul Reynolds, Lee Ross, Kelda Holmes, Lucy Benjamin
Original broadcaster | ITV
Award | 1 BAFTA
For fans of . . . | *Drop The Dead Donkey* (1990)

Although *Press Gang* was originally created for ITV's children's schedule, the series later found an older audience through repeats on Channel 4. Many of its adult fans were too old to have seen it when it was first broadcast in the afternoon, but they now became members of an ardent cult following. The series marked the TV debut of Steven Moffat, later the cocreator of *Coupling* (2000) and *Sherlock* (2010) and the lead writer on the rebooted *Doctor Who* (2005).

Over five seasons of *Press Gang* saw the development of the difficult relationship between the two main characters, Lynda (Julia Sawalha), editor of the *Junior Gazette*, and delinquent reporter Spike (Dexter Fletcher). Spike loved Lynda, but had to accept that her first love would always be the paper and that she wasn't afraid to manipulate her friends in order to achieve success. Lynda also managed to bring out hidden depths in Spike, who hid behind sassy jokes and quick put-downs, but who had a natural eye for a good lead and was capable of smart logical leaps.

Rarely has a children's drama been so well written and performed or dealt so grittily with serious social issues, such as drug abuse. Sawalha would later play Jennifer Saunders' daughter in *Absolutely Fabulous* (1992), while Fletcher (already a familiar face from the movie *Bugsy Malone*, 1976) would feature in the ensemble cast of Guy Ritchie's debut movie *Lock, Stock and Two Smoking Barrels* (1998) before directing his own first feature, *Sunshine on Leith* (2013). **JS**

Traffik

Drama | UK | 1989

A tangled web of heroin trading ensnares parallel lives in several countries

Cast | Bill Paterson, Lindsay Duncan, Jamal Shah, Julia Ormond, Talat Hussain
Original broadcaster | Channel 4
Awards | 4 BAFTAs, 1 Emmy
For fans of . . . | *The Wire* (2002)

Traffik, about the human impact of drug trafficking, was among the most successful dramas to be made by Channel 4. That it picked up several gongs for Britain's fourth TV station was just reward for a complex, layer-cake drama in which the three lead actors (Bill Paterson, Lindsay Duncan, and Jamal Shah) created separate narratives, in London, Hamburg, and Pakistan.

Over its six episodes, the series showed the end-to-end impacts of the drug industry. It spanned the opium-producing poppy fields of upland Pakistan and the addictive use of their derivative, heroin, by secret users such as Caroline (Julia Ormond, in her first major role), the daughter of British government minister Jack Lithgow (Paterson), who is responsible for approving a program designed to deter heroin production in Pakistan. Meanwhile, in Germany, trophy wife Helen (Duncan), initially shocked to find her businessman husband on trial for trafficking, takes ever more ruthless measures to protect her lifestyle and family. In Pakistan, the army's destruction of one village's poppy fields drives farmer Fazal (Shah) to work for the druglord Tariq (Talat Hussain). All of them faced personal losses and dangerous dilemmas.

Traffik went into daringly downbeat territory for production company Carnival Films, which launched its more mainstream hit *Poirot*, plus *Jeeves and Wooster*, within a year of the serial's release. Carnival would go on to produce *Downton Abbey* (2010) and become Britain's leading drama production house. **MWy**

Seinfeld

Comedy | USA | 1989–98

Comedy phenomenon that held the United States spellbound

Cast | Jerry Seinfeld, Julia Louis-Dreyfus, Jason Alexander, Michael Richards
Original broadcaster | NBC
Awards | 7 Emmys, 3 Golden Globes
For fans of . . . | *Curb Your Enthusiasm* (2000)

Famously described as "a show about nothing," *Seinfeld* was, in fact, anything but. Rarely had any series delved so deeply into the nature of things to present plots of fine and intricate detail in which multiple story lines would intersect at various unlikely points and where the minutiae of modern life (off-the-cuff remarks, forgotten names, wardrobe malfunctions) seemed almost malevolently to contrive ways to create chaos.

In the eye of every storm was Jerry Seinfeld, a successful New York stand-up comedian surrounded by a close-knit trio of friends who were always hanging around his apartment. Elaine (Julia Louis-Dreyfus) was Jerry's ex, now a platonic friend, and neurotic in a New York way, but free of any romantic hangups about Jerry. The short, disillusioned, anger-fueled George (Jason Alexander) was an old school-friend of Jerry's; his neighbor Kramer (Michael Richards) was a tall, constantly optimistic, fizzing bundle of energy.

Cocreated by Seinfeld and Larry David, the show belied its surface simplicity to deliver surprisingly complex situations through which the central character would often stroll unscathed while his friends endured various setbacks and disasters. Central to *Seinfeld*'s success was a wilful avoidance of any of the sentimentality that normally characterized prime time TV. This "warts and all" approach paid off and propelled the show to the top of the ratings. **DF**

❱ Kramer, George, Jerry, and Elaine stare in shock at the latest "nothing" to bring chaos into their lives.

Television had brought us reports from other wars, but the (first) Iraq war placed us right in the face of Scud missiles. We witnessed the collapse of the Soviet Union, Nelson Mandela's release, and the funeral of Princess Diana. The old networks were challenged by new subscription services such as Sky and HBO, while Hollywood's finest began to notice that TV offered them a much broader palette: while the real US president was being impeached, *The West Wing* brought us a world leader we could all believe in, and *The Sopranos* totally changed the face and the pace of narrative TV.

1990s

◄ Matthew Perry (Chandler Bing), Courteney Cox (Monica Geller), and David Schwimmer (Ross Geller) lark around in *Friends* (1994).

Beverly Hills, 90210

Drama | USA | 1990–2000

Will twins Brandon and Brenda sink or swim when they are thrown in at the deep end at West Beverly Hills High?

Cast | Jason Priestley, Shannen Doherty, Luke Perry, Jennie Garth, Tori Spelling, Brian Austin Green, Ian Ziering, Gabrielle Carteris   **Original broadcaster** | Fox **For fans of . . .** | *Beverly Hills Teens* (1987), *Dawson's Creek* (1998)

When twins Brandon and Brenda Walsh moved from the Midwest to the bright lights of Beverly Hills, they encountered not only culture shock, but also plenty of drama at West Beverly Hills High.

Although *Beverly Hills, 90210* faced low ratings during its first season, it grabbed large audiences on reruns during the summer of 1991, and remained a hit throughout the decade. Casting perhaps the oldest teenagers in the world (sixteen-year-old Andrea Zuckerman was played by twenty-nine-year-old Gabrielle Carteris), the show made heartthrobs of male stars Jason Priestley (Brandon) and Luke Perry (Dylan McKay). A generation of teenage girls fought over the advantages of clean-cut Team Brandon or bad-boy Team Dylan.

The show initially focused on the twins' struggle to fit in with their rich and beautiful classmates. In later seasons, it became an ensemble piece, with the pressures of leading a glamorous California lifestyle pushed to the fore. Part of the show's popularity was its willingness to confront issues and everyday problems faced by real teens, from fraught relationships with parents and peer pressures to rape, suicide, drug abuse, and eating disorders—often revolving around the beautiful Kelly Taylor (Jennie Garth).

The show spawned a significant franchise and was remade in 2008 as *90210*, with many members of the original cast reappearing. There were also some spin-offs: *Melrose Place* (1992, remade in 2009) and *Models Inc.* (1994). **EB**

Classic episode
Commencement 1 | *Season 3, episode 30*. As graduation looms, the gang looks back on the past and forward to the future. Which college will they go to? While some decide on Yale, Brenda decides on the University of Minnesota.

◉ Luke Perry as bad boy Dylan McKay and Shannen Doherty as Midwest newcomer Brenda Walsh.

Harry Enfield's Television Programme

Comedy | UK | 1990–92; 1994–97

What a thoroughly bloody nice bloke!

Cast | Harry Enfield, Paul Whitehouse, Kathy Burke, Gary Bleasdale, Mark Moraghan, Jon Glover
Original broadcaster | BBC One
For fans of . . . | *The Dick Emery Show* (1963), *The Fast Show* (1994), *The Catherine Tate Show* (2004)

Harry Enfield voiced characters for the satirical puppet series *Spitting Image* (1984) and performed on the revue show *Saturday Live* (1985). For his own *Television Programme* (rechristened *Harry Enfield & Chums* in 1994), he was joined by Kathy Burke and his cowriter Paul Whitehouse in a series of sketches, many of which managed to contribute to everyday language in Britain.

Among the recurring characters were the Scousers (soccer fans from Liverpool, whose perms, mustaches, and cries of "Ay! Ay! Calm down!" became the bane of the city's real soccer supporters), Wayne and Waynetta Slob (a dim-witted couple who named their children Frogmella and Spudulika), the morbid Old Gits, Tim Nice-But-Dim (a posh twit who considered everyone he met a "bloody nice bloke"), and Mr. Cholmondley-Warner, whose public information films provided such sound advice as "Women—know your place!"

Several creations took on lives of their own. Smashie and Nicey—nauseating disc jockeys name-dropping "showbiz mates" who do good work for "charidee"—appeared in their own spin-off and all but finished off the careers of a few real DJs. Most successful was Kevin —initially called "Annoying younger brother" until he hit puberty and became a sulky, parent-tormenting brat. With Perry (Burke) as his sole pal, the pair graduated to their own movie, *Kevin & Perry Go Large* (2000).

Whitehouse became a driving force of rival sketch comedy *The Fast Show* (1994) but revived his partnership with Enfield for 2007's more cynical *Harry & Paul.* **JS**

The Mary Whitehouse Experience

Comedy | UK | 1990–92

That's you, that is . . .

Cast | David Baddiel, Rob Newman, Hugh Dennis, Steve Punt, Melanie Hudson
Original broadcaster | BBC Two
For fans of . . . | *Newman and Baddiel in Pieces* (1993), *The Imaginatively Titled Punt & Dennis Show* (1994)

Mary Whitehouse was a tireless campaigner against lax morals in Britain, who could be relied upon to condemn anything from Dennis Potter plays to *Doctor Who*. However, any program she judged as "filth" could expect a bump in the ratings the following week.

The ironically titled *The Mary Whitehouse Experience* made its debut on radio. Of its ensemble of rising comic stars—including Jo Brand, Jack Dee, and Mark Thomas—only four survived the transfer to TV: Steve Punt, Hugh Dennis, David Baddiel, and Rob Newman.

Within topical monologues were character sketches that became the show's most enduring elements. Mr. Strange (Dennis) had an unsettling obsession with dairy products, muttering "Milky milky," and sending shivers down the spines of the audience. Ray (Newman) was cursed with terminal sarcasm, and his misadventures were forever characterized as "a personal disaster." Most successful of all was "History Today," in which Newman and Baddiel played pompous professors whose discussions always descended to schoolyard taunts: "That's you, that is." Recurring references to The Cure's frontman Robert Smith culminated in a cameo by Smith himself.

The team splintered after just two seasons. Newman and Baddiel took "History Today" to *Newman and Baddiel in Pieces* (1993) and to Britain's arenas until their relationship strained to breaking point. Meanwhile, Punt and Dennis fronted their own series before returning to radio in 1998 to host the satirical *The Now Show.* **JS**

The Fresh Prince of Bel-Air

Comedy | USA | 1990–96

Now this is a story all about how my life got flipped, turned upside down . . .

Cast | Will Smith, Alfonso Ribeiro, Joseph Marcell, James Avery, Karyn Parsons, Tatyana Ali, Jeff Townes
Original broadcaster | NBC **For fans of . . .** | *The Beverly Hillbillies* (1962)

Capitalizing on the popularity of rapper Will Smith, NBC devised a sitcom in which he could play a version of himself—albeit based on the experiences of producer Benny Medina (and with a few years knocked off Smith's age—he was twenty-one when the show began).

The setup was detailed in an addictive theme song cowritten by Smith and his DJ (and occasional guest) "Jazzy Jeff." Sent by his mother to stay with relatives in rich Californian suburb Bel-Air, Will's live-in-the-moment attitude and street-smart immaturity contrasted with the kind but strict Uncle Phil (James Avery), droll butler Geoffrey (Joseph Marcell), and uptight cousin Carlton (Alfonso Ribeiro, whose much-mocked gyrations were based on those of Courteney

Cox in Bruce Springsteen's "Dancing in the Dark" video, and Eddie Murphy's "white people dancing" routine).

The joyful show never took itself too seriously. The recasting of Will's aunt, for example, prompted numerous in-jokes about her new appearance. Crucial to the show's success, though, was the fact that, as well as comedy, there was always heart. **IF**

Classic episode
Papa's Got a Brand New Excuse | *Season 4, episode 24.* Will's absentee father (Ben Vereen, Emmy-nominated for *Roots*) shows up. A powerful and moving climactic scene featured unscripted elements by Smith and James Avery.

⊘ Rage in the cage: Will Smith and Alfonso Ribeiro as Will's cousin, Carlton Banks.

Jeeves and Wooster

Comedy | UK | 1990–93

A jolly good literary adaptation

Cast | Stephen Fry, Hugh Laurie, Robert Daws, Richard Dixon, Mary Wimbush **Original broadcaster** | ITV
Awards | 2 BAFTAs **For fans of . . .** | *Downton Abbey* (2010), *Blandings* (2013)

There is a comforting repetitiousness about the literary misadventures of P.G. Wodehouse's dim-but-lovable Bertie Wooster and his peerless valet, Jeeves. Misunderstandings abound in many convoluted combinations, which are routinely picked apart by the imperturbable Jeeves with nothing more than a calmly delivered "Very good, Sir." Having Hugh Laurie and Stephen Fry play the gentleman and manservant was television's best literary casting of all time.

Writer Clive Exton and producer Brian Eastman were already collaborating on Agatha Christie's *Poirot* when they turned their attention in 1990 to Wodehouse. The BBC had previously adapted the Jeeves stories for *The World of Wodehouse* (1965), but *Jeeves and Wooster* took a more sumptuous approach to the 1930s detail. Exton dramatized all twenty-three hour-long episodes, combining several short stories or extracting sections of full-length novels. Impeccably acted out by Laurie and Fry, they are a master class in adaptation, capturing the essence of what makes Wodehouse so charming, enjoyable, and uproariously funny. **MW**

Classic episode
Pearls Mean Tears | *Season 2, episode 3.*
Bertie is pulled into Aunt Agatha's plan to marry him off to a nice quiet girl, a pearl necklace goes missing, and Jeeves appears unwilling to help arrange a union for one of Bertie's wayward pals.

⬙ Valet larking: Hugh Laurie as Bertie Wooster and Stephen Fry as Jeeves.

One Foot in the Grave

Comedy | UK | 1990–2000

Comedy about aging that gave Britain the catchphrase "I don't believe it!"

Cast | Richard Wilson, Annette Crosbie, Doreen Mantle, Angus Deayton, Janine Duvitski
Original broadcaster | BBC One
Awards | 3 BAFTAs
For fans of . . . | *Jonathan Creek* (1997)

Perpetually frustrated with bad service from every business he encountered, Victor Meldrew (Richard Wilson) became a consumer vigilante whose explosive, vivid vocabulary let customer service departments know exactly what he thought of them. Inevitably, events conspired against him. As his wife Margaret (Annette Crosbie) took pains to tell one of his critics, Victor was surprisingly compassionate and sensitive. His exasperation came from a belief that things really should be better, easier, and more reliable, not perplexing, overcomplicated, and bafflingly inept.

Creator David Renwick's exceptional scripts were packed with detail. The most minor elements would have a bearing on the conclusion—and not always in a comedic way. A deep vein of tragedy runs through much British comedy, and *One Foot in the Grave* mined a lot of it. The suggestion that Victor and Margaret lost a child was revealed in a brief aside, but it was one of many cues that they were real people, no matter how farcical their lives were. Even Victor's most ludicrous plights—whether it was finding a flat cap inside a loaf of bread, a dead cat in his freezer, or a lawn covered in garden gnomes—remained the right side of plausible.

Renwick's choice to kill off both the series and Victor was a brave one, but going out on a high ensured that neither outstayed their welcome. The show made a household name of Wilson after decades in the business, and bequeathed a catchphrase to Britain in the form of Victor's oft repeated, "I don't *believe* it." **JS**

Twin Peaks

Fantasy/Horror/Sci-Fi | USA | 1990–91

The show about a mind-bending small-town mystery that became a cultural juggernaut

Cast | Kyle MacLachlan, Michael Ontkean, Madchen Amick, Dana Ashbrook, Lara Flynn Boyle
Original broadcaster | ABC
Awards | 2 Emmys, 2 Golden Globes
For fans of . . . | *American Horror Story* (2011)

For fourteen months in the early 1990s, the United States was haunted by a single question: who killed Laura Palmer? The answer, as it turned out, was not straightforward—but nothing in *Twin Peaks* was.

When a pretty, popular high school senior is found dead on a lake shore, nude and wrapped in a plastic tarp, her hometown, the rural Twin Peaks, is shattered. FBI Special Agent Dale Cooper (Kyle MacLachlan) uncovers a horrifying undercurrent of corruption, violence and drugs beneath the town's sleepy surface, suggesting that Laura's death was only the tip of an iceberg. Cooper's unusual investigative methodology, which focuses as much on dreams and divination as on forensic analysis, sends Twin Peaks into a tailspin as the townsfolk scramble to keep their secrets hidden.

With its high production values and compelling central mystery, *Twin Peaks* was an overnight success. By the end of its short first season, it had transformed into a cultural juggernaut as fans analyzed the tiniest of clues in the hope of figuring out who killed Laura Palmer before Cooper did. The show's creators, David Lynch and Mark Frost, never intended to reveal the killer, but yielded to pressure going into the second season and resolved the mystery, after which the show's intimate tone and rich mythology proved unable to sustain the momentum it had gained. *Twin Peaks* was canceled after its second season, following a shocking cliff-hanger ending—although Lynch announced a continuation to the series in late 2014. **AP**

Twin Peaks centered on the murder of Laura Palmer (Sheryl Lee). ❯

Waiting for God

Comedy | UK | 1990–94

Raise hell—no matter how close you get to it

Cast | Graham Crowden, Stephanie Cole, Daniel Hill, Janine Duvitski, Andrew Tourell, Sandra Payne
Original broadcaster | BBC One
For fans of . . . | *Last of the Summer Wine* (1973), *One Foot in the Grave* (1990)

Former photojournalist Diana Trent (Stephanie Cole) missed the days when she would hang from helicopters while warlords shot at her. She was sentenced to life at Bayview Retirement Home, a place where her sharp wit and desire for excitement were met with indifference by a world that regarded her as terminally out to pasture.

Enter Tom Ballard (Graham Crowden). Interned at Bayview by his boring son and vile daughter-in-law, he seemed to be a batty old man prone to ridiculous flights of fantasy. However, as Diana discovered, Tom was as sharp as ever. "They all think we go barmy after seventy," he reasoned. "Exploit it, I say." The acid-tongued, world-weary Diana befriended the gleeful, good-natured Tom and together they fought for dignity and respect—for themselves, their fellow inmates, and all senior citizens. With pitch-perfect performances by Crowden and Cole, *Waiting for God* didn't sugarcoat the realities of aging: the infirmity, the loneliness, and the way Western society regards its elders as a nuisance to be hidden away. It could be depressing, but razor-sharp gallows humor and its love of life, mischief, and sheer tenacity made a defiantly subversive concoction.

Tom and Diana ran rings around Bayview's profit-hungry manager Harvey Bains (Daniel Hill), his simpering assistant Jane (Janine Duvitski), and every relative, politician, and official who came to regret crossing their path. Viewers couldn't help but hope that, when their time came, they would follow the pair's example and rage against the dying of the light. **RM**

Fort Boyard

Game show | France | 1990–present

Feel the fear and do it anyway

Cast | Patrice Laffont, Jean-Pierre Castaldi, Olivier Minne, André Bouchet, Alain Prévost
Original broadcasters | Antenne 2, France 2
For fans of . . . | *The Krypton Factor* (1977), *The Crystal Maze* (1990), *La carte aux trésors* (1996)

When *Fort Boyard* made its debut—as the swiftly abbreviated *Les clés de Fort Boyard*, created by Jacques Antoine—few could have foreseen just how big a small-screen phenomenon it would become. Having spawned 1,600 episodes over almost 150 seasons in more than thirty countries, it has established itself as a true TV force to be reckoned with.

The original show was named after a Napoleonic outpost off France's west coast, once used as a clue in Antoine's *La chasse aux trésors* (1968, remade in the UK as 1982's *Treasure Hunt*). It was conceived as an international coproduction, although British partner Channel 4, finding that the rundown fort's conversion to a TV location had yet to be completed, forged ahead instead with the very similar *The Crystal Maze* (1990).

Fort Boyard's premise is essentially the same around the world: contestants tackle mental and physical challenges to win keys and gain access to the titular fort's "treasure room." These games have changed over the years—and ranged from arm wrestling to trying to stay off the floor of a perilous haunted room—but have lost none of their edge. (A legendarily racy variant that initially slipped past British censors involved clues tattooed on a woman mostly naked but for body paint.)

Internationally, various celebrities have enjoyed a fresh lease on life on *Boyard*, including retired soccer player Peter Schmeichel in the Danish variant, and Leslie Grantham ("Dirty" Den in *EastEnders*) and Christopher Ellison (*The Bill*'s Frank Burnside) in Britain. **CW**

Northern Exposure

Comedy/Drama | USA | 1990–95

Welcome to Cicely, Alaska—the quirkiest town in America

Cast | Rob Morrow, Janine Turner, Barry Corbin, John
Cullum, Darren E. Burrows, John Corbett
Original broadcaster | CBS
Awards | 2 Golden Globes, 8 Emmys
For fans of . . . | *Twin Peaks* (1990)

Dr. Joel Fleischman (Rob Morrow), late of New York City,
was an unwilling transplant to tiny Cicely, Alaska, bound
to practice there for four years to repay an Alaska state
student loan. What was he to make of the Aurora
Borealis, seasonal ice breakup, nude men running down
main street to celebrate the coming of the spring, and a
general store owner who never heard of bagels?

Whether he wanted it or not, he was welcomed by
the townspeople, primarily by beautiful, tomboyish
bush pilot Maggie McConnell (Janine Turner),
living proof that opposites attract, whose constant
arguments with Fleischman belied their deep mutual
attraction. Others included Maurice Minnifield, a
former astronaut with 15,000 acres of land he'd like to
develop; home-brew philosopher Chris Stevens, DJ at
the local radio station; the May–December lovers Shelly
Tambo and Holling Vincoeur; and aspiring filmmaker
Ed Chigliak, who traveled between universes to battle
a demon on a mountaintop to save an innocent life.

In Cicely, such magic was always just around the
corner. When Dr. Fleischman himself left the series
half a season before its conclusion, he naturally
traveled through a mystic portal that deposited him
back in New York City. There was just as much magic
in *Northern Exposure* as there was in *Twin Peaks* (1990),
but here it was either beneficial or neutral in form,
and the inhabitants of Cicely had learned to embrace
it. Likewise, the viewers had no problem embracing
Northern Exposure back for six whole seasons. **RBA**

Classic episode
Cicely | *Season 3, episode 23*. Dr. Fleischman and
his friends receive a firsthand account from a
centenarian of how lesbian couple Cicely and
Roslyn founded the town. The show's main cast
appears in alternate roles as early settlers.

◉ Another fine moose. Rob Morrow as Joel Fleischman is a creature
out of water, more gefilte fish than Alaskan salmon.

Mr Bean

Comedy | UK | 1990–95

Behold the man who is a Bean

Cast | Rowan Atkinson, Matilda Ziegler
Original broadcaster | ITV
For fans of . . . | *The Silent Show* aka *Eugene* (1957), *Not the Nine O'Clock News* (1979), *Mr Bean: The Animated Series* (2002)

Before two blockbuster movies and an animated incarnation, *Mr Bean* was simply a sitcom . . . albeit one that up to eighteen million viewers watched, and that revolved around barely a handful of characters— essentially Rowan Atkinson's title character, Matilda Ziegler as his girlfriend, and a teddy bear. "Mr. Bean is very, very self-contained . . ." Atkinson explained to IGN, "because he's so introspective and so selfish and self-centered that there's no particular need to have another person in the scene." And with very little dialogue, *Mr Bean* is closer to the work of vintage comedians Charlie Chaplin and Buster Keaton than to any contemporary sitcom. The wonderfully physical Atkinson inhabited Bean's childlike awkwardness and innocence. The comedy drew on these qualities, as mundane tasks such as going to the laundromat, playing miniature golf, swimming, and cooking Christmas dinner went awry.

This visual style of comedy meant its appeal crossed generations and cultures. Bean is, Atkinson confirmed to theartsdesk.com, "as well known in Shanghai as he is in Venezuela as he is in Wolverhampton." After all, who in the world wouldn't laugh at Bean struggling to change into swimwear at the beach without a fellow beachgoer seeing him naked, only to realize that the person in question was blind? Indeed, it was near impossible to watch *Mr Bean* with a straight face. "He is a child trapped in a man's body and that's what's funny about it," Atkinson noted. "His selfishness and his instinctive anarchy are funny to watch." **LH**

Keeping Up Appearances

Comedy | UK | 1990–95

"It's pronounced 'Bouquet' . . ."

Cast | Patricia Routledge, Clive Swift, Judy Cornwell, Geoffrey Hughes, Mary Millar, Josephine Tewson
Original broadcaster | BBC One
For fans of . . . | *I Love Lucy* (1951), *Ain't Misbehavin'* (1994), *Upwardly Mobile* (1995)

Hyacinth Bucket (Patricia Routledge) would like you to pronounce her last name "Bouquet." And, if you were very nice (not to mention wealthy, and/or part of the British upper class), she might invite you to one of her famous candlelight suppers. But if she did, you might want to run for the hills.

Last of the Summer Wine (1973) writer Roy Clarke's batty, obliviously snobbish character was brought to life by Routledge, an award winner for *Objects of Affection* (1982) and BAFTA-nominated for *Talking Heads* (1987). "To live with it must be murder," Clarke noted of his creation, "but to watch it is funny." A strong supporting cast—including Clive Swift as Hyacinth's long-suffering husband, Richard; Judy Cornwell and Mary Millar as her working-class sisters, Daisy and Rose; and Geoffrey Hughes as her lager-guzzling brother-in-law Onslow— made *Keeping Up Appearances* a show to remember. Alongside sharp and sophisticated dialogue, there was frequent physical comedy, for which Routledge played against type to perfection.

Clarke wrote every episode until, after five seasons, it was brought to an end to enable Routledge to move on (to *Hetty Wainthropp Investigates*) without being typecast. Before that, however, it won great success in Britain and overseas, including on public television in the United States (Routledge described Hyacinth as "the monster who has become such a success around the world"). It was later adapted as a stage play, and is fondly celebrated as a British TV comedy great. **SL**

◀ "I'm aware of the rewards of doing it," Rowan Atkinson remarked of *Mr. Bean*, "and they're not just financial."

Law & Order

Crime/Mystery | USA | 1990–2010

Both sides of the criminal justice coin

Cast | Chris Noth, Sam Waterston, S Epatha Merkerson
Original broadcaster | NBC
Awards | 6 Emmys
For fans of . . . | *Kojak* (1973), *Hill Street Blues* (1981), *NYPD Blue* (1993)

Some shows rely on great characterization, others on long story arcs or fantastic performances. While *Law & Order* was no slouch when it came to creating three-dimensional characters, its real strength lay in its strong, steady weekly storytelling. A winning combination of police procedural and courtroom drama, *Law & Order's* plotting was always immaculate.

Many of its best story lines were taken directly from the news—it was often clear-eyed and sometimes funny on difficult issues. The first season featured an episode based on the case of the Menendez brothers, who murdered their parents. An episode in season eight reconstructed the kidnapping of JonBenét Ramsey. After Mel Gibson's notorious anti-Semitic outburst, *Law & Order* ran an episode in which a racist actor (played by Chevy Chase) is accused of murdering a Jewish television producer.

The show had a starry roster of guest actors, and a wonderful recurring cast, including Benjamin Bratt, Sam Waterston, and S. Epatha Merkerson as tough-but-fair Lieutenant Van Buren. It bore cast changes better than many shows, perhaps because New York City itself was always the real star.

When *Law & Order* was first broadcast, New York still had the air of a crime capital dating from its dangerous reputation in the 1970s. By 2010, when the show ended, the city had been cleaned up and pushed its seedier elements to the fringes. The show too changed over the years but never lost its Big Apple core. **RL**

Classic episode
Mayhem | *Season 4, Episode 17*. Three separate homicides are called in within twelve hours. With a ripped-from-the-headlines Lorena Bobbitt-esque crime at its heart and a devastating ending, it's a *Law & Order* tour de force.

⊘ Peter Riegert as Jerold Dixon undergoes a polygraph test with Jill Hennessey as ADA Claire Kincaid overseeing the procedure.

Oranges Are Not the Only Fruit

Drama | UK | 1990

Controversial because of its depiction of sex, but really a sharp critique of religious practices

Cast | Charlotte Coleman, Emily Aston, Kenneth Cranham, Geraldine McEwan, Cathryn Bradshaw
Original broadcaster | BBC Two
Awards | 3 BAFTAs
For fans of . . . | *Orange is the New Black* (2013)

Jess (Emily Aston, Charlotte Coleman) grew up in a small town in northern England, adopted by a middle-aged couple with strong ties to the local church. Her early life was all about conformity, following instructions from her parents—particularly her domineering mother (Geraldine McEwan)—and the pastor (Kenneth Cranham). Her spare time was spent praying for the poor in Africa and learning the Bible. Stepping out of her community for the first time to attend school, she found herself out of sync with other children of her age. She became friends with Melanie (Cathryn Bradshaw), a relationship that eventually became sexual. When their affair was discovered, it scandalized her community and pushed her mother to take drastic steps to rid Jess of sin and temptation.

Jeanette Winterson adapted her own novel for this three-part serial. Much of the more fantastical allegorical sections of the book were ditched in favor of a more direct, realistic approach. The lesbian sections were diluted, too, not that this shielded the series from complaints. Viewed today, it's less the sexuality of the characters that surprises than the depiction of people with faith. For Jess, the vision of God as presented by her mother and the pastor did not match her own growing understanding of love and compassion. In Jess, the viewers saw a denial of purely black-or-white existences; driven to leave the church, she discovered a sense of her own individuality and realized that love can never be a sin. **JS**

Classic episode
Episode 2. The adults discover that Jess and Melanie are more than just good friends. The pastor denounces them before a packed congregation and demands that the girls turn their backs on Satan.

◉ Emily Aston as Jess, and Geraldine McEwan as the stern and overbearing woman who adopted her.

Have I Got News For You

Game show | UK | 1990–present

Topical satire in a quiz-show format

Cast | Angus Deayton, Ian Hislop, Paul Merton **Original broadcaster** | BBC Two
For fans of . . . | *Mock the Week* (2005), *8 out of 10 Cats* (2005)

The format is two teams of two: the captains are Ian Hislop, editor of satirical magazine *Private Eye*, and comedian Paul Merton; each has a different guest panelist in every episode; he or she is usually a politician, a media celebrity, or a journalist. The teams face a series of questions based on the week's news; the answers are amusing rather than factual, and, although points are awarded, there's little evidence that the scores are kept accurately. In this show it is not the winning that matters, but the taking apart of the inflated reputations of people in the public eye.

For the first twelve years, the show was hosted by actor and comedian Angus Deayton, but he was dropped after scandalous revelations about his private life. Since then, the question master has changed each week; actor Alexander Armstrong has occupied the chair most often; Jeremy Clarkson, former host of *Top Gear* (2002), has also been a regular returnee.

Have I Got News For You runs the risk of infringing English libel laws, but Hislop has made a running gag out of adding "allegedly" to controversial remarks. **GL**

Classic episode
Season 17, episode 7. Guest Jimmy Savile engages in banter with Ian Hislop about his private life. It seemed innocent at the time, but appeared in a different light after subsequent revelations about the DJ's sexual proclivities.

⊙ (L–R) Angus Deayton, Ian Hislop, and Paul Merton in an early publicity still for the long-running show.

House of Cards

Drama | UK | 1990–95

I couldn't possibly comment...

Cast | Ian Richardson, Susannah Harker, Diane Fletcher, Colin Jeavons   **Original broadcaster** | BBC One
Awards | 2 BAFTAs, 1 Emmy   **For fans of . . .** | *The Good Wife* (2009), *Scandal* (2012)

Francis Urquhart (known by the intentionally provocative initials "F.U.") was chief whip for the British government: a puppet-master role that afforded him great power and knowledge of the secrets of prominent party members. This enabled him to swerve every potential trap—and, when called for, to destroy all opposition. With the support of his wife, Elizabeth (Diane Fletcher), Urquhart seduced a young and naive reporter, Mattie Storin (Susannah Harker), using her to manipulate the press and the world around him. Soon he would be prime minister—and then who would stop him?

Although he had appeared in *Tinker Tailor Soldier Spy* (1979), Ian Richardson was primarily a stage star—making him ideal to turn Shakespearean antihero Urquhart into a charismatic TV villain. He broke the fourth wall to address the audience, and his "You might very well think that; I couldn't possibly comment" has become part of the British political lexicon. Adapted from Michael Dobbs' novels by Andrew Davies (*A Very Peculiar Practice*, *Mother Love*), the *House of Cards* trilogy continued with *To Play the King* (1993) and *The Final Cut* (1995). It also courted controversy by making play with real events, notably staging a funeral for former prime minister Margaret Thatcher (who, at the time, was still alive). Asked for his verdict on the 2013 American remake with Kevin Spacey, Davies responded with the Urquhart-esque, "I'm not allowed to say something bad about the show so I won't say anything." **JS**

Ian Richardson as Francis Urquhart, perhaps the most evil occupant of the official home of the British prime minister.

Drop the Dead Donkey

Comedy | UK | 1990–98

Satirical situation comedy referring to events in real-life current affairs

Cast | Robert Duncan, Jeff Rawle, Haydn Gwynne, Neil Pearson, David Swift, Stephen Tompkinson
Original broadcaster | Channel 4
Awards | 1 BAFTA, 2 Emmys
For fans of . . . | *The Newsroom* (2012)

Drop the Dead Donkey—a fictional term for the last item of a news broadcast—blended sitcom with satire, filtered through the staff of cable network GlobeLink.

Razor-sharp writers Andy Hamilton and Guy Jenkins had an impressive track record in TV comedy, including the cornerstone of British satire *Spitting Image* (1984). *Drop the Dead Donkey*'s unique selling point was the filming of episodes, each script peppered with gaps on the eve of transmission, allowing the inclusion of topical gags about the news of the day. This created a vibrancy that has rarely been replicated.

It was also a first-rate sitcom, the newsroom setting creating well-drawn and well-played characters. Never-seen media mogul Sir Royston Merchant demanded a sensationalist approach to news gathering, a message enforced by business-speak addict Gus (Robert Duncan). Hypochondriac editor George (Jeff Rawle) was unable to stand up to him, leaving hard decisions to his tough deputy Alex (Haydn Gwynne) and, later, Helen (Ingrid Lacey). Other characters included conscience-free reporter Damien Day (Stephen Tompkinson), womanizing Dave Charnley (Neil Pearson), and elder statesman broadcaster Henry Davenport (David Swift).

Drop the Dead Donkey riffed on changes wrought in the industry by cable news and moguls such as Rupert Murdoch, although the final seasons eschewed satire to focus on the staff as they prepared for life outside GlobeLink. A haul of international awards was testament to the show's innovation and quality. **MW**

It

Fantasy/Horror/Sci-fi | USA | 1990

Clowning around with Pennywise, Stephen King's horror creation

Cast | Tim Curry, Richard Thomas, Harry Anderson, Tim Reid, John Ritter, Dennis Christopher, Richard Masur
Original broadcaster | ABC
Award | 1 Emmy
For fans of . . . | *American Horror Story* (2011)

With over twenty million viewers for its first broadcast, *It* won a following well beyond that of most miniseries. Stephen King's vast, 1,000-page novel followed small-town characters through three decades as they battled prejudice, bullying, and a supernatural, shape-shifting creature that preferred the form of Pennywise the Clown.

Lawrence D. Cohen, who wrote the screenplay for the 1976 movie adaptation of King's *Carrie* (1974), and director Tommy Lee Wallace, a protégé of horror legend John Carpenter, adapted *It* into two ninety-minute installments. Streamlining the novel's multiple perspectives, shifting time frame, and metaphysical climax, they set the first episode in 1960 and the second in 1990. (Instructed to cut down his original, six-hour screenplay, Cohen inadvertently jettisoned the miniseries' intended director, zombie maestro George Romero—who, King himself told *Fangoria*, "threw up his hands and walked because he didn't think it was enough space.") Dispensing gore that was graphic for the time, and with several of the scariest moments shown from the monster's point of view, Pennywise was a second iconic role for Tim Curry after Dr. Frank-N-Furter of *The Rocky Horror Picture Show* (1975). He was initially reluctant to take it because of the lengthy makeup process.

It's rare for TV horror to create characters as enduring as Michael Myers or Freddy Krueger. But Pennywise the Clown truly was the stuff of nightmares, lingering on into the bad dreams of the twenty-first century. "I think of him," remarked Curry, "as a smile gone bad." **MM**

Tim Curry as the evil, shape-shifting Pennywise the Clown. ❯

The Jerry Springer Show

Talk show | USA | 1991–present

The show that changed TV talk shows forever—"Go Jerry! Go Jerry!"

Cast | Jerry Springer, Steve Wilkos, Jason Brandstetter
Original broadcaster | Syndication
For fans of . . . | *Sally* (1983), *The Oprah Winfrey Show* (1986), *Geraldo* (1987), *Ricki Lake* (1993), *The Jeremy Kyle Show* (2005), *The Steve Wilkos Show* (2007)

Sober and restrained, the debut episode of the talk show hosted by Jerry Springer, a former mayor of Cincinnati, discussed news stories in the style of the venerable Phil Donahue. However, unimpressive ratings forced his team to rethink their approach, and a spectacle was born. *The Jerry Springer Show* made staple ingredients of the raciest and most controversial elements of the talk show format: family disputes, infidelity, extreme behavior, and fighting. In the show's heyday, it was a rare week in which a punch would not be thrown, prompting the introduction of security guards—notably Steve Wilkos and Jason Brandstetter—to keep warring guests apart. When fights broke out, or when the host made a wisecrack or pithy observation, the audience would break into chants of "Jerr-y! Jerr-y" or "Go Jerry! Go Jerry!" This new format, while prompting outrage in some quarters, turned *The Jerry Springer Show* into a global brand.

In the years since the show found its groove, Springer has become a byword for dysfunctional America. When, in the second Austin Powers film, Dr. Evil and his estranged son appear on the show, it is taken as read that the audience will understand that *The Jerry Springer Show* is where the modern world's messy family arguments play out. However, each show is capped off by a sober address from Springer, directly addressing the camera and the viewers at home with a moralizing "final thought," hilariously at odds with the turmoil of the previous hour. **WM**

Classic episode
The Sound and the Fury | Season 16, episode 41.
Any episode featuring the Ku Klux Klan is usually vintage, but drag queen and fan favorite Jason Hartshorn takes the prize with an episode in which he attacks the executive producer.

◉ Jerry Springer's sensationalist style and subject matter have set the template for his type of family talk shows the world over.

Dark Season

Fantasy/Horror/Sci-Fi | UK | 1991

Atmospheric school-based serial

Cast | Ben Chandler , Kate Winslet, Victoria Lambert, Brigit Forsyth, Grant Parsons, Jacqueline Pearce
Original broadcaster | BBC One
For fans of . . . | *Doctor Who* (1963), *The Demon Headmaster* (1996)

Russell T. Davies' credits include *Queer as Folk* (1999) and the relaunch of *Doctor Who* in 2005. But he started his career in children's television and, with no *Doctor Who* being produced in the early 1990s, he set out to make the next best thing: *Dark Season*.

As a surrogate Doctor, we have Marcie Hatter (Victoria Lambert), an idiosyncratic teenager who carries a lacrosse stick in her bag, notices the smallest detail, and acts twenty years older than her age. Attempting to keep up with her are schoolfriends Thomas (Ben Chandler) and Reet (a young Kate Winslet, five years before her first Oscar nomination) and teacher Miss Maitland (Brigit Forsyth).

Dark Season was effectively two three-part serials. The first saw the gang investigating a company that was giving free computers to their school. In the second serial, the kids discovered a powerful relic of the Second World War buried in the school grounds and battled a group of neo-Nazis for control of it. They were pitted against two *Doctor Who*-style villains: the evil Mr Eldritch (Grant Parsons) and Miss Pendragon (Jacqueline Pearce).

What the production lacked in budget it made up for in style: director Colin Cant shot it as creatively as possible, with frequent Dutch tilts down corridors, creating an unsettling atmosphere.

With its witty script, eccentric characters and fun sci-fi ideas, *Dark Season* spawned Davies's second spooky series: *Century Falls* (1993). **WH**

Nummer 28

Reality | Holland | 1991

Arguably the starting point of reality TV

Cast | Sander Buckers, Jan Jaap Weidema, Deborah Fernald, Brenda van der Linden, Rowena Kerkhove, Carolien Wolff Schoenmaker
Original broadcaster | KRO
For fans of . . . | *The Real World* (1992)

In truth, this show was more notable for its groundbreaking format than for its content: as the first reality soap ever, it sparked the wide array of reality TV programs that flood the networks worldwide today. *Nummer 28* ran for only one season, and is little known even in its country of origin, the Netherlands. However, a year later the very similarly formatted MTV reality series *The Real World* would impact a generation. And beyond that, the worldwide smash hit *Big Brother* (1997), also a Dutch production, surely owes a debt to this more modestly set-up predecessor.

The premise of *Nummer 28* was that seven students aged between sixteen and twenty-one of varying backgrounds and characters were put together in a house in Amsterdam and were followed by cameras as they took their first strides toward independent living. Unlike later reality shows, there was no game element, and the housemates were not isolated from the outside world. There was a small studio where the housemates could record a video diary. The events of each week were edited together in twenty-minute episodes and supplied with a snappy soundtrack.

Dutch producer Erik Latour, who came up with the concept of *Nummer 28*, has striven to get recognition for his original idea; however, documentary maker Jon Murray, one of the creators of *The Real World*, has maintained that the MTV program was inspired to a large extent by observational documentary *An American Family* (1973). **PW**

Bottom

Comedy | UK | 1991–95

Violent and chaotic slapstick comedy

Cast | Rik Mayall, Adrian Edmonson
Original broadcaster | BBC Two
For fans of . . . | *The Comic Strip Presents* (1982),
The Young Ones (1982), *The New Statesman* (1987),
Men Behaving Badly (1992)

Rik Mayall and Adrian Edmonson first made their mark on British TV in *The Young Ones*, an anarchic, violent and subversive punch in the gut of traditional sitcoms. *Bottom* takes the cartoon violence of *The Young Ones* and turns the dial up to maximum. It has none of the satirical political commentary of the previous series, however, and is in many ways quite conventional.

Not that that is to its detriment: *The Young Ones* is in many ways both comic actors' finest hour, with the physical comedy for which they had become famous here strongly augmented by flights of verbal fancy as they rant at each other over the most inconsequential and preposterous matters.

The title of each episode was one word appended to "Bottom"—"Bottom Smells," "Bottom's Up," "Bottom Gas," etc. The internal structure of every show was loose enough to maximize the room for mayhem— for example, in "Bottom Holy," Richie (Mayall) finds a baby on Christmas Day and convinces himself that, since he's the child's parent by default, he must be the Virgin Mary. He and his flatmate, Eddie Elizabeth Hitler (Edmonson), then shower the child with gifts in a parody of the Three Wise Men.

In "Bottom Dough," the two losers print counterfeit banknotes but then have to win a pub quiz in order to pay their accomplice. They cheat their way to victory, but it turns out that their £5,000 prize money is also in forged notes. Finally they discover why their creditor is known as "Skullcrusher." **LH**

The House of Eliott

Historical drama | UK | 1991–94

A frisson of fashion in 1920s London

Cast | Stella Gonet, Louise Lombard, Aden Gillett
Original broadcaster | BBC One
Awards | 1 BAFTA, 1 Emmy
For fans of . . . | *Upstairs, Downstairs* (1971),
Downton Abbey (2010)

It was a coup when the BBC secured the cocreators of *Upstairs, Downstairs* (1971), Jean Marsh and Eileen Atkins, as creative figureheads for a new period drama. *The House of Eliott* delved into the world of 1920s haute couture, following sisters Beatrice (Stella Gonet) and Evangeline (Louise Lombard) Eliott in their quest to establish a London fashion house, after their father's death left them penniless. While Marsh and Atkins would not appear in the series, their telling of the sisters' plight and rich period detail bore their hallmarks.

The House of Eliott was the last major drama to be shot in the multicamera studio setting of BBC Television Centre in London, with location filming in Bristol and Gloucestershire. Throughout the three seasons, the sisters struggled—as many women did in the 1920s —to be taken seriously, but Bea's relationship with photographer Jack (Aden Gillett) provided the funds to set up their own business. For thirty-four episodes the sisters loved and lost, and saw acclaim in the fashion world turn to failure before their success with the House of Eliott became more stable.

Season three ended with an uncertain future for Bea, Evie, and the business they had built up. Producers were not expecting cancellation, hence the open-ended finale. With *Downton Abbey* (2010) setting a vogue for costume drama, Marsh's desire for a revival of *The House of Eliott*, updated to the 1950s, was reported in the press. Whether the Eliott sisters will live to stitch another day remains to be seen. **MW**

❷ Beatrice (Gonet) and Evie (Lombard) plan the rise of the House of Eliott over champagne, with Yvette (Larrieu) and Gilles (Valota).

Familie

Soap opera | Belgium | 1991–present

Unlikely family misfortunes

Cast | Jacky Lafon, Annie Geeraerts, Jef De Smedt, Martine Jonckheere, Karel Deruwe, Ronny Waterschoot, Ray Verhaeghe, Silvia Claes
Original broadcaster | VTM
For fans of . . . | *Thuis* (1995), *Sara* (2007)

The most successful product of Herman Verbaet's Studio-A, *Familie* (*Family*) initially focused on the Van den Bossche clan, whose ranks were thinned by death, divorce, and kidnapping. So far, so soap. But this series upped the ante by resurrecting the presumed-deceased and putting new actors in established roles to an extent that made *Roseanne*'s two Beckys seem scarcely worthy of comment. At the heart of *Familie* for more than twenty-three years was Belgian actress Jacky Lafon as black sheep Rita Van den Bossche, whose alcoholism, doomed offspring, recurring spouses and health woes made her an enduring icon of Flemish popular culture.

The show has weathered several storms. In 2009, as familiar faces gave way to new, Verbaet raged that VTM's tinkering with the format had cost *Familie* a quarter of a million viewers. In 2012, actress Anne Somers—who had played Véronique Van den Bossche every year bar 1996–2001, when Ann-Christine Hendrickx took the role—grumbled once too often in public about Lafon and was promptly replaced by Sandrine André, star of *Sara* (2007). Of her ever-changing cohorts, Lafon observed in 2014, "They are all super-sweet and talented [but] it does not feel like my family." She duly asked to be written out of the series but implored the producers "not to let me die." Her last appearance to date was in February 2015, but if the history of *Familie* is anything to go by, even death does not preclude further appearances. **BM**

The Brittas Empire

Comedy | UK | 1991–97

Everything goes wrong, every time

Cast | Chris Barrie, Harriet Thorpe, Julia St John, Pippa Haywood, Judy Flynn, Michael Burns, Tim Marriott, Russell Porter
Original broadcaster | BBC One
For fans of . . . | *Fawlty Towers* (1975)

The Brittas Empire was unashamedly silly and full of puerile jokes, ridiculous characters, and situations you have to watch through your fingers. But under the surface there was cleverly constructed farce.

Andrew Norriss and Richard Fegen cut their teeth on children's series before creating the accident-prone Gordon Brittas, played with nasal gusto by Chris Barrie of *Red Dwarf* (1988). The setting was Whitbury Newtown Leisure Center, and Brittas was the well-intentioned but monstrous new manager, out to inspire his staff and customers, whether they liked it or not.

Weird and wonderful employees surrounded Brittas. Janitor Colin (Michael Burns) displayed injuries and pustules you wouldn't want anywhere near your swimming pool. The permanently apologetic receptionist Carole (Harriet Thrope) couldn't get childcare so kept her children in a desk drawer. Brittas's secretary Julie (Judy Flynn) had no interest in doing what she was told and didn't care who knew it. Gavin and Tim (Tim Marriott and Russell Porter) were a gay couple but kept their relationship secret from Brittas. Meanwhile, Gordon's wife Helen (Pippa Haywood) declined into alcoholism and drug abuse. The only sane member of the team was Laura, the deputy manager (Julia St John), who was calm, unflappable, and knew how to handle her boss.

Like all the best farces, an episode of *The Brittas Empire* let us think things couldn't get any worse and then proved us wrong. **WH**

Brides of Christ

Historical drama | Australia | 1991

"When you spat, complained, and argued, they returned love"

Cast | Brenda Fricker, Sandy Gore, Josephine Byrnes, Lisa Hensley, Kym Wilson, Naomi Watts
Original broadcaster | Australian Broadcasting Corporation
For fans of . . . | *Call the Midwife* (2012)

The 1960s was a time of revolution, not least for women who were seeking and winning liberation from many social restrictions. The anticommunist war in Southeast Asia raged, as did antiwar demonstrations in Australia. The Catholic Church shook off centuries of tradition under Vatican II. The Church's progressive social justice work was felt even in Australia, where the it's conservative Irish roots dominated.

This Australian coproduction with the United Kingdom's Channel 4 and Irish TV station R.T.E. told the stories of a small group of women and girls against this backdrop of significant social change. Each of the six fifty-minute episodes focused, in turn, on young women who wanted to become nuns, and the older nuns who ran a school for girls in Sydney. Episodes also revealed the tension between the younger and older nuns, and their mother superior's arguments with the more conservative order members and senior male counterparts. Issues of faith in a time of questioning were examined in personal terms.

Brides of Christ featured a top-notch cast, and some, such as Naomi Watts and Russell Crowe, went on to pursue successful international film careers. The miniseries was created and produced by Penny Chapman and Sue Masters, both of whom were powerhouses in Australian TV drama production. The series brought humanity to women often viewed as inhumanly pious and, at times, abusively cruel; for all it showed the divisive social reality of the 1960s. **SJG**

Classic episode
Diane | Episode 1. Still grieving for her father, Diane breaks off her engagement and embarks on a new life journey—as a nun. She struggles to come to terms with the strict order of the convent and her new friendships.

◉ Three brides of Christ and two of their young charges.

G.B.H.

Drama | UK | 1991

A labyrinth of shady dealings and job action

Cast | Robert Lindsay, Michael Palin, Julie Walters, Lindsay Duncan, Tom Georgeson, Andrew Schofield
Original broadcaster | Channel 4 **Awards** | 2 BAFTAs **For fans of . . .** | *Boys From the Blackstuff* (1982)

A critical success for Channel 4, *G.B.H.* told a story ripped from the headlines then deliciously twisted by polemic writer Alan Bleasdale. Ambitious, self-serving Labour politician Michael Murray (Robert Lindsay) wanted to protest against the Conservative government, so he called a citywide day of strikes, as much to raise his profile as to cause agitation. However, when a teacher (Michael Palin) opened a school to care for disturbed children, Murray saw this as crossing the picket line and a threat that must be crushed.

The real-life influence on this drama was Derek Hatton, deputy leader of Liverpool City Council in the 1980s and a member of the far-left militant movement. However, Bleasdale gave viewers a fictional equivalent much more complex than Hatton. In the hands of Lindsay, Murray was both a bullying brute and a bedevilled little boy; viewers couldn't take their eyes off him. Bleasdale avoided cliché, so the plot unfolded in dramatic and unexpected ways. At times tense and emotional, at others laugh-out-loud funny or surreal, *G.B.H.* was full of passion, attack, and attitude. **IF**

Classic episode
Message Sent | Season 1, Episode 4. Murray is haunted by his past, pulled in different directions by confidants, surrounded by sci-fi geeks, and all aflutter thanks to a sexy newcomer in his life—hilarious farce.

◍ Michael Palin as pacifist schoolteacher Jim Nelson.

Maigret

Crime/Mystery | France | 1991–95

The great fictional French detective brought to life in his native land

Cast | Bruno Crémer, Jean-Claude Frissung, Erick Desmarestz, Anne Bellec, Alexandre Brasseur, Eric Prat, Pierre Diot, Jean-Paul Bonnaire, Jean-Pierre Gos **Original broadcaster** | Antenne 2 **For fans of . . .** | *Maigret* (1960)

When Georges Simenon, author of seventy-five novels and twenty-eight short stories about the eponymous Parisian police inspector, first met Rupert Davies, who played the role in the 1960 BBC One adaptation, he reputedly exclaimed: "You are Maigret!"

Unfortunately, the novelist died in 1989, before this French version hit the television screens. It is easy to imagine that he would have thought Bruno Crémer an even better choice than the British actor. Simenon had described Maigret as "a solid block; everything had to break against it"; after the first episode was screened, the reviewer for French newspaper *Le Monde* wrote that Crémer had "the massive allure of an oak, and the fragility of a reed"—exactly what the role required.

Crémer was well supported throughout, especially by Jean-Pierre Gos as Maigret's assistant, Lucas.

Each episode was faithful to a particular novel, and the location scenes (many of which were shot in Budapest, Hungary) captured the atmosphere of postwar France. Of all the Maigrets (and there have been many), this was the best. **GL**

Classic episode
Maigret et le corps sans tête (Maigret and the Headless Corpse) | *Season 1, episode 5.* When a man's body is fished out of a canal, suspicion falls on the woman who runs a nearby bistro, but this is no open-and-shut case.

◎ Bruno Crémer as Maigret rests between takes in Paris.

Prime Suspect

Crime/Mystery | UK | 1991–2006

Grisly murders and a prickly detective whose life was as complex as her cases

Cast | Helen Mirren, Tom Bell, John Benfield, Richard Hawley, Jack Ellis, Philip Wright, Craig Fairbrass
Original broadcaster | ITV
Awards | 4 BAFTAs
For fans of . . . | *Cracker* (1993)

Although she was determined and hardworking, Detective Inspector Jane Tennison (Helen Mirren) was a deeply flawed character. Tactless and often unsympathetic, she had a drinking problem and an on-off relationship with cigarettes. She formed brief but ultimately doomed relationships with men, who were either too safe or too unreliable for her, and even her own family didn't quite understand her. Yet she won viewers over through her strength, tenacity, and determination to see justice done.

In her first case, Jane took over an investigation that her late predecessor had felt was almost complete. As she picked apart the evidence, she alienated her team and her superiors, and was forced to release their suspect, George Marlow, without charge. Only with the help of evidence from prostitutes from across the country was Jane able to strengthen the case against him and reveal that his crimes were far more numerous than they had first suspected.

In each season, Jane had to use all the resources available to sift through the evidence and identify a viable suspect. Sometimes, she got it tragically wrong. Writer Lynda La Plante spoke to real high-ranking police officers to create Jane, and the part made Mirren a huge international star. Although La Plante left the series after the third run, it continued without her. The final two impressive and nerve-shredding seasons came close to competing with La Plante's attention to detail and eye for character. **JS**

2point4 Children

Comedy | UK | 1991–99

A middle-aged woman tries to juggle home life with working with her best friend

Cast | Belinda Lang, Gary Olsen, Julia Hills, John Pickard, Clare Buckfield, Kim Benson, Georgina Cates, Liz Smith, Sandra Dickinson
Original broadcaster | BBC One
For fans of . . . | *One Foot in the Grave* (1990)

When Andrew Marshall's *2Point4 Children* first hit British screens, it was compared to *Roseanne* (1988) with only the slightest justification (mainly Gary Olsen's burly build as lumberjack-shirted Ben). Admittedly, like *Roseanne*, it survived the recasting of the eldest daughter, and had occasional lapses into surrealism, but there the similarities ended. Initially, the ongoing story concerned a flirtation between hardworking middle-aged mom Bill (Belinda Lang) and a motorcycle courier whom she kept meeting unexpectedly. Thankfully, Marshall realized that Bill did not need an affair to liven up her life, not when she had hypersensitive vegetarian daughter, Jenny (Clare Buckfield); ghoulish son, David (John Pickard); and a husband, Ben, who was an overgrown kid himself. Bill also had to contend with her sex-mad best friend, Rona (Julia Hills).

At its peak, *2Point4Children* was pulling in more than twelve million viewers. Like another sitcom of the time, *One Foot in the Grave* (written by Marshall's former writing partner David Renwick), much of the comedy came from farcical events affecting the very normal family. What gave *2Point4 Children* the edge was a willingness to go a bit strange occasionally. Christmas specials often featured musical numbers, and a couple of episodes focused on Ben's ongoing war with a rival businessman, Jake Klinger (Roger Lloyd Pack). In one installment, Ben woke up in a strange village populated by sinister weather balloons: a stunt organized by Jake in tribute to classic cult serial *The Prisoner* (1967). **JS**

◖ Helen Mirren won a best actress BAFTA for her role as Jane Tennison in *Prime Suspect*.

Julie Lescaut

Crime/Mystery | France | 1992–2014

A cerebral sleuth who can do everything except convince her colleagues and loved ones that she's good at what she does

Cast | Véronique Genest, Mouss Diouf, Jérôme Anger, Renaud Marx, Jennifer Lauret, Joséphine Serre, Alexis Desseaux, Claude Brécourt, Jean-Paul Rouve
Original broadcaster | TF1
For fans of . . . | *Cagney & Lacey* (1982)

As a female police officer, Julie Lescaut (Véronique Genest) faced all the problems one might have anticipated. Policemen didn't think she was up to the job, and speculated uncharitably about how she might have got it: through a misguided equal opportunities directive, through positive discrimination, or perhaps by sleeping with the bosses. Even after she'd demonstrated that she was every bit as good as they were, they were not placated; indeed, they resented her even more. Meanwhile, at home, Julie was bringing up two daughters, Sarah (Jennifer Lauret) and Babu (Joséphine Serre), who never managed to come to terms with the way their mother put her work before all other considerations.

Viewers who tuned in to *Julie Lescaut* in the expectation of fast action and reliably regular violence were disappointed. This was seldom a spectacular show, but one that dwelt at a leisurely place on the heroine's problems of reconciling life and work, and of her struggles to undermine sexist stereotypes. It also concentrated more on the psychological motivations of the criminals than on their shoot-'em-up deeds.

If you think that sounds like a recipe for failure, think again: *Julie Lescaut* ran for more than 100 episodes, and regularly returned viewing figures of around the six million mark. The audience was predominantly female, understandably, but the show also appealed to everyone who preferred cerebral drama to simplistic cops-and-robbers tales. **GL**

Classic episode
Cougar | *Season 21, episode 2.* After two fashion models are stabbed to death on consecutive days, Julie suspects the work of a serial killer. But the true explanation is different, and even more sinister.

◉ Véronique Genest as Julie Lescaut: she knew how to handle a handgun, but seldom chose to use it.

A Touch of Frost

Crime/Mystery | UK | 1992–2010

Casting a favorite British comedy actor in the central role helped create one of the most popular detective dramas in the history of British TV

Cast | David Jason, Bruce Alexander, Caroline Harker, Arthur White, John Lyons, David Gooderson
Original broadcaster | ITV
For fans of . . . | *Bergerac* (1981), *Inspector Morse* (1987), *Pie in the Sky* (1994)

Novelist R.D. Wingfield's Inspector William "Jack" Frost was untidy, disorganized, and lacked respect for authority—common police procedural tropes loved by viewers. The character was in good hands when he was transferred to the screen, as many of the writers and directors on *A Touch of Frost* had worked on *Inspector Morse*. But ITV's master stroke was casting David Jason, a household name from BBC sitcoms, as Frost. While Jason was best known for comedy, he had already moved toward drama with *Porterhouse Blue* (1974) and *The Darling Buds of May* (1991). In *Frost*, the scales tipped even farther, though a dry humor helped to take the edge off the often dark subject matter.

In a small recurring cast of police officers (including Jason's brother, Arthur White, as archivist Ernie Trigg), Frost was paired with a changing lineup of subordinates, each with his or her own foibles. Notable actors included Neil Stuke, Russell Hunter, Susannah Doyle, Philip Jackson, Cherie Lunghi, and Robert Glenister.

Jack Frost was widowed and living for his job. His lack of respect made him unpopular with his superintendent—"Horn-Rimmed Harry"—but his George Cross medal won for bravery (and a knack for solving cases) made him hard for the force to retire.

A wide range of mysteries and strong guest actors helped the show along, but it's hard to imagine the series being as successful without Jason's central performance as the lonely, righteous detective with a twinkle in his eye. **WH**

Classic episode
No Other Love | *Season 5, episode 4*. Frost and Barnard look into an armed robbery at a pawn shop and the subsequent murder of its proprietor. Their investigation uncovers a family's shocking history of child abuse.

◬ (L–R) David Jason (Frost), Matt Bardock (Barnard), and Bill Rourke (Sergeant Hanlon) examining the latest evidence.

Melrose Place

Drama | USA | 1992–2009

Prime-time soap opera for the 1990s

Cast | Heather Locklear, Thomas Calabro, Marcia Cross, Laura Leighton, Josie Bissett, Courtney Thorne-Smith, Jack Wagner
Original broadcaster | Fox
For fans of . . . | *Dallas* (1978)

A spin-off from the teen-targeting *Beverly Hills, 90210* (1990), *Melrose Place* started out as an adult-orientated look at the day-to-day problems of young professionals who all lived in the eponymous apartment complex in Los Angeles. It touched on topics such as fidelity, work–life balance, and friendship, and dealt with them with a seriousness that many critics thought was verging on the heavy-handed.

Such worthiness seemed to have booked the show a one-way ticket to early cancelation until a sudden sharp thematic U-turn halfway through the first season transformed it from a classy but portentous character drama into serial soap nirvana. *Melrose Place* reemerged as the go-to prime-time drama of the 1990s. At its core, Heather Locklear, as ruthlessly ambitious advertising exec Amanda Woodward, was surrounded by a growing cast of characters, including a serial philanderer, a live-in prostitute, and a psychotic surgeon who blew up the building.

As the years unfolded, it increasingly looked as if anything was possible as long as it had shock value. In one famous season finale, a hand suddenly popped out of a shallow grave. This wasn't an original coup de théâtre—it recalled the end of Brian De Palma's movie *Carrie* (1976)—but it sent the ratings skyrocketing. Though never a critical success, *Melrose Place* became one of television's guiltiest pleasures for millions of viewers during its seven-year run and was briefly resurrected in 2009. **SL**

Classic episode
Asses to Ashes | *Season 7, episode 35*. Sexual jealousy runs amok. Amanda confesses to a homicide, but maintains that it was in self-defense. Meanwhile her enemies hatch a plot to kill her.

◬ Heather Locklear as Amanda Woodward.

The Real World

Reality | USA | 1992–present

The putative daddy of all TV reality shows

Cast | Various
Original broadcaster | MTV
For fans of . . . | *An American Family* (1973), *Big Brother* (2000), *The Real Housewives of Orange County* (2006), *The Real Housewives of Beverly Hills* (2010)

The Real World takes seven or eight ordinary young people, carefully selected to represent a wide cross section of races, sexual orientations, and political and religious beliefs, and puts them together in a house for several months during which they are constantly filmed. The early seasons were acclaimed for their insights into contemporary social attitudes, but more recently the series has evolved into a showcase for exhibitionists and media wannabes.

Some people have regarded this as an unwelcome development, but it has done nothing to reduce the show's popularity: the thirtieth season, set in Chicago (the location changes every year), premiered on December 16, 2014, and there is no reason to suppose that it will be the last.

The producers originally planned a scripted show, but found that the cost of writers, actors, and costume designers was prohibitive. So they came up with this cheap alternative. Little did they realize that it would inspire a plethora of similar reality shows, which have now dominated popular viewing worldwide for almost a quarter of a century.

The show has a long record of giving unknowns their first breaks in showbiz and the media. Several former housemates, including Jamie Chung and Eric Nies, now make their livings as actors; Kevin Powell has become a poet; Heather B. Gardner is a successful hip-hop artist; other *Real World* veterans have subsequently been photographed for *Playboy* magazine. **RP**

Gute Zeiten, schlechte Zeiten

Soap opera | Germany | 1992–present

A good times, bad times soap for young adults

Cast | Andreas Elsholz, Jeanette Biedermann, Oliver Petzsokat, Yvonne Catterfeld, Wolfgang Bahro, Daniel Fehlow, Felix von Jascheroff
Original broadcaster | RTL
For fans of . . . | *Verbotene Liebe* (1995)

Before Germany's reunification, East Berlin's Babelsberg Studios—the oldest large-scale film studios in the world—had faded into oblivion. But when Berlin regained its former status as capital of Germany in 1990, the country's cultural life gravitated toward it, too, and Babelsberg rose from the ashes.

Gute Zeiten, schlechte Zeiten (Good Times, Bad Times), known as GZSZ, was one of the first postreunification TV shows to be made in Babelsberg. An unremarkable soap opera by international standards, it stood out in Germany because it tackled issues that concerned young people, such as drug addiction, bulimia, and underage drinking. Its initial concept was based on the Australian soap *The Restless Years* (1977), which followed the lives of young adults in Sydney, and it simply adapted the Australian scripts for the first year. GZSZ also spawned a Dutch version, *Goede tijden, slechte tijden* (1990). Both shows are the most successful soap operas in their country, with more than 5,000 episodes broadcast in each case. To mark the show's 1,500th episode in 1998, the producers pulled out all the stops with a fairy-tale wedding between two of the main characters. Among the guests was Germany's then chancellor, Gerhard Schröder, an indication of the show's popularity.

Many GZSZ actors—including Jeanette Biedermann and original cast member Andreas Elsholz—have also launched successful singing careers. The good times are continuing well into the show's third decade. **DH**

Absolutely Fabulous

Comedy | UK | 1992–2012

Sex and drugs and rock 'n' roll; the world according to Eddy and Patsy

Cast | Jennifer Saunders, Joanna Lumley, Julia Sawalha, Jane Horrocks, June Whitfield
Original broadcasters | BBC Two, BBC One
Award | 1 BAFTA
For fans of ... | *Men Behaving Badly* (1992)

From British comedy legends Jennifer Saunders and Dawn French came these tales of Edina Monsoon (Saunders) and Patsy Stone (Joanna Lumley), aging best friends who fed off each other's vice and excess, while indulging their obsessions with fashion and fad. *Absolutely Fabulous* chronicled their madcap adventures; the series was often shameless and sometimes heartless in its humor, but it was always breathtakingly funny because of its core cast, notably Julia Sawalha as Edina's austere and judgmental daughter, June Whitfield as her wily mother, and Jane Horrocks as her dotty, fashion-victim assistant.

Absolutely Fabulous achieved international fame, and was particularly popular in the United States after a successful run on Comedy Central. Originally running for three seasons in the mid-1990s, the show attracted a cavalcade of famous guest stars from the worlds of television, film, and popular culture (among them Idris Elba, Jean-Paul Gaultier and Debbie Harry); it has returned on five occasions for additional seasons and specials.

The impact of *Absolutely Fabulous* has been global, especially among gay communities and in the world of fashion. The Pet Shop Boys' song "Absolutely Fabulous," with a video featuring the two stars of the series, was originally released in 1994 for Comic Relief and is still played in dance clubs today. Persistent rumors of a film version strongly suggest that the world has not yet seen the last of the monstrous Eddy and Patsy. **SL**

Between the Lines

Drama | UK | 1992–94

Inside the Complaints Investigation Bureau of the London Metropolitan Police

Cast | Neil Pearson, Siobhan Redmond, Tom Georgeson, Lesley Vickerage, Jaye Griffiths
Original broadcaster | BBC One
Award | 1 BAFTA
For fans of ... | *Prime Suspect* (1991)

Detective Superintendent Tony Clark (Neil Pearson) was seconded reluctantly to the Complaints Investigation Bureau (CIB), the internal watchdog of London's Metropolitan Police. Despised by rank-and-file officers, who viewed the CIB as traitors, Tony's small team comprised Detective Inspector Harry Naylor (Tom Georgeson) and Detective Sergeant Mo Connell (Siobhan Redmond), who often had to help Tony balance his work and his messy private life.

Between the Lines found a new niche among police procedural dramas, a genre that underwent a major revival and proliferated in the 1990s. Each episode presented the investigators with both the details of the case and the challenge of sifting through the various prejudices of anyone connected to it. While allegations of excessive force were commonplace against police officers, each one had to be investigated thoroughly, but the mere presence of CIB often muddied the waters further. One additional ongoing complication was that Tony was having an affair with a young policewoman who later gave evidence in a case Tony's team was handling. Another was the revelation that his boss was corrupt.

Many critics believe that the exceptional first and second seasons were let down by the third season, in which Tony, Harry, and Mo quit the force and set themselves up as security advisers. It was generally agreed that the concluding episode's explosive ending came as a blessed release. **JS**

◔ (L–R) Jennifer Saunders (Edina Monsoon), Julia Sawalha, Jane Horrocks, and Joanna Lumley (Patsy Stone).

Red Shoe Diaries

Drama | USA | 1992–97

Duchovny-narrated, soft focus sexcapades for the MTV generation

Cast | David Duchovny, Brigitte Bako, Matt LeBlanc, Audie England
Original broadcaster | Showtime
For fans of . . . | *The Secret Diary of a Call Girl* (2007), *Lip Service* (2009)

Zalman King, creator of *9 1/2 Weeks* (1986) and a long-running, late-night series of glossy, softcore films blending erotica and fantasy, produced the made-for-TV movie, *Wild Orchid III: Red Shoe Diaries* (1992). The movie starred Brigitte Bako as Alex, an interior designer involved with two men, her fiancee Jake (a pre-*The X-Files* David Duchovny), and blue-collar worker Tom. Following her suicide, Jake came upon secret diaries in which she had chronicled her infidelities.

The diaries launched the format of the Showtime TV series. Seeking to heal his broken heart, Jake began reading the secret diaries of other women, in the hope of gaining insight into what Alex had done. To acquire the stories, he placed an ongoing newspaper ad. Each of the thirty-minute episodes (sixty-six in total) was taken from a woman's secret diary, narrated by Jake. Most of the episodic plots involved the woman's sexual awakening.

The acting left a lot to be desired, with the cast an odd roster of talent (most either on their way up or down the career ladder), from former Bond girl Maryam D'Abo to a pre-*Friends* Matt LeBlanc). The storytelling ranged from corny to contrived, but it had a certain kitsch value with its stilted melodrama, MTV-style soft-focus porn (more titillating than explicit), and the early 1990s fashions. It also deserved some credit for presenting a female perspective on various sexual issues, more than twenty years before the mainstream success of *Fifty Shades of Grey* (2015). **JGT**

Men Behaving Badly

Comedy | UK | 1992–98

Crude, rude, hilarious laddish comedy that reacted against the "New Man" zeitgeist

Cast | Martin Clunes, Neil Morrissey, Caroline Quentin, Leslie Ash, Harry Enfield
Original broadcasters | ITV (1992–94), BBC One (1994–98)
For fans of . . . | *Absolutely Fabulous* (1992)

This sitcom put some much-needed bite back into a genre that was beginning to lose its edge in the early 1990s because of contemporary concerns about political correctness.

The show began with Harry Enfield starring alongside Martin Clunes, but viewing figures were poor. ITV dropped it after two seasons, and Enfield left. But BBC One picked it up, introduced a new character played by Neil Morrissey, and soon had a hit on its hands. The title said it all: Gary (Clunes) and Tony (Morrissey) were bachelor roommates and poster boys for arrested adolescence. Gary's long-suffering girlfriend, Dorothy (Caroline Quentin), somehow managed to put up with his coarse and crass behavior. Meanwhile, the single Tony lusted after Deborah (Leslie Ash), a beautiful blonde who lived in the apartment upstairs. As usual in these situations, the women came across as (mostly) sophisticated and adult, while the lads were portrayed as cloddish louts. Here, it was done to perfection, with rollicking humor. As the series progressed it even managed to reveal some of the characters' underlying pathos. The men were great fun to be with and eventually the audience saw why Dorothy put up with Gary and why Deborah finally hooked up with Tony. The characters had first appeared in a novel by the show's writer/creator Simon Nye, who based them on students he'd observed at a London university. It certainly captured the zeitgeist, although a US version (1996) failed to replicate the British success. **DF**

Martin Clunes as Gary in *Men Behaving Badly.* ❯

Shortland Street

Soap opera | New Zealand | 1992–present

A popular Kiwi hospital drama that frequently pushes the boundaries

Cast | Karl Urban, Marton Csokas, Rene Naufahu, Michael Galvin, Angela Bloomfield, Paul Gittins, Martin Henderson, Karl Burnett, Elizabeth McRae
Original broadcaster | TV2
For fans of . . . | *Casualty* (1986)

Originally conceived as a Kiwi version of Australian soaps such as *Neighbours* (1985) and *Home and Away* (1988), New Zealand's longest-running soap, *Shortland Street*, follows the lives of staff at Shortland Street Hospital and their relatives. While Australian soaps have come under fire for lack of positive representation of minorities, *Shortland Street* quickly became notable for the diversity of its cast, reflecting that of its Auckland setting. Rene Naufahu, a Polynesian actor, was cast as a paramedic at a time when New Zealand had only one Pacific Islander performing this role for real. The show has also been praised for employing a Maori advisor.

In addition to the usual melodramatic plots involving serial killers, pregnancies, and love affairs, the show takes opportunities to celebrate New Zealand. When the country hosted the 2011 Rugby World Cup, for example, several members of the home team made cameo appearances, and characters were shown discussing the previous night's game.

Shortland Street is known for pushing boundaries. It featured a controversial sex scene in its first episode, and has included a range of openly LGBT characters. Some scenes have been criticized for being too violent and it has received warnings for graphic content.

The show has aired globally and continues to be shown in Australia, Fiji, the Cook Islands, and Ireland. Past stars who have moved on to Hollywood include Karl Urban (*Lord of the Rings,* 2002, and *Star Trek,* 2009) and Marton Csokas (also *Lord of the Rings*). **EB**

As Time Goes By

Comedy | UK | 1992–2002

Gentle romance that showed you're never too old to fall in love

Cast | Judi Dench, Geoffrey Palmer, Joan Sims, Frank Middlemass, Moyra Fraser, Paul Chapman, Janet Henfrey, Tim Wylton
Original broadcaster | BBC One
For fans of . . . | *One Foot in the Grave* (1990)

Love can come along at any time, but there is a special melancholy sweetness to a romantic relationship that burgeons in the autumn years of one's life. Jean Mary Pargetter (Judi Dench) and Lionel Hardcastle (Geoffrey Palmer) had fallen in love thirty-eight years before the action begins, when she was a nurse and he was a soldier heading to Korea, but due to a mix-up they never heard from one another again. After a lifetime spent with other partners now absent or dead, Jean and Lionel were reunited when he hired an assistant from her secretarial agency to help with the manuscript of his memoirs.

Created by Colin Bostock-Smith, who originally intended Jean Simmons to play Dench's role, the series was first titled *Winter with Flowers*, but a protest by the cast, when production began, forced the change, which everyone ultimately agreed was an improvement. The show's warmth, mild humor, and leisurely pace perfectly accompanied the gradual development of Jean and Lionel's new friendship as it slowly grew into a deep love. At the end of the show's nine-season run, the two were finally married. Along the way, they wrestled with the problems that came with romance past middle age, as well as the reactions of their families and friends.

The series was so popular that it inspired a radio adaptation in 1997, which ran on BBC Radio Two for three seasons. As for the TV show itself, a two-part 2005 reunion special wrapped up the story. **ATB**

The Larry Sanders Show
Comedy | USA | 1992–98

The late-night talk show wars captured in a postmodern satirical comedy

Cast | Garry Shandling, Jeffrey Tambor, Rip Torn, Penny Johnson, Janeane Garofalo, Jeremy Piven
Original broadcaster | HBO
Awards | 1 BAFTA, 3 Emmys
For fans of . . . | *Curb Your Enthusiasm* (2000)

The Larry Sanders Show is frequently lauded as a lasting and innovative television achievement, with an undeniable influence on other shows that engaged in media metacommentary and featured celebrities as parodies of their own personas. Created by Garry Shandling and Dennis Klein, the series was based on the former's experiences as guest host on *The Tonight Show* (1954) and his previous Showtime sitcom *It's Garry Shandling's Show* (1986).

Here neurotic talk show host Larry Sanders dealt with professional and personal problems on either side of the camera, accompanied by insecure and overbearing sidekick Hank Kingsley (Jeffrey Tambor) and profanity-spewing producer Artie (Rip Torn). With more than 150 guest stars from movies, music, and TV, many of whom appeared as unflattering versions of themselves, the show blended videotaped segments of Sanders' talk show—staged as it would be produced and with a live studio audience early in the run—with filmed behind-the-scenes material that carried the story offstage into the back offices and into Sanders' home.

The Larry Sanders Show paved the way for the free use of more profanity than had ever previously been regarded as acceptable on TV. Early episodes were filmed in two versions, one for HBO, the other for broadcast syndication, but as the series became more successful the guest stars became less willing to reshoot a sanitized version of the original, and thus heralded the dawn of the age of the onscreen oath. **ATB**

Classic episode
Everybody Loves Larry | *Season 5, episode 1*. Larry is terrified that *The X-Files'* star David Duchovny (playing himself) is in love with him. Duchovny does nothing to disabuse the talk show host of this silly notion.

◉ Garry Shandling as Larry at his on-air desk.

Boy Meets World

Comedy | USA | 1993–2000

A boy's eye view of the ups and downs of high school life and adolescence

Cast | Ben Savage, William Daniels, Rider Strong, Danielle Fishel **Original broadcaster** | ABC
For fans of ... | *The Wonder Years* (1988), *Heartbreak High* (1994)

Boy Meets World was a right-of-passage comedy. It premiered just as *The Wonder Years* (1983) drew to a close and was cut from the same cloth—a cozy sitcom following its likable protagonist's journey through adolescence, with protective parents, overbearing brother, inseparable best friend, kooky girlfriend Topanga (Danielle Fischel), and a gently moralistic tone. The boy, Cory Matthews, was played by Ben Savage, younger brother of *The Wonder Years* star Fred Savage.

Providing support was William Daniels, who played Mr. George Feeny, Cory's long-suffering history teacher (and later principal), who happened to be Cory's neighbor. Surreal metafiction and in-jokes were added for more culturally savvy viewers.

In 2014, the Disney Channel launched *Girl Meets World*, centering on Cory and Topanga's twelve-year-old daughter Riley. Savage and Fischel reprised their roles, with several others from *Boy Meets World* in recurring roles or in cameos. The spin-off was warmly received, and Disney Channel announced it was renewing the series for a second season, set to premiere in 2015. **JG**

> **Classic episode**
> *I Was a Teenage Spy* | *Season 3, episode 19. Back To The Future* meets *Happy Days* when a freak accident sends Cory back to 1957, where he meets a gum-smacking Topanga and is accused of being a Russian spy.

⬥ William Daniels as Mr. Feeny, Cory's teacher and neighbor, and Ben Savage as Cory Matthews.

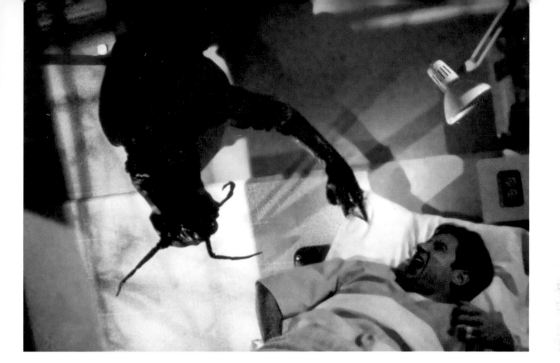

The X-Files

Fantasy/Horror/Sci-Fi | USA | 1993–2002

Paranoid conspiracy thriller that taught us to trust no one

Cast | Gillian Anderson, David Duchovny, Mitch Pileggi, Robert Patrick, Annabeth Gish
Original broadcaster | Fox **Awards** | 5 Golden Globes **For fans of . . .** | *The Twilight Zone* (1959)

The foremost cult series of the decade, *The X-Files* broke out into the mainstream in a way that few other genre shows have, with two feature films and two top-ten singles. The creator, Chris Carter, also produced similar shows *Millennium* (1996) and *The Lone Gunmen* (2008).

The series charted investigations into paranormal activity by FBI agents Fox Mulder (David Duchovny) and Dana Scully (Gillian Anderson). Their growing attraction to one another brought a human dimension to what was at first a "monster of the-week" show, with werewolves, mutants, and ghosts. Later seasons made increasing use of a secondary cast of characters to suggest a huge conspiracy to hide the existence of aliens from the American public.

Originally filmed in the uncharted wastes of Canada, production later moved to Los Angeles. The style thereafter became more conventional and led to declining ratings; the series was canceled in 2002. However, in 2008 *The X-Files* was revived for a second movie and a new six-part mini-series with Duchovny and Anderson is now scheduled for 2016. **MM**

Classic episode
The Erlenmeyer Flask | *Season 1, episode 24*. The agents get a chance to uncover the government conspiracy and prove the existence of alien life, but miss their opportunity. This episode proved that none of the show's cast was indispensible.

◉ Hospital hygiene hits a new low as a giant insectlike creature attempts to slow David Duchovny's recovery.

Walker, Texas Ranger

Action/Adventure | USA | 1993–2001

Chuck Norris thwarts Texan crime with his trademark brand of rough-and-ready justice

Cast | Chuck Norris, Clarence Gilyard, Sheree J. Wilson
Original broadcaster | CBS
For fans of . . . | *Shadow Warriors* (1980), *The A-Team* (1983), *Sidekicks* (1986), *Martial Law* (1998), *The Legend of Bruce Lee* (2008)

A mash-up of good old-fashioned American law enforcement, Westerns, and martial arts, *Walker, Texas Ranger* was a relentlessly (and sometimes ridiculously) entertaining action adventure series, perfectly suited to its kick-ass movie star lead, .former Tae Kwon Do champion Chuck Norris.

Norris kicked and punched his way through 203 episodes in which he played Sergeant Cordell Walker, former Marine turned law enforcer. With a strict moral code inspired by the Old West, Walker would bring down various criminals—from drug cartels to insane cannibals—using his own brand of natural justice. Norris had turned down numerous offers to do a TV show, but was impressed by the concept (originally codeveloped by J. Michael Straczynski, creator of *Babylon 5*, 1993) and also by the fact the show would be filmed close to his ranch. While the show's selling point was undoubtedly Norris's martial arts skills, the emphasis was on action rather than on violence; Walker's roundhouse kicks would disable his hapless villains without spilling any blood. As a result, the show found a family audience, even though it sometimes featured dark and outlandish story lines.

A huge success throughout its original eight-year run, the show returned for a TV movie in 2005, but a change of policy at CBS scuppered plans for any further continuation. The show gained a surprising second life in the twenty-first century thanks to Conan O'Brien, who would show brief clips during his NBC talk show. **SO**

Classic episode
The Assassin | *Season 2, Episode 22*. Walker has to hunt down an assassin targeting a US Senator, and is aided by a former Texas Ranger who is also seeking the assassin to avenge the murder of his son.

⊛ Justice, Texas-style: Chuck Norris as Cordell Walker.

Homicide: Life on the Street

Crime/Mystery | USA | 1993–99

Groundbreaking police procedural

Cast | Andre Braugher, Richard Belzer, Melissa Leo, Kyle Secor, Yaphet Kotto, Clark Johnson
Original broadcaster | NBC
Awards | 4 Emmys
For fans of . . . | *Oz* (1997), *The Wire* (2002)

Baltimore Sun newspaper reporter David Simon spent four years trailing the city's homicide cops and then wrote a book about his experiences. *Homicide: A Year on the Killing Streets* (1991) won an Edgar and became an instant true-crime classic. Within two years the book was fictionalized for television, with Simon as producer and writer. *Homicide: Life on the Street* was a critical success but failed to attract a big audience. Nevertheless, it remained on the air for seven years and generated an incalculably important legacy in US television. Simon, creator of *The Corner* (2000), *The Wire*, *Generation Kill* (2008), and *Treme* (2010), is one of several writers, directors, producers, and stars who, after cutting their teeth on *Homicide*, would redefine the police procedural in the decades that followed.

Intended as a corrective to the myth of the homicide cop as a kind of modern-day Sherlock Holmes, *Homicide* focused on the minutiae of policework from the perspectives of the detectives involved, from the procedures that make up their day-to-day work to the soul-crushing misery of unsolved cases. *Homicide*'s characters were complex, fully-realized human beings, who struggled with departmental ennui, personal demons, and systemic abuse.

Homicide's tenor changed in later seasons, as the network and the writers wrangled over plot points and story arcs. One of its characters, Detective John Munch (Richard Belzer), was later incorporated into Dick Wolf's *Law & Order: Special Victims Unit* (1999). **AP**

Late Show with David Letterman

Talk show | USA | 1993–2015

A grand master of the talk show genre

Cast | David Letterman, Alan Kalter, Bill Wendell
Original broadcaster | CBS
Awards | 9 Emmys
For fans of . . . | *The Tonight Show* (1962), *The Daily Show* (1996)

After numerous guest appearances on Johnny Carson's *The Tonight Show* and a short-lived morning program, David Letterman acquired his own late-night talk show on NBC in 1982. An experienced writer and comedian, Letterman won audiences with his quick wit, unorthodox approach, and a knack for asking his guests the questions his viewers were thinking.

When Carson retired from *Tonight*, many felt that Letterman was his natural successor (Carson himself later revealed he'd thought the same), but the position went to Jay Leno. Letterman left NBC to set up *The Late Show* at CBS, taking announcer Bill Wendell and his house band with him—Paul Shaffer's World's Most Dangerous Band was renamed The CBS Orchestra.

Recorded at the Ed Sullivan Theater in New York, each episode of Letterman's show was structured around his opening monologue, his topical Top Ten list, letters from viewers, and banter with the house band. Comedy sketches and the main guest would lead into the musical act that closed the show. Like all good hosts, Letterman had his favorites: Bill Murray was a regular guest and he often cited the Foo Fighters as his favorite band. His old mentor, Johnny Carson, sent him jokes and Letterman would mime a golf swing after the punch line of any that he used. In 2013, Letterman surpassed Carson's record of being the longest serving talk show host in history. In 2015, he bowed out just shy of thirty-five years in the role, handing over the show to Stephen Colbert. **JS**

Iron Chef

Reality | Japan | 1993–99

Cuisine without financial constraint

Cast | Takeshi Kaga, Chen Kenichi, Yutaka Ishinabe, Hiroyuki Sakai, Masahiko Kobe, Rokusaburo Michiba, Koumei Nakamura
Original broadcaster | Fuji Television
For fans of . . . | *MasterChef* (1990)

In this amazing show, Takeshi Kaga—the self-styled "Iron Chef" of Japan—challenged other great chefs to produce dishes that surpassed those produced by him and his team in presentation and flavor. Each task was against the clock, and the time limit was normally one hour, the length of each broadcast, but the show was sometimes extended if the cooking times were longer than the scheduled time slot.

The recipes were often forbiddingly complicated and demanding. In one episode, a challenger spent more than $1,000 (on lobster to flavor his asparagus. The total amount spent on ingredients over the lifetime of the show was in excess of $7 million.

Typically, four dishes had to be prepared for each meal, but sometimes the rules of engagement demanded as many as eight. They had to be presented in six servings: one each for the chairman and the four judges (Jackie Chan was one of them for a time), and another for the photographers. In the event of a tie, the contestants had to create an extra dish from their leftover ingredients; these "overtime battles" were aired on subsequent occasions.

Few of the challengers beat the Iron Chef, but of those who did one of the most notable was Kyoko Kagata, who was both the first woman ever to appear and the youngest victor. The show, which was originally called *Ryôri no tetsujin*, was successful not only in Japan but also in North America, where it ran on the Food Network in a dubbed English version. **GL**

Snowy River: The McGregor Saga

Drama | Australia | 1993–96

A turn-of-the-century frontier saga

Cast | Andrew Clarke, Wendy Hughes, Brett Climo, Guy Pearce, Sheryl Munks
Original broadcasters | Nine Network Australia/ Family Channel
For fans of . . . | *Little House on the Prairie* (1974)

There's more than one Wild West, as this saga of family rivalries and romances in a burgeoning Australian town showed. The period setting (around 1900) was a photogenic asset, as were the members of the cast.

Andrew Clarke starred as upstanding widower Matt McGregor, a mature version of the Man from Snowy River, a character in a famous Australian bush ballad of 1890. The McGregors were pivotal to the little town of Paterson's Ridge (named after the ballad's author). Matt became its member of parliament and one of his children was the pastor (played by Brett Climo). Guy Pearce was in the saddle as his other son throughout the series, well after his breakout movie *The Adventures of Priscilla, Queen of the Desert* (1994). Wendy Hughes played Kathleen, an equally principled childhood friend of Matt, who ran the school and local paper, while the family's main long-term rivals were the scheming and wealthy Blackwoods. Notable guest stars included Hugh Jackman, Dean Stockwell, and Olivia Newton-John.

What made *Snowy River* so refreshing, for all its apparent simplicity, was its deftness in showing a small community evolve in the inhospitable bush through, for example, the building of the railroad from Melbourne. By tussling with the social and moral undercurrents of a now-remote way of life rather than focusing on fisticuffs and gunplay (although *Snowy River* often did that, too), this good-hearted series showed the McGregors live through many compelling adventures. **MWy**

Lipstick on Your Collar

Music/Musical | UK | 1993

This witty and moving musical drama was among the last works of one of British TV's most respected and original writers

Cast | Giles Thomas, Ewan McGregor, Louise Germaine, Douglas Henshall
Original broadcaster | Channel 4
For fans of . . . | *Pennies from Heaven* (1978), *The Singing Detective* (1986)

The third in Dennis Potter's loose trilogy of historical musical dramas, *Lipstick on Your Collar* followed on from *Pennies from Heaven* and *The Singing Detective*. Set in 1956, during the run-up to the Suez crisis, in which Britain was forced to realize it was no longer a world power, it followed two young clerks in London's War Office. In contrast to Potter's darker earlier work, the series was considered something of a romantic comedy, despite its portrayal of an abusive marriage that culminated in an unexpected act of violence.

Much of the story was driven by the shy, studious Private Francis's attraction to Sylvia, the wife of the brutal Corporal Berry. With its stultifying atmosphere, the War Office formed part of an old order, its staff—played by an ensemble of character actors, all visibly enjoying themselves—forced to make way for the rock'n'roll generation, epitomized by Private Hopper, played by a then-unknown Ewan McGregor. In a device familiar from Potter's earlier serials, Hopper's daydreams represented by popular songs interspersed the drama. The actors lip-synched to songs of the era, including "The Great Pretender," "Earth Angel," and "Your Cheatin' Heart."

The show was the last of Dennis Potter's television plays to be broadcast in his lifetime. He died in 1994, but two connected series, *Karaoke* and *Cold Lazarus*, were broadcast posthumously in 1996. Although not as groundbreaking as some of his earlier work, *Lipstick on Your Collar* was a fitting final act to the career of one of British television's most distinctive voices. **HE**

Classic episode
Season 1, episode 3. Private Hopper daydreams about life and love, and shares his thoughts with new recruit Private Francis. Suddenly, the "red telephone" rings, reminding the pair about the impending Suez crisis.

◬ Ewan McGregor as the iconoclastic Private Hopper.

Cracker

Crime/Mystery | UK | 1993–96

An egotistical psychologist is hired by police to help with murder investigations

Cast | Robbie Coltrane, Barbara Flynn, Geraldine Somerville, Christopher Eccleston, Ricky Tomlinson
Original broadcaster | ITV
Awards | 6 BAFTAs
For fans of . . . | *Prime Suspect* (1991), *Luther* (2010)

Writer Jimmy McGovern imagined Fitz, the main character in *Cracker*, as a quiet, wiry individual, but the casting of heavy-set Robbie Coltrane took the role in a different direction. Coltrane made Fitz an intellectual bully, an alcoholic gambler whose addictions drove his family away. He was contemptuous of the police, and thought he could solve cases better than they could. In his first association with Detective Chief Inspector Bilborough (Christopher Eccleston), he succeeded only in proving their one suspect innocent (the real culprit was revealed to the audience, but escaped undetected), while his goading of a murderer through the press resulted in the violent death of an officer.

For all Fitz's faults, there was something seductive about his rudeness; the viewers approved of his refusal to obey the rules at the "nine items or less" checkout line in the grocery store and his baiting of a sexist officer. His relationship with Detective Sergeant Jane Penhaligon (Geraldine Somerville) was more complicated. He enjoyed teasing her, but shared her frustration that she was often overlooked because of her gender.

Cracker was never comfortable viewing. Like its ITV stablemate *Prime Suspect* (1991), it explored some of the darkest areas of the human psyche. Nevertheless, every episode was gripping, none more so than the season two opener, "To Be a Somebody." In 1997, *Cracker* was remade as *Fitz* for American TV with Robert Pastorelli in the title role. It lost much of the appeal of the original, and lasted only one season. **JS**

Classic episode
True Romance Part 1 | *Season 3, episode 6.* At the opening of this two-parter, a university lab technician starts electrocuting students. Fitz discovers that she's doing it in order to attract his attention.

⊘ Hold that train of thought: Fitz (Robbie Coltrane) has a chat with a suspect.

NYPD Blue

Crime/Mystery | USA | 1993–2005

*Even racist homophobic drunks
sometimes make good cops*

Cast | Dennis Franz, David Caruso, Jimmy Smits,
Kim Delany, Gordon Clapp, Ricky Schroder
Original broadcaster | ABC
Awards | 20 Emmys, 4 Golden Globes
For fans of . . . | *Hill Street Blues* (1981)

NYPD Blue was the brainchild of Steven Bochco and David Milch, writer–producers who had previously had great success with *Hill Street Blues* (1981) and now wanted to develop a show with a single lead character rather than an ensemble cast. Their idea was originally to create a starring vehicle for David Caruso, who had come to their attention in a supporting role as a police officer in the movie *King of New York* (1990).

They also wanted to see how much grittier they could make a new police procedural series. At the planning stage, their ideas were rather more radical than those of the ABC network, and consequently the show had a protracted gestation period during which the parties wrangled over how much violence, nudity, and profanity were acceptable.

The finished product was thus a compromise, and although it pulled more punches than perhaps the creators would have liked, it still caused a few storms. Not the least of these was that surrounding the character of Detective Andy Sipowicz (Dennis Franz), a mean drunk and a bigoted homophobic racist, who was constantly at odds with everybody in the precinct. Although he was always number two to a conventionally good-looking lead actor (first Caruso, then Jimmy Smits, and finally Ricky Schroder), Franz was really the star of the show throughout its twelve seasons as he deftly charted Sipowicz's gradual redemption. Sipowicz became—and remains—one of the most beloved TV cops of all time. **JH**

Goodnight Sweetheart

Comedy | UK | 1993–99

*Sitcom about a time traveler between
the present day and wartime London*

Cast | Nicholas Lyndhurst, Victor McGuire, Dervla
Kirwan, Michelle Holmes, Elizabeth Carling, Emma
Amos, Christopher Ettridge
Original broadcaster | BBC One
For fans of . . . | *Birds of a Feather* (1989)

What would you do if you found a portal that took you back to the Second World War? Modern-day Londoner Gary Sparrow (Nicholas Lyndhurst) got another girlfriend/wife and pretended to be an MI5 agent. *Goodnight Sweetheart* derived its humor from the conflict that arose from this double life as he flitted between his sarcastic modern wife, Yvonne (Emma Amos), and his feisty landlady, Phoebe (Elizabeth Carling).

The series changed halfway through its run when the actresses who originally played Gary's lovers both left the show. Thereafter, the dynamic altered: Yvonne became a successful millionaire businesswoman with little time for Gary; Phoebe became mother to Gary's son, which made Gary's choice, in the end, very straightforward. Two other characters were fixtures in the show from start to finish: Gary's best friend, Ron (Victor McGuire), and lovably stupid policeman Reg Deadman (Christopher Ettridge). Ron was the only person who knew of Gary's timetraveling escapades. He also printed his wartime money and generally offered sage advice, which Gary often ignored. Reg, the butt of most of the jokes in the wartime sections, was played with childlike innocence by Ettridge. He joins characters such as Trigger from *Only Fools and Horses* (1981) in the pantheon of great sitcom fools.

Viewed objectively, Gary was a dreadful person, but scriptwriters Laurence Marks and Maurice Gran made him as sympathetic as one of their earlier comic monsters, Alan B'Stard in *The New Statesman* (1987). **LH**

Beavis and Butt-Head

Animation | USA | 1993–97, 2011

Animation in which two idiotic teenagers outsmart most other things on TV

Cast | Mike Judge, Tracy Grandstaff **Original broadcaster** | MTV
For fans of . . . | *The Simpsons* (1989), *Family Guy* (1999), *The Inbetweeners* (2008)

In 1992, animator Mike Judge made a short film for MTV that featured two boys playing baseball—as wholesome a topic as the viewer could wish for, you might think. But both boys were puerile, sniggering, heavy metal-obsessed delinquents, and they were playing the game with a live frog. Beavis and Butt-Head had arrived, and their brand of immaculate stupidity quickly became a global phenomenon.

Butt-Head—the dark-haired one with braces—was the marginally more intelligent of the two, and thought of himself as a ladies' man, which he patently wasn't. Beavis—the blonde one with the underbite—was prone to wild outbursts and mood swings. Their world was divided into things that were "cool" (rock music,

vandalism, and arson) and things that "sucked" (school, teachers, and their smart classmate, Daria).

The show ran for four years until Judge retired the pair with a hit full-length movie, *Beavis and Butt-Head Do America* (1996). They returned for one more season in 2011, before Judge started work on the live-action comedy *Silicon Valley* (2014). **WM**

Classic episode
1-900 Beavis | *Season 4, episode 9.* The duo attempt to call a sex chat line, and spend most of the call sniggering nervously in their trademark fashion, overawed by the prospect of actually speaking to a real-live woman.

⊘ (L–R) Butt-Head and Beavis get wood in California; no holds were barred in the groundbreaking comic animation.

Frasier

Comedy | USA | 1993–2004

Sitcom about two snobbish brothers that matches the original on which it is based

Cast | Kelsey Grammer, David Hyde Pierce, John Mahoney, Jane Leeves, Peri Gilpin
Original broadcaster | NBC **Awards** | 37 Emmys **For fans of . . .** | *Curb Your Enthusiasm* (2000)

Has there ever been a spin-off sitcom as successful as *Frasier*? Taking the snobby, intellectual psychiatrist Dr. Frasier Crane (Kelsey Grammer) from *Cheers* (1982), which was set in Boston, and sending him to Seattle to live with his football-loving, retired-cop father, Martin (John Mahoney), and Martin's "psychic," kooky physical therapist, Daphne Moon (Jane Leeves), must surely count as one of the smartest moves in TV history. The addition of Frasier's even-more-neurotic brother, Niles (David Hyde Pierce), and Roz (Peri Gilpin), the sexually liberated producer of Frasier's therapy radio show, created a hitherto unrivaled sitcom lineup of the overrepressed and the underrepressed, the awkward and the even more awkward.

Among the joys of the show were the weekly call-ins to Frasier's radio program—often voiced by famous actors doing brilliant cameos. The central joke was that Frasier was a psychiatrist who could not take his own advice. His problems could easily be sorted out if he just said what he meant, but he never did until his reticence had caused chaos. **RL**

Classic episode
Ski Lodge | *Season 5, episode 14*. Frasier, Niles, and Daphne take a skiing trip together and farce ensues. Everyone in their cabin takes a fancy to someone else, but never the right someone. A masterpiece of bed-swapping comedy.

○ The hypnotic parent: John Mahoney puts his fictional children (David Hyde Pierce and Kelsey Grammer) to sleep.

Lois and Clark: The New Adventures of Superman

Action/Adventure | USA | 1993–97

Comic-book adventure focusing on the relationship between the two leads instead of the famous red cape

Classic episode
Fly Hard | Season 1, Episode 20. Terrorists storm the offices of the *Daily Planet* building and take the journalists hostage. Clark has the power to save them, but how can he do so without revealing his secret identity?

⊘ Faintly ridiculous: Lois collapses into Clark's arms. (L–R) K Callan, Teri Hatcher, Lane Smith, and Dean Cain.

Cast | Dean Cain, Teri Hatcher, Lane Smith, Justin Whalin, Eddie Jones, K Callan
Original broadcaster | ABC
For fans of . . . | *Doctor Who* (1963), *Buffy the Vampire Slayer* (1997), *Angel* (1999)

For four seasons spread over five years, viewers fell for the sparkling chemistry between leads Dean Cain and Teri Hatcher and followed their on–off relationship. It was this focus that separated *Lois and Clark* from other screen adaptations of the DC comic books. Each episode kept to a minimum the amount of Superman the viewers saw and concentrated primarily on the two main characters' developing romance.

Lois and Clark kept its tongue firmly in its cheek, from riffing on Superman lore (how does Lois never realize that Clark is Superman?) to some wonderfully over-the-top comic-book villains: gangsters made an army of robot fighters; a bunch of smart kids took over Metropolis; a time-traveling H.G. Wells and a villain from the future, Tempus, wreaked havoc. It was a marvelous feat of the show that no matter how ridiculous the villain, the show remained grounded, which came down to the relationship between Lois and Clark.

Aside from Lois and Clark, honorable mentions must go to Lane Smith, the best ever on-screen *Daily Planet* editor-in-chief, Perry White. His double act with Justin Whalin as the photographer Jimmy Olsen provided many amusing scenes. Clark's parents were also a charming presence. BBC executives later said that *Lois and Clark* was one of the inspirations behind their *Doctor Who* revival in 2005, with its warmth of character, great villain-of-the-week stories, and ongoing plots all tying together to provide a perfect fantasy show that the whole family could watch together. **LH**

I Love My Family

Comedy | China | 1993–94

Widely regarded as the first domestically produced Chinese sitcom

Cast | Xingyu Wen, Dandan Song, Lixin Yang, Ling Guan, Yunqiao Li, Tian Liang, Chang Shen, Mingming Zhao, Yongqiang Zhang, Yaqin Jin
Original broadcaster | China Central Television
For fans of . . . | *My Family* (2000)

I Love My Family's claim to fame stands either as China's first television sitcom or as the nation's first to have been filmed with more than a single camera. It was also the first such show to have been made in Mandarin. Its main characters were six members of a family living in Beijing, and the action was principally concerned with their everyday lives as they went about their work in the Chinese capital.

Although the show contained all the classic elements of sitcom, on first viewing it came across as a series of short sketches; some of them comic, others emotionally charged. Many sitcom viewers—especially those whose only experience of the genre had been of its highly stylized Western form—needed to see a number of episodes to recognize that there was ultimately a thematic link between all the apparently disjointed parts. Indeed, one of *I Love My Family*'s many virtues was its demonstration of the fact that the Anglo-American model was not the only one possible.

Of the 198 episodes, 120 were directed by Da Ying; the remainder were the work of Cong Li. There were eighteen credited scriptwriters, the most prolific of whom were Zuo Liang and Shuo Wang, who are each credited as author or coauthor of 120 shows.

The star of *I Love My Family* was Wen Xingyu as the laidback, affectionate paterfamilias; he was already well known in China as a comic actor. His later work included the movie *Spicy Love Soup* (1997) and the TV series *Qian Wang* (2002) and *Jia You Er Nu* (*Grandpa*, 2005). **GL**

Century Falls

Fantasy/Horror/Sci-Fi | UK | 1993

An atmospheric and disturbing drama from the mind of Russell T. Davies

Cast | Bernard Kay, Mary Wimbush, Eileen Way, Simon Fenton, Catherine Sanderson, Emma Jane Lavin
Original broadcaster | BBC One
For fans of . . . | *Doctor Who* (1963), *Dark Shadows* (1966), *Sapphire and Steel* (1979)

When Tess Hunter (Catherine Sanderson) and her pregnant mother moved to the isolated village of Century Falls, they were unaware that no child had been born there in forty years. But they were not the only newcomers: the wayward Ben (Simon Fenton) and his sister Carey (Emma Jane Lavin) had been brought to the village by their uncle (Bernard Kay), and the three of them were part of a plot to correct mistakes of the past.

Over six brooding twenty-five-minute episodes, the secret of Century Falls was gradually uncovered: the villagers were psychic, and an earlier attempt to pool their collective minds into human form ended in tragedy and had terrible ongoing effects; their shame had since caused the miscarriage of every unborn child. But now the psychic mind was reasserting its influence, and this time it intended to succeed.

Inventively filmed, complex, layered, and bleak, *Century Falls* put most psychological horror dramas to shame. It is surprising, therefore, that it was broadcast in a teatime slot (between 5pm and 7pm), and that the BBC ordered no cuts to even its bleakest moments. However, writer Russell T. Davies relieved some of the darkness with optimism and ensured that private human drama took precedence over shock effects.

Century Falls lingered in the memory long after its satisfying, if bittersweet, conclusion. By being unsettling rather than downright scary, and by dealing in the supernatural while emphasizing human relationships, the series remained a truly remarkable TV landmark. **RM**

Star Trek: Deep Space Nine

Fantasy/Horror/Sci-Fi | USA | 1993–99

Staying boldly, at warp speed

Cast | Avery Brooks, Nana Visitor, Rene Auberjonois, Terry Farrell, Colm Meaney, Armin Shimerman
Original broadcaster | Syndication   **For fans of . . . |** *Babylon 5* (1994)

This third *Star Trek* spin-off was, in the view of many, the most successful of them all. *Deep Space Nine* explored the human condition and the emotional ties that bind individuals to a family. Benjamin Sisko (Avery Brooks), widower and father, was brought to an isolated outpost on the borders of the fragile Federation. There he came to realize both his place in the universe and his status as the mysterious emissary of the neighboring world of Bajor, which had thrown off the shackles of an oppressive occupier after half a century. He enlisted the aid of a core group of regular supporting members of the franchise cast.

While never as popular as its flashier predecessor, *Star Trek: The Next Generation* (1987), *Star Trek: Deep Space Nine* nevertheless served a loyal fan base attracted to deeper and darker topics than any *Star Trek* before or since. It remains the only *Star Trek* series fully to embrace serialized storytelling, with sweeping story arcs, including a nine-episode finale. Going boldly into the unknown is not always reliant upon a spaceship, after all. **SL**

Classic episode
Far Beyond the Stars | *Season 6, episode 13*. Sisko finds himself in another reality—1950s Earth, as a struggling writer. This is a serious take on racial inequality and an unexpected departure into metafiction.

◬ Avery Books as Ben Sisko and Nana Visitor as Kira Nerys; his weapon is small but remarkably effective.

Babylon 5

Fantasy/Horror/Sci-Fi | USA | 1994–98

A sprawling science fiction novel for television

Cast | Bruce Boxleitner, Michael O'Hare, Claudia Christian, Mira Furlan, Andreas Katsulas, Peter Jurasik
Original broadcasters | Syndication, TNT **Awards** | 2 Emmys **For fans of . . .** | *Game of Thrones* (2011)

Destiny and sacrifice, loyalty and betrayal, and the universal truths that bring us all together: these were the hallmarks of *Babylon 5*. Set in the not-too-distant future, the series told the story of humanity's next steps after a devastating interstellar war. In doing so, it defined a new genre of science-fiction storytelling arcs: events set in motion in the opening act would come to fruition years later, as the show's human characters forged alliances, learned secrets, and uncovered plans set in motion eons ago in the long struggle between good and evil. *Babylon 5* was also an early pioneer of CGI imagery.

The series suffered numerous disruptive cast and production changes, and was even canceled once midseason before earning a last-minute reprieve. It survived, however, mainly through the strength and determination of its creator, J. Michael Straczynski, and was eventually followed by a sequel series, *Crusade* (1999), and several made-for-TV films. With *Buffy the Vampire Slayer* (1997), it helped to reestablish serial drama as a viable American television medium. **SL**

Classic episode

The Coming of Shadows | *Season 2, episode 9*.
Londo Mollari (Peter Jurasik) makes a decision that sets in motion a devastating war and seals his people's fate—this is the focal point of the entire five-year series.

⚠ Londo (Peter Jurasik) argues with G'Kar (Andreas Katsulas) with poor Vir (Stephen Furst) stuck in the middle.

Riget

Fantasy/Horror/Sci-Fi | Denmark | 1994–97

Lars von Trier's supernatural horror set in a hospital at the gateway to hell

---

Cast | Ernst-Hugo Järegård, Kirsten Rolffes, Holger Juul Hansen, Søren Pilmark
Original broadcaster | DR
For fans of . . . | *A Ghost Story For Christmas* (1971), *The Killing* (2007), *Borgen* (2010)

Director Lars von Trier has never been funnier, more human, or more frightening than in *Riget* (*The Kingdom*). Made before subtitled Danish drama found international acclaim, *Riget* had more death than *The Killing* (2007), darker conspiracies than *Borgen* (2010), and more infuriatingly complicated antiheroes than *The Bridge* (2011). It delighted in nail-biting cliff-hangers, surreal laughs, and sheer terror.

The Kingdom was Denmark's best hospital, but it hid a very dark secret. Hypochondriac psychic Mrs. Drusse (Kirsten Rolffes) found every excuse not to leave, staying to investigate the murder of a ghostly girl. She crossed swords with belligerent neurosurgeon Stig Helmer (Ernst-Hugo Järegård). He had problems of his own; in trying to cover up malpractice and charge his electric car, he became intimately involved in the hospital's murky underbelly, which included a mysterious secret society, a trade in cancers, and a devil dog. Events were narrated by two kitchen workers with Down syndrome, both of whom had a connection to the terrible forces being reborn in the hospital.

The first season was chilling; the second was bizarre. Ghostly messages appeared in a doorman's pornography stash, a nymphomaniac lesbian sex clinic became possessed by demons, and everyone was surprisingly accepting of an undead staff member. Death himself checked arrivals at the hospital. Auteur von Trier appeared, in a tuxedo, to give a talk over the closing credits of each episode. **JG**

Due South

Comedy/Drama | Canada/USA | 1994–99

Surreal buddy crime series about a Mountie, a wolf, and a hard-bitten cop

---

Cast | Paul Gross, David Marciano, Callum Keith Rennie, Leslie Nielsen
Original broadcasters | CBS, CTV
For fans of . . . | *Northern Exposure* (1990), *Walker, Texas Ranger* (1993)

The hero, Royal Canadian Mounted Police officer Benton Fraser (Paul Gross) set the scene: "I first came to Chicago on the trail of the killers of my father and, for reasons which don't need exploring at this juncture, I have remained, attached as liaison to the Canadian consulate."

Due South was the story of a morally upright Mountie adrift on the mean streets of the Windy City. His only friends were a wolf and a tough cop called Ray (David Marciano). What started out as a fairly routine crime drama took increasingly bizarre detours into the genres of romance, the supernatural, and musical comedy.

The show's development was steered by Gross, who became one of the series' most accomplished writers, producers, singers, and songwriters. Increasingly, the characters became more important than the crimes: Ray was a shabby lounge lizard; Fraser was an impossibly noble figure, and his wolf, Diefenbaker, was deaf. Leslie Neilsen played a Mountie superhero with gastric trauma; Fraser had a "will they, won't they" relationship with his boss, Margaret Thatcher (Camilla Scott); and when Callum Keith Rennie arrived in season three claiming to be Ray, only Fraser batted an eyelid.

When CBS dropped the show, further seasons were funded enthusiastically by Canadian CTV and the BBC. International audiences couldn't get enough of Fraser's good looks and impeccable manners, the show's rich soundtrack, and its occasional departures into utter lunacy. **JG**

All-American Girl

Comedy | USA | 1994–95

Cultures clash in this comedy about a Korean-American woman's determination to live life on her own terms, whatever her mother thinks

Cast | Margaret Cho, Amy Hill, Jodi Long, Clyde Kusatsu, Maddie Corman, Judy Gold
Original broadcaster | ABC
For fans of . . . | *The Fresh Prince of Bel-Air* (1990), *Fresh Off the Boat* (2015)

While *All-American Girl* was primarily devised to capitalize on the growing success of the popular Korean-American comedian Margaret Cho, it was also an attempt to bring some cultural diversity to American prime-time comedy.

The series focused on Cho's character Margaret, a young Korean-American student embracing the American dream, who came into conflict with her traditional Korean parents, especially her mother Katherine, played with great gusto by Jodi Long. The key focus was on Margaret's fight against her mother's insistence that she live her life in line with Korean culture and values. However, for a series riding on the back of Cho's popularity as a stand-up comedian, the show failed to incorporate her own idiosyncratic humor. Cho had little creative input to the scripting and direction of the series. As a result, it fell back on clichés and stereotypes prevalent in American sitcoms of the period.

The series received a mixed reaction, with particular criticism leveled at the poor characterization and story lines, though there was also disappointment that Cho was the only Korean-American actor in the principal cast. Despite attempts to amend the format in later episodes, *All-American Girl* came to an end after nineteen episodes and was not renewed for a second season. Nevertheless, the excitement that Asian-Americans felt at seeing themselves represented on prime-time American television was considerable and significant. **SO**

Classic episode
Pulp Sitcom | *Season 1, episode 18*. Quentin Tarantino guest stars as Margaret's boyfriend Desmond, although the burgeoning relationship comes to an end when she discovers he deals in pirated VHS cassettes.

◉ Jodi Long as Katherine Kim works with Margaret Cho as Margaret Kim at a cosmetics counter.

Cadfael

Crime/Mystery | UK | 1994–98

Historical crime drama with a gentle heart

Classic episode

The Potter's Field | *Season 1, episode 2.* When a man takes holy orders in Shrewsbury Abbey after the sudden death of his wife, the monks suspect that he has killed her with an overdose of Cadfael's herbal potions.

◬ Derek Jacobi and Sean Pertwee as medieval crime-solvers.

Cast | Derek Jacobi, Michael Culver, Terrence Hardiman, Mark Charnock, Sean Pertwee
Original broadcaster | ITV
For fans of . . . | *Sharpe* (1993), *Murdoch Mysteries* (2008), *Sherlock* (2010), *Copper* (2012)

The vogue for feature-length crime dramas was rife on British television in the 1990s. One of the very best of these was *Cadfael*, based on the popular historical novels of Ellis Peters, concerning a twelfth-century monk with a penchant for investigation. There had been three Cadfaels on BBC Radio prior to the television adaptations: Ray Smith (1977), Glyn Houston (1979), and Philip Madoc (1991). All three were of Welsh birth, in keeping with Cadfael's nationality in the books. This trend was bucked in casting an Englishman, Derek Jacobi, as the eponymous monk for television, but he was perfect for the role in every way.

Cadfael, a former soldier of the Crusades and a sailor, entered the monastic life at Shrewsbury Abbey, tending to the weak and injured with his herbalist skills. He had a strong sense of justice, and often aidED those seeking sanctuary within the abbey—much to the dismay of the Abbot (Terrence Hardiman). Murder was a frequent visitor, and Cadfael had help—and often hindrance—from Sheriff Hugh Beringar (Sean Pertwee/Eoin McCarthy/Anthony Green) in his investigations. The series was shot on location in Hungary and combined the best traits of British historical/costume drama with the long tradition of crime series.

Thirteen episodes of *Cadfael* were produced. All were adapted from Peters' books, leaving seven original novels unfilmed. The series was sold around the world, and broadcast by PBS in North America as part of the *Masterpiece Mystery!* anthology. **MW**

Heartbreak High

Soap opera | Australia | 1994–99

Teenage angst in an urban Sydney high school

Cast | Alex Dimitriades, Emma Roche, Lara Cox, Luke Jacobz, Katherine Halliday, Salvatore Coco, Scott Major, Ada Nicodemou, Rupert Reid, Nina Liu
Original broadcaster | Network Ten
For fans of . . . | *Freaks and Geeks* (1999)

Deriving from the 1993 film *The Heartbreak Kid*—itself based on a play in which a young teacher falls in love with one of her teenage students—*Heartbreak High* followed the lives of a group of students at Hartley High School, in Sydney. It was notable for its multicultural cast, praised by critics for reflecting a more accurate view of Australia than other exports, such as *Neighbours* and *Home and Away*—as had the film, which explored racial tensions in Sydney's Greek Australian community.

Showing teens facing universal problems—sex, alcohol, love, and loss—*Heartbreak High* promptly became a hit with teenagers worldwide. Perhaps most notable was its popularization of the unusual phrase "rack off," used in lieu of swearing for a family-friendly audience, and soon synonymous with the show itself.

Unusually, compared to more glossy offerings, such as *Beverly Hills, 90210*, the show often took a realistic tone where plot points and crises could not be neatly wrapped up at the end of an episode. The ensemble cast, while predictably being mostly in their twenties rather than actual teenagers, felt like an ordinary group of students, which cemented the show's appeal with an audience feeling its own share of self-consciousness and general angst. This was a series that understood alienation in all its forms and was not just about the beautiful people. *Heartbreak High* aired in thirty different countries worldwide, and significantly throughout Europe and the Americas, making it one of Australia's most notable televisual exports. **EB**

Kommissar Rex

Crime | Austria/Italy | 1994–present

A dog and male models solve crimes

Cast | Santo vom Haus Zieglmayer ("Beejay"), Rhett Butler, Henry, Gedeon Burkhard, Tobias Moretti, Francesco Arca
Original broadcaster | ORF
For fans of . . . | *Skippy the Bush Kangaroo* (1966)

The premise is laughable. A mildly gifted German shepherd solves crimes with assistance from a succession of damaged yet soulful and athletic male detectives. It's an internationally successful franchise that has been running for more than twenty years and starred three different canines in the title role.

Rex is a dog that works with the Viennese homicide squad. He has a great sense of smell and wonderful tracking ability. He likes ham rolls and dislikes women and vets. His partners are the kind of broken detectives that TV drama adores, but through their relationship with Rex they become healed—it raises the question of how Morse or Tennison might have turned out if they had only had the love of a faithful dog.

What makes the show work is that, superficially at least, it takes itself seriously—Rex investigates serial killers, drug smugglers, and organized crime. Murders are grim and protracted, and Rex's partners frequently come to grisly and explosive ends.

Kommissar Rex is one of Austria's most popular shows, and there's a highly successful Polish version. The series' international popularity was great enough to save it from cancellation when ratings dipped in the German-speaking world. After the original run ended in 2004, Italian funding brought it back, provided that Rex moved to Rome, where he immediately learned Italian and dedicated himself to rounding up the Mafia. So far only one of his handsome partners has died in a car bombing, but it's hard to believe he will be the last. **JG**

ER

Drama | USA | 1994–2009

Vibrant and lauded medical drama that redefined a genre

Cast | Anthony Edwards, George Clooney, Sherry Stringfield, Noah Wyle, Julianna Margulies, Eriq La Salle
Original broadcaster | NBC **Awards** | 23 Emmys **For fans of . . .** | *House* (2004), *Grey's Anatomy* (2005)

The lives of the staff in the emergency room of Chicago's County General Hospital became the preoccupation for an international audience, and for many years *ER* formed the cornerstone of NBC's Thursday night "must-see TV" schedule.

ER endured a long gestation. Michael Crichton wrote the book *Five Patients* in 1970, based on his experiences as an MD in the late 1960s. In 1974, he wrote a movie screenplay set in an emergency room, but the script remained untouched until Crichton collaborated with Steven Spielberg on a big-screen adaptation of his 1990 novel *Jurassic Park*. Spielberg suggested that *ER* be filmed as a feature-length TV pilot rather than a movie. NBC bought it and commissioned six episodes.

ER started as the second most popular show on US TV, and soon took over top position from *Seinfeld* (1989). It has achieved a bigger audience share than any show since *Dallas* (1978). It also made stars of its principal cast, including Anthony Edwards as chief resident Mark Greene, George Clooney as pediatrician Doug Ross, and Julianna Margulies as Nurse Carol Hathaway. **MW**

Classic episode
Love's Labor Lost | *Season 1, episode 19*
In this winner of five Emmy Awards, Dr. Mark Greene endures a long and emotional night that ends in tragedy as he treats a pregnant woman with serious complications.

◉ (L–R) Anthony Edwards, Sherry Stringfield, Ellen Crawford, Noah Wyle, Christine Elise, Deezer D, Julianna Margulies, George Clooney.

The Stand

Fantasy/Horror/Sci-Fi | USA | 1994

An apocalyptic tale of small-town folk facing a terrifying life-or-death choice

Cast | Gary Sinise, Molly Ringwald, Jamey Sheridan, Ruby Dee, Ossie Davis, Laura San Giacomo, Miguel Ferrer
Original broadcaster | ABC **Awards** | 2 Emmys **For fans of ...** | *Golden Years* (1991), *Storm of the Century* (1999)

One man trying to escape a deadly virus on a military base is the catalyst for the last days of humanity as we know it. As groups of survivors come to terms with their losses and the enormity of their situation, some begin to experience visions—either of a kindly old black woman or a persuasive blond man dressed in denim.

Two parties of survivors make their way across the United States with different goals: the hope of peace and security in Nebraska with Mother Abigail (the black woman played by Ruby Dee) or the promise of salvation from destruction with the demonic Randall Flagg (the blond man played by Jamey Sheridan) in Las Vegas. The crushed and dejected must take a stand and decide the fate of the world.

Adapted from Stephen King's novel, this epic four-part miniseries bore many of the tropes familiar to fans of King's work. The body count was high and the victims were often the characters we most wanted to survive. In an impressive cast, Sheridan played against his all-American family man type as the initially seductive but increasingly terrifying Flagg. **JS**

Classic episode
Episode 1, the opening titles. The camera pans across bodies sprawled across desks and a Ping-Pong table in a military base. Outside, a black crow pecks at a child's rag doll. All to the sound of "Don't Fear the Reaper" by Blue Öyster Cult.

◎ Gary Sinise as Stu Redman, one of the virus-immune survivors of a mysterious plague, who follow Mother Abigail westward.

Tous les garçons et les filles de leur âge

Drama | France | 1994

French teenagers come of age

Cast | Elodie Bouchez, Grégoire Colin, Claire Keim, Virginie Ledoyen
Original broadcaster | Arte
For fans of . . . | *Skins* (2007), *The Inbetweeners* (2008), *Fresh Meat* (2011), *Bad Education* (2012)

Tous les garçons et les filles de leur âge (*All the Boys and Girls of Their Time*) is a collection of nine TV films framed around the theme of adolescence, each produced by nine different filmmakers: André Téchiné, Chantal Akerman, Claire Denis, Olivier Assayas, Laurence Ferreira Barbosa, Patricia Mazuy, Émilie Deleuze, Cédric Kahn, and Olivier Dahan. While each story was about teenagers coming to terms with their adulthood, it also reflected the changes in France between the 1960s and 1990s. With its authentic depiction of the pain and confusion of the teenage years, and the use of rock soundtracks, the series rendered evocative snapshots of the evolution of French society over thirty years.

The series was the brainchild of Chantal Poupard, who had the idea for making a program about teenagers from different eras when comparing her own memories of adolescence with the experiences of her sons, then aged fourteen and eighteen. Although each story was independent, they were united by the sense that being a teenager is the same whenever you experience it.

Poupard gave the filmmakers strict guidelines: The action had to take place at a party of some sort, a device that allowed the introduction of rock music specific to the era. The low budget meant that the films caught several now well-known actors at the beginning of their careers, including Elodie Bouchez, Virginie Ledoyen, and Grégoire Colin. *Tous les garçons et les filles de leur âge* is essential viewing for anyone interested in French cinema. **MS**

Space Ghost Coast to Coast

Talk show | USA | 1994–2004

Celebrities interviewed by a superhero

Cast | George Lowe, C. Martin Croker, Andy Merrill, Don Kennedy
Original broadcasters | Cartoon Network (1994), Adult Swim (2001)
For fans of . . . | *Mystery Science Theater 3000* (1988)

Space Ghost (1966), an animated show about the adventures of an alien superhero, was one of many short-lived Hanna-Barbera series rerun by Cartoon Network in the 1990s. It was, however, the only one whose hero landed his own late-night talk show.

The brainchild of producer Mike Lazzo, *Space Ghost Coast to Coast* recycled and revoiced animation from the original show, setting it against the backdrop of a TV studio in space. Celebrity guests appeared on a screen, initially bemused but increasingly in on the joke as the show's eight-season run progressed. The interviews were carried out in advance, with questions and answers edited in the broadcast version to provide maximum surreal humor. The formerly heroic Space Ghost was characterized as charmless, egotistical, and completely unsuited to the job of hosting the show. Like *The Larry Sanders Show* (1992), *Space Ghost Coast to Coast* focused on backstage tensions: since the crew were supervillains—including producer Moltar, a man made from molten lava, and bandleader Zorak, a giant mantis—these were inevitably bizarre.

The great popularity of the series led directly to the establishment of Cartoon Network's comedy offshoot, Adult Swim, whose initial programming included *The Brak Show*, a sitcom based on another Space Ghost foe. After *Space Ghost Coast to Coast* finished its TV run in 2004, Space Ghost and his associates continued to appear in special online episodes and in Cartoon Network linking material. **IK**

My So-Called Life

Drama | USA | 1994–95

Sophisticated teen drama that focused on the emotional lives of a group of high-school students

Cast | Claire Danes, Jared Leto, A. J. Langer, Wilson Cruz, Devon Gummersall, Bess Armstrong, Tom Irwin, Lisa Wilhoit
Original broadcaster | ABC
For fans of . . . | *Freaks and Geeks* (1999)

At fifteen years of age, we feel everything keenly. Every defeat is crushing, every victory intoxicating; every emotion, big or small, is felt intensely. Few dramas have attempted to portray teen life in this way, and none has done so as successfully as *My So-Called Life*.

Angela Chase (Claire Danes) had two loving parents and a younger sister, and went to high school with her new best friend, Rayanne (A. J. Langer), her crush Jordan (Jared Leto), and her bisexual friend Ricky (Wilson Cruz). All of this sounds routine for teen drama, but it was the richness of the characters that made this series remarkable. Everything that happened was obsessed over and picked apart, and everything was a big deal to the characters, who had rich and brittle inner lives. In the pilot episode, Angela dyed her hair red, and the fallout from this action, and the effect it had on her personality, yielded more than enough material to keep the show bubbling along for that first hour.

The characters were typical, but never stereotypical. Angela was unconfident and not as nice as she thought she was. Rayanne struggled with her self-image and eventually had sex with Jordan, who was virtually illiterate. The show's underdog, Brian Krakow (Devon Gummersall), had an unrequited crush on Angela.

Disappointingly, *My So-Called Life* ran for just one season and ended on a cliff-hanger that was never resolved. However, its influence on subsequent teen dramas has been pervasive, and it has become something of a cult classic. **WM**

Classic episode
Life of Brian | **Episode 11.** Told entirely from the perspective of Brian, as he meets a girl he likes and ultimately spurns her attentions to focus on his ongoing crush, Angela—who, of course, remains completely indifferent to him.

◉ Clare Danes and Jared Leto—in the days before superstardom beckoned for them both.

Friends

Comedy | USA | 1994–2004

A group of close friends share their lives together in New York

Cast | Jennifer Aniston, Courteney Cox, Lisa Kudrow, Matt LeBlanc, Matthew Perry, David Schwimmer
Original broadcaster | NBC
For fans of . . . | *Man About The House* (1973), *Three's Company* (1977), *The Big Bang Theory* (2007)

The basic scenario was nothing very remarkable: six close friends, including the siblings Ross (David Schwimmer) and Monica (Courteney Cox), shared their lives together in New York City. It was the add-ons that turned the show into a decade-long international smash hit. The most important of these was the interplay of the characters' relationships: they were linked by more than just friendship; *Time* magazine correctly identified that although the show "called itself *Friends*, [it] was really about family."

Of no less significance were the sassy scripts, which put expressions and turns of speech into the English language: often-out-of-work actor Joey (Matt LeBlanc) would introduce himself to attractive women with a slightly lascivious "How you doin'?"; soon everyone was saying it; likewise, the whole cast's use of "so," as in "It so isn't," became, for a while, the most widely used intensifer in the English language.

Also important were the actors' dress and general appearance, most notably Jennifer Aniston's much-coveted hairstyle—extremely straight and heavily layered—which for a while became known almost universally as "the Rachel" (the name of her character).

All these qualities enabled the vast and loyal viewing audience to overlook some of the show's less credible elements, such as how characters in such low-paid jobs could live in opulent Manhattan surroundings. **JS**

◐ (L-R) Rachel, Joey, Ross, Phoebe, Chandler, and Monica. For more than a decade, they were the world's best friends.

The Fast Show

Comedy | UK | 1994–97, 2000, 2014

Running gags, and short, sharp sketches that piled laugh upon laugh throughout each episode

Cast | Paul Whitehouse, Charlie Higson, John Thomson, Simon Day, Mark Williams, Caroline Aherne
Original broadcaster | BBC Two
Awards | 2 BAFTAs
For fans of . . . | *Monty Python's Flying Circus* (1969)

Harry Enfield had dominated the sketch-comedy genre for several years. Paul Whitehouse had written and performed in many of Enfield's shows and stockpiled a few sketches that were little more than a single punchline. Whereas a standard sketch show might contain nine or ten scenes, *The Fast Show* would churn out almost thirty per episode, some as short as ten seconds long, few longer than three minutes.

Old British radio classics, such as *It's That Man Again* (*ITMA*, 1939), were full of characters that were defined by catchphrases. *The Fast Show* revived this tradition with a host of recurrent characters who always said the same thing: a woman interrupted dramatic scenes to ask "Does my bum look big in this?"; a teenager rambled through various locations declaring everything "brilliant!"; a pair of gentlemen's outfitters suggestively said "Suits you!" to a customer; a weather reporter from an undefined foreign country declares everywhere in the region will be "scorchio."

These catchphrases became part of the language of the 1990s in ways that were baffling to outsiders. Fans would tell their friends about a night out that left them "very, very drunk" or follow up news of spectacularly good fortune with " . . . which was nice." The series spawned spin-offs, including one for car salesman Swiss Toni ("Selling a car is like making love to a beautiful woman") and another that focused on the uncomfortable relationship between bumbling aristocrat Ralph and his elderly groundsman, Ted. **JS**

Classic episode

The Fast Show | *Series 3, episode 8*. One character performs a play that he claims has been specially written for him by Samuel Beckett. Others go white-water rafting, and Ralph makes a moving speech at a funeral.

◉ The cast of *The Fast Show* in their typically diverse array of attire from the costume department.

The Vicar of Dibley

Comedy | UK | 1994–2007

Fish-out-of-water comedy in an English village

Cast | Dawn French, Gary Waldhorn, James Fleet, John Bluthal, Roger Lloyd-Pack, Emma Chambers
Original broadcaster | BBC One
For fans of . . . | *French and Saunders* (1987), *Doc Martin* (2004), *Rev.* (2010)

In 1993, for the first time in history, the Church of England permitted the ordination of women. Writer Richard Curtis at once began developing a television show about a female vicar.

Immediately following her ordination, the Reverend Geraldine Granger (Dawn French) took up her post as the vicar of Dibley, a village in Oxfordshire. Despite the reservations of her flock, who were taken aback as much by her jovial and irreverent nature as by her gender, Geraldine soon became an integral part of local life. Her duties included overseeing regular meetings of the parish council, at which her progressive politics and outsized personality were pitted against the conservative, irascible, and oddball personalities of the other members. *The Vicar of Dibley* placed as much emphasis on gentle running jokes as it did on fish-out-of-water comedy, and although it poked fun at all its characters, each drawn with the broad strokes of traditional sitcom, it rarely looked down on them.

The show mined the bulk of its humor from Geraldine's good-natured entanglements with her strange congregation. French led but did not dominate a stellar cast of character actors with impeccable comic timing. Perhaps the stand-out gag from the series' run was the joke played over each episode's closing credits: Geraldine tells her absurdly literal-minded verger, Alice (Emma Chambers), a joke, and then has to explain it in enormous detail when Alice inevitably misunderstands the punch line. **AP**

Blue Heelers

Crime/Mystery | Australia | 1994–2006

Rural community policing at its finest

Cast | Julie Nihill, John Wood, Martin Sacks, Lisa McCune, Paul Bishop, Jane Allsop, Ditch Davey
Original broadcaster | Seven Network
For fans of . . . | *Dixon of Dock Green* (1955), *The Bill* (1984), *Heartbeat* (1992)

Set in a fictional semirural town in Victoria, Australia, *Blue Heelers* was a popular police procedural. It followed the lives and work of Mount Thomas' police officers, known colloquially as "blue heelers" after the Australian blue cattle dog, which is renowned for its intelligence and fierce loyalty to its owner.

Police work is not all about solving murders. Mostly it is routine enquiries, checking the stories of witnesses and suspected offenders, and keeping the peace. In a rural setting, the pace of life is slower than in the city, and policing is all about the community. People know each other. Every now and again, though, the city's influence comes to town, bringing with it strangers and organized crime. *Blue Heelers* brought the best of both worlds to millions of Australian viewers for forty-odd weeks each year for twelve years. All the stories were told from the perspectives of the men and women in blue, who worked hard to keep the peace and sort out any problems, before going off to relax in the country pub with the bar staff.

Producer Hal McElroy wanted the show to be told firmly from the police officers' points of view and not that of the offenders. In that regard it was similar to the long-running British police procedural show, *The Bill*. Compared by critics to *Heartbeat*, the other British police procedural popular in the 1990s, *Blue Heelers* successfully mixed modern policing, crime, and domestic drama with likable characters played by a strong ensemble cast. **SJG**

The Day Today
Comedy | UK | 1994

Satirical masterpiece that changed the way we watch the news

Cast | Chris Morris, Steve Coogan, Rebecca Front   **Original broadcaster** | BBC Two   **Award** | 1 BAFTA
For fans of . . . | *Brass Eye* (1997)

The Day Today made us see news bulletins in all their pompous and often ill-informed glory. Based on the BBC radio show *On The Hour* (1991), *The Day Today* brought a visual dimension to what was already a razor-sharp pastiche and refined the characters who took the viewers through a succession of absurd invented news items. The standout was inept sports reporter Alan Partridge (Steve Coogan), who went on to have two shows of his own, but others were equally memorable: Peter O'Hanrahanrahan (Patrick Marber), the economics reporter bullied into admitting his ignorance on air by Chris Morris' anchor; Barbara Wintergreen (Rebecca Front), whose gruesome reports satirized the prurience of local news in the United States; the Collaterlie Sisters

(Doon Mackichan—it's one character that sounds like two), whose nonsensical business news was delivered with intense conviction. *The Day Today* took the language of news broadcasts and twisted it to reveal its absurdity. Its graphics were highly detailed and brilliantly uninformative. The show ran for only six episodes, but each was near perfect and endlessly rewatchable. **RL**

Classic episode
Big Report | Episode 2. Highlights include a report on horse racing by Alan Partridge, an exposé of dentists practicing illegally under bridges, a day in the life of a swimming pool, and a family with webcams installed in their heads.

⬣ Alan Partridge (Steve Coogan) went on to host his own spoof chat show, *Knowing Me, Knowing You* (1994).

Ellen

Comedy | USA | 1994–98

Goofy sitcom about a gay bookstore owner and her friends in Los Angeles

Cast | Ellen DeGeneres, David Anthony Higgins, Clea Lewis, Joely Fisher, Jeremy Piven, Arye Gross, Holly Fulger, Maggie Wheeler **Original broadcaster** | ABC **Awards** | 3 Emmys **For fans of ...** | *The Lucy Show* (1962)

Ellen is most famous as the first US prime-time comedy with an openly gay lead actress and title character. It took four seasons to lead up to that revelation in "The Puppy Episode." Until then, *Ellen* had been little different from *Friends* (1994) and other 1990s sitcoms.

ABC originally commissioned a series titled *These Friends of Mine*. The setup was simple: Ellen (Ellen DeGeneres) lived in Los Angeles and goofed around with a small group of friends and her roommate Adam (Arye Gross). It was reworked slightly for its second year and renamed *Ellen*. A host of new characters were introduced, and they were often played by guest movie stars, including Emma Thompson, Carrie Fisher, Martha Stewart, Bea Arthur, Mary Tyler Moore, Eddie Fisher, and

Ron Palillo. Mostly, though, the show was a vehicle for DeGeneres, previously an established stand-up comedian, whose brand of observational humor, often verging on the surreal, was always delivered deadpan.

In 2008, DeGeneres married her long-term partner, Portia de Rossi, and later hosted a hugely popular light entertainment and talk show. **SJG**

Classic episode

The Puppy Episode | *Season 4, episode 22.* The title was meant to keep its subject matter secret, but *Time* magazine splashed the news ahead of the broadcast: Ellen DeGeneres was gay, and her character in the series was also coming out.

◉ Ellen DeGeneres (R) receives a visit from Sherry (Andrea Bendewald), one of her numerous quirky friends.

Frontline

Comedy | Australia | 1994–97

Don't let truth get in the way of a good story

Cast | Rob Sitch, Jane Kennedy, Tiriel Mora, Alison Whyte, Santo Cilauro, Anita Smith, Linda Ross, Pip Mushin, Trudy Hellier, Torquil Neilson
Original broadcaster | ABC
For fans of . . . | *Drop the Dead Donkey* (1990)

Frontline, known as *Breaking News* in the United States, was set in the studio of a fictional current affairs TV show. It provided a comical and cynical take on the lengths to which newshounds and producers would go to get a story, and took a no-less skeptical view of their morality. All the worst abuses of press freedom were here—illegal use of hidden cameras, deceiving people in order to gain access to places to which reporters have no right of entry, and paying outrageous sums of money for prurient kiss-and-tell exposés.

In the workplace, there was a strict hierarchy, in which almost all the journalists kowtowed to executives and people from whom they hoped to derive advantage, and bullied everyone in a subordinate role. Meanwhile, they were always on the lookout for ways to undermine their superiors in the hope of taking their jobs once they'd been fired.

Many of the plots were based on recent or well-known news stories, which lent the show a strong topicality. If *Frontline* had a moral, it was the paradox that it's not only in war that truth is the first casualty: it's also quick to be sacrificed in a newsroom as hacks struggle to fill air time.

Since its run ended, the show has regularly been voted one of the best home-grown Australian TV productions. Its core seriousness is attested to by its inclusion on media studies courses and in a year-twelve English examination module entitled "Representation and Text: Telling the Truth." **GL**

Knowing Me, Knowing You

Comedy | UK | 1994–95

Spoof talk show hosted by a deluded presenter

Cast | Steve Coogan, Rebecca Front, David Schneider, Doon Mackichan
Original broadcaster | BBC Two
For fans of . . . | *The Larry Sanders Show* (1992), *The Day Today* (1994)

The character of Alan Partridge first appeared in *On The Hour* (1991), a British radio comedy. He was the mock news program's sports reporter, whose self-importance was matched only by his lack of sporting insight. Alan proved popular, and BBC Radio 4 gave him a spin-off—a spoof weekly talk show titled *Knowing Me, Knowing You* after a hit song by Abba. After *On The Hour* was remade for TV (as *The Day Today,* 1994), writers Steve Coogan, Armando Iannucci, and Patrick Marber pulled the same trick with *Knowing Me, Knowing You.*

The TV show featured numerous guests played by a brilliant stock company of actors from *The Day Today*. They played foils to Alan's tangential questioning and self-satisfied arrogance. Sublimely played by Coogan—a skilled impressionist as well as a comedian—Alan was a mighty buffoon, committing faux pas, missing the point, and insulting his guests with outrageous aplomb. Over six episodes and a Christmas special, the result was never anything less than hilarious.

Even though his talk show was fictionally axed, the character of Alan lived on. From 1997, he was the basis of a critically acclaimed sitcom, the twelve-episode *I'm Alan Partridge*, which tracked the rapid decline of his broadcasting career. Living in a budget hotel and working on local radio, he tried in vain to get his TV show recommissioned. Periodic specials and webcasts followed, as did a very funny movie, *Alan Partridge: Alpha Papa,* in 2013. **IF**

Ah-haah! It's Alan Partridge, the least self-aware sports presenter in the UK. ❯

Der Bulle von Tölz

Crime/Mystery | Germany | 1995–2009

Humor and social commentary made this German crime drama far from ordinary

Cast | Ottfried Fischer, Ruth Drexel, Katerina Jacob, Katharina Abt   **Original broadcasters** | Sat.1, ORF
For fans of . . . | *Tatort* (1970)

With its quaint Alpine setting, lack of violence, and affable inspector who still lives with his mom, *Der Bulle von Tölz* (*The Bull of Tölz*) seemed to be at the gentle end of the crime drama spectrum. However, this series packed a punch on a cerebral level, with well-constructed and plausible plots, as well as a certain degree of social criticism delivered in a humorous way.

Set in Bad Tölz, a sleepy town in Bavaria, the show revolved around the exploits of its heavily overweight crime-scene investigator Benno Berghammer (Ottfried Fischer), whose widowed mother, Resi (Ruth Drexel), had identified Benno's colleague, Sabrina Lorenz (Katerina Jacob), as the woman who would one day take over her role in caring for Benno. However, Benno

viewed Sabrina in a strictly platonic way, resulting in a long and tense on-screen chemistry between the two protagonists—until Jacob left in 2006 and her character was replaced by a new female investigator.

While the show didn't have explicit messages, its writers frequently addressed double standards in German society, especially within the Church. **DH**

Classic episode
Tod Im Internat | *Season 1, episode 2*. At a private school for boys, the daughter of the caretaker is found dead. The headmistress and the local police officer insist it was an accident, but Benno sets out to prove a murder.

◉ Ottfried Fischer as criminal investigator and mama's boy Benno Berghammer.

Star Trek: Voyager

Fantasy/Horror/Sci-Fi | USA | 1995–2001

Lost in the darkness of the final frontier

Cast | Kate Mulgrew, Robert Beltran, Jeri Ryan, Robert Picardo, Tim Russ, Roxann Dawson, Ethan Phillips
Original broadcaster | UPN **Awards** | 7 Emmys **For fans of . . .** | *Lost in Space* (1965)

Star Trek: Voyager charted the return of Captain Kathryn Janeway (Kate Mulgrew) and her starship crew from the far side of the galaxy, a projected seventy-five year journey during which they stopped off frequently to savor the sights. Although it was not the best of the franchise's spin-offs, it had many moments and characters to savor, including the repeated challenges to Janeway's authority posed by a woman rescued from the clutches of the vile Borg, and the ship's doctor, a crotchety emergency medical hologram who, over time, achieved full consciousness.

In addition to a host of alien life forms, the *Voyager* experienced several dangerous natural phenomena, including the Void (a vast area of empty space).

With a crew of only 150, the *Voyager* was smaller than other United Star Ships, and could land on most of the planets it encountered en route. This was a mixed blessing. It saved time because the ship did not have to go into orbit around a planet and then beam its crew down to the surface; conversely, it often delivered the whole mission straight into alien clutches. **SL**

Classic episode

Flashback | *Season 3, episode 2. Voyager* celebrates the thirtieth anniversary of *Star Trek* through the eyes of the Vulcan officer Tuvok, who recalls his days serving under Captain Sulu (a welcome return appearance by George Takei).

Kate Mulgrew as Captain Kathryn Janeway on the bridge of the starship *Voyager*—immaculate hair, even in dire situations.

Band of Gold

Drama | UK | 1995–97

*Women in mortal danger on the streets
of a British city*

Cast | Cathy Tyson, Geraldine James, Barbara Dickson,
Samantha Morton, Ray Stevenson, Lena Headey,
David Schofield, Rachel Davies
Original broadcaster | ITV
For fans of . . . | *Widows* (1983), *Bad Girls* (1999)

This dark drama, which spanned three seasons,
followed a group of prostitutes working on the grim
"lanes" of Bradford. It packed a punch from the start.
Heavily in debt to loan sharks and with nowhere else
to turn, a desperate Gina was lured into the dangerous
profession of streetwalking. Despite warnings from
Carol, who has worked the lanes for years, Gina was
soon out of her depth and ultimately paid the price
when she was murdered. Looking for answers, her
husband, Steve, and mother, Joyce, find themselves
drawn into the murky world of joyless sex. While Steve
was angry and bitter at what his wife resorted to, Joyce
reached out to the women.

As the police investigation intensified, the band of
women—Rose, Tracy, and Anita—were running scared.
They still worked the streets even though Gina's killer
was still at large and may strike again at any time.

Writer Kay Mellor cleverly gave each of the women a
good backstory and avoided all the clichés that many
dramas fall into when depicting prostitutes. There was
enough heart, tragedy, and compassion in the narrative
for the viewers to feel for the individual woman as she
confronted her own history and demons. The lead actors
were all given time to shine and this freedom helped
to launch the Hollywood careers of Samantha Morton
(*Minority Report*) and Lena Headey (*Game of Thrones*).
Band of Gold had the feel of a documentary, and had
us totally immersed until the end, when the surviving
women tried to leave their old lives behind. **JV**

Bugs

Fantasy/Horror/Sci-Fi | UK | 1995–99

*Gadgets and gizmos are at the heart
of this lighthearted adventure series*

Cast | Jaye Griffiths, Jesse Birdsall, Craig McLachlan,
Jan Harvey
Original broadcaster | BBC One
For fans of . . . | *The Avengers* (1961), *The Professionals*
(1977), *Primeval* (2007)

Sci-fi adventure had once been a staple ingredient of
Saturday night British TV schedules, but by the mid-
1990s it had all but vanished. *Bugs* led the big revival.

The series was the brainchild of Brian Eastman and
Stuart Doughty with advice from Brian Clemens, the TV
veteran who made a huge hit of *The Avengers* (1961) and
created *The Professionals* (1977). The result was a show
driven by gadgets and technology. Security consultant
Ros Henderson (Jaye Griffiths), former spy Nick Beckett
(Jesse Birdsall), and helicopter pilot Ed (Craig McLachan)
use their skills to fight crime.

While the episodes were mostly stand-alone, the
series featured some story arcs, notably in season
two, when a villain imprisoned by the team was seen
influencing the events of each episode from his cell
before making his escape and executing his final plan
in the two-part finale.

The series gained a sleek, futuristic look by shooting
on location in London's newly rebuilt Docklands—
although for the purposes of overseas sales, it tried to
avoid direct references to the city.

When McLachlan left, the producers decided that Ed
could not be written out in the middle of a story line,
so Steven Houghton took over the character (who was
suddenly not Australian). The final season ended on
a cliffhanger, with the team kidnapped at a wedding.

Bugs brought action drama to a new generation of
family audiences, and paved the way for shows like
Strange (2003) and *Primeval* (2007). **WH**

Xena: Warrior Princess

Fantasy/Horror/Sci-Fi | USA | 1995–2001

Bold and brassy adventure series that broke the mold for TV action heroines and may be the mother of all twenty-first-century female-led popular drama

Cast | Lucy Lawless, Renee O'Connor, Ted Raimi, Kevin Smith, Hudson Leick
Original broadcaster | Syndication
For fans of . . . | *Buffy the Vampire Slayer* (1997), *Dark Angel* (2000)

Television never had another heroine like Xena (Lucy Lawless), the ancient Greek warrior-turned-do-gooder, whose exploits were sometimes high tragedy and sometimes low comedy, but always wildly entertaining. Female-led action shows are commonplace today, but in 1991, *Xena: Warrior Princess* was groundbreaking, and set the template for many shows that followed.

Xena made her first appearance in *Hercules* (1995), a cheesy syndicated action drama that reimagined the exploits of the legendary hero. When the show's creators began to consider a spin-off, she was a natural figure to helm it. They paired her with innocent bard-in-training Gabrielle (Renée O'Connor) and hapless wannabe warrior Joxer (Ted Raim) and sent them on a six-season whistle-stop tour of an ancient world—filmed in lush New Zealand—in which Julius Caesar, the Norse gods, and the angels and demons of Christian mythology all rubbed shoulders. The show didn't take itself seriously and its willingness to be playful with its format led to a musical outing, absurd doubles of Xena, and an episode set in the present day featuring clones of Xena and Gabrielle being induced to remember their past by watching clips of their own show. It took postmodernism to a new level, yet remained emotionally engaging and heartfelt throughout.

Were Xena and Gabrielle friends or lovers? The show never explicitly revealed the answer, but its depiction of an intense and supportive female friendship remains unmatched on television to this day. **RL**

Classic episode
Been There, Done That | *Season 3, episode 2*.
Groundhog Day comes to ancient Greece as Xena, Gabrielle, and Joxer find themselves living the same day over and over. Xena figures out what she must do to free them all.

◉ The redoubtable Xena (Lucy Lawless) and Gabrielle (Renee O'Connor)—icons for a new generation.

Sliders

Fantasy/Horror/Sci-Fi | USA | 1995–2000

Mind-bending adventures through alternate realities

Cast | Jerry O'Connell, Cleavant Derricks, Sabrina Lloyd, John Rhys-Davies **Original broadcasters** | FOX (Seasons 1–3), Sci-Fi Channel (Seasons 4–5) **For fans of . . .** | *Doctor Who* (1963), *Quantum Leap* (1989)

Physics student Quinn Mallory (Jerry O'Connell) devised a way to travel to alternate Earths by "sliding" through a vortex opened with a handheld timer, which also told the sliders how long they had left to visit that reality before they must move on. Accompanied by Professor Arturo (John Rhys-Davies), Wade Wells (Sabrina Lloyd), and singer Rembrandt Brown (Cleavant Derricks), the "Sliders" spent two seasons visiting realities in which history went a different way . . . and then encountered the dual threats of the Kromagg species and the Fox Network, which took closer creative control of the show in its third season.

Series cocreator Tracy Tormé was hoping to offer viewers a cerebral exploration of a solid science-fiction concept. Unfortunately, what began as a clever and often intriguing adventure quickly degenerated into pastiches of popular films like *Jurassic Park* (1993) and *Twister* (1996). Tormé left, and the show moved to the Sci-Fi Channel. The final season ended on a cliff-hanger in which Rembrandt attempted to save Earth Prime from the Kromagg threat. **ATB**

Classic episode

Fever | *Season 1, episode 2*. On an Earth suffering from an apocalyptic infection, Wade gets sick and faces death. Arturo invents penicillin, and Quinn is taken into custody by the California Health Commission, a Nazi-like organization.

◬ (L–R) Time travelers Rembrandt (Derricks), Maggie (Wuhrer), Quinn (Jerry O'Connell), and Colin (Charlie O'Connell).

Murder One

Crime/Mystery | USA | 1995–97

Landmark legal drama containing greater detail than any courtroom drama before or since

Cast | Daniel Benzali, Anthony LaPaglia, Mary McCormack, Stanley Tucci   **Original broadcaster** | ABC
Awards | 1 BAFTA, 2 Emmys   **For fans of . . .** | *L.A. Law* (1986), *Broadchurch* (2013)

By the time he made *Murder One*, co-creator and producer Steven Bochco had already had success with *Hill Street Blues* (1981), *L.A. Law*, and *NYPD Blue* (1993). But while they were master classes in keeping multiple story lines in play, *Murder One* spent an entire season following just one case from crime to verdict.

In season one, "The Goldilocks Murder," Hollywood actor Neil Avedon (Jason Gedrick) was charged with the murder of his teenage girlfriend. He was defended by the intimidating Ted Hoffman (Daniel Benzali) and his team of associates. A gripping and complex mystery developed, but what made season one so captivating were the performances. Hoffman's prizefighter image masked a formidable legal brain and uncompromising moral authority. In the opposite corner, Stanley Tucci played Richard Cross, a charismatic but corrupt billionaire, whose malign influence often drove the many twists in the plot. Over twenty-three complex episodes, during which witnesses and suspects were cross-examined, fresh leads pursued, and the truth finally exposed, the tension never failed to mount. **HE**

Classic episode
Season 1, episode 10. As the jury is assembled for the Avedon trial, the prosecution and defense try to outmaneuver each other and secure the jurors most likely to be sympathetic to their cases.

⬆ Anthony LaPaglia, who replaced Daniel Benzali as Jimmy Wyler in season two.

Father Ted

Comedy | UK | 1995–98

A surreal sitcom about three Roman Catholic priests and their housekeeper, who live together in a remote Irish community

Cast | Dermot Morgan, Ardal O'Hanlon, Frank Kelly, Pauline McLynn
Original broadcaster | Channel 4
For fans of . . . | *Fawlty Towers* (1975), *Green Wing* (2004)

Just off the coast of Ireland, the remote Craggy Island was home to Father Ted Crilly (Dermot Morgan), a priest somewhat disappointed with the direction of his life. He shared the presbytery with Father Dougal (Ardal O'Hanlon), a young novice with a very simplistic view of the world; Father Jack (Frank Kelly), a foul-mouthed whiskey-drinking priest with occasional moments of lucidity (prone to outbursts of "Drink! Feck! Arse!"); and their housekeeper, Mrs. Doyle (Pauline McLynn), who was habitually oversolicitous with her offers of warm refreshing beverages ("Have a cup of tea. Ah, go on, go on, go on, go on . . .").

This much-loved comedy from writers Arthur Mathews and Graham Linehan followed the great tradition of exposing authority figures as idiots. Even Ted, the brightest of the bunch, was tainted with a tragic flaw that prevented him from escaping the island. The lead characters were like the Three Stooges with dog collars, a mix of cartoon violence and sweet, innocent stupidity. In one celebrated scene, a bishop asked Father Dougal if his faith was ever tested. He replied: "Well, you know the way God made us . . . and then his son came down and saved everyone and all that . . . and when we die, we're all going to go to heaven? . . . Well, that's the part I have trouble with."

The team had already decided to bring *Father Ted* to a close at the end of the third season, but the sudden death of Morgan soon after production ended, cast a shadow over the final episode. **JS**

Classic episode
The Passion of Saint Tibulus | Season 1, episode 3.
The Vatican condemns a film as blasphemous. Ted and Dougal picket a screening at their local movie theater and are dismayed to discover that their protest attracts even more people to the film.

◉ (L–R) Pauline McLynn as Mrs. Doyle, Frank Kelly as Father Jack, Dermot Morgan as Father Ted, and Ardal O'Hanlon as Father Dougal.

Hollyoaks

Soap opera | UK | 1995–present

The surprisingly glamorous world of British teenagers

Cast | Nick Pickard, Jeremy Edwards, Yasmin Bannerman, Kieron Richardson
Original broadcaster | Channel 4
For fans of . . . | *Brookside* (1982), *Home and Away* (1988), *Sunset Beuch* (1997)

In general, American soaps are shiny and beautiful, full of fashion designers and oil barons. British soaps, by contrast, tend to feature blue-collar workers who are socially excluded and downtrodden. *Hollyoaks*, however, is the exception to this rule.

Created in the 1990s as a soap specifically aimed at teenagers, *Hollyoaks* is aspirational. Its characters—mainly students and young business owners—instead of mundanely struggling to put food on the table, are ducking and weaving to escape stalkers and serial killers. Rarely a month goes by without an explosion or a train wreck. In other soaps, if a character dies it's newsworthy. In *Hollyoaks*, it's a surprise if one of the impossibly sexy characters doesn't leave in a coffin.

Hollyoaks is unconventional in other ways, too. It was showing text messages on-screen long before *Sherlock* (2010). For a period, many episodes opened with a fantasy sequence. It's the soap opera that does what it wants and doesn't care what the grown-ups think.

But it's not all glamour and gloss. The show is celebrated for story lines about anorexia, drug abuse, homosexuality, and other issues that directly affect its audience. Teenagers don't want to watch dreary government information films, but they are much more likely to tune into a mad, attractive show and hence stand a better chance of receiving its underlying messages about serious topics. And that, in summary, is the brilliance of *Hollyoaks*; it teaches without being pedantic. **JL**

Hamish Macbeth

Crime/Mystery | UK | 1995–97

A quirky and atypical police comedy drama with an appealing central character

Cast | Robert Carlyle, Ralph Riach, Shirley Henderson
Original broadcaster | BBC One
Award | 1 BAFTA
For fans of . . . | *Heartbeat* (1992), *Midsomer Murders* (1997), *Justified* (2010)

The picture-postcard Scottish Highland scenery, colorful characters, the charm of the leading man, and his lovable pet dog could suggest a middle-of-the-road drama in the style of *Midsomer Murders*, but *Hamish Macbeth* had a subversive streak that took it out of the mainstream into a subgenre all its own.

Hamish Macbeth (Robert Carlyle) was the sole policeman in Lochdubh, a picturesque village on the west coast of Scotland. He was far from a conventional TV cop, preferring to avoid enforcing the law for petty crimes, such as poaching or after-hours drinking, and resisting interference from the nearby Inverness police. His role in the village was more counselor than law enforcer, and he yearned for the simple things, enjoying village life and even smoking marijuana. However, this idyll proved difficult to maintain because of his complicated love life, the bizarre eccentricities of some of the locals, and the occasional invasion by serious villains. *Hamish Macbeth* was based on the novels by M.C. Beaton, but the TV series moved away from murder mystery and became a sort of morality play where things were never what they seemed. The series was beautifully realized with endearingly witty scripts, but it also had a dark undercurrent that added an ominous shade to the glittering environment.

The program showcased the talents of Carlyle, who later became a Hollywood star. *Hamish Macbeth* lasted only a short time, but it was a mesmerising piece of TV drama. **DF**

Verbotene Liebe

Soap opera | Germany | 1995–present

The tribulations of the aristocracy in a purportedly classless society

Cast | Nina Bott, Konrad Krauss, Gabriele Metzger, Isa Jank, Andreas Brucker, Valerie Niehaus
Original broadcaster | Das Erste **For fans of . . .** | *Gute Zeiten, schlechte Zeiten* (*Good Times, Bad Times*, 1992)

In a country that abolished the aristocracy almost a century ago, *Verbotene Liebe* (*Forbidden Love*) occupies a strange place. On the one hand, the German soap opera portrays this hereditary system (somewhat ironically) as something to aspire to. On the other hand, it also sometimes addresses contemporary social issues, such as LGBT, drug addiction, and mental health.

The show's title translates as "forbidden love," which initially referred to the affair between a couple who discover that they were twins separated at birth. But with five episodes broadcast each week, *Verbotene Liebe* soon had to introduce other plots to keep going. These also frequently revolve around young people's problematic, or indeed unacceptable, relationships.

The program's other overarching theme is the contrast between different social groups, exemplified by the noble von Anstetten family and their middle-class counterparts, the Brandners.

TV station Das Erste planned to cancel *Verbotene Liebe* in early 2015, but the German state-owned channel stepped in to save it. **DH**

Classic episode

Season 1, episode 67. Having learned that his girlfriend is his twin, Jan Brandner ends their affair without telling her why. But when she requires a bone marrow donor, their mother has to reveal the truth.

⬙ Location shooting for the long-running show in 2014: Mirja Du Mont and Martina Servatius.

Pride and Prejudice

Historical drama | UK | 1995

Benchmark costume drama that set the standard for literary adaptation

Cast | Jennifer Ehle, Colin Firth, Benjamin Whitrow, Alison Steadman   **Original broadcaster** | BBC One
For fans of . . . | *Cranford* (2007), *Downton Abbey* (2010)

Pride and Prejudice marked the coming-of-age of costume drama. Of the many adaptations of Jane Austen's novel, this is the one against which all are measured. It released the genre from the confines of studio-bound videotape to become truly sumptuous, and made a star of future Oscar winner Colin Firth.

Dramatist Andrew Davies and producer Sue Birtwistle wanted to adapt *Pride and Prejudice* as early as 1986, but the new version had to wait until a cofinancing deal was struck between the BBC and North America's A&E Network. Davies' adaptation injected a modern energy and dialogue into the tale, but it was the central relationship and battle of wits between Elizabeth Bennet (Jennifer Ehle) and the arrogant and upper-class Mr. Darcy (Colin Firth) that fired the narrative to sizzling levels. Ehle and Firth were key, their chemistry complex and undeniable, making Darcy's eventual declaration of love and rebuttal from Elizabeth truly breathtaking. The six-part series is among the BBC's most feted and successful productions, and twenty years on, it is the adaptation that producers dream to outclass. **MW**

Classic episode

Pride and Prejudice | *Episode 4.* The iconic moment of the series occurs when Darcy (Firth) models a drenched shirt following a cleansing dive into a lake, after which he has a sexually charged encounter with Elizabeth (Ehle).

⚠ Spoiler alert (for those who haven't read this 200-year-old book): Elizabeth (Ehle) and Darcy (Firth) finally tie the knot.

Water Rats

Crime/Mystery | Australia | 1996–2001

Still waters run deep

Cast | Colin Friels, Catherine McClements, Steve Bisley, Toni Scanlan, Jay Laga'aia, Aaron Pedersen
Original broadcaster | Nine Network
For fans of . . . | *Patrol Boat* (1979), *Home and Away* (1988), *Blue Heelers* (1994)

With its blue waters, bridge, and opera house, Sydney makes a beautiful backdrop for dramas of all genres, including crime. *Water Rats* was the first to put cops on the water, basing its characters on the New South Wales Police force's harbor team. Chases—both aquatic and on land—dominated the show.

At the heart of the show was the relationship between two detectives: Frank Holloway (Colin Friels) and Rachel "Goldie" Goldstein (Catherine McClements), both wisecracking, deeply cynical, and dealing with dysfunctional home lives. Their family relationships provided long-running story lines in the years in which they led the show, while *Water Rats* reveled in their tough-but-fair policing. Holloway was investigated by Internal Affairs more than once—including for a murder charge—which added to his hard-edged larrikin nature. Both characters left during the fourth season, to be replaced by detectives Jack Christey (Steve Bisley) and Alex St. Clare (Dee Smart).

Created by Tony Morphett (*Blue Heelers*) and John Hugginson (*Home and Away*), *Water Rats* also boasted an innovatively diverse cast of characters. Constable Tommy Tavita (Jay Laga'aia) was from the Pacific Islands, Sergeant Helen Blakemore (Toni Scanlan) was openly gay, and Constable Michael Reilly was played by Aborigine actor Aaron Pedersen. Sydney's harbor, though, was the real star of the show, providing a supremely serene veil for murder, mayhem, and car and boat chases. **SJG**

3rd Rock from the Sun

Comedy | USA | 1996–2001

Lightning-fast comedy with a sci-fi twist

Cast | John Lithgow, Kristen Johnston, Jane Curtin, French Stewart, Joseph Gordon-Levitt
Original broadcaster | NBC
Awards | 8 Emmys, 2 Golden Globes
For fans of . . . | *Mork & Mindy* (1978)

Mining comedy from extraterrestrials struggling to understand the ways of the humans is nothing new: *My Favorite Martian* (1963) and *Mork & Mindy* did it in the 1960s and 1970s. However, few shows have matched *3rd Rock from the Sun* for sheer comedic invention.

Four aliens, charged with the task of assessing humanity, arrived on Earth in the guise of an average family: father figure Dick (John Lithgow); his sister, Sally (Kristen Johnston); brother, Harry (French Stewart); and son, Tommy (Joseph Gordon-Levitt). Dick became a professor, but his otherworldly knowledge baffled his students. Sally, once a powerful warrior, retained many warlike traits. Tommy, although technically the eldest member of the team, was in a teenager's body and at the mercy of his hormones. Harry was simply profoundly odd, misreading every earthly situation.

Dick embarked on an unlikely relationship with off-kilter professor Mary (Jane Curtin), while Sally enjoyed romance with dumb, overweight cop Don (Wayne Knight), who consistently failed to detect her alien nature. Tommy eventually got a steady girlfriend and even Harry saw action with their landlady's daughter.

The show was created by Bonnie and Terry Turner, who honed their ideas for aliens-among-us comedy with the *Saturday Night Live* sketch favorites the Coneheads (one of whom was played by Curtin). The cast was uniformly excellent, although Lithgow's towering performance as the humility-free, egomaniacal Dick was truly spectacular. **DF**

(L–R) Rock stars Kristen Johnston, Jane Curtin, John Lithgow, French Stewart, and Joseph Gordon-Levitt. ❯

Ballykissangel

Drama | UK | 1996–2001

Gentle romance that for a time topped Sunday night ratings in Britain

Cast | Stephen Tompkinson, Colin Farrell, Dervla Kirwan, Frankie McCafferty, Joe Savino, Niall Toibin, Robert Taylor, Tony Doyle   **Original broadcaster** | BBC One   **For fans of . . .** | *Heartbeat* (1992)

A Roman Catholic priest, Father Peter Clifford (Stephen Tompkinson) was transferred from Manchester, England, to Ballykissangel, a fictional village in Ireland that is described early on in the piece as "the back of beyond." Local life there revolved around two buildings: the church and the pub. The latter was run by Assumpta Fitzgerald (Dervla Kirwan), who didn't like the clergy, and wasn't afraid to say why not.

The relationship that developed between these two main characters was quintessential British Sunday night family viewing: warm and gentle. The two bickered, but came to adore each other. It was a love story without beginning or end, because Father Peter's was a celibate vocation. Both he and Assumpta always knew that.

The show was a great success until Tompkinson and Kirwan left it at the end of season three, reportedly because they were bored. Thereafter, it struggled on, but the magic was gone, and the arrival of a replacement priest, Australian Father Vincent Sheahan (Robert Taylor), did little to recapture it. *Ballykissangel* was canceled at the end of season six. **GL**

Classic episode

Fallen Angel | *Season 1, episode 4*. Father Peter needs to learn to drive, so he asks Assumpta for lessons. It's his birthday, but he's kept that a secret—so how come everybody hears about it on a local radio station?

⊘ Niall Toibin as Father Frank MacAnally and Stephen Tompkinson as Father Peter Clifford enjoyed mass appeal.

The Daily Show

Talk show | USA | 1996–present

When news breaks, they fix it

Cast | Jon Stewart, Stephen Colbert, John Oliver, Craig Kilborn, Trevor Noah
Original broadcaster | Comedy Central   **Awards** | 20 Emmys   **For fans of . . .** | *The Colbert Report* (2005)

The Daily Show achieved the seemingly impossible: to enthuse and educate a young generation about politics without hectoring or resorting to empty rhetoric.

Bolder and more brazen in their interviewing than any other TV crew, longtime host Jon Stewart and his "best f@cking news team ever" cover stories from foreign policy to federal funding, finding the comedy in each. On one occasion, correspondent Samantha Bee critiqued television talk shows through the medium of expressive dance. On another, they reported a senator being caught having sex in a bathroom by having a crooner sing R. Kelly's "Trapped in the Closet."

The show launched two other "fake news" reporters: Stephen Colbert of *The Colbert Report* and Jon Oliver of *Last Week Tonight*. Together, they have changed the landscape of debate, injecting humor and color into the driest of subjects. For many Americans, *The Daily Show* is the most trusted source of current affairs information—which, even more than the content of the show, vindicates its argument that mainstream American news culture is profoundly corrupt. **RL**

Classic episode
Episode 1651 | March 18, 2010. In a bravura impression of libertarian media personality Glenn Beck, Jon Stewart scribbles on a chalk board and "proves" that Bert from *Sesame Street* is in the vanguard of Nazism.

◬ Barack Obama became the first sitting president to guest on *The Daily Show*. Jon Stewart addressed him as "sir" and "dude."

Dalziel and Pascoe

Crime/Mystery | UK | 1996–2007

A pair of mismatched police detectives work together to solve murders in Yorkshire—an odd couple, but a peerless professional combination

Classic episode
Houdini's Ghost | *Season 10, episode 1*. Pascoe attends the scene of a death that looks like suicide. Dalziel knew the victim's ex-wife and sabotages the investigation to protect her. Annoyed, Pascoe opens a murder investigation.

◉ Colin Buchanan as Inspector Peter Pascoe and Warren Clarke as Superintendent Andy Dalziel.

Cast | Warren Clarke, Colin Buchanan, David Royle, Jennifer James, Wayne Perrey, Susannah Corbett, Joe Savino
Original broadcaster | BBC One
For fans of . . . | *Inspector Morse* (1987)

Take an aging detective who rose through the ranks doing police work the old-fashioned way; pair him with a young university graduate on the force's fast-track program; the result—*Dalziel and Pascoe*.

Andy Dalziel—pronounced Dee-el and effortlessly played by Warren Clarke—was a solid copper of tradition: larger than life, a heavy smoker, a heavier drinker, and a consumer of cholesterol-packed traditional Yorkshire food that is likely to kill him. His blunt, forthright manner hid a keen mind.

Peter Pascoe (Colin Buchanan) was the academically clever modern detective heading straight for the top of his profession. His girlfriend, Ellie (Susannah Corbett), disapproved of him becoming a policeman. She married him at Dalziel's suggestion and they had a child, but she left him and emigrated to the United States.

The two detectives were antagonistic—often openly hostile—but the tension between them was creative; they bounced ideas off each other in the search for solutions to the seemingly impossible forensic problems posed by a succession of one-off murders, serial killers, deaths that at first looked like suicides, and cold cases that reemerged to haunt the present.

Forty-six episodes of *Dalziel and Pascoe* were made in twelve seasons. The first three seasons and half of the fourth season were based on the novels of English crime writer Reginald Hill. All but one of the remaining episodes were original screenplays; the exception was season seven's two-parter "Dialogues of the Dead." **SJG**

Our Friends in the North

Drama | UK | 1996

The state of Britain in the late twentieth century reflected in the disparate experiences of three young men and a woman

Cast | Christopher Eccleston, Gina McKee, Daniel Craig, Mark Strong, Peter Vaughan, Malcolm McDowell
Original broadcaster | BBC Two
Awards | 2 BAFTAs
For fans of . . . | *The Long Firm* (2004)

This miniseries was based by writer Peter Flannery on his 1982 stage play of the same name. Each of its nine episodes had the title of the year in which it was set and charted the lives over a thirty-one year period of Dominic "Nicky" Hutchinson (Christopher Eccleston), Mary Soulsby (Gina McKee), George "Geordie" Peacock (Daniel Craig), and Terry "Tosker" Cox (Mark Strong).

The fortunes of these four main characters were mixed, and inextricably intertwined with contemporary political and social events. In the opening episode, "1964," for example, Nicky has just returned from the United States, where he became involved in the Civil Rights movement. Later the viewers witnessed the 1984 UK miners' strike, which attempted in vain to prevent the government from dismantling the British coal industry, and the momentous storm of 1987 that caused unprecedented damage throughout the country. A runnning theme throughout was the fate of their native city, Newcastle-upon-Tyne, as it endured the trauma of deindustrialization and embarked gingerly on the process of regeneration. The proximity of some of the fiction to real people and events made the BBC anxious about legal action against them.

Much of the dramatic material was in striking contrast to the fortunes of the leading actors, for whom *Our Friends in the North* was a springboard to further success and in two cases stardom: in 2005, Eccleston became the ninth Doctor Who, and in the following year Craig became the seventh James Bond. **BM**

Classic episode
1967 | *Episode 3*. The marriage of Mary and Tosker collapses. Geordie puts himself in danger when he has an affair with one of the mistresses of a pornographer (a rare television appearance by Malcolm McDowell).

⊙ Step back in Tyne: (L–R) Christopher Eccleston (Nicky), Gina McKee (Mary), Mark Strong (Tosker), and Daniel Craig (Geordie).

Die Wochenshow

Comedy | Germany | 1996–2002; 2011

This irreverent sketch show breathed new life into German comedy

Cast | Ingolf Lück, Anke Engelke, Bastian Pastewka, Marco Rima, Annette Frier, Dominik Kuhn
Original broadcaster | Sat.1   **For fans of . . .** | *Not the Nine O'Clock News* (1979)

With its irreverent humor and large cast of young comedians, *Die Wochenshow* (*The Week's Review*) felt like a breath of fresh air in Germany in the mid-1990s. Featuring sketches about current affairs and famous people, and parodies of well-known TV programs, the show was a modern version of *Rudis Tagesshow* presented by Rudi Carrell (a Dutch entertainer much loved in Germany), which was itself based on the UK's *Not the Nine O'Clock News* (1979). However, unlike its German predecessor, *Die Wochenshow* was much more anarchic. It wasn't afraid to offend people with personal attacks or politically incorrect humor. Among its most popular recurring characters was Sex TV host Brisko Schneider (Bastian Pastewka).

The program's catchphrases became part of young Germans' everyday speech, and the show made stars out of many previously unknown comedians. However, after some of the most popular performers, including Anke Engelke, Bastian Pastewka, and Markus Maria Profitlich, left in the early 2000s; audiences dwindled, and the show was canceled in 2002.

Old episodes continued to be aired on German television, ensuring that the show wasn't forgotten. The success of such repeats led to a relaunch of the show in 2011. Eight new episodes, with original host Ingolf Lück, were broadcast, but they were as poorly received as the last few installments of the original series, and the show was canned for good. **DH**

⬥ Anke Engelke plays the part of a prostitute in a sketch with Marco Rima.

This Life

Drama | UK | 1996–97

Sex, drugs, and drama

Cast | Jack Davenport, Amita Dhiri, Andrew Lincoln, Daniela Nardini, Jason Hughes, Luisa Bradshaw-White
Original broadcaster | BBC Two **Awards** | 2 BAFTAs **For fans of . . .** | *Teachers* (2001)

This Life was among the first British productions in the 1990s to take TV drama to a new level, pointing the roving eye of fly-on-the-wall documentaries at scripted performances. Without traditional blocked-out and rehearsed moves, the cameras struggled to keep up with the actors' naturalistic movements, creating a fast-moving, energetic show that left some viewers queasy. Much TV is made this way today, but, in 1996, it was something special.

The show's roots were in reality TV—specifically *The Real World* (1992), MTV's precursor to *Big Brother* (1999). In *This Life,* the housemates knew each other, but didn't necessarily get along. Ambitious Milly (Amita Dhiri) was in a relationship with Egg (Andrew Lincoln,

later in *The Walking Dead*), who hated his job and felt directionless until he found his niche in catering. Egg's coworker Warren (Jason Hughes) was a dull, naive, closeted gay man, while sparks flew between arrogant and selfish Miles (Jack Davenport) and his ex-girlfriend, ruthless and chaotic Anna (Daniela Nardini). In its second season, the story opened up to include peripheral characters, such as Warren's cousin Kira (Luisa Bradshaw-White) and various coworkers.

The one-off *This Life +10* (2007) reunited the gang for their tenth anniversary, but a decade is a long time in TV. Viewers were less likely to be shocked by casual sex and recreational drug use, and the characters had grown up, making the sequel feel rather tame. **JS**

⊘ Jack Davenport and Daniela Nardini as ex-couple Miles and Anna who share a house with other friends in London.

Never Mind the Buzzcocks

Game show | UK | 1996–present

Mock 'n' roll will never die

Classic episode

Episode 173 | February 14, 2007. Samuel Preston, of uncelebrated indie band The Ordinary Boys, stalks off the set after host Simon Amstell reads extracts from his wife—and *Celebrity Big Brother* winner—Chantelle Houghton's autobiography.

⊙ Team captain Phill Jupitus (right, with guest comedian Greg Davies) has notched up the most appearances on *Buzzcocks*.

Cast | Mark Lamarr, Simon Amstell, Noel Fielding, Phill Jupitus, Bill Bailey, Sean Hughes, Rhod Gilbert
Original broadcaster | BBC Two
For fans of . . . | *Shooting Stars* (1995), *Pop-Up Video* (1996), *Celebrity Juice* (2008)

A dazed Amy Winehouse slurring, John Barrowman challenging the host to "a gay-off," Fun Lovin' Criminals frontman Huey Morgan smashing a mug in annoyance, Josh Groban urging viewers not to buy his album, Jamelia calling fellow R&B singer Javine Hylton "a slag." *Never Mind the Buzzcocks* has rarely been short of irreverence, comedy, and headline-grabbing moments.

Its predecessors include the BBC's prosaically titled *Pop Quiz* (1981), hosted by DJ Mike Read. However, *Buzzcocks*—its title nodding to the punk band of that name and the Sex Pistols album *Never Mind the Bollocks* —does not pretend to be a serious game show; instead it requires its panelists to imitate song introductions, to pick minor members of minor bands from identity parades, and to keep up with the acerbic wit of initial host Mark Lamarr and his successor Simon Amstell.

Best equipped to deal with the hosts' barbs were team captains Phill Jupitus, Sean Hughes, Bill Bailey, and *The Mighty Boosh*'s Noel Fielding. However, several guests have risen to the challenge. Ryan Jarman of The Cribs claimed to have invented Live Aid despite being five at the time, former Spice Girl Mel C outwitted Amstell in banter about condoms, and Josh Groban proved so ready to mock himself that he returned as a guest host. Other memorable hosts include David Tennant, who aimed repeated jokes at his *Doctor Who* rival John Barrowman, David Hasselhoff; and comedian Rhod Gilbert, who took the chair on a more permanent basis in 2014. **BM**

La Carte aux trésors

Game show | France | 1996–2009

Rapide, à l'hélicoptère!

Cast | Sylvain Augier, Marc Bessou, Nathalie Simon
Original broadcaster | France 3
For fans of . . . | *La chasse aux trésors* (1981), *Treasure Hunt* (1982), *Blue Thunder* (1984), *Fort Boyard* (1990), *La quête* (2007)

Helicopters helped game shows to no end, untethering them from studios. In *La Chasse aux trésors* (1981), contestants remained in a studio, but sent a host in a helicopter scrambling across France to solve clues on their behalf. This format was co-opted by Britain's *Treasure Hunt* (1982), starring Anneka Rice, which was rebooted in 2002 with Suzi Perry. But *La Carte aux trésors* (*The Treasure Map*) put a spin on the format; now the contestants were in helicopters.

Racing in rival choppers, the participants breathlessly harangued bemused locals to help them solve riddles. As the show evolved, they were presented with increasingly complicated physical challenges—climbing towers, crawling through caves, leaping into boats, riding horses across lakes, racing against time and each other, desperate to solve the final riddle and find the treasure—with the show's host on their tail.

The real star of the show was the country of France itself. Breathtaking aerial photography made the most of chateaux (to be explored), vineyards (to be raced through), and, memorably, Mont Blanc (to be scrambled across). In later seasons, the show ventured farther afield into French territories, such as New Caledonia, and the challenges became increasingly grueling but also more cultural—enlisting locals to learn war dances, botany, and fishing.

The show's successors include *La quête*, which was essentially *La Carte aux trésors* meets *Game of Thrones*, sadly minus helicopters and dragons. **JG**

Pop-Up Video

Music/Musical | USA | 1996–2002; 2011–12

Videos accompanied by "popping" info bubbles

Cast | None
Original broadcaster | VH1
For fans of . . . | *MTV Video Music Awards* (1991), *Shooting Stars* (1995), *Never Mind the Buzzcocks* (1996), *Celebrity Juice* (2008)

Pop-Up Video featured old and new music videos, but had a twist: as the video played, information bubbled "pop up" on-screen with factoids about the video or band, pop-culture trivia, and ironic commentary (for example, making fun of Alanis Morissette's misuse of the word "ironic"). It was also educational—in the video for "Land Down Under" by Men at Work, the viewers learned that the fine for torturing a koala in 1996 was $300.

The creators of *Pop-Up Video* put hours of research into the fact bubbles, but despite this, artists such as Mariah Carey and Billy Joel took exception to the show's irreverent tone. Nevertheless, it was terrifically popular, put the network VH1 on the map, and quickly became one of the network's most-watched original shows.

In an era before social networking, *Pop-Up Video* was arguably the original live-tweeting platform, with each bubble big enough to hold only around one hundred and twenty characters, providing running commentary to the viewers. It met the demand for concise pop-culture trivia in a way that anticipated the list-based phenomenon Buzzfeed, and other ephemeral sites.

Many popular TV shows, from *Sabrina the Teenage Witch* (1996) to *Will & Grace* (1998) have referenced *Pop-Up Video*, confirming its cult status. It was rebooted in 2011 with sixty new episodes populated with fresh nuggets of brain candy. Second time around, the show also popped-up hip-hop videos in addition to the pop and rock clips that had dominated the series in its first incarnation. **JG**

Millennium

Crime/Mystery | USA | 1996–99

It's always darkest before the end of days

Cast | Lance Henriksen, Terry O'Quinn, Megan Gallagher, Brittany Tiplady, Bill Smitrovich, Klea Scott
Original broadcaster | Fox **For fans of . . .** | *The X-Files* (1993), *Harsh Realm* (1999), *The Lone Gunmen* (2001)

For anyone who found *The X-Files* (1993) insufficiently grim and paranoid, its creator Chris Carter delivered *Millennium,* a series about a broken man hunting serial killers at the close of the twentieth century. In one of the darkest shows ever made, sometimes the only thing you could see through the murk was the blood.

Lance Henriksen played Frank Black, a forensic profiler haunted by visions of the deeds of the damned. Black swam through the dying light of the world; his marriage crumbling; his only hope in the smiles from his daughter. His cases became entwined with the Millennium Group—but whose side were they on? Could the apocalypse be averted? Apparently not; after two seasons, the show closed with the end of the world.

However, Fox ordered a third season. How did it row back from the apocalypse? With difficulty. Season three moved away from serial killers, toward a conspiracy theory so complicated that even *X-Files* fans would scratch their heads . . . which they did when *Millennium* was canceled and the arc had to be wrapped up in a baffling crossover episode of *The X-Files.* **JG**

Classic episode
Jose Chung's Doomsday Defense | Season 2, episode 9. Writer/director Darin Morgan—responsible for *The X-Files'* finest hours—delivers a funny and even moving satire of belief systems, Scientology, and *Millennium* itself.

⏏ Lance Henriksen as Frank Black, a character name borrowed from one used by Charles Francis of indie rock legends Pixies.

Silent Witness

Crime/Mystery | UK | 1996–present

Every dead body tells a story

Cast | Amanda Burton, William Gaminara, Tom Ward, Emilia Fox, David Caves
Original broadcaster | BBC One **For fans of . . .** | *CSI: Crime Scene Investigation* (2000)

Gruesome detail and puzzling mysteries have made *Silent Witness* one of the longest-running forensic-science dramas. It was first set in Cambridge, England, where pathologist Sam Ryan (Amanda Burton) had a knack for annoying the police when science suggested foul play. Early stories also featured her troubled relationships with family members and past loves.

In its fourth season, the show relocated to London and was bolstered by William Gaminara as Leo Dalton—who replaced Ryan at the helm—and Tom Ward as Harry Cunningham. Emilia Fox joined in season eight as Nikki Alexander, and her character's African background took the show to Zambia and South Africa. When Leo and Harry departed, Nikki remained to mentor a new team.

Silent Witness was created by former police officer (and researcher on *Our Friends in the North*) Nigel McCrery, who worked with forensic pathologists on murder investigations. Exposing the truth, even at personal cost, is a hallmark of the series, as is the use of realistic cadavers—a combination that seems set to help carry the show into its third decade. **SJG**

Classic episode

A Time to Heal | *Season 8, episodes 1 and 2.* The team is summoned to Northern Ireland to investigate two bodies who may be victims of the Troubles. The second half marked Amanda Burton's final appearance as Sam Ryan.

◕ Can I get a witness? Amanda Burton as Sam Ryan, with John McGlynn as Cambridge police investigator Tom Adams.

Sous le soleil

Soap opera | France | 1996–2008

The lives and romances of three close friends on the French Riviera

---

Cast | Tonya Kissinger, Bénédicte Delmas, Adeline Blondieau
Original broadcaster | TF1
For fans of . . . | *Dallas* (1978), *EastEnders* (1985), *The Bold and the Beautiful* (1987)

Sous le soleil (*Under the Sun*) was a long-running soap opera set in Saint-Tropez on the sun-soaked, opulent French Riviera. One of the most exported French TV shows of all time, it was broadcast in 135 countries, gaining huge audiences not only in France but throughout Europe and Latin America, where it was better known as *Saint-Tropez*. It focused on the lives, romances, and friendships of three women, Laure (Bénédicte Delmas), Caroline (Adeline Blondieau), and Jessica (Tonya Kissinger). In authentic soap-opera style, it combined silliness, glamour, love interest, and a succession of labyrinthine plot twists.

One of the cornerstones of the show's success was its apparently unerring ability to incorporate something for almost everyone, and nowhere was that more clearly reflected than in the diverse characters of the three principal women. Laura was a clever and sensitive doctor; Caroline a professional singer who, triggered by a life-changing loss, became a lawyer; Jessica was an American blonde bombshell who worked as a barmaid, a model, and a dancer. The tone was mainly light, although darkness sometimes lurks beneath the glossy surface. The characters must cope with complex family situations and emotional dilemmas, and regularly faced major life choices.

The amazing popularity of the original series inspired a spin-off entitled *Sous le soleil de Saint-Tropez*, which features the original lead actresses and has been running on TF1 since 2013. **MS**

The Newsroom

Comedy | Canada | 1996–97; 2003–5

Devastatingly funny Canadian satire of TV news team

Cast | Ken Finkleman, Peter Keleghan, Karen Hines
Original broadcaster | Canada CBC
Award | 1 Emmy
For fans of . . . | *Drop the Dead Donkey* (1990), *The Larry Sanders Show* (1992)

It may come as a surprise to some that the screenwriter of movies such as *Grease 2* and *Who's That Girl?* would create a superbly dark, single-camera comedy satirizing a TV news team, but that is what Ken Finkleman achieved with this Canadian sitcom.

The Newsroom explored the tensions and sensitivities within the team that was charged with pulling together the evening news show. It focused on three main characters; self-obsessed executive producer George Findlay (Ken Finkleman), facile anchorman Jim Walcott (Peter Keleghan), and committed producer Karen Mitchell (Karen Hines). These characters were observed in such detail—and played perfectly—that they came across as authentic, even amid the outrageous satirical story lines they inhabited. Findlay, in particular, was a genius creation, and Finkleman called him his "unedited id." He would spend as much time avoiding his mother's calls as he would sensationalizing stories to increase ratings. The character of Findlay appeared in three different Finkleman-produced series.

The show was well received and was resurrected as a TV movie, *Escape from the Newsroom,* in 2002. This was followed by two more seasons, both of which maintained the high standard of the original. A searing swipe at the battling egos at play in a highly pressured environment, it laid to rest the myth that all sitcom characters had to be likable. *The Newsroom* is a hidden gem, and deserves to be better known outside of Canada. **SO**

La Femme Nikita

Action/Adventure | Canada | 1997–2001

Compelling psychological thriller in which a reluctant female assassin tries to escape her employers

Cast | Peta Wilson, Roy Dupuis, Eugene Robert Glazer, Alberta Watson, Matthew Ferguson, Don Francks, Cindy Dolenc
Original broadcaster | USA Network
For fans of . . . | *Alias* (2001), *24* (2001)

With all the ambition of a US network TV action series but little of its budget, this cable reboot of Luc Besson's 1990 film of the same name focused on character and clever storytelling to engage the audience.

While the movie Nikita was a teenage criminal, this one was a homeless woman convicted of a murder she did not commit. She was taken from prison by secret counter-terrorism organization Section One, which forced her to work as an assassin.

The series tackled the paradox of using terrorist methods to prevent terrorist activity, a theme that was given even greater prominence in creator Joel Surnow's subsequent project, *24*. *La Femme Nikita* was a bleak, complex affair, with its reliance on dialogue making unusually rigorous demands on the viewers' attention. Peta Wilson made a strong impression in the lead, convincingly conveying Nikita's inner conflict, but all of the cast—regulars and special guest stars alike—made the most of the intelligent script.

In later seasons the series suffered from network interference and reduced financial support, which set up a vicious circle: less money produced an inferior product; an inferior product reduced the viewing figures; reduced viewing figures led inevitably to calls for cancellation. *La Femme Nikita* was duly axed after season four, but a fan campaign forced the creation of a fifth (albeit shortened) run. And there it ended, although a revival—*Nikita*—emerged on The CW network in 2010 and ran for four seasons. **SO**

Classic episode
Spec Ops | *Season 2, episode 2*. Recaptured by Section One after a brief breakout, Nikita is forced to undergo evaluation by special operations agent Jurgen. Can she stop him from uncovering the circumstances of her escape?

⌖ Peta Wilson, as the titular heroine Nikita, proves that looks can kill.

Ally McBeal

Comedy/Drama | USA | 1997–2002

An eccentric, humorous, and dramatic show notable for its surrealistic fantasy sequences

Cast | Calista Flockhart, Greg Germann, Jane Krakowski, Peter MacNicol, Gil Bellows, Courtney Thorne-Smith
Original Broadcaster | Fox **Awards** | 2001 Golden Globe, 2001 Emmy **For fans of . . .** | *LA Law* (1986)

Written by David E. Kelley, *Ally McBeal* starred Calista Flockhart as the eponymous young lawyer working for Cage and Fish, a fictional law firm in Boston. At first glance this was a legal drama, but in reality the main focus of the series was the personal and love lives of the main characters, with the legal proceedings serving as little more than plot devices to reinforce a character's own drama. Legal arguments were often used to brief the audience about a variety of social issues.

The series was notable for its collection of entertaining running jokes. Whenever Ally met an attractive man she could be relied upon to fall over, and frequent reference was made to Richard Fish's wattle fetish and the self-serving mottos he devised, or

to John Cage's tics and improbable legal success. The show digressed into vivid fantasy sequences to express Ally's and other characters' wishful thinking, and there were regular visits to a local bar, haunt of singer Vonda Shepard. The show's ratings began to decline in the third season, but stabilized in the fourth after Robert Downey, Jr. temporarily joined the cast. **RP**

Classic episode

Ally McBeal | *Season 1, episode 12.* This episode saw the first appearance of the Dancing Baby, a metaphor for the ticking of Ally's biological clock. The same animation was shown on several episodes as a recurring hallucination.

◭ Ally McBeal (Calista Flockhart) characteristically struggles to reconcile odd external events with the thoughts crowding her mind.

Stargate SG-1

Fantasy/Horror/Sci-fi | USA | 1997–2007

Saving the world, one episode at a time

Cast | Richard Dean Anderson, Amanda Tapping, Michael Shanks, Christopher Judge, Ben Browder, Don Davis, Claudia Black, Beau Bridges **Original broadcasters** | Showtime, Sci-Fi Channel **For fans of . . .** | *Babylon 5* (1994)

Spawned by Roland Emmerich's 1994 movie *Stargate,* this record-breaker launched a franchise of its own.

MacGuyver hero Richard Dean Anderson inherited the lead role (from the film's Kurt Russell) of Jack O'Neill, a colonel who led Earth's first conflict against the Go'auld, a race of slavers who controlled much of the galaxy. Using "stargates" that provide instantaneous travel, O'Neill and his associates—including scientists Daniel Jackson (Michael Shanks) and Samantha Carter (Amanda Tapping), and alien Teal'c (Christopher Judge) —battle enemies, learn secrets, and advance human knowledge and technology to prevent Earth's downfall. (The show was later retooled with new stars, including *Farscape* alumni Ben Browder and Claudia Black.)

Discontinued by Showtime but revived by Sci-Fi, *SG-1* spawned its own spin-offs. The cast made cameos (and, in Tapping's case, became a regular) in *Stargate Atlantis* (2004) and made-for-DVD movies. But neither *Atlantis* nor the later *Stargate Universe* (2009) enjoyed the longevity of *SG-1*—whose ten seasons made it North America's longest running sci-fi show. **SL**

Classic episode
Wormhole X-Treme! | *Season 5, episode 12.* In an ambitious slice of self-mockery, the SG-1 team find themselves the subject of a sci-fi series based on their adventures. In-jokes abound in the show's one-hundredth episode.

⬨ Galactic gate-hoppers Michael Shanks (Jackson), Amanda Tapping (Carter), and Richard Dean Anderson (O'Neill).

Jonathan Creek

Crime/Mystery | UK | 1997–2014

Head-scratching mysteries? Call the conjurer

Classic episode

The Problem at Gallows Gate | **Season 2, episodes 4–5.** At a party, several people witness a wealthy young man commit suicide. Several days later, a girl is found strangled with his fingerprints on her. *Utopia's* Alistair Petrie guests.

⦿ Caroline Quentin as Maddy Magellan and Alan Davies as Jonathan Creek—British TV's very own Scooby and Shaggy.

Cast | Alan Davies, Caroline Quentin, Julia Sawalha, Sheridan Smith, Sarah Alexander, Stuart Milligan
Original broadcaster | BBC One
Award | 1 BAFTA
For fans of . . . | *Scooby-Doo, Where Are You!* (1969)

The locked-room mystery is as old as the crime genre itself, but David Renwick is the writer of some of the most ingenious takes on the genre. Best known for creating *One Foot in the Grave* (1990), Renwick gave *Jonathan Creek* a real comic edge. This was aided by Alan Davies' laconic portrayal of the hero, whose profession is developing magic tricks. His attendant skill for unpicking mundane elements from the fantastical enabled him to solve even the most baffling of crimes.

Of a succession of female sidekicks, best was the formidable Maddy Magellan (*Men Behaving Badly's* Caroline Quentin). Liking and irritating each other in equal measure, she and Creek had a sparkling rapport that complemented the show's strongest mysteries. Touches of old-school gothic horror—deals with the Devil, murderous ghosts, vanishing murderers—added to the atmosphere before Creek, in true Scooby-Doo-cum-Agatha Christie style, solved the mysteries and revealed the truth to those involved.

Later seasons edged closer to comedy with the introduction of *The Young Ones'* Adrian Edmondson as a bumbling TV executive and *Coupling's* Sarah Alexander as Creek's wife, who wants him to give up solving crimes. But it continued to be one of British TV's best murder mystery shows, with Renwick consistently creating well-rounded, interesting characters who were also engaging and funny. So, for all the seemingly supernatural strangeness of the stories, the enduring success of his formula was no mystery at all. **LH**

Brass Eye

Comedy | UK | 1997–2001

The small screen's most vicious satire

Cast | Chris Morris, Mark Heap, Kevin Eldon, Doon Mackichan, Julia Davis, Gina McKee, Claire Skinner
Original broadcaster | Channel 4
For fans of . . . | *The Day Today* (1994), *Jam* (2000), *Stewart Lee's Comedy Vehicle* (2009)

The greatest satire is utterly vicious and no show was as cruel—and, consequently, as funny—as *Brass Eye*. Building on his BBC news parody *The Day Today* (which brought Steve Coogan's Alan Partridge to TV), creator and star Chris Morris refined that show's elements into a format so controversial that, ultimately, members of parliament called for it to be banned.

Not since *Fawlty Towers* (1975) had a comedy cut such a swathe with so few episodes. The initial run, in 1997, consisted of just six: "Animals," "Drugs," "Science," "Sex," "Crime," and "Decline," each exploring topics beloved of the British tabloid press with its insatiable hunger for moral outrage. Sketches featuring fake newscasters and documentary makers expanded upon—or, more commonly, obscured—each subject, but the true highlights were what got the show's makers into the most trouble. Posing as genuine journalists, they persuaded celebrities and politicians to hold forth about each show's theme, often inducing them to read out prepared statements whose absurdity would have been obvious if the clueless marks had spent even a moment thinking about them. This was precisely the show's point: in our news culture, we want to be outraged more than we want to be informed.

With 2001's one-off "Paedophilia," *Brass Eye* didn't so much push the boundaries of taste as demolish them. Offensive? Absolutely, but never without purpose. This unforgettable indictment of all that's wrong in our news culture was fueled by righteous anger. **RL**

Midsomer Murders

Crime/Mystery | UK | 1997–present

Murder mystery in the deadly English countryside

Cast | John Nettles, Neil Dudgeon, Daniel Casey, Jason Hughes, Gwilym Lee
Original broadcaster | ITV
For fans of . . . | *Shoestring* (1979), *Bergerac* (1981), *Inspector Morse* (1987)

The cozy eccentricities of rural Middle England provided the UK's ITV network with its most enduring drama hit of the last two decades—and one of the biggest international television exports. The "Chief Inspector Barnaby" book series of Caroline Graham was the basis for *Midsomer Murders*, providing titles and foundations for the first five feature-length episodes, including a successful 1997 pilot.

The series was developed by producers Betty Willingale and Brian True-May, along with Anthony Horowitz, who penned many of the early screenplays. The series delves into the dark underbelly of village life in the fictional county of Midsomer, the officers of Causton CID unearthing convoluted and multiple murder plots behind tea, scones, and village cricket teams. There isn't much edge to *Midsomer Murders*, but it is easy viewing with a wicked, almost subversive charm beneath the sunny backdrops. The series is gifted with the casting of John Nettles as the easygoing Detective Chief Inspector Barnaby, a major contrast to his other major TV role as the tortured Bergerac (1981).

Nettles handed in his warrant card after thirteen seasons in 2011, replaced by Neil Dudgeon as cousin DCI John Barnaby; the new Barnaby has since been joined by Sergeant Charlie Nelson (Gwilym Lee). *Midsomer Murders* has sold to numerous international territories, and while it may no longer enjoy the ratings high of its peak during the early 2000s, it remains a popular and highly entertaining TV staple. **MW**

Buffy the Vampire Slayer

Fantasy/Horror/Sci-Fi | USA | 1997–2003

In every generation, there is a chosen one . . .

Cast | Sarah Michelle Gellar, Alyson Hannigan, James Marsters, Nicholas Brendon, Anthony Stewart Head
Original broadcasters | The WB, UPN
Awards | 2 Emmys
For fans of . . . | *Angel* (1999), *Being Human* (2008)

As a movie in 1992, *Buffy the Vampire Slayer* flopped— too few of those involved understood that writer Joss Whedon was trying to subvert horror clichés, not reinforce them. But, resurrected as a TV show for a minor network, it became a hugely influential hit that challenged and ultimately rewrote those conventions.

Sunnydale student Buffy Summers (Sarah Michelle Gellar) refused to abide by rules set out by her guide, stuffy librarian Giles (Anthony Stewart Head), and gravitated to geeky underdogs Xander (Nicholas Brendon) and Willow (Alyson Hannigan). Early episodes erred on the side of "monster of the week," but foes were often metaphors for adolescent alienation, loneliness, romantic betrayal, and peer pressure. Buffy's boyfriend Angel (David Boreanaz) was a vampire with a soul, a prospective stepfather was a murderous robot, and Willow's thirst for magical knowledge was revealed to be as deadly and destructive as drug addiction.

Characters died, often horribly, though some were allowed back. Angel was killed (by Buffy, though she had a good excuse) then resurrected, before leaving for his own series. Buffy herself died twice, only to return and land in the bed of Sid Vicious-style vampire Spike (James Marsters). But even in the darkest hours, there were laughs—often juxtaposed, especially in the last two of the seven seasons, with moving moments. "We paved the way for young heroines, for shows that can revolve around a three-dimensional female character," Gellar observed. "I really feel like we started that." **JS**

Classic episode
Hush | *Season 4, episode 10.* This exceptionally eerie tale was largely dialogue-free, yet was the only episode to be nominated for an Emmy for writing. Snubbed year after year, *Buffy* earned Emmys only for its music and makeup.

⊙ Camden Toy, who played one of the Gentlemen in *Hush,* returned in season seven as an "über-vamp" foe of Buffy (Sarah Michelle Gellar).

Un gars, une fille

Comedy | Canada | 1997–2002

This fresh and clever comedy about a Québec couple's constant bickering hit a chord

Cast | Guy A. Lepage, Sylvie Léonard, Norman Helms, Louise Richer
Original broadcaster | Radio-Canada Télé
For fans of . . . | *Till Death Us Do Part* (1965), *The Fast Show* (1994)

One guy plus one girl equals . . . lots of little arguments. That was the simple math behind this quickfire sitcom with a cult following, whose simple formula was copied around the world. The French-Canadian original tapped into a near-universal understanding of the frequent disagreements that punctuate domestic bliss. Comedy actors Guy A. Lepage and Sylvie Léonard played a couple with their own forenames— Guy and Sylvie—whose fondness for each other constantly had to absorb their everyday differences about the smallest things.

Une gars, une fille (*A Guy, a Girl*) began life in 1995 as a series of sketches on Lepage's daily radio show. Turned into a weekly TV series, it proved a runaway success. Much of this was due to the fractious chemistry between Lepage and Léonard, but the series also benefited from its fresh and contemporary style. Rather than having a standard unbroken narrative, a typical half-hour contained three acts, divided into a handful of scenes. It was similar to the urgency of *The Fast Show,* the BBC's hit sketch show of the 1990s, with a hint of MTV.

The show had many guest characters, who were sometimes cropped out of shot, so that Guy and Sylvie appeared to be addressing the (often static) camera, as they interacted with dinner guests, callers at their door, train passengers, and so on—encounters that would invariably spark off another squabble. By keeping the focus on the central couple's reactions, the show cleverly kept hitting the bull's-eye. **MWy**

Classic episode
À la Bibliothèque | *Season 1, episode 2.* Guy and Sylvie visit the local library. Confusion begins when Sylvie disappears upstairs, leaving Guy to return her library books, which the librarian thinks are his.

◉ Sylvie Léonard and Guy A. Lepage as a couple who were rarely on the same page.

Little Dieter Needs to Fly

Documentary | Germany | 1997

A pilot returns to the places he bombed in Vietnam

Cast | Dieter Dengler, Werner Herzog, Eugene Deatrick
Original broadcaster | ZDF
For fans of . . . | *The World at War* (1973), *Vietnam: A Television History* (1983)

At heart this is a simple story: a US pilot, shot down in Vietnam, is captured and tortured, then escapes and is hailed a hero. He claims he enlisted simply because he wanted to learn to fly, and it never really sank in that there were people in the villages he was bombing and that they might not treat him in accordance with the Geneva Convention. To complicate matters further, this US pilot was born German, and director Werner Herzog's remarkable documentary is both one man's story and an epic account of what war does to people.

Dieter Dengler was inspired to become a pilot when Second World War planes bombed his village. He and Herzog discuss the hunger of their youth, when stolen wallpaper made a nourishing meal. This experience haunts Dengler when he recounts the starvation he underwent at the hands of his captives. Herzog takes him back to Vietnam, and villagers help to re-enact the torments and privations Dengler experienced until he eventually escaped. (Herzog returned to the story for 2006's *Rescue Dawn,* starring Christian Bale as Dengler.)

The documentary is layered with redemption. It is about a child growing up in Nazi Germany who wants to be an American; about Dieter's acceptance by his squadron; about the hero's welcome he received on his return to the United States; about the friendships he forms with the Vietnamese hired for the re-enactment. And, detailing his obsessive opening of doors, and the basement he keeps full of emergency food, it is about the scars that remain on Dieter's body and mind. **JG**

Oz

Drama | USA | 1997–2003

Conflict in a maximum security prison

Cast | Terry Kinney, J.K. Simmons, Lee Tergeson, Ernie Hudson, Eamonn Walker, Dean Winters, Adewale Akinnouye-Agbaje
Original broadcaster | HBO
For fans of . . . | *Orange is the New Black* (2013)

Not to be mistaken for its cheery, Munchkin-packed namesake, *Oz* was a groundbreaking series set in a maximum security prison. The "Emerald City" is a special unit of the Oswald State Correctional Facility, or "Oz." Its warden, Tim McManus (Terry Kinney), brought together some of its most hardened criminals in an attempt to do the impossible: to rehabilitate them.

McManus's experiment became a microcosm of the greater problems in society as a whole. *Oz* portrayed a broken world filled with conflict on every level: between races, religions, and individuals, as well as between the inmates and their wardens. The show came complete with deliberately theatrical (and occasionally finger-wagging) introductions to drive home each episode's theme.

Oz presented prison not as a system for rehabiliation, but for transformation—and very rarely for the better. The conflicts between various individual prisoners were engrossing. The best were those between Tobias Beecher (Lee Tergeson)—Harvard law school graduate, successful attorney, family man, drunk-driving killer—and Vern Schillinger (J.K. Simmons), a hardened racist. Another was that between Muslim leader Kareem Said (Eamonn Walker) and Nigerian gangster Simon Adebisi (Adewale Akinnouye-Agbaje), who vied for the souls of Oz's African-American inmates.

The prison life depicted here was filled with violence, rape, manipulation, and sadism. *Oz* was not for the faint of heart or the claustrophobic. **AP**

King of the Hill

Animation | USA | 1997–2010

Propane and pleasure deep in the heart of Texas

Cast | Mike Judge, Kathy Najimy, Pamela Adlon, Brittany Murphy, Johnny Hardwick, Stephen Root
Original broadcaster | Fox
Awards | 2 Emmys
For fans of . . . | *The Simpsons* (1989)

Debuted as a midseason replacement for *Ned & Stacey* (1995), *King of the Hill* was a runaway success. Created by Mike Judge, father of *Beavis and Butt-Head* (1993), and Greg Daniels, it confirmed, alongside stalwarts such as *The Simpsons* (1989), *South Park* (1997), and *Family Guy* (1999), that cartoons were no longer just for kids.

King of the Hill was very much a family-oriented show, with jokes aimed at all ages. Propane-obsessed salesman Hank Hill lived a fairly ordinary lifestyle with wife Peggy, son Bobby, and teenage niece Luanne, in the fictional town of Arlen, Texas. *King of the Hill*, avoiding the surreal situations often explored in other animated series, remained anchored in reality, and followed a much more traditional dramatic format.

Much of the humor stemmed from Hank's traditional values; for example, he was afraid to show affection in public, even to his wife. The fact that Bobby often showed interest in such "feminine" things as dolls and fashion prompted the show's catchphrase, "That boy ain't right." When the then twelve-year-old (*King of the Hill* was unusual for a cartoon in having its characters age) dated a fourteen-year-old girl in the Emmy Award–winning episode "And They Call It Bobby Love," Peggy worried about the age gap, while Hank was mainly concerned that "vegetarians can't be trusted."

King of the Hill ran for thirteen years, during which time it attracted a huge range of guest stars, including Alan Rickman, Christopher Lloyd, Meryl Streep, and The Dixie Chicks. **EB**

Classic episode
Hank's Dirty Laundry | *Season 2, episode 17*.
After being refused a credit application, Hank discovers he has an outstanding debt for a pornographic movie. Insisting he did not rent the tape, he has to fight to save his reputation.

◉ Patch Boomhauer (voiced by Brad Pitt) makes an impression on Hank Hill and the ladies of Arlen in *King of the Hill*'s 150th episode.

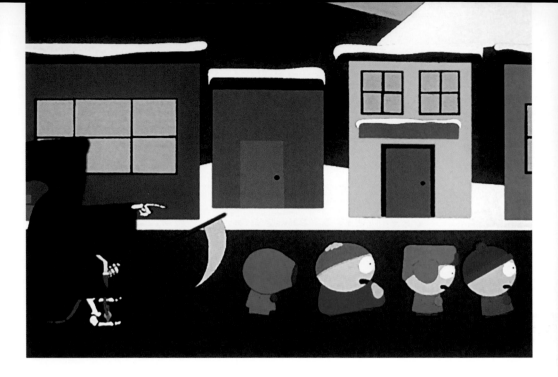

South Park

Animation | USA | 1997–present

Four boys. One f**ked up town

Cast | Trey Parker, Matt Stone, Mary Kay Bergman, Isaac Hayes, Mona Marshall, April Stewart
Original broadcaster | Comedy Central **Awards** | 5 Emmys **For fans of . . .** | *Aqua Teen Hunger Force* (2000)

College students Trey Parker and Matt Stone's 1992 short titled *Jesus vs Frosty* caught the eye of Fox executive Brian Graden, who paid the duo to create an animated Christmas card. The resultant *Jesus vs Santa* (later rebranded with its predecessor as *The Spirit of Christmas*) was one of the internet's first viral videos and led to the development of *South Park:* the often insane exploits of third—later fourth—graders Stan (based on Parker), Kyle (based on Stone), Kenny (who died in most episodes for the first five years), and hateful bigot and opportunist Cartman. (Parker and Stone adapted their crude, construction paper-based technique—inspired by Monty Python's Terry Gilliam—to be rendered by computer animation in the same simple style.)

South Park goes where other shows fear to tread, tackling contentious topics with surprising profundity, albeit masked by scatological and surreal humor. With stars such as Jennifer Aniston and Radiohead providing guest voices, it relentlessly crusades against political correctness, corporate greed, and religious fervor, to the delight of its fans and fury of its critics. **ATB**

Classic episode
Imaginationland | Season 11, episodes 10–12.
In this Emmy-winning trilogy, a portal to a realm of pure imagination is breached, and a terrorist attack ensues. Can Butters—initially a successor to the forever fated Kenny—save the day?

◉ The grim reaper guests alongside (L–R) Kenny, Cartman, Kyle, and Stan in season one's *Death*, a precursor to the *South Park* movie.

Cold Feet

Comedy/Drama | UK | 1997–2003

Boy meets girl. Boy loses girl. Boy wins girl back

Cast | James Nesbitt, Helen Baxendale, Hermione Norris, John Thomson, Fay Ripley, Robert Bathurst
Original broadcaster | ITV **Award** | 1 BAFTA **For fans of . . .** | *Friends* (1994), *This Life* (1996)

Other shows courted aspirational twentysomethings, but *Cold Feet* focused on working professionals. Initially detailing the friendships of three couples, the show—like *Friends*—defined a cross-section of the audience.

Commissioned to write a one-off production for Granada Television, Mike Bullen created *Cold Feet*, depicting the blooming romance between Adam Williams (James Nesbitt) and Rachel Bradley (future *Friends* star Helen Baxendale). Adam's friends Pete (John Thomson) and Jenny (Fay Ripley) are trying to start a family, while Rachel's middle-class chums Karen (Hermione Norris) and David (Robert Bathurst) are considering a second child and a nanny. The show won a Rose d'Or award in 1997 and a series duly followed.

The show grew darker as infidelity corroded the couples. The core cast remained until Fay Ripley left during the fourth season, but ratings remained high as the show wound toward its shocking climax. (There was a short-lived US remake in 1999.) Ultimately, *Cold Feet* proved cathartic for a demographic that British TV has since struggled to pin down in the same way. **MW**

Classic episode
Season 2, episode 11 | October 24, 1999. This episode showcases *Cold Feet*'s deft balance of light and dark. Adam learns that he has testicular cancer—a plight that prompts Pete and Jenny to give their marriage another try.

 John Thomson (Pete) and Helen Baxendale (Rachel) dance the night away.

Dawson's Creek

Soap opera | USA | 1998–2003

Will they, won't they teen drama—"Just make a decision"

Cast | James Van Der Beek, Katie Holmes, Michelle Williams, Joshua Jackson
Original broadcaster | WB
For fans of . . . | *Beverly Hills, 90210* (1990), *Party of Five* (1994), *The O.C.* (2003)

This is *Scream* (1996) writer Kevin Williamson's take on the teen soap, centering on the loves and lives of four fresh-faced youths in high school: would-be film director Dawson Leary (James Van Der Beek), Joey Potter (Katie Holmes), Jen Lindley (Michelle Williams), and Pacey Witter (Joshua Jackson)—living in the fictional coastal town of Capeside, Massachusetts.

With its easy on the eye cast and scenery as well as a cool teen soundtrack, it became a huge global success, especially in Australia and in the United Kingdom where, scheduled on Sunday mornings, it became the perfect hangover cure. Kerr Smith's coming-out story line garnered praise, but the big draw was the love triangle at its core. Would Dawson be the one to take his former sleepover pal, Joey (that's a girl), down the aisle or would bad boy Pacey capture her heart? It was a story line that would enthral and frustrate for six seasons, culminating in a two-hour finale.

The show was not without its critics and much was made of the fact that these supposed teenagers (clearly in their later twenties) had all swallowed the same multi-volumed dictionary to enable them to spout their almost Shakespearean angst. References to shows such as *The Mary Tyler Moore Show* (1970) and *The Dick Van Dyke Show* (1961) also seemed greatly at odds with the age of the characters. However, that did not bother the audience, who were more concerned that Joey would make up her mind and pick the one with the floppy hair and big forehead. **DJ**

Classic episode

All Good Things . . . Must Come to an End |
Season 6, episodes 23/24. Flashing forward five years, Dawson is a successful TV producer. Joey returns from Paris and realizes she still has feelings for her two childhood sweethearts.

⚉ The fab four: (L–R) Michelle Williams, James Van Der Beek, Joshua Jackson, and Katie Holmes.

All Saints

Drama | Australia | 1998–2009

Popular Aussie medical drama

Cast | Judith McGrath, Georgie Parker, Tammy Macintosh, Erik Thomson, Conrad Coleby, Martin Lynes, Ben Tari, John Howard, Libby Tanner, Wil Traval
Original broadcaster | Seven Network
For fans of . . . | *Casualty* (1986), *Blue Heelers* (1994)

Primarily set in Ward 17 of All Saints Western General Hospital in the fictional Sydney suburb of Clydesbridge, *All Saints* followed the lives of the hospital workers and their patients in classic hospital drama style. Nicknamed "the garbage ward," as it was where all the undesirables in the city seemed to end up, Ward 17 offered valuable life lessons to both patients and staff. The show was well received for its realistic portrayal of medical issues. It was considered more akin to BBC's *Casualty* (1986) than NBC's *E.R.* (1994).

In 2004, to arrest declining ratings and accusations of repetitive story lines, *All Saints* underwent a major realignment, with the focus shifted from Ward 17 to the hospital's high-drama emergency department. Rejuvenated by the change, the show ran for another five years. Producers tried this trick again in 2009, adding a medical response unit to introduce action and stunt sequences, and renamed the show *All Saints: Medical Response Unit*. This time, however, the change proved less successful and the series was canceled shortly after.

In addition to hosting a range of much loved Australian actors as guest stars, including Anne Charleston *(Neighbours)* and Anthony Brandon Wong *(The Matrix Reloaded)*, *All Saints* was a hotbed for young Australian talent who went on to achieve success in Hollywood, including Eric Bana *(Star Trek)*, Adelaide Clemens *(The Great Gatsby)*, and Mia Wasikowska *(Alice in Wonderland)*. **EB**

Ultraviolet

Fantasy/Horror/Sci-Fi | UK | 1998

"Our free range days are over"

Cast | Jack Davenport, Susannah Harker, Stephen Moyer, Idris Elba, Philip Quast, Fiona Dolman, Corin Redgrave
Original broadcaster | Channel 4
For fans of . . . | *Apparitions* (2008), *True Blood* (2008)

Across the pond, the successful and popular Buffy was kicking ass with stakes and spells. But in the United Kingdom, *Ultraviolet* took a very different approach to vampire slaying: a dark, innovative version of the bloodsucker mythos with a thoroughly modern twist. When copper Michael's best friend Jack goes missing on the eve of his wedding, he finds himself sucked into the shadowy world of a government-sponsored organization tasked with hunting down vampires. The "ministry" is forced to recruit Michael when he realizes that Jack has been corrupted and infected by the new vampire threat. Michael's investigations make him question where his loyalties lie, and he is soon faced with some very difficult choices.

Writer and director Joe Ahearne cleverly explores very dark themes in *Ultraviolet*, such as HIV contaminating the blood supply (food chain), vampires experimenting with humankind as we would lab rats, abortion, paedophilia, and enemy forces infiltrating positions of power. Each episode is a self-contained story along the arc of Michael's journey. The producers use the stylish backdrop of London to its maximum potential in driving the action, and with the use of superb lighting and filters it adds a very seedy and eerie tone to the script. Widely embraced by the loyal audience it built over the six episodes and well received by critics, *Ultraviolet* lasted for only one series, but Ahearne made it a classic cult favorite that still stands its ground now. **JV**

Hornblower

Historical drama | UK | 1998–2003

Rip-roaring nautical adventure—"Exceptional shot, if I may say so sir"

Cast | Ioan Gruffudd, Robert Lindsay, Paul McGann
Original broadcaster | ITV **Awards** | 2 Emmys **For fans of . . .** | *Sharpe* (1993)

The beloved series of books by C.S. Forester charting the adventures of Horatio Hornblower in the British navy received the TV adaptation it deserved and the charismatic handsome lead it required in young Ioan Gruffudd. It is a grand adventure, with swashes buckled and villains defeated, but its greatest achievement was to make old-fashioned virtues seem modern.

Over eight TV movies, *Hornblower* charts Horatio's growth from fumbling lieutenant to confident captain as he takes part in some of the defining action of the Napoleonic Wars. Filming on water is notoriously expensive and that the show managed to look so authentic on a TV budget is a testament to its ingenuity and its skilled use of scale models as well as full-size sailing ships. Horatio was the perfect hero, modest about his own abilities and fervent in his desire to see right done. Ioan Gruffudd was excellent in the role, managing to convey diffidence and self-doubt at one moment and steely authority at another. The supporting cast of British drama stalwarts brought color to even the smallest roles. **RL**

Classic episode
The Even Chance | Season 1, episode 1. The show hits the ground running as viewers are introduced to a seasick young Hornblower. Soon at odds with his tyrannical captain, he is caught up in a duel that threatens his career and his life.

◬ Robert Lindsay brought gravitas as Sir Edward Pellew to balance out Ioan Gruffudd's more youthful enthusiasm.

That '70s Show

Comedy | USA | 1998–2006

Reimagining the scintillating seventies—"That kid's on dope!"

Cast | Topher Grace, Ashton Kutcher, Laura Prepon, Mila Kunis, Kurtwood Smith, Debra Jo Rupp
Original broadcaster | Fox   **Award** | 1 Emmy   **For fans of . . .** | *Happy Days* (1974)

Imagined as a slice-of-life sitcom about the adventures of 1970s teenagers, seen through the filters of early 21st-century TV, *That '70s Show* is perhaps remembered more for its style than for its substance. It also launched the illustrious careers of several of its cast members.

Set in the sleepy rural town of Point Place, Wisconsin, *That '70s Show* focused on the coming of age of its young stars, led by Topher Grace and Laura Prepon as young lovestruck Eric and Donna, and breakout cast member Ashton Kutcher as the airheaded Kelso. Along with their friends and parents, they experience for the first time much of what is now looked back upon as a decade of kitsch: disco music, *Star Wars* obsessions, early video games, and marijuana use (surprisingly,

the teenagers would often sit around the table quite obviously high).

An unexpected hit for the Fox network, the show ran for eight seasons, with a variety of cast changes and additions as well as a slowing of its own timeline. A short-lived UK version for ITV titled *Days Like These* was seen in 1999. **SL**

Classic episode

Dine & Dash | *Season 3, episode 13*. Kelso is in the money so invites his friends out for a slap-up lobster dinner. He expects them all to run away without paying the bill, and he is the first to dash. Payback comes the next day.

⊘ Will Mila Kunis succumb to the charms of Ashton Kutcher? Probably not.

Goodness Gracious Me

Comedy | UK | 1998–2014

Goodness gracious, how audacious

Cast | Sanjeev Bhaskar, Meera Syal, Kulvinder Ghir, Nina Wadia, Dave Lamb
Original broadcaster | BBC Two
For fans of . . . | *The Fast Show* (1994), *The Kumars at Number 42* (2001)

The theme tune to *Goodness Gracious Me* had once been a hit in the UK singles chart for Peter Sellers (playing an apologetic Asian alongside the sophisticated Sophia Loren). Rearranged by Nitin Sawhney, the tune took on an air of ironic authenticity that matched perfectly the attitude of the show. The first ever British-Asian sketch comedy, *Goodness Gracious Me* hit the ground running with a scene that mocked the English habit of getting drunk and going into an Indian restaurant to be as rude and obnoxious as possible. Here at last was a comedy written and performed by second-generation British Asians who encouraged the audience to laugh with them, not at them.

It wasn't aggressive or wildly political, but it had something to say about post-colonial British culture that wasn't being said anywhere else. It was also inclusive: viewers saw the archetypes of snobbery in the Kapoors, who insisted their name was "Cooper" and tried to out-English their neighbors; the Bhangra Muffins were like any other teens trying to mimic US rap culture, but this time interspersed with words they'd learned at home from their parents; and we identified with the son whose boastful Indian father insisted that every great Western invention actually came from India.

Sanjeev Bhaskar and Meera Syal continued the cross-cultural comedy with *The Kumars at Number 42*, a pastiche chat show in which Sanjeev Kumar interviews celebrities in the front room of his house, with his family interjecting and embarrassingly hilarious results. **JS**

Dinnerladies

Comedy | UK | 1998–2000

Serving bittersweet moments and belly laughs

Cast | Victoria Wood, Julie Walters, Anne Reid, Thelma Barlow, Andrew Dunn, Duncan Preston, Shobna Gulati, Maxine Peake, Celia Imrie
Original broadcaster | BBC One
For fans of . . . | *Victoria Wood: As Seen on TV* (1985)

British comedian, writer, and actor Victoria Wood wrote, starred in, and coproduced this sitcom gem set in a work canteen. Although Wood's role, as deputy manager Bren, was central, she formed part of a large ensemble of experienced actors and rising stars, a familiar Wood formula that she used in other shows. Many of the lead and supporting roles in *Dinnerladies* were performed by regulars in the popular ITV soap *Coronation Street* (1960), a slice of working-class life in Manchester, where *Dinnerladies* was also set, while other roles were played by Wood's regular collaborators, such as Celia Imrie (who played human resources manager and soft southerner Philippa), Duncan Preston (handyman Stan), and Julie Walters (Bren's fanciful, flatulent mother Petula, who lived in a caravan behind a gas station).

Wood's *As Seen On TV* sketch show from 1985 had included short fly-on-the-wall documentaries about tragicomic figures, and *Dinnerladies* occasionally mined the same seam. This was often seen in episodes about Bren's difficult relationship with Petula, whose unpredictability continually thwarted Bren's chance of happiness. Other poignant moments included the time Bren's blossoming romance with canteen manager Tony was threatened by his treatment for cancer, and when the mother of an abandoned baby was revealed to be a member of the team. As in many of the best British comedies, laughter and heartbreak often ran hand in hand. **JS**

Charmed

Fantasy/Horror/Sci-Fi | USA | 1998–2006

The power of three will set you free

Cast | Holly Marie Combs, Alyssa Milano, Shannen Doherty, Rose McGowan, Brian Krause, Dorian Gregory, Julian McMahon, Drew Fuller, Kaley Cuoco
Original broadcaster | WB
For fans of . . . | *Buffy the Vampire Slayer* (1997)

From TV impresario Aaron Spelling came *Charmed*, a San Francisco-set series focusing on the Halliwell sisters—Prue (Shannen Doherty), Piper (Holly Marie Combs), and Phoebe (Alyssa Milano)—who possessed the "power of three," secretly protecting the world from evil and juggling magical adventures with everyday woes. Their *Book of Shadows* was a constant resource, as was their guardian angel "Whitelighter"—later Piper's husband—Leo (Brian Krause). Phoebe's troubled relationship with half-demon Cole (Julian McMahon) provided years of additional dramatic developments.

Doherty departed under a cloud of controversy at the end of the third season and was replaced by half-sister Paige (Rose McGowan). The show provided a series conclusion with the seventh season finale, *Something Wicca This Way Goes . . .?* but when it was renewed for one more year thanks to fan outcry, season eight brought fledgling witch Billie (Kaley Cuoco) and another finale, "Forever Charmed."

The impact of *Charmed* on pop culture and academia was far-reaching, and the show had a reputation for representing a new era in female empowerment on TV. It also inspired later witchcraft-influenced series such as *Hex* (2004), *American Horror Story* (2011), and *The Originals* (2013). Long after its conclusion, the show continued to rank highly in on-demand and streaming services, enchanting new viewers every year with its blend of magic and melodrama. Plans for a reboot have failed to weave the same spell. **ATB**

Classic episode
All Hell Breaks Loose | *Season 3, episode 22.*
The truth about the Halliwells' magical powers becomes public knowledge. Time must be turned back to restore their secret, and one of the sisters must make a tragic sacrifice.

◉ (L–R) Alyssa Milano, Shannen Doherty, and Holly Marie Combs as the Halliwell sisters—their mother always told them they were special.

Sex and the City

Comedy | USA | 1998–2004

Are you a Carrie, a Miranda, a Samantha, or a Charlotte?

Cast | Sarah Jessica Parker, Kim Cattrall, Kristin Davis, Cynthia Nixon   **Original broadcaster** | HBO
Awards | 7 Emmys, 8 Golden Globes   **For fans of . . .** | *Desperate Housewives* (2004), *Girls* (2012)

Four single women facing the trials of living and dating in New York City. It's a simple premise, but *Sex and the City* ("SATC"), relishing the freedom provided by a cable network, added envelope-pushing spice and created a phenomenon. Created by Darren Star, and based on Candace Bushnell 's columns in the *New York Observer*, the series centered on the strong friendship between the four women: columnist and narrator Carrie (Sarah Jessica Parker), sex-mad Samantha (Kim Cattrall), romantic Charlotte (Kristin Davis), and work-focused Miranda (Cynthia Nixon). They talked candidly about sex, men, relationships, and friendship, including with gay men. There were quite a few heterosexual men along the way, the most significant of whom was

Chris Noth's Mr. Big, Carrie's on-off paramour. One very important character was New York City itself.

The show had a huge impact on fashion and popular culture of the time. Manolo Blahnik shoes became a household name and Cosmopolitan cocktails the drink of choice for the savvy urban woman. The show also led to two movies. **KB**

Classic episode
Ex and the City | *Season 2, episode 18*. Carrie tries to be friends with her ex, Mr. Big, and brings season two to a close by telling him "Your girl is lovely, Hubble," a quote from the Streisand–Redford romance *The Way We Were*.

◉ Willie Garson (Stanford), Parker (Carrie), Davis (Charlotte), Cattrall (Samantha), and Nixon (Miranda).

Who Wants to Be a Millionaire

Game show | UK | 1998–2014

Ask the audience—phone a friend—win a fortune

Cast | Chris Tarrant (UK), Regis Philbin (USA) **Original broadcaster** | ITV
Award | 1 BAFTA **For fans of . . .** | *The $64,000 Question* (1955), *The Million Pound Drop* (2010)

Who Wants to Be a Millionaire was a huge success because it combined a simple format with a life-changing prize. Contestants had to answer only fifteen multiple choice questions correctly to win the top prize—£1 million. It was presented by Chris Tarrant, who was a supportive host, encouraging those in the hot seat and willing them to win. Contestants were helped by three lifelines: ask the audience for their opinion on an answer; remove two of the four possible answers; and phone a friend.

There were two hurdles to overcome in order to reach the money ladder. First, contestants had to get on the show. Instead of the traditional quiz show audition, there was a premium rate telephone line to call—which funded the prizes on offer. Once past this obstacle, it was necessary to win a "fastest finger first" round against nine other contestants: the fastest person to answer the question correctly got the chance to play for the money. It was an instantly successful format, and eventually Judith Keppel became the first of the show's millionaires (her £1 million question was which English king was married to Eleanor of Aquitaine). *Who Wants to Be a Millionaire* was a hit around the world, notably in the United States and India, where it became the inspiration for the Academy Award-winning movie *Slumdog Millionaire* (2008). Some countries tweaked the format, but the core attraction remained the same: the biggest cash prize on TV. **WH**

⊙ *Who Wants to Be a Millionaire* host Chris Tarrant (right) made it all seem so easy.

Cupid

Comedy | USA | 1998–99

The god of love and Jeremy Piven were a match made in Chicago

Cast | Jeremy Piven, Paula Marshall, Jeffrey D. Sams, Paul Adelstein
Original broadcaster | ABC
For fans of . . . | *Moonlighting* (1985), *Miss Match* (2003)

Many screenwriters have had their heart broken by a TV network canceling their show, but Rob Thomas was doubly unfortunate in having his smart, romantic comedy *Cupid* canned twice by the same network.

Jeremy Piven starred as Trevor Hale, a charismatic man who believed he was Cupid, the Roman god of love, exiled to Earth (and more specifically, to a mental hospital in Chicago). After telling his psychologist Claire Allen (Paula Marshall) that his only way back to Mount Olympus was by uniting one hundred couples, she agreed to help him in the hope that acting out his mission would aid his recovery. Trevor found most of his targets at the bar where he worked and at Claire's relationship therapy group, but while his matchmaking attempts were largely successful, his aim wasn't always true.

What may sound a corny concept on paper was lifted by smart writing and acting. Piven stole the show, though Marshall's flirtatious crosstalk also provided lots of laughs. The inspired plotting ensured the stories didn't always go as the audience expected.

While well received by critics, the show fared less well with viewers and was canceled after fifteen episodes. Piven went on to star in the comedy drama *Entourage*, while Thomas created the critically acclaimed whodunit *Veronica Mars*, after which he rebooted *Cupid*, again for ABC, in 2009. But this revival, filmed in New York and featuring a new cast, was also short-lived, with only six episodes actually aired. **SO**

The Royle Family

Comedy | UK | 1998–2012

Watching television through a thick fug of cigarette smoke

Cast | Ricky Tomlinson, Sue Johnston, Caroline Aherne, Craig Cash, Ralf Little, Jessica Hynes, Liz Smith
Original broadcaster | BBC One
Awards | 4 BAFTAs
For fans of . . . | *Brookside (1982), The Office* (2001)

Caroline Aherne had been a member of *The Fast Show* (1994) team and had kept viewers on the edge of their seats with her portrayal of an elderly chat show host, Mrs Merton. Writing, directing, and starring in *The Royle Family*, she subverted the whole notion of the sitcom with a documentary-style approach. Long pauses in the dialogue were actually scripted, as were the family's interactions with the TV—*Gogglebox* style. Whole episodes went by without major incident and the drama, what there was of it, mainly came from the everyday nonsense that the family said to one another to pass the time: Jim's outrage at a telephone bill; what Dave and Denise had for tea; how their neighbor Cheryl's diet was going; whether Anthony's vegetarian girlfriend could eat wafer-thin ham.

Ricky Tomlinson and Sue Johnston had already played husband and wife in the soap opera *Brookside*, and here they consolidated their unofficial roles as British TV's most believable couple. The guest cast consisted of familiar faces from soap operas and other sitcoms, such as *Coronation Street*'s Geoffrey Hughes as Jim's friend Twiggy, and the younger cast included early roles for Jessica Hynes as dumpy Cheryl from next door and Sheridan Smith as Anthony's girlfriend Emma. Barbara's mother, played by Liz Smith, would often visit the Royle household. In a heartbreaking special episode, she spent her last months in a spare bed erected at the back of the living room. A sublime, subtle sitcom that drips in Northern humor and pathos. **JS**

Manchester's TV-fixated family: (L–R) Aherne (Denise), Cash (Dave), Tomlinson (Jim), Little (Anthony), Johnston (Barbara). ❷

Sports Night

Comedy/Drama | USA | 1998–2000

This workplace sitcom about making television heralded a new golden age for American TV

Cast | Josh Charles, Peter Krause, Felicity Huffman, Joshua Malina, Sabrina Lloyd, Robert Guillaume
Original broadcaster | ABC **Awards** | 3 Emmys **For fans of . . .** | *The West Wing* (1999), *30 Rock* (2006)

After finding success with *A Few Good Men* (1992) on Broadway and *The American President* (1995) for Hollywood, Aaron Sorkin wrote *Sports Night* for television, a workplace sitcom about making a sports-centered news show on cable. Despite critical applause, the show struggled to find an audience and was canceled after two seasons, freeing Sorkin to work on his next project—*The West Wing* (1999).

Sports Night featured what would become hallmarks of Sorkin's TV writing—whip-fast banter, competing conversations, and the so-called "walk and talk," when characters converse while moving through a set. The show focused on the relationships between the main characters, especially the two anchors, Dan Rydell (Josh Charles) and Casey McCall (Peter Krause), their producer (Felicity Huffman), the show's managing editor (Robert Guillaume), and the network brass who regularly interfered with the show's production. *Sports Night* was infused with its characters' love of sports reporting and the writers' clear affection for—and frustration with—the process of producing content for television. **AP**

Classic episode

Quo Vadimus | *Season 2, episode 22.* The show is at risk of being canceled as the station faces closure, freeing the crew to consider what their lives would be like without *Sports Night.* Then a mysterious buyer appears.

ⓐ Peter Krause (Casey), Felicity Huffman (Dana), and Robert Guillaume (Isaac) in an episode from 1998.

Will & Grace

Comedy | USA | 1998–2006

Where there's a Will there's a Grace

Cast | Eric McCormack, Debra Messing, Megan Mullally, Sean Hayes   **Original broadcaster** | NBC
Awards | 16 Emmys   **For fans of . . .** | *Gimme Gimme Gimme* (1999)

Centered on the relationship between gay lawyer Will Truman (Eric McCormack) and Grace Adler (Debra Messing), a Jewish, straight, interior designer, the sitcom *Will & Grace* focused on the stereotypical ups and downs of dating, marriage, divorce, and casual sex experienced by four seemingly disparate New Yorkers. Continually threatening to steal the limelight from the title characters are their friends Karen Walker (Megan Mullally), a rich socialite, and Jack McFarland (Sean Hayes), a struggling gay actor/singer/dancer who has numerous other brief careers and boyfriends.

All four stars won an Emmy for their performances, making *Will & Grace* one of only three sitcoms to achieve this feat. Since the final episode aired, the show

has been credited with improving public opinion of the LGBT community. In 2014 the Smithsonian Institution added an LGBT history collection to their museum, which included items from *Will & Grace*. Curator Dwight Blocker Bowers stated that the sitcom used "comedy to familiarize a mainstream audience with gay culture" that was "daring and broke ground" in US media. **RP**

Classic episode
A.I.: Artificial Insemination | *Season 4, episode 25*.
When Grace misplaces the sperm sample, she decides to try to get pregnant the old-fashioned way: by having sex, with Will. Jack quits acting, but has a rethink when he is "visited" by Cher.

◉ (L–R) Emmy award winners Sean Hayes, Eric McCormack, and Debra Messing.

Bad Girls

Soap opera | UK | 1999–2006

Bribery, corruption, rape . . . and that's just the screws

Cast | Dannielle Brent, Jack Ellis, Helen Fraser, Linda Henry, Mandana Jones, Claire King, Simone Lahbib, Debra Stephenson
Original broadcaster | ITV
For fans of . . . | *Orange Is the New Black* (2013)

Bad Girls was not the first UK TV show to be set in a women's prison—*Within These Walls* in the mid-1970s was the first—but it owed much to Australia's *Prisoner* (aka *Prisoner: Cell Block H*, 1979) because it focused on the inmates rather than on the prison officers. One of the show's greatest strength is that it is that rare thing: a female-centered drama, with the creators (Maureen Chadwick, Eileen Gallagher, and Anne McManus) and the majority of its writers and cast all being women. It is also dramatic—sometimes melodramatic—harrowing, and occasionally humorous, with a strong emotional content. There are heroes and villains on both sides of the bars: prison officer/governor Jim Fenner (Jack Ellis) is more of a criminal than most of the woman incarcerated. *Bad Girls* is often thought-provoking as it reveals the backgrounds of characters and the relentless spirals of misfortune and bad judgment that have brought them to fall foul of the law, but it also packs a powerfully unpleasant punch in its consideration of inmates who are not far short of evil, such as child trafficker Natalie Buxton (Dannielle Brent).

There are few happy endings in Larkhall Prison's G Wing. Even the most sympathetic characters suffer, and it is definitely not a show for the faint hearted, with drugs, rape, torture, child abuse, murder, and decomposing corpses liberally strewn throughout eight seasons. No subject was off the table: lesbianism, bisexuality, and transsexuality—and the prejudices these attract—were all part of the show. **JR**

Classic episode
Mistaken Identity | Season 2, episode 5.
Claustrophobic new inmate Barbara Hunt is put in solitary confinement and murderer "Mad" Tessa Spall assumes her identity. Hysterical Barbara is left to suffer as Tessa spreads terror.

◬ Debra Stephenson (center front) plays top dog Shell Dockley.

Strangers with Candy

Comedy | USA | 1999–2000

A forty-something gets a second chance

Cast | Amy Sedaris, Stephen Colbert, Paul Dinello, Greg Hollimon, Deborah Rush, Larc Spies
Original broadcaster | Comedy Central
For fans of . . . | *Parker Lewis Can't Lose* (1990), *Rude Awakening* (1998)

Jerri Blank (Amy Sedaris) was forty-six years old, living with her catatonic father, stepmother Sara, and tormenting stepbrother Derrick, and starting her freshman year at Flatpoint High School after more than thirty years as "a boozer, a user, and a loser." But her rich life experiences didn't help her negotiate the pitfalls. She found herself turning snitch for the school principal, Onyx Blackman (Greg Hollimon), and concocting a game of elimination to secure the position of prom queen. Although Jerri was not the prettiest woman in school, and her fashion sense made her look like a golfer, she strove to gain the attention of the school's top hunks and coolest girls. In the end, though, she would always be forced to return to her real friends.

Creators and costars Amy Sedaris, Stephen Colbert, Paul Dinello—along with fellow writer Mitch Rouse— were inspired by old public information programs, often shown after school, in which people who'd made bad life choices returned to school to tell the kids what they had learned. Their version turned this morality on its head and gave it a cynical modern edge. In one episode, for example, Jerri learned that eating disorders can help a girl become an alpha female, while in a story from season three, she was surprised to discover that "the sexier you are, the more freedom you deserve."

Low ratings resulted in *Strangers with Candy* being pulled after three seasons, though a movie prequel was released in 2006, with most of the series cast reprising their roles. **JS**

All Stars

Comedy/Drama | Netherlands | 1999–2001

It's definitely the taking part that matters

Cast | Roeland Fernhout, Dirk Zeelenberg, Daniël Boissevain, Kees Boot, Raymi Sambo
Original broadcaster | VARA
Award | 1 Emmy
For fans of . . . | *Dream Team* (1997), *Playmakers* (2003)

Based on a 1997 film that was a box-office success in Dutch cinemas, *All Stars* comfortably straddled the line between drama and sitcom, and certainly did not shy away from big themes, such as homosexuality, immigration, and religion. Scriptwriter Jean van de Velde has remarked that having the viewpoints of a whole soccer team of characters to play with gave him the freedom to address a range of controversial themes in a humorous fashion.

The setup was this: seven friends have played since childhood for local amateur football team Swift Boys 8 with more enthusiasm than accomplishment. Each episode started with team captain Bram telephoning all the players to try to motivate them for the upcoming training session or match. The lives of the main characters off the field were just as fraught as on it: none of them was very successful at anything. Most of the narrative took place on and around the playing field, with a locker-room shower scene being another fixture.

The series was remade in Belgium, Germany, and Italy, and the first season especially garnered critical acclaim, with the pilot episode, "Alle Menschen werden Brüder" ("All Men Will be Brothers") winning an Emmy in the drama category. *All Stars* had its share of stereotypes and clichés, but these were as much a part of real life as twists of fate, and fortunately there was no shortage of them in the series, either. *All Stars* remained engaging and thought-provoking from its first broadcast to its thirty-ninth and final episode. **PW**

Family Guy

Animation | USA | 1999–present

Uncut, un-PC, and unsuitable for kids

Cast | Seth MacFarlane, Alex Borstein, Seth Green, Mila Kunis, Mike Henry, Patrick Warburton
Original broadcaster | Fox **Awards** | 5 Emmys **For fans of . . .** | *The Simpsons* (1989), *American Dad!* (2005)

Fox Television has become synonymous with "pushing the envelope," but *Family Guy* takes things one step further. The show can be juvenile and banal, but it tempers that with sophisticated meta humor and human insight. Gags can run long and be disconnected from the main plot, but they often mirror life.

The show centers around the well-meaning Griffin family: crass Peter, caring but slightly kinky Lois, wide-eyed son Chris, and awkward (and unnecessarily targeted for derision) daughter Meg. But the true heart of the Griffins is the double act of infant Stewie, an effete and slightly homicidal diapered tactician, and Brian, the family's double martini-swilling, aspiring novelist talking dog; with gadgets and time machines

galore, their adventures are always the most offbeat and fun. *Family Guy* was canceled after three seasons and revived several years later due to viewer demand and healthy DVD sales. With *The Simpsons*, it is the anchor of Fox's Sunday night "animation domination" block: one of the strongest and most stable viewing blocks of the US TV week. Giggity! **SL**

Classic episode

Back to the Pilot | *Season 10, episode 5*. In order to uncover the whereabouts of Brian's favorite bone, buried in the Griffins' back yard ten years previously, Stewie and Brian use the time machine to travel back to the series pilot.

⬥ Peter decides to home school his children in an episode titled *Foreign Affairs* from season 9.

Inspector Montalbano

Crime/Mystery | Italy | 1999–2013

A slow-burn Italian police drama with a drop-dead gorgeous setting

Cast | Luca Zingaretti, Cesare Bocci, Angelo Russo, Katharina Böhm
Original broadcaster | RAI   **For fans of . . .** | *Inspector Morse* (1987), *Midsomer Murders* (1997)

Few TV crime dramas make policing look as effortless as *Inspector Montalbano*. But the endless sunshine, alfresco lunches, and romantic liaisons are a beguiling foil for darker undercurrents at play in this absorbing series.

Based on novels by Andrea Camilleri, the series focuses on the police force of the fictional town of Vigàta in Sicily, led by police chief Salvo Montalbano. Over the course of each two-hour episode Montalbano tries to solve a typically elliptical mystery while keeping interfering mafiosi elements at bay. Luca Zingaretti, as the titular character, anchors the series, ably supported by a strong regular cast, with Angelo Russo providing comic relief as the bumbling officer Catarella. Salvo's personal life adds flavor to the mix, as his long-distance relationship with Livia (Katharina Böhm) is complicated by an almost constant temptation to stray. The beautiful Sicilian scenery and laid-back pace of life help to draw the viewer into the slow-burn storytelling.

The overseas success of the series led to a prequel, *The Young Montalbano,* showing Salvo as the newly appointed police chief. **SO**

Classic episode
The Goldfinch and the Cat (Gatto e cardellino) | *Season 4, episode 4.* Montalbano finds that seemingly unrelated incidents—a series of muggings, a missing doctor, and a father's attack on a hospital—are linked, but he can't see how.

◈ Luca Zingaretti (Commissario Montalbano) and Margareth Madè as Angelica Cosulichr, Montalbano's lover.

Angel

Fantasy/Horror/Sci-Fi | USA | 1999–2004

Good battles evil in the City of Angels

Cast | David Boreanaz, Alexis Denisof, Charisma Carpenter, J. August Richards, Andy Hallett, Amy Acker, Vincent Kartheiser, Julie Benz, James Marsters, Christian Kane **Original broadcaster** | The WB
For fans of . . . | *Buffy the Vampire Slayer* (1997)

Patrolling the streets of Los Angeles was a rare being—a vampire with a soul. Though he tried to live the life of a loner, he habitually attracted friends: a spoiled but penniless heiress trying her luck as an actress; an Irish demon plagued by visions; a disgraced English vampire hunter desperate for redemption; a former gangster compelled to hunt demons; a bright-green and stylish host of a demonic karaoke bar; and a mousy academic rescued from another dimension by the gang. Together, they formed the Angel Detective Agency, specializing in supernatural cases, many of which emanated from the powerful corporation Wolfram and Hart.

This surprisingly successful spin-off from the cult hit *Buffy the Vampire Slayer* (1997) transplanted Buffy's brooding boyfriend Angel to Los Angeles. An innovative twist on the Chandleresque gumshoe thriller, *Angel* was more adult than the dark but essentially teenage *Buffy*. What the loyal Buffy fans got was an insight into how messed up grown-ups are, too. Early episodes struggled to fulfill the promise that a Joss Whedon production would offer, but by its second season *Angel* was often hitting harder and more regularly than the series that spawned it.

The growing threat from demonic legal firm Wolfram and Hart became the primary focus in later seasons. *Angel*'s ultimate demise, after five seasons and strong ratings, appeared to be a political move at The WB, but a deliberately ambiguous ending left fans with hope of a future return. **JS**

Shooting the Past

Drama | UK | 1999

A love letter to photography

Cast | Lindsay Duncan, Timothy Spall, Liam Cunningham, Billie Whitelaw, Emilia Fox, Arj Barker, Blake Ritson
Original broadcaster | BBC Two
For fans of . . . | *The Lost Prince* (2003)

The staff at the Fallon Photo Library and Collection had high hopes when Mr. Anderson (Liam Cunningham), the representative of their new owners, arranged to pay them a visit. Anderson, however, was not happy. He couldn't understand why the library was still operational when he had relayed explicit instructions: the best photo collections were to be boxed up, the rest destroyed, and the entire building was to have been vacated before his arrival. The news hits the team hard, especially head of staff Marilyn Truman (Lindsay Duncan). It soon became clear that Anderson's message had been intercepted by the library's eccentric curator, Oswald Bates (Timothy Spall), in the vain hope that the problem would go away. Marilyn comes up with a plan to save not only the team's jobs but the heart of the collection, too. In order to do that, she needs to find out more about Mr. Anderson . . .

Stephen Poliakoff's love letter to photography managed to be sentimental without ever descending into mawkishness. Moreover, it had a confidence that, in a time when the editing of dramas was getting faster and faster, an audience could still be seduced by what amounts to a series of monologues over montages of static snapshots. In *Shooting the Past*, Poliakoff used Marilyn, narrating Oswald's collections, to beguile the frosty Anderson and draw him ever deeper into understanding the true value of the collection's ten million assets. It's a trick he successfully pulled off again with his next project, *Perfect Strangers* (1986). **JS**

The League of Gentlemen

Comedy | UK | 1999–2002

"We don't bother the outside world, we don't want it bothering us"

Cast | Mark Gatiss, Steve Pemberton, Reece Shearsmith
Original broadcaster | BBC2
Awards | 2 BAFTAs
For fans of . . . | *Little Britain* (2003)

Written by Jeremy Dyson, Mark Gatiss, Steve Pemberton, and Reece Shearsmith, *The League of Gentlemen* began as a stage show and a radio series before transferring to TV. Set in the remote northern town of Royston Vasey, all of the main residents are played by Gatiss, Pemberton, and Shearsmith, thus creating the impression of a place where inbreeding is rife. In fact, that is probably the least freaky and upsetting charge to be leveled at the demented and deranged residents.

Visitors to Royton Vasey might arrive with local cab driver Barbara, a post-op transsexual who is happy to describe her procedure in agonizing detail. There is a butcher's shop that specializes in "special meat," a vet who has an unfortunate track record of accidentally killing his patients, and a job center where the terrifying Pauline bullies the job seekers. An obsessive compulsive couple, the Dentons, keep prize toads and maintain strict rules about the use of their towels. Up on the moors is "a local shop for local people," run by Tubbs and Edward, a husband and wife responsible for a number of disappearances in the region. And passing through occasionally is a circus performer called Papa Lazarou with a collection of unwilling wives. *The League of Gentlemen* Christmas special took inspiration from the BBC's *Ghost Stories for Christmas* by taking the form of a portmanteau of connected short stories. A feature film in 2005 didn't quite capture the disturbing magic of the series, but the cast has gone on to create similarly chilling comedies in the form of *Psychoville* (2009). **JS**

Classic episode
Welcome to Royston Vasey | *Season 1, episode 1*. When a hitchhiker goes missing, a policeman calls at the local shop, run by in-bred husband and wife Edward and Tubbs. Panicked by the questions, Tubbs reveals "we didn't burn him!"

⊘ (L–R) Reece Shearsmith as Judee and Mark Gatiss as her cleaner Iris: "He has made me do things that would make a whore blush."

Queer as Folk

Drama | UK | 1999–2000

What to do when a one-night stand won't go away

Cast | Aidan Gillen, Craig Kelly, Charlie Hunnam, Denise Black, Antony Cotton, Carla Henry, Andy Devine
Original broadcaster | Channel 4   **For fans of . . .** | *Looking* (2014)

When fifteen-year-old schoolboy Nathan (Charlie Hunnam) takes his first steps onto the Manchester gay scene, one night spent with the handsome and successful executive Stuart (Aiden Gillen) convinces him that he is in love. But the only person Stuart loves is himself—and doesn't his best friend Vince (Craig Kelly) know it.

Written by *Doctor Who*'s Russell T. Davies, this drama about young people living in and around Manchester's gay quarter was uncompromising from the start: *Queer as Folk* depicted a lifestyle not previously seen on British TV, certainly not in such vivid detail. For some, the graphic scenes of same-sex intercourse and very strong language were too much, and in the British gay press, the series was attacked for not depicting a more positive view of homosexuality. *However, Queer as Folk* remains relevant precisely because Davies didn't pander to concerns about representation or heavy-handed issues; these weren't archetypes spouting queer propaganda, they were fully rounded characters with none of the edges smoothed off. **JS**

Classic episode
Episode 9 | February 15, 2000. Stuart is forced to come out to his parents when his nephew threatens to blackmail him. Their reactions are mixed. Vince quits his job and sets off into the sunset with Stuart—sort of.

⊙ (L–R) Craig Kelly, Aiden Gillen, and Charlie Hunnam: three's a crowd?

The West Wing

Drama | USA | 1999–2006

Right place, right time, right man

Cast | Martin Sheen, Allison Janney, Dulé Hill, Rob Lowe, Janel Moloney, Richard Schiff, Jimmy Smits
Original broadcaster | NBC **Awards** | 2 Golden Globes, 26 Emmys **For fans of . . .** | *House of Cards* (1990)

With fast dialogue, an accomplished cast, and an optimistic portrayal of top-level politics, this dramatization of the workings of the White House won over viewers easily. Creator Aaron Sorkin borrowed many elements from his movie *The American President* (1995), a romantic comedy about a widowed president. The president's chief of staff was Josiah Bartlet (Martin Sheen), promoted in *The West Wing* to the Oval Office. Sheen was intended to appear in only a few episodes, with the focus on his staff and in particular Sam Seaborn (Rob Lowe), but President Bartlet swiftly moved to the heart of the show. Despite the office setting, lead director Thomas Schlamme gave *The West Wing* a dynamic visual style, and its "walk and talk" approach was much parodied.

The show found a new direction in its sixth year when it began to focus on the campaigns to replace Bartlet, an angle it had only touched on before. Although it tended toward an idealized view of politics, *The West Wing* created positive role models for a new generation of politicians and a likable array of characters you wished really were running the White House. **WH**

Classic episode

Noël | Season 2, episode 10. This episode depicts the effects of post-traumatic stress disorder. We discover that Josh has been behaving erratically, shouting at the president, panicking at a Christmas party, and somehow injuring his hand.

◉ (L–R) Martin Sheen, Richard Schiff, and Rob Lowe in the emotional episode *Two Cathedrals*.

The Sopranos

Crime/Mystery | USA | 1999–2007

Meet Tony Soprano. If one family doesn't kill him . . . the other family will

Cast | James Gandolfini, Lorraine Bracco, Edie Falco, Michael Imperioli, Steven Van Zandt, Tony Sirico
Original broadcaster | HBO
Awards | 21 Emmys, 5 Golden Globes
For fans of . . . | *The Wire* (2002)

What would a gangster share with his therapist without incriminating himself? How would he encapsulate the pressure of managing people with limited intelligence and volatile temperaments? How might he describe his ambitious wife, high-flying daughter, listless son, or joyless mother, who claims she would do anything for her family—but once tried to have him killed?

Although *The Sopranos* invites obvious comparisons with *Goodfellas* (1990) and *Analyze This* (1999), it also had roots in the original Italian melodrama *I Claudius* (the clue is Tony's toxic mother, Livia). Family includes not only blood relatives but also those with whom Tony Soprano surrounds himself: the Italian-American foot-soldiers who fight against the stereotypes they perpetuate. Then there are the external pressures: the Feds who keep Tony's operations under surveillance.

David Chase's writing made fine use of HBO's lack of rigid scheduling to tell stories at the pace they required. Some episodes are like European art films, in the way they allow the audience to watch a character slowly fall apart, only to flinch at another instance of brutality. In truth, everyone is tainted by Tony's activities, including the viewer. We will him on to avoid being caught out—and if he drags us into another unbelievably violent act, we want it to be over swiftly. Often the best episodes are those in which nothing happens and viewers can breathe a hefty sigh of relief. **JS**

⊙ (L–R) Steven Van Zandt, James Gandolfini, and Tony Sirico in season seven.

Roswell

Fantasy/Horror/Sci-Fi | USA | 1999–2002

There's truth to every rumor

Cast | Jason Behr, Shiri Appleby, Brendan Fehr, Colin Hanks, Katherine Heigl, Majandra Delfino, Tess Haters
Original broadcasters | WB, UPN
For fans of . . . | *Buffy the Vampire Slayer* (1997), *The X-Files* (1993)

It is easy to see the appeal of a "Buffy" show with aliens. Showcasing the alienation felt by many high school students by making your central characters aliens, literally, may not be the most sophisticated metaphor. However, there was a lot of mileage in a group of outsiders who just wanted to fit in, despite being able to raise the dead.

Whereas *Buffy the Vampire Slayer* was an effortless blend of teen angst and vampire slaying, *Roswell*'s development was more uneasy. Season two saw the arrival of writer Ronald D. Moore (later to go on to *Battlestar Galactica*), who added more aliens to the mix. Lots more aliens. Gradually the love affair between alien king Max (Jason Behr) and normal girl Liz (Shiri Appleby) took a back seat to clone twins, shape-shifting assassins, intergalactic dynastic struggles, and invasions. Colin Hanks (son of Tom) briefly became very famous and then left to do a movie. This was problematic because he was integral to the cast, but the producers' solution of making his disappearance an alien conspiracy theory was a masterclass in how to deal with these situations. *Roswell*'s third series wrapped things up with a happy ending. The show's lasting gift to viewers was Dido. Her haunting theme song ("Here With Me") rapidly became a ubiquitous hit and is a rare case of a show's title music being better known than the program itself. *Roswell* also featured Katherine Heigl as alien diva Isabel: a demanding and prickly character with no sense of humor. **JG**

Classic episode
A Roswell Christmas Carol | *Season 2, episode 10.*
It's Christmas. Max struggles to use his healing power and avoid being exposed by those searching for him. Isabel is in love with Christmas. And it snows. In New Mexico.

◑ Human or alien?: (L–R) Tess Haters, Brendan Fehr, Jason Behr, Katherine Heigl.

Gimme Gimme Gimme

Comedy | UK | 1999–2001

Loud and crude and as offensive as possible

Cast | Kathy Burke, James Dreyfus, Beth Goddard,
Rosalind Knight, Brian Bovell, Doña Croll
Original broadcaster | BBC One
For fans of . . . | *Birds of a Feather* (1989),
Little Britain (2003)

The flatshare has always been a popular situation for a comedy, putting a couple of mismatched characters in a small set and hoping for drama. This abrasive series by Jonathan Harvey (*Beautiful Thing, Coronation Street*) brought together James Dreyfus as Tom Farrell, an overdramatic and vain out-of-work actor living in hope that his agent might find him work more fulfilling than being an extra on *Eastenders*, and his flatmate, Linda La Hughes (Kathy Burke), a myopic, grotesque sex-obsessed woman with few boundaries and a complete lack of self-awareness. Linda's approach to dating was unsubtle: pounce first and ask questions later. She was also not the brightest of women and often failed to notice that her love techniques tended to repel most prospective suitors.

Tom and Linda begin the series with a strange man in their kitchen. As the pair struggle with hangovers and try to piece together which of them has managed to bring the guest home the previous night, the stranger's wife (Beth Goddard) arrives and they discover that he is in fact their new neighbor, Jez (Brian Bovell). Dreyfus and Burke milked the single entendres out of each vile exchange, yet their equal delusions—that Linda was "drop-dead gorgeous" and Tom was a professional actor—gave them a strange vulnerability that prevented them from being totally hateful. Even so, viewers felt relieved that the pair had found one another, to prevent anyone else from being unhappy with either of them. **JS**

Big Brother

Reality | Netherlands | 1999–present

Who is watching you?

Cast | Bridget Maasland, Ruud de Wild, Rolf Wouters,
Daphne Deckers
Original broadcaster | Veronica
For fans of . . . | *Celebrity Big Brother* (2001),
I'm a Celebrity . . . Get Me Out of Here! (2002)

Inspired by the constant surveillance in George Orwell's novel *Nineteen Eighty-Four* (1949), *Big Brother* debuted in the Netherlands. Its phenomenal success there led to copies in Germany and Spain before the United States and the United Kingdom unveiled their own versions. Each country has its own distinct approach. In the United States, it was possible for the least popular housemate to win through clever strategy; the UK version resembled a Roman amphitheater with viewers voting in their millions to let each contestant know of their displeasure. Within its first few years, more than twenty countries had their own *Big Brother*.

The basic format remains the same: contestants are locked into a purpose-built compound under constant surveillance. They live together 24/7, undergo tasks set by an unseen Big Brother, and, away from the other housemates, they share their thoughts with the viewers via a diary room. Each week, they nominate the housemate they wish to be evicted until eventually a winner remains. Many *Big Brother* finals have seen young people voting in greater numbers than in their nation's general elections. This is not too surprising for a show that pumps out more broadcasting minutes than the news. However, the hysteria surrounding *Big Brother* has now passed its peak, and some territories have quietly closed it down. The more media-aware housemates always know how to play the game, but the machinations of Big Brother ensure that there are still plenty of surprises. **JS**

Futurama

Animation | USA | 1999–2003; 2008–13

Matt Groening's follow-up to The Simpsons *was an animated sci-fi show with nine lives*

Cast | Billy West, Katey Sagal, John DiMaggio, Lauren Tom, Phil LaMarr, Tress MacNeille, Maurice LaMarche
Original broadcaster | Fox **Awards** | 6 Emmys **For fans of . . .** | *Star Trek* (1966), *Community* (2009)

On New Year's Eve, 1999, slacker pizza delivery boy Philip J. Fry was accidentally cryogenically frozen for a thousand years. Upon waking, he discovered that New York was now New New York, and his only living descendent was an elderly scientist who ran an intergalactic delivery company. Fry spent the rest of the series trying to adjust to life in the distant future, a weird place where the wheel was obsolete, self-serve suicide booths lined street corners, and hell was run by a robot.

Futurama, Matt Groening's follow-up to *The Simpsons*, employed writing staff with advanced degrees and was notable for jokes that referenced math, science, history, science fiction, and broader geek culture, yet it was anchored by solid human stories.

Canceled after four seasons following low ratings, the show found new life in reruns and on DVD. Cable network Comedy Central then commissioned four movie-length episodes, sold initially on DVD and then broken up into shorter episodes to air on television. Following that success, it brought *Futurama* back to the air for two more seasons. **AP**

Classic episode
Jurassic Bark | *Season 4, episode 7.*
Fry discovers the fossilized remains of his beloved dog Seymour and remembers his former life. He also reflects on what will happen to his own fossilized remains in the future.

 Fry grabs a ride with Leela, captain of Planet Express.

Farscape

Fantasy/Horror/Sci-Fi | Australia/USA | 1999–2003

A space flight from danger leads to even greater jeopardy

Cast | Ben Browder, Claudia Black, Virginia Hey, Anthony Simcoe, Gigi Edgley, Paul Goddard, Lani John Tupu
Original broadcasters | Nine Network (Australia), Sci-Fi Channel (USA) **For fans of . . .** | *Stargate SG-1* (1997)

Farscape was set on the spacecraft *Moya*, in which the heroes were fleeing from sinister oppressors who called themselves the Peacekeepers. They were joined first by US astronaut John Crichton (Ben Browder), who had accidentally entered their dimension through a space wormhole, and then by a stranded Peacekeeper, Aeryn Sun (Claudia Black). The main story lines concerned the crew's efforts to evade capture and Crichton's search for a way back into his own time and space.

The original concept was developed by Hallmark Entertainment with Jim Henson Productions, which was responsible for styling the show, particularly the physical appearance of the numerous aliens. Unfortunately, *Farscape* was never as successful as the makers had hoped, and it was canceled after four seasons. However, by the time the producers reached this decision, the fifth season was well in progress and therefore provided the material for a three-hour miniseries, *Farscape: The Peacekeeper Wars* (2004). In 2014, it was reported that a movie version was in an advanced planning stage. **GL**

Classic episode
The Flax | *Season 1, episode 12*. When Crichton and Aeryn go flying together, they are caught in a net by space pirates. They wait for the *Moya* to rescue them, but the crew is distracted by other, more pressing, concerns.

⬆ *Moya*'s pilot, who was voiced by Lani John Tupu.

Terra Nostra

Historical drama | Brazil | 1999–2000

After landing in South America, star-crossed lovers endure years of separation

Cast | Thiago Lacerda, Ana Paula Arósio, Marcello Antony, Carolina Kasting, Ângela Vieira, Raul Cortez
Original broadcaster | Rede Globo
For fans of . . . | *Cabocla* (1979), *Os Imigrantes* (1981), *O Clone* (2001), *Da Cor do Pecado* (2004)

Terra Nostra (*Our Land*) shot the Portuguese-language telenovela—in which serial meets soap—into the twenty-first century. Paradoxically, it did so with a story set in the late-nineteenth century. Aboard a ship to Brazil, Italian emigrants Matteo (Thiago Lacerda) and Giuliana (Ana Paula Arósio) meet, make love, and moot marriage. But these best-laid plans go awry when one is taken to work on a coffee plantation, the other whisked to a millionaire's mansion. Will they be reunited? In 125 hours, you'll find out.

Written by Benedito Ruy Barbosa, *Terra Nostra* swapped soapy excesses for an elegant examination of class differences that was more akin to period drama. Epic production values, complemented by archive footage, and a soundtrack of traditional Italian songs, ensured that the sights and sounds matched the story.

The result was a smash in Italy and Spain—neither normally a noted consumer of such TV fare. The show's immigrant theme influenced the Arab-oriented *O Clone* (which, unluckily, debuted shortly after the terrorist attacks on the United States on September 11, 2001) and its success hastened Jayme Monjardim's progress to directing a mainstream movie (*Olga*, 2004). After seventy countries had bought *Terra Nostra*, broadcasters Globo commissioned a sequel. Initially reluctant to write more, Barbosa eventually came up with *Esperança* (2002), which told the tales of some of the other passengers on board the ship that had made the original journey across the Atlantic Ocean. **BM**

Yo soy Betty, la fea

Soap opera | Colombia | 1999–2001

One of the world's most popular telenovelas proves that beauty is only skin deep

Cast | Ana María Orozco, Jorge Enrique Abello, Ricardo Vélez, Natalia Ramírez, Luis Mesa
Original broadcaster | RCN Television
For fans of . . . | *Melrose Place* (1992), *Desperate Housewives* (2004)

Turning the traditional telenovela formula on its head, *Yo soy Betty, la fea* (*I Am Betty, the Ugly Girl*) followed the professional and personal tribulations of a "homely" but smart woman in the fashion world. Previously, telenovelas had tended to follow a strict, predictable pattern, showing exclusively beautiful people in romantic entanglements.

The series follows Beatriz "Betty" Pinzón Solano (Ana María Orozco), a trained economist, who works for a fashion design firm, EcoModa. Balancing comedy with traditional soap melodrama, the show creates empathy for its characters by never crossing the line into pure farce. Like the earlier US series, *Models Inc.* (1994), *Yo soy Betty, la fea* runs amok in the often ridiculous world of the fashion industry, but while plot lines often revolve around business intrigue, Betty's supposed ugliness remains a vehicle for emphasizing the moral side of the industry. For example, EcoModa is able to triumph on the catwalk by using Betty's circle of friends, called *el cuartel de las feas* (club of the ugly ones) as the models rather than traditional beauties. The series was a massive hit throughout the world during its initial run, gathering audiences of more than 80 million viewers. There have been eighteen international adaptations, including the highly successful US version, *Ugly Betty*.

Although the show was accused of abandoning its principles toward the end, when Betty is revealed as a secret beauty (all it took was a haircut, new glasses, and a good waxing, apparently), the show remained devoted to the principle that beauty is only skin deep. **LN**

Freaks and Geeks

Comedy | USA | 1999–2000

This sharply written comedy only lasted one season but it acquired cult status among fans and proved to be a springboard for a host of new talent

Cast | Linda Cardellini, John Francis Daley, James Franco, Samm Levine, Seth Rogan, Jason Segel
Original broadcaster | NBC
Award | 1 Emmy
For fans of . . . | *Futurama* (1999), *Party Down* (2009)

Critical darling *Freaks and Geeks* lasted only one season, with the network NBC airing only twelve of the eighteen episodes it produced. But the show immediately attracted a fervent fanbase and has since been recognized as one of the best television shows of the early 2000s, as well as serving as the breakthrough platform for future stars such as Linda Cardellini *(Scooby-Doo, ER)*, Rashida Jones *(The Office)*, James Franco *(Spider-Man)*, and others.

Taking place over the course of a school year in 1980, in the small town of Chippewa, Michigan, the show followed the lives of a sister and brother, Lindsay (Linda Cardellini) and Sam Weir (Samm Levine), as they navigated the pitfalls of high school. While Lindsay threw over her nerdy friends to start hanging out with the slackers, the "freaks" of the title, freshman Sam and his friends, the "geeks," tried to fit into a social system that made fun of them for their weird hobbies and interests. Both Lindsay and Sam struggle to reevaluate themselves in light of the adults they're becoming.

The stories were handled sensitively and with gentle humor, and the writing never made light of its young characters and their struggles. Lindsay's sweet romance with the earnest Nick (Jason Segel) was a particular highlight, as was Sam's first foray into dating. Although *Freaks and Geeks* was canceled before it hit its prime, it never had to struggle with flagging story lines. Audiences can watch eighteen near-perfect episodes that end on a lovely, if bittersweet, note. **AP**

Classic episode
Discos and Dragons | *Episode 18.* In the final episode of the series Lindsay is torn about whether to accept a scholarship to an academic summer camp, and Sam teaches bad-boy Daniel how to play Dungeons & Dragons.

ⓐ Lindsay (played by Linda Cardellini) gets to know Nick (Jason Segel) better in episode six.

Spaced

Comedy | UK | 1999–2001

Sitcom splattered with surrealism and recreational drug use

Cast | Simon Pegg, Jessica Hynes, Nick Frost, Julia Deakin, Mark Heap
Original broadcaster | Channel 4
For fans of . . . | *Black Books* (2000), *The IT Crowd* (2006), *The Big Bang Theory* (2007)

Procrastinating journalist Daisy (Jessica Hynes) and wannabe comic book artist Tim (Simon Pegg) keep bumping into one another in a run-down London café. They soon bond over their frustration at trying to find an apartment they can afford in the free ad newspapers. They hit upon the idea of posing as a couple to nab a strict "couples only" pad. The con works, and they move into Marsha's house. So far, so straightforward, as long as you remember they are not a couple.

Pegg and Hynes added to the mix a splattering of references to their favorite cult films, and director Edgar Wright ran with this idea, using Hollywood's tropes and techniques to great effect. With its fantasy sequences and otherworldliness (not to mention the inclusion of clubbing and recreational drug taking) the series resonated with the twentysomethings that it portrayed. In the process a house style was created, one that Pegg and Wright would hone for their trilogy of films *Shaun of the Dead* (2004), *Hot Fuzz* (2007), and *The World's End* (2013), all co-starring Nick Frost and capitalizing on the pairs' on-screen bromance.

Despite its critical and cult following, an oft-talked about third series never materialized, and a Fox remake was canned, mainly because the producers were not keen to involve its creators. However, there was the briefest of *Spaced* scenes in *Shaun of the Dead,* when Pegg and Frost's zombie-fighting gang bump into a rival gang featuring Hynes and do a double-take. **DJ**

Walking with Dinosaurs

Documentary | UK | 1999

Innovative and visually stunning prehistoric wildlife documentary

Cast | Kenneth Branagh
Original broadcaster | BBC One
Awards | 3 BAFTAs, 2 Emmys
For fans of . . . | *Life on Earth* (1979), *Primeval* (2007), *Frozen Planet* (2011)

Inspired by the movie *Jurassic Park,* producer Tim Haines wanted to create a wildlife documentary with a difference with *Walking with Dinosaurs.* While appearing to be a David Attenborough–style fly-on-the-wall nature series, with a narrative, it used animatronics and computer animation on top of real locations to re-create a visual and factual tour de force that enthralled audiences all over the world.

The show consulted more than a hundred scientists to ensure it was as accurate as possible, delving into little-explored areas, such as how dinosaurs urinated and mated. Haines said "None of these stories are testable—we will never know 100 percent whether they are right—but we were absolutely determined that nothing would be provably wrong." The series started in the Triassic period with Coelophysis and ended with the Tyrannosaurus of the Cretaceous period, and the extinction of the dinosaurs sixty-five million years ago. Not only did it deal with the history of the dinosaurs themselves but also with the world they inhabited, from the supercontinent of Pangea to landmasses resembling the continents of today.

The innovative "fake documentary" style has inspired other series, such as sister shows *Walking with Beasts* and *Walking with Monsters,* and more recently the BBC's *Planet Dinosaur.* While continuing research may eventually invalidate some of *Walking with Dinosaurs'* details, it remains a stunning work and a superb overview of the Age of Reptiles. **JR**

❯ Creatures such as the Placerias appeared to have been brought back to life in *Walking with Dinosaurs.*

The sight of the "Twin Towers" collapsing in New York City brought the Western world to a standstill. Reality hit home in other ways too, as TV schedules were filled with wannabes, hopefuls, and arch manipulators in *Big Brother*, *Survivor*, and the resurrection of the talent show. Though many predicted the end of linear TV with the arrival of online, on-demand services such as the BBC iPlayer, traditional broadcasting was still producing must-see television that reflected uncertain times. Both *24* and *Spooks* showed us a more cynical, brutal approach to the spy drama, using our fear of modern terrorism as a basis for entertainment.

2000s

◄ Kiefer Sutherland as Counter Terrorist Unit (CTU) agent Jack Bauer in *24* (2001), a series given credibility by the events of 9/11.

At Home with the Braithwaites

Drama | UK | 2000–03

A family wins the lottery and thinks all its troubles are over—but they're only just beginning

Cast | Amanda Redman, Peter Davison, Sarah Smart, Sarah Churm, Keeley Fawcett, Julie Graham
Original broadcaster | ITV
For fans of . . . | *Last Tango in Halifax* (2012), *Happy Valley* (2014)

Alison Braithwaite (Amanda Redman) was gifted a ticket for the European Lottery for her fortieth birthday and unexpectedly won £38 million. Fearing the effects this life-changing event would have on her family—husband David (Peter Davison) and daughters Virginia (Sarah Smart), Sarah (Sarah Churm), and Charlotte (Keeley Fawcett)—Alison chose to keep it a secret. She established a fake name and set up a charity to help people through her good fortune. This laudable enterprise was doomed to failure and by season two, the Braithwaites were installed in a country mansion.

Sally Wainwright showed continuing mettle as a first-class writer of offbeat, funny, and edgy television. Her scripts explored the effects of sudden wealth on a dysfunctional family and how it emphasized the fracture lines already there. David had been having an affair with his secretary, Virginia was obsessed with neighbor Megan (Julie Graham), Sarah embarked on a series of ill-advised relationships, while Charlotte was a quiet loner. Across the four seasons, relationships evolved, ended, were reconciled, or terminated in bitter acrimony, but Wainwright's subversive humor was ever present, and was perhaps at its freshest here. Redman and Davison proved their skill as TV leads, Davison especially showing his underrated range; further lead roles awaited him in the years to follow. *At Home with the Braithwaites* enjoyed consistently high ratings across its run, and the final episode left the family as much of the series saw them—arguing! **MW**

Classic episode
Season 1, episode 1. Alison Braithwaite wins the lottery, but keeps the £38-million win secret and founds a philanthropic foundation. In this first script, Sally Wainwright cleverly sets up a slow fall into human nature's reaction to wealth.

◈ A gun appears as family life takes a turn for the (even) worse.

My Family

Comedy | UK | 2000–11

The amusingly tormented life of a dentist and his family

Cast | Robert Lindsay, Zoë Wanamaker, Kris Marshall, Daniela Denby-Ashe, Gabriel Thomson
Original broadcaster | BBC One
For fans of . . . | *2point4 Children* (1991), *Outnumbered* (2007)

There is a popular train of thought that British TV comedy is best delivered short and sweet, but this isn't always the case. While shows such as *Fawlty Towers* (1975), *The Office* (2001), and *Miranda* (2009) are cited as prime examples of first-class comedy, they are rarely said to have defined their decade. *My Family* was a show that looked for easy laughs, but it was also successful in its own right. And for the millions who tuned in every week over eleven series, it was arguably the most successful British sitcom of the 2000s.

A traditional family sitcom, *My Family* was a show that wore its heart on its sleeve, confident in its ability to set up immediate laughs in comfortable surroundings. However, its longevity gave it additional strengths. The five-strong Harper family shared the decade with their viewers, and as our families grew and moved on, so did theirs. Lovable idiot son Nick became charmingly independent, and rebellious daughter Janey became a loving yet unconventional mother. However, it was youngest son Michael's story that made *My Family* one to remember. A program that spans more than a decade is very often the story of its youngest child. Viewers saw Michael grow from smart, geeky teenager to a young man at ease with his developing sexuality.

My Family appeals to a wide audience because although the situations are often exaggerated the relationships are not. It is a program that viewers can grow up with: a warm and reliable friend you can return to time and time again. **PPW**

The Corner

Crime/Mystery | USA | 2000

Pioneering crime show that sowed the seeds for what became The Wire

Cast | T.K. Carter, Khandi Alexander, Sean Nelson, Clarke Peters
Original broadcaster | HBO
Award | 1 Emmy
For fans of . . . | *The Wire* (2002)

The creator of this seminal six-part series was David Simon, a former crime reporter on the *Baltimore Sun* daily newspaper and the author of two books, one of which formed the basis of the long-running TV series *Homicide: Life on the Street* (1993).

Simon was delighted by the success of this venture, but felt that the show was constrained by the conventions of detective drama: a crime is committed, police seek and arrest the felon; the end. He wanted to create a more realistic product that clearly showed the deprivation of the poor in his home city, with the emphasis that, in real life, there are seldom clear-cut conclusions, and those stories that do have proper endings seldom have happy ones.

This show, the product of his labors, chronicled the lives of a family whose home was at the intersection of North Monroe (US Route 1) and West Fayette—the corner of the title—where there was a brisk open-air drug market. The police would bust the area from time to time, but the dealing stopped only for as long as the flashing blue lights were visible; as soon as they left, trade would resume as normal. All the characters had some involvement with drugs, whether as pushers, users, law enforcement agents, or merely the people who had to step over discarded needles on their way to and from low-paid blue-collar jobs.

The Corner was critically acclaimed but not a popular success until after its successor, *The Wire*, blazed its own trail and became a global phenomenon. **GL**

Survivor

Reality | USA | 2000–present

Outwit, outplay, outlast . . . and produce outstanding television

Cast | Jeff Probst
Original broadcaster | CBS
Awards | 7 Emmys
For fans of . . . | *The Amazing Race* (2001), *The Island with Bear Grylls* (2014)

A group of contestants marooned on a desert island, in a jungle, or at another exotic location compete against one another for the chance to win a million dollars—seems easy enough. However, *Survivor* is all about the complications, and for this reason it has achieved legendary status across the globe.

Hosted by Jeff Probst, each season features a different group of contestants: most often average Americans from all walks of life, occasionally celebrities staying under the radar, and sometimes cast members from previous seasons. The contestants are split into two (or more) "tribes" and given only a few bare essentials; it is up to the ingenuity, skill, and determination of the players to create shelter, to find food, and to survive against the odds. Various competitions and tests of stamina make or break the players, and their actions are judged by their peers. Over thirty-nine days, the number of contestants is whittled down until there is only one survivor.

Based on the Swedish reality series titled *Operation Robinson*, *Survivor* debuted to stellar ratings for CBS in 2000. The format has been utilized for versions in more than forty additional countries, including a brief run in the United Kingdom on ITV in the early 2000s. The original Swedish edition is also still running. A number of contestants of the US version have achieved TV fame (or notoriety, in the case of first season winner Richard Hatch, who later was jailed on tax evasion charges) due to their appearances on the show. **SL**

CSI

Crime/Mystery | USA | 2000–present

Sin never sleeps . . . in this show, it never even takes a nap

Cast | Ted Danson, Elisabeth Shue, George Eads, Marg Helgenberger, William Petersen, Laurence Fishburne
Original broadcaster | CBS
Awards | 6 Emmys
For fans of . . . | *Without a Trace* (2002)

Writer Anthony Zuiker's *CSI* franchise has created a programming phenomenon that is outliving each and every *Star Trek* incarnation and is currently beaten only by Dick Wolfe's *Law & Order*. It is a fairly standard idea: let the police find a crime and then wait for the crime scene investigators to solve it using forensic science. The series showcases the very latest technology and, although the scenes sometimes stretch the truth a little, the majority of the equipment used has its feet firmly grounded in reality. Throw in some of the most intelligent, complex scripts (*CSI* never treats its audience as idiots) and well-rounded characters and you have a success story. So much so that three spin-offs (*CSI: Miami*—10 seasons, *CSI: New York*—9 seasons, and the forthcoming *CSI: Cyber*) have each gained their own fierce followings independent of the parent show.

CSI has a successful revolving door of characters, which keeps the series refreshed and unique. (By the end of the 2014/15 series, no one from the first episode will be still around.) A brave example of this policy is the very first story, in which viewers are introduced to the world of crime and the CSI team through the eyes of Holly Gibbs (Chandra West) on her first day. Then the tables turn, Holly becomes the murder victim, and the team must find her killer. It was a clever move: to throw the audience off and say "this show is not quite what you think it is." The BBC did something similar with the character of Helen Flynn in the second episode of *Spooks* (2002)—but *CSI* did it better. **GR**

❯ In the season four episode "Jackpot," William Petersen as Gil Grissom investigates the discovery of a decapitated body.

Clocking Off

Drama | UK | 2000–03

*Ensemble drama following the workers
of a Manchester textile factory*

Cast | Sarah Lancashire, Christopher Eccleston,
Siobhan Finneran, Philip Glenister, Sophie Okonedo
Original broadcaster | BBC One
Awards | 2 BAFTAs
For fans of . . . | *Last Tango in Halifax* (2012)

Clocking Off was an ensemble drama par excellence,
with each episode following the life of a different
worker in Mackintosh textiles factory, from the lowliest
forklift truck driver to the millionaire business owner,
exploring issues of class, race, and wealth along
the way. With characters and themes interlinking
throughout the four seasons, each episode also stood
alone in its own right.

While the factory was the glue binding the
characters together, their lives were very different,
and the show effectively highlighted the often
stark contrasts between the roles people play in the
workplace and the reality of their private lives. Work
was a refuge and everyone had secrets they were
desperate to hide, from unhappy marriages leading to
misguided affairs, to criminal behavior, to alcoholism.

The cast was universally strong, and many of its
members have had significant careers since. Part of the
show's genius lay in giving each performer a chance
to shine in an individual episode, and this allowed a
wealth of strong characters throughout the series, even
in episodes where they made little more than cameo
appearances. Themes merged and wove throughout
interlinking stories, and a throwaway line in one scene
could later become the basis of an entire episode.

Writer Paul Abbott went on create to *State of Play*
(2003) and *Shameless* (2004), while the influence of the
show went on to be seen in later ensemble dramas,
such as *The Street* (2006) and *The Syndicate* (2012). **EB**

Black Books

Comedy | UK | 2000–04

*Surreal comedy in a bookshop that is
always "Closed"*

Cast | Dylan Moran, Bill Bailey, Tamsin Greig
Original broadcaster | Channel 4
Awards | 2 BAFTAs
For fans of . . . | *Father Ted* (1995), *Spaced* (1999),
The IT Crowd (2006)

One half of the creative team behind *Father Ted*,
Graham Linehan joined forces with comedian Dylan
Moran to craft a darkly hilarious comedy about Bernard
Black (Moran, in an extension of his own stage persona),
a belligerent drunk who hated the living soul of every
customer who entered his bookshop and was not
afraid to tell them so. Bernard's bad attitude with his
customers was hugely liberating, like a petulant child,
only drunk. Highly stressed accountant Manny (Bill
Bailey) came looking for *The Little Book of Calm*, but
after joining Bernard on a drinking binge he accepted
a job at the shop managing Bernard's account books.
Manny's optimistic enthusiasm for everything was
beautifully at odds with his new surroundings: a bleak,
untidy store that might also be home to an ever-
increasing pile of dead animals. Help came from Fran
(Tamsin Greig), Bernard's oldest/only friend, who ran a
craft shop next door. Although Fran appeared to be
the sensible one of the trio, she had a knack for finding
herself in cringe-making situations. Together, Manny
and Fran conspired to get the inebriate shopkeeper to
step outside and discover the world.

The guest cast read like a who's who of British
comedy at the turn of the twenty-first century, with
the likes of Nick Frost, Simon Pegg, Lucy Davis, Olivia
Colman, and Rob Brydon all making appearances. Like
its stablemate *Spaced*, there was always something a
bit *Twilight Zone* about the series, where logic seemed
to be a bendable force. **JS**

Queer as Folk

Drama | USA | 2000–05

This trailblazing drama chronicling the trials and tribulations of a group of gay friends in Pittsburgh, Pennsylvania, was vibrant, witty, and frank

Cast | Hal Sparks, Gale Harold, Randy Harrison, Michelle Clunie, Thea Gill, Scott Lowell, Peter Paige, Sharon Gless, Robert Gant, Jack Wetherall
Original broadcaster | Showtime
For fans of . . . | *Sex and the City* (1998), *Looking* (2014)

Adapted from the British show of the same name made by Russell T. Davies, *Queer as Folk* followed the antics of a group of gay friends in Pittsburgh. Michael (Hal Sparks) was a supermarket manager and a fan of comic books; Michael's best friend, and secret crush, Brian (Gale Harold) was a narcissistic advertising executive with a torrid sex life. One of Brian's conquests, seventeen-year-old Justin (Randy Harrison), fell in love with him, to Brian's unease. Brian was also the father of a baby boy, the product of a sperm donation to his friend Lindsay (Thea Gill) and her partner Melanie (Michelle Clunie). Acting as agony aunt to the gang was Michael's mother, Debbie (Sharon Gless), a gay rights campaigner who was more comfortable with her son's sexuality than he himself was.

Though the series followed many of the same plots as the British show, its longevity (eighty-three episodes over five seasons) enabled it to widen its range of characters and explore some new themes. It featured fairly explicit gay sex, tackled issues such as same-sex marriage, and included a plot about homophobia. Unlike its British counterpart, it also covered HIV.

In the character of Michael, *Queer as Folk* also mined the humor to be found in the comic-book geek. A world away from the stereotypes later seen in *The Big Bang Theory* (2007), Michael was a socially able adult who happened to like superheroes (during the course of the series, he opened a comic book store). Sparks effectively re-created Michael for a brief encounter with Spidey in a cameo role for *Spider-Man 2* (2004). **JS**

Classic episode
Bowling for Equality | *Season 2, episode 19.*
Michael is faced with a dilemma when he catches a friend making out with someone other than his regular partner. Meanwhile Debbie organizes a gay bowling team.

⬥ (L–R) Peter Paige (Emmett), Randy Harrison (Justin), and Gale Harold (Brian) in the US version of *Queer as Folk*.

Waking the Dead

Crime/Mystery | UK | 2000–11

A dedicated team of detectives solves a string of cold cases

Cast | Trevor Eve, Sue Johnston, Wil Johnson, Holly Aird, Claire Goose, Tara Fitzgerald
Original broadcaster | BBC One
Award | 1 Emmy
For fans of . . . | *Silent Witness* (1996)

Trevor Eve's performance as Detective Superintendent Peter Boyd was key to the success of *Waking the Dead*. Although it was an ensemble show, his skillful presence permeated this popular crime drama. Its plots may have been labyrinthine, but its stylish look and well-cast ensemble helped it log nine seasons.

The show was created by Barbara Machin and the pilot was broadcast in the fall of 2000. In this episode, Boyd mobilized his cold case team—profiler Dr. Grace Foley (Sue Johnston), DS Spencer Jordan (Wil Johnson), DC Mel Silver (Claire Goose), and forensic pathologist Dr. Frankie Wharton (Holly Aird)—into having a second attempt at cracking a five-year-old murder case. The pilot set the tone for the next nine series as Boyd's actions flushed out the killer but placed members of his team in danger. He flouted rules and was prone to explosive outbursts of temper, but Grace was always there to provide a soothing conscience.

Each series of *Waking the Dead* comprised between four and six individual stories. The plots were frequently dense, and the directing punchy and fast, but this did not deter viewers. By series four, the show was pulling in very high ratings and its place in the schedules was assured for years to come. *Waking the Dead* remained popular to the end, and it was felt by Trevor Eve that his show was canceled slightly ahead of its time. Only weeks after the final episode, Tara Fitzgerald headlined a spinoff, *The Body Farm*; it lasted one season, eight shy of *Waking the Dead*'s impressive run. **MW**

Deal or No Deal

Game show | Netherlands | 2000–present

Open a box, any box, and see if you've won a star prize or a pig in a poke

Cast | Noel Edmonds (UK), Howie Mandel (USA), Beau van Erven Dorens (Netherlands)
Original broadcaster | TROS RTL 4
For fans of . . . | *Who Wants to be a Millionaire* (1998), *Golden Balls* (2007)

Most game shows involve a certain amount of trivia knowledge or physical ability at the very least. *Deal or No Deal* relies on random luck, yet manages to ramp up the drama of the moment to often torturous levels.

The show began in the Netherlands and was originally the final round in the game show *Miljoenenjacht*, which translates as "Hunt for Millions." *Deal or No Deal* offers less money, but the format is very simple. A series of sealed boxes each contain a different sum of money, from the insignificant 1p to the life-changing £250,000 in the United Kingdom. The contestant chooses a box for themselves, and then has to open the rest one by one to reveal the amount of money within. After every few boxes an anonymous banker offers the contestant a sum of money to purchase their chosen box and stop them playing the game. The contestant must decide whether to take the offer (deal) or play on (no deal). The skill is in knowing whether to quit while you are ahead.

The show has now been exported around the world to more than seventy countries on every continent. Different countries have slightly different variations of the game, and over time extra elements have been added. For example, the opportunity to win prizes in a separate side game, or the introduction of an additional box offering the risky chance to double winnings or to lose everything. However, the show's success really stems from a deep human need: ultimately viewers want to know exactly what fate lies in that final box. **DJO**

◔ The "cold case" team reunited: (L–R) Trevor Eve (Peter Boyd), Holly Aird (Frankie Wharton), and Sue Johnston (Dr. Grace Foley).

Jackass

Reality | USA | 2000–02

Stupid, pointless, and just plain dangerous—hilarity guaranteed

Cast | Johnny Knoxville, Chris Pontius, Steve-O, Bam Margera, Ryan Dunn, Preston Lacy, Dave England
Original broadcaster | MTV **For fans of . . .** | *The Young Ones* (1982), *Beavis and Butt-Head* (1993)

Jackass roared onto screens in 2000, after producer Jeff Tremaine brought together a bunch of skateboarders who all had some pedigree in pointless, stupid stunts: Bam Margera and his crew were already the stars of a series of home-made skateboard videos, and Johnny Knoxville, Chris Pontius, and others had worked for a skateboard magazine. Completing the *Jackass* team was Tremaine's friend, film director Spike Jonze.

Over the course of three series, the boys bobbed for jellyfish, crashed golf buggies, skateboarded off a variety of structures, stapled their butts, and a thousand other eye-watering things, all in the name of gonzo entertainment. All this could have been incredibly crass and boorish, but, largely because the gentlemanly Knoxville and pals approached every stunt with the utmost sincerity, *Jackass* came across almost as heroic. The boys always looked like they were genuinely having fun, and their stunts were never vindictive. The joke was always on them, often very painfully so. This is why the *Jackass* formula has proved so difficult to replicate. **WM**

Classic episode
Episode 1 | April 12, 2000. The "poo cocktail" stunt, in which Johnny Knoxville is locked inside a portaloo full of human waste, is a mission statement for the entire series. You will laugh and squirm in equal measure.

⊘ Members of the extreme team: (L–R) Johnny Knoxville, Bam Margera, and Steve-O.

Malcolm in the Middle

Comedy | USA | 2000–06

Chaotic family life of a boy genius

Cast | Frankie Muniz, Bryan Cranston, Jane Kaczmarek, Christopher Masterson, Justin Berfield, Erik Per Sullivan
Original broadcaster | Fox   **Awards** | 7 Emmys   **For fans of . . .** | *The Simpsons* (1989)

The third of four (later five) boys, twelve-year-old Malcolm struggled to get attention in his chaotic and noisy family. Oldest brother Francis was sent away to military school and moved to Alaska. Older brother Reese was a bully and youngest brother Dewey was simply annoying, but developed into a musical prodigy later in the show. With an IQ of 165, Malcolm struggled to cope with being different, and even his parents, Lois and Hal, sometimes turned to him for moral support.

Unusually for a modern US prime-time sitcom, *Malcolm in the Middle* did not use a studio audience or laugh track. This allowed its young cast freedom to stretch their acting talents, and the show's writers to be more experimental with the format.

The show culminated in Malcolm's graduation from high school. In later seasons, the focus pulled away from him and on to the family as a whole; a fifth son, Jamie, was added in the fourth season. Both Bryan Cranston (later of *Breaking Bad*) and Jane Kaczmarek welcomed the chance to explore their comic talents in the show, becoming increasingly prominent in later seasons. **EB**

Classic episode
Bowling | Season 2, episode 20. This multiple Emmy Award–winning episode spoofs the movie *Sliding Doors* as parallel story lines see Hal or Lois take Malcolm and Reese bowling. Romance and a potential perfect game are all on the cards.

⬥ Frankie Muniz (Malcolm) in the middle, flanked by his brothers Justin Berfield (L) as Reese, and Erik Per Sullivan as Dewey.

Rejseholdet

Crime/Mystery | Denmark | 2000–02

Tense and stylish Nordic crime dramas took the world by storm in the 2000s, and Rejseholdet *from Denmark was one of the first*

Cast | Charlotte Fich, Waage Sandø, Mads Mikkelsen, Lars Brygmann, Trine Pallesen, Erik Wedersøe
Original broadcaster | D.R.1
Award | 1 Emmy
For fans of . . . | *Criminal Minds* (2005)

An early example of Nordic noir—predating *The Bridge* (2011), *Borgen* (2010), and *The Killing* (2011)—*Rejseholdet* (*Unit One*) featured an elite, mobile police unit that was sent into local police forces to investigate brutal and complex crimes. Their dedication bordered on obsession and often affected their personal lives.

The first of the four series kicked off with the introduction of a tough new leader to the tight-knit team: ambitious Ingrid Dahl (Charlotte Fich), temporarily promoted from internal affairs. There were hints that her promotion was the result of positive discrimination, but she soon earned her spurs, in spite of the gruff ire of her colleague Ulf (Erik Wedersøe). Ingrid took the only other woman on the team—Gaby (Trine Pallesen)—under her wing.

Evocatively shot in different parts of Denmark (it also visited Sweden, Iceland, Germany, and the United Kingdom), the stories were based on real-life crimes, including murders, kidnaps, and sex trafficking. Political corruption was never far from the surface, and occasionally erupted with devastating consequences for the unit. The complicated relationships between the characters ran through all four series, and at times adversely affected the investigations.

Although *Rejseholdet* featured a strong ensemble cast, many of whom went on to work on other noir dramas, Mads Mikkelsen, now best known as Hannibal Lecter in the series *Hannibal* (2013), stood out as the brilliant yet frustrated detective Allan Fischer. **SJG**

Classic episode
Assistancemelding A-17/00 | *Season 1, episode 7.*
Fischer's family holiday on the North Sea coast is ruined when the local police receive an anonymous tip-off that a homicide has been committed in the neighborhood.

◉ Mads Mikkelsen, who played *Rejseholdet*'s Allan Fischer.

Coupling

Comedy | UK | 2000–04

This inspired comedy about a group of thirty-somethings had truth running through its veins

Cast | Jack Davenport, Sarah Alexander, Gina Bellman, Richard Coyle, Kate Isitt, Ben Miles
Original broadcaster | BBC Two
For fans of . . . | *Joking Apart* (1991), *Friends* (1994), *Cold Feet* (1998)

Coupling told the funny, filthy story of Susan (Sarah Alexander) and Steve (Jack Davenport), their developing relationship, and their friends' self-interested attempts to support them. It had all the hallmarks of writer Steven Moffat's work, in particular, complex plotting and autobiographical content.

One of Moffat's previous sitcoms, *Joking Apart*, was inspired by the breakup of his marriage, and it was no coincidence that the protagonists in *Coupling* had the same first names as Moffat and his producer and new partner Sue Vertue. The characters around Susan and Steve drove much of the comedy. Jeff (Richard Coyle) was eccentric, unlucky in love, and full of unhelpful advice; Patrick (Ben Miles), Susan's ex, was confident and obscenely well-endowed; Sally (Kate Isitt) was a vain beautician terrified of getting older; and Jane (Gina Bellman), Steve's ex, verged on being unstable. The two trios represented the id, ego, and superego of a typical human being.

The show ran for four years and won a prestigious Silver Rose at the Rose d'Or festival in Montreux. It suffered from comparisons to the American sitcom *Friends*, although the similarities didn't go much beyond an attractive cast of three men and three women aged around thirty.

Coupling's ingenious plotting and frank attitude to sex worked alongside great jokes. The strong cast led by Davenport and Alexander delivered a painfully humorous show. **WH**

Gilmore Girls

Comedy | USA | 2000–07

A heartwarming screwball comedy about mothers and daughters

Cast | Lauren Graham, Alexis Bledel, Edward Herrmann, Kelly Bishop, Melissa McCarthy
Original broadcaster | The WB
Award | 1 Emmy
For fans of . . . | *Dawson's Creek* (1998), *Bunheads* (2012)

Following an unplanned pregnancy at age sixteen, Lorelai Gilmore (Lauren Graham) ran away from her chilly, privileged life to raise her daughter, Rory (Alexis Bledel), on her own terms. Sixteen years later, Lorelai had it all: a comfortable home in a quirky New England town, a great job, and a quietly brilliant daughter with ambitions to go to Harvard. When Rory was accepted at an expensive prep school, however, Lorelai was forced to approach her estranged parents, Emily and Richard (Kelly Bishop and Edward Herrmann), for financial help. Her parents agreed to loan her the money, providing she and Rory start coming to dinner once a week.

Gilmore Girls was a critically lauded hit for its young network, The WB. For seven years audiences tuned in to watch Lorelai anxiously bounce off her parents while her daughter forged a deep relationship with them. *Gilmore Girls* also featured one of recent TV's great "will they, won't they" relationships in the palpable chemistry between Lorelai and Luke Danes (Scott Patterson), the grumpy diner owner with a heart of gold, who kept her in coffee and burgers. *Gilmore Girls* also provided a significant early role for Melissa McCarthy (*Bridesmaids*, *The Heat*), who played Lorelai's best friend.

Following the departure of *Gilmore Girls'* creator Amy Sherman-Palladino after the sixth season, the show suffered a drop in quality and was finally canceled. In the seven years it was on the air, though, the show never moved away from the warm lived-in relationships at its heart. **AP**

Curb Your Enthusiasm

Comedy | USA | 2000–present

Everyone has a bit of Larry David, but most people keep it on the inside

Cast | Larry David, Cheryl Hines, Jeff Garlin, Susie Essman
Original broadcaster | HBO
Awards | 2 Emmys, 1 Golden Globe
For fans of . . . | *Seinfeld* (1989), *Extras* (2005)

In *Curb Your Enthusiasm*, *Seinfeld* creator Larry David plays a fictionalized version of himself, and while not a mockumentary, the show is very much shot as if the events are being documented rather than created. This real-life element is enhanced by the lack of a laughter track, and it also helps that all the dialogue is improvised by the cast. This adds a spontaneity and truth to the performances and the humor.

Curb Your Enthusiasm is certainly one of the funniest comedies to have been made in the United States in the last fifteen to twenty years. Although it can take a while to adjust to the style of humor, it is worth getting in tune with Larry David because once you do, you won't be able to stop laughing. The show focuses on the minutiae of life that annoy Larry in everyday situations—having to mingle at a dinner party, for example—but where most people suffer in polite and embarrassed silence through awkward social situations, Larry openly rants and raves and says all the things we wish we could say. These rants lead to more severe social awkwardness and embarrassment, usually felt worst by Larry's long-suffering wife, Cheryl.

In truth it is easy to see why the critically acclaimed *Curb Your Enthusiasm* is so popular: we all want to be Larry David. He fights the fight against silly social rules so that we don't have to, and it's all done in the most brutally funny way. **LH**

◗ Susie Essman and Larry David improvise in season six.

Alias

Action/Adventure | UK | 2001–06

"Only one other person knows the truth"

Cast | Jennifer Garner, Michael Vartan, Ron Rifkin, Bradley Cooper, Carl Lumbly, Merrin Dungey
Original broadcaster | ABC
Award | 1 Golden Globe
For fans of . . . | *Lost* (2004), *Chuck* (2007)

Sydney Bristow was a girl with a secret: by day she was a college student, by night she was working for a black ops division of the CIA—which turned out not to be the CIA, but an international terrorist organization bent on world domination. So Sydney became a double agent for the real CIA, trying to take down the evil fake CIA while also trying to come to terms with the death of her fiancé as well as the ridiculous commotions caused by her roommate, Francine. And that was just the pilot episode. *Alias* really burned through plot like every episode was a season finale.

Thankfully, creator/producer J.J. Abrams (*Lost*, *Star Trek*, *Star Wars*) kept a tight hand on the reins, so the show never veered too far into ridiculousness. *Alias* was the seminal Abrams series, containing all the motifs that carried through his subsequent works, including red spheres, bizarre machinery, numerology, crazy twists, and weekly what's-in-the-box mysteries, allowed to breathe here in a series that was designed around them. As Sydney, Jennifer Garner walked a tightrope between emotional femininity and hard-nosed spy.

The show ultimately proved Abrams' rule that once you open the box, the contents can never be as wonderful as the expectations, and *Alias* zoomed off in ever more ludicrous directions from the third season onward. However, the show can never be accused of being boring; stunt casting (Ricky Gervais as a terrorist) and increasingly zany plots continued until the oddly satisfying finale. **LB**

A Grande Família

Comedy | Brazil | 2001–14

Blue-collar comedy, Brazilian-style

Cast | Marco Nanini, Marieta Severo, Pedro Cardoso, Guta Stresser, Lúcio Mauro Filho
Original broadcaster | Rede Globo
For fans of . . . | *Bread* (1986), *Roseanne* (1988), *The Simpsons* (1989), *Os Normais* (2001)

Until *A Grande Família* (*The Big Family*) and *Os Normais* (*The Regulars*) came along in 2001 and kickstarted a trend for comedy, the soapy telenovela dominated Brazil's schedules. Although *Normais* lasted for only three seasons, *Família*, reported *Variety*, became "the third most popular regularly scheduled show on broadcast television, behind TV Globo's prime-time telenovela and its evening newscast *Jornal Nacional*."

Essentially, *Família* was about a lower-middle-class family struggling to make ends meet. At its head were Lineu Silva (Marco Nanini, star of 1999's telenovela *Andando Nas Nuvens*) and his beloved Nené (the much-garlanded Marieta Severo). Forever at odds with Lineu was his impish son-in-law Agostinho (Pedro Cardoso), an audience favorite. The family was completed by daughter Bebel (Guta Stresser) and teenage son Tuco (Lúcio Mauro Filho).

The animated opening titles led into the comic theme for that episode—ranging from pregnancies to pet stores, via time travel and kidnapping. All eventualities were faced, noted Severo, "with good humor, affection, solidarity, and understanding." The characters' on-screen chemistry was fueled by the camaraderie of the cast. The show became Brazil's highest-rated and longest-running sitcom, even becoming a TV movie in 2007 (which found a place for veteran singer Roberto Carlos, the subject of a running gag about sexual arousal). It came to a close only after fourteen seasons and nearly 500 episodes. **BM**

The Amazing Race

Reality | USA | 2001–present

It's not how far they go . . . it's more what happens along the way

Cast | Phil Keoghan
Original broadcaster | CBS
Awards | 15 Emmys
For fans of . . . | *Whicker's World* (1958), *Survivor* (2000), *I'm a Celebrity . . . Get Me Out of Here!* (2002)

The Amazing Race is a reality competition show in which teams compete against one another in a grueling race around the world. It was created by Elise Doganieri and Bertram van Munster, and international versions of the show have been shown in more than ten countries.

There are usually eleven teams comprising two players each. Most often the pairs of players are best friends, dating or married couples, or work colleagues, and they have to follow clues that will lead them through multiple countries and various challenges over the course of a few weeks. The clues can send them traveling locally, traveling to a new country, or competing in a challenge to earn the next clue. Teams face options such as "detours," in which they have to choose between two tasks, and "roadblocks," where only one member of the team can complete a task. The types of tasks are very varied, such as climbing tall buildings, eating strange foods, and dancing; the variety is limited only by the imaginations of the producers.

To some extent, *The Amazing Race* gives viewers the chance to learn a little about the countries and cultures that feature in the race. The producers try to incorporate local culture in many of challenges, and this has led to some interesting tasks such as participating in a Japanese game show and rolling cheese down a hill (one of the funniest segments ever). The show has won all but two of the Emmy awards for outstanding reality competition program since the inception of the category in 2003. **KB**

Classic episode
Mow 'em Down Like Grass | *Season 7, episode 8*.
A particularly hairy task sets the stage for one of the favorite teams, Uchenna and Joyce, to continue to the finale with a nail-biting finish and the downfall of a much-disliked team.

⊘ Phil Keoghan explains the rules to the teams in Los Angeles.

Beckett on Film

Drama | UK | 2001

*A true treasure trove of plays
by Samuel Beckett*

Cast | Michael Gambon, John Hurt, Julianne Moore, Barry McGovern, David Thewlis, Timothy Spall, Alan Rickman, Kristin Scott Thomas, Penelope Wilton
Original broadcaster | Channel 4
For fans of . . . | *The Singing Detective* (1986)

Irish writer Samuel Beckett produced nineteen dramatic works in his career. The best-known are full-length plays, such as *Waiting for Godot* (1953), a biting comedy about the hopelessness of the human condition; and *Endgame* (1957), which focuses on a small group who may be the last family on Earth, and whose emotional ties are as stubborn and bitter as they are complex. Until 2000, nobody had ever attempted to film all nineteen of Beckett's works, much less put them on TV.

Beckett on Film was the brainchild of Michael Colgan, artistic director of Dublin's Gate Theatre. Every effort was made to make the plays as definitive as possible, with a top-notch cast matched to each piece. Key casting included Michael Gambon as the obstreperous Hamm and David Thewlis as the rebellious Clov in *Endgame*, and John Hurt as the eponymous narrator, trapped by his own memories, in *Krapp's Last Tape* (1958). Big names were also attached to the more experimental pieces, with Julianne Moore turning her hand to the terrifying monologue *Not I* (1972). In addition to a stellar cast, high-profile directors such as Anthony Minghella, David Mamet, Atom Egoyan, and Neil Jordan took their turn behind the camera.

Samuel Beckett was notoriously exacting about the finer details of his plays whenever they were staged, for fear that his unique, stark vision might be diluted. This ambitious yet respectful project managed to stay true to the playwright's intentions and the spirit of his work as a whole. **WM**

24

Drama | USA | 2001–14

*A lot can happen in a day, and this
is a day like no other*

Cast | Kiefer Sutherland, Mary Lynn Rajskub, Carlos Bernard, Elisha Cuthbert, Dennis Haysbert
Original broadcaster | Fox
Awards | 20 Emmys, 2 Golden Globes
For fans of . . . | *Mission: Impossible* (1966)

Debuting on US TV eight weeks to the day after the 9/11 attacks, terrorism thriller *24* was timely. An instant success both in the ratings and in its impact on popular culture, it was innovative, modern, and addictive. Creators Joel Surnow and Robert Cochran spotted the correlation between a standard US TV season (twenty-four episodes) and the hours in a day, so formatted their new drama to take place in real time: each episode was one hour of story; each season was one twenty-four-hour period. The judicious use of split screens showed viewers events that were occurring simultaneously, while a ticking clock appeared on screen at key moments. Every episode ended on a monster of a cliffhanger.

Cast in the lead role was movie star Kiefer Sutherland, who attacked every episode, every scene, every line with full-blooded intensity. Jack Bauer was the head agent of the counter-terrorist unit, tasked with foiling bombers, hostage takers, and hostile spies. Subplots revealed other points of view—most famously, those of a succession of US presidents. Also, Jack's private life often got caught up in the crises.

Initially set in Los Angeles, the show migrated in later years to Washington, New York, a fictional African country (in the one-off special *Redemption*) and, after a hiatus, to London. But what remained the same was the almost unbearable tension of every situation—this was a drama about life and death, torture and freedom, impossible dilemmas and huge sacrifices. Viewers couldn't take their eyes off the screen. **IF**

❷ Kiefer Sutherland as Jack Bauer in *24: Live Another Day* (2014).

Smallville

Drama | USA | 2001–11

How Superman fell to Earth—the long-running story of the superhero's origins as a small-town teenager in Kansas and his path to becoming a legend

Cast | Tom Welling, Michael Rosenbaum, Kristin Kreuk, Allison Mack, Sam Jones III, Annette O'Toole
Original broadcaster | The WB
Awards | 3 Emmys
For fans of . . . | *Heroes* (2006), *Arrow* (2012)

The longest-running North American science-fiction series, *Smallville* had an unbeatable premise: Superman before he becomes super, as just an ordinary teenager in small-town Kansas. Except, of course, Clark Kent is anything but an ordinary teenager.

Smallville dealt with the fallout of the event that brought the infant Clark Kent (Tom Welling) to Earth—a meteor storm that hit the farming community of Smallville and killed a number of people, including the parents of his future girlfriend Lana (Kristin Kreuk). As Clark grew up, learned of his alien origins, and struggled to control his burgeoning powers, he also had to make peace with his violent arrival on the planet. With the support of his friends, who gradually learned his secret, particularly Lex Luthor (Michael Rosenbaum), Clark navigated the perils of high school and then early adulthood, and developed into not just a superhero, but a good person.

Drawing upon nearly eight decades of Superman mythology as well as a rich tradition of teen dramas, *Smallville* was a ratings success for its network, The WB, with its debut drawing 8.4 million viewers. Audiences responded to both elements of the show, enjoying the high school–set trials and tribulations of its characters as well as strands of the original *Superman* story that the show incorporated. The friendship between Clark and his future nemesis, a young Lex Luthor, became a fan favorite, as the show explored Luthor's background as delicately and thoughtfully as it did Kent's. **AP**

Classic episode
Red | *Season 2, episode 4.* Clark buys an expensive ring without realizing that the stone mounted on it is made of red Kryptonite, the only substance that can weaken him. The results are almost catastrophic.

⊘ Tom Welling as a young Clark Kent and Kristin Kreuk as Clark's first girlfriend Lana Lang.

Bob & Rose

Drama | UK | 2001

Rose is the only woman for Bob, and Bob is the only man for Rose, even though he's gay

Cast | Alan Davies, Lesley Sharp, Jessica Stevenson, Penelope Wilton
Original broadcaster | ITV
For fans of . . . | *Will & Grace* (1998), *Queer as Folk* (1999)

Bob Gossage (Alan Davies) was gay and increasingly weary of the Manchester scene. Rose Cooper (Lesley Sharp) was disillusioned with her safe boyfriend. A chance meeting brought them together and marked the beginning of a touching love story that neither of them was expecting.

For writer Russell T. Davies (best known for *Doctor Who*), *Bob & Rose* marked a natural progression from his seminal *Queer as Folk*, broadcast two years earlier, and brought a fresh and original love story to the mainstream ITV network. A drama featuring a homosexual lead was considered controversial for ITV in some quarters, including in the gay community, where some felt that the depiction of a gay man falling for a straight woman delivered the wrong message. This misconception of Davies' typically eloquent script does *Bob & Rose* a great disservice. There is ultimately no ambiguity to Bob's sexuality: he is gay and maintains that he will die gay, but he falls for Rose completely as a person. It is such a simple yet complex story, rendered brilliantly and compellingly watchable thanks to six idiosyncratically textured scripts from Davies, brought to life by the ensemble cast. Despite some weighty issues woven into the narrative, *Bob & Rose* is laugh-out-loud funny. Alan Davies and Lesley Sharp are note perfect, performing their roller-coaster relationship with a warm likability. The supporting cast run with their own affecting story lines, thereby giving the series a fully rounded and satisfying sense of reality. **MW**

The Blue Planet

Documentary | UK | 2001

A stunningly beautiful exploration of life in the ocean depths

Cast | Sir David Attenborough
Original broadcaster | BBC One
Awards | 2 BAFTAs, 2 Emmys
For fans of . . . | *Life on Earth* (1979), *Planet Earth* (2006), *Frozen Planet* (2011)

The Blue Planet may last only 400 minutes in total, but it took five years to make—a mammoth undertaking of exploration by the filmmakers. Its eight episodes dealt with every aspect of marine life from the tiny krill to the gigantic blue whale, taking in creatures such as turtles, dolphins, penguins, albatross, and every form of fish and marine invertebrate. They included some creatures never before caught on camera, and some that had not been known to exist. More than 70 percent of the Earth is sea, and with the ocean making up 97 percent of the Earth's inhabitable space by volume, it is unsurprising that there is so much to be discovered. More people, narrator Sir David Attenborough explained, have traveled into space than have ventured into the depths of the ocean. This series went a long way to filling the gaps in our collective knowledge.

The cinematography was stunning—viewers could watch the series with the volume turned off and still be enthralled. Each episode had a different focus: the unexplored deep; predators; the Arctic and Antarctic; the seasons; coral reefs; tidal seas; and coastal ecosystems. Throughout, the viewer was made aware of the oceans' impact on humankind—and vice-versa. Sir David Attenborough and producer Alastair Fothergill went on to make the series *Planet Earth* and *Frozen Planet* to a similar template. There have been other documentaries tackling similar marine subjects but *The Blue Planet* remains unmatched for sheer scale and beauty. **JR**

Band of Brothers

Historical drama | USA | 2001

War brings out the extraordinary qualities of ordinary men

Cast | Damian Lewis, Ron Livingston, Donnie Wahlberg, Scott Grimes
Original broadcaster | HBO
Awards | 6 Emmys, 1 Golden Globe
For fans of . . . | *The Winds of War* (1983)

Band of Brothers perfectly encapsulated the very best qualities of cable broadcaster HBO, and was exactly the kind of TV that the major networks were wary of attempting in the modern era. It was also reportedly the most expensive series ever mounted by any TV network at the time of production, with a budget in the region of $125 million. Tom Hanks and Erik Jendresen (with Steven Spielberg) developed *Band of Brothers* from Stephen E. Ambrose's book of the same name. A well-crafted and critically lauded miniseries, it depicted the final months of the Second World War through the eyes of a tight-knit unit of soldiers, known as Easy Company.

Band of Brothers was highly praised for its visceral depiction of warfare, and its battle sequences were directed with a taught and realistic visual style. The large ensemble cast effectively portrayed the full emotional response of men at war, their camaraderie melded together through pre-filming bootcamp training. British actor Damian Lewis deserves special credit for his performance as Major Richard "Dick" Winters, eventual commander of Easy. His flawless accent and calm manner gave good account of the pressures of a commanding officer. Talking-head interviews with the real men of Easy Company—whose identities were not revealed until the final episode—added poignancy throughout. **MW**

◀ Damian Lewis (left) was nominated for a Golden Globe and won several Best Actor awards for his portrayal of Richard D. Winters.

McLeod's Daughters

Drama | Australia | 2001–09

Giving the lie to anyone who says you need men to run a farm

Cast | Bridie Carter, Lisa Chappell, Rachael Carpani, Jessica Napier
Original broadcaster | Nine Network
For fans of . . . | *Dallas* (1978), *The Alice* (2005), *Land Girls* (2009)

When asked about her inspiration for *McLeod's Daughters,* creator Posie Graeme-Evans said she'd been annoyed at how women were portrayed on TV. "They used to say," she said, "that there were three ages of women on screen: babe, mom, and district attorney— and, I would add, girlfriend. We're just so much more than that, and that's what I wanted to show."

The result was a 1996 TV movie that introduced half sisters inheriting their late father's farm, overcoming both their unfamiliarity with each other and the condescension of the farm workers. Although the movie achieved record ratings, the TV spin-off was delayed, in part, by misgivings about the viability of female-driven drama. Ultimately, however, the show proved a hit. The grittiness of the movie gave way to gloss, but viewers flocked to the tales of family, friends, and foes. By 2003, it was Australia's most popular TV drama, making stars of Bridie Carter and Lisa Chappell (sisters Tess and Claire respectively) and Rachael Carpani (farmhand Jodi Fountain).

The show's popularity survived the killing-off of Chappell's character, but soapy silliness eventually got the better of quality drama and the ax fell in 2009. At its height, however, the series broke fresh ground. Unusually for an Australian export, it acquired a dedicated following in the United States. At home, it was the first prime-time drama to emerge from South Australia—whose landscapes, as captured by painter Hans Heysen, had helped inspire the concept. **BM**

Perfect Strangers

Drama | UK | 2001

Bringing people together through old photograph albums

Cast | Michael Gambon, Lindsay Duncan, Matthew Macfadyen, Claire Skinner, Toby Stephens, Jill Baker
Original broadcaster | BBC Two
Award | 1 BAFTA
For fans of . . . | *Shooting the Past* (1999)

Award-winning scriptwriter Stephen Poliakoff had already explored the power of photography in his miniseries *Shooting the Past.* Set at a large family reunion in a glamorous hotel in London, this companion piece also reveled in the emotional connection to the past that photographs can bring—specifically two sets of images that revealed long-forgotten moments to both the black sheep of the family, Raymond Symon (Michael Gambon), and his son, Daniel (Matthew Macfadyen). For Raymond, the image depicted an occasion on which his father had made him and his brother laugh; for Daniel, the photograph was of himself at a children's costume party that he couldn't remember attending, dressed in a costume he was sure he had never worn.

Poliakoff used these photographs—brought to the family gathering by family archivist Stephen Symon (Anton Lesser)—to weave a series of spellbinding and unsettling stories about family members who were mostly strangers to one another. It is riveting TV, played out at an unusually slow pace and in great detail. As Daniel uncovered more of his own mystery, he also discovered the increasingly curious stories of his family, such as the three elderly sisters and their experiences during the war, the tragic reason for the rift between his glamorous cousins Rebecca (Claire Skinner) and Charles (Toby Stephens) and his enigmatic aunt Alice (Lindsay Duncan), and ultimately his own role in piecing together the family's greatest secret of all. **JS**

Scrubs

Comedy | USA | 2001–10

This medical sitcom had zip as well as heart and delighted viewers with its exhilarating, sometimes surreal, flights of fancy

Cast | Zach Braff, Sarah Chalke, Donald Faison, Neil Flynn, Ken Jenkins, John C. McGinley, Judy Reyes
Original broadcaster | NBC
Awards | 2 Emmys **For fans of . . .** | *M*A*S*H* (1972), *St. Elsewhere* (1982), *ER* (1994), *The Office* (2001)

A workplace comedy about a group of newly minted doctors feeling their way through their first years of practice, *Scrubs* had a theme and leaned on it hard: laughter is the best medicine. But *Scrubs* had more to offer than treacly lessons about the mutability of life. From its inception, creator Bill Lawrence was interested in exploring the experiences of young medics with sensitivity and thoughtfulness as well as the playful weirdness that would come to define the show.

Narrated in an ongoing voice-over by young attending physician John Michael "J.D." Dorian (Zach Braff), *Scrubs* opened on the first day of his residency at Sacred Heart Teaching Hospital and followed him through his professional and personal life: with prickly mentor Dr. Perry Cox (John C. McGinley), his best friend and roommate Turk (Donald Faison) and his terrifyingly efficient girlfriend Carla (Judy Reyes), with his on-again-off-again love interest Elliot (Sarah Chalke), and with his nemesis, the nameless janitor (Neil Flynn).

Scrubs wore its heart on its sleeve. No thought or feeling went uncommunicated, and no good deed went unpunished. But the show leavened this with screwball comedy. In its final season, a new cast was introduced in an effort to return the show to its roots—exploring the lives of young medics at the start of their careers. The switch was not wholly successful and the show aired its final episode in 2010, but it left behind a lesson in the power of a single-camera sitcom and a taste for surreal workplace comedy. **AP**

Classic episode
My First Day | *Season 1, episode 1.* The inaugural episode introduces most of the characters and elements (rivalry between teams, the fear of accusations of malpractice), including J.D.'s voice-over, that would define the show.

◉ Zach Braff (J.D.) and Donald Faison (Turk).

Six Feet Under

Drama | USA | 2001–05

The darkly comic lives and loves of the Fisher family, who run a funeral parlor in Los Angeles

Cast | Peter Krause, Michael C. Hall, Frances Conroy, Lauren Ambrose, Rachel Griffiths, Freddy Rodriguez, Matthew St. Patrick, Jeremy Sisto, James Cromwell
Original broadcaster | HBO **Awards** | 9 Emmys, 2 Golden Globes **For fans of . . .** | *Breaking Bad* (2008)

Like *The Sopranos* (1999), *Six Feet Under* was at the vanguard of the rise of "premium cable" channels, such as HBO ,as rivals to the traditional TV networks. Freed from the main networks' restrictions when portraying adult content, HBO was able to create in *Six Feet Under* a series that spoke right to the heart of its audience about things that really mattered—life, sex, family, relationships, and (most importantly) death.

After the sudden death of their father Nathaniel in a car crash, brothers Nate and David Fisher took over the family's undertaking business. The family, still in shock after Nathaniel's death, reacted in different ways. Sullen teenager Claire headed to college to study art. Mother Ruth sought some joy for herself as a widow. David, already in a relationship with police officer Keith, finally found the courage to come out to his family. And Nate embarked on a relationship with a woman he bumped into on the way back home for his dad's funeral.

Created and occasionally written by *American Beauty* film director Alan Ball, *Six Feet Under* was both sophisticated and character-focused. It broke boundaries by placing death at the center of the series. Stories of the week mixed with lengthy ongoing plot lines for the regular characters, with many surprising events and shocking character developments. Happy to show that happiness and sadness are two sides of the same coin, *Six Feet Under* was a groundbreaking series that paved the way for many of the more adult and intelligent programs we enjoy today. **PC**

Caméra Café

Comedy | France | 2001–03

The whole of human life in a long series of three-minute episodes

Cast | Bruno Solo, Yvan Le Bolloc'h, Alain Kappauf
Original broadcaster | M6
For fans of . . . | *The Office* (2001), *30 Rock* (2006), *Community* (2009), *Parks and Recreation* (2009), *Outsourced* (2010)

The concept was brilliant in its simplicity: set up a camera inside a coffee vending machine and film office staff as they chat while waiting for their cups to fill. Each episode lasted for only three minutes—the time it took between them choosing their beverage and taking it back to their desks.

The scripts covered not only every topic that people habitually discuss in the workplace—pay and conditions, the management, the colleagues they like and dislike, holidays, clothes shopping, books, movies, parents, children, sport—but also political and philosophical subjects, such as gay marriage, the disabled, US foreign policy, and the purpose of life.

No other show has ever incorporated so much material into so small a space. *Caméra Café* was wildly successful in its native land, where seven hundred episodes were made, and the format was adapted in twenty other countries—Algeria, Australia, Belgium, Brazil, Cambodia, Canada, Chile, Colombia, Indonesia, Ireland, Italy, Luxembourg, Morocco, the Philippines, Poland, Spain, Switzerland, Tunisia, Turkey, and Vietnam.

The conspicuous absentees from this list are Britain and the United States. This is unaccountable—even the obvious objection that the length of the episodes offers insufficient gaps between commercial breaks is untenable, because several of the countries that have developed their own versions have spliced together several different coffee breaks to make programs of the normal duration. **GL**

⊗ Peter Krause and Michael C. Hall as Nate and David Fisher in their professional habitat.

Teachers

Comedy/Drama | UK | 2001–04

Poor behavior, habitual lateness, almost total lack of effort—and that's just the teachers

Classic episode
Episode 9 | March 13, 2002. Simon is given control of a class full of high-achievers, which terrifies him. Two new teachers arrive and Susan finds herself with a crush on the very young new French teacher, JP.

◉ Andrew Lincoln stars as newly qualified teacher Simon Casey.

Cast | Andrew Lincoln, Ursula Holden Gill, Gillian Bevan, Lloyd McGuire, Ellen Thomas, Adrian Bower, Navin Chowdhry, Vicky Hall, Raquel Cassidy
Original broadcaster | Channel 4
For fans of . . . | *This Life* (1996)

Teachers was one of a number of programs that blurred the line between sitcom and drama. Although it included many farcical elements and the kind of heightened melodrama of a comedy, it was shot like a drama, without a studio audience. Created by Tim Loane, it followed the activities in and out of school of a group of twenty-something schoolteachers who were trying to find some direction in their lives.

The first season focused on Simon Casey (Andrew Lincoln), who was serving his probationary period at Summerdown Comprehensive. He often found himself making excuses for not doing work in the same way that his students would explain away their lack of homework. At heart, he wanted to be one of the kids and resented the imposition of grown-up things such as responsibility, punctuality, and conformity. He eventually left the school with the hope of traveling the world, but briefly returned to teaching after wasting his year out. Simon's similarly immature friends, Kurt and Brian, weren't much better: always ready for a drinking session and realizing on one occasion that they had forgotten to prepare for a parent-teacher evening.

As new characters came in during the third series, the original cast drifted away. In the final season, an amalgamation of schools saw the remaining teachers facing rivalries between pupils while trying to organize Gay and Lesbian Awareness Week, Fat Week, and Racial Awareness Week—all the while being undermined by their lack of enthusiasm for their own subjects. **JS**

Peter Kay's Phoenix Nights

Comedy | UK | 2001–02

"I have a dream. If we build it, they will come"

Cast | Peter Kay, Dave Spikey, Neil Fitzmaurice, Paddy McGuinness, Toby Foster, Steve Edge, Archie Kelly, Janice Connolly, Beatrice Kelley, Justin Moorhouse
Original broadcaster | Channel 4
For fans of . . . | *Max & Paddy's Road to Nowhere* (2004)

Brian Potter (Peter Kay) owned The Aquarius Club, until it flooded. His second venue, The Neptune, burned down. And then he had The Phoenix Club, and he was determined to make it the best venue in Bolton. Unfortunately, he was surrounded by staff most kindly described as inept. Confined to a wheelchair as a result of an accident during the flood, Potter was obsessed with Den Perry (Ted Robbins), the successful proprietor of The Banana Grove. It was a rivalry that could only end in tears—or more accurately, ashes.

The character of Brian Potter first graced British TV screens in *That Peter Kay Thing* (2000), a comedy anthology in which Kay played different roles starring in fly-on-the-wall documentary films. *Phoenix Nights* was cowritten by Kay with Dave Spikey and Neil Fitzmaurice (who played DJ Ray Von). Although it only ran for two short seasons, *Phoenix Nights* was something of a cult hit. A follow-up series, *Max & Paddy's Road to Nowhere*, saw the former doormen on a road trip on the run from hitmen. As Kay's star began to rise, largely thanks to his sell-out stand-up comedy tours, he resurrected Potter for a one-off duet with Matt Lucas as Lou (also in a wheelchair) from *Little Britain*, singing a cover of The Proclaimers' "500 Miles" in aid of the Comic Relief charity telethon. In 2014, the phoenix once again rose from the ashes as Peter Kay announced a UK-wide arena tour of "Phoenix Nights Live." Fans are undoubtedly hoping this will lead to a return of the TV show in the near future. **JS**

The Secret Life of Us

Drama | Australia/UK | 2001–05

Life's a beach in St. Kilda, Melbourne

Cast | Claudia Karvan, Samuel Johnson, Deborah Mailman, Abi Tucker, Joel Edgerton, Sibylla Budd,
Original broadcasters | Network Ten (Australia), Channel 4 (UK)
For fans of . . . | *Tales of the City* (1993), *This Life* (1996)

Set in Melbourne's St. Kilda, a hip beach suburb with a bohemian approach to life, *The Secret Life of Us* focused on a revolving door of smart young adults living in the same apartment block. They negotiated love and work, pondered the meaning of life, studied, and, above all, had fun. The show quickly attracted a loyal audience both in Australia and the United Kingdom; its first three seasons were coproduced by the UK's Channel 4.

Three characters in the apartment block were central: Evan Wylde, played by Samuel Johnson, was a would-be novelist. Alex Christensen, played by rising star Claudia Karvan, longed to work in England, and Kelly Lewis, played by Deborah Mailman, was a student and the only character who remained in the block for the run of the show. The three friends frequented a local bar, where they befriended Simon, played by David Tredinnick, who topped them up with beer and wine as required.

Episodes were accompanied by a pithy commentary, and pulsated with a soundtrack showcasing the cream of Australian independent music at the time. Featured artists included Genevieve Maynard, Stella One Eleven, and Something for Kate.

The young audience identified with the characters' preoccupations and also with their appetite for love and life. Even when things did not go according to plan for them, the music and surfing backdrop suggested that life could never be that bad, and kept the whole thing chilled. **SJG**

The Office

Comedy | UK | 2001–03

"You just have to accept that some days you are the pigeon, and some days you are the statue"

Cast | Ricky Gervais, Martin Freeman, Mackenzie Crook, Lucy Davis, Patrick Baladi, Stirling Gallacher
Original broadcaster | BBC Two
Awards | 6 BAFTAs, 2 Golden Globes
For fans of . . . | *Parks and Recreation* (2009)

The real genius of *The Office* is that many people believed it to be a real documentary when they first saw it, such is the level of skill in the writing and directing. The show came at a time when reality TV was making huge stars out of the people who appeared on it, such as Jane McDonald from *The Cruise* and Jeremy Spake from *Airport*. And so Ricky Gervais and Stephen Merchant created David Brent (played by Gervais), the boss of Wernham Hogg: a paper merchant in the dreary town of Slough in the south of England. Brent wanted to be funny, he wanted to be popular, and he wanted to be famous. And it was through his awkward, embarrassing, and painful attempts to achieve these things that most of the humor came.

The characters that surrounded Brent were each fantastically observed in their own right: there was gangly Territorial Army soldier Gareth (Mackenzie Crook); Tim, the only sane member of the team (a wonderful debut performance from Martin Freeman); and receptionist Dawn (Lucy Davis). Tim and Dawn's Romeo and Juliet romance started out as a subplot, but by the final episode it was the main reason why many viewers tuned in: it was so beautifully written and performed. The arrival of *The Office* changed comedy forever, and its influence can be seen in gems such as *The Thick of It* (2005) and *Gavin & Stacey* (2007). What better epitaph can there be for a sitcom? **LH**

❯ Ricky Gervais as David Brent performs his now-notorious workplace dance routine.

Firefly

Fantasy/Horror/Sci-Fi | USA | 2002

Science-fiction adventures in the new wild frontier

Cast | Nathan Fillion, Gina Torres, Morena Baccarin, Adam Baldwin, Jewel Staite, Alan Tudyk
Original broadcaster | Fox **Award** | 1 Emmy **For fans of . . .** | *Star Trek* (1966), *Buffy the Vampire Slayer* (1997)

After his success with *Buffy the Vampire Slayer* and *Angel*, Joss Whedon wanted to try something different; a blend of sci-fi and Western. He pitched *Firefly* to Fox as "Nine people looking into the blackness of space and seeing nine different things."

Set aboard the freighter *Serenity* (a Firefly-class spaceship), the series told the story of brooding captain Malcolm Reynolds (Nathan Fillion) and his makeshift crew: soldiers, fortune-seekers, wide-eyed innocents, and fugitives from dark powers, with a preacher and a prostitute thrown in for good measure.

Fox executives bought it on the basis of Whedon's track record but were too nervous to throw their whole weight behind it. They launched it without its expository two-hour pilot show in a graveyard slot on Friday nights. Perhaps unsurprisingly therefore ratings were poor and *Firefly* ended after only a few months on the air. But later an unprecedented bonanza in its DVD sales, along with a dedicated fan base, led to *Serenity* (2005), a cinema revival that tied up many loose ends from the TV series and achieved cult status. **SL**

Classic episode
Out of Gas | *Season 1, episode 5*. A string of flashbacks to the recent and distant past fill in the background to the story, showing how Mal Reynolds originally acquired *Serenity* and assembled his crew.

⬙ Nathan Fillion and Summer Glau on the edge of an uncertain future.

Footballers' Wives

Drama | UK | 2002–06

In the houses—and the beds—of the women behind the men of British soccer

Cast | Gillian Taylforth, Zöe Lucker, Alison Newman, Chad Shepherd, Gary Lucy, Jesse Birdsall, Lewis Till
Original broadcaster | ITV **For fans of . . .** | *The Only Way Is Essex* (2010)

The fictional Earls Park Football Club (known as "The Sparks") welcomed a new signing in 2002—Ian Walmsley, who struggled with his new-found success. His wife, Donna, was desperate to find her son, who was put up for adoption by her parents when she was just a teenager. Donna's younger sister Marie was having an affair with The Sparks' star player, the roguish Jason Turner, who at the time was married to Tanya—and nobody ever crossed Tanya and got away with it.

This was the setup in the first season of British TV's most wilfully crass, headline-grabbing, and often hilarious drama ever. Tanya Turner emerged as the show's star player, murdering a rival for her husband, having affairs with other footballers, killing her second

husband though a heady mix of alcohol, Viagra, cocaine, and very aggressive sex, and swapping her newborn baby for that of her love rival, Amber Gates (a scheme that backfired when her own son was accidentally suffocated by Amber's pet dog). The exploits of the women and men surrounding the team were tabloid-baiting and lowest common denominator. Infidelity was rife, sexuality changeable, and morality low.

Every season featured at least one kidnapping and a murder or two. Somehow, it was compelling; it was the very worst that trashy TV could be—and for a time the viewers loved it. But *Footballers' Wives* would come to an end in April 2006, the victim of poor ratings and strong opposition from the BBC's *Hotel Babylon*. **JS**

⚉ Zöe Lucker (Tanya) and Alison Newman (Hazel) bubble with intrigue and soccer-related gossip.

Berlin, Berlin

Comedy/Drama | Germany | 2002–05

Like Friends *but with emotionally mature and articulate Germans*

Cast | Felicitas Woll, Jan Sosniok, Matthias Klimsa, Sandra Borgmann, Rhea Harder, Matthias Schloo
Original broadcaster | ARD
Award | 1 Emmy
For fans of . . . | *Caroline in the City* (1995)

While the "twentysomething in a big city" trope may now seem as old as the New York coffee shop Central Perk, writer David Safier regarded it as largely unexplored territory on German TV. He duly located his fictional heroine, Carlotta "Lolle" Holzmann (Felicitas Woll), in his nation's capital. Her bid to establish new relationships, while experiencing life's highs and lows, in "the most exciting city in Germany" made for an ideal blend of comedy and drama.

The first season opened with Lolle tracking a boyfriend from her hometown on the Baltic coast to Berlin, where she discovered his infidelity, and decided to stay with her cousin Sven (Jan Sosniok). The core cast was rounded out by their friends Hart (Matthias Klimsa) and Rosalie (Sandra Borgmann). By the close of the season, Rosalie had decamped to the United States, and Lolle had fallen for Sven. The latter scenario evolved into a love triangle involving the couple and Lolle's new love, art student Alex (Matthias Schloo).

Laugh-out-loud funny yet frequently moving, defiantly quirky—notably in its sprinkling of animation—and with refreshingly strong heroines, *Berlin, Berlin* gave Germany its very own *Friends* (albeit with a lead actress playing a character her own age, unlike half of the US show's cast). Safier chose to write from a female perspective because, unlike his gender, women "have learned to talk about their feelings"—and the result was an eighty-six-episode hit over four seasons. **BM**

Wire in the Blood

Crime/Mystery | UK | 2002–08

Dysfunctional criminal psychologist teams up with ambitious police to solve murders

Cast | Robson Green, Hermione Norris, Simone Lahbib, Mark Letheren, Emma Handy
Original broadcaster | ITV
For fans of . . . | *Cracker* (1993), *Profiler* (1996), *Criminal Minds* (2005)

Wire in the Blood is a series of whodunits in which murders are investigated by Dr. Tony Hill (Robson Green), an eccentric criminal psychologist who carries a blue shopping bag.

The first four episodes were based on Val McDermid's popular series of novels, set in the fictional Yorkshire town of Bradfield, in which the central drama was derived from the relationship between Hill and police Detective Inspector (DI) Carol Jordan (Hermione Norris). Later, however, the television series took on a life of its own, and the remainder of the series (a further twenty episodes) featured Hill and Scottish DI Alex Fielding (Simone Lahbib) in new, original stories.

Dr. Hill is a complex character, his forensic genius disguised by a childlike innocence. He speaks rather incoherently, an impediment that often makes it hard for the police to rely on his judgment. But they learn to trust him as he demonstrates time and again that he has a unique ability to understand the tormented minds of the killers. His insights are achieved at great personal cost, however: his empathy is psychologically damaging and on more than one occasion almost gets him killed.

The success of *Wire in the Blood* on television then inspired McDermid to write more books about Hill and Jordan. The author even appeared in one episode in the first TV series: she had a brief role as a newspaper reporter, which was one of her first jobs in real life after leaving university. **SJG**

Robson Green at a departmental brainstorming meeting in season five of *Wire in the Blood.* ❯

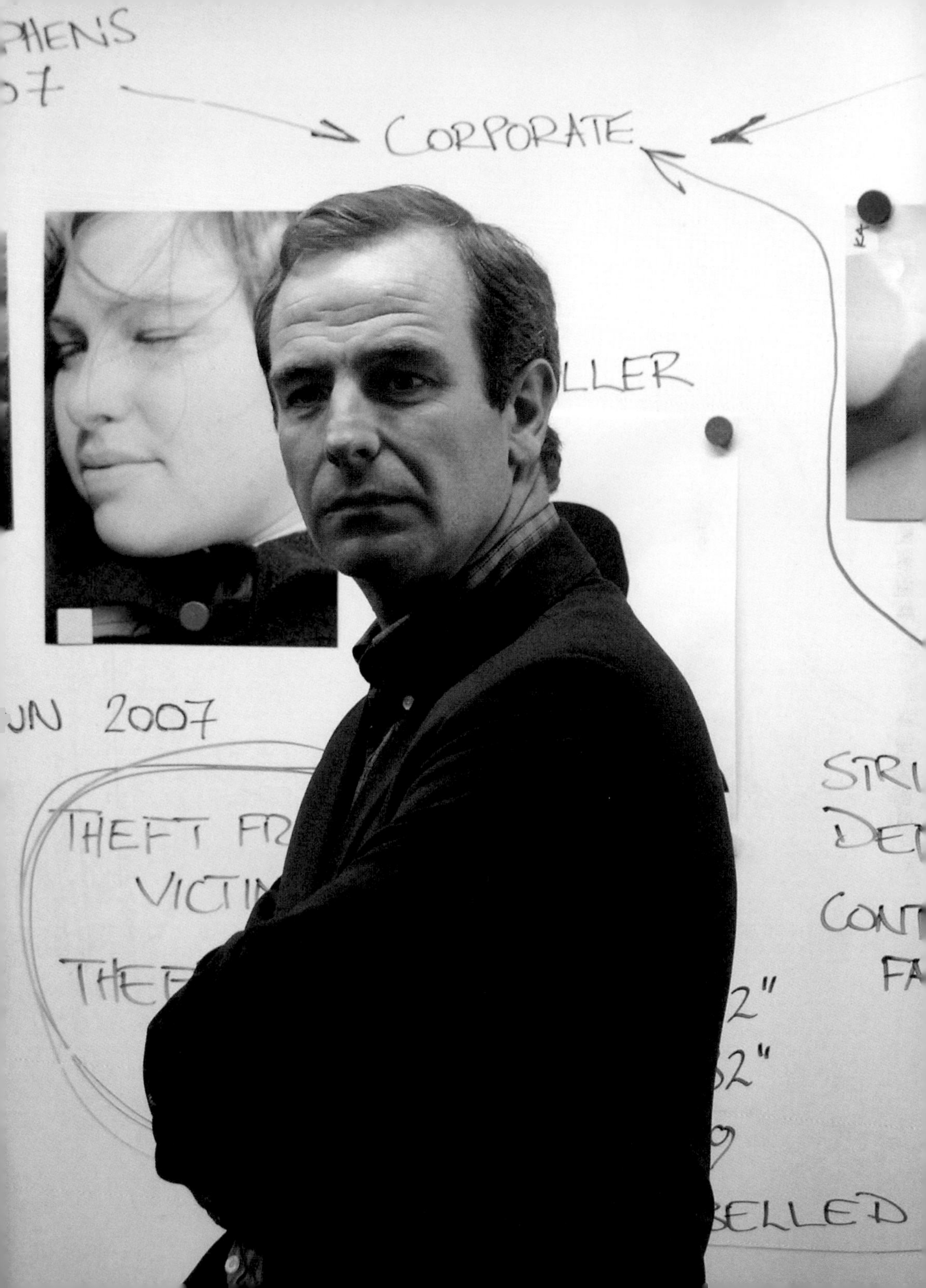
CORPORATE

Foyle's War

Historical drama | UK | 2002–present

Classy wartime detective drama

Cast | Michael Kitchen, Honeysuckle Weeks, Anthony Howell   **Original broadcaster** | ITV
Award | 1 BAFTA   **For fans of . . .** | *Endeavour* (2012)

After the end of *Inspector Morse* in 2002, ITV sought another cerebral sleuth to fill the void. Into the breach stepped Chief Superintendent Christopher Foyle (Michael Kitchen), walking a wartime beat on Britain's home front during the Second World War.

Developed by writer Anthony Horowitz, *Foyle's War* opens with a feature-length episode in which the hero is turned down for military service and has to resign himself to remaining in the police force for the duration of the conflict. With the help of his driver, Sam Stewart (Honeysuckle Weeks) and Detective Sergeant Paul Milner (Anthony Howell), Foyle tackles corruption, murder, Foreign Office cover-ups, art forgery, and more as the conflict allows increased criminal activity.

Foyle's War looks simply gorgeous, the period detail is usually pin-sharp, and episodes are punctuated with historical events. The plots are well structured and packed with variety, and Kitchen, Weeks, and Howell form an attractive trio. The series is popular all over the world, particularly, in North America, where it is broadcast as part of the PBS Mystery! strand. **MW**

> **Classic episode**
> *The Hide* | *Season 6, episode 3*. Foyle resigns from the police force but his departure is delayed when he intervenes on behalf of troubled youth James Devereux, who faces a charge of treason, a capital offense.

⬿ Michael Kitchen as Christopher Foyle in season eight of the award-winning show.

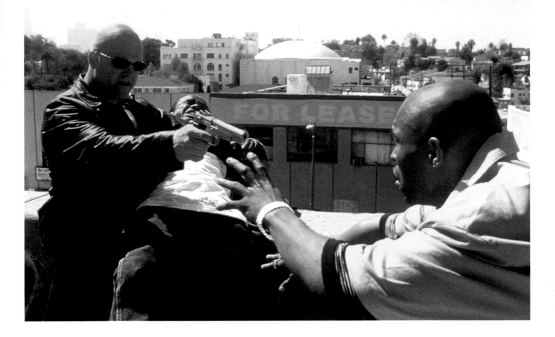

The Shield

Drama | USA | 2002–08

Hard-hitting cop show that demonstrated what cable drama could deliver

Cast | Michael Chiklis, C.C.H. Pounder, Walton Goggins
Original broadcaster | FX **For fans of . . .** | *The Wire* (2002)

At the start of the twenty-first century, American television drama was beginning to push the boundaries of what it could show and say on-screen. The cop drama was at the leading edge of this trend, and while *The Wire* may be the best-known example, *The Shield* was daring and brutal and equally instrumental in blazing a trail for other shows.

The central story, loosely inspired by a real-life scandal, concerns the Task Force, a small group of cops entrusted with tackling gang violence in Los Angeles. Vic Mackey (Michael Chiklis), the strike team's leader, seems a classic antihero, but the show didn't make the mistake of falling in love with his villainy. As its coherent story unfolded over seven tightly plotted seasons, we saw the terrible price paid for his crimes by both his family and his colleagues. And the show offered a moral heart to counterpoint his spiritual emptiness: Detective Claudette Wyms, a world-weary but upright character of the type traditionally portrayed as male but here, groundbreakingly, by a black woman, Guyanese-born C.C.H. Pounder. **RL**

Classic episode
Pilot | Season 1, episode 1. A drug bust and an investigation into the disappearance of a child during which Vic displays both his steely hold over the team and the lengths to which he will go to protect their extra-legal activities.

⊘ Michael Chiklis (L) demonstrates his reluctance to compromise in the fight against crime.

Tipping the Velvet

Historical drama | UK | 2002

A young Victorian woman's romance with a female stage performer

Cast | Rachael Stirling, Keeley Hawes, Anna Chancellor, John Bowe
Original broadcaster | BBC Two
For fans of . . . | *Oranges Are Not the Only Fruit* (1989), *Fingersmith* (2005)

British writer Sarah Walters' debut novel, *Tipping the Velvet*, told the story of a young woman in the 1890s who fell for a male impersonator and was drawn into an intoxicating London counterculture. Numerous publishers turned the book down before it finally found a home in 1998, and when the BBC produced a three-part television adaptation four years later, the drama attracted controversy due to its subject matter.

The script—by Andrew Davies, author of a recent successful version of Jane Austen's *Pride and Prejudice*—replicated the sexual and personal awakening lead character Nan felt as she came to London to work with theater star Kitty Butler.

Walters admitted that, to some extent, she'd invented the world in which Nan moved—lesbianism in Victorian London went unrecorded by history—yet the TV series made it all appear authentic. The entire cast—including *Spooks* star Keeley Hawes as Kitty, Anna Chancellor as hedonistic widow Sapphie, and Benedict Cumberbatch as Nan's early boyfriend—was terrific. But it was Rachael Stirling, daughter of Diana Rigg, who shone especially brightly. As Nan, she held the whole piece together with charm and star quality.

The series faithfully reproduced the novel's liberal depiction of sex (lesbian and otherwise), and thus drew viewer complaints. The BBC stood firm, however, defending the show. Quite right too: this was an inventive, engrossing and erotic rites-of-passage story that demanded to be seen. **IF**

Winter Sonata

Drama | South Korea | 2002

Landmark series that blazed the trail for Korean shows into the wider world

Cast | Bae Yong-joon, Choi Ji-woo, Park Yong-ha, Park Sol-mi, Lee Hye-eun, Ryu Seung-soo, Kwon Hae-hyo, Song Ok-sook, Jung Dong-hwan
Original broadcaster | KBS2
For fans of . . . | *Stairway to Heaven* (2003)

Joon-sang (Bae Yong-joon) is a talented teenager who moves from Seoul to the provinical city of Chuncheon, ostensibly to further his education, but in reality to search for the father he has never known. His mother, Kang Mi-hee (Song Ok-sook), has told him he is dead, but he does not believe her.

At school, he falls in love with fellow pupil Jeong Yoo-jin (Choi Ji-woo), but she is then injured in an automobile crash, and cannot remember anything about her life before the accident. Mi-hee, who has been jealous of her son's girlfriend, is now inspired by the thought that the past can be erased, and sends Joon-sang to a psychiatrist whose therapy causes the boy to forget his own backstory. Mi-Hee then takes Joon-sang to the United States and gives him a new name, Lee Min-hyeong, and a whole new identity. His teachers and friends in Korea are told that he is dead.

Fast forward a decade; Lee Min-hyeong, now a successful architect, returns to Korea, and there encounters Yoo-jin. He somehow reminds her of her long-lost first love, and so strong are her feelings toward him that she breaks off her engagement to a local man. But in the intervening period, Lee Min-hyeong has made other emotional commitments.

This beautifully crafted and psychologically intense study of love, deception, estrangement, and reconciliation brought South Korean TV and cinema to the attention of the wider world; the nation's industry has never looked back since. **GL**

Monk

Crime/Mystery | USA | 2002–09

Mystery series that blended gentle comedy and crime drama to become a long-running cable hit

Cast | Tony Shalhoub, Bitty Schram, Jason Gray-Stanford, Ted Levine, Traylor Howard
Original broadcaster | USA Network
Awards | 8 Emmys, 1 Golden Globe
For fans of . . . | *Columbo* (1971)

Sharing many elements with one of its principal inspirations—the stories of Sherlock Holmes—this series followed three main characters: former detective-turned-consultant Monk (Tony Shalhoub), a brilliant but obsessive-compulsive individual whose techniques often irritated close friends and colleagues; San Francisco police captain Leland Stottlemeyer (Ted Levine), and nurse Sharona (Bitty Schram). Always pursuing the unknown bomber who murdered his wife Trudy and led to his nervous breakdown and subsequent departure from the police force, Monk solved crimes to try to bring order to the world while battling germophobia and a plethora of other fears.

Created by Andy Breckman and originally developed at ABC for *Seinfeld*'s Michael Richards, *Monk* was a deft blend of comedy and procedural drama with a quirky and endearing central character, whose habit-heavy behavior and razor-sharp attention to detail enabled him to solve the most twisted of crimes. Like *Columbo*, *Monk* often gave viewers a look at the actual crime before the investigation began, inverting the traditional approach in which the culprit was not known until the conclusion of the story.

Following contract disputes, Schram was fired from the series in its third season and Traylor Howard joined the cast as Monk's new assistant, Natalie. The show later spawned a series of tie-in novels and numerous webisodes, most notably a ten-episode flashback spin-off, *Little Monk* (2009). **ATB**

Classic episode
Mr. Monk and the End | *Season 8, episode 16*. In the series finale—at the time the most watched scripted drama in cable history—Monk solves the mystery of his wife Trudy's murder and discovers a daughter he never knew she had.

◉ Tony Shalhoub in "Mr. Monk Meets Dale the Whale" (season one, episode four).

The Wire

Crime/Mystery | USA | 2002–08

Both sides of the war on drugs played out in a Baltimore community

Cast | Dominic West, Wendell Pierce, Sonja Sohn, Clarke Peters, Andre Royo, Michael Kenneth Williams, Frankie Faison, J.D. Williams, Idris Elba
Original broadcaster | HBO
For fans of . . . | *The Sopranos* (1999)

Even for viewers familiar with police procedurals, *The Wire* could be hard work. There was little exposition in the early episodes, and the dense street slang of the hustlers and pushers did nothing to help our understanding. But patience was rewarded midway through the first series when it became clear how all the plot stands were interwoven.

Across five exquisitely crafted series, we witnessed the corruption, indolence, and self-serving politics that polluted the entire infrastructure of Baltimore—its police force, harbor board, city council, newspapers, and educational services.

At the heart of the action was McNulty (Dominic West), an adulterous, hard-drinking, lazy cop who was redeemed by his determination to do good, even if that meant inventing a serial killer to draw attention to the plight of the homeless. The wire itself was the police's covert surveillance team of phone-tappers led by Lester Freeman (Clarke Peters).

We also got a close-up view of the drug gangs who battled for control of the street corners. The foot soldiers thought only in the short term; their bosses dealt with strategy in their struggle to outthink rival criminals. We even found ourselves admiring some of them, including Stringer Bell (Idris Elba), who applied his business-school strategy to his situation as the right-hand-man to a psychotic gangster. **JS**

❯ (L–R) Clarke Peters checks a victim's wrist; Sonja Sohn takes notes; Wendell Pierce looks at his cell; Dominic West looks puzzled.

Without a Trace

Drama | USA | 2002–09

Series focusing on a Manhattan FBI team whose job it is to find missing people against a ticking clock

Cast | Anthony LaPaglia, Eric Close, Poppy Montgomery, Marianne Jean-Baptiste
Original broadcaster | CBS
For fans of . . . | *Law & Order: Special Victims Unit* (1999), *Cold Case* (2003), *CSI: NY* (2004)

Procedural crime dramas focusing on special units that locate missing people weren't new to television, but what made *Without a Trace* different from any of its predecessors was that it came from the Jerry Bruckheimer stable, hot on the heels of *CSI*. Like that show, *Without a Trace* relied on effective visual gimmickry for many of its effects. It used on-screen captions to indicate how long each person had been missing, thus increasing the tension of the race against time. It also, quite daringly, featured as many tragic endings as happy ones.

The lead characters of *Without a Trace* were in some ways as vulnerable as the people they sought to help. There were interdepartmental relationships that went wrong, messy divorces, serious illnesses and at least two of the leads suffered post-traumatic stress as a result of their work—in the case of Jack Malone (Anthony LaPaglia), it was a major thread that ran through several seasons.

Even after seven seasons, *Without a Trace* showed no signs of losing its original power. But it is a hallmark of Jerry Bruckheimer's shows that they never outstay their welcome, so that was the end of it. However—again characteristically—the final episode, in which the longstanding on-off affair between Danny (Enrique Murciano) and Elena (Roselyn Sanchez) at last culminated in their marriage, left open the possibility of a subsequent revival of the series at some future date: there are many worse things that could happen. **GR**

Classic episode

Our Sons and Daughters | *Season 2, episode 6*.
In the search for a missing teenage boy, the team uncovers a den of underage sex orgies. For broadcasting this episode at family-viewing times, CBS was fined a then-record $3.6m.

◉ Martin (Eric Close) and Danny (Enrique Murciano) prepare to storm a warehouse as they search for a missing woman.

City of Men

Drama | Brazil | 2002–05

Show about the gap between rich and poor and white and black in Rio de Janeiro

Cast | Darlan Cunha, Douglas Silva, Thiago Martins, Camila Monteiro, Pierre-Augustin Crenn, Roberta Rodrigues, Phellipe Haagensen, Jonathan Haagensen
Original broadcaster | TV Globo
For fans of . . . | *Diff'rent Strokes* (1978)

Extraordinary brutality proved no obstacle to success for Fernando Meirelles' and Kátia Lund's 2002 movie *Cidade de Deus* (*City of God*), which broke box-office records for a homegrown feature in Brazil and became an international hit. Its story of life on the streets of Rio de Janeiro's most notorious slum was duly spun off into this four-season, nineteen-episode series that picked up the tales of characters from contrasting ends of the social spectrum.

At its heart were slum-dwelling young teens Luis "Acerola" Cunha (Douglas Silva) and Uólace "Laranjinha" da Silva (Darlan Cunha). (The characters had first appeared in a 2000 episode of the anthology series *Brava Gente*, in which Silva played Laranjinha and Cunha played Acerola.) Their lives were compared with the life of middle-class, white thirteen-year-old João Victor (Thiago Martins), with whom Acerola and Laranjinha eventually crossed paths. The duo's preoccupations otherwise centered on hip-hop, drug-dealing relatives, and girls—principally Laranjinha's beloved Camila (Camila Monteiro).

Gritty yet humorous (a final, animated show envisioned how the characters might grow up), the show drew 35 million viewers. Most of the cast and their stories resurfaced in a 2007 movie of the same name, which made liberal use of clips from the series as flashbacks. But perhaps its key legacy was to put Brazil's unrepresented African population on screen, helping to weaken a long-held color bar. **BM**

Takeshi's Castle

Game show | Japan | 1986–89; 2002–04

Physical endurance competition with knockabout games

Cast | Takeshi Kitano, Michiru Jo, Hayato Tani
Original broadcasters | Tokyo Broadcasting System (Japan), Challenge TV (UK)
For fans of . . . | *It's a Knockout* (1966), *Tarrant on TV* (1990), *Total Wipeout* (2009)

Takeshi's Castle was an insane, fast, crazy, dangerous, and very funny series of physical challenges, in which upward of one hundred contestants per season were ordered by General Tani, at the same time, to get through various challenging obstacles and endurance tests in order to earn the chance to storm Count Takeshi's Castle and win a prize of one million Japanese yen ($8,250). All along the way they were relentlessly battered, attacked, and impeded by Count Takeshi's crew.

The challenges faced by contestants of both sexes and all ages were many and various. They included having to run across lakes via a series of rolling cylinders; pole-vaulting across a river; riding down white-water rapids in plastic teacups; swinging across a void while wearing a fly costume and then letting go to become stuck on a horizontal Velcro-covered board; and climbing a pyramid while being shot at by water cannons. With each challenge, the contestants were gradually whittled down in number, until only a few were left to go into the final battle against Takeshi's army in laser-firing tanks.

Originally transmitted in Japan from 1986 to 1989, the show has aired in various formats in twenty-seven different countries and territories around the world. In the UK, it was substantially reedited and provided with a new narration by actor and comedian Craig Charles, and the resultant shows were first transmitted from 2002 to 2004. **DJH**

I'm a Celebrity . . . Get Me Out of Here!

Reality | UK | 2002–present

Marvel as celebrities are humiliated in the Australian jungle

Cast | Anthony McPartlin, Declan Donnelly, Tony Blackburn, Kerry Katona, Carol Thatcher
Original broadcaster | ITV **Awards** | 2 BAFTAs **For fans of . . .** | *Survivor* (2000), *Celebrity Big Brother* (2001)

I'm a Celebrity . . . Get Me Out of Here! was evidently the show that the British public had longed for. There's something perversely satisfying about watching a host of celebrities humiliated in the name of entertainment. The format sees famous contestants flown to the Australian jungle to live in a specially constructed camp, surviving on basic rations and without any of the comforts to which they are accustomed. Each day they compete in grueling "Bushtucker Trials"—a series of harrowing tasks that include both brutal physical challenges and eating revolting jungle-related foods.

For the viewers, the main draw is the eating trials, where contestants are forced to eat platters of stomach-churning substances in order to win regular meals for their camp mates. Menu items have included cooked pigs' brains, kangaroo penises, live insects, and fish eyes.

The British public votes for who it wants to complete the trial the following day, often cruelly subjecting the same contestant to numerous repeat repasts (in season seven, Janice Dickinson completed ten such ordeals). The King or Queen of the Jungle is also crowned by public vote.

Like many large-scale reality television shows, the franchise operates globally, with several other nations' versions using the same purpose-built Outback camp. It seems that watching humiliated celebrities eat animal genitals has become a universal pastime. **MB**

⬣ (L–R) Jungle contestants Kendra Wilkinson and Melanie Sykes face their fears in the Critter Conveyor Bushtucker Trial.

The Bachelor

Reality | USA | 2002–present

An attractive man is awarded as a reality show prize

Cast | Chris Harrison
Original broadcaster | ABC **For fans of . . .** | *The Dating Game* (1965), *Blind Date* (1985), *Take Me Out* (2010)

The Bachelor introduced a new premise to the concept of dating shows. Antecedents such as *Blind Date* and *The Dating Game* had presented contestants on an equal footing, but *The Bachelor* introduced the unusual concept of a man as both prize and judge, with contestants battling for the ultimate prize of a proposal.

Twenty-five women compete for the affections of the eponymous bachelor. He takes each out on a date, presenting a rose to those he wishes to remain in the competition. As the weeks go by, rivalry between the contestants intensifies as they gradually get closer to the Bachelor, who himself tends to have difficulty choosing who to eliminate week by week. Rivalries between the women often boil down to who is

there for the "right reasons." Being on television to be seduced by an attractive, lucrative man is considered to be a more legitimate aim than seeking to further a career in the media or looking for a free vacation.

The Bachelor led to a slew of shows offering a desirable man as the prize—and *The Bachelorette*, in which men compete for a woman's affections. **EB**

> **Classic episode**
> *After the Final Rose* | *Season 13, episode 13*.
> Bachelor Jason Mesnick chose Melissa Mycroft as his winner, but on this live follow-up show, he publicly broke it off with her and begged runner-up Molly Malaney for a second chance.

◉ Juan Pablo Galavis, the former Venezuelan soccer player, begins his search for his soulmate, choosing one of twenty-seven women.

Look Around You

Comedy | UK | 2002–05

*Spot-on spoof of vintage schools'
science programmes*

Cast | Peter Serafinowicz, Robert Popper, Nigel
Lambert, Olivia Colman, Josie D'Arby, Edgar Wright
Original broadcaster | BBC Two
For fans of . . . | *Hale and Pace* (1986), *Parks and
Recreation* (2009)

This series set out to parody the educational
programmes that appeared on British television in the
1970s and 1980s. However, familiarity with the original
is not required to appreciate the humor: *Look Around
You* contains many tropes that are universal to all similar
attempts to educate through the medium of video.

The main joy of the production was its painstaking
attention to detail, with its wonderful recreation of
the strangely dull sets of the period and the stilted
way in which the narrators and presenters addressed
the audience. The title also was perfectly chosen,
mimicking those of the time but also allowing a wide
range of subjects to be included (diverse themes such
as "Calcium" and "Music" in the first season). Each ten-
minute edition was a miniature masterpiece, with
the humor emanating as much from the discipline
of maintaining the authenticity as from the more
outlandish experiments or propositions on offer.
There was also an undeniable affection for the source
material which itself (being viewed thirty or more years
later) can seem outlandish, dated and unintentionally
funny. The second season (of 30-minute episodes)
featured greater interaction between the presenters
and guest stars, including Harry Enfield, Simon Pegg,
David Walliams, and Matt Lucas.

Look Around You was the brainchild of Peter
Serafinowicz and Robert Popper, who together and
separately have used their distinctive comedic skills
on a numerous other projects for TV and movies. **DF**

The Osbournes

Reality | USA | 2002–05

*At home with the Prince of Darkness
and his oddball family*

Cast | Ozzy Osbourne, Sharon Osbourne,
Jack Osbourne, Kelly Osbourne
Original broadcaster | MTV
Award | 1 Emmy
For fans of . . . | *The Real World* (1992)

When *The Osbournes* first arrived on screens, Ozzy
Osbourne was known—mostly by heavy metal fans—
as the hard-living front man of Black Sabbath. By the
time the run ended in 2005, he was known as the put-
upon patriarch of the wildest family on TV.

The Osbournes introduced viewers to Ozzy's wife/
manager Sharon, son Jack, and daughter Kelly. It did
not, however, introduce daughter Aimee, who declined
to be part of the show.

Over four seasons, the show had Ozzy attempt to
cope with a controlling spouse, near out-of-control
teenagers, and a Beverly Hills mansion–filling menagerie
of pets whose excreta featured in many episodes—
often after having being trodden in by "Mr. O."

Rather than simply featuring outrageous car-crash
moment followed by further chaos, *The Osbournes*
provided several surprising insights into the life of the
family. Episodes often featured typical parental topics,
such as Ozzy dealing with Jack upon learning that he
was leaving the house carrying a knife. Conversely, a
single season four installment showed Kelly struggling
with rehab while Jack celebrated his newly attained
sobriety. Sharon's diagnosis of colon cancer was
covered, with her treatment featuring in a few episodes,
as was a life-threatening ATV accident.

That's not to say there wasn't mania and mayhem,
including an unfortunate incident of canicide. It's little
wonder that *The Osbournes* became the highest-rated
program in MTV history. **ST**

Spooks

Drama | UK | 2002–11

Smash hit series suggesting that life in the British security service can be complicated, frightening, and short

Cast | Peter Firth, Matthew Macfadyen, Keeley Hawes, David Oyelowo, Hugh Simon, Rupert Penry-Jones
Original broadcaster | BBC One
Award | 1 BAFTA
For fans of . . . | *Mission: Impossible* (1966), *24* (2001)

Spooks found a setting for a TV drama that was a change from the usual fare of police stations and hospitals. Creator David Wolstencroft hit upon the idea of the security service; not the sexy spy stuff of James Bond but the backroom operatives who have to juggle life-threatening investigations while maintaining double (or even triple) lives to protect themselves and their country. *Spooks* served notice early on that its body count would be high—a trainee agent had his face plunged into a deep-fat fryer and was then shot in the back of the head. When characters left the show, it was usually in a body bag.

The production team worked with a trio of former security agents from MI5, the CIA, and the KGB to develop plots around probable security threats. In the post-9/11 world, Cold War spy games were superseded by a preoccupation with terrorist activity. A second-season episode about suicide bombers drew complaints from Islamic groups concerned about their perception in the media; two years later, real suicide attacks brought London to a standstill.

In 2009, BBC Three launched a spin-off series. *Spooks: Code 9* was set in a near future where a small group of young adults were recruited to help protect a country paralyzed after a nuclear attack. *Spooks* was retitled *MI-5* in North America, where each 60-minute episode was cut by almost a quarter to make room for adverts. When the series ended, the story continued with the feature film *Spooks: The Greater Good* (2015). **JS**

Classic episode
Season 3, episode 4. Middle East peace talks are derailed when the UN chief negotiator is abducted. The agency tries to find her, but their efforts are hindered by an Israeli extremist who wants to ensure that no agreement is reached.

◉ Peter Firth filming on location in London.

Kath & Kim

Comedy | Australia | 2002–07

Mock fly-on-the-wall documentary about a very strange mother and daughter

Cast | Gina Riley, Jane Turner, Magda Szubanski, Glenn Robbins, Peter Rowsthorn
Original broadcaster | ABC **For fans of . . .** | *Summer Heights High* (2007)

Kath & Kim took Australia by storm in 2002; it took the rest of the world some time to catch up, but catch up it did. It is a pseudo-fly-on-the-wall documentary that follows the lives of Melbourne mother Kath and her daughter Kim. The show is full of righteously spoken mispronunciations, mixed metaphors, rhyming wordplay ("Does it make me a crim to keep myself trim, Kim?") and cuttingly observed characters, many played by Gina Riley and Jane Turner (the Kim and Kath of the title) themselves. Nothing about suburban life is sacred: the show's main satirical target is pretentiousness.

Self-centered Kim keeps leaving her husband Brett and returning home. But Kath has fallen for "purveyor of fine meats" Kel and there is no longer room for

Kim in the family home. Kim's friend Sharon (Magda Szubanski) loyally does all she can for Kim and Kath. Between the three women, and their menfolk, lots of trouble abounds although they remain oblivious to the carnage left in their wake.

A sign of the show's success was the large number of its catchphrases that entered common parlance. **SJG**

Classic episode
The Wedding | *Season 1, episode 8.* Kel is convinced that Kath is going to leave him at the altar, and a horse gets the hots for Kim. Mostly told in flashbacks that explain why Kath, Kim, and Sharon are in hospital after the big day.

⊘ Jane Turner as Kath and Gina Riley as Kim. Their satire on suburban Australia struck a chord all over the world.

Top Gear

Sports | UK | 2002–present

How three car nuts conquered the world with their competitive banter and outrageous road trips

Cast | Jeremy Clarkson, Richard Hammond, James May   **Original broadcaster** | BBC Two
Award | 1 Emmy   **For fans of . . .** | *Wheeler Dealers* (2003), *Counting Cars* (2012)

To produce a car show that is adored by people who have no interest in automobiles is an extraordinary achievement—but that's what BBC's *Top Gear* has done. As well as reviewing new models and covering driving-related news, it invites celebrity guests to drive timed laps, and embarks on chaotic road trips to places like Botswana and Iraq. The emphasis is on entertainment, fun, and the interaction of the hosts.

The original *Top Gear*, a straightlaced consumer-affairs show, was axed in 2001. Former presenter Jeremy Clarkson, however, saw potential. Along with producer Andy Wilman, he pitched a new format to the BBC: retain the car reviews and motoring news, add a studio audience, and build up the jokey rivalry of three presenters—Richard Hammond (from season two), James May, and Clarkson himself.

Top Gear is now shown in almost every country in the world. But pranks that have backfired and politically incorrect banter have caused controversy. In spring 2015, Clarkson was dismissed after a fracas with a producer, and the show faced an uncertain future. **IF**

Classic episode

Christmas Special 2009. The 2009 Bolivia Special was a road trip across South America. Beginning in Bolivia, the team raced each other in battered old cars through jungles and across mountains to the Pacific Ocean.

◉ (L–R) Richard Hammond, Jeremy Clarkson, and James May, whose lighthearted rivalry became a trademark of the show.

Still Game

Comedy | UK | 2002–07

*Pensioners live out their final years on a
run-down housing estate outside Glasgow*

Cast | Ford Kiernan, Greg Hemphill, Paul Riley, Mark
Cox, Jane McCarry, Sanjeev Kohli, Gavin Mitchell
Original broadcaster | BBC Scotland
For fans of . . . | *Last of the Summer Wine* (1973),
Rab C Nesbitt (1988), *Waiting for God* (1990)

If you live anywhere in the world but Scotland, you
can be forgiven for never having heard of *Still Game*.
The show was little broadcast outside its native land.
That was no doubt partly because the characters speak
a broad Glaswegian dialect. But regional accents are
not impenetrable—listeners get used to them;
remember *The Wire*—and the effort to understand is
well rewarded because the show is one of the most
consistently funny British sitcoms of the century
so far. When it was eventually shown in England, it
outperformed much better-known comedies.

Ford Kiernan and Greg Hemphill star as the
cantankerous, eternally bickering lifelong friends Jack
Jarvis and Victor McDade, residents of a dilapidated
tower block. They and their friends Wilson and Tam
are regulars at the local pub, where landlord Bobby
is usually the butt of their merciless jokes. The local
corner shop is run by the amiable Navid (Sanjeev
Kohli), and it's here that incorrigible gossip Isa (Jane
McCarry) can usually be found with the latest updates
on everybody else's news.

Jack, Victor and their friends had previously featured
in a Scottish sketch show, *Chewin' the Fat* (1999), in
which they sang bawdy songs with memorable gusto.
The rough edges and expletives were retained for *Still
Game*, whose razor-sharp script and strong characters
endured through forty-four episodes. Since the show
concluded its run there have been rumors of a new
series, but so far no contracts have been signed. **JS**

Nikolaj og Julie

Comedy/Drama | Denmark | 2002–03

*Proof that Scandinavians can do light
as well as dark*

Cast | Peter Mygind, Sofie Gråbøl, Dejan Cukic, Sofie
Stougaard, Jesper Asholt, Therese Glahn
Original broadcaster | DR1
Award | 1 Emmy
For fans of . . . | *thirtysomething* (1987), *Cold Feet* (1998)

A former mayor hosts *The Jerry Springer Show*, and *Silver
Spoons*' child star Ricky Schroder grew up to feature
on *24*. So perhaps it's not surprising that the creator of
Borgen and the writer of *Forbrydelsen* (*The Killing*) won
their big break with a romantic drama.

Created by Adam Price (*Borgen*) and helmed by
Søren Sveistrup (*Forbrydelsen*), *Nikolaj og Julie* (*Nikolaj
and Julie*) concerned the everyday struggles of thirty-
somethings in Copenhagen. Peter Mygind and future
Forbrydelsen lead Sofie Gråbøl played the titular pair,
and their social circle i consisted of conservative
husband-and-wife Frank (Jesper Asholt) and Karina
(Sofie Stougaard), troubled actress Søs (Therese Glahn),
and player-about-town Philip (Dejan Cukic).

Gråbøl, Asholt, and Stougaard had starred in *Mifunes
sidste sang* (*Mifune's Last Song*, 1999), a formative entry
in Denmark's Dogme 95 filmmaking movement. If
Nikolaj og Julie was far removed from work associated
with Dogme, traces of its integrity could be found
in Gråbøl's commitment to her role. Julie, she told
Autograf, was "a woman with ambitions, a job,
children, wants to be a good mother, stressed out.
Very feminine in her approach to all the problems.
She was so feminine that she was institutionalized at a
mental hospital out of pure feelings of pure femininity.
When we were finished, I thought for a brief second
that I never wanted to make TV again. I lost forty-four
pounds and was completely exhausted." But then *The
Killing* called . . . **BM**

Little Britain

Comedy | UK | 2003–06

A willfully perverse and twisted view of the inhabitants of the British Isles—not for the politically correct or the faint-hearted

Cast | David Walliams, Matt Lucas, Tom Baker, Anthony Head
Original broadcaster | BBC Three
Awards | 4 BAFTAs
For fans of . . . | *The League of Gentlemen* (1999)

Little Britain started on BBC radio before a successful transfer to TV. David Walliams and Matt Lucas played all the major parts, most of which were extreme grotesques whose power came as much from uncomfortable invasions of space as from genuine laughs: rubber-clad Daffydd insisted that he was "the only gay in the village" despite contradictory evidence; government aide Sebastian maintained an obsessive infatuation with his boss, the prime minister (Anthony Head); Marjorie Dawes was the bullying organizer of a "fat fighters" group; unhelpful computer operator Carol justified her bad service with a blunt "Computer says 'no'"; argumentative Vicky Pollard began each exchange with "Yeah, but no, but yeah, but . . ."; and Bubbles was a chronically obese heiress with an unwelcome habit of stripping naked. The series was narrated by former Doctor Who Tom Baker, whose authoritative voice clashed beautifully with an outrageous script that denounced fat people as "vermin" and accused the audience of being "either a woman, a gay, or a mental."

The most popular creations were Lou Todd, well-meaning but patronizing care assistant to Andy Pipkin, a wheelchair user with limited vocabulary (usually "Yeah, I know," "I want that one" and "I don't like it") who always manages to get his own way and is much more mobile than Lou ever realizes. The final series of the show, *Little Britain in the USA*, took the cast farther afield. A spin-off series, *Come Fly with Me* (2010), was a mockumentary about air travel **JS**

Classic episode
Season 11, episode 1. As Lou discusses Andy's care needs with a pool attendant, Andy steps out of his wheelchair, climbs the ladder of a diving board and dive-bombs into the pool, returning to his chair before Lou turns around.

◆ Matt Lucas and David Walliams, for whom taboos exist only to be broken.

Peep Show

Comedy/Drama | UK | 2003–present

Comedy based on inner monologue as voiceover

Cast | David Mitchell, Robert Webb, Olivia Colman, Matt King
Original broadcaster | Channel 4
Awards | 2 BAFTAs
For fans of . . . | *The Office* (2001)

Mark (David Mitchell) is a timid office worker hopelessly pursuing his colleague Sophie (Olivia Colman), a sensible, down-to-earth woman who just might, under the right circumstances, agree to date him if he doesn't blow it by trying too hard and being overbearing. Jeremy, aka Jez (Robert Webb) sees himself as something of a rebel and is determined to make it big on the music scene, like his pal Super Hans (Matt King) seems to have done. On the surface, Jeremy and Mark—flatmates in a high-rise apartment block—appear not to be very nice people, but underneath they're even worse. We know this because we are privy to their secret thoughts, heard in voice-overs, which often contradict their spoken statements and are littered with sexual desperation, bitterness, bile, and obscene fantasies.

Quirky, clever, and extremely dark, *Peep Show* was high-grade theater of embarrassment. Aside from the inner monologue device, another innovation was to force the viewer to witness the action through the characters' eyes: many shots from their points of view, sometimes in extreme close-up, gave the show a curious intimacy and added a level of intensity to the already in-your-face scenes of anger and madness. The lead actors pulled off the difficult trick of making their fundamentally loathsome characters oddly appealing.

Peep Show was not for the faint-hearted but it provided fantastic fun for viewers with strong stomachs—and there were millions of them. **DF**

The Lost Prince

Historical drama | UK | 2003

The true story of a forgotten child of the British royal family

Cast | Daniel Williams, Matthew James Thomas, Brock Everitt-Elwick, Gina McKee, Michael Gambon
Original broadcaster | BBC One
Awards | 1 BAFTA, 3 Emmys
For fans of . . . | *Perfect Strangers* (1986)

Stephen Poliakoff wrote and directed this drama based on the short life (1905–19) of Prince John, the youngest child of the British King George V and Queen Mary, a largely forgotten royal whose name is omitted from all but the most detailed histories of the early twentieth century.

The prince, known as Johnnie (played as a child by Daniel Williams and as a youth by Matthew James Thomas), had severe learning difficulties and was prone to bouts of epilepsy, as a result of which it was decided that he should live in isolation, away from the rest of his family. His only constant companion was Lalla (Gina McKee), a nanny tasked with looking after him and keeping his sickness hidden from guests, other household servants, and even his own relatives. After Johnnie's personal tutor loses hope of ever teaching him anything, Lalla takes on responsibility for his education, never giving up hope that he might one day be accepted and take his place in the wider world.

The two-part miniseries told its story from the boy's perspective. He is close to his grandfather, Edward VII (Michael Gambon), a kindly old man who loves children. It is at the old king's funeral that Johnnie discovers that he is related to all the ruling families of Europe: his father's uncle is the King of Greece, his cousin Bill is the Emperor of Germany.

The Lost Prince synthesizes the small, private world of the tragic youth with the broader canvas of a Europe that is sleepwalking into the First World War. **JS**

Angels in America
Drama | USA | 2003

The 1980s from the perspective of gay people in the United States

Cast | Al Pacino, Meryl Streep, Patrick Wilson, Mary-Louise Parker, Emma Thompson, Justin Kirk, Jeffrey Wright
Original broadcaster | HBO   **Awards** | 5 Golden Globes   **For fans of . . .** | *Philadelphia* (movie) (1993)

This two-part series, told in six chapters, is based on Tony Kushner's seven-hour play of the same name. It is a no-punches-pulled commemoration of the twenty-fifth anniversary of the first recognized case of AIDS.

The story follows the complicated adventures of two women and five men, three of whom are "out," the other two of whom are in the closet. They are all linked in some way to Roy Cohn (Al Pacino), a wheeler-dealer right-wing lawyer who is also gay but won't admit it. After living through the worst years of the disease, they finally come together in Central Park, New York, to talk of the gradual emergence of hope from despair: people can now live with HIV, rather than, as previously, inevitably die of AIDS.

Several members of the cast take several roles, most notably Meryl Streep, who plays plays a rabbi, an angel, and Ethel Rosenberg, who was executed for espionage in 1953; and Emma Thompson, who plays an angel, a tramp, and a nurse. Mike (*The Graduate*) Nichols directed the piece in a theatrically gorgeous yet timeless way. **SJG**

Classic episode
Millennium Approaches | *Season 1, episode 1.*
Powerful and riveting opener in which one of the lead characters is diagnosed with AIDS and Roy Cohn checks in to a hospital for reasons that he doesn't want revealed.

⬢ Emma Thompson as The Angel America appears before Al Pacino as Roy Cohn.

Carnivàle

Drama | USA | 2003–05

This slow-burning drama about a traveling freak show achieved cult status

Cast | Nick Stahl, Clancy Brown, Clea DuVall, Amy Madigan **Original broadcaster** | HBO **Awards** | 5 Emmys
For fans of . . . | *Twin Peaks* (1990), *Deadwood* (2004), *American Horror Story: Freak Show* (2011)

Set in the poverty-stricken Depression of 1930s America, *Carnivàle* was about the struggles faced by members of a freak show run by Samson (*Twin Peaks*'s Michael J. Anderson). The characters were unusual to say the least. There were Ben Hawkins (Nick Stahl), who began to manifest supernatural powers, an insane clergyman (Clancy Brown) and his odd sister (Amy Madigan), and a blind professor (Patrick Bauchau). The story became progressively more supernatural, and gradually evolved into a full-blown battle between Good and Evil, Heaven and Hell, with the writers drawing on tarot cards, the Knights Templar, Freemasonry, and gnosticism.

Carnivàle won a devoted fan base for its stunning visuals, subtle use of musical motifs, period setting, intense performances, and rich mythological themes. Its first episode attracted 5.3 million viewers, but despite winning awards and a large cult following, it didn't sustain these early ratings. With a $2 million per episode budget, the writing was on the wall. Its legacy, however, was considerable. It blazed a trail for the likes of *Boardwalk Empire*, *Fringe*, and *True Detective*. **JGT**

Classic episode
Pick a Number | *Season 1, episode 6.* In a tense and sinister episode, the travelers carry out their own brand of carnival justice. The shocking revelation of Dora Mae's ultimate fate is disturbingly unforgettable.

Michael J. Anderson (Samson) and Nick Stahl (Ben Hawkins) in an episode from season one.

America's Next Top Model

Reality | USA | 2003–present

Mega-successful, fast-paced, high-fashion modeling competition hosted by legendary supermodel Tyra Banks

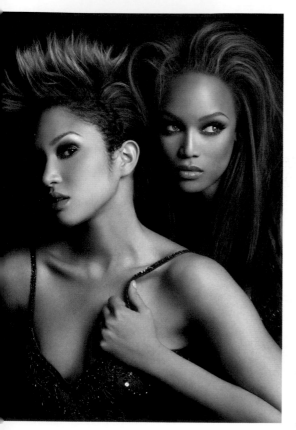

Cast | Tyra Banks, Janice Dickinson, J. Alexander, Twiggy, Kelly Cutrone
Original broadcaster | UPN, The CW
For fans of . . . | *Project Runway* (2004), *RuPaul's Drag Race* (2009)

In 2003, reality television shows were not a new concept, but neither was the genre as saturated as it subsequently became. *America's Next Top Model* was a critical and commercial success from the start as supermodel Tyra Banks took the reins in a nationwide search to launch the career of a new global face.

The format has always been pretty simple: a number of women (and, in seasons twenty and twenty-one, men) compete in various fashion-based challenges to avoid elimination. Each week the aspiring models are tasked with performing in various studio-based and on-location photo shoots, styled and aided by the show's creative director, Jay Manuel. Makeovers are provided early on in each season. These transformations—which usually include dramatic haircuts and colors—are one highlight of the show. Another is the foreign excursions: each season, contestants are whisked away to glamorous locations such as Bali, São Paulo, and Santorini. At the end of each episode the contestants are judged on their best photograph and their overall demeanor and performance throughout. Grand final prizes have included modeling contracts and spreads in global fashion magazines. The judging panel, headed by Tyra and including some of the most vivacious characters from the world of fashion, is as much of a draw as the contestants and challenges themselves.

The format is modified slightly every season, but never fails to hold the audience spellbound. **MB**

Classic episode
The Girl Who Pushes Tyra Over the Edge | *Season 4, episode 7*. At the episode's climax, Tiffany and Rebecca are both eliminated, the first time in the show's history that two contestants rather than one are sent home.

⏺ Naima Mora, winner of season four, and Tyra Banks.

Dae Jang Geum

Historical drama | South Korea | 2003–04

*An epic story of a woman's success
in a male-dominated society*

Cast | Lee Yeong-ae, Ji Jin-hui, Im Ho, Hong Ri-na
Original broadcaster | MBC
For fans of . . . | *The Forsyte Saga* (1967), *Upstairs,
Downstairs* (1971), *The Tudors* (2007), *Downton Abbey*
(2010), *Wolf Hall* (2015)

Historical TV dramas set in the time of the Joseon Dynasty are many, varied, and popular in Korea. Over fifty-four episodes, *Dae Jang Geum* (*The Great Jang-geum*) captivated not only domestic viewers, but also pulled in a worldwide audience. A fictionalized account based on records of a real person living around the turn of the sixteenth century, this epic costume drama followed the turbulent life of Jang-geum (Lee Yeong-ae), a young woman born of low status who rose to become the king's first personal female physician.

Jang-geum was chosen to work in the palace, where she proved to be a diligent kitchen hand with an exceptional palate. Cooking competitions provided a showcase for exquisite Korean dishes fit for the king, and were used to court royal approval. These events were tense affairs laden with backstairs politics, and as a result of one such intrigue Jang-geum was dismissed from service. After various turns of fate, she returned to the palace as an assistant doctor, eventually gaining the trust and affection of King Jungjong (Im Ho), who bestowed on her the honorific title "Dae" ("The Great"). A wealth of subplots and characters enriched the epic story line: notably that concerning Jang-geum's ever-supportive lover, Jeong-ho Min (Ji Jin-hui).

The popularity of *Dae Jang Geum* inspired both a spin-off animated TV series, *Jang Geum's Dream*, and a stage musical. Lee went on to star in Park Chan-wook's crime thriller movie *Sympathy for Lady Vengeance* (2005). **SH**

Jake 2.0

Drama | USA | 2003–04

*A scientist's body is invaded by microscopic
machines that turn him into a superhero*

Cast | Christopher Gorham, Philip Anthony-Rodriguez, Marina Black, Miranda Frigon
Original broadcaster | United Paramount Network
For fans of . . . | *The Six Million Dollar Man* (1974)

Jake 2.0 follows the exploits of Jake Foley (Christopher Gorham), a National Security Agency (NSA) computer technician who's more interested in working in the field than in the labs. When he gets caught in crossfire during a battle between NSA guards and an industrial saboteur he is showered with an experimental serum containing nanomites. These tiny machines enter his bloodstream and transform him into a super being with amazing strength, speed, hearing, vision, and the ability to communicate with computers.

Of course, the NSA realizes this, and plans to use Jake for its own purposes. His situation is complicated by the fact that his girlfriend, Sarah Carter (Marina Black), is part of an investigation into how the serum was developed in the first place.

This short-lived series (only sixteen episodes) failed to attract much interest in the United States on its original airing, and indeed was pulled from transmission with four episodes unaired due to poor ratings. These episodes were included in a run on UK television, however, and have since been shown in syndication on the SciFi Channel.

Among the episodes that were originally broadcast was "Double Agent," in which actor Lee Majors plays Richard "Dick" Fox, a retired agent. Majors was hired specifically so that his appearance on screen would echo his most celebrated role as Steve Austin, the original Bionic Man in the television series *The Six Million Dollar Man*. **DJH**

Slings & Arrows

Comedy | Canada | 2003–06

When it comes to staging Shakespeare, the real show takes place backstage

Cast | Paul Gross, Martha Burns, Mark McKinney, Susan Coyne, Stephen Ouimette, Rachel McAdams
Original broadcasters | Movie Central, The Movie Network
For fans of . . . | *Due South* (1994), *Extras* (2005)

What is it with Paul Gross and ghosts? In *Due South* (1994), as Mountie Benton Fraser, he was haunted by his father; in *Slings & Arrows*, as actor Geoffrey Tennant, he couldn't escape the specter of director Oliver Welles (Stephen Ouimette). As in *Due South*, however, the supernatural element was very much secondary to finely judged and occasionally moving comedy about, as *Variety* noted, "the politics and lunacy surrounding a Shakespearean stage troupe." Key characters alongside Tennant and Welles included passive-aggressive actress Ellen Fanshaw (played by Gross' wife Martha Burns) and young hopeful Kate McNab (Rachel McAdams).

Created by stage actors Susan Coyne and Bob Martin, with former *Kids in the Hall* star Mark McKinney, the three seasons (the first of which was remade in Brazil as 2009's award-winning *Som e Fúria*) followed the cast through productions of *Hamlet*, *Macbeth*, and *King Lear*. "They had to be plays that people had some passing familiarity with," Coyne observed to A.V. Club. "We couldn't do *Cymbeline* or something."

Influenced by the British *House of Cards* (1990), the creators envisioned Shakespearean asides to the camera, but decided that Ouimette's ghostly Oliver provided sufficient commentary. And despite initial critical misgivings that the show might appeal to no one outside Ontario—site of the annual, Shakespeare-oriented Stratford Festival—*Slings & Arrows* proved a smash that confirmed Canadian comedy had no need to take its cues from Stateside models. **BM**

Dead Like Me

Drama | USA | 2003–04

Only George knows when your time on Earth is up . . .

Cast | Ellen Muth, Callum Blue, Jasmine Guy, Cynthia Stevensen, Mandy Patinkin, Britt McKillip, Christine Willes, Laura Harris, Greg Kean.
Original broadcaster | Showtime
For fans of . . . | *Reaper* (2007), *Grimm* (2011)

The show is narrated by and follows the character of Georgia "George" Lass (Muth) who is killed early in the first episode by a flaming toilet seat that plummets to Earth from the passing Mir Space Station. She is reincarnated as a "Reaper," a group of dead humans who have the task of "reaping" the souls from the living just before they die, thus ensuring that any death trauma is spared them. Her new friends and fellow Reapers are Rube (Patinkin) who runs the group and who passes out post-it notes with names, places, and times of death of those they need to reap; Daisy Adair (Harris), a movie starlet who claims to have had sexual relations with many stars of the silver screen; Mason (Blue) a stoner who uses drink as a crutch to his own perceived inadequacies; and Roxy (Guy) a strong-willed woman who is initially working as a traffic warden, but then becomes a police officer. Although they are dead, they still have to "live" and so have jobs to earn money to survive in the real world. For George, this survival also means coming to terms with the family she left behind.

Although nominally a dark comedy, *Dead Like Me* is a well-observed, enjoyable series, covering eternal themes of life and death. It can be harsh at times, and some of the deaths that George has to deal with are not pleasant. Over the course of twenty-nine episodes, all the characters grow and develop, and George in particular changes from an unlikable eighteen year old, to a more mature young woman, better able to cope with all that death can throw at her. **DJH**

One Tree Hill

Drama | USA | 2003–12

Small-town teenage love and loss . . . and basketball

Cast | Chad Michael Murray, James Lafferty, Bethany Joy Lenz, Sophia Bush, Lee Norris, Paul Johansson, Hilarie Burton
Original broadcaster | The WB
For fans of . . . | *Dawson's Creek* (1998), *The O.C.* (2003)

Set in the fictional town of Tree Hill, North Carolina, half-brothers Lucas (Chad Michael Murray) and Nathan (James Lafferty) were rivals both on and off the basketball court. Gradually, the two become friends, facing the neverending realm of teenage high school dramas side by side—gun crime, teenage pregnancy, murder, and drug addictions were just a handful.

After squeezing four seasons out of the final two years of high school, the actors were exponentially older than their teenage counterparts, and the show suddenly jumped forward four years into the future. This allowed the show to escape the difficult high school to college transition often seen in teen shows where the characters all inexplicably decide to stay in their hometown. Shifting the focus to the characters returning to Tree Hill, unsure what to do next after graduation, allowed *One Tree Hill* a realistic portrayal of the difficulties faced by millennials in the "real world." A series reboot of sorts, new characters were introduced and events of the four unseen years were alluded to, giving the characters a chance to mature and grow, having finally escaped high school.

The show continued to play with time in ever creative ways, with the season eight finale episode spanning an entire year, with the final episodes taking place approximately fifteen years after the show's 2003 inception. *One Tree Hill* was also an early adopter of interactive media, allowing viewers to determine the outcome of a story line as early as season two. **EB**

Classic episode
With Tired Eyes, Tired Minds, Tired Souls, We Slept | *Season 3, episode 16.* In this controversial episode, *One Tree Hill* tackled the topic of shootings at high schools in a nuanced and sensitive fashion.

⬤ Chad Michael Murray as Lucas snuggles down with Sophia Bush as Brooke.

Arrested Development

Comedy | USA | 2003–13

A demanding comedy that made viewers concentrate

Cast | Jason Bateman, Jeffrey Tambor, Jessica Walter, Portia de Rossi, Will Arnett, Alia Shawkat
Original broadcaster | Fox
Awards | 6 Emmys
For fans of . . . | *30 Rock* (2006), *Modern Family* (2009)

Conceived by Ron Howard (*Happy Days*) and Mitchell Hurwitz, narrated by Howard and featuring a flawless cast of actors—anchored by Jason Bateman as Michael Bluth, the moral center of a wealthy and very dysfunctional family suddenly torn asunder by a criminal scandal—*Arrested Development* was a critical triumph, even if the ratings never truly caught up.

The beauty of the series was in its clever writing matched by its direction; the comedy lay not within just the words, but also in the sight gags (witness hapless Tobias and his quest to become part of the famed Blue Man Group by covering himself in blue body paint; blue fingerprints all over the Bluth model home continued the gag for weeks) A steady stream of film and television stars, including Ben Stiller and Liza Minnelli, made cameo appearances that added to the credentials of the series, which is often credited as one of the best sitcoms in American television history.

Although canceled after only three seasons, *Arrested Development* became so popular on DVD that Netflix revived the series for one further season, which required even more concentration than its predecessors: episodes were set in the same time period as others but told from different points of view. Eventually sixty-eight episodes were made. At the time of publication of this book, producers were considering a film version, a fifth season, or possibly both. **SL**

❯ Jason Bateman (Michael) and Will Arnett (Gob) in "Colony Collapse" from season four.

Monkey Dust

Comedy | UK | 2003–05

A darkly disturbing animated sketch comedy that's definitely not for kids

Cast | Simon Greenall, Sharon Horgan, Morwenna Banks, Rebecca Front, Frances Barber, Simon Pye
Original broadcaster | BBC Three
For fans of . . . | *Brass Eye* (1997), *The League of Gentlemen* (1999), *Robot Chicken* (2005)

The brainchild of Harry Thompson and Simon Pye, *Monkey Dust* consisted of a series of animated sketches about sexual practices. There is little doubt that none of the material would have been broadcastable in live action form.

In this world, sex was always something either demeaning or heartbreakingly disappointing: a voice-over actor's pillow talk was so bland and passionless that his wife became convinced that he was faking interest; a pathetic balding man concocted preposterous excuses for being late home to conceal from his wife yet another shameful act of extramarital debauchery.

The series made much of British tabloid newspaper obsessions: a demonic Paedofinder General staged public executions of innocent people, including musical theater star Topol (because of his *Fiddler on the Roof* character's desire to "diddle diddle dum" all day long); three teenage boys had fun in a Muslim terrorist cell; and a team of TV executives created a new reality series called *People on the Toilet*.

The standout character of the series was the childlike Ivan Dobsky, an inmate at Crowmarsh Prison who was notorious as "the Meat-Safe Murderer." When DNA evidence revealed his innocence, he was released into society, along with his best friend, a sentient space hopper called Mr. Hoppy, who the viewer learned had been the real murderer all along.

The third season of *Monkey Dust* was its last, after Thompson's death in 2005. **JS**

The Venture Bros.

Animation | USA | 2003–present

In a weird world, good and evil swap roles unpredictably to keep you guessing

Cast | James Urbaniak, Patrick Warburton, Michael Sinterniklaas, Christopher McCulloch, Doc Hammer, Steven Rattazzi, Dana Snyder
Original broadcaster | Cartoon Network
For fans of . . . | *Squidbillies* (2005), *Robotomy* (2010)

This immensely successful, long-running show is largely based on characters from the comic book *Jonny Quest*. An animated series starring Jonny Quest himself had been produced in 1964 by Hanna-Barbera, but *The Venture Bros.* is broader in scope and features encounters with numerous superheroes and supervillains, some of whom were taken from the original, others from a variety of other sources.

At the focal point of the action are Dr. Rusty Venture and his teenage twin sons, Hank and Dean. As the story unfolds, the viewers learn that both boys have been killed numerous times, but have subsequently been regenerated; they have no memory of their previous existences.

Lining up with this trio are the family bodyguards: first, Brock Samson, and then, from season four, Sergeant Hatred, a reformed supervillain pedophile.

The agents of evil who oppose them are all members of the Guild of Calamitous Intent. The worst of them are The Monarch and his companion Dr. Girlfriend, a female with a man's voice who used to go out with another leading baddie, Phantom Limb, but chucked him because he wasn't evil enough.

The continuing success of this bizarre show is due in part to the protean nature of all its characters: slayers can become saints, slimy double dealers can become loving single parents, and torturers can be tormented by conscience. Fans expect—indeed, they demand—the unexpected, and they are seldom disappointed. **GL**

Newlyweds: Nick and Jessica

Reality | USA | 2003–05

A celebrity couple let a film crew in on their private life to create a massive hit series and a disastrously failed marriage

Cast | Nick Lachey, Jessica Simpson, Drew Lachey, Tina Simpson, Lea Lachey, Cacee Cobb, Joe Simpson, Ashlee Simpson
Original broadcasters | MTV (US), MuchMusic (Canada)
For fans of . . . | *The Osbournes* (2002)

The public's growing appetite for reality television turned singers Nick Lachey (former frontman of boy band 98 Degrees) and Jessica Simpson into genuine A-list celebrities as a result of the popularity of their show *Newlyweds: Nick and Jessica.*

Originally conceived as a vehicle for Michael Jackson and his then-wife Priscilla Presley in 1994, the project was shelved by MTV until Jessica's father, Joe Simpson—who managed both Nick and Jessica— pitched the idea of a reality show to the network. The series debuted in conjunction with the release of Jessica's album *In This Skin*, but not much synergy was immediately noticeable, as the album quickly fell down the charts. But then Jessica's "dumb blonde" persona caught on with viewers, and the show became car-crash viewing for reality show buffs. When Jessica's next single, "With You," was released, *In This Skin* began rising in the charts again and spent eight weeks in the Top Ten. Millions of viewers tuned in to *Newlyweds* on a weekly basis for three years to watch Nick and Jessica, their family members, and friends attempt the kind of "normal" life that only the very rich can manage, with Jessica's trademarked ditzy comments and Nick's aggravated responses making them the Gracie Allen and George Burns of the 2000s.

But the couple's arguments on screen were all too real. The final episode of *Newlyweds: Nick and Jessica* aired on March 30, 2005, and the couple filed for divorce on December 16 that same year. **RBA**

Classic episode
Newlyweds Decorate | *Season 1, episode 7.* While Jessica is on a book tour promoting *Jessica Simpson I Do: Achieving Your Dream Wedding*, Nick starts redecorating. On her return to the marital home she is less than pleased.

◉ Jessica Simpson and Nick Lachey keep smiling.

QI

Game show | UK | 2003–present

British quiz show that rewards interesting answers over correct ones

Cast | Stephen Fry, Alan Davies   **Original broadcaster** | BBC Four
For fans of . . . | *Whose Line Is It Anyway?* (1988), *Mock the Week* (2005)

Which country is the world's largest supplier of bibles? The correct answer is China, but you might win points on *QI* if you know something interesting about bibles. Or book production. Or countries that begin with the letter C. Or, frankly, anything. Short for "Quite Interesting," *QI* is a panel/quiz show hosted by Stephen Fry, who asks a rotating selection of panelists baffling questions with no easy answers. Points are awarded for interesting responses and deducted for easy or obvious ones; researchers ("QI elves") are on hand at all times to check the facts.

QI was conceived as a radio show, but during development producer John Lloyd (*Blackadder*, *Not the Nine O'Clock News*) reworked his concept for television.

Every season is themed around a letter of the alphabet, with individual episodes sometimes relating to a single word. Although the panels change from episode to episode, Alan Davies (*Jonathan Creek*), is the one permanent fixture besides Fry, and he provides a good-natured foil to the occasionally over-the-top intellectualism the show cheerfully indulges. **AP**

> **Classic episode**
> *Films and Fame* | *Season 6, episode 11*. David Mitchell, John Sessions, and Emma Thompson join Fry and Davies in a cinema-themed episode that veers off memorably into a discussion about giant tortoises.

⊛ (L–R) Alan Davies, David Mitchell, host Stephen Fry, Rob Brydon, and Dara Ó Briain.

Reno 911!

Comedy | USA | 2003–09

Heavily improvised "mockumentary" of law enforcement reality shows

Cast | Cedric Yarbrough, Niecy Nash, Robert Ben Garant, Thomas Lennon, Kerri Kenney-Silver, Carlos Alazraqui, Wendi McLendon-Covey   **Original broadcaster** | Comedy Central   **For fans of . . .** | *The State* (1993)

Relying on skeletal scripts that set up the basic story but left the details to the actors, *Reno 911!* utilized the well-honed improvisational skills of its cast and guest stars to create a madcap stream of consciousness revolving around the lunatic antics of an inept team of law-enforcement officers from the fictional Reno Sheriff's Department. Parodying reality shows like *COPS*, the series featured the team playing up their exploits for the cameras and lamenting the fact that none of their successes seemed to make the final cut.

Standout recurring characters included Nick Swardson as a flamboyant troublemaker; Patton Oswalt as a passionate gamer whose exploits frequently went awry; Keegan-Michael Key as a hugely suspicious "Theoretical Criminal"; and Oscar Nuñez as criminal mastermind "Spanish Mike" Alvarez.

In 2007 the series transferred to the big screen in *Reno 911!: Miami*. Several of the regular characters were killed off in the sixth TV series, but the producers later regretted that decision and there has since been talk of a revival that resurrects the dead officers. **ATB**

> **Classic episode**
> *Terrorist Training* | *Season 1, episode 12*. The start of a two-parter in which the Office of Homeland Security sends Captain Hernandez and Officer Kim to drill the Reno Sheriff's Department in terror preparedness.

◉ (L–R) Cedric Yarbrough, Kerri Kenney-Silver, Ian Roberts, Thomas Lennon, Niecy Nash, Robert Ben Garant.

The Second Coming

Fantasy/Horror/Sci-Fi | UK | 2003

*What if the Messiah returned,
not to the Holy Land but to modern Britain?*

Cast | Christopher Eccleston, Lesley Sharp,
Mark Benton
Original broadcaster | ITV
For fans of . . . | *Jesus of Nazareth* (1977), *Casanova*
(2005), *Cucumber* (2015)

Writer Russell T. Davies made his name with *Queer as Folk* (2000), set in the gay community in Manchester. He retained a Manchester setting for this drama, although the subject matter could hardly have been more different. *The Second Coming* is an examination of issues of faith and morality, based on a simple premise—what if the Messiah returned to Earth?

Stephen Baxter (Christopher Eccleston) is a pretty average man—he works in a video shop and enjoys a pint with his mates. Then one day, he suddenly vanishes to nearby Saddleworth Moor for forty days and forty nights. When he returns, he claims to be the Son of God. Reactions range from anger to pity, but Stephen is deadly serious, and, during a gathering at a Manchester stadium, he performs a bona fide miracle by transforming night into day. There can be no doubt—this is the Second Coming. Stephen issues an ultimatum: humanity has five days to produce a third testament, or face Judgment Day.

Eccleston made a manic, vulnerable Messiah, by turns arrogant and wracked with self-doubt; Lesley Sharp was excellent as a woman whose humanity might just redeem us all. In its depiction of overwhelming issues and their impact on the lives of ordinary people, *The Second Coming* was bold, challenging, and breathtakingly imaginative. Davies and Eccleston would team up again the following year to re-create another savior of the world in the rebooted and revitalized *Doctor Who*. **WM**

Two and a Half Men

Comedy | USA | 2003–15

*Two adults, one kid, no grown-ups:
millions of viewers*

Cast | Charlie Sheen, Jon Cryer, Angus T. Jones,
Conchata Ferrell, Holland Taylor, Melanie Lynskey
Original broadcaster | CBS
Awards | 9 Emmys
For fans of . . . | *The Big Bang Theory* (2007), *Mom* (2013)

Chuck Lorre (*Roseanne*, *Grace Under Fire*, *Cybill*) and Lee Aronsohn (*The Love Boat*) were hired to write a show about two brothers. In what turned out to be a stroke of brilliance, they added a third lead, a precocious scene-stealing juvenile.

The setup was this: Alan was married with a young son, Jake; his brother Charlie was a self-indulgent and footloose bachelor. When Alan divorced, Charlie had to take care of his nephew, and soon found that his new duties cramped his hedonistic lifestyle. The sparks came from the three males' efforts to forge new relationships with one another.

The scenario was good, but the real key to the show's enormous success lay in the casting of Charlie Sheen as Charlie and Angus T. Jones as Jake. Sheen's private life was reputedly not unlike that of the character he was playing; although Jones was only nine years old when shooting started, he was already a veteran of *ER* (1994). This duo was well complemented by Jon Cryer as Alan and Conchata Ferrell as the men's sharp-speaking housekeeper, Berta.

From 2005 through 2010, *Two and a Half Men* was the most watched comedy on US television. After eight seasons, however, the show crashed and burned spectacularly. Jones—now a born-again Christian—decried it as "filth"; Sheen needed substance rehab and was fired. Ashton Kutcher stepped into the breach, but the magic vanished from the final four seasons and the last of the 262 episodes aired in 2015. **BM**

❷ Charlie Sheen (Charlie Harper) goes shopping with his young nephew Angus T. Jones (Jake Harper).

Tru Calling

Fantasy/Horror/Sci-Fi | USA | 2003–05

The dead ask Tru Davies for help, causing her to relive each victim's last day on Earth in the hope of saving them

Cast | Eliza Dushku, Zach Galifianakis, Shawn Reaves, Jason Priestley
Original broadcaster | Fox
For fans of . . . | *Dollhouse* (2009), *Quantum Leap* (1989)

Tru Davies (Eliza Dushku) had hopes of becoming a doctor until a prized internship at a local hospital failed to materialize. Determined to grasp any connection to her chosen profession, she accepted a job at the city morgue. On her first day there, a dead body spooked her by asking her for help. Suddenly she found herself catapulted back to the beginning of the day, trying to save that person from death.

The premise of the show was that select individuals who got "The Calling" were destined to relive times past and right the balance of the universe, as in a morbid *Groundhog Day*. A challenge came with the arrival of Jack Harper (Jason Priestley), whose role was to prevent Tru from changing events, to set the course of fate back on its tracks and ensure that the dead stayed dead—but which of them would get to the recently departed first?

That *Tru Calling* survived to a second season can be attributed to the genuine chemistry between the ensemble cast and some thought-provoking writing from a team led by Jon Harmon Feldman. The series had a novel take on the notions of time travel and the paranormal, and, after a shaky start, began to draw in strong ratings. Celebrations were premature though, as the show was canceled during production of the sixth episode of season two.

Disappointed fans were later relieved when writer Doris Egan posted a blog that provided them with the uncompleted story arcs. **MC**

Classic episode
'Twas the Night Before Christmas . . . Again | *Season 2, episode 6.* The last-ever episode delivered new plot devices, new connections, and touching performances. The cast knew the series was canceled as they filmed it.

⬙ Eliza Dushku does dialogue with the dead.

NCIS

Drama | USA | 2003–present

Long-running drama about US navy cops tracking down criminals and fighting terrorists

Cast | Mark Harmon, Michael Weatherly, Pauley Perrette, David McCallum, Cote de Pablo, Rocky Carroll
Original broadcaster | CBS
For fans of . . . | *Moonlighting* (1985), *JAG* (1995)

With a winning combination of action, humor, and character depth, crime drama *NCIS* has been one of American television's monster hits. Clever case-of-the-week stories are the show's backbone, but it's more than a standard police procedural. The interplay and complexity of the regular cast mean audiences have cared deeply for its members for more than a decade.

In the eighth season of US military-lawyer drama *JAG*, a special two-part story focused on a team of agents from the Naval Criminal Investigative Service (NCIS). This "backdoor pilot" introduced us to Special Agent Leroy Jethro Gibbs (Mark Harmon), a no-nonsense but compassionate widower and former Marine who investigates crimes perpetrated against or by US Navy personnel. His original team contained charismatic man-child Tony DiNozzo, Goth-fan forensics expert Abby Sciuto, and cultured medical examiner Donald "Ducky" Mallard. When promoted to their own series a few months later, the group grew with the gradual addition of ex-Secret Service agent Caitlin Todd, computer geek Timothy McGee, damaged Israeli operative Ziva David, and country girl Ellie Bishop.

Although a show about terrorism and murder, character comedy is never far away. Running jokes have built up over the years, such as Gibbs' set of unbreakable rules for life, Abby's addiction to energy drinks, and Ducky's long-winded anecdotes. *NCIS* has become an enormous success, amassing huge viewing figures and giving birth to two further spin-offs. **IF**

State of Play

Drama | UK | 2003

The investigation into the murder of an MP's researcher uncovers political corruption

Cast | John Simm, David Morrissey, Bill Nighy, Philip Glenister, James McAvoy, Marc Warren, Rory McCann
Original broadcaster | BBC One
Awards | 3 BAFTAs
For fans of . . . | *House of Cards* (1990), *Spooks* (2002)

A young man is murdered; in a separate incident at around the same time a woman is killed after falling under the wheels of a subway train. At the outset there seems to be no connection between the two deaths, the first a drug-related slaying, the second no more than a tragic accident. But while the police uncover nothing in either case, a newspaper investigation reveals that both the deceased were victims of a corrupt scheme hatched by oil tycoons and British government ministers. Piece by piece, the journalists complete the jigsaw: they know who committed the crimes, but can they prove it? And if they can, will someone powerful prevent them from doing so?

Scriptwriter Paul Abbott had risen through the ranks at Granada TV, where he had credits for *Coronation Street*, *Children's Ward*, and *Cracker*, before creating *Clocking Off* and *Linda Green* for the BBC. *State of Play* was Abbott's response to a challenge by BBC drama boss Jane Tranter to write something on a bigger scale than his previous works.

The six-part thriller was hailed by critics as one of the top dramas of 2004, and Abbott was commissioned to write a second serial before the first had been broadcast. Ultimately, that follow-up never materialized; instead Abbott created *Shameless*, a new drama for Channel 4. In 2009, Russell Crowe, Ben Affleck, and Helen Mirren starred in a big-screen adaptation of *State of Play*, in which the action was transposed from London to Washington, D.C. **JS**

Nip/Tuck

Drama | USA | 2003–10

Tell me what you don't like about your body, and I'll fix it

Cast | Dylan Walsh, Julian McMahon, John Hensley, Joely Richardson, Roma Maffia, Linda Klein, Kelsey Batelaan
Original broadcaster | FX   **Awards** | 1 Emmy, 1 Golden Globe   **For fans of . . .** | *Six Feet Under* (2001)

Plastic surgeons Sean MacNamara and Christian Troy were best friends, who ran a successful clinic in Miami, Florida (later relocated to LA). While Sean juggled his family life with his career, and aimed to be the moral voice of the two, Christian was a party animal, who took advantage of his high-status job to seduce women. Often blunt, he told a model he slept with in the pilot episode exactly what surgery he would recommend to remove her flaws and take her from an "eight" to a "ten."

The show became known for its graphic depiction of plastic surgery, from mundane work, such as nose and breast jobs, to increasingly fashionable procedures, including vaginal rejuvenation, which led to extensive award nominations for the makeup and prosthetics team. *Nip/Tuck* reflected the increasing acceptability of cosmetic surgery, and did not moralize. Each episode was named after the patient being treated that week.

When it first aired, *Nip/Tuck* was the highest rated new cable series in the United States and at its peak had domestic ratings of nearly six million. It was sold to more than seventy countries. **EB**

> **Classic episode**
> *Joan Rivers* | *Season 2, episode 16*. In an example of the dark humor that ran through the show, Joan Rivers wants her face returned to what it should have been had she never embarked on plastic surgery.

⊘ Dylan Walsh (Dr. Sean MacNamara) and Julian McMahon (Dr. Christian Troy) size up their patient.

The O.C.

Drama | USA | 2003–07

Prime-time soap opera focusing on the teen generation

Cast | Ben McKenzie, Adam Brody, Peter Gallagher, Kelly Rowan, Mischa Barton, Rachel Bilson, Melinda Clarke
Original broadcaster | Fox   **For fans of . . .** | *Melrose Place* (1992), *Dawson's Creek* (1998)

Ryan Atwood (Ben McKenzie), an edgy boy from the wrong side of the tracks, is adopted by the Cohens, a wealthy Newport Beach family. That was the launch point of *The O.C.*, a prime-time soap whose title initials stand for "Orange County," a rich district of California.

Created by Josh Schwartz (*Gossip Girl*, *Chuck*) and executive produced by prolific filmmaker McG, *The O.C.* became an enormous hit and launched the careers of its four young leads (McKenzie, Adam Brody, Mischa Barton, and Rachel Bilson). Its first season was regarded as the best, on the strength of both its appealing young actors and the charismatic performances of Peter Gallagher as idealistic lawyer/doting father Sandy Cohen and Kelly Rowan as his wife Kirsten.

The O.C. was not without its shortcomings— meandering story lines; ham-fisted dialogue—and off-screen scandal, especially that surrounding Barton's controversial departure at the end of the third season. Nevertheless, the show inspired the development of numerous similar drama series aimed at 1990s children approaching their teenage years. **SL**

Classic episode
The Ties That Bind | *Season 1, episode 27*.
Fearing that the one person he's ever wanted— Summer—has been lost for good, Seth Cohen sets out on his own . . . leaving the future of the show's most popular relationship in jeopardy.

◉ Ben McKenzie (Ryan) and Mischa Barton (Marissa Cooper), his sexually ambivalent neighbor.

The Mighty Boosh

Comedy | UK | 2004–07

The bizarre comic fantasy adventures of a jazz fan, a fashion victim, a mystic, and their gorilla

Cast | Julian Barratt, Noel Fielding, Michael Fielding, Dave Brown, Rich Fulcher
Original broadcaster | BBC Three
For fans of . . . | *Monty Python's Flying Circus* (1969), *The Goodies* (1972)

"Come with us now on a journey through time and space . . . to the world of the Mighty Boosh": so began each episode of the cult comedy, as "jazz maverick" Howard Moon (Julian Barratt), and "King of the Mods" Vince Noir (Noel Fielding) brought the viewers their craziest, zaniest adventures, full of pop-culture references, psychedelic visuals, and musical interludes. In season one, the duo worked as zookeepers in the dilapidated "Zooniverse" under a manager who knew nothing about animals; in season two they shared an apartment with Bollo the talking gorilla; in season three they assisted at the Nabootique, a magic shop. Along the way, Vince saved Howard from some monstrous threats, which could be anything from the ancient, abominable Yeti to Old Gregg, the deep sea transexual (many of these unique and crazy characters were played by the leads themselves). Perhaps the finest comic creations were the simple-minded, happy Moon and a disembodied pink-headed shaman with tentacles sprouting from his neck.

The second and third seasons of *The Mighty Boosh* took the characters even further into the surreal, the wacky, and the outright grotesque, with the accompaniment of increasingly zany a capella songs, but the show always remained at heart a modern variation on the classic odd-couple theme.

Production ended after twenty episodes, but there have since been persistent rumors of a full-length movie version. **IDG**

Dog the Bounty Hunter

Reality | USA | 2004–12

Criminals pursued by an agent of justice and a camera crew

Cast | Duane "Dog" Chapman, Beth Chapman, Cecily Barmore-Chapman, "Baby" Lyssa Rae Chapman, Duane Lee Chapman Junior, Leland Chapman
Original broadcaster | A&E
For fans of . . . | *Justice* (2006)

The idea for this long-running show came from the 2002 appearance on *Take This Job*, a series about people with out-of-the-ordinary occupations, of Duane "Dog" Chapman, who made a living out of capturing fugitives from justice.

Dog the Bounty Hunter was mainly high-octane action involving fights, fast-car chases, and confrontations, but it also treated the human stories behind the criminality. Dog was tough—he had served time in prison himself—but he was not heartless: he believed in the possibility of redemption, and that even the worst felon deserves a second chance.

Set predominantly in Hawaii and Colorado, the series followed Dog, his wife Beth, and assorted offspring, all working for Dog's company to track down wanted men and women. A typical episode would see leather-clad Chapman and his team follow leads and clues that led them to the inevitable capture of the villain of the week in the final scene. There was also conflict between Dog and his family—some of the confrontations were played out on screen, while others that blew up in private were deliberately leaked to the news media in order to keep the show in the spotlight.

Dog the Bounty Hunter was later parodied in *Family Guy* and *South Park*, thus cementing its place in the collective consciousness of the viewing public. Although the series ended in 2012, a spin-off—*Dog and Beth: On the Hunt*—continued in production for Country Music Television (CMT). **RJH**

Battlestar Galactica
Fantasy/Horror/Sci-Fi | USA | 2004–09

A dynamic reimagining for a new generation

Cast | Edward James Olmos, Mary McDonnell, Katee Sackhoff, Jamie Bamber, Tricia Helfer, James Callis
Original broadcaster | Sci-Fi Channel **Awards** | 3 Emmys **For fans of . . .** | *Babylon 5* (1994)

A controversial "reimagining" of a short-lived but hugely popular 1970s science-fiction entertainment, *Battlestar Galactica* beat all the odds. Immensely popular with critics and celebrated for its writing and acting, it became the most acclaimed show on the Sci-Fi Channel and proved that genuine science fiction could be received positively without resorting to cliché or bug-eyed monsters.

Galactica breathed new life into the original characters—the last survivors of an attack by the vicious Cylons, consigned to a small fleet of ships in search of a lost colony of mankind called Earth. At its core was a brilliant cast, anchored by Edward James Olmos as stoic ship commander Bill Adama, and

Mary McDonnell as steadfast teacher Laura Roslin, who was thrust begrudgingly into the political arena. Written by a team led by *Star Trek* alumnus Ronald D. Moore, *Galactica* probed the depths of moral relativity, religious conviction, sacrifice, and human spirit: a saga of a broken people cast out of Paradise, left to their base instincts to seek only survival. **SL**

> **Classic episode**
> *33* | *Season 1, episode 1.* The first regular episode remains one of the best: it is a taut thriller pitting the exhausted crew against the clock to discover the secret behind their enemy's attacks, which take place at thirty-three-minute intervals.

⊘ Jamie Bamber as Capt. Lee "Apollo" Adama and Bodie Olmos as Lt. Brendan "Hot Dog" Costanza.

Entourage

Comedy | USA | 2004–11

An A-list actor and his buddies navigate the shark-infested waters of Hollywood

Cast | Kevin Connolly, Adrian Grenier, Jeremy Piven, Kevin Dillon, Jerry Ferrara   **Original broadcaster** | HBO
Awards | 1 BAFTA, 6 Emmys, 1 Golden Globe   **For fans of . . .** | *Californication* (2007), *Suits* (2011)

Entourage is a study of five men charting their course through the Hollywood scene. It was developed by series creator Doug Ellin from the experiences of actor/former rap star Mark Wahlberg.

At the start of *Entourage* we meet actor Vincent Chase (Adrian Grenier), fresh off a blockbuster film and looking to make his next move. Chase, who grew up relatively poor in a rough part of Queens, New York, has three friends (some might say sycophants): Eric Murphy (Kevin Connolly), his confidante; Turtle (Jerry Ferrara), his driver; and Johnny (nicknamed "Drama"), his older brother, a faded TV actor, played by Kevin Dillon. Vince is managed by Ari Gold (a multi-award-winning performance by Jeremy Piven), a sharp-tongued agent

who is loyal to his clients but always most concerned about his own financial advancement.

Entourage was a mainstay of HBO's rotating schedule for eight seasons. It featured guest appearances by numerous celebrities—among them movie directors James Cameron, Peter Jackson, and Martin Scorsese—some of whom played themselves. **SL**

> **Classic episode**
> *One Day in the Valley* | *Season 3, episode 2.*
> Stuck in LA's suburban San Fernando Valley after a series of misadventures, the guys crash a pool party thrown by unsupervised high school kids. Needless to say, maturity goes out the window.

⦿ (L–R) Adrian Grenier (Chase), Jerry Ferrara (Turtle), Kevin Connolly (Murphy), and Kevin Dillon ("Drama").

Blackpool

Comedy/Drama | UK | 2004

Big-time dreams, small-town corruption, and a detective who is not entirely guiltless

Cast | David Morrissey, Sarah Parish, David Tennant, Georgia Taylor, Thomas Morrison, John Thomson, Steve Pemberton
Original broadcaster | BBC One
For fans of . . . | *The Singing Detective* (1986)

Blackpool, Lancashire, northwest England: home of the pleasure beach, nightclubs, drag shows, and amusement arcades. Loud and brash, the place drew revelers, straight and gay, from all over Britain. It also attracted businesspeople looking to make money from the leisure industry.

Told over six one-hour episodes, *Blackpool* followed a murder investigation in the newly opened amusement arcade owned and run by entrepreneur Ripley Holden (David Morrissey). Holden was the chief suspect. Sexist and homophobic, he lived like a wheeling and dealing Nashville wannabe. People either instantly loved or hated him, and Scottish police detective Carlisle (David Tennant) found him repulsive. He fell for Holden's wife, Natalie (Sarah Parish), who at first resisted the fantasy that her life would be fine with him and not her husband. The Holdens' children—Shyanne (Georgia Taylor) and Danny (Thomas Morrison)—had their problems in love: Shyanne with a man who went to school with her dad, and Danny with a prostitute who worked in one of his dad's apartments. Both kids really wanted nothing more than their father's approval.

The soundtrack was filled with pop and rock tunes that the cast of larger-than-life characters broke into dance routines to and sang along with. Laced with dark humor, the series was more drama than comedy or musical. Background characters all came to life as well, bringing a vibrancy to the tale of family love torn asunder by strangers and sex. **SJG**

Green Wing

Comedy | UK | 2004–07

Lightning-paced and surreal, this show was a fresh take on situation comedy

Cast | Tamsin Greig, Julian Rhind-Tutt, Stephen Mangan, Mark Heap, Michelle Gomez
Original broadcaster | Channel 4
Award | 1 BAFTA
For fans of . . . | *Scrubs* (2001)

Created by the team that delivered the fast-paced, female-driven sketch show *Smack the Pony* (1999), this series took elements of that program and added a linking story line to create a fresh TV comedy. Although set in a hospital, it mostly ignored medical matters and instead concentrated on the intertwined lives of a disparate group of strange and flawed characters.

Central to it all was Dr. Caroline Todd (Tamsin Greig), a newcomer confronted by a menagerie of colorful eccentrics, including two would-be suitors, handsome surgeon Mac (Julian Rhind-Tutt) and the soulless egocentric Guy Secretan (Stephen Mangan). Elsewhere the viewers encountered the intense Dr. Alan Statham (Mark Heap), an active volcano of spluttering insecurities and barely contained lust; the unsettling staff-liaison officer Sue White (Michelle Gomez), who belittled those seeking her help; and Joanna Clore (Pippa Heywood), the highly strung human relations officer who was sexually involved with Dr. Statham. Although sitcom type plots could be found in the sixty-five-minute long episodes, they mainly operated as lines on which to hang sketches.

Green Wing was an ambitious hybrid show that incorporated a flashy style (slo-mo and speeded up film were used to link scenes) and favored a system whereby scriptwriters incorporated improvisation worked out by the actors beforehand, which encouraged them to push back boundaries. Certainly, many of the characters were unusually extreme. **DF**

Veronica Mars

Drama | USA | 2004–07

Beautifully written noir detective drama set in a high school where all is not as lovely as it appears from the outside

Cast | Kristen Bell, Jason Dohring, Enrico Colantoni
Original broadcaster | UPN, The CW
For fans of . . . | *Buffy the Vampire Slayer* (1997), *Dawson's Creek* (1998), *Freaks and Geeks* (1999), *Gossip Girl* (2007), *Top of the Lake* (2013)

Veronica Mars put its teenage characters into tough adult situations and dealt with real-life concerns; in that respect it was rather like *Buffy the Vampire Slayer*. It was funny, too, with a sharp-witted and quip-filled script that was worthy of the best sitcoms.

It was neo-noir, a private-dick show set in Neptune High, a Californian school attended by the children of the uberwealthy . . . and by the children of their household staff. As the show began, Veronica's friend Lilly had been murdered, and while investigating that crime throughout the whole first season, Veronica uncovered the dark secrets in those immaculate homes, and grapples with her own issues.

The standout performance was that of Kristen Bell in the title role. Again like Buffy, Veronica had something she had to do in the world, something more than simply find a boy and fall in love. She resisted love on the grounds that it might distract her from her greater purpose, make her contented, and take away her drive. In that, it's as relevant to real life as any drama ever has been.

The show lasted only three seasons, each of which had a different central mystery, but six years after its cancellation its creator, Rob Thomas, asked for $2 million of crowdfunding to make a movie that would wrap up the story. The Kickstarter project raised almost $6 million and the movie premiered in Los Angeles in 2014—proof that studio moguls no longer have the final say in whether a show will run or fall. **RL**

Classic episode
A Trip to the Dentist | *Season 1, episode 21*.
By reconstructing various subtly different accounts of the same events, Veronica finally manages to identify the man who raped her at a party the previous summer.

⊙ Kristen Bell as Veronica shows who's in charge.

Desperate Housewives

Comedy/Drama | USA | 2004–12

The lives and loves of suburban American wives and their families

Cast | Felicity Huffman, Teri Hatcher, Marcia Cross, Eva Longoria, James Denton, Ricardo Antonio Chavira, Doug Savant, Brenda Strong **Original broadcaster** | ABC **For fans of . . .** | *Dallas* (1978), *Dynasty* (1981)

Desperate Housewives began with a bang, literally: the suicide of a housewife, who subsequently became the show's primary voiceover.

The overarching story focused on the lives, loves, and social circles of four women: unassuming Susan Mayer (Teri Hatcher), who had recently moved in to the show's Wisteria Lane locale; calculating Bree Van de Camp (Marcia Cross); Gabrielle Solis (Eva Longoria), an iron-willed Latina with a jealous husband and a secret tryst with her gardener; and Lynette Scavo (Felicity Huffman), a hard-pressed mother forced to go back to work after her husband loses his job. The four became friends and remained together through eight seasons of scandal, intrigue, and murder.

The show became ABC's Sunday night anchor for nearly a decade. Creator Marc Cherry supervised the series throughout its entire run; he was also at the center of a highly publicized casting battle involving recurring player Nicolette Sheridan, whose role as thrice-married femme fatale Edie was written out in the fifth season. **SL**

Classic episode
Free | *Season 4, episode 17*. The season finale marking the series' halfway point settles up its current ongoing story lines and then makes an unexpected and shocking jump five years into the future for its final act.

◕ (L–R) Eva Longoria (Gabrielle), Felicity Huffman (Lynette), Marcia Cross (Bree), and Teri Hatcher (Susan) .

The 4400

Fantasy/Horror/Sci-Fi | USA | 2004–07

Abductees return after sixty years with strange powers

Cast | Joel Gretsch, Jacqueline McKenzie, Mahershalalhashbaz Ali, Billy Campbell, Conchita Campbell
Original broadcaster | USA Network **For fans of . . .** | *Dark Skies* (1996), *Roswell* (1999), *Threshold* (2005)

In 1946, eight-year-old Maia Rutledge (Conchita Campbell) was abducted, making her the first of more than 4,000 people to disappear over a period of six decades. When a giant ball of light dropped them all back into 2004, the US National Threat Assessment Command discovered that some of the returnees exhibit paranormal abilities: precognition, telekinesis, telepathy, and even the power to resurrect the dead.

Anyone hoping for a straightforward alien abduction story must have been thrown by the conclusion of the first season, when it was revealed that the returnees were snatched by humans from the future. In later seasons the viewers learned that their special attributes were generated by a neurotransmitter.

Low ratings and the ongoing Writers Guild of America strike in 2007 made cancellation inevitable, and though fans ran an inventive campaign to maintain interest in their favorite show—they sent sunflower seeds to the network—they were ultimately unsuccessful. They could, however, follow the ongoing stories in a series of spin-off novels. **MR**

Classic episode
Life Interrupted | *Season 2, episode 6.* A time-shift diversion from the main narrative, the viewers see how the main characters' lives would have panned out if they had not been missing for more than half a century.

⊙ (L–R) Tom Verica (Dr. Max Hudson), Jacqueline McKenzie (Diana Skouris), and Joel Gretsch (Tom Baldwin) in "Mommy's Bosses."

The Catherine Tate Show

Comedy | UK | 2004–06

Sketch comedy featuring a host of outrageous characters, some of whose expressions passed into common usage

Classic episode

Series 1, episode 5. Nan visits a discount store and finds nothing to her liking; Lauren copes in her own inimitable way with the discovery that she has not been invited to a friend's party; and a host of other sketches.

⊙ Catherine Tate as argumentative schoolgirl Lauren Cooper.

Cast | Catherine Tate, Mathew Horne, Niky Wardley, Derren Litten, Angela McHale, Ella Kenion, Andy Dennehy, Lee Ross
Original broadcaster | BBC One
For fans of . . . | *Little Britain* (2003)

Catherine Tate's series of character-based sketches showcased her genius for accents. Her physical appearance was often changed for different roles through the extensive use of makeup and often comical prosthetics.

She did a nice line in parody, particularly of police procedural dramas, but her most memorable creations were eccentric (and usually deranged) imagined (but strangely recongizable) individuals. Among the most celebrated of these were Derek Farr, an effeminate middle-aged gentleman who exclaimed "How very dare you!" whenever anyone made the natural assumption about his sexuality; a hyper-tense woman who screamed in fright at the sudden noise of her husband's breakfast cereal; and Lauren, an insolent, disengaged schoolgirl who responds to every rebuke with "Am I bovvered?" "Bovvered?" soon passed into common parlance, and was named Word of the Year in 2007.

All of Tate's characters were well observed. Many were comfortable stereotypes, but some were controversial, none more so than Joannie Taylor, aka Nan, an elderly woman whose long-suffering grandson Jamie (Mathew Horne) would come to visit, only to hear her spew a litany of objectionable and obscene opinions about anyone and anything.

After the series ended, Tate went on to take major roles in the revival of *Doctor Who* and the US version of *The Office*. **JS**

Bodies

Drama | UK | 2004–06

Dark and disturbing visceral drama about medical practitioners

Cast | Max Beesley, Patrick Baladi, Keith Allen, Neve McIntosh
Original broadcaster | BBC Three
For fans of . . . | M*A*S*H (1972), _House_ (2004), _Line of Duty_ (2012)

Bodies was an unsettling, emotional rollercoaster of a series, often agonizingly bleak but elsewhere shot through with a rich vein of jet-black humor.

Idealistic young doctor Rob Lake (Max Beesley) takes up a new post at an obstetrics and gynaecology department in a monolithic infirmary. He soon realizes that his boss, consultant Roger Hurley (Patrick Baladi), is dangerously incompetent and gets by on self-confidence, good looks, and charm. Lake contemplates becoming a whistle-blower but is warned by (among others) Nurse Donna Rix (Neve McIntosh) that it would do no good and result only in damaging or destroying Lake's own career. Lake gets no help either from another colleague, consultant Tony Whitman (Keith Allen), a brilliant surgeon who is aware of Hurley's shortcomings but is more concerned with making money. Lake's moral dilemma and deteriorating relationship with Hurley form the basis of the ongoing story, although the various (romance-free) sexual trysts between the staff provide interesting sideshows.

Creator/writer (and ex-doctor) Jed Mercurio here delivered an uncompromising tour de force based on his own book in which he observed that incompetent doctors get away with it for years as their colleagues turn blind eyes. That cynicism was brought more into focus by the graphic, sometimes horrific, surgical sequences and their gory consequences. _Bodies_ was not for the squeamish, but those with the stomach for it were rewarded with a memorable experience. **DF**

North and South

Historical drama | UK | 2004

Pride and Prejudice _for the age of the Industrial Revolution_

Cast | Daniela Denby-Ashe, Richard Armitage, Tim Pigott-Smith, Lesley Manville, Sinead Cusack, Brendan Coyle, Anna Maxwell Martin
Original broadcaster | BBC One
For fans of . . . | _Bleak House_ (2005), _Cranford_ (2007)

This striking adaptation of Elizabeth Gaskell's classic 1855 love story, set against the background of mid-nineteenth-century British industrial upheaval, established a high-water mark for the BBC's costume dramas in the twenty-first century.

Following a crisis of conscience, clergyman Richard Hale (Tim Pigott-Smith) leaves the Church of England, uproots his wife Hannah (Lesley Manville) and nineteen-year-old daughter Margaret (Daniela Denby-Ashe) from their comfortable existence in the rural south of England and moves them to the industrial town of Milton (a fictionalized Manchester). While caring for her ailing parents there, Margaret gains firsthand experience of the strained relationship between the social classes as farm laborers move to the urban area in search of work. She observes the efforts of local mill workers to form trade unions and the social and economic threat of industrial strikes. Meanwhile she struggles with diminishing success to resist her growing attraction to handsome mill owner John Thornton (Richard Armitage).

Many screen versions of classic novels are criticized for anachronism, but here the attention to period detail was unfalteringly superb. The central perfomances were all outstanding, but if one had to be singled out for special praise it would be that of Armitage. A virtual unknown when he took the role, he was acclaimed Best Actor of 2004 in a BBC poll and went on to star in _Spooks_ (2002) and _The Hobbit_ (2012). **AP**

Boston Legal
Drama | USA | 2004–08

Slick, multilayered, and funny, this legal drama outshone the show from which it was spun

Cast | James Spader, William Shatner, Candice Bergen, Julie Bowen, Mark Valley
Original broadcaster | ABC **Awards** | 1 Golden Globe, 5 Emmys **For fans of . . .** | *Rumpole of the Bailey* (1978)

A spin-off from David E. Kelley's *The Practice* (1997), *Boston Legal* developed an irreverent, postmodern style all its own. Alan Shore (James Spader) and Denny Crane (William Shatner) comprised one of legal drama's finest partnerships. The final seven episodes of *The Practice* served as the pilot for the series, with Spader going to work for the brilliant but erratic litigator Denny Crane of Crane, Poole, & Schmidt. Other staff included senior partner Shirley Schmidt (Candice Bergen), managing partner Paul Lewiston (Rene Auberjonois), and Brad Chase (Mark Valley). The show played fast and loose with narrative and often broke the fourth wall, with characters aware they were in a TV show. Denny even mentioned having captained his own spaceship.

This fast-moving, hugely entertaining drama was a revolving door for the cast. Only Spader, Shatner, and Bergen stayed the distance. Despite respectable ratings, *Boston Legal* was curtailed after a shortened fifth season. Most episodes finished on the balcony of Denny's office, with Alan and Denny smoking cigars and ruminating on the day. **MW**

Classic episode
Son of the Defender | *Season 3, episode 18*.
Fifty years ago, Denny and his father successfully represented a murderer—and the son of the victim holds Denny hostage and forces him to retry the case.

⊘ (L–R) Candice Bergen (Shirley Schmidt), William Shatner (Denny Crane), and James Spader (Alan Shore).

Project Runway

Reality | USA | 2004–present

A reality show in which aspiring fashion designers face a panel of demanding judges

Cast | Heidi Klum, Tim Gunn, Nina Garcia, Michael Kors, Zac Posen **Original broadcaster** | Bravo
For fans of . . . | *America's Next Top Model* (2003), *RuPaul's Drag Race* (2009)

Created by Eli Holzman, *Project Runway* is a fashion design competition in which contestants create clothing with restrictions on time, materials, and theme.

Each episode's challenge requires the designers to develop new clothing to be presented at a runway show. The requirements vary from week to week: the contestants may have to use non-traditional materials, design for a corporate fashion line, or incorporate a particular feature. The designers are mentored by consultant Tim Gunn.

At the end of each episode, the designers dress their models, select their hair, makeup, and accessories, and send their creations down the runway. Resident judges Heidi Klum (who hosts the show), Nina Garcia,

and Michael Kors, along with celebrity guest judges, eliminate usually one designer per episode until three or four remain. After the final challenge, the remaining designers are told to prepare a complete collection to be presented at New York Fashion Week. The ultimate winner is selected by the judges, and receives significant prizes. **RP**

> **Classic episode**
> *En Garde!* | *Season 4, episode 8.* In an avant-garde gown challenge, teammates Chris March and Christian Siriano fused their skill sets and produced an epic, towering, breathtaking creation that appeared to defy gravity.

◬ (L–R) Designer Michael Kors, singer/designer Victoria Beckham, and model/host Heidi Klum judge a runway show.

House

Drama | USA | 2004–12

Medical drama featuring an irascible modern-day Sherlock Holmes

Cast | Hugh Laurie, Robert Sean Leonard, Jennifer Morrison, Lisa Edlestein, Omar Epps, Jesse Spencer
Original broadcaster | Fox
Awards | 2 Emmys, 2 Golden Globes
For fans of . . . | *Jeeves and Wooster* (1990)

Inspired by the success of the *CSI* franchise, Paul Attanasio and David Shore first pitched their new series as a medical mystery in which doctors diagnose the undiagnosable. Although initially conceived of as a traditional ensemble show, the creators eventually settled on a central character—a brilliant diagnostician who would work at cross-purposes with his team to make controversial assessments of baffling cases. Ultimately, the character of Dr. Gregory House (Hugh Laurie) emerged, a painkiller-addicted misanthrope with undeniable genius and a hair-trigger temper.

Most episodes of *House* were formulaic: a patient was admitted to the Princeton-Plainsboro Teaching Hospital with an illness that was either already mysterious or about to become so. House and his team then entered a race against the clock, frantically trying to diagnose the problem before it became worse, while House's unconventional methods put him at odds with his staff and the hospital's administration. Although House usually managed to diagnose the mystery illness correctly, he did not always do so in time. The darkness of the show's subject matter was leavened by an ongoing subplot in which House was forced to pit his formidable intellect against walk-in patients with rather less than mysterious medical issues.

In 2008, *House* was the most-watched television show in the world. **AP**

◉ Hugh Laurie (Dr. Gregory House) brings his unique brand of tough love to another patient.

The Eagle: A Crime Odyssey

Crime/Mystery | Denmark | 2004–06

The secret lives of Danish spies

Cast | Jens Albinus, Marina Bouras, Steen Stig Lommer, Janus Nabil Bakrawi, David Owe
Original broadcaster | DR
Award | 1 Emmy
For fans of . . . | *Spooks* (2002)

In this series, Danish national television combined terrorism, high-tech gadgets, espionage, and semi-obscure references to Greek mythology to create a crime odyssey of grand ambition and epic proportions.

Written by Mai Brostøm and Peter Thorsboe, the show revolves around an elite police unit and its enigmatic leader, Hallgrim "Ørnen" Hallgrimsson. A man of natural authority on the outside but a human in slow emotional decay on the inside, Hallgrim has to deal with international crime, a childhood trauma, and doomed romances as he leads his team all over northern Europe.

One of the most ambitious projects in Danish TV history, the show had slick cinematography, explosive action, and plenty of cloak-and-dagger. The production crew practically shut down one of the runways at Copenhagen airport just to film a sequence for the first episode, and the constant changes of scenery—from the streets of Copenhagen and Berlin to the stunning landscapes of Norway, Sweden, and Hallgrim's native Iceland—gave the piece a truly international feel. Clever writing also kept the drama going at high speed as one small incident from a previous episode precipitated an international catastrophe in the next.

The combination of all the above, served with a tasty helping of Nordic noir, made the show unique as a spy drama. Perhaps even more interesting are the ways in which it foreshadowed the dominance of Scandi-drama in the years to come. **JH**

Who Do You Think You Are?

Documentary | UK | 2004–present

Famous faces explore their family trees

Cast | Kim Cattrall, Jeremy Clarkson, Alan Cumming, Stephen Fry, Jeremy Irons, J.K. Rowling, Jerry Springer, David Tennant, and others
Original broadcaster | BBC Two
For fans of . . . | *Finding Your Roots* (2012)

Most families have secrets, lost relatives, and scandals. While the idea of exploring genealogy isn't original, the celebrity aspect of *Who Do You Think You Are?* adds an extra level of intrigue: how far back do we need to go to find relatives of the rich and famous who are as poor as the rest of us? If the evidence is to be believed, not all that far at all.

Inevitably, the series turned up stories of families lost in the Holocaust or the First World War trenches, of illegitimacy and of prison terms. Author J.K. Rowling had always believed her grandfather had been awarded the Legion of Honour in France. Though this turned out not to be the case, he had in fact been given the civilian equivalent, the Croix de Guerre. Actor John Hurt was disappointed to learn that the Irish roots he'd always been proud of were just a family myth. Comedian Alexander Armstrong discovered that he was a descendant of William the Conqueror. And actress Kim Cattrall returned to her native Liverpool to uncover what happened to a grandfather who abandoned his family and disappeared.

The format has been exported to Poland, Canada, Australia, Germany, Ireland, and South Africa. One of the most successful versions has been in the United States, to which it was brought by actress Lisa Kudrow, who was a fan of the British shows and was executive producer for the remake. Among those who have appeared in this version are Sarah Jessica Parker, Kelly Clarkson, and Kelsey Grammer. **JS**

Garth Marenghi's Darkplace

Fantasy/Horror/Sci-Fi/Comedy | UK | 2004

Pastiche of cheaply made sci-fi/horror captures the essence of B movies in all their absurd glory

Cast | Matthew Holness, Richard Ayoade, Matt Berry, Alice Lowe
Original broadcaster | Channel 4
For fans of . . . | *The Office* (2001), *The Mighty Boosh* (2004)

Garth Marenghi's Darkplace was first aired late at night with next to no publicity; it attracted very few viewers. That it has since grown into a huge cult hit will come as no surprise to those who did tune in back in 2004. A show within a show, it features the fictional 1980s series "Darkplace," starring author Garth Marenghi (Matthew Holness) as Rick Dagless, MD, his publicist Dean Leaner (Richard Ayoade) as Thornton Reed, and actor Todd Rivers (Matt Berry) as Dr. Lucien Sanchez. Marenghi introduces each appallingly bad episode, which is interspersed with "modern-day" interviews with Marenghi, Learner, and Rivers about their "visionary and groundbreaking" masterpiece.

The attention to detail is superb, from the use of the 1980s television ident to the grading of the film and the terribly cheap special effects. It is also an excellent pastiche of B-movie sci-fi and horror. The humor is bizarre, and Richard Ayoade is outstanding as Dean Learner/Thornton Reed. Garth Marenghi is full of his own brilliance and self-importance without any hint of awareness of how ridiculous and pompous he is.

Due to its poor ratings, *Darkplace* never got a second series, but it later developed into a cult success on DVD. Dean Learner and Garth Marenghi both appeared again as characters in *In Conversation with Dean Learner*, a fictional chat show developed by Holness and Ayoade, but if you want to see these characters in their full majesty, you really should venture deep into the original *Darkplace*. **LH**

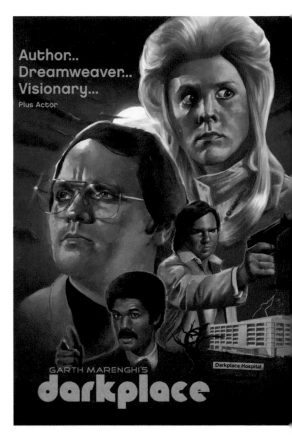

**Author...
Dreamweaver...
Visionary...**
Plus Actor

Darkplace Hospital

GARTH MARENGHI'S
darkplace

Classic episode
The Creeping Moss from the Shores of Shuggoth | *Season 1, episode 6*. Dagless and Reed save Sanchez after a woman he falls for infects him with cosmic broccoli. With an awful 1980s-style song and an absurd fight in a saloon bar.

◎ The publicity posters maintained the pretence that this was a movie rather than a TV show.

Lost

Fantasy/Horror/Sci-Fi | USA | 2004–10

Time-jumping tale of plane crash survivors stranded on a mysterious island

Cast | Matthew Fox, Jorge Garcia, Daniel Dae Kim, Yunjin Kim, Evangeline Lilly, Terry O'Quinn
Original broadcaster | ABC
Awards | 11 Emmys , 1 Golden Globe
For fans of . . . | *24* (2001), *Fringe* (2008)

The premise is simple enough: a group of strangers survive an airplane crash and have to live together on a remote island while they wait to be rescued. But then come the twists. The island has polar bears, deadly smoke, and scientific research stations. It turns out that many of the passengers have crossed paths before. And their fates seem to be connected to a set of six numbers: 4, 8, 15, 16, 23, and 42.

The writers insisted that they knew the answers to all the island's mysteries from the very beginning; viewers were skeptical, but they were hooked by the show's deft use of cliff-hangers and eventually rewarded with a series that kept reinventing itself. The flashbacks that were the backbone of the early seasons later gave way to flashes forward and sideways.

The most common theory posited when the series began was that the characters had died and the island was a kind of limbo. The final episode—which resolved some of the mysteries—confirmed that this was not the case. But the choice to show the characters reuniting after death sowed much confusion, with many viewers believing they had been right all along.

Lost paved the way for more long-form storytelling on TV, but it also made viewers wary of investing in vague mysteries. Its biggest legacy, though, is the career of creator J.J. Abrams, who went on to direct *Star Trek* and *Star Wars* movies. **WH**

◑ (L–R) Dominic Monaghan (Pace), Yunjun Kim (Sun Kwon), Daniel Dae Kim (Jin Kwon), Jorge Garcia (Hurley), and Josh Holloway (Sawyer).

Rescue Me

Drama | USA | 2004–11

Unflinching take on firefighters dealing with the aftermath of the 9/11 terrorist attacks on New York

Cast | Denis Leary, Andrea Roth, John Scurti
Original broadcaster | FX
Award | 1 Emmy
For fans of . . . | *Third Watch* (1999), *The Job* (2001), *Damages* (2007), *Chicago Fire* (2012)

The terrible attack on the World Trade Center on September 11, 2001, has left a lasting scar on the US consciousness, but one of its positive outcomes has been the widespread recognition of the sheer bravery of the firefighters during the darkest hours. The searing *Rescue Me* focused on these amazing people to tell the story of post-9/11 America.

Cocreated by and starring stand-up comedian Denis Leary, the series followed New York City firefighter Tommy Gavin, his work colleagues, and his family as they tried to come to terms with the aftermath of the terrorist attack. Tommy's personal life was a mess; he was separated, an alcoholic, and suffering from survivor guilt—he escaped the collapse of the Twin Towers, but his cousin Jimmy and many colleagues did not make it. Leary cleverly incorporated his acerbic stand-up persona into his performance as Tommy, which brought some humor into this often bleak drama. The title of the series has a double meaning—while he risks his life to save others, who will save him? This was the question which drove the narrative through seven seasons. *Rescue Me* was not always an easy watch, but it offered real catharsis as Tommy and his loved ones tackled their demons head-on.

Probably the first TV series to attempt to capture the impact of 9/11 on the American people, *Rescue Me* was an uncompromising piece of quality drama that is poignant without being sentimental, and which offered hope in the bleakest of circumstances. **SO**

Classic episode
Justice | *Season 2, episode 13*. A family tragedy sends a grief-stricken Tommy in search of revenge, which in turn jeopardizes his reunion with his wife, Janet. Meanwhile, his colleague Sean starts to question his faith in God.

◬ Denis Leary as haunted New York firefighter Tommy Gavin.

Plus belle la vie

Drama | France | 2004–present

Soap opera plus crime drama equals
unprecedented success

Cast | Colette Renard, Serge Dupire, Dounia Coesens,
Cécilia Hornus, Sylvie Flepp, Michel Cordes, Rebecca
Hampton, Laetitia Milot
Original broadcaster | France 3
For fans of . . . | *Sous le soleil* (1996)

At the start of the twenty-first century, the conventional
wisdom was that soap operas did not play well in
France. Of the nation's few sorties into the genre, *Cap
des Pins* (*Tide of Life*, 1998) lasted only two years and was
held up by TV executives as an awful warning against
any future such undertakings. *Sous le soleil* (1996) had
had its moments, but was now losing viewers.

Undeterred by this, producer Hubert Besson hired
four experienced scriptwriters to create a show that
was more city-focused than *Cap des Pins* (a rustic idyll
set in a remote village in Brittany), and not preoccupied
with women's issues, so as to avoid comparisons with
Sous le soleil.

The setting is Le Mistral, a fictional suburb of
Marseille with a mixed population of rich and poor
living close together. The name—the same as that
of the harsh wind that blows for much of the year in
Southern France—is aptly chosen, because it reflects
the adversity and frequent changes of circumstance
faced by its main characters. Some of the story lines
are standard soap fodder—love affairs, infidelities,
squabbles over possessions—but what lifts *Plus belle
la vie* out of the ordinary is its willingness to incorporate
criminal intrigues of the kind for which Marseille is
notorious—drug smuggling, gun-running, race crime.

Viewing figures were poor at first, but gradually
increased until the show was regularly watched by
five million people. The two-thousandth episode was
broadcast in 2012, and the series is still going strong. **GL**

Stargate: Atlantis

Fantasy/Horror/Sci-Fi | USA | 2004–09

Second time's the charm for MGM's
Stargate *franchise*

Cast | Joe Flanigan, David Hewlett, Torri Higginson,
Rachel Luttrell, Jason Momoa, Amanda Tapping
Original broadcaster | Sci-Fi Channel
For fans of . . . | *Star Trek* (1966), *Stargate SG-1* (1997),
Game of Thrones (2011)

In *Stargate SG-1*, the Sci-Fi Channel demonstrated
that fans were amenable to a show with its own fully
fleshed-out fictional history and mythology. The
station and the producers then attempted to capture
lightning a second time.

Adapting the winning formula of a small team
exploring the unknown, cut off from Earth, *Stargate:
Atlantis* recounted the experiences of a group of
soldiers and scientists sent to the distant Pegasus
Galaxy. There they encountered the Wraith, a vicious
race of space vampires.

The show avoided the temptation to take itself too
seriously; indeed, it embraced the preposterous, with
increasingly outlandish story lines about the voyagers'
efforts to hold the line against the would-be invaders
of Earth. It benefited further from a strong cast,
including David Hewlett as a slightly buffoonish but
brilliant scientist, *Game of Thrones'* Jason Momoa as a
soft-speaking warrior, and Amanda Tapping, reprising
her popular role from the original series as Sam Carter.
Rotating cast changes persisted throughout the series'
whole run.

Stargate: Atlantis eventually met an untimely end, not
at the hands of the Wraith but at those of Sci-Fi and
MGM, who canceled the series (even though it was still
quite popular) to make way for *Stargate Universe* (2009).
However, this new spin-off ran for only two seasons
before it too was axed; a planned *Atlantis* follow-up
film never materialized. **SL**

Deadwood

Western | USA | 2004–06

Nasty, brutish, and far-too-short Western

Cast | Timothy Olyphant, Ian McShane, Molly Parker, Jim Beaver, Brad Dourif **Original broadcaster** | HBO
Awards | 3 Emmys, 1 Golden Globe **For fans of . . .** | *The Wire* (2002), *Carnivàle* (2003), *Justified* (2010)

A far cry from the Westerns of TV's Golden Age, *Deadwood* was a gritty, revisionist take on life at the fringes of civilization. Based loosely on historical events, it was set in the settlement of the same name in 1870. Over the show's three seasons, Deadwood grew from a rough camp into a town.

As in all Westerns, there were white hats and black hats, but here the lines were often blurred. Seth Bullock (Timothy Olyphant) arrived with aspirations of a profitable life in business, but events conspired to force him into donning the sheriff's badge. His intentions were honorable—avenge a friend, protect a widow, nurture the town's growth—but he often strayed from the path of righteousness.

The undisputed boss of Deadwood was Al Swearengen (Ian McShane), owner of the saloon. Aggressive and foul-mouthed, he ruled with an iron fist and his ambitions quickly came into conflict with Bullock's idealism. The two wavered between impassioned rivalry and reluctant alliance as their dreams alternately collided and intertwined. **JS**

Classic episode
Here Was a Man | *Season 1, episode 4.* A close-up on sharpshooter and gambler Wild Bill Hickok as he struggles to live up to his own legend, which is important not only to him but also to the townspeople of Deadwood.

⊛ (L–R) Ian McShane (Swearengen), Timothy Olyphant (Bullock), W. Earl Brown (Dority), and Sean Bridgers (Burns).

Hex

Fantasy/Horror/Sci-Fi | UK | 2004–05

Witches and demons run riot in a girls' school

Cast | Christina Cole, Jemima Rooper, Jamie Davis, Laura Pyper, Michael Fassbender, Joseph Beattie
Original broadcaster | BSkyB/Sky One **For fans of . . .** | *Buffy the Vampire Slayer* (1997)

Cassie (Christina Cole) and Thelma (Jemima Rooper) are boarders at Medenham Estate school. Cassie is posh and uninterested in Thelma, who holds a romantic torch for her. Then Thelma is killed, and comes back as a ghost that only Cassie (who is a witch) can see. Together they try to unravel the mystery of the school's murky past and the role in it all of the demon Azazeal (Michael Fassbender).

Although nominally a series for young adults, the content of *Hex* is quite grown up. The two main characters have a lesbian relationship, and there is some limited nudity and other sexual content.

The first season, dominated by the relationship between Cassie and Thelma, is more effective than the second. Once Cassie and Azazeal leave, we follow the 500-year-old "anointed one" Ella (Laura Pyper) and Azazeal's son Malachi (Joseph Beattie) as Thelma struggles to prevent their evil from prevailing. The plot is complex and convoluted, but always entertaining. *Hex* introduces demon slayers and knights that would later become the stock-in-trade of teen TV. **DJH**

Classic episode
Life Goes On | *Season 1, episode 2.* Thelma helps Cassie to interpret her mysterious dreams. Subsequent revelations lead the pair deeper into the horrors that lurk beneath the surface of the rich-kids' school.

⬙ (L–R) Jemima Rooper (Thelma), Laura Pyper (Ella), Michael Fassbender (Azazeal), and Christina Cole (Cassie).

Shameless

Drama | UK | 2004–13

A charming and captivating series about charmless and repellent people

Cast | David Threlfall, James McAvoy, Maxine Peake, Anne-Marie Duff   **Original broadcaster** | Channel 4
For fans of . . . | *Dallas* (1978), *Threads* (1984), *The Royle Family* (1998)

Shameless was controversial. Were the characters criminals or heroes, devils or saints? Was the show a comedy or a drama, a satire or a memoir?

Paul Abbott's script—based partly on his own chaotic working-class upbringing—showed how the Gallagher family somehow made ends meet in spite of their addictions, crimes, and violence. In some ways, it was a fairy story, in which gifted daughter Fiona (Anne-Marie Duff) escaped from her impoverished roots after meeting a dashing car thief (James McAvoy). Dominating the show was the monster-savant Frank Gallagher (David Threlfall), a looming, incontinent presence, offering unwanted advice, occasional kindness, and headbutts.

Wildly different from anything else on television, *Shameless* became a magnetic success. The problem was that almost the entire cast moved on, several of them to stardom. Frank remained behind, so drunk that he was oblivious to the changes around him, but later seasons degenerated into comic-book poverty porn. At its best, though, *Shameless* was compulsive and hilarious. **JG**

Classic episode
Affairs | *Season 1, episode 5*. Frank has concurrent affairs with his son's girlfriend and her mother. When the boy finds out, there's a generational confrontation that gives a fresh twist to the legend of Oedipus.

◈ David Threlfall as Frank Gallagher—an example to us all of how not to behave—and Johnny Bennett as Liam Gallagher.

The L Word

Drama | USA/Canada | 2004–09

The challenges of being gay

Cast | Jennifer Beals, Laurel Holloman, Leisha Hailey, Katherine Moennig, Pam Grier, Mia Kirshner, Erin Daniels, Eric Mabius, Sarah Shahi **Original broadcaster** | Showtime **For fans of . . .** | *Queer as Folk* (2000)

The initial in the title stands for "lesbian," and the main focus of the show was on Bette and Tina (Jennifer Beals and Laurel Holloman), a long-established lesbian couple who wanted a child.

Their women friends dealt with their own sexuality in different ways: some, like Carmen (Sarah Shahi), a self-confident disc jockey, were out and proud; others, like tennis pro Dana (Erin Daniels), were in the closet and tormented by the possible consequences of revealing their true orientation; Jenny (Mia Kirshner) was an annoying narcissist; journalist Alice (Leisha Hailey), was simply desperate for love.

Yet *The L Word* was not a niche show; it also featured heterosexuals, notably Tim (Eric Mabius), who was married and divorced in season one, dated several women in season two, and married again in season three. More importantly, it revealed the humanity of all the characters, and the viewers recognized that it was primarily about relationships, and that the sexuality of the participants was never more than a secondary concern, and sometimes actually irrelevant. **GL**

Classic episode
Lifeline | *Season 3, episode 5.* As Bette and Tina struggle to get along, the former considers adopting Buddhism while the latter hooks up with men online in sex chat rooms. Meanwhile, Alice dates a lesbian vampire.

⊕ (L–R) Katherine Moennig (Shane), Leisha Hailey (Alice), and Karina Lombard (Marina).

Strictly Come Dancing

Reality | UK | 2004–present

A reality show that pairs celebrities with professional dancers in a knockout contest

Cast | Bruce Forsyth, Tess Daly, Claudia Winkleman, Zoë Ball, Len Goodman, Bruno Tonioli, Craig Revel Horwood, Arlene Philips, Alesha Dixon, Darcey Bussell
Original broadcaster | BBC One
For fans of . . . | *Dancing on Ice* (2006)

A kaleidoscope of sequins, choreography, music, and pizzazz, *Strictly Come Dancing* has played a huge role in the re-emergence of popular Saturday-night television in the UK. Each season, several celebrities are paired with professional dancers and given a series of routines to master. As the weeks go by, they're whittled down by public vote until the last couple standing are crowned champions. As each celeb is a novice at the start, we get excellence, calamity, and drama in equal measure. But because the competitors are successful in their own fields, no one treats it as if it were life or death. Having fun is the order of the day.

The original *Come Dancing* was a long-running BBC series (1949–98) that presented ballroom culture to the masses. For the current series, an adverb was borrowed from Australian movie *Strictly Ballroom* to spice things up. The hosts were initially showbiz veteran Bruce Forsyth and former model Tess Daly; Forsyth stood down after the 2013 season, replaced by the quick, witty Claudia Winkleman. A panel of judges—including avuncular Len Goodman, outrageous Bruno Tonioli, and picky Craig Revel Horwood—comment on and score every performance, then their rankings are combined with the result of a public vote. Each week's "dance-off" sees the bottom two couples perform again, with one being picked by the panel to stay.

Knowledge of ballroom or Latin dancing is never essential for the viewer—it's the inbuilt drama that keeps the viewers hooked year after year. IF

The X Factor

Reality | UK | 2004–present

Members of the public sing before a panel of judges as solo artists or groups

Cast | Simon Cowell, Louis Walsh, Sharon Osbourne, Dermot O'Leary, Cheryl Fernandez-Versini, Gary Barlow, Nicole Scherzinger, Tulisa, Kate Thornton
Original broadcaster | ITV
For fans of . . . | *New Faces* (1973), *Pop Idol* (2001)

After two years of ITV's successful *Pop Idol*, a show designed to find new singing talent, its famously caustic judge, Simon Cowell, wanted a piece of the pie. He pitched his own version to the network: *The X Factor*, which became a colossal hit, not only in the UK but also abroad with country-specific remakes. Regularly topping the ratings charts, it has produced numerous new pop stars and established itself as a key influence in modern British culture.

The format has been tweaked over the years, but the basic talent-show structure has remained. After a round of auditions, a "bootcamp" session whittles down the pool of talent. Four celebrity judges are then assigned a category each—usually boys under 24, girls under 24, groups, and over-25s—and at an exotic location they reveal which acts they want to appear in the weeks of knockout finals. The interplay between the judges has often been the show's biggest selling point, and their rivalries and backstage gossip about them have kept the show a tabloid and social media favorite.

The number of hopeful contestants queuing to audition each season has reached hundreds of thousands, all of them fighting for a £1 million recording deal. Winners have included Leona Lewis, Alexandra Burke, and Little Mix; huge success has also come to other finalists such as One Direction, Olly Murs, and Cher Lloyd. But almost as significant to the show's popularity have been the failures: *The X Factor* revels in the desperate and the deluded. IF

Schillerstrasse

Comedy | Germany | 2004–11

German TV found international success with this unscripted show set in someone's living room

Cast | Cordula Stratmann, Jürgen Vogel, Annette Frier, Martin Schneider, Michael Kessler, Ralf Schmitz, Tetje Mierendorf
Original broadcaster | Sat.1
For fans of . . . | *Loriot* (1976), *Berlin, Berlin* (2002)

Germany has struggled to find an international audience for its original productions. Even its most popular programs rarely find traction with viewers beyond Austria or Switzerland. However, in the mid-2000s, the improvisational comedy show *Schillerstrasse* became a surprise hit at home and abroad.

Humorous, unscripted, and largely unedited, *Schillerstrasse* couldn't be more at odds with the earnest eighteenth-century philosopher after whom the fictitious street in the title was named. Its setting was the lounge of a lodger at No. 9 Schillerstrasse. The lodger, initially played by Cordula Stratmann, later by Jürgen Vogel, was visited by friends and relatives. These guest actors were not given names or scripted lines, but they were aware of the topic of the show, which could be quite bizarre (for example, Halloween, the driver's license, or the shelf), and received some individual directions through an earpiece, which was shared with the television audience. They might be asked to reveal surprising developments in their personal lives or to start crying whenever someone said something mildly upsetting. Apart from that, the actors had to improvise a humorous plot. Even when things went wrong, the result was rarely cut from the thirty-minute broadcast. Although *Schillerstrasse* was canceled in Germany in 2011, its success prompted Fox to snap up the format. Versions are also planned for the United Kingdom, France, Russia, Israel, South Africa, Australia, and the Netherlands. **DH**

Classic episode
Das shooting | November 2010. Maddin (Martin Schneider) wants to see if Jürgen (Jürgen Vogel) could make it as a male model. He invites him home to an advertising shoot, and little does Jürgen know that he will have to strip off.

◉ Cordula Stratmann with improvisation specialist John Hudson on the fictitious Schillerstrasse.

Hustle

Comedy/Drama | UK | 2004–12

Tongue-in-cheek and extremely glamorous drama about a gang of con artists

Cast | Adrian Lester, Marc Warren, Robert Glenister, Matt Di Angelo, Kelly Adams, Jaime Murray, Robert Vaughan
Original broadcaster | BBC One
For fans of . . . | *Spooks* (2002), *Mad Dogs* (2011)

The success of films such as *The Sting* and *Ocean's 11* in all its incarnations demonstrates that there's always a public appetite for drama based around con artists and the tricks they perform. Although clearly inspired by these movies, *Hustle* isn't derivative; it's full of interesting and quirkily original characters, glamorous locations, clever plots, and funny dialogue. It has a similarly cinematic feel to that of other dramas produced by independent company Kudos, such as *Spooks* and *Life on Mars*.

Hustle principally concerns a group of long-con artists led by Mickey Stone (Adrian Lester). (A long con is one that involves lots of preparation, deep deception, and skill, and which has huge rewards.) Each week the gang finds a new "mark" (potential victim), works out his or her biggest weakness (which is usually insatiable greed) and then exploits it. Most weeks it appears that the con has gone wrong in some way, but it always comes right in the end. Each episode concludes with a stylish tailpiece that reveals in flashback how the hustlers pulled it off.

That we never disapprove of the heroes' criminality is partly down to the fact that the victims are always much more evil than the gang could ever be. But it also says much for the unflagging quality of the script (by former *EastEnders* head writer, Tony Jordan) and the performances of the leading actors. Rarely has British television been so glamorous, so cinematic, or as much fun to watch. **LH**

MasterChef Goes Large

Reality | UK | 2005–present

Cooking doesn't get tougher or more competitive than this

Cast | John Torode, Gregg Wallace, India Fisher
Original broadcaster | BBC Two
For fans of . . . | *Iron Chef* (1993), *Food Network Challenge* (2005), *Hell's Kitchen* (2005), *Cupcake Wars* (2009), *The Great British Bake-Off* (2010)

MasterChef Goes Large took competitive culinary expertise to a new level, transforming the sedate Sunday afternoon format of the original *Masterchef* (1990–2001) into a top-rating global television franchise.

The revised format, developed by Franc Roddam, the show's original creator, and John Silver, ran for five consecutive nights and showed six amateur chefs put through a battery of exercises to test their prowess. One by one the contestants are eliminated until the last chef standing is the winner.

Among the keys to its appeal are the fast cutting, the pulsing music, and the tense narration, together with the contrasting judges—former retailer Gregg Wallace, a chirpy lover of desserts, and restaurateur John Torode, a softer presence with a preference for Middle Eastern dishes. Their descriptions of the dishes they are served can be laugh-out-loud funny, but they're never callous in their criticisms, and are always mindful of the contestants' feelings.

When Wallace says "Cooking doesn't get tougher than this," he's right, and that's another reason why the show's popularity has increased with every season. The "Goes Large" suffix was dropped in 2008 and in the following year it was transferred from the minority channel BBC Two to the mainstream BBC One.

Masterchef later spawned three spin-off series in Britain—*Celebrity MasterChef*, *MasterChef: The Professionals*, and *Junior Masterchef*—as well as numerous international iterations. **MW**

Supernatural

Fantasy/Horror/Sci-Fi | USA | 2005–present

Troubled brothers fight the unnatural in a quest to set the world to rights and understand their own dark destinies

Cast | Jared Padalecki, Jensen Ackles, Misha Collins, Mark Sheppard, Katie Cassidy, Lauren Cohan
Original broadcaster | The WB/The CW
For fans of . . . | *Buffy the Vampire Slayer* (1997), *Angel* (1999)

When *Supernatural* appeared, viewers could have been forgiven for letting out a yawn. The tale of brothers fighting a creepy menace of the week felt like a format that had been done many times before, but after a solid but ordinary opening season, the show found its own voice and niche.

Heart and soul of the show are the Winchester brothers, Sam (Jared Padalecki) and Dean (Jensen Ackles), whose mother was killed by a demon and whose father set them on the path to fighting otherworldly monsters. It never shies away from outright horror, from parasitic changelings sucking the life force from their mother to some truly nasty witches, but its true power comes from the larger story it reveals about Sam's origins and his role in a coming apocalypse. In later seasons the show pits pitiless demons against unempathetic angels in a novel take on Judeo-Christian mythology. Perhaps its greatest strength is its willingness to be playful with its own text and tropes. When it's revealed that Sam and Dean are the heroes of a series of books chronicling the adventures we've seen on screen and possibly scripted by God himself, the show is poking fun at itself and its fans.

Supernatural pulls off the difficult trick of telling apocalyptic stories seriously while remaining aware of its own absurdity. And in a world in which the spooky is so often defeated only by the middle class, it is refreshing to see two blue-collar heroes kicking butt and listening to classic rock as they do it. **RL**

Classic episode
The French Mistake | *Season 6, episode 15*. Meta-textual hijinks as the Winchester brothers are transported by an angel to a parallel world in which unflattering versions of the stars play the leads in a show called . . . "Supernatural."

⊘ Ax-wielding monsters were typical of the adversaries faced by Sam and Dean.

American Dad!

Animation | USA | 2005–present

Another garish cartoon tour de force from the creative team behind Family Guy

Cast | Seth MacFarlane, Wendy Schaal, Scott Grimes
Original broadcaster | Fox **For fans of . . .** | *Family Guy* (1999)

Stan Smith is a bigoted right-wing zealot who works for the CIA. Despite his values, he proves remarkably naive and is easily persuaded by any ideology that passes. He is married to Francine, who has a background in crime and sexual permissiveness (especially with rock stars).

The Smiths have two children, a sex-obsessed virgin called Steve and the rebellious, pot-smoking Hayley. They are also the custodians of Klaus, a one-time East German skiing champion whose brain has been transplanted (by the CIA) into a goldfish. Rounding out the household is the alien Roger whom Stan has liberated from top-secret Area 51 in Nevada. An alcoholic, money-motivated egomaniac, Roger amuses himself by impersonating characters who trick unsuspecting strangers.

The *Family Guy* comedy style is ever present, with humor squeezed from sexual innuendo, bloody violence, bad-taste dialogue, near-slanderous put-downs of celebrities, and farcical plots building toward surreal denouements. Seth MacFarlane, the driving force of *Family Guy*, voices Stan and Roger and weaves his dark but brilliant comedy through every episode. **DF**

> **Classic episode**
> *Bullocks to Stan* | *Season 1, episode 8.*
> Regular guest star Patrick Stewart (voicing Stan's CIA boss Avery Bullock) is a standout in this story of the unlikely sexual relationship between Bullock and Stan's daughter, Hayley.

◉ The family listens to an announcement from Hayley in the episode "Honey, I'm Homeland."

Robot Chicken

Animation | USA | 2005–present

Sketch comedy show starring stop-motion action figures and toys

Cast | Seth Green **Original broadcaster** | Adult Swim **Awards** | 3 Emmys
For fans of . . . | *Mystery Science Theater 3000* (1988)

Robot Chicken is a bizarre satiric, sketch comedy show that builds on a plethora of pop culture references shared largely by the generation that grew up on a steady diet of TV shows and cartoons. Every episode features gags that could sometimes last mere seconds as an array of action figures and dolls from recognizable franchises act out bizarre non-sequitur encounters, make sexually charged or scatological jokes, or play out longer and more elaborate satires of the shows from which the given characters were derived.

Created by Seth Green and Matthew Senreich, and based on a print feature in *ToyFare* magazine, the series features fast-paced 11-minute episodes, except for one special 30-minute installment focusing on *Star Wars* and featuring guest voice George Lucas. The premise is that a robot chicken is forced to watch a variety of shows on TV and keeps flipping channels—hence the quickfire approach. Some sketches recur throughout the run of the show, as well as a joke that accompanies nearly every season finale in which the network announces the series' cancelation. **ATB**

> **Classic episode**
> *Chirlaxx* | *Season 3, episode 60*. Among the highlights of this show, dedicated to the people it had killed, was the search by the Japanese makers of a fungal infection cream for a big-name celebrity to front their TV ads.

◉ Mad Scientist and Robot Chicken team up to push back the frontiers of comedy.

BeTipul

Drama | Israel | 2005–08

Riveting drama in which the psychotherapist needs therapy

Cast | Assi Dayan, Gila Almagor, Meirav Gruber, Ayelet Zurer **Original broadcaster** | HOT
For fans of . . . | *The Human Jungle* (1963), *In Treatment* (2008)

Few dramas gain the attention and acclaim that *BeTipul* (*In Therapy*) garnered when first broadcast in Israel. This unique piece of television distilled drama to its purest form, making compelling and thought-provoking viewing out of two people sitting in a room talking.

Rueven Dagan (Assi Dayan) was a psychotherapist who met his regular clients at the same time every week, before attending a session with his own therapist, Gila (Gila Almagor). As he guided his clients through their problems, Dagan coped with an unravelling home life and his own psychological demons. The pace was slow, but *BeTipul* insidiously burrowed under the viewer's skin in a series of thirty-minute episodes. Co-creator and director Hagai Levi had perfected his

craft in popular Israeli telenovelas and soaps. As a long-time advocate of psychotherapy, he felt the discipline deserved a more serious approach on screen than the caricatured depictions routinely seen in, for example, the films of Woody Allen. The result was a drama that became a television phenomenon and was showered with awards from the Israeli Television Academy. **MW**

> **Classic episode**
> *Gila* | *Season 1, episode 40*. Reuven goes on the offensive against Gila, his own therapist, and berates her for concealing the shortcomings of her own relationships. Gila reminds him that that is not the role of the counselor.

🔺 Assi Dayan as Rueven Dagan (center) and a selection of his clients.

Rome

Historical drama | USA | 2005–07

The corrupt politics of the Roman Empire, viewed through the eyes of two lowly centurions

Cast | Kevin McKidd, Ray Stevenson, Polly Walker, James Purefoy, Kerry Condon, Max Pirkis, Ciarán Hinds
Original broadcaster | HBO **For fans of . . .** | *I, Claudius* (1976), *The Tudors* (2007), *Game of Thrones* (2011)

The backdrop to this lavish series is the period covered in Shakespeare's *Julius Caesar* and *Antony and Cleopatra*. We meet Caesar, Antony, Brutus, Cassius, and their families. The real heart of the story, though, comes from two centurions, the conscientious Lucius Vorenus (Kevin McKidd) and the rather base Titus Pullo (Ray Stevenson). Through them we learn of the Roman underclass, the slaves and footsoldiers.

Rome has plenty of sex and violence but always manages to stay classy. There's a merciful lack of the kind of cod-Shakespearian dialogue that often makes historical drama inaccessible; Titus Pullo in particular speaks with modern rhythms that provide many intentionally comic moments.

As an accessible way of getting to grips with Roman history, this series is an eye-opening (if occasionally eye-watering) glimpse of a society with a very different moral code from ours. Epic in scale and with a budget to match, *Rome* is a guilty pleasure. And historically speaking, the story of the main characters feeds almost directly into the classic BBC series *I, Claudius*. **JS**

Classic episode
How Titus Pullo Brought Down the Republic |
Season 1, episode 2. With tensions high in Rome, Pullo's involvement in an ongoing bar brawl is both a symptom and a partial cause of the city's descent toward civil war.

⌕ Roman legionaries set out to conquer and civilize Western Europe and North Africa.

It's Always Sunny in Philadelphia

Comedy | USA | 2005–present

Cult pitch-black comedy hit

Cast | Rob McElhenny, Glenn Howerton, Charlie Day, Kaitlin Olson, Danny DeVito
Original broadcasters | FX, FXX
For fans of... | *Futurama* (1999), *Shameless* (2004), *Archer* (2010)

While most shows feature characters who grow and change for the better, *It's Always Sunny in Philadelphia* takes a different approach: the lazy, self-absorbed characters who make up The Gang don't learn and improve from episode to episode or season to season, but instead become steadily worse. Every episode features a frantic race-to-the-bottom as siblings Dennis and "Sweet Dee" Deandra, their father Frank, and their friends Charlie and Mac plumb new depths of depravity in their ongoing efforts to do whatever they must in order to do as little as possible. For example, in the early episode "Dennis and Dee go on Welfare," Dennis and Deandra cultivated addictions to crack cocaine, thinking that substance dependence will help them successfully apply for welfare.

The Gang own and nominally run Paddy's, a seedy bar in Philadelphia, which serves as their home base as they run any number of get-rich-quick schemes, humiliate and sell each other out, and generally wreak havoc in the lives of those unfortunate enough to come into contact with them. No topic is taboo, and no plan can be conceived without immediately being escalated to absurd heights.

It's Always Sunny evolved into its final form at the beginning of season two, when Danny DeVito joined the cast as Frank Reynolds, nominally the father of Dennis and Dee—and possibly of Charlie as well. **AP**

❷ Kaitlin Olson as Dee and Glenn Howerton as Dennis.

Criminal Minds

Crime/Mystery | USA | 2005–present

The FBI hunts serial killers, kidnappers, and terrorists

Cast | Mandy Patinkin, Thomas Gibson, Shemar Moore, Matthew Gray Gubler, A.J. Cook, Kirsten Vangsness, Paget Brewster   **Original broadcaster** | CBS   **For fans of . . .** | *Rejseholdet* ("Unit One") (2000)

There are probably more serial killers in fiction than in reality. In the 1990s they caught the imagination of popular culture and inspired numerous books, movies, and television series. Quite a few of these stories feature FBI agents. Most focus on one or two maverick agents, damaged by their run-ins with evil genius.

Criminal Minds features the Bureau's Behavioral Analysis Unit (BAU), which responds to serial murders, rapes, and abductions. Its agents travel the length and breadth of the United States by private jet. Many of the stories refer to real crimes; this provides an air of authenticity. But, it is not a documentary series, nor even pseudo-documentary. It is a police procedural crime drama with occasional forays into espionage.

The team is usually led by the ambitious Aaron Hotchner (Thomas Gibson). Expert hacker Penelope Garcia (Kirsten Vangsness), the technical analyst, flirts constantly with the intense Morgan (Shemar Moore), while Dr. Spencer Reid (Matthew Gray Gubler) dispenses facts and figures like a walking encyclopedia. J.J. (A.J. Cook) is their cool liaison with the media. **SJG**

Classic episode

The Slave of Duty | *Season 5, episode 10.* The piece begins with the funeral of Hotchner's ex-wife, Hayley, killed protecting their son from serial killer Foyet. At the wake, his team is called into action against another killer.

(L–R) Thomas Gibson (Hotchner), Shemar Moore (Morgan), and Matthew Gray Gubler (Reid) inspect a victim.

The Colbert Report

Talk show | USA | 2005–14

Satirical skewering of pundit-led political talk shows

Cast | Stephen Colbert   **Original broadcaster** | Comedy Central
Awards | 6 Emmys   **For fans of . . .** | *The Daily Show* (1996)

The series was created by Stephen Colbert, Jon Stewart, Ben Karlin, and Joe Antonetti as a spin-off based on Colbert's clueless conservative right-wing commentator of the same name featured on Stewart's *The Daily Show*. *The Colbert Report* parodied real political pundit television shows such as *The O'Reilly Factor*, and utilized real news stories presented through the distorted lens of Colbert's idiotic ideology. It featured monologues, interviews with real guests from the worlds of politics and entertainment, and structured sketches including Colbert's "The Word," based on O'Reilly's "Talking Points Memo."

Taping four days a week apart from holiday breaks, the show unfolded on a set emblazoned with over-the-top American iconography and a consistent use of Colbert's "C" initial to reinforce the character's patriotism and massive ego. Although characterized as a "fake" news show, *The Colbert Report* had an impact on real politics, with the "Colbert Nation" of viewers supporting Colbert in two presidential bids as well as attending a National Mall rally. **ATB**

> **Classic episode**
> *December 8, 2014.* This edition had an interview with President Barack Obama, who also delivered the segment normally entitled "The Word" but renamed "The Decree" for the occasion.

⊘ Stephen Colbert waits to begin taping an episode of his long-running show.

Bones

Drama | USA | 2005–present

Crime drama with heart and wit in which the leading characters' growing romantic attachment overshadows the abundant gore

Cast | Emily Deschanel, David Boreanaz, Michaela Conlin
Original broadcaster | Fox
For fans of . . . | *Quincy* (1976), *Silent Witness* (1996), *Messiah* (2001)

Crime and romance have been melded before, but never as seamlessly as in *Bones*, a stylish drama that pairs ruled-by-her-head forensic anthropologist Temperance "Bones" Brennan (Emily Deschanel) with tough, pragmatic FBI agent Seeley Booth (David Boreanaz). Together they solve a succession of increasingly bizarre and intriguing murder cases. An ensemble of lovable eccentrics help them week by week as they examine stomach-churning corpses, swap charming banter, and fall in love.

Bones was originally billed as an adaptation of the crime novels of forensic anthropologist Kathy Reich, but as the series progressed it owed less to its source material and more to the wild inventiveness of creator Hart Hanson and the gruesome humor he added to the format. It follows a case-of-the-week format, but wrapped around those are season-long story arcs about the emotional lives of the geeky "squints" at the fictional Jeffersonian Institute Medico-Legal Lab. Each character is fully developed with a rich internal and external life, but Booth and Brennan's classic opposites-attract relationship is at the heart of it all, and the contrast of her cool intellectualism with his passionate realism is perfect. The result is that rarest of things: a drama that survived the resolution of its central will they/won't they romance.

The leads' chemistry is outstanding and the entire cast brings a warmth and vivacity to a set-up that could have been much too grim. **RL**

Classic episode
The Woman in the Sand | *Season 2, episode 8.*
After a body is uncovered in the desert outside Las Vegas, Brennan and Booth go undercover at a casino, posing as a trashy high-rolling couple "engaged to be engaged."

⊛ Emily Deschanel (Brennan) and David Boreanaz (Booth) interview a suspect.

Mandrake

Crime/Mystery | Brazil | 2005–07; 2012

Legally Bond—brilliant lawyer mixes business and pleasure

Cast | Marcos Palmeira, Marcelo Serrado, Luís Carlos Miele, Virginia Cavendish, Marcelo Adnet, Érika Mader, Maria Luísa Mendonça
Original broadcaster | HBO Latin America
For fans of . . . | *Matlock* (1986), *Suits* (2011)

Amoral yet alluring, Paolo Mandrake was the James Bond of Brazil, albeit a criminal lawyer rather than a secret agent. Switching effortlessly between his high-class clients and Rio de Janeiro's underbelly, he solved cases with seemingly minimal effort and maximum suavity. And what *Mandrake* lacked in authenticity, it more than made up in tongue-in-cheek cool.

Based on stories by influential Brazilian writer Rubem Fonseca, and adapted by his son José Henrique, *Mandrake* benefited from such customary HBO traits as a quality cast and a liberal attitude toward sex and violence. As the hero, Marcos Palmeira earned an international Emmy nomination to add to his homegrown award tally for shows including the 1990 drama *Barrela: Escola de Crimes*. Érika Mader (mistress Bebel), Maria Luísa Mendonça (girlfriend Berta), and Virginia Cavendish (secretary Verônica) played the most regular of his female sparring partners. Best of all was Luís Carlos Miele as Mandrake's legal associate and father figure Léon Wexler, the cynical but philosophical voice of reason.

After thirteen episodes over two seasons in 2005 and 2007, *Mandrake* returned for two episodes in 2012 and a TV movie in 2013. Performed in Portuguese, all were dubbed into Spanish to win popularity beyond Brazil's borders. And in a world where his spiritual brother Harvey Specter of *Suits* continues to outwit criminals and weaken knees, it's hard to imagine that we won't see the high-flying legal eagle once more. **BM**

Outrageous Fortune

Drama | New Zealand | 2005

When Wolf West is put away, his wife vows the family will go straight

Cast | Robyn Malcolm, Grant Bowler, Antony Starr, Siobhan Marshall, Antonia Prebble, Kirk Torrance
Original broadcaster | TV3
For fans of . . . | *Arrested Development* (2003), *Shameless* (2004), *Weeds* (2005)

When viewing figures on Rachel Lang's medical drama *Mercy Peak* began to slide, she decided that it was because the characters were too nice. She vowed that she wouldn't make the same mistake again with *Outrageous Fortune*. And she didn't.

Cheryl West (Robyn Malcolm) is the trophy wife of Auckland crime-lord Wolf West (Grant Bowler). When he's sent to prison, she tries to put the family on the straight and narrow but they have problems staying there. While Cheryl sets up the "Hoochie Mama" lingerie range, her four offspring follow in their father's footsteps. Of the twins (both played by Antony Starr), Jethro becomes a devious lawyer and Van a sofa-bound hoodlum; Pascalle (Siobhan Marhsall) inherits her father's genius at making contacts with local criminals, but she sleeps with them; Loretta (Antonia Prebble) has all her dad's skills and learns safe-cracking from grandpa. Then there's Wolf's nemesis, Detective Sergeant Judd (Kirk Torrance). Cheryl finds herself falling in love with him.

Outrageous Fortune was a complex story of shifting allegiances and family feuds that took six series to reach a resolution. It delighted in throwing its characters into bed together, and the numerous couplings complicated the plot and increased the viewing figures in comparable measure.

The name of the show is a quotation from *Hamlet*, and every one of the 107 episodes had a title taken from a line by Shakespeare. **JG**

My Lovely Sam-soon

Drama | South Korea | 2005

A unique woman's pursuit of love and cake

Cast | Kim Sun-a, Kim Seon-ah, Hyun Bin, Jeong Ryeo-won, Daniel Henney
Original broadcaster | MBC
For fans of . . . | *Just Good Friends* (1983), *May to December* (1989)

Kim Sam-soon (Kim Sun-a), a less than classically beautiful, slightly chubby single woman in her thirties, tries to make her way in modern-day Korea and perhaps meet the unlikely man of her dreams. In view of which it is hardly surprising that *My Lovely Sam-soon* has often been dubbed a Korean *Bridget Jones's Diary*.

Publicly dumped by her boyfriend, talented pastry chef Sam-soon seeks real independence. She quickly secures a good job in a five-star restaurant, albeit more by accident than design. The handsome, arrogant restaurant owner, Jin-heon (Hyun Bin) is desperate to avoid the interminable blind dates arranged for him by his domineering mother, and offers to pay Sam-soon extra to act as his girlfriend. Needing the money, she accepts this bizarre arrangement, but over time this sham relationship grows ever more genuine, only to be complicated by the unexpected reappearance of Jin-heon's ex-girlfriend.

The sixteen episodes offered a captivating mix of social realism, romance, and moments of dark humor. Sam-soon's quest to become a successful career woman—with her direct manner and endearing social awkwardness—had wide appeal, as did the "will they, won't they" love story.

After major success on Korean TV, a stage version followed. Further afield, *My Lovely Sam-soon* was also broadcast in various Asian countries and remade with local emphasis in the Philippines. Daniel Henney went on to appear in *X-Men Origins: Wolverine* (2009). **SH**

Classic episode
Episode 15. Against her better judgment, Sam-soon allows Jin-heon to go to the United States with his old flame. Will he return? Has she lost him forever? Prepare for twanging heartstrings.

◉ KIm Sun-a stars as the eponymous heroine, a Bridget Jones with added Seoul.

Prison Break

Crime/Mystery | USA | 2005–09

A man orchestrates his own imprisonment in order to break his innocent big brother out of jail

Cast | Wentworth Miller, Dominic Purcell, Robin Tunney, Peter Stormare, Robert Knepper
Original broadcaster | Fox
Award | 1 Golden Globe
For fans of . . . | *Oz* (1997), *Breakout Kings* (2011)

Lincoln Burrows (Dominic Purcell) has been sentenced to death for the murder of the US Vice President's brother—a crime he did not commit but for which he was framed as part of a larger anti-establishment conspiracy. What the powers behind the cover-up don't count on are the ties of blood and family, and how Lincoln's younger brother, Michael Scofield (Wentworth Miller), will do anything to free his sibling and prove his innocence.

Michael orchestrates an armed robbery in order to get put into the same prison as his brother. Once inside, he builds alliances with inmates and prison staff in order to execute his escape plan—a plan which he has tattooed on his entire upper body but which only he can interpret.

When the brothers escape, they go on the run with the convicts who helped them, only to be eventually captured and incarcerated in Central America. This time, the US government promises Michael and Lincoln full pardons if they can break another inmate out of their latest prison.

Sometimes changes of location and cast can be a big turn-off for previously loyal viewers, but the new setting in Panama and the greatly altered dramatis personae gave *Prison Break* a massive boost.

Knowing well in advance that the show was coming to the end at the end of season four, the creators were able to tie up loose ends ahead of a memorable movie-length finale. **MR**

Classic episode
Riots, Drills and the Devil: Part 1 | *Season 1, episode 6*. The real-life cost of freedom for the brothers is highlighted starkly here when it's proved that no one, no matter how clever, can plan for every eventuality.

◉ Wentworth Miller (Michael Scofield) gets imprisoned so that he can spring his brother.

Dancing with the Stars
Reality | USA | 2005–present

Celebrities hone their ballroom dancing skills in a perennially popular competition

Cast | Tom Bergeron, Erin Andrews, Len Goodman, Carrie Anne Inaba, Julianne Hough, Bruno Tonioli
Original broadcaster | ABC **For fans of . . .** | *Strictly Come Dancing* (2004)

Here's a format that has become one of the most familiar on TV all over the world, thanks to the success of the BBC's *Strictly Come Dancing* (2004). This US version of the show has the same format: celebrities team up with professional dancers to learn a variety of ballroom and Latin routines. One couple is voted off every week until just three pairs are left to fight it out in the final for the mirrorball trophy. The main difference is that, while Britain gets only one season a year, American audiences get two, one in spring and the other in the fall. The quality of celebrities is undeniably variable (few viewers will have heard of all the contestants), but there are always enough participants of true star quality to keep it all fresh and exciting.

Over the years the series has dished up its fair share of memorable winners—with the likes of Jennifer Grey (2010), Nicole Scherzinger (2010), Donny Osmond (2009), and more recently (in 2014) *Fresh Prince* star Alfonso Ribeiro—but aside from the starry lineup, it's the quality of the dancing that makes this show: at their best, the routines are simply thrilling. **CW**

Classic episode
Season 18, episode 10. Having seen off her ice dancing partner Charlie White in an earlier round, Meryl Davis trounced actress Candace Cameron Bure and Paralympic snowboarder Amy Purdy in the spring 2014 final.

Italian TV hostess Simona Ventura makes a guest appearance on the show.

Medium

Crime/Mystery | USA | 2005–11

Woman with psychic powers helps police to solve crimes

Cast | Patricia Arquette, Jake Weber, Miguel Sandoval, Sofia Vassilieva, Maria Lark, David Cubitt
Original broadcaster | NBC **Award** | 1 Emmy **For fans of . . .** | *Jonathan Creek* (2004), *Ghost Whisperer* (2005)

Medium was loosely based on *Don't Kiss Them Good-bye* (2005), the memoirs of Allison DuBois, a self-styled medium and psychic who used extrasensory perception to help various criminal investigations (although the police disputed her claims).

In the show, the character of the same name, played by Patricia Arquette, was a medium who worked for the district attorney's office in Phoenix, Arizona. She used her power to communicate with the dead to explain unsolved mysteries, and her prophetic dreams to forestall criminal conspiracies and spontaneous crimes of passion. Her three children all shared their mother's psychic powers, and helped to interpret her premonitions when she herself could not make sense

of them. The first season of *Medium* was a massive hit—it netted nearly 14 million viewers and its audience share was larger than any other show at the time apart from *CSI: Miami*. Gradually, though, the novelty wore off, and by the end of season seven, when fewer than 8 million people were watching each episode, the producers decided to pull the plug. **GL**

Classic episode
The Song Remains the Same | *Season 2, episode 2.*
A song stuck in Allison's head provides a clue to the whereabouts of a missing coed. She tries to enlist the help of the girl's priest, but he refuses to divulge what she told him at confession.

◉ Even psychics need the Internet: Patricia Arquette as Allison and Jake Weber as her husband, Joe.

Casanova

Historical drama | UK | 2005

A sideways look at the life and loves of the eighteenth-century Italian adventurer

Cast | David Tennant, Peter O'Toole, Laura Fraser, Rupert Penry-Jones, Nina Sosanya, Shaun Parkes, Rose Byrne, Freddie Jones, Clare Higgins
Original broadcaster | BBC Three
For fans of . . . | *Pride and Prejudice* (1995)

The BBC had tackled the story of Giacomo Casanova before, back in the early 1970s, in a version starring Frank Finlay with a script by Dennis Potter. Russell T. Davies' three-part adaptation of the hero's own twelve-volume memoirs was a little more irreverent, using modern idioms and delivered with a knowing wink to the audience. Peter O'Toole played the septuagenarian Casanova, working as a librarian and keeping a young servant girl shocked and intrigued by stories of his many sexual conquests as a younger man.

Davies covered his subject's promiscuity, but also looked at his achievements, one of which was the invention of the lottery, a ruse concocted by the penniless Venetian to make his way in Paris. Above all, though, the series was a giddy romp through Italy, France, and England, fast-cut and often farcical. In one standout scene, Casanova confesses his deeds to a priest (Freddie Jones), listing his various encounters with sisters, their mother, a pair of nuns, and even a woman who he'd thought was a man until she produced her fake penis. When he finished his confession, he saw that the priest had collapsed, overcome with shock.

The story is also a romance, following the protagonist's doomed affair with Henriette, a beautiful woman already promised to the Duke of Grimaldi.

The younger Casanova was played by David Tennant, who would star in Davies' next production, the resurrection of British sci-fi classic *Doctor Who*. **JS**

Help

Comedy | UK | 2005

A promising show that was dropped when one of its stars was sent to prison

Cast | Paul Whitehouse, Chris Langham, Alison King, Mark Williams, Olivia Colman
Original broadcaster | BBC Two
For fans of . . . | *Frasier* (1993), *Harry Enfield and Chums* (1994), *The Sopranos* (1999), *Monk* (2002)

Peter Strong (Chris Langham) was a psychotherapist who was infatuated with his receptionist (Alison King), but too uptight to proclaim his love to her. During each working day, he saw a string of patients, including a taxi driver with Alzheimer's disease, a TV host, a magician, and an ordinary man who just wanted to get away from his wife for the duration of each session on the couch. Most of these parts were played by Paul Whitehouse, who also took the role of Strong's own analyst, whom he visited regularly. The series—cowritten by the two leads—had provisionally been entitled *Crazy*.

Help was generally well received by critics, and viewing figures were encouraging. The BBC was widely reported to have been contemplating a second season, but abandoned its plans as soon as Langham was charged with possessing child pornography; he was subsequently jailed for that offense.

Under the circumstances, it seems almost inconceivable that the show will ever be revived in Britain, but the format has been successfully exported to Sweden as *Hjälp!* (2007). In this version, which ran for three seasons and may again be recommissioned, the psychologist was played by Stina Ekblad (the coroner in the Swedish *Wallander*, 2005). Each of the patients was played by different actors, including Chevy Chase as a US television journalist who has been ditched by his wife and left penniless, passportless, and clinically depressed in Stockholm. **GL**

Archangel

Drama | UK | 2005

Riveting conspiracy thriller about the uncovering of Stalin's last secret by an Oxford historian

Cast | Daniel Craig, Yekaterina Rednikova, Gabriel Macht, Konstantin Lavronenko
Original broadcaster | BBC One
For fans of . . . | *Tinker Tailor Soldier Spy* (1979), *Edge of Darkness* (1985)

The publication in 2003 of *The Da Vinci Code* changed both literature and film. The runaway success of Dan Brown's thriller, which attempts to unravel an alternative religious history, sent publishers and filmmakers hunting for similar fare. *Archangel* is an excellent example of the genre. This two-part miniseries was based on Robert Harris' thriller of the same name, published in 1998. The novel was a thematic follow-up to the same author's *Fatherland* (1992) and *Enigma* (1995), both of which had been concerned with the murky history of the Second World War. Set in a postcommunist Russia coming to terms with its Soviet past, *Archangel* used a quest for Joseph Stalin's secret diary to delve into the terrible legacy of the dictator.

The BBC adaptation starred a just pre–James Bond Daniel Craig as Fluke Kelso, a historian whose research took him on a bloody journey to the Russian city of Archangel. There he uncovered far more than just Stalin's notebook; he made a terrible discovery that could change the world. Gritty and rich in location filming in Moscow and Latvia, *Archangel* looked very like a movie, which was what it was originally intended to be. Writers Dick Clement and Ian La Frenais (better known for writing comedies such as *The Likely Lads* and *Porridge*) had bought the rights to the Harris' book, but struggled for years to get their film funded until the success of Dan Brown's *The Da Vinci Code* sent the BBC out in search of similar alternative histories. **JG**

Classic episode
Episode 2. Deep in the forests of northern Russia, Kelso locates the missing diary. He also discovers to his horror that Stalin's legacy is alive and threatening to return to the driving seat in the Kremlin.

◉ Daniel Craig as Fluke Kelso, the historian who learns that the past is not over.

The Office

Comedy | USA | 2005–13

Long-running mockumentary about life and rivalries in a boring workplace

Cast | Steve Carell, Rainn Wilson, John Krasinski, Jenna Fischer, B.J. Novak, Mindy Kaling, James Spader
Original broadcaster | NBC
Awards | 4 Emmys, 1 Golden Globe
For fans of . . . | *Parks and Recreation* (2009)

Following the critical and commercial success of the original British *The Office*, countries around the world began to develop the formula for their own markets. The most successful and longest-running of these was the US version, which ran for nine seasons and made stars out of many of its writers and actors.

The Scranton, Pennsylvania headquarters of paper company Dunder Mifflin was almost exactly like any other office: it was staffed by people who were comfortable if not totally happy in their jobs, and boiling over with minor disagreements and irritations. What it had that most offices did not was Michael Scott (Steve Carell), self-proclaimed world's best boss and enthusiastic man-child who was more interested in being his employees' friend than their supervisor. Encouraged by his assistant, Dwight (Rainn Wilson), Scott spent his days trying—and failing—to make the office a better, funnier place. Balancing Scott's manic energy were slacker salesman Jim (John Krasinski) and grounded receptionist Pam (Jenna Fischer).

Lighter in tone than its UK counterpart, the US version of *The Office* featured the same cringeworthy situational humor, but developed its characters and story lines in ways the original did not. By the second season the show found its own voice, exploring the gentle humor and fundamental goodness of its characters even as it poked fun at them. **AP**

❯ Steve Carell as the boss from Hell in the company that no one wants to work for.

Doctor Who

Fantasy/Horror/Sci-Fi | UK | 2005–present

He's back. And it's all about time…and space

Cast | Christopher Eccleston, David Tennant, Matt Smith, Peter Capaldi, Billie Piper, Freema Agyeman, Catherine Tate, Karen Gillan, Jenna Coleman **Original broadcaster** | BBC One **Awards** | 2 BAFTAs **For fans of . . .** | *Farscape* (1999), *Fringe* (2008)

When the BBC announced it was going to revive classic sci-fi series *Doctor Who*, the program had been off TV screens for fifteen years. Traditional TV audiences were fragmenting, particularly on Saturday nights, and many anticipated a massive flop. But thanks to the creative genius of showrunner Russell T. Davies (and later Steven Moffat), the new *Doctor Who* was a massive hit. Ten years on, it still commands huge ratings and is seen around the world, from Brazil to South Korea and India.

The revival of the series continued the story of the Doctor, a friendly alien traveling through time and space fighting villains and monsters with a human companion by his side. This new series played up the emotional impact of the adventures on the Doctor and his companions—and sometimes on the companions' families, too. The first new companion, Rose (Billie Piper), actually fell in love with the Doctor, and it seemed that the Doctor had fallen for a human as well. For the first time, the show attracted many avid female fans.

Over the course of ten years (and counting), the Doctor has died a series of heroic deaths, and each time has regenerated with a new face. Companions have been stranded in parallel worlds, had their memories wiped, or traveled in time to live their lives in the past. Throughout it all, the rip-roaring adventures, the strong sense of morality, and the cheeky sense of humor have never flagged. The Doctor has now claimed a place alongside Sherlock Holmes and James Bond among the great heroes of British fiction. **PC**

Classic episode
The Fires of Pompeii | *Season 4, episode 2*. The Doctor (David Tennant) and Donna (Catherine Tate) arrive in Pompeii. Donna wants the Doctor to save a family from the imminent eruption of Vesuvius, but aliens lurk inside the volcano.

◉ David Tennant (the Doctor) and Billie Piper (Rose).

Matroesjka's

Crime/Mystery | Belgium | 2005–08

Adventures in the flesh trade

Cast | Peter Van den Begin, Axel Daeseleire, Tom Van Dyck, Luk Wyns, Eugenia Khirivskaya, Zemyna Asmontaite, Vilma Raubaite
Original broadcaster | VTM
For fans of . . . | *Svetlana's Journey* (2004)

A boom in dramas about the global trade in young women by gangsters included the British *Sex Traffic* (2004), with John Simm and the US *Human Trafficking* (2005), starring Donald Sutherland. But none was as acclaimed as Guy Goossens' and Mark Punt's *Matroesjka's*, broadcast internationally as *Matrioshki* or *Russian Dolls: Sex Trade*. The story began in Lithuania, where Belgian businessmen led by Raymond Van Mechelen (Peter Van den Begin) approached friends Daria (Zemyna Asmontaite) and Kasandra (Vilma Raubaite). Offered work as dancers in Belgium and Holland, Kasandra was skeptical, but Daria was keen to flee poverty and domestic abuse.

Gritty, not glorified, the series was more *Sopranos* than *Showgirls*. Van Mechelen and his fellow gangster Vincent Dockx (Tom Van Dyck) were repulsive but not entirely unsympathetic. The former's doomed relationship with Russian girl Kalinka (Eugenia Khirivskaya) proved pivotal to the story. The show's unswerving look at the sex trade attracted admiration from Amnesty International, who reportedly used scenes from the show in a documentary urging caution by schoolgirls in Eastern Europe.

The eight-hour first season was followed in 2007 by *Matroesjka's 2*, which followed Van Mechelen and Eddy Stoefs (Luk Wyns) to Thailand in search of their partner Jan Verplancke (Axel Daeseleire), only to become embroiled once more in the exploitation of vulnerable young women. **BM**

Marian, Again

Drama | UK | 2005

A woman vanishes then reappears: is it magic?

Cast | Stephen Tompkinson, Kelly Harrison, Owen Teale, Samantha Beckinsale
Original broadcaster | ITV
For fans of . . . | *The Price* (1985), *Marion and Geoff* (2000), *The Honourable Woman* (2014)

Based on the 1977 US kidnapping of Colleen Stan, *Marian, Again* is a riveting story of abduction and torture played out in the suburbs of Manchester, England.

It begins when happily married Chris (Stephen Tompkinson) gets lost on the way to his daughter's piano exam. He pops into a supermarket to ask for directions and spots Marian (Kelly Harrison), the love of his life. She suddenly disappeared 15 years ago and he never got over it. When he confronts her, she's adamant that her name is Susie. She's the wife and assistant of Bernie (Owen Teale), a plumber and part-time magician who can only get gigs in old people's homes where even the senile aren't entertained. Chris recognizes Bernie as a rival from when he first met Marian. What is she doing living with him now? How has the vivacious girl become so withdrawn? He decides to investigate and invites Bernie round to do some plumbing. When Bernie notices Chris's attractive teenage daughter, he thinks he may have a vacancy for a new assistant.

This compelling psychological drama is made all the more convincing by the mundane nature of its characters. Bernie's magic act is truly awful, his trick cabinet an old formica wardrobe on cheap castors. This makes him even more terrifying, and the torments he subjects Marian to all the more horrific. Tompkinson is equally good as a decent man trying to come to terms with the sudden realization that Bernie stole his old life and now threatens his new one. At the drama's heart is Harrison's hauntingly empty portrayal of Marian. **JG**

Engrenages

Drama | France | 2005–present

Murder, sex crimes, and political corruption in Paris tackled by police, lawyers, and an investigating judge

Cast | Caroline Proust, Grégory Fitoussi, Philippe Duclos, Thierry Godard, Fred Bianconi, Audrey Fleurot
Original broadcaster | Canal+
For fans of . . . | *Law & Order* (1990)

Paris, usually depicted as romantic and beautiful, has a dark underbelly caught in a spiral of escalating violence. *Engrenages* (*Spiral*) follows the lives and work of a small police team, two young lawyers, and an investigating judge as they battle vicious criminals, other police, and the political and legal systems. Bureaucracy often obstructs them, so they have to bend the law from time to time; the show is morally gray throughout.

The stories are told in a series of interlinking serials. Each serial follows a particular police investigation and a particular judicial investigation. Just as in real life, other unconnected crimes and cases emerge and need to be dealt with. At times the judicial and criminal cases intersect beyond the official working relationship between Judge Roban (Philippe Duclos) and police captain Laure Berthaud (Caroline Proust). Events from their past come to light and threaten to derail their quests for justice. Both Berthaud and her lieutenant Gilou (Thierry Godard) often push the boundaries of acceptable police procedure.

The cases are brutal and have included a serial killer, human trafficking, international arms dealing, domestic violence, and small town corruption with links to the very top of French politics. Filmed in a gritty and realistic style, the series never lets up in examining both crime and the methods used to tackle it. Like the investigating judge's approach to difficult cases, the moral implications of the characters' actions are never without dire consequences. **SJG**

Classic episode

Season 3, episode 9. Berthaud hunts Mexican Ronaldo Fuentes, suspected to be the Butcher of La Villette, against the orders of Judge Roban. She and her team track an Albanian crime gang who they suspect are hiding Fuentes.

◈ Caroline Proust stars as tough police captain Laure Berthaud, who doesn't always play by the rules.

Bleak House

Historical drama | UK | 2005

A galaxy of stars in a series of short, sharp episodes that effectively brought a vast Victorian novel to a twenty-first century audience

Cast | Anna Maxwell Martin, Denis Lawson, Carey Mulligan, Gillian Anderson, Timothy West
Original broadcaster | BBC One
Awards | 5 BAFTAs, 2 Emmys
For fans of . . . | *Pride and Prejudice* (1995)

The Jarndyce and Jarndyce case had dragged on for decades as lawyers contested contradictory versions of one man's will. Eventually almost all of his estate was consumed by legal fees. In the final generation of potential beneficiaries were John Jarndyce, his wards (Richard Carstone and Ada Clare), and Lady Dedlock. Lady Dedlock had a secret—an illegitimate child who she believed had died but had in fact been raised by Lady Dedlock's sister. When the child, Esther Summerson, came of age, she too fell under the guardianship of John Jarndyce. That was when all the mysteries were finally solved.

The BBC had dramatized *Bleak House* once before, in an eight-episode version in 1985. This adaptation into 15 soap-opera-style 30-minute episodes had a far bigger budget and featured numerous stars of film and TV, including Charles Dance and Timothy West, who appeared alongside young actors who were about to become very famous indeed. Anna Maxwell Martin won a BAFTA for her performance as the optimistic ingenue Esther, while Carey Mulligan, who played Ada Clare, was just a few years away from her first Oscar nomination for *An Education*. For Gillian Anderson, the role of Lady Dedlock was pivotal in her move away from *The X-Files* and back to her native Britain; within a few years of *Bleak House*, she played Miss Havisham in a new adaptation of another Dickens novel, *Great Expectations*, before taking the lead in powerful police procedural *The Fall*. **JS**

Classic episode
Episode 12. The creepy lawyer Tulkinghorn is found murdered. Inspector Bucket investigates and soon makes an arrest, but the case is not as open-and-shut as he would like to think, and the plot of the novel thickens even further.

◭ Gillian Anderson as Lady Honoria Dedlock, an aristocrat with a dark secret.

Sugar Rush

Drama | UK | 2005–06

This coming out drama perfectly captures the pangs of first love

Cast | Olivia Hallinan, Lenora Crichlow, Sarah-Jane Potts, Andrew Garfield, Richard Lumsden
Original broadcaster | Channel 4
Award | 1 Emmy
For fans of . . . | *The L Word* (2004)

Based on a novel by Julie Burchill, an enfant terrible of British journalism during the 1980s, *Sugar Rush* followed the trials and tribulations of a gauche fifteen-year-old called Kim as she fell in love with her best friend Maria "Sugar" Sweet. As well as being heterosexual, Sugar was a notorious troublemaker and Kim was enthralled—blind to her faults and head over heels in love.

Struggling with her family's recent move to the seaside town of Brighton from London, naive Kim turned to Sugar for support. Wasting no time in using Kim's infatuation to her advantage, Sugar persuaded her friend to steal a car and drive to London. At the end of season one, Sugar was arrested and sent to a young offenders institution. In season two, Kim tried to move on from her first obsession and embark on a relationship with sex shop owner Saint, while constantly wondering "what if" about Sugar.

Perfectly capturing the exquisite pain of first love and the fact that teenage girls are just as sex-obsessed as their male counterparts, the show became a huge hit with its teenage audience. Its young stars went on to future success, with Olivia Hallinan later taking a recurring role in the BBC costume drama *Lark Rise to Candleford* (2008), and Lenora Crichlow starring in *Being Human* (2008). Andrew Garfield, seen here in a minor role as Tom, Kim's socially awkward next door neighbor and first romantic conquest, has since conquered Hollywood and is now best known to global audiences for *The Amazing Spider-Man* (2012). **EB**

Threshold

Fantasy/Horror/Sci-Fi | USA | 2005–06

The fight against an invasion by DNA-altering "bodyforming" aliens

Cast | Carla Gugino, Peter Dinklage, Brent Spiner, Charles S. Dutton, Brian Van Holt, Rob Benedict
Original broadcaster | CBS
For fans of . . . | *Star Trek: The Next Generation* (1987), *Star Trek: Voyager* (1995)

Threshold concerns the activities of a US government organization that works to prevent extraterrestrial invasions of Earth. It is headed by Dr. Molly Anne Caffrey (Carla Gugino) and her "Red Team" of experts including hard-drinking and womanizing mathematics and linguistic genius Arthur Ramsey (future *Game of Thrones* star Peter Dinklage) and NASA microbiologist Nigel Fenway (*Star Trek: The Next Generation*'s Brent Spiner).

The attack duly comes, but it takes a form the scientists have not anticipated: the humans on board a space freighter are hit by a form of radiation; some are killed immediately, but those who survive are regenerated with the strength and hostile intentions of the aliens—the concept is reminiscent of the Cybermen in *Doctor Who*. They land in the United States and start regenerating; they must be stopped before they become so numerous that they can take over the world—this is the threshold of the title.

Critical reaction to the series was generally favorable but muted; ratings started off low and remained poor even after CBS made it the first show to be offered via Internet streaming on its website.

The makers soon abandoned their original plans for a three-year run and canceled *Threshold* after only nine episodes. The four further episodes that had already been produced were later shown on Sky1 in Britain. The whole series came out on DVD in 2006 and was catchable in the United States for several years but was unavailable at the time of publication of this book. **BA**

Numb3rs

Crime/Mystery | USA | 2005–10

A brilliant mathematician helps his brother, an FBI agent, to solve crimes using equations and formulas

Cast | David Krumholtz, Rob Morrow, Judd Hirsch, Alimi Ballard, Sabrina Lloyd, Peter MacNicol
Original broadcaster | CBS
For fans of . . . | *CSI: Crime Scene Investigation* (2000), *Bones* (2005), *Scorpion* (2014)

"We all use math every day. To predict weather . . . to tell time . . . to handle money. Math is more than formulas and equations. It's logic; it's rationality. It's using your mind to solve the biggest mysteries we know." This handy mission statement by Professor Charlie Epps (David Krumholtz) served as an opener to each episode and filled fans and math-geeks alike with excitement: solving crimes, it seems, is all in the numbers.

FBI Agent Don Epps (Rob Morrow) initially sought the help of his brilliant mathematician brother Charlie to plan a "hot zone" in a bid to catch a rapist for the Los Angeles Violent Crimes Squad. Their uneasy relationship resulted in a number of successfully solved cases. The boys' father, Alan (Judd Hirsch), mediated between hot-headed Don and cool, calculating Charlie with well-chosen words of wisdom.

Show creators Nicolas Falacci and Cheryl Heuton admitted that they never let the math get in the way of a good story, but the number work was genuine, and some of it is even used in real life by the FBI. The series has been used as a teaching tool in US schools.

This shouldn't make *Numb3rs* appear impenetrable; the math wasn't always in the front seat, and it was the strength of the relationships between the characters that made the show compulsive viewing.

Produced by Ridley and Tony Scott, this was the most successful and critically acclaimed foray into television for the film-directing brothers until *The Good Wife* (2009). **MR**

Classic episode
When Worlds Collide | *Season 4, episode 18*.
Two men are kidnapped by terrorists, and the brothers solve the case through their unique synthesis of procedural investigation and the judicious application of mathematical principles.

⊘ Rob Morrow as Don and Alimi Ballard as David, his unit's second-in-command.

Extras

Comedy | UK | 2005–07

The hilarious, celebrity-filled follow-up to The Office

Cast | Ricky Gervais, Stephen Merchant   **Original broadcaster** | BBC Two   **Award** | 1 Emmy
For fans of . . . | *Curb Your Enthusiasm* (2000), *The Office* (2001), *Episodes* (2011)

In this follow-up to *The Office*, Ricky Gervais and Stephen Merchant both wrote and acted in a satirical take on the world of film and television. The former plays Andy Millman, author and star of "When the Whistle Blows," a TV sitcom set in a factory canteen. The show is a critical flop but a major hit with ordinary viewers; Millman isn't happy with any of it: nothing he writes turns out in performance the way he expected or wanted it to. Merchant is Darren Lamb, Millman's ineffective agent, who nearly always agrees with whoever he happens to be talking to and often negotiates his client out of lucrative deals that were his for the asking.

Appearing with them in cameo roles are a host of stars—including David Bowie, Robert De Niro, Samuel L. Jackson, Daniel Radcliffe, Diana Rigg, Ben Stiller, and Kate Winslet—who all play twisted, offbeat versions of their real selves.

Extras ran for 13 episodes over two series. It was internationally celebrated and cemented the reputations of Gervais and Merchant as two of the best comedy writers of their generation. **LH**

Classic episode
The Extra Special Series Finale | *Season 2, episode 7.* In this Christmas special, writers Gervais and Merchant adopt cinematic techniques to produce the funniest and most moving piece in the whole series.

◬ The final episode of *Extras* featured cameos from a host of actors and celebrities.

The Thick of It

Comedy | UK | 2005–12

Sharp political comedy that brought us Malcolm Tucker and the term "omnishambles"

Cast | Peter Capaldi, Chris Langham, Rebecca Front, Roger Allam, Chris Addison, Joanna Scanlan, James Smith
Original broadcaster | BBC Four   **Awards** | 5 BAFTAs   **For fans of . . .** | *Yes, Minister* (1980), *Veep* (2012)

Malcolm Tucker (Peter Capaldi) is the British government's firebrand director of communications. Whenever there's a ministerial cock-up, he is there with some extraordinarily angry, verbose, and largely profane put-down of whoever is responsible.

Tucker is the star of the show, but the supporting cast of weak politicians and sycophantic political aides and civil servants each have sublime moments in the spotlight. Rebecca Front is especially good as pleasant but weak and inefficient minister, Nicola Murray. She constantly clashes with Malcolm over her personal life and her public persona.

The Thick of It is fantasy, but there is about Tucker a strong air of authenticity as he devotes all of his energy and powerful personality into covering up scandals and discouraging negative media coverage. The depiction of ministers as weak-willed timeservers is also equally as plausible.

The team behind *The Thick of It* also produced a film version (*In the Loop*) and later created the hugely successful *Veep* in the United States. **LH**

Classic episode

Season 4, episode 6. Concerned about leaks to the press, the British government holds a public inquiry. At the head of it is an eminent jurist with a keen forensic intelligence, but he is no match for the slippery Tucker.

⊘ Peter Capaldi (Malcolm Tucker, standing) watches on a monitor as one of the politicians in his care performs badly in a TV interview.

Wallander

Crime/Mystery | Sweden | 2005–13

Classy Scandinavian crime drama with an intriguing lead

Cast | Krister Henriksson, Johanna Sällström, Ola Rapace, Mats Bergman
Original broadcaster | TV4 **For fans of . . .** | *Forbrydelsen* (*The Killing*) (2007)

The global success of Henning Mankell's novels about Kurt Wallander—the opera-loving, junk food-eating police inspector in the provincial Swedish town of Ystad—made it inevitable that they would be adapted for the screen. First came nine cinema movies, starring Rolf Lassgård. They were followed by thirty-two feature-length television films with Krister Henriksson in the title role.

Only one of these shows was developed from a pre-existing book; all the others were TV originals based on suggestions by Mankell.

While this series was running, the makers filmed English-language versions of *Wallander* that used many of the same production personnel as the Swedish original and starred Kenneth Branagh. When this series arrived in Britain in 2008, digital channel BBC Four broadcast both it and the original Swedish episodes, allowing audiences to compare Henriksson and Branagh. Some viewers had a strong preference for one or the other, but many fans became equally hooked on both. **MW**

> **Classic episode**
> *Tjuven* (*The Thief*) | *Season 2, episode 17.*
> The people of Ystad form a vigilante group after a string of house burglaries. Wallander becomes suspicious that there has been a double murder, but he cannot find the bodies.

Ⓐ (L–R) Ola Rapace (Stefan Lindman), Krister Henriksson (Kurt Wallander), and Johanna Sällström (Linda Wallander).

Grey's Anatomy

Drama | USA | 2005–present

It's a beautiful day to save lives

Cast | Ellen Pompeo, Sandra Oh, Katherine Heigl, T. R. Knight, Patrick Dempsey, Kate Walsh, Chandra Wilson
Original broadcaster | ABC   **Awards** | 4 Emmys, 2 Golden Globes   **For fans of . . .** | *ER* (1994), *Scrubs* (2001)

Originally aired as a midseason replacement for *Boston Legal*, *Grey's Anatomy* was created by Shonda Rhimes as a medical drama focused on equality, with strong women of all races competing in a hospital in Seattle.

The title is a play on words, referring both to the classic medical student textbook *Gray's Anatomy* and the main character and narrator, Meredith Grey (Ellen Pompeo), who started as an intern and was rapidly promoted. The show explores the relationships between a range of medics and their patients. Their lives are full of drama, mayhem, and illness, from cancer to plane crashes or being hit by a bus. In a work environment with such stress and pressure, affairs and romances are rife.

The show was remade in Turkey as *Doktorlar* (*Doctors*, 2006) and in Colombia as telenovela *A Corazón Abierto* (*An Open Heart*, 2010). In 2009 it even became a video game for a variety of platforms.

Private Practice (2007) was a spin-off series following Dr. Addison Montgomery (Kate Walsh) when she moved to private practice in Los Angeles. **EB**

Classic episode
Sanctuary | Season 6, episode 23. The hospital goes into lockdown when it is revealed a gunman is on the loose and everyone is at risk. Meanwhile, Meredith learns that she is pregnant by Dr. Derek Shepherd (Patrick Dempsey).

◎ (L–R) Katherine Heigl (Izzie Stevens), Justin Chambers (Alex Karev), Sandra Oh (Cristina Yang), and Ellen Pompeo (Meredith Grey).

How I Met Your Mother

Comedy | USA | 2005–14

Have you met Ted?

Cast | Josh Radnor, Alyson Hannigan, Jason Segel, Neil Patrick Harris, Cobie Smulders
Original broadcaster | CBS **Awards** | 9 Emmys **For fans of . . .** | *Friends* (1994)

Years into the future, Ted Mosby (voiced by Bob Saget) sits his children down to tell them the story of how he met their mother. The main story then returns to the present day, following the exploits of Ted (Josh Radnor), loving couple Marshall (Jason Segel) and Lily (Alyson Hannigan), womanizer Barney (Neil Patrick Harris), and local newsreader Robin (Cobie Smulders), who has an on-off relationship with Ted.

The continuity within the show was incredibly tight, with jokes and references set up for payoffs months, sometimes years later. In the season nine episode "How Your Mother Met Me," the mother's story was recounted in flashback, often interacting with previous story lines of the show, her path almost crossing time

and time again with Ted's. *How I Met your Mother* was also unafraid to challenge the traditional sitcom format, such as season eight's "The Time Travelers," in which Ted and Barney met their older selves.

Though the show ended in 2014, rumors persist of a spin-off series, which was provisionally titled *How I Met Your Dad*. **EB**

> **Classic episode**
> *Slap Bet* | *Season 2, episode 9*. Marshall and Barney bet on why Robin won't go to a mall. The winner gets to slap the other whenever he wants. They discover a secret from Robin's past, and Barney is forever after in fear of being hit.

⊙ (L–R) Neil Patrick Harris (Barney), Cobie Smulders (Robin), Josh Radnor (Ted), Jason Segel (Marshall), and Alyson Hannigan (Lily).

Weeds

Drama | USA | 2005–12

Darkly humorous drama with a smoky undercurrent

Cast | Mary-Louise Parker, Elizabeth Perkins, Justin Kirk, Kevin Neal
Original broadcaster | Showtime **For fans of . . .** | *Breaking Bad* (2008)

After her husband died suddenly of a heart attack while out jogging, Nancy Botwin (Mary-Louise Parker) wanted to maintain her affluent lifestyle so started selling marijuana around a gated middle-class community in the fictional town of Agrestic, California. She clashed with Celia (Elizabeth Perkins), her image-obsessed friend and president of the local PTA. She then opened a bakery as a front for her drug dealing and became romantically involved with a man who was, unknown to her, a DEA agent.

Having started out as a dark comedy, *Weeds* got even blacker at the end of season three, when Nancy burned down her home and set off with her two sons to start a new life running drugs across the US–Mexico border.

In later episodes Nancy spent time in prison, before the family went back to the West Coast in the final, eighth season.

The first twenty-two of the 102 episodes were written by the series' creator, Jenji Kohan, whose subsequent credits included acclaimed drama *Orange Is the New Black* (2013). MW

Classic episode
Cooking with Jesus | *Season 2, episode 2*.
Afraid that her boyfriend will discover she's a drug dealer, Nancy tries to end their relationship. Celia announces that she's running for the city council and asks Nancy to back her campaign.

◆ Mary-Louise Parker (Nancy) taps into a lucrative but illegal source of income.

Infinite Challenge

Reality | South Korea | 2005–present

Popular, broad-based entertainment show that combines comedy, variety, and competitive games

Cast | Yoo Jae-suk, Park Myeong-su, Jeong Jun-ha, Jeong Hyeong-don, HaHa, Hwang Kwanghee
Original broadcaster | MBC
For fans of . . . | *Strong Heart* (2009), *Hwasin—Controller of the Heart* (2013)

Aired at peak time every Saturday night, *Infinite Challenge* has been the top free-to-air show on Korean television for more than a decade. At the heart of each episode are games in which contestants compete for prizes. Some of the events are winnable, but others are not—in the case of the latter, the fun lies in watching people attempt to achieve impossible targets. In one game, "Ah-ha," the quizmaster says a word and the contestants must then say it backward; if they fail to do so correctly, they get hit over the head. The show's six hosts say that the criteria for all their games are that they should be "dirty, dangerous, and difficult."

There are also secretly filmed insights into the participants' lives, usually in amusing or embarrassing situations, and *Candid Camera*–style pranks on members of the public. Interspersed between the challenges are numerous comedy sketches by members of the cast. Among the most popular of these is a running dialogue between characters named Ha (Jeong Jun-ha) and Soo (Park Myeong-su). Ha is strident and aggressive; Soo is simple-minded and suggestible. Their exchanges are reminiscent of those between Peter Cook and Dudley Moore in *Not Only . . . But Also* (1964) and Mel Smith and Griff Rhys Jones in *Alas Smith and Jones* (1984).

Cast members come and go—for example, host Haha left in 2008 to do military service—but the show's popularity is undiminished because it is so much more than the sum of its parts. **GL**

Classic episode
Midsummer-Day Special | *Season 4, episode 63*.
On this typically zany evening, some participants turn up at a company's offices at midnight to offer their services as security guards. Others have to camp in the lobby of MBC headquarters.

⊘ Jeong Jun-Ha, Yoo Jae-Suk, and No Hong-Chul take a photo before a street racing challenge.

Ugly Betty
Comedy | USA | 2006–10

The adventures of a fish out of water in the big city touch on some serious issues, such as the assimilation of Hispanic people into US society and the significance of physical appearance

Cast | America Ferrera, Eric Mabius, Vanessa Williams, Ana Ortiz, Tony Plana, Alan Dale, Becki Newton
Original broadcaster | ABC
Awards | 3 Emmys
For fans of . . . | *Modern Family* (2009)

From the moment she steps into the world of fashion, Betty Suarez (America Ferrera) knows she's in over her head, but she has a strong character and preternatural resilience. Silvio Horta's inspiring, occasionally hilarious, and surprisingly insightful remake of the Colombian telenovela *Yo soy Betty, la fea* (*I Am Betty, the Ugly One*) focused on Betty's adventures as the assistant of Daniel Meade, a rich playboy given responsibility by his overbearing father for running glamorous fashion magazine *Mode*. The two become friends and allies against threats from both outside and within.

Lauded for its smart writing and production design, as well as for its positive portrayal of the Latina lead character, *Ugly Betty* pivoted on a large and diverse cast, from the far-from-one-dimensional Meade family to Wilhelmina Slater, Daniel's nemesis at *Mode* played to perfection by Vanessa Williams. The series also notably featured two gay lead characters, the flamboyant assistant Marc and Betty's young teenaged nephew Justin, whose first same-sex kiss was promoted as a major event in the show's fourth and final season.

Although a strong ratings grabber in its first two years, *Ugly Betty*'s shifting timeslot on the ABC schedules eventually led to a decline in viewing figures and ultimately to cancellation, although the series' major storylines were all wrapped up by the finale. A movie version has long been rumored but at the time of publication of the present volume had yet to be officially announced. **SL**

Classic episode
Million Dollar Smile | *Season 4, episode 17*. After four seasons, Betty finally has her braces removed. As the big moment approaches, she ponders how her life would have been if she had never worn them at all.

⬤ America Ferrera as Betty Suarez in the first day of her new job with *Mode* magazine.

30 Rock

Comedy | USA | 2006–13

Farcical sitcom about a late-night sketch comedy show

Cast | Tina Fey, Alec Baldwin, Tracy Morgan, Jane Krakowski, Jack McBrayer
Original broadcaster | NBC
Awards | 16 Emmys
For fans of . . . | *Drop the Dead Donkey* (1990)

There is a special kind of madness to *30 Rock*—a sitcom about a sketch series. Created by Tina Fey, fresh from a much-lauded run as actress and writer on NBC's *Saturday Night Live*, *30 Rock* is based partly on her experiences with that show, but with just the right amount of madcap, over-the-top performances and shenanigans to keep it fresh and unpredictable.

The right show at the right time, *30 Rock* debuted as a critics' darling and never lost its luster. Fey stars as Liz Lemon, the head writer of show-within-a-show *TGS with Tracy Jordan*, on which she is surrounded by neurotic method actress friend Jenna Maroney (Jane Krakowski), impossible and even more neurotic film buffoon/strip club devotee Tracy Jordan (Tracy Morgan), NBC's charmingly slick head of East Coast television (and microwave oven programming) Jack Donaghy (Alec Baldwin), a hapless hillbilly page/television fanatic Kenneth Parcell (Jack McBrayer), and a seasoned supporting cast running the gamut from lazy sketch-writers to wizened members of the Jordan entourage. The plotline mostly centers on Liz's forays into one love affair after another, and her relationship with mentor/boss/friend Jack.

The brilliance of the performances is matched by the quality of the writing. *30 Rock* is a rich tapestry of fun, a once-in-a-generation sitcom without equal, and a series that bears repeated revisits. **SL**

➦ (L–R) Tracy Morgan as Tracy Jordan, Jane Krakowski as Jenna Maroney, and Tina Fey as Liz Lemon.

America's Got Talent

Reality | USA | 2006–present

Britain's Got Talent *became a worldwide phenomenon, but this show is where it all began*

Cast | Nick Cannon, Howie Mandel, Heidi Klum, Mel B, Howard Stern
Original broadcaster | NBC **For fans of . . .** | *Pop Idol* (2001), *The X Factor* (2004)

Americans embraced the "Got Talent" format before the Brits or anyone else got their hands on it. Thus *America's Got Talent* is a must-watch, not only for the wackiness of some of the acts but also for the purposes of comparison with the versions that later appeared all over the world.

The US show has been through a string of presenters and judges: the former have included Jerry Springer and Nick Cannon; among the latter have been Howard Stern, Howie Mandel, Mel B, Heidi Klum, Piers Morgan, and David Hasselhoff (but no Simon Cowell, even though he is the brains behind the whole thing).

As with similar US talent shows, the genuinely talented acts seem bigger and better than in many of its foreign counterparts. The less able acts are as hopeless and as laughable as they are across the rest of the world. The format of the US final is unique—it all ends up with a week in Las Vegas and $1m for the winner—but overall the original series is much the same—and every bit as entertaining—as the numerous imitations it went on to inspire. **CW**

> **Classic episode**
> *Season 9, quarter-finals, 2014.* Two teenage tap dancers from Chicago rock the audience but leave the judges unmoved; guitarist Miguel Dakota gets unanimous acclaim for his version of The Beatles'"Come Together."

⬥ (L–R) Judges Piers Morgan, Sharon Osbourne, and David Hasselhoff enjoy the acts.

The Street

Drama | UK | 2006–09

A series of short plays about the residents of one Manchester street

Cast | Timothy Spall, Jim Broadbent, Anna Friel, Bob Hoskins, Jody Latham, Jane Horrocks
Original broadcaster | BBC One **Awards** | 2 BAFTAs, 4 Emmys **For fans of . . .** | *Play for Today* (1970)

The Street was very much the realization of writer Jimmy McGovern's commitment to producing realistic, socially relevant drama with a credible working-class setting. Each episode focused on the occupants of a different house in an unnamed Manchester street as they faced some form of crisis. McGovern used the anthology format of the series—every episode told a self-contained story—to revive the stand-alone television play, once a staple of British broadcasting but something of a rarity since the early 1990s.

Although the situations the characters found themselves in were frequently harrowing—a young soldier returns from Afghanistan badly scarred; a teacher falls under suspicion of being a sex offender;

a single mother becomes a prostitute to make ends meet—*The Street* found hope, redemption, and even humor in their stories, all without compromising the series' realism. An inspired updating of the kitchen sink drama tradition, *The Street* showcased the work of one of Britain's best, and most overtly political, television writers and that of many fine British actors. **HE**

Classic episode
The Promise | *Season 2, episode 12.* A young man's life is overshadowed by the terrible crime he committed as a child. Unexpectedly, he comes into contact with the woman whose own life was shattered by his actions.

⊘ (L–R) Jody Latham, Timothy Spall, Christine Bottomley, Jane Horrocks, and Jim Broadbent.

Life on Mars

Crime/Mystery | UK | 2006–07

Postmodernist take on 1970s cop shows

Cast | John Simm, Philip Glenister, Liz White, Dean Andrews, Marshall Lancaster
Original broadcaster | BBC One
Awards | 1 BAFTA, 2 Emmys
For fans of . . . | *The Sweeney* (1975)

"My name is Sam Tyler. I had an accident, and I woke up in 1973. Am I mad, in a coma, or back in time?" So opens each episode of *Life on Mars*, a show that straddles the genres of science fiction, historical drama, and police procedural. Originally conceived by Matthew Graham and Ashley Pharoah as a comedy series with the working title "Ford Granada," *Life on Mars* took eight years to sell because it proved so difficult to categorize. However, when it eventually hit TV screens in 2006, its unique concept proved an immediate success.

The first episode has twenty-first century detective Sam Tyler involved in a hit-and-run car accident, and baffled to wake up in 1970s Manchester. Surprise quickly turns to horror when he realizes that his new boss is DCI Gene Hunt, described by Sam as an "overweight, over-the-hill, nicotine-stained, borderline alcoholic homophobe with a superiority complex and an unhealthy obsession with male bonding." Appalled by the prejudice and corruption of policing in the 1970s, Sam embarks on a dual mission: to clean up his department and find a way back to 2006. Sam's by-the-book methods and sensitivity frequently cause clashes with Hunt's bullish corner-cutting, but the two eventually form an unstoppable team.

Life on Mars embraces the style of unreconstructed drama series such as *The Sweeney* while at the same time critiquing their outdated attitudes. It spawned a UK sequel, *Ashes to Ashes*, set in the 1980s, and both US and Russian remakes. **MW**

Charlie Brooker's Screenwipe

Comedy | UK | 2006–09

The news mocked by a grumpy couch potato

Cast | Al Campbell, David Firth, Aisleyne Horgan-Wallace, Tim Key, Doug Stanhope, Diane Morgan, Brian Limond
Original broadcaster | BBC Four
For fans of . . . | *Harry Hill's TV Burp* (2002)

Charlie Brooker's TV review column for the British *Guardian* newspaper established him as a pessimistic curmudgeon who ranted inventively against the people responsible for television's worst excesses. *Screenwipe* was an extension of this, depicting him alone in his apartment, directing his razor-sharp wit at the lowest of the low from around the world. His persona was one of frustrated bafflement—how had things been allowed to get this bad?—but his bile was alleviated by insightful discourses on how TV works, such as the way selective editing makes "reality" TV one of the least truthful formats.

Within the *Screenwipe* format, "Newswipe" targeted the way the media selects its stories, with experts helping Brooker shine a light on such topics as how the reporting of massacres in American schools actually contributes to the problem. "Gameswipe" took Brooker back to his roots as a videogame reviewer, while "Charlie Brooker's Weekly Wipe" highlighted current news stories.

One of the show's most subversive tricks was to mock TV's use of "talking heads" to explain the context of various topics. Among those appearing with Brooker were Barry Shitpeas (series director Al Campbell), a slackjawed pundit who understood less about the world than any viewer, vacuous Philomena Cunk (Diane Morgan), and the bewildered Glaswegian Limmy (Brian Limond). The series also featured contributions from American comedian Doug Stanhope. **JS**

◉ John Simm rests on the hood of a 1970s Ford.

Planet Earth

Documentary | UK | 2006

BBC documentary about our home, shown around the world

Cast | Sir David Attenborough (UK, worldwide); Sigourney Weaver (US)
Original broadcaster | BBC Two
Awards | 5 Emmys
For fans of . . . | *Cosmos* (2014)

Planet Earth was as as big as the world itself—a sprawling eleven-part documentary series voyaging across our forests and deserts and oceans to examine their splendors and the fragile lives that inhabit them. Its viewership was as impressive as its scope—it was screened in more than two-thirds of the world's countries within a year of broadcast, and widely released on DVD and Blu-Ray.

Gorgeously shot in high-definition over five years, *Planet Earth* encompassed everything from the vast peaks of the Himalayas to the trenches of the Pacific Ocean, from the fragile ecosystems of the poles to the complexity of its rainforests. Its story was not only that of biology and ecology, but also of humans; the way we impact our world.

Planet Earth was originally broadcast in the UK. Each episode was narrated by naturalist David Attenborough and accompanied by a ten-minute "behind the episode" documentary-within-a-documentary. BBC Worldwide sold the series overseas to CBC in Canada, Australia's ABC, and a variety of other broadcasters. Discovery Networks, which purchased the series for US audiences, made minor edits to the broadcast and chose actress Sigourney Weaver to replace Attenborough's narration. It also compiled all the original featurettes into a full additional episode. *Earth*, a film re-edited from the series, later achieved great success as one of the highest-grossing feature documentaries ever made. **SL**

Waterloo Road

Soap opera | UK | 2006–15

The best days of your life couldn't get any more dramatic than they do at Waterloo Road

---

Cast | Neil Pearson, Angus Deayton, Philip Martin Brown, Jason Done, Denise Welch, Jill Halfpenny, Chelsee Healey, Neil Morrissey, Elizabeth Berrington
Original broadcaster | BBC One
For fans of . . . | *Grange Hill* (1978), *Teachers* (2001)

Over the years, the eponymous Waterloo Road school has merged with the local private school, been razed to the ground, been set upon by a rogue digger, and even been relocated 200 miles (320 km) north to Glasgow, with a coach crash along the way.

Produced by Ann McManus and Maureen Chadwick, the team behind ITV's *Bad Girls* (1999) and *Footballers' Wives* (2002), the show was the spiritual descendant of BBC's *Grange Hill*. Portraying students and teachers in an equal light, it dramatized the problems faced by both. Aired in a midevening slot, it aimed for a family audience, with topics ranging from addictions to eating disorders and child abuse, as well as gender and sexuality issues. It also touched on wider education concerns such as excessive bureaucracy, frequent threats of closure, and teacher stress.

A number of notable actors have cut their teeth in the series, including *Doctor Who*'s Jenna Coleman, Sophie McShera (*Downton Abbey*'s Daisy), and Chelsee Healey (*Casualty*'s Honey Wright).

The show ran for nine series, dodging the ax on a number of occasions. An online spin-off, *Waterloo Road Reunited*, was produced in 2011, following the post-school lives of a number of well-loved students as they faced the challenges of the real world beyond the school gate. *Waterloo Road* aired across Europe, Southeast Asia, and the Middle East on international BBC channels, as well as in Australia, New Zealand, and South Africa. **EB**

Big Love

Drama | USA | 2006–11

An uncompromising examination of the institution of marriage in the Church of Jesus Christ of Latter-day Saints

Cast | Bill Paxton, Jeanne Tripplehorn, Chloë Sevigny, Ginnifer Goodwin, Amanda Seyfried, Douglas Smith
Original broadcaster | HBO
Award | 1 Golden Globe
For fans of . . . | *The Sopranos* (1999)

Bill Hendrickson (Bill Paxton) and his wife Barb (Jeanne Tripplehorn) had what appeared to be a fairly ordinary marriage: a house, kids, the usual. What was less usual, however, was that in two other houses Bill had two other wives and two other families. The family were polygamous Mormons, and although only Barb was recognized by law as Bill's wife, both second wife Nicki (Chloë Sevigny) and third, and the youngest, wife Margie (Ginnifer Goodwin) were equally important in his life. The extended setup had to be kept secret from the wider, nonunderstanding world.

A major focus of the show was the power play between the sister wives—although all three were victims of a patriarchal world, they were forced to focus inward and challenge each other, rather than rage against the system. Although they were sometimes jealous of one another, there was an affection among them based on their shared experiences, with Margie in particular looking up to "head wife" Barb, who became almost a mother figure for the entire extended family.

The show didn't shy away from the potential negatives of polygamy. While the relationships at the heart of the show were shown to be reasonably positive for all involved, season two in particular looked at the abuse that can happen within these situations. This was explored mostly through Barb's eyes, brought up a Mormon but an outsider to the polygamous world, unlike Nicki, the daughter of one of her father's fourteen wives. **EB**

Classic episode
The Ceremony | *Season 1, episode 12.* Life and religious faith collide in this season finale, in which Barb is nominated for the Mother of the Year award, but she is uncertain whether it is right for her to compete.

◉ (L–R) Ginnifer Goodwin (Margie), Chloë Sevigny (Nicki), Bill Paxton (Bill), and Jeanne Tripplehorn (Barb).

Jericho

Fantasy/Horror/Sci-Fi | USA | 2006–08

Fans of this cult, postapocalyptic survival drama pleaded for more

Cast | Skeet Ulrich, Lennie James, Ashley Scott, Kenneth Mitchell, Brad Beyer   **Original broadcaster** | CBS
For fans of . . . | *Threads* (1984), *Jeremiah* (2002), *Survivors* (2008), *Revolution* (2012)

When Jake Green (Skeet Ulrich) saw an atomic mushroom cloud on the horizon, somewhere in the direction of Denver, he headed home to Jericho, where he found his estranged father murdered by convicts who had escaped their prison transport when the bomb fell. News of a similar nuclear attack in Atlanta spread, and it gradually materialized that twenty-three states had been attacked—but by whom?

In the ensuing struggle for survival, ruthless self-interest trounced community cooperation. Eventually, a sinister police state, the Allied States of America, took power, provoking Jake and a mysterious newcomer Robert Hawkins (Lennie James), who was aware of the shocking origins of the original attack, to take action.

While *Jericho* debuted well, ratings declined sharply, perhaps because of its slow pace. The show's fans campaigned for a second season, even sending 20 tons of peanuts to CBS. They gained another seven episodes, but ratings continued falling and the show was canceled. An attempt to interest other networks failed, though the story eventually continued in comic-book form. **MR**

Classic episode
A.K.A. | *Season 1, episode 18.* The slow-burning drama takes a twist when the clandestine reasons for a new world order are revealed to Jake, and he discovers some of the secrets in Hawkins' background.

◉ Lennie James (Robert Hawkins) and Skeet Ulrich (Jake Green) join forces.

Torchwood

Fantasy/Horror/Sci-Fi | UK | 2006–11

The members of a secret organization protect the Earth from alien menace

Cast | John Barrowman, Eve Myles, Burn Gorman, Naoko Mori, Gareth David-Lloyd, Kai Owen, Mekhi Phifer
Original broadcasters | BBC Three, Starz **For fans of . . .** | *Doctor Who* (1963), *Fringe* (2008)

A rift in time surges through Cardiff, Wales, causing extraterrestrial and interdimensional phenomena that fall under the remit of Torchwood, a secret organization with a royal charter to protect the UK. The team is led by Captain Jack Harkness (John Barrowman), a former time traveler cursed with an inability to die (and whose resurrections are agonizingly painful). Police officer Gwen Cooper (Eve Myles) comes close to uncovering the group's activities but instead finds herself recruited.

Creator Russell T. Davies challenged London-centric TV by making a production that promoted the Welsh capital and showcased local talent. The title is an anagram of "*Doctor Who*," in which Captain Jack first appeared in 2005, but unlike its progenitor, which was always aimed at the whole family, *Torchwood* is decidedly adult, with strong language, sex scenes, and gory violence.

By trying too hard to target "grown-ups," some early episodes seemed a little forced, but the series soon settled down to provide some of the creepiest drama seen on British television in recent years. **JS**

> **Classic episode**
> *Children of Earth: Day One* | *Season 3, episode 1.*
> Decades ago, a bargain was made with an alien race known only as "the 456." Now, they have returned to collect their bounty—one in ten of all the children on planet Earth.

⬧ (L–R) Jack Harkness (John Barrowman), Gwen (Eve Myles), Ianto (Gareth Lloyd-Davies), Owen (Burn Gorman), Toshiko (Naoko Mori).

The Unit

Drama | USA | 2006–09

A celebrated US playwright displays his mastery of drama in a show about soldiers and their families back home

Cast | Dennis Haysbert, Regina Taylor, Scott Foley
Original broadcaster | CBS
For fans of . . . | *Soldier Soldier* (1994), *The Shield* (2002), *Ultimate Force* (2002), *Strike Back* (2010), *Homeland* (2011)

A TV action drama may seem a strange departure for a playwright acclaimed for his idiosyncratic take on American culture, but if you look more closely, you can see that *The Unit* allowed David Mamet—author of *Glengarry Glen Ross* (1984) and *Speed-the-Plow* (1988)—to deal with his perennial themes in a new medium.

Based on a book by former operative Eric L. Haney, the show focused on the members of a top-secret military force as they conducted dangerous operations all over the world. Crucially, it also followed the lives of their families back home. It was this split narrative that allowed Mamet to tell his stories about real-life Americans, and the sacrifices made—on both sides—for the good of the country. As you would expect from a US network show, the action was lavishly mounted and had real pace, but this was nicely balanced by the human stories. The soldiers grappled with the dichotomy of being fathers and killers, while their wives dealt with the absence of their loved ones, and the constant fear that they may never see them again. Mamet and fellow executive producer Shawn Ryan—creator of *The Shield* (2002)—tapped into the feelings of a nation that was fighting a war in the Middle East.

The producers contemplated a fifth season, but the *The Unit* was eventually canceled at the end of season four after sixty-nine episodes. Mamet later posted online an account of the development of the show that has become an authoritative guide to good TV screenwriting. **SO**

Classic episode
Five Brothers | *Season 3, episode 7*. The Unit travels to Beirut to rescue a journalist who has been kidnapped. Back home, the wives join forces to help Tiffy when her car is impounded by a vindictive tow service operator.

◉ Dennis Haysbert as Jonas on a mission to Brazil to stop a drug baron from selling missiles.

(A Town Called) Eureka

Drama | USA | 2006–12

Set in an Oregon town filled with super-geniuses who make things that explode, this is a soft-focus drama that sometimes displays a harder edge

Cast | Colin Ferguson, Salli Richardson-Whitfield, Erica Cerra, Neil Grayston, Joe Morton, Chris Gauthier, Jordan Hinson, Niall Matter, Ed Quinn
Original broadcaster | SyFy
For fans of . . . | *Warehouse 13* (2009), *Alphas* (2011)

Sheriff Jack Carter (Colin Ferguson) moves into a small American town populated solely by geniuses, and finds that he can help them when they can't help themselves. A fish out of water there, his groundedness saves the day on many occasions.

Eureka shares much of its DNA with shows such as *Northern Exposure* and *Due South*, seasoning light drama with comedy. However, it occasionally and oddly changes its tone and deals with much darker themes, including cold-blooded murder.

In the fourth season, the show refocused itself in a soft reboot, as five of the main characters travel back in time to 1947. When they return to the present day, they find that they have created an alternative timeline which persists for the rest of the show's run.

This new timeline retained the overall premise—a normal(ish) man in a town of geniuses—but many of the characters' relationships changed, a shift that allowed the show to focus on its strengths, to discard some previous assumptions, and to explore the ramifications of the changes created by altering history.

Although *Eureka*'s ratings were high, the show was not profitable enough to allow the commissioning of a sixth season. The decision to scrap it came late in the day, and after a cliff-hanger finale to the fifth season was already in production. Fortunately, the producers were able to write and shoot a final closing episode, "Just Another Day," to satisfy fans and provide a resolution to the series. **PB**

Classic episode
Founder's Day | Season 4, episode 1. Five people travel back to 1947. With the aid of Eureka's founder, Dr. Trevor Grant (*Battlestar Galactica*'s James Callis), they return to their own time without anyone realizing they've been away.

⊙ Jack (Colin Ferguson) and Henry (Joe Morton) inspect a burnt corpse as people of the town mysteriously start to combust.

Time Trumpet

Comedy | UK | 2006

This spoof documentary set in the future looked back in laughter at today's world

Cast | Armando Iannucci, Richard Ayoade, Matthew Holness, Adam Buxton, Jo Enright, Stewart Lee, Jo Neary, Mark Watson
Original broadcaster | BBC Two
For fans of . . . | *The Day Today* (1994)

This short-lived but highly original BBC mockumentary created by British satirist Armando Iannucci looked back on the first thirty years of the twenty-first century from the perspective of 2031. It was partly inspired by the many specials about popular culture in past decades that peppered British TV schedules at the time.

Supported by archive footage, modern-day celebrities played by actors (and aged by twenty-five years) reflected on their own experiences of the period and expounded on events that had impacted their lives—David Beckham explained why he had a vagina stitched into his arm, Jamie Oliver reflected on his move into cooking human flesh, David Cameron reminisced on how he had courted publicity by learning to break dance. "Expert" talking heads, played by comedians Richard Ayoade, Matthew Holness, Jo Enright, and others, discussed the absurdities that had apparently come to pass (a hugely successful TV series called *Rape an Ape*, the revelation that the 2012 London Olympics had been a hoax, and the rise of the All-Bacon Home Shopping Channel).

Time Trumpet was a surreal, dystopian future-history that painted a bizarre picture of how the worst aspects of the modern world had run amok. Some of the material could be quite savage, but the intentionally anodyne mood of the series somewhat blunted the impact and probably allowed Iannucci to explore areas that would have been more controversial in a more orthodox satirical setting. **DF**

Friday Night Lights

Drama | USA | 2006–11

Frank, brutal and acclaimed depiction of a small-town high-school football team

Cast | Kyle Chandler, Connie Britton, Gaius Charles, Zach Gilford
Original broadcaster | NBC
Awards | 3 Emmys
For fans of . . . | *Nashville* (2012)

That *Friday Night Lights* was never a mainstream hit may be counted as one of the greatest crimes in broadcast history. Peter Berg's five-season trawl through Middle America, seen through the fortunes of a high-school football team, is world class, but its brutal and honest outlook was perhaps too uncompromising for a prime-time NBC audience.

Berg originally made it as a big-screen movie based on *Friday Night Lights: A Town, a Team, a Dream,* H.G. Bissinger's book about a season in the life of the Permian Panthers of Odessa, Texas. He then created a new version for television in which the rhythms of a college football season developed over multiple episodes as coach Eric Taylor (Kyle Chandler) takes on the Dillon Panthers. Connie Britton and Brad Leland had appeared in the movie, and Berg cast them in similar roles here; Britton as high-school counselor and Taylor's wife Tami, and Leland as booster Buddy Garrity.

Friday Night Lights never quite took hold on NBC. It's more than a drama about a sports team; it's a social document that examines the disaffection of youth, high-school funding, racism, corruption, and how the fortunes of the team are linked to the morale of a small town. The shooting is loose and edgy, and cast members are encouraged to play scenes instinctively; the avoidance of soundstages gives a solid authenticity. After season two, NBC premiered subsequent episodes of *Friday Night Lights* on DirecTV's 101 Network, which earned the show another three series. **MW**

Kyle Chandler as football coach Eric Taylor. ❯

Real Housewives of Orange County

Reality | USA | 2006–present

Hit reality show about the idle rich

Cast | Vicki Gunvalson, Tamra Judge, Heather Dubrow, Shannon Beador, Lizzie Rovsek
Original broadcaster | Bravo
For fans of . . . | *Desperate Housewives* (2004), *Made in Chelsea* (2011)

The Real Housewives of Orange County documents "real life" in the wealthy gated community of Coto de Caza in Southern California. With a nod toward the comedy-drama *Desperate Housewives*, it follows the personal and professional lives of five women, all of whom bask in the benefits and advantages that affluence brings. In interviews, the executive producers said they consider it to be more of a soap opera than a reality show. In truth, it's probably an amalgam of both.

While the show holds a mirror up to wealth in some of its more outlandish aspects, it also celebrates some of the hard work that went into acquiring and holding on to it. Businesses demand tough decisions, marriages need to be worked at, and kids need teaching about the lessons of life—the viewers see all of this, and no matter whether they envy, admire, or disapprove of the lives depicted, the show sparks discussion.

Over the years the lineup has been expanded and rotated; at the time of publication of the present volume, sixteen housewives had appeared. Only one member of the original quintet has been ever-present: Vicki Gunvalson.

The show's success spawned spin-off series about the lives of rich housewives in other parts of the United States—New York City, Atlanta, New Jersey, Washington, D.C., Beverly Hills, and Miami. They have all performed well in the ratings, but in the view of many the original is best: its decadence is addictive, and its drama compelling. **PPW**

Brothers & Sisters

Drama | USA | 2006–11

A family coping with the loss of its patriarch

Cast | Sally Field, Calista Flockhart, Rachel Griffiths, Rob Lowe, Matthew Rhys, Ron Rifkin, Patricia Wettig
Original broadcaster | ABC
Award | 1 Emmy
For fans of . . . | *Cold Feet* (1997), *Six Feet Under* (2001)

Advance publicity and trailers for this series made much of the fact that it starred Tom Skerritt, who played William Walker, paterfamilias and proud owner of Ojai Foods. But the character drops dead in first episode, and as his surviving relatives set about untangling his estate they discover that he had been keeping secrets throughout his life. *Brothers & Sisters* charts the effect of these revelations on his widow Nora and their children: unhappily married Rachel, brash and outspoken Kitty, gay but lonely Kevin, jealous Tommy, broken Justin.

Sally Field made her long-awaited return to network television (after replacing Betty Buckley in a last-minute recasting) to headline ABC's Sunday-night foray into soap-opera intrigue (created by actor/producer Ken Olin). With an impressive cast and sumptuous set design, the series spent five seasons wringing the Walker clan through one heart-rending drama after another, including the discovery of a secret daughter who bonds with the family, turns out not to be a daughter after all, and finally enters into a relationship with one of the sons. Most episodes ended, if not happily, with an upbeat restatement of the basic tenet that the family would stay together no matter what fate hurled at it.

Later story lines branched away from the core family, especially after the sale of Ojai Foods, but the series retained much of its appeal for four seasons. By the end of the fifth, however, makers and viewers agreed that it had run its course. **SL**

Wild at Heart

Drama | UK | 2006–12

A happy British family relocates to Africa to live and work with animals on a beautiful game reserve

Cast | Stephen Tompkinson, Amanda Holden, Dawn Steele, Lucy-Jo Hudson, Olivia Scott-Taylor, Hayley Mills, Deon Stewardson, Nomsa Xaba
Original broadcaster | ITV1
For fans of . . . | *Where the Heart Is* (1997)

With stunning scenery and an array of exotic animals, *Wild at Heart* was a hit with audiences from the start. The show followed the adventures of Danny Trevanion (Stephen Tompkinson), a veterinarian who, after treating a rare monkey at his practice in England, traveled with his extended family to release it into the wild. After falling in love with South Africa, the family decided to relocate there permanently, to work on a reserve for wild animals.

Filmed on location in Glen Afric Country Lodge, Broederstroom, the show focused on the challenges faced by the family in this fish-out-of-water scenario. Not only did they have to adjust to life on a different continent, but also to the dangers of working with wild animals and the stresses of dealing with an endless stream of guests and visitors. After the death of Danny's wife Sarah (played by Amanda Holden, who left the show) at the end of season three, *Wild at Heart* refocused slightly with the arrival of a new veterinarian, Alice Collins (Dawn Steele).

The show was remade by The CW for American audiences in 2007 as *Life Is Wild*, starring D.W. Moffett and Stephanie Niznik, but this version was less successful than the original and was canceled after just one season.

In a slight change of direction, moving away from heartwarming family dramas, creator Ashley Pharoah is now best known for *Life on Mars* (2006) and *Ashes to Ashes* (2008). **EB**

Classic episode
Season 1, episode 5. The resort's first paying guests arrive in the midst of chaos, including a horde of rampaging elephants. Danny and Sarah's marriage is under strain due to interference and rumors.

⊘ Exit, pursued by a pachyderm: Stephen Tompkinson (Danny) outruns a psychologically troubled elephant.

Türkisch für Anfänger

Comedy | Germany | 2006

A comedy about the culture clash between two families

Cast | Josefine Preuß, Elyas M'Barek, Anna Stieblich, Pegah Ferydoni, Adnan Maral
Original broadcaster | Das Erste
For fans of . . . | *Mind Your Language* (1977), *Arrested Development* (2003)

Türkisch für Anfänger (*Turkish for Beginners*) starts with a plane crash. Stranded on a desert island, the spoiled and lost Lena meets wannabe gangsta rapper Cem. And it is loathe at first sight. Once they are rescued, things get even worse. It turns out that Cem's strict policeman father has fallen madly in love with Lena's spiritual therapist mother. They're moving in together, which means the disaffected German girl and the Turkish boy will be spending lots of time with each other. It's a disaster. Lena has to share a room with Cem's devoutly Muslim sister, and Cem has to cope with Lena's brother Nils, a loner who likes rockets.

If you've ever seen a romantic comedy, then you'll know what happens next. Cem and Lena start to fall in love. Then out of love. Then back in love. The genius of this sharply-observed, warm-hearted and spiteful series is how funny it is. Clever sight gags, outrageous putdowns, vicious flashbacks, and carefully-constructed payoffs ensure that each episode delivers proper out-loud laughs. Creator Bora Dağtekin drew on his own experiences growing up in a Turkish–German household, and gleefully plundered the rulebook of every successful US sitcom to ensure that this is compulsively hilarious viewing.

The show ran for two series and ended on a typically cruel, downbeat note. This wasn't good enough for the fans, and after a two-year hiatus, a final series appeared which belatedly gave the audience the happy ending they had been crying out for. **JG**

Classic episode
Die, in der ich meine Freiheit verliere (*The One Where My Freedom Is Lost*) | *Season 1, episode 1.*
Pitch-perfect pilot in which Cem and Lena are thrown together, and the supporting characters are firmly and hilariously established.

⊘ Josefine Preuß (Lena) speaks to the camera for her video diary.

Brotherhood

Drama | USA | 2006–08

A tale of sibling rivalry and crime that impressed the critics

Cast | Jason Isaacs, Jason Clarke, Fionnula Flanagan, Annabeth Gish, Kevin Chapman, Ethan Embry, Brían F. O'Byrne, Fiona C. Erickson, Stivi Paskoski
Original broadcaster | Showtime
For fans of . . . | *The Black Donnellys* (2007)

The main characters on this TV show were the Caffee brothers—Tommy (Jason Clarke) and Michael (Jason Isaacs)—who found their fortunes in different places: the former as a Rhode Island politician, the latter in organized crime, as a leading member of New England's Irish Mob. Writer and producer Blake Masters based the concept on the real-life tale of the Bulger brothers: William M. Bulger, who was president of the Massachusetts Senate in the 1970s, and James J. Bulger, who was big in the Winter Hill Gang until 2011, when he was imprisoned for life for eleven murders.

In *Brotherhood*, Tommy Caffee spent so much time pursuing his personal ambitions and so little with his wife, Eileen (Annabeth Gish), that she had an affair with a mailman. Their daughter, Mary Rose (Fiona Erickson), having been caught stealing and taking drugs, turned for advice to her uncle Michael, who had come back to his hometown to escape a hit man and had plenty of experience with law enforcement agencies. Tommy hated all this. The other prominent family member was the brothers' mother, Rose (Fionnula Flanagan), who was part fearsome matriarch—her boys were tough, but would never stand up to her—and part needy, lonely old lady.

Brotherhood pleased the critics, many of whom compared it favorably with *The Sopranos* (1999) and *The Wire* (2002), but it failed to capture a big enough audience, and the show was canceled at the end of season three. **GL**

Classic episode
Uneasy Lies the Head | *Season 3, episode 1.*
It's Rose's birthday and she is determined to hide her health problems from her family and feuding sons. Tommy orders a corruption investigation and is tempted to leave politics.

◉ Jason Clarke stars as Tommy Caffee.

Dexter

Crime/Mystery | USA | 2006–13

Principled serial killer Dexter also works as a crime-scene analyst for the Miami police

Cast | Michael C. Hall, Jennifer Carpenter, David Zayas, James Remar, Lauren Vélez, C.S. Lee
Original broadcaster | Showtime
Awards | 2 Golden Globes
For fans of . . . | *The Sopranos* (1999), *Hannibal* (2013)

Dexter Morgan has a secret. Seemingly an affable guy with a solid relationship with his girlfriend, he's actually a sociopath and a serial killer. Using forensic skill to carry out and then hide his crimes, he ritualistically murders people and disposes of their bodies. But his victims are not chosen at random. Dexter lives by a code, taught to him at an early age by his father: kill only people who deserve it. So he targets murderers and rapists who are otherwise evading justice. And he does all this while holding down his day job as a blood-splatter analyst for the local police force.

The first season of this scintillating drama, which broke viewing-figure records for US network Showtime, was based on Jeff Lindsay's best-selling 2004 novel *Darkly Dreaming Dexter*. Adapting it for television, the producers took the book's part-kooky, part-terrifying concept and created something quite extraordinary. Former *Six Feet Under* star Michael C. Hall played Dexter, one of the toughest acting jobs on TV, and made him scary and sympathetic in equal measure. As well as a strong supporting cast—including Jennifer Carpenter, whom Hall married while making the show, as Dexter's sister—there were big-name guest stars such as Jaime Murray, Keith Carradine, Jimmy Smits, John Lithgow, Julia Stiles, Edward James Olmos, and Colin Hanks. Many played killers that Dexter hunted in gripping season-long story arcs. **IF**

⊘ Michael C Hall as Dexter, the killer with a conscience.

The IT Crowd

Comedy | UK | 2006–13

The technical support team of a large corporation fail to connect to the outside world

Cast | Chris O'Dowd, Richard Ayoade, Katherine Parkinson, Chris Morris, Matt Berry, Noel Fielding
Original broadcaster | Channel 4   **Awards** | 3 BAFTAs   **For fans of . . .** | *Father Ted* (1995)

When Jen (Katherine Parkinson) came to Reynholm Industries, a lie on her application saw her conscripted as manager of the IT department. Her two underlings, the slacker Roy (Chris O'Dowd) and the ultra-nerdy Moss (Richard Ayoade), immediately realized that Jen had no idea about computers and set about exposing her as a fraud, but a friendship soon developed, between them, albeit one that was motivated in part by the threat of dismissal if they didn't stop moaning about her. This new-found allegiance didn't prevent Moss and Roy from convincing Jen that a small black box with a flashing light on top of it was actually "the Internet," on loan to the department from the top of Big Ben.

The IT Crowd was written by Graham Linehan, and had the same playful relationship with reality as one of his previous hits, *Father Ted*. While much of its humor appealed mainly to people from a technological background, it remained accessible enough for those of us who still struggle with anything more complicated than a TV remote control. **JS**

> **Classic episode**
> *The Work Outing* | *Season 2, episode 1*. Roy and Moss accompany Jen on her date with a man from work who they all assume is gay. When Roy is caught using a disabled toilet, he finds himself telling a terrible lie. . . .

◉ (L–R) *IT Crowd* artists Matt Berry, Katherine Parkinson, Richard Ayoade, and Chris O'Dowd.

Heroes

Drama | USA | 2006–10

This early runner in the new-wave superhero dramas held audiences spellbound

Cast | Greg Grunberg, Robert Knepper, Ali Larter, James Kyson Lee, Masi Oka, Hayden Panettiere, Adrian Pasdar
Original broadcaster | NBC **Awards** | 1 BAFTA, 1 Emmy **For fans of . . .** | *Buffy the Vampire Slayer* (1997)

Riding the crest of the ordinary-people-turned-superhumans dramas of the 2000s, *Heroes* set a high standard for the genre. The critically acclaimed series brought NBC its largest audience for drama for half a decade. However, viewers' frustrations led to declining ratings in subsequent seasons, and the show was quietly canceled four years after it premiered.

The story began with a solar eclipse, after which people around the globe discovered superpowers, from near-invulnerability to teleportation and shape-shifting. While they struggled to come to terms with their new abilities, a secret organization, The Company, set out to find and control (or destroy) them. At the same time, they were being hunted by one of their own.

Creator Tim Kring conceived of *Heroes* as a televised comic book, featuring a large cast of major characters and multiple overlapping story lines. Although this style occasionally left individual characters uninvolved in the show's larger story, it anticipated the larger casts and scope of shows that would follow, including *Game of Thrones* (2011). **AP**

Classic episode
How to Stop an Exploding Man | *Season 1, episode 23.* The first season's many plot threads come together as Peter Petrelli (Milo Ventimiglia) finally confronts Sylar (Zachary Quinto) to discover whether the world can ever be saved.

⬥ (L–R) Milo Ventimiglia, Hayden Panettiere, Jack Coleman, and, in the foreground, Zachary Quinto.

Satisfaction

Drama | Australia | 2007–09

Shining a clear new light on the world's oldest profession

Cast | Kestie Morassi, Madeline West, Alison Whyte, Diana Glenn, Bojana Novakovic, Peta Sergeant
Original broadcaster | Showcase
For fans of . . . | *Prisoner Cell Block H* (1979), *Sex and the City* (1998)

Set in the glitzy heart of Melbourne, *Satisfaction* sent shockwaves around Australia when it first aired. Centered on a group of beautiful, desirable women, the group of six all had one thing in common: they were prostitutes, working at "232," an upmarket brothel. Particularly notable was the inclusion of soap star Madeline West, best known as Dee Bliss, the tragic wife of Jarrod "Toadfish" Rebecchi in *Neighbours* (1985).

The producers were keen to keep the show as realistic as possible, veering away from portraying the profession as part of an aspirational Cinderella story, à la *Pretty Woman* (1990), and avoiding the "dead hooker in a dumpster" trope often seen in crime dramas. Free from cliché, the group were depicted as ordinary women who could be your friends or neighbors, with a secret you would never suspect.

To prepare for their roles, the cast members visited a number of brothels and met with sex workers to see the realities of their clandestine world. One of the show's strengths was its ensemble cast, a group of women fully in charge of their sexuality and using it to empower themselves. Friendship was at the fore, and they refused to be victims, holding down relationships and parenthood alongside their working lives.

Several members of the cast went on to Hollywood success, most notably Liam Hemsworth (*The Hunger Games*), who played a teenage rent boy.

Despite its controversial subject matter, *Satisfaction* was sold to more than twenty countries worldwide. **EB**

Wilfred

Comedy | Australia | 2007–10

What happens when man's best friend actually hates you?

Cast | Adam Zwar, Jason Gann, Cindy Waddingham, Fiona Gubelmann, Dorian Brown, Alison Mack
Original broadcaster | SBS One
For fans of . . . | *The Muppet Show* (1976), *Mongrels* (2010)

Based on an award-winning 2002 short film (itself loosely based on a real-life experience of writer Adam Zwar), *Wilfred* was the story of new couple Sarah and Adam, and her dog Wilfred, who was jealous and over-protective. While everyone else saw Wilfred as just an ordinary dog, Adam saw him as a full-grown man in a not-particularly-convincing dog costume. Wilfred was foul-mouthed, drank beer, and smoked marijuana, and hated Adam. Adam, in his turn, was baffled by Wilfred's attempts to foil his relationship at every turn.

Wilfred was torn between wanting to have Adam as his new "daddy," and being highly suspicious of his relationship with Sarah. Gradually, Wilfred and Adam begrudgingly learned to accept each other, becoming an odd couple, much to the bemusement of Sarah. The show was criticized in Australia for using government funding to create a comedy with lewd elements.

The show was remade for US audiences and first aired in 2011, taking a very different tone to the dark surrealism of the original Australian story. This starred Elijah Wood as Ryan, alongside the original Wilfred, Jason Gann, and took more of a buddy-comedy approach to the shaggy dog story. The adaptation ran for four seasons, making it the most successful US adaptation of an Australian series. In 2012 it was announced that a Russian-language version, *Charlie*, would be produced for the Commonwealth of Independent States, starring Maksim Averin as human Nikita and Maksim Stetskov as Charlie. **EB**

Burn Notice

Action/Adventure | USA | 2007–13

Compelling conspiracy-driven cable action adventure series that retained a loyal audience for seven years

Cast | Jeffrey Donovan, Gabrielle Anwar, Bruce Campbell, Sharon Gless, Coby Bell
Original broadcaster | USA Network
For fans of . . . | *Leverage* (2008), *Covert Affairs* (2010), *Homeland* (2011)

When Michael Westen (Jeffrey Donovan)—a spy so feared by the Russians that they believed him to be multiple operatives working under a single code name—was "burned" (disavowed) and left with no identity or resources, he turned to self-employment, offering his unique skills to the people of Miami in their fight against an array of underworld types engaged in every manner of criminal activity. Aided by his mother Madeline (Sharon Gless), ex-girlfriend Fiona (Gabrielle Anwar), aging lothario and former Navy SEAL Sam (Bruce Campbell), and later fellow "burned" agent Jesse Porter (Coby Bell), Westen meanwhile also investigated his own termination.

Created by Matt Nix (who is heard telling Westen that he's been "burned" in the opening of every episode), the series employed voice-over narration as Westen took us through the details of his exploits and provided advice as if imparting his wisdom to others who might follow him into the world of covert operations. Westen frequently cobbled together elaborate or inventive gadgetry to help with his work that would make fellow gadget-mad TV hero MacGyver jealous. Donovan himself was involved in the construction of Westen's devices and performed many of his own stunts.

A 2011 TV-movie prequel directed by Donovan, *Burn Notice: The Fall of Sam Axe*, threw the spotlight on Westen's partner and also led into the show's fifth season, in the final episode of which Westen learns the truth about his own fate. **ATB**

Classic episode
Psychological Warfare | *Season 7, episode 7.*
Westen endures extreme torture that revives old memories and makes him realize that the abuse he suffered at his father's hands may have given him the tools to survive.

⌂ Jeffrey Donovan as Michael Westen.

Britain's Got Talent

Variety | UK | 2007–present

*Extraordinary and entertaining members
of the British public are given a global stage*

Cast | Anthony McPartlin, Declan Donnelly, Simon
Cowell, Amanda Holden, Piers Morgan, Alesha Dixon,
David Walliams
Original broadcaster | ITV
For fans of . . . | *America's Got Talent* (2006)

Britain's Got Talent celebrates the best (and during the
early stages, the worst) of the nation's entertainers.
Several weeks of auditions, all of which are aired,
precede live semi-finals and a grand final. Contestants
are gradually eliminated through a combination of
the verdicts of four celebrity judges and public vote.
The winner is decided by public vote alone and given
the chance to perform before the Queen at the annual
Royal Variety Performance in London.

The format was devised in Britain, but contractual
obligations delayed its first broadcast, which eventually
came later than the US equivalent, *America's Got
Talent*. The British show has launched the careers
of many performers, most famously Susan Boyle,
a previously unrecognized middle-aged singer.
She was runner-up in the competition, but her
version of "I Dreamed a Dream" from the musical
Les Misérables propelled her to global celebrity.
The winners that season, Diversity, an all-male
dance troupe, also had some success, but nothing
like that of the woman who became internationally
known as SuBo.

Among the other winners who went on to greater
things were opera singer Paul Potts, who won season
one with his performance of "Nessun Dorma," an aria
from Puccini's opera *Turandot*; Ashleigh and Pudsey,
woman and a dancing dog; and young street dancer
George Sampson. The . . . *Got Talent* format has since
been adopted in more than fifty countries. **MB**

Jekyll

Fantasy/Horror/Sci-Fi | UK | 2007

*Modern take on the classic literary tale
of an experiment gone horribly awry*

Cast | James Nesbitt, Michelle Ryan, Gina Bellman,
Paterson Joseph, Denis Lawson, Meera Syal,
Fenella Woolgar
Original broadcaster | BBC One
For fans of . . . | *Doctor Who* (1963), *Sherlock* (2010)

It's hard to put a fresh new spin on a story as well
known as that of Robert Louis Stevenson's *Strange Case
of Dr. Jekyll and Mr Hyde* (1886). And yet this all-too-short
television version (only six episodes) breathed new life
into the dual identity premise by positioning itself as
both revisionist adaptation and sequel.

Dr. Tom Jackman (James Nesbitt) began exhibiting
an alternate, dangerous personality and isolated
himself from his family in order to research his own
condition. Hiring nurse Katherine Reimer (Michelle
Ryan) to assist him, Jackman struggled to understand
and control his other self while his wife Claire (Gina
Bellman) sent a private investigator, Miranda Callendar
(Meera Syal), to track him down. Jackman eventually
learned that he was descended from the real-life Henry
Jekyll immortalized by Stevenson's "fictionalized"
account, and that a corrupt biotechnology company
sought to trigger the emergence of his "Hyde" persona.

Particularly effective were the prosthetics used
to turn Nesbitt into Hyde. The transformation was
achieved via a daily one-hour makeup process that
involved dropping the actor's hairline lower than
normal, extending his nose and chin with prosthetic
appliances, and using black contact lenses to create a
demonic look that was effective but subtle compared
to some film and TV incarnations of Hyde.

With powerful performances and atmospheric
production, *Jekyll* revived an old horror trope and left
viewers pining for more. But they never got it. **ATB**

Benidorm

Comedy | UK | 2007–present

Full of warmth, charm, and fun in the sun, this comedy about the British abroad has proved a smash hit

Cast | Steve Pemberton, Janine Duvitski, Siobhan Finneran, Sheila Reid, Oliver Stokes, Kenny Ireland, Elsie Kelly, Johnny Vegas
Original broadcaster | ITV
For fans of . . . | *Gavin and Stacey* (2007)

The "Sunny Special" has long been a sitcom tradition—most long-running shows have at least one episode in which familiar, well-rounded characters are thrown into unfamiliar situations abroad. But when *Benidorm* creator Derren Litten made this feature the main event, setting his sitcom around and often in a swimming pool in Spain, he knew he was onto a surefire winner. Since its debut in 2007, *Benidorm* has regularly drawn audiences of more than seven million.

The show focuses on the adventures of a group of British folk on vacation at the Solana holiday resort in Benidorm, Spain. Central to it all are the members of the Garvey family—husband and wife Mick and Janice (Steve Pemberton and Siobhan Finneran), teenage daughter Chantelle (Hannah Hobley) and eight-year-old son Michael (Oliver Stokes)—who bring with them on their first foreign vacation all the classic Little Englander prejudices about the wider world.

But they are not the only ones: the success of the show stems from its broad range of characters, who are either people in the pool or the people around it whom the members of the inner circle recognize and dread. Every character has his or her idiosyncrasies, from chain-smoking, permatanned Madge (Sheila Reid) to transvestite barman Les/Lesley (Tim Healy). Although the humor is often coarse and politically incorrect, a grain of truth runs through it all. We may not be a Garvey or an Oracle (Johnny Vegas), but we all know somebody like them. **PPW**

Classic episode
Hello Benidorm | *Season 1, episode 1.*
Viewers meet the vacationers as they meet each other. The Garvey family arrives at Benidorm's Solana resort, but don't realize their daughter Chantelle is hiding a big secret.

⊙ Johnny Vegas as Oracle visits Madge's boyfriend in hospital.

Forbrydelsen

Crime/Mystery | Denmark | 2007–12

A murder hunt and its effects on all involved

Cast | Sofie Gråbøl, Mikael Birkkjær, Nicolas Bro, Ann
Eleonora Jørgensen, Søren Malling, Lars Mikkelsen,
Morten Suurballe
Original broadcaster | DR1
For fans of . . . | *Broadchurch* (2013)

A series focusing on just one murder was not an
innovation. Nor was procedural policing new to Danish
television. But *Forbrydelsen* (*The Killing*, or, literally,
"The Crime") combined its ingredients to create
something that broke out of Denmark and brought
the world a gripping new genre: Nordic noir.

Like *Twin Peaks* before it, *Forbrydelsen* begins with
the death of a schoolgirl. Like Lynch's series, it takes
as much interest in the effect on the community as
it does in the identity of the killer. But where Agent
Cooper was light-heartedly eccentric, detective Sarah
Lund (Sofie Gråbøl) is cold and distant.

Lund was a refreshing creation: a female detective
as flawed as her hard-drinking, not-by-the-book male
counterparts. Her romances and family relationships fall
apart because she's obsessed with her work. Gråbøl
gives a captivating central performance, somehow
managing to make this sometimes incompetent police
officer likable in spite of her numerous evident faults.

Forbrydelsen also incorporated political intrigue,
but with uneven success. Nevertheless it was the
whodunit in each season that provided the watercooler conversation after each episode. Wisely, the
series didn't repeat itself, with each season focusing on
a very different crime. The show helped to inspire *Broen*
(*The Bridge*, 2011) and *Broadchurch* (2013) and spawned
an American remake (2011–14). **WH**

❯ Sofie Gråbøl's performance as a conflicted police detective
turned her into an international star.

Primeval

Fantasy/Horror/Sci-Fi | UK | 2007–11

Time-bending dinosaur adventures

Cast | Douglas Henshall, Lucy Brown, Andrew-Lee Potts, Hannah Spearritt, Ben Miller, Jason Flemyng, Alexander Siddig, Juliet Aubrey **Original broadcaster** | ITV **For fans of . . .** | *Walking with Dinosaurs* (1999)

After *Doctor Who*'s rip-roaring revival on the BBC in 2005, ITV responded with this heady mix of sci-fi, time-travel adventure and dinosaur action. *Primeval* lacked the staying power of its rival show, but for several years it achieved good ratings with early evening audiences.

After *Walking with Dinosaurs* demonstrated that prehistoric creatures could be unleashed on a TV budget, Adrian Hodges and Tim Haines developed *Primeval* with the BBC, but their high-concept creation eventually went to the commercial station.

The plot concerns the efforts of Professor Nick Cutter (Douglas Henshall) to find out what has caused the appearance in modern Britain of terrifying creatures from prehistory and the far future.

With its mix of strong characters and effectively realized monsters of the week, *Primeval* was hugely popular for three seasons. It then tailed off, but two further series aired after a co-production deal was secured with UK cable channel Watch. A Canadian spin-off, *Primeval: New World*, debuted on Space in 2012, but lasted only one season. **MW**

> **Classic episode**
> *Season 1, episode 6.* A twisty-turny temporal paradox in which a terrifying predator from the future is on the loose. Cutter realizes that his opposition to it is doomed to failure because of past events that he cannot alter.

◉ Professor Nick Cutter (Douglas Henshall) avoids becoming collateral damage in a dinosaur fight.

Damages

Drama | USA | 2007–12

Edgy legal drama with a powerhouse central performance

Cast | Glenn Close, Rose Byrne, Tate Donovan, Ted Danson **Original broadcaster** | FX
For fans of . . . | *The Good Wife* (2009)

Manipulation abounds in this legal drama that eschewed courtroom dynamics in favor of subterfuge and dominance in a New York law firm. The ruthless Patty Hewes (Glenn Close) plays power games with her reluctant protégé Ellen Parsons (Rose Byrne); the supporting cast is full of other powerful women.

Creators Daniel Zelman and the brothers Glenn and Todd A. Kessler centered each season of *Damages* on a different high-profile case, although the legal actions largely play second fiddle to the relationship between Hewes and Parsons. The non-linear narrative is compelling, even though it takes thirteen episodes to establish why Ellen is running blood-soaked and half-naked through the New York streets while her boyfriend lies bludgeoned to death in their apartment. This approach almost renders the legal cases irrelevant, but with guest stars such as Ted Danson, William Hurt, Lily Tomlin, and Martin Short, *Damages* never feels anything less than finely honed in every area.

The final season featured a running plot inspired by the WikiLeaks scandal of 2010. **MW**

> **Classic episode**
> *Because I Know Patty* | *Season 1, episode 13*.
> The first season closes with Ellen acquitted of murder and a high-profile case brought to a resolution. Ellen returns to work for Patty, but does she have an ulterior motive?

◉ Glenn Close (left) as legal eagle Patty Hewes and Rose Byrne as Ellen Parsons, her trainee.

Chuck

Comedy | USA | 2007–12

A slick comedy about a small-time computer nerd who grows in stature when he becomes a reluctant spy in the United States' war on terror

Cast | Zachary Levi, Yvonne Strahovski, Joshua Gomez, Sarah Lancaster, Adam Baldwin
Original broadcaster | NBC **Awards** | 2 Emmys
For fans of . . . | *Freaks and Geeks* (1999), *Alias* (2001), *Heroes* (2006)

The premise of *Chuck* was simple and unbeatable: Chuck Bartowski (Zachary Levi) was a failed computer whiz and modest IT assistant at a big-box technology store in Los Angeles. After being exposed to the Intercept, a device that downloads into his brain every spy secret in the United States, Chuck suddenly found himself an unwilling asset in the country's war on terror. In an effort to keep Chuck and his secrets safe, the CIA and the NSA sent two agents to watch over him: the terrifying John Casey (Adam Baldwin), who went undercover as Chuck's coworker, and the beautiful but ruthless Sarah Walker (Yvonne Strahovski), who posed as Chuck's girlfriend.

In its early seasons, *Chuck* mined the bulk of its humor from the increasingly absurd situations into which it dropped its hapless protagonist. Chuck regularly found himself out of his depth in his efforts to back up his handlers, but became increasingly confident in his abilities even as he struggled to keep his real life and his spy life separate, and his growing feelings for Sarah under control. In later seasons Chuck came into his own as a spy, but the show continued to employ geek-oriented, fish-out-of-water comedy to balance its increasingly complex backstory.

The cast was notable for its excellent acting and exceptional chemistry, but *Chuck*'s greatest strength lay in its leading man. Levi played his unwilling spy with goofy bonhomie and a gentle sweetness, making Chuck Bartowski an easy character to root for. **AP**

Classic episode

Chuck versus the Lethal Weapon | *Season 2, episode 16*. Chuck, Sarah, and Casey must rescue Perseus, a defense department scientist who designed the Intersect. Chuck hopes Perseus will be able to remove the Intersect from his brain.

○ Yvonne Strahovski (Sarah Walker), and Zachary Levi (Chuck) in "Chuck Versus the Role Models," 2010.

Skins

Drama | UK | 2007–13

This unflinching drama about the secret lives of British teenagers had it all—authentic characters and compelling story lines, not to mention a heady mix of sex, drugs, and alcohol

Cast | Nicholas Hoult, Dev Patel, Hannah Murray, April Pearson, Mike Bailey, Joe Dempsie, Mitch Hewer, Larissa Wilson, Kaya Scodelario, Dakota Blue Richards
Original broadcaster | E4 **Award** | 1 BAFTA
For fans of . . . | *Gossip Girl* (2007), *Misfits* (2009)

Skins courted controversy even before it premiered, thanks to a suggestive marketing campaign that presented its teenage characters in a highly sexualized manner. It followed through with its story lines: characters slept around, lied to their parents, and used drugs indiscriminately. Yet the stories were presented sensitively for all their controversy, and the show was an immediate critical and commercial success.

The show specifically focused on sixteen- to eighteen-year-olds as they navigated the pitfalls of modern life. Led in the first two seasons by the Machiavellian Tony (Nicholas Hoult, star of the movie *About a Boy*), each episode focused on an individual character while furthering the overlapping plotlines of the others. The show was notable for subverting audience expectations about characters, presenting them first from the outside as stereotypically self-absorbed teenagers with little perspective or insight, and then, in spotlight episodes, exploring their individual circumstances.

Every two years the main cast was replaced by the next "generation," as characters graduated into the wider world. The show was created by father-and-son writing team Bryan Elsey and Jamie Brittain, and the average age of the *Skins* writing team was twenty-one, which lent the show a distinct and authentic voice. It presented its teenaged characters as dark, uncertain, and complex, and took their problems as seriously as any adult drama would. **AP**

Classic episode
Maxxie and Anwar | *Season 1, episode 6.*
On a college trip to Russia, Anwar (Dev Patel) struggles to come to terms with the homosexuality of his best friend Maxxie (Mitch Hewer).

◉ Nicholas Hoult (Tony) and other semi-clad revelers enjoy a typically wild party scene in an episode from 2007.

Summer Heights High

Comedy | Australia | 2007

Show about a troubled breakdancer, a spoiled girl, and an egomaniac drama teacher

Cast | Chris Lilley
Original broadcaster | ABC
For fans of . . . | *The Office* (2001), *Kath & Kim* (2002), *Modern Family* (2009), *Mrs Brown's Boys* (2011), *Twenty Twelve* (2011)

Chris Lilley had shown what he could do in *We Can Be Heroes* (2005), in which he played five roles. In *Summer Heights High* he reprised one of these characters, the spoiled brat Ja'mie, and also played Mr. G, a crazed drama teacher, and Jonah, a delinquent breakdancer from Tonga.

Whether this is to your taste or not depends on how comfortable you are with a middle-aged white man playing a teenage girl and a Polynesian. What's remarkable is that Lilley portrays all three grotesques so well and so differently. Jonah is too surly to say even the F-word properly (despite extensive sessions at Gumnut Cottage remedial class). Ja'mie is a monster who organizes a school prom so expensive that she has to fake an AIDS fundraiser to pay for her own ticket. Mr G throws all of his energy and none of his talent into staging a spectacularly tasteless school musical.

Summer Heights High succeeds because Lilley's performances are never cringe-inducing and always aware of the heart hidden somewhere inside his grotesques. He's also helped out by the deadpan playing of the rest of the cast. Ja'mie may really be a man in his mid-30s, but her posse's placid acceptance of her reign of terror makes her all the more believable.

Ja'mie later returned in the acclaimed *Ja'mie: Private School Girl* (2013). In *Jonah From Tonga* (2014), Lilley wore heavier makeup to disguise the face that he was now 40. This show was branded "racist", "degrading," and "inherently creepy" by the Tongan community. **JG**

Classic episode
Season 1, episode 8. Mr. G is directing a new play. Ja'ime is preparing for the school social but is having trouble with her date. And Jonah learns that he has been expelled from school and takes it out on the cars in the parking lot.

◍ Chris Lilley as Mr. G, the drama teacher.

Two Days and One Night

Reality | South Korea | 2007–present

Sunday evening entertainment reality show

Cast | Cha Tae-hyeon, Kim Ju-hyeok, Kim Jun-ho, Defcoon, Jeong Jun-yeong, Kim Jong-min
Original broadcaster | KBS
For fans of . . . | *I'm a Celebrity . . . Get Me Out of Here!* (2002)

With no evictions—so no chance of escape—this reality show takes six regular celebrities way out of their urban comfort zones, often to lesser-known, wilder areas of South Korea, where they must survive for the stated period. Having completed the sometimes challenging journey, the contestants play games of chance to win food and/or comfortable lodgings; the losers are forced to go hungry and sleep rough. In early shows, participants usually went alone, but in subsequent seasons they traveled with others: real-life friends, for instance, famous chefs, or even selected viewers. With competitors unconstrained by rigid scripting, it is their unrehearsed responses to discomfort, mild humiliation, and cruel twists of fate that provide the main entertainment. The action is punctuated by frequent animated captions and cartoon sound effects.

One of the producers of the show, Nah Yeong-seok, later revamped the format to make a range of other hit reality shows, including *Grandpas Over Flowers* (2013), in which contestants go backpacking over longer distances, and *Three Meals a Day* (2014), in which participants are left in a remote rural village and challenged to find their own food.

After the phenomenal success of *Two Days and One Night* in Korea, the format was exported to China in 2013. Along with *Infinite Challenge* (2013), this long-running mix of variety and reality show set the standard for light entertainment on Korean TV in the early twenty-first century. **SH**

Outnumbered

Comedy | UK | 2007–present

Perfectly captures family dynamics

Cast | Hugh Dennis, Claire Skinner, Tyger Drew-Honey, Daniel Roche, Ramona Marquez
Original broadcaster | BBC One
For fans of . . . | *2point4 Children* (1991), *Malcolm in the Middle* (2000)

Never work with animals or children: you can't control them and they won't be able to learn their lines. *Outnumbered* gave the lie to the second part of this old theatrical adage by turning the youth of its three child actors—aged six, eight, and eleven a the start of the series—into its major strength.

Claire Skinner and Hugh Dennis play harried parents Pete and Sue Brockman, who are outnumbered by their three young children. Their solid, skillful, and emotionally truthful performances hold the show together—they move the plot along as they attempt to retain control of their brood. But it's in the brilliant work of the young cast that the comedy really lies. Tyger Drew-Honey as Jake, Daniel Roche as Ben, and Ramona Marquez as the relentlessly critical, quizzical, argumentative and knowing Karen constantly say what they shouldn't say, do what they shouldn't do, and behave in a way that is recognizably like actual children—in the process revealing how rare this is in movies or TV.

The secret is in the method by which writers Andy Hamilton and Guy Jenkin—who previously collaborated on *Drop the Dead Donkey* (1990)—constructed the young actors' performances, mostly from material the children had improvised themselves.

The show deals with the normal problems of family life—aging grandparents, sibling troubles, and job woes—but the brilliant lunacy of the children makes everything that happens, both tragic and comic, more real than any sitcom family has ever been before. **RL**

Reaper

Fantasy/Horror/Sci-Fi | USA | 2007

Compelling but underrated series that highlights ways in which the Devil looks after his own

Cast | Bret Harrison, Tyler Labine, Rick Gonzales, Missy Peregrym, Andrew Arlie, Ray Wise, Donovan Stinson, Allison Hossack
Original broadcaster | CW Television Network
For fans of . . . | *Dead Like Me* (2003)

Largely overlooked, *Reaper* is a magnificent series, showcasing Ray Wise as the Devil in a performance which is magnetic and impressive. Added to this is a quartet of superb performances from the other leads and some very good writing.

The premise of the show is simple. Sam Oliver's parents sold his soul to the Devil when he was a baby, and now the Devil is back to make his claim, which is that Sam (Brett Harrison) should reap souls for him. But not just any souls. The Prince of Darkness wants only the souls of people who have escaped from his clutches in hell—demons and monsters and killers and evildoers of all persuasions.

Every time Sam sets out on a mission, he takes with him a specially tailored "vessel" to assist him. This might be a toaster or a plastic toy, a horn or a plastic gun, but in each case it has the ability to harvest the soul. Aiding and abetting Sam are his friends: stoner Bert (Tyler Labine); tech-minded Ben (Rick Gonzales); and Sam's major love Andi (Missy Peregrym). Together they help to reap the souls and thus keep Sam from the Devil's clutches.

Reaper ran for two seasons, and its imaginative power remains on full throttle throughout all thirty-one episodes. The romantic element is present throughout, but remains in the background, and the interplay between Sam and the Devil as the former tries to get out of the contract that his parents sold him into is unfailingly witty and engaging. **DJH**

> **Classic episode**
> *Coming to Grips* | *Season 1, episode 15*.
> When Andi sees Sam decapitate an apparently blameless victim, she thinks it is a murder. Sam has to renegotiate his pact with the Devil in order to prevent her from calling the cops.

◓ Tyler Labine and Bret Harrison.

Cranford

Historical drama | UK | 2007–09

Practically perfect costume drama

Cast | Eileen Atkins, Judi Dench, Julia McKenzie, Philip Glenister, Imelda Staunton
Original broadcaster | BBC One
For fans of . . . | *Pride and Prejudice* (1995), *Lark Rise to Candleford* (2008)

The BBC again showed its celebrated skill for costume drama in this delightful adaptation of Elizabeth Gaskell's 1853 novel. It stars the cream of British acting talent in a production of wit and lightness of touch among sumptuous detail, focusing on the social trials of the women of the eponymous Cheshire village.

Gaskell's work had been adapted for the screen previously by the BBC in 1951 and 1972, and a fresh take seemed overdue. Audiences were not disappointed when *Cranford* debuted shortly before Christmas 2007. England in the 1840s is in the midst of the Industrial Revolution, but the residents of Cranford are resistant to change. At the heart of village life are spinster sisters Deborah and Matty Jenkyns (Eileen Atkins and Judi Dench), along with a large cast of colorful and eccentric characters. Following the sudden death of her sister, Matty faces financial ruin, while the specter of the railroad being built through the nearby countryside feels like a very real threat.

Less rigid and serious than some historical dramas, Heidi Thomas' scripts capture the arch camp inherent in Gaskell's original. But this is no bawdy comedy: there's tragedy and poverty and a sense of fear at the changes taking place.

There were only seven episodes of this very special series, but they were all as perfectly formed as costume drama gets. It inspired a sequel, *Return to Cranford*, which reunited the original cast and aired in 2009 as a two-part Christmas special. **MW**

The Graham Norton Show

Talk show | UK | 2007–present

Outrageous chat with the impish Irish comic

Cast | Graham Norton
Original broadcaster | BBC Two
Awards | 3 BAFTAs
For fans of . . . | *Sticky Moments* (1989), *The Tonight Show Starring Jimmy Fallon* (2014)

In 2009, Graham Norton took over from fellow Irishman Terry Wogan in providing UK commentary for the Eurovision Song Contest. It seemed a natural succession, as Norton was also poised to take the place once occupied by Wogan as the BBC's most popular talk show host.

Norton moved to the BBC from Channel 4 in 2007. The guests for his Channel 4 talk shows—*So Graham Norton* (1998–2002) and the short-lived nightly *V Graham Norton* (2002–03)—were chosen more for their amusement value than their topicality, but his BBC series has moved closer to talk show convention, with guests promoting their latest film, play, album, or TV series, though Norton's approach remains the same. As well as intimate, ribald chat with celebrity guests, there are hidden camera jokes, visits to the more bizarre corners of the Internet, and participation from the studio audience, who are regularly called upon to confess their most embarrassing moments. One difference of the BBC show is that the guests are interviewed collectively, allowing them to interact with one another as well as with Norton.

The defection of talk show host Jonathan Ross to ITV in 2010 led to Norton's show being promoted to a Friday night slot on BBC One, attracting even bigger stars. As well as being a staple of the Friday night schedule, Norton's cheeky brand of chat is now a mainstay of the BBC's festive programming, with a special edition of his show broadcast every New Year's Eve. **IK**

Hotel Babylon

Drama | UK | 2006–09

This slick drama opened the "Staff Only" door of a fictional top London hotel

Cast | Tamzin Outhwaite, Max Beesley, Dexter Fletcher, Natalie Mendoza
Original broadcaster | BBC One
For fans of . . . | *Hotel* (1983), *Hustle* (2004), *The Paradise* (2012), *Mr. Selfridge* (2013)

This fun and frothy drama about life in the fast lane of a five-star hotel was based on a book by Imogen Edwards-Jones and an anonymous coauthor from the hotel industry. Although *Hotel Babylon* never took itself too seriously, it purported to sail close to reality.

In the show, Rebecca Mitchell (Tamzin Outhwaite) was general manager of the exclusive Hotel Babylon. Her unruly team caused her as many problems as the well-heeled guests, but supported by deputy manager Charlie (Max Beesley), she kept the glamorous facade intact, whatever the problem (suicide, prostitution, theft), despite also having a marriage away from the hotel that was heading for the rocks.

The linchpins of the series were Charlie and head concierge Tony Casemore (Dexter Fletcher). Tony knew more about the hotel than anyone. He saw everything and everyone, and it was often his streetwise quick thinking that saved the day.

Undemanding but highly watchable, the show was given a prime-time Friday night slot. After a hard week at work, viewers in search of escapism lapped up its glossy luxury and vicarious pleasures. By the end of season three, however, Outhwaite and Beesley had left the cast. Audience figures then slumped and even the introduction of Nigel Harman—formerly a star of the BBC soap opera *EastEnders*—as the hotel's new owner could not arrest the decline. *Hotel Babylon* closed its doors for the final time after thirty-two hugely entertaining and glitzy episodes. **MW**

Gossip Girl

Drama | USA | 2007–12

The privileged lives of Upper East Side teens provided shameless escapism for millions

Cast | Blake Lively, Leighton Meester, Penn Badgley, Taylor Momsen, Chace Crawford
Original broadcaster | The CW
For fans of . . . | *The O.C.* (2003), *Skins* (2007), *90210* (2008)

A story of gorgeous young people living impossibly glamorous lives, *Gossip Girl* was based on Cecily von Ziegesar's series of young adult novels of the same name. The show's prime mover and shaker was sultry sixteen-year-old Serena van der Woodson (Blake Lively). To the viewer, she was an empathetic, if privileged teen; to fellow characters she was a transcendent, unapproachable "It" girl, who inspired both awe and jealousy. While Serena wanted to have fun and be "normal," she was scrutinized for everything she did, said, and especially wore.

Gossip Girl's six seasons began with Serena's return to her Upper East Side prep school after a lengthy and mysterious absence. Where had she been? Why had she left in the first place? And, most importantly, would Serena's return derail the Machiavellian social machinations of her BFF—Blair Waldorf (Leighton Meester)? (The two girls' on–off friendship provided years of great drama.)

No matter how tough things got with guys, grades, or gowns, Serena and Blair's charm anchored the show, and the rest of the cast were no less likable. In spite of their privileges, the girls resolved their problems with decency, which made the show heartwarming.

The titular Gossip Girl was, of course, the show's overarching mystery. She was a manipulative, anonymous character (voiced perfectly by Kirsten Bell), who acted as a viewer substitute; judging, envying, and enjoying the characters' glorious antics. **JS**

Secret Diary of a Call Girl

Drama | UK | 2007–11

A tongue-in-cheek look under the covers of the world's oldest profession, starring a family favorite of British TV

Cast | Billie Piper, Cherie Lunghi, Iddo Goldberg, Ashley Madekwe
Original broadcaster | ITV2
For fans of . . . | *Sex and the City* (1998), *Satisfaction* (2007), *The Client List* (2012)

As *Doctor Who*'s feisty companion Rose Tyler in the 2005 revival of the eponymous sci-fi serial, Billie Piper was the breakout star. Her decision to follow this success by playing a high-class prostitute surprised many.

Based on a real-life blog by Belle de Jour, *Secret Diary of a Call Girl* followed Hannah Baxter as she tried to keep her double-life as a respectable university graduate and a call girl under control. While maintaining an angelic image for her family, she spent the evenings in hotel rooms, as Belle. Hannah's mentor in prostitution was Stephanie Charlton (Cherie Lunghi), who dispensed wisdom with waspish delight, while her best friend Ben (Iddo Goldberg) offered support and a moral conscience.

The show had a lightly humorous tongue-in-cheek tone, while the stylized direction brought artistic flair to the many sex scenes. Not only did Hannah narrate, but she also directly addressed the audience.

Piper brought real verve to the show, and even some respectability to the topic of prostitution. Lunghi and Goldberg offered sterling support, while Toyah Willcox, Colin Salmon, and Matt Smith were just some of the guest stars who crossed Hannah's path.

Reaching four successful seasons, the show was the first drama specially commissioned for ITV2 and was that channel's first big hit. Piper's brave decision to take such a controversial role paid off, as it was proof of her versatility as an actress. Her career has continued to develop successfully. **SO**

Classic episode
Season 1, episode 7. Hannah is hired by a couple to celebrate their twentieth wedding anniversary with a foursome. This gives Ben the opportunity to experience Hannah's job firsthand, making him reconsider his opinions.

⊙ Billie Piper as part-time sex worker Belle de Jour.

Flight of the Conchords

Comedy | USA | 2007–09

The musical adventures in New York of a two-man band from New Zealand

Cast | Jemaine Clement, Bret McKenzie, Rhys Darby, Kristen Schaal, Arj Barker
Original broadcaster | HBO
For fans of . . . | *Fame* (1982), *Glee* (2009), *The Sing-Off* (2009)

Flight of the Conchords stars the real-life duo of Jemaine Clement and Academy Award-winner Bret McKenzie, playing fictionalized versions of themselves. The series centers on the day-to-day lives and loves of two shepherds–turned–folk musicians who have uprooted themselves from their native New Zealand to try to make it big in the United States.

The two have frequent appointments with their officious and ineffectual manager, Murray Hewitt, a deputy cultural attaché at the New Zealand embassy. Jemaine and Bret constantly fend off the amorous attentions of Mel, a married woman who is their sole fan and stalker. Their friend Dave Mohumbhai works at a pawn shop and gives them advice on dealing with American women and culture. Other recurring characters include their landlord, Eugene, Bret's short-term girlfriend Coco, Jemaine's and Bret's ex-girlfriend Sally, and Murray's put-upon assistant Greg. The antagonists outside of this small group are usually either their other girlfriends or Australians. Jemaine or Bret break into song in each episode.

Typically, at least once per show, a song is shot in the form of a music video. As the series evolved, other main characters also had their own musical interludes. The songs enable them to express their inner feelings in ways that they never do in spoken discourse, which is always low-key and slightly inhibited. **RP**

❷ Jemaine Clement (L) and Bret McKenzie meet the infatuated Mel (Kristen Schaal) while trying to make it big in New York.

Californication

Drama | USA | 2007–14

Adult-oriented drama about a novelist battling writer's block and relationship traumas

Cast | David Duchovny, Natasha McElhone, Evan Handler, Madeline Martin, Pamela Adlon
Original broadcaster | Showtime **For fans of . . .** | *Thirtysomething* (1987)

In this forthright series, created by former *Dawson's Creek* writer Tom Kapinos, David Duchovny battled down-to-earth problems centered on sex, drugs, and rock'n'roll. It ran on US television for seven seasons.

Duchovny played Hank Moody, a writer with a string of successful novels to his name who now struggled to produce anything good. To make matters worse, a diluted movie adaptation of one of his books was on general release. He also faced a mixture of emotions in response to the plans of his long-time lover Karen (Natasha McElhone) to marry someone else. Feeling the pressure, Hank's severely low temptation threshold repeatedly got him into trouble—and in this area, the show really pushed the boundaries.

Scenes and discussions of nudity, sex, masturbation, and drug-taking attracted criticism from conservative groups. But these elements were vital for a story about adults facing adult problems. Hank was a sex addict, and his favorite pastime always had severe consequences. Never dull, always daring, *Californication* was addictive television. **IF**

> **Classic episode**
> *So Here's the Thing* | *Season 3, episode 7*. Hank decides to clean up his act and divest himself of all the extraneous women in his life. But they don't share his views on the desirability of breaking up, and his will is anything but iron.

⬥ (L–R) Evan Handler (Charlie Runkle), David Duchovny (Hank Moody), and guest RZA, co-founder of hip-hop group Wu-Tang Clan.

Gavin & Stacey
Comedy | UK | 2007–10

Warm, family-based comedy with a surreal edge

Cast | Mathew Horne, Joanna Page, James Corden, Ruth Jones, Larry Lamb, Alison Steadman, Rob Brydon, Melanie Walters   **Original broadcaster** | BBC Three   **Awards** | 2 BAFTAs   **For fans of . . .** | *Just Good Friends* (1983)

Gavin & Stacey told the story of how a working-class girl from Barry Island in Wales and a middle-class boy from Essex in England fell in love and married in spite of their different backgrounds. It was a bit like *Romeo and Juliet* without the corpses.

Written by two of the cast, James Corden and Ruth Jones, this isn't a straight-down-the-line sitcom: there's no laughter track; jokes aren't always explained, and the main families carry the names of notorious British serial killers (West, Sutcliffe and Shipman). There's also the main source of surreal humor in the form of Stacey's best friend Nessa (Jones), who drives a truck and claims to have had relationships with almost every famous man who gets mentioned.

Gavin & Stacey is beautifully observed from start to finish; the dialogue and the relationships between the characters are all judged to perfection, and the plot twists always seem natural, never forced. There are very few shows on TV these days that don't feel cynical in any way, but this is one of them. Its numerous fans still watch it tirelessly on DVD. **LH**

> ### Classic episode
> *Season 1, episode 6.* Gavin and Stacey get married. All the characters come together, there are revelations, laugh-out-loud moments (the best man's speech), and moments that bring a tear to the eye (Stacey's dad's letter).

◔ Mathew Horne and Joanna Page lose no opportunity to show how they feel about each other.

Sea Patrol

Drama | Australia | 2007–11

*Australian action drama following the crew
of a Navy patrol ship*

Cast | Ian Stenlake, Lisa McCune, Kristian Schmid
Original broadcaster | Nine Network
For fans of . . . | *The Flying Doctor* (1959), *Blue Heelers*
(1994), *Water Rats* (1996), *Stingers* (1998), *NCIS* (2003),
Surf Patrol (2007)

Created by Hal and Di McElroy—best known for their
involvement in previous hits such as *Blue Heelers* (1994)
and *Water Rats* (1996)—*Sea Patrol* followed the crew of
HMAS *Hammersley*, an Australian Navy patrol boat, as
it protected the country's borders. The quality of the
stories of the week was variable, swapping from the
serious—drug trafficking—to the almost ridiculous—a
radioactive island. However, most seasons had an
overarching story line that provided cohesion.

Filming a sea-based series completely on location
was no small undertaking, and this was reflected in
the budget, which was AUS$1 million (US$750,000)
per episode. It is a credit to the cast and crew that the
authenticity of the environment was captured so well
on-screen, especially when one considers that the sixty-
person production crew filmed in sweltering heat on a
ship built for only twenty-four crew members.

Sea Patrol initially came in for some criticism
regarding its characterization and scripting, but the
viewers' response improved as the series continued.
The show came to an end after five seasons and sixty-
eight episodes. This decision was not due to loss of
popularity, but to budgetary concerns; the makers had
benefited from government rebates that were limited
to the first sixty-five episodes.

Sea Patrol demonstrated a growing ambition in
Australian TV drama, and its success paved the way for
the bolder productions that have emerged from the
country since. **SO**

The Guild

Comedy | USA | 2007–13

*Webcast comedy created by gamers, about
gamers, that appealed to a much wider market*

Cast | Felicia Day, Vincent Caso, Jeff Lewis, Amy
Okuda, Sandeep Parikh, Robin Thorsen, Brett
Sheridan, Wil Wheaton, Teal Sherer
Original broadcaster | YouTube
For fans of . . . | *Parks and Recreation* (2009)

The Guild is on online series with episodes of variable
length anchored by the show's creator, Felicia Day,
as Codex, a young woman whose minor troubles in
real life are complicated by major troubles among
her gaming friends, a guild known collectively as the
Knights of Good. Each episode begins with Codex
recording a webcam entry in a video diary; in her first
entry she confesses that her therapist just "fired" her.
When Zaboo, one of her gaming friends, shows up
at her door with expectations of an instant deep and
meaningful relationship, she turns to the other Knights
of Good for help.

Day is an appealing lead with superb comic timing.
The nuanced expressiveness in her face is of particular
importance when the video diary entries in each
episode usually feature nothing but her character
talking to the camera. The rest of the cast are gifted and
have the benefit of inhabiting well-defined characters
who are stereotypes on one level but capable of
realistic growth beyond their initial constructs. Among
the many stars who have made guest appearances are
Wil Wheaton, Erin Gray, Stan Lee, and Nathan Fillion.

Prima facie *The Guild* may seem like it would appeal
only to gamers, but the story, characters, and themes
are of universal interest. It is an ensemble piece that
bears favorable comparison with such network
smashes as *The Office* and *Parks and Recreation*. Even
though it's only available online, great comedy is great
comedy, no matter where you find it. **SWH**

Keeping Up with the Kardashians

Reality | USA | 2007–present

The living proof that people who are not rich themselves love watching the adventures of those who are

Cast | Kris Jenner, Bruce Jenner, Kourtney Kardashian, Kim Kardashian, Khloé Kardashian, Rob Kardashian, Kendall Jenner, Kylie Jenner
Original broadcaster | E!
For fans of . . . | *Kourtney and Kim Take Miami* (2009)

This immensely popular reality show follows the lives of the siblings Kim, Kourtney, Khloé, and Rob Kardashian, their mother, Kris Jenner, and stepfather, Bruce Jenner, a former Olympic decathlon champion. Also featured prominently are Jenner's daughters, Kendall and Kylie, and his sons, Brody and Brandon. All these children have numerous boyfriends and girlfriends, many of whom are well known in the world of entertainment: Kim's lovers have included the rapper Ray J and basketball player Kris Humphries. She married the latter, but left him after only ten weeks, by which time she was pregnant by another rapper, Kanye West; in 2012 she gave birth to a daughter named North.

However, the show is not all about the affairs of the Kardashian–Jenners; it also observes their professional development. Kim worked as a stylist and later became personal shopper to movie star Lindsay Lohan. She then, with her sisters, opened a boutique named D-A-S-H in Southern California.

As a promotional vehicle for the families, *Keeping Up with the Kardashians* is unimprovable; as a TV show, it has attracted criticism for approving the conspicuous consumption of the idle rich. Some people say that the Kardashians are famous only for being famous. But that's a matter of opinion; the viewing figures are facts. More than one million people tune in regularly, and the season five premiere, "Kim's House Party," drew an audience of more than four-and-a-half million in the United States. The series is also a hit in export markets. **GL**

Classic episode

Botox and Cigarettes | *Season 5, episode 5*.
Kim wants to get rid of facial wrinkles, but soon after receiving a protein injection, her eyes turn purple. Kris is discovered smoking and Kourtney tries to persuade her to quit.

⬣ (L–R) Kris with her daughters Khloé, Kourtney, and Kim.

The Big Bang Theory
Comedy | USA | 2007–present

The geeks shall inherit the Earth in this era-defining sitcom

Cast | Johnny Galecki, Jim Parsons, Kaley Cuoco, Simon Helberg, Kunal Nayyar, Melissa Rauch, Mayim Bialik
Original broadcaster | CBS
For fans of . . . | *Two and a Half Men* (2003)

The Big Bang Theory is about four nerdy science whizzes whose lives are turned upside down when the girl of their dreams moves in across the hall. It was created by veteran sitcom writers Chuck Lorre and Bill Prady, but CBS rejected their first pilot so they reshot it with actors Johnny Galecki and Jim Parsons as physicists and roomies Leonard Hofstadter and Sheldon Cooper. With the addition of Kaley Cuoco as Penny, the girl next door, and Simon Helberg and Kunal Nayar as Leonard's and Sheldon's colleagues Howard and Raj, the ensemble clicked and a 13-episode season was secured.

The result was a heady mix of fast one-liners, sass, and pop culture nods to comics, movies, and TV shows. As the series progresses, the four scientists become less nerdy and Penny matures from struggling actress–waitress into a mature character in a relationship with Leonard. But there are no miracle transformations, and at heart, the geeks are still geeks and the Nebraska party girl is still a Nebraska party girl.

The show grows with the characters. The additions of Bernadette (Melissa Rauch) and Amy (Mayim Bialik) as love interests for Howard and Sheldon add new dimensions as we go along.

After a slow-burn start, *The Big Bang Theory* went stratospheric, its seventh season (2013/14) finishing in the number-two slot for highest-rated shows. And even after all this time, it shows no sign of decline. **MW**

◐ (L–R) Johnny Galecki, Jim Parsons, Brooke D'Orsay, and Simon Helberg in season one, episode seven, "The Dumpling Paradox."

Pushing Daisies

Comedy/Drama | USA | 2007–09

Ned is a pie-maker who can bring back the dead; Chuck is the love of his life he can never touch

Cast | Lee Pace, Anna Friel, Chi McBride, Kristin Chenoweth, Swoosie Kurtz **Original broadcaster** | ABC
For fans of . . . | *The Avengers* (1961), *Fraggle Rock* (1983), *Torchwood* (2005), *Hannibal* (2013)

In the first episode of *Torchwood*, Captain Jack brought back the dead for a minute with his Resurrection Glove. A year later the idea resurfaced in the magic fingers of pie-maker Ned, translated from the rain-soaked streets of Cardiff to a technicolor American dream.

In an era when other shows majored in ochre and beige, director Barry Sonnenfeld pushed for tartrazine and made *Pushing Daisies* the brightest dark comedy ever. But it wasn't just good to look at—writer Bryan Fuller created a quirky world of endlessly lovable characters hunting down ruthless serial killers.

Critically lauded yet strangely unwatched, the show was a victim of the scheduling and production turbulence caused by the 2007 strike by the Writers

Guild of America. Fans couldn't get enough of it; the network couldn't wait to get rid of it. It (more or less) managed two seasons before coming to an abrupt end. Fuller's previous series (the equally quirky *Wonderfalls* and *Dead Like Me*) suffered similar fates. His next project, a remake of *The Munsters*, didn't make it beyond a pilot. His next goer was *Hannibal*. **JG**

> **Classic episode**
> *Bitter Sweets* | *Season 1, episode 8.* Is a man with a doll for a girlfriend a serial killer? Or is it the doll? Ned seeks answers to these questions while facing rivalry to his pie-making business from a newly opened candy store over the road.

◉ (L–R) Anna Friel (Charlotte "Chuck" Charles), Chi McBride (Emerson Cod), and Lee Pace (Ned) contemplate the dead.

The Tudors

Historical drama | USA | 2007–10

The life and all the loves of King Henry VIII of England in just four seasons

Cast | Jonathan Rhys Meyers, Joely Richardson, Natalie Dormer, Jeremy Northam, Sam Neill
Original broadcaster | Showtime **For fans of . . .** | *Rome* (2005)

The Tudors was rightly criticized for its historical inaccuracies, but it has an energy that sweeps the audience along on a whistle-stop tour through the reign of English King Henry VIII (Jonathan Rhys-Meyers).

The series often plays fast and loose with the facts, firmly establishing itself as drama rather than document. The first two seasons form an exuberant depiction of life in Henry's court, the political and religious chicanery, with its dramatic backbone being Henry's courting of Anne Boleyn and his divorce from Catherine of Aragon. The series' aesthetic is writ large in the casting of Jonathan Rhys Myers as Henry and Natalie Dormer as Anne, their pairing charged with a passionate chemistry that drives early episodes.

The final two seasons speed through Henry's physical decline, and are perhaps diminished by the loss of Dormer following Anne Boleyn's execution at the end of season two. Yet *The Tudors* remains enjoyable throughout, and there are notable guest cameos by, among others, Sam Neill, Peter O'Toole, and Max von Sydow. **MW**

Classic episode

Problems in the Reformation | *Season 3, episode 5.* Following the death of his third wife, Jane Seymour, Henry enters seclusion with his Fool. Affairs of state fade into the background as the king descends briefly into madness.

Henry VIII (Jonathan Rhys Meyers) with the last of his six wives, Catherine Parr (Joely Richardson).

Mad Men

Drama | USA | 2007–15

*Advertising agents at the dark heart
of the American dream*

Cast | Jon Hamm, Elisabeth Moss, John Slattery,
Vincent Kartheiser, January Jones, Christina Hendricks
Original broadcaster | AMC
Awards | 2 BAFTAs, 15 Emmys, 4 Golden Globes
For fans of . . . | *The Sopranos* (1999), *House of Cards* (2013)

Cable network AMC's entry into the prestige drama
ring, *Mad Men* hit the ground running with a stylish,
beautifully realized setting, compelling storytelling,
and a breakout star in Jon Hamm, its square-jawed
lead. Eschewing nostalgia in favor of a clear-eyed
consideration of the fluidity of identity in a changing
world, *Mad Men* did not shy away from uncomfortable
confrontations with the darker aspects of the American
dream, from the rampant and socially acceptable
racism and sexism to the casual alcoholism and marital
infidelity that typified the early to mid-1960s.

Decorated Korean War veteran Don Draper (Hamm)
seemed to have it all: he was a partner and head of
the creative department at a well-regarded advertising
agency in the heyday of American consumerism. A self-
made man from a humble background, Draper had a
good salary, a beautiful wife, and two perfect children.
But Don Draper was a man with secrets: he was an
inveterate womanizer with a drinking problem, whose
entire life was founded on a single, terrible lie.

It is easy to overlook the darkness at the heart of
Mad Men's examination of mid-century America.
The production design is astonishing, and partially
responsible for a recent resurgence of interest in
classic mid-century design, while the advertising
industry appears—at least superficially—as elegant
and cosmopolitan as it imagines itself to be. **AP**

❯ (L–R) Jon Hamm (Don Draper), John Slattery (Roger Sterling),
Kevin Rahm (Ted Chaough), and Harry Hamlin (Jim Cutler).

The Mentalist

Crime/Mystery | USA | 2008–15

Police procedural with a "psychic" twist and a serialized mythology—let the mind games begin

Cast | Simon Baker, Robin Tunney, Tim Kang, Owain Yeoman, Amanda Righetti, Rockmond Dunbar, Emily Swallow, Joe Adler, Josie Loren
Original broadcaster | CBS
For fans of . . . | *Psych* (2006)

Patrick Jane (Simon Baker) had been successful as a celebrity psychic medium, but the very real skills and insights that he honed in observing and manipulating people through his work came in handy when his wife and daughter were murdered by a crafty killer who operated under the name "Red John." Jane offered his services to the California Bureau of Investigation (CBI) as a consultant, and he not only helped them with their casework, but labored to track down his family's murderer and bring him to justice.

Created by executive producer Bruno Heller, the series juggled the more traditional anthological approach of a police procedural with an ongoing plot concerning Jane's pursuit of Red John. That story, and the show's tradition of naming every episode with a reference to the color red, ended with a brutal final confrontation between Red John and Jane eight episodes into the sixth season. The series then engineered a somewhat surprising narrative shift in one week, picking up two years later when a reclusive Jane, living quietly after his revenge was satisfied, was drawn back into the world of criminal investigation.

The resolution of the Red John story may have been satisfying to many viewers, but it left the series without the primary driving force that had sustained it for so long. Perhaps more jarring for some—yet equally welcomed by others—was the development of a romantic relationship between Jane and CBI team leader Teresa Lisbon (Robin Tunney). **ATB**

Classic episode
Strawberries & Cream | *Season 3, episodes 23/24.*
The CBI team investigate the death of a thief and uncover a link that might lead them to Red John. Jane looks forward to a potentially explosive encounter with his arch-nemesis.

⊛ Simon Baker as Patrick Jane in "Red Sky in the Morning," the season two finale.

Apparitions

Fantasy/Horror/Sci-Fi | UK | 2008

"Does for the Catholic Church what Spooks *did for MI5"*

Cast | Martin Shaw, Rick Warden, Siobhan Finneran, John Shrapnel, Michelle Joseph, Shaun Dooley, David Gyasi, Elyes Gabel
Original broadcaster | BBC One
For fans of . . . | *Ultraviolet* (1998), *Spooks* (2002)

Following the critical success of *Ultraviolet*, its creator Joe Ahearne (with cowriter Nick Collins) produced a contemporary tale of possession, exorcism, miracles, and murders. Father Jacob, played superbly by Martin Shaw (*The Professionals*, *Judge John Deed*) headed the Congregation for the Causes of Saints, which presented cases of miracles that could lead to canonization. And there was one in particular that would shake the foundations of the Church forever. The past case involved the alleged possession and attack of Mother Teresa shortly before her death and the apparent cure of a destitute child's leprosy. The child, Vimal, pledged his life to the Church and as an adult finished his training for priesthood at Jacob's seminary.

It was there that a young girl asked them to perform an exorcism on her father, and despite fierce opposition from within the Church, Jacob obliged. However, the exorcism was not successful, and the demon went on to possess a vagrant, Michael. This set off a chain of events that cost Vimal his life. Jacob not only had to fight the political factions within the Church, but he also had his own personal battles against the demons.

Never shy of tackling controversial subjects, Ahearne drew in viewers with an imaginative story that used contemporary issues that a modern-day Church and other religions face. Outstanding performances came from Rick Warden (who gave great depth to the troubled Michael) and *Downton Abbey*'s Siobhan Finneran as Sister Ruth. **JV**

Dead Set

Fantasy/Horror/Sci-Fi | UK | 2008

A reality TV show is taken over by glassy-eyed, brain-dead monsters—yes, really

Cast | Jaime Winstone, Andy Nyman, Kevin Eldon, Adam Deacon, Davina McCall, Warren Brown, Riz Ahmed, Beth Cordingly, Kathleen McDermott
Original broadcaster | E4
For fans of . . . | *The Walking Dead* (2010)

For the first decade of the twenty-first century, Channel 4 in the United Kingdom handed over its summer schedule to the reality show *Big Brother*. Tabloids were full of stories about the contestants, and everyone had an opinion even if they had not watched the program. By setting a zombie apocalypse within the actual *Big Brother* compound, writer Charlie Brooker created the ultimate satire.

Firstly, there was the distressing sight of the hugely popular *Big Brother* host Davina McCall succumbing to a zombie attack, and then joining their number. Secondly, the cast of characters selected as the fictional housemates were entirely credible. Finally, Brooker's script made viewers wholly complicit in wanting one set of characters to survive over another. This was a natural extension of the *Big Brother* machine, which cons viewers into thinking that they have a better insight into who should survive than the people in the compound. Jaime Winston shone as the resourceful production company runner who suddenly found herself in the *Big Brother* house, while Andy Nyman stole the show as the manipulative TV producer who remained contemptible to the bloody end.

Dead Set can be seen as a perceptive metaphor for the modern TV landscape: screens filled with vacuous reality stars destroying life as we know it for the sake of entertainment. It is also an exceptional take on the zombie myth. Extremely gory and terrifyingly nihilistic, it is everything a zombie apocalypse should be. **JS**

Being Human

Fantasy/Horror/Sci-Fi | UK | 2008–13

Flatmates by day—undead by night

Cast | Lenora Crichlow, Russell Tovey, Aidan Turner, Sinead Keenan, Michael Socha, Damien Molony, Kate Bracken, Jason Watkins **Original broadcaster** | BBC Three **For fans of . . .** | *Buffy the Vampire Slayer* (1997)

Being Human was first broadcast within a series of pilots in which the most popular one was rewarded with a full commission. It was billed as a comedy drama, although this rather undersold its roots in horror lore set down in previous vampire, ghost, and werewolf fiction. Writer Toby Whithouse cherry-picked the best elements of the genre without being slavish to what had gone before. His vampires could move around quite comfortably in daylight, but were still vulnerable to wooden stakes. When the series began, it focused on Mitchell, an ancient vampire trying to avoid his murderous past; George, a nervous hospital porter and werewolf; and Annie, a ghost initially trapped within the walls of the house where she died.

The third season was accompanied by an online spinoff, *Becoming Human*, about a teenage vampire and a werewolf school friend who solved the mystery of the death of their ghost classmate. A US remake of *Being Human* took plot elements from the first season, relocated the action to Boston, and largely diverged from its source to become its own beast. **JS**

Classic episode

Bad Moon Rising | *Season 1, episode 6*. Mitchell is still weak after a near-fatal attack, George wants to start a new life with Nina, and Annie has rejected the chance to move onto the other side. None of them is safe while Herrick still lives.

⬥ Aidan Turner and Russell Tovey in the opening episode of season two.

Leverage

Crime/Mystery | USA | 2008–12

Sometimes bad guys make the best good guys

Cast | Timothy Hutton, Gina Bellman, Christian Kane, Beth Riesgraf, Aldis Hodge
Original broadcaster | TNT **For fans of . . .** | *Mission: Impossible* (1966), *Hustle* (2004)

Former insurance investigator Nate Ford (Timothy Hutton) sought revenge for the misfortunes that had befallen him and became the leader of a gang of reformed criminals, each with their own specialized skill set. The roles of the team were grifter, hacker, hitter, and thief, with Nate acting as the mastermind who planned and operated each con.

Although often seen as a counterpart to the UK show *Hustle*, *Leverage* was much more highly focused, and every week the team used their skills to bring justice to those who had destroyed the lives of the less fortunate through greed. It is reminiscent of *Mission: Impossible*, which also featured a team of specialized regulars who caused a target to bring about their own destruction.

The show consisted mostly of standalone episodes and had a strong pulp sensibility: in effect viewers got to see a miniature heist movie each week. And like any heist movie, much of the pleasure was in watching how each con was actually pulled off through cleverness and misdirection, a twist usually revealed in a series of flashbacks at the end of the episode. **PB**

Classic episode
The Bottle Job | *Season 2, episode 11.* The team has to run the classic con known as "The Wire" (the same con that is at the heart of *The Sting*) in the bar from which they work. During a wake. In less than two hours.

○ Timothy Hutton (right) as Nate Ford in the season three episode "The Jailhouse Job."

Ashes to Ashes

Crime/Mystery | UK | 2008–10

Fire up the Audi Quattro for a trip to the dark side of the 1980s

Cast | Philip Glenister, Keeley Hawes, Dean Andrews, Marshall Lancaster, Monserrat Lombard, Joseph Long, Amelia Bullmore, Adrian Dunbar, Daniel Mays
Original broadcaster | BBC One
For fans of . . . | *Dempsey and Makepeace* (1985)

When actor John Simm decided to quit the role of Sam Tyler after only two series of retro cop show *Life on Mars* (2006), creators Matthew Graham and Ashley Pharoah took the opportunity to reinvent the format for the 1980s. They brought DCI Gene Hunt (Philip Glenister) and his team down from Manchester to London, and introduced a new time-traveling character, DI Alex Drake (Keeley Hawes). Alex was shot during a hostage negotiation in 2008 and woke up in 1981, where Hunt mistook her for a high-class call girl. Their initial antagonism developed into a will they, won't they flirtation, undermined by Alex's suspicion of Hunt and his role in Tyler's disappearance. In addition to having to confront the outdated attitudes of her new colleagues, Alex was constantly searching for answers as to why she had been transported back to the past, and hoping that she could return to 2008 and her daughter, Molly. Episodes took place against the backdrop of the wedding of Prince Charles and Lady Diana, the Falklands War, and Margaret Thatcher's re-election as UK prime minister, while the music of the New Romantics lent a genuine period flavor.

The well-received *Life on Mars* was a tough act to follow, but despite initially lukewarm reviews *Ashes to Ashes* became an iconic show in its own right, eventually making a TV legend out of Hunt and his unmistakable Audi Quattro. After three series, *Ashes to Ashes* concluded in 2010 with one of British TV's most anticipated final episodes. **MM**

Little Dorrit

Historical drama | UK | 2008

A Dickens blockbuster brought to the screen by a master of period drama

Cast | Claire Foy, Matthew Macfadyen, Tom Courtenay, Emma Pierson, Alun Armstrong, Judy Parfitt
Original broadcaster | BBC One
Awards | 7 Emmys
For fans of . . . | *Bleak House* (2005)

Amy Dorrit had lived in the Marshalsea Debtors' Prison all her life. There, she cared for her proud but unreliable father while working as a seamstress for sour-faced Mrs.Clennam. Then Mrs. Clennam's son Arthur returned from China with news that his dying father had tasked him with putting right a family wrong. Aided by a private investigator, his quest uncovered a family secret, an inheritance, and the realization that love had its own reward, though having money in the bank didn't hurt.

Less familiar to audiences than *Oliver Twist* and *Great Expectations*, *Little Dorrit* was one of Dickens's most political novels, a critique on the hypocrisy of London society and the trap of the debtors' prison where, once inside, it was near-impossible to repay the debts (Dickens's own father had spent time in one). In adapting the novel for the screen, Andrew Davies structured it like a British soap, with thirty-minute episodes bookended by extended opening and closing installments.

The impressive ensemble cast produced fine performances. Andy Serkis played the villain, Rigaud, an unscrupulous French blackmailer and murderer, while Tom Courtenay captured the tragic dignity of Amy's father fleeing England in the hope it will help his family escape the taint of his former debts.

The production was generally well received, though after fourteen tightly packed episodes, the rush to tie up the many diverse plot strands left some less attentive viewers confused. **JS**

True Blood

Drama | USA | 2008–14

Long-running HBO show that capitalized profitably on the recently revived appeal of the vampire legend

Cast | Anna Paquin, Stephen Moyer, Alexander Skarsgard, Ryan Kwanten, Rutina Wesley
Original broadcaster | HBO
Awards | 2 Emmys, 1 Golden Globe
For fans of . . . | *Buffy the Vampire Slayer* (1997)

Bon Temps, Louisiana, was a quaint southern hamlet with a supernatural underside: it was at the center of hundreds of years of demonic possession, faerie magic, and vampire legend . . . and the setting of one of HBO's most prominent shows.

Based on *The Southern Vampire Mysteries* (2001–13), a thirteen-novel series by Charlaine Harris, *True Blood* was more than a horror show; it was a sprawling saga of the intertwined lives of numerous characters, only some of whom are human. At its emotional center was Sookie Stackhouse, Harris' heroine, played initially as a wide-eyed waitress by Oscar winner Anna Paquin. Sookie's destiny was linked to that of Bill Compton (Stephen Moyer), one of thousands of centuries-old vampires whose simultaneous emergence throughout the United States and elsewhere might be interpreted as an allegory of the emerging rights of gays and lesbians. Sookie, Bill, and their allies, acquaintances, and rivals endured heartache, distress, and retribution as they confronted the shapechangers, maenads, and politics of the fledgling vampire dominion.

True Blood was a ratings champion for HBO until the departure of series creator Alan Ball at the end of the fifth season. The show subsequently moved away from its literary sources and rapidly lost popularity as a result. HBO put an end to it in 2014 in a finale that featured Harris herself in a cameo appearance and tied up the story with a flash forward to four years after the end of the tale. **SL**

Classic episode
Strange Love | *Season 1, episode 1.* The show's opening episode brings waitress Sookie Stackhouse into her first contact with Bill Compton, the man (at least in appearance) whose destiny would be tied to hers.

◭ Anna Paquin (Sookie) and Stephen Moyer (Bill): pure love meets blood lust.

Breaking Bad

Crime/Mystery | USA | 2008–13

Unstable, volatile, dangerous. And that's just the chemistry in this show that raised the bar of moral jeopardy to a previously unimagined height

Cast | Bryan Cranston, Aaron Paul, Anna Gunn, Dean Norris, Bob Odenkirk, Betsy Brandt, R.J. Mitte
Original broadcaster | FX
Awards | 16 Emmys, 2 Golden Globes
For fans of . . . | *The Sopranos* (1999)

The very best TV can be difficult to watch. This can occur when it is coarse and uninviting and when it challenges viewers to think outside their comfort zone, sometimes even bidding them to sympathize with very extreme characters and behavior (*The Sopranos* springs to mind). In the rare times that it works, it is extraordinary.

With *Breaking Bad*, creator and producer Vince Gilligan created a story that challenged viewers' loyalties to the extreme: the fall of terminally ill high school chemistry teacher Walter White (masterfully portrayed by Bryan Cranston), who entered the world of illicit drug manufacture ostensibly to secure his family's future. Along the way, viewers witnessed his slow and painful metamorphosis from hero to villain, and the impact that his descent into the depths of human depravity made on his family and on Jesse Pinkman (an equally impressive Aaron Paul), who became his partner in crime. As Walter traded his chemistry lab for a mobile methamphetamine laboratory, and set himself among the worlds of hard-core street crime and high-stakes drug trafficking, *Breaking Bad* remained the story of the human condition itself: the struggle against death and life in equal measure; the quest to justify and maintain increasingly immoral choices.

At its heart, *Breaking Bad* is the antithesis of a tale of redemption, but one that is crafted brilliantly, acted and written superbly, and is ultimately intensely satisfying. It was a triumph for the FX network, which believed in the source material and watched it flourish. **SL**

Classic episode

ABQ | *Season 2, episode 13.* After an entire season, viewers finally discover that the damaged pink bear floating in the pool is part of the debris from an airplane crash indirectly caused by Walter and Jesse. Priceless.

◓ Aaron Paul as Jesse and Jesse Plemons as Todd.
◓ Bryan Cranston as Walt realizes how much money he can make.

In Plain Sight

Drama | USA | 2008–12

A classic tale of police officers struggling to enforce the law and keep their own lives on track

Cast | Mary McCormack, Fred Weller, Nichole Hiltz, Lesley Ann Warren, Paul Ben-Victor, Rachel Boston
Original broadcaster | USA Network
For fans of . . . | *Cagney & Lacey* (1982), *Burn Notice* (2007), *Covert Affairs* (2010)

Mary Shannon (Mary McCormack) was a deputy US Marshal in Albuquerque, New Mexico, who worked on the Federal Witness Security Program. Her professional life would have been demanding even if all her circumstances had been auspicious, but they were not. She was the child of addictive parents— her father a gambler who deserted the family after robbing a bank; her mother, Jinx (Lesley Ann Warren), a reformed alcoholic—and that background made it hard for her to form loving relationships. She had regular disagreements with her working colleague, Marshall Mann (Fred Weller), about the best way to approach the job. Their worst disputes were mediated by their boss, Stan McQueen (Paul Ben-Victor), a just and decent man who calmed them both. The other main influence on Mary's life was her younger sister, Brandi (Nichole Hiltz), the apple of Jinx's eye.

At various times during the show's five seasons, Mary was shot, abducted, and rescued, and had an adulterous affair with an FBI agent and a brief fling with her ex-husband, after which she became pregnant. Meanwhile, it emerged that her arguments with Marshall were sublimating their attraction to each other, but nothing ever came of it; he was in a relationship with Detective Abigail Chaffee (Rachel Boston).

Intelligently scripted, convincingly acted, and beautifully filmed, mainly on location in New Mexico, *In Plain Sight* became USA Network's biggest hit since *Psych* (2006). **GL**

Classic episode
Duplicate Bridge | *Season 2, episode 7.* A bridge collapses and the architect is taken under police protection, but fakes his suicide so that he can take revenge on the head of the construction company. Mary and Marshall must find him fast.

◉ Mary McCormack as Mary Shannon.

Merlin

Fantasy/Horror/Sci-Fi | UK | 2008–12

*The darkest hour is just before the dawn
of the age of magic*

Cast | Colin Morgan, Bradley James, Angel Coulby,
Katie McGrath, Richard Wilson, Anthony Head
Original broadcaster | BBC One
Award | 1 BAFTA
For fans of . . . | *Game of Thrones* (2011)

All magic had been banned in the Kingdom of Camelot
at the command of Uther Pendragon (Anthony Head),
who had imprisoned the last of the powerful dragons
beneath the great castle. It was into this dangerous
world that young Merlin (Colin Morgan) arrived to work
with court physician Gaius (Richard Wilson). When Merlin
was squired to young Prince Arthur (Bradley James), the
forging of the greatest legend ever told began.

After several abortive attempts, the BBC finally
brought a new take on the legend of Merlin, the
magician, and Arthur, the greatest king of England, to
TV. It was epic but not dour, and the young cast and
fast-moving plots were seasoned with impressive visual
effects to attract a lucrative family audience. Morgan
was note-perfect as Merlin; his striking, awkward looks
gave the young magician an almost gothic appeal. This
contrasted with the handsome, straight-jawed James
as the youthful future king. Merlin faced his destiny at
the behest of the last dragon (voiced by John Hurt),
often placing himself in great danger to protect Arthur.

Merlin mixed romance, epic quests, magical
creatures, adventure, and destiny, served up in an
entertaining modern package. Its five-season run
was greeted with critical acclaim and high ratings
in the face of strong competition on home soil. The
final two-part story wrapped up the origins of the
world's greatest legend in some style, but its devoted
international audience hoped that one day Merlin and
Arthur would ride into battle once more. **MW**

Sense & Sensibility

Historical drama | UK | 2008

*Love, money, and heartache
in Regency England*

Cast | Hattie Morahan, Charity Wakefield, David
Morrissey, Dan Stevens, Janet McTeer, Lucy Boynton,
Mark Williams, Mark Gatiss, Claire Skinner
Original broadcaster | BBC One
For fans of . . . | *Pride and Prejudice* (1995)

Following the success of his TV adaptation of *Pride and
Prejudice*, writer Andrew Davies embarked on an Austen
rework for the twenty-first century. Opening with a sex
scene and derided by the Jane Austen Society for being
"too raunchy," the plot captured the intricacies of desire
in eighteenth-century society.

There are no huge surprises in the plot for those
even passingly familiar with Austen—three sisters, a
little poor (they can afford only two servants), try to
find love. Forced to move out of their family home after
their half brother inherits the property, they move to
a small cottage in Devonshire. The oldest sister Elinor
("Sense") pines for Edward Ferrars, who is engaged to
another woman; the middle, and sillier, sister Marianne
("Sensibility") attracts the eye of older Colonel
Brandon, although she greatly prefers the company
of the younger, better-looking Mr. Willoughby. Suffice
to say, the course of true love does not run smooth
and Marianne falls head over heels for a wrong'un
before finding love with a much more sensible—and,
importantly, richer—gentleman.

Davies's sparkling adaptation not only brought out
the human side of the romance but also the wit and
warmth of Austen's original work. The scenes involving
the three male romantic leads were embellished to add
greater depth to their characters, in particular Colonel
Brandon being portrayed as a sensitive yet strong man,
rather than merely as a taciturn and a distinctly inferior
choice for Marianne. **EB**

In Treatment

Drama | USA | 2008–10

Stark, simple, and rivetingly powerful tales from the office of an unhappy psychiatrist

Cast | Gabriel Byrne, Dianne Wiest, Melissa George, Blair Underwood, Mia Wasikowska, Josh Charles, Embeth Davidtz   **Original broadcaster** | HBO   **For fans of . . .** | *My So-Called Life* (1994), *Help* (2005)

The psychiatrist's office has long been a setting both for comedy—from Woody Allen's movies to *Analyze This* and *Frasier*—and for drama such as *The Sopranos*. *In Treatment* was different. In episode after episode, we simply saw one or two patients talking with Dr. Paul Weston (Gabriel Byrne) at his office. Practically nothing happened, yet each story was immediately compelling, leading us either to laugh out loud or weep. Each episode followed one psychiatry session, and in the first season, HBO rearranged its schedule to have the half-hour episodes run nightly. Mondays were Laura's sessions, Tuesdays were Alex's, and so on. Friday nights were the exception: those were Dr. Weston's session with his own therapist, Dr. Gina Toll (Dianne Wiest).

Back then, it was genuine appointment-to-view television. Consuming it now as a box set, you will struggle not to binge-watch, and you'll have to fight the temptation to skip ahead and see what happens next with this patient or that. The individual episodes do work on their own, and so do the entire stories per patient, but the seasons also tell an overall tale. **WG**

Classic episode
Season 2, episode 2. Yes, stroppy student April always has a problem, but here it is not just some character in some plot; this is a real person, and you are feeling her pain. You don't just want to see what happens next—you want to help her.

🅰 Gabriel Byrne as Dr. Paul Weston displays his concerned bedside manner with a hospital patient.

The Inbetweeners

Comedy | UK | 2008–10

Inspired a whole new language for teenagers—Beep be de beep beep beep!

Cast | Simon Bird, Joe Thomas, James Buckley, Blake Harrison
Original broadcaster | Channel 4 **Award** | 1 BAFTA **For fans of . . .** | *The Big Bang Theory* (2007)

Put simply, the main reason for the success of *The Inbetweeners* was how wickedly funny it was. Damon Beesley and Iain Morris created one of the best comedies in years, in terms of both visual and written gag rates. It was pretty much impossible to stifle your laughter as Jay (James Buckley) pretended to be Australian, as Will (Simon Bird) attempted to buy alcohol, or as Simon (Joe Thomas) walked the runway. Pretty much any sentence that Neil (Blake Harrison) uttered was hilarious. The show also had a great number of genuinely funny supporting characters, including a worryingly accurate representation of a teacher. Mr. Gilbert stole practically every scene he was in, particularly those in which he came up against

nerdy Will. There was also liar Jay's dad, and chronically embarrassed Simon's perpetually randy dad, among many others. The series spawned two hugely successful feature film releases. Both movies were as amusing as the series, which was highly unusual for film versions of TV sitcoms. This success speaks volumes about the quality of the source material here. **LH**

Classic episode
Exam Time | *Season 2, episode 6.* The boys are sitting their school exams and Will has been over-indulging in energy drinks to see him through. The consequence is a laugh-out-loud episode of the highest order.

◉ (L–R) Simon Bird, Blake Harrison, James Buckley, and Joe Thomas made viewers cringe and laugh in equal measure.

Packed to the Rafters

Comedy | Australia | 2008–13

The Australian clan whose members may go but who often return like boomerangs

Cast | Rebecca Gibney, Erik Thomson, Jessica Marais, Hugh Sheridan, Michael Caton
Original broadcaster | Seven Network
For fans of . . . | *The Brady Bunch* (1969), *Neighbours* (1985), *At Home with the Braithwaites* (2000)

How exactly do you refer to a series that is packed full of drama but is also rich in comedy? One that features the complicated domestic turmoil of a suburban family and their friends, assailed by constant trials and turbulent love lives? The easiest answer is to call it a soap opera, but *Packed to the Rafters* is more than that. It is paced more thoughtfully and it is beautifully shot.

Over its six series, *Packed to the Rafters* told the story of the Rafter clan. Julie (Rebecca Gibney) and Dave (Erik Thomson) had been married for twenty-five years. Their children were grown-up but had not necessarily moved on: their son Ben (Hugh Sheridan) left home . . . and moved in next door. Gradually all their children returned and then Julie's dad moved in, too. Did the family ever get a moment's peace? Well, no, but they found happiness. Sometimes. *Packed to the Rafters* took all the familiar soap story lines—death, infidelity, fights, and house fires—but played them out long and slow. The sale of a beloved car absorbed several episodes and became a plot every bit as poignant as the fallout from a love affair. Each episode was narrated by a different character, and the show loved a long flashback.

After six seasons, 122 episodes, and very impressive ratings, *Packed to the Rafters* came to an end in 2013. However, that was not the end of the family. The program's makers vowed that the Rafters' adventures would continue in occasional TV movies and specials. And the show's devoted audience will be furious if it doesn't happen. **JG**

Tutti pazzi per amore

Soap opera | Italy | 2008–12

How a new kind of soap shook up Sunday evening schedules in Italy

Cast | Antonia Liskova, Emilio Solfrizzi, Stefania Rocca, Neri Marcorè, Giuseppe Battiston, Sonia Bergamasco,
Original broadcaster | RAI
For fans of . . . | *Un medico in famiglia* (1998), *Cesaroni* (2006)

In many ways, *Tutti pazzi per amore* (*All Crazy About Love*), broadcast over three seasons from 2008 to 2012, was a classic Italian soap. Shown on Sunday evening, the traditional time for mainstream family drama in Italy, it featured Paolo (Emilio Solfrizzi), a widower with a teenage daughter, and Laura (Antonia Liskova), a divorcée with two sons. Having met in the elevator of their apartment building, the pair fell in love. Their attempt to build a new life together, and the ripples this sent through their family, friends, and neighbors, formed the main meat of the narrative.

However, in a successful attempt to draw in younger audiences (before the start, the show was promoted using YouTube), the series employed three narrative devices that made it innovative: It used imaginary dream sequences, in the style of shows such as *Ally McBeal* and *Scrubs* (2001), to explore what might happen to the character if his or her thoughts became a reality; it employed an intermittent voice-over in the form of Dr. Freiss (Giuseppe Battiston), who explained the problems faced by the protagonists; and it included liberal bursts of Italian pop music, which, in addition to inspiring the title of each episode, were incorporated into the narrative itself to convey emotion or to alleviate or ramp up tension. Sometimes characters would act out well-known video clips. The music could also be enjoyed independently from the unfolding drama and was often picked out and posted on social media. **SM**

John Adams

Historical drama | USA | 2008

A lavish prestige biopic of the president who succeeded George Washington and united the states of America

Cast | Paul Giamatti, Laura Linney, Stephen Dillane, David Morse, Danny Huston, Tom Wilkinson
Original broadcaster | HBO
Awards | 13 Emmys, 4 Golden Globes
For fans of . . . | *North and South* (1985)

Based on the book by David McCullough, and starring Paul Giamatti in the title role, *John Adams* chronicled most of US President John Adams' political life and his role in the founding of the United States. The series was directed by Tom Hooper (Kirk Ellis wrote the screenplay) and it won more Golden Globe and Emmy awards than any other miniseries in TV history.

The action spanned the years 1770 to 1826, from the Boston Massacre, when Adams was a lawyer, through his years in the continental congresses, where he showed a passion and bluntness as he helped to shape and ignite the revolution with George Washington, Benjamin Franklin, Thomas Jefferson, and other founding fathers. Adams traveled to Paris and the Netherlands, and was appointed the first US ambassador to the United Kingdom after the Revolutionary War. He then returned to America for the first presidential election, where he was chosen as vice president, and eventually the second president.

Against the backdrop of the birth of a nation, the home life of Adams was as successfully dramatized and engrossing as his impressive and combative political career. One of the miniseries' more fantastic moments—the scenes in which political rivals yet lifelong friends Adams and Thomas Jefferson died mere hours apart on the fiftieth anniversary of the Declaration of Independence (July 4)—was a real-life event. Jefferson was aged eighty-three; Adams was ninety. **RP**

Classic episode
Unnecessary War | *Season 1, episode 6.*
Political conflict is at the heart of this long episode as Adams insists on maintaining neutrality between France and England, despite opposition inside his own cabinet.

◉ Paul Giamatti as a determined John Adams.

Wallander

Crime/Mystery | UK | 2008–present

A British take on the Swedish sleuth that was in some ways even more brooding and melancholic than the original

Cast | Kenneth Branagh, Sarah Smart, Tom Hiddleston
Original broadcaster | BBC One
Awards | 6 BAFTAs
For fans of . . . | *Wallander* (2005), *Hinterland* (2014)

The UK version of *Wallander* is at first a dislocating watch, with its English-speaking and accented characters firmly entrenched in the Swedish landscape and culture. But it slowly draws the viewers in, rewarding them with textured and assured storytelling.

The series follows Kurt Wallander (Kenneth Branagh), a troubled police detective based in the town of Ystad, as he and his team try to solve a number of baffling crimes involving corruption, racism, religious fanaticism, and murder. This *Wallander* relies more than the first Swedish series on the original novels of Henning Mankell. It is also, perhaps surprisingly, more evidently in the tradition of Swedish cinema, with brooding landscapes and similar silences that are reminiscent of—and indebted to—the work of Ingmar Bergman. In the title role, Branagh achieves the remarkable feat of conveying internal conflict through minimal expression; his quiet performance does not dominate, but never fails to grasp the attention.

While the second Swedish version starring Krister Henriksson is widely regarded as the definitive retelling, the UK version of *Wallander* is truer to the spirit of the novels, bringing out the commentary on Swedish society that is so characteristic of Mankell's writing. Many fans have watched all three versions with pleasure; each has its merits, and it would be invidious to rank them. However, there is no doubt that this series is an astonishing fusion of two different cultures, and a richly rewarding viewing experience. **SO**

Classic episode
One Step Behind | *Season 1, episode 3*. A case involving three missing teenage girls becomes personal for Wallander when his colleague is murdered after investigating the same case under his own initiative.

⊘ Kenneth Branagh filming in Gothenburg, Sweden.

Romanzo Criminale

Drama | Italy | 2008–10

An epic series about Italian criminal organizations

Cast | Francesco Montanari, Vinicio Marchioni, Alessandro Roja, Marco Bocci, Daniela Virgilio, Andrea Sartoretti, Antonio Gerardi
Original broadcaster | Sky Cinema Uno
For fans of . . . | *The Sopranos* (1999), *Gomorrah* (2014)

Romanzo Criminale (*Criminal Novel*), based on judge Giancarlo De Cataldo's book, was previously adapted for the screen in 2005 by Michele Placido. The series, set from 1977 to 1989, told of a criminal group—inspired by a real gang, the Banda della Magliana—controlling Rome's heroin trade. The language of the series was Italian mixed with the Romanesco dialect. The leaders were three friends, Libanese, Freddo, and Dandi, who in their struggle for power faced personal and "business" problems, as well as opposition from the dogged Inspector Scialoja, the Italian secret services, the Camorra, and the Mafia. Apparently tough and invincible, the characters had weaknesses that became apparent as the series progressed: they needed love and had harsh childhoods, which were shown as the root cause of their delinquency.

Libanese was a natural leader—focused, cold-blooded, and with a sound business sense; Freddo was the most "democratic" and realistic of the gang, and he started having second thoughts when he fell in love with Roberta; Dandi, who just wanted to be surrounded by luxury and feel important, was obsessed with Patrizia, a prostitute whose good looks and charm also won over Inspector Scialoja.

Romanzo Criminale was tough and violent, but many feared that it glamorized criminality, and adduced as evidence the fact that soon after the show opened, Italian websites and forums were suddenly full of nicknames inspired by those of the characters. **SDG**

Man v. Food

Reality | USA | 2008–12

Will viewers want to watch people eating until they are fit to burst? They certainly will

Cast | Adam Richman
Original broadcaster | Travel Channel
For fans of . . . | *I'm a Celebrity, Get Me Out of Here!* (2002), *Bizarre Foods with Andrew Zimmern* (2006), *Man vs. Wild* (2006), *The Trip* (2010)

There is something about an extreme challenge—one that pushes the body to the limits of its capabilities—that is always going to win a captive audience, and TV personality Adam Richman proved no exception when he launched his own particular quest to consume as many oversized delicacies as possible over the course of one TV series. Indeed, *Man v. Food* was irresistible to watch, as Adam headed across the United States to track down some of the craziest meals on offer at diners and then attempted to finish every last mouthful. Be they overstuffed sandwiches (really, really overstuffed), exceptionally hot curries, or just dishes with an awful lot of calories, nothing proved too much of a challenge for the intrepid host. Except in those instances where, as he put it, food won.

Richman brought the show to an end in 2012, shedding an awful lot of weight in the process, but *Man v. Food* is still a regular fixture on-screen and stands up to repeat viewings. Much of the appeal came from Richman himself, with his likable personality, obvious love of food (the competitive eating was only one part of the show, the rest focused on restaurants and diners and what they had to offer), and realistic approach to the challenge at hand. The fact that some of the time he failed to beat food at its own game only added to the fun, which suggests that he did it more for entertainment value than to show off. And it's that, more than anything, which makes this such a guilty viewing pleasure. **CW**

Childrens Hospital

Comedy | USA | 2008–present

"Prescribe only silliness and slapstick. That is all"

Cast | Malin Åkerman, Lake Bell, Rob Corddry, Erinn Hayes, Rob Huebel, Ken Marino, Megan Mullally
Original broadcasters | TheWB.com, Adult Swim
Awards | 2 Emmys
For fans of . . . | *A Touch of Cloth* (2012)

There are several medical dramas to watch before you die, and all these shows deal with important issues in life. But *Childrens Hospital* is the best and the funniest. This hilarious Emmy award-winning show operates on shows such as *ER* (1994), *Scrubs* (2001), and *House* (2004) to produce a sublime parody, both instantly recognizable and gloriously absurd.

The show began life in 2008 as a web series before being picked up by Adult Swim in 2010. It centers on the staff of Childrens Hospital, named (of course) after Dr. Arthur Childrens, and features Rob Corddry as Dr. Blake Downs, always dressed in clown makeup, and Megan Mullally as Chief, expertly channeling *ER*'s fiery Kerry Weaver on acid. *Childrens Hospital* is not a show that viewers would watch once. It is a program that they gorge on, pushing themselves to watch one more episode just to see how weird things can get. As soon as they think they know what's to come, the plot spins on its head once again. It is a show in the tradition of *Police Squad!* (1982), in which no visual gag is missed and no plot is too random. Every single episode is a series of finely tuned sketches, each masterful one hitting its mark to take the audience to places they would never expect (and possibly places they've always done their best to avoid).

Sure, watch other medical shows—you'll need some context, after all—but, when you're feeling down, *Childrens Hospital* is true to its original and offbeat premise: laughter really is the best medicine. **PPW**

Lark Rise to Candleford

Historical drama | UK | 2008–11

Old ways live forever in the human heart

Cast | Julia Sawalha, Olivia Hallinan, Claudie Blakley, Brendan Coyle, Linda Bassett, Mark Heap
Original broadcaster | BBC One
For fans of . . . | *Cranford* (2007), *Call the Midwife* (2012)

Based on classic historical fiction, this adaptation of Flora Thompson's novels—*Lark Rise, Over to Candleford,* and *Candleford Green,* published between 1939 and 1943—was well rounded, treading a line between homespun homilies and drama showing the hardships of rural communities. The links between the village of Lark Rise and the affluent market town Candleford provided much of the plot: the hard-working Lark Rise villagers often felt beholden to Candleford, and young villager Laura (Olivia Hallinan), who left the rural Oxfordshire hamlet of Lark Rise to take up a job with her cousin, Dorcas Lane (Julia Sawalha), in the Post Office of Candleford, was frequently seen as having ideas above her station as she adapted to town life. There was also comedy to be had in a brilliant performance from Mark Heap as postman Thomas Brown.

Lark Rise bubbled merrily along with a series of problem-of-the-week plots. Themes of the old world colliding with industrial progress were never far away, which gave a sense of time marching and the series its through line. Above all, it looked wonderful, with the countryside and town rendered picture perfect by excellent direction and production design. Despite remaining a reliable ratings winner, *Lark Rise to Candleford* was axed after a shortened fourth season. Fans protested, but no reprieve was granted. The departure of creator Bill Gallagher was cited as the ultimate reason, but this was little consolation to fans who had warmed to the drama. **MW**

Fringe

Drama | USA | 2008–13

Trippy sci-fi epic about the perils of evil science

Cast | Anna Torv, Joshua Jackson, John Noble
Original broadcaster | Fox
For fans of . . . | *The Twilight Zone* (1959), *The X-Files* (1993), *24* (2001), *Lost* (2004), *Prison Break* (2005), *Heroes* (2006)

The first significant J.J. Abrams project after the huge success of *Lost*, the mind-bending sci-fi thriller *Fringe* was originally dismissed as an *X-Files* clone—but it won over critics and viewers with its unique storytelling. Taking its name from the exploration of fringe science, the show focused on the core relationship between Agent Olivia Denham (Anna Torv), genius scientist Walter Bishop (John Noble), and the latter's son Peter Bishop (Joshua Jackson) as they investigated strange events under the auspices of the FBI's Fringe Division. Many of these events were related to experiments previously carried out by Walter, and his need to atone for his earlier hubris led to the team fighting against the inhabitants of an endangered Alternate Earth and the mysterious Observers.

The series started off as a "weird mystery of the week" procedural, backed up by some serialized elements, but the decision to concentrate on the series mythology allowed it to blossom. *Fringe* wasn't afraid to play with the format, with some episodes partially animated and a run of episodes alternately swapping between Earth and the Alternate Earth. The main cast is uniformly excellent. Jackson plays Peter with charming warmth, while Noble rightly won plaudits as the amusing but troubled genius Walter. However, it is Torv who is the revelation here, pulling off every demand the writers threw at her. Somewhat underrated, this compelling and emotional series is a box-set experience you will not regret. **SO**

Classic episode
White Tulip | *Season 2, episode 18.* The Fringe team investigate a professor trying to travel back in time to save the life of his late fiancée, while Walter grapples with the prospect of telling Peter about how he saved his life as a boy.

⊘ Joshua Jackson (Peter Bishop; left) investigates another peculiar occurrence.

Underbelly

Crime/Mystery | Australia | 2008–present

Australia's dark past and present reunited in dramatic form

Cast | Caroline Craig, Dieter Brummer, Peter O'Brien, Gyton Grantley, Chelsie Preston Crayford, Danielle Cormack, Peter Phelps, Sigrid Thornton
Original broadcaster | Nine Network
For fans of . . . | *True Crimes* (1991), *The Wire* (2002)

They say that truth is stranger than fiction. Certainly it can be as violent, chaotic, weird, and volatile as a story. For the *Underbelly* series, the writers mined some of the most brutal and hard-hitting elements of Australia's colorful criminal past to create fascinating drama. Each series was told in a gritty, semi-documentary style that did not hold back from the sex, drugs, and extreme violence that characterized Antipodean organized crime. And none of the significant murders were without emotional consequences.

The show explored the seductive power of particular criminal gangs, their criminal lifestyles, and the cops who either joined them, ruled them, or tried to stop them. Two episodes, *Razor* and *Squizzy*, explored the gangsters who invented Australian organized crime during the Roaring Twenties. The narration was often provided by those related to the events, such as a female cop from the state of Victoria who was involved in the first story. The New Zealand serial was narrated by a male cop who featured in the case against the so-called "Mr. Asia" heroin smuggling syndicate.

Although each series drew closely from real events, some dramatic license was needed in order to protect witnesses. Despite this, the scripts remained remarkably faithful to the facts of the cases depicted, as far as anyone still alive knew the truth about some of the most brutal episodes of Australasian criminal history. "It's a jungle out there . . ." observed the TV theme tune. **SJG**

Only Connect

Game show | UK | 2008–present

Lateral thinking required in the most mind-stretching quiz on TV

Cast | Victoria Coren-Mitchell
Original broadcaster | BBC Four
For fans of . . . | *Have I Got News for You* (1990), *QI* (2003), *Eggheads* (2003), *Mock the Week* (2005), *Pointless* (2009)

Traditionally, TV game and quiz shows have relied on a very narrow skill set, usually the ability to remember or retain facts and trivia. Not so with *Only Connect*, a quiz that rewards lateral thinking. For in *Only Connect*, as the name suggests, contestants not only have to be au fait with science, the arts, literature, music, and a healthy dose of trivia, but they also have to make connections between things that appear, at first, to be entirely unrelated.

Each episode consists of four rounds. In the first round, four connected clues are given, with the amount of points awarded for the answer decreasing with each clue. In the second round, three clues form a sequence, and the teams have to guess the fourth item in the chain. The third round is the fiendish "Wall," where the teams must sort sixteen items into logical groups of four, a task made harder by the fact that the four categories always overlap. In the final round, the team must guess well-known phrases and names that have had their vowels removed and the remaining consonants moved about. This cerebral assault course is designed to test lateral thinking skills to the limit.

The program began on the digital channel BBC Four in 2008, presented by Victoria Coren-Mitchell, daughter of the writer Alan Coren. The format was an immediate hit and has not changed since, with Coren-Mitchell continuing to host as the show proved popular enough to make the move to the more mainstream BBC Two in 2014. **WM**

Star Wars: The Clone Wars

Fantasy/Horror/Sci-Fi | USA | 2008–14

Animated adventures that breathed new life into the perennially watchable saga of life in a galaxy far, far away

Cast | Matt Lanter, Ashley Eckstein, James Arnold Taylor, Dee Bradley Baker, Tom Kane
Original broadcaster | Cartoon Network/Netflix
Awards | 4 Emmys
For fans of . . . | *Futurama* (1999)

Cashing in on the tremendous success of the *Star Wars* film series revival in the early 2000s, Lucasfilm Animation brought the saga to TV as a regular series. *Star Wars: The Clone Wars* was set between the second and third films. Ignoring the fact that its principal character was destined to turn evil and wreak havoc on the galaxy (as the villainous Darth Vader), the series was an attempt to create an animation that was aimed at both a young audience and the older generations that the brand would undoubtedly attract. After a widely panned theatrical debut, *Star Wars: The Clone Wars* began in earnest in 2008 and never looked back; its wide canvas told tales of dashing deeds and thrilling adventures with Anakin Skywalker, his young assistant Ahsoka Tano, the heroic Obi-Wan Kenobi, and fan favorite diminutive Jedi master Yoda.

While enjoying a five-season run on the Cartoon Network, the series was preemptively ended when Disney purchased Lucasfilm. The Netflix streaming video service came to the rescue, debuting the limited run of sixth season stories that had been completed (more or less) before cancellation as "The Lost Missions." Among the many guest actors lending voices to the series were Liam Neeson (reprising his "Phantom Menace" role), *Star Trek*'s George Takei, *Doctor Who*'s David Tennant, *Battlestar Galactica* alumnus Katee Sackhoff, and original *Star Wars* star Mark Hamill. Many members of the production moved over to Lucasfilm/Disney's new entry, *Star Wars Rebels* (2014). **SL**

Classic episode
The Lawless | Season 5, episode 16. Darth Maul takes command of Death Watch and edges closer to creating a vast criminal empire. Obi-Wan Kenobi travels to Mandalore to try and rescue Duchess Satine.

◉ Weapons at the ready.

Sons of Anarchy

Drama | USA | 2008–14

The story of bikers who'd rather be free than bound by convention

Cast | Charlie Hunnam, Ron Perlman, Katey Sagal, Maggie Siff, Mark Boone Junior
Original broadcaster | FX
Award | 1 Golden Globe
For fans of . . . | *The Shield* (2002)

Ranking as one of FX's highest-rated shows, *Sons of Anarchy* was an unyielding drama centered on a renegade motorcycle club (SoA) based in Charming in California's Central Valley. Jackson "Jax" Teller (Charlie Hunnam) was the club's vice president, and his uneasy relationship with his stepfather and club president Clay Morrow (Ron Perlman) caused conflict as ties of family and community clashed with the club's ethos.

Sons of Anarchy was not pretty. It was a raw, sweaty, taut portrayal of a tight-knit Californian community, and its even tighter-knit motorcycle club. It shared the same tone as *The Shield*, another FX big-hitter on which *Sons of Anarchy* creator Kurt Sutter served time as writer and producer. It was more personal, though: the conflict for Jax as he took on family responsibilities tested his commitment to SoA and to Clay. The club kept Charming safe and free from outsiders through intimidation and bribery, with a gun-running operation on the side. Each season was charged with drama that frequently took its protagonists to the limit, handling complex story lines and weaving the lives of Jax and his family together with deftness and heart-in-mouth resolutions—as well as a final reckoning for Jax and Clay that was truly shocking. Whisperings of a prequel set in the 1960s have been heard in Hollywood; should it happen, it will be hard pushed to match the stone-cold brilliance of the original. **MW**

◁ (L–R) Tommy Flanagan (Chibs), Kim Coates (Tig), Theo Rossi (Juice), David Labrava (Happy), and Charlie Hunnam (Jax) in season six.

Archer

Animation | USA | 2009–present

Uber-black animation set in the ludicrous world of espionage

Cast | H. Jon Benjamin, Judy Greer, Amber Nash, Chris Parnell, Aisha Tyler, Jessica Walter
Original broadcaster | FX **For fans of . . .** | *American Dad!* (2005)

Sterling Archer is the self-proclaimed greatest secret agent in the world. He works for a spy agency owned by his mother, Malory, whose less-than-maternal instinct has left him with a long list of psychological hangups. His prowess with a gun is matched by his insatiable appetite for alcohol and women. Each mission sees Archer aided or hindered by his coworkers, including Lana, a super-efficient agent with whom he has an off-off relationship. The series is set in a deliberately anachronistic time period, and Cold War paranoia clashes with modern technology. While the characters might look like they have stepped from an early Bond movie, the humor is very much twenty-first century, with the same level of postmodern approaches to sexism, racism, bodily functions, and violence common to other animated comedies such as *American Dad!*. However, *Archer* has a more realistic approach: characters suffer permanent disability from their exploits and a cancer scare for Archer spans several episodes. None of this dents the deeply sarcastic and extremely quotable dialogue, full of crude innuendo and bitchy one-liners. **RM**

> **Classic episode**
> *Honeypot | Season 1, episode 5.* Archer must seduce a gay Cuban agent who is in possession of a sex tape involving Archer's mother, Malory. Can Archer successfully pose as gay and seduce the blackmailer? Duh and/or hello!

◉ Sterling Archer (voiced by H. Jon Benjamin) in the season four episode titled "Coyote Lovely."

Misfits

Fantasy/Horror/Sci-Fi | UK | 2009–13

Juvenile delinquents with superpowers

Cast | Antonia Thomas, Iwan Rheon, Robert Sheehan, Nathan Stewart-Jarrett, Lauren Socha, Matthew McNulty
Original broadcaster | E4 **Awards** | 3 BAFTAs **For fans of . . .** | *It's Always Sunny in Philadelphia* (2005)

Following a mysterious electrical storm, five teenagers who had been stuck outside doing community service suddenly found themselves possessed of extraordinary powers: everything from being able to rewind time to sending people into a sexual frenzy. Initially delighted by their abilities, the teenagers used their new-found gifts for personal gain, but they gradually realized that having superpowers was a terrible burden.

A darkly funny revisionist take on the usual superhero mythologies, *Misfits* found glory in throwing its difficult characters into stereotypical superhero situations and watching them react with all the cowardice, greed, and selfishness of typical teenagers rather than with the selfless nobility of more traditional characters such as

Superman and Spider-Man. One of the show's strengths was the superb acting and fantastic chemistry between its leads. However, following Robert Sheehan's departure after the second season, *Misfits* struggled to find a way to replace his character, Nathan, whose swaggering bravado had helped balance the show's humor with its more serious subject matter. **AP**

Classic episode
Episode 1 | *November 12, 2009*. The traditional superhero origin story introduces a bunch of misfits on a community payback scheme. During an unexpected storm, some unexpected powers are revealed. Cue murder number one.

⊕ (L–R) Nathan Stewart-Jarrett (Curtis), Antonia Thomas (Alisha), Robert Sheehan (Nathan), Lauren Socha Kelly), and Iwan Rheon (Simon).

Being Erica

Comedy | Canada | 2009–11

Time travel enables the "me" generation to right the wrongs it has committed

Classic episode
Leo | *Season 1, episode 13*. After traveling back in time to say goodbye to her deceased brother one last time, Erica cannot resist the temptation to change the future, with heartbreaking consequences.

◉ In the season finale, Erin Karpluk as Erica ends up right back where she started.

Cast | Erin Karpluk, Michael Riley, Reagan Pasternak, Tyron Leitso, Adam Fergus, Sebastian Pigott, Morgan Kelly
Original broadcaster | CBC
For fans of . . . | *Saving Grace* (2007)

Wouldn't life be perfect if you could wave a magic wand and fix all your mistakes? That was exactly the opportunity that thirtysomething Erica Strange (Erin Karpluk) was offered by therapist Dr. Tom (Michael Riley), when he gave her the power to travel back in time to undo her many regrets. However, Erica soon realized that some things needed to happen for a reason. Gaining a sense of perspective and agency throughout her re-experiences, she was able to learn from her past and accept responsibility for her actions.

Rejecting the "will they, won't they" conceit of many shows with male and female leads, *Being Erica* revelled in having a clearly non-sexual relationship between Erica and Dr. Tom. Importantly, the characters grew with the show, and what could have been a shallow initial premise was handled with warmth and humor by the writers. Family and friendship were key throughout, with Erica's "do overs" centering as much on the needs of others as on her own, sometimes selfish, wishes. Although the initial focus was on Erica's past life, *Being Erica* became increasingly confident in its time travel rhetoric, sending its protagonist into the future and alternate realities. Despite the sci-fi trappings, modern Toronto life had rarely been shown as vibrantly as it was in *Being Erica*, happily rejecting stereotypes of religion, sexuality, and race. Sold worldwide to thirty-five countries, with plans for both US and UK remakes, the show was one of Canadian TV's most successful exports: funny, quirky, and uplifting. **EB**

United States of Tara

Drama | USA | 2009–11

Just your average mother, teenager, biker dude, housewife . . .

Cast | Toni Collette, Rosemarie DeWitt, John Corbett, Keir Gilchrist, Brie Larson
Original broadcaster | Showtime
Awards | 2 Emmys, 1 Golden Globe
For fans of . . . | *Weeds* (2005), *Californication* (2007)

Tara Gregson (Toni Collette) had suffered for most of her life from dissociative identity disorder, in which she experienced a transition into a number of alternative personalities whose characteristics were informed by Tara's life experiences. Consequently, life was never dull. Her condition was kept in check by medication, but Tara sometimes tried to do without the pills in an effort to live her life in a normal way. This could came across as irresponsible to her family, especially to her sister Charmaine (Rosemarie DeWitt), who felt that her older sister's attention-grabbing behavior had overshadowed her entire life.

When Tara was stressed, her alternate personalities (or "Alters" as they were referred to) came out almost as a defense mechanism. The problem was that some of the Alters thought they should have dominance over Tara and live their own lives. Alice, a matriarchal self-styled 1950s wife and a devout Catholic, held the strongest claim to be permanently in control.

The show originated from Steven Spielberg, and it was handed to movie screenwriter Diablo Cody to realize. Diablo's previous work on the films *Juno* (2007) and *Jennifer's Body* (2009) demonstrated her ability to write strong, touching, and believable characters while deriving dark comedic moments out of everyday situations. Australian actress and Academy Award nominee Toni Collette agreed to star in the TV show, marking a return to the small screen for the first time since her acting debut almost twenty years earlier. **MC**

Classic episode
Transition | *Season 1, episode 6.* Man's-man Buck drunkenly opens the episode, Tara's parents visit her with the hope of taking their grandchildren home with them, and a new (fourth) alter ego called Gimme closes the episode with a shock!

◬ Toni Collette as Tara Gragson's teenage alter ego T in season three.

Castle

Crime/Mystery | USA | 2009–present

A successful novelist works with hard-bitten police officers to solve crimes: murder has seldom been such fun

Cast | Nathan Fillion, Stana Katic, Susan Sullivan, Molly C. Quinn
Original broadcaster | ABC
For fans of . . . | *Murder She Wrote* (1984), *Moonlighting* (1985)

Richard Castle (Nathan Fillion) is a celebrated crime novelist who kills off his successful book character, just as a copycat serial killer starts a murder spree based on the deaths in his books. Only by teaming up with Detective Kate Beckett (Stana Katic) can Castle clear his own name, solve the crime, and embark on a new literary endeavor that brings him closer to Beckett.

Debuting in 2009 as a mid-season replacement, *Castle* did well enough to warrant an immediate order for a full second season. The premise of a novelist being allowed to shadow a New York detective for writing inspiration could have had a limited shelf-life. But across seven seasons, *Castle* has grown in popularity and its ratings have risen steadily. Much of this is down to the expert casting of Castle and Beckett. Nathan Fillion is the epitome of likable, clownish charm as Castle, while Stana Katic is an excellent detective and more than a capable foil for Castle's wisecracking. Around this central duo is ranged a solid ensemble that creates a very grounded and watchable crime drama.

Romance between lead characters in other shows has historically led to swift cancellation, but the growing attraction between Castle and Beckett is the driving force here, their relationship allowed to develop over several seasons without dominating the line and length of investigative stories. At the close of season six, Castle and Beckett were set to marry, but a cliff-hanger ending left Castle's life in doubt, his car a burning wreck. Will the writer and the cop ever tie the knot? **MW**

Classic episode
After the Storm | *Season 5, episode 1*. It's the morning after the night before for Castle and Beckett. While they contemplate their next move, they must track down the killer responsible for the murder of Beckett's mother. And fast.

⊙ Nathan Fillion as Castle in the season one episode "A Death in the Family."

Lie to Me

Crime/Mystery | USA | 2009–11

He knows when you're lying, even when you don't answer the questions: your every movement is a giveaway

Cast | Tim Roth, Kelli Williams, Brendan Hines, Monica Raymund, Hayley McFarland, Mekhi Phifer
Original broadcaster | Fox
For fans of . . . | *Numb3rs* (2005), *Bones* (2005), *Sherlock* (2010)

Much as the popular Fox series *Bones* was based loosely on scientist Kathy Reichs' life and writings, its network companion, *Lie to Me,* was based on the work of Professor Paul Ekman, the world's foremost expert on facial expression recognition, who worked as an advisor to police departments and government agencies.

Driven by guilt over not realizing that his mother was planning to commit suicide, Dr. Cal Lightman (Tim Roth) learned to study microexpressions. These expressions are extraordinarily brief, only a fraction of a second, but they convey a full range of human emotions, from joy to contempt, from sadness to shame. Some people are naturally gifted at reading microexpressions, and Dr. Lightman hired a group of talented individuals to work as consultants to various law enforcement agencies. From these facial microexpressions and involuntary body language, in conjunction with standard interrogation techniques, Lightman and his team could procure answers from people who did not utter a word.

Although well-liked by critics, *Lie to Me* never quite caught on in the United States. A production team shake-up did not help, as long-running plot threads were dropped and characters began to behave differently. Dr. Lightman went from lovable misanthrope to mean-spirited jerk. Although the end of the third season showed things getting back on track, this didn't happen quickly enough for the Fox network, and *Lie to Me*'s final episode aired in 2011. **RBA**

Classic episode
Blinded | *Season 1, episode 12.* As a copycat serial rapist blinds his victims, Cal Lightman must play verbal cat and mouse with the original rapist—a master at deception—to gain clues that will help the FBI profile the copycat.

◉ Tim Roth as Dr. Cal Lightman in the pilot episode of this undervalued series.

Better Off Ted

Comedy | USA | 2009–10

Veridian Dynamics—you either work for us or against us

Cast | Jay Harrington, Portia de Rossi, Andrea Anders, Jonathan Slavin
Original broadcaster | ABC **For fans of . . .** | *Arrested Development* (2003), *30 Rock* (2006)

Spookily like a comedy version of *Fringe* (2008), *Better Off Ted* was the story of products manager Ted and Veridian Dynamics, a faceless evil corporation intent on world domination. They made killer robots, artificial life, and weaponized pumpkins. The show was about people trapped inside a system that they knew was wrong. They knew they were making the world worse, and yet they couldn't help being obsessed by their bonus packages or the new sweetener in the kitchens. Jay Harrington's Ted was clearly a wonderful person to work for, but Portia de Rossi's Veronica was the highlight of the show. A microwaved mix of Servalan and Darth Vader, she ruled with a cold, velvet fist. Charming and chilling in equal measure, *Better Off Ted* made serious points about modern morals and workplace politics. It was warmly narrated by Ted, and viewers were left hoping that he found happiness—even if he did bring about the end of the world. The show was interrupted frequently by brilliant fake adverts for Veridian Dynamics, blending genuine cheesy corporate stock video footage with creepy slogans. **JG**

> **Classic episode**
> *Racial Sensitivity* | *Season 1, episode 4*. Veridian Dynamics installs new motion sensors, but they can't see black employees. "It's actually the opposite of racist," insists Veronica, "because it's not targeting black people. It's just ignoring them."

◉ Jay Harrington as Ted (with tray) and his team in the season 2 episode "Beating a Dead Workforce."

Party Down

Comedy | USA | 2009–10

Out-of-work actors moonlight for a catering company

Cast | Adam Scott, Jane Lynch, Ken Marino, Ryan Hansen, Martin Starr, Lizzy Caplan, Megan Mullally
Original broadcaster | Starz **For fans of . . .** | *The Office* (2001), *Parks and Recreation* (2009), *Archer* (2009)

Creators Rob Thomas (*Veronica Mars*, 2004), Dan Etheridge, and Paul Rudd (*Parks and Recreation*, 2009) struck gold with *Party Down*, a comedy about out-of-work actors who worked at a small-time catering company. The show followed Henry Pollard (Adam Scott), who had found minor success early in his career when he appeared in a well-known beer ad, but couldn't land a job afterward. Finally, dispirited and broke, Henry decided to give up acting and rejoined Party Down, a catering company where he had once worked. For two seasons, Henry went from event to event playing the straight man to his oddball colleagues and clients, and nursing a crush on his insecure aspiring comedian workmate Casey (Lizzy Caplan). *Party Down* delighted in dropping its characters into increasingly uncomfortable situations, constantly forcing them to re-evaluate their priorities. The show's dry, dark humor never overwhelmed its cast, and the actors brought true warmth and chemistry to their roles. Although the entire cast was superb, Jane Lynch (*Glee*, 2009) was a standout as a manic, clueless former actress. **AP**

Classic episode
Willow Canyon Homeowners' Party | Season 1, episode 1. When Steve Guttenberg (playing himself) forgets to cancel his own birthday party, he invites the Party Down team to hang out and enjoy themselves at his house.

◈ (L–R) Adam Scott (Henry), Lizzy Caplan (Casey), Megan Mullally (Lydia), Ken Marino (Ron), and Martin Starr (Roman).

Modern Family

Comedy | USA | 2009–present

One big—straight, gay, multicultural, traditional—happy family

Cast | Ed O'Neill, Ty Burrell, Julie Bowen, Jesse Tyler Ferguson, Sofía Vergara, Eric Stonestreet
Original broadcaster | ABC
Awards | 21 Emmys, 1 Golden Globe
For fans of . . . | *Arrested Development* (2003)

The Pritchett clan is fairly diverse. In the first season, patriarch Jay (Ed O'Neill) is married to Gloria (Sofía Vergara), a fiery Latina woman half his age; at home with them they have a baby son and Manny (Rico Rodriguez), a fourteen-year-old from Gloria's previous marriage. Also in the picture, but no longer in the parental home, is Jay's grown-up daughter Claire (Julie Bowen), her assiduously immature husband, real-estate agent Phil (Ty Burrell), and their three demanding children: Haley (Sarah Hyland), Alex (Ariel Winter), and Luke (Nolan Gould). In another part of Los Angeles, Jay's son Mitchell (Jesse Tyler Ferguson), a lawyer, and his husband Cameron (Eric Stonestreet) have adopted a Vietnamese baby. It may not be a typical American family, but it certainly is a funny one.

Modern Family was an immediate success for ABC, winning many high-profile awards in its first season. This is in no small part due to the brilliant core cast, particularly sitcom veteran Ed O'Neill (*Married with Children*, 1987), breakout star Sofía Vergara as his firebrand wife, and Ty Burrell as the classic "cool father" who sometimes demonstrates as little sense as his dimwit son. Often crass but always very funny, and poignant glimpse into the nature of family life in the twenty-first century, the series has been widely lauded for its writing and sharp direction. Its pseudo-documentary style is reminiscent of *The Office* (2001). **SL**

◀ The season five finale covers one of the most chaotic wedding ceremonies in the history of matrimony.

Bored to Death

Comedy | USA | 2009–11

Quirky private-eye comedy with the emphasis on character, not crime

Cast | Jason Schwartzman, Ted Danson, Zach Galifianakis
Original broadcaster | HBO **For fans of . . .** | *Moonlighting* (1985), *Rake* (2010)

For viewers who like metafiction, *Bored to Death* was a comedy by Jonathan Ames about a writer named Jonathan Ames. Set in Brooklyn, the fictional Ames (Jason Schwartzman) was a struggling author who decided to become a private detective. Though his initial cases were easily resolved, he was soon forced to call for backup from his friends—frustrated comic-book writer Ray Hueston (Zach Galifianakis) and narcissistic magazine editor George Christopher (Ted Danson). The series focused on these characters and their relationship, to the point that the crime-solving took a backseat. This was not a bad thing, since these three characters—and indeed the supporting cast—were so compelling. They all struggled in different ways—

although they all shared a keenness for marijuana—and their clumsy attempts at detective work were a real delight.

Running for twenty-four episodes over three seasons, *Bored to Death* was a wickedly subversive comedy that ended much too soon. However, a TV movie is currently in development. **SO**

> **Classic episode**
> *The Case of the Missing Screenplay* | *Season 1, episode 3*. Jonathan gets the opportunity to submit a screenplay to director Jim Jarmusch, but leaves it in a therapist's office when he has a romantic liaison with the therapist's daughter.

⊘ (L–R) Ted Danson as George Christopher, Zach Galifianakis as Ray Hueston, and Jason Schwartzman as Jonathan Ames.

The League

Comedy | USA | 2009–present

A fantasy football league that brings out the worst in the participants

Cast | Mark Duplass, Nick Kroll, Stephen Rannazzisi, Paul Scheer, Jon Lajoie, Katie Aselton
Original broadcaster | FX   **For fans of . . .** | *It's Always Sunny in Philadelphia* (2005)

In this comedy, six friends compete in their version of the popular game in which each player picks an imaginary team of real-life major league footballers, and scores points for their achievements on the pitch.

Salesman Pete (Mark Duplass) has his eye so firmly on the prize that he'll stoop to anything to outdo his rivals. Assistant district attorney Kevin (Stephen Rannazzisi) knows nothing about football and gets his information from his wife, Jenny (Katie Aselton), who also participates. Lawyer Rodney (Nick Kroll) is convinced that everyone is out to get him, but this isn't paranoia, it's an evidentially based conclusion. Plastic surgeon Andre (Paul Scheer) knows little and understands less. The other team member is Kevin's kid brother, Taco (Jon Lajoie).

While the fantasy league is the focal point of the show, plenty of comedy comes from the main characters' relations with work colleagues and past, present, and prospective lovers. Outstanding among a strong roster of stars making occasional guest appearances is Jeff Goldblum as Rodney's witheringly sarcastic father, Rupert. **GL**

Classic episode

The Guest Bong | *Season 3, episode 11.* Pete's new girlfriend tries to influence his team lineup, but does she know what she's talking about? Meanwhile, an autocorrect error on an email gets all six friends into trouble.

◑ The ensemble cast in an episode from season five titled "The Credit Card Alert."

Dollhouse

Fantasy/Horror/Sci-Fi | USA | 2009–10

You can wipe away a memory, but can you wipe away a soul? Joss Whedon's cult series was more interested in the question than the answer

Cast | Eliza Dushku, Harry Lennix, Fran Kranz, Tahmoh Penikett, Enver Gjokaj, Dichen Lachman, Olivia Williams, Miracle Laurie, Amy Acker, Reed Diamond
Original broadcaster | Fox
For fans of . . . | *Firefly* (2002)

Writer and director Joss Whedon's return to TV after *Firefly* opened a window onto a dark world in which mind-wiped people, known as dolls, were used as repositories for the memories and skills of others. Initially focusing on the dolls fulfilling the fantasies of wealthy clients, the show later concentrated more on the ethics and morality of the Dollhouse itself.

Dollhouse was a fascinating challenge of a series. Many of the major characters began as blank slates, taking on the memories and personalities of the characters that they were imprinted with for each episode. The show starred Eliza Dushku as series lead Echo, best-known at that time for her role as Faith in *Buffy the Vampire Slayer* (1997). As Echo returned from her missions, she found that the memory-wiping process used between assignments wasn't working, and she began to develop her own personality.

The first half of season one concentrated on mission-of-the-week style episodes for Echo, and it was only after these introductory stories had passed that the series engaged fully with its theme. What are the ethical implications of being human, and if we had the technology to move our sense of self from one body to another, what effects would that have on the world? If a new personality is created in someone's body, what rights ought that new person to have? *Dollhouse* depicted a world in which people were used as tools and playthings for the rich and powerful. If that makes you uncomfortable—it should. **PB**

Classic episode
Epitaph One | *Season 1, episode 13*. Twenty years into the future, we learn the fate of the Dollhouse and of the human race, as well as where the memory-imprinting technology leads. It isn't pretty.

◉ Eliza Dushku as Echo in the season one episode "Gray Hour."

Un village français

Drama | France | 2009–present

Resistance and collaboration in occupied wartime France

Cast | Robin Renucci, Audrey Fleurot, Marie Kremer, Francis Renaud, Nicolas Gob, Richard Sammel
Original broadcaster | France 3
For fans of . . . | *Moonstrike* (1963), *Clochemerle* (1972), *Spiral* (2005)

Un village français (*A French Village*) is a year-by-year study of the inhabitants of Villeneuve, a fictional hamlet on the Franco–German frontier, after the Nazi invasion of France in 1940.

The local residents react to the Occupation in many different ways. Some attempt to ignore the disruption, and carry on their lives as normal; others actively and willingly collaborate with the Germans, either because they sympathize with their aims, or merely to stay out of trouble. Those who are implacably opposed to the enemy forces join the Resistance and go into hiding.

The German troops have similarly mixed motives and feelings. Some are conscripts who would rather be at home; some disapprove of Hitler. Others, however, are enthusiastically brutal: the Gestapo is active in the village, crushing known and suspected opponents, and scouring the countryside for saboteurs. Even more ruthless than the Nazi secret police is Heinrich Müller (Richard Sammel), an SS officer who is later put in charge of Villeneuve.

As the tide of the Second World War turns against the Nazis, more and more of the village's resources are siphoned off for frontline troops. Meanwhile, there is increasing pressure to fulfill the requisite quotas of Jews for deportation to concentration camps.

Un village français is undeniably bleak, but it shows human responses to adversity in all its forms. It has been a hit in France, and has been exported to Belgium, Canada, South Korea, and Switzerland. **GL**

Nurse Jackie

Drama | USA | 2009–15

The problems of running a family and a substance habit

Cast | Edie Falco, Merritt Wever, Paul Schulze, Eve Best, Dominic Fumusa, Anna Deavere Smith, Peter Facinelli
Original broadcaster | Showtime
Awards | 5 Emmys
For fans of . . . | *Scrubs* (2001), *No Angels* (2004)

Jackie Peyton (Edie Falco) was a wife, a mother, and a nurse at All Saints Hospital; she was also addicted to prescription drugs. Keeping all the plates spinning as well as the lies wasn't easy, but Jackie just about pulled it off. It was her compassion, acerbic wit, and relationships with her work colleagues, mixed with the toxic decline of addiction, which brought such dark humor and drama to this series.

There was Eddie (Paul Schulze), the hospital pharmacist, who unwittingly assisted Jackie with her habit; Zoey (Merritt Wever), the intern who had a very ditzy view on life; Ellie O'Hara (Eve Best), who was the polar opposite to the caring nurse; Dr. Fitch Cooper (Peter Facinelli), who had a very interesting Tourettes response to stressful situations; Thor (Stephen Wallem) the gentle giant of a nurse looking for the love of a good man; and Akalitis (Anna Deavere Smith), the hospital administrator who did things by the book. Jackie's balancing act with husband Kevin (Dominic Fumusa), who ran a bar, and their children, who were developing dysfunctional habits of their own, only added to the complexities of her double life.

On paper it would appear to be hard to feel any sympathy for Jackie, an accident looking for a place to happen, but Falco gave all those flaws and imperfections such a level of humanity that the viewer couldn't help but fall in love with her. Best and Wever were perfect foils, adding depth to their characters with unfailingly brilliant comic timing and subtle pathos. **JV**

Getting On

Comedy | UK | 2009–12

Bleakly satirical comedy about the staff and patients of a geriatric ward

Cast | Jo Brand, Vicki Pepperdine, Joanna Scanlan, Ricky Grover
Original broadcaster | BBC Four
Award | 1 BAFTA
For fans of . . . | *The Thick of It* (2005)

Situation comedy has found many successes in unlikely settings—a prison, a Korean War field hospital, the office of a stationery supplier—but none is quite as unlikely as the National Health Service geriatric ward that formed the backdrop to *Getting On*. But against this unpromising, often bleak background, its three writers and lead actresses produced something remarkable: a believable take on hospital life that was never less than brilliantly funny across its fifteen episodes.

For all its darkness, *Getting On* remained very much a traditional sitcom in one crucial respect: it was driven by the sharply observed relationships between its beautifully written and played main characters. The mutual antipathy between the high-handed and insensitive Dr. Pippa Moore and the ward's nursing staff was palpable but a master class in understatement. The awkward—and terribly misguided—developing romance between Sister Den Flixter and the ward's male matron, Hilary Loftus, was both agonizing and touching. Throughout, there was no "playing for laughs"; every line and look was delivered straight.

Getting On carved itself a place in a strong satirical tradition in contemporary British comedy. As *The Thick of It* is to Westminster politics and *W1A* is to the BBC, *Getting On* is to the modern NHS. With these immaculately judged scripts and performances, Jo Brand, Vicky Pepperdine, and Joanna Scanlan have created a sitcom with something to say that merits a place alongside the very best of the genre. **HE**

RuPaul's Drag Race

Reality | USA | 2009–present

It takes a showbiz legend. . . to make a drag superstar

Cast | RuPaul, Michelle Visage, Santino Rice, Merle Ginsberg
Original broadcaster | Logo
For fans of . . . | *The Dame Edna Experience* (1987), *Big Brother* (2000), *Survivor* (2000)

RuPaul—the actor, musician, and performer who more than anyone bridged the gap between the art of female impersonation and mainstream viewership, beginning in the late 1980s with the dance club hit "Supermodel"—is the executive producer and host of this reality series, which crosses the cutthroat maneuvers of *Survivor* with the fashion-conscious wit of *Project Runway*.

Bringing between twelve and fourteen unknowns to the stage in order to give them the opportunity to show their charisma, uniqueness, nerve, and talent, *RuPaul's Drag Race* offers a modern look at the art of female impersonation. The contestants' appearance counts for something, of course, but it is not the be-all and end-all: the competition also requires proficiency in many areas: wardrobe design, makeup, presentation skills and the ability to work under pressure. At the same time, it asks important questions about gender roles in society.

Although it's not exactly high art, the appeal of *RuPaul's Drag Race* is both in the cavalcade of drag personalities and the plenitude of guest judges: joining regulars RuPaul, actress/musician Michelle Visage and designer Santino Rice have been the likes of Paula Abdul, Pamela Anderson, Neil Patrick Harris and Sharon Osbourne. However, it's really all about RuPaul and conveys a clear message about acceptance, which he summarized as: "If you can't love yourself, how the hell are you gonna love somebody else?" **SL**

India—A Love Story

Drama | Brazil | 2009

Caste is no insuperable barrier to romance in this series exploring the pride and pitfalls of love across the tracks

Cast | Juliana Paes, Márcio Garcia, Letícia Sabatella, Cléo Pires, Laura Cardoso, Christiane Torloni
Original broadcaster | TV Globo
Award | 1 Emmy
For fans of . . . | *Terra Nostra* (1999), *Love Story* (2008)

Having hit big with writer Glória Perez's *O Clone* (2001) and *Amazônia: De Galvez a Chico Mendes* (2007), Brazilian broadcaster TV Globo ensured its next collaboration with the author would become event television. At its heart was a story of forbidden love between Maya (Juliana Paes), from a traditional, rich Indian family, and Bahuan (Márcio Garcia), from an untouchable lower caste. Drawing on India's history, and adding a telenovela's cocktail of intrigue and romance, *India—A Love Story* was epic in scale.

At $80 million (£55 million), it was among the most expensive and ambitious telenovelas ever made. Shooting began in Brazil—where two Indian towns were built on a backlot—before moving to India and Dubai. The resulting 160 hours aired between January and September 2009, conjuring images of, as *Variety* noted, "a colorful India complete with mystic figures, magnificent palaces and temples, and chaotic traffic."

The premise was far from bulletproof, with no guarantee that Brazilian viewers would take to an across-the-tracks romance in a different country. "We had to focus a lot on gestures to help the people in Brazil understand and connect with the story," Paes told *The Times of India*. Yet the show's final episode secured an 81-percent audience share, and broadcasting rights were sold to more than ninety countries. "I have done several shows, but the impact has never been this great," Paes observed. "Women were like, 'Oh my god, we need an Indian husband!'" **BM**

Classic episode
Episode 1 | *January 19, 2009*. Confirming Globo's "event televison" vision, the show proved a ratings smash from its first episode. Far from being turned off by overseas characters, the viewers were spellbound as the story unfolded.

◉ Juliana Paes with two of her numerous male admirers.

Community
Comedy | USA | 2009–present

Genre-bending comedy that proves it really is chic to be geek

Cast | Joel McHale, Gillian Jacobs, Donald Glover, Danny Pudi, Alison Brie, Chevy Chase, Rob Corddry
Original broadcaster | NBC/Yahoo Screen   **Award** | 1 Emmy   **For fans of . . .** | *New Girl* (2011)

Created by writer Dan Harmon, the show is deliberately reminiscent of teen classics such as *The Breakfast Club* (1985). There's Troy the sports hero, Abed the weird one, Shirley the comforting one, Jeff the cool one, Britta the political one, Annie the pretty one, and Pierce, the grinchy one. The cast is very strong, and the relationship between Troy and Abed is particularly delightful (modeled on the relationship between Geordie and Data in *Star Trek: The Next Generation*). The invocation of *Star Trek* is only the start of the media in-jokes, though. Where *Community* stands head and shoulders above other TV shows is in its brilliantly clever and playful use of characters and set pieces from other shows and movies. From "A Fistful of Paintballs", a riff

on the Western set during a paintball tournament, to "Epidemiolog," in which the dean's use of mystery meat sets off a zombie plague, and from the chicken finger-based mafia movie episode "Contemporary American Poultry," to the tangled plots of "Conspiracy Theories" and "Interior Design," *Community* has been consistently the smartest take on TV to be found on TV. **RL**

Classic episode
Remedial Chaos Theory | *Season 3, episode 4.*
Jeff rolls a dice to see who's going for pizza, and Abed points out that this has created six alternate time lines. Shows what the group would be like without each member in turn.

⊘ Rob Corddry as Alan Connor and Joel McHale as Jeff Winger in the opening episode of season five, titled "Repilot."

The Good Wife

Drama | USA | 2009–present

His scandal, her story—as smart as it is witty

Cast | Julianna Margulies, Josh Charles, Christine Baranski, Archie Panjabi, Matt Czuchry, Chris Noth
Original broadcaster | CBS   **Awards** | 5 Emmys, 1 Golden Globe   **For fans of . . .** | *Revenge* (2011)

The legal drama seemed played out, but then along came *The Good Wife*. The titular wife is Alicia Florrick (Julianna Margulies), who was left as a single mum when her high-profile husband was sent to prison on corruption charges. Forced to return to work as a lawyer after years away, she starts at the very bottom alongside super-competitive youngster Cary Agos (Matt Czuchry). She faces week-by-week trials in court and season-long political arcs that rival *The West Wing* (1999) at its best. Around her is one of the best ensemble casts on TV, supported by a host of memorable recurring characters. Michael J. Fox as shady lawyer Louis Canning is just one of the star-turn guests that the show's top-quality writing is able to

attract. Moral compromises are at the heart of *The Good Wife*, and it is seeing Alicia struggling to make the "right" choice when none truly exists that often propels the narrative. But in a TV era in which moral ambiguity is often twinned with nihilism and brutality, *The Good Wife* is that rarest of all things: a show that can be light about being serious. **RL**

Classic episode
Red Team, Blue Team | *Season 4, episode 14.*
Seething resentments and dishonesties threaten to tear Lockhart apart, as Alicia and Cary's fake courtroom conflict with Will and Diane becomes all too real. Wicked David Lee stirs the pot.

Julianna Margulies as Alicia Florrick and Chris Noth as Peter Florrick share a rare moment together onstage.

Parks and Recreation

Comedy | USA | 2009–15

Public servants struggle to cut administrative red tape

Cast | Amy Poehler, Rashida Jones, Aziz Ansari, Nick Offerman, Chris Pratt, Adam Scott, Rob Lowe
Original broadcaster | NBC
Awards | 1 Emmy, 1 Golden Globe
For fans of . . . | *The Office* (2005), *30 Rock* (2006)

This satire on local government was filmed in the manner of a fly-on-the-wall documentary. The protagonist was Leslie Knope (Amy Poehler), deputy director of the Parks and Recreation Department in the fictional town of Pawnee, Indiana. The action began when a local resident demanded that an abandoned construction pit be filled in because it was a danger to health and safety. Leslie approved the plan, but then faced opposition from her boss, Ron Swanson (Nick Offerman), a right-wing libertarian.

Early episodes produced a tepid critical response and discouraging viewing figures. The producers responded by instructing the writers to work in topical references, often at the last minute before filming. Their move turned a potential flop into a huge success.

In season six, the neighboring town of Eagleton went bankrupt, and was absorbed into Pawnee. This inspired further machinations, as public servants in both places competed to get the best they could.

The underlying theme of *Parks and Recreation* was that most people are well intentioned, but that their best-laid plans are often subverted, sometimes by dishonesty, but more often by intractable bureaucracy.

In 2014, Poehler won a Golden Globe for her role as Leslie. Among other outstanding performances was that of Rob Lowe, who appeared in seventy-seven episodes as state auditor Chris Traeger. **GL**

◐ Chris Pratt as Andy Dwyer, Adam Scott as Ben Wyatt, and Amy Poehler as Leslie Knope.

Garrow's Law

Historical drama | UK | 2009–12

Period legal drama introduces the principle of innocent until proven guilty

Cast | Andrew Buchan, Lyndsey Marshal, Rupert Graves, Alun Armstrong, Aidan McArdle, Michael Culkin, Sean Biggerstaff, Martin Savage
Original broadcaster | BBC One
For fans of . . . | *Foyle's War* (2002), *City of Vice* (2008)

Garrow's Law gave BBC One a chance to combine its skill at period pieces with the popularity of legal fiction. The show was inspired by eighteenth-century barrister William Garrow, a real-life reformer of legal processes of the United Kingdom. His aggressive defense techniques led to the development of the adversarial system still used in courts today (before this system, the accused had to defend themselves). He introduced the concept of "innocent until proven guilty," which remains the backbone of the modern global judiciary.

Filmed on location in Edinburgh and Glasgow, each episode started with a real trial, sourced from accounts of contemporaneous Old Bailey trials—it was the publication of these online in 2008 that led to the rediscovery of Garrow's work. The introductory trials cemented the show's basis within historical fact before segueing into fictional cases, often based on real events—such as that of James Hadfield, accused of attempting to assassinate King George III.

Thankfully for the purposes of drama, William Garrow's private life was not entirely without scandal, and the show relished exploring his relationship with Sarah Dore, with whom he had two illegitimate children before finally marrying her a decade later. For modern audiences, however, this was not quite scandal enough. For the purposes of fiction in *Garrow's Law*, Sarah Dore was married off to Sir Arthur Hill—in real life they had a child but never married—and much drama was wrung out of this subplot. **EB**

Classic episode

Season 1, episode 3. Garrow successfully defends Edgar Cole for raping a servant, despite his obvious guilt. Later, Garrow has the opportunity to take revenge on Forrester, a thief-catcher who caused Garrow's first client to lose his life.

Legal eagles: Andrew Buchan (William Garrow) and Alun Armstrong (John Southouse).

Whitechapel

Crime/Mystery | UK | 2009–13

The nightmare of Jack the Ripper lasted less than a year in 1888; now it begins again

Cast | Rupert Penry-Jones, Philip Davis, Steve Pemberton, Claire Rushbrook
Original broadcaster | ITV
For fans of . . . | *Wire in the Blood* (2002), *Wallander* (2008), *Ripper Street* (2012)

When *Whitechapel* premiered it seemed that it would be no more than a three-part crime drama following a group of detectives who find themselves investigating a sequence of modern murders that ape the infamous Jack the Ripper killings. However, the show was such a success—its characters so compelling and its darkly sinister depiction of East London so mesmerizing—that it returned for more short-run series, each more gloriously ghastly than the last.

Jack the Ripper was hardly an original inspiration for crime fiction, and *Whitechapel* had to fight hard to stand out from the crowd. It helped that the central detective partnership between obsessive-compulsive loner Chandler (Rupert Penry-Jones) and his down-to-earth sergeant, Miles (Philip Davis), was so unexpectedly touching. They anchored the viewer in a show that was genuinely terrifying at times, especially when it trod the line between realism and out-and-out supernatural chills. As the cases expanded to include one that was very similar to the crimes of the notorious Kray twins and then three wholly fictional but deeply twisted murders, the true breadth of the premise—that new crimes follow old patterns—was revealed.

It is extraordinary that in the crowded field of detective dramas *Whitechapel* managed to feel entirely unique. It succeeded by being absolutely committed to its own gothic horror aesthetic, bringing a Victorian look and feel to the modern East End that worked astonishingly well. It was grim, gripping, and strangely fun. **RL**

Classic episode
Episode 9 | February 13, 2012. A gruesome opening sees a fox running through the dark London streets with a severed human arm in its mouth. As more parts of the dismembered body are found, Chandler and the team close in.

◑ Rupert Penry-Jones as DI Joseph Chandler and Philip Davis as DS Ray Miles in season four.

The Vampire Diaries

Fantasy/Horror/Sci-Fi | USA | 2009–present

Love triangle involving one innocent young girl and two aged vampires

Cast | Nina Dobrev, Paul Wesley, Ian Somerhalder, Steven R. McQueen, Sara Canning, Kat Graham
Original broadcaster | The CW **For fans of . . .** | *Buffy the Vampire Slayer* (1997), *Angel* (1999), *True Blood* (2008)

Based on the eponymous book by L.J Smith, this has proven to be one of the most popular supernatural "young adult" shows around. It has won multiple Teen Choice awards, gained a band of loyal followers, and to date has run for seven seasons. The series follows young protagonist Elena Gilbert (Nina Dobrev) as she falls madly in love with 163-year-old vampire Stefan Salvatore (Paul Wesley), which in turn drags her into a supernatural world. When Stefan's sinister brother Damon (Ian Somerhalder) arrives on the scene, Elena cannot help falling in love with him, too.

The pilot episode of *The Vampire Diaries* attracted the The CW network's biggest audience for any series since it began to operate in 2006; it remains its most-watched

series. Somerhalder, one of the show's standout stars, has gained both critical acclaim and many awards.

Less overtly adult and sexual than similarly themed programs such as *True Blood*, *The Vampire Diaries'* die-hard fan base and visually pleasing cast make for a winning combination in a time when pop culture feels a bit swamped by vampire romance fiction. **JE**

> **Classic episode**
> *1912* | *Season 3, episode 16.* Stefan and Damon recall the year in which a serial killer terrorized Mystic Falls. Stefan drinks human blood on Damon's instruction, and Elena later sees him bite the neck of a girl.

⊘ Nina Dobrev, Ian Somerhalder, and Kelly Hu in "Children of the Damned," a flashback episode in season one.

Glee

Comedy/Drama | USA | 2009–15

Join the club—amazinglee, excitinglee, surprisinglee

Cast | Chris Colfer, Jane Lynch, Kevin McHale, Lea Michele, Matthew Morrison, Amber Riley, Cory Monteith, Dianna Agron **Original broadcaster** | Fox **Awards** | 6 Emmys, 4 Golden Globes **For fans of . . .** | *Fame* (1980)

The brainchild of Ryan Murphy, Brad Falchuk, and Ian Brennan, *Glee* revolved around New Directions, the William McKinley High School glee club, which competed on the show choir competition circuit while its numerous members dealt with relationships, bullying, physical and mental disabilities, sexuality, and social issues, and learned to become an effective team.

The initial twelve characters included a club director and Spanish teacher and his wife, a cheerleading coach, a guidance counselor, and eight student club members. In later seasons the main cast expanded to fourteen and fifteen members. A highlight of *Glee* was its performances of musical numbers, a clever mix of show tunes and chart hits. A breakout hit that spanned

generations, *Glee* was genuinely new in the way it wove musical performances into the show proper—a technique that had succeeded in movies but not on TV. The music also made the show's social messages more digestible, heightening audience responses to learning of villain Sue's soft spot for her mentally disabled sister, for example, or watching Kurt's coming-out process. **RL**

> **Classic episode**
> *The Quarterback* | *Season 5, episode 3*. A tribute episode to actor Cory Monteith, who had died months earlier. Monteith's character, Finn, was eulogized by current and returning characters and cast members.

◭ Darren Criss as Blaine takes centerstage as the Glee club gives it their all in rehearsal.

Warehouse 13

Fantasy/Horror/Sci-Fi | USA | 2009–14

Absurd sci-fi capers in which the unknown has an address

Cast | Joanne Kelly, Eddie McClintock, Saul Rubinek, Allison Scagliotti, Aaron Ashmore
Original broadcaster | Syfy **For fans of . . .** | *Stargate: Atlantis* (2004), *Eureka* (2006), *Misfits* (2009)

The Syfy network had found critical success with *Battlestar Gallactica* (2004), but it struggled to find a true breakout hit until *Warehouse 13* came along. It quickly became the highest-rated show on the channel and proved that quality did not correlate with budget as its charming cast and sharply written capers worked alongside cheap and cheerful special effects. The premise of the show was that a warehouse existed where all the weird and whacky artifacts in the world were taken for safe-keeping. Government agents were tasked with tracking down these artifacts, which were often ridiculous and sometimes genuinely sinister. Whether the agents were on the trail of acid trip-inducing reading glasses or an orchid that could infect the world with a lethal fever, they were always having fun. *Warehouse 13* was a show bursting with joyous silliness and genuine heart beneath its knowing absurdity. There was also a slow-burn "will they, won't they" romance between lead agents Pete (Eddie McClintock) and Myka (Joanne Kelly), but essentially this was a show about friendship and its power to overcome any obstacle. **RL**

Classic episode
Love Sick | *Season 3, episode 3*. As Artie and Claudia struggle to deal with a virtual virus with strangely real-world effects, Pete and Myka wake up in bed together—with absolutely no memory of how they got there.

⊗ Eddie McClintock as Pete and Joanne Kelly as Myka in the pilot.

Braquo

Crime/Mystery | France | 2009–present

Gritty, violent, morally gray crime drama justly praised as France's answer to The Wire

Cast | Jean-Hugues Anglade, Nicolas Duvauchelle, Joseph Malerba, Karole Rocher
Original broadcaster | Canal + **Award** | 1 Emmy **For fans of . . .** | *The Wire* (2002)

Braquo (from the French *braquage*, meaning "violent robbery") is a modern crime drama created by former police officer Olivier Marchal. In the depressed suburbs of Hauts-de-Seine on the outskirts of Paris, Eddy Caplan (Jean-Hugues Anglade) is a flawed hero whose heart is good but whose actions can be brutish. His colleagues too are complex: Walter Morlighem (Joseph Malerba) has a thuggish demeanor that conceals emotional depth; Théo Vachewski (Nicolas Duvauchelle) is a tattooed, coke-snorting womanizer, the very soul of French existentialism; and Roxane Delgado (Karole Rocher), the sole recurring female character, is a chain-smoking ice queen, whose tough exterior hides inner sadness. When their friend and colleague Max

Rossi (Olivier Rabourdin) is falsely accused of criminal misconduct in the line of duty, he commits suicide, thus proving his guilt in all but the eyes of those closest to him. The four police officers swear to do whatever is necessary to clear his name. The show was an immediate hit, breaking record audience figures for an original drama produced by Canal+. **MS**

> **Classic episode**
> *La ligne jaune* (*The Yellow Line*) | *Season 1, episode 2.* The group comes under pressure. Vachewski discovers that he's been betrayed by his own attorney. Morlighem asks Caplan to help him clear his gambling debts.

◎ Eddy Caplan (Jean-Hugues Anglade, standing) and his loyal crew.

Ratings have shrunk with the arrival of more TV stations, yet we remain loyal to the same type of stories viewers enjoyed fifty years ago. We still love detectives like Sherlock, science fiction shows like *Doctor Who*, and historical epics like *Game of Thrones*. With so many demands on our leisure time, this is the age of the TV box set, when we binge on entire series in one long sitting. But with the entire history of TV to choose from on DVD or online, we can be in Westeros one minute and in the Twilight Zone the next. A new Golden Age? It could be…

2010s

◐ Bob Odenkirk (kneeling) in trouble again as Saul Goodman in the *Breaking Bad* spin-off and prequel *Better Call Saul* (2015).

Hatufim

Drama | Israel | 2010–12

This show was successful in its own right and the progenitor of an even bigger hit in the United States—Homeland

Cast | Ishai Golan, Yoram Toledano, Gal Zaid, Yael Eitan, Salim Dau, Sendi Bar, Hadar Ratzon Rotem, Yaël Abecassis, Mili Avital, Assi Cohen, Mickey Leon, **Original broadcaster** | Channel 2
For fans of . . . | *Homeland* (2011), *Tyrant* (2014)

Gideon Raff's formative forays into Hollywood were less than auspicious. He was the assistant director on *Mr. & Mrs. Smith* (2005), then directed *The Killing Floor* (2007), a B-movie with *Buffy*'s Marc Blucas and *Roswell*'s Shiri Appleby. A feeling of exile then inspired him to create *Hatufim* (*Kidnapped*), a tale of prisoners of war coming home after an enforced absence. Among other benefits, the concept enabled him to return to his native Israel.

His pilot script was snapped up by *24* producers Howard Gordon and Alex Gansa. "We started meeting in Los Angeles to discuss turning it into an American show," Raff later explained. "A lot of the changes came down to differences between the two countries. In Israel, we negotiate with terrorists to get prisoners released. The US don't . . . [and] I wanted to show broken soldiers." While Gordon and Gansa transformed this idea into *Homeland*, Raff developed his tale of two Israeli soldiers (played by Ishai Golan and Yoram Toledano) who returned to their families after seventeen years imprisoned in Syria. While they tried to readjust to everyday living, a military investigation probed disparities in their accounts.

Considerably lower budget and grittier than its US counterpart, *Hatufim*—aka *Prisoners of War*—had no less impact. "*Homeland* is certainly exciting," author Stephen King conceded to *Entertainment Weekly*, "but, to my mind, it has never come close to the emotional resonance of the Israeli original." **BM**

Classic episode
Mivtza Yehuda | *Season 2, episode 13.* In the penultimate episode, a soldier's kidnapping has a profound and disturbing effect on Nimrod Klein (Yoram Toledano), one of the show's original pair of protagonists.

◉ Mickey Leon as Yaakov "Yaki" Zach, brother of one of the returned prisoners of war.

Accused

Crime/Mystery | UK | 2010–12

Self-contained, uncompromising dramas about people who find themselves on trial

Cast | Christopher Eccleston, Juliet Stevenson, Sean Bean
Original broadcaster | BBC One
Awards | 1 BAFTA, 2 Emmys
For fans of . . . | *Criminal Justice* (2008)

Accused had much in common with creator Jimmy McGovern's earlier anthology series, *The Street* (2006), not least in following closely his maxim: "The only way to tell stories on TV is to convince people that what they are seeing is actually happening now and is real." Each episode told the story of a different character on trial, gradually revealing what brought them to the dock. Each story stood alone, but the final episode, set in a young offenders' institution, drew together the stories of characters encountered in previous episodes.

Accused was not interested in the police procedural detail common to most crime-based drama. Instead, it focused on the interplay of character, circumstance, and social context that led to the crime. The crimes were rooted in contemporary social concerns, including gang violence, corporate negligence, and—controversially at the time of broadcast— military bullying in Afghanistan. Each episode was a shining example of the storyteller's art; over an hour of television, the pieces fell into place and the action was propelled toward its—frequently grim—climax.

McGovern and his cowriters rarely offered neat or comforting conclusions, and it was often the injustice of the situation that stayed with the viewer. *Accused*'s combination of compelling performances, unsparing but tender writing, and the way it saw each case through to its conclusion, however painful, made the series a striking entry in TV's long tradition of crime and legal drama. **HE**

The Voice

Reality | Netherlands | 2010–present

Singers aim to make judges spin around, purely on the basis of their talent

Cast | Christina Aguilera, Jessie J, Tom Jones, Ricky Martin, Gwen Stefani, Rachel Stevens, Will.i.am, Pharrell Williams
Original broadcaster | RTL4
For fans of . . . | *The X Factor* (2004)

Created by globe-conquering Dutch television producer John de Mol (see also *Big Brother* and *Deal or No Deal*), *The Voice* has rapidly spread worldwide since its inception in 2010 as a rival to the *X Factor* and *Idol* franchises. There are currently fifty-two *The Voice* franchises worldwide, plus twenty-four children's versions. With some franchises covering multiple countries, the total global audience stands at approximately eighty countries.

The premise is simple. Four judges sit in high-backed chairs, facing away from the stage while the performer sings. If they like what they hear, they spin around. The appeal of this is that the singer is judged purely on their voice, rather than theatricality or appearance. This has led to some notable scenes; for example, partially sighted UK singer Andrea Begley did not even know if any of the judges had spun their seats. In Italy, Cristina Scuccia gave the judges a shock when they spun to find a singing nun dressed in full habit. Both these memorable performers went on to win their season.

The judges are an integral part of the show, with many well-known and often contemporary celebrities taking part. If multiple judges choose a singer in the initial blind audition, the onus is on the performer to pick the judge that they wish to mentor them throughout the rest of the process. This can lead to sometimes unintentionally hilarious begging from prospective celebrity mentors if they find a singer they would particularly love to cultivate. **EB**

An Idiot Abroad

Comedy | UK | 2010–12

Or a puppet on a string

Cast | Karl Pilkington, Ricky Gervais, Stephen Merchant, Warwick Davies   **Original broadcaster** | Sky 1
For fans of . . . | *The Ricky Gervais Show* (2010), *Paul Merton's Adventures* (2011)

In 2005 Ricky Gervais and Stephen Merchant got together with their old XFM radio producer, Karl Pilkington, to release a series of podcasts. Although titled *The Ricky Gervais Show*, there was only ever one star: Karl. His bizarre outlook on the world and a propensity to say ridiculous things, combined with world-weariness beyond his years, proved comedy gold and a cult figure was born.

An Idiot Abroad was a travel program with a difference, in that Karl would visit the Pyramids of Giza and conclude that they were similar to a "massive game of Jenga that had got out of hand," for example. Each season had a theme: the Seven Wonders of the World, the bucket list, and the Marco Polo route (which he did

on a motorcycle with Warwick Davies). However, the instructions were never quite as simple as "visit Machu Picchu" or "swim with dolphins" because Gervais and Merchant devised ways to take Karl completely out of his comfort zone, and this was where much of the humor lay. There was no spin with Karl: he told it how it was, which was as refreshing as it was hilarious. **LH**

> **Classic episode**
> *Brazil* | *Season 1, episode 6*. Karl visits a gay beach, meets a drag artist, and stays in a youth hostel on the eve of carnival. He finally sees Christ the Redeemer and is surprisingly positive (except about its chin).

◬ Warwick Davis (left) and Karl Pilkington land roles in a Bollywood movie.

The Pillars of the Earth

Historical drama | USA/UK | 2010

Nothing is sacred

Cast | Rufus Sewell, Ian McShane, Matthew Macfadyen, Eddie Redmayne, Hayley Atwell, Donald Sutherland
Original broadcasters | USA, Starz; UK, Channel 4   **Award** | 1 Emmy   **For fans of . . .** | *Game of Thrones* (2011)

Based on Ken Follet's best-seller of the same name, *The Pillars of the Earth* told the story of the many lives that became intertwined as construction of a grand cathedral got under way in the fictitious town of Kingsbridge in twelfth-century Britain. It was partly based on true events surrounding the succession crisis at the end of Henry I's reign after his son and natural heir died when their ship sank in 1120. This threw the country into a period of lawlessness as several powerful factions fought for the throne.

The Pillars of the Earth was long considered by many, including Follet, to be almost impossible to turn into a movie or TV drama. Then Ridley Scott and David Zucker (*Numb3rs*, *The Good Wife*) got involved and developed the book into an eight-hour miniseries. They brought in director Sergio Mimica-Gezzan, who had previously worked with Steven Spielberg, and together they created an almost Hollywood-like quality for the show. Scott's unique aesthetic vision and passion for historical drama, in particular, were clearly visible throughout each episode. JH

Classic episode
Battlefield | *Season 1, episode 4*. Rivals, assassins, and hostages. Torture and betrayal. Important hostages are taken at the battle between King Stephen and Princess Maud. The former is tortured into a confession.

Ian McShane (Waleran), Sarah Parish (Regan), David Oakes (William), and Gordon Pinsent (Archbishop) in "Battlefield."

Boardwalk Empire

Historical drama | USA | 2010–14

The rise and fall of a notorious early twentieth-century racketeer

Cast | Steve Buscemi, Michael Pitt, Kelly Macdonald, Michael Shannon, Shea Whigham, Stephen Graham
Original broadcaster | HBO
Awards | 18 Emmys, 2 Golden Globes
For fans of . . . | *The Sopranos* (1999)

This show was inspired by a book of the same title by Nelson Johnson about real-life criminal Enoch L. Johnson, treasurer and political boss of Atlantic City, New Jersey, from the end of the First World War until the mid-1930s. After Prohibition was introduced in 1920, Enoch Johnson enriched himself by taking bribes from every speakeasy and brothel in his hometown. He became a Mafia boss, and remained powerful until jailed in 1941 for tax evasion.

The TV series was created by Terence Winter, who had previously been a writer and producer on *The Sopranos* (1999). The lead role of Nucky Thompson was played by Steve Buscemi, who had played Tony Soprano's cousin in that same show.

The pilot of *Boardwalk Empire*, directed by Martin Scorsese, cost $18 million, and set the tone for the whole fifty-six-episode, five-season run: it was moody, atmospheric, and frequently bloody.

Of all the real people depicted in the show, the most famous was mobster Al Capone, here brilliantly played by British actor Stephen Graham. One scene in particular stuck in the memory; when Capone was about to go to jail, he told his deaf son, Sonny (Alex Eckstein): "Be a good boy. Remember all I did was for you," and the boy responded with a touching gesture of affection. It was just one of many poignant moments in a series that was universally acclaimed. **GL**

> Steve Buscemi as Nucky Thompson, whose sad eyes were also those of a killer.

Borgen

Drama | Denmark | 2010–13

Show that succeeded in making Danish politics more interesting than any domestic power struggle

Cast | Sidse Babett Knudsen, Birgitte Hjort Sørensen, Pilou Asbæk, Søren Malling, Benedikte Hansen
Original broadcaster | DR
For fans of . . . | *House of Cards* (1990), *Forbrydelsen* (*The Killing*, 2007), *The Bridge* (2011)

Unexpected events turned Birgitte Nyborg (Sidse Babett Knudsen), leader of a small political party, into the first female prime minister of Denmark. In her new role, she struggled to hold both her family and her fragile coalition together. With the latter, she had help from her spin doctor, Kasper Juul (Pilou Asbæk).

A surprise hit in several countries, *Borgen* created riveting character-based drama. Viewers became experts at the power plays that took place behind the scenes in order to keep a loose alliance of political rivals working together in one government. In no small part, the success of the show is due to Knudsen's stellar central performance. She was neither as tough as nails, nor was she weak and vulnerable, but something completely credible in between. There were times when her party and her family suffered from her decisions, but all her actions were reasonable and motivated by the desire to do the right thing.

In October 2011, just after the second season of *Borgen* had been broadcast, Denmark elected its first ever female prime minister, Helle Thorning-Schmidt. Was this life imitating art, or merely coincidence? There is no way of knowing, but neither is there any doubt that *Borgen* captured the zeitgeist.

Borgen (*The Castle*) is the nickname for Christiansborg Palace, the seat of Danish government. It's used extensively for location filming, so as a visitor to Copenhagen you can have great fun spotting where scenes were shot. **PC**

Classic episode
The First Tuesday in October | *Season 1, episode 10.*
After a year in office Birgitte's life is in ruins. Her government is about to fall. Her husband is on the verge of divorcing her. The pressures of a job she never wanted are mounting.

◉ Sidse Babett Knudsen as Birgitte Nyborg, the fictional first female premier of Denmark.

The Only Way Is Essex

Reality | UK | 2010–present

Real-life soap opera following the turbulent lives of the vibrant citizens of Essex

Cast | Mark Wright, Amy Childs, Kirk Norcross, Lauren Goodger, Gemma Collins, Joey Essex
Original broadcaster | ITV
Award | 1 BAFTA
For fans of . . . | *The Hills* (2006), *Made in Chelsea* (2011)

Scripted reality was not a new television concept when the outspoken characters of Brentwood, Essex first appeared on our screens. *The Only Way Is Essex*, like *The Hills* and *Jersey Shore* (2009) before it, offered a glimpse of real life among a group of friends and enemies.

The first season explored the tempestuous relationships between the show's most enduring characters: nightclub promoter Mark Wright and on/off partner Lauren Goodger, and club owner Kirk Norcross and then girlfriend Amy Childs. Many supporting characters have been introduced along the way, including Lady Gaga fan Harry, Wright's lovable grandmother Nanny Pat, larger-than-life Gemma Collins, and the hilariously naive self-styled Joey Essex. The format has remained the same over the show's duration, with two episodes a week filmed only days before broadcast. The outlandish fashions of Essex residents, their commitment to rigorous beauty regimes, and the endearing, guileless ignorance of the characters has ensured the show's success. It's a wonderful snapshot of our time and beneath the hilarious facade the show explores some deeply sensitive issues, from relationships to body image to homosexuality. It introduced us to the vajazzle (crystal genital decoration), while many of the characters' catchphrases and idioms have been adopted by the British press and the viewers alike. It was a world we suspected existed, but hadn't previously had the pleasure of fully engaging with. **MB**

Terriers

Drama | USA | 2010

A cut-short-too-soon story of money, power, and corruption on the West Coast

Cast | Donal Logue, Michael Raymond-James, Laura Allen, Kimberly Quinn, Jamie Denbo
Original broadcaster | FX
For fans of . . . | *The Rockford Files* (1974), *Ultraviolet* (1998), *Firefly* (2002)

Terriers lasted for just one short season of thirteen episodes. It followed the lives of two unlicensed California private investigators—recovering alcoholic and ex-detective Hank Dolworth (Donal Logue) and retired breaking-and-entering specialist Britt Pollack (Michael Raymond-James)—as they scratched a living serving writs and tracking down bail jumpers. But when they got involved with a rich land developer who had been sleeping around, it led them into a season-long mystery that might just get them killed.

With superficially seedy but morally unimpeachable heroes who provided a counterpoint to affluent West Coast life—apparently glitzy but deeply corrupt—*Terriers* was recognizably indebted to the novels of Raymond Chandler, particularly to his private eye Philip Marlowe. But the show was no rip-off: it had a clear inspiration of its own; the writing was consistently sharp, and the acting was never less than excellent.

So why did it fail? The smart money is on the name. Who would imagine that a show called *Terriers* was an interrogation of the difference between the rich and the poor and the relation between the powerful and the powerless, as well as a smart crime show?

Once you've started watching *Terriers*, its charm and wit and sense of fun soon get you hooked, but not enough people sampled the series, and despite critical acclaim, its exceptionally poor ratings—averaging just a touch over half a million viewers each week—led to its swift cancellation. **PB**

The Trip

Comedy | UK | 2010–14

Lunch has never been so funny

Cast | Steve Coogan, Rob Brydon **Original broadcaster** | BBC Two **Award** | 1 BAFTA
For fans of . . . | *Knowing Me, Knowing You with Alan Partridge* (1994), *Episodes* (2011)

Actors Steve Coogan and Rob Brydon played exaggerated, often unlikable avatars of themselves, meandering through improvised conversations over a series of gourmet restaurant meals. It shouldn't have worked, but somehow *The Trip* defied self-indulgence to make a sharp and insidiously watchable show. When Coogan was commissioned by a newspaper to write a travelogue review of restaurants in the north of England, he extended an invitation to fellow actor Brydon to join him. Cue six episodes of one-upmanship, arguments, jealousy, humiliation, and Sean Connery impressions—the insecurities of the actor writ large.

The Trip was at its best when Coogan and Brydon were left to pick at the threads of their insecurities.

On the page, a scene in which two men attempt to outdo one another with impressions of Michael Caine is bewildering, but in the hands of Coogan and Brydon it was melancholic and laugh-out-loud funny. Subversive, bittersweet, and uproariously funny, *The Trip* was a uniquely British creation featuring two of the country's finest acting talents at the height of their powers. **MW**

Classic episode
L'Enclume | *Season 1, episode 2*. A Hollywood dream, a tortuous telephone call, a rendition of Kate Bush's "Wuthering Heights," and a duel of comedic impressions over dinner. Coogan and Brydon can banter for Great Britain.

⊘ Rob Brydon (left) fails to impress Steve Coogan at breakfast in a country hotel.

Carlos

Biography | France/Germany | 2010

Biopic thriller depicting the life of terrorist Carlos the Jackal

Cast | Edgar Ramírez, Alexander Scheer, Fadi Abi Samra, Lamia Ahmed   **Original broadcaster** | Canal +
Award | 1 Golden Globe   **For fans of . . .** | *The Price* (1985), *The Honourable Woman* (2014)

Carlos was a three-part television biopic by French director Olivier Assayas about Venezuelan terrorist Carlos the Jackal (Ilich Ramírez Sánchez). It was later made into a feature film. There are 338- and 319-minute versions, as well as shorter ones for the German and US markets.

The first episode documented Ramírez Sánchez's early association with Palestinian freedom fighters and his attacks in London and at the French Embassy in the Hague. The second part focused mainly on the infamous siege of the OPEC headquarters in 1975. Failing to escape, Ramírez Sánchez was forced to exchange hostages for money, regaining his freedom but failing in the mission given to him by the head

of the PFLP. This marks the end of Ramírez Sánchez's ideological terrorism and the beginning of his life as a mercenary behind the Iron Curtain. The final episode set the decline of Ramírez Sánchez against the backdrop of the failing Eastern Bloc. The fall of the Berlin Wall put an end to most of his clients. While on the run in Syria and suffering from a chronic testicular condition, he was finally arrested.

Widely acclaimed, the series ran into legal difficulties when Ramírez Sánchez himself threatened to sue the filmmakers for potentially prejudicing juries in future criminal trials. The case was thrown out by a judge and as the present volume went to press Ramírez Sánchez was still awaiting trial for four attacks in France. **MS**

◉ Badih Abou Chakra as Sheikh Yamani and Edgar Ramírez as Carlos the Jackal.

Raising Hope

Comedy | USA | 2010–14

A female serial killer leaves a former lover with nothing but Hope

Classic episode
Jimmy's Fake Girlfriend | *Season 2, episode 14.* Virginia and Burt persuade Jimmy to invent a fake girl friend in order to make Sabrina jealous. Mary-Louise agrees to play the part but the plan backfires. Obviously.

⊘ A scene from "The Chance Who Stole Christmas/Bee Story."

Cast | Lucas Neff, Martha Plimpton, Garret Dillahunt, Cloris Leachman
Original broadcaster | Fox
For fans of . . . | *Everybody Loves Raymond* (1996), *The Middle* (2009)

Jimmy Chance (Lucas Neff) was a clueless happy-go-lucky guy who brought home a girl he had just met. In the morning, the girl joined him and his family for breakfast, which was when they learned from the TV news that she was a serial killer wanted by the police. They knocked her out and called 911. While facing the death penalty, the girl gave birth, and custody of the child was granted to Jimmy, who named her Hope. The good-hearted young father soon discovered just how difficult it was to raise a child on his own.

Fortunately for him, help was on hand from his parents Virginia (Martha Plimpton) and Burt (Garret Dillahunt), who lived together in a house owned by Virginia's grandmother, Barbara June (Cloris Leachman), aka "Maw Maw." They had been kicked out of her house six years earlier, on Jimmy's eighteenth birthday, but they moved back in when Maw Maw's mental health began to deteriorate. She frequently mistook Jimmy for her late husband Wilfred, and made amorous advances toward him.

The popularity of the show was founded partly on its in-references—for example, Lucy's prisoner number, 24601, was the same as Jean Valjean's in *Les Misérables*—but mainly on its consistently amusing but never insensitive treatment of an inexperienced young man thrown into single parenthood. *Raising Hope* was a success not only in the United States but also in Britain, Canada, the Czech Republic, Germany, Finland, Italy, Portugal, and throughout Latin America. **MR**

Rake

Crime/Mystery | Australia | 2010–14

The life and times of a self-destructive barrister in need of more help than his desperate clients

Cast | Richard Roxburgh, Russell Dykstra, Danielle Cormack
Original broadcaster | ABC1
For fans of . . . | *North Square* (2000), *Boston Legal* (2004), *Judge John Deed* (2007)

Many courtroom TV dramas feature charismatic legal eagles, but not many have them defending clients charged with such outrageous crimes as cannibalism, bestiality, and severing penises. It was this unabashed approach that gave *Rake* a uniquely Australian flavor.

Cocreated by lead actor Richard Roxburgh, *Rake* followed the exploits of Cleaver Greene, brilliant barrister and walking disaster zone, as he battled his personal demons and tried every trick in the book to save his usually guilty clients from prison. The character of Greene was inspired by the real-life escapades of infamous Sydney barrister Charles Waterstreet, while the outlandish plots were often inspired by real-life news items. As Greene fell into bed with various women and fell out of favor with underworld enforcers, the breathtaking boldness of the storytelling was delivered with such devastating charm that even puritanical viewers came to envy Greene's chaotic and self-destructive lifestyle. Roxburgh's charismatic performance captivated throughout, but did not overshadow the other members of the engaging ensemble cast.

Rake was a critical and ratings hit in Australia throughout its three seasons. The US remake starring Greg Kinnear, which aired on Fox in 2014, fared less well, and was canceled after one season. However, the memory and legacy of the original series have survived, with its trademark audacity setting a new benchmark for quality Australian drama. **SO**

Classic episode
R vs Chandler | *Season 1, episode 5*. Greene agrees to defend his friend Dr. Bruce Chandler after police receive evidence that the doctor has been indulging in truly inappropriate activities with the family pet.

⊛ Richard Roxburgh stars as criminal lawyer Cleaver Greene.

Downton Abbey

Historical drama | UK | 2010–15

A genteel period drama that became a worldwide phenomenon

Cast | Hugh Bonneville, Maggie Smith, Dan Stevens, Michelle Dockery, Jim Carter
Original broadcaster | ITV
Awards | 2 BAFTAs, 11 Emmys, 3 Golden Globes
For fans of . . . | *Upstairs Downstairs* (1971)

When Gareth Neame of Carnival Films required a writer to develop a new period drama set in an English country house, Julian Fellowes, already an Oscar winner for his screenplay for *Gosford Park* (2001), was the obvious choice. Fellowes provided Neame with the outline for what would become the first season of *Downton Abbey*—a saga about life above and below stairs in a stately home in post-Edwardian England.

The story began in April 1912, with the Grantham estate in financial trouble and in need of a male heir, forcing Lord Grantham (Hugh Bonneville) to turn to distant cousin Matthew Crawley (Dan Stevens). Below stairs, butler Carson (Jim Carter) oversaw an unruly retinue of footmen, chamber maids, and cooks, while the wider world was changing at an alarming pace, as war loomed.

Since it premiered, *Downton Abbey* has amassed an estimated global audience of 120 million. It is among the most successful British television productions of all time. The departure of Dan Stevens as Matthew in the 2012 Christmas Special caused uproar among *Downton*'s loyal fans, and it's a testament to the production that, by and large, it has maintained a large ensemble cast over five seasons. *Downton*'s essential Britishness, its sumptuous depiction of the class divide, and fine cast have made the fate of every character the preoccupation of a worldwide audience. **MW**

◐ (L–R) Sir Richard (Iain Glen) joins star-crossed lovers Lady Mary (Michelle Dockery) and Matthew Crawley (Dan Stevens) for a shoot.

Justified

Crime/Mystery | USA | 2010–present

"I shot people I like more for less"

Cast | Timothy Olyphant, Walton Goggins, Joelle Carter
Original broadcaster | FX **Awards** | 2 Emmys **For fans of . . .** | *Deadwood* (2004)

Elmore Leonard is a modern master of American crime fiction, so there were high hopes for the TV adaptation of his works about US Marshal Raylan Givens, but no guarantee that it could capture the hard-bitten, laconic charm of the original. A lot hung on the performance of Timothy Olyphant in the title role, and he delivered in spades, providing a breakout hit for FX and a corrective to the plethora of antihero narratives on TV at that time. And then there was Givens' childhood friend, sometime adult nemesis, and kingpin of local wrongdoing Boyd Crowder, superbly played by Walton Goggins. The men's fraught relationship is the motor for much of the show's action as they battle over a woman and for control of the county.

In a TV landscape that is perceived by some to be increasingly slanted toward a left-wing, Democratic Party view of the world, *Justified* is seen as an antidote: a proudly right-leaning show set among the neglected white underclass of the South. In fact, it transcends politics, and its empathy for all its characters, even the most monstrous, is of universal appeal. **RL**

Classic episode
Brother's Keeper | *Season 2, episode 9*. The season's conflicts reach boiling point, its villains show their hands, and its heroes face their toughest tests as bitter, unloved Coover takes revenge on Loretta.

⊘ Elmore Leonard described Timothy Olyphant as "the kind of guy I saw when I wrote his lines."

Louie

Comedy | USA | 2010–present

Hybrid of auteur-driven comedy and drama

Cast | Louis C.K., Pamela Adlon, Hadley Delany, Ursula Parker, Robert Kelly, Edward Gelbinovich, Ricky Gervais
Original broadcaster | FX **Awards** | 3 Emmys **For fans of . . .** | *Lucky Louie* (2006)

A viewer would have to enjoy comedian Louis C.K.'s unique blend of self-deprecating humor and nihilistic worldview to appreciate this show, but anyone not watching the series would be missing one of the most amazing achievements in TV production since the medium began. Produced, written, directed and edited by, and starring C.K., the series is a singular vision shaped by one creator—with collaborative input from cast and crew—and he weaves stand-up sequences with vignettes of various lengths that are often as funny as they are steeped in pathos. C.K. portrays a version of himself as he juggles his comedy career with his responsibilities as a divorced parent of two daughters. Some episodes presented multiple short sketchlike stories in a single installment, while later seasons were more serialized and dramatic, showcasing C.K.'s evolving skills as the sole driving force of his own series. He produces every episode as an individual work that stands on its own regardless of whether it fit seamlessly with the rest of the series. The results are wildly diverse in tone . . . much like life itself. **ATB**

Classic episode
Barney/Never | *Season 3, episode 6*.
Guest starring Robin Williams. Louie meets a kind stranger at the funeral for a comedy club owner. They are surprised to discover that the dead man found family in the strangest of places.

◉ In the season four episode "Pamela Part 3," Louis C.K. confesses his love for Pamela.

Luther

Crime/Mystery | UK | 2010–present

Grand Guignol hanging by a Wire

Cast | Idris Elba, Ruth Wilson, Warren Brown, Dermot Crowley, Paul McGann, Nikki Amuka-Bird
Original broadcaster | BBC One
Award | 1 Golden Globe
For fans of . . . | *The Wire* (2002), *Good Cop* (2012)

"Something horrible is bound to happen," wrote the *Guardian* of *Luther*'s third season. "And then something horrible does happen, and it's even more horrible than you expected, and as the title sequence rolls you're trying to work out how comprehensively you just evacuated your bowels. It's good to have *Luther* back."

The BBC had increasingly tapped an HBO-esque vein of danger in the twenty-first century, with gruesome moments earning tabloid headlines for *Spooks* (2002) and *Silent Witness* (1996). *Luther*, however, took British crime drama further from *Midsomer Murders* (1997) than ever before. "I keep a 'nightmare tally' of the number of people who've confessed that my work has kept them up all night," gloated creator Neil Cross (who wrote for *Spooks*) to *Venue*. "Since (season two), I've also kept a list of people who've said they'll never again get in a lift with a motorcycle courier; that they'll never again fill their tank after dark; that they now double-check they've locked all the doors and windows before going to bed. . . ."

The nerve-shredding show was made compelling by *The Wire*'s Idris Elba as a hero so unhinged that it was unclear whether we should be more alarmed by him or his foes. The first black actor to lead a British crime series, Elba earned awards and famous fans. On meeting Barack Obama, he told the *Sun,* "I said, 'Mr. President, I hear I am not your favorite character in *The Wire*,' and he said, 'Well, yeah, but *Luther*—that's me.'" **BM**

⊙ "Luther will always be that guy who can't help seeking out those bad people," remarked Idris Elba. "He'll never get peace."

The Pacific

Historical drama | USA | 2010

Hell was an ocean away

Cast | James Badge Dale, Joseph Mazzello, Jon Seda, Tom Hanks
Original broadcaster | HBO
Awards | 8 Emmys
For fans of . . . | *Band of Brothers* (2001)

It was lavish, it was visceral, and it had the names of Steven Spielberg and Tom Hanks above the door as executive producers. However, *The Pacific* marched an alternative route to *Band of Brothers* (2001), highlighting the differences in the theaters of Europe and the Pacific.

The narrative was wide as the ten-part series followed three marines: Eugene Sledge (Joseph Mazzello), Robert Leckie (James Badge Dale), and John Basilone (Jon Seda), all in different regiments of the 1st Marine Division. The action moved from 1942 and the landings on Guadalcanal to the end of the war after the surrender of Japanese forces. In early episodes, Sledge was desperate to enlist and join the war effort, while Leckie and Basilone were already in action, arriving in Australia and then moving on to the pivotal Battle of Peleliu. The Peleliu landing was depicted with typical verve and hard-nosed honesty, and it was easy to see in microcosm why *The Pacific* cost in excess of $200 million to produce.

Filming of the series took place in Australia from 2007 to 2008, utilizing numerous locations to re-create the Pacific Theater of Operations in intense detail. *The Pacific*'s size and scope is evidenced in the range of co-production, which brought together many international broadcasters to make the show a reality. The result was affecting and heartfelt TV, with little left to the imagination in its depiction of the horrors of war. **MW**

Classic episode
Peleliu Landing | *Season 1, episode 5*. A showcase for *The Pacific*'s frenetic and furious filming style. Bullets zip across the soundscape, dying men scream in agony, and limbs are ripped away. It isn't pretty, but it's thoroughly compelling.

⏺ James Badge Dale (Leckie) said that the boot camp training for the role was so grueling that he has repressed all memory of it.

The Great British Bake Off

Reality | UK | 2010–present

Everyone loves Mary Berry—and cake

Cast | Mel Giedroyc, Sue Perkins, Mary Berry, Paul Hollywood
Original broadcaster | BBC Two
Award | 1 BAFTA
For fans of . . . | *Masterchef* (1990), *Survivor* (2000)

Only the BBC could take something as inoffensive as baking and turn it into a true ratings champion and cultural phenomenon. From humble beginnings on a minority channel and set in a marquee, this elimination contest between a group of amateur bakers has become the preoccupation of a nation.

The concept is very simple. Each week contestants are subjected to a trio of baking challenges based around a particular theme, ranging from pastry and bread to celebration cakes and pies. A signature bake is followed by a technical challenge using a recipe previously unseen by the contestants, before a "showstopper" round finishes the heat. One contestant is crowned Star Baker, and another is sent home based on their overall performance that week.

The appeal of the show is a combination of many elements working together. The hosting by comedians Mel Giedroyc and Sue Perkins is humorous and engaging, while the comments of judges Mary Berry and Paul Hollywood can be brutally honest. However, the show has transformed the careers of Berry and Hollywood, and launched several more on the fortunes of the contestants. Overall, *The Great British Bake Off* works because of the emotional investment in the contestants. Baking disasters lead to tears and the odd tantrum, epitomized in the so-called "Bingate" of 2014: a rival contestant allegedly removed Iain Watters' baked Alaska from a freezer. It melted; he binned it. The nation was gripped and baking fever reigned. **MW**

The Big C

Drama | USA | 2010–13

Living, dying, laughing, and crying with cancer

Cast | Laura Linney, Oliver Platt, John Benjamin Hickey, Gabriel Basso, Gabourey Sidibe
Original broadcaster | Showtime
Awards | 1 Emmy, 1 Golden Globe
For fans of . . . | *Arrested Development* (2003)

A middle-aged married mother had her life blown apart when she was told she had skin cancer. Initially Cathy kept her illness from her husband and teenaged son. She got unlikely help and support from her difficult neighbor, with whom she struck up a friendship. Over the four seasons, Cathy's journey saw her go through a marriage crisis, teenaged angst, death, and trauma, but always she managed to maintain spirit and humor. She embraced the freedom that terminal illness gave her, fighting for all causes, lost or otherwise.

A TV show about cancer may seem a total turn-off, but from the outset *The Big C* wasn't scared to fly in the face of the fear of cancer, confronting it with humor, humanity, and reality. At times the show had the audience laughing out loud, then bawling like a baby, but it never became overly sentimental. The construction of a swimming pool at Cathy's home served as a motif that allowed the audience to follow her timeline toward its inevitable conclusion.

Laura Linney gave a stunning performance in this show. She gave Cathy a spirit and humor that was neither flippant nor crass. The supporting cast were not slouches either. The ever-brilliant Oliver Platt sparked wonderfully with his leading lady, and all the regulars gave life to their characters, making it easy to care about their lives. There were also some top-class guest performances, notably from Alan Alda, Susan Sarandon, and Allison Janney. *The Big C* took cancer seriously but managed to avoid taking itself too seriously. **CR**

Parenthood

Drama | USA | 2010–15

The circle of life goes around and through a single family

Cast | Craig T. Nelson, Bonnie Bedelia, Peter Krause, Lauren Graham, Erika Christensen, Dax Shepard
Original broadcaster | NBC   **For fans of . . .** | *Brothers & Sisters* (2006)

Created by Ron Howard, who directed the movie *A Beautiful Mind* (2001), *Parenthood* (loosely based on the 1999 film of the same name) examined the dynamics of three—and, ultimately, four—generations of the Braverman family: Zeek and Camille (Craig T. Nelson and Bonnie Bedelia), their four grown-up children, and their children's nine offspring.

Most of their dealings were unremarkable: they went to ball games together or separately, according to circumstance; they babysat each other's progeny; they gave, and sometimes gratefully received, help and advice. Their main distinguishing feature—and the one that gained the most publicity for the show—was that grandson Max (Max Burkholder) had Asperger's syndrome, but gradually came to terms with his condition and embarked on a career as a photographer.

The Waltons was idealistic and sentimental; *The Simpsons* is funny and rude; *Parenthood* was sometimes all those things, but it was also tinged throughout with the sadness that comes from the knowledge that everyone must die, as Zeek did in the final episode. **GL**

> **Classic episode**
> *In-Between* | *Season 3, episode 8.* Adam and his wife try to revive their love life for the first time since becoming parents. Crosby, another of Zeek and Camille's children, worries when his son tells him he'd prefer someone else as his father.

◬ The Bravermans at dinner. At the head of the table is Peter Krause as Adam, the oldest son of Zeek and Camille.

This is England '86

Drama | UK | 2010

"It's still bleak, as you'd expect. At times touching, at others funny"

Cast | Vicky McClure, Joseph Gilgun, Joe Dempsie, Thomas Turgoose, Rosamund Hanson, Johnny Harris
Original broadcaster | Channel 4   **Awards** | 2 BAFTAs   **For fans of . . .** | *Boys from the Blackstuff* (1982)

Shane Meadows' critically acclaimed film *This Is England* (2006)—set in 1983 in the aftermath of the Falklands War—revolved around Shaun (Thomas Turgoose), a troubled teen who fell in with a gang of older youths and in particular the charismatic, persuasive, and racist Combo (Stephen Graham). *This is England '86* picked up on the action three years later, with the gang still coming to terms with events in the film.

The TV show focused on the difficult relationship between the prickly Lol (Vicky McClure) and her directionless boyfriend Woody (Joseph Gilgun), who got as far as the registry office before getting cold feet and admitting he wasn't ready to get married. Then Lol learned that her father Mick (Johnny Harris) had

been released from prison and had reunited with her mother. Although Mick swore that he was a reformed man, Lol was unable to forgive him for abusing her and was afraid he could be capable of doing the same thing to her younger sister. After her friend Trev (Danielle Watson) confessed that Mick had raped her, too, Lol took drastic action, only to receive support from an unlikely source.

The series could be oppressively grim at times, but the performances of the cast rang painfully true. McClure shone in particular; also in the follow-up *This Is England '88* (2011), in which she had a baby daughter. The series also boasted an epic soundtrack of songs contemporary with the setting of each series. **JS**

ⓐ Joe Gilgun (Woody) and Vicky McClure (Lol, front) with the cast at a promotional photo shoot.

Treme

Drama | USA | 2010–13

How New Orleans recovered from one of the worst natural disasters in US history

Cast | Khandi Alexander, John Goodman, Michiel Huisman, Melissa Leo, Lucia Micarelli, Clarke Peters, Wendell Pierce, Steve Zahn **Original broadcaster** | HBO **Award** | 1 Emmy **For fans of . . .** | *The Wire* (2002)

This series—named for Tremé, a neighborhood of New Orleans—was a fictionalized account of the efforts of ordinary people in the city to rebuild their homes and businesses after Hurricane Katrina destroyed them and caused widespread flooding in August 2005.

The show was created by David Simon, who cast several of the actors with whom he had worked on previous TV projects: Melissa Leo from *Homicide: Life on the Street* (1993); Khandi Alexander from *The Corner* (2000); and Clarke Peters and Wendell Pierce from *The Wire* (2002). Many of the minor roles were played by local people, a significant boost to the city's morale.

One of the greatest merits of *Treme* was the music, which honored the city's jazz tradition and fit perfectly with the narrative. Pierce played trombone in the show, but the star was Kermit Ruffins, an accomplished trumpeter and real-life chef.

Treme was always at risk of sensationalizing or trivializing the plight of the hurricane victims for purposes of entertainment, but it avoided both traps and was unfailingly sensitive and politically acute. **GL**

> **Classic episode**
> *Shame, Shame, Shame* | *Season 1, episode 5*.
> Albert (Clarke Peters) lobbies a city councilman to reopen the housing projects. Davis (Steve Zahn) assembles a group of local musicians to cut a campaign CD.

◓ (L–R) Khandi Alexander, Venida Evans, and Melissa Leo wrestle with the implications of their extreme circumstances.

Pretty Little Liars

Drama | USA | 2010–present

Everybody has secrets…

Cast | Troian Bellisario, Ashley Benson, Lucy Hale, Shay Mitchell, Sasha Pieterse, Laura Leighton, Janel Parrish, Tyler Blackburn, Holly Marie Combs **Original broadcaster** | ABC Family **For fans of . . .** | *Revenge* (2011)

Based on a series of young adult novels first published in 2006 by Sara Shepard, *Pretty Little Liars* is a mystery thriller following a group of teenagers: Spencer, Hanna, Aria, and Emily, whose clique fell apart when their "leader" Alison disappeared. A year later, they are reunited as they all start receiving messages from the mysterious "A," who threatens to reveal secrets they thought only Alison knew. After Alison's body is found the girls reunite to work out who is trying to ruin their lives, and how. In particular they want to hide "the Jenna thing," an incident they were all involved in that led to the blinding of one of their classmates.

Conceived as a *Desperate Housewives* for teens, the show, while melodramatic to its core, strongly depicts the angst of being a twenty-first-century teenage girl, with secrets, lies, and friendships being the absolute most important things in life. Of course, being a US drama, everyone is beautiful, and half the characters seem to be sleeping with one another. A spin-off, *Ravenswood*, was made in 2013 but canceled after only one season. **EB**

> **Classic episode**
> *This Is a Dark Ride* | *Season 3, episode 13*.
> In this Halloween episode, the girls are stalked by a mysterious presence while on a ghost train. The only thing for certain is that somebody won't be making it out alive.

◬ The girls are spooked by the latest eerie event in their increasingly complicated lives.

Sherlock

Crime/Mystery | UK | 2010–present

A new sleuth for the twenty-first century

Cast | Benedict Cumberbatch, Martin Freeman, Una Stubbs, Rupert Graves, Louise Brealey, Mark Gatiss
Original broadcaster | BBC One
Awards | 13 BAFTAs, 7 Emmys
For fans of . . . | *Elementary* (2012)

Sherlock Holmes (Benedict Cumberbatch) is a wealthy, well-connected eccentric, whose brilliance and ability to see threads that connect seemingly disparate elements is matched only by his complete lack of empathy for everybody else. Events brought him in league with John Watson (Martin Freeman), a military doctor no longer on duty after a stint in Afghanistan, and it's here that Holmes aficionados will recognize how surprisingly close to Sir Arthur Conan Doyle's original premises these modern reworkings are.

Inspired by movies starring Basil Rathbone that transplanted the Victorian investigator to the 1940s, writers Steven Moffat and Mark Gatiss crafted a Holmes for the twenty-first century—even with a deerstalker on his head. Though this Holmes claims to be ignorant of modern technology, the series doesn't shy from the leaps in forensic science and technology—the first episode's innovative visualization of text messaging has been much copied ever since.

Each season is a short three episodes long—albeit with feature-length episodes—and the writers cruelly tease their audience. The climax of the second season had viewers perplexed as to how Sherlock survived a lethal fall—only for the next season to refuse to reveal how he cheated death (though there were multiple possible solutions, from the highly improbable to the fan-pleasingly ridiculous). The show made a star of Cumberbatch, who finely balances arrogance and aspects of Asperger's syndrome with engaging wit. **JS**

Classic episode
The Reichenbach Fall | *Season 2, episode 3.*
Holmes' nemesis Moriarty (Andrew Scott) has turned the detective into public enemy number one. With his reputation in tatters, Sherlock takes the plunge. *Silent Witness'* Jaye Griffiths guests.

⊙ Benedict Cumberbatch as Sherlock Holmes.
⊙ Watson (Martin Freeman) hunts for the hounds of Baskerville.

Spartacus

Action/Adventure | USA | 2010–13

Some legends are written in blood

Cast | Andy Whitfield, Liam McIntyre, Lucy Lawless, Daniel Feuerriegel, John Hannah, Manu Bennett
Original broadcaster | Starz
For fans of . . . | *Heroes* (2006), *Game of Thrones* (2011), *Vikings* (2013)

Spartacus, the tragic story of the failed revolt by Roman slaves led by a heroic gladiator, was itself marred by tragedy when lead actor Andy Whitfield was diagnosed with lymphoma and died before filming of the second season could begin. It could have been the end of the show, but replacement Liam McIntyre ably led the series through to its action-packed conclusion.

On paper, *Spartacus* was a ratings winner, but not a show that would attract much critical love. It covered the same ground as the beloved 1960 film, utilized the same virtual sets and excessively gory special effects as the much-mocked *300* (2006), and aired on Starz, a network not known for its restraint. And yet all this worked in its favor. Yes, the screen was often filled with blood or was writhing with naked flesh, but the show turned what could have been exploitative erotica into a serious study of the powerlessness of slaves. John Hannah and Lucy Lawless played Batiatus and Lucretia, the master and mistress of the gladiatorial school where the story began, and their alternately loathsome and empathetic performances anchored the show.

Spartacus painted its story in big, broad strokes, but it was as great a story as any on TV. And while the gory reimagining of ancient Rome may have taken historical liberties in its details, it absolutely captured the decaying soul of the status- and wealth-obsessed ancient Republic. **RL**

❯ Manu Bennett as Crixus the Gaul, one of Rome's top gladiators.

Weissensee

Drama | Germany | 2010–present

Set in the good-old, bad-old days of preunification Berlin, Weissensee *has been a huge hit*

Cast | Florian Lukas, Stephan Grossmann, Katrin Sass, Uwe Kockisch, Jörg Hartmann
Original broadcaster | Das Erste   **For fans of . . .** | *Doctor's Diary* (2008)

While few people would want to live in a society where their movements are restricted and their homes bugged, there is a nostalgia among some former East Germans for days of yore behind the iron curtain. There is a demand for defunct brands from the former GDR and for drama that portrays everyday life there, such as the Academy Award–winning movie *The Lives of Others* (2006).

The series *Weissensee*, named after an area in Berlin, came out of this *Ostalgie*. Set in the 1980s, it follows the lives of two families, the apparatchik Kupfers and the freethinking Hausmanns. Both Hans Kupfer and his son Falk work for the Ministry for State Security (better known as Stasi), while singer Dunja Hausmann writes

protest songs and tries to give her daughter Julia a liberal education. When Julia meets Hans's other son, Martin, the two fall in love, causing problems for both families and uncovering various secrets and lies.

Weissensee has been a critical success throughout Germany, and not just among those viewers who feel a strong sense of *Ostalgie*. **DH**

Classic episode
Season 1, episode 5. Afraid that his brother's affair with Julia Hausmann will ruin his career at the Stasi, Falk Kupfer attacks Martin and says he will try to destroy him and his girlfriend, who is about to find out that she's pregnant.

⊘ Dunja Hausmann (Katrin Sass) records the songs that an oppressive regime has banned her from performing.

Mongrels

Comedy | UK | 2010–11

"I'm a cat and I'm stuck up a tree! I'm such a cliché"

Cast | Rufus Jones, Dan Tetsell, Lucy Montgomery, Katy Brand, Paul Kaye, Tony Way   **Original broadcaster** | BBC Three   **For fans of . . .** | *The Muppet Show* (1976), *South Park* (1997), *Family Guy* (1999), *Archer* (2009)

As fast as humans have changed the environment, animals have had to adapt, too. Urban fox Nelson, residing in the backyard of a London pub, had adapted well; sensitive and educated, he described himself as an "urbane" fox. He lived near his best friend, Marion, a Persian cat whose naivety had left him with only two of his nine lives. Joining them by the bins were Destiny, a vain Afghan hound, and Kali, a street-smart pigeon. Between them they found that, even in an urban landscape, the laws of the jungle still applied.

Sharp and edgy, *Mongrels* was where *The Muppet Show* met *Family Guy*. Expressive puppets were imbued with vivid characters and given inventive scripts that blended surreal flashbacks with large doses of pop-culture references, as well as packs of celebrities lining up to be ridiculed in quick-fire cameos. Each episode's highlight was the song, in which the musical style was as likely to be Mary Poppins as Lady Gaga. Subjects ranged from the gentrification of the East End ("No One's Been Stabbed Here Since Friday") to the age-of-consent laws ("What a Difference a Day Makes"). **RM**

> **Classic episode**
> *Nelson the Naughty Arsonist* | *Season 1, episode 6.*
> It's bonfire night—or as the animals know it, "5/11"—and Marion is duped by a radicalized hedgehog into blowing up the pub. Only one thing is for sure; this episode is not about religion.

⊘ (L–R) Destiny, Nelson, Kali, Marion, and Vince—*Mongrels* was a comedy with plenty of bite.

The Walking Dead

Fantasy/Horror/Sci-Fi | USA | 2010–present

Fight the dead, fear the living

Cast | Andrew Lincoln, Jon Bernthal, Sarah Wayne Callies, Melissa McBride, Madison Lintz, Laurie Holden
Original broadcaster | AMC
Awards | 2 Emmys
For fans of . . . | *Supernatural* (2005)

Before the debut of *The Walking Dead*, the notion of a violent horror series about zombies airing on a commercial TV network was barely a sensible thought. However, within its first six episodes, the show had captivated TV viewers and catapulted the zombie genre—already a popular and ubiquitous subcategory of horror in post-9/11 pop culture—to an unheard-of level of mainstream awareness and success. Within a few years, *The Walking Dead* has become one of the most popular shows on TV, crossing all demographic boundaries.

Adapted from the Image comic book series created by Robert Kirkman in 2003, the show was developed by Frank Darabont, with Kirkman's active involvement, and quickly established its own approach to the material, borrowing characters and plot threads from the comic while forging its own path through a postapocalyptic landscape of reanimated corpses (Walkers) and deadly living humans desperate to make their way through a treacherous and uncertain future. As with all good zombie stories, the focus is always firmly on the survivors, led by former sheriff's deputy Rick Grimes (Andrew Lincoln), with the flesh-hungry corpses— expertly designed and executed by a special-effects team led by longtime horror makeup maestro Greg Nicotero—as the rotting lenses through which human nature is dissected and examined every week **ATB**

◑ Former cop Rick Grimes (Andrew Lincoln) witnesses the horror of a zombie apocalypse

Any Human Heart

Drama | UK | 2010

The twentieth century seen through the eyes of one man

Cast | Jim Broadbent, Matthew Macfadyen, Sam Clafin, Samuel West, Gillian Anderson, Kim Cattrall
Original broadcaster | Channel 4
Awards | 2 BAFTAs
For fans of . . . | *White Heat* (2010)

Following Logan Mountstuart from childhood until his death, and adapted by William Boyd from his 2002 novel of the same name, *Any Human Heart* was the epic tale of an extraordinary life. Rather than burden an unfortunate actor with aging makeup, the producers decided to have four actors each play Logan at a different stage of life: Conor Nealon was the child, Sam Clafin the idealistic youngster, Matthew Macfadyen the middle-aged man, and Jim Broadbent the elderly Logan who looked back with nostalgia at lost times and lost loves as he wandered around an empty house in France and made the viewers anxious to know how the cocksure Oxford student reached this point in his dotage. His best friend, Peter Scabius (Freddie Fox and Samuel West), wrote awful popular novels, but was rich and successful, while Logan was barely known.

The quartet of actors deftly underlined the central theme—that one changes so much throughout one's life that one almost becomes an entirely different person with each passing year, "a collection of selves." While the novel was written as a series of chronological journals, with the amazing and mundane presented side by side, for television the focus was fixed by the external anchors on Logan's life: chiefly his loves and losses and the sometime overlap between each.

It was revealed throughout that Logan has led an incredible life, with shades of Forrest Gump at times as he rubbed shoulders with famous real people, including Ernest Hemingway and Ian Fleming. **EB**

Maison close

Drama | France | 2010–13

The hard lives of prostitutes in nineteenth-century Paris

Cast | Anne Charrier, Valérie Karsenti, Jemima West, Catherine Hosmalin, Clemence Bretécher, Deborah Grall, Blandine Bellavoir
Original broadcaster | Canal+
For fans of . . . | *Secret Diary of a Call Girl* (2007)

Maison close was about a brothel named Paradise in the outskirts of Paris. The action was set in 1871, a year of great social and political upheaval, shortly after the French had been defeated in the Franco-German War and the government of Napoleon III had fallen. Prostitution was illegal, and women walking in the street alone or accompanied by different men on different occasions could be arrested by the often overzealous police vice squad. Consequently, the sex trade had to move into private houses, such as this one.

The main focus of the narrative was on three women. Hortense (Valérie Karsenti), owner of the establishment, had to keep staff and customers happy, and at the same time deal with the protection racketeers who demanded a regular cut of her earnings to prevent them from denouncing her to the authorities.

Vera (Anne Charrier) was thirty-five years old; her beauty was fading and she was approaching the end of her working life as a prostitute. She had naively set her heart on a pension from her main client, Baron du Plessis (Quentin Baillot).

Rose (Jemima West) came to Paris in search of her mother, who had been forced into prostitution, but ironically suffered the same fate as her parent.

Maison close was a success, but less of one than its makers had hoped. Critics remarked that the show's problem was its excessive seriousness—true, the workers were enslaved and exploited, but even gallows humor would have offered some light relief. **GL**

The Fades

Drama | UK | 2011

Creepy supernatural goings-on proliferate when teenager Paul Roberts discovers that he can see the dead

Cast | Iain De Caestecker, Daniel Kaluuya, Tom Ellis, Natalie Dormer, Lily Loveless
Original broadcaster | BBC Three
Award | 1 BAFTA
For fans of . . . | *Misfits* (2009), *In the Flesh* (2013)

It is unlikely that even the biggest fan of *The Fades* would claim that the idea on which it was based is original. Teenager Paul (Iain De Caestecker) discovered that he could see the spirits of the dead (the Fades) and soon learned that they had a grudge against the living. The source of their grievance was that they had been prevented from "ascending," as they were conventionally entitled to do, because there were not enough portals in the sky to process them and they felt they were being kept on Earth against their will. Gradually, they were resuming human form, and when they achieved it they planned to get back the world that had held them captive by bringing about the Apocalypse. Paul's job was to stop them, but the problem was that no one would believe his story—no one, that was, apart from a few people who shared his strange powers, a small group known as the Angelics.

There is no such thing as a new story, but even the oldest yarns can be revitalized in the telling, and that's where *The Fades* really shone. Among its standout features were Jack Thorne's brilliantly savage scripts and Farren Blackburn's direction, which used dark and light in an object lesson for anyone who doubted the truth of the dictum "show, don't tell."

This drama about death was full of life, but in the wake of the world banking crisis, the BBC was constrained by reduced budgets and decided not to recommission it. It was not the only victim of austerity, but it was the one whose parting many people most mourned. **GR**

Classic episode
Episode 5. Growing more powerful by the day, the Fades lay siege to a building full of Angelics. Paul astonishes those around him with his ability to kill the attackers. It emerges that humans can be "reborn" as Fades by eating their own species.

⊙ In *The Fades*, the behavior of birds alerts Paul (Iain De Caestecker) to the arrival of unnatural forces that threaten humanity.

Arne Dahl

Crime/Mystery | Sweden | 2011–present

Mismatched Nordic cops tackle grisly crimes in this nail-biting crime drama

Cast | Shanti Roney, Irene Lindh, Malin Arvidsson
Original broadcaster | Sweden Sveriges Television   **For fans of . . .** | *Those Who Kill* (2011)

While audiences worldwide are rightly impressed by the intricate, longform style of series such as *The Killing* and *The Bridge,* Scandinavia continues to produce traditional crime dramas such as *Arne Dahl.*

Taking its name from the pen name of author Jan Arnald (and based on his books), the series follows the A Unit, a crack team of disparate detectives brought together to solve unusual crimes. A Unit is led by Jenny Hultin, a tough but fair boss who has to control a team not only in conflict with each other, but also with their inner demons; much is made of the personal issues each member faces, but not at the expense of the main narrative. The violent nature of the crimes adds to a general bleakness. Arnald's aim in the books was

to show that Swedish society has moved away from its progressive ideals, and this is reflected in the series.

With each story spread across two 90-minute episodes, the show moves at breakneck speed yet the characters are given space to develop. Though not as revered as some thrillers in the Nordic stable, *Arne Dahl* certainly keeps viewers on the edge of their seats. **SO**

Classic episode

Bad Blood | Season 1, episodes 3/4. Hultin and the A Unit join forces with the FBI to track down the Kentucky Killer, an American serial killer who has traveled to Sweden to increase the number of his victims.

⊘ Shanti Roney (Paul Hjelm) and Malin Arvidsson (Kerstin Holm) bring justice to the harbor area of Stockholm.

Mrs. Brown's Boys

Comedy | Ireland/UK | 2011–13

A family survives because—and often in spite—of its head, who's played by a man in drag

Cast | Brendan O'Carroll, Jennifer Gibney, Paddy Houlihan, Danny O'Carroll **Original broadcasters** | RTÉ One (Ireland), BBC One (UK) **Awards** | 2 BAFTAs **For fans of . . .** | *Till Death Us Do Part* (1965), *Father Ted* (1995)

Critics hated *Mrs. Brown's Boys*, but in many parts of the United Kingdom and Ireland it became essential viewing; it was especially popular with older people. Much of it was derived from pantomime; its lead character, Agnes Brown (played by writer Brendan O'Carroll) spoke directly to the audience, and goofs and gaffes were left in as part of the story, resulting in the characters veering off-script. With half of the cast related to O'Carroll, either directly or by marriage, it was very much a family affair.

Some of the humor was coarse but overall the show was highly traditional. Family-based sitcoms fell out of favor in the 1990s, but the enduring appetite for them was evidenced by the ratings for the 2012 Christmas Special, which had twelve million UK viewers.

O'Carroll originally unveiled Agnes Brown ("Browne," as she was then) on Irish radio in 1992. He later wrote a series of books about her and toured with a stage show in which she starred. The success of the TV series spawned a full-length feature film in 2014; more recently it was announced that an animated series was in production. **JS**

> **Classic episode**
> *Mammy's Break* | *Season 3, Episode 6.* Agnes is desperate for a vacation, but cannot leave the house until she has found someone to look after Grandad. No one is keen, but no one is a match for Mrs. Brown.

◒ Brendan O'Carroll drags up as the popular Irish mammy, Agnes Brown, reviving the pantomime tradition long moribund on TV.

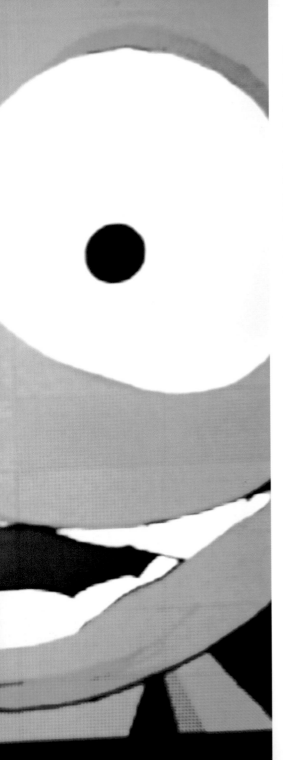

Black Mirror

Drama | UK | 2011–present

Dark, thought-provoking anthology series
about the bleak prospects of the human race

Cast | Charlie Brooker, Jesse Armstrong, Konnie Huq
Original broadcaster | Channel 4
Award | 1 Emmy
For fans of . . . | *The Twilight Zone* (1959), *Brass Eye*
(1997), *10 O'Clock Live* (2011)

Black Mirror is an anthology series with self-contained
dramas unified by a single theme: the effects on
our lives of new technologies. The show—its title
a reference both to the screens on cell phones and
to the darkness of the envisioned future—was the
brainchild of Charlie Brooker, a satirist who had carved
a niche taking sardonic looks at the modern world,
especially its increasing reliance on technology and
global twenty-four-hour media. Brooker had previously
written and presented several shows exploring these
themes (*Screenwipe*, *Newswipe*, *How TV Ruined Your Life*)
and created the comedy series *Nathan Barley* (2005)
and *A Touch of Cloth* (2012). He was also the creator
of *Dead Set* (2008), a horror-comedy serial featuring a
zombie attack on the *Big Brother* house.

   The stories in *Black Mirror* are set in a nightmarish
near future in which people have electronic implants to
record their every experience; the dead can be partially
resurrected by accessing their online identities; every
individual is responsible for generating his or her own
power; obese people are considered second-class
citizens; and dating coaches can communicate directly
with their clients and talk them through a seduction
as it happens.

   Black Mirror is outrageous, irreverent, haunting, and
archly clever. Each different story features a new cast,
including many highly regarded names. **DF**

◗ Daniel Rigby as a failed comedian who performs the voice
and movements of a blue cartoon bear in "The Waldo Moment."

Bob's Burgers

Animation | USA | 2011–present

Animated comedy about a hapless family running a burger joint in a seaside tourist town

Cast | Dan Mintz, Eugene Mirman, Kristen Schaal, H. Jon Benjamin, John Roberts   **Original broadcaster** | Fox
Award | 1 Emmy   **For fans of . . .** | *The Simpsons* (1989)

Bob's Burgers, created by Loren Bouchard, centers on the Belchers, who run a struggling hamburger joint on Ocean Avenue in a seaside community. The diner's biggest rival is Jimmy Pesto's nearby pizzeria.

Bob and Linda Belcher are an average blue-collar couple raising three eccentric kids. Their oldest, Tina, is preoccupied with unicorns, zombies, and her newly formed boobs. She also writes erotic "friend fiction," which is often about Jimmy Pesto Jr. Gene, the dim-witted middle child, blasts everyone with his music. Louise, the youngest and feistiest, is always planning her next prank and is never without her bunny ears.

The restaurant is situated between a funeral home and a condo building where tenants come and go on a regular basis. The Belchers live in an apartment above the premises.

Critics thought the show vulgar, but it has been hugely popular with viewers who enjoy the way in which the strength of the Belcher family's bonds keeps them together in spite of the endless series of disasters that befall them. **RP**

> **Classic episode**
> *Bad Tina* | *Season 2, episode 8.* Tina is assigned to show new girl Tammy around her school. Tammy finds Tina's precious erotic friend fiction, which repeatedly mentions Jimmy Jr. and his butt, and tries to blackmail her with it.

⚓ Bob the father with his children (L–R) Louise, Gene, and Tina, and wife Linda.

New Girl

Comedy | USA | 2011–present

Who's that quirky girl? It's Jess!

Cast | Zooey Deschanel, Jake Johnson, Max Greenfield, Lamorne Morris   **Original broadcaster** | Fox
For fans of . . . | *Friends* (1994), *Happy Endings* (2011)

The kooky character is a staple of many sitcoms—think *Friends'* Phoebe and *Seinfeld's* Kramer—but *New Girl* differs in that it puts the zany one center stage.

Following a breakup with her boyfriend, teacher Jess (Zooey Deschanel) ends up sharing an apartment with bartender Nick, marketer Schmidt, and former basketball player Winston. The series follows the thirtysomething friends as they negotiate the transition between youth and maturity. Serious topics, such as breakups and cancer scares, underpin laugh-out-loud moments.

Writer Elizabeth Meriwether's background as a playwright brings a freshness to the story lines, and characters are bold and rounded as opposed to gag-a-minute ciphers. Deschanel makes Jess a relatable figure—buoyant yet fragile, she's best friend material for female viewers, while being a girl-next-door figure for the guys. Lamorne Morris' Winston is the show's secret weapon, acting as the conscience of the group. A single-camera sitcom without a laugh track, *New Girl* impresses with its winning performances, strong writing, and assured take on friendship. **SO**

Classic episode
Cooler | *Season 2, episode 15*. Nick, Schmidt, and Winston go out to meet women, but when Jess gets scared, the guys and their dates return. Party games ensue, forcing Jess and Nick to face up to their feelings for each other.

◉ The cast of *New Girl*, a comedy about four thirtysomethings who still want to have fun.

Scott & Bailey

Crime/Mystery | UK | 2011–present

Gender-busting police procedural on the streets of Greater Manchester

Cast | Suranne Jones, Lesley Sharp, Amelia Bullmore
Original broadcaster | ITV
For fans of . . . | *Cagney & Lacey* (1981), *Murder in Suburbia* (2004), *Happy Valley* (2014)

Deftly balancing detailed police procedural with character-driven drama, *Scott & Bailey* pushes the lives of its trio of female protagonists to the fore with liberal dashes of caustic humor. This exception to the male-dominated examples of the genre has led to critical acclaim and ratings success.

Scott & Bailey was co-created by Sally Wainwright and Diane Taylor, but the series was based on an idea by actress (and series star) Suranne Jones and her former *Coronation Street* colleague Sally Lindsay. Jones wanted a female-led show with characters who were not defined as wives, mistresses, or sidekicks. It would have been easy for *Scott & Bailey* to cast its male characters disparagingly, but detective constables Rachel Bailey and Janet Scott are both as capable and flawed in their personal and professional lives as the men.

The investigations of the Syndicate 9 Major Incident Team of the Manchester Metropolitan Police could descend into gritty realism—there is an atypical working-class motif within most episodes—but the show's honest gallows humor lifts *Scott & Bailey* above this. Combined with a forensic attention to detail, thanks to cocreator Diane Taylor's previous experience as a detective inspector, the disparate elements of the series work together to make viewing that is at once compelling and entertaining. With stars Jones, Lesley Sharp, and Amelia Bullmore (who is also one of the writers) in high demand, the future of *Scott & Bailey* remains uncertain. **MW**

Twenty Twelve

Comedy | UK | 2011

A comedy of the zany sort that only the British could make

Cast | Hugh Bonneville, Amelia Bullmore, Jessica Hynes, Olivia Colman, Vincent Franklin, Karl Theobald
Original broadcaster | BBC Four
Awards | 2 BAFTAs
For fans of . . . | *The Office* (2005)

There's something delightfully British about *Twenty Twelve*, a spoof documentary tracking the work of the London 2012 Olympic Deliverance Commission, headed by the beleaguered Ian Fletcher (Hugh Bonneville). With his barely competent team, Fletcher steered the Games toward the opening ceremony (the final episode aired just three days before the event itself). Uncannily, fact and fiction sometimes coincided. In the opening episode, for example, an Olympic countdown clock, unveiled on the bank of the Thames, failed to operate. The day after the episode aired, London's real-life countdown clock malfunctioned.

The show's success was in the brilliantly poker-faced acting. As well as Bonneville, Amelia Bullmore was totally believable as out-of-her-depth Head of Sustainability Kay Hope, and there was great humor from Vincent Franklin's plain-speaking Nick Jowett. The biggest hit was Jessica Hynes, who brought a savage reality to hateful PR executive Siobhan Sharpe.

Twenty Twelve was well received by viewers and critics alike. Once London 2012 was over, Ian Fletcher found himself a new job as Head of Values at the British Broadcasting Corporation in *W1A* (the show took its title from the postal district of BBC's Broadcasting House), which pokes fun at its own paymaster. Fletcher has a new team, but there is one relic of the Olympics he is shackled to—Siobhan Sharpe. With a second season of *W1A* commissioned for broadcast in 2015, it's a partnership that could run and run. **MW**

Borgia

Historical drama | France | 2011–14

There was ambition and passion by the bucketload in this acclaimed drama about the powerful Borgia dynasty that shaped Renaissance Italy

Cast | John Doman, Mark Ryder, Isolda Dyachauk, Stanley Weber, Marta Gastini,
Original broadcaster | Canal+
For fans of . . . | *I, Claudius* (1976), *Rome* (2005), *Casanova* (2005), *The Tudors* (2007)

Chronicling the rise of the powerful Borgia family in sixteenth- and seventeenth-century Italy, *Borgia* was an authentic account of the dynasty's ruthless ambition. The lavishly mounted drama was made all the more compelling by the performances. John Doman fascinated as Cardinal Rodrigo Borgia, a man locked in an eternal battle with his rivals, his children, and himself, in his overriding desire to become Pope, while Isolda Dyachauk delivered a standout performance as Rodrigo's harlot daughter Lucrezia.

Before making the series, writer Tom Fontana—the creative force behind the breakout HBO series *Oz*—immersed himself in the historical detail of the time. It was a very different approach from Neil Jordan's melodramatic rival series *The Borgias* produced for Showtime around the same time. (Fontana met with Jordan prior to production to explore the potential of merging the two projects, but they failed to agree on an approach.) Fontana's *Borgia* was visceral, carnal, and often brutal, with characters driven by faith, sex, and death. It showed the violence of the period without being gratuitous, and the sex was graphic without being glamorized.

Borgia showed how human frailty, insecurity, and paranoia can drive people to make disastrous decisions, and lead to Machiavellian behavior that can devastate lives. The series was a searing morality tale, made unique by its period detail while dealing in themes that resonate today. **SO**

Classic episode
Legitimacy | *Season 1, episode 6*. Christopher Columbus discovers America. In a masterly sleight of hand, Rodrigo Borgia carves up the new lands between Spain and Portugal, favoring the former while appearing neutral.

◉ Isolda Dyachauk as Lucrezia Borgia, a dangerous femme fatale.

Portlandia

Comedy | USA | 2011–present

Satirical sketch comedy series based in a uniquely quirky American town

Cast | Fred Armisen, Carrie Brownstein **Original broadcaster** | IFC **Award** | 1 Emmy
For fans of . . . | *Parks and Recreation* (2009)

Co-produced by *Saturday Night Live*'s Lorne Michaels and costarring its creators, Fred Armisen and Carrie Brownstein, *Portlandia* is a postmodern sketch comedy.

Growing out of an Internet comedy project, the series was produced in Portland, Oregon, and some locations, such as a feminist bookstore, appear without alteration. The show drew powerhouse guest stars from the worlds of film and television, many of whom either played against type or showcased their sometimes previously unknown comedic side. The likes of Steve Buscemi, Pearl Jam's Eddie Vedder, director Gus Van Sant, and tennis champion Martina Navratilova all crossed paths with the multitude of characters played by Armisen and Brownstein. One memorable sketch featured Kyle MacLachlan as the mayor and ex-Monkee Michael Nesmith as his father, who is secretly financing construction initiatives for his son's benefit.

The main object of the satire is Portland itself, in all its Pacific Northwest quirkiness, but the city never objected; indeed, it took the show to its heart, as did much of the rest of the world. **ATB**

Classic episode
One Moore Episode | *Season 2, episode 2.*
A couple gets roped into buying a unique artisanal gift by a beguiling shop owner. Another couple tracks down the creator of *Battlestar Galactica* in order to make him write more episodes.

◉ (L–R) Carrie Brownstein and Fred Armisen freak Portland out with an act of ecoterrorism.

Episodes

Comedy | UK/USA | 2011–present

Comedy about the difficulties of remaking a British sitcom in the United States

Cast | Matt LeBlanc, Stephen Mangan, Tamsin Greig, John Pankow   **Original broadcasters** | BBC Two (UK), Showtime (USA)   **Award** | 1 Golden Globe   **For fans of . . .** | *Curb Your Enthusiasm* (2000), *Extras* (2005)

The premise of *Episodes* is this: on the strength of their critically acclaimed UK sitcom *Lyman's Boys*, happily married couple Sean and Beverly Lincoln (Stephen Mangan and Tamsin Greig) are invited by American TV exec Merc Lapidus (John Pankow) to remake their show for a US audience. Before long there's lots of studio interference with the original format; Matt LeBlanc, ex-*Friends* (a twisted version of himself, a TV star whose twin obsessions are sex and remaining in the public eye), is forced on them as the lead, and the show is renamed *Pucks!* It's a massive flop.

Episodes covers much of the same ground as *Extras* (2005), but what differentiates it from Ricky Gervais' show is its warmheartedness. The viewers are made to care about Sean and Beverly as their marriage deteriorates. Meanwhile another wickedly funny scene is never far away. *Episodes* is thus something of a paradox: a successful Anglo-American co-production that is founded on the often accurate assumption that attempts to bridge the transatlantic culture and humor gap are doomed to failure. **LH**

Classic episode

Season 2, episode 9. Merc's Man of the Year celebrations turn into a huge brawl, where Matt dislocates his shoulder. Revelations tumble out and Sean finally starts trying to fix his marriage with Beverly.

⬥ (L–R) Matt LeBlanc (as a version of himself), Stephen Mangan (Sean), and Kathleen Rose Perkins (Carol, head of programming).

Vampire Prosecutor

Fantasy/Horror | South Korea | 2011–12

A smart vampire uses his powers to solve gruesome crimes

Cast | Yeon Jeong-hun, Lee Yeong-ah, Lee Won-jong, Kim Joo-young
Original broadcaster | OCN
For fans of . . . | *Buffy the Vampire Slayer* (1997), *Angel* (1999)

Veering far away from the teenage romance of the *Twilight* series, this tense modern vampire tale delivered horror, mystery, and crime, in twenty-three gripping episodes. The story started with a spectacular car crash, during which suave prosecutor Min Tae-yeon (Yeon Jeong-hun) was bitten by a vampire. Inevitably, he became one himself—but with unexpectedly useful powers. After drinking some blood of a murder victim, he was able to visualize the events leading up to the killing. From then on, working with his scruffy sidekick, detective Hwang Sun-beom (Lee Won-jong), who knew his true nature, he exploited his affinity with blood to catch criminals. However, new female prosecutor, Yu Jeong-in (Lee Yeong-ah), who favored logical reason to solve crimes, became suspicious of her strange colleagues and their bizarre behavior.

Kim Tae-seong, cinematographer for *War of the Arrows* (2011), delivered stylish imagery throughout the series, using computer-generated technology to visualize Tae-yeon's retrospective views of crimes, and to reiterate the prosecutor's vampiric nature. Scenes shot from odd angles, shaking images, and upbeat background music complemented the action. Due to popular demand a second season of eleven shows followed in 2012, directed by Yu Seon-dong, director of Korean horror film *Death Bell 2: Bloody Camp* (2010).

Vampire Prosecutor was a fast moving visual feast, starring a supercool modern vampire with no fatal sunlight, garlic, or crucifixes to cramp his style. **SH**

Bref

Drama | France | 2011–12

A young man's existential angst as he sees his middle age looming ahead

Cast | Kyan Khojandi, Mikaël Alhawi, Alice David, Dédo, Blanche Gardin, Jonathan Cohen, Kheiron, Keyvan Khojandi, Bérengère Krief, Baptiste Lecaplain
Original broadcaster | Canal+
For fans of . . . | *Peep Show* (2003)

This eighty-two-episode series of two-minute films depicted the experiences of a man as he approached and passed the age of thirty. The unnamed protagonist was played by Kyan Khojandi, a French comedian of Iranian heritage, who also wrote most of the scripts.

The hero's existence was generally mundane and lacking in purpose. He was bored and unfulfilled; he idly surfed the Internet; he procrastinated, then worried about procrastinating. But then he got a job, even though the interviewer saw through all the lies he told on his application form. The work was boring, so he quit. The only activity that motivated him was the pursuit of women. It seemed to him that musicians got the best girls, so he took up the guitar. At first, the instrument was merely a prop for his pick-up routine, but gradually he became serious about it.

He had a string of sexual encounters, but the women he really desired didn't want to know. Eventually, he narrowed down his hit list to two women: Maria, his longstanding friend with benefits, and Sarah, his true love. He wisely chose Sarah, but later had another fling with Maria, and thus ruined everything.

Throughout the series, Khojandi's main confidant was Keyvan, his brother both in the fiction and in fact. The two men were presented as having a telepathic rapport that enabled them to understand each other instinctively, often without speaking.

Bref was a great success in France, with an audience that peaked at 2.5 million viewers. **GL**

Broen

Drama | Denmark/Sweden | 2011–present

*Scandinavian cop drama that took
the world by storm*

Cast | Sofia Helin, Kim Bodnia, Dag Malmberg,
Rafael Pettersson, Puk Scharbu
Original broadcaster | SVT1/DR1
For fans of . . . | *Wallander* (2005), *Forbrydelsen*
(*The Killing*, 2007), *Mammon* (2014)

From the opening moments of *Broen* (*The Bridge*), when
a murdered body is discovered on the bridge between
Copenhagen in Denmark and Malmö in Sweden, it
was clear the show was going to be different. When
detectives Saga Norén of Malmö (Sofia Helin) and Martin
Rohde (Kim Bodnia) of Copenhagen investigated the
crime, they found that the head and torso belonged to
one woman, while the legs were those of another, and
the join had been placed precisely on the border of the
two countries. As the killing is revealed to be the work of
a serial killer, two police forces are obliged to cooperate,
giving rise to entertaining culture clashes.

The plot of the first season was gripping, dark, and
strange, and took viewers on a tour of high and low
places in Scandinavian society. It included the torture of
a homeless man live-streamed on the Internet, and the
deliberate withholding of drugs to psychotic patients.

The pitch-perfect characterization in *Broen* is a
triumph, especially in the leather-wearing Saga, who is
plain-speaking to the point of hilarity, while also dimly
aware that this makes her unpopular. She picks up men
in bars for casual sex and is then puzzled when they
want to talk about their feelings. Martin, the Danish
cop, a bear of a man with a wife and family, is her polar
opposite. By the end of a season, the viewers want the
crimes to be solved at least as much for Martin and
Saga as for themselves. **RL**

❯ Cross-border cooperation in the opening episode of *Broen*.

Silk

Drama | UK | 2011–14

British legal drama exploring the human side of a profession having to balance the moral with the pragmatic

Classic episode
Season 1, episode 4. Martha defends a police officer accused of racism. The pupils prepare to hear whether they have made the grade. Clive receives some news that could change his own life and the lives of everyone in chambers.

◉ Maxine Peake (Martha Costello) and Rupert Penry-Jones (Clive Reader) wrestle with their legal and personal issues.

Cast | Maxine Peake, Rupert Penry-Jones, Neil Stuke, Frances Barber, Alex Jennings
Original broadcaster | BBC One
For fans of . . . | *Kavanagh QC* (1995), *North Square* (2000)

Prior to *Silk*'s first broadcast, creator Peter Moffat declared that "life at the bar is the richest possible drama territory." The resulting series, based on Moffat's own experiences in the legal world, was full of the pressures, rivalries, Machiavellian deals, sacrificed principles, sex, and drinking that form everyday life at a busy London legal chambers.

The title refers to "taking silk," the moment a barrister attains Queen's Counsel in the British legal system and is permitted to wear a different gown. Set in Shoe Lane Chambers, Moffat's series focused chiefly on top barristers Martha Costello (Maxine Peake) and Clive Reader (Rupert Penry-Jones), both competing for QC. Senior clerk Billy Lamb (Neil Stuke) assigned cases and kept the chambers afloat, while Costello and Reader dealt with mentoring two trainee barristers.

Silk developed themes from Moffat's *North Square* (2000), and there are parallels in both chambers-based formats. Peake portrayed a driven, talented barrister who had to run that bit faster in the still-male dominated legal world; Frances Barber joined the cast as QC Caroline Warwick for season two, bringing another strong female presence to proceedings. BBC Radio 4 broadcast a sequel drama, *Silk: The Clerks Room*, in 2014, featuring Neil Stuke, and it was announced in late 2014 that ABC was making a US version of the series, with Moffat's input. *Silk* ended after three seasons, with Moffat and Peake maintaining it was essential to go out on a high, but many felt it went before its time. **MW**

Winners & Losers

Comedy | Australia | 2011–present

Female losers win big in this rags-to-riches comedy drama with a moral message

Cast | Melissa Bergland, Zoe Tuckwell-Smith, Virginia Gay, Melanie Vallejo
Original broadcaster | Australia Seven
For fans of . . . | *Sex and the City* (1998), *At Home with the Braithwaites* (2000)

Everyone hates bullies, and seeing them get their comeuppance is a popular theme for drama. The four female friends in *Winners & Losers* achieve this in style thanks to a lottery win, but their attempt to reinvent themselves is not as easy as they expect.

This Australian comedy follows quirky Jenny, lively Bec, straight-laced Frances, and smart Sophie, who were all considered losers in high school. This changes when they are reunited in their twenties and win the Australian Lotto. However, their windfall only complicates their already complex lives, with consequences for their closest relationships.

Creator Bevan Lee wanted the show to explore how we all carry the inner loser inside ourselves, no matter how great life gets. As the series develops, it's clear that the girls' dissatisfaction comes from their need for approval from others, when they would be happier by being true to themselves.

Winners & Losers is a frothy confection, but underpinned by a serious theme and a hint of melancholy. The four leads have a great on-screen rapport, undoubtedly helped by the time they spent together prior to filming, as demanded by the show's makers. The writing and performances combine to show the gap between expectation and reality that we all experience, but is demonstrated more keenly here by the sadness and frustration of the girls, who can't seem to get to where they want to be, despite their wealth. **SO**

Human Planet

Documentary | UK | 2011

A worldwide anthropological survey of Homo sapiens *in all its scope and spectacle*

Cast | John Hurt
Original broadcaster | BBC One
Awards | 2 BAFTAs, 1 Emmy
For fans of . . . | *The Ascent of Man* (1973), *Life on Earth* (1979)

Human beings are one of the most successful species ever to have occupied the Earth, and, almost uniquely among living things, they have adapted to inhabit all of the planet's climates and regions. *Human Planet* was an ambitious attempt to document the many and varied indigenous populations.

The series took three years to make, during which time film crews from the BBC Natural History unit and BBC Wales spent weeks and months in some of the world's most hostile environments, filming remote tribes and peoples. The results were spectacular.

Each of the program's eight episodes focused on the people of a particular habitat, ranging from jungles and mountains to oceans and rivers; from the ice-bound wastes of the Arctic to the most arid and hostile deserts of Asia, Africa, Australia, and the Americas.

Viewers were treated to some truly unforgettable sights. Among the highlights were whale hunters off the Indonesian island of Lembata; Piaroa children in Venezuela catching and eating goliath bird-eating tarantulas, the largest spiders in the world; Buddhist monks in the ruined Angkor temples deep in the Cambodian jungle; and beggars scavenging on the vast Kibarani dump just outside Mombasa, Kenya. This was humanity in all its richness and strangeness, and *Human Planet* let us see ourselves clearly, as if we were outside observers of our own species—the most curious, contradictory, and remarkable one that has ever lived. **WM**

Enlightened
Drama | USA | 2011–13

Woman slays her own demons, then sets about those of the company she works for

Cast | Laura Dern, Luke Wilson, Diane Ladd, Sarah Burns, Timm Sharp, Mike White
Original broadcaster | HBO **Award** | 1 Golden Globe **For fans of . . .** | *Breaking Bad* (2008)

Enlightened opened with the departure of Amy Jellicoe (Laura Dern) from the holistic treatment clinic at which she had spent a month recuperating after a mental breakdown. She moved in with her mom, Helen (Diane Ladd, Dern's real-life mother), and went back to work for her previous employer, but in a much less responsible job than the one she had left. She worried that this was a move toward constructive dismissal.

Processing data at her new desk, she came to see the company from a whole new perspective and with fresh eyes, rapidly uncovering a web of corporate corruption. The old Amy was neurotic and driven and probably would have turned a blind eye to such abuses in the interests of her own career. The new Amy was cool,

balanced, and detached, and decided that she must expose the wrongdoing. As the drama unfolded, the microcosmic changes that she had made in her own life catalyzed macrocosmic changes in the company: by the end, everyone was enlightened.

The show was created by Dern and Mike White; the latter wrote all eighteen episodes. **GL**

Classic episode
The Weekend | *Season 1, episode 4*. In an effort to build bridges with her ex-husband, Levi (Luke Wilson), Amy suggests they go on a camping trip. Soon after they reach their destination, she finds a stash of drugs in his case.

⊙ Amy (Laura Dern) is determined to become enlightened—at any cost. Watch out Levi (Luke Wilson)!

Once Upon a Time

Fantasy/Horror/Sci-Fi | USA | 2011–present

Fractured fairy tale set in the real world

Cast | Jennifer Morrison, Ginnifer Goodwin, Lana Parrilla, Robert Carlyle, Jared S. Gilmore, Emilie de Ravin, Colin O'Donoghue **Original broadcaster** | ABC **For fans of . . .** | *Smallville* (2001), *Grimm* (2011)

The success of Tim Burton's *Alice in Wonderland* in 2010 spawned numerous new takes on classic fairy tales, including *Tin Man* (Syfy) and *Grimm* (NBC). ABC here draws on the backlist of its parent company, Disney, to produce a compelling show that shows the relevance of ancient narratives to contemporary life.

Once upon a time, in a land far away, beautiful princesses and heroic princes battled wizards, sorcerers, and evil stepmothers. Regina (Lana Parrilla), who's both a wicked stepmother and an evil queen, cursed the Enchanted Forest, and transported all of its inhabitants (including herself) to Storybrooke, a small town in rural, modern-day Maine. Snow White, Cinderella, and Red Riding Hood now led quiet lives with no memory of

their magical pasts. But Regina's adopted son, Henry (Jared S. Gilmore) believed that something was not right and went in search of his birth mother, Emma (Jennifer Morrison), who, it turns out, is the long-lost daughter of Snow White and Prince Charming. Henry brings Emma back to Storybrooke and Emma finds herself at the center of a prophecy she hardly understands. **AP**

Classic episode
Skin Deep | Season 1, episode 12. After a cat-burglar robs the modern-day home of Mr. Gold (Robert Carlyle), Emma fears that the victim is going to take retribution into his own hands. With flashbacks to the Enchanted Forest.

⊘ In season three, the main characters hunt the witch who landed them in twenty-first century Maine.

Vera

Crime/Mystery | UK | 2011–present

Pensive, obsessive, and a little bit crotchety, this middle-aged female detective has earned her place in the ranks of favorite British sleuths

Cast | Brenda Blethyn, David Leon, Kenny Doughty, Paul Ritter, Cush Jumbo
Original broadcaster | ITV
For fans of . . . | *Inspector Morse* (1987), *Prime Suspect* (1991), *A Touch of Frost* (1992)

Based on the books of crime novelist Ann Cleeves, *Vera* has proved a hit with audiences since its debut in 2011. With a brilliant central performance from twice-Oscar-nominated Brenda Blethyn, the series is a character-driven crime drama set against the stark backdrop of northeast England. It is captivating viewing.

Producer Elaine Collins came across a copy of the little-sold novel *The Crow Trap* by Ann Cleeves in a thrift store. She knew that its intelligent, middle-aged, female protagonist would translate well to television. Complex and obsessive, Detective Chief Inspector Vera Stanhope frequently battles her own demons in the midst of an investigation. Her often disrespectful attitude to her colleagues, especially Sergeant Joe Ashton (David Leon), is unusual, but Blethyn's skill makes her likable despite the rough edges.

Vera is a police drama that is light on action, high on sleuthing, with the moody Northumberland countryside well utilized. Mixing adaptations of Cleeves' novels with wholly original work, the feature-length investigations have a common theme. The cases are born out of simple human failings, often within close-knit communities. It's a trait shared with the BBC's Shetland, adapted by the same production company from another series of novels by Cleeves. Vera Stanhope has earned her place alongside Inspector Morse, Jack Frost, and DCI Jane Tennison as one of Britain's most popular TV detectives. **MW**

Classic episode
On Harbour Street | *Season 4, episode 1*. DS Joe Ashton's daughter Jessie (Olivia Armstrong) witnesses the death of a retiree on a train. The murder brings Vera to the coastal town of Mardle and an investigation into the past.

◉ Brenda Blethyn in the role of DCI Vera Stanhope.

Fresh Meat

Comedy | UK | 2011–present

Raunchy comedy based on social interaction and sexual shenanigans in an English student house-share

Cast | Jack Whitehall, Zawe Ashton, Charlotte Ritchie, Kimberley Nixon, Greg McHugh
Original broadcaster | Channel 4
For fans of . . . | *Green Wing* (2004), *The Inbetweeners* (2008), *Bad Education* (2012)

The most successful comedic take on student life since *The Young Ones* in the 1970s, *Fresh Meat* was an absorbing and amiable mix of comedy and drama populated by rich characters and enlivened by snappy dialogue.

The title refers to five first-year students sharing a house in Manchester: arrogant would-be lothario J.P. (Jack Whitehall); tough, carefree slacker Vod (Zawe Ashton); desperate-to-be-cool Oregon (Charlotte Ritchie); sweet on the surface but sour underneath Josie (Kimberley Nixon); and the genial and charming, though self-doubting, Kingsley (Joe Thomas), who has a stormy romance with Josie. The sixth member of the household is Howard (Greg McHugh), a socially awkward, older character who is already established at the university.

Stories revolve around their relationships, with the comedy and drama arising from the facts that all the characters were beset by neuroses and all had created facades of the people they wanted to be. The show is vulgar, but also has great heart. In spite of the housemates' obvious differences, there is a warmth among them, which results in an unusually realistic depiction of friendship.

Fresh Meat was created by Sam Bain and Jesse Armstrong (writers of *Peep Show*) with a team of writers who developed the series into a classy production that has grown stronger with each episode. The gifted cast pulls off the difficult trick of creating characters that are likable even when they are doing unlikable things. **DF**

Classic episode
Season 3, episode 8. In the finale of the third season many of the show's long-running plotlines reach critical points with the housemates' friendships threatened from all sides. The perfect mix of comedy and drama.

⬆ Jack Whitehall joins a demonstration of student power.

Dem som Dræber

Crime/Mystery | Denmark | 2011

A show about serial killers that was deemed too violent for screening in its native Denmark

Cast | Laura Bach, Jakob Cedergren, Lars Mikkelsen, Lærke Winther Andersen, Frederik Meldal Nørgaard, Iben Dorner **Original broadcaster** | TV2 **For fans of . . .** | *Forbrydelsen* (*The Killing*, 2007)

Not wishing to be outdone by Danish DR after its success with *Forbrydelsen* (*The Killing*), its compatriot station TV2 put together its own crime drama featuring a dedicated detective and her partner, a criminal profiler, who head a special unit of the Copenhagen police that has been set up to catch serial killers and other wrongdoers in and around the Danish capital.

The show was the brainchild of crime writer Elsebeth Egholm. It got off to a flying start in Denmark when the first episode pulled in nearly 1.5 million viewers, but the increasing level of violence depicted on-screen was inversely proportional to its ratings. It attracted serious criticism, not just for its sadism and gore, but also for the time it aired, when children were still watching TV.

In other countries, however, *Den som dræber* (*Those Who Kill*) fared better and won acclaim that had eluded the show in Denmark. Nevertheless, international success didn't prevent TV2 from canceling the show after its first season. The final episode was subsequently released as a feature film in theaters.

The show contained some powerful performances, especially by guests such as Kim Bodnia (who starred as Martin Rohde in *The Bridge*) and Ulrich Thomsen (later Kai Proctor in *Banshee*); most of the other guest stars played criminals. While *Den som dræber* may not have been the success it was intended to be in its native Denmark, it remains one of the top Nordic noir dramas, as well as one of the darkest. **JH**

⊘ Lærke Winther Andersen investigates one of the grim events that was to embroil *Den som draeber* in controversy.

Falling Skies

Fantasy/Horror/Sci-Fi | USA | 2011–15

A former history professor joins freedom fighters to find out why his son was taken by aliens

Cast | Noah Wyle, Moon Bloodgood, Maxim Knight, Mira Sorvino, Will Patton, Doug Jones, Sarah Carter
Original broadcaster | TNT **For fans of . . .** | *Earth: Final Conflict* (1997), *The Walking Dead* (2010)

One of the greatest of this show's many strengths was that several seasons passed before the viewers got to see the aliens who had invaded Earth—an unknown foe is always scarier than a visible one. Since no one knew what they called themselves, they were referred to by a variety of nicknames, including "Skitters," "Mechs," and "the Overlords."

The main narrative peg was the protagonist's search for his missing son, but the show did not concentrate exclusively on this thread—it broadened out to encompass the lives of several of the freedom fighters. *Falling Skies* undoubtedly benefited from a big budget and probably also from the creative input of Steven Spielberg, who was the series' executive producer. This was the acclaimed director's first return to near-future television since *SeaQuest DSV* ended in 1996.

Fans of *Falling Skies* will recall that one of its most memorable and terrifying aspects was the "harness" that the aliens attached to children, which then fused with them and made them controllable and alienlike—every parent's nightmare. **MR**

Classic episode
Shall We Gather at the River | *Season 2, episode 2.*
Having spent time with the aliens, the hero, Tom, begins to wonder if they have tampered with his mind. His self-doubt makes the freedom fighters doubt him, too.

◉ Tom (Noah Wyle) aims for the skies, not through personal ambition but to save the Earth from extraterrestrial invasion.

Unforgiven

Drama | UK | 2009

Bleak story and bleak landscape make great television drama

Cast | Suranne Jones, Peter Davison, Siobhan Finneran, Emily Beecham, Matthew McNulty
Original broadcaster | ITV
For fans of . . . | *Last Tango in Halifax* (2012), *Happy Valley* (2014)

Before *Last Tango in Halifax* and *Happy Valley*, writer Sally Wainwright brought a bleak, one-off drama to the hills of Halifax in *Unforgiven*. It shared common ground with the dark *Happy Valley*; the story of Ruth coming to terms with life on the outside after fifteen years in prison following a conviction for murder as a teenager was bleak stuff. As Ruth, Suranne Jones gave a sensitive performance, revealing a range that confirmed her status as one of Britain's top-flight actresses.

For *Unforgiven*, Wainwright returned to the hills and towns of West Yorkshire where she was born. The landscape, contrasting ugly tower blocks with old farmhouses, was painted in muted tones, bleached to a dirty tobacco yellow. The main thrust of the drama came from Ruth's adjustment to life on the outside and a desire to find her sister, who was adopted. She was helped by lawyer John Ingram (Peter Davison), and the story was punctuated by the father of one of Ruth's victims seeking revenge on his son's killer. *Unforgiven* was raw character drama at its best, the relationships complicated and nuanced. Wainwright created Ruth with Jones in mind, and there was an isolation and quietness to the character that was engaging and encouraged investment in Ruth's plight.

The drama was tightly focused over three episodes into a taught, compelling story, and it was all the more appealing for its one-off status. While it may have set the stall for *Happy Valley*, *Unforgiven* stands as one of Wainwright's most affecting pieces of work. **MW**

Southland

Crime/Mystery | USA | 2009–13

A steep learning curve in Los Angeles as rookie cop wises up to stay alive

Cast | Ben McKenzie, Kevin Alejandro, Arija Bareikis, Michael Cudlitz, Shawn Hatosy
Original broadcaster | NBC/TNT
Awards | 2 Emmys
For fans of . . . | *The Shield* (2002), *Stalker* (2014)

On his first day as a police officer in the Los Angeles Police Department, Ben Sherman (Ben McKenzie) was taken under the wing of training officer John Cooper (Michael Cudlitz) and straight out into a baptism of fire on the streets. As the show progressed, the lives of homicide detectives Lydia Adams and Russell Clarke and gang squad detectives Sammy Bryant and Nate Moretta became intertwined with the crimes being investigated. The second season saw a trimming down of the cast roster and a focus on the relationships of this small group of officers, as some of the narrative became more personal and backstories were explored. In the final season, Sherman was responsible for overseeing a rookie officer out on patrol. In contrast to his own early days on the force, he encountered difficulties imparting his experience, because the new recruit was a military veteran with fixed ideas.

Commissioned for broadcast network NBC as an ensemble police drama rather than a procedural show like *CSI: Crime Scene Investigation* (2000), *Southland* garnered critical praise for its authentic look and "bold contemporary tone." Despite this, NBC canceled the show after watching the first four episodes of the sophomore season and deciding it was too dark; showrunners announced the news to cast and crew on set. Cable network TNT stepped in and took the six already filmed episodes, and also ordered another seven. *Southland* remained with TNT until the end of its run in 2013. **MC**

❯ Michael Cudlitz as John Cooper in the episode "See the Woman."

Suits

Drama | USA | 2011–present

Smart, well-tailored drama with exceptional texture

Cast | Gabriel Macht, Patrick J. Adams, Gina Torres, Meghan Markle, Rick Hoffman, Sarah Rafferty
Original broadcaster | USA Network
For fans of . . . | *L.A. Law* (1986), *Ally McBeal* (1997), *Boston Legal* (2004), *The Good Wife* (2009)

Harvey Specter (Gabriel Macht) is a brilliant attorney, and his boss, Jessica (Gina Torres), thinks he's the person to take over when she retires. But he's a lone wolf, and that's not a great quality in a leader. She thinks he needs to learn empathy and that the best way to teach it to him is by forcing him to take on an associate.

Enter stoner Mike Ross (Patrick J. Adams). A bright young man with street smarts and a photographic memory, he should have been a Harvard graduate, but he made a stupid mistake and blew his chances. Harvey really likes him and hires him, but the two men have to conceal the fact that he doesn't have the necessary qualifications for the job.

Mike and Harvey complement each other perfectly, but their colleagues also interweave effortlessly. Each has his or her own agenda, changing loyalties, and insecurities, which are either resolved or—more often—cripple their ambitions. The fan favorite, however, is Donna (Sarah Rafferty), Harvey's personal assistant; sharp, sassy, and a force to be reckoned with, she is fiercely loyal to Harvey and, eventually, to Mike.

Suits focuses more on the politics of personal relationships than on the law. It is part buddy-comedy and part slick power-drama, and succeeds most when it unpicks the threads that bind unlikely colleagues together and stitches them together again in new ways. And it manages that feat week after week. **RM**

◀ Harvey Specter (Gabriel Macht) and his protégé Mike Ross (Patrick J. Adams) face-off in this classy, well-dressed drama.

Game of Thrones

Fantasy/Horror/Sci-Fi | USA | 2011–present

Civil war tears a world apart in a bloody, treacherous fantasy—plus dragons!

Cast | Lena Headey, Peter Dinklage, Maisie Williams, Emilia Clarke, Kit Harington, Iain Glen, Sophie Turner
Award | 1 Golden Globe   **Original broadcaster** | HBO
For fans of . . . | *The Tudors* (2007), *Legend of the Seeker* (2008), *Outlander* (2014), *Black Sails* (2014)

This unprecedentedly successful series combines all the best elements of historical drama in a compelling package that contains something for almost everyone.

The show is based on *A Song of Ice and Fire*, a series of fantasy novels by George R.R. Martin, the first volume of which was entitled *A Game of Thrones*. In Martin's imagined world there are two continents, Westeros and Essos, which sometimes cooperate, sometimes ignore each other, and sometimes come into conflict.

There are three main narrative arcs. The first concerns a civil war in Westeros for the Iron Throne of the Seven Kingdoms. The second concerns the ongoing threats—both real and perceived—to the people of Westeros by the barbaric peoples of the northlands and Essos. The third strand follows the attempts of a deposed and exiled monarch to reclaim her crown. Much of the material is inspired by events in medieval English history, notably the Hundred Years' War (1351–1453) and the Wars of the Roses (1455–85).

The show was keenly anticipated even before its first broadcast, and thereafter went from strength to strength on account of its nudity and violence (which were controversial, but attractive to many), and its judicious use of special effects. Among its most innovative features were Dothraki and Valyrian, languages specially created by US linguist David J. Peterson and subtitled on screen. **JS**

◉ Jack Gleeson (Joffrey) and Charles Dance (Tywin) in "The Bear and the Maiden Fair" from season three.

Grimm

Fantasy/Horror/Sci-Fi | USA | 2011–present

And you thought the Brothers Grimm only did fairy tales . . .

Cast | David Giuntoli, Russell Hornsby, Bitsie Tulloch, Silas Weir Mitchell, Sasha Roiz, Reggie Lee, Bree Turner, Claire Coffee **Original broadcaster** | NBC **For fans of . . .** | *Dead Like Me* (2003), *Reaper* (2007)

This series updates the fairy tales of the Brothers Grimm into a modern context. Here humans coexist with the Wesen, monstrous creatures that resemble humans, but whose true nature emerges when they become agitated. Nick Burkhardt (David Giuntoli) is a homicide detective, and he is also a Grimm—one who can see the Wesen beneath the skin. The show follows his life and relationships with his girlfriend, Juliette (Bitsie Tulloch), his wolflike best friend, Monroe (Silas Weir Mitchell), and Monroe's literally foxy girlfriend, Rosalee (Bree Turner).

The trio's main adversaries are police chief Renard (Sasha Roiz), who is part-Wesen, and Adalind (Claire Coffee), a witch with a long-standing grudge against Nick for depriving her of her powers.

Grimm has moments of classic, stylized horror, but it is no straightforward battle between good and evil. The series is subtly nuanced so that the Wesen are sometimes more appealing than the humans, and this ambivalence about the rights and wrongs of the drama gives the series much greater credibility than its title alone might suggest. **DJH**

Classic episode

Mr. Sandman | *Season 2, episode 15*. Nick is attacked by a fly-like Wesen that can make its victims blind. Monroe and Rosalee discover that to save Nick's sight they need the eye of a Wesen taken while the creature is in undisguised form.

⊕ David Giuntoli as detective Nick Burkhardt in the episode "Highway of Tears."

Teen Wolf

Fantasy/Horror/Sci-Fi | USA | 2011–present

Who knew werewolves could be sexy?

Cast | Tyler Posey, Crystal Reed, Dylan O'Brien, Tyler Hoechlin **Original broadcaster** | MTV
For fans of . . . | *Buffy the Vampire Slayer* (1997)

Superficially, *Teen Wolf* may appear to be a formulaic creation in which a good-looking protagonist fights monsters. But there's much more to it than that.

It's the characters that make it special. One of the central female figures appears to be a standard, played-for-laughs, fashion-obsessed bimbo. But she's also the cleverest student at school, and as the series develops she becomes the heart of the show. Why shouldn't a clever girl like fashion? There's a gay character who doesn't just act camp. He plays lacrosse, he goes to gay clubs, and he has boyfriends, and viewers even see some intimacy between him and one of them. He's treated exactly the same as a straight character, which was still a rare thing on television in 2014.

With a frenetic soundtrack and some beautiful direction, *Teen Wolf* looks fantastic, and the scripts are consistently smart and witty. It has much in common with *Buffy the Vampire Slayer* (1997): both have plenty of villains, but they are fundamentally not about the battle of good and evil; they are about rites of passage and growing up. **JL**

Classic episode
Party Guessed | *Season 1, episode 9*. At her birthday party, Lydia is forced to spike the punch with a drug that makes people hallucinate their worst fears. The consequences for some of the guests are devastating.

◉ Tyler Posey as Scott McCall, who has to balance diurnal life as a high school student with nocturnal existence as a monster.

Revenge

Drama | USA | 2011–15

An edge-of-the-seat tale that keeps viewers hooked with its impossibly wealthy characters, surface glitter, and endlessly dazzling twists

Cast | Emily VanCamp, Madeleine Stowe, Henry Czerny, Gabriel Mann, Nick Wechsler, Josh Bowman, James Tupper
Original broadcaster | ABC
For fans of . . . | *Scandal* (2012)

When Emily Thorne (Emily VanCamp) arrived among the affluent socialites summering in the Hamptons, she came bearing a dark secret: She was really the daughter of David Clarke (James Tupper), a man framed for financing a terrorist act, who was later brutally killed and silenced. Having learned the truth from his journals, Emily returned to ruin those who destroyed him.

By combining a conspiracy to commit a terrorist attack on American soil with the repercussions of the 2008 global financial crisis, this effective retelling of Alexandre Dumas' *The Count of Monte Cristo* instantly resonated with audiences.

In the early episodes, Emily systematically targeted and destroyed someone responsible for either downing Flight 197 or incriminating her father. But unexpected revelations and emotional ties soon upset Emily's plans, and pushed the story in unexpected directions. The nominal villains proved to be as capable of loyalty, decency, and regret as they are of deception, betrayal, and ruthless self-preservation. In particular, Emily's nemesis—the icy Victoria Grayson (Madeleine Stowe)—inspired sympathy as she wrestled with the fallout from betraying David, a man she loved, and battled to keep her children safe.

With a fine line in bristling and knowing dialogue, and a flair for grandly operatic storytelling, *Revenge* was a helter-skelter drama, and the tumbling succession of audacious twists ensured you never could tell what would happen next. **RM**

Classic episode
Execution | *Season 3, episode 22.* The long-awaited showdown between Victoria and Emily comes near the end of a thrilling episode. But the jaw-dropping final scene sets the show on course for a very different fourth season.

⬓ Emily VanCamp as Emily Thorne, righter of wrongs.

The Crimson Petal and the White

Historical drama | UK | 2011

A lavish costume drama set in England in the Victorian era, based on the novel of the same name by Dutch Australian author Michel Faber

Cast | Romola Garai, Chris O'Dowd, Amanda Hale, Richard E. Grant, Gillian Anderson, Mark Gatiss
Original broadcaster | BBC Two
Award | 1 BAFTA
For fans of . . . | *The Mystery of Edwin Drood* (2012)

This drama, set in 1870s London, told the story of a young prostitute, Sugar (Romola Garai), who climbed the social ladder by becoming the mistress of successful businessman William Rackham (Chris O'Dowd).

The key focus of the story was the contrast between the worldly-wise Sugar and Rackham's uptight wife, Agnes (Amanda Hale) who, typically for the period, was very repressed regarding matters sexual, and barely even acknowledged her own daughter. Sugar inveigled herself into Rackham's life and began to manipulate herself into high society.

The drama explored the different outlets that many of the characters used to vent their feelings. When viewers first saw Sugar, she was writing a novel about the clients whom she despised. Rackham also fancied himself as a novelist, although he was less adept at this than Sugar. His pious brother, Henry Junior (Mark Gatiss), wrote sermons because he wanted to become a clergyman. Agnes kept a diary.

The series' re-creation of the era was extremely authentic, and it is no surprise that it won design and costume awards. Although there are obvious limitations in transferring a long, dark novel to the screen, director Marc Munden portrayed the seedy underworld of Victorian London with an appropriately hazy, lurching sense of movement through dark alleyways. The cast was also exceptional, with O'Dowd receiving praise from author Michel Faber for making Rackham more sympathetic on the screen than on the page. **AN**

Classic episode
Episode 3. William moves Sugar into his home, where she is to work as a governess to his neglected daughter, Sophie. Soon afterward, Agnes' health deteriorates; Sugar promises to help with her recovery.

⊛ Romola Garai as Sugar, who is not as sweet as her name suggests.

The Hour

Historical drama | UK | 2011–12

1950s-set drama about the intertwining worlds of broadcasting and politics

Cast | Dominic West, Romola Garai, Ben Whishaw, Anton Lesser, Anna Chancellor   **Original broadcaster** | BBC Two   **For fans of . . .** | *Mad Men* (2007)

The Hour was a multilayered period piece depicting the pressures of bringing a new program to air on TV. On the surface, with its issues of censorship and romantic liaisons, it's a 1950s British version of *The Newsroom* (1996), but underneath there are political schemes, cover-ups, and an overarching story line that could have been lifted from the pages of a novel by John le Carré.

Disillusioned producer Freddie Lyon (Ben Whishaw) was drafted by Bel Rowley (Romola Garai) to head up the domestic news desk of *The Hour*, a hard-hitting current affairs show she was setting up at the BBC under her mentor Clarence Fendley (Anton Lesser). Lyon felt that domestic news was beneath him, especially when the show's anchor was the vapid Hector Madden

(Dominic West). As *The Hour* struggled onto the air, the team battled management interference and low ratings, Bel and Hector began an affair, and Lyon became embroiled in a murder that linked one of his colleagues to a Cold War espionage plot.

The first season of *The Hour* was creditably successful; the second was a flop; there was never a third. **MW**

Classic episode
Season 1, episode 6. The producers of *The Hour* are warned not to criticize the government, but they go ahead anyway. As a consequence the show is canceled and some of those involved with it are fired.

⊙ (L–R) Anna Chancellor (Lix), Ben Whishaw (Freddie), Romola Garai (Bel), Dominic West (Hector), and Oona Chaplin (Marnie).

Happy Endings
Comedy | USA | 2011–13

A twentysomething buddy comedy that was offbeat and funny

Cast | Eliza Coupe, Elisha Cuthbert, Zachary Knighton, Damon Wayans Jr., Casey Wilson, Adam Pally
Original broadcaster | ABC **For fans of . . .** | *How I Met Your Mother* (2005), *New Girl* (2011)

When a couple separates, it presents many difficulties, not least for their friends. *Happy Endings* took this problem as its starting point—could all parties stay friends or would they take sides?

The series focused on six best friends who were forced to reevaluate their relationships with one another when the couple at the center of their group, Dave (Zachary Knighton) and Alex (Elisha Cuthbert), break up. Initial difficulties included the etiquette of postbreakup dating, the removal of couple tattoos, and dealing with anniversaries.

The series gradually moved away from its original conceit, allowing characters to generate offbeat and funny story lines of their own. The neat and knowing use of cultural references gave the show a unique identity, preventing it from turning into a *Friends* clone.

Although it fell victim to low ratings in its third and final season, *Happy Endings* attracted a keen following and positive notices from critics. A subsequent sitcom from its creator David Caspe—*Marry Me*—lives in the same universe, with some of the same characters. **SO**

Classic episode
Dave of the Dead | Season 1, episode 7.
The friends become obsessed with the threat of a zombie apocalypse, leading Max and Jane to test out potential survival plans, while Penny tries to keep up with her new hipster boyfriend.

◎ *Happy Endings'* successful formula mixed bittersweet humor and slapstick.

Homeland

Drama | USA | 2011–present

Who is true—a decorated military hero or a lone CIA operative who believes he is a traitor?

Cast | Claire Danes, Damian Lewis, Morena Baccarin, David Harewood, Mandy Patinkin
Original broadcaster | Showtime
Awards | 5 Golden Globes, 8 Emmys
For fans of . . . | *Allegiance* (2015)

Marine Sergeant Nicholas Brody (Damian Lewis) returns to the United States more than eight years after being imprisoned by al-Qaeda. However, one person at the CIA, Carrie Mathison (Claire Danes) doesn't believe Brody's story, because a contact in Iraq has warned her that a captured soldier had been turned by the terrorist organization and would be used to attack the United States. Unfortunately for Carrie, an unauthorized operation resulting in the deaths of innocent people combined with her deteriorating mental health leads everyone to doubt her, including herself. But her mentor Saul Berenson (Mandy Patinkin) keeps faith.

Meanwhile, Brody's reintegration into family life is difficult. His family, believing him to be dead, have moved on. His daughter suspects her father has changed when she discovers him praying toward Mecca. Over the course of the seasons, the viewers witness the destruction of the CIA, an attempt on the president's life, and Carrie being deployed back into the field, though this time to Pakistan as a station chief who will do anything and use anyone to complete her mission.

The show is based on the Israeli series *Hatufim* (*Prisoners of War*) produced by Keshet in 2010. While the show is generally praised by critics in the United States and Britain, it has come under fire for its negative portrayal of Muslims. Lebanon threatened to sue the producers for damage to its tourism industry. **MR**

◉ Claire Danes takes aim as Carrie Mathison in *Homeland*.

Mad Dogs
Drama | UK | 2011–13

Darkly funny drama with a bleak undertone

Cast | Max Beesley, Philip Glenister, John Simm, Marc Warren   **Original broadcaster** | Sky 1
For fans of . . . | *Hustle* (2004), *Life on Mars* (2006)

Mad Dogs was about friendship. It was about growing older, seeing where one has been and where one might go. It was about that impending midlife crisis. It was also about crime, murder, and deceit. It was wickedly, darkly funny and blessed with a superb cast.

Cris Cole's scripts brought together four friends—Baxter (John Simm), Rick (Marc Warren), Woody (Max Beesley), and Quinn (Philip Glenister)—for a reunion at the Majorcan villa of Alvo (Ben Chaplin). After Alvo was murdered, the four were mistaken for drug dealers, fell foul of corrupt local police officers, and, following a siege at the villa, escaped by ferry to Ibiza with €3 million. Across the four seasons, the friends became embroiled in ever-more labyrinthine situations, never quite getting ahead. David Warner provided a highlight of season two, guest starring as the British expatriate behind the drug operation.

Viewers could never be sure where the plot was going next, at least not until the fantastical and bleak two-part ending in which the four friends plunged toward hell in a car following their execution on a beach. **MW**

Classic episode
Season 1, episode 4. Believing they are under threat from the Serbian Mafia, the friends spend a tense night in the villa. They eventually work out that there is no Mafia and they are dealing with corrupt local police.

⌾ (L–R) Max Beesley (Woody), Philip Glenister (Quinn), Ben Chaplin (Alvo), Marc Warren (Rick), and John Simm (Baxter).

The Wonders of the Universe

Documentary | UK | 2011

Physicist Brian Cox's four-part exploration of the workings of the universe

Cast | Brian Cox **Original broadcaster** | BBC Two **For fans of . . .** | *Cosmos: A Personal Journey* (1980), *Wonders of the Solar System* (2010)

The Wonders of the Universe was a giant leap forward for popular science on British television. It focused on massive, complex subjects, such as the birth of reality and the nature of light—but it was never anything other than accessible and inclusive. With 13.7 billion years to cover since the Big Bang, host Professor Brian Cox skillfully boiled down his story and, like all great teachers, made it fun as well as fascinating.

The series was made with a huge sense of scale. Cox and his crew traveled to exotic locations—from Zambia's Victoria Falls to an ancient temple in Peru built to match the movement of the Sun—which were all beautifully photographed. (If the science bamboozles you, the scenery will melt your heart.) But this was no waste of money or self-indulgent folly. Cox, a former member of pop band D:Ream, knows exactly how to tell a story; he used the beauties of planet Earth to illuminate the beauties of the cosmos. As in his earlier show *Wonders of the Solar System* (2010), he took advantage of found objects, such as rocks, sand, and abandoned buildings, to explain the science behind the ideas. **IF**

Classic episode
Stardust | Episode 2. Science and religion meet in a nonconfrontational way as Cox reconciles faiths that believe in the reconstitution of matter with the cyclical nature of the physical world.

⊛ Professor Brian Cox filming on location at Start Point, the most southerly point in Devon, England.

Shameless

Comedy/Drama | USA | 2011–present

American adaptation of British series about a young woman raising her siblings

Cast | William H. Macy, Emmy Rossum, Justin Chatwin, Jeremy Allen White, Cameron Monaghan, Shanola Hampton, Joan Cusack
Original broadcaster | Showtime
For fans of . . . | *Nurse Jackie* (2009)

Adapting such a popular, long-running, and idiosyncratically British show was always going to be tricky. However, the US *Shameless* succeeds precisely because it doesn't attempt to reproduce the original note for note, but concentrates on the universal issues of alcoholism, poverty, and familial love.

By transplanting the action to Chicago's working-class South Side, the show benefits from the bleak atmosphere of the miserable Midwestern weather. Humor is less overt here than in the UK version, but virtuosic performances by native Chicagoan Joan Cusack as the paranoid, agoraphobic Sheila Jackson, and William H. Macy as Frank Gallagher are masterpieces of comic timing. Frank's eldest daughter Fiona (Emmy Rossum) struggles to keep her family afloat despite his constant attempts to drag them into further poverty. The humanity of the characters is the show's biggest draw.

Time and again the characters do things that we may regard as unforgivable, but then they reveal a human frailty that brings them back into our hearts. Viewers root for the Gallaghers in spite of themselves. The show's ratings have increased throughout its run, as has its critical acclaim. The later seasons moved away from comedy into more dramatic territory, but there has been no decline in the quality of the work, and viewers are still tuning in in their millions. **LN**

❯ William H. Macy as Frank the Plank falls foul of faulty handcuffs.

American Horror Story
Fantasy/Horror/Sci-Fi | USA | 2011–present

Twisted and brutal series revitalized the horror genre on television

Cast | Jessica Lange, Sarah Paulson, Evan Peters, Frances Conroy, Lily Rabe, Kathy Bates, Zachary Quinto
Original broadcaster | FX **Awards** | 4 Emmys, 1 Golden Globe **For fans of . . .** | *The X-Files* (1993)

After their success as writers and producers of *Glee* (2009), Ryan Murphy and Brad Falchuk made a sharp change of direction with this amazing gore-fest. One of the interesting things about *American Horror Story* is its anthology format, with each season featuring a different self-contained story set in a different place and at a different time. Season one was set in a haunted house in modern-day California; season two in a 1960s insane asylum; season three in a witches' coven in modern-day New Orleans; and season four in a 1950s circus freak show. Each year focuses on different types of horror—both human and supernatural. There are serial-killer clowns, Nazi doctors, ghostly teenagers, aliens, and much, much more.

But it's not just blood, gore, and ghouls; viewers genuinely care about each world's inhabitants. The standout performance is usually provided by Jessica Lange, who is mesmerizing in each of her roles. With a setting and story change each year, *American Horror Story* never feels stale and could run on indefinitely, which is the ultimate aim of any serial format. **LH**

Classic episode
Madness Ends | *Season 2, episode 13*. Sister Jude (Jessica Lange) is emancipated and sets out on a new life. Lana Winters (Sarah Paulson) discovers the truth about her son and brings the season to an end on an emotional high.

◍ Jessica Lange has played a pivotal character in each season; here she is the ambitious boss of a struggling freak show in season four.

Marchlands

Fantasy/Horror/Sci-Fi | UK | 2011

Supernatural drama that affects three families in the same house in three separate decades

Cast | Alex Kingston, Dean Andrews, Jodie Whitaker, Shelley Conn, Elliot Cowan, Jamie Thomas King, Tessa Peake-Jones, Anne Reid **Original broadcaster** | ITV **For fans of . . .** | *Afterlife* (2005), *Remember Me* (2014)

Marchlands was both a ghost story and a mystery. It opened in 1967 with the death by drowning of young Alice Bowen near the eponymous family home. Her parents, Ruth and Paul, could not understand why she wandered off into danger. In an effort to escape their sad memories, they moved out.

But Marchlands was now haunted by Alice's ghost, who visited the subsequent owners of the house. First she appeared to Helen and Eddie, who moved in with their young family in the 1980s, and then to Mark and his pregnant wife, Nisha, in the present day.

Each decade's haunting was subtly different. Ruth and Paul were consumed by grief and the ubiquitous reminders of Alice; Helen's and Eddie's young daughter befriended the ghost of Alice; Nisha was disturbed by supernatural occurrences after she decided to name her new daughter Alice. Nisha was later kept company in the largely empty Marchlands by a much older Ruth, who returned to get the truth about what happened to Alice. The show was full of echoes down the ages but never became repetitive. **LH**

Classic episode
Episode 5. We discover what really happened on the night Alice died, and Ruth finally achieves a form of closure. The Bowens leave Marchlands in a poignant, yet remarkably upbeat, ending to a lovely series.

⬥ Helen (Alex Kingston) and Eddie Maynard (Dean Andrews) realize the haunting is getting close to home . . .

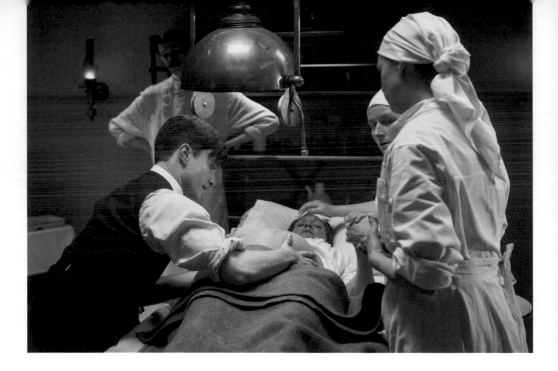

A Young Doctor's Notebook

Comedy | UK | 2012–13

A naive medical student struggles with life in rural Russia

Cast | Jon Hamm, Daniel Radcliffe, Rosie Cavaliero, Vicki Pepperdine, Adam Godley, Margaret Clunie
Original broadcaster | Sky Arts **For fans of . . .** | *The Knick* (2014)

Based on the memoirs of Mikhail Bulgakov, author of the novel *The Master and Margarita* (1967), *A Young Doctor's Notebook* depicted Dr. Vladimir Bomgard, both as an adult in 1933 in a remote village hospital, and as a naive and idealistic medical student in Moscow sixteen years previously. The older man was played by Jon Hamm, famous for his role as Don Draper in *Mad Men* (2007); the younger was Daniel Radcliffe, star of the *Harry Potter* movies (2001–11).

A dark comedy, the program did not shy away from the bleak humor often used by medical practitioners. The young doctor put away the childish things he loved in the Russian capital and became a responsible adult. Much was left unsaid about the intervening years, and

the viewers are left to decide for themselves how the rise of Stalinism would have affected the young man's change into the older.

The first season was broadcast on Sky Arts in Britain. US cable channel Ovation took over the second, which covered the Russian Revolution and the rise of communism in the Soviet Union. **EB**

Classic episode
Season 1, episode 4. After becoming famous, the young doctor struggles to cope with the influx of patients clamoring for him to treat them, and becomes further enthralled by the temptations of morphine after failing to save a patient's life.

◭ Daniel Radcliffe as a young doctor tending to a patient in Moscow at the time of the Russian Revolution.

Scandal

Drama | USA | 2012–present

Complex and compelling political drama featuring a mesmerizing lead actress

Cast | Kerry Washington, Tony Goldwyn, Darby Stanchfield, Katie Lowes, Guillermo Diaz, Jeff Perry
Original broadcaster | ABC   **For fans of . . .** | *The West Wing* (1999), *The Good Wife* (2009)

Smart, sassy, and sexy, *Scandal* slow-burned its way to the top of the North American TV drama ratings within three years of debuting with an intriguing ensemble of characters, centered on the political crisis management services of Olivia Pope (Kerry Washington) in Washington, D.C.

Scandal is based on the experiences of former White House press aide Judy Smith, who serves as coexecutive producer. Shonda Rhimes' production begins with Pope leaving her job as White House Communications Director to President Fitzgerald Grant (Tony Goldwyn) and setting up her own business. As her team, including investigator Abby Whelan (Darby Stanchfield) and troubled ex-CIA operative Huck

(Guillermo Diaz), work to protect the image of the great and good of American politics, Olivia finds her emotional links to Grant are hard to break.

Kerry Washington became the first African American woman since 1995 to be nominated for Outstanding Lead Actress in a Drama Series at the 2013 Emmy Awards. A win seems only a matter of time. **MW**

> **Classic episode**
> *A Woman Scorned* | *Season 2, episode 20*. Melody Grant (Bellamy Young) threatens to expose her husband's extramarital affair with Olivia to the American people—but President Grant thinks she's bluffing.

◐ (L–R) Tony Goldwyn (Fitzgerald Grant), Kerry Washington (Olivia Pope), and Jeff Perry (Cyrus Beene).

A Touch of Cloth

Comedy | UK | 2012–present

Gag-heavy police spoof with an unrelenting barrage of jokes

Cast | John Hannah, Suranne Jones, Julian Rhind-Tutt, Navin Chowdhry
Original broadcaster | Sky 1
For fans of . . . | *Car 54, Where Are You?* (1961), *Police Squad!* (1982), *The Thin Blue Line* (1995)

A Touch of Cloth is far from subtle. Charlie Brooker's comedy riffs on the procedures of the British police service, often bludgeoning the audience in the face with its visually signposted humor and wordplay. The show is clever, yet highly juvenile; the characters are clichéd, which is entirely the point. Viewers never know whether to laugh or groan.

Detective Inspector Jack Cloth (John Hannah) heads up the investigation into a series of murders that have targeted jurors. Cloth is partnered with Detective Constable Anne Oldman (Suranne Jones), and Assistant Chief Constable Tom Boss (Julian Rhind-Tutt) pushes them for a quick result. The pressure is on. Hannah is perfectly cast as the tortured Cloth, having previously played troubled detective Rebus in 2000. Cloth and Rebus could be carbon copies of one another if it were not for the comedy in *A Touch of Cloth*, and the irony is not lost. It is to the credit of Brooker, the writer, that the schoolboy humor, which is seldom seen on modern TV, works well, as does the relationship between Cloth and Oldman (her surname is indicative of the level of humor to be found here).

In 2013, Cloth was called back to work by Boss for a second investigation—despite the fact that his superior was revealed as the murderer in season one. A third case was broadcast in 2014. With a debt of gratitude to *Police Squad!* (1982), *A Touch of Cloth* bursts the pomposity of the British police service—and if Jack Cloth won't do it, who will? **MW**

Video Game High School

Action/Adventure | USA | 2012–14

A boy wins his way into a prestigious school with a curriculum of video games

Cast | Josh Blaylock, Johanna Braddy, Cynthia Watros, Jimmy Wong, Nicole Wyland
Original broadcaster | FreddieW
For fans of . . . | *Deadly Games* (1995), *Level Up* (2012), *King of the Nerds* (2013)

This series of webisodes mixed live action with gaming footage to great effect. *Video Game High School* was set in the near future, where video gaming was the world's most competitive sport. The protagonist, BrianD (Josh Blaylock), accidentally fell into the application process for the prestigious school for gifted gamers after beating one of its alumni in a televised contest through a mixture of luck and skill. His new friends then coached him in the ways of the school, and one of them became his love interest, Jenny Matrix (Johanna Braddy).

This show was a labor of love for its creators. As self-confessed geeks, they wanted to bring together their passion for gaming with YouTube clips laden with special effects. Freddie Wong and Brandon Laatsch already had a successful channel on the online video platform where they released their own self-shot short videos, so they teamed up with Matt Arnold to expand on a concept dreamed up by Will Campos and Chris Pappavaselio.

The team created their own original concept games to be used for battling in the show, and thus saved themselves from having to pay huge amounts of money to license other games. The bespoke games also provided pertinent plot devices.

Video Game High School easily captured its prime target audience, computer nerds, but its appeal spread much further than that, because it's also about eternal themes of love and friendship. **MR**

Nashville

Drama | USA | 2012–present

Although set in the country music scene, this show appeals to anyone who likes romance and dramatic intrigue

Cast | Connie Britton, Hayden Panettiere, Clare Bowen, Eric Close, Charles Esten, Robert Wisdom, Powers Boothe, Will Chase, Oliver Hudson
Original broadcaster | ABC
For fans of . . . | *Rock Follies* (1976), *Tutti Frutti* (1987)

The country music capital of the world is brought to life in *Nashville*, which combines character drama with original and authentic music from an ensemble of attractive stars. In Connie Britton and Hayden Panettiere, the series has two leads who revel in the rivalry and insecurities of two stars of the country scene—fading "Queen of Country Music" Rayna James and the younger, hipper Juliette Barnes.

In *Nashville* Oscar-winning screenwriter Callie Khouri (*Thelma and Louise*, 1991) swapped cinema for television as series creator. The narrative thrust of season one is provided by Juliette and Rayna, who team up on a national tour to revive the latter's fortunes. As the series develops, peripheral characters come more into play—Rayna's politically ambitious husband Teddy (Eric Close), her domineering father Lamar (Powers Boothe), former lover Deacon Claybourne (Charles Esten), and his shy niece Scarlett (Clare Bowen), taking her first steps into the music business.

What sets *Nashville* apart is its effective use of authentic country music. The songs punctuate the drama, but are never forced. With Khouri's husband T. Bone Burnett producing songs for season one and acclaimed lyricists such as Elvis Costello providing subsequent material, the music of *Nashville* has enjoyed chart success and added a revenue stream to the show's profitability. Fundamentally, however, *Nashville* is a show about rivalry, jealousy, and love—but the songs are a great bonus. **MW**

Classic episode
I'll Never Get Out of This World Alive | *Season 1, episode 21*. Deacon discovers he's the father of Rayna's eldest daughter, Maddie. Turning back to the bottle for comfort, he causes a horrific automobile collision.

◉ Country superstar Juliette (Panettiere) in the recording studio.

Äkta människor

Fantasy/Horror/Sci-Fi | Sweden | 2012–present

What would happen if sophisticated androids were integrated into human society?

Cast | Lisette Pagler, Pia Halvorsen, Kåre Hedebrant, Johan Paulsen, Natalie Minnevek
Original broadcaster | SVT-1   **For fans of . . .** | *Battlestar Galactica* (1978), *Black Mirror* (2011)

One of the luxuries of living in an age where the viewers are familiar with science fiction is that concepts such as parallel universes and mass-produced robots can be introduced with little fanfare. This is good news for *Äkta människor* (*Real Humans*), which features both concepts. Freed from the burden of exposition, the makers of this show explore the effects that a mass-produced android workforce could have on modern society.

Set in present-day Sweden, the population is integrated with androids known as Hubots. However, the inclusion of synthetic humans into everyday life throws up many questions: legal, emotional, spiritual, and sexual. There is even a pressure group that campaigns against the plastic people. Initially, the action

was centered around the Engman family, who took charge of their first Hubot, Anita, in episode one. The Engmans reacted to Anita in various ways, struggling to accommodate this strange new presence in their lives. However, Anita has a big secret that will change everything. *Real Humans* explores this fascinating idea in a thoughtful and thorough way. **WM**

> **Classic episode**
> *Break In, Break Loose* | *Season 1, episode 1.*
> The pilot episode effortlessly invites the viewers into a world where androids are commonplace, beginning with an old man running over a pedestrian who turns out to be synthetic.

⊘ Lisette Pagler is outstanding as the Hubot named Anita that challenges assumptions about human identity.

Les Revenants

Fantasy/Horror/Sci-Fi | France | 2012–present

The European arthouse Walking Dead

Cast | Yara Pilartz, Jenna Thiam, Pierre Perrier, Céline Sallette **Original broadcaster** | Canal+
Award | 1 Emmy **For fans of . . .** | *Twin Peaks* (1990)

Residents of a small mountain town are oblivious, but the dead are coming back. Sounds like your typical zombie horror show, right? It isn't. *Les Revenants* (*The Returned*) is a drama about grief. But it's not just about the grief of the living. It's also about the pain of coming back from the dead and discovering that your loved ones are simply getting on with their lives.

The show works because it's underplayed. The music, by Scottish band Mogwai, is subtle and chilling. The direction is still and simple and the actors play it straight. It's quiet and unshowy. It's the complete opposite of anything you'd expect from something that could be categorized as a zombie drama. It's a series set firmly in the real world.

With a murder in the first episode and water draining out of a nearby dam revealing dead animals and a submerged town, the mystery elements of the series are as gripping as the emotional reality. We want to know how and why the dead have returned. But mostly we're fascinated by what their return means for everyone, the living and the dead. JL

Classic episode
Camille | *Season 1, episode 1*. A bus full of schoolchildren driving along a mountain road suddenly swerves to avoid an unseen something before careering off over a precipice. A simple, real, brutal, and chilling start.

◬ The past resurfaces in one of several publicity images in which objects are handed to the living by the underwater dead.

Arrow

Action/Adventure | USA | 2012–present

Five years on a desert island transform playboy Oliver into Arrow—the hooded vigilante

Cast | Stephen Amell, Emily Bett Rikards, David Ramsey, Colton Haynes, John Barrowman
Original broadcaster | The CW **For fans of . . .** | *Smallville* (2001)

Five years after disappearing in the same boat accident that claimed his father's life, bad-boy billionaire Oliver Queen (Stephen Amell) returned to Starling City. Before the accident, Oliver was an arrogant wastrel, but his experiences surviving on a dangerous island made him mature and thoughtful. Determined to make up for the past, he became Arrow, a hooded vigilante with impressive archery skills, taking revenge against those he considers to have failed the city.

He is initially determined to operate alone, but was soon joined by ex-soldier John Diggle (David Ramsey), IT whiz Felicity Smoak (Emily Bett Rikards), and Roy Harper (Colton Haynes). Family secrets complicate matters, as does Oliver's relationship with his ex-girlfriend Laurel Lance (Katie Cassidy), whose detective father is determined to catch the unknown vigilante.

Arrow operates in two time frames, with the modern-day adventures interspersed with flashbacks to Oliver's missing years. It is gritty and complex, with flawed characters, enlivened by fine performances and brilliant action sequences. **DF**

Classic episode
Unthinkable | *Season 2, episode 23*. In this all-action season finale, Oliver's no-kill rule is tested when his nemesis Slade threatens to kill someone close to him. It also marks the end of Oliver's island flashbacks.

⬤ Stephen Amell as Oliver Queen demonstrates his prowess with the bow that inspired the name of his alter ego, Arrow.

Line of Duty
Crime/Mystery | UK | 2012–present

Watching the detectives has never felt so real

Cast | Lennie James, Keeley Hawes, Martin Compston, Vicky McClure, Adrian Dunbar, Craig Parkinson, Mark Bonnar, Neil Morrissey **Original broadcaster** | BBC Two **For fans of . . .** | *The Wire* (2002), *Broadchurch* (2013)

This unusual cop show portrays what takes place when the anticorruption unit of the police turns its attentions to one of its own. In season one, Superintendant Ted Hastings (Adrian Dunbar) and his team investigate DCI Tony Gates (Lennie James); is he the perfect copper, or could he have a much more sinister side? In season two, the same unit investigates DI Lindsay Denton (Keeley Hawes), the only survivor of a police squad traveling in convoy to accompany a woman under witness protection. Why was Denton alone left alive?

Written by Jed Mercurio, the award-winning creator of British medical dramas *Cardiac Arrest* (1994), *Bodies* (2004), and *Critical* (2015), *Line of Duty* is notable for the sheer believability it brings to the cop show formula.

The first season was a huge success for BBC Two, but the second surpassed it. A key factor was Hawes' performance in a role that was a million miles from her typically glamorous ones. Throughout the six episodes, audience figures increased week after week. The stunning final episode was enough to convince the BBC to commission two more seasons. **PC**

> **Classic episode**
> *Season 2, episode 1.* Denton is physically assaulted and ostracized by her workmates. Her only hope of persuading them of her innocence is that the only other survivor of the attack, the protected witness, can corroborate her story.

⊘ (L–R) DCI Tony Gates (Lennie James), DC Kate Fleming (Vicky McClure), and DS Steve Arnott (Martin Compston) in season one.

Parade's End

Historical drama | UK | 2012

The tribulations of an English gentleman during the First World War

Cast | Benedict Cumberbatch, Roger Allam, Rupert Everett, Miranda Richardson, Janet McTeer
Original broadcasters | BBC One (UK), HBO (USA)
Award | 1 BAFTA
For fans of . . . | *The Good Soldier* (1981)

As well as coping with mental and physical scars from fighting in the First World War, civil servant Christopher Tietjens (Benedict Cumberbatch), embodiment of the repressed, stiff-upper-lipped English gentleman, had to contend with the cruelty and infidelity of his wife, Sylvia (Rebecca Hall), and embarked on a hesitant romance with the young suffragette Valentine Wannop (Adelaide Clemens). Meanwhile, his reputation was being destroyed by groundless but persistent rumors.

Based on four novels by Ford Madox Ford, *Parade's End* was a lavish five-part BBC/HBO co-production with a star-filled cast and a script by one of Britain's greatest dramatists: Tom Stoppard. Ford's novels took place inside the heads of just the main characters, but Stoppard expanded the other characters to give a full picture of a Britain on the brink of change. Cumberbatch expertly conveyed the vulnerability beneath Tietjens' rocklike exterior, and Hall was superb as Sylvia, her existence far removed from the horrors her husband experienced. There was also tremendous support from Roger Allam as Tietjens' disapproving godfather and Miranda Richardson as Valentine's wise novelist mother.

Parade's End painted a vivid, believable portrait of Britain before, during, and after the First World War, and Tietjens' experiences at the front were rendered in harrowing detail. It was perhaps too complex for mass appeal, but was lavished with critical acclaim and achieved a slew of award nominations. It was one of the twenty-first century's most intelligent TV adaptations. **IK**

Continuum

Fantasy/Horror/Sci-Fi | USA | 2012–15

Terrorists escape from the future into present-day Vancouver

Cast | Rachel Nichols, Erik Knudsen, Stephen Lobo, Victor Webster, Lexa Doig, Omari Newton
Original broadcaster | Showcase
For fans of . . . | *Time Trax* (1993), *Terminator: The Sarah Connor Chronicles* (2008)

Sentenced to death for their part in a terrorist attack that killed thousands, criminals from the group Liber8 used a time-travel device to escape their fate, dragging law enforcement officer Kiera Cameron (Rachel Nichols) through time, too, from 2077 to 2012. Once there, they planned to engineer and change events of the future.

Kiera arrived in present-day Vancouver equipped with a hand weapon and a bodysuit that served as armor, camouflage, and a boost to her innate abilities. She made contact with Alec Sadler (Erik Knudsen), who, in his later life, would create the technology that built the future from which she came. The two then worked to neutralize the terrorist threat and preserve the future.

Not all of the criminals who traveled back in time shared the same agenda. Once in the present day, Matthew Kellog (Stephen Lobo) decided that he enjoyed not being on the run, and engineered a rich and comfortable life for himself. He and Kiera became tentative allies.

The show was initially presented from Kiera's point of view, but as it progressed, it was revealed that the future she believed was right to save may not have been the best of all worlds. Corporations ruled the dystopian future, and it seemed that the aims of Liber8 may have been just, despite their methods. This raises the age-old question: can the end justify the means?

An extra plus is that the city of Vancouver was represented as itself rather than, as is so often the case, an American city. **PB**

◐ Benedict Cumberbatch as Christopher Tietjens gets to experience the mud of the trenches in *Parade's End*.

Last Tango in Halifax

Drama | UK | 2012–present

An evergreen love story that captured a nation's heart

Cast | Derek Jacobi, Anne Reid, Sarah Lancashire, Nicola Walker **Original broadcaster** | BBC One
Awards | 3 BAFTAs **For fans of . . .** | *Brothers and Sisters* (1979), *Happy Valley* (2007)

Last Tango in Halifax ignored the obsession with youth and featured two mature protagonists. In the romance between Alan (Derek Jacobi) and Celia (Anne Reid), Sally Wainwright crafted one of the most affecting, funny, and real love stories of modern drama. The show was inspired by Wainwright's observations of her mother's happiness in a second marriage to a friend she had not seen for decades. In the series, Alan and Celia lost touch when she moved away from their hometown of Halifax as a teenager. Both married, had children, and were widowed, then reconnected through social media more than fifty years later. Shortly after meeting again they announced they were to marry—to the horror of his daughter Gillian (Nicola Walker) and her daughter

Caroline (Sarah Lancashire). There is something wicked beneath *Last Tango in Halifax* as a natural comedy develops. This positive depiction of life in the twilight years was intended as a one-off, six-part drama, but audiences took to this endearing couple in their millions. The show was described by the *LA Times* as "the best new show of the fall" in 2013. **MW**

> **Classic episode**
> *Season 1, episode 6.* Celia struggles to cope with Caroline's newfound love, Kate. Alan is shocked by Celia's behavior at a family dinner and calls off the wedding. Celia tries to make amends, but the stress causes Alan to have a heart attack.

◉ (L–R) Anne Reid (Celia), Derek Jacobi (Alan), Nicola Walker (Gillian), and Sarah Lancashire (Caroline).

Veep

Comedy | USA | 2012–present

A scathing satire of the vice-presidential position and the US political class

Cast | Julia Louis-Dreyfus, Anna Chlumsky, Matt Walsh **Original broadcaster** | HBO **Awards** | 4 Emmys
For fans of . . . | *Yes, Minister* (1980), *The West Wing* (1999), *Commander in Chief* (2005), *The Thick of It* (2005)

The position of vice president has been a national joke since long before Tom Lehrer sang "Whatever Became of Hubert," about then-incumbent VP Hubert Humphrey. The person nearest the president is one of the least influential politicians in the United States. With an eye for the absurd, *Veep*'s creator Armando Ianucci (writer of the British political comedy *The Thick Of It*, 2005) and actress Julia Louis-Dreyfus created in Selina Meyer a character who is aware that her job is really a consolation prize. She is supported—or undermined—by her team of self-important half-wits, including loyal bagman Gary (Tony Hale) and workaholic Amy (Anna Chlumsky).

Episodes revolve around Meyer's attempts to position herself well with the media, political donors, or party grandees, which go wrong in hilarious ways. Meyer is wealthy, and has lost touch with ordinary people. Estranged from her husband, she tries to make her family appear normal to the press, while still arranging her sex life. She is a terrible person, but her character is slickly written and performed brilliantly, bringing an irreverent realism to this portrayal of US politics. **RL**

Classic episode
Clovis | *Season 3, episode 4*. Selina visits Clovis, a combination of Facebook, Google, and Apple run by a modern billionaire. Clovis introduce Selina to a porn site dedicated to her and tell her they consider themselves "post tax."

🔊 Listening up: Julia Louis-Dreyfus as Selina Meyer and Matt Walsh as her director of communcations, Mike McLintock.

Puberty Blues

Drama | Australia | 2012–present

Classic coming-of-age story, retold for the twenty-first century

Cast | Ashley Cummings, Brenna Harding, Charlotte Best, Sean Keenan, Claudia Karvan, Jeremy Lindsay Taylor, Susie Porter, Roger Knight, Rodger Corser
Original broadcaster | Network Ten
For fans of . . . | *The Inbetweeners* (2008)

In 1979, when Gabrielle Carey and Kathy Lette published their novel about the lusts and loves of two teenage girls, it quickly became a wonderful guilty secret for adolescents around the world: a book to read under the sheets and explore the pubescent dream. This television version not only captures perfectly the novel's account of awkward first steps into a new and sexually active world, but also allows the viewers to look back to the 1970s and compare it with the world of today. The evidence is mixed; some things are better, some are worse; many are not much different in anything other than their external trappings.

Puberty Blues is the story of Debbie Vickers (Ashleigh Cummings) and Sue Knight (Brenna Harding), teenage friends growing up in an Australian beachside suburb. They spend every day together and every night on the phone with each other. When we meet them they're naive outsiders, convincing themselves they're one step closer to acceptance and popularity, but as the series advances so does their maturity and empowerment. The show exudes authenticity, and every aspect of the language, dress, and art direction is steeped in vintage realism that rings true in every scene.

But this realism brings with it uncomfortable truths: sex, drugs, smoking, and the attention of the opposite sex are trophies to prove acceptance. *Puberty Blues* is as relevant to life and youth in this century as it was in the last. The series underlines the old truth that the more things change, the more they stay the same. **PPW**

Derek

Comedy/Drama | UK | 2012–14

Sentimental comedy about the life of lovable Derek and his elderly charges

Cast | Ricky Gervais, Karl Pilkington, Kerry Godliman, David Earl, Tim Barlow, Arthur Nightingale
Original broadcaster | Channel 4
For fans of . . . | *The Office* (2001), *Extras* (2005), *Getting On* (2009), *Life's Too Short* (2011)

He gave the world David Brent, and followed it up with the equally sharp *Extras* (2005) and *Life's Too Short* (2011), but by the time *Derek* aired, Ricky Gervais' deadpan humor was starting to divide viewers, and some wondered whether he was capable of more. This show proved that he did have more strings to his bow, and was capable of pathos and sentimental comedy-drama.

Here, Gervais played the title character, Derek, a simple and lovable middle-aged man who worked in a retirement home, often going above and beyond the call of duty to help the residents he clearly loved. He was one of life's misfits, and the same could have been said of those around him, including Dougie (Karl Pilkington) the caretaker, and his friend Kev (David Earl). The mockumentary style would have been familiar to those who had seen Gervais' previous shows, but the tone—alternating between high comedy and genuine triple-handkerchief moments—trod new territory.

The show initially caused controversy, as some suggested that Gervais mocked the disabled with his portrayal of Derek—claims he later refuted, saying the show was about how the character's quirks had led him to be ostracized from society and how those around him had suffered a similar fate. Derek was sympathetic and likable, which strengthened these claims. It was hard not to warm to him and his childlike outlook, to the extent that the viewers would laugh and cry along with him, not to mention log on to YouTube to check those viral videos he was obsessed with. **MW**

● Ricky Gervais as care worker Derek Noakes.

Ripper Street

Crime/Mystery | UK | 2012–present

The hard edge of crime and detection in Victorian London's East End

Cast | Matthew Macfadyen, Jerome Flynn, Adam Rothenberg, MyAnna Buring
Original broadcaster | BBC One
Award | 1 BAFTA **For fans of ...** | *Whitechapel* (2009), *Peaky Blinders* (2013)

It was London in 1889, six months after Jack the Ripper's reign of murder in Whitechapel. The detectives of H Division continued to police this lawless area. Inspector Edmund Reid (Matthew Macfadyen) and Sergeant Bennet Drake (Jerome Flynn) tackled murder, corruption, and prostitution, joining forces with former US Army surgeon Homer Jackson (Adam Rothenberg), who brought a forensic approach to their work.

Ripper Street, a co-production between Tiger Aspect, BBC, and BBC America, established a loyal fan base on its first broadcast. It was a slick, historical, crime-drama, stylized with believable performances. Macfadyen, Flynn, and Rothenberg play their parts with little mirth, while MyAnna Buring completes the ensemble as brothel madam Long Susan. Victorian London is brilliantly evoked; Whitechapel was recreated in Dublin's Clancy Barracks. There are routine crime-of-the-week story lines with running arcs alongside: Reid's strained relationship with his wife following the death of their daughter, Drake's liaisons with a local prostitute, and the ever-present specter of Jack the Ripper.

A second season was ordered due to good ratings— although it faced criticism over its two-dimensional depiction of women. But when it was announced that a third season would not be forthcoming because of disappointing ratings, online campaigns mobilized. After negotiations between Tiger Aspect and LoveFilm, season three debuted exclusively online in 2014; the law had not yet deserted Whitechapel. **MW**

Classic episode
A Man of My Company | *Season 1, episode 7.*
Inspector Abberline (Clive Russell) discovers the remains of a woman beneath the floorboards of Jackson's lodgings and accuses the surgeon of being Jack the Ripper.

◉ (L–R) Adam Rothenberg, Matthew Macfadyen, and Jerome Flynn rush to where a police officer has been impaled on railings.

Elementary

Crime/Mystery | USA | 2012–present

Contemporary American update of the much-loved Sherlock Holmes story—set in New York

Classic episode

The Woman | **Season 1, episode 23.** Sherlock is reunited with the woman he loves, and finally comes face to face with his archenemy, Moriarty, who is in this iteration transformed from Conan Doyle's man into a woman (Natalie Dormer).

◉ Lucy Liu (Watson) brings music to Jonny Lee Miller (Sherlock).

Cast | Jonny Lee Miller, Lucy Liu, Aidan Quinn, Jon Michael Hill, Ophelia Lovibond
Original broadcaster | CBS
For fans of . . . | *Murder, She Wrote* (1984), *Sherlock* (2010)

Two years after the BBC launched *Sherlock* (2010), its modern retelling of Sherlock Holmes, CBS came up with its own version of the characters created by Sir Arthur Conan Doyle—whose works were by now conveniently out of copyright.

The two shows are superficially similar but very different in style and content. *Elementary* replaces Dr. John Watson with Joan Watson (Lucy Liu), a former surgeon who works as a sober companion to recovering drug addicts—in this case, Sherlock Holmes (Jonny Lee Miller). Holmes is still a British consulting detective, but the action takes place in New York. The series is episodic, with a case of the week to investigate, but there are long plot arcs dealing with the leads' relationship, Joan's transformation into a detective in her own right, Sherlock's past in London, and his addiction and recovery.

Among the regular supporting cast are Aidan Quinn as Captain Tommy Gregson and Sean Pertwee as Gareth Lestrade, for whom Holmes previously consulted at Scotland Yard. Notable special guests have included former soccer player Vinnie Jones as Sebastian Moran, Natalie Dormer of *Game of Thrones* (2011) as Irene Adler, and Rhys Ifans of the movie *Notting Hill* (1999) as Sherlock's brother Mycroft.

Sharp scripts, engaging mysteries, and the fascinating dynamic between Miller's Holmes and Liu's Watson produce a series that stands head and shoulders above the standard police procedural. **WH**

Salamander

Crime/Mystery | Belgium | 2012–present

Secrets and lies abound in a violent gripping tale of deceit in the corrupt heart of modern Europe

Cast | Filip Peeters, Koen De Bouw, Mike Verdrengh, Violet Braeckman, Lucas Van den Eynde, Jo De Meyere, Koen van Impe, Warre Borgmans
Original broadcaster | Eén
For fans of . . . | *Edge of Darkness* (1985), *Witse* (2004)

Amid an onslaught of Nordic noir, Belgium fought back with this twelve-part tale of police investigating the theft of safety deposit boxes from a Brussels bank. The loot was not money, but sensitive material that linked the country's elite to Salamander, an organization whose vested interests were shrouded in secrecy.

Written by novelist Bavo Dhooge and *Witse* screenwriter Ward Hulselmans, *Salamander* was directed by Frank van Mechelen, award-nominated for his *Midnight Express*–style movie thriller *De hel van Tanger* (2006). Filip Peeters, who appeared in that movie, starred as Paul Gerardi, a police inspector whose investigation has both personal and political repercussions.

Domestic audiences, who had lived through four years of political instability in Belgium from 2007 to 2011, were unsurprisingly receptive. Elsewhere, *Salamander* earned a mixed reception from the newfound audience for international productions. Nordic partisans, accustomed to thoughtful drama and strong women, were sniffy about its old-school male lead and occasionally stretched credibility. But as an example of a quality thriller produced for a more overtly commercial market than its Scandinavian sisters, *Salamander* delivered on its promise of gripping mystery.

A second season was given the green light in early 2015. Meanwhile Dhooge—whose penchant for titles beginning with the letter "S" earned him the nickname "S-Express"—turned out the origins novel *Salamander—Shot in the Dark* (2013). **BM**

Classic episode
Season 1 episode 2. The postheist story gets underway. Paul Gerardi is suspended after refusing to accept the official explanation for the robbery, and intrigue mounts—with fatal consequences.

◉ Detective Paul Gerardi (Filip Peeters) can trust no one.

Call the Midwife

Historical drama | UK | 2012–present

*Deceptively subversive historical drama
set in 1950s London*

Cast | Jessica Raine, Miranda Hart, Jenny Agutter, Pam
Ferris, Judy Parfitt, Stephen McGann
Original broadcaster | BBC One
Awards | 2 BAFTAs
For fans of . . . | *The Crimson Field* (2014)

Based on memoirs by Jennifer Worth, *Call the Midwife*
was a breakout hit from the first episode. It falls between
inoffensive historical drama and social commentary on
life in a deprived London district in the 1950s. The lives
and work of the midwives of Nonnatus House has found
an appreciative worldwide audience, to become the
BBC's biggest drama hit in years and one of its most
successful exports.

Newly qualified midwife Jenny Lee (Jessica Raine)
arrives at Nonnatus House to work with the order
of nuns and other staff in Poplar, East London. With
her fellow midwives—Chummy (Miranda Hart), Trixie
(Helen George), and Cynthia (Bryony Hannah)—she
struggles not to become involved in the lives of the
patients. The show reveals the trials that women faced
during the 1950s, as childbirth rates soared, and Jenny
and her colleagues attempt to keep their charges safe
and healthy.

The young midwives and nuns must also find
their way in the world, which again highlights the
difficulties for women in the 1950s. Even in 2015, the
predominantly female cast makes *Call the Midwife*
atypical for prime-time drama, and its subversive social
commentary and personal story lines strike a chord
with audiences everywhere. Even with the departure
of star Jessica Raine in 2014, the series' future seems
assured. **MW**

❯ Midwives to the rescue: (L–R) Bryony Hannah (Cynthia Miller),
Jessica Raine (Jenny Lee), and Helen George (Trixie Franklin).

Girls

Comedy | USA | 2012–present

A cutting-edge comedy about a group of women in their twenties living in New York

Cast | Lena Dunham, Allison Williams, Jemima Kirke, Zosia Mamet, Adam Driver, Alex Karpovsky
Original broadcaster | HBO
Awards | 1 Emmy, 2 Golden Globes
For fans of . . . | *Sex and the City* (1998)

Created by and starring Lena Dunham, *Girls* was inspired by some of Dunham's real-life experiences. Her character, Hannah Horvath, is a narcissistic aspiring writer who lives in Brooklyn and navigates her twenties "one mistake at a time," supported by her circle of friends. They include her best friend and roommate Marnie (Allison Williams), a level-headed art gallery assistant, and her college friend Jessa (Jemima Kirke), an unpredictable world traveler with an attitude. When Jessa returns to New York, she struggles to cope with her marriage and ends up in rehab. Her bubbly cousin and roommate Shoshanna (Zosia Mamet) is a math major at New York University, and, while seemingly naive, reveals herself to be the most grounded of the group, maturing as the series progresses. Hannah's boyfriend, Adam (Adam Driver), a seemingly aloof young man, is as defensive as Hannah is when it comes to his personal feelings, but Hannah and the audience learn that there's more to him than it seems.

Critics praised the show for its raw nature, humor, and refreshing tone, applauding its realistic portrayal of women and their relationships. Often heralded as *Sex and the City* (1998) for the twenty-first century, *Girls* is a realistic and somewhat idealistic take on what it is like for the millennial generation as they try to find their places in the world. **RP**

❯ Jemima Kirke (Jessa), Lena Dunham (Hannah), and Zosia Mamet (Shoshanna) in season one.

Hatfields & McCoys

Historical drama | USA | 2012

Realistic miniseries detailing a legendary family feud in the late nineteenth century

Cast | Kevin Costner, Bill Paxton, Tom Berenger, Matt Barr, Jena Malone, Sam Reid, Powers Boothe
Original broadcaster | History Channel
Awards | 5 Emmys, 1 Golden Globe
For fans of . . . | *The Life and Legend of Wyatt Earp* (1955)

Hatfields & McCoys was the History Channel's first scripted programming to be broadcast in the United States. A three-part miniseries (in two-hour-long segments), it was directed by Kevin Reynolds (*Robin Hood: Prince of Thieves*, 1991) and gained critical acclaim as well as setting the record (at the time) for the most watched nonsports event ever on basic cable—14.3 million viewers.

Based closely on America's most famous family feud and set along the Tug Fork river, part of the state line separating Kentucky (home of the McCoys) and West Virginia (home of the Hatfields), the miniseries delved deeply into the origins of the quarrel and the events that fueled it as the years went by. No simple rivalry, this feud involved murder, arson, and other violence.

Familial power struggles and revenge schemes have always made for good storytelling. This particular tale has been told in many different ways via many media but never before with such depth and authority. Kevin Costner and Bill Paxton gave great performances as the heads of the families, and the viewers were treated to beautiful cinematography (most of the location filming was in Romania) and exemplary attention to detail in the production design's authenticity. The pacing was sometimes uneven and there was an abundance of gunplay, but even with a total running time of nearly five hours, it effortlessly fascinated and provided even greater reward to viewers paying attention to all aspects of its production. **SWH**

Classic episode
Part 2. The McCoys murder Anse's younger brother. The Hatfields swear vengeance and set out on the warpath. Neighboring families take sides in the dispute, and West Virginia and Kentucky are brought close to war.

◉ The devil incarnate? Kevin Costner in his award-winning role, as head of the family "Devil" Anse Hatfield.

The Paradise

Historical drama | UK | 2012–13

Life, loves, and shopping in a pleasing historical drama set in the north of England

Cast | Joanna Vanderham, Sarah Lancashire, Emun Elliott, Sonya Cassidy, Ben Daniels
Original broadcaster | BBC One
For fans of . . . | *Cranford* (2007), *Lark Rise to Candleford* (2008), *Mr Selfridge* (2013)

Based on Émile Zola's novel *Au Bonheur des Dames* (*The Ladies' Paradise*, 1883), *The Paradise* transplanted the action from Paris to a northern English town, but the department store backdrop was much the same. The BBC series beat ITV's similarly shop-based drama *Mr. Selfridge* (2013) to the screens by several months.

It was 1875. Denise Lovett (Joanna Vanderham) arrived to work in her uncle's draper's store to find the business in trouble and the trade of local shops affected by The Paradise department store. Denise found work in the ladieswear department at The Paradise, under the exacting Miss Audrey (Sarah Lancashire), but once the widowed storeowner John Moray (Emun Elliott) noticed her, life was never the same again. Their blossoming relationship and "will they, won't they" tension drove the show.

In developing *The Paradise*, the creator, Bill Gallagher, swapped the rural setting of *Lark Rise to Candleford* (2008) for an urban backdrop. The two shows share many traits: a varied cast of textured characters, story lines of romance, and the plight of working people in a rapidly changing world.

There was a major cast change in season two. Lancashire's Miss Audrey departed in episode two and Ben Daniels arrived as Tom Weston, the dynamic new owner of The Paradise, adding a pleasing rivalry for Moray. The show secured respectable ratings and sales abroad, but the BBC decided against a third season. The Paradise closed its doors in December 2013. **MW**

Classic episode
Season 1, episode 8. Moray's marriage to Katherine looms, but his heart is not in it. When Denise returns to The Paradise, Moray jilts Katherine and declares his feelings for Denise. The first season comes to a close as they share a kiss.

⊘ Joanna Vanderham as Denise Lovett before a window of her uncle's department store, The Paradise.

The Newsroom

Drama | USA | 2012–14

Current affairs and heartache combine in this ethical TV studio

Cast | Jeff Daniels, Emily Mortimer, Sam Waterston, John Gallagher Jr., Alison Pill, Dev Patel
Original broadcaster | HBO
Award | 1 Emmy
For fans of . . . | *The West Wing* (1999)

Writer/producer Aaron Sorkin (*The West Wing*, 1999) returned to scripted television with *The Newsroom*, a drama set in the offices of a fictional cable news network that had lost its direction. Will McAvoy (Jeff Daniels) was the everyman anchor, whose passion had folded with increasingly higher paychecks and viewer numbers. In the opening scene of the pilot, Will railed against America's place in the world, before reminiscing about the nation's lost moral integrity in days of yore.

Sorkin assembled a strong cast that included a touching and crotchety performance from Sam Waterston as the head of news programming, and several guest appearances by Jane Fonda as the network's wealthy owner. The show touched upon current events at the time, and began with the then-developing Deepwater Horizon oil disaster in the pilot. These events served both as backdrop to the interpersonal stories between the characters as well as markers of the show's place in history.

The first season of *The Newsroom* received mixed reviews, therefore it was retooled for the second season, to incorporate a more cohesive narrative across the season as a whole. The show was later renewed for a third and final season. Never among HBO's most popular offerings, and sometimes criticized for its political diatribes, it nevertheless remains an example of classic Sorkin drama. **SL**

◑ Jeff Daniels as Will McAvoy and Olivia Munn as Sloan Sabbith.

Duck Dynasty

Reality | USA | 2012–present

Catfish, commerce, and comedy in the Deep South

Cast | Willie Robertson, Phil Robertson, Jase Robertson, Si Robertson, Kay Robertson, Korie Robertson, Missy Robertson   **Original broadcaster** | A&E   **For fans of . . .** | *The Real Housewives of Orange County* (2006)

For a true picture of success, look no further than the Robertsons from Louisiana, stars of the most watched nonfiction cable series in history: *Duck Dynasty*. Phil Robertson founded the multimillion-dollar Duck Commander company, and this is a tale about the joys of a family business told in a unique way. At first glance, *Duck Dynasty* meets expectations about redneck millionaires—long beards, conservative values, huntin', shootin', and fishin'. But it is a story about real people who love their lives and work with people they love.

The more time the viewers spend with the Robertsons, the more likable they become. It is easy to envy their lifestyle, even if some of the realities of life in the Deep South are uncomfortable. Unlike other reality TV shows, the viewers leave each episode wishing they were friends with the Robertsons.

It would be easy to dismiss *Duck Dynasty* as simple redneck voyeurism, but it is the story of a smart, savvy business that keeps true to its roots. Each episode ends with Phil giving thanks; his family's smiles grow around the table, showing what true success looks like. **PPW**

Classic episode

Till Duck Do Us Part | *Season 4, episode 1*. The wives plan a surprise ceremony for Phil and Miss Kay to renew their vows. Si is sent to occupy the couple for a day, but his plan to take them down Memory Lane ends up with several wrong turns.

◬ Kay and Phil Robertson renew their wedding vows in a surprise ceremony attended by the whole family.

Last Resort

Action/Adventure | USA | 2012–13

A US Navy submarine commander goes rogue to stop a new world war

Cast | Andre Braugher, Scott Speedman, Daisy Betts, Michael Ng   **Original broadcaster** | ABC
For fans of . . . | *The Last Ship* (2014)

While off the coast of Pakistan on a secret mission, Captain Marcus Chaplin (Andre Braugher) ordered the USS *Colorado* to collect a US Navy SEAL team from the mainland. Chaplin then received orders via an antiquated communication system to launch nuclear ballistic missiles at Pakistan. Questioning this action, Chaplin asked for orders to be sent via the official channels—a request that led to his removal from command. The submarine was declared an enemy of its own country and the attack on Pakistan took place, regardless.

With no home to go to, and wrongly blamed for the attack, the crew of the *Colorado* headed for a NATO outpost on the island of Sainte Marina in the Indian Ocean. Their family in America, convinced of their innocence, worked to clear their names, but uncovered a far-reaching conspiracy within the US government.

The debut episode of *Last Resort* garnered great acclaim for pacing and story, but the initial high ratings were difficult to maintain. ABC let the show's creators know when the show would end, allowing them to write a solid conclusion to the series. **MC**

Classic episode
Damn the Torpedoes | *Season 1, episode 11.* The conspiracy in Washington, DC picks up pace, while on the island, uneasy alliances are forged out of necessity as the crew liaises with the Chinese government.

◉ (L R) Daisy Betts (Shepard), Michael Ng (Pitts), Scott Speedman (Kendal), and Andre Braugher (Chaplin) prepare for nuclear war.

House of Cards

Drama | USA | 2013–present

A wry thriller centered on a manipulative politician at the White House

Cast | Kevin Spacey, Robin Wright, Michael Kelly, Nathan Darrow, Mahershala Ali, Michael Gill
Original broadcaster | Netflix
Awards | 4 Emmys, 2 Golden Globes
For fans of . . . | *The West Wing* (1999)

This version of the 1996 British original stars Kevin Spacey as Francis Underwood, a powerful man at the heart of Washington, D.C. The audience sees him playing a long game of revenge, positioning his pawns, and bringing them into his game when it suits him. Even seeming acts of kindness are strategic moves with one ultimate goal—to unseat the president and take his place.

Though the beats of the plot come from the BBC series and the novel (1989) by Michael Dobbs that inspired it, this *House of Cards* dances to a different rhythm. It retains the conceit of Underwood addressing the audience directly, where he reveals his true feelings and motivations, but the biggest change is in its pace. It benefits hugely from its distribution model, released via Netflix in one go, to satisfy the appetite for "box set binges." Without the limitations of a traditional TV schedule time slot, the duration of each "chapter" varies from forty-five to sixty minutes, depending on how much time the story needs to develop.

The biggest shift in focus is with Francis' wife (Robin Wright), who is no longer a taciturn accessory. Claire Underwood has her own agenda, whether securing funding for her charity, making a bid for her own political future, or turning a tabloid scandal to her advantage by revealing a terrible secret from her past. She is revealed over time to be almost as skillfully manipulative as her husband. Almost. **JS**

◀ Kevin Spacey (Francis Underwood), Robin Wright (Claire Underwood), and Michael Kelly (Doug Stamper).

Wentworth

Drama | Australia | 2013–present

Brutal, gritty, and uncompromising reworking of a kitsch 1980s soap, also set in a penitentiary

Cast | Danielle Cormack, Nicole da Silva, Pamela Rabe, Kate Atkinson, Celia Ireland, Shareena Clanton, Aaron Jeffrey, Robbie Magasiva, Katrina Milosevic
Original broadcaster | SoHo/Foxtel
For fans of . . . | *Orange Is the New Black* (2013)

Just as *Battlestar Galactica* (2004) "reinvented" itself from a fondly remembered yet "of its time" show of 1978, so *Wentworth* is a "reimagining" of the characters and setting of *Prisoner: Cell Block H* (1979). *Wentworth* centers on the story of Bea Smith (Danielle Cormack), a housewife and mother who, finally snapping after years of domestic violence, tries to kill her husband, after which she is sent to Wentworth Correctional Centre to await trial. There she realizes very quickly that she will have to toughen up to resist a variety of unwanted attentions—not only from her sometimes violent fellow inmates, but also from the corrupt and self-interested prison officers in charge.

The *Prisoner* series was renowned for its prison gates that wobbled alarmingly when they were being closed, and its occasional overacting. In contrast, *Wentworth's* acting is uniformly magnificent, with particular praise owed to protagonists Cormack, Nicole da Silva as the charismatic yet violent "top dog" Frankie Doyle, and (from season two) Pamela Rabe as the terrifying new governor of the prison, Joan Ferguson. The writing, too, is undeniably powerful, with the almost all-female cast getting the chance to portray a huge range of realistic, well-rounded, and three-dimensional characters.

Not many Australian prime-time dramas become international hits nowadays, but *Wentworth* has carved out a name for itself around the globe, with fans in the United Kingdom, Poland, Sweden, Russia, and the United States lining up for more incarceration. **PC**

Classic episode
Fear Her | *Season 2, episode 12*. Bea's plan to get revenge for her daughter Debbie's death reaches its shattering conclusion, and Joan "The Freak" Ferguson realizes that her hold over the prison is not as strong as she believed.

◉ Danielle Cormack, who plays Bea Smith, posing with a model during a special presentation of *Wentworth* in Melbourne, Australia.

The Tractate Middoth

Fantasy/Horror/Sci-Fi | UK | 2013

A Christmas ghost story with a CGI finale

Cast | Sacha Dhawan, Louise Jameson, John Castle, Roy Barraclough, Una Stubbs, David Ryall, Nicholas Burns, Eleanor Bron, Charlie Clemmow
Original broadcaster | BBC Two
For fans of . . . | *A Ghost Story for Christmas* (1971)

In this thirty-five-minute BBC adaptation of a short story by M.R. James—published in 1911—young fogey librarian William Garrett is approached by an elderly man, John Eldred, to find a collection of Hebrew writings entitled *The Tractate Middoth*. Garrett duly searches the shelves of the dusty library, but before he can find the volume he comes into contact with a terrifying ghostly apparition. So disturbed is he by the experience that he leaves town to recover at a country guest house. Here he discovers that his landlady, Mary Simpson, is a cousin of Eldred, whom she believes cheated her of her rightful inheritance. She believes that her uncle, Dr. Rant, hid his will within the pages of a book, and Garrett realizes that the volume now sought by Eldred must be the lost book. But what Eldred does not suspect is that *The Tractate Middoth* harbors not only the will but also a deadly secret.

As young Garrett, Sacha Dhawan (*The History Boys*, 2006) captured just the right degree of wide-eyed terror and determined curiosity. Writer and director Mark Gatiss surrounded him with experienced character actors like John Castle as the greedy Eldred, Louise Jameson (*Tenko*, 1981) as Mary Simpson, and Eleanor Bron as her ominous housekeeper, Mrs. Goundry. Gatiss perfectly captured the mood and style of older BBC adaptations of M.R. James stories, where the atmosphere was created more by the use of sound and light than outright gore, but the ghostly apparition's final appearance was genuinely horrific. **JS**

The Tunnel

Crime/Mystery | UK/France | 2013–present

Slick adaptation of a Scandinavian original

Cast | Stephen Dillane, Clémence Poésy, James Frain, Tobi Bakare, Joseph Mawle
Original broadcasters | Sky Atlantic (UK); Canal+ (France)
For fans of . . . | *The Bridge* (2011)

The vogue for Nordic noir inspired numerous imitations that tried to demonstrate that darkness is not exclusively confined to Scandinavia. Just as the cable channel AMC turned the Danish *Forbrydelsen* (2007) into *The Killing* in the United States, Sky Television and Canal+ rebranded *Bron/Broen* (*The Bridge*) for Anglo-French audiences. But *The Tunnel* was no slavish, literal translation; it added considerable originality to recycled material.

When the torso of a French politician and the lower body of a British prostitute are discovered in the Channel Tunnel, midway between France and England, a cross-jurisdiction investigation was launched. Karl Roebuck (Stephen Dillane), an experienced British detective, was paired with young French detective Elise Wasserman (Clémence Poésy). They developed a spiky relationship as they worked their way through the list of likely suspects. The investigation eventually became a hunt for a killer known as the Truth Terrorist (James Frain), who posted videos to taunt the police, and was confident that they would never catch him.

Much of the first episode was a carbon copy of the original, but as the drama unfolded, the intricate plot took its own direction. *The Tunnel* was well-written and well-paced, and even though some critics found it too close to *The Bridge* for comfort, it attracted enough viewers for the networks to contemplate a follow-up. It was reported that the two production companies involved—Kudos and Shine France—are developing a second season for Sky. **MW**

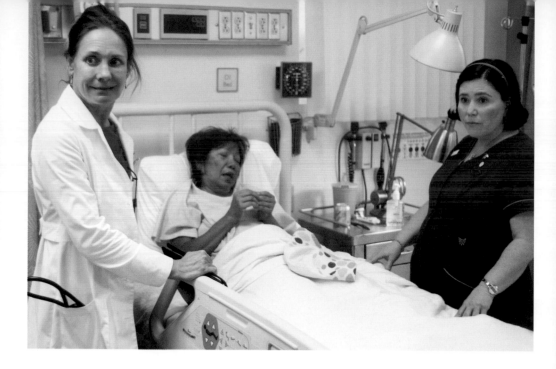

Getting On

Comedy | USA | 2013–present

A dark comedy about the lives and loves of the staff in an extended-care hospital unit

Cast | Laurie Metcalf, Alex Borstein, Niecy Nash, Mel Rodriguez
Original broadcaster | HBO   **For fans of . . .** | *The Thick of It* (2005)

Getting On, developed by Mark V. Olsen and Will Scheffer, deals with life in a hospital ward in all its aspects: both the everyday drudgery and the moments of beauty and compassion that come from a small staff working with a group of elderly, sick, and dying patients. Based on a British series of the same name, the US version is set in the Billy Barnes Extended Care Unit of the down-and-out Mount Palms Memorial Hospital in Long Beach, California.

Getting On is at once deadly serious and uncomfortably funny. Alex Borstein stars as Dawn, a put-upon yet determined nurse who wants to do right for her patients and build a life for herself, preferably with her supervisor Patsy (Mel Rodriguez), a male nurse

whose mixed signals leave her, and the audience, trying to figure out if he's gay. Laurie Metcalf is Dr. Jenna James, a self-absorbed gerontologist who wants to further her career.

The residents in the ward are played by a who's who of actresses of a certain age, including June Squibb, K. Callan, Lynn Cohen, and Ann Morgan Guilbert. **RP**

Classic episode

Is Soap a Hazardous Substance? | *Season 2, episode 6.* The introduction of a hospice program gets a mixed reception from staff and patients. One of the latter, an alcoholic, tries to find ways around the ward's drink ban.

⊕ Dr. Jenna James (Laurie Metcalf) and nurse Dawn Forchette (Alex Borstein) tend to the needs of their patients as best they can.

The Americans

Drama | USA | 2013–present

Soviet spies in Washington, DC, during the Reagan administration

Cast | Keri Russell, Matthew Rhys, Noah Emmerich, Margo Martindale **Original broadcaster** | FX
For fans of . . . | *Tinker, Tailor, Soldier, Spy* (1979), *Spooks* (2002)

The Americans harks back to days of the Cold War, when the United States' main enemy was the Soviet Union. Phil and Elizabeth Jennings (Matthew Rhys and Keri Russell) are a young couple with two children. They run a travel agency and give every appearance of being a happy pair of patriotic Americans. The only problem is that beneath their deep cover, they are Soviet agents whose socialist views have led them into espionage for idealistic reasons.

Created by former CIA officer Joe Weisberg, *The Americans* often leaves the viewer rooting for the bad guys as Phil and Elizabeth try to maintain a normal family life while simultaneously involving themselves in plots and counterplots.

Outstanding among a strong supporting cast are some of the Jennings's local handlers (including the brilliant Margo Martindale as Claudia, their kindly, almost grandmotherly—but also ruthlessly deadly—Russian contact), and Stan Beeman (Noah Emmerich), the FBI counterintelligence agent who lives across the street from them. **SL**

Classic episode

Comrades | *Season 2, episode 1*. A routine mission goes wrong and threatens to blow the Jennings' cover. To make matters worse, their children start to suspect that there is more to the family business than they have been told.

⌾ Keri Russell and Matthew Rhys as Elizabeth and Phil Jennings, who don't look like Reds, but are.

Bluestone 42

Comedy | UK | 2013–present

Comedy set in a bomb disposal unit in Afghanistan

Classic episode
Season 1, episode 6. Nick tries to learn the tango in order to impress Mary, and Bird's budding romance with the new vet is interfered with by the rest of the team as they form a committee to determine whether he's good enough for her.

⌕ Laura Aikman (ATO Ellen Best) and Matthew Lewis (Corporal Gordon House, aka "Towerblock") soldiering in season three.

Cast | Kelly Adams, Oliver Chris, Tony Gardner, Scott Hoatson, Katie Lyons, Jamie Quinn, Stephen Wight, Keeno Lee Hector, Matthew Lewis, Laura Aikman
Original broadcaster | BBC Three
For fans of . . . | *M*A*S*H* (1972), *Blackadder* (1983)

Bluestone 42—pronounced "four two," never "forty-two"—is the call sign of a bomb disposal unit based in Helmand Province, Afghanistan. Ammunition Technical Officer (ATO) Nick Medhurst (Oliver Chris) must disable or destroy the improvised explosive devices planted all over the region by the Taliban. A known aficionado of casual sex, Nick has his heart set on finding his way into the pants of the new female Padre, Mary (Kelly Adams).

It may seem odd, or perhaps even a little distasteful, to have a situation comedy set in a conflict that at the time of first broadcast was still going on, but the laughs are derived mainly from the daily minutiae of army life—the food, the work environment, the bureaucracy, how to find or make your own entertainment. This to some extent reflects a sense of mystification about the overall purpose of the war, but *Bluestone 42* is not a political work in the same way *M*A*S*H* (1972) was a commentary on Vietnam (albeit Vietnam disguised in a Korean setting). It is basically a traditional production full of the usual comic stereotypes, including the Stupid One, the Narcissist, and the Fool Who Thinks He Knows Best.

While the heart of *Bluestone 42* is the darkly humorous banter between the principal characters at base camp, the show also features action scenes, filmed on location in South Africa, with bomb disarming, firefights, explosions, and the occasional casualty. And with its army setting, the show also features military-grade swearing. **PB**

In the Flesh

Fantasy/Horror/Sci-Fi | UK | 2013–14

The inhabitants of a small town prepare for the return of their cured relatives

Cast | Luke Newberry, Emily Bevan, Harriet Cains,
Stephen Thompson, Ricky Tomlinson, Kenneth
Cranham, Steve Evets, Marie Critchley, Wunmi Mosaku
Original broadcaster | BBC Three
For fans of . . . | *The Walking Dead* (2010)

The best zombie stories are never about the undead,
but about society. *In The Flesh* examined mob mentality,
small-town prejudices, homophobia, religious dogma,
and local politics, all on a very small scale. When "the
uprising" was in full swing, few people hesitated to
call the living dead "rotters," but once a cure for their
condition was found and they began their rehabilitation
within the communities they terrorized, their condition
became known as partially deceased syndrome (PDS).
Some former zombies wore makeup and contact lenses
to hide their condition, though a brave few celebrated
their condition by walking about "au naturel" as a
provocation to those who once hunted them.

The success of *In The Flesh* was in making its low
budget an asset; free from the excesses of a Hollywood
production, the series focused on human questions,
such as the reasons PDS sufferers struggled with their
resurrection. Some did because they had painful
memories of what they had done in their rabid state;
others because they'd already made an active choice
to die rather than face living in an insular small town.

The first season introduced recently returned
Kieren, whose family tried to help him readjust to
normal life, while his sister Jem comes to terms with
the lives she ended while part of the Human Volunteer
Force, a group of vigilantes. In the second season, the
characters fell under the influence of Maxine Martin, a
charismatic and ambitious politician whose extremism
toward PDS sufferers concealed ulterior motives. **JS**

Classic episode
Season 1, episode 1. New medication enables
zombies to return at least partially to a normal
life. The disease is now under control, but old
resentments toward sufferers will not be
banished overnight.

◉ Two sufferers of Partially Deceased Syndrome: Amy (Emily Bevan)
and her brother, Keiren (Luke Newberry).

Broadchurch

Crime/Mystery | UK | 2013–present

Murder mystery series focusing on a small town's reaction to the murder of a young boy

Cast | David Tennant, Olivia Colman, Jodie Whittaker, Andrew Buchan, Arthur Darvill, Pauline Quirke
Original broadcaster | ITV
Awards | 3 BAFTAs
For fans of . . . | *Forbrydelsen (The Killing)* (2007)

The first season of *Broadchurch* covered much of the same ground as the first season of the Danish thriller *Forbrydelsen (The Killing)*. Both shows focus on a family's grief after the murder of a child and the reaction of the community. *Broadchurch* also owes a debt to *Twin Peaks* (1990), particularly in the character of the psychic in season one played by Will Mellor, but the British production is no pale imitation of anything; it has freshness and originality all of its own.

Much of *Broadchurch*'s power is drawn from the performances, above all that of Jodie Whittaker as Beth Latimer, the heartbroken mother who knows that she must find a way to cope in order to support her family, but just cannot see through the pain.

David Tennant's character Alec Hardy leads the investigation and Olivia Colman plays his assistant, Ellie Miller. The scene in which Ellie discovers the truth of what has happened is nothing short of mind-blowing. David Tennant is also superb as Alec Hardy, an underwritten role that he imbues with a wonderful sense of world-weariness and loss.

The first season of *Broadchurch* was so successful that a second was immediately commissioned. It was also remade in the United States as *Gracepoint* (2014), in which Tennant again starred. The power-house acting duo of Olivia Colman and David Tennant turned Broadchurch into one of ITV's biggest hits in years. **LH**

❯ Olivia Colman as Detective Superintendent Ellie Miller and David Tennant as Detective Inspector Alec Hardy.

Bates Motel

Fantasy/Horror/Sci-Fi | USA | 2013–present

A compelling contemporary prequel to Psycho, *Alfred Hitchcock's classic 1960 horror movie*

Cast | Vera Farmiga, Freddie Highmore, Max Thieriot, Olivia Cooke, Nestor Carbonell
Original broadcaster | A&E **For fans of . . .** | *American Horror Story* (2011), *Hannibal* (2013)

Bates Motel chronicles the tormented lives of Norman Bates and his mother, Norma, prior to the events portrayed in Alfred Hitchcock's classic film of Robert Bloch's popular novel *Psycho*. The characters are those of the original, but the action is relocated from Fairvale, California, to another fictional town, White Pine Bay, Oregon, and the setting is contemporary.

Developed for television by Carlton Cuse, Kerry Ehrin, and Anthony Cipriano, each episode is filled with suspense, eerie plotlines, and a lot of murder. This smart, creepy drama series begins with Norma's purchase, straight after the death of her husband, of the infamous motel. Some locals welcome the Bateses, but others aren't quite so friendly, and White Pine Bay isn't

as peaceful as it at first appears. Also, Norma's eldest son, Dylan (Norman's half-brother), who has long been estranged from his mother, returns to trouble the pair.

Bates Motel unfurls a terrifying portrayal of Norman's psyche, revealing his dark, twisted backstory and the intense and often uncomfortably close relationship that he has with his mother. **RP**

Classic episode

The Truth | *Season 1, episode 6*. It's revealed that it may be Norman, not Norma, who killed his father, further reinforcing the hypothesis of Norman's dual personality and his mother's unyielding devotion to her son.

⊘ Don't tell lies to your mother! Vera Farmiga as Norma Bates and Freddie Highmore as her crazy, mixed-up son, Norman.

The Village

Drama | UK | 2013–present

The United Kingdom in the twentieth century, as experienced by one small rural settlement

Cast | John Simm, Maxine Peake, Rupert Evans, Joe Armstrong, Derek Riddell, Juliet Stephenson, Tome Varey, Chloe Rowley   **Original broadcaster** | BBC One   **For fans of . . .** | *Heimat: A Chronicle of Germany* (1984)

The Village began its journey through British history with the arrival of the first bus to travel to a small village in Derbyshire. Writer Peter Moffat conceived the show as a working-class drama to counterbalance programs such as *Downton Abbey* (2010), focusing on farmers and laborers rather than the aristocracy. As a consequence, the show is often bleak and uncompromising.

The first and second seasons were introduced by a present-day version of one of the characters, Bert Middleton (David Ryall). From the distance granted by old age, he spoke about the changes that came to the village. Certainly, one of the pleasures of the series is to see characters change dramatically but realistically over the course of the years. For example, John Middleton

(John Simm) discovers God, rejects alcohol, and ceases to be a drunken, abusive husband.

The Village was inspired by the German miniseries *Heimat: A Chronicle of Germany* (1984), whose eleven episodes originally ran from 1919 to 1982. *The Village* is currently planned to have a forty-two-episode run and to cover one hundred years of British history. **PB**

Classic episode
Season 1, episode 4. The Middletons' son is ill, and John takes desperate measures in an attempt to win him a miracle cure. Meanwhile at another house, a new doctor uses brutal and unsavory methods to cure a woman's hysteria.

⬥ John and Grace Middleton (John Simm and Maxine Peake) are flanked by Bert and Mary Middleton (Tom Varey and Chloe Rowley).

Da Vinci's Demons

Historical drama | USA | 2013–present

Slick, pretty, and inventive Renaissance drama about the life of the greatest mind of all time

Cast | Tom Riley, Laura Haddock, Blake Ritson, Elliot Cowan, Lara Pulver
Original broadcaster | Starz   **For fans of . . .** | *Spartacus* (2010)

It may throw historical accuracy to the wind, but *Da Vinci's Demons* is a stylish confection that charts the life of a young, sexy Leonardo da Vinci (Tom Riley) as he cuts a swathe through fifteenth-century Florence. Political skulduggery, religious scandal, battles, and quests all have a place in this slick, good-looking entertainment that has the air of a fast-moving Renaissance espionage series with steampunk undertones. It has been sold to more than one hundred territories worldwide.

In the first episode Leonardo encountered a mysterious Turk, who tasked him with finding the Book of Leaves. The artist's inquiries were hindered by Count Riario (Blake Ritson), and a potential romance sizzled in his relationship with Lucrezia Donati (Laura Haddock).

Da Vinci's Demons has stunning production design and punchy, video-game-influenced direction. Story arcs run across the series—one recurring plot line concerns the whereabouts of Leonardo's missing mother—and it is frequently implied that the events depicted in the series will never be mentioned in history. How convenient! **MW**

Classic episode
The Sins of Daedalus | *Season 2, episode 10*. It emerges that the Book of Leaves may have been in Constantinople all along, while the Labyrinth has turned Riario. In the climactic moments, the identity of Leonardo's mother is revealed.

◉ Tom Riley as ambidextrous Leonardo da Vinci in the opening episode, "The Hanged Man."

Sleepy Hollow

Fantasy/Horror/Sci-Fi | USA | 2013–present

A soldier reawakens 200 years after his death to discover that he still has work to do

Cast | Tom Mison, Nicole Beharie, Orlando Jones, John Noble   **Original broadcaster** | Fox
For fans of . . . | *Point Pleasant* (2005), *Hemlock Grove* (2013), *Forever* (2014)

This show is a modern-day adaptation of American essayist Washington Irving's short story "The Legend of Sleepy Hollow" (1820). The first season of thirteen episodes was so popular that it was soon followed by a second season of eighteen episodes.

In the 1780s a headless rider, who turned out to be one of the Four Horsemen of the Apocalypse, terrorized Sleepy Hollow, NY, until young Colonial spy Ichabod Crane (Tom Mison) killed him, but died of his own wounds. Two hundred and thirty years later, a coven of witches resurrected both combatants and soon afterward, a series of beheadings took place across New York. Police lieutenant Abbie Mills (Nicole Beharie) leads the investigation and is helped by Crane. And it emerged that Crane's eighteenth-century wife was a witch, and that it was she who placed her husband in suspended animation.

Crane's view of the present from his two-hundred-year-old perspective provided much of the show's early humor, but the underlying fear of dark forces was never dissipated and gradually intensified. **MR**

Classic episode
Necromancer | *Season 1, episode 8.* The show's mythos takes an interesting twist by weaving itself further into the work of the founding fathers and examining the real motives of the Headless Horseman.

Tom Mison (playing Ichabod Crane) leads Nicole Beharie (Lieutenant Abbie Mills) further into trouble.

Endeavour

Crime/Mystery | UK | 2012–present

Prequel crime drama telling the origins of a much-loved television mainstay

Classic episode
Fugue | Season 1, episode 2. A serial killer terrorizes Oxford with apparently random attacks. He leaves no clues, but Morse intuitively surmises that the perpetrator must be an opera lover; it takes one to know one.

⚉ Shaun Evans as Endeavour Morse and Roger Allam as his mentor, Detective Inspector Fred Thursday.

Cast | Shaun Evans, Roger Allam, Anton Lesser, Sean Rigby
Original broadcaster | ITV
For fans of . . . | *Maigret* (1960), *Inspector Morse* (1987), *Spender* (1991)

Between 1987 and 2000, *Inspector Morse* was a cornerstone of British television. With the character ultimately killed off, and actor John Thaw dying in 2002, the producers now looked to the past in a prequel about the detective's early history.

The title was taken from Morse's seldom-used and long-unrevealed Christian name. Shaun Evans was cast as young Morse for a feature-length TV film portraying the awkward and solitary young detective constable being seconded to a murder case in the university city of Oxford (the usual setting for *Inspector Morse*) in the mid-1960s. Morse is mentored by Inspector Thursday (Roger Allam), who sees potential in the young man, despite his inability to fit in with his colleagues. The success of this pilot led to a series commission the following year.

Endeavour is influenced by the Scandinavian noirs that were popular at the time but true to the spirit of the original. Evans' performance—influenced, he said, more by Colin Dexter's novels than by Thaw's earlier interpretation—bring out some of the seediness that was previously hinted at but never stated. The stories reveal the background to Morse's love of opera and beer, and two of the supporting characters—Max (James Bradshaw) and P.C. Strange (Sean Rigby)—feature in two seasons.

In the closing shot of the pilot, an image of Thaw's Morse looks back at his younger self in a rear-view mirror. Somehow, it felt right. **MW**

The Following

Drama | USA | 2013–15

Dark thriller pitting an FBI agent with unorthodox methods against an army of serial killers

Cast | Kevin Bacon, James Purefoy, Shawn Ashmore, Natalie Zea, Annie Parisse
Original broadcaster | Fox
For fans of . . . | *24* (2001), *Criminal Minds* (2005), *Crossing Lines* (2013)

Lone serial killers are a staple element of many TV crime dramas, but the idea of multiple serial killers working together is a different proposition altogether. That's what made *The Following* terrifying yet utterly compelling viewing.

Created by Kevin Williamson (*Dawson's Creek*, 1998, and *The Vampire Diaries*, 2009), *The Following* starred Kevin Bacon as former FBI agent Ryan Hardy, called back into service when the serial killer he brought to justice, Joe Carroll (James Purefoy), escaped from prison. As Hardy pursued Carroll, he discovered that Carroll had spent his incarceration building up a cult of followers, ready to act upon his instructions. The central conceit of Carroll creating a cult of murderous acolytes in his own image was unsettling, and the surprising levels of violence reinforced the bleak tone. The frenetic pace and Hardy's willingness to go to extremes were elements that have drawn parallels with *24*.

Bacon was an inspired lead; he brought real gravitas to the role of the loose-cannon cop, and offered a reassuring presence among the horrors on offer. Purefoy was a disconcerting on-screen presence, and his interactions with Bacon showed both actors at their best. While some critics have criticized *The Following* for being too violent, it has received praise for its concept and the performances. It was a bold series that divided opinion, but it was a welcome and largely successful exercise in bringing the horror and suspense genre to the small screen. **SO**

Classic episode
The Final Chapter | *Season 1, episode 15*. Agent Debra Parker has been buried alive, and Hardy has to track her down before her oxygen runs out. Meanwhile, Carroll prepares to face Hardy for the final time.

⬤ Kevin Bacon (Hardy) and Annie Parisse (Parker), FBI specialists in cult behavior. Can they stop a super-group of serial killers?

Hannibal

Drama | USA | 2013–present

Everyone's favorite serial killer is having friends for dinner

Cast | Mads Mikkelsen, Hugh Dancy, Laurence Fishburne, Caroline Dhavernas, Scott Thompson, Aaron Abrams, Gillian Anderson
Original broadcaster | NBC
For fans of . . . | *American Horror Story* (2011)

Dr. Hannibal Lecter first appeared as a supporting character in Thomas Harris' 1981 police procedural novel *Red Dragon*, which was released in 1986 by Michael Mann as *Manhunter*. It was Jonathan Demme's 1990 adaptation of Harris' *Silence of the Lambs* with Anthony Hopkins that made Lecter an unlikely cult hero. A further sequel, a remake of *Red Dragon* (2002), and a prequel solidified Lecter's place as the world's favorite consumer of well-cooked human flesh.

This TV series extrapolated details from Harris' novels to create a new story. One of the biggest changes is the character of FBI profiler Will Graham (Hugh Dancy), who is a peripheral figure in the novels, but here takes center stage. As played by Dancy, he has a profound empathy for his suspects, and reconstructs each gruesome killing in his mind. Will's compassion for the victims is matched by a reluctant emotional connection to the killers, leading him to question whether there's a murderer within him, too. Hannibal (Mads Mikkelsen) and Will develop an uneasy friendship: Hannibal provides insights into disturbing murder cases while taking a vicarious pleasure in the gory details.

Hannibal is not for the squeamish; each victim is horrifically mutilated and through Will's visions the viewers see the murders in vivid detail. And occasionally they see how Hannibal's own murderous career results in interesting choices for his dining table. **JS**

❯ Mads Mikkelsen as evil Hannibal Lecter.

Hemlock Grove

Fantasy/Horror/Sci-Fi | USA | 2013–15

A boy who happens to be a werewolf teams up with a rich kid to track down a serial killer

Cast | Famke Janssen, Bill Skarsgård, Dougray Scott, Penelope Mitchell, Landon Liboiron
Original broadcaster | Netflix
For fans of . . . | *Dark Shadows* (1966), *The Gates* (2010), *Teen Wolf* (2011)

When two teenage girls were found dead in the depressed town of Hemlock Grove, police pulled in Peter (Landon Liboiron), a local Roma boy who was rumored to be a werewolf. Determined to prove his innocence, Peter teamed up with the son and heir to the estate of the richest family in town, Roman (Bill Skarsgård), to whom he revealed that he really was a werewolf—although he promised that he had never actually killed anyone.

Meanwhile, Roman's cousin Letha (Penelope Mitchell) was pregnant and claimed that the father of the baby was an angel. Roman's mother Olivia (Famke Janssen) had a dark secret of her own and a familial history that placed Roman on a dark path, meaning that he was destined to fight his newfound friend.

With a very large budget—$45 million was spent on the first season alone—and the prolific horror film director Eli Roth as executive producer, *Hemlock Grove* was full of incredible, and often disturbing, monster special effects.

Thanks to the roots provided by the book on which it was based (by Brian McGreevy, who helped to adapt it for television), there was a rich hinterland of lore to be explored—it turned out that the town was a haven for supernatural creatures and a prejudiced cult that was determined to destroy any nonhumans. The backstory enabled the show to become darker and more fantastical as it progressed, and to reach a firm resolution at the end of its third and final season. **MR**

Classic episode
Children of the Night | *Season 1, episode 12.* A Vargulf is a mentally unstable werewolf. Peter and Roman know there is one in their midst, but the revelation of its true identity is one of the biggest shocks in the whole series.

⊘ Famke Janssen as Olivia Godfrey, chief scientist at the laboratory that is thought to be the cause of all the sinister occurrences.

Stella

Comedy/Drama | UK | 2012–present

A warm-hearted family drama about village life in the Welsh valleys

Cast | Ruth Jones, Craig Gallivan, Catrin Stewart, Justin Davies, Steve Speirs, Elizabeth Berrington
Original broadcaster | Sky 1
For fans of . . . | *Nighty Night* (2004), *Gavin & Stacey* (2007), *Nurse Jackie* (2009), *Last Tango in Halifax* (2012)

Following the success of *Gavin & Stacey* (2007), cowriter and star Ruth Jones was in great demand with TV producers around the United Kingdom. Jones was courted by Sky and almost two years to the day since the finale of *Gavin & Stacey* aired, *Stella* debuted on Sky 1 as a flagship comedy-drama. Cocreated by Jones with husband David Peet, *Stella* is warm and quirky, occupying a regular place in the UK cable schedule.

Stella Morris (Jones) is a single parent living in the village of Pontyberry in the Welsh valleys. A cheerful soul, Stella deals with the challenges unleashed by her children, their fathers, and an extensive roster of eccentric friends. Her eldest son, Luke (Craig Gallivan), is serving a prison sentence, while her daughter, Emma (Catrin Stewart), and youngest son, Ben (Justin Davies), give her frequent cause for concern. Stella's sister-in-law, Paula (Elizabeth Berrington), runs the local funeral home, her ex-husband is in a relationship with a younger woman, and gentle giant Alan (Steve Speirs) has been smitten with her since their school days. *Stella* displays Jones' talent for writing quirky characters with depth. Pontyberry feels like a real village, and the story lines stay plausible and never stray into melodrama.

In early 2015, Sky had commissioned four seasons of *Stella*, as the series established a loyal UK audience. *Stella*'s lack of cynicism, the tight scripting, and, above all, a warm, likable central turn from Jones herself made it a worthy hit. Stella is a character that the viewers root for, which keeps them coming back for more. **MW**

Classic episode
Season 2, episode 10. Stella faces a life-changing decision in the season finale when Rob (Mark Lewis Jones) offers her the opportunity of a new life in Canada. When Sean (Kenny Doughty) re-enters her life, she is unsure which way to turn.

🔺 Ruth Jones (Stella) joins Craig Gallivan (Luke) and Bethan Witcomb (Zoe) on their wedding day.

Utopia

Drama | UK | 2013–14

A complex and disturbing conspiracy thriller

Cast | Alexandra Roach, Nathan Stewart-Jarrett, Geraldine James, Fiona O'Shaughnessy
Original broadcaster | Channel 4
For fans of . . . | *Edge of Darkness* (1985), *The Shadow Line* (2011)

Four comic-book fans were brought together through an online forum where they discussed the lost sequel to a cult graphic novel, *The Utopia Experiments*. Finding themselves in possession of the manuscript, they were pursued by the mysterious and ruthless Network. Gradually, they learned the secrets of the manuscript and the true—global and shocking—ambitions of the Network. Dennis Kelly's *Utopia* was one of the most imaginative thrillers ever made for British television.

As well as giving a fresh twist on the paranoid conspiracy mystery, *Utopia* was set apart by its claustrophobic soundtrack and distinctive aesthetic. Its violence, of which children were often the victims or perpetrators, made *Utopia* the subject of controversy, and it undoubtedly made for unsettling viewing. But the flashes of brutality, the blank remorselessness of Network hitman Arby (brilliantly played by Neil Maskell), and the succession of disturbing revelations all fed a tension that bordered on dread and gripped views up until the final scene.

Meanwhile, the decidedly unheroic heroes, hopelessly out of their depth, wondered who to trust as allegiances shifted, unsuspected connections emerged, and the Network's terrifying plan proved unexpectedly seductive to one of them.

Channel 4 announced in 2014 that there would not be a third season, but HBO is planning its own version, which will be written by Gillian Flynn and directed by David Fincher. **HE**

My Mad Fat Diary

Comedy/Drama | UK | 2013–present

Teen drama with an overweight protagonist

Cast | Sharon Rooney, Jodie Comer, Ciara Baxendale, Dan Cohen, Ian Hart, Claire Rushbrook, Nico Mirallegro
Original broadcaster | E4
For fans of . . . | *Skins* (2007), *The Inbetweeners* (2008)

Based on the teenage diaries of British writer and broadcaster Rae Earl, *My Mad Fat Diary* charts the author's attempts to find her way in the outside world after leaving a psychiatric hospital, where she has been living for the last few months.

Funny, sweet, and truthful, the series, which is set in Lincolnshire, shows what it's like to be an overweight and mentally ill teenager. But crucially, it also demonstrates that these are not the traits that define her; instead this is a story about the life of a teenager who just happens to be "mad" and "fat."

The majority of episodes feature Rae's voice-over as she reads out her diary entries to the viewers, and the action on the screen regularly freezes to show Rae's often scatological doodles over the picture. The music selection is also a strong feature of the series and the soundtrack is lush with Britpop classics of the mid-1990s.

Rae is funny and filthy in all the right ways, and her attempts to discover how boys work and to be accepted, and to accept herself, are the main plot drivers. As well as dealing with her friends, the series also explores Rae's problematic relationship with her family when her mother's Tunisian boyfriend moves in.

Although Rae's original diaries were written in 1989, the series updates the setting to 1996, imposes a story structure on the life of the main character, and makes people in general just a bit nicer than they came across in the original book. **PB**

Brooklyn Nine-Nine

Comedy | USA | 2013–present

An action comedy series set in a New York City Police Department in Brooklyn

Cast | Andy Samberg, Stephanie Beatriz, Terry Crews, Melissa Fumero, Joe Lo Truglio, Andre Braugher
Original broadcaster | Fox
Awards | 2 Golden Globes
For fans of . . . | *Police Squad!* (1982)

Serious and stern Captain Ray Holt (Andre Braugher) takes over Brooklyn's 99th precinct, which includes Detective Jake Peralta (Andy Samberg), a talented, carefree, but immature detective who is used to doing whatever he wants. Jake comes into immediate conflict with his new commanding officer, who is literally gay but often serves as the proverbial straight man.

Around them is a large ensemble cast, including Detective Amy Santiago (Melissa Fumero), Jake's overachieving and competitive partner; Rosa Diaz (Stephanie Beatriz), a tough detective who keeps to herself; Detective Charles Boyle (Joe Lo Truglio), Jake's quirky best friend, who has crush on Rosa; Detective Sergeant Terry Jeffords (Terry Crews), who became so anxious after the birth of his twin girls that he's incapable of leaving the station to go out on patrol; and Gina Linetti (Chelsea Peretti), the precinct's sarcastic civilian administrator.

Brooklyn Nine-Nine's confidence in its central conceit was evident when, in its first episode, it plunged Holt into a fully-formed comic world, populated by personalities that have stayed relatively constant since. With the minimum of exposition, but a hilarious series of flashbacks, especially those in which bald Holt is seen with an afro, the characters and their relationships are the essence of a show that epitomizes the next generation of the traditional workplace comedy. **RP**

◑ Joe Lo Truglio and Andy Samberg get to grips with Father Christmas felons in a festive episode of season one.

Africa

Documentary | USA/UK/Chile/France | 2013

Masterpiece about the continent's wildlife

Cast | David Attenborough (narrator, UK), Forrest Whitaker (narrator, USA)
Original broadcaster | BBC One
For fans of . . . | *Life on Earth* (1979),
The Blue Planet (2001)

Throughout a career spanning almost half a century, naturalist David Attenborough has been behind many outstanding nature programs, each of which has been even better than its predecessors. *Africa* was perhaps his masterpiece: every episode focused on a particular area and its indigenous species—from chimpanzees in the Congo basin to silver ants in the Sahara desert. Each episode also featured a fifteen-minute tailpiece about how the crew captured the spectacular footage.

Coproduced by the BBC Natural History Department, The Discovery Channel, China Central Television, and France Télévision, this was a triumph of production. The project was four years in the making, and involved complex logistics and exposure to great danger; the result was unfailingly beautiful photography, jaw-dropping encounters with animals, and informative narration. The series was also remarkable in that it covered not only the wild animals themselves but also the dangers facing them, such as poaching, climate change, and population growth. The viewers get to see firsthand what the conservationists and scientists are doing to try to save endangered species, such as the black rhino and the mountain gorilla. If watching this show doesn't inspire people to change, especially after having fallen in love with every creature over the course of this majestic series, nothing will. *Africa* shifted perceptions, and thrilled and stunned its viewers— while very slightly changing the world we live in for the better. **LH**

The Wrong Mans

Comedy/Drama | UK | 2013–14

Fast-paced serial lampooning action-film clichés

Cast | James Corden, Mathew Baynton, Sarah Solemani, Dawn French
Original broadcaster | BBC Two
Award | 1 BAFTA
For fans of . . . | *Chuck* (2007)

Phil (James Corden) and Sam (Mathew Baynton) were local council workers whose lives changed dramatically when they answered a ringing phone they found at the scene of a road accident. The voice on the other end threatened to kill a hostage unless a rendezvous was met, and Phil convinced Sam that they had to make the meeting to save the girl. This decision kickstarted a series of unlikely and dangerous events bringing the "wrong mans" into contact with all manner of underworld characters, murderous lunatics, and globe-trotting spies. Somehow they survived these lethal situations despite (and sometimes because of) Phil's reliance on his knowledge of action films to dictate their every move. With sterling support from Sarah Solemani (as Sam's ex-girlfriend) and Dawn French (as Phil's off-kilter mother) and a host of guest stars (including Dougray Scott, Emilia Fox, and Rebecca Front), the series benefited from the likable leads and the classy production values.

A second season the following year continued the same story with our heroes hidden away in Texas on a witness protection program but once again becoming embroiled in situations not of their making, hinging on misunderstandings and cases of mistaken identity.

The Wrong Mans (its title deliberately clumsy to indicate its comic intent) was a well-received, fast-moving romp that brought a breath of fresh air to the TV lineup and succeeded brilliantly in the tricky art of combining laughs with thrills. **DF**

Under the Dome

Fantasy/Horror/Sci-Fi | UK | 2013–present

Chester's Mill, a small settlement in Maine, may be the unluckiest place on Earth

Cast | Mike Vogel, Dean Norris, Rachelle Lefevre, Britt Robertson, Natalie Martinez, Alexander Koch, Colin Ford
Original broadcaster | CBS
For fans of . . . | *The Stand* (1994)

Chester's Mill is warm and friendly, its citizens tightly knit, its downtown quaint and folksy. That is, until a giant, invisible, impenetrable dome appears over the town. Suddenly the small New England town is isolated from the rest of civilization and becomes a hotbed of conspiracy and subterfuge.

Based on Stephen King's 2009 eponymous novel, *Under the Dome* focuses on several characters, residents and visitors, trapped by the dome-shaped force field, including the mysterious Dale Barbara (Mike Vogel), journalist Julia Shumway (Rachelle Lefevre), sheriff Linda Esquivel (Natalie Martinez), teenaged everyman Joe McAlister (Colin Ford) and his older sister Angie (Britt Robertson), and local alderman "Big Jim" Rennie (Dean Norris). Big Jim begins to envision himself as the community's leader and savior, but has to deal not only with his own insecurities but also the creepy moves made by his son Junior (Alexander Koch), whose antics include trapping Angie in a bomb shelter. Against the backdrop of the dome, hampered by its prisonlike isolation as well as the otherworldly clues received both in prophetic visions and resurrections of the dead, the town's inhabitants struggle to stay alive and solve all the mysteries.

The show was recommissioned after a successful first run, but the second season lacked cohesion and lost some of its original popularity. It is now the task of a third season, in production as the present volume went to press, to recover the lost viewers. **SL**

Classic episode
Curtains | Season 1, episode 13. In the first season's finale, Big Jim decides on Dale Barbara's fate. There is a hanging, a shower of butterflies, and long-prophesied pink stars rising from an onyx egg.

◈ Rachelle Lefevre as Julia Shumway and Mike Vogel as Dale "Barbie" Barbara.

Orange Is the New Black

Drama | USA | 2013–present

Piper Chapman is sent to a women's federal prison after her past catches up with her

Cast | Taylor Schilling, Kate Mulgrew, Jason Biggs,
Laura Prepon, Michael Harney, Laverne Cox
Original broadcaster | Netflix
Awards | 3 Emmys
For fans of . . . | *Oz* (1997), *Wentworth* (2013)

Piper Chapman (Taylor Schilling) had everything: a fiancée, a great life, great friends, and a future free from worries except for first-world problems, like sourcing ethical Arabica beans. Then her life collapsed around her when she was put in prison for fifteen months because of the activities of a former girlfriend.

Chapman swiftly realized how ill-prepared she was for her new environment. As she tried to school herself on prison-related issues, she made a catastrophic mistake in insulting matriarch and head cook Red (Kate Mulgrew), and as a result she was given a "used tampon sandwich." To make matters worse, Chapman's ex-girlfriend Alex Vause (Laura Prepon) was also housed in the same facility, a constant reminder to Chapman (and, via flashback, to the viewers) of just how she came to be spending her days in prison orange.

As the season progressed, the audience discovered the backstories of other characters in the prison. Alliances and dynamics changed thanks to Chapman's naive honesty, which often left her vulnerable to manipulation but also helped to soften many of the prisoners' cynical attitudes toward her.

Netflix optioned Piper Kerman's 2010 memoir, *Orange Is the New Black: My Year in a Women's Prison*, about her own experiences. The show received wide critical acclaim for its frankness, especially its portrayal of a transgender inmate (Laverne Cox). MR

❯ Taylor Schilling (right) as Piper Chapman contemplating her life in prison and thinking of all the places she'd rather be.

Atlantis

Fantasy/Horror/Sci-Fi | UK | 2013–present

An impressive modern take on ancient Greek mythology

Classic episode

Pandora's Box | *Season 1, episode 9.*
Medusa (Jemima Rooper) is kidnapped, and the ill-fated and and oddly matched relationship between her and Hercules frames a dramatic race against time for friendship and love.

⊙ Swords and boots drama: (L–R) Pythagoras (Robert Emms), Jason (Jack Donnelly), and Hercules (Mark Addy).

Cast | Mark Addy, Jack Donnelly, Robert Emms, Jemima Rooper, Alexander Siddig
Original broadcaster | BBC One
For fans of . . . | *Hercules: The Legendary Journeys* (1995), *The Odyssey* (1997), *Merlin* (2008)

Conceived by Howard Overman—creator of *Misfits* (2009) and scriptwriter for *Hotel Babylon* (2006) and *Merlin* (2008)—*Atlantis* brought to the small screen yet another reworking of Greek mythology, this time set in the legendary lost city of the title.

Oceanographer Jason (Jack Donnelly) took a one-man submarine down to the seabed in the hope of tracking down the source of a deep-sea disturbance that caused the disappearance of his father when Jason was a child. As Jason approaches his father's last known location, his submarine began to shut down. He lost consciousness and was pulled into a white light. Waking on a beach in Atlantis, he was befriended by Pythagoras (Robert Emms) and an out-of-shape former prize fighter Hercules (Mark Addy).

Atlantis effectively mixed present-day idioms with the trappings of fantasy, while the rich mythos of characters and plots made a welcome change from similar shows that tend to focus on—and often exhaust—a single legend. Here the Oracle, Orpheus, Medusa, and the Cyclops all made appearances.

The show was initially welcomed on both sides of the Atlantic and recommissioned soon after the first season began its run. But the second season suffered from a significant cast change, a shift in the ongoing story arc, and the introduction of a number of new central characters. The producers hoped that this reboot would enable newcomers to join the show, but viewing figures slumped and the show was canceled. **MR**

The Doctor Blake Mysteries

Crime/Mystery | Australia | 2013–present

Big crimes in small-town Australia

Cast | Craig McLachlan, Nadine Garner, Cate Wolfe, Joel Tobeck, Rick Donald
Original broadcaster | ABC
For fans of . . . | *Perry Mason* (1957), *Quincy, M.E.* (1976)

Lucien Blake (Craig McLachlan) was born in Australia, but went to Scotland in the 1930s to study medicine. On his way home he stopped off in Asia, where he married and fathered a child, but had to abandon his family when Singapore fell to the Japanese in 1942. After the Second World War he returned to his native Ballarat, a picturesque gold-rush town in the State of Victoria, and established a medical practice. But since this is a crime drama, he ends up doing more detection than prescription. This isn't a world of heroes and villains, but a murky slice of 1950s noir re-created for the twenty-first century. Stories reach a resolution, rather than a happy ending, and frequently the wrong people live to fight another day.

In the title role, McLachlan is transformed utterly from the pop star who made his name as an actor in the Australian soap operas *Neighbours* (1985) and *Home and Away* (1988). Here he appears convincingly rumpled and haunted by his unhappy past. He is assisted in all his endeavors by two equally down-at-heel colleagues— receptionist Jean Beazley (Nadine Garner) and district nurse Mattie O'Brien (Cate Wolfe)—and by two police officers—Chief Inspector Matthew Lawson (Joel Tobeck) and Constable Daniel Parks (Rick Donald).

An international hit, *The Doctor Blake Mysteries* is a refreshing change of tone from Australia's previous successful crime drama export, *Miss Fisher's Murder Mysteries* (2012), a much more conventional series about a glamorous private detective. **JG**

Ja'mie: Private School Girl

Comedy | Australia | 2013

Observational comedy

Cast | Chris Lilley, Lester Ellis Jr., Georgie Jennings, Laura Grady, Phoebe Roberts, D'arci Buckerfield
Original broadcaster | ABC
For fans of . . . | *Gossip Girl* (2007), *Mrs. Brown's Boys* (2011)

After nearly seven years, Chris Lilley resurrected Ja'mie King, the brattish star of *We Can Be Heroes* (2005) and *Summer Heights High* (2007). This time viewers followed Ja'mie as Queen Bee of Hillford School, an institution where she had been Head Girl for nearly a decade.

Ja'mie's efforts to stay ahead were as appalling as ever. She forced her parents to adopt a Ugandan, shocked the school with a highly sexualized dance routine, and terrorized her classmates by deciding who was fat and who was a lesbian (by the end of the series, Ja'mie had put on weight and showed an increasing interest in women). Ja'mie had discovered sex and used it as another weapon of intimidation and humiliation, taunting her rival Madison (Lester Ellis Jr.) with a photograph she'd received from Madison's boyfriend and saying "he says you've got fat."

Ja'mie: Private School Girl demonstrated that Lilley has kept up with the modern day, even if Ja'mie was still from the Dark Ages. Ja'mie's phrases and strops were pure Tumblr fodder, and the show had a sharp eye on how awareness of social media drives behavior among teenage girls. Still surrounded by a deadpan cast playing it completely straight, Lilley wasn't afraid to push Ja'mie to bigoted, racist, sexist extremes. If it seemed initially strange that the sharpest observer of the awful pressures of being an adolescent girl was a middle-aged man, this became eventually reassuring. After all, it was just a vicious man in a skirt and a wig. Predators like Ja'mie can't really exist, can they? **JG**

The Blacklist

Drama | USA | 2013–present

*Labyrinthine, murky, and violent
neo-noir thriller*

Cast | James Spader, Harry Lennix, Megan Boone,
Diego Klattenhoff
Original broadcaster | NBC
Award | 1 Emmy
For fans of . . . | *The Sopranos* (1999)

The Blacklist opened with master criminal Raymond
"Red" Reddington (James Spader) handing himself in
to the FBI in order to make a deal: in exchange for
immunity from prosecution, he would provide vital
information on a comprehensive list of criminals and
terrorists with whom he had been associated. The
level of threat from those figures was so high that
Bureau chief Harold Cooper (Harry Lennix) reluctantly
agreed, knowing full well that he was "dealing with
the Devil." Red had one other condition: he would
work only alongside rookie agent Elizabeth Keen
(Megan Boone), but he refused to say why.

Drawn into a web of deceit, Keen soon realized that
she hadn't been chosen at random—her past was
somehow intertwined with Red's. It also became clear
that Red had his own agenda, and was using the FBI to
rid himself of some troublesome adversaries.

One of the principal strengths of the show is
that it manages complexity without confusing the
viewers. That is a rare feat. Another is the apparent
ease with which it develops new mysteries as others
approach their solutions: by the time we discover
the link between Reddington and Keen, whole new
story arcs are keeping us tuned in. And at the heart of
these compelling plot twists and character revelations
lies a mesmerizing central performance by James
Spader as Red. **DF**

◗ James Spader as "Red" Reddington wonders whether Ramsey
Farrahgallah as Ali Hassan is clubbable.

Marvel's Agents of S.H.I.E.L.D.

Action/Adventure | USA | 2013–present

A covert security organization that handles cases too hot for superheroes

Cast | Clark Gregg, Chloe Bennet, Ming-Na Wen, Brett Dalton, Iain De Caestecker, Elizabeth Henstridge
Original broadcaster | ABC **For fans of . . .** | *Spooks* (2002), *Gotham* (2014)

Introduced to modern audiences in the first *Iron Man* feature film (2008), the Strategic Homeland Intervention, Enforcement and Logistics Division (S.H.I.E.L.D.) appeared to be a *Men in Black*–style home for backroom geeks and accountants. In *Marvel's The Avengers*, the audience saw one particular agent, the mild-mannered Phil Coulson (Clark Gregg), meet a bloody end at the hands of an Asgardian deity with a point to prove.

But death never stands in the way of a TV spin-off. A resurrected Agent Coulson assembled a team of misfits with a variety of skills, including computer hacking and proficiency in the martial arts. But each played to his or her own agenda. Even Coulson wasn't entirely honest.

A superhero TV show without superheroes was a risky move, and even fans of Marvel comics found the early episodes hard going. But those who kept the faith were well rewarded as the bigger story began to unfold. Those who stayed with it into the second season found themselves hooked on a series that had now masterfully hit its stride. **JS**

Classic episode
End of the Beginning | *Season 1, episode 16.*
While his team follows the trail of The Clairvoyant, Coulson finds evidence to suggest that their target is a high-ranking member of S.H.I.E.L.D.

◬ The three main agents: Clark Gregg as Phil Coulson, Chloe Bennet as Daisy Johnson, and Ming-Na Wen as Melinda May.

Peaky Blinders

Crime/Mystery | UK | 2013–present

Stylish and violent gangster period piece, set in post–First World War Birmingham, England

Cast | Cillian Murphy, Helen McCrory, Sam Neill, Annabelle Wallis, Tom Hardy, Noah Taylor
Original broadcaster | BBC Two   **Awards** | 2 BAFTAs   **For fans of . . .** | *The Wire* (2002), *Ripper Street* (2012)

Created by British screenwriter and director Steven Knight, this riveting and fast-paced drama romps through rackets, robbery, betting scams, family feuds, murder, and sexual shenanigans with a rich and heady mix of stylish cinematography and charismatic performances, backed by a contemporary soundtrack from Nick Cave, Jack White, and P.J. Harvey.

At its heart is war veteran Tommy Shelby (Cillian Murphy), who heads a family of notorious criminals in the English Midlands, and their powerful local gang, the Peaky Blinders. They make their money from illegal betting, protection rackets, and the black market, but Tommy wants to move up in the world and run legitimate operations. His ambition brings him into deadly conflict with rival gangs and his would-be nemesis, the righteous Chief Inspector Chester Campbell (Sam Neill). As their personal war develops, Tommy and Campbell battle for the affections of the beautiful and mysterious Grace Burgess (Annabelle Wallis), recruited by Campbell to spy on Tommy.

As viewers follow the story of the Shelby family through the 1920s, a determined Tommy expands the empire into London, encountering Jewish gangster Alfie Solomons (Tom Hardy) and psychotic Italian mobster Darby Sabini (Noah Taylor). Meanwhile, the family matriarch Polly (Helen McCrory) tries to prevent the sins of the adults from being visited on the younger generation. **IDG**

⊘ Tommy Shelby (Cillian Murphy) oversees the expansion of the Peaky Blinders' empire.

Masters of Sex

Drama | USA | 2013–present

Period piece about the medical researchers who gave birth to the sexual revolution

Cast | Michael Sheen, Lizzy Caplan, Caitlin Fitzgerald, Allison Janney
Original broadcaster | Showtime **Award** | 1 Emmy **For fans of . . .** | *Mad Men* (2007)

This series is based on Thomas Maier's biography of the lives and works of Dr. William Masters and his research assistant Virginia Johnson, who in the 1950s and 1960s researched the nature of sexual relations between Americans of all sorts—from naive newlyweds in hospital laboratories to self-pleasuring prostitutes in brothels and pretty much everyone in between.

Viewers expecting titillation from *Masters of Sex* will be disappointed by the lack of bedroom activity, but they will be hooked by the series' wry look at the very different people who conducted such groundbreaking research into the sexual revolution. Masters (Michael Sheen) is an uptight, repressed physician caught in a loveless marriage. Johnson (Lizzie Caplan) is free-spirited and ambitious. They make an odd couple, but they complement each other perfectly and make a real contribution to the fund of human knowledge.

Masters of Sex has few thrills, cheap or otherwise. It is real adult storytelling, uncompromising but shot through with truth, and presented with humor and great panache. **SO**

Classic episode

Catherine | *Season 1, episode 5.* With his wife Libby pregnant after he told her she could not conceive, William has to help her deliver their stillborn baby—an experience that causes him to react in an unexpected way.

⬥ Lizzy Caplan as Virginia Johnson explains exciting new technology in season two, episode two, "Kyrie Eleison."

The Fall

Crime/Mystery | UK | 2013

Atmospheric thriller pitting a female detective against a Belfast serial killer

Cast | Gillian Anderson, Jamie Dornan, John Lynch, Bronagh Waugh, Archie Panjabi, Colin Morgan
Original broadcaster | BBC Two (UK), RTÉ (Ireland) **Award** | 1 BAFTA **For fans of . . .** | *Prime Suspect* (1991)

Serial killer dramas, in film and on TV, too often present women as victims. While the violence in *The Fall* is indeed mostly against women, the series goes out of its way to present a more feminist angle. Writer and creator Allan Cubitt avoids glamorizing the crimes on the show and, in Superintendent Stella Gibson (Gillian Anderson), makes a great addition to television's gallery of memorable detectives.

Not that a female lead investigator is itself groundbreaking. From Jane Tennison in *Prime Suspect* to Sarah Lund in *Forbrydelsen* (*The Killing*, 2007), the path has been trod before, and Gibson is, like them—and like many male TV detectives—a driven, forceful loner with a messy personal life. But Gibson differs from them

in her powerful sexuality. It's not that she uses sex to get what she wants; when sex is what she wants, she gets it, ensnaring whichever colleague she chooses.

The Fall may not completely achieve all of its author's and producers' stated aims, but each episode entices you back to follow this tense game of cat and mouse to its thrilling conclusion. **WH**

Classic episode
Dark Descent | *Season 1, episode 1*. A well-known young bereavement counselor with an apparently normal family life turns out to be a sexual predator who goes out at night to murder women.

◬ The hunter and the hunted: between D S Stella Gibson (Anderson) and psychopath Paul Spector (Dornan), which is which?

Mr. Selfridge

Historical drama | UK | 2013–present

Sumptuous historical biography of the world-famous retailer

Cast | Jeremy Piven, Frances O'Connor, Katherine Kelly, Ron Cook, Tom Goodman-Hill, Aisling Loftus
Original broadcaster | ITV **For fans of . . .** | *Downton Abbey* (2010), *The Paradise* (2012)

This series was based on Lindy Woodhead's *Shopping, Seduction & Mr. Selfridge* (2007) a biographical study of the life, loves, and excesses of the larger-than-life founder of the London store that bears his name.

The series charts the struggles of American Harry Selfridge (Jeremy Piven) to introduce his innovative retail methods to Britain and open the world's biggest department store in the nation's capital. There was a large ensemble of characters that fuel the scripts, from the Selfridges shopgirls and executive backroom staff to the aristocrats and society figures by whom Harry craved to be accepted.

The period detail is astonishing—the backlot re-creation of the Selfridges store frontage and interior is stunning in its execution; the building is almost a character in itself. *Mr. Selfridge* was one of the most popular shows on UK television for three seasons, and the series has been sold in numerous international territories. The life of Harry Selfridge did not end happily, but the story of his rise, decline, and fall makes for compelling television. **MW**

Classic episode
Season 2, episode 10. Multiple plot strands come to a head in a season finale that sees the Selfridge family hit by tragedy. Staff are on the move—two of them quit to take on a restaurant—and Harry's wife has more bad news

⬥ Harry Selfridge (Jeremy Piven) holds court in Selfridges, the new temple he has dedicated to the gods of retail.

Vicious

Comedy | UK | 2013–present

Barbed comedy centered on Stuart and Freddie, an elderly gay couple of almost fifty years

Cast | Derek Jacobi, Ian McKellen, Frances de la Tour, Iwan Rheon, Marcia Warren, Phillip Voss
Original broadcaster | ITV **For fans of . . .** | *Will & Grace* (1998), *Gimme Gimme Gimme* (2001)

The melodramatically long-suffering Stuart Bixby (Derek Jacobi), a former barman, and his acerbic life partner Freddie Thornhill (Ian McKellen), an erstwhile actor, spend their days bickering and ranting as they endeavor to cope with each other, visits from much-loved but infuriating friends, and the distractions provided by their young and handsome neighbor. The episodes veer from broad farce to the darkly comic, and provide a stream of pithy put-downs and crisply deadpan witticisms.

Originally written as *Vicious Old Queens* (a title ultimately deemed too extreme), the series was devised by award-winning playwright Mark Ravenhill. However, his commitments to the Royal Shakespeare Company prevented full-time scripting duties and Gary Janetti, renowned for his work on series such as *Will & Grace* (1998), was brought on board. Although the lead characters are gay, Janetti has stated that he was more concerned with portraying older characters in a long-term relationship and the ways in which they interact with the modern world, which is primarily represented by neighbor Ash (Iwan Rheon), the series' straight man, in both senses of the term.

The scripts, written specifically for the leads, draw heavily on their real-life characters (both are openly gay), and allow them full rein for campness and cattiness. Filmed mainly on a single set, *Vicious* is a classic, character-driven British situation comedy. **JJJ**

◎ Ian McKellen and Derek Jacobi exchange loving looks that obscure the edgy discomfort of their characters' relationship.

Top of the Lake

Drama | New Zealand/UK/USA | 2013

The search for a missing girl leads to shocking discoveries

Cast | Elisabeth Moss, Holly Hunter, Peter Mullan, David Wenham, Thomas M. Wright, Genevieve Lemon **Original broadcasters** | BBC UKTV (New Zealand); BBC Two (UK); Sundance (USA) **Awards** | 4 Emmys, 1 Golden Globe **For fans of . . .** | *Twin Peaks* (1990)

Writer and director Jane Campion was inspired to make this six part miniseries by the New Zealand landscape near the Routeburn Track. In the richly textured crime drama, co-written with Gerard Lee and co-directed with Garth Davis, the vast mountains, lush forests, and deep lakes were as much characters as the human players. There was a tone of foreboding as it cast a reflective eye on gender, sexuality, family, and love.

When detective Robin Griffin (Elisabeth Moss, star of *Mad Men*, 2007) visited her dying mother in Laketop, her childhood town, she investigated the case of twelve-year-old Tui Mitcham, who tried to drown herself in a vast lake and was secretly five months pregnant. Her father Matt, the local hard man and drug dealer, demanded an abortion, and as Tui claimed that "no one" was her baby's father, Robin faced uncomfortable questions about incest and rape within the male-dominated township. Matt was also furious when a women's group, led by their self-styled guru, "GJ," (played in an androgynous, beguiling manner by Holly Hunter), bought land and set up a refuge nearby. With the battle lines of the sexes drawn, Campion cleverly explored notions of feminism and the portrayal of women in the media and in a patriarchal society.

Global success led to a further six episodes being put into production, again written by Campion and Gerard Lee, set in Sydney, Australia. **IDG**

❯ David Wenham as Detective Al Parker and Elisabeth Moss as the increasingly unsettled Robin Griffin.

Our Girl

Drama | UK | 2013–present

Female-led army drama exploring the final days of British involvement in the twenty-first-century Afghanistan conflict

Cast | Lacey Turner, Iwan Rheon, Ben Aldridge, Matthew McNulty, Sean Gallagher, Kerry Godliman, Arinze Kene, Lawrence Walker, Ade Oyefeso
Original broadcaster | BBC One
For fans of . . . | *Tour of Duty* (1987)

Putting a twist on the traditional *bildungsroman*, *Our Girl* follows eighteen-year-old Molly Dawes' progression from truculent beauty therapist to skilled combat medical technician. Starting as a one-off ninety-minute television movie, *Our Girl* proved so popular that the BBC quickly commissioned a series, following Molly's deployment on a six-month tour of Afghanistan (which was re-created on location in South Africa).

Molly constantly has to battle the expectations of others—from the army recruitment officers and her new captain, who low-rate her, to her friends and family, who mock her attempts to better herself. She seeks a surrogate family within the army, seeing it as a way to the happiness that has thus far eluded her.

As the only woman in her platoon, Molly struggles to prove her worth in a testosterone-fueled environment. This is set sharply against the role of women under the Taliban regime. Befriending eleven-year-old local girl Bashira brings the realities home. Molly couldn't be bothered to attend school; Bashira isn't allowed to.

Molly's life back in London is also shown, with due emphasis placed on the tensions that arise from xenophobic and racist attitudes in the poor areas within a multicultural society.

Importantly, *Our Girl* makes no attempt to eulogize the conflict in Afghanistan. The day-to-day anxieties of the recruits in 2 Section, fighting alongside soldiers from the Afghan National Army, are shown frankly alongside the horrors of war. **EB**

Classic episode
Season 1, episode 1. Sent with little warning to Camp Bastion, Molly gets her first taste of active combat with her new platoon. Forced to prove herself in the toughest circumstances, can her training help her overcome her fears?

◔ Before and after: the aspirational Molly Dawes (Lacey Turner) was to seek fulfillment far from the streets of London.

My Love from the Star

Fantasy/Horror/Sci-Fi | South Korea | 2013–14

After 400 years of isolation on Earth, alien Doh Min-jun finally finds the true love who will banish his loneliness

Cast | Kim Soo-hyun, Jun Ji-hyun, Park Hae-jin, Yoo In-na
Original broadcaster | SBS
For fans of . . . | *I Dream of Jeannie* (1965), *Lois & Clark: The New Adventures of Superman* (1993)

After being deposited on Earth in 1609, alien Doh Min-jun (Kim Soo-hyun) had to wait more than 400 years before he could return to his home planet. While looking perfectly human, he had a wide range of superpowers: teleportation, telekinesis, enhanced hearing and sight, and an ability to pause time. Also, his body did not age, so he lived through many created identities over the years, much like the immortal Connor MacLeod in the movie *Highlander* (1986).

In the seventeenth century, Min-jun loved a girl who sacrificed herself to save his life. Following this tragedy, he studiously avoided close relationships. This worked well for him until self-important Korean movie star, Cheon Song-i (Jun Ji-hyun), moved in next door, wondering why her strange, frosty neighbor seemed immune to her unsubtle charm. Set in modern-day Seoul, with frequent flashbacks to various points in time, *My Love from the Star* mainly tracked the last three months of Min-jun's stay.

The twenty-one beautifully shot episodes blended science fiction, romance, and fantasy, all further enriched by top-quality visual effects. The ill-matched intellects of the alien visitor and the beautiful but vacuous actress offered lighter comic moments, too, as did the various nods to Hollywood movies including *E.T.: The Extra-Terrestrial* (1982), *Mission: Impossible* (1996), *Notting Hill* (1999), and *The Time Traveler's Wife* (2009). ABC has recently commissioned an adaptation for initial release in the United States. **SH**

Classic episode
Episode 21. Min-jun Doh must depart from Earth, and their farewell kiss is terribly sad, for Song-i Cheon and most fans of the show alike. But after three years Min-jun learns how to teleport back to Earth and he meets Song-I again.

🔺 Close encounter of an extraordinary kind: Kim Soo-hyun as the alien Min-jun with Jun Ji-hyun as Song-i, his earthbound love.

Ray Donovan

Crime/Mystery | USA | 2013–present

He's the man Hollywood calls to fix its problems—if only he could fix his own

Cast | Liev Schreiber, Paula Malcomson, Eddie Marsan, Jon Voight, Elliott Gould, Hank Azaria, James Woods
Original broadcaster | Showtime **Award** | 1 Golden Globe **For fans of . . .** | *The Sopranos* (1999)

Employed by a top legal firm, Ray Donovan (Liev Schreiber) is a "fixer" sent to do Hollywood's dirty work: protect the reputations of the rich and famous by solving problems and removing obstacles by (almost) any means. When his father, Mickey (Jon Voight), was released after twenty years in jail, Ray was adamant that he didn't want him back in his life. Mickey served time for the murder of a priest suspected of molesting young boys, including his sons. But Ray knows that Mickey killed the wrong priest—and Mickey knows that someone is trying to bring down Ray's entire organization.

Ray Donovan is like a made-for-TV version of the movie *L.A. Confidential* (1997), with all the same sleaze and corruption that lurks beneath the surface of Hollywood's glitz and glamour. Taking his first leading role for television, Schreiber embodies the cold, silent type popularized in 1950s Westerns. Voight makes a menacing presence as Mickey, but he's also hilariously inappropriate, especially with his grandchildren. British actor Eddie Marsan also excels as Ray's socially awkward brother Terry. **JS**

> **Classic episode**
> *A Mouth is a Mouth | Season 1, episode 2.*
> With his private life in turmoil, Ray takes on two cases, as an actor's home is invaded by a stalker and a blackmailer threatens to destroy an action hero's reputation.

◬ Liev Schreiber as Ray Donovan warns Eddie Marsan as Terry that he shouldn't count too much on brotherly love.

Hinterland

Crime/Mystery | UK | 2013–15

Atmospheric detective series made in both Welsh and English

Cast | Richard Harrington, Mali Harries, Aneirin Hughes   **Original broadcaster** | S4C/BBC Four
For fans of . . . | *Forbrydelsen* (*The Killing*, 2007)

The police procedural crime series has long been a staple of TV drama, but *Hinterland* proved that the genre still had something fresh to offer. Set in Aberystwyth on the Welsh coast, the series followed the cases of Detective Chief Inspector Tom Mathias, who was in retreat from a difficult—but initially unexplored—past, about which viewers could surely expect to learn more as the series developed. Although the program's inception undoubtedly owed much to the success of Nordic noir serials such as *The Killing* (2007), it has its own distinctive aesthetic and identity, owing much to the stark beauty of the Welsh landscape.

Also at the heart of why *Hinterland* works so well was Richard Harrington's understated but charismatic performance as Mathias, which was all the more remarkable for being a double performance—delivered once in English and once in Welsh. His investigations made for downbeat and even disturbing viewing; the opening episode, for example, was a grim story rooted in a case of institutional child abuse, which very much set the show's tone. But Mathias, isolated and obviously troubled yet still deeply moral and compassionate, was the ideal guide through the darkness.

The show's Welsh title, *Y Gwyll*, or *The Dusk*, nicely captures the series' twilit atmosphere, at once melancholy and sinister. *Hinterland* was a striking new development in TV crime drama, and Tom Mathias was a truly distinctive detective for the small screen. **HE**

◉ Richard Harrington as Detective Chief Inspector Tom Mathias and Mali Harries as Detective Inspector Mared Rhys.

Vikings

Drama | Ireland/Canada | 2013–present

The Vikings depicted not as monsters or savages, but as a complex, brutal society

Cast | Travis Fimmel, Katheryn Winnick, Jessalyn Gilsig, Clive Standen, George Blagden, Gustaf Skarsgård
Original broadcaster | History
For fans of . . . | *Rome* (2005), *Game of Thrones* (2011)

Vikings is a radical break from the traditional TV image of Norsemen as horn-helmeted savages; the producers made sure that all the series' content was closely based on historical fact and showed as much of the intricacies of Viking society and family life as possible.

When we first meet Ragnar (Travis Fimmel), he is a poor farmer, albeit one with a burning ambition and a powerful sense of destiny. His desire spurs him on, but makes him powerful enemies, not the least of whom is his brother Rollo (Clive Standen), who secretly desires Ragnar's wife, the beautiful Lagertha (Katheryn Winnick). Ragnar's world is one of brutal politics, constant war, widespread fear and superstition, and submission to the will of capricious and powerful gods.

Fimmel makes Ragnar a fine hero—a man driven by a code of honor and an unshakable sense of purpose. While capable of extreme savagery, Ragnar remains sympathetic to the viewers, and is portrayed always as a man doing what it takes to make his way in a violent and treacherous world. By the end of the second season, he has realized his ultimate ambition to become king, but has left a trail of bodies in his wake.

Vikings is the history lesson as kick-in-the-pants, a reminder that we don't always need the fictional excesses of fantasy dramas like *Game of Thrones* to thrill us when our own real-life history is so rich in battles, blood, and excitement. **WM**

❷ It's not all murder and pillaging: Rollo (Standen), Bjorn Lothbrok (Ludwig), and Ragnar Lothbrok (Fimmel).

Orphan Black

Fantasy/Horror/Sci-Fi | Canada | 2013–present

A masterly thriller that takes conspiracy to a new level of intrigue

Cast | Tatiana Maslany, Jordan Gavaris
Original broadcasters | Space (Canada),
BBC America (USA)
For fans of . . . | *24* (2001), *Dollhouse* (2009),
Sherlock (2010)

Con artist Sarah Manning (Tatiana Maslany) witnessed a woman jumping to her death—a woman who looked just like her. She took on the woman's identity and, by the end of the first episode, had met another doppelganger. As the series progresses, Sarah discovers that she is a clone and, together with the other clones, she must fight to stay alive and free.

The clones, including sweet gay geek Cosima and uptight suburban mom Alison, are all individual and distinct. Each of them is so convincing that it's easy to forget that they are all played by Maslany. Sarah's adopted brother, Felix (Jordan Gavaris), is a gay artist who, with his dry wit, always manages to keep the series human and down-to-earth, no matter how strange the situation may become. He's also indicative of the finest element of the show—its character development. Sarah was quite unlikable in the opening episodes. She wanted her daughter back but she had no concern about the woman who died in front of her and didn't want to investigate the mystery. However, later her attitude changed. Alison and Felix are complete opposites, but gradually she brought out his sweet caring side and he helped her to loosen up.

That's what makes *Orphan Black* so special. In a world where so many conspiracy thrillers feature bland, stock figures, this clone show has some of the strongest characterization on television. **JL**

◉ Tatiana Maslany as Sarah Manning, a woman who assumes numerous different identities.

Happy Valley

Crime/Mystery | UK | 2014–present

Hard-as-nails police sergeant and grandmother tackles the seedy underbelly of her picturesque home territory

Cast | Sarah Lancashire, Siobhan Finneran, Steve Pemberton, George Costigan, James Norton, Derek Riddell, Shane Zaza, Joe Armstrong, Jill Baker
Original broadcaster | BBC One
For fans of . . . | *Prime Suspect* (1991), *Fargo* (2014)

When the first TV trailers for *Happy Valley* were broadcast, viewers thought they knew what to expect—a whimsical, lighthearted police drama set in the north of England. How wrong they were. "Happy Valley" is the real-life police nickname of a beautiful part of Yorkshire that, uncomfortably, is blighted by poverty and drugs, and this series twists from one shocking development to another, leaving the audience gasping and desperate to find out what happens next.

At the heart of it all is a towering performance from Sarah Lancashire. She plays Police Sergeant Catherine Cawood, a woman still trying to recover from the suicide some years previously of her daughter after she was raped. When the daughter of a local businessman is kidnapped and held for ransom by a group of incompetent yet lethally dangerous criminals, Catherine's personal history rapidly catches up with her.

Written by multiaward-winning Sally Wainwright, *Happy Valley* became a word-of-mouth blockbuster on its first transmission, with ratings increasing through each of its six weeks. Dark comedy sits side-by-side with nail-biting tension and moments of extreme and brutally realistic-looking violence. The cast is also uniformly excellent, with Siobhan Finneran—the devious lady's maid O'Brien in *Downton Abbey* (2010)— almost unrecognizable as Catherine's ex-heroin addict sister, and Steve Pemberton outstanding as the weak accountant whose plan to extort money from his boss sets the whole chain of events in motion. **PC**

Classic episode

Season 1, episode 4. The tension escalates to almost unbearable levels as Catherine tracks down the location of the kidnapped girl. However, she is not alone: kidnapper Tommy Lee Royce has also arrived at the scene.

◉ A stern look from Sarah Lancashire as Police Sergeant Catherine Cawood, doughty law enforcer of *Happy Valley*.

The Flash

Action/Adventure | USA | 2014–present

A remake of a much-maligned comic-book series, placing the character within the wider DC Comics Universe

Cast | Grant Gustin, John Wesley Shipp, Tom Cavanagh, Candice Patton, Rick Consett
Original broadcaster | The CW
For fans of . . . | *The Flash* (1990), *Smallville* (2001), *Arrow* (2012)

An experimental particle accelerator exploded, and gave superhuman powers to an unknown number of people. Bumbling crime scene investigator Barry Allen (Grant Gustin) awakened from a coma caused by the explosion to find that he could move extremely fast. He was approached by Star Labs to help them to locate and, in some cases, subdue the other supercharged victims of the accident—known as "metahumans." The viewers learned that Allen also suffered tragedy as a child when he witnessed the murder of his mother and the wrongful arrest of his father, Harry (John Wesley Shipp, who starred as Barry Allen in the original TV series).

The Flash is no mere spin-off from *Arrow* (2012), as its detractors have claimed; the two shows occupy different spaces. *The Flash* lightens the tone a little, falling back on a rhythm similar to that of *Smallville* (2001) for villain-of-the-week plots and an ongoing story arc about resolving a family issue. Attention to detail provides a wealth of little extras for fans of the original 1990 show and also for readers of DC Comics.

The success of this show and its precursor demonstrates that there is an appetite for "shared universe" content, with the crossover episodes not only scoring highly with fans and critics, but actually adding texture to the story lines of both shows. With DC Comics adding more shows to the roster for Netflix, expect to see a proliferation of interseries character interaction to create a truly universal feel. **MR**

Classic episode
Power Outage | *Season 1, episode 7*. Barry finally gets his superhero name, and a bubbling-under story arc breaks wide open and provides a hint of the great adventures to come. Wonderfully good episodic writing.

◉ Grant Gustin as Barry Allen, aka The Flash, the critically underrated superhero.

Cosmos: A Spacetime Odyssey

Documentary | USA | 2014

A journey through time, space, and reality

Cast | Neil deGrasse Tyson
Original broadcaster | Fox/National Geographic Channel
Awards | 4 Emmys
For fans of . . . | *Cosmos: A Personal Voyage* (1980)

Thirty-four years after the great American astronomer and astrophysicist Carl Sagan introduced us to an incredible journey of discovery in the landmark *Cosmos: A Personal Voyage* (1980), which became PBS's most watched series in the world, Fox Television teamed up with the National Geographic Network to produce a one-season companion series that updated that journey for a new generation.

Neil deGrasse Tyson, acclaimed astrophysicist and director of New York's Hayden Planetarium, joined with Ann Druyan (widow of Dr. Sagan) and Seth MacFarlane, creator of *Family Guy* (1999), among others, to produce *Cosmos: A Spacetime Odyssey*. Unlike its predecessor, the series was shown in prime time on a major broadcast network and achieved critical acclaim for its storytelling craft. Featuring animated reconstructions of historical events crucial to modern human understanding of the Earth and space, it was also a lightning rod for criticism from religious leaders who decried its neglect of biblical chronology (which, Tyson would respond, was precisely the point).

The series featured an extensive supporting cast of voices for its animated sequences. Although only mildly successful in its initial television run, *Cosmos* has been seen widely around the world, thanks to the local distributive powers of the Fox Network and the National Geographic Channel. **SL**

❯ Host Neil deGrasse Tyson surveys one of the mysteries of the universe.

Gotham

Drama | USA | 2014–present

The pre-Batman years of America's darkest, dirtiest, craziest city

Cast | Ben McKenzie, Donal Logue, David Mazouz, Zabryna Guevara, Sean Pertwee, John Doman
Original broadcaster | Fox **For fans of . . .** | *Arrow* (2012), *The Flash* (2014)

The history of Gotham has been written and rewritten in graphic novels ever since the first appearance of Batman in 1939. Set roughly a decade before the Caped Crusader began his life of crime-fighting, this series follows rookie detective Jim Gordon (Ben McKenzie) as he encounters various characters whom fans will recognize as nascent versions of Gotham's greatest villains. Prime among them is Oswald Cobblepot, an odious creep known mockingly as "Penguin," who lurks near the bottom of the city's underworld. There's also an opportunist teenage thief who calls herself "Cat" and a riddle-obsessed police forensic expert called Edward Nygma. The city is held in the balance by three families. The wealthy philanthropist Waynes

and warring mob clans the Falcones and the Maronis. When Thomas and Martha Wayne are gunned down by an unknown mugger, their young son Bruce (aided by butler and guardian Alfred Pennyworth) begins to figure out just how corrupt Gotham really is. This series effectively blends the gritty reality of a lawless city with comic-book effects. **JS**

> **Classic episode**
> *The Spirit of the Goat* | *Season 1, episode 6.*
> Gordon's partner, Harvey Bullock, is disturbed when a murder bears all the hallmarks of a serial killer he knows to be dead. Is this a copycat crime or something more sinister?

⊛ (L–R) Benjamin McKenzie (Gordon), Donal Logue (Bullock), and Cory Michael Smith (Nygma) tackle Gotham's seedy underbelly.

The 100

Fantasy/Horror/Sci-Fi | USA | 2014–present

Young offenders are sent to Earth to see whether resettlement is possible after nuclear war

Cast | Eliza Taylor, Henry Ian Cusick, Paige Turco, Isaiah Washington, Ricky Whittle
Original broadcaster | The CW   **For fans of . . .** | *Survivors* (1975, 2008), *Jericho* (2006), *Revolution* (2012)

It is ninety-seven years since a nuclear war on Earth and the last humans are living on a supersized space station named "The Arc," which was cobbled together from the smaller stations that were orbiting the planet at the time of the disaster. Food, air, and living quarters are at a premium, so almost all criminals are "floated" into space—all, that is, except for the station's transgressing children, who are imprisoned for their crimes. These young people, one hundred in total, are sent down to Earth to see whether it is safe to recolonize.

The 100 is certainly glossy—everyone looks like a glamour model with perfect teeth—but it is also surprisingly hard-hitting, and addresses some serious social issues. Above all, though, it's thrilling: The Arc is

deteriorating rapidly and must soon be evacuated; the young people on Earth realize that they are not alone on the surface of the planet.

After a mesmerizing final two episodes of the first season, the second season opened up a world of possibilities after hard decisions were made and more surviving factions were brought into play. **MR**

Classic episode
Twilight's Last Gleaming | *Season 1, episode 5*.
Most of the action takes place on the space station, where the occupants decide that the only way that any of them can survive is by further reducing their number.

◉ Eliza Taylor as Clarke Griffin, one of a small group of humans to have survived a nuclear holocaust.

Fargo

Drama | USA | 2014–present

A self-contained miniseries that transcends the movie on which it is based

Cast | Martin Freeman, Allison Tolman, Billy Bob Thornton, Colin Hanks, Kirsten Dunst
Original broadcaster | FX
Awards | 2 Emmys, 1 Golden Globe
For fans of . . . | *Twin Peaks* (1990), *Six Feet Under* (2001)

With a complex relationship to the 1996 film of the same name—part remake, part sequel—FX's anthology show *Fargo* had a dangerous, daring, and downright devious first season. Across ten episodes it told the story of various people in small-town America whose lives intertwined after a brutal murder. Each week, the drama became more macabre, the comedy more barbed, and the characters richer and more interesting.

Eighteen years after *Fargo* (the sixth movie produced and directed by the brothers Joel and Ethan Coen), writer/producer Noah Hawley created this TV show, which, though based on the original, was clearly no ordinary adaptation. The situations and characters echoed those of the movie, yet there were vital differences—the viewers learned that the two stories actually take place in a shared fictional universe.

Hawley's vision was of a collection of related miniseries in the manner of *True Detective*, which debuted in the same year. Therefore, at the end of the first season, the story was concluded and viewers said good-bye to a sensational cast, including Martin Freeman, Billy Bob Thornton, and newcomer Allison Tolman. Season two switched to new characters in the 1970s and explored tangentially connected events already referenced in year one. The story combines violence, surrealism, melancholy, gallows humor, and unpredictable, but never incredible, plot twists. **IF**

◀ Martin Freeman as Lester Nygaard, insurance salesman and one of life's natural victims.

The Strain

Fantasy/Horror/Sci-Fi | USA | 2014–present

Reinvigorating the vampire legend for a new generation

Classic episode
Creatures of the Night | *Season 1, episode 8*.
Setrakian discovers he's been infected by the parasitic worms. His companions are trapped in a gas station convenience store with a group of vampires massing outside.

◬ Corey Stoll (Dr. Ephraim Goodweather) turns against the worms.

Cast | Corey Stoll, David Bradley, Mia Maestro, Kevin Durand, Jonathan Hyde, Richard Sammel, Sean Astin, Jack Kesy, Natalie Brown, Miguel Gomez, Ben Hyland
Original broadcaster | FX
For fans of . . . | *The Walking Dead* (2010)

Based on a trilogy of novels by horror filmmaker Guillermo del Toro and author Chuck Hogan, *The Strain* is a dark sci-fi/fantasy/horror series that combines elements of classic vampire and zombie storytelling to create a modern apocalyptic saga, blending cutting-edge gory effects and monstrous mutations with old-style folklore.

When a plane brought a mysterious worm-borne contagion to New York, disease investigators led by Dr. Ephraim Goodweather (Corey Stoll) teamed up with a Holocaust survivor and Professor Abraham Setrakian (David Bradley) to track down an ancient evil that threatened to consume the city and then the world.

The Strain began in book form after del Toro's original plans to develop a television series didn't work out. Following publication of the final volume in the trilogy, the FX network took up the TV rights.

The show's look was designed to replicate a comic-book visual style via "saturated monochrome," with a reliance on two dominant colors—amber (day) and cyan (night)—with red for the vampire aspects of the plot. Elements of more realistic police procedural series were utilized to create a world that felt more like ours, with the unfolding story slowly transforming it into a nightmarish landscape falling to the vampire invaders.

The promotional poster artwork depicted a parasitic worm entering a victim's eyeball. FX soon agreed to withdraw the ad, but it had already succeeded in horrifying—or at least disgusting—the public. **ATB**

About a Boy

Comedy | USA | 2014–present

Feel-good but also thoughtful viewing

Cast | David Walton, Minnie Driver, Benjamin Stockham, Al Madrigal, Annie Mumolo
Original broadcaster | NBC
For fans of . . . | *Diff'rent Strokes* (1978), *Growing Up Fisher* (2014)

The critical acclaim that greeted *About a Boy* when it premiered on NBC in 2014 shouldn't have been surprising. Nick Hornby's original novel of 1998, about the friendship between a socially awkward eleven-year-old boy and the urbane and cynical Will Freeman, captured the mood of the late 1990s perfectly. Then the movie adaptation in 2002 was nominated for an Oscar. The most surprising thing about the TV version was not its success, but that it took so long to be made.

David Walton played Will, the writer of a classic Christmas song who never has to work again. In his pursuit of attractive women, he got the idea that they might be even more impressed by him if they thought he was a single father. With this in mind, he struck a deal with Marcus (Benjamin Stockham), the charmingly naive new kid who lived next door. Marcus pretended to be his son, and in return got to chill at Will's house, doing all the things Marcus's hippie mother (Minnie Driver) wouldn't allow. The charade didn't last long, but the two struck up a warm friendship. Will became a role model for Marcus, who himself became an inspiration for Will. As time went on, they explored the world around them and surprised each other with the decisions they made and the lessons they learned.

About a Boy was, in a sense, a traditional culture clash comedy, but the chemistry between the three leads enchanted every episode. The show's heart lay in the discovery of what it meant to grow up and change, so if you think you know the story, think again. **PPW**

Fleming: The Man Who Would Be Bond

Drama | UK | 2014

The life of the creator of 007

Cast | Dominic Cooper, Lara Pulver, Samuel West, Anna Chancellor, Pip Torrens
Original broadcaster | BBC America
For fans of . . . | *Tinker, Tailor, Soldier, Spy* (1979), *Spooks* (2002)

"Everything I write has a precedent in truth," started each episode of this four-part miniseries about the life of Ian Fleming, creator of James Bond, during the Second World War.

Fleming came from a wealthy and influential London family. He regarded himself as "the lesser Fleming," very much in the shadow of his older brother, Peter. On the outbreak of war in September 1939 he landed a job in naval intelligence through his parents' friendship with Winston Churchill. He became a Royal Navy commander—the same rank as that of the fictional hero he would later create. He was forbidden from going on any missions, but claimed to have seen action on two occasions, although there were no witnesses to either deployment and his commanding officer, like many others, regarded him as a fantasist. Stuck in London, Fleming yearned for adventure, but had to make do with his rich, glamorous, right-wing social set. He fell in love with Anne O'Neil, girlfriend of Esmond Rothermere, owner of the *Daily Mail* newspaper. Their relationship prefigured the cruel streak that would be apparent in Bond.

The end credits noted that certain facts and names were changed for dramatic effect. Fleming did have a record of exaggerating, of adding flair. Great for Bond, Fleming's lasting legacy, and great for this miniseries about the author's wartime experience. This was not the only dramatic biography of Fleming, but it was easily one of the more exciting ones. **SJG**

Penny Dreadful

Fantasy/Horror/Sci-Fi | USA | 2014–present

Sumptuous and sinister horror drama with literary origins

Cast | Timothy Dalton, Olivia Llewellyn, Eva Green, Josh Hartnett, Harry Treadaway, Billie Piper **Original broadcasters** | Showtime (USA), Sky One (UK) **For fans of . . .** | *Whitechapel* (2009), *American Horror Story* (2011)

Penny Dreadful takes classic literary horror as its inspiration, mining the works of Bram Stoker, Mary Shelley, and Oscar Wilde and fusing their material into one of Showtime's finest original dramas.

The overarching story concerns the efforts of Sir Malcolm Murray (Timothy Dalton) to find his daughter, Mina (Olivia Llewellyn), who has been kidnapped by supernatural forces. Enlisting the services of psychic Vanessa Ives (Eva Green), gunslinger Ethan Chandler (Josh Hartnett), and scientist Victor Frankenstein (Harry Treadaway), Murray sets about banishing evil from the streets of London.

This is blisteringly good stuff—*Penny Dreadful* is such a good idea it's almost too obvious. Some might see it as derivative, but everything that is copied is embellished with a skill and love for the genre that confounds negative criticism.

The viewing public was in no doubt. After the success of the first season, Showtime immediately commissioned a second season; *Penny Dreadful* looks set to run and run. **MW**

> **Classic episode**
> *Demimonde* | *Season 1, episode 4*. Dorian Gray attends a performance of *The Transformed Beast*, a werewolf play, at the Grand Guignol theater. Meanwhile, Sir Malcolm confronts an intruder in his home.

◉ (L–R) Sembene (Danny Sapani), psychic Vanessa Ives (Green), Sir Malcolm Murray (Dalton), and Dr. Victor Frankenstein (Treadaway).

The Last Ship

Fantasy/Horror/Sci-Fi | USA | 2014–present

A ship's crew tries to save what's left of the world after a nuclear holocaust

Cast | Eric Dane, Rhona Mitra, Adam Baldwin, Charles Parnell, Travis Van Winkle, Sam Pruell, Marissa Neitling, Christina Elmore, John Paper-Ferguson **Original broadcaster** | TNT **For fans of . . .** | *The Walking Dead* (2010)

Spare a thought for the USS *Nathan James* and her hapless crew. In the original novel *The Last Ship* by William Brinkley, published in 1988, the guided missile destroyer survives a global thermonuclear war by virtue of having been on patrol in the Barents Sea in the Arctic. In this television series based on the book, the *Nathan James*, again on patrol in the Arctic and under radio silence for several months, discovered that the world has been stricken by a pandemic that has wiped out most of its population. This was the unluckiest naval vessel since the giant submarine *Seaview* in *Voyage to the Bottom of the Sea* (1964).

As the last hope for humanity, the crew started searching for a cure, but before long their vessel came under a surprise attack by a breakaway faction of the Russian Navy.

Wide-scale visuals, top-notch special effects, and the use of real naval vessels as sets make *The Last Ship* look more like a theatrical film than a TV show. TNT soon commissioned a second season, which was in production as the present volume went to press. **RB**

> **Classic episode**
> *Dead Reckoning | Season 1, episode 3.*
> The *Nathan James* faces off against a Russian cruiser and then tries to escape by stealth; two crew members go on a mission to disable their adversary.

◉ Eric Dane (left) takes the lead as Tom Chandler, commanding officer of the USS *Nathan James*.

Jonah From Tonga

Comedy | Australia | 2014

Is there hope for a Polynesian bad boy?

Cast | Chris Lilley
Original broadcaster | ABC
For fans of . . . | *Summer Heights High* (2007), *Angry Boys* (2011), *Mrs. Brown's Boys* (2011), *Ja'mie: Private School Girl* (2013)

A sequel to *Summer Heights High* (2007), *Jonah From Tonga* featured further adventures of the disruptive Polynesian schoolboy, played by the very Caucasian comedian Chris Lilley.

Jonah is now living with his uncle and determined to hit the big time. He couldn't decide if this would be through a life of crime or by winning the "Feel Da Beats" song competition with his friends, the "Fobbaliscious" crew. His good angels included teachers, nuns, prison guards, and painfully earnest Christian counselor Kool Kris. His demons were street criminals and his own family. Would petty crime and a spell in prison prevent him from winning through in the end?

Jonah's return appearance featured heavier makeup to help disguise the fact that Chris Lilley was now forty years old playing a fourteen-year-old. This was not a universally well-received move; it was branded "racist," "degrading," and "inherently creepy" by Australia's Tongan community, who objected to being depicted as a crime-riddled, foul-mouthed minority by a man in blackface. However, if you can put those objections to one side (and it's a big if), *Jonah From Tonga* argued passionately against racism and for the good in people: many critics acknowledged that the creator's aim had been not to make light of prejudice, but to castigate it by holding it up to ridicule. Unusually for a Lilley show, subsidiary characters played a strong part, and the overall effect was sweet, earnest, and well-meaning, with some entertainingly puerile jokes about genitals. **JG**

Last Week Tonight... With John Oliver

Comedy | USA | 2014–present

Part comedy, part chat show

Cast | John Oliver
Original broadcaster | HBO
For fans of . . . | *The Daily Show* (1996), *Real Time with Bill Maher* (2003), *John Oliver's New York Stand-Up Show* (2010)

The work of writer/satirist John Oliver as both correspondent and fill-in host on the landmark Comedy Central series *The Daily Show* (1996), along with his turn as master of ceremonies on the same network's *New York Stand-Up Show* (2010), led to the creation of *Last Week Tonight*. Conceived as a half-hour hybrid of talk show and social commentary, the series has increased the cachet of its broadcaster, HBO, and addressed potentially explosive topics with a courage that has sometimes courted controversy—it never shies away from combustive issues, such as Palestine, Islamic terrorism, and racial tension in the United States.

The series is partly satirical—see, for example, its item on "space geckos," a send-up of Russian satellite experiments, or its attack on the royal house of Thailand that offended the nation's crown prince—but there is much more to it than that, as it welcomes as guests champions of human rights, such as Ugandan LGBT activist Pepe Julian Onziema, and science educator Bill Nye. Meanwhile, Oliver's take on topics such as election fraud, payday loan outfits, and the perceived corruption of world soccer governing body FIFA and the Miss America pageant have led to viral success on YouTube and increased scrutiny by journalists.

Last Week Tonight currently has a two-series commitment from HBO with options for more, which may include expanding the series' format to a full hour, giving Oliver extended opportunities to ask the important questions of the day. **SL**

John Oliver has an idiosyncratically British take on US affairs. ❯

Inside No. 9

Comedy/Drama | UK | 2014–present

An anthology of chilling tales, set at different addresses with the same number on the door

Cast | Reece Shearsmith, Steve Pemberton, Julian Rhind-Tutt, Anna Chancellor, Timothy West, Oona Chaplin, Julia Davis, Denis Lawson
Original broadcaster | BBC Two
For fans of . . . | *The League of Gentlemen* (1999)

Steve Pemberton and Reece Shearsmith had already provided viewers with comic chills, first in *The League of Gentlemen* (1997) and later in their disturbing *Psychoville* (2009). With *Inside No. 9*, they created a series of one-off tales of the macabre and thus resurrected the horror anthology, a genre that had been missing from British TV screens for several decades.

Pemberton and Shearsmith starred in all but one episode of the first season, taking on different characters who all found themselves in various locations—houses, apartments, dressing rooms—each of which had a number nine on the door. The first episode was set in a large house where a group of adults were playing a game of Sardines. The characters were introduced in turn as each found the hiding place—a dusty old wardrobe—and forced their way in to join the others already in there. But one of the participants had a particularly nasty fate in mind for all of them.

Among the other self-contained stories were the tale of a man who, having taken in a hobo, found that his guest thanked him for his generosity in the same way as the cuckoo repays the crow; the granting of a wish to a terminally ill child; a revenge comedy played out behind the scenes in a theater; and the fate of two teenaged girls who were paid to spend the night in a haunted mansion.

Every one of these episodes was a gleeful blend of horror and comedy, although ultimately the horror won out with a chilling twist in each tale. **JS**

Jane the Virgin

Comedy | USA | 2014–present

Venezuelan telenovela immaculately reconceived for US television

Cast | Gina Rodriguez, Andrea Navedo
Original broadcaster | The CW
Award | 1 Golden Globe
For fans of . . . | *Desire* (2006), *Fashion House* (2006), *Ugly Betty* (2006), *American Heiress* (2007)

The telenovela—a finite long-form serial drama—is a popular format in Asia, Latin America, and Spain, but it took *Ugly Betty* (2006)—itself based on a Colombian series—to make the United States see this storytelling format as a rich source of new and interesting ideas.

Based on the Venezuelan telenovela *Juana la virgen*, (2002), *Jane the Virgin* concerns a devoutly religious Latina who wants to be a teacher and remain a virgin until she is married. But her plans are left in tatters when a mix-up at a routine medical examination results in her being artificially inseminated. To add insult to injury, she discovers that the sperm donor is her boss. A slightly ludicrous concept that would almost be de rigueur in a telenovela or a trashy soap is here transformed into a warm and clever prime-time drama by creator Jennie Snyder Urman and her team. The series combines the proud Latino heritage of the characters with the culture of the modern United States to create a refreshing tale of ordinary people in an extraordinary situation; it provides a real insight into what has been an underrepresented group on US prime-time television. What really helps are the winning performances on display; particularly that of Gina Rodriguez who really captures the confusion and conflict that Jane experiences, and shows how she grows as a result of her circumstances.

Jane the Virgin is a bold contemporary take on the family unit, and a new approach that is a welcome and popular addition to prime-time network television. **SO**

The Honourable Woman

Drama | UK/USA | 2014

We all have secrets. We all tell lies. Sometimes the former are revealed and we are called to account for the latter

Cast | Maggie Gyllenhaal, Stephen Rea, Lubna Azabal, Andrew Buchan, Janet McTeer, Philip Arditti, Eve Best, Tobias Menzies, Genevieve O'Reilly
Original broadcasters | BBC Two (UK), Sundance TV (USA)
For fans of . . . | *The Shadow Line* (2011)

Those who saw Hugo Blick's award-winning *The Shadow Line* (2011) will know that the writer/director/producer doesn't shy away from uncompromising or complex plotting. With *The Honourable Woman* he presented an even more ambitious and satisfying eight-part drama, touching on politics, the security services, shady business, and questions of loyalty to family and state.

Maggie Gyllenhaal starred as Nessa Stein, the British daughter of a murdered Israeli arms dealer, who, having shifted her father's company toward more peaceful telecommunication endeavors in the West Bank, was given a life peerage. But Nessa had secrets, and when Kasim, the son of a close Palestinian friend was kidnapped, those secrets threatened to come to light. As viewers learned in flashbacks of Nessa's abduction and rape eight years earlier, it became clear that she might have been hiding the facts for the right reasons, but they were costing people their lives. Nessa was never in control, and as greater powers pulled the strings around her, all she could ultimately do was try to keep her family safe. Blick drew powerful performances from an impressive cast. Gyllenhaal shouldered the drama throughout with a truly three-dimensional character and a faultless British accent. Other standouts were Stephen Rea as the tired old dog of a spy who put the pieces of the puzzle together, and Janet McTeer as his boss at MI6.

The Honourable Woman was a slow burn, but gradually combusted into an engrossing tale that reflected many of the political tensions in the modern world. **DJO**

Classic episode
The Ribbon Cutter | *Episode 4*. Halfway through the story, we finally see what has thus far only been alluded to: Nessa's suffering while held captive in Gaza. We also learn of her tormentors' plans for her after her release.

⌂ Maggie Gyllenhaal (R) as Nessa Stein, with Genevieve O'Reilly as Frances Pirsig, her private secretary.

How to Get Away with Murder

Drama | USA | 2014–present

Rollercoaster legal drama

Cast | Viola Davis, Jack Falahee, Alfred Enoch, Matt McGorry, Karla Souza, Aja Naomi King, Tom Verica, Marcia Gay Harden, Megan West, Conrad Ricamora
Original broadcaster | ABC
For fans of . . . | *Scandal* (2012)

For any student, starting school is daunting, but for law students at Middleton University it is even harder because their lecturer is formidable attorney Annalise Keating (Viola Davis). Five students selected to shadow their professor on her cases soon find themselves involved in a twisted mystery with Annalise herself right at its heart.

How to Get Away with Murder is told out of sequence, past and present unpeeled with every episode. From the very first scene the students are involved with covering up a murder, and Annalise's husband Sam (Tom Verica) is soon implicated in the death of Lila Stangard (Megan West), a student with whom he was having an affair. While the murders are clearly linked, new information repeatedly spins the story off in unexpected directions.

The compelling story line is complemented by some brilliant performances, particularly that of Davis, who portrays not only the toughness of a hard-hitting attorney but also the private heartbreak of a woman whose life is falling apart. The students, too, are complex; initial superficialities evaporate quickly as the desperate situation leads them to realize what matters to them most. Jack Falahee in particular impresses as the smooth man-whore Connor whose slow breakdown leads him to rebuild his world around eventual boyfriend Oliver (Conrad Ricamora). **RM**

❯ (L–R) Matt McGorry, Karla Souza, and Aja Naomi King in "She's A Murderer," season 1, episode 12.

Mammon

Crime/Mystery | Norway | 2014

A journalist uncovers his brother's shady dealings

Cast | Jon Øigarden, Terje Strømdahl, Ingjerd Egeberg, Alexander Tunby Rosseland
Original broadcaster | NRK **For fans of . . .** | *House of Cards* (1990), *State of Play* (2003), *Borgen* (2010)

Sibling rivalry has always been a rich source of inspiration for drama. That rivalry took a much darker turn in this Norwegian thriller. Set over the course of six days, with each episode covering one day, *Mammon* told the story of a journalist investigating an embezzlement scandal involving his own brother. Slowly, a web of lies and deceit started to unravel, putting both the journalist and his family in danger.

Drawing heavily on the great political thrillers that came before it, *Mammon* has been favorably compared to both *All The President's Men* (1976) and *State of Play* (2003), but creator Gjermund Eriksen has also admitted to having been heavily influenced by the biblical tale of Cain and Abel, as well as his own relationship with

his brother, Vegard, who produced the show, and with whom he had plenty of creative arguments. Fox bought the rights for a US remake almost a year before the show premiered—which looks like a sound investment in view of the fact that the first episode of *Mammon* later grabbed a 60 percent audience share, the second highest figure in Norwegian TV history. **JH**

Classic episode
The Awakening | *Episode 2*. After five years of fruitless investigation, the journalist finds the secret at the heart of a dishonest business deal, which involved his brother and seems to have pushed him to take his own life.

◉ Jon Øigarden as the truth-seeking newshound, Peter Verås.

Star Wars Rebels

Animation | USA | 2014–present

Star Wars *returns to its roots: a single team at the start of a revolution*

Cast | Freddie Prinze Jr., Jason Isaacs, Vanessa Marshall, Tiya Sircar, David Oyewolo, Steve Blum, Taylor Gray
Original broadcaster | Disney XD   **For fans of . . .** | *Star Wars: The Clone Wars* (2008)

Star Wars Rebels is a prequel set several years before the fictional date of the first movie in the series. It follows the adventures of the motley crew of the spaceship *Ghost*—idealistic privateers who are destined to form the Rebel Alliance—whom the viewers see through the eyes of fifteen-year-old Ezra Bridger, a street orphan with a burgeoning affinity for the mystical Force. Together, the crew begins a guerrilla conflict against the vile Empire, all the while attempting to avoid the Inquisitor, a dark disciple of Darth Vader charged with destroying the last vestiges of Jedi power.

Beautifully crafted in 3-D animation by many of the artists who produced *Star Wars: The Clone Wars* (2008), *Star Wars Rebels* is stunning to look at, but its visuals do not overwhelm strong performances by a cast that includes several returnees from previous chapters in the saga, including Anthony Daniels, Frank Oz, and Billy Dee Williams (as C-3PO, Yoda, and Lando Calrissian, respectively). In an extended version of the series pilot, James Earl Jones reprised his celebrated turn as the voice of Darth Vader. **SL**

> **Classic episode**
> *Visions of Hope* | *Episode 12.* Having received intelligence about an Imperial plan to capture an exiled diplomat who wants to hold a rally on the planet Lothal, the crew of *Ghost* intervenes to thwart the enemy.

🅐 Kanan senses the presence of the Inquisitor.

True Detective

Crime/Mystery | USA | 2014–present

Two warring police detectives spend seventeen years trying to crack a murder case

Cast | Matthew McConaughey, Woody Harrelson, Michelle Monaghan, Michael Potts, Tory Kittles
Original broadcaster | HBO
Awards | 5 Emmys
For fans of . . . | *The Wire* (2002)

HBO's innovative police drama came to screens to much critical acclaim. Compelling and full of twists and revelations, it was near impossible to review without spoiling a number of major plot points, but things were further complicated by the announcement that *True Detective* had been planned as an anthology: the second season would have nothing to do with the first.

That first season was told across multiple time frames. In 2012, former police detective "Rust" Cohle (Matthew McConaughey) and detective Marty Hart (Woody Harrelson) were interviewed separately about their respective roles in the investigation into the ritualistic murder of a prostitute some years previously. Still working as a detective, Marty recalled how his chaotic and selfish lifestyle at the time put a strain on his relationship with his wife and daughters, though he partly explained away his conduct as a response to the distressing details of the case. Rust, meanwhile, was a dropout, having left the force in disgrace due in part to ongoing substance abuse and mental health issues.

As the eight-part story unfolded, flitting back and forth from the past to the almost-present, small details were revealed that teased the viewers into not quite being sure what the situation actually was. While *True Detective* stayed close to its pulp-fiction roots, it was this constant expectation of the unexpected that kept the audience hooked until the nail-biting conclusion. **JS**

◀ Detection in action: Woody Harrelson as Marty Hart and Matthew McConaughey as "Rust" Cohle.

The Leftovers

Drama | USA | 2014–present

The aftermath of a global event that caused the disappearance of millions of people

Cast | Justin Theroux, Amy Brenneman, Christopher Eccleston, Liv Tyler, Chris Zylka, Margaret Qualley, Carrie Coon, Ann Dowd, Scott Glenn
Original broadcaster | HBO
For fans of . . . | *Under the Dome* (2013)

Created by Damon Lindelof and Tom Perrotta, and based on the latter's 2011 novel of the same name, *The Leftovers* takes place three years after the "Sudden Departure," an event in which two percent of the world's population just inexplicably disappeared.

A slow-paced drama that doesn't offer up any quick answers (or many answers at all), *The Leftovers* centers on police chief Kevin Garvey (Justin Theroux) and the residents of Mapleton as they try to adjust to the new reality. Garvey's wife (Amy Brenneman) has joined "The Guilty Remnant," a cultlike group whose members have vowed to do whatever is necessary to ensure that the remaining population never forget what they have lost. Their daughter (Margaret Qualley)—torn between her allegiance to her father, her longing for her mother, and her compassion for Kevin's father's mental breakdown—struggles to cope with teenage angst. Their son (Chris Zylka) finds a new family in a group of followers led by a seemingly benevolent yet somewhat menacing messiah figure. While struggling to keep his own sanity, Kevin also tried to keep the peace within his own family and between the population of his town and the Guilty Remnant.

The Leftovers is a meditation on family, love, responsibility, and loss, often punctuated by displays of uncontrollable grief, shocking brutality, and unspeakable acts of emotional terrorism. It is a thought-provoking and unflinching look at the everyday through the prism of the extraordinary. **RP**

The Musketeers

Action/Adventure | UK | 2014–present

Sexy, swashbuckling adventures with Alexandre Dumas's quartet of heroes

Cast | Tom Burke, Santiago Carbrera, Howard Charles, Luke Pasqualino, Tamla Kari, Peter Capaldi
Original broadcaster | BBC One
For fans of . . . | *Merlin* (2008), *Atlantis* (2013), *Da Vinci's Demons* (2013)

While there has been a glut of film adaptations of Alexandre Dumas's *The Three Musketeers* (1844) to keep Hollywood well fed for a century, TV iterations have been few and far between. That changed with BBC One's *The Musketeers*, a modern, somewhat breathless take on Dumas's novels featuring Athos, Porthos, Aramis, and their young charge D'Artagnan.

The Musketeers' first-season opener followed the same path as the novel. D'Artagnan (Luke Pasqualino) arrived in Paris in 1630 to take revenge on Athos (Tom Burke), the Musketeer he believed murdered his father. Aramis (Santiago Carbrera) and Porthos (Howard Charles) coopted D'Artagnan into helping to prove that Athos was framed. By episode's end, D'Artagnan joined the trio of Musketeers with a hope of earning a commission into the regiment. Other familiar elements were present—a cunning Cardinal Richelieu (Peter Capaldi), his agent Milady de Winter (Maimie McCoy), a vain King Louis (Ryan Gage), and put-upon Queen Anne (Alexandra Dowling). D'Artagnan became involved with Constance Bonacieux (Tamla Kari), while flirtation developed between Aramis and Queen Anne. The scene was set for ten episodes of slick action and stunts, shrewd political chicanery from the Cardinal, and ongoing plots that came to a head in a season finale that revealed Richelieu's treachery. The series' appeal lies not only in the action and rich detail, but also in the well-crafted relationships that develop throughout. **MW**

The Crimson Field

Historical drama | UK | 2014

A drama of rare quality that entertains and raises awareness about the conflict that was mistakenly called "The War to End All Wars"

Cast | Oona Chaplin, Hermione Norris, Suranne Jones, Kerry Fox
Original broadcaster | BBC One
For fans of . . . | *Upstairs, Downstairs* (1971), *Tenko* (1981), *Birdsong* (2012)

In 2014, to commemorate the centenary of the outbreak of the First World War, the BBC commissioned a number of documentaries and dramas. *The Crimson Field* told the story of a group of women who worked as medics in a field hospital and how their actions impacted on the men they treated.

Writer Sarah Phelps' soap opera background—she wrote numerous episodes of *EastEnders* (1985) as well as many works for theater—shone through in this unashamedly populist series. In the opening scene three well-to-do, beautifully dressed women arrived on a ship, looking thrilled to be doing their bit for Blighty. Then, after the opening titles the viewers see a horrifically injured man take his last breath and die. The contrast was, of course, deliberately shocking.

It was the characters who made *The Crimson Field* special. They weren't stiff-upper-lipped, stock war-drama characters—these people, both for good and for ill, were flawed and interesting. This meant that rather than watching some remote historical drama, the viewers felt involved in something real—a war of which few people approved and even fewer understood the aims.

Many television series have attempted to re-create the horror of the first global conflict; the inventory includes straightforward histories, costume dramas, and even comedies, such as *Blackadder Goes Forth* (1989). *The Crimson Field* bears favorable comparison with even the best of them. JL

Classic episode
Episode 1. Just as the viewers have come to respect Sister Margaret Quayle, she sends a sick man back to the trenches and eats a cake that a fellow nurse had made for the dying patients. A masterful series opener.

◉ Oona Chaplin as nurse Kitty Trevelyan feels the pain of the walking wounded at a First World War field hospital.

Outlander

Drama | USA/UK | 2014–present

Love across the centuries in an engrossing historical fantasy seasoned with grit, swords, and kilts

Cast | Caitriona Balfe, Sam Heughan, Tobias Menzies, Graham McTavish   **Original broadcasters** | Starz (USA), Amazon Prime (UK)   **For fans of . . .** | *Doctor Who* (1963), *Poldark* (1975), *Game of Thrones* (2011)

Superficially *Outlander* may resemble a Scottish-flavored *Game of Thrones* (2011) with added time travel. But that description does scant justice to this genre show and the source material it's based on. Taking Diana Gabaldon's popular novels, *Outlander* weaves historical fiction, political unrest, and a central romance between a 1940s nurse and an eighteenth-century Jacobite into a multifaceted tale that eschews the gender stereotyping that remains common even in modern TV.

Having spent time apart during the Second World War, nurse Claire Randall (Caitriona Balfe) and husband Frank (Tobias Menzies) rekindle their relationship with a trip to the Highlands of Scotland. Their time together is cut short by Claire's passage through time—via a stone circle—to the year 1743. She finds herself caught in the simmering tensions between English Redcoats and the MacKenzie clan. Viewed with suspicion, Claire is entangled in the business of the clan, married off to young Jamie Fraser (Sam Heughan) and scrutinized by Black Jack Randall (Menzies again), infamous ancestor of her husband. Claire's desire to get home drives the narrative of Ronald D. Moore's series, roughly following the plot of Gabaldon's first novel.

Outlander's first sixteen-episode season was split in two; the success of the first block led to an order for a second season just days after its premiere in August 2014. *Outlander* may be hard to categorize generically, but commercially it's a resounding success. **MW**

⊕ Sam Heughan as Jamie and Caitriona Balfe as Claire (both on horseback), with attendants to the rear.

Silicon Valley

Comedy | USA | 2014–present

Proving that the technology world isn't all fun, games, and Google

Cast | Thomas Middleditch, T.J. Miller, Zach Woods, Christopher Evan Welch, Martin Starr, Kumail Nanjiani
Original broadcaster | HBO   **For fans of . . .** | *Beavis and Butt-Head* (1993), *Arrested Development* (2003)

In its first season, *Silicon Valley* attracted a great deal of attention—not all of it for the right reasons. Halfway through filming, one of the lead actors—Christopher Evan Welch, in a terrific performance as a quirky venture capitalist—passed away. His remaining scenes were expertly tailored in a new direction by Mike Judge, series creator and the man behind MTV's *Beavis and Butt-Head* (1993) and Fox's *King of the Hill* (1997). The final product was a fine comic take on California's technology industry that attracted rave reviews.

Set among a small team of programmers with big dreams of success and fortune, *Silicon Valley* spoofs the battle between frantic fly-by-night startup companies and the pleasantly sophisticated—yet unsurprisingly cutthroat—big tech companies. T.J. Miller gives a brilliant, and oftentimes raucously obscene, performance as the head of the incubator house with an oncoming date with destiny.

Silicon Valley managed to tell a terrific and (thankfully) mostly complete story line in a single season, while leaving loose plot threads for a possible follow-up. **SL**

Classic episode
Fiduciary Duties | *Season 1, episode 4.*
At a riotous toga party, Richard (Thomas Middleditch) promises to make Erlich (T. J. Miller) a board member, but later feels that he has spoken in haste.

◈ (L–R) Martin Starr (Gilfoyle), Kumail Nanjiani (Dinesh), and Thomas Middleditch (Richard) at their classic toga party.

Wolf Hall

Historical drama | UK | 2015

Glossy and gripping retelling of the political machinations of Thomas Cromwell, advisor to King Henry VIII of England

Cast | Mark Rylance, Damian Lewis, Claire Foy, Bernard Hill, Anton Lesser, Joanne Whalley, Jonathan Pryce, Thomas Brodie-Sangster, Jessica Raine
Original broadcaster | BBC Two
For fans of . . . | *I, Claudius* (1976), *The Tudors* (2007)

A historical drama that was more interested in the drama than the history, *Wolf Hall*, for all its incongruities and inaccuracies, was sumptuous television. Central to its success was Mark Rylance's measured performance as Thomas Cromwell, playing the real historical figure as a mild-mannered hero who always saves the day just in time. While Cromwell was no superman, there's joy to be found watching him trying to keep his world—in King Henry VIII's court—turning. There was steel in Rylance's performance, too. This was a hard world, with death and disease as prevalent as treachery, and Cromwell was a match for any man who stood in his way. Such was the way that Cromwell was portrayed that you would believe a politician can be a good guy.

Based on the award-winning novels *Wolf Hall* (2009) and *Bring Up the Bodies* (2012) by Hilary Mantel, and adapted by Peter Straughan—screenplay writer of the Oscar-nominated *Tinker Tailor Soldier Spy* (2011)—the six-part series had a leisurely pace that focused on character rather than action, giving each actor a chance to shine. Jessica Raine as Jane Boleyn (Anne's sister) and Bernard Hill as the foul-mouthed Duke of Norfolk were particularly notable; so too was Mark Gatiss as Stephen Gardiner, one of Cromwell's many enemies.

Wolf Hall was one of the most popular and critically acclaimed dramas ever to have been broadcast by the BBC. Of course, it had its detractors, most of whom drew attention to errors of fact; but this was a work of the imagination, not an annal. **NC**

Classic episode
Season 1, episode 5. Second wife Anne Boleyn incurs Henry's displeasure for failing to produce a male heir. When the king is injured at a joust, Cromwell performs cardiopulmonary resuscitation to save his life.

◬ Mark Rylance looks grave as Thomas Cromwell.

Cucumber

Drama | UK | 2015

Modern gay life in Manchester—a desperate tale that is very, very funny

Cast | Vincent Franklin, Julie Hesmondhalgh, Freddie Fox, Cyril Nri, James Murray, Anjli Mohindra, Con O'Neill, Fisayo Akinade, Ceallach Spellman
Original broadcaster | Channel 4
For fans of . . . | *This Life* (1996), *Queer as Folk* (1999)

Henry (Vincent Franklin) and Lance (Cyril Nri) were a middle-aged gay couple with a big house, secure jobs, and a great bunch of friends. When Henry rejected Lance's surprise marriage proposal, his life began to fall apart: he lost his partner, home, job, and savings. Henry befriended a pair of teenagers and joined them in an apartment that, he discovered, was little more than a glorified squat, home to a varied bunch of misfits, all with their own stories to tell. As Lance began a friendship with a new colleague at work, Henry became drawn to one of his new roommates, the confident and unattainable bisexual Freddie (Freddie Fox). A tragic event prompted Henry to rebuild his life and he began to understand what it means to be a forty-something gay man in the twenty-first century.

Having already written *Queer as Folk* (1999), Russell T. Davies returned to Manchester's gay village for an altogether more melancholy tale. Just as challenging, provocative, witty, and abrasive as his earlier series, this story spanned the generations and the spectrum of sexuality, with teenagers exploring their own identities just as a middle-aged man began to examine his.

Cucumber formed part of a triple whammy for Channel 4; also in 2015, on sister-channel E4, a spin-off series, *Banana*, looked at the back stories of some of the supporting characters, while More4, the channel's on-demand online service, offered *Tofu*, a series of real-life interviews with a wide range of people discussing issues around sex and sexuality. **JS**

Battle Creek

Drama | USA | 2015

Engaging cop drama created by two TV heavyweights

Cast | Josh Duhamel, Dean Winters, Kal Penn, Janet McTeer, Aubrey Dollar
Original broadcaster | CBS
For fans of . . . | *White Collar* (2009), *The Good Guys* (2010)

The runaway success of *Breaking Bad* meant that its creator, Vince Gilligan, became hot property, and inevitably broadcasters showed new interest in his unproduced ideas. One such concept was *Battle Creek*, a police drama script that had been under consideration at CBS in the early 2000s but had fallen through. CBS were interested in reviving the project, with David Shore, creator of *House* (2004), brought on board as showrunner.

Sticking closely to the premise of Gilligan's original script, the series followed old-fashioned Detective Russ Agnew (Dean Winters) as he was drafted in to partner newcomer FBI agent Milton Chamberlain (Josh Duhamel). The pair combined their very different skills and approaches—cunning in the case of Agnew, and technology for Chamberlain—to tackle crime in Battle Creek, Michigan. Cases included drug dealing, murder, and arson. Buddy cop shows such as this live or die on the chemistry between the leads, and Duhamel and Winters pulled it off skillfully, while also bringing some levity to the serious story lines.

While Gilligan cowrote the pilot—directed by Bryan Singer—it was Shore's steady hand on the tiller for the series as a whole. Luckily, Shore's and Gilligan's sensibilities found common ground, which particularly came out in the series' quirkier moments. Combining the idiosyncrasies of its creators with the traditional storytelling style of the CBS network, *Battle Creek* made for satisfying viewing. **SO**

Empire

Drama | USA | 2015–present

Grittiness and glamour to a hip-hop beat

Cast | Terrence Howard, Taraji P. Henson, Trai Byers, Jussie Smollett, Byshere Y. Gray, Naomi Campbell
Original broadcaster | Fox   **For fans of . . .** | *Dynasty* (1981)

Former drug dealer turned rapper Lucious Lyon is now a hugely successful music mogul, but when he is diagnosed with amyotrophic lateral sclerosis (ALS) he realizes he must appoint one of his sons to take over Empire Entertainment—even though, in his eyes, none has what it takes. Then his ex-wife is unexpectedly released from prison, and she's set on getting a piece of the company he founded with her drug money.

Empire's premise is decidedly Shakespearean—Lucious' son Jamal compares their situation to *King Lear*—and with its riches, family feuds, and boardroom politics it is easy to see why it has been dubbed "the black *Dynasty*." Yet *Empire* is fresh, brimming with confidence, attitude, and fun, with an array of complex, nuanced characters. A strong social context underpins the drama, too, as poverty, homophobia, and mental illness are frankly—and occasionally brutally—tackled.

Debuting at the start of 2015, *Empire* was an instant hit. Charting strongly for Fox, and becoming the first show in twenty years to increase its ratings week on week, it was recommissioned almost instantly.   **RM**

Classic episode
Unto the Breach | *Season 1, episode 9*. When Empire Records comes under attack from Lucious' long-term rival, the Lyon family pull together to bolster the company's reputation and keep artists from defecting.

◆ Terrence Howard as Lucious Lyon, whose youthful transgressions are coming back to haunt him.

Unbreakable Kimmy Schmidt

Comedy | USA | 2015–present

The kooky and adorable survivor of an underground cult hits NYC

Cast | Ellie Kemper, Tituss Burgess, Jane Krakowski, Carol Kane   **Original broadcaster** | Netflix
For fans of . . . | _Arrested Development_ (2003), _30 Rock_ (2006)

From Tina Fey and Robert Carlock, the driving forces behind _30 Rock_ (2006), _Unbreakable Kimmy Schmidt_ is instantly quotable, packed full of visual gags, satirical, heartwarming, and hilarious. It centers on the titular Kimmy (Ellie Kemper), who has spent most of her adult life as a prisoner in an underground doomsday cult. Once she's released, she is determined to be more than a victim and starts a new life in New York. She gets an apartment with struggling actor Titus Andromedon (Tituss Burgess) and a job as a nanny for New York socialite Jacqueline Voorhees (Jane Krakowski). These two become her best friends, and the interactions with them provide much of the show's warmth and funniest moments.

Much of the humor focuses on Kimmy's struggles to adjust to being a free woman in a world of which she has no previous experience. She is particularly baffled by the latest technology and the terms used to describe it. _Unbreakable Kimmy Schmidt_ is kooky, charming and may make you wonder how you've coped so long without a Netflix subscription. **LH**

Classic episode
Kimmy Goes to School | _Season 1, episode 6._
Kimmy enrolls in an adult education class to get the schooling she missed while in the bunker. Titus tries to make a video to promote his song "Pinot Noir."

◈ Tituss Burgess as Titus Andromedon and Ellie Kemper as Kimmy on location on the streets of Manhattan.

Vinyl

Drama | USA | 2016–present

Inside the illegal highs and lows of the 1970s record industry

Cast | Bobby Canavale, Olivia Wilde, P. J. Byrne, Juno Temple, Max Casella, James Jagger
Original broadcaster | HBO
For fans of . . . | *The Sopranos* (1999), *Boardwalk Empire* (2010)

It is New York in 1973, and record label president Richie Finestra (Bobby Canavale) is panicking. His label is in trouble, music is in a rut, and he is considering signing his whole company over to a German rival. But then he has an epiphany when he sees the New York Dolls performing—and he emerges recharged. With a healthy dose of cocaine never far from his nose, Richie is on the hunt for the future of rock'n'roll and woe betide anyone who gets in his way—whether that be his staff, his rivals or his wife Devon (Olivia Wilde).

Considering that legendary movie director Martin Scorsese has also built up an acclaimed back catalog of music documentaries, it is surprising that it has taken him quite so long to create a fictionalized account of the heady days of the 1970s music industry. Scorsese, along with fellow executive producers Mick Jagger and Terence Winter, has cracked open a peephole into this simultaneously seductive and repellent world. Weaving the new fictional characters throughout a real historical tapestry (David Bowie, Andy Warhol, and Led Zeppelin all feature) creates a show that never feels anything less than grimily authentic.

As you would expect, the soundtrack to the series is superb, and Bobby Canavale's central performance is riveting. With such a rich setting and impressive cast attached to the project, Vinyl looks set to be a long-playing success for HBO. **PC**

◗ **Bobby Canavale as Richie Finestra, the beleaguered president of music label Century Records.**

Index by Genre

Contributors

Benjamin Adams (BA) has written short stories and essays for anthologies, such as the Bram Stoker Award-winning *Horrors! 365 Scary Stories*, *Blood Muse*, and *Doctor Who Short Trips: The Centenarian*. He also co-edited the anthology *Children of Cthulhu*.

John Ainsworth (JA) has written reviews, interviews, and features on TV and film as well as working for the BBC, the Sci-Fi Channel, and Carlton. He also produces science fiction and fantasy talking books and radio drama.

Karen Baldwin (KB) was born in the USA, lives in the UK, and is a lifelong fan of TV (the good, the bad, and the ugly) from both sides of the Atlantic. Among her many "likes" are college basketball and The Muppets.

Piers Beckley (PB) worked for the BBC, produced plays, wrote about fictional spaceships, and made forays into games writing and design. He lives in London, south of the river. Most of the monsters there are gone now. Most of them.

Lee Binding (LB) has worked in the TV industry for most of his life, either writing about it or doing pictures for it. He often reminds his parents that they told him to "turn that telly off, it'll never get you a job."

Arnold T. Blumberg (ATB) is an author and designer with decades of experience in pop culture criticism, especially in science fiction, horror, and comics. He teaches university courses in zombies and Marvel superheroes.

Erykah Brackenbury (EB) got away with writing about *Doctor Who* for her English Literature dissertation. As a journalist, she now edits postgraduate psychiatry exams and watches too much Netflix.

Matt Bramford (MB) works for *What's on TV* magazine, which brings TV listings, news, and features to more than three million UK readers. He also writes about fashion and art and is based in London, UK.

Alessandra Caporale (AC) is a Community Video trainer. In 2012 she won a prize for the documentary *Penelope's Threads*. She is a lecturer in Audiovisual Ethnography in Feminist Research Methodology and holds a Phd in Visual Anthropology.

Sang Hee Choi (SHC) was a film journalist for several years for various online and print magazines in Korea, including *Film 2.0*. In the UK, she has worked as a freelance writer, foreign correspondent, and translator specializing in film and media.

Paul Condon (PC) has written articles and reviews about TV and film for a variety of magazines, and written books on popular culture, the movies of Alfred Hitchcock, the show *Six Feet Under*, the *Matrix* series, and a comprehensive history of TV.

Neil Corry (NC) has worked for many UK publishers, specializing in film and TV. He is a self-employed writer and editor involved in partwork magazines. Neil has one single solitary review in this magnum opus. See if you can find it.

Sara Di Girolamo (SDG) is a scout, editor, and publishing consultant. She holds a BA in Semiology of Cinema, and is a regular contributor and copy editor for the online magazine *Inkroci*, for which she runs the column "The Vertical Thought."

Jane Elsmore (JE) is a half-Thai, Sussex-born actress living in London with a keen interest in martial arts, a background in modeling and several years in the niche entertainment industry.

Hywel Evans (HE) is an editor and reviewer who works mainly on academic books but with occasional diversions into popular culture. He lives in London.

Ian Farrington (IF) has written more than a dozen short stories and edited numerous fiction and factual books. He has produced audio dramas, written for *Doctor Who*

Magazine, and is production editor of *All About Soap* magazine.

Dick Fiddy (DF) is a writer and researcher who has happily immersed himself in TV history for thirty years and currently works for the British Film Institute in London.

Ian Garrard (IG) has produced award-winning websites for the BBC, ITV, and NBC Universal. Brought up on classic children's TV and 1970's drama, he is a huge fan of Dennis Potter. He has interviewed a range of people, including June Brown, Patrick Moore, Kylie Minogue, and Louis Theroux.

James Gent (JGT) is a writer, tutor, and graphic designer. He has contributed to various websites and publications about cult TV and wrote the biography for the official *Monty Python* website.

James Goss (JG) used to edit the BBC's *Cult TV* website. He has also written for the *Guardian*, *Gay Times*, and *The Times*, as well as radio plays and novels. He is currently Douglas Adams's rather baffled ghostwriter.

Sarah J. Groenewegen (SJG) was born in Australia and lives in England. She holds a Masters degree by thesis, which was on TV audiences, and has worked for fifteen years in law enforcement in Australia, the Netherlands, the UK, and the USA.

Katharina Hahn (KH) was born in Vienna and lives in London. She is a sub-editor at Condé Nast and has previously edited a number of illustrated books for various publishing houses, including Thames & Hudson and Dorling Kindersley.

Jesper Hauerslev (JH) is a games producer and writer hoping to write the next big science fiction epic: not easy when there are so many games, movies, TV shows, and books, to play, watch, read, and write about.

Richie J. Haworth (RH) has written for telefantasy publications and governmental periodicals. He studied Theology, which goes some way to explaining his interest in melodrama and political intrigue.

Laurie Hooper (LH) developed a love of vintage TV at a young age, especially the work of John Sullivan and 1970s BBC TV dramas. He hosts discussion panels at classic TV events, and loves nothing more than dissecting the latest plotlines.

David J. Howe (DJH) has been a journalist and freelance writer for thirty years. He worked on the *Radio Times Guide to Science Fiction* and was contributing editor of *Starburst Magazine*. He is now editorial director of Telos Publishing, which specializes in cult TV and film.

Will Howells (WH) has written for several BBC Radio comedy series, contributes to a TV magazine, and has written and script edited several audio dramas based on *Dark Shadows*. He has appeared on *Only Connect*, *University Challenge*, and *Mastermind*.

David Hutter (DH) was born and raised in Germany, and lived in Italy and France before studying Creative Writing in London, where he has worked as a writer and editor ever since. He is currently the managing editor of a magazine.

John J. Johnston (JJ) is an Egyptologist, classicist, and cultural historian. He lectures in the UK and has contributed to academic and popular publications. His introductory essay to *Unearthed* (2013) was a British Science Fiction Association Award finalist.

Darren Jones (DJO) is a screenwriter and author who has written for many familiar TV characters, such as *Bob the Builder*, *Doctor Who*, and *Sabrina the Teenage Witch*.

Daniel Judd (DJ) has worked for the BBC on TV websites as diverse as *Comic Relief*, *EastEnders*, and *Strictly Come Dancing*. He loves old programs with a murder or spaceship in them (or sometimes both).

Ivan Kirby (IK) is the mind behind *TV Minus 50*, a blog about what was on British TV fifty years ago each week. He commutes to the present day but wouldn't want to live there.

Nicole Kuderer (NK) used to work for several publishers in the UK, but now lives and works as an art director in Berlin. Being a TV show junkie and German native speaker, she enjoyed writing about the German TV shows of her childhood.

Rebecca Levene (RL) has been a writer and editor of games, books, and TV for twenty years. She was a script consultant on China's first soap and an editor of the *Doctor Who* books. She is working on book three of her fantasy series, *The Hollow Gods*.

George Lewis (GL) was for several years the TV critic of a Financial Times' magazine.

Winnie M. Li (WL) produced four feature films and an Oscar-nominated® short. She has programmed for the Doha Tribeca Film Festival, written for *The Huffington Post*, and is completing her debut novel. She holds degrees from Harvard, Goldsmiths, and is a PhD candidate at LSE.

Joseph Lidster (JL) has written scripts for theatre, radio, and TV, including episodes of *Torchwood*, *The Sarah Jane Adventures*, *Wizards Vs. Aliens* and *Millie Inbetween*.

Shaun Lyon (SL) has written two books about the return of *Doctor Who*, as well as short stories and articles. He lives in Los Angeles with a husband and three cats, and he's still waiting for his close-up, Mr. DeMille.

Bruno MacDonald (BM) has written about TV for *Radio Times*, *Time Out*, *OK!*, and *Closer*. He can quote large chunks of *Friends* and *Buffy* dialogue, and swears by *Weeds*, *The Walking Dead*, *The Sopranos*, *Family Guy*, and *Rastamouse*.

Will Maclean (WM) has been writing for TV for eight years, and has worked on

numerous comedy and children's shows. His earliest TV memory is being terrified by Sooty and Sweep at the age of three.

Sara Martin (SM) teaches History of Television and New Media at the University of Udine and is chief editor of the academic journal "Cinergie. Il Cinema e le altre arti." She has written several books.

Matthew Michael (MM) holds down three jobs in seven countries and occasionally finds time to watch some of his growing pile of DVDs. He is a regular contributor to *Doctor Who Magazine*.

Rob Morris (RM) is a telly addict and has sometimes written articles for TV magazines just to call it "research." His first dramatic work "The Curse of Shurafa"—part of a series continuing the gothic soap *Dark Shadows*—was released in 2015.

Louis Niebur (LN) teaches music and media at the University of Nevada, Reno, where he is head of the music department. He writes about the legacy of the BBC's Radiophonic Workshop when not torturing his friends with old black and white shows.

Stephen O'Brien (SO) is a scriptwriter, author, and blogger who has written about TV, music, and film for twenty years. There are three entries in this book he wanted to write, and he's thrilled he got one of them.

Robb Pearlman (RP) is an associate publisher at Rizzoli and has acquired books about *Star Trek*, *The Princess Bride*, *Game of Thrones*, and *Family Guy*. He has also written *The Wit and Wisdom of Star Trek* and the upcoming *He-Man's Guide to Life*.

Anne C. Perry (AP) is a professional editor. Her fiction and non-fiction have been published by Pornokistch, Tor.com, Adventure Rocketship, and others.

Paul Phipps-Williams (PPW) trained as a filmmaker, so naturally spent fourteen years in the public sector. A freelance writer, he is working on his second novel. He has more TVs in his house than is healthy.

Jacqueline Rayner (JR) has written thirty books, many of them TV-related. She writes a column for *Doctor Who Magazine*.

Marc Robinson (MR) has written reviews and opinion pieces for a decade. He watches the first episode of every US show, and never tires of discussing the virtues of the lucky few that become regular viewing.

Charlie Ross (CR) is a writer, broadcaster, and stand-up comedian. He has presented on BBC Radio Scotland and BBC 5Live, written for *Doctor Who Magazine*, *City Life*, and is a published author. He has also appeared in the *Doctor Who* audio plays.

Gary Russell (GR) has written more than thirty five books on cult TV and movies, edited magazines, written for TV shows and video games, script-edited *Doctor Who* and *Torchwood*, and is executive producer at Planet 55 Studios in Australia.

Jim Sangster (JS) has written books on *Friends*, *Spooks*, *24*, Alfred Hitchcock, and Martin Scorsese. He has also been a talking head on documentaries about science fiction, the supernatural, and police dramas.

Marion Serre (MS) was born in France and moved to the UK to pursue a career in publishing. When not reading or writing, she spends her days (and quite a lot of her nights) binge-watching TV series.

Jared Shurin (JS) writes about books with dragons, sleuths, and superheroes in them for Pornokitsch and Tor.com. His ten-year-old self is super-duper proud of him.

Andrew Spokes (AS) has three ambitions: for someone to make toy Krotons from *Doctor Who*, to be a contestant on a game show, and to get up close to a tiger. The last two preferably not at the same time.

Sam Tennant (ST) is a Scottish/Northern Irish/Mancunian who enjoys playing rugby (when not wiping out the weekend with TV box sets and retro video games).

Jim Vogiatzis (JV) worked on the BBC *EastEnders* website for a couple of years and was PA to June Brown who plays Dot Branning (née Cotton) on the soap. An avid collector of films with a wide interest in TV drama, old and new.

Paul Vyse (PV) has more time for old TV than new. He worked for twelve years as art editor for *What's On TV* magazine. He has written reviews and articles for a variety of

publications and is now a freelance magazine designer and exhibiting artist.

Steven Warren Hill (SWH) is a classic film and TV buff living in Chicago. He has written two books on horror films (*Silver Scream* vol. 1 and 2) and is the owner of the popular online "Gallifrey Base" *Doctor Who* forum.

Caroline Westbrook (CW) has written about TV and film for BBC News Online, *Empire*, and *Radio Times*. She is an entertainment reporter for *Metro* Online, where her Eurovision obsession proves useful.

Dandis Wong (DW) is a movie critic in Shanghai doing PhD work in Shanghai Theatre Academic. He's also a film selector for the Shanghai International Film Festival.

Mark Wright (MW) is a *Sunday Times* best-selling author, screenwriter, and journalist. He has worked on audio drama, radio production, comics, stage plays, short films, and has written for characters from *Doctor Who* and *Blake's 7* to the *Power Rangers*.

Mark Wyman (MWy) worked with creative talent at BBC TV Centre and contributed to British TV and film magazines. He was the reviewer for *Buffy the Vampire Slayer* and *Starburst* for *TV Zone* and worked with Oliver Postgate on his interactive autobiography.

Picture Credits

22 Popperfoto/Getty Images **24** SNAP/REX **25** Getty Images/Silverscreen/Moviepix **26** Everett Collection/REX **27** CBS Photo Archive/Getty Images **29** NBC/Getty Images **30** CBS Photo Archive/Getty Images **33** ABC Photo Archives/Getty Images **34** J. R. Eyerman/Life Magazine/The LIFE Picture Collection/Getty Images **36** ZUMA Press, Inc./Alamy **39** Silver Screen Collection/Getty Images **40** Silver Screen Collection/Getty Images **41** AF archive/Alamy **42** Pictorial Press Ltd/Alamy **43** John Pratt/Keystone Features/Hulton Archive/Getty Images **44** CBS Photo Archive/Getty Images **45** Deutsche Presse-Agentur **46** CBS Photo Archive/Getty Images **49** Popperfoto/Getty Images **50** NBC/Getty Images **52** Hulton Archive/Getty Images **53** Archive Photos/Getty Images **54** CBS Photo Archive/Getty Images **55** Ronald Grant/Mary Evans Picture Library **56** Allan Grant/The LIFE Picture Collection/Getty Images **59** ABC Photo Archives/Getty Images **60** ABC Television/Getty Images **63** Ralph Crane/The LIFE Picture Collection/Getty Images **65** Silver Screen Collection/Getty Images **66** ABC Photo Archives/Getty Images **67** CBS Photo Archive/Getty Images **68** Ronald Grant/Mary Evans Picture Library **72** CBS Photo Archive/Getty Images **73** United Archives GmbH/Alamy **74** Popperfoto/Getty Images **75** Archive Photos/Getty Images **76** AF archive/Alamy **77** NBC/Getty Images **78** Moviestore Collection/Alamy **80** Popperfoto/Getty Images **81** CBS Photo Archive/Getty Images **82** Ronald Grant/Mary Evans Picture Library **83** Ronald Grant/Mary Evans Picture Library **85** NBC/Getty Images **86** CBS Photo Archive/Getty Images **87** Silver Screen Collection/Getty Images **88** NBC/Getty Images **89** NBC/Getty Images **91** John Rodgers/Redferns/Getty Images **92** Ronald Grant/Mary Evans Picture Library **95** CBS Photo Archive/Getty Images **97** ABC Photo Archives/Getty Images **98** Ronald Grant/Mary Evans Picture Library **99** Popperfoto/Getty Images **100** CBS Photo Archive/Getty Images **101** Silver Screen Collection/Getty Images **102** Mondadori Portfolio/Getty Images **104** ABC Photo Archives/Getty Images **105** Don Cravens/The LIFE Images Collection/Getty Images **106** Everett/REX Shutterstock **107** Ron Howard/Redferns/Getty Images **108** NBC/Getty Images **109** Silver Screen Collection/Getty Images **110** Moviestore Collection/Alamy **111** AF archive/Alamy **112** NBC/Getty Images **114** CBS Photo Archive/Getty Images **115** CBS Photo Archive/Getty Images **117** Allan Grant/The LIFE Images Collection/Getty Images **118** Moviestore Collection/REX **119** John Shearer/The LIFE Picture Collection/Getty Images **120** Hulton Archive/Getty Images **121** Ray Green/Keystone Features/Bob Thomas/Getty Images **122** Yale Joel/The LIFE Picture Collection/Getty Images **124** ABC Photo Archives/Getty Images **125** CBS Photo Archive/Getty Images **126** CBS Paramount Television/Getty Images **128** Michael Ochs Archives/Getty Images **129** Silver Screen Collection/Getty Images **131** Popperfoto/Getty Images **132** Courtesy Everett Collection/REX **133** Mary Evans Picture Library **134** Silver Screen Collection/

Getty Images **135** Silver Screen Collection/Getty Images **136** REX **139** Popperfoto/Getty Images **140** CBS Photo Archive/Getty Images **141** Ronald Grant/Mary Evans Picture Library **142** Popperfoto/Getty Images **143** Ronald Grant/Mary Evans Picture Library **144** CBS Photo Archive/Getty Images **145** NBC/Getty Images **147** NBC/Getty Images **149** AF archive/Alamy **151** AF archive/Alamy **152** Ronald Grant/Mary Evans Picture Library **153** Rolf Adlercreutz/Alamy **154** ABC Television/Getty Images **155** ABC Television/Getty Images **156** Peter Bischoff/Getty Images **160** ABC Television/Getty Images **161** AF archive/Alamy **162** Hulton Archive/Getty Images **163** GAB Archive/Redferns/Getty Images **165** Michael Putland/Getty Images **166** Michael Putland/Getty Images **167** CBS Photo Archive/Getty Images **169** Peter Bischoff/Getty Images **170** Ronald Grant/Mary Evans Picture Library **171** Ronald Grant/Mary Evans Picture Library **172** Ronald Grant/Mary Evans Picture Library **173** NBC/Getty Images **174** CBS Photo Archive/Getty Images **176** FremantleMedia Ltd/REX **177** Mirrorpix **178** Photos 12/Alamy **179** Michael Ochs Archives/Getty Images **180** NBC/Getty Images **181** Silver Screen Collection/Getty Images **182** Ronald Grant/Mary Evans Picture Library **183** Ronald Grant/Mary Evans Picture Library **184** INA Georges Galmiche **185** CBS Photo Archive/Getty Images **186** ITV/REX **187** Keystone-France/Gamma-Keystone/Getty Images **188** FremantleMedia Ltd/REX **190** 20th Century Fox/Everett/REX **191** 20th Century Fox/Everett/REX **192** United News/Popperfoto/Getty Images **194** Silver Screen Collection/Getty Images **196** Peter Bischoff/Getty Images **199** dpa picture alliance/Alamy **200** Keystone/Getty Images**201** Photos 12/Alamy **202** dpa picture alliance/Alamy **203** AF archive/Alamy **204** CBS Photo Archive/Getty Images **207** Silver Screen Collection/Getty Images **208** Michael Marks/Michael Ochs Archives/Getty Images **209** Silver Screen Collection/Getty Images **210** CBS Photo Archive/Getty Images **211** Peter Bischoff/Getty Images **212** Moviestore Collection/Alamy **213** CBS Photo Archive/Getty Images **214** Michael Ochs Archives/Getty Images **215** Ronald Grant/Mary Evans Picture Library **217** United News/Popperfoto/Getty Images **218** Silver Screen Collection/Getty Images **220** NBC/Fotos International/Getty Images **221** ABC Photo Archives/Getty Images **223** AF archive/Alamy **224** AF archive/Alamy **225** Silver Screen Collection/Getty Images **226** Dana Edelson/NBC/Getty Images **227** Dana Edelson/NBC/Getty Images **228** Moviestore Collection/Alamy **230** FremantleMedia Ltd/REX **231** CBS Photo Archive/Getty Images **233** Mary Evans Picture Library **234** Silver Screen Collection/Getty Images **235** Columbia/Everett/REX **237** Olycom SPA/REX **238** Express Newspapers/Getty Images **240** Moviestore Collection/REX **241** ABC Photo Archives/Getty Images **242** Jean-Claude Deutsch/Paris Match/Getty Images **244** NBC/Getty Images **246** Ltd/REX Shutterstock **248** Michael Ochs Archives/Getty Images **249** CBS Photo Archive/Getty Images **251** Interfoto/Alamy **252** Everett Collection/REX **253** Mary Evans Picture Library **254** ABC Photo Archives/Getty Images **255** NBC/Getty Images **256** ABC Photo Archives/Getty Images **257** NBC/Getty Images **258** ABC Photo Archives /Jim Britt/Getty Images **260** NBC/Getty Images **261** ABC Photo Archives/Getty Images **262** Chris Capstick/REX **263** ABC Photo Archives/Getty Images **264** Ronald Grant/Mary Evans Picture Library **267** CBS Photo Archive/Getty Images **268** Hulton Archive/Getty Images **269** Pictorial Press Ltd/Alamy **270** NBC/Getty Images **273** Ronald Grant/Mary Evans Picture Library **274** CBS Photo Archive/Getty Images **275** CBS Photo Archive/Getty Images **277** Mary Evans Picture Library **278** AF archive/Alamy **280** Moviestore Collection/Alamy **281** BBC **282** NBC/Getty Images **283** Ronald Grant/Mary Evans Picture Library **284** The Kobal Collection/BBC/Paramount **286** Everett Collection/REX **290** Interfoto/Mary Evans Picture Library **291** Moviestore Collection/Alamy **293** Silver Screen Collection/Getty Images **294** CBS Photo Archive/Getty Images **295** Interfoto/Mary Evans Picture Library **296** Ronald Grant/Mary Evans Picture Library **297** Courtesy of Television.AU **298** ABC Photo Archives/Getty Images **299** Ronald Grant/Mary Evans Picture Library **300** Moviestore Collection/Alamy **302** NBC/Getty Images **304** Moviestore Collection/Alamy **305** Mary Evans Picture Library **306** ABC Photo Archives/Getty Images **307** Interfoto/Mary Evans Picture Library **309** Mike Hollist/Associated Newspapers/REX **311** David McGough/DMI/The LIFE Picture Collection/Getty Images **313** Paramount/Getty Images **314** AF archive/Alamy **316** Geoffrey Taunton/Alamy **317** Ronald Grant/Mary Evans Picture Library **318** FremantleMedia Ltd/REX **319** Photos 12/Alamy **320** IPC Magazines: What's On TV/REX **321** Everett Collection/REX **322** NBC/Getty Images **324** NBC/Getty Images **325** ITV/REX **327** Ronald Grant/Mary Evans Picture Library **328** BBC **331** Everett Collection/REX **332** Richard Blanshard/Getty Images **335** Mary Evans Picture Library **336** NBC/Getty Images **339** Photos 12/Alamy **340** ITV/REX **341** ITV/REX **342** Al Levine/NBC/Getty Images **343** AF archive/Alamy **344** AF archive/Alamy **346** Everett Collection/REX **347** Victor Watts/Alamy **348** ABC Photo Archives/Getty Images **349** NG Collection/ Mary Evans Picture Library **350** Fremantle Media Ltd/REX **351** BBC **353** Pictorial Press Ltd/Alamy **354** Moviestore Collection/Alamy **355** POO/AFP/Getty Images **356** ABC Photo Archives/Getty Images **359** Paul Drinkwater/NBC/Getty Images **360** Mary Evans Picture Library **363** Interfoto/Mary Evans Picture Library **364** Mary Evans Picture Library **365** Trinity Mirror/Mirrorpix/Alamy **367** Gene Trindl/NBC/Getty Images **368** AF archive/Alamy **370** AF archive/Alamy **371** Mary Evans Picture Library **372** Terry O'Neill/Getty Images **373** Mary Evans Picture Library **375** Mary Evans Picture Library **376** ABC Photo Archives/Getty Images **378** CBS Photo Archive/Getty Images **379** Chrysalis Visual/REX **380** Mary Evans Picture Library **382** Hemant Pithwa/The India Today Group/Getty Images **383** ABC Photo Archives/Getty Images **384** CBS Photo Archive/Getty Images **385** Craig Sjodin/ABC Photo Archives/Getty Images **386** British Film Institute **388** Toronto Star/Getty Images **390** Moviestore Collection/REX **391** Mirrorpix **392** Mary Evans Picture Library **394** 20th Century Fox/Everett/REX **397** FremantleMedia Ltd/REX **398** NBC/Getty Images **400** NBC/Getty Images **404** Spelling/Everett/REX **406** Paul Drinkwater/NBC/Getty Images **407** ITV/REX **409** Mary Evans Picture Library **411** CBS Photo Archive/Getty Images **412** Paul Greaves/REX **414** Robert Gilberg/NBC/Getty Images **415** Mary Evans Picture Library **416** Mike Floyd/Daily Mail/REX **417** Mary Evans Picture Library **419** Everett Collection/REX **420** Ron Galella, Ltd/WireImage **423** BBC **425** Everett Collection/REX **426** Moviestore Collection/REX **427** Hubert Fanthomme/PARISMATCH/SCOOP **428** ITV/REX **430** SIPA/REX Shutterstock **431** ITV/REX **432** Ronald Grant/Mary Evans Picture Library **434** Photos 12/Alamy **437** Fremantle Media Ltd/REX **439** AF archive/Alamy **440** ABC Photo Archives/Getty Images **441** Ronald Grant/Mary Evans Picture Library **442** Moviestore Collection/REX **445** Mary Evans Picture Library **446** ITV/REX **448** Mary Evans Picture Library **449** Moviestore Collection/Alamy **450** Getty Images **452** Everett Collection/REX **453** Moviestore Collection/REX **455** ABC Photo Archives/Getty Images **456** Photos 12/Alamy **458** NBC/Getty Images **459** United Archives GmbH/Alamy **461** Mark Seliger/ABC Photo Archives/Getty Images **462** NBC/Getty Images **464** Mary Evans Picture Library **466** Mary Evans Picture Library **467** ABC Photo Archives/Getty Images **469** BBC **470** Peter Bischoff/Getty Images **471** CBS Photo Archive/Getty Images **473** Getty Images **474** Larry Newberg/NBC/Getty Images **475** Mary Evans Picture Library **476** Mary Evans Picture Library **478** Andreas Rentz/Getty Images **479** Mary Evans Picture Library **481** NBC/Getty Images **482** REX **483** Roger L. Wollenberg-Pool/Getty Images **484** Mary Evans Picture Library **485** Mary Evans Picture Library **486** Mary Evans Picture Library **487** Moviestore Collection/Alamy **488** Brian J. Ritchie/TalkbackThames/REX **490** Photos 12/Alamy **491** AF archive/Alamy **493** AF archive/Alamy **494** AF archive/Alamy **495** AF archive/Alamy **496** BBC/Mary Evans Picture Library **498** AF archive/Alamy **499** Société Radio Canada/Ponopresse/Gamma **501** 20th Century Fox/Everett/REX **502** Getty Images **503** ITV/REX **504** Getty Images **506** ITV/REX **507** AF archive/Alamy **509** Getty Images **510** Hulton Archive/Getty Images **511** Mary Evans Picture Library **513** ITV/REX Shutterstock **514** ABC Photo Archives/Getty Images **515** AF archive/Alamy **516** AF archive/Alamy **518** 20th Century Fox/Everett/REX **519** Ernesto Ruscio/Getty Images **521** BBC/Mary Evans Picture Library **522** Mary Evans Picture Library **523** Mary Evans Picture Library **524** HBO/Everett/REX **526** 20th Century Fox/Everett/REX **528** 20th Century Fox/Everett/REX **529** Everett Collection/REX **531** NBC/Getty Images **533** AF archive/Alamy **536** ITV/REX **539** Robert Voets/CBS Photo Archive/Getty Images **541** AF archive/Alamy **542** BBC/Allstar **544** Frank Micelotta/ImageDirect **545** 20th Century Fox/Everett/REX **546** Miklos Szabo/Rex Features **548** HBO/Everett/REX **551** Robert Voets/CBS Photo Archive/Getty Images **552** Robert Voets/CBS Photo Archive/Getty Images **554** Michael Courtney/Warner Bros./Getty Images **556** Gamma Rapho/Getty Images **559** Richard Cartwright/ABC Photo Archives/Getty Images **560** Moviestore Collection/REX **562** REX **564** BBC

566 Snap Stills/REX 567 AF archive/Alamy 569 ITV/REX 570 ITV/REX 571 AF archive/Alamy 573 Steve Wilkie/USA Network/NBC/Getty Images 574 HBO/Everett/REX 576 Craig Blankenhorn/CBS 578 REX 579 Rick Rowell/ABC Photo Archives/Getty Images 581 WENN Ltd/Alamy582 Sundance/ Everett/REX 583 Barbara Lindberg/REX 585 Mary Evans Picture Library 586 Mary Evans Picture Library 588 HBO/Everett/REX Shutterstock 589 Photos 12/ Alamy 590 Jim De Yonker/CBS Photo Archive/Getty Images 593 Fred Norris/Warner Bros./Getty Images 594 Netflix/Everett Collection/REX 597 Theo Wargo/WireImage 598 Brian J. Ritchie/TalkbackThames/REX 599 ComedyC/Everett/REX 601 AF archive/Alamy 602 Photos 12/Alamy 604 Moviestore Collection/REX 605 Everett Collection/REX 606 BBC 608 Carole Segal/NBC/Getty Images 609 Roland Grant/Mary Evans Picture Library 611 UPN/Everett/REX 612 AF archive/Alamy 613 Photos 12/Alamy 614 Dave Hogan/Getty Images 616 AF archive/Alamy 617 Stephen Lovekin/Getty Images for IMG 618 NBC/Getty Images 621 MoviePoster DB 622 AF archive/Alamy 624 Startraks Photo/REX 626 HBO/Everett/REX 627 AF archive/ Alamy628 Mary Evans Picture Library 629 Showtime Network 631 Interfoto/Mary Evans Picture Library 633 Sergei Bachlakov/Warner Bros./Getty Images 634 FOX/Getty Images 635 Everett/REX Shutterstock 636 www.haaretz.com 637 RAI Fiction/Getty Images 638 FXNetwork/Everett/REX 640 CBS Photo Archive/Getty Images 641 Brendan Smialowski/Getty Images 642 FOX/Getty Images 644 imgkid.com 645 Everett/Rex Shutterstock 646 NurPhoto.com/Alamy 647 Photos 12/Alamy 649 BBC 650 Justin Lubin/NBC/Getty Images 652 Rex Shutterstock 654 REX 655 Mary Evans Picture Library 657 Monty Brinton/CBS Photo Archive/Getty Images 658 Mary Evans Picture Library 659 BBC 660 Photos 12/Alamy 661 AF archive/Alamy 662 Ron P. Jaffe/CBS Photo Archive/Getty Images 663 Showtime/Everett/REX 664 Sci-Fi/Everett/REX Shutterstock 665 AF archive/Alamy 666 Ali Goldstein/NBC/Getty Images 668 Trae Patton/NBC/Getty Images 669 ITV/REX Shutterstock 670 Mark Campbell/REX Shutterstock 673 HBO/Everett/REX Shutterstock 674 Greg Schwartz/CBS Photo Archive/Getty Images 675 Ronald Grant/Mary Evans Picture Library 676 Bill Inoshita/CBS/Getty Images 677 Ilgan Sports/Multi-Bits/Getty Images 679 Bill Records/Getty Images 681 ITV/REX Shutterstock 682 fanpop.com 683 AF archive/Alamy 684 AF archive/Alamy 686 AF archive/Alamy 687 Mary Evans Picture Library 689 ITV/REX Shutterstock 691 ITV/REX Shutterstock 692 Moviestore/REX 694 Chris Haston/NBC/Getty Images 695 Ronald Grant/Mary Evans Picture Library 696 Jordin Althaus/NBC/Getty Images 697 a Company Pictures / Stormdog Production for E4 698 The Kobal Collection/Princess Pictures 700 Everett/REX Shutterstock 703 ITV/REX Shutterstock 704 AF archive/Alamy 706 Everett/REX Shutterstock 707 REX Shutterstock 709 MoviePoster DB 710 REX Shutterstock 712 AF archive/Alamy 713 Everett/REX Shutterstock 714 AMC/Everett Collection/REX 716 Eric McCandless/CBS Photo Archive/Getty Images 718 Photos 12/Alamy 719 TNT/Everett/REX Shutterstock 721 AF archive/Alamy 722 AMC/Everett Collection/REX 723 AF archive/ Alamy 724 Cathy Kanavy/USA Network/NBC/Getty Images 726 Moviestore Collection/Alamy 727 AF archive/Alamy 729 HBO/Everett/REX Shutterstock 730 © Left Bank Pictures (Television) Limited. Photographer: Laurence Cendrowicz. 732 Moviestore Collection/Alamy 733 MoviePoster DB 735 MoviePoster DB 736 Everett/REX Shutterstock 738 Everett/REX Shutterstock 739 MoviePoster DB 740 Stephen Scott/SOAPnet/Getty Images 741 Everett/REX Shutterstock 742 ABC Inc/Everett/REX Shutterstock 743 WENN Ltd/Alamy 744 ABC/Everett/REX Shutterstock 745 Starz/Everett/REX Shutterstock 746 Peter "Hopper" Stone/ABC Photo Archives/ Getty Images 748 HBO/Everett/REX Shutterstock 749 Everett/REX Shutterstock 750 Everett/REX Shutterstock 753 MoviePoster DB 754 Justin Lubin/NBC/Getty Images 755 David Giesbrecht/CBS Photo Archive/Getty Images 756 Steve Jennings/NBC/Getty Images 758 MoviePoster DB 759 ITV/REX Shutterstock 760 Justin Lubin/NBC/Getty Images 762 Everett/REX Shutterstock 763 FOX/Getty Images 764 Sci-Fi/Everett/REX Shutterstock 765 MoviePoster DB 768 Hulu/Everett/REX Shutterstock 770 Barcroft India/Barcoft Media/Getty Images 771 Starz/Everett/REX Shutterstock 772 AF archive/Alamy 774 Photos 12/Alamy 776 AF archive/Alamy 777 AF archive/Alamy 779 Everett/REX Shutterstock 780 AF archive/Alamy 782 Photos 12/Alamy 783 Everett/REX Shutterstock 784 Robert Viglasky/ BBC 786 BBC 788 Ben Cohen/NBC/Getty Images 789 Photo by Dean Rogers © Warp Films 790 Photos 12/Alamy 791 Eric McCandless/ABC Family/Getty Images 793 Photos 12/Alamy 794 AF archive/Alamy 796 RD/Julia Terjung 797 Moviestore Collection/Alamy 798 Moviestore Collection/Alamy 801 MoviePoster DB 802 © Filmlance International AB Photo: Johan Paulin 803 MoviePoster DB 804 Hal Shinnie 805 20th Century Fox/Everett/REX 806 FOX/Getty Images 809 Jens Kalaene/dpa/Alamy 810 Everett/REX Shutterstock 811 Showtime/Everett/REX 812 MoviePoster DB 814 AF archive/Alamy 816 BBC 818 AF archive/Alamy 819 Jack Rowand/ABC Photo Archives/Getty Images 820 ITV/REX Shutterstock 821 McPix Ltd/REX Shutterstock 822 http://www.signesejlund.com 823 NT/Everett Collection/REX 824 AF archive/Alamy 826 HBO/Everett/REX Shutterstock 828 Scott Green/NBC/ Getty Images 829 AF archive/Alamy 830 AF archive/Alamy 831 MoviePoster DB 832 Photos 12/Alamy 833 Photos 12/Alamy 834 Showtime/REX 836 MoviePoster DB 837 David Bagnall/Alamy 838 Showtime/Everett/REX/Company Pictures for Channel 4 840 Everett/REX Shutterstock 841 Everett/ REX Shutterstock 842 AF archive/Alamy 843 Richard Cartwright/ABC Photo Archives/Getty Images 845 AF archive/Alamy 846 MoviePoster DB 847 MoviePoster DB 848 AF archive/Alamy 849 MoviePoster DB 850 HBO/Everett/REX 852 Red Production Company/BBC 853 Photos 12/Alamy 855 Ray Burmiston 856 tidyproductions.com 857 WENN Ltd/Alamy 858 Giovanni Rufino/CBS Photo Archive/Getty Images 859 MoviePoster DB 860 Laurence Cendrowicz/© Neal Street Productions 2011 861 HBO/Everett/REX 862 AF archive/Alamy 864 AF archive/Alamy 865 MoviePoster DB 866 HBO/Everett Collection/REX 868 A&E/Everett Collection/REX 869 Mario Perez/ABC Photo Archives/Getty Images 870 Netflix/Everett Collection/REX 872 EPA European Pressphoto Agency/Alamy 874 HBO/Everett/REX 875 Everett/REX Shutterstock 876 BBC 877 MoviePoster DB 878 ITV/REX 880 A&E/Everett Collection/REX 881 Stuart Wood/Company Pictures/BBC 882 Starz!/Everett/REX 883 20th Century Fox/Everett/REX 884 ITV/REX 885 Everett/REX Shutterstock 886 Brooke Palmer/NBC/Getty Images 888 Netflix/Everett Collection/REX 889 20th Century Fox/Everett/REX 890 20th Century Fox/Everett/REX 893 Brownie Harris/CBS Photo Archive/Getty Images 894 Netflix/Everett Collection/REX 896 © Urban Myth Films Ltd. Photography Ray Burmiston. Design Alicia Kulikowski 898 Will Hart/NBC/Getty Images 900 ABC 901 WENN Ltd/Alamy 902 Showtime Networks Inc./REX 903 MoviePoster DB 904 ITV/REX 905 REX 906 Sundance Channel/Everett Collection/REX 907 Sundance Channel/courtesy Everett Collection/REX 908 MoviePoster DB 909 Popperfoto/Getty images 910 Showtime Networks Inc./Everett Collection/REX 911 EPA European Pressphoto Agency/Alamy 912 History Channel/Everett Collection/REX 914 AF archive/Alamy916 MoviePoster DB 917 MoviePoster DB 918 FOX/Getty Images 920 20th Century Fox/Everett/REX 921 CW Network/Everett Collection/REX 922 Everett/REX Shutterstock 924 FX/Everett/REX 926 Showtime Networks Inc./Everett/REX 927 TNT/Everett/REX 929 Sixteen String Jack Productions/Avalon TV/The Kobal Collection 931 Simon James/FilmMagic 932 Nicole Rivelli/ABC Photo Archives/Getty Images 934 Everett Collection/REX 935 LUCASFILM 936 HBO/Everett/REX 939 Allstar/BBC 940 REX Shutterstock 941 HBO/Everett/REX 942 Joan Wakeham/REX Shutterstock/ Company Pictures and Playground Entertainment for BBC2 944 Everett/REX Shutterstock 945 Steve Sands/ GC Images 946 Paramount/Jagged Films/HBO/The Kobal Collection

Acknowledgments

With huge thanks to ever-suffering housemates Laurie, David, Neil, and Jim for putting up with long absences, moody silences, and the odd hangover. Massive appreciation to my moral support—the Notplayers, All Creatures, Dan, and many, many more. You've kept me sane. And biggest thanks of all to my family—in particular to those who have brainwashed me into a lifetime of telly-loving—notably Mum (miss you!), Dad, Joan, Sandra, and Yvonne. I'm blaming you all.